D1253731

**adolescent
development**

mc graw-hill
series in psychology

BUCKNER AND MC GRATH *Vigilance: A Symposium*

COFER *Verbal Learning and Verbal Behavior*

COFER AND MUSGRAVE *Verbal Behavior and Learning: Problems and Processes*

CRAFTS, SCHNEIRLA, ROBINSON, AND GILBERT *Recent Experiments in Psychology*

DAVITZ *The Communication of Emotional Meaning*

DEESE *The Psychology of Learning*

DOLLARD AND MILLER *Personality and Psychotherapy*

ELLIS *Handbook of Mental Deficiency*

EPSTEIN *Varieties of Perceptual Learning*

FERGUSON *Statistical Analysis in Psychology and Education*

FORGUS *Perception: The Basic Process in Cognitive Development*

GHISELLI *Theory of Psychological Measurement*

GHISELLI AND BROWN *Personnel and Industrial Psychology*

GILMER *Industrial Psychology*

GRAY *Psychology Applied to Human Affairs*

GUILFORD *Fundamental Statistics in Psychology and Education*

GUILFORD *The Nature of Intelligence*

GUILFORD *Personality*

GUILFORD *Psychometric Methods*

GUION *Personnel Testing*

HAIRE *Psychology in Management*

HIRSCH *Behavior Genetic Analysis*

HIRSH *The Measurement of Hearing*

HURLOCK *Adolescent Development*

HURLOCK *Child Development*

HURLOCK *Developmental Psychology*

JACKSON AND MESSICK *Problems in Human Assessment*

KARN AND GILMER *Readings in Industrial and Business Psychology*

KRECH, CRUTCHFIELD, AND BALLACHEY *Individual in Society*

LAZARUS *Adjustment and Personality*

LAZARUS *Psychological Stress and the Coping Process*

LEWIN *A Dynamic Theory of Personality*

LEWIN *Principles of Topological Psychology*

MAHER *Principles of Psychopathology*

MARX AND HILLIX *Systems and Theories in Psychology*

MESSICK AND BRAYFIELD *Decision and Choice: Contributions of Sidney Siegel*

MILLER *Language and Communication*

MORGAN *Physiological Psychology*

NUNNALLY *Psychometric Theory*

PAGE *Abnormal Psychology*

RETHLINGSHAFER *Motivation as Related to Personality*

ROBINSON AND ROBINSON *The Mentally Retarded Child*

SCHERER AND WERTHEIMER *A Psycholinguistic Experiment on Foreign Language Teaching*

SHAFFER AND LAZARUS *Fundamental Concepts in Clinical Psychology*

SHAW AND WRIGHT *Scales for the Measurement of Attitudes*

SIDOWSKI *Experimental Methods and Instrumentation in Psychology*

SIEGEL *Nonparametric Statistics for the Behavioral Sciences*

STAGNER *Psychology of Personality*

TOWNSEND *Introduction to Experimental Methods for Psychology and the Social Sciences*

VINACKE *The Psychology of Thinking*

WALLEN *Clinical Psychology: The Study of Persons*

WARREN AND AKERT *The Frontal Granular Cortex and Behavior*

WATERS, RETHLINGSHAFER, AND CALDWELL *Principles of Comparative Psychology*

WINER *Statistical Principles in Experimental Design*

ZUBEK AND SOLBERG *Human Development*

JOHN F. DASHIELL was Consulting Editor of this series from its inception in 1931 until January 1, 1950. CLIFFORD T. MORGAN was Consulting Editor of this series from January 1, 1950 until January 1, 1959. HARRY F. HARLOW assumed the duties of Consulting Editor from 1959 to 1965. In 1965 a Board of Consulting Editors was established according to areas of interest. The board members are HARRY F. HARLOW (physiological, experimental psychology), NORMAN GARMEZY (abnormal, clinical), HAROLD W. STEVENSON (child, adolescent, human development), and LYLE V. JONES (statistical, quantitative).

adolescent development

elizabeth b. hurlock, ph.d.
Graduate School of Education
University of Pennsylvania

THIRD EDITION

McGraw-Hill
Book Company
New York
St. Louis
San Francisco
Toronto
London
Sydney

**adolescent
development**

Library of Congress Catalog Card Number
66–23277

3 1 4 5 5

1 2 3 4 5 6 7 8 9 0   UL   7 3 2 1 0 6 9 8 7 6

Photographs by ANN ZANE SHANKS. *Photo for Chapter 3 Courtesy* THOMAS JEFFERSON JUNIOR HIGH
SCHOOL, *Teaneck, New Jersey.*

TO MY HUSBAND,
irland mcknight beckman

preface

The original edition of this book appeared in 1949, and the revised edition in 1955. Since then, such radical changes have taken place in American adolescents that an almost completely new approach to a study of characteristic adolescent interests, values, and behavior patterns is mandatory. This third edition of ADOLESCENT DEVELOPMENT has attempted to give the reader as complete and as accurate a picture as possible of today's American adolescent and to show why he is different, in many respects, from adolescents in other cultures.

The approach of this edition is, therefore, new. In addition, three other major revisions have been made. First, significant new material related to areas of adolescent interests and behavior has been introduced. Major areas that have been added or greatly expanded include: levels of aspiration; effects of success and failure on the adolescent's self-concept and on his subsequent behavior; adolescent interest in and preoccupation with status symbols; the new type of interest adolescents have in education; personal and social problems stemming from social mobility; reasons for the discrepancy between moral knowledge and moral behavior, as shown by the rise in misdemeanors and juvenile delinquency; and difficulties adolescents—especially girls—have in accepting the traditional roles for their sex.

The second major change in this revision is the introduction of paragraphs or sections designed to show the reader how a particular area of behavior adjustment, or lack of adjustment, influences the adolescent's personal and social adjustments as he grows older as well as during adolescence. The purpose of emphasizing the long-term effects is to discourage any tendency the reader may have to regard a particularly troublesome form of adolescent behavior as a "passing phase" which the adolescent will "outgrow" or to think of it as "kid stuff" characteristic of all adolescents at a certain stage of their development. An attempt is made to explain the seriousness of such behavior and to show how it often can become the adolescent's characteristic method of adjusting to problems. Although the reader may not always agree with the interpretations offered or may even feel that the proverbial mountain is being made out of a molehill, if what is presented here stimulates controversy and a critical attitude on the part of the reader, it will be well worth the space devoted to it.

The third major change is the presentation of references in an inconspicuous manner. All names of authors are omitted, except when specific mention is made of their studies or when their works are quoted. To show the source from which the material of the text has been taken, numbers have been inserted within or at the end of a paragraph. These refer to studies listed alphabetically in the bibliography at the end of each chapter. When two or more numbers are given, the authors referred to have reported similar findings in their research studies, and the present writer has made use of their findings, either directly or indirectly, in the statement preceding the reference. It is hoped that this method of presenting references will prove to be less distracting to the reader than the method previously used but equally effective as a guide to further information about the topic.

I wish to take advantage of this opportunity to thank the editors of textbooks and scientific journals for their permission to reproduce material in this book and to use some of their illustrations. I am deeply grateful to the many readers of the second edition of this book—both instructors and students—who have written to me and have suggested topics to be enlarged upon or new topics to be added. Their suggestions have been most helpful in planning this third edition. My special gratitude goes to my colleagues in the American Psychological Association for their many helpful criticisms and suggestions.

ELIZABETH B. HURLOCK

contents

CHAPTER 1
adolescence:
age of
transition

"Adolescence" comes from the Latin verb *adolescere,* which means "to grow," or "to grow to maturity." As Horrocks has defined it, "Adolescence is both a way of life and a span of time in the physical and psychological development of an individual. It represents a period of growth and change in nearly all aspects of the child's physical, mental, social, and emotional life. It is a time of new experiences, new responsibilities, and new relationships with adults as well as peers" (89).

The changes which occur in adolescence lead to the goal of maturity. To an adolescent, being mature means having the rights and privileges of an adult—the freedom to do as he pleases when he pleases. The symbol of maturity for today's adolescents is owning a car—the symbol of freedom (127). In their desire to create the impression that they are adults, adolescents "copy all the adult vices and dissipations—smoking, drinking, staying up late, omitting milk and nutritious food from diets, experimenting sexually—as the only way they can discover to be grown-up" (53).

To an adult, by contrast, a mature person is one who is independent of others and able to manage his affairs without help or guidance from others. He is honest with himself and presents himself as he is to others; he is realistic about what he can and cannot do, especially vocationally; and above all, he is capable of steering his own course through life, and willing to do so, accepting the blame if things do not work out to his liking (12,173). In describing a mature person, Cole (34) has emphasized the characteristics associated with maturity in the following way:

> A true adult is, then, a person of adequate physical and mental development, controlled emotional reactions, and tolerant attitudes; he has the ability to treat others objectively; he is independent of parental control, reasonably satisfied with his point of view toward life, and reasonably happy in his job; he is economically independent; he is not dominated by the opinions of those about him, nor is he in revolt against social conventions; he can get along in ordinary social situations without attracting unfavorable attention; and, above all, he has learned to accept the truth about himself and to face reality instead of either running away from it or making believe that it is not there.

age of adolescence

Broadly speaking, adolescence extends from sexual maturity until the age when independence from adult authority is legally assured. American society recognizes the individual as mature at the age of 21 years and gives him at this age the right to vote and to be responsible for his own behavior. We may, therefore, regard the age of 21 as the legal age of maturity and hence the end of adolescence. Marking off the beginning of adolescence is more difficult because the age of sexual maturing varies so greatly. For the average American girl of today, sexual maturing comes during the thirteenth year, and for boys, during the fourteenth. Within the sex groups, however, marked individual differences may be found. This means that, on the average, adolescence extends from 13 to 21 years for girls, and for boys, from 14 to 21. Thus, girls have a year longer to be adolescents and a year less to be children.

Until recently, adolescence was regarded as a single period in the life span. However, studies of adolescents have revealed that there is a marked difference in the behavior patterns of the young and of the older adolescent. Consequently, adolescence may be divided into two subdivisions, early and late. The dividing line between early and late adolescence is 17 years. This holds true for boys who mature later than girls just as it does for girls (47).

The dividing line between early and late adolescence is not determined by physiological status but by changes in behavior patterns. In the American culture of today, the adolescent who has progressed through the school grades according to the standard ages becomes a senior in high school at some time during his seventeenth year. The status of a senior is markedly different from that of the underclassmen; it is more prestigeful and it has rights, privileges, and responsibilities not given to underclassmen. From the point of view of the student body, the seniors are the big wheels who run everything (117). When an adolescent becomes a senior in high school, his status in the home likewise becomes more clearly defined and more prestigeful. Parents suddenly realize that in a year's time their adolescent son or daughter will be away at college, in a vocational training school, in the Army, married, or earning a living. Awareness of the imminent change that will be taking place in their children's lives leads parents to grant them privileges and responsibilities they formerly withheld. Even by younger siblings, a senior in high school is treated differently from a sophomore or junior.

With the changed status in the home and school, the adolescent tries to live up to social expectations. This change often comes suddenly, generally over the summer between the junior and senior years in high school. Many teachers report that boys and girls put away childish things and grow up at this time. The motivation to do so comes from their recognition of their new status and the social expectations that this new status brings.

Labels of Subdivisions While the usual names applied to the subdivisions of adolescence are "early" and "late," they are called by other names also. The young adolescent is commonly referred to as a "teenager"; the older adolescent is sometimes called a "youth" but, more often, a "young man" or a "young woman." Because "teenager" has become a stereotype label for an unstable, unpredictable, and unsocial person, the older adolescent resents being called a teen-ager. Even young adolescents resent this label.

The term "youth" has likewise acquired unfavorable connotations and is often associated with lack of sophistication or lack of control over sex behavior. Because the descriptive adjectives "callow" and "flaming" are so often applied to youth, the older adolescent resents being called a youth almost as much as he resents being called a teen-ager (163). He cannot, however, correctly be called a "man" until he is 21 years of age. But the prefix, "young," suggests that his behavior is more like that of an adult than a child. Being referred to as a "man" implies a maturity of behavior which is pleasing to him (46,68).

Long versus Short Adolescence Regardless of when the child matures sexually, late adolescence normally begins for him at the age of 17 years. This means that a late-maturing child will have a shorter-than-average early adolescence while an early maturer will have a longer-than-average one. It also means that, as girls mature earlier than boys, for the average girl early adolescence will cover a span of 4 years—from 13 to 17—while for the average boy it will cover

only 3 years—from 14 to 17. An academically accelerated child will reach senior status at the age of 16 or earlier. Hence, late adolescence will begin for him sooner than for the average student. The academically retarded child, by comparison, will be treated according to the standards for his academic level. Consequently, he will not have the status in school or in the home which will encourage him to acquire behavior patterns characteristic of the older adolescent.

There are both advantages and disadvantages to a longer-than-average or to a shorter-than-average adolescence. A child who matures early is subjected to the indefinite status associated with early adolescence longer than his age-mates; this affects him unfavorably. On the other hand, a shorter-than-average early adolescence may be a handicap because it deprives the adolescent of the time needed to learn the social skills his age-mates have been learning over a longer period of time. Once the adolescent achieves senior status in school, his status in the group will be the same as that of his classmates, regardless of when he matured.

Adolescence versus Puberty Adolescence should not be confused with "puberty," the period when sexual maturing occurs. Puberty is an overlapping period; approximately one-half of it overlaps the end of childhood, and one-half, the early part of adolescence. On the average, it takes 4 years for the child to be transformed into an adult. Of this time, about 2 years will be spent in preparing the body for reproduction while the other 2 years will be spent in completing it.

The first two years of puberty, the time which overlaps childhood and before the sex organs have started to function, is known as "preadolescence." The individual is called a "preadolescent" or a "pubescent child." He is not an adolescent, because according to the criterion of adolescence, an adolescent is a person who is sexually mature. Nor is he characteristically a child. Many of the physical features and behavior patterns of the child have begun their t formation to those of an adult. The last half of puberty overlaps the early part of early adolescence.

Puberty, thus, is a part of adolescence but is not synonymous with it; adolescence includes *all* phases of maturing, not physical maturing alone. Among primitive peoples and also among civilized peoples in early times, adolescence meant sexual maturing alone. For that reason, it was a short period of time as compared with adolescence today. A further distinction between adolescence and puberty will be given in the following chapter.

traditional beliefs about adolescence

Tradition holds that radical changes take place in the individual as he emerges from childhood into maturity. He is supposed to shed, automatically, the undesirable traits acquired during childhood and to develop, in some mysterious way and with little or no effort, desirable traits that will serve him well when he reaches maturity. The mentally retarded child, for example, is supposed to leave behind his mental deficiency and become normal; the selfish child is expected to turn into a considerate, kindly adult; and the careless, to develop habits of neatness and orderliness.

This point of view was popularized early in the twentieth century by G. Stanley Hall, usually called the "Father of Child Study in America." According to Hall, adolescence was the time when a "new birth" occurred in the individual's personality. Rapid and marked changes were believed to take place at this time, transforming the child into a totally new personality. These changes, according to Hall, resulted from sexual maturing and were, thus, biologically generated. Because these changes are so rapid and pronounced, Hall described the period as one of "storm and stress," a time when the individual is erratic, emotional, unstable, and unpredictable (72).

Evidence from Scientific Research Interest in the problem of adolescence, aroused by the work of Hall and his followers, led to studies by psychologists, sociologists, and anthropologists of large groups of adolescents from different social classes, from different cultures, and from different economic levels. One of the pioneer studies of this type, made by Hollingworth shortly after the First World War, refuted the idea that all children are changelings who, at puberty, develop into new and different personalities (87). Gradually, scientific research has brought together evidence to disprove these earlier points of view. No longer is it possible to hold out hope that a metamorphosis will take place in the adolescent years. Rather, there is ample evidence to show that traits present in childhood will become more deep-rooted with the passage of time (107).

If storm and stress were biologically generated, then it would follow that these disturbances would be found in all adolescents and the same characteristics would mark adolescence in all civilizations. Such is not the case. Studies of the relationship of sexual maturing to emotional tensions have shown that emotional tensions persist long after sexual maturing has been completed. Furthermore, they have revealed that social and economic conditions and pressures are largely responsible for the difficulties the individual has in passing from childhood into adulthood (29,124,148).

That adolescent storm and stress is caused by socioeconomic rather than physical conditions is shown by the fact that among primitive people and in ancient civilizations no such condition existed. In Samoa, for example, adolescence is a pleasant age with none of the stress and strain that American youth experience. In Samoa, the period of maturing is short and the individual becomes mature almost overnight. He does not have to wait for 5 or more years to pass before he can have the rights and privileges, as well as the responsibilities, that are associated with a physically mature body (127).

Each year, as scientific research brings to light new data regarding the adolescent, we find added justification for discarding the traditional beliefs, which, until recently, were widely accepted and which, in turn, were responsible for many of the misunderstandings existing on the part of both adults and adolescents (132). Garn (63) stressed this change in point of view when he said:

> Traditionally, in our culture, adolescence is a period of stress and strain but there is no physiological reason for it. Twenty milligrams of testosterone is not unsettling except to a few dozen sebaceous glands. "Adolescent rebellion" occurs in the hypogonadal lad as well as in the normal boy. Growth, itself, does not result in awkwardness. Despite a raft of elementary textbooks, an overnight increase of two-hundredths of an inch hardly unsettles the balance of Joe, or Pete, or Tom, or Dick. We cannot blame undesirable adolescent behavior on growth, genes, or glands, but only on a culture that has no meaningful place for the adolescent. This, however, does not lessen the vicissitudes of adolescent growth and its effect on the adult-to-be. The fat adolescent is unhappy in a lean milieu. . . . In the sports-oriented school the lean or nonmuscular boy may gravitate into an intellectual corner, or into a mischievous group. Lacking muscular outlets the muscular lad is more likely to find prestige in an antisocial gang. Differences in growth rate, physique, and fat-patterning may have tremendous repercussions on the adolescents themselves.

present-day attitudes toward adolescence

Since the beginning of recorded history, adolescence has been regarded as a troublesome age—a time in the life span when the person is hard to live or work with. In the past, when authoritarian child training prevailed, the troublesome youth was made to toe the mark by punishment or threat of punishment. While he might complain of the restrictions placed on him by the adult members of society, open rebellion would not have been tolerated.

With a shift from authoritarian to more democratic methods of child training,

adolescence has become a more troublesome age for the adolescent as well as his parents and teachers. After a long period of relatively stable behavior, the child suddenly becomes unbalanced, unpredictable, and unstable as he emerges into adolescence. As Harris has pointed out, adolescents are "excitable, show a high level of activity and drive, have little regard for official social norms, are iconoclastic, and exhibit marked contrasts and inconsistencies in attitudes and behavior" (75). If judged by adult standards, normal, healthy adolescents are "notably psychopathic, manic, and schizoid in their psychological make-up and behavior" (75). As Josselyn has stressed, the "normal adolescent is inevitably a mixed-up person, but not at all in the sense of being a psychologically sick person" (105).

While their behavior makes them difficult to live or work with, most adolescents come through this period with relatively little difficulty and make relatively good personal and social adjustments to adult life. Those who have breakdowns, on the other hand, are generally adolescents who have a history of maladjustment going back to early childhood years (11).

Adult Concern Adult concern about adolescents generally centers around three major problems. First, most parents are concerned about the unattractiveness of the adolescent's *appearance* and *manners*. Adolescence, it has been said, "reminds one of pimply boys and giggling girls, of the period when our youngsters lose the appealing naïveté of the uninhibited child, but have not yet acquired the veneer of the young adult" (116). Typically, the adolescent is homely because he is out of proportion; he is unsure of himself and this makes him say and do things in a gauche manner. For the parent who had hoped for improvement, this can be a source of great concern.

The second source of concern centers around adolescent *defiance of adult authority*. While older children begin to challenge authority, the real challenge comes during adolescence. Many adolescents go out of their way to do the opposite of what they have been told to do (46). This is the age when you "can tell an adolescent because you can't tell him anything. That is the way exasperated adults sometimes feel about teen-agers who refuse to listen to reason—adult reason. In calmer moments, we adults recognize that when young people seem difficult, they are displaying symptoms which commonly go along with growing up" (143).

The third major area of concern centers around the question of what will happen to the adolescent in the *future*. As parents watch their adolescent children go downhill academically, as they watch them hanging around the popular teen-age spots with their classmates, idling their time away in talking or arguing with their friends, and as they see them looking off into space when they are presumably studying, they wonder how these patterns of behavior will prepare the adolescents for the competitive world in which they will soon find themselves. The more parents try to impress the adolescent with the seriousness of preparing himself for adult life, the more resistant he is likely to become.

Adult Dread of Adolescence Many parents and teachers dread this period in the child's life because of the countless problems it presents. Parents are often predisposed to react even more unfavorably than they otherwise would because they approach each new problem with a preconceived idea of how difficult it will be and how helpless they will be meeting the challenge successfully. Because the early part of adolescence is generally regarded as the most difficult of all, the junior high schools are constantly faced with a shortage of teachers. Experienced teachers refuse, far too often, to teach in the junior high schools, while inexperienced teachers approach a teaching assignment at this level with a strong feeling of inadequacy.

Adolescence has, in recent years, been called the "terrible teens" and "teen-ager" has become the "journalistic equal of 'hoodlum, gangster, junior public enemy'" (115). With this stereotype, it is not surprising that adults have developed a dread of their children's adolescent years. This dread has been intensified by reports of the rise in juvenile delinquency, motor accidents, sex delinquencies, dope addictions, school dropouts, shotgun marriages, illegitimate births, and teen-age marriages which fill our newspapers, magazines, radio and television programs, and even sermons (11,15,92). As Hess and Greenblatt have pointed out, "With the possible exception of old age, no other phase of individual development is so clearly marked by negative connotations and lack of positive sanctions" as is adolescence (85).

Adolescent Dread of Adolescence Adults are not the only ones who dread adolescence; the adolescents themselves dread it, even though they may not verbalize their feelings. While looking forward to being grown up with the freedom they associate with an adult status, they have a mixed feeling of anticipation and fear. They often wonder if they are capable of assuming the responsibilities that go with freedom. Certainly parental anxiety and concern about the adolescent's ability to cope with his problems and to achieve a satisfactory adult status do not increase the adolescent's self-confidence. Instead, they increase his anxiety and lead to even stronger negative feelings about himself and his abilities.

Furthermore, knowing how adults feel about adolescence makes adolescents resentful toward adults. They feel they are being prejudged or judged unfairly because a handful of their age-mates have attracted nationwide publicity for their antisocial behavior. As Hess and Greenblatt have stressed, adolescents frequently believe that, as a group, they are "subject to condemnation, criticism, and general devaluation by adults and that there exists among adults a stereotype of adolescents as sloppy, irresponsible, unreliable, inclined toward destructive and antisocial behavior" (85).

As a matter of fact, adult ratings of adolescents are not so unfavorable as adolescents believe. However, believing that they are leads many adolescents to play the role, resentfully, assigned them by the adult group—the role of junior public enemy.

Other adolescents may be motivated by this unfavorable adult attitude to prove that they are not juvenile delinquents in order to win adult support for their interests and activities (70,85,145).

pattern of development

Like the development that takes place during the childhood years, development in adolescence follows an orderly sequence or pattern. The changes that occur in pre-adolescence and early adolescence are greater than those which take place later. They accompany the rapid physical changes that occur at that time. As physical development slows down, changes in behavior are slower in making their appearance. Within the period of late adolescence, physical changes are almost at a standstill. This, however, is not true to the same extent of behavioral changes. Both physical and behavioral changes do occur, but at a slower rate than in the early years of adolescence.

Because all adolescents follow much the same pattern of development, it is possible to observe certain characteristic forms of behavior in them. Almost all adolescents, for example, are rebellious against family requirements and prohibitions; they are anxious and insecure; they are seeking reassurance from their own age group and they are inclined to be snobs, excluding those who are not members of their clique. All adolescents are eager to be approved and accepted by those a little older than they, they are confused and worried about their masculine or feminine roles, they are fearful of sex, and they have a feeling of strong loyalty and devotion to their group (34,55,90).

Developmental Tasks Since the pattern of development is similar for all, with slight individual differences, every cultural group expects individuals of a given age to do the things they are capable of doing. These expectations are expressed in the form of "developmental tasks"—behavior patterns a person must learn if he is to be reasonably successful and happy (5,8,45,64). The following developmental tasks must be mas-

tered by adolescents in our culture if they are to be happy and well adjusted (77):

1 *Achieving new and more mature relations with age-mates of both sexes*
2 *Achieving a masculine or feminine social role*
3 *Accepting one's physique and using the body effectively*
4 *Achieving emotional independence of parents and other adults*
5 *Achieving assurance of economic independence*
6 *Selecting and preparing for an occupation*
7 *Preparing for marriage and family life*
8 *Developing intellectual skills and concepts necessary for civic competence*
9 *Desiring and achieving socially responsible behavior*
10 *Acquiring a set of values and an ethical system as a guide to behavior*

Successful achievement of the developmental tasks for a certain period in life leads to success with later tasks, while failure not only leads to personal unhappiness and disappointment but also to difficulties with later tasks. Good achievement on a particular developmental task at one age is followed by good achievement on a similar task at later ages. Furthermore, good achievement on one developmental task is generally associated with good achievement on other tasks at the same age. Good peer relationships, for example, link with success in other developmental tasks and vice versa for that age level (28,38,60,155).

Because adolescence is a long period, there is little motivation for most adolescents to master the developmental tasks for this age at first. As a result, little progress is made during early adolescence. However, by the time adolescents reach the senior year in high school, they realize that adulthood is rapidly approaching; this provides them with the necessary motivation to prepare themselves for this new status As a result, they make greater strides toward the goal of maturity than they did in early adolescence. Whether or not the developmental tasks will be fully mastered by the time they reach legal maturity will depend partly upon how strong their motivation is, partly upon their opportunities for learning, and partly upon the type of foundations they have when they reach adolescence (80).

transition from childhood to adulthood

Adolescence is a period of transition between childhood and adulthood. Sorenson (163) has described adolescence thus:

> Adolescence is much more than one rung up the ladder from childhood. It is a built-in, necessary transition period for ego development. It is a leave-taking of the dependencies of childhood and a precocious reach for adulthood. An adolescent is a traveler who has left one place and has not reached the next . . . . It is an intermission between earlier freedoms . . . and subsequent responsibilities and commitments . . . a last hesitation before . . . serious commitments concerning work and love.

Transition always means change. With change, comes a need for adjustment to this change. The more rapidly changes come, the harder it is to adjust to them. However, all change, whether it comes slowly or rapidly, means breaking old habits of thought and action and establishing new ones. Owing to the stress that change brings, an upset in homeostasis occurs. Stress is often increased by parental expressions of anxiety or by discontent with the way the adolescent is adjusting to the change (44).

The onset of puberty brings rapid changes in body size and structure. Accompanying these physical changes are changes in interests. No longer do childhood playmates or play activities interest the adolescent. He finds himself taking a new interest in the other sex, in movies, in social activities, and even in books of a type that he formerly scorned. He thus passes from childish behavior to mature behavior, from childish interests to mature interests, and from childish attitudes to mature attitudes. This is illustrated in Figure 1–1.

Furthermore, more new problems arise than the adolescent has ever had to solve in so short a time before. He realizes that because he looks like an adult he is expected to behave as an adult. But he does not know how to do so. As he moves away from the home into the peer group, he no longer has models of desirable behavior so readily available nor does he have a stable environment to facilitate identification. In addition, he must learn to stand on his own feet and face the world without his parents and teachers to act as buffers, as they did when he was a child. Because he is on the threshold of adulthood, he must make decisions and adjustments that will have far-reaching implications for his future (4, 112).

Whether he likes it or not, the child cannot remain a child forever. When physical development reaches a certain point he must grow up psychologically and put away childish things. But this is too big a task for a short time. Therefore, he must have time to make this change. That is the function of adolescence. In commenting on adolescence as a time society provides for the transition from childhood to adulthood, Stone and Church have pointed out that it is a "way station" in development, and as such, its most "universal and pervasive feeling is of being out of step" (168).

Under any circumstances and at any time in life, adjusting to change is difficult; the more radical the change, the more difficult it is. In discussing the difficulties of growing up, Keniston (109) has stressed how universal these difficulties are:

> Growing up is always a problem, whether in Samoa, Nigeria, or Yonkers. It entails abandoning those special prerogatives, world views, insights and pleasure that are defined by the culture as specifically "childish" and substituting for them the rights, responsibilities, outlooks, and satisfactions that are suitable for the culturally defined "adult." Although the concepts of "childish" and "adult" differ from one culture to another, every culture requires some change in the child's habitual ways of thinking, feeling, and acting—a change which involves psychic dislocation and therefore constitutes a "problem" for the individual and the culture. . . . In societies where the transition to adulthood is unusually painful, young people often form their own "youth cul-

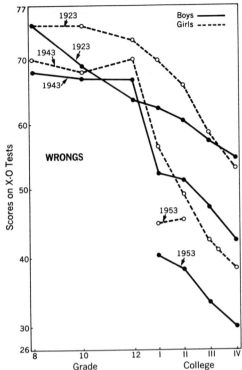

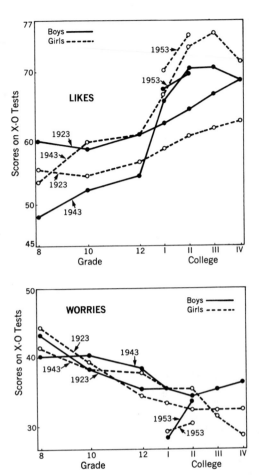

FIGURE 1–1 Changes in attitudes with age. (Adapted from S. L. Pressey and A. W. Jones: 1923–1953 and 20–60 age changes in moral codes, anxieties, and interests, as shown by the "X-O Tests." *J. Psychol.*, 1955, **39**, 485–502. Used by permission.)

ture" with a special set of antiadult values and institutions in which they can at least temporarily negate the feared life of the adult. But somehow children must be induced to accept their roles as adults if the society is to continue.

difficulties in making the transition

Some children find the transition from childhood into adulthood relatively easy; others find it difficult, even to the point where they give up the struggle and revert to the dependency state of childhood. How easy it will be will depend partly upon the individual, partly on environmental aids or obstructions, and partly on adult expectations. As a result, adolescence may be easy and pleasant or difficult and unpleasant

(109,135). Of the many factors that influence the ease or difficulty the adolescent experiences, the following have been found to be the most important.

Speed of Transition Changing roles is never easy. When the change must be made abruptly, as it must at adolescence, it is hard to adjust to. At no time in life does the individual undergo such a sudden and drastic change in so short a time and at no time is he less prepared to cope with the problems this change brings. This is especially true when the adolescent goes to work. In discussing this problem, Lane and Logan (116) point out:

Change from school to work is one of the greatest they ever experience. One week the adolescent is a carefree schoolchild, learning

under the kindly eye of a teacher; the next week he is a number that clocks in at the factory gate, works in a gang with his own eye on the boss, and scurries off home when the whistle blows.

Length of Transition Too much time can produce as many difficulties in going from the status of a child to that of an adult as can too little time. Rapid maturers, who literally grow up overnight, find adjustment to adult expectations more difficult than do those who mature at the average rate or slightly more slowly. The reason for this is that the adolescent is expected to behave like an adult before he has had time to learn to do so just because he looks, suddenly, more like an adult than like a child (131).

On the other hand, a prolonged adolescence also brings problems. One of these is that the adolescent gets into the habit of being dependent, which, like all habits, is difficult to break later (11). By the time boys and girls reach the end of high school, they want to become adults. However, a vocational aspiration that makes them dependent on their parents blocks the transition into adulthood. Thus, "living in the twilight of an arrested transition renders the adolescent self-conscious and ashamed" (21).

Discontinuities in Training The status of the child is different from that of the adult in most cultures. In our culture, we go to great extremes in emphasizing this difference. Only occasionally does the training of the child not involve discontinuities. As a child, he is encouraged to be nonresponsible but later is expected to assume a responsible adult role. The transition from a submissive to an independent role is difficult because he has been trained to behave in a submissive way, and then suddenly he is expected to behave in an independent way. Much of the stress and strain of adolescence is due to the discontinuities in the child's training.

This is in direct contrast to the training given children in primitive cultures; it helps to explain why the transition from

childhood to adulthood is so much easier for them than for children in our culture (17,127). However, when training is marked by continuities, as is true in the socialization of children in suburban communities, where the pattern of training is in preparation for adult life in a suburban environment, transition to adulthood is not too difficult, provided the individual remains in a similar environment. Should he go into a rural or urban environment, he would find the training for suburban living unsatisfactory preparation. This would interfere with the success of his adjustments (189).

The adolescent whose childhood has been a gradual preparation for the independent status of an adult will have far less difficulty in adjusting to adulthood than the one who has received little training or encouragement to be independent (81). Consequently, if the transition is to be facilitated, it is apparent that "it is the very early years that count most. If they are good ones, the chances that adolescence will go smoothly are significantly increased" (59).

Degree of Dependency How dependent the individual will be when he reaches adolescence will depend mainly on the type of training he has received in childhood, how much encouragement he has had to be independent, and how successfully he has been able to handle the independence he has been granted (170). Parents often feel that adolescents have not shown, up to that time, sufficient evidence that they can assume responsibility for their own behavior to warrant granting them the desired privileges. As a result, many adolescents find it difficult to make the transition to adulthood (23,134,185).

The transition is facilitated by work experience which helps the adolescent to achieve some measure of independence, adds to his self-confidence, and eliminates many of the conflicts with parents which dependency gives rise to (75,126,152). Girls, as a rule, are encouraged to be more dependent than boys and they have more severe conflicts with their parents if they try to achieve independence. As a result, they find the transition into adulthood more difficult than do boys. Lower-class children, from early childhood, are encouraged to be more independent than are children from the middle and upper socioeconomic groups. This facilitates their transition into adulthood (10,16,42,43).

Ambiguous Status In tradition-bound societies, the child is expected to follow in the footsteps of his parents; this gives him a pattern of behavior to imitate (56). In a democratic society, by contrast, it is assumed that every individual should be free to choose his own pattern of self-development. As a result, he is deprived of the guidance and help given in tradition-bound societies where the behavior of youth is regulated by a defined code (46). Furthermore, because of his desire for independence, the adolescent in a democratic culture has loosened his ties with his parents. He therefore cannot turn to them for help or rely upon them as he did when he was a dependent child (104,146).

While it is true that all cultures, to some extent, hold confusion for the adolescent, the fact that adolescents in the American culture today lack a defined role tends to increase the confusion (105). As Hess and Greenblatt (85) have pointed out:

> Adolescents occupy an ambiguous position in American society. As a phase in personal and social development adolescence is a recognized period experienced by every American youth. As a status in the social structure, however, it is loosely defined at both entry and exit transition points and offers a set of vague and often conflicting roles. The age behaviors expected of adolescents by adults are viewed by society with ambivalence and anxiety.

Conflicting Demands The adolescent is confronted with conflicting demands from his parents, teachers, contemporaries, and the community. He is confused and exasperated by being told, "You are old enough to know better," and then, in almost the next breath, "You are not old enough to do this or that." He is told to take responsibilities, to show some judgment, and to make decisions. Then he is treated as a child and is expected to be submissively obedient to his parents and teachers. He is told, "in effect to grow up—to achieve an undefined state. He is not told *how* to grow up" (56). Parents and teachers expect him to be a diligent worker and a serious student; the peer group prefers an irresponsible pleasure-seeker (159). As Gardner has stressed, adolescents must be considered with "due emphasis upon the pressures and value systems of the groups that surround them, and with emphasis upon the sometimes sharply conflicting values of the multiple roles they must assume" (62).

This is even more true of girls than of boys. Having had similar training and privileges as boys during childhood, the girl discovers at adolescence that her role will from then on be very different from that of the boy and that the privileges granted to boys will be withheld from her. This adds to the confusion that all adolescents experience and increases the difficulty the girl encounters in growing up (54,92).

Degree of Realism Thinking unrealistically about themselves and their futures starts for most adolescents during childhood. At that time, they develop definite concepts of what they will be and have when they are grown up. Furthermore, they far too often believe that with the physical changes will come psychological changes that will make them into the type of adults they want to be. Young adolescents are more optimistic about reaching their ideals than are older adolescents who have discovered that change is not always in the desired direction (147,170).

When the adolescent begins to look like an adult, he discovers that life begins to open up for him and that he is permitted an added degree of freedom. This far too often encourages him to set unrealistic goals for himself, to believe that the obstacles in his way, once removed, will no longer be a barrier and that now he can be and do what he has always wanted to (37, 50,144). But when given the opportunity to play the adult role, adolescents often discover that they are not ready, either physically or psychologically, to do so. As a result they are not satisfied with themselves or their lives. This weakens their motivation to try to achieve an adult status (124,165, 169).

Motivation In most cultures, prestige is associated with age. Children look forward eagerly to the time when they are grown up with the rights and privileges this status brings them. This provides them with a strong source of motivation to grow up. However, when the time comes, the adolescent finds it far less easy and pleasant than he had anticipated. Furthermore, he had not, in his unrealistic thinking about adulthood, realized that rights and privileges are normally accompanied by responsibilities. Before granting him privileges, he discovers, society tests him to see if he can and will assume responsibilities (134,149).

The adolescent goes through a period of wondering how he will meet the new problems life presents. He would like to grow up but he is unsure of his ability to cope with adulthood. So long as this feeling of insecurity exists, there will be little motivation to make the transition into adulthood. Howard (91) has described the uncertainty the adolescent feels about growing up thus:

> From the adolescent's troubled vantage point, he remembers his childhood as a peaceful time, or longs for the day when he will be an adult, feeling that things will be different then.

As the barriers to growing up are lowered or removed by parents, teachers, and society, the adolescent can see the possibility of reaching the goal of adulthood. As a result, motivation to make the transition is normally increased. The exception to this general rule comes when parental encouragement to remain dependent blocks the transition the adolescent attempts to make or when lack of preparation for achieving adult status undermines the adolescent's confidence that he can achieve it. Under such conditions, there is a tendency to cling to the security of childhood (91,150, 170).

effects of transition

A period of transition always leaves its mark on the individual's behavior and personality. How great and how persistent this mark will be depends mainly on the degree of difficulty he experiences in making the transition. Most adolescents make the transition from childhood to adulthood without any serious emotional upset though few do so without any "emotional scars." Sometimes the emotional scars are damaging enough to affect their entire future. Others give up the struggle and remain immature for the rest of their lives.

However, regardless of individual differences, certain effects of the transition from childhood to adulthood are almost universal in the American culture of today.

INSTABILITY

Instability comes from feelings of insecurity, and insecurity, in turn, results when the individual must abandon habitual patterns and substitute new ones. No longer can the adolescent do things as he did when he was younger. But he is unsure of his ability to do what society now expects of him. Having had the security of adult guidance and help during his childhood, he now is deprived of this by declaring that he is capable of managing his own affairs. This further adds to the feelings of inadequacy that lead to instability (91,128,150).

Feelings of insecurity are always accompanied by emotional tension; the individual is worried and concerned or he is angry and frustrated. Rarely is he happy when insecure because he realizes that his behavior reflects his lack of confidence in himself. Emotional tension may express itself outwardly or inwardly; the adolescent may be aggressive, self-conscious, or withdrawn. He goes to extremes because he is afraid he will be unable to prove his all-round competence. Some overwork in school, others throw themselves feverishly into school sports, while others devote their time almost exclusively to social activities.

Being deprived of status in society leads to a state of chronic frustration, in which irritability and emotionality are intensified. Frustration, in turn, leads to aggression, which may take many forms, the most common of which are exaggerated demands for independence, generalized contempt for adults and established values, conceit, arrogance, a defiance of authority, and a stereotyped hostile attitude toward parents and elders (44,54,67).

Instability is to be expected in early adolescence. It shows that the individual is growing up and is trying out new patterns of behavior to find which meet his needs best. Should instability not appear, it is generally an indication that the adolescent is clinging to childish dependency and to childish forms of behavior. This may be his fault or it may be the fault of his environment. If he has met with too many failures in too rapid succession in his attempts to be independent, he may become intimidated and seek the protection of childhood. On the other hand, lack of instability may mean that he has been overprotected and subjected to such authoritarian child-training methods that he is not permitted to try to be independent. Reasonable instability is a sign of mental and social maturity (195).

As adolescence progresses, greater stability is gradually achieved. As a result, the older adolescent can be counted on more than the younger, and he, as well, can count on himself. How early and how successfully he will achieve stability depends partly on how strong his motivation is to speed up his transition to maturity and partly on how much opportunity he has to do so. When he discovers that people regard his instability unfavorably, this may provide him with the necessary motivation to become more stable and dependable (183).

Opportunities to make his own decisions, free from parental interference, are most likely to occur when the adolescent has a chance to be away from home—in school, camp, college, or in the Armed Forces—for a long enough time to learn to be independent. Studies have revealed that adolescents who grow up in large families, where more is expected of them and where parents are less overprotective, become more stable and at an earlier age than do adolescents from small families (25).

With increasing stability, the adolescent makes better personal and social adjustments. As a result, he is happier and freer from emotional tensions. On the other hand, long-continued and pronounced instability and inconsistency indicate that the individual is having difficulties—either through his own fault or the fault of his environment—in breaking off childish habits and establishing more mature ones. As a result, he will make poorer adjustments than one could anticipate for his age level (44, 67,128).

Stresses and strains "are normal to adolescence—they are the rapids and cascades in the stream of growth" (196). If one maintains a proper perspective, it will readily become apparent that the characteristic behavior of this transitional period is not serious unless it becomes permanent. This need for perspective was emphasized by Gardner (61) when he said:

> My main therapeutic approach to the parents of adolescents—my main treatment, advice, and prescription to them in the face of such behavior—is the tried-and-true phrase of the men of the ancient church who, when beset by the unpredictable and the seemingly uncontrollable, comforted themselves and one another with the words, "It will pass. It will pass."

PREOCCUPATION WITH PROBLEMS

Adolescence is widely accepted as a "problem age." This label has a twofold meaning: first, that the adolescent has many problems that occupy his time and attention, and second, that he is a problem to his parents, teachers, and society in general. *Problems* arise in any situation which the individual feels incapable of dealing with *to his satisfaction.* The more important a matter or condition is to him, the more of a problem it will seem to be. Because the adolescent tends to be unrealistic about his abilities, he often feels more inadequate about handling his problems than he actually is. Until the adolescent can solve his problems both to his satisfaction and to that of the social group, he cannot be happy or successful (141).

Adjustment to new situations at any age brings problems. However, at adolescence, the problems seem worse than they actually are or than they would seem at other ages. There are several reasons for this. First, the problems of adolescence cover a wider scope and affect more people than do the problems of childhood, and hence they seem proportionally more serious. Then, second, because the transition to adulthood is rapid at first, many problems are likely to pile up at once, giving the adolescent insufficient time to adjust to one before he is deluged by others. And third, the adolescent has had little experience in handling his problems *alone*. In childhood, he sought help from parents. Now he must learn to assume responsibility for the solution of his own problems (41, 175).

Adolescents of today are faced with problems not present when their parents and many of their teachers were teen-agers. As a result, adults do not always understand how serious the problems are to the adolescent, nor do they feel that they are capable of helping him with them (3,66,142,194).

Adolescents who have been brought up by democratic child-training methods are generally better equipped to meet the problems that come with transition into adulthood than are those brought up in authoritarian homes. This is true partly because the former have had more experience in coping with problems under guidance and partly because the atmosphere of the democratic home encourages an adolescent to ask his parents for help with problems he cannot cope with alone (92). As Landis (114) has pointed out:

> In every crucial situation the child from the democratic home has a big advantage over his brow-beaten counterpart in the authoritarian family. . . . The iron hand of the authoritarian home is not conducive to the development of such traits (quick thinking and self-assurance): the child from such a home has two strikes on him from the start.

Types of Problems The problems that occupy the time and attention of adolescents fall, roughly, into two major categories, personal problems and problems characteristic of adolescence. Many of the *personal* problems the adolescent is faced with are not new; they are carry-overs of problems he experienced during childhood but which he has not, as yet, solved to his satisfaction. In adolescence, they re-present themselves, often in more serious forms than during childhood. Characteristic of such problems are achieving greater independence from parental domination and becoming more popular with members of the peer group (190).

Some personal problems may be new in the sense that the adolescent never experienced them or experienced them in such minor forms in childhood that they were of little concern to him. The adolescent who, as a child, had little competition with classmates for the top academic position in his class may discover, in a large high school where competition is keener, that he no longer can maintain his position at the top of his class. Or he may discover that belonging to a minority group now is a barrier to social acceptance while in childhood it was not.

At every age level, there are problems *characteristic* of it; they arise from the developmental tasks the social group expects the individual to master and are general throughout the culture.

As most of the developmental tasks for the adolescent involve, either directly or indirectly, social relationships, the type of problem the typical American adolescent today must cope with is social in nature; it involves learning to adjust to other people and to new and different social situations. Because these are usually far more complex than any he has met in his childhood days and because social maturity lags behind physical maturity, the adolescent can be expected to face many problems similar to those of other adolescents in his cultural group (156).

Variations in Problems Different adolescents have different childhood experiences and develop the values of the particular cultural groups with which they are associated; therefore, different adolescents have different problems. Even when they have similar problems, they may vary in severity according to the value an adolescent associates with the situation. If having money for status symbols, such as clothes, a car, and an impressive home, is important to an adolescent, a break in the family caused by divorce or death will be a greater problem for him than it would be were economic or material values not important.

Because the developmental tasks in every *cultural group* differ in minor or major respects from those of other cultures, the problems arising from these tasks will likewise differ (110,186). American adolescents, for example, are more concerned with problems relating to behavior of a personal and individualistic nature while British adolescents who are more concerned with their obligations to others, have more problems of a social nature (79).

When the social and economic structure of society changes, so does the relative emphasis on problems. In a comparison of the life interests and problems of adolescents in the mid-1950s with those in the mid-1930s, it was found that while adolescents in both eras had similar problems, the severity of these problems varied. Health, for example, was less of a problem to the adolescents of the fifties than of the thirties, though mental health was more of a problem. The new emphasis on mental health and the new drugs to cure disease are largely responsible for the shift. Similarly, recreation proved to be more of a problem for today's adolescents because today's homes provide fewer opportunities for recreation (73). (See Figure 1–2.)

Problems change as the individual grows *older* (1). Studies of high school students' problems have revealed that the problems of sophomores, juniors, and seniors differ not so much in type as in the

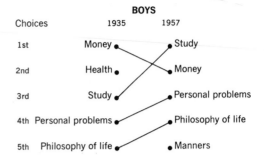

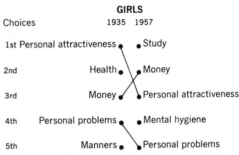

FIGURE 1–2 The severity of adolescent problems changes as the social and economic structure of society changes. (Adapted from L. Cole and I. N. Hall: *Psychology of adolescence.* 6th ed. Holt, Rinehart and Winston, 1964. Used by permission.)

emphasis the students place on the problems. Seniors, for example, rate getting a job as their most important problem, while juniors and sophomores rank preparing for their vocation higher than getting a job. Similarly, boy-girl problems increase in emphasis from the ninth to the twelfth grades, as do school problems (142,172).

The number and severity of problems vary according to the adolescent's *previous success* in adjustments to them. An adolescent who was unsuccessful in solving his problems in childhood is not likely to find it easy to meet the more complicated problems that present themselves at an older age. Comparisons of groups of socially accepted and socially unaccepted high school students have revealed that the unaccepted had more problems and more serious problems than the accepted. Furthermore, there was a difference in the type of problem the two groups reported. In the case of the unaccepted, not feeling well, being overweight, lack of status, and being unhappy were the most commonly reported problems, while for the more accepted, moral problems in their relationship with members of the opposite sex, problems about future education, and problems about jobs proved to be of special concern (65,113).

Because every cultural group has different expectations for members of the two *sexes*, it is understandable that the problems of boys differ from the problems of girls. There are more problems among girls than among boys. The number of problems that girls face increases with age, while for boys the number decreases (1,65,73,74, 142). Sex differences in the relative importance of different problems commonly found among young adolescents are shown in Figure 1–4, page 17.

There are also marked sex differences in the problems facing the older adolescent in college. Social problems trouble girls more than boys, as do problems related to morals, religion, sex, and marriage, and problems centered around personal attractiveness. Boys are especially disturbed about matters relating to money and sex and delays in starting work and marriage. While both boys and girls of college age report problems relating to family relationships, the most serious for boys are conflicts with their parents over educational and vocational plans and independence. For girls, major conflicts with parents are over finances, vocational and educational plans, and independence (34,89,172,192).

Problems of *bright* adolescents differ from those of average or below-average intelligence. Bright adolescents are usually more keenly aware of their problems and feel more intensely about them. Furthermore, since it is often assumed that they can work out their problems unaided, they receive less help than those of lesser ability (24, 82). Brightness also gives rise to certain problems. Because of the wide range of vocational choices open to those who are very bright, the problem of vocational decision is greater than for those whose intellectual abilities limit them to a narrower range. Very bright adolescents tend to have more problems with their parents because few parents understand the bright child as well as the child of average ability (171).

Adolescents who *differ* from the school group with which they are associated have more problems and more serious problems than those who are more similar to the group. College students who are younger than their age-mates have more social adjustment difficulties than those who are approximately the average age for their classes (111). Married college students have problems similar to those of their unmarried classmates though their concerns are mainly centered on problems related to the present while their unmarried classmates' problems center more on the future (102).

Members of a minority group in school or college have problems similar to those of their majority-group classmates, but they emphasize the problems that are intensified by their minority-group status, such as social acceptance and recreational activities (119, 186). Rural students in an urban or suburban school have different problems from those they would have were they in a rural school with students whose backgrounds were more similar to theirs. When rural students are made to feel that they are different by such labels as "country bumpkin" or "country hick," it intensifies their social problems (76,162).

Common Problems of Adolescence What the typical problems of American adolescents are has been determined by many means: by asking them, having them check their problems in order of difficulty on a checklist, studying their wishes and resolutions to reform, and the free expression of their interests. When, for example, the individual lists owning material possessions, such as a car, high among his interests and rates self-improvement low, it means that his problems center more on material possessions than on self-improvement (2,99). Similarly, New Year's resolutions that center around self-improvement suggest that the individual regards self-improvement as one of his major problem areas (197). In Figure 1–3 are shown the common wishes of boys and girls at different ages in childhood and adolescence. Note that interest in material objects, as expressed in their wishes, declines with age, while wishes for self-improvement increase sharply during the years of early adolescence (33).

A number of studies have been made of the problems of junior and senior high school students during the *early adolescent* years. Typical problems for this age are shown in Figure 1–4. Their problems, for the most part, center around physical appearance, health and physical development, schoolwork, relationships with members of their families, their teachers, and peers of both sexes, the choice of a vocation, money, personal adjustment, morals, and sex—their own sexual behavior and adequacy rather than sex per se (2,6,94,128,136,194).

The studies of the problems facing the *older adolescent* have, to date, been limited to those of college students. What problems face the older adolescent whose life is in the world of work are still unknown. Many of the problems of the college student can be traced to the fact that the older adolescent is still in a state of dependency on his family. Some of the problems, as a result, are created by home and family situations, while others arise from the college environment in which the older adolescent finds himself.

The older adolescent is concerned with problems relating to his college grades, his ability to graduate, and how to study effectively; problems related to selecting a career, his ability for the chosen career, the training needed, and the opportunities available; social adjustment problems relating to shyness, feelings of inferiority, social sensitivity, and making friends; family problems centered on parental discord, divorce or separation of the parents, adjustment to the remarriage of a parent, and conflicts with parents; problems related to money, especially money needed for status symbols; and sex problems related to conduct, behavior, and experience (41,136,151,177,192,197).

Solution of Problems Solving a problem is never easy. It is especially difficult for young adolescents who, far too often, have been accustomed to having their problems

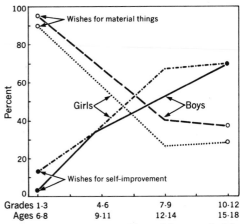

FIGURE 1–3 Changes in wishes of boys and girls from childhood to adolescence. (Adapted from L. Cole and I. N. Hall: *Psychology of adolescence.* 6th ed. Holt, Rinehart and Winston, 1964. Used by permission.)

solved for them by parents or teachers. As a result, many adolescents feel incapable of handling their problems alone. While many would like to go to their parents, they hesitate to do so. They feel that their parents may not understand their problems, that they will not be sympathetic; even worse, they fear that they will create the impression that they are incapable of being independent, thus jeopardizing what independence they have been able to achieve.

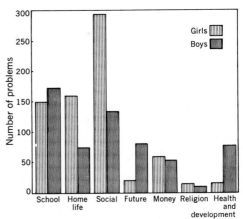

FIGURE 1–4 Typical problems of young adolescent boys and girls. (Adapted from O. Y. Lewis: Problems of adolescents. *Calif. J. second. Educ.,* 1949, **24**, 215–221. Used by permission.)

Others regard their parents as symbols of the childhood they want to leave behind (142).

As a result of cutting themselves off from the source of help they habitually relied on during childhood, many adolescents feel themselves adrift and in need of new sources of help. Some adolescents turn to teachers, ministers, older siblings, adult relatives, and family friends. Others regard all adults as authority figures and want to avoid putting themselves in a position of submission to them. They then turn to members of the peer group for help. Or lacking confidence in the help they get from their peers, they may turn to unseen advisers, getting their help by mail, through the advice columns in newspapers, magazines, or over radio and television (26,51,142).

Even when they turn to parents for help, adolescents tend to be more cautious about which parent they will go to and what problems they will be willing to discuss than they were when they were younger. Both boys and girls prefer to go to their mothers; they feel that their mothers are more tolerant and understanding (93).

How much the adolescent will turn to his parents for help depends not upon the type of relationship he has with them as much as the type and seriousness of the problem. The more serious the problem the more resistant he is to seeking help from them. Problems relating to sex, to boy-girl relationships, or to religious doubts are least likely to be discussed with parents (85,88, 136).

While most adolescents want to discuss their problems with others, they do not want to be told how to solve them. Even when they turn to peers, they resist being forced into solving the problem as someone else thinks it should be solved. On the other hand, they do not want to be told that its "your problem" and receive no help. Instead, they want a middle-of-the-road approach—specific suggestions and advice and then an opportunity to make the final decision for themselves. Only when the adolescent feels too inadequate to make the decision will he be willing to accept a ready-made decision from another (31,88,142).

By the time the adolescent reaches his senior year in high school, he generally feels adequate to cope with his problems; as a result, he seeks less and less help from others. Even though he may continue to turn to others for advice, he becomes more selective than he was when he was less sure of himself and would take advice from anyone who would give it to him (27,151).

However, some adolescents, either because of lack of help or feelings of inadequacy, fail to cope with their problems to their satisfaction. As a result, they continue to be preoccupied with them long beyond the age when other adolescents are beginning to turn their attention outward. This causes them to be self-bound and disinterested in anything that does not relate to them personally. The outcome of this turning inward usually takes one of two common forms. The adolescent may develop such feelings of inadequacy or inferiority that he works below his level in whatever he does, or he may revert to childish dependency, hoping in this way to free himself of the burden of solving his problems (118,154).

PROBLEM BEHAVIOR

Behavior at any age is regarded as "problem behavior" if it causes trouble for others. Certainly at no time in the growing-up process are there more instances of behavior causing trouble for others than at adolescence. The fundamental reason for believing that adolescence is a problem age is that the adolescent is too often judged by adult standards rather than by standards for adolescents.

To make the situation worse, too many studies by psychologists and psychiatrists have emphasized the behavior of the poorly adjusted adolescent. The result has been a widespread impression that *all* adolescents are problem cases.

The young adolescent is even more of a problem to himself than to others. He is not adjusted to his new role in life, and as a result, he is confused, uncertain, and anxious. Instead of being expected to behave in a way that is consistent with his level of development, he is sometimes treated like a child and sometimes is expected to behave like an adult (9). Consequently, in addition to his own problems he finds that "adults and their unreasonable ways and points of view are really the problems" he must cope with (89). While he remains in this state of confusion about what society expects of him, he is tense, nervous, ready to fly off the handle at the slightest provocation, or he is moody, grumpy, and generally unhappy (44,56,67,172). As adolescence progresses, this problem behavior gradually diminishes; the adolescent becomes less of a problem to himself and to the social group.

UNHAPPINESS

It is difficult to be happy when one is burdened with problems. Consequently it is questionable whether there is much truth to the traditional belief that adolescence is a "happy, carefree age." Adolescence is not carefree for the typical adolescent in our culture nor is it a happy time of life. While there are, of course, moments of happiness, these far too often are overshadowed by the frustrations, disappointments, and heartbreaks that accompany growing up.

Studies of happiness at different ages during the life span have revealed that adolescence stands close to the top of the list of unhappy ages. For most people, happiness depends mainly on feelings of adequacy to do what society expects of them; it means freedom from worry and responsibility, combined with the achievement of one's hopes and ambitions. Because of the problems the adolescent must face and the conflicts that arise when he is prevented from achieving the status he feels entitled to, it is understandable that it would be difficult for adolescents in the American culture of today to find adolescence a truly happy age (13,181,193). That unhappiness in adolescence is mainly environmental in cause is shown by the fact that it is far from universal. In most primitive cultures, adolescence is one of the happiest periods of life (127). In many civilized cultures, it is a far happier period than in ours (13).

Variations in Happiness During adolescence, unhappiness is generally greater among boys than among girls. While boys are given greater freedom than girls, more demands are placed on them. As a result, they feel greater pressure to live up to expectations beyond their capacities than do girls. By contrast, many girls, especially those from middle- and upper-class families, regard adolescence as a happy age because they are protected, fewer demands are placed on them, and they are encouraged to have a good time as a stepping-stone to meeting the "right people" and making a successful marriage (129,193).

Adolescents from unfavorable home environments which have low socioeconomic status or frictional family relationships have fewer happy experiences and fewer happy memories of their childhood than have adolescents from more favorable environments (48,86,133). Normally, happiness as shown in an optimistic outlook on life increases as adolescence progresses. As Tuddenham has pointed out, "Increased optimism is a usual concomitant of passage from stormy adolescence to serene maturity" (182).

Causes of Unhappiness There is no one cause of unhappiness in adolescence but many. Of these, the most common are described in the following paragraphs and are shown in Figure 1–5.

social pressures The social group expects the adolescent to master the develop-

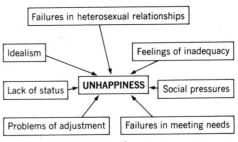

FIGURE 1–5 Unhappiness has many causes.

mental tasks it sets for the age level before adolescence ends, and no adolescent can be happy if he feels that he has fallen short of these expectations (7,22). Social pressures from the peer group cause as much unhappiness as pressures from parents, teachers, and other adults. A boy, for example, who has aspirations for a career that will require a long and expensive education is made unhappy when the peer group puts pressures on him to date, to go steady, or even to marry early. If he conforms to peer expectations, he will be unhappy because he feels that he is wasting time that could better be spent on preparing for his future career or he will live in fear that he will be "trapped by a dame" and this will jeopardize his future career (193). If he fails to live up to peer expectations, he will lack acceptance by the group and this will make him unhappy.

problems of adjustment Adjustment is always accompanied by anxiety. The most intense anxiety shows itself in the area of development most recently established. How the adolescent reacts to adjustment problems will determine how happy he is. The adolescent whose maturity rate differs from that of his age-mates finds it especially difficult to cope with the normal adjustment problems of adolescence and, consequently, he tends to be even more unhappy than his age-mates (184).

Normally, in the latter part of adolescence there are better adjustments between the adolescent and his family as well as better adjustments with his friends and adults outside the home. As a result, there is less stress and anxiety and, consequently, less unhappiness (13,86,184). Any abnormal condition in the adolescent's life, such as a home broken by death or divorce of the parents, increases the adjustment difficulties. This is especially true for girls, because the home plays a more important role in girls' social acceptance than in boys' (14).

lack of status Boys and girls expect a change in their families' attitudes toward

them when they become sexually mature. Furthermore, the adolescent no longer enjoys the freedom from responsibilities he had as a child, nor does he have the rights and privileges of an adult. This uncertain status is bound to make him unhappy. The adolescent whose vocational aspirations require a long period of education with the accompaniment of prolonged dependency, continues to be unhappy beyond the age when unhappiness normally is replaced by increasing happiness (124). As Blos has pointed out, "Living in the twilight of an arrested transition renders the adolescent self-conscious and ashamed" (21).

idealism Every adolescent has high aspirations for himself, his family, his friends, his community, and his country. Because identity with them reflects on him, he wants them to be ego boosters. Then, when they fall short of the ideals he has set for them, he is unhappy; he feels that they have let him down and that they have too little interest in him to try to make him happy.

Nothing will make an adolescent unhappy more easily than being dissatisfied with himself. And nothing will make him dissatisfied more quickly than gaps between his aspirations for himself and his achievements. Because early adolescence is a time of unrealistic thinking and idealism, and because the young adolescent is less likely to be able to come up to his ideals than the older adolescent, the young adolescent is more unhappy due to self-dissatisfaction than is the older adolescent (97,124).

feelings of inadequacy Because the adolescent generally has unrealistic concepts of his abilities, he is bound to feel inadequate when he falls short of the goals he set for himself. Competition with others in school, in athletics, in social affairs, and in all areas of his life becomes increasingly severe as each year passes. Few adolescents find themselves at the top or even near the top. This often proves to be a crushing blow to their egos and makes them look upon themselves as total failures.

defeats in heterosexual relationships Love affairs can be happy experiences for an adolescent, but few are. And because the major part of adolescence is the "age of romance," few adolescents find the happiness from their romantic experiences that they have dreamed of since their fairy-tales days, when all romances ended with "the couple lived happily ever after."

meeting of needs At every age, there are certain fundamental needs which must be met to a person's satisfaction if he is to be happy. While these needs may vary in intensity from one person to another, they are generally fairly universal within a cultural group. Among American adolescents, the fundamental needs are for acceptance, achievement, affection, approval, belonging, conformity, dependence, independence, dominance, recognition, self-realization, and being understood (123). Many of these, especially during the early years of adolescence, are only partially met or are not met to the adolescent's satisfaction. The more needs that remain unmet, the less will be the adolescent's chances for happiness.

Effects on Behavior The unhappiness of adolescence manifests itself in different patterns of behavior. One of the most common forms is *disorganization of behavior*, as shown by inability to focus on the specific task at hand, shifts in mood, and inefficiency in both mental and physical activities. The adolescent cannot focus his attention on what he is doing; thus he spends more time on a task and gets poorer results than he would if he were able to concentrate on it (54).

Disorganization of behavior leads to recklessness, either of speech or behavior. The adolescent may say things without stopping to consider how they sound to others or how they will affect others. Rudeness, swearing, slang, and sarcastic, derogatory comments are common expressions of recklessness. It may also be expressed in accidents or impulsive acts that lead to juvenile delinquency. The unhappy adolescent, thinking of his unhappiness, does things which lead to trouble for him or for others —things which he would not do were he less self-bound (44).

A common form of disorganized behavior is in the area of *emotionality*. The unhappy adolescent is moody; he broods, is secretive about his personal affairs, and refuses to communcate with others. Then, for no apparent reason, he flies into a rage, often as disorganized in behavior as a young child. If he feels that he is receiving little attention or that he is being frustrated in what he wants to do, he may turn to smashing things as he did when he was younger, or he may hurt himself or others (44,54, 67).

An emotionally disturbed person is usually *quarrelsome*. Quarrelsomeness generally comes in the early adolescent period —reaching its peak between 15 and 17 years. Quarrelsomeness is especially strong in the home, though it is not limited to the home. The unhappy adolescent has a chip on his shoulder toward *all* people, though the members of his family usually bear the brunt of his attacks because he knows they will have to accept him whatever his behavior. The mother is generally the target for the adolescent's attacks; he depreciates her, belittles her in arguments, and accuses her of doing all she can to make his life unhappy (105,124,137).

Quarrelsomeness leads to *antisocial behavior*; the adolescent goes out of his way to behave in a way contrary to what he knows society expects of him. This is his retaliation for the imagined wrongs society has done to him. He shows an intolerance toward others, especially the younger members of his family, members of minority groups, and those of lower intellectual or socioeconomic status than he; he demands money to spend as he wishes, regardless of the financial sacrifices this may impose upon his family; he resists advice, frequently doing just the opposite of what he has been advised to do; he shows less appreciation and affection for his family than ever before; he scorns sentiment of all kinds; and he delights in eccentric methods of dressing, going to the extreme of wearing shabby, dirty garments, or of overdressing (7,67,172).

Perhaps the most antisocial behavior the unhappy adolescent shows is *scapegoating*. Instead of accepting the blame for the things that have made him unhappy, he projects the blame on others. The adolescent claims, for example, that it is not his fault when he does not achieve the independence society expects of him at his age. Instead, he argues, it is the fault of his parents who baby him (35,158).

Escape from a situation that gives rise to unhappiness is a common way of meeting it. Many adolescents run away from home, drop out of school, marry in the hope that they will find happiness that they have not found in their own homes, go to work so they can be financially independent and thus free from the restrictions their families place on them, or travel to faraway places, hoping to leave behind the reminders of their unhappiness. Escape into the daydream world is, perhaps, the most common form because it is easiest and requires the least courage. In the daydream world, the adolescent can have things just as he wants them, thus being happy so long as he remains shut away from the real world (19, 107,157,164).

Many adolescents are unhappy to the point of developing personality disorders (49, 105). However, personality disorders resulting from unhappiness in adolescence often appear to be worse than they later turn out to be (58). When unhappiness is intense, many adolescents talk about suicide; some threaten to commit suicide, and a few actually carry out their threats. In fact, many of the so-called "accidents" of adolescents are suicides. When suicide does occur in adolescence, it is generally impulsive and motivated by a desire to punish parents or others thought to be responsible for the adolescent's unhappiness. It may also be motivated by a desire to force those in authority to do what the adolescent wants them to do "or else." Girls more often threaten or attempt suicide, while boys more often carry through their threats and commit suicide (40,95,179,180).

success in making the transition

Some adolescents are successful in mastering the developmental tasks of adolescence before they reach the age of legal maturity, some lag behind the norm for their age level, and some never make the grade. As a result, they remain immature for the rest of their lives. The majority of American adolescents, especially those from middle- or upper-class homes, reach legal maturity with some "unfinished business" of adolescence which they eventually finish during the early years of adulthood. In commenting on the unfinished business the adolescent carries into adulthood, Jersild (98) has pointed out:

> The adolescent not only continues many tasks of life that he began in earlier years; he also leaves unfinished many tasks that are the business of adolescence but are carried over into adult life. There is something of the uncompleted work of adolescence in every adult. The big issues with which the adolescent strives—issues relating to his attitudes toward himself and others, issues pertaining to his relationship to authority, sex, responsibilities he should seek to carry or to shirk—are not completely settled just because he officially has finished the adolescent years. There are issues he must face as long as he lives. Even some of the issues that seem to have been settled—such as the choice of a vocation and even the choice of a mate—are not as completely settled as they seem to be.

For most adolescents, unfinished business is limited to certain of the developmental tasks, not to all of them. The ones that are finished are generally those which the individual is encouraged and helped to master; the unfinished ones, by contrast, have been particularly difficult or have been played down by parents as of little value (187).

Because of the high value the American culture of today places on popularity, most middle-class adolescents are encouraged to master the developmental tasks of learning how to get along with age-mates of both sexes. With the trend toward vocational specialization and the long period of training this requires, adolescents are encouraged at home or in school to select and prepare for an occupation. By contrast, they are given little training either in the home or the school in preparing for marriage and family life. Nor are they encouraged, in far too many homes, to achieve emotional independence of parents and other adults. Because preparing for a chosen life career often requires financial dependency, adolescents of both sexes are handicapped in achieving a socially approved masculine or feminine role in society (80).

Variations in Unfinished Business Boys, more often than girls, enter adulthood with attitudes and behavior patterns that conform to adult norms. They are not only encouraged to master the developmental tasks to prepare them for adulthood but they are given guidance and help in doing so. Just the opposite happens to girls. Middle- and upper-class adolescents of both sexes find it more difficult to achieve maturity than do those of the lower social classes; they are more overprotected and overindulged emotionally than are those from the lower classes.

In discussing the immaturity of behavior that is characteristic of teen-agers, Bernard has stressed that this is mainly found among adolescents of higher socioeconomic backgrounds. Adolescents in the civilian labor force, in the armed services, or who are married, are chronologically but not necessarily "teen-agers." She claims that (20):

They are neophytes in the adult culture of our society. They may share some aspects of teen-age culture, but, for the most part, they are expected to perform adult roles in adult dress. . . . Youngsters of the lower socioeconomic classes are in the teen-age culture only in their early teens. They are more likely than children of the higher socioeconomic class to enter the labor force or the armed forces or to get married soon after high school and, thus, to disappear into the adult world.

A large family makes "babying" of any child impossible. As a result, adolescents who have grown up in a large family, especially if they are among the oldest children of the family, tend on the whole to enter adulthood with a maturity of attitudes and behavior that suggest "completed business." In fact, many of them have mastered the developmental tasks of adolescence even before they reach legal maturity and have made their transition into adulthood before they are granted the status of adults (25).

Transition in Primitive Peoples Unfinished business would not be permitted among adolescents in primitive cultures. If it did occur, the disgrace to the adolescent and his family would be so great that the adolescent could never hope to be a respected member of the cultural group nor could his parents ever again hope to have the social esteem they formerly enjoyed. Unlike such civilized cultures as the American culture of today, most primitive cultures have firmly established social expectations of approved adult behavior. Every adolescent is then tested to see if he will come up to these expectations before the status of adulthood is granted him.

The testing of the adolescent occurs in the "puberty rites"—ceremonials in which the boy or girl is tested by the elders of the group in the activities they consider essential for him to have mastered successfully before they will grant him the status of adulthood. What these developmental tasks are varies from one cultural group to another and depends on what each group has found to be essential for success in adult living in that group. In a warlike tribe, for example, success in fighting is a more highly valued activity than success in hunting or fishing—tasks which are more highly valued in peace-loving tribes (127).

When parents know what will be expected of children, whether male or female, they begin to train them in the developmental tasks of their cultural group as soon as the children are capable of learning. Furthermore, knowing that they will be tested when they reach puberty to see how they have mastered these tasks, children have a strong motivation to master them. If they fail to do so, their unfinished business will not be unnoticed. Under such conditions, neither the child nor his parents can afford to let any unfinished business exist.

Few civilized cultures have any means of testing the readiness of the adolescent for adult status. When he reaches the chronological age that has been set for the transition into adulthood, whether it be 16 or 18 or 21, he is automatically granted the status of an adult. Under such conditions, the motivation on the part of the adolescent or of his parents to be prepared for adulthood is often weak. The result is that many adolescents in civilized cultures are neither trained nor motivated to master the developmental tasks the social group expects them to master. That is why they often carry unfinished business into adulthood (17,90,127,191).

Seriousness of Unfinished Business Even though the adolescent in civilized cultures is not submitted to a testing procedure similar to that of the pubescent child in a primitive culture, and even though the status of an adult is not withheld if he has not mastered the developmental tasks the cultural group expects, it does not mean that unfinished business is of no consequence. It is.

There are two reasons for this. First, the individual who is immature at adulthood has, more likely than not, been immature throughout adolescence. If he has been a late maturer and has not had either the environmental encouragement or the motivation to learn what his age-mates have learned, he has doubtless developed a feeling of personal inadequacy which has been expressed in one of two common ways, either by aggressive attempts to be allowed the status of his age-mates or by withdrawal tendencies which are expressed in working below his capacity in whatever he undertakes.

The second serious consequence of unfinished business at adulthood is that the habit of being immature may and often does become so strong that the individual continues to be immature throughout his adult life. Studies of adults at middle and old age have revealed that their pattern of adjustment is similar to that of their adolescent years. Those who made poor adjustments in adolescence, for example, continued to do so as adults (41,166,183).

At adolescence, the individual is at the "crossroads of life." Even before he reaches adulthood, he must make decisions as to which road he will take. Once the decision has been made, it is not always possible to change to another road. As Havighurst has pointed out, the adolescent "stands at the frontier of adulthood, with the happiness of a life time at stake" (78). If he does not take the right road—the road that will lead to behavior the social group expects of him —he will develop feelings of inadequacy which will color the pattern of his future adjustments. Should he, on the other hand, take the right road, he will be more acceptant of himself because the social group will be more acceptant of him (97,164).

Aids in Making the Transition Most adolescents will eventually make the transition from childhood to adulthood. But by doing so, they may develop psychological scars that will color their outlook on life throughout the adult years. If making the transition is more difficult and longer than necessary, the psychological damage will be mainly in the form of feelings of inadequacy. Even adolescents who make the transition without undue stress cannot hope to escape some of the psychological scars of feelings of inadequacy and unhappiness. These scars may be only temporary. But while they last, they will interfere with the achievement of the developmental tasks the social group imposes on the individual (187).

Left to his own devices, the adolescent is likely to employ a trial-and-error approach to mastering the developmental tasks essential to transition to adulthood. While he may learn from his mistakes, in doing so he wastes valuable time that might be spent in more constructive activities and he weakens his self-confidence and motivation to carry through with tasks that have proved to be difficult for him. In time, this may lead to a shunning of the difficult tasks and a concentration on the easier ones; thus he reaches adulthood with unfinished business in certain important areas (96,106).

As in all learning, guidance is valuable in learning the developmental tasks necessary for successful transition to adulthood. A clue to the value of guidance comes from studies of adolescents in many primitive cultures. Primitive parents, as has already been stressed, do not expect their children to make the transition into adulthood unaided. They know the demands of the social group are great and that failure to meet them may leave a life-long scar on their children's chances for happiness and success.

To avoid the possibility of failure, they guide their children in preparation for the tests they must pass in the puberty ceremonials before they will be granted the coveted status of adulthood. Instead of placing obstacles in the way of their children's learning, they guide and encourage their learning, thus building up confidence in their children that they can do what is expected of them. By so doing, they also eliminate the possibility of many failures their children might otherwise encounter if the learning were left to trial and error. As a result of this guidance, the unhappiness so characteristic of American adolescents is almost unheard of among adolescents of primitive cultures. In fact, adolescence is one of the happiest periods of their lives.

The more complex the culture, the more guidance the individual needs in meeting new demands. That guidance is essential if the transition is to be made successfully and with minimum psychological damage has been stressed by Anderson, "Our task with adolescents is to facilitate the movement from the security of childhood to the responsibility of adult life" (4).

This responsibility is not limited to parents; it is a responsibility that must be assumed by all who live or work with adolescents. Because the school plays such an important role in the American adolescent's life, the responsibility of the school in guiding the transition into adulthood is especially great. Frank has pointed out that the

guidance should be primarily in helping the individual adolescent with problems arising in the areas in which he, personally, has encountered difficulties. As he has commented (54):

> The schools should not try to prepare them for future living by specific instruction and training for tasks they will meet later, but help them to meet their present adolescent problems. . . . Here, as in all other ages, the best preparation for tomorrow is to live adequately today, to deal with today's requirements so as to be able to go forward without too much "unfinished business."

Because each adolescent has his own individual problems in making the transition from childhood into adulthood, no universal system of aid can hope to meet the needs of every adolescent adequately. This has been tried in the so-called "youth movements" in Italy under Mussolini, in Germany under Hitler, and more recently, in Russia and in Israel. In every case, the purpose was not to help the young people make the transition into adulthood so much as it was to indoctrinate them with a political philosophy in keeping with the philosophy of the government in power at the time. Furthermore, a planned program, meant for all adolescents of a cultural group without regard for individual differences "always runs the danger of subverting them in one direction and causing them to develop along too narrow lines" (90).

More in tune with democratic principles—principles that respect individual differences and the rights of the individual to develop along the lines that will bring him the greatest satisfaction—are suggestions for facilitating the transition of the American adolescent of today. These combine guidance with motivation on the adolescent's part to do his share of making the transition. Chapman (32) has suggested the following four principles which illustrate this democratic approach:

> 1 Couple a restriction with a privilege. This will motivate the adolescent to assume responsibility for his acts while, at the same time, emphasizing his responsibility to the social group.

2 *Couple a liberty with a responsibility.
When the adolescent learns that liberties
and responsibilities go hand-in-hand, it
will help to slow down his demands for
liberties until he is capable of handling
them successfully.*

3 *Couple a compliment with a criticism
and a criticism with a compliment. Too
many compliments may lead to cocky
self-confidence which will lessen the adolescent's motivation to conform to social
expectations while too few compliments
and too much criticism will weaken his
self-confidence and this, too, will lessen
his motivation. A wholesome balance between the two will, on the other hand,
increase his motivation to learn what society expects him to learn and will
strengthen his confidence in his ability to
do so.*

4 *Link the adolescent's demands with his
earning capacity. There is no quicker way
to motivate the adolescent to break his
ties of dependency and to develop patterns of independent thought and action
than to provide him with the motivation
needed to do what he is developmentally
ready to do.*

In summary, Chapman has suggested
"three basic L's" for making the transition
into adulthood easier and happier for the
adolescent, "Love, limitations, and let them
grow up."

BIBLIOGRAPHY

1 ADAMS, J. F.: Adolescent personal problems
as a function of age and sex. *J. genet.
Psychol.*, 1964, **104**, 207–214.

2 AMATORA, SISTER M.: Free expression of adolescents' interests. *Genet. Psychol. Monogr.*,
1957, **55**, 173–219.

3 AMOS, R. T., and R. M. WASHINGTON: A comparison of pupil and teacher perceptions of
pupil problems. *J. educ. Psychol.*, 1960, **51**,
255–258.

4 ANDERSON, J. E.: Behavior and personality.
In E. Ginzberg, *The nation's children*. New
York: Columbia, vol. 2, *Development and
Education*, 1960, pp. 43–69.

5 ANGELINO, H.: Developmental tasks and
problems of the middle adolescent period.
Education, 1955, **76**, 226–231.

6 ANGELINO, H., and E. V. MECH: "Fears and
worries" concerning physical changes: a preliminary survey of 32 females. *J. Psychol.*,
1955, **39**, 195–198.

7 AUSUBEL, D. P.: *Theory and problems of
adolescent development.* New York: Grune
& Stratton, 1954.

8 AUSUBEL, D. P.: Acculturative stress in modern Maori adolescence. *Child Develpm.*,
1960, **31**, 617–631.

9 BANHAM, K. M.: Obstinate children are
adaptable. *Ment. Hyg., N.Y.*, 1952, **36**, 84–
89.

10 BARCLAY, D.: The battle of the "ages."
The New York Times, Feb. 11, 1962.

11 BARNES, M. W.: The nature and nurture of
early adolescents. *Teach. Coll. Rec.*, 1956,
57, 513–521.

12 BARRETT-LENNARD, G. T.: The mature person. *Ment. Hyg., N.Y.*, 1962, **46**, 98–102.

13 BARSCHAK, E.: A study of happiness and unhappiness in childhood and adolescence of
girls of different cultures. *J. Psychol.*, 1951,
32, 175–215.

14 BARTLETT, C. J., and J. E. HORROCKS: A
study of the needs status of adolescents from
broken homes. *J. genet. Psychol.*, 1958, **93**,
153–159.

15 BEALER, R. C., F. K. WILLITS, and P. R.
MAIDA: The rebellious youth subculture—a
myth. *Children*, 1964, **11**, 42–48.

16 BELL, R. R., and J. V. BUERKLE: The daughter's role during the "launching stage." *Marriage fam. Living*, 1962, **24**, 384–388.

17 BENEDICT, R.: Continuities and discontinuities in cultural conditioning. *Psychiatry*,
1938, **1**, 161–167.

18 BERNARD, H. W.: *Adolescent development in
American culture.* New York: Harcourt,
Brace & World, 1957.

19 BERNARD, H. W.: *Human development in
western culture.* Boston: Allyn and Bacon,
1962.

20 BERNARD, J.: Teen-age culture: an overview.
Ann. Amer. Acad. pol. soc. Sci., 1961, **338**,
1–12.

21 BLOS, P.: Prolonged adolescence: the formulation of a syndrome and its therapeutic implications. *Amer. J. Orthopsychiat.*, 1954, **24**, 733–742.

22 BLOS, P.: *On adolescence*. New York: Free Press, 1962.

23 BOEHM, L.: The development of independence: a comparative study. *Child Develpm.*, 1957, **28**, 85–92.

24 BONSALL, M. R.: Introspections of gifted children. *Calif. J. educ. Res.*, 1960, **11**, 159–166.

25 BOSSARD, J. H. S., and E. S. BOLL: The *sociology of child development*. 3d ed. New York: Harper & Row, 1960.

26 BOYER, W. H.: A survey of the attitudes, opinions, and objectives of high school students in the Milwaukee area. *J. educ. Sociol.*, 1959, **32**, 344–348.

27 BROWN, D.: Helping teen-agers with their family living problems. *Marriage fam. Living*, 1959, **21**, 389–391.

28 BUCHER, C. A.: The atomic age strikes youth. *Education*, 1955, **76**, 203–205.

29 BURTON, W. H.: The preadolescent: rebel in our society. *Education*, 1955, **76**, 222–225.

30 CARLSON, H. B.: Psychiatric casualties in college. *Educ. Admin. Supervis.*, 1955, **41**, 270–276.

31 CARLSON, M. B., and E. T. SULLENGER: A study of certain areas in which high school youth desire counseling. *J. educ. Sociol.*, 1958, **31**, 179–182.

32 CHAPMAN, A. H.: On managing adolescents. *J. Amer. med. Ass.*, 1960, **174**, 1954–1957.

33 COBB, H. V.: Role-wishes and general wishes of children and adolescents. *Child Develpm.*, 1954, **25**, 161–171.

34 COLE, L., and I. N. HALL: *Psychology of adolescence*. 6th ed. New York: Holt, 1964.

35 COLLIER, R. M., and H. P. LAWRENCE: The adolescent feeling of psychological isolation. *Educ. Theory*, 1951, **1**, 106–115.

36 CORNELL, E. L., and C. M. ARMSTRONG: Forms of mental growth patterns revealed by reanalysis of the Harvard growth data. *Child Develpm.*, 1955, **26**, 169–204.

37 CRANE, A. R.: Stereotypes of the adult held by early adolescents. *J. educ. Res.* 1956, **50**, 227–230.

38 DALES, R. J.: A method for measuring developmental tasks: scales for selected tasks at the beginning of adolescence. *Child Develpm.*, 1955, **26**, 111–122.

39 DAVIE, J. S., and R. M. RUST: Personal problems of college students. *Ment. Hyg.*, N.Y., 1961, **45**, 247–257.

40 DESPERT, J. L.: Suicide and depression in children. *Nerv. Child*, 1952, **9**, 378–389.

41 DIXON, M. M.: Adolescent girls tell about themselves. *Marriage fam. Living*, 1958, **20**, 400–401.

42 DOUVAN, E.: Independence and identity in adolescence. *Children*, 1957, **4**, 186–190.

43 DOUVAN, E.: Sex differences in adolescent character processes. *Merrill-Palmer Quart.*, 1960, **6**, 203–211.

44 DUNBAR, F.: Homeostasis during puberty. *Amer. J. Psychiat.*, 1958, **114**, 673–682.

45 EISENSTADT, S. N.: Youth, culture and social structure in Israel. *Brit. J. Sociol.*, 1951, **2**, 105–121.

46 ENGLAND, R. W.: A theory of middle class juvenile delinquency. *J. crim. Law Criminol. police Sci.*, 1960, **50**, 535–540.

47 ENGLISH, H. B.: Chronological divisions of the life span. *J. educ. Psychol.*, 1957, **48**, 437–439.

48 EPSTEIN, R.: Social class membership and early childhood memories. *Child Develpm.*, 1963, **34**, 503–508.

49 ERIKSON, E. H.: Youth and the life cycle. *Children*, 1960, **7**, 43–49.

50 FARBER, M. L.: New Year's resolutions in England and the United States: implications for national character. *Psychol. Rep.*, 1957, **3**, 521–524.

51 FARWELL, G. T., and H. J. PETERS: Social-personal concerns: guidance implications. *Understanding the Child*, 1957, **26**, 110–112.

52 FORER, R.: The impact of a radio program on adolescents. *Publ. Opin. Quart.*, 1955, **19**, 184–194.

53 FRANK, L. K.: This is the adolescent. *Understanding the Child*, 1949, **18**, 65–69.

54 FRANK, L. K.: Personality development in adolescent girls. *Monogr. Soc. Res. Child Develpm.*, 1951, **16**, no. 53.

55 FRANK, L. K., and M. H. FRANK: *Your adolescent, at home and in school*. New York: Viking, 1956.

56 FRICK, W. B.: The adolescent dilemma: an interpretation. *Peabody J. Educ.*, 1955, **32**, 206.

57 FRIEDENBERG, E. Z.: *The vanishing adolescent.* Boston: Beacon Press, 1959.

58 GALLAGHER, J. R.: Various aspects of adolescence. *Yale J. biol. Med.*, 1950, **22**, 595–602.

59 GALLAGHER, J. R.: The doctor and other factors in adolescents' health and illnesses. *J. Pediat.*, 1961, **59**, 752–755.

60 GALLAGHER, J. R., and F. P. HEALD: Adolescence. *Pediatrics*, 1956, **18**, 119–125.

61 GARDNER, G. A.: The mental health of normal adolescents. *Ment. Hyg., N.Y.*, 1947, **31**, 529–540.

62 GARDNER, G. E.: Present-day society and the adolescent. *Amer. J. Orthopsychiat.*, 1957, **27**, 508–517.

63 GARN, S. M.: Growth and development. In E. Ginzberg, *The nation's children.* New York: Columbia, vol. 2, *Development and education*, 1960, pp. 24–42.

64 GARRISON, K. C.: Developmental tasks and problems of the late adolescent period. *Education*, 1955, **76**, 232–235.

65 GARRISON, K. C., and B. V. CUNNINGHAM: Personal problems of ninth grade pupils. *School Review*, 1952, **60**, 30–33.

66 GEIST, H.: Adolescents and parents talk it over. *Understanding the Child*, 1955, **24**, 98–102.

67 GESELL, A., F. L. ILG, and L. B. AMES: *Youth: the years from ten to sixteen.* New York: Harper & Row, 1956.

68 GOLDMAN, S.: Profile of an adolescent. *J. Psychol.*, 1962, **54**, 229–240.

69 GOTTLIEB, D., and C. RAMSEY: *The American adolescent.* Homewood, Ill.: Dorsey, 1964.

70 GRAMBS, J. D.: The community and the self-governing adolescent group. *J. educ. Sociol.*, 1956, **30**, 94–105.

71 GRINDER, R. E. (ed.): *Studies in adolescence: a book of readings.* New York: Macmillan, 1963.

72 HALL, G. S.: *Adolescence.* New York: Appleton-Century-Crofts, 1904.

73 HARRIS, D. B.: Life problems and interests of adolescents in 1935 and 1957. *School Review*, 1959, **67**, 335–459.

74 HARRIS, D. B.: Sex differences in the life problems and interests of adolescents, 1935 and 1957. *Child Develpm.*, 1959, **30**, 453–459.

75 HARRIS, D. B.: Work and the adolescent transition to maturity. *Teach. Coll. Rec.*, 1961, **63**, 146–153.

76 HATHAWAY, S. R., E. D. MONACHESI, and L. A. YOUNG: Rural-urban adolescent personality. *Rural Sociol.*, 1959, **24**, 331–346.

77 HAVIGHURST, R. J.: *Human development and education.* New York: Longmans, 1953.

78 HAVIGHURST, R. J.: Poised at the crossroads of life: suggestions to parents and teachers of young adolescents. *School Review*, 1953, **61**, 329–336.

79 HAVIGHURST, R. J.: *Studies of children and society in New Zealand.* Christ Church, N.Z.: Canterbury University College Publication, 1954.

80 HAVIGHURST, R. J.: Research on the developmental-task concept. *School Review*, 1956, **64**, 215–223.

81 HAVIGHURST, R. J., and K. FEIGENBAUM: Leisure and the life-style. *Amer. J. Sociol.*, 1959, **64**, 396–404.

82 HAYS, D. G., and J. W. M. ROTHNEY: Educational decision-making by superior secondary-school students and their parents. *Personnel Guid. J.*, 1961, **40**, 26–30.

83 HECHINGER, G., and F. M. HECHINGER: *Teen-age tyranny.* New York: Morrow, 1963.

84 HEMMING, J.: *Problems of adolescent girls.* London: Heinemann, 1960.

85 HESS, R. D., and I. GREENBLATT: The status of adolescents in American society: a problem in social identity. *Child Develpm.*, 1957, **28**, 459–468.

86 HILL, J. T.: Attitudes toward self: an experimental study. *J. educ. Sociol.*, 1957, **30**, 395–397.

87 HOLLINGWORTH, L. S.: *The psychology of the adolescent.* New York: Appleton-Century-Crofts, 1928.

88 HOLMAN, M.: Adolescent attitudes toward seeking help with personal problems. *Smith Coll. Stud. soc. Wk.*, 1955, **25**, 1–31.

89 HORROCKS, J. E.: What is adolescence? *Education*, 1955, **76**, 218–221.

90 HORROCKS, J. E.: *The psychology of adolescence.* 2d ed. Boston: Houghton Mifflin, 1962.

91 HOWARD, L. P.: Identity conflicts in adoles-

cent girls. *Smith Coll. Stud. soc. Wk.*, 1960, **31**, 1–21.

92 HSU, F. L. K., B. G. WATROUS, and E. M. LORD: Culture patterns and adolescent behavior. *Int. J. soc. Psychol.*, 1961, **7**, 33–53.

93 JACKSON, P. W.: Verbal solutions to parent-child problems. *Child Develpm.*, 1956, **27**, 339–349.

94 JACKSON, P. W., J. W. GETZELS, and G. A. XYDIS: Psychological health and cognitive functioning in adolescence: a multivariate analysis. *Child Develpm.*, 1960, **31**, 285–298.

95 JACOBZINER, H. J.: Attempted suicides in children. *J. Pediat.*, 1960, **65**, 519–525.

96 JENSEN, B. T.: Adolescence: implications for the teacher. *Education*, 1955, **76**, 239–241.

97 JERSILD, A. T.: Self-understanding in childhood and adolescence. *Amer. Psychologist*, 1951, **6**, 122–126.

98 JERSILD, A. T.: *The psychology of adolescence.* 2d. ed. New York: Macmillan, 1963.

99 JERSILD, A. T., and R. J. TASCH: *Children's interests and what they suggest for education.* New York: Teachers College, Columbia University, 1949.

100 JONES, H. E., and M. C. JONES: *Growth and behavior in adolescence.* Berkeley, Calif.: University of California Press, 1957.

101 JONES, M. C.: A comparison of the attitudes and interests of ninth-grade students over two decades. *J. educ. Psychol.*, 1960, **51**, 175–186.

102 JONES, W. R.: Affective tolerance and typical problems of married and unmarried college students. *Personnel Guid. J.*, 1958, **37**, 126–128.

103 JOSSELYN, I. M.: Psychological problems of the adolescent. *Soc. Casewk.*, 1951, **32**, 183–190.

104 JOSSELYN, I. M.: Social pressures in adolescence. *Soc. Casewk.*, 1952, **33**, 187–193.

105 JOSSELYN, I. M.: Psychological changes in adolescence. *Children*, 1959, **6**, 43–47.

106 KABACK, G. R.: An examination of teacher reaction to adolescent needs. *Education*, 1955, **76**, 242–245.

107 KAGAN, J., and H. A. MOSS: *Birth to maturity: a study in psychological development.* New York: Wiley, 1962.

108 KELLEY, E. C.: *In defense of youth.* Englewood Cliffs, N. J.: Prentice-Hall, 1962.

109 KENISTON, K.: Alienation and the decline of Utopia. *Amer. Scholar*, 1960, **29**, 161–200.

110 KIRKPATRICK, M. E.: The mental hygiene of adolescence in the Anglo-American culture. *Ment. Hyg., N.Y.*, 1952, **36**, 394–403.

111 KOGAN, N.: A study of young students in college. *J. counsel. Psychol.*, 1955, **2**, 129–136.

112 KUHLEN, R. G.: *The psychology of adolescent development.* 2d ed. New York: Harper & Row, 1963.

113 KUHLEN, R. G., and H. S. BRETSCH: Sociometric status and personal problems of adolescents. *Sociometry*, 1947, **10**, 122–132.

114 LANDIS, P. H.: The ordering and forbidding technique and teen-age adjustment. *Sch. Soc.*, 1954, **80**, 105–106.

115 LANE, H.: The meaning of disorder among youth. *Education*, 1955, **76**, 214–217.

116 LANE, R. S., and R. F. L. LOGAN: The adolescent at work. *Practitioner*, 1949, **162**, 287–298.

117 LANGWORTHY, R. C.: Community status and influence in high school. *Amer. sociol. Rev.*, 1959, **24**, 537–539.

118 LARSON, J. L.: Implications of adolescent problems for the school administrator. *Education*, 1955, **76**, 236–238.

119 LEVINSON, B. M.: The problems of Jewish religious youth. *Genet. Psychol. Monogr.*, 1959, **60**, 309–348.

120 LIMBERT, P. H.: New light on the needs of adolescents. *Relig. Educ.*, 1950, **45**, 287–291.

121 LLOYD-JONES, E.: Women today and their education. *Teach. Coll. Rec.*, 1955, **57**, 1–7.

122 LORAND, A. S., and H. L. SCHNEER (eds.): *Adolescents.* New York: Harper & Row, 1961.

123 LUCAS, C. M., and J. E. HORROCKS: An experimental approach to the analysis of adolescent needs. *Child Develpm.*, 1960, **31**, 479–487.

124 LUCHINS, A. S.: On the theories and problems of adolescence. *J. genet. Psychol.*, 1954, **85**, 47–63.

125 MATLOCK, J. R.: Counseling as students see it. *J. nat. Ass. Deans Women*, 1954, **18**, 7–12.

126 MC CLUSKY, H. Y.: The status of youth in our culture. *Education*, 1955, **76**, 206–209.

127 MEAD, M.: *Male and female*. New York: Morrow, 1952.

128 MEISSNER, W. W.: Some anxiety indications in the adolescent boy. *J. gen. Psychol.*, 1961, **64**, 251–257.

129 MELTZER, H.: Age and sex differences in workers' perceptions of happiness for self and others. *J. genet. Psychol.*, 1964, **105**, 1–11.

130 MOHR, G. H., and M. A. DESPRES: *The stormy decade: adolescence*. New York: Random House, 1958.

131 MUSSEN, P. H., and M. C. JONES: Self-conceptions, motivations, and interpersonal attitudes of late- and early-maturing boys. *Child Develpm.*, 1957, **28**, 243–256.

132 MUUSS, R. E.: *Theories of adolescence*. New York: Random House, 1962.

133 PATTIE, F. A., and S. CORNETT: Unpleasantness of early memories and maladjustment of children. *J. Pers.*, 1952, **20**, 315–321.

134 PELTZ, W. L., and M. GOLDBERG: A dynamic factor in group work with post-adolescents and its effect on the role of the leader. *Ment. Hyg., N.Y.*, 1959, **43**, 71–75.

135 PITT, W. J.: Psychological aspects of adolescence. *J. soc. Hyg.*, 1954, **40**, 226–231.

136 POMEROY, W. B.: An analysis of questions on sex. *Psychol. Rec.*, 1960, **10**, 191–201.

137 POWELL, M.: Age and sex differences in degree of conflict within certain areas of psychological adjustment. *Psychol. Monogr.*, 1955, **69**, No. 2.

138 PRESSEY, S. L., and R. G. KUHLEN: *Psychological development through the life span*. New York: Harper & Row, 1957.

139 RADKE-YARROW, M.: Problems of methods in parent-child research. *Child Develpm.*, 1963, **34**, 215–226.

140 RAINES, G. N.: Adolescence: pattern for the future. *Geriatrics*, 1956, **11**, 159–162.

141 REMMERS, H. H.: Cross-cultural studies of teenagers' problems. *J. educ. Psychol.*, 1962, **53**, 254–261.

142 REMMERS, H. H., and D. H. RADLER: *The American teenager*. Indianapolis: Bobbs-Merrill, 1957.

143 REMMERS, H. H., and L. M. SPENCER: All young people have problems. *J. nat. Educ. Ass.*, 1950, **39**, 182–183.

144 RESNICK, J.: Toward understanding adolescent behavior. *Peabody J. Educ.*, 1953, **30**, 205–208.

145 ROGERS, D.: *The psychology of adolescence*. New York: Appleton-Century-Crofts, 1962.

146 ROSE, A. M.: Parental models for youth. *Sociol. soc. Res.*, 1955, **40**, 3–9.

147 ROSE, A. M.: Acceptance of adult roles and separation from family. *Marriage fam. Living*, 1959, **21**, 120–126.

148 ROSENTHAL, I.: Reliability of retrospective reports of adolescence. *J. consult. Psychol.*, 1963, **27**, 189–198.

149 ROUCEK, J. S.: Age as a prestige factor. *Sociol. soc. Res.*, 1958, **42**, 349–352.

150 RUBÉ, P.: Adolescence: 1. Is there a problem of adolescence? *Amer. J. Psychother.*, 1955, **9**, 503–509.

151 RUST, R. E., and J. S. DAVIE: The personal problems of college students. *Ment. Hyg., N.Y.*, 1961, **45**, 247–257.

152 SCALES, E. E., and P. W. HUTSON: How gainful employment affects the accomplishment of developmental tasks of adolescent boys. *School Review*, 1955, **63**, 31–37.

153 SCHNEIDERS, A. A.: *Personality development and adjustment in adolescence*. Milwaukee: Bruce, 1960.

154 SCHOEPPE, A.: Implications of adolescent problems for teacher-training programs. *Education*, 1955, **76**, 253–256.

155 SCHOEPPE, A., and R. J. HAVIGHURST: A validation of development and adjustment hypotheses of adolescence. *J. educ. Psychol.*, 1952, **43**, 339–353.

156 SCHUTZ, R. E.: Patterns of personal problems of adolescent girls. *J. educ. Psychol.*, 1958, **49**, 1–5.

157 SEIDMAN, J. M. (ed.): *The adolescent: a book of readings*. Rev. ed. New York: Holt, 1960.

158 SHAFFER, L. F., and E. J. SHOBEN: *The psychology of adjustment*. 2d. ed. Boston: Houghton Mifflin, 1956.

159 SIMPSON, R. L., and I. H. SIMPSON: The school, the peer group, and adolescent development. *J. educ. Sociol.*, 1958, **32**, 37–41.

160 SLATON, T. F.: *Dynamics of adolescent adjustment*. New York: Macmillan, 1963.

161 SMITH, E. A.: *American youth culture*. New York: Free Press, 1962.

162 SMITH, P. M.: Problems of rural and urban

Southern Negro children. *Personnel Guid. J.*, 1961, **39**, 599–600.

163 SORENSON, R.: Youth's need for challenge and place in society. *Children*, 1962, **9**, 131–138.

164 SPIVACK, S. S.: A study of a method for appraising self-acceptance and self-rejection. *J. genet. Psychol.*, 1956, **88**, 183–202.

165 STERN, H. H.: A follow-up study of adolescents' views on their personal and vocational future. *Brit. J. educ. Psychol.*, 1961, **31**, 170–182.

166 STEWART, L. H.: Social and emotional adjustment during adolescence as related to the development of psychosomatic illness in adulthood. *Genet. Psychol. Monogr.*, 1962, **65**, 175–215.

167 STIER, L. D.: Adolescents and other Western cultures. *J. second. Educ.*, 1961, **36**, 398–405.

168 STONE, L. J., and J. CHURCH: *Childhood and adolescence.* New York: Random House, 1957.

169 STRANG, R.: How children and adolescents view their world. *Ment. Hyg., N.Y.*, 1954, **38**, 28–33.

170 STRANG, R.: Adolescents' views on one aspect of their development. *J. educ. Psychol.*, 1955, **46**, 423–432.

171 STRANG, R.: Gifted adolescents' views on growing up. *Except. Children*, 1956, **23**, 10–15, 20.

172 STRANG, R.: *The adolescent views himself.* New York: McGraw-Hill, 1957.

173 SUPER, D. E.: Dimensions and measurement of vocational maturity. *Teach. Coll. Rec.*, 1955, **57**, 151–163.

174 SUTTON-SMITH, B., B. G. ROSENBERG, and E. F. MORGAN: Historical changes in the freedom with which children express themselves on personality inventories. *J. genet. Psychol.*, 1961, **99**, 309–315.

175 SYMONDS, P. M.: Implications for the counselor. *Education*, 1955, **76**, 246–248.

176 SYMONDS, P. M., and A. R. JENSEN: *From adolescent to adult.* New York: Columbia, 1961.

177 TATE, M. T., and V. A. MUSICK: Adjustment problems of college students. *Soc. Forces*, 1954, **33**, 182–185.

178 THRESSELT, M. E.: The adolescent becomes a social person. *J. soc. Hyg.*, 1954, **40**, 130–134.

179 TOOLAN, J. M.: Suicide and suicidal attempts in children and adolescents. *Amer. J. Psychiat.*, 1962, **118**, 719–724.

180 TUCKMAN, J., and H. E. CONNON: Attempted suicide in adolescents. *Amer. J. Psychiat.*, 1962, **119**, 228–232.

181 TUCKMAN, J., and I. LORGE: Perceptual stereotypes about life adjustments. *J. soc. Psychol.*, 1956, **43**, 239–245.

182 TUDDENHAM, R. D.: Constancy of personal morale over a fifteen-year interval. *Child Develpm.*, 1962, **33**, 663–673.

183 TYLER, F. H.: Stability of intra-individual patterning of measures of adjustment during adolescence. *J. educ. Psychol.*, 1957, **48**, 217–226.

184 WALL, W. D.: Happiness and unhappiness in childhood and adolescence of a group of women students. *Brit. J. Psychol.*, 1948, **39**, 191–208.

185 WALTERS, J., F. I. STROMBERG, and G. LONIAN: Perceptions concerning development of responsibility in young children. *Elem. Sch. J.*, 1957, **57**, 209–216.

186 WATERS, E. W.: Problems of rural Negro high school seniors on the Eastern shore of Maryland: a consideration for guidance. *J. Negro Educ.*, 1953, **22**, 115–125.

187 WATSON, W. C.: Helping adolescents to achieve maturity. *Chicago Sch. J.*, 1963, **44**, 209–216.

188 WATTENBERG, W. W.: *The adolescent years.* New York: Harcourt, Brace & World, 1955.

189 WESTLEY, W. A., and F. ELKIN: The protective environment and adolescent socialization. *Soc. Forces*, 1957, **35**, 243–249.

190 WHEELER, D. K.: Expressed wishes of students. *J. genet. Psychol.*, 1963, **102**, 75–81.

191 WHITING, J. W. M., and I. L. CHILD: *Child training and personality: a cross cultural study.* New Haven, Conn.: Yale, 1953.

192 WILLIAMS, C. D.: College students' family problems. *J. Home Econ.*, 1950, **42**, 179–181.

193 WILSON, F. M.: The best in life at every age. *Ment. Hyg., N.Y.*, 1955, **39**, 483–488.

194 WITHEY, S. B.: What boys see as their problems. *Education*, 1955, **76**, 210–213.

195 WRIGHT, J. C., and B. B. SCARBOROUGH: Re-

lationship of the interests of college freshmen to their interests as sophomores and as seniors. *Educ. psychol. Measmt.*, 1958, **18**, 153–158.

196 ZACHRY, C. B.: Customary stresses and strains of adolescence. *Ann. Amer. Acad. pol. soc. Sci.*, 1944, **236**, 136–144.

197 ZELIGS, R.: Trends in children's New Year's resolutions. *J. exp. Educ.*, 1957, **26**, 133–150.

CHAPTER 2

the
changed
body

In no area is the transition from childhood to adulthood more readily apparent than in the individual's appearance. In a relatively short time, the child's body changes on the exterior and interior into that of an adult. The exterior change is often so radical that the adolescent may not be recognized at first glance by those who have not seen him recently. The changes that take place within the body—in the size, shape, and functioning of the different organs and glands—are not visible, but are equally as marked.

Throughout the adolescent years, these physical changes are taking place. However, the major part of the changes comes in the early part of adolescence—the puberty phase. "Puberty," from the Latin word *pubertas*, meaning "age of manhood," is the time when the reproductive organs mature and begin to function. The word "phase" suggests that the transition from child to adult, from an asexual to sexual body, occurs in a relatively short time. Accompanying the changes in the reproductive organs are changes in the rest of the body; these, in turn, lead to changes in interests, attitudes, and behavior. Physical development continues after sexual maturity has been attained, but at a progressively slower rate; consequently, it will lead to less pronounced psychological and behavioral changes (37).

early recognition of puberty

Among primitive peoples, there is almost universal recognition of the fact that at predictable ages, the body of the boy or girl will change into that of a man or woman. There is also awareness of the behavioral changes that accompany the physical changes. Consequently, it has become customary to expect certain patterns of behavior when the child has been transformed into an adult in appearance and to test him in order to see if the social expectations have been fulfilled (157).

The first recorded reports of puberty changes go back to the days of Aristotle. In his *Historia animalium* Aristotle refers to the fact that when boys are "twice seven years old," they begin to "engender seed." With this change comes the appearance of hair on the pubes; the voice alters, getting harsher, more uneven, and of a somewhat shrill tone. Girls at the same age experience the first menstrual flow. When this occurs, Aristotle said, the breasts have, in the majority of cases, swelled to the height of two fingers' breath. At this time, the girl's voice changes to a deeper tone. Aristotle noted also that behavioral changes accompany these changed physiological states. He mentioned among other behavioral changes the tendencies to be ardent, irritable, passionate, and sanguine. Girls at this age, according to Aristotle, are in need of constant surveillance because of their developing sex impulses.

This early recognition of the effects of a changed body on attitudes and behavior

has been borne out by scientific studies. When changes are rapid, the individual cannot make adequate adjustments to them and, as a result, is confused and insecure. Bühler, who has labeled this period of adolescence the "negative phase," has helped to focus scientific attention on the marked behavioral changes that come with sexual maturing (26). These changes are, for the most part, unfavorable and are expressed in confusion, feelings of insecurity, and "anti" attitudes toward life. They lead to poor personal and social adjustments. This is a time of "predictabilities and unpredictabilities," a time when no one, not even the young person himself, knows what he will say or do next (143). Generally, however, the worst of the negative-phase behavior is over when girls become sexually mature, at the time of the "menarche," or first menstruation. The same holds true for boys when their sex organs reach a level of functional maturity.

age of puberty

Puberty begins with the beginning of the transformation of the child's body into an adult's and ends when the transformation has been completed. It is an overlapping period in the sense that part of puberty occurs in the later years of childhood and part, in the early years of adolescence. A child is considered a "child" until he is sexually mature; he is then called an "adolescent."

Among primitive peoples and even among civilized peoples in earlier times, puberty and adolescence were synonymous. When the child had been transformed physically into an adult, it was assumed that he was also transformed psychologically. The more complex the culture, the longer the time needed to learn to think, act, and feel like an adult; consequently, the transitional period for psychological maturity has been lengthened. As a result, adolescence today is a longer period in the life span of the human child than it was in the past, extending several years beyond the end of puberty.

Criteria of Sexual Maturity To be able to determine the age of puberty, one must have reasonably accurate criteria to tell when the transformation of the body begins, when it has been completed, and when the child has become sexually mature. At the present time, the most dependable single criterion of sexual maturity in boys and girls is the assessment of the state of their *bone development* by means of X rays. Studies of boys and girls have revealed that genital growth always occurs at a certain point in the bone development of the individual. X rays of the long bones of the hands and knees, taken at different times during the preadolescent growth spurt, make it possible to determine just when puberty begins and at what rate it is progressing. The maturity determiners in the bones are successive changes in the outline of the shaft ends and in the contour of epiphysical ossification centers (see Figure 2–1). Some years before puberty, X rays of the hand will distinguish children who will mature early from those whose maturation will be delayed (79,88).

Among girls, the menarche, or first menstruation, has been used for centuries as the best single criterion of sexual maturity. Scientific studies have shown that the menarche comes at neither the beginning nor at the end of the period of physical changes taking place at puberty. Instead, the menarche may be regarded as the midpoint of puberty. This is justified by evidence that there is a period of "adolescent sterility" following the menarche. This period lasts for 6 months or longer when the time between menstrual periods ranges from 2 to 6 months and when "ovulation," or the ripening and release of a ripe ovum from a follicle in the ovary, does not occur. This is evidence that sexual maturing has not been completed (119,154).

Among boys, the first "nocturnal emission," or "wet dream," has been popularly used as a criterion of the boy's sexual maturity. During sleep, the penis sometimes becomes erect and "semen," or fluid containing sperm cells, spurts out. This is the normal way for the male reproductive organ to rid itself of excessive amounts of

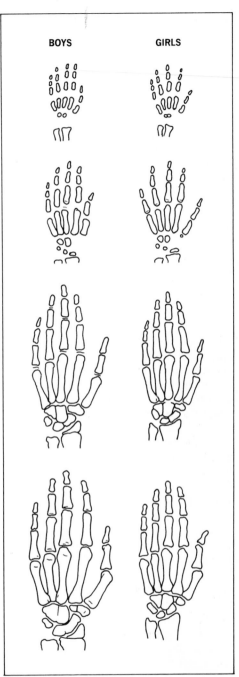

FIGURE 2–1 Ossification of the hand and wrist bones is used as a criterion of sexual maturity. (Based on unpublished material of N. Bayley. Adapted from F. K. Shuttleworth: The adolescent period: a graphic atlas. *Monogr. Soc. Res. Child Develpm.*, 1949, **14**, no. 1. Used by permission.)

semen. However, nocturnal emissions have been found to occur after some pubertal development has taken place and therefore cannot be used as a criterion of the onset of puberty. Furthermore, not all boys experience this phenomenon, or not all recognize it as such (118).

Stages in Puberty Development The puberty phase is usually divided into three subdivisions: (1) the "prepubescent," or immature, stage when bodily changes are taking place, when the secondary sex characteristics, or physical features that distinguish the two sexes, are beginning to develop, but the reproductive function is not yet developed; (2) the "pubescent," or maturing, stage when sex cells are produced in the sex organs but the bodily changes are not yet complete; and (3) the "postpubescent," or mature, stage in which the sex organs are functioning in a mature way, the body has attained its adult height and proportions, and the secondary sex characteristics are well developed (231).

At the present time, approximately 50 percent of all American girls are sexually mature or pubescent between the ages of 12.5 and 14.5 years, with an average of 13 years for girls of the middle and upper socioeconomic groups and 13.5 for girls of the lower groups. Boys, on the average, mature approximately a year later than girls. Thus, the average age for sexual maturing in boys falls between 14 and 15.5 years, with an average age of 14.5 years. The other 50 percent of boys and girls are about equally distributed between ages below and above the averages. Those who mature earlier than the average are known as "early maturers"; those who mature later than the average are called "late maturers" (15,155,165,169). Figure 2–2 shows the distribution of age of maturing for boys and girls.

Differences between the sexes are especially marked between the ages of 12 and 14 years, when there are many more mature girls than there are mature boys. This difference shows itself not only in the larger and more mature bodies of girls but also in their more mature, more aggressive, and more sex-conscious behavior. Furthermore, differences in ages of maturing within a sex group cause many social problems for several years. This occurs during the junior and early senior high school ages. These problems cause trouble for the teacher and for the students, thus resulting in poorer quality of work and more disciplinary problems than usual.

Variations in the Ages of Maturing As Johnston has pointed out, "The time clock that governs the developmental process in children is an individual one" (105). Variations in age of sexual maturing are due to variations in the functioning of the *endocrine glands* which are responsible for the transformation of the child's body. Functioning of the endocrine glands, in turn, is influenced by a hereditary factor as well as by intelligence, general health conditions, and emotional tension. Thus, no one factor alone is responsible for the age of sexual maturing (29,65).

Age of maturing seems to "run in the family," thus showing the influence of *heredity*. Mothers, for example, who menstruated early tend to have daughters who menstruate early while mothers who were late maturers tend to have late-maturing daughters. A definite relationship between the age of the menarche in sisters has also been reported (124,178). Age of sexual maturity is likewise influenced by level of *intelligence*. Children of superior intelligence mature sexually earlier than those of average intelligence. The greater the degree of mental deficiency, the greater the retardation in sexual development (159,214).

Good health, due to good prenatal and postnatal care and good nutrition, results in earlier maturing among boys and girls of today than in the past. Better health conditions are greatly influenced by *nutrition.* A predominately protein diet, more characteristic of children of the higher than of the lower socioeconomic groups, leads to early maturing while a predominately carbohydrate diet, usually found in the lower socioeconomic groups, leads to late maturing (65,119,122).

Because health is influenced by care as well as by nutrition, it is not surprising that children from *urban* environments, where there are better medical and child-care facilities, mature earlier than children from rural environments. Furthermore, because of differences in medical care and nutrition, children from poor *home backgrounds* mature later and are more variable as a group in the age at which they mature than children from well-to-do homes (29,155,169, 231). The later sexual maturing of boys and girls from the Tropical and Arctic zones may be due more to nutritional and care factors than to *climatic conditions,* as was formerly believed (56,64,119,153).

Body size in childhood has a tremendous influence on the age at which boys and girls become sexually mature. Children who are taller and fatter than their age-mates are more advanced in physical maturity, and thus reach the age of sexual maturity earlier. They are also more advanced in their bone development. Obese children reach puberty about a year earlier than the average (122,228). By contrast, children from less well-nourished families are small in childhood, their physical and osseous development is delayed, and they are later than the average in reaching sexual maturity. Because of the close relationship between body size and age of maturing, it is understandable that children from the better *socioeconomic* groups would, on the average, reach sexual maturity sooner than children of the poorer groups where both nutrition and physical care are less favorable (48,65, 73,104,231).

Body build has as much influence on age of maturity as does body size. Children with feminine-type bodies (broad hips and short legs), tend to be early maturers while those with masculine-type bodies (broad shoulders and long legs) tend to be late maturers (87,122). Children who are predominantly ectomorphic (tall and slender) are usually late maturers and there is little variation in the age at which they mature. By contrast, mesomorphs (persons with a muscular build) tend to be early maturers, though they are more variable in the age at which they mature than are the ectomorphs. The two types that are most variable of all are, first, the endomorphs (short,

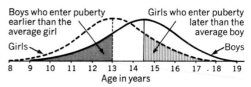

stocky build), and second, the deviant maturers (those who are either markedly early or late in maturing as compared with the average) (15,22,98,103,136,231).

Race was formerly believed to have a marked influence on the age of sexual maturity with white children reaching puberty earlier than children of other racial groups. However, more recent studies have contrasted the age of puberty in groups where comparable health, nutrition, and medical care existed. As a result of control over these variables, it is now questionable whether there are racial differences in age of puberty. When differences do exist, they are more likely to be due to socioeconomic factors than to race per se (94,95,211).

Effect on Body Development The pattern of development differs according to whether the child matures earlier or later than the average age for his sex group or at approximately the average age. In the late maturer, growth is usually irregular and asymmetrical, with growth of the body dimensions and of the internal organs lagging behind growth in stature. This is in direct contrast to the early maturer whose growth is more regular and there is less organic imbalance. The ultimate size of late maturers does not show as extreme differences as it did in late childhood when late maturers seemed to be abnormally small (207).

Age of maturing affects the pattern of development of different body tissues as well as the pattern of development of body dimensions. Early-maturing girls, for example, are larger than late-maturing girls in total breadth of calf and in the breadths of fat, muscle, and bone within the calf. The same difference is shown in boys who mature early, though to a lesser degree than in girls (179).

time needed for maturing

Children's bodies are not transformed into adult bodies overnight. In fact, it takes much longer than most adults realize to make the change. For the pubescent child or the young adolescent, it sometimes seems that the time is interminable. There are such marked variations in the time needed for the transformation that it is impossible to give an exact estimate of how long it will take. Approximately 1 to 2 years are needed for the preliminary changes from an asexual to a sexual state, during which time changes in preparation for sexual maturity are taking place throughout the body (231). After the sex organs have reached a point in their development where they begin to function, another year or two will be required to complete their development and the changes throughout the entire body which accompany maturity of the sex organs. This means that the average child requires from 2 to 4 years to make the transition. However, some children require less than the average time just as others require more than the average. Those who require less than the average are known as "rapid maturers"; those who require more are called "slow maturers" (15,16,100,204).

Variations in Rate Certain patterns are characteristic of the maturing of members of both *sexes*. Girls require on the average 3 years to mature and they do so more or less uniformly. Boys, on the other hand, are far less uniform in the way they develop. They require from 2 to 4 years to complete the process, with more taking a longer time than girls. However, within each sex group there are marked individual variations. The age at which the child matures likewise influences the time needed for maturing. Once they get started, late maturers develop more rapidly than either the early maturers or those who mature at the average age. On the other hand, early maturers need more time than the average or the late maturers

to complete their development. As a rule, late and rapid maturing go hand in hand, and early and slow. There are, however, many exceptions to this rule (16,100,172).

The *body build* of the child affects the rate of maturing. Those of rugged muscular build and those who are fat are usually rapid maturers; those with finely and delicately constructed physiques tend to be the slow maturers (4). Mesomorphs usually mature at the average rate, endomorphs at a slow rate, and ectomorphs at a rapid rate. However, mesomorphs have a far wider range of maturational rate than ectomorphs and endomorphs, both of whom are more homogeneous in their rates of maturing (22,98, 136).

Effect on Development The pattern of development at puberty is markedly influenced by the speed at which the development takes place. The rapid maturers have greater spurts of rapid growth; their periods of acceleration and of stopping come abruptly; and they attain adult proportions very quickly. The sex organs and secondary sex characteristics develop early, and the osseous development is accelerated.

Slow maturers, by contrast, have less intense periods of acceleration; their growth is more even and gradual; and it continues for a longer time. The sex organs and secondary sex characteristics develop at a slower rate than in the average maturer, thus reaching their mature level later. The osseous development is also later. At maturity, the slow maturers are usually larger than the rapid maturers (16,73,150,207,210).

causes of puberty changes

For centuries the exact cause of sexual maturation was completely unknown. Aristotle referred to the fact that the physical changes of puberty in boys were dependent upon some activity of the testes because, when boys were castrated, their voices remained high-pitched and pubertal hair did not appear. People knew that, in some mysterious manner, the bodies of little boys and girls began to change. But what lay back of these changes and how it happened that they occurred in such a regular, predictable manner were questions for which no answer had been discovered.

In recent years a partial answer to the mystery of sexual maturation has come from the research work of endocrinologists who have discovered that a close relationship exists between the pituitary gland, located at the base of the brain, and the gonads, or sex glands.

Role of the Pituitary The anterior lobe of the pituitary gland produces two hormones, which are closely related to puberty development. These two hormones are the *growth* hormone, which is an influential factor in determining the size of the individual, especially of the limbs, and the gonad-stimulating, or *gonadotropic*, hormone, which, when acting on the gonads, stimulates them to increased activity.

There is evidence that just before puberty there is a gradual increase in the gonadotropic hormone. At the same time there is an increasing sensitivity of the gonads to this hormone. The combination of these two conditions initiates puberty. What in turn is responsible for the increased supply of the gonadotropic hormone or the increased sensitivity of the gonads to this hormone, at the more or less predictable age at which puberty changes occur, has not yet been fully explained. Some hereditary factor is unquestionably at work.

Role of the Gonads The gonads, the second of the endocrine glands to play an active role in bringing about puberty changes, are the sex glands. The female gonads are called the "ovaries," and the male, the "testes." Just before puberty the gonadotropic hormone from the pituitary gland is produced in sufficient quantity to cause the immature gonads of boys and girls to grow and develop into mature testes and ovaries. With their development comes the production of germ cells, as well as hormones that bring about sex changes in the growth and development of the *genital organs* and *secondary sex characteristics*.

As the ovaries develop, their primary function is to produce germ cells, called "ova," for the perpetuation of the race. In addition to this, they produce two regulatory hormones, "theelin" and "progestin," which initiate and bring to completion the period of pregnancy. At puberty two internal secretions are produced, the "follicular" hormone and that of the *corpus luteum*. The sex hormones in the girl stimulate breast development, which results from the growth of the mammary glands. Likewise, changes occur in the reproductive organs, such as the development of the uterus, the Fallopian tubes, and the vagina. Accompanying these changes comes cyclic menstrual bleeding or menstruation. In addition to these developments there is the development of the secondary sex characteristics of the female body.

The male gonads, or testes, like the female ovaries, are stimulated to development at puberty by the gonadotropic hormone. The testes have a dual function. They produce "spermatozoa," or sex cells, which are needed for reproduction, and they produce one or more hormones that control the physical and psychological adjustments necessary in the carrying out of the reproductive function. The physical adjustment includes the development of secondary sex characteristics, as well as the testes themselves, the prostate gland, the seminal vesicles, and the penis.

Interaction of Gonads and Pituitary After the gonadal sex hormones are stimulated by hormones from the pituitary gland, they in turn act on the pituitary and cause a gradual reduction in the amount or the effectiveness of the growth hormone. The gonadal sex hormones eventually stop the action of the growth hormone completely. If there has not been enough of the growth hormone in late childhood and early puberty, the individual's growth will be arrested and he will be below average in height. If, on the other hand, production of the gonad hormones in adequate quantity is delayed, the individual's growth continues for too long and his body, especially his limbs, becomes too large. It is thus obvious that the pituitary gland and the gonads must function in a reciprocal manner, with properly timed action on the part of both, if growth is to be normal (119,158,169,187).

Abnormal Functioning An inadequate supply of gonadal hormones *delays puberty* and prevents normal development of the sex organs and of the secondary sex characteristics. In delayed puberty, the secondary sex characteristics in girls are normal but the uterus is small and undeveloped. Boys are somewhat effeminate in appearance, while girls tend to be somewhat masculine in their looks and ways. They usually have a childish appearance and often seem immature (183,187).

Accelerated puberty known as "puberty precox," comes from an excessive supply of the gonadotropic hormone during the early years of childhood. This, in turn, affects the gonads, and the individual matures too soon, even to the production of spermatozoa and ova. While there is no evidence, to date, of what causes the excessive supply of gonadotropic hormone at an early age, there is evidence that it is not caused by inheritance (116).

Medical records of puberty precox have given a picture of what effects precocious puberty has on the mental and physical development of the individual. Height and weight approximate the "adolescent spurt," only at an abnormally early age. By the time the individual reaches maximum growth in height, his pubic hair has assumed adult characteristics. The appearance of axillary and facial hair is delayed. Facial growth is on an infantile level. The teeth and central nervous system are the least advanced in the maturation of all bodily systems. The individual's mental age is near the level for his chronological age. There is also no indication of pubescent personality and behavior. There is, thus, evidence that individuals who experience precocious puberty do not pass though a normal puberty. They do not start to walk at an earlier age than those whose development is normal, though their strength is superior to that of individuals whose development follows a normal pattern. In puberty precox, there is no evidence of a premature drive to heterosexual behavior, a fact which suggests that this drive comes more from learning than from increased gonadal hormone secretion (57, 173,187,192).

physical transformation at puberty

The child's body is not transformed into an adult body all at one time or at the same rate in all areas. Because the entire body, both externally and internally, is changed, a convenient classification of the changes can be made by subdividing them into four major categories: growth in body size, changes in body proportions, development of the primary sex characteristics, and development of the secondary sex characteristics. While there are marked individual differences in the rate of the changes, the pattern of the changes is similar for all children and, hence, predictable.

GROWTH IN BODY SIZE

At puberty, there is a growth spurt during which time the body grows to its adult size. While there may be an addition of weight with advancing age, the *normal* weight for the body height and build is achieved during the puberty growth spurt. Puberty is one of the two periods of accelerated growth during the human life span. The first occurs during the 9 calendar months of prenatal life and in the first 6 postnatal months. From then until 6 months to a year before pubescence sets in, growth is slow and relatively regular.

With the beginning of changes in the sex organs comes the second period of accelerated growth. And like the first, this second growth spurt is relatively short in duration. It lasts for a year or two before the sex organs become functionally mature and for 6 months to a year after that. This is commonly referred to as the "adolescent growth spurt." However, because the most rapid growth occurs in the preadolescent period, it more correctly should be called the "preadolescent growth spurt."

The growth spurt for girls begins between the ages of 8.5 and 11.5 years, with a peak of rapidity in growth occurring, on the average, at 12.5 years. After this, the rate declines until it gradually comes to a standstill between 15 and 16 years. Boys have a similar pattern of rapid growth, but they start later and grow for a longer time than girls. The average pattern is a beginning of the spurt between 10.5 and 14.5 years, with a peak of rapidity around 14.5 years, then a gradual decline until 17 or 20, when growth is completed (16,139,204).

Variations in the growth spurt are due, in part, to *hereditary influences* and, in part, to environmental factors. Children with large-chested parents, it has been reported, are taller, heavier, and more advanced in skeletal development than are children of narrow-chested parents (71). With advancing age, there is an increasing similarity between the child's and his parents' pattern of development (14). Body build likewise influences the growth spurt, with persons of mesomorphic build reaching a peak in the pubertal spurt in both height and weight one year earlier, on the average, than those of ectomorphic build (52).

Of the *environmental* factors, the most important is nutrition. Poor nutrition in the childhood years may delay the appearance of the puberty growth spurt. The reason for this is that a diminished production of the pituitary growth hormone can be caused by diminished intake of calories. Severe malnutrition can interfere with the entire pattern of growth because of an inadequate ingestion of the essential ingredients for the development of new tissue, ingredients such as minerals, vitamins, and proteins (209). Emotional tension during the growth years causes nutritional disturbances and they, in turn, affect growth. When emotional tension is chronic, as in the case of anxiety, there is an overproduction of adrenal steroids which inhibit growth by acting to antagonize the growth hormone from the pituitary (186).

Growth in body size is measured in terms of height and weight. The characteristic pattern for each is described below.

Height Height is regulated by the growth hormone from the anterior lobe of the pituitary gland. In adequate amounts it enables healthy well-nourished children to attain their maximum normal size. In the absence of an adequate amount of the growth hormone, dwarfism occurs in more or less pronounced forms, depending upon the degree of deficiency of the hormone. Too much of the growth hormone has the opposite effect and produces giantism. The most important fact about the growth hormone is that it *must be produced at the right time* if the child is to grow normally (133).

pattern of growth Growth in height follows a fairly regular pattern and usually, though not always, precedes that in weight. This pattern differs somewhat for boys and girls. For *girls*, there is an average annual increase in height of 2.9 inches in the year preceding the menarche. A 5- or 6-inch gain at that time, however, is not unusual. The next greatest increase, 2.6 inches, comes 2 years before the menarche. This means an average increase of 5.5 inches in height during the 2 years preceding the menarche. After the menarche the rate of growth decelerates and the annual gains are very small (64,69,79,210,231). (See Figure 2–3.)

Among *boys*, the greatest increase in height comes in the year when the boy passes from the pubescent to the postpubes-

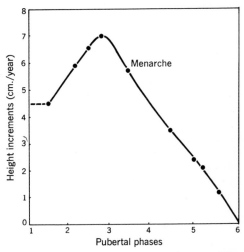

FIGURE 2–3 Growth in girls slows down rapidly after the menarche. (Adapted from H. B. Young, A. Zoli, and J. R. Gallagher: Events of puberty in 111 Florentine girls. *Amer. J. Dis. Children,* 1963, **106**, 568–577. Used by permission.)

cent stage. The beginning of the spurt in height comes from 10.4 to 15.75 years, with an average at 12.88 years. It ends between 13.1 and 17.5 years, with an average at 15.33 years. The apex of velocity in growth in height falls between the ages of 11.9 and 16.65 years, with a mean at 13.99. It takes boys longer, on the average, to attain their mature height than it does girls. However, when they achieve their mature height, they are taller, as a group, than girls (16,79, 204).

effect of age of maturing Girls who mature early are taller between the ages of 8 and 12 years than those whose maturing begins later. But the late-maturing girls continue to grow after the growth of the early-maturing girls has come to an end. After the age of 13 years, the position of early- and late-maturing girls is reversed, with those maturing late taller than those maturing early (4,25,52,108).

Boys who reach puberty late are likely, on the average, to be shorter than their earlier-maturing contemporaries. The reason for this is that they have not had as long a time to grow as their earlier-maturing contemporaries have had. However, boys who mature early complete their growth early while late maturers complete their growth late (108,204). Boys who mature very early and, to a lesser extent, those who mature later than the average show less variation in height than boys who are somewhat early in sexual maturing (135).

mature height How tall or short the individual will be when his growth is completed depends upon many factors. Children tend, on the whole, to resemble their parents in height. This means that tall parents tend to have tall children rather than short ones (14,17,137). Adolescents with ectomorphic builds are taller, as adults, than those with mesomorphic builds. This difference exists throughout the growth years but becomes more pronounced after the puberty changes have been completed (52).

Of the environmental influences on adult height, nutrition is the most important single factor. Children from the higher economic groups, on the average, become taller adults than those from the lower groups because they have better nutrition and care during the growth years (75,224). For persons to attain the maximum height potential, it is essential to "remove any accumulated growth debt before the epiphyses and diaphes of the major long bones undergo fusion" (47). Poor nutrition in the growth years prevents this, with the result that the child fails to attain his expected height when his growth spurt has been completed in adolescence (48,170). Because calories are "growth-promoting," better-nourished children during the growth years become taller as adults than less well-nourished persons of the same racial stock (75).

The average American woman of today is 65 to 66 inches tall. Most of this height has been achieved at 14 years of age. From then until 18 years of age, gain is at a very slow rate. After 18, there is little or no gain in height. The average American boy of today measures 69.5 inches at 18 years. However, boys continue to grow, at a progressively slower rate, until they are 21 or 22 years old; thus the difference in height between males and females in adulthood is greater than the difference at 18 years (124). While girls become taller sooner than boys during the adolescent years, boys become taller than girls when their growth has been completed (16).

Adolescents of all economic groups are larger than adolescents of the same groups in past generations, though those of the upper groups have not shown so great an increase in average height as those from the lower economic groups (59). A comparison of college students of this era with those of their parents' era revealed that girls of today are about 1 inch taller, and boys, 2 inches taller, than their parents were at the same ages (153).

Age of maturing likewise influences the ultimate height of both boys and girls. By the age of 15 years, differences between early and late maturers begin to disappear. After that, late maturers not only catch up with their early-maturing contemporaries but usually outstrip them. The result is that late maturers are taller as adults than their childhood measures would have indicated, while early maturers have shorter-than-expected adult stature (4,15,87,143). Children who mature at a slow rate are generally taller as adults than those who mature at a more rapid rate (108, 153).

Weight Increase in weight during adolescence is due largely to growth in the bones and in the muscles. The *bones* grow larger as well as heavier. They change in shape, proportions, and internal structure. The cartilage and fibrous tissue of the child's bones are now replaced by a harder tissue created by the conversion of cartilage into bone. This comes from the increased supply of thyroid hormone. By the time the girl is 17 years old, her bones are mature or nearly mature in size and ossification; boys' bones are completed in their development approximately 2 years later. At maturity, about 16 percent of the body weight is provided by the bones (144,215).

In childhood, the *muscles* contribute approximately one-fourth of the total body weight and, by maturity, approximately 45 to 50 percent. Muscles contribute more to body weight in boys than in girls; in girls fat is a heavier contributor than in boys. The most pronounced increase in muscle tissue comes between 12 and 15 years for girls and between 15 and 17 years for boys (90,124,180,204).

At the very time when weight increases most rapidly during puberty, adolescents look their scrawniest. At this time, their bony framework is rapidly enlarging so that their shoulders, legs, and arms make their bodies appear bigger than before. With the increase in their muscles and bones comes an increase in body weight. Only when the body is covered with fat tissue does it look fat (215).

pattern of development Because weight increase is closely associated with sexual maturing, the greatest increase in weight comes early in adolescence, after the child has become sexually mature. Between the ages of 10 and 15 years, girls are generally heavier than boys of the same ages. The reason for

this is that girls at these ages are further advanced in their sexual maturing than boys are. However, fat increase for girls comes nearly to a standstill by the time they are 16 years old, while for boys, the increase continues until they are 17 or 18, but at a slower rate (54,75,204). The weight of boys and girls up to about 11 years comes from comparable proportions of fat and muscle; after the age of 11, boys have proportionally more muscle weight, and girls, proportionally more fat weight (72).

There are *sex differences* in the distribution of fat during puberty. Relative skinfold thickness in the neck, thorax, abdomen, the front, and the back increases more in boys than in girls. Boys also show greater gains in fat in the lumbar region than do girls. There is a spurt in the lower thorax before the spurt in puberty growth. Girls show a fairly uniform increase in fat from childhood on; relative fat thickness decreases during puberty in the neck, abdomen, the total front, and the front of the thorax, but it increases in the back of the thorax and the total back (74,195). Gain in weight at puberty, as is true in childhood, comes in cycles, with the greatest gain coming between June and December (49).

The period when girls make their greatest gain in weight is just before and just after puberty. The greatest increase, an annual average gain of 14 pounds, occurs in the year before puberty, and the next largest gain, 10 pounds, 2 years before puberty. The same average gain comes in the year following puberty. This means that in 3 years the average increase in weight for girls is 34 pounds.

For boys, the weight spurt comes a year or two later than for girls. Their pattern of weight increase varies more than does that for height. The mean gain during the pubertal period has been found to be 39.92 pounds, with a range from 17.2 to 64.81 pounds. The maximum growth in weight is with or after the maximum growth in height (64,124,204). Weight increase for boys and girls during puberty is influenced by their *body builds*. Mesomorphs, at every age, are heavier than ectomorphs, with an average difference of between 16 and 23 pounds between the ages of 13 and 17 years (52).

Age of maturing affects the pattern of weight increase during puberty. Early maturers are heavier at the same chronological ages than are those who mature later. This difference appears several years before sexual maturing takes place. Early-maturing girls are 33.6 percent heavier than late-maturing girls at the point of greatest contrast, which falls between the ages of 11.5 and 12.5 years. Among boys, those who mature before their fourteenth birthdays are heavier than those who mature later, and those who mature between their fourteenth and fifteenth birthdays are heavier at all ages than those who mature after their fifteenth birthdays (25,106). Figure 2-4 shows weight comparisons for boys who matured early and late.

The average American woman today weighs 135 pounds and the average American man, 152 pounds. The major part of this weight has been achieved by girls at the age of 16 years, and by boys, at 18 or 19 years. The mature weight is greatly influenced by the body build of the individual as well as by his eating habits. Mesomorphic males, at maturity, for example, have been reported to be 21 pounds heavier, on the average, than ectomorphs (52). Regardless of body build, those who watch their diets will weigh less than those who eat what they want, when they want (17,124).

As is true of height, the weight of American adults of today is greater than it was in past generations. Women of this generation average 6 pounds heavier, and men, 10 pounds heavier, than women and men of the preceding generation. The greatest proportional increase has come in the lower socioeconomic groups where, as a result of better nutrition and care during the growth years, today's adults, in both height and weight, are above the averages for their parents' and grandparents' generations (35,59,224). In spite of this increase in weight, adults of today appear to be more slender than adults of past generations. The reason for this is that the proportional increase has been greater in height than in weight; the adult of today thus looks thinner because he is taller (124).

puberty fat period It is common for both boys and girls to experience a "fat period" early in their sexual maturing. This is due in part to the hormonal dislocation that accompanies sexual maturing and in part to the increased appetite that accompanies rapid physical growth. This fat look normally disappears as height increases and as hormonal balance is restored (15,138, 219).

In boys, the fat period comes at or near the onset of the period of rapid growth for height and the onset of the spurt in penis growth. At this time, boys tend to have marked accumulations of fat around the nipples and over the abdomen, hips, and thighs. The facial appearance is altered by increase of fat about the cheeks, neck, and jaw. This fat period lasts for approximately 2 years, after which the body regains its normal proportions (204,219).

The fat period among girls comes with the onset of puberty. At this time, appetite increases, and the girl often overeats. Like the boy, the girl develops fat in areas of the body where fat is considered inappropriate, especially over the abdomen and hips. As puberty development continues, the fat appearance of the girl generally disappears, in spite of the fact that her weight may not

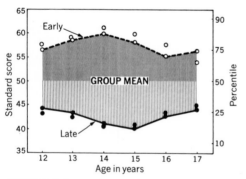

FIGURE 2-4 Increase in weight follows a different pattern for early- and late-maturing boys. (Adapted from M. C. Jones: The later careers of boys who were early- and late-maturers. *Child Develpm.,* 1957, **28,** 113–128. Used by permission.)

change. This occurs when her legs lengthen and her whole body becomes taller (130, 219,227).

Relatively few adolescents remain fat. Most are well enough adjusted to be willing to adopt a new nutritional pattern and take enough exercise to enable them to retain reasonably slim bodies. Those who continue to be fat or who become even fatter as they grow taller are generally poorly adjusted; relatively few suffer from glandular upsets or any other physical cause for obesity. The poorly adjusted adolescent often turns to overeating and inactivity as ways of avoiding threatening and ego-deflating social experiences. Such an adolescent is usually overdependent and feels intensely deprived at the slightest provocation. He then alternates between ascetic denial and abandoned gorging. Some obese adolescents are the product of faulty family eating habits which they have never had the motivation to revise; some suffer from emotional tension arising from pressure of work. Whatever the cause, the prolongation of the fat period beyond the time when it normally occurs will prove to be a serious social handicap (23,24,28,85,104,138).

CHANGES IN BODY PROPORTIONS

Growth at puberty is asynchronous in the sense that the peak rates of growth in various physical characteristics do not necessarily occur at the same time. Spurt in grip strength, for example, comes later than the spurt in weight (219).

Not only do the different parts of the body grow at different rates but they reach their maximum development at different times. However, while each part of the body has its own peculiar pattern of development, all parts conform in a general way to the patterns for growth in height and weight. Consequently, changes in body proportions are predictable (145,204,219,221).

Body build varies according to *age of maturing*. Late-maturing boys are characteristically of slender build, long-legged at all ages, and relatively weak at the ages when they are lagging in size behind their contemporaries. Early-maturing boys, on the contrary, are usually large, strong, and with broad hips. Late-maturing girls have slightly broader hips than those who mature early. Late-maturing individuals of both sexes tend to have slightly broader shoulders than those who mature early (16,108,233). Figure 2–5 shows the influence of age of maturing on the body proportions of three girls, all 18 years old, but who matured differently.

Changes in Body Exterior As different areas of the body exterior reach their mature size and shape, there are changes in the exterior of the body and changes in appearance. Until all parts of the body have grown to their mature levels, it is never possible to predict what the mature appearance of the adolescent will be.

The *head* at birth is one-fourth the total length of the body as compared with the adult proportion of one-sixth of the body length. By the time the individual reaches the age of 13 or 14 years, about 5 or 6 percent of growth in circumference remains uncompleted. Mature head size is attained about 1 year earlier in early- than in late-maturing girls. But the length of the head of the late-maturing girl finally approximates, or even slightly exceeds, that of the early-maturing girl (53,77).

In the *face*, disproportions in the rela-

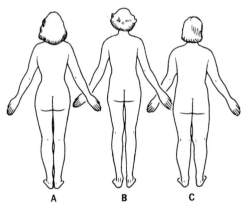

FIGURE 2–5 Effects of different types of maturing on the adult body build of girls. A was accelerated; B was retarded; C's growth was irregular. (Adapted from N. Bayley: Individual patterns of development. *Child Develpm.*, 1956, **27**, 45–74. Used by permission.)

tive sizes of the different features are especially marked in the early part of adolescence, when growth in the length of the face is rapid while growth in width is slower. The low forehead of childhood becomes higher and wider in adolescence. There is a spurt in nose growth before the child's puberty changes are under way; nose growth is nearly complete by the time sexual maturity occurs. Other facial features are not near their adult size until maximum height has been attained (151).

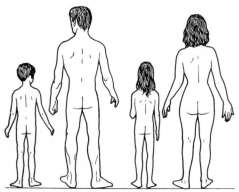

FIGURE 2–6 Changes in body proportions as children mature.

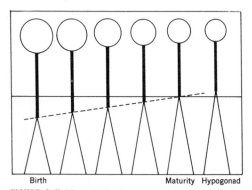

Birth   Maturity Hypogonad

FIGURE 2–7 Normal body proportions from birth to maturity. At maturity, the lower measurement equals the upper. If growth continues beyond the time at which maturation normally occurs, the lower measurement will exceed the upper. The result is the hypogonad figure. (Adapted from M. S. Margolese: Mental disorders in childhood due to endocrine disorders. *Nerv. Child*, 1948, **7**, 55–77. Used by permission.)

The mouth widens, and the flat lips, characteristic of childhood, become fuller. The jaw is the last of the facial features to attain adult size. The slightly receding chin of the child later juts out. There are very slight changes in the eyes during adolescence, and there are no marked, or by any means universal, changes in vision (196). When the face is completely developed, the contour of the boy's face is more rugged than that of the girl. The boy's jaw lines are sharper and squarer, while the girl's face is less angular, somewhat oval, and with a less harsh expression.

At maturity the *trunk* is three times as long and wide as at birth, and not quite two and one-half times as thick. In early adolescence a waistline develops, but it appears to be high because the trunk has grown less than the legs. As the trunk lengthens, the waistline drops and adult proportions are attained. See Figure 2–6. Rapid growth in shoulder width is characteristic for boys, while rapid increase in hip width is characteristic for girls. As a rule, boys who mature early have broader hips than boys who mature late. Girls have slightly broader hips when they mature late. The typical masculine figure, with its slender hips and broad shoulders, seems to be that of the late-maturing boy. Late-maturing girls, like late-maturing boys, have broader shoulders (15,204).

At puberty, the *legs* are four times as long as they were at birth, and at maturity, five times as long. Just before puberty the legs become relatively longer than the trunk. In late-maturing children the leg growth continues longer, and at maturity the individual is long-legged. The legs of an early-maturing individual have a tendency to be stocky, while those of a late-maturing person are generally slender (15,79,230). Figure 2–7 shows the relationship of the trunk to the legs at different ages.

Legs change in shape as well as in length. The straight legs characteristic of a child become noticeably curved during adolescence. The female leg is larger in mean breadth of fat, while the male leg is larger in mean breadth of muscle and fat (181,

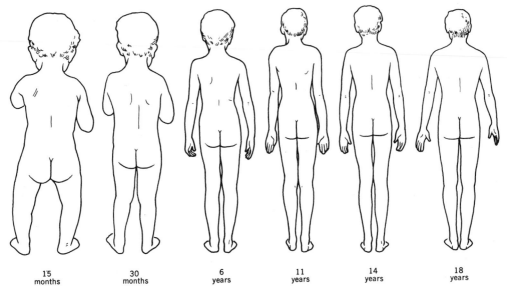

| 15 months | 30 months | 6 years | 11 years | 14 years | 18 years |

FIGURE 2–8 Changes in body proportions during the growth years. The same boy at 15 months, 30 months, 6 years, 11 years, 14 years, and 18 years. (Adapted from N. Bayley: Individual patterns of development. *Child Develpm.*, 1956, **27**, 45–74. Used by permission.)

204). The short, shapeless *arms* of childhood begin to lengthen in the years before and immediately after puberty. Their growth precedes the rapid spurt of growth of the trunk, with the result that for a short time the youth appears to have disproportionately long arms. Early-maturing individuals have a tendency to have short arms because the growth of the arms is arrested by the onset of puberty. The opposite is true of the late maturing (36,204).

The *hands* and *feet* of both boys and girls reach their mature size before the arms and legs. As a result, they seem disproportionately large. Growth of the foot is completed 4 to 5 years before maximum stature has been attained. Much the same is true of the hands (7,36,145). Figure 2–8 shows changes in body proportions in the same child from the age of 15 months until he has achieved adult size at 18 years.

Changes in Body Interior   Internal growth is not so readily apparent as external growth but it is just as pronounced. It is closely correlated with growth in height and weight and, like external growth, is asynchronous, with different organs reaching their peak growth at different ages. The pattern of these changes is just as predictable as the pattern of changes in the exterior of the body. Because the different internal organs grow at different rates and reach their mature levels at different ages, adolescence is characterized by a temporarily increased physiological instability (55,111,145).

There is a change in the relative size of the organs of the *digestive system* at puberty. The stomach becomes longer and less tubular in shape than it was in childhood; thus its capacity increases. The intestines grow in length and circumference, and the smooth muscles in the stomach and intestinal walls become thicker and stronger; this results in stronger peristaltic movements. The esophagus increases in length and the liver in weight. At the end of puberty, the major part of the growth has taken place; after that, growth is at a progressively slower rate (21,145).

In the *circulatory system*, there is an

increase in the size of the heart and in the length and thickness of the walls of the blood vessels. The heart grows so rapidly that, in the 17- or 18-year-old, it is twelve times as heavy as it was at birth. The increase in the veins and arteries during this time, by contrast, is only 15 percent. By the end of adolescence, the ratio of the size of the heart to the arteries is 290 to 61, as compared with a ratio of 25 to 20 at birth (21,90,145). This means that a large heart must pump blood through small arteries. Until this condition is corrected, late in adolescence, too strenuous exercise may cause an enlargement of the heart or result in a valvular disease. Furthermore, tension in the arteries, resulting from disproportions in the size of the heart and of the arteries, causes much of the restlessness characteristic of this age (21,90,145).

As a result of growth in the lungs, there are marked changes in *respiration* during adolescence. Breathing is slower than in childhood, though the volume of inhaled and exhaled air is greater. Up to the age of 14 years, there is not much difference between the sexes in lung capacity; after that, boys surpass girls. The greater oxygen consumption of boys after puberty is caused by the fact that they have more muscle than fat tissue, not because of their larger bodies (72,90,149).

There is a temporary imbalance of the entire *endocrine system* during adolescence. The different glands of the endocrine system grow at different rates and reach their mature level at different ages. The adrenal glands, attached to the kidneys, lose weight during the first year of life and do not regain their birth weight until the middle of adolescence. The thyroid glands, located in the throat, enlarge in girls at the time of the menarche; this produces irregularities in the basal metabolic rate. The gonads of both boys and girls grow rapidly at puberty and reach their adult size late in adolescence or early in adulthood (90,158).

DEVELOPMENT OF PRIMARY SEX CHARACTERISTICS

The primary sex characteristics are the sex organs proper; their function is to pro-

duce offspring. During childhood the sex organs of both boys and girls are small, inconspicuous, and do not produce cells for reproduction. With the onset of puberty all this is changed. The period at which functional maturity occurs, the "pubescent stage," is the true dividing line between the sexually immature and the sexually mature individual.

Male Sex Organs The male sex organs consist of both external and internal genitalia. Those on the outside of the body are the penis and the scrotum, or sac containing the testes, while inside the body are the vas deferens and its associated parts, the prostate gland and the urethra. For most boys, growth of the primary sex characteristics is predictable and follows a pattern similar for all, even though the timing of the different stages varies according to the rate of maturing. In this pattern, five stages have been found to occur. They are (165):

STAGE I. *Penis, testes, and scrotum are essentially the same as in early childhood.*

STAGE II. *Testes and penis have noticeably enlarged: highly pigmented downy hair has appeared.*

STAGE III. *The penis has appreciably lengthened: downy hair is interspersed with straight, coarse pigmented hair.*

STAGE IV. *Larger testes and penis of increased diameter are apparent. Pubic hair looks adult but its area is smaller.*

STAGE V. *Genitalia are adult in size and shape; pubic hair is adult.*

nocturnal emissions When the male reproductive organs are mature in function, nocturnal emissions generally occur. This is a normal way for the reproductive organs to rid themselves of excessive amounts of semen. The first nocturnal emission occurs most frequently between the ages of 12 and 16 years, though by the age of 15 years, only approximately half the boys have experienced nocturnal emissions. Up to the age of 15 years, nocturnal emissions are most frequent among boys who mature early. After this age, early-maturing boys depend upon other sources of outlet, such as masturbation and heterosexual coitus.

The nocturnal emission may be caused by a number of different circumstances. Sometimes a dream of sex excitement gives rise to it, or it may be set off by other stimulating circumstances, such as being too warmly covered, sleeping on the back, wearing tight pajamas, having a full bladder, or having constipated bowels. The boy may not be conscious of what is taking place until he sees the telltale spot on his bedclothes or pajamas. The first ejaculation of a pubescent boy generally comes from either masturbation or nocturnal emission (118).

Female Sex Organs The female reproductive organs lie mostly inside the body. In the prepuberty years, the growth of the reproductive organs may result in the enlargement of the abdomen, which is the source of much embarrassment and concern to the girl. Gradually, as the bony framework enlarges, there is sufficient space in the abdominal cavity for these enlarged organs. The abdominal wall then flattens, and the pouchy "tummy" of the prepubescent girl disappears.

The most important part of the female reproductive apparatus consists of two ovaries, the organs producing the ova or eggs. They begin a spurt of rapid growth between the ages of 12 and 18 years, which continues for some time. When the girl reaches puberty, the eggs begin to ripen, one approximately every 28 days, or every menstrual cycle. It enters the Fallopian tube, or passageway from the ovary to the uterus, and then passes into the uterus, or womb. It later passes through the vagina, or passage leading from the uterus to the outside genital opening.

The uterus grows rapidly during puberty. In a girl of 11 or 12 years, the average weight of the uterus is 5.3 grams, and of 16 years, 43 grams. After that, there is little further increase. The ovaries go through a similar growth spurt during puberty. However, the ovaries do not reach their mature weight and size until the girl is 20 or 21 years old, even though they start to function in approximately the middle of the puberty period (119,145,169,182).

menarche The first definite indication a young girl has of her sexual maturity is the menarche, or first menstruation. This is the beginning of a series of periodic discharges from the uterus that will occur with greater or less regularity every 28 days. A seasonal trend has been noted in the menarche, with peaks of frequency coming in the summer and winter (119,178).

A period of "adolescent sterility" follows the menarche. At this time the endocrine glands do not pour their hormone into the bloodstream with proper intensity to make ovulation and reproduction possible. The duration of this period in the human female ranges from 1 month to 7 years and is extremely variable. Even after several menstrual periods, it is questionable whether a girl's sexual mechanism is mature enough to make it possible for her to conceive. There is some evidence that the period of adolescent sterility is shorter for late maturers than for early maturers (155, 169).

menstruation "Menstruation" comes from the Latin word menses, meaning "month." It refers to the lunar month of 28 days, not the calendar month of 30 or 31 days. The menstrual discharge is made up of four different ingredients. They are: (1) blood released from the capillaries of the uterus lining, which totals approximately 2 ounces during the entire period; (2) mucus similar to that discharged from the nose when one suffers from a head cold; (3) lime and other minerals intended for the nourishment of the egg, should it be fertilized; and (4) broken-down cell tissue. The mucus makes up the major part of the menstrual flow, especially toward the end of the period when the discharge is light in color. In the menstrual period of 3 to 5 days, the total discharge is only 4 to 5 tablespoonfuls.

In the early stages of the menstrual flow, there is great variability in the time interval between each period. In the summer months there are more long cycles than in the winter. Younger girls more often miss periods than do older ones. However, at every age there are great variations among girls, with no instance of an absolutely "regular" case. Decrease in variability of length comes with age.

There are likewise marked variations in the length of the period of the flow. In the first few menstrual periods, it is not at all uncommon for the flow to last only a day or even less. Later, it may last from 1 to 14 days, with a mean between 4.6 and 4.85 days. There has been found to be a relationship between body build and menstruation. Girls of feminine build rarely have unduly long intervals between periods, unduly long periods, or severe discomforts during the period.

It is not at all uncommon for menstruation during the first few years following puberty to be accompanied by physical discomfort or actual pain. The most common disturbances, which are fairly universal among all pubescent girls, are headaches, backaches, cramps, or severe abdominal pains. These are often accompanied by vomiting, fatigue, bladder irritability, soreness of the genital organs, pain in the legs, swelling of the ankles, and skin irritations. As the menses become more regular, the disturbances become less and less severe. Circulatory congestion, which is relieved by the menstrual flow, is partially responsible for these disturbances (119,145,155,169).

DEVELOPMENT OF SECONDARY SEX CHARACTERISTICS

Beginning around the tenth year, girls start to look more feminine, and boys, a year or two later, look more masculine. What is responsible for increasingly different appearances of the two sexes in the next few years is the development of "secondary sex characteristics," or physical features that indirectly play an important role in mating, though not directly related to reproduction. The hormones from the gonads not only stimulate the growth of the sex organs—the primary sex characteristics—but they are responsible for the development of the secondary sex characteristics.

Pattern of Development Not all secondary sex characteristics develop at the same rate, nor do they reach their mature stage

at the same age. Furthermore, the pattern of development differs for members of the two sexes. Early maturers follow much the same pattern as those who mature at the average age for their sex group, though the different characteristics appear earlier. Similarly, late maturers do not vary in the order in which the secondary sex characteristics appear as much as in the time of their appearance. Figure 2–9 shows a timetable for the typical sequence of appearance of secondary sex characteristics in boys and girls.

Secondary Sex Characteristics of Girls Studies of girls have revealed a maturational sequence in the development of the secondary sex characteristics. The pattern most frequently observed is as follows (87,165, 169,182):

1 Increase in width and roundness of the hips, caused partly by the enlargement of the pelvic bone and partly by the development of subcutaneous fat.
2 Beginning of breast development.
3 Appearance of pubic hair.
4 The menarche. This usually, but not always, precedes appearance of axillary hair.
5 Appearance of axillary hair and a slight down on the upper lip.
6 Change in voice from a high-pitched, childish tone to a lower-pitched, more melodious tone. This change comes just before or just after the menarche.
7 Broadening of the shoulders.
8 Arms and legs take on a definite shape, due to heavier musculature, and hair appears on them.

Each of the important secondary sex characteristics develops according to a predictable pattern. In the case of the female *breast*, for example, there are four stages.

Papilla stage This is characteristic of early childhood in which only the papilla, or nipple, is slightly elevated.

Bud stage This is attained by the tenth or eleventh year. At this time there is greater elevation in the nipple and surrounding areola.

Primary breast stage In this stage the development is due principally to an increase in the amount of fat underlying and

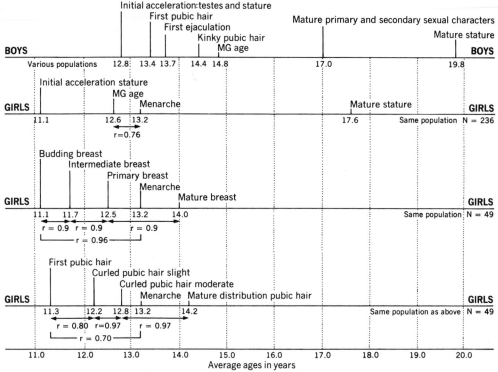

Initial acceleration:testes and stature
First pubic hair
First ejaculation
Kinky pubic hair
MG age
Mature primary and secondary sexual characters
Mature stature

BOYS   **BOYS**

Various populations   12.8   13.4   13.7   14.4   14.8   17.0   19.8

Initial acceleration stature
MG age
Menarche
Mature stature

GIRLS   **GIRLS**

11.1   12.6   13.2   17.6   Same population N = 236
r = 0.76

Budding breast
Intermediate breast
Primary breast
Menarche
Mature breast

GIRLS   **GIRLS**

11.1   11.7   12.5   13.2   14.0   Same population N = 49
r = 0.9   r = 0.9   r = 0.9
r = 0.96

First pubic hair
Curled pubic hair slight
Curled pubic hair moderate
Menarche   Mature distribution pubic hair

GIRLS   **GIRLS**

11.3   12.2   12.8   13.2   14.2   Same population as above N = 49
r = 0.80   r = 0.97   r = 0.97
r = 0.70

11.0   12.0   13.0   14.0   15.0   16.0   17.0   18.0   19.0   20.0
Average ages in years

FIGURE 2–9 Typical sequence and interrelation of events in the process of sexual maturation of boys and girls. (Adapted from F. K. Shuttleworth: The adolescent period: a graphic atlas. *Monogr. Soc. Res. Child Develpm.*, 1949, **14**, no. 1. Used by permission.)

immediately surrounding the papilla and areola. This causes the areola to be raised above the level of the chest wall, in a conical shape.

Secondary, or mature breast, stage When this stage is reached, the breast is larger and rounder, because of the development of the tissue of the mammary glands. The areola is incorporated in the breast itself, so that only the papilla protrudes (165, 207).

Regardless of when they are reached, the major part of the breast development, the mature stage, comes after the menarche. It takes nearly 3 years after development starts before the papilla projects above the level of the surrounding structures (165,207).

There are several important changes taking place in the *skin* at puberty and during the remaining years of adolescence. The soft, delicate, transparent skin of the child gradually becomes thicker and coarser as the individual matures sexually. At the beginning of puberty, there is a definite increase in the thickness of subcutaneous tissue. The pink-and-white coloring that accompanies the transparent skin of the child then gives way to a sallowness. The pores of the adolescent's skin enlarge, and the soft down on the child's skin not only grows heavier with age but is supplemented by coarse and more pigmented hair in regions of the body where in childhood no hair grew.

Shortly before puberty the "apocrine" *sweat glands* begin to enlarge, but they do not attain their full development until puberty is well advanced. The functioning of these glands, especially in the axillae, or armpits, begins even before the axillary hair makes its appearance. The characteristic odor of axillary perspiration may be detected first at puberty. It becomes more pronounced during the early years of adolescence. Increased secretion from these glands occurs during the premenstrual and menstrual portions of the menstrual cycle.

The "sebaceous," or *oil-producing, glands*, become especially large and active at puberty. They are for a time associated with disproportionately small ducts. This causes a temporary maladjustment in their functioning, which continues until the maturation process is completed. The result is a skin disturbance known as "acne." When the matter from the sebaceous glands cannot drain properly because of the disproportionately small ducts leading from the temporarily too large glands, it forms into hard plugs in the pores at the openings of the gland ducts. These are known as "comedones" or "blackheads." They are most often found on the nose, the chin, and the center of the forehead. When the plugged pores are overfilled, they easily become inflamed, and pimples appear on the surface of the skin.

Pubic hair does not appear in any considerable quantity until breast and hip development are well under way. A few unpigmented hairs may, however, appear at the beginning of the pubertal changes. These are generally found on the outer lips of the vulva. For a number of months this scanty amount of hair will remain unchanged; then suddenly the hair becomes more pigmented, changes from straight to kinky, and becomes much more luxuriant in quantity (51,87,165).

Facial hair follows a pattern of development that is similar for members of both sexes. A slight down first appears on the upper lip. This is followed by down on the upper part of the cheeks, and finally on the sides and lower border of the chin. These areas are less heavily covered than in boys, and the hair is of a finer texture and less pigmented. Girls of brunet coloring, as a general rule, have darker and heavier down on their faces than do girls whose coloring is blond.

When the development of the pubic hair is nearly completed, *axillary hair* begins to appear. The first axillary hairs are fine, straight, and only lightly pigmented.

It takes at least a year before many hairs of the adult type are present. As is true of facial hair, axillary hair is generally coarser and darker in brunets than in blonds. *Body hair* is the last hair to develop during puberty. Girls have far less hair on their arms and legs than do boys. Only in cases of glandular disturbance do girls have hair on their chests, shoulders, and backs (87,119, 165,169,182).

Secondary Sex Characteristics of Boys The different secondary sex characteristics of boys, as is true of girls, develop according to their own predictable patterns (80). When the growth of the testes and penis is well under way, *pubic hair* begins to develop. The pattern of development and the mean ages at which changes in pubic hair occur are as follows (183).

1 Infantile stage
2 First appearance of pubic hair, pigmented, usually straight, sparse, at base of penis—12.2 years
3 Slight curl, slight spread, usually darker—13.3 years
4 Curled, moderate amount and spread, not yet extended to thighs—13.9 years
5 "Adult" in type, profuse, forming an inverse triangle, extending to thighs—16.1 years

At puberty, the downy hairs at the corners of the upper lip become conspicuous because of their size and pigmentation. Gradually these hairs spread to the middle of the lip. This eventually results in the formation of a mustache. The "juvenile mustache" is made of rather fine hair, which is longer, coarser, and darker than the vellus it replaced. Toward the end of adolescence, the hairs of the mustache become coarser and more heavily pigmented. Most boys do not have enough face hair to necessitate shaving before they are 16 or 17 years old.

While the juvenile mustache is developing, the vellus over the upper part of the boy's cheek increases. Following the appearance of vellus on the cheeks, the area surrounding the midline, just below the lower lip, begins to get hair. Later, a scanty growth of long, coarse, well-pigmented hairs along the sides and lower border of the chin appears. There are also hairs on the sides of the face, just in front of the ears, and on the throat. These hairs on the throat and side of the face gradually become coarser and more heavily pigmented, developing into a beard.

Studies of the *hairline* have shown that it changes at puberty. It has, therefore, been referred to as a secondary sex characteristic of boys. In immature boys and in both girls and women, the hairline takes the form of an uninterrupted bowlike curve. In mature males, the curved line is interrupted by two wedge-shaped indentations, one over each lateral frontal region. These have been named the *calvities frontalis adolescentium* (80).

Body hair in males follows a fairly predictable growth pattern. Hairs on the limbs and trunk begin to appear early in adolescence, with rapid growth at first. By the end of adolescence the growth has slowed down and continues at a slow rate until middle life. Terminal hairs appear first on the upper half of the forearm, later on the sides of the lower arms, and still later, on the back of the hand. Hair growth on the legs begins after it is well under way on the arms. The hair gradually spreads upward toward the knee; by late adolescence terminal hair is moderate to heavy on the thighs, legs, and buttocks.

The change in the boy's *voice*, which is one of the most obvious indications of pubertal maturing, is due to the rapid growth of the larynx (Adam's apple) and to the lengthening of the vocal cords that stretch across it. The vocal cords become, in time, nearly double their former length. This results in the drop of an octave in pitch. There is also an increase in volume, and the tonal quality is pleasanter than that of the high-pitched childish voice. It is rather unusual for the beginning of the change to occur before some pubic hair is present. Huskiness precedes actual change in pitch, while vocal instability and loss of control of the voice do not come until the change in tone is one octave in extent. The boy's voice does not begin to acquire the deeper tone characteristic of a mature male

until the boy reaches his fifteenth birthday, but roughness of tone and unexpected changes in pitch continue until he is 16 or 18 years old (41,118,204,206).

Between the ages of 12 and 14 years, *breast knots*, or slight knobs around the male mammary gland, appear. They last for only a few weeks and then decrease rapidly in number and size. They are occasionally painful. The male mammary gland, which persists throughout life as a rudimentary structure, begins to enlarge in one or both of the breasts early in puberty. The areola becomes larger and more deeply pigmented. This is due to hormonal action. The enlargement, however, lasts for only a short time, after which the breasts again become flat (118,174,204).

psychological significance of body transformation

One of the major developmental tasks of adolescence is the individual's acceptance of his changed body. The adolescent must adjust to the normal physical changes that accompany puberty and must accept his size and shape as the physique he will have for the remainder of his life. Sooner or later, most adolescents do this (42,68,197, 204).

In spite of the fact that most children look forward eagerly to the day when they will be grown up, changes in their bodies frequently cause more distress than pleasure. Many adolescents report that they would like to change their physical characteristics and that they know specific ways in which they would like to be different (8,197,226).

Dissatisfaction with appearance is generally at its height shortly after sexual maturity has been achieved, during the high school age. After that, adolescents who are well adjusted show an increasingly more acceptant attitude toward themselves and their appearance. While boys tend to have a less favorable opinion of their abilities than girls have, girls tend to have a less favorable opinion of their appearance (5,66).

"Body cathexis," or degree of feeling of satisfaction with the body or its various parts, is more important to girls than to boys because society places more value on appearance in girls. Unless the adolescent girl is satisfied with her body after the transformation of puberty has taken place, it will lead to anxiety and feelings of insecurity. This is true of boys also, but to a lesser extent because of the lesser value boys place on physical attractiveness (193). There is more improvement in the self-concept as adolescence progresses among persons of the middle and upper socioeconomic groups than among those of the lower. This is because adolescents of the middle and upper groups have more opportunity to dress in a way that camouflages the areas of their appearance that are most disturbing to them and because they automatically have the social prestige that is attached to upper-class identification (66,96).

CAUSES OF PSYCHOLOGICAL EFFECTS

How marked are the psychological effects of adolescent physical changes will depend upon many factors, the most important of which are described below.

rapidity of change Rapid growth and changes in the body make a revision of the physical self-image necessary. The adolescent is frequently unprepared for these changes, and he does not always recognize their true meaning. Furthermore, he may overestimate the value of physical characteristics (97,197,232).

lack of preparation How much foreknowledge and forewarning the adolescent has had of the physical changes will influence markedly his attitude toward such changes. Not knowing that the age for maturing varies from one individual to another, many adolescents are seriously concerned about their normality when their maturing is accelerated or delayed. This concern is likely to be intensified if parents and other significant people in his life verbalize their concern (8,189).

In no area is lack of preparation likely to have so great an influence as in the area of sex-organ functioning. The menarche in girls or the first nocturnal emission in boys is likely to be a traumatic experience if the pubescent child has not been prepared ahead of time. This is especially true of early maturers, whose parents had not anticipated the need for early instruction, and of boys and girls in the lower socioeconomic groups (9,95,131).

childhood ideal Every child has, as has been pointed out before, an image of himself as he will be when he is grown up. Few individuals, unfortunately, ever achieve this ideal. The further away from this ideal they are when their body growth is complete or nearly complete, the more disturbed and distressed they will be. Any feature that deviates markedly from their ideal will be the source of marked concern.

social expectancy The social group expects certain physical characteristics to appear as children mature sexually just as they expect behavioral changes. The adolescent's attitude toward his body and facial features is greatly influenced by what he *believes* significant people in his life, especially his parents and members of the peer group, think of them. If their attitudes are negative, his are likely to be also; if positive, he will be better satisfied with his appearance, and this will be reflected in the quality of his behavior (46,89,112,204).

stereotypes Stereotypes play an important role in determining what the social group expects. If, for example, wide lips are believed to be an indication of friendliness, the adolescent will want to have wide lips. Because the heroes in books and on the screen are broad-shouldered, the adolescent boy's attitudes toward self will be colored by how closely his own shoulders conform to this stereotype (114,115,213). Body builds or facial features associated with unfavorable stereotypes lead to unfavorable self-concepts with their accompaniment of unsocial behavior (38,117).

social insecurity Every adolescent is aware of the fact that physical appearance aids or interferes with social acceptance. How closely related social insecurity and physical appearance are may be seen in a study of nicknames. Those disliked most by adolescents are the ones that refer to some unfortunate physical characteristic such as fatness (81,184).

AREAS OF EFFECT

The psychological effects of body changes may be divided roughly into two categories: those which are *sources of concern* and those which affect *behavior*. The concern the adolescent has about his changing body is primarily responsible for the effect the body changes have on his behavior.

Sources of Concern All adolescents have a lively interest in their developing bodies. They constantly compare themselves with their contemporaries and are distressed when their own development falls short. As Havighurst (89) has pointed out, "It is a rare youngster who is never worried during this period with the question: Am I normal?" Physical conditions are a source of concern, of anxiety, or worry, because they represent either real or fancied social handicaps. From the point of view of adjustment, it is of little importance whether the handicap is real or imagined. So long as it exists, it will influence the adolescent's behavior (8,68).

Studies of sources of concern have revealed that the adolescent is generally disturbed by *one physical characteristic* which he feels is homely or disproportionate, which is sex inappropriate, or which does not come up to social standards. He may also be concerned because of a personal dislike for the trait, arising mainly from the fact that it does not come up to his childhood ideal (67,101,152,184). Of the different physical traits that cause the greatest concern in adolescence, the following are the most important:

sex organ changes There is a widespread belief that small male genitalia imply sexually inappropriate development. When a boy's sexual maturing is slow, undeveloped genitalia prove to be a source of embarrassment and concern to him. It is not uncommon for boys to wear tight bands or supporters over what they consider to be too prominent sex organs, or to add artificial padding when the sex organs are too small (97,118,204).

The changes in a girl's body, especially in the external genitalia, are not so pronounced as in boys. A girl, therefore, does not have so continual a reason for distress as the boy. However, her monthly disturbance, resulting from her menstrual period, is frequently so intense that it more than compensates for the slighter disturbances endured day after day by the boy (68,119, 169).

secondary sex characteristics When the secondary sex characteristics begin to appear, they are naturally in an undeveloped state. This will persist for many months. Not realizing that this is the normal pattern of growth, the pubescent child imagines that he will look as he now does for the rest of his life; this is very disturbing to him. Typically, *hair* is more widely distributed over boys' bodies than over girls'. As a result, hairiness of the body has come to be associated with maleness. When the growth of pigmented hair on the body and face is delayed or scanty, it is disturbing to both boys and their parents.

To a boy the change in tonal quality of his *voice* and his lack of control over it causes so much embarrassment that he often will not recite in class. Or he is silent in the presence of those he is afraid might ridicule him. Many adults are very tactless about this matter and further increase the boy's embarrassment by their remarks or amused smiles.

As the *breasts* and *hips* develop, the young girl becomes embarrassed about her changing body. She realizes that the curves of her breasts show through her dresses or sweaters, especially when she walks or runs. To hide her new curves, she may wear a tight brassiere or she may slump her shoulders and develop poor posture. Poor posture, she soon discovers, helps also to distract attention from her broadening hips. She may even go on a rigid diet in the hope that her hips will become less prominent, or she may wear a rigid, heavily boned girdle.

The slight *down* that grows on a girl's face at puberty is very distressing to a brunet. Evening dresses and sport clothes today are so designed that the *axillary hairs* show. To eliminate the hairs from under her arms, the young girl uses any and every method she hears of. The growing girl is spared the embarrassment and humiliation that the boy experiences when his *voice* changes. She can count on her voice and has no reason to fear its pitch when she gets up to recite in class (48,67,169).

The effect the secondary sex characteristics have on a girl is closely related to how important they are to her. As Parker has pointed out, secondary sex characteristics are the girl's "badges of femininity, the basis of her physical attractiveness, and she yearns for their perfection. Her inability to achieve her ideal of perfection in these is the source of most of her problems during this age" (169). Of the different secondary sex characteristics, the breasts have the "greatest psychological significance to her" because they are the feature that distinguishes the girl most readily from members of the opposite sex (169).

the menarche The girl who has had little or no preparation for the menarche often has a marked emotional reaction to it. She is apt to believe that she is having a hemorrhage or that some other dreadful thing is happening to her. Even after she discovers that it is a perfectly normal function of her body, the initial fright, together with the secrecy that surrounds menstruation, tends to build up an unfavorable attitude. This attitude may persist throughout the girl's life (9,95,131).

menstruation From the earliest times, the menstrual period has been surrounded with ideas of danger, horror, and fear. These ideas have led to feelings of shame and guilt on the part of the girl and to strict taboos limiting her activities at the time of the menstrual period. The culture in which the girl lives unquestionably influences her attitude toward menstruation. In America today, there is still the belief among many people that menstruation is a physiological phenomenon of which one should be ashamed. Members of the older generation usually refer to it as "being sick," while the younger generation calls it "the curse." Neither name suggests that it is a normal function of the female body (2,120,203).

The most common ways in which American girls of today react to menstruation are (205):

Dreading the physiological changes and being frightened by them

Resenting the limitations imposed by menstruation

Being embarrassed when they cannot go swimming or play vigorous games with the boys

Being merely secretive about it

Being proud of this sign of maturity as a woman

Regardless of what physical discomforts accompany menstruation, the girl's attitude toward it is more influenced by social and cultural factors than by physical. If she has learned to accept menstruation as a normal physiological function, she will adjust to the temporary discomfort it brings and will not allow it to upset her emotionally, to interfere with the quality of her work in school, or to make her unsocial in her attitudes and behavior (93,185, 225). However, even well-adjusted girls who normally adhere to the rules and regulations of the home and school often become "naughty girls" during their menstrual periods (169).

nocturnal emissions A problem of great concern to most pubescent boys is that of nocturnal emissions. According to tradition, the nocturnal emission may result in loss of strength and manliness, or even worse, some maintain that it is caused by disease. Modern scientists scoff at these traditions. They maintain that nocturnal emissions are perfectly normal. However, many pubescent boys are unaware of modern scientific facts, and as a result, they are greatly influenced by the stories they are told about the cause and effect of nocturnal emissions (118, 204).

skin disturbances There is a superstitious belief, quite prevalent even today, that skin eruptions come from excessive masturbation or from one of the "social diseases," such as syphilis or gonorrhea. Many adolescents either believe this superstition or are afraid that other people will interpret their skin blemishes as resulting from such causes. Even those adolescents who do not associate blemishes on their skin with such causes are greatly concerned by their disfiguring influence (97,204).

Changes in the glands of the skin, especially in the armpits, are accompanied by excessive *perspiration*. With emotional tension, perspiration is increased. The result is a telltale stain on the girl's dress or the boy's shirt. To make the situation even more embarrassing for them, there is an odor to the perspiration that they can easily detect, and they are afraid others will detect it also. Some adolescents are also troubled by excessive perspiration of the palms of their hands, especially when they are emotionally disturbed. This, combined with the perspiration in the armpits, leads them to shun social functions in the belief that they are not "socially acceptable" (8,197).

body build The social ideal for the male is to be tall, strong, broad-shouldered, and with well-developed masculine sex characteristics. The female ideal is that of the petite person, with small hands and feet, a slender body, and a nonathletic appearance (114,187). Gross size is associated with physical prowess in males and the petite body with beauty and delicate femininity. A body that is taller than that of a girl is a cultural "must" for the adolescent boy (18,70,164).

Adolescents who do not measure up to these cultural ideals are dissatisfied. Boys are especially concerned about being short and lacking strength while girls are concerned when they are large, tall, or overweight. Small boys and large girls show poorer adjustment and greater dissatisfaction than do those who more closely approximate the norms for the cultural group (30,46,127,218). Sex-inappropriate facial features are just as much a source of dis-

content among boys as sex-inappropriate bodies (18,70,119).

Among girls sex inappropriateness is of as great concern as it is among boys. A face or figure that does not conform to their ideals of womanliness disturbs them greatly. Sources of concern to them are large hands, feet, or ankles; underdeveloped or very large breasts; pigmented hair on the face in the form of a beard or whiskers; hairiness of the arms and legs; and massive body build. They want to be "exotic," to conform to the standards of feminine beauty set by the movies or cover girls (112,169). Because few girls can achieve the body build they would like to have, they tend to be even more rejectant of their bodies than boys. Furthermore, because appearance is more important to girls, dissatisfaction with their bodies has more damaging psychological effect on them than it has on boys (113, 115,188).

physical defects Physical defects, no matter how slight they may be, are disturbing to an adolescent. A broken front tooth, glasses, a slight limp, a scar or birthmark on the face, or any similar defect are all sources of great concern and may lead to marked feelings of inferiority. The adolescent whose physical defect is a source of great concern to him is faced with the general problems of adjustment characteristic of his age level *plus* the more specific problems that arise from his handicap (78,142,168).

Because most physical defects cannot be eliminated, the well-adjusted adolescent gradually learns to acquire wholesome attitudes toward them and does his best with clothes and beauty aids to cover them up. If he fails to do this, the handicap may give rise to emotional and personality disturbances which interfere with personal, social, marital, and vocational adjustments as the adolescent grows older (32,128).

If the physical characteristic that troubles the adolescent is merely temporary, such as a too large nose or a body that towers over his classmates, the adolescent is better able to acquire a healthy attitude if he realizes that the condition is only temporary. If, on the other hand, the physical characteristic that disturbs the adolescent is permanent, the effect can be persistent and increasingly more damaging as the adolescent becomes aware of social attitudes. As Abel has said, "In a world that virtually equates physical beauty with social survival, disfigurement is often short of tragic" (1).

fat One of the most common physical defects that disturb the pubescent boy or girl is obesity. As Strang has pointed out, "It is bad enough to be fat and forty, but to be fat and fourteen is still harder to bear" (205). While most pubescent children and young adolescents experience a puberty fat period, some are actually obese. As a result of being overweight, the adolescent is unable to engage in the sports and other activities his contemporaries enjoy. Consequently, his concept of himself and his social adjustments suffer (24,202).

Contrary to popular belief, fat boys are not happy boys. Of even greater importance, the psychological effects continue even after the boy has attained a sexually appropriate physique. As Stolz and Stolz have written, "There is evidence that in such cases the early adolescent fat period experience continued to affect personality development unfavorably for many years after the somatic stigma had disappeared" (204).

Nearly all girls, at puberty, acquire an increased fat padding around the lower part of the trunk and upper part of the thighs. As a general rule, the fat begins to disappear soon after the girl is sexually mature. However, while it lasts, it is a source of great distress to her, because her ideal is the pencil-slim body in style at the present time. Girls, more often than boys, go on strenuous reducing diets to get rid of their excess fat, and as a result they are disturbed by it for a shorter time than is generally true of boys (170,193,208).

health Concern about health is centered mainly on two aspects: the effect it has on appearance and the degree to which it interferes with what the adolescent wants to do. During adolescence, there is a decline in illness as compared with childhood.

However, there is a tendency for the pubescent to feel tired and listless. This is due to the rapidity of his growth, to faulty eating and sleeping habits which are developed as part of his generalized resistance to adult authority, and to the endocrine disturbances that occur when the gonads begin to play a major role in the endocrine system. Most of the illnesses of adolescence are not serious enough to interfere with the adolescent's activities, though they tend to decrease his efficiency and to lessen his motivation to do as much as he is capable of (10,200,218).

Many adolescents have some chronic condition, such as eye impairment, diseased tonsils and adenoids, dental decay, orthopedic disabilities, anemia, chronic digestive disturbances, constipation, and nervousness resulting from calcium deficiency. So long as these disturbances are minor, they will not be of great concern. If, however, they are serious enough to interfere with the activities the adolescent wants to engage in and if they make him dependent on his parents when he is trying to achieve independence, the psychological effect on the adolescent as well as on his family can be devastating (11,121,140).

A certain amount of poor health in adolescence is imaginary and is used as a means of escape from difficult school or social situations. The tendency to imagine that one is in poor health is more common among girls than among boys. Another source of poor health in adolescence is worry and anxiety resulting from any one of many causes, such as romances that are not turning out satisfactorily, home friction, unpopularity with schoolmates, or poor schoolwork. If pronounced and continued over a period of time, these worries may lead to loss of appetite, digestive upsets, headaches, and sleeplessness. In addition they predispose the adolescent to general nervous tension and irritability (201).

Adolescents are notoriously careless about their health. They neglect almost every hygiene rule and regard the common precautions taken in childhood as unnecessary or even silly. Neglect of health at this age sometimes results from the adolescent's hesitancy to report minor ailments to parents, teachers, or even doctors. This may come from shame on the adolescent's part, as in the case of reporting constipation; from fear that there is something seriously wrong; from the belief that it is babyish to complain about not feeling well or that it is not masculine; or from the fear that parents wil use this as a means of reimposing some of the restrictions on the adolescent's behavior that they have been persuaded to withdraw (76,127,129).

uneven growth For several years during adolescence the youth has certain bodily features that are proportionally too large. Big feet and hands are especially embarrassing to girls because of the feeling that a "lady" has small feet and small delicate hands. While the girl can, with the aid of hand lotions, make her hands look delicate and well kept, there is nothing she can do about their size except to keep them hidden as much as possible (68,92).

Fashion makes it possible for a girl to camouflage the size of her feet by wearing high-heeled shoes. Another common way in which girls show their concern about their too large feet is by cramping them into shoes that are too tight and too short. Because fashion decrees that boys' shoes must be low-heeled and plain in design, the boy's only hope for covering up his conspicuously large feet is by wearing shoes that cramp his feet. Many boys do this.

Not realizing that the nose attains its mature size earlier than the other features, the adolescent is greatly concerned that his looks will be marred by a nose protruding too far from the face. To make the matter even worse, he realizes that there is nothing he can do to conceal the large nose or make it less conspicuous. Gradually, as the chin and other facial features reach their mature sizes, the adolescent sees that his nose is not out of proportion after all, and his concern about it ceases.

sex differences in development Because girls develop more rapidly than boys, girls and boys are out of step for a period of from 2 to 5 years. Boys are embarrassed because they are shorter, smaller, and less developed than girls, a fact that is a blow to their masculine egos at a time when they have convinced themselves that they are the superior sex. The girl in early adolescence is disturbed because she no longer enjoys childish forms of play but cannot find companions to share with her the forms of recreation she now craves. Many girls, not understanding why boys do not want to dance and date, believe that they lack attractiveness and appeal for the boys (234).

Effects on Behavior Most of the changes in behavior that accompany the onset of puberty are unfortunately of an unpleasant sort. The child seems to go in reverse in that many socially desirable traits, built up during late childhood, disappear. In their places are unsocial forms of behavior. Charlotte Bühler has given the name "negative phase" to this period of growth (26). The period when the child's behavior is markedly affected by his sexual maturing is relatively short, 6 to 12 months in duration. It immediately precedes puberty.

The effects on behavior are more pronounced when puberty is rapid than when it progresses at a slower rate. Girls, as a whole, are more affected by puberty changes than boys, partly because girls mature more rapidly and partly because girls are more often thwarted in their desires to do things than boys. Poor health in childhood, poor parent-child relationships, and lack of preparation for the changes that are taking place in the body at this time all intensify the effects puberty changes have on behavior (67,76,99).

As the boy or girl reaches the end of the prepubescent stage just before sexual maturity is actually achieved, all forms of unsocial behavior seem to intensify. The few months before the menarche in girls and before nocturnal emissions, pubic hair, and other signs of sexual maturing in boys are unquestionably among the most difficult of the whole growth pattern. While the prepubescent child does nothing seriously wrong, he is troublesome and irritating. At this time, friction between parent and child generally reaches its peak of both frequency and intensity (4,50,67,76,111).

When sexual maturity has been achieved, the pattern of unsocial behavior characteristic of the negative phase changes. However, this is not done suddenly. As Josselyn has emphasized, "Practically every child is somewhat overwhelmed for a short period by the effects of the physiological maturing process. His defenses are inadequate to deal with the strain to which he is exposed" (111). Remmers and Radler have further emphasized this (177):

> Growing up isn't a steady, smooth process. On the way to adult poise, Jerry and Susie pass through awkward misery. Their erstwhile smooth-working bodies turn into gangly, ill-coordinated machines. Their noses, growing faster than the rest of their bodies, threaten to topple them forward. Their rosy cheeks, glowing just a moment ago with the bloom of childhood, now look to them like some nightmare field of black pits and erupting volcanoes. This newly strange body of theirs is the battleground for spiritual upheaval. Mother and Dad fall off their pedestals. They don't know everything after all—they're not always right. Maybe teachers are wrong, then, too. Maybe—dare they think it?—maybe even the church is wrong!

Gradually, however, the young adolescent, now a sexually mature person, adjusts to these physical and psychological upheavals. He then becomes more energetic and shows a desire for strenuous activity and competitive sports; he shows an interest in social activities, an interest in members of the opposite sex, in clothes and appearance, better emotional control, less restlessness, less boredom, a less critical attitude toward family and friends, and a stronger motivation to do things. In each successive month of the postpubescent period, there are evidences of improved behavior and shifts from negative to positive social attitudes (45,76, 141).

Common Behavior Patterns   During the transition from the negative phase behavior to the more mature behavior characteristi-

cally found in older adolescents, certain patterns of behavior are common. Of the many, the following are the most common.

shyness   During the period of shooting up in height, the adolescent may, for a period of a year or two, be very self-conscious about his size. This often leads to eccentricities in gait and posture. It also makes him shy in the presence of others and gives rise to a desire to withdraw from all social situations or to remain as inconspicuous as possible when he must be with others. Figure 2–10 shows the characteristic pattern of shyness for boys and girls, with the peak at 12 years of age for members of both sexes. Then, for boys, there is an abrupt drop, because shyness is regarded as sex inappropriate. For girls, however, the peak persists until after sexual maturity has been achieved (141).

Once boys and girls become accustomed to their newly enlarged bodies, there is a marked decrease in shyness and an increase in self-importance. No longer is it necessary to look up when they speak to adults. Now they can meet them on an equal footing physically; for that reason, they soon come to expect the rights and privileges that adults enjoy. If these rights and privileges are withheld, the friction with parents and teachers, which was at a high pitch during the negative phase, increases.

preoccupation with sex   While the body is changing, the adolescent's self-consciousness about his body is intensified. Furthermore, the changes focus his attention on sex and the new sensations he experiences. Knowing that his parents and contemporaries are aware of his changing body serves to heighten his interest; this leads to a preoccupation with sex that never appeared during the childhood days. This may take many different forms, the earliest of which is usually exploring the body and engaging in masturbation (118,119,229).

Even before the body transformation has been completed, interest in sex is turned outward and is revealed in the increased attention the adolescent gives to members of the opposite sex, in impressing them with his newly changed body and sexually appropriate appearance, and in showing them that he is no longer a child but a near adult. Girls often try to attract the attention of boys with coyness, affected mannerisms, and a showing off of their feminine physical characteristics, especially their breasts. Boys put more emphasis on their masculine strength and prowess. The reserve that accompanied the early changes in the body gives way to sexual showing off as puberty draws to a close (141). Much of the conversation and most of the day-dreams of the young adolescent center around sex (39,67).

awkwardness The cause of awkward-ness may be traced to muscle growth. During childhood, growth is moderate and relatively uniform. With the sudden rapid growth of bones and muscles at puberty, the bones bear a new ratio to one another. Furthermore, the muscles are elongated and pulled into new patterns. The result is an upset in the built-in motor achievements acquired during childhood (58).

How awkward the adolescent is will depend largely upon how rapid the growth spurt has been and how seriously his patterns of behavior have been dislocated. Awkwardness is more likely to accompany the rather sudden beginnings of growth than later and more rapid growth (199). Body build likewise has an influence on the degree of awkwardness the individual experiences. Because children with endomorphic builds tend to be relatively inactive and to devote their time to passive play rather than to active sports and games, they have less control over their bodies when they reach the "awkward age" than do children with ectomorphic or mesomorphic builds. As a result, they tend to be more awkward during adolescence than those whose body control was better when they were younger (194).

Boys, more often than girls, go through a period of conspicuous awkwardness. This is primarily because their growth spurt is greater than that of girls. Furthermore, because boys tend to be emotionally disturbed

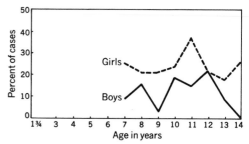

FIGURE 2–10 Characteristic patterns of development of shyness in boys and girls. (Adapted from J. Macfarlane, L. Allen, and M. P. Honzik: *A developmental study of the behavior problems of normal children between twenty-one months and fourteen years.* Berkeley, Calif.: University of California Press, 1954. Used by permission.)

by their awkwardness, they are more likely than girls to withdraw from situations where their awkwardness will make them conspicuous. Girls, by contrast, make it their business to try to overcome their awkwardness by engaging in physical education and dancing not so much for the fun of the activities as for the aid they will give in overcoming awkwardness (19,76).

restlessness Tension in the arteries, resulting from disproportions between the size of the heart and of the arteries, causes the adolescent to be restless and incessantly active, with a desire to consume his newly released energy. But because the adolescent is frequently aware of his awkwardness, he restrains this desire. As a result, he twitches and squirms like a child. Because the adolescent feels very strong and energetic, he believes that his supply of energy is inexhaustible. He therefore burns the candle at both ends by too much exercise, work, and social life, thus wearing down his great vitality and frequently predisposing himself to illness (48,67,76).

pride in achievement Pride in strength and physical achievements of all sorts is great during adolescence. Few adolescents realize that increased prowess is a direct outgrowth of sexual maturing. They believe that it is a personal attainment for which they should receive credit. This results in a feeling of smug satisfaction and a desire to show off either in competitive games or in individual contests (20,82,146).

The feeling of superiority that boys have in their relations with girls comes partly from the realization that they are stronger than girls. In any game or sport in which the two sexes take part, the boys are invariably the easy victors. Once again, boys do not realize that this difference is part of their sex-hereditary endowment for which they deserve no personal credit. Their behavior which stems from a feeling of superiority of the masculine sex, reflects clearly the belief that attainment of physical superiority is accompanied by superiority along other lines (34,67,76,223).

eating Because of the rapid growth of the body, the adolescent needs more nourishment than the child. The enlarged capacity of his stomach and the changes in glandular activity brought on by puberty result in a ravenous appetite. Typically, the adolescent's daily intake is twice as great as that of the adult who does manual work, not necessarily in amounts but in calorie content. From 2,800 to 5,000 calories a day are not unusual, especially during early adolescence. The period of greatest dietary needs for girls is concentrated in a 2- to 3-year period of their growth spurt (23,76, 90,141).

While the appetite is generally large, there are times when it is poor and finicky. A rapid shift from overeating to undereating is quite common. Because emotional disturbances interfere with appetite, adolescents who are subject to emotional ups and downs find that their appetites vary as their emotional states vary (198).

Between-meal eating, which is usually discouraged or forbidden during childhood, is common in adolescence. It is more the rule than the exception for adolescents to eat before school, at recess, during school, after school, and while they are watching television in the late afternoon or evening. Few go to bed without a good, hearty snack. Boys, as a rule, eat more than girls between meals and during meals partly because they need more food for their greater growth and partly because they are less weight-conscious than girls. In fact, girls often go on such strict diets to lose weight that they literally starve themselves. Then, when they reach a point where hunger is greater than they can comfortably endure, they go on "food benders," often gorging themselves on carbohydrates because they satisfy hunger quickly and are pleasanter than the energy-producing foods for a person who has deprived herself of food she craves (24,85,145,171).

The young adolescent often appears more slender when he eats large quantities of food than he did when he ate far less. The reason for this is that so long as the body is growing in height, there will not be an appearance of overweight even though there is an increase in actual weight (104, 124,209).

During adolescence, old likes and dislikes give way to new ones. To a certain extent the new independence that accompanies growing up and the feeling that certain foods are "grown up" influences the change in food likes and dislikes. Food dislikes are often the result of vague discomforts resulting from too much or ill-chosen food. A craving for certain foods and for unusual combinations and mixtures is common during the adolescent years (104,170, 171).

effects of deviant development

There is nothing that gives a young adolescent a greater feeling of security and self-confidence than being so much like the members of the peer group that there is nothing to call attention to him. On the other hand, there is nothing so disturbing as being different, especially when the difference is ever present and readily apparent, as in physical appearance. The child who looks like a young adult while his classmates still look like children is so embarrassed that he would rather receive failing grades than get up to recite in class so that his near-adult body will be in full view (166,167).

The seriousness of being different in appearance from one's age-mates, owing to deviant sexual maturation, has been emphasized thus by Bayley (12):

> Being different from the group with whom one is thrown is always a possible hazard in social and emotional adjustments, but especially so during the adolescent years of growing into adulthood, when there seems to be a hypersensitivity to any deviations from the accepted norm. The physical differences which are thrust on some children by the mere difference in their velocities of maturing are among those hazards.

The reason for the concern the deviant maturer experiences is that being different is invariably interpreted by children and adolescents to mean "inferior"; so long as they are like their age-mates, they regard themselves as normal. A slight difference causes no real concern; a conspicuous difference, on the other hand, leads the adolescent to wonder what is the matter. While there are problems arising from being out of step with one's age-mates, lagging behind them is often interpreted as being less bright than they and, hence, inferior. This concern is often exaggerated by parental concern (31,130).

The psychological significance of deviant sexual maturing differs for early and late maturers. Boys and girls who are early in maturing have a shorter period of childhood and, therefore, less chance to enjoy the relative freedom that comes with childhood. But, on the other hand, early maturers have a longer adolescence; that, in turn, offers more opportunity for social and emotional adjustments needed for successful adulthood. Late maturing cuts down the adjustment period and limits the individual to a shorter time than his peers have for preparing themselves for adult life. Adults tend to treat children in accordance with their physical age rather than their chronological age. This makes deviant development difficult for both early and late maturers. Too much is expected of the former, while, on the other hand, too little is expected of the latter (144,157,187).

DIFFERENTIAL EFFECTS

While early and late maturing affect the individual differently, they also affect the members of the two sexes in a slightly different way. On the whole, early maturing is more advantageous to boys, and late maturing is less damaging to girls. However, under no circumstances can one say that there is a greater advantage to being a deviant maturer than to being an average maturer; it is a matter of which causes less psychological damage. A summary of results of studies of early and late maturers among boys and girls will highlight the advantages and disadvantages of each.

Effect on Boys Studies of the effects of age of sexual maturing on boys have revealed that the most marked contrast in physical characteristics comes between the ages of 13 and 15 years. At this time, early-maturing boys are tall, strong, well muscled, and masculine in build, while late-maturing boys are small, slender, poorly muscled, and childish in build. The greatest difference in psychological characteristics, on the other hand, comes between the ages of 15 and 16 years. Early-maturing boys are consistently rated as superior in *physical attractiveness, grooming,* and *expressiveness* in terms of animation and eagerness, while late-maturing boys are rated as superior in *attention-seeking behavior, bossiness, restlessness,* and *immaturity of behavior* (108,161).

Because of their larger and better-developed bodies, early-maturing boys are able to achieve greater athletic success than their average- or late-maturing age-mates. Because of the social prestige linked with athletic success, the early maturer gains a more favorable reputation and is more widely accepted both by boys and girls than are those who are less skilled in athletics (33,103,125, 146,176). As a result of their greater acceptance, they are likely to be selected for leadership roles in activities unrelated to athletics. This gives them a more favorable attitude toward themselves and leads to better personal as well as social adjustments (82,86,132). In addition, it generally leads to superior achievement in school, not because of higher IQs but because of better adjustment (20). From the ranks of early-maturing boys come most of the outstanding leaders in curricular as well as extracurricular activities (108,146).

While it is true that early-maturing boys may have some of the disturbing accompaniments of rapid growth, such as severe acne, they are usually accepted and treated by adults and their age-mates as mature individuals. Consequently, they have little need to strive for status or little reason to feel that they are being treated unfairly.

The *late-maturing* boy is often shy, timid, and secretive. He will not undress in front of his contemporaries for fear they will ridicule his undeveloped body, and therefore he will not enter many sports. He feels self-conscious and inferior about his lack of strength and will not compete with his more mature friends in sports. As a result, he withdraws from all activities in which physical strength is needed. Sometimes he compensates by excelling in academic work. The late-maturing boy exhibits many forms of relatively immature behavior, owing partly to the fact that others treat him as a child and partly to his trying to counteract his physical disadvantage by greater activity and striving for attention or by withdrawing (108,156).

Boys who mature later than their contemporaries usually develop negative self-concepts; they have profound feelings of being rejected by others, strong affiliative needs, especially for heterosexual affiliation, prolonged dependency needs, and a rebellious attitude toward parents and all adults in authority. Being aware of the fact that they are at a disadvantage makes them anxious and insecure—feelings which are reflected in unfavorable patterns of behavior. As a result, they are more likely to be personally and socially maladjusted during adolescence than are early or average maturers. As Mussen and Jones (162) have emphasized:

Apparently in our culture, the physically retarded boy is more likely to encounter a socio-psychological environment which may have adverse effects on his personality development. The early-maturer's experiences, on the other hand, seem to be more conducive to good psychological adjustment.

Figure 2–11 shows the difference in personality adjustments as reflected in self-acceptance (being relaxed, unaffected, and matter-of-fact) in early- and late-maturing boys.

Effect on Girls While it is impossible to say that early maturing is *always* an advantage to boys and late maturing is *always* a disadvantage, the trend is in those directions. Similarly, it is impossible to say that early maturing is *always* a disadvantage to girls, and late maturing, *always* an advantage. There is, however, evidence that these are the trends. Stated in other terms, this means that the advantages boys derive from early maturing prove to be disadvantages to girls, while the disadvantages to boys of lagging behind their age-mates prove to be assets to a girl.

For boys, large, well-developed, masculine bodies are an asset. Early-maturing girls are not only taller and more mature in appearance than their female age-mates but also than most of the boys in their class. They are conspicuously large, and this is *not* an asset for girls in our culture. Consequently, girls look upon their large bodies as a physical stigma. Furthermore, early-maturing girls, when their growth has been completed, tend to have broad and stocky builds which are culturally less admired than the tall, slender physiques of late maturers (15,16,109,150,195).

Interest in members of the opposite sex accompanies sexual maturity. Because girls, as a group, mature earlier than boys, they show an interest in boys earlier than boys show an interest in girls. When her age-mates are beginning to be sexually aggressive, the girl who shows an interest in boys will not be conspicuous; she will be following the crowd. However, the early-maturing girl who shows an interest in boys before her age-mates do and before the boys in her class are interested in girls is likely to win the reputation of being "fast" or "not nice." Frequently, because of emotional immaturity and lack of social experiences, early-maturing girls do things which lead to sexual delinquency (119,144,173). In commenting on the seriousness of sex interests in the early-maturing girl, Jones and Mussen have pointed out (109):

> The early-maturing girl quite naturally has interests in boys and in social usages and activities more mature than those of her chronological age group. But the males of her own age are unreceptive, for while she is physiologically a year or two out of step with the girls in her class, she is three or four years out of step with the boys—a vast and terrifying degree of developmental distance.

A slightly precocious sexual development, on the other hand, may give the girl prestige in the eyes of her classmates, especially during the junior high school years when girls tend to have crushes on older girls who show a social sophistication they envy. Being able to wear more mature clothes than they and to show a poise in social situations which they lack adds to the glamour the more mature girls have for their less mature classmates. However, envy does not always lead to prestige. Like the jealous person, the one who shows envy may express it by the sour-grapes mechanism—by making derogatory comments about the things she craves but finds are out of her reach. Thus, the early-developing girl is in a precarious position; if she watches her step and behaves with great restraint she may win the admiration of her age-mates. An act that can be misinterpreted as "fast," on the other hand, can quickly tarnish any prestige she has achieved from her earlier-than-average social sophistication.

Delayed puberty often leads to psychological misfits because of the girl's excessive height, lack of secondary sex characteristics, and emotional immaturity. Like the late-maturing boy who is likely to be treated as a child when his age-mates are treated in a more mature way, the late-maturing girl develops negative self-concepts, tends to be negativistic in her attitudes toward others, and is often rebellious and demanding of

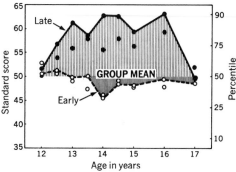

FIGURE 2–11 Differences in the personality characteristic of "eagerness" of boys who were early and late maturers. (Adapted from M. C. Jones: The later careers of boys who were early- and late-maturers. *Child Develpm.*, 1957, **28**, 113–128. Used by permission.)

attention. This behavior creates the impression that she is emotionally immature (109, 157).

Girls who are slower than the average in sexual maturing, though not slow enough to be conspicuously out of step with the age-mates, are the most favorably affected by deviant sexual maturing. They are out of step only enough to make them want to assert themselves and win a place in the group they might not otherwise have (109, 157).

In Figure 2–12 are shown the differences in effects of deviant sexual maturing on boys and girls in their social attitudes and behavior as judged by how much recognition they receive from the peer group in

	EARLY MATURING		LATE MATURING	
	High mention	No mention	High mention	No mention
BOYS	33%	11%	0%	55%
GIRLS	11%	33%	42%	8%

FIGURE 2–12 The relation of "newsworthiness" of adolescents and the age at which they mature sexually. (Adapted from M. C. Jones: A study of socialization patterns at the high school level. *J. genet. Psychol.*, 1958, **93**, 87–111. Used by permission.)

the school newspaper. Those who are mentioned most frequently are the most socially active and popular; those mentioned least or not at all are the most withdrawn and less popular. As may be seen in this figure, early-maturing boys are mentioned much more than are late maturers. By contrast, early-maturing girls are most often in the no-mention category while late maturers dominate the high-mention category (107).

LONG-TERM EFFECTS
In most cases, the effects of deviant ages of sexual maturing have disappeared by the end of the high school age. However, when the deviation from the average has been more than a year, the effects do not disappear so quickly or so completely.

The *psychological scars* left by deviant age of maturing are often persistent. How long they will persist is not yet known, though genetic studies, following the careers of early and late maturers into the mid-thirties, have shown that there is little or no evidence of the fading of the scars by then. The reason for this is the effect deviation has on the adolescent's concept of self. This, in turn, is influenced by the way significant people in his life—mainly his parents, siblings, and members of the peer group—treat him. And how they treat him will depend on his physiological age—how old he looks—rather than on his chronological age. Because the adolescent who matures sexually ahead of or behind his age-mates will have time to develop a healthy or unhealthy self-concept, this is likely to be persistent and to affect the quality of his behavior long after the circumstances that led to the self-concept have disappeared.

The long-term effects of early or late maturing have been studied in the case of a group of men up to the mid-thirties. In this group it was found that those who had been early maturers were socially more active and more often held leadership roles in their communities than did the late maturers. As Ames stressed, "Early maturers tend to either become or remain socially active in adulthood, whereas late maturers tend to either remain or become less socially active as a group" (6).

Early-maturing men have been reported to be more dominant, to make better impressions on others, to be more self-controlled and more willing and able to carry social responsibilities than are those who were late maturers. They create the impression of being more mature and are often chosen for leadership roles in both community and business affairs. As a result, they are more successful vocationally than the late maturers. The pattern of behavior of late maturers, based on unfavorable self-concepts developed during adolescence, is seen in their adult behavior. They tend to be rebellious, touchy, impulsive, self-indulgent, and lacking in self-insight—characteristics of immaturity which are reflected in poorer personal, social, and vocational adjustment than is usually found among the earlier maturers (106,107,109,162).

To date, there have been no reports of the long-term effects of deviant sexual maturity among girls. Consequently, it is only possible to speculate about its effects, basing our speculation on the information about the long-term effect on boys and the short-term on girls. If girls develop feelings of embarrassment because they appear to be so grown up that they suspect their age-mates will think them stupid because they are in a class with boys and girls who appear to be much younger than they, there is little reason to believe that these feelings of personal inadequacy will disappear when the early-maturing girl's contemporaries finally catch up to her. In fact, they do not disappear during the high school years and there is little evidence that they disappear later (89,107,157).

Furthermore, reputations, once established, tend to become persistent. Should the early-maturing girl acquire the reputation of being "fast" or "not nice" because her behavior is different from that of her age-mates—even though it is in accordance with her physiological development—it will not be easy for her to live down this reputation nor will her contemporaries or their parents quickly forget that they disapproved of her behavior when she was, according to her chronological age, "too young to behave that way."

Markedly delayed sexual maturing cannot fail to leave psychological scars which are difficult if not impossible to erase. After a period of being different and of being treated as inferior, boys develop an unfavorable self-concept which is so firmly reinforced that, as was pointed out above, their personal, social, and vocational adjustments are affected even into the mid-thirties. There is little reason to believe that girls would be any less seriously damaged.

It must be stressed that the effects of deviant maturing *need not* do temporary or permanent damage to the individual. What effect the impact of age of maturing will have depends partly on the early foundations and partly on the treatment the individual receives from the significant people in his life during puberty and throughout the adolescent years. It need not be inevitable that late-maturing boys or both late- and early-maturing girls be either temporarily or permanently damaged psychologically by virtue of the fact that they deviated from the norm for their age and sex group in the time at which they matured sexually (161).

It should also be stressed that deviant age of sexual maturity per se is not responsible for the temporary or permanent psychological scars or advantages both boys and girls who are early or late maturers may experience. The early-maturing boy, for example, is not made more outgoing, self-confident, poised, and mature in his behavior just because he matured several years sooner than his age-mates or even because this provided him with a headstart in acquiring mature social skills. It was due, in part, to social expectations of more mature behavior and opportunities provided him to learn to behave in a more mature way. As Jones and Bayley have stressed, there is "clear evidence of the effect of physical maturing on behavior. Perhaps of greater importance, however, is the repeated demonstration of the multiplicity of factors, psychological and cultural as well as physi-cal, which contribute to the formation of basic personality patterns" (108). This same point of view was expressed by Jones and Mussen when they said, "Each individual's personality structure is determined by a complex of interacting variables, including rate of maturation" (109).

BIBLIOGRAPHY

1 ABEL, T. M.: Figure drawings and facial disfigurement. *Amer. J. Orthopsychiat.*, 1953, **23**, 253–264.

2 ABEL, T. M., and N. F. JOFFEE: Cultural backgrounds of female puberty. *Amer. J. Psychother.*, 1950, **4**, 90–113.

3 ACHESON, R. M.: A method of assessing skeletal maturity from radiographs. *J. Anat.*, 1954, **88**, 498–508.

4 ACHESON, R. M., and C. W. DUPERTUIS: The relationship between physique and rate of skeletal maturation. *Hum. Biol.*, 1957, **29**, 167–193.

5 AMATORA, SISTER M.: Developmental trends in preadolescence and in early adolescence in self-evaluation. *J. genet. Psychol.*, 1957, **91**, 89–97.

6 AMES, R.: Physical maturing among boys as related to adult social behavior. *Calif. J. educ. Res.*, 1957, **8**, 69–75.

7 ANDERSON, M., M. BLAIR, and W. T. GREEN: Growth of the normal foot during childhood and adolescence. *Amer. J. phys. Anthrop.*, 1956, **14**, 287–308.

8 ANGELINO, H., and E. V. MECH: "Fears and worries" concerning physical changes: a preliminary survey of 32 females. *J. Psychol.*, 1955, **39**, 195–198.

9 ANGELINO, H., and E. V. MECH: Some "first" sources of sex information as reported by sixty-seven college women. *J. Psychol.*, 1955, **39**, 321–324.

10 BARKER, L. S., M. SCHOGGEN, P. SCHOGGEN, and R. G. BARKER: The frequency of physical disability in children: a comparison of three sources of information. *Child Develpm.*, 1952, **23**, 215–226.

11 BAYER, L. M., and M. M. SYNDER: Illness ex-

perience of a group of normal children. *Child Develpm.*, 1950, **21**, 93–120.

12 BAYLEY, N.: The long and short of it. *Educ. Leadership*, 1945, **2**, 331–335.

13 BAYLEY, N.: Some psychological correlates of somatic androgyny. *Child Develpm.*, 1951, **22**, 47–60.

14 BAYLEY, N.: Some increasing parent-child similarities during the growth of children. *J. educ. Psychol.*, 1954, **45**, 1–21.

15 BAYLEY, N.: Growth curves of height and weight by age for boys and girls scaled according to physical maturity. *J. Pediat.*, 1956, **48**, 187–194.

16 BAYLEY, N.: Individual patterns of development. *Child Develpm.*, 1956, **27**, 45–74.

17 BAYLEY, N., and S. R. PINNAU: Tables for predicting adult height from skeletal age: revised for use with Greulich-Pyle hand standards. *J. Pediat.*, 1952, **40**, 423–441.

18 BEIGEL, H. G.: Body height in mate selection. *J. soc. Psychol.*, 1954, **39**, 257–268.

19 BELL, M., and C. E. WALTERS: Attitudes of women at the University of Michigan toward physical education. *Res. Quart. Amer. Ass. Hlth. Phys. Educ. Recr.*, 1953, **24**, 379–391.

20 BIDDULPH, L. G.: Athletic achievement and the personal and social adjustment of high school boys. *Res. Quart. Amer. Ass. Hlth. Phys. Educ. Recr.*, 1954, **25**, 1–7.

21 BRECKENRIDGE, M. E., and E. L. VINCENT: *Child development.* 5th ed. Philadelphia: Saunders, 1965.

22 BROVERMAN, D. M., I. K. BROVERMAN, W. VOGEL, R. D. PALMER, and E. L. KLAIBER: Physique and growth in adolescence. *Child Develpm.*, 1964, **35**, 857–870.

23 BRUCH, H.: Developmental obesity and schizophrenia. *Psychiatry*, 1958, **21**, 65–70.

24 BRUCH, H.: Psychological aspects of obesity in adolescence. *Amer. J. Pub. Hlth.*, 1958, **48**, 1349–1353.

25 BRYAN, A. A., and B. C. GREENBERG: Methodology in the study of the physical measurements of school children: II. Sexual maturation—determination of immaturity points. *Hum. Biol.*, 1952, **24**, 117–144.

26 BÜHLER, C.: *Das Seelenleben der Jugendlichen.* Stuttgart: Gustav Fischer Verlag KG, 1927.

27 BULL, K. R.: An investigation into the rela-

lationship between physique, motor capacity, and certain temperamental traits. *Brit. J. Educ.*, 1958, **28**, 149–154.

28 BURCHINAL, L. G., and E. S. EPPRIGHT: Test of psychogenic theory of obesity for a sample of rural girls. *Amer. J. clin. Nutrit.*, 1959, **7**, 288–294.

29 BURRELL, R. J. W., M. J. HEALY, and J. M. TANNER: Age at menarche in South African Bantu school girls living in the Transkei Reserve. *Hum. Biol.*, 1961, **33**, 181–190.

30 CALDEN, G., R. M. LUNDY, and R. J. SCHLAFER: Sex differences in body concepts. *J. consult. Psychol.*, 1959, **23**, 378.

31 CAPLAN, H.: The role of deviant maturation in the pathogenesis of anxiety. *Amer. J. Orthopsychiat.*, 1956, **26**, 94–107.

32 CARLSEN, A. H.: Vocational and social adjustment of physically handicapped children. *Except. Children*, 1957, **23**, 364–367, 398.

33 CLARKE, H. H., and D. H. CLARKE: Social status and mental health of boys as related to their maturity, structural, and strength characteristics. *Res. Quar. Amer. Ass. Hlth. Phys. Educ. Recr.*, 1961, **32**, 326–334.

34 CLARKE, H. H., and E. W. DEGUTIS: Comparison of skeletal age and various physical and motor factors with the pubescent development of 10, 13, and 16 year old boys. *Res. Quart. Amer. Ass. Hlth. Phys. Educ. Recr.*, 1962, **33**, 356–368.

35 CLEMENTS, E. M. B.: Changes in the mean stature and weight of British children over the past seventy years. *Brit. med. J.*, 1953, **48**, 897–902.

36 COLE, L., and I. N. HALL: *Psychology of adolescence.* 6th ed. New York: Holt, 1964.

37 CORNELL, E. L., and C. M. ARMSTRONG: Forms of mental growth patterns revealed by reanalysis of the Harvard growth data. *Child Develpm.*, 1955, **26**, 169–204.

38 CORSINI, R. J.: Appearance and criminality. *Amer. J. Sociol.*, 1959, **65**, 49–51.

39 CROW, A.: Parental attitudes toward boy-girl relations. *J. educ. Sociol.*, 1955, **29**, 126–133.

40 CROW, L. D., and A. CROW: *Adolescent development and adjustment.* 2d ed. New York: McGraw-Hill, 1965.

41 CURRY, E. T.: Hoarseness and voice change in male adolescents. *J. speech hear. Disord.*, 1949, **14**, 23–25.

42 DALE, R. J.: A method for measuring de-

velopmental tasks: scales for selected tasks at the beginning of adolescence. *Child Develpm.*, 1955, **26**, 111–122.

43 DALTON, K.: Effect of menstruation on school girls' weekly work. *Brit. med. J.*, January, 1960, pp. 326–328.

44 DALTON, K.: School girls' behavior and menstruation. *Brit. med. J.*, December, 1960, pp. 1647–1649.

45 DAVIDSON, H. L., and L. S. GOTTLIEB: The emotional maturity of pre- and postmenarcheal girls. *J. genet. Psychol.*, 1955, **86**, 261–266.

46 DENO, E.: Self-identification among adolescent boys. *Child Develpm.*, 1953, **24**, 269–273.

47 DREIZEN, S., C. CURRIE, E. J. GILLEY, and T. D. SPIES: The effect of nutritive failure on the growth patterns of white children in Alabama. *Child Develpm.*, 1953, **24**, 189–202.

48 DREIZEN, S., R. M. SNODGRASSE, H. WEBB-PEPLOE, and T. D. SPIES: The retarding effect of protracted undernutrition on the appearance of the postnatal ossification centers in the hand and wrist. *Hum. Biol.*, 1958, **30**, 253–264.

49 DUBOIS, F. S.: Rhythms, cycles, and periods in health and disease. *Amer. J. Psychiat.*, 1959, **116**, 114–119.

50 DUNBAR, F.: Homeostasis during puberty. *Amer. J. Psychiat.*, 1958, **114**, 673–682.

51 DUPERTUIS, C. W., W. B. ATKINSON, and H. ELFTMAN: Sex differences in pubic hair distribution. *Hum. Biol.*, 1945, **17**, 137–142.

52 DUPERTUIS, C. W., and N. B. MICHAEL: Comparison of growth in height and weight between ectomorphic and mesomorphic boys. *Child Develpm.*, 1953, **24**, 203–214.

53 EICHORN, D. H., and N. BAYLEY: Growth in head circumference from birth through young adulthood. *Child Develpm.*, 1962, **33**, 257–271.

54 EICHORN, D. H., and J. P. MC KEE: Oral temperature and subcutaneous fat during adolescence. *Child Develpm.*, 1953, **24**, 235–247.

55 EICHORN, D. H., and J. P. MC KEE: Physiological stability during adolescence. *Child Develpm.*, 1958, **29**, 255-268.

56 ELLIS, R. W. B.: Age of puberty in the tropics. *Brit. med. J.*, 1950, **1**, 85–89.

57 ENGSTROM, W. W., and P. L. MUNSON: Pre-cocious sexual and somatic development in boys due to constitutional and endocrine factors. *Amer. J. Dis. Children*, 1951, **81**, 179–192.

58 ESPENSCHADE, A., R. R. DABLE, and R. SCHOENDUBE: Dynamic balance in adolescent boys. *Res. Quart. Amer. Ass. Hlth. Phys. Educ. Recr*, 1953, **24**, 270–275.

59 ESPENSCHADE, A., and H. E. MELENEY: Motor performances of adolescent boys and girls of today in comparison with those of 24 years ago. *Res. Quart. Amer. Ass. Hlth. Phys. Educ. Recr.*, 1961, **32**, 186–189.

60 FALKNER, F.: Skeletal maturation: an appraisal of concept and method. *Amer. J. phys. Anthrop.*, 1958, **16**, 381–396.

61 FAUST, M. S.: Developmental maturity as a determinant in prestige of adolescent girls. *Child Develpm.*, 1960, **31**, 173–184.

62 FERRIS, B. G., and C. W. SMITH: Maximum breathing capacity and vital capacity of female children and adolescents. *Pediatrics*, 1953, **12**, 341–352.

63 FERRIS, B. G., J. L. WHITTENBERGER, and J. R. GALLAGHER: Maximum breathing capacity and vital capacity of male children and adolescents. *Pediatrics*, 1952, **9**, 659–670.

64 FOLL, C. A.: Physical development of school girls in upper Burma. *Arch. Dis. Childh.*, 1958, **33**, 452–454.

65 FOLL, C. A.: The age at menarche in Assam and Burma. *Arch. Dis. Childh.*, 1961, **36**, 302–304.

66 FRANK, L. K.: Personality development in adolescent girls. *Monogr. Soc. Res. Child Develpm.*, 1951, **16**, no. 53.

67 FRANK, L. K., and M. H. FRANK: *Your adolescent, at home and in school.* New York: Viking, 1956.

68 FRAZIER, A., and L. K. LISONBEE: Adolescent concerns with physique. *School Review*, 1950, **58**, 397–405.

69 FRIED, R. F., and E. E. SMITH: Postmenarcheal growth patterns. *J. Pediat.*, 1962, **62**, 562–565.

70 GALLAGHER, J. R., and C. D. GALLAGHER: Some comments on growth and development in adolescents. *Yale J. biol. Med.*, 1953, **25**, 334–348.

71 GARN, S. M., A. CLARK, L. LANDKOF, and L. NEWELL: Parental body build and develop-

mental progress in the offspring. *Science,* 1960, **132**, 1555–1556.

72 GARN, S. M., and L. C. CLARK: The sex difference in the basal metabolic rate. *Child Develpm.,* 1953, **24**, 215–224.

73 GARN, S. M., and J. A. HASKELL: Fat and growth during childhood. *Science,* 1959, **130**, 1711–1712.

74 GARN, S. M., and J. A. HASKELL: Fat changes during adolescence. *Science,* 1959, **129**, 1615–1616.

75 GARN, S. M., and J. A. HASKELL: Fat thickness and developmental status in childhood and adolescence. *Amer. J. Dis. Children,* 1960, **99**, 746–751.

76 GESELL, A., F. L. ILG, and L. B. AMES: *Youth: the years from ten to sixteen.* New York: Harper & Row, 1956.

77 GOLDSTEIN, M. S.: Development of the head in the same individuals. *Hum. Biol.,* 1939, **11**, 197–219.

78 GREENBERG, H. M., L. ALLISON, M. FEWELL, and C. RICH: The personality of junior high and high school students attending a residential school for the blind. *J. educ. Psychol.,* 1957, **48**, 406–410.

79 GREULICH, W. W.: The rationale of assessing the developmental status of children from roentgenograms of the hand and wrist. *Child Develpm.,* 1950, **21**, 33–44.

80 GREULICH, W. W., R. I. DORFMAN, H. R. CATCHPOLE, I. C. SOLOMON, and C. S. CULOTTA: A handbook of methods for the study of adolescent children. *Monogr. Soc. Res. Child Develpm.,* 1942, **7**, no. 3.

81 HABBE, S.: Nicknames of adolescent boys. *Amer. J. Orthopsychiat.,* 1937, **7**, 371–377.

82 HALE, C. J.: Physiological maturity of Little League baseball players. *Res. Quart. Amer. Ass. Hlth. Phys. Educ. Recr.,* 1956, **27**, 276–284.

83 HALE, J. G.: Changing growth patterns in the American child. *Education,* 1958, **78**, 467–470.

84 HAMILTON, D. M.: Character development of the girl from seven to fourteen. *Ment. Hyg., N.Y.,* 1948, **32**, 568–577.

85 HAMPTON, M. C., L. R. SHAPIRO, and R. L. HUENEMANN: Helping teen-age girls improve their diets. *J. Home Econ.,* 1961, **53**, 835–838.

86 HANLEY, C.: Physique and reputation of junior high school boys. *Child Develpm.,* 1951, **22**, 247–260.

87 HANSEMAN, C. F., and M. M. MARESH: A longitudinal study of skeletal maturation. *Amer. J. Dis. Children,* 1961, **101**, 305–321.

88 HARDING, V. V.: A method of evaluating osseous development from birth to 14 years. *Child Develpm.,* 1952, **23**, 181–184, 247–271.

89 HAVIGHURST, R. J.: *Human development and education.* New York: Longmans, 1953.

90 HEALD, F. P., M. DAUGELA, and P. BRUNSCHYBER: Physiology of adolescence. *New England J. Med.,* 1963, **268**, 192–198, 243–252, 299–307, 361–366.

91 HEALD, F. P., R. P. MASLAND, S. H. STURGIS, and J. R. GALLAGHER: Dysmenorrhea in adolescence. *Pediatrics,* 1957, **20**, 121–127.

92 HELLERSBERG, E. F.: Unevenness of growth in its relation to vulnerability, anxiety, ego weakness, and the schizophrenic patterns. *Amer. J. Orthopsychiat.,* 1957, **27**, 577–586.

93 HENDRIKSEN, E.: Medical report. *Today's Hlth.,* January, 1957, p. 15.

94 HENTON, C. L.: A comparative study of the onset of menarche among Negro and white children. *J. Psychol.,* 1958, **46**, 65–73.

95 HENTON, C. L.: The effect of socioeconomic and emotional factors on the onset of menarche among Negro and white girls. *J. genet. Psychol.,* 1961, **98**, 255–264.

96 HILL, J. T.: Attitudes toward self: an experimental study. *J. educ. Sociol.,* 1957, **30**, 395–397.

97 HORROCKS, J. E.: *The psychology of adolescence.* 2d ed. Boston: Houghton Mifflin, 1962.

98 HUNT, E. E., G. COCKE, and J. R. GALLAGHER: Somatotype and sexual maturation in boys: a method of developmental analysis. *Hum. Biol.,* 1958, **30**, 73–91.

99 HURLOCK, E. B., and S. SENDER: The "negative phase" in relation to the behavior of pubescent girls. *Child Develpm.,* 1939, **6**, 325–340.

100 JENSEN, K.: Physical growth and physiological aspects of development. *Rev. educ. Res.,* 1950, **20**, 390–410.

101 JERSILD, A. T.: *In search of self.* New York: Teachers College, Columbia University, 1952.

102 JERSILD, A. T.: *The psychology of adoles-*

cence. 2d ed. New York: Macmillan, 1963.

103 JOHNSON, B. L.: Influence of pubertal development on responses to motivated exercise. *Res. Quart. Amer. Ass. Hlth. Phys. Educ. Recr.*, 1956, **27**, 182–193.

104 JOHNSON, M. L., B. S. BURKE, and J. MAYER: Relative importance of inactivity and overeating in the energy balance of obese high school girls. *Amer. J. clin. Nutrit.*, 1956, **4**, 37–44.

105 JOHNSTON, F. E.: Individual variation in the rate of skeletal maturation between five and eighteen years. *Child Develpm.*, 1964, **35**, 75–80.

106 JONES, M. C.: The later careers of boys who were early- or late-maturers. *Child Develpm.*, 1957, **28**, 113–128.

107 JONES, M. C.: A study of socialization patterns at the high school level. *J. genet. Psychol.*, 1958, **93**, 87–111.

108 JONES, M. C., and N. BAYLEY: Physical maturing among boys as related to behavior. *J. educ. Psychol.*, 1950, **41**, 129–148.

109 JONES, M. C., and P. H. MUSSEN: Self-conceptions, motivations, and interpersonal attitudes of early- and late-maturing girls. *Child Develpm.*, 1958, **29**, 491–501.

110 JOSSELYN, I. M.: *The adolescent and his world.* New York: Family Service Association of America, 1952.

111 JOSSELYN, I. M.: Psychological changes in adolescence. *Children*, 1959, **6**, 43–47.

112 JOURARD, S. M., and R. M. REMY: Perceived parental attitudes, the self, and security. *J. consult. Psychol.*, 1955, **19**, 364–366.

113 JOURARD, S. M., and R. M. REMY: Individual variance scores: an index of the degree of differentiation of the self and the body image. *J. clin. Psychol.*, 1957, **13**, 62–63.

114 JOURARD, S. M., and P. F. SECORD: Body size and body-cathexis. *J. consult. Psychol.*, 1954, **18**, 184.

115 JOURARD, S. M., and P. F. SECORD: Body-cathexis and the ideal female figure. *J. abnorm. soc. Psychol.*, 1955, **50**, 243–246.

116 JUNGEK, E. C., W. H. BROWN, and N. CARMONA: Constitutional precocious puberty in the male. *Amer. J. Dis. Children*, 1956, **91**, 138–143.

117 KAUFMAN, I., and L. HEIMS: The body image of the juvenile delinquent. *Amer. J. Orthopsychiat.*, 1958, **28**, 146–159.

118 KINSEY, A. C., W. B. POMEROY, and C. E. MARTIN: *Sexual behavior in the human male.* Philadelphia: Saunders, 1948.

119 KINSEY, A. C., W. B. POMEROY, C. E. MARTIN, and P. H. GEBHARD: *Sexual development in the human female.* Philadelphia: Saunders, 1953.

120 KLAUSNER, S. Z.: Sacred and profane meanings of blood and alcohol. *J. soc. Psychol.*, 1964, **64**, 27–43.

121 KOEGLER, R. R.: Chronic illness and the adolescent. *Ment. Hyg., N.Y.*, 1960, **44**, 111–114.

122 KRALJ-CERCEK, L.: The influence of food, body build, and social origin on the age at menarche. *Hum. Biol.*, 1956, **28**, 393–406.

123 KROGMAN, W. M.: The concept of maturity from a morphological viewpoint. *Child Develpm.*, 1950, **21**, 25–32.

124 KROGMAN, W. M.: The physical growth of the child. In M. Fishbein and R. J. R. Kennedy (eds.), *Modern marriage and family living.* Fairlawn, N. J.: Oxford, 1957, pp. 417–425.

125 KROGMAN, W. M.: Maturation age of 55 boys in the Little League World Series, 1957. *Res. Quart. Amer. Ass. Hlth. Phys. Educ. Recr.*, 1959, **30**, 54–56.

126 KROGMAN, W. M.: How your child grows. *Saturday Evening Post*, July 14, 1962, pp. 50–53.

127 KUHLEN, R. G.: *The psychology of adolescent development.* 2d ed. New York: Harper & Row, 1963.

128 LAIRD, J. T.: Emotional disturbances among the physically handicapped. *Personnel Guid. J.*, 1957, **36**, 190–191.

129 LANTAGNE, J. E.: Health interests of 10,000 secondary school students. *Res. Quart. Amer. Ass. Hlth. Phys. Educ. Recr.*, 1952, **23**, 330-346.

130 LANTZ, B.: Children's learning, personality, and physiological interactions. *Calif. J. educ. Res.*, 1956, **7**, 153–158.

131 LARSEN, V. L.: Sources of menstrual information: a comparison of age groups. *Family Life Coordinator*, 1961, **10**, 41–43.

132 LATHAM, A. J.: The relationship between pubertal status and leadership in junior high school boys. *J. genet. Psychol.*, 1951, **78**, 185–194.

133 LAVINE, L. S., M. L. MOSS, and C. R. NOBACK: Digital epiphyseal fusion in adolescence. *J. Pediat.*, 1962, **61**, 571–575.

134 LEVIN, V. E.: Studies in physiological anthropology: III. The age of onset of menstruation of the Alaska Eskimos. *Amer. J. phys. Anthrop.*, 1953, **11**, 252.

135 LIVSON, N., and D. MC NEILL: Variability in male stature as function of adolescent maturation rate. *Science*, 1961, **133**, 708–709.

136 LIVSON, N., and D. MC NEILL: Physique and maturation rate in male adolescents. *Child Develpm.*, 1962, **33**, 145–152.

137 LIVSON, N., D. MC NEILL, and K. THOMAS: Pooled estimates of parent-child correlations in stature from birth to maturity. *Science*, 1962, **138**, 818–819.

138 LOWREY, G. H.: Obesity in the adolescent. *Amer. J. Pub. Hlth.*, 1958, **48**, 1354–1358.

139 LUND, F. H.: Biodynamics vs. Freudian psychodynamics. *Education*, 1957, **78**, 41–54.

140 LUND, F. H., E. R. YEOMANS, and E. A. GEIGS: Health indices in relation to age, sex, race, and socioeconomic status. *J. soc. Psychol.*, 1946, **24**, 111–117.

141 MACFARLANE, J., L. ALLEN, and M. P. HONZIK: *A development study of the behavior problems of normal children between twenty-one months and fourteen years.* Berkeley, Calif.: University of California Press, 1954.

142 MAC GREGOR, F. C.: Some psycho-social problems associated with facial deformities. *Amer. sociol. Rev.*, 1951, **16**, 629–638.

143 MARESH, M. M.: Linear growth of long bones of extremities from infancy through adolescence. *Amer. J. Dis. Children*, 1955, **89**, 725–742.

144 MARGOLESE, M. S.: Mental disorders in childhood due to endocrine disorders. *Nerv. Child*, 1948, **7**, 55–77.

145 MARTIN, P. C., and E. L. VINCENT: *Human development.* New York: Ronald, 1960.

146 MC CRAW, L. W., and J. W. TOLBERT: Sociometric status and athletic ability of junior high school boys. *Res. Quart. Amer. Ass. Hlth. Phys. Educ. Recr.*, 1953, **24**, 72–80.

147 MC GUIGAN, F. J.: *Biological basis of behavior.* Englewood Cliffs, N. J.: Prentice-Hall, 1963.

148 MC HUGH, G., and J. K. WASSER: Application of the Thurstone-Chave attitude rating technique to attitudes toward menstruation. *Psychol. Rep.*, 1959, **5**, 677–682.

149 MC KEE, J. P., and D. H. EICHORN: Seasonal variations in physiological functions during adolescence. *Child Develpm.*, 1953, **24**, 225–234.

150 MC NEILL, D., and N. LIVSON: Maturation rate and body build in women. *Child Develpm.*, 1963, **34**, 25–32.

151 MEREDITH, H. V.: A time series analysis of growth of nose height during childhood. *Child Develpm.*, 1958, **29**, 19–34.

152 MEYER, E., W. E. JACOBSON, M. T. EDGERTON, and A. CANTER: Motivational patterns in patients seeking elective plastic surgery. *Psychosom. Med.*, 1960, **22**, 193–203.

153 MILLS, C. A.: Temperature influence over human growth and development. *Hum. Biol.* 1950, **22**, 71–74.

154 MONTAGU, A.: The existence of a sterile phase in female adolescence. *Complex*, 1950, **1**, 27–39.

155 MONTAGU, A.: *Human heredity.* New York: Harcourt, Brace & World, 1959.

156 MOODY, C. B.: Physical education and neurotic behavior disorders. *Understanding the Child*, 1952, **21**, 20–24.

157 MORE, D. M.: Developmental concordance and discordance during puberty and early adolescence. *Monogr. Soc. Res. Child Develpm.*, 1953, **18**, 1–128.

158 MORGAN, C. T.: *Physiological psychology.* 3d ed. New York: McGraw-Hill, 1964.

159 MOSIER, H. D., H. J. GROSSMAN, and H. F. DINGMAN: Secondary sex development in mentally deficient individuals. *Child Develpm.*, 1962, **33**, 273–286.

160 MUSSEN, P. H.: *Developmental psychology.* Englewood Cliffs, N. J.: Prentice-Hall, 1963.

161 MUSSEN, P. H., and M. C. JONES: Self-conceptions, motivations, and interpersonal relationships of late- and early-maturing boys. *Child Develpm.*, 1957, **28**, 243–256.

162 MUSSEN, P. H., and M. C. JONES: The behavior-inferred motivations of late- and early-maturing boys. *Child Develpm.*, 1958, **28**, 61–67.

163 NANDA, R. S.: Eruption of human teeth. *Amer. J. Orthodontics*, 1960, **46**, 363–378.

164 NASH, H.: Assignment of gender to body regions. *J. genet. Psychol.*, 1958, **92**, 113–115.

165 NICHOLSON, A. B., and C. HANLEY: Indices of

physiological maturity: derivation and inter-relationships. *Child Develpm.*, 1953, **24**, 3–38.

166 NISBET, J. D., and R. ILLESLEY: The influence of early puberty on test performance at age eleven. *Brit. J. educ. Psychol.*, 1963, **33**, 169–176.

167 NISBET, J. D., R. ILLESLEY, A. E. SUTHERLAND, and M. J. DOUSE: Puberty and test performance: a further report. *Brit. J. educ. Psychol.*, 1964, **34**, 202–203.

168 NORRIS, H. J., and W. M. CRUICKSHANK: Adjustment of physically handicapped adolescent youth. *Except. Children*, 1955, **21**, 282–288.

169 PARKER, E.: *The seven ages of woman.* Baltimore: Johns Hopkins, 1960.

170 PECKOS, P. S.: Nutrition during growth and development. *Child Develpm.*, 1957, **28**, 273–285.

171 PECKOS, P. S., and F. F. HEALD: Nutrition of adolescents. *Children*, 1964, **11**, 27–30.

172 PROVIS, H. S., and R. W. B. ELLIS: An anthropometric study of Edinburgh school children. *Arch. Dis. Childh.*, 1955, **30**, 328–337.

173 RAFFERTY, F. T., and E. S. STEIN: A study of the relationship of early menarche to ego development. *Amer. J. Orthopsychiat.*, 1958, **28**, 170–179.

174 RAMSEY, G. V.: The sexual development of boys. *Amer. J. Psychol.*, 1943, **56**, 217–233.

175 RAMSEY, G. V.: Sexual growth of Negro and white boys. *Hum. Biol.*, 1950, **22**, 146–149.

176 REICHERT, J. L.: Competitive athletics for pre-teen-age children. *J. Amer. med. Ass.*, 1958, **166**, 1701–1707.

177 REMMERS, H. H., and D. H. RADLER: *The American teenager.* Indianapolis: Bobbs-Merrill, 1957.

178 REYMERT, M. L., and H. JOST: Further data concerning the normal variability of the menstrual cycle during adolescence and factors associated with age of menarche. *Child Develpm.*, 1947, **18**, 169–179.

179 REYNOLDS, E. L.: Sexual maturation and the growth of fat, muscle, and bone in girls. *Child Develpm.*, 1946, **17**, 121–144.

180 REYNOLDS, E. L.: The distribution of subcutaneous fat in childhood and adolescence. *Monogr. Soc. Res. Child Develpm.*, 1950, **15**, no. 2.

181 REYNOLDS, E. L., and P. GROTE: Sex differences in the distribution of tissue components in the human leg from birth to maturity. *Anat. Rec.*, 1948, **102**, 45–53.

182 REYNOLDS, E. L., and J. V. WINES: Individual differences in physical changes associated with adolescence in girls. *Amer. J. Dis. Children*, 1951, **82**, 329–350.

183 REYNOLDS, E. L., and J. V. WINES: Physical changes associated with adolescence in boys. *Amer. J. Dis. Children*, 1951, **82**, 529–547.

184 ROFF, M., and D. S. BRODY: Appearance and choice status during adolescence. *J. Psychol.*, 1953, **36**, 347–356.

185 ROSE, A. A.: Menstrual pain and personal adjustment. *J. Pers.*, 1949, **17**, 287–300.

186 ROSENBAUM, M.: The role of psychological factors in delayed growth in adolescence: a case report. *Amer. J. Orthopsychiat.*, 1959, **29**, 762–771.

187 SCHEINFELD, A.: *The human heredity handbook.* Philadelphia: Lippincott, 1956.

188 SCHNEIDERMAN, L.: The estimation of one's own bodily traits. *J. soc. Psychol.*, 1956, **44**, 89–100.

189 SCHONFELD, W. A.: Deficient development of masculinity. *Amer. J. Dis. Children*, 1950, **79**, 17–29.

190 SCHONFELD, W. A.: Inadequate physique. *Psychosom. Med.*, 1950, **12**, 49–54.

191 SCHONFELD, W. A.: Gynecomastia in adolescence. *Amer. Arch. gen. Psychiat.*, 1961, **5**, 46–54.

192 SECKEL, H. P. G.: Six examples of precocious sexual development. *Amer. J. Dis. Children*, 1950, **79**, 278–309.

193 SECORD, P. F., and S. M. JOURARD: The appraisal of body-cathexis: body-cathexis and the self. *J. consult. Psychol.*, 1953, **17**, 343–347.

194 SILLS, F. D., and P. W. EVERETT: The relationship of extreme somatotypes to performance in motor and strength tests. *Res. Quart. Amer. Ass. Hlth. Phys. Educ. Recr.*, 1953, **24**, 223–228.

195 SKERLJ, B.: Further evidence of age changes in body form based on material of D. A. W. Edwards. *Hum. Biol.*, 1954, **26**, 330–336.

196 SLOANE, A. E., and J. R. GALLAGHER: Changes in vision during adolescence. *Amer. J. Opthalmol.*, 1950, **33**, 1538–1542.

197 SMITH, W. D., and D. LEBO: Some changing

aspects of the self-concept of pubescent males. *J. genet. Psychol.*, 1956, **88**, 61–75.

198 SMITH, W. I., E. K. POWELL, and S. ROSS: Food aversions: some additional personality correlates. *J. consult. Psychol.*, 1955, **19**, 145–149.

199 SOLLEY, W. H.: Ratio of physical development as a factor in motor co-ordination of boys ages 10 to 14. *Res. Quart. Amer. Ass. Hlth. Phys. Educ. Recr.*, 1957, **28**, 295–304.

200 STATON, W. M.: The adolescent: his physical growth and health. *Rev. educ. Res.*, 1954, **24**, 19–29.

201 STATON, W. M., and J. A. RUTLEDGE: Measurable traits of personality and incidence of somatic illness among college students. *Res. Quart. Amer. Ass. Hlth. Phys. Educ. Recr.*, 1955, **26**, 197–204.

202 STEFANIK, P. A., F. P. HEALD, and J. MAYER: Caloric intake in relation to energy output of obese and nonobese adolescent boys. *Amer. J. clin. Nutrit.*, 1959, **7**, 55–62.

203 STEPHENS, W. N.: A cross-cultural study of menstrual taboos. *Genet. Psychol. Monogr.*, 1961, **64**, 385–416.

204 STOLZ, H. R., and L. M. STOLZ: *Somatic development of adolescent boys.* New York: Macmillan, 1951.

205 STRANG, R.: *The adolescent views himself.* New York: McGraw-Hill, 1957.

206 STUART, H. C.: Normal growth and development during adolescence. *New England med. J.*, 1946, **234**, 666–672, 693–700, 732–738.

207 STUART, H. C.: Physical growth during adolescence. *Amer. J. Dis. Children*, 1947, **74**, 495–502.

208 SUMMERSKILL, J., and C. D. DARLING: Emotional adjustment and dieting performance. *J. consult. Psychol.*, 1955, **19**, 151–153.

209 TANNER, J. M.: *Growth at adolescence.* Springfield, Ill.: Charles C Thomas, 1962.

210 TANNER, J. M.: The regulation of human growth. *Child Develpm.*, 1963, **34**, 817–847.

211 TANNER, J. M., and B. O'KEEFFE: Age at menarche in Nigerian school girls, with a note on their heights and weights from age 12 to 19. *Hum. Biol.*, 1962, **34**, 187–196.

212 TANNER, J. M., and R. H. WHITEHOUSE: Standards of height and weight of British children from birth to maturity. *The Lancet*, 1959, **2**, 1096–1098.

213 TAYLOR, C., and G. G. THOMPSON: Age trends in preferences for certain facial proportions. *Child Develpm.*, 1955, **26**, 97–102.

214 TERMAN, L. M., and M. H. ODEN: *The gifted child grows up.* Stanford, Calif.: Stanford, 1947.

215 TROTTER, M.: Variable factors in skeleton weight. *Hum. Biol.*, 1956, **28**, 146–153.

216 TUDDENHAM, R. D.: Studies in reputation: I. Sex and grade differences in school children's evaluation of their peers. II. The diagnosis of social adjustment. *Psychol. Monogr.*, 1952, **66**, no. 1.

217 TYLER, F. T.: Organismic growth: some relationships within the individual among cycles of growth in physical characteristics. *Child Develpm.*, 1957, **28**, 55–63.

218 VALADIAN, I., H. C. STUART, and R. R. REED: Studies of illnesses of children followed from birth to eighteen years. *Monogr. Soc. Res. Child Develpm.*, 1961, **26**, no. 3.

219 VAMBEROVA, M. P., and J. TEFRALOVA: The effect of puberty on the development of obesity. *Child Develpm. Abstr.*, 1963, **38**, no. 36.

220 VINCENT, E. L.: Physical and psychological aspects of puberty and adolescence. *J. nat. Ass. Deans Women*, 1955, **19**, 3–10.

221 VINCENT, E. L., and P. C. MARTIN: *Human psychological development.* New York: Ronald, 1961.

222 WATTENBERG, W. W.: *The adolescent years.* New York: Harcourt, Brace & World, 1955.

223 WEAR, C. L., and K. MILLER: Relationship of physique and developmental level to physical performance. *Res. Quart. Amer. Ass. Hlth. Phys. Educ. Recr.*, 1962, **33**, 615–631.

224 WHITACRE, J., and E. T. GRIMES: Some body measurements of native-born white children from seven to fourteen years in different climatic regions of Texas. *Child Develpm.*, 1959, **30**, 177–209.

225 WICKHAM, M.: The effects of the menstrual cycle on test performance. *Brit. J. Psychol.*, 1958, **49**, 34–41.

226 WINKER, J. B.: Age trends and sex differences in the wishes, identifications, activities, and fears of children. *Child Develpm.*, 1949, **20**, 191–200.

227 WOLFF, E., and L. M. BAYER: Psychosomatic disorders of childhood and adolescence. *Amer. J. Orthopsychiat.*, 1952, **22**, 510–521.

228 WOLFF, O. H.: Obesity in childhood: a study of the birth weight, the height, and the onset of puberty. *Quart. J. Med.*, 1955, **24**, 109–123.

229 WOLMAN, B.: Sexual development in Israeli adolescents. *Amer. J. Psychother.*, 1951, **5**, 531–559.

230 WORCESTER, J., and O. M. LOMBARD: Predictability of leg length. *Child Develpm.*, 1948, **19**, 159–166.

231 YOUNG, H. B., A. ZOLI, and J. R. GALLAGHER: Events of puberty in 111 Florentine girls. *Amer. J. Dis. Children*, 1963, **106**, 568–577.

232 ZACHRY, C. B.: *Emotion and conduct in adolescence*. New York: Appleton-Century-Crofts, 1940.

233 ZUK, G. H.: The plasticity of the physique from early adolescence through adulthood. *J. genet. Psychol.*, 1958, **92**, 205–214.

234 ZUK, G. H.: Sex-appropriate behavior in adolescence. *J. genet. Psychol.*, 1958, **93**, 15–32.

CHAPTER 3
emotions
in adolescence

Traditionally, adolescence is the age of *Sturm und Drang*, the stage G. Stanley Hall referred to as the period of "storm and stress" (66). The word "storm" suggests that anger with its accompaniment of temper outbursts is one of the dominant, if not *the* dominant, emotion at this age. "Stress" means "anything which in a relatively extreme form tends to disrupt normal func-

tioning"; it refers to a generally upset condition which leads to deterioration of functioning, both physical and mental (56, 98).

When a condition exists that suggests storm and stress, it is symptomatic of trouble. To the psychologist, heightened emotionality extending over a period of time is what fever is to a doctor—a danger signal.

And, like fever, its effects may be far-reaching. The adolescent who, for example, is experiencing an unhappy ending to a romance is nervous and tense not only in situations related to the romance but in his home, school, and social relationships. His schoolwork suffers, he quarrels with his friends and family, and in a general way he makes himself thoroughly obnoxious to all with whom he comes in contact.

Most investigators of adolescent emotions agree that adolescence is a period of heightened emotionality. However, few are willing to label this emotionality "storm and stress." Josselyn has emphasized that the "normal adolescent is inevitably a mixed-up person, but not at all in the sense of being a psychologically sick person" (78). In studying the happiness of adolescents, Barschak has found no evidence that adolescence is a period of storm and stress, though there is more unhappiness during adolescence than in childhood. But this is only transitory. In other words, there is no evidence that adolescence is such an emotionally disturbed time that unhappiness is either universal or persistent (14).

Instead, there is evidence that heightened emotionality is limited to a small portion of the adolescent span. It generally occurs during periods of developmental change. This is limited to the last year or two of childhood and the first year or two of adolescence. The more sudden and pronounced the physical changes, the greater the disturbance to body homeostasis and, in turn, the greater the likelihood of heightened emotionality (42,49). As development slows down, heightened emotionality normally subsides. Studies of adolescents over a period of time have revealed that heightened emotionality generally reaches its peak between the ages of 11 and 12 years. Thirteen- to fourteen-year-olds are often irritable and get excited easily (see Figure 3–1). In addition, they are more likely to explode emotionally than to control their feelings. A year later, there is a definite attempt on the part of the young adolescent to cover up his feelings; this leads to moodiness. By the time the adolescent is 16 years old, he "doesn't believe in

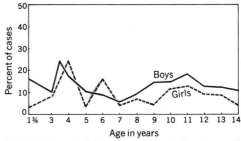

FIGURE 3–1 Irritability increases at the time of puberty. (Adapted from J. Macfarlane, K. Allen, and M. P. Honzik: A *developmental study of the behavior problems of normal children between twenty-one months and fourteen years.* Berkeley, Calif.: University of California Press, 1954. Used by permission.)

worrying," with the result that he takes a calmer approach to his problems (58).

Furthermore, not all adolescents are, by any means, subject to storm and stress. As was pointed out in Chapter 1, adolescents in many primitive as well as civilized cultures find adolescence one of the happiest periods in life. Even in our present-day American culture, not all adolescents are subject to emotional stress. While it is true that all, unquestionably, experience emotional instability from time to time, it is also true that this is characteristic of people of all ages, not of adolescence alone. During adolescence, those who deviate markedly from the norm for sexual maturing for their sex group are the ones most likely to experience heightened emotionality of a severe and prolonged type. This is not because of the maturing itself but because of the many personal and social problems deviant sexual maturing brings (30,49,55,77).

evidence of heightened emotionality

"Heightened emotionality" means more than the normal emotionality for a *given person.* The criterion of whether or not the individual is experiencing heightened emotionality is how he reacts emotionally as compared with his usual pattern. A calm, unemotional person when experiencing heightened emotionality may appear to be behaving in a relatively calm, unemotional manner; in comparison with others, he is calm. However, in comparison with his usual behavior, he is emotionally disturbed.

Heightened emotionality is never hidden; it expresses itself in some form of behavior though it may not always be readily recognized as such. Gesell has labeled periods of heightened emotionality as periods of "disequilibrium"—times when insecurities, tensions, indecisions, and similar forms of problem behavior are readily recognized. They are times when the individual is "out of focus," when his behavior causes more problems for others than is normal and when he is less happy and well adjusted than usual. However, no two individuals express their disequilibrium in exactly the same way: instead, each has his own characteristic method of expression (58).

EXPRESSIONS OF HEIGHTENED EMOTIONALITY

A number of the most common ways in which heightened emotionality is shown are discussed below and shown in Figure 3–2.

Specific Nervous Habits Nervous habits may be divided, roughly, into four categories: "oral," such as sucking the thumb or a finger, biting nails, tongue protrusion, and sucking or biting the lips; "nasal," such as picking, scratching, or wrinkling the nose; "hirsutal," such as pulling or twisting the hair or scratching the head; and "facial," such as picking the face, touching the face with the hand, or leaning the face on the hand (124,173,174).

Of all the different specific nervous habits, nail biting in adolescence is the most common. While most adolescents bite their nails occasionally during periods of emotional stress, those who are poorly adjusted are generally the most persistent nail biters. At puberty, there is likely to be an increase in nail biting. This is generally followed by a drop in frequency as tension eases and as the adolescent becomes more appearance-conscious. Up to the age of 10, there is no significant sex difference in the frequency of nail biting. However, the peak for girls comes earlier than for boys—at 11

years for girls and at 13 for boys. Girls, as a rule, give up nail biting sooner than boys, owing not to less emotional tension but rather to an earlier social consciousness (107,108).

General Nervous Tension The individual who experiences heightened emotionality is generally nervous, tense, edgey, and "jittery." He finds it difficult to relax and enjoy himself and he often suffers from insomnia. This general emotional tension is not directed toward anyone or anything; instead, it is a generalized state (42,58,78).

Marked Mood Swings The individual who is experiencing heightened emotionality is generally subject to marked mood swings. He goes from pleasant to unpleasant, or from one unpleasant to another unpleasant mood without any apparent reason or without awareness as to why he does so. Because he is in an emotionally stirred-up state, it is easy for changed conditions in his environment or within himself to give rise to a new emotional state, often as intense as the one it is replacing (49,107).

Predisposition to Emotional Outbursts Just as heightened emotionality is often expressed in mood swings, so it tends to predispose the individual to emotional outbursts out of all proportion to the type of stimulus that gave rise to them. A comic situation, for example, may give rise to giggling and screaming which is far more intense than the humor of the situation justifies (58). Similarly, in times of emotional stress, the adolescent will respond with grief reactions out of all proportion to the situation that gave rise to the grief (1).

Quarrelsomeness Heightened emotionality predisposes the individual at every age to be quarrelsome; adolescence is no exception. The height of parent-adolescent conflicts comes during the early part of puberty, at which time heightened emotionality is pronounced (138). The young adolescent seems to have a chip on his shoulder and to

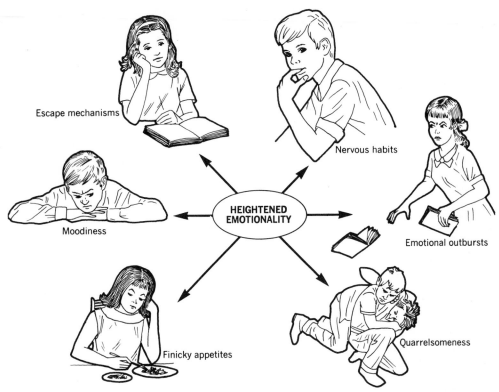

Escape mechanisms

Nervous habits

Moodiness

HEIGHTENED
EMOTIONALITY

Emotional outbursts

Finicky appetites

Quarrelsomeness

FIGURE 3–2 Common expressions of heightened emotionality.

be predisposed to pick fights with anyone at the slightest provocation (58).

Finicky Appetites One of the common accompaniments of heightened emotionality is the tendency to have a finicky appetite and to pick at food. Studies of the relation of anxiety to eating have revealed that those who experience high anxiety have a large number of food aversions and show a tendency to reject food they formerly liked. Girls suffer more from food aversions and finicky appetites than boys (155).

Escape Mechanisms Many adolescents try to escape from the anxieties and frustrations in daily life by withdrawal into the world of daydreams. Here, temporarily, they can be free of the emotional stress that plagues them. Studies of unhappiness, of problems, of worries, of mental disease, and of suicide all show some increase in emotional tension at adolescence. Because

heightened emotionality is more characteristic of early adolescence than of later, these escape mechanisms are more common in the early adolescent period (59,146).

Moodiness Perhaps the most common way in which heightened emotionality expresses itself is in moodiness. A "mood" is a drawn-out or prolonged emotion. In his attempt to conceal his feelings and to behave in a socially approved manner, the adolescent, figuratively speaking, bottles up his emotions inside himself where they smolder away for hours or days at a time. The better the emotional control of the adolescent, the moodier he will be. And since the emotions that are most likely to be subjected to control are those which are regarded by the social group as unpleasant or socially unacceptable, such as fear, anger, envy, and jealousy, adolescent moods are typically of the gloomy, morbid sort (58, 72).

causes of heightened emotionality

Heightened emotionality results from the necessity of breaking off old habits of thought and action and establishing new. While the adjustment is taking place, the adolescent is emotionally disturbed. After the adjustment has been made, he settles down, and emotionality disappears (58). As Kuhlen (89) has pointed out:

> *Evidence seems to indicate that adolescence is not to be thought of as an unduly stressful period. Rather, what does characterize adolescence is a particular group of adjustment problems which in the American culture are typically faced in the teens, and which may thus typically produce anxiety and stress in the teens.*

PREDISPOSING CAUSES OF EMOTIONALITY

There are a number of common causes of feelings of insecurity and uncertainty on the part of the adolescent: These feelings predispose him to heightened emotionality. They are mainly the product of environmental and social factors. For that reason, one can safely conclude that heightened emotionality during adolescence is attributable to social factors, not glandular, as was formerly believed.

The factors that predispose the adolescent to intense emotionality are described below.

Physical Condition When body homeostasis is disturbed, heightened emotionality is almost inevitable. And the maintenance of homeostasis is especially difficult during periods of developmental change, such as occurs during the early part of adolescence (49). Similarly, emotional tension, in the form of anxiety or frustration, will cause nutritional disturbances and these, in turn, will intensify and prolong the emotional tension (42,145). Improper amounts or unbalanced combinations of nutrients are likely to predispose the individual to emotional tension. Unquestionably, poor nutri-

tion is "at the basis of some of the stresses and strains of adolescence" (134).

Anemia from iron deficiency causes apathy, accompanied by increased anxiety and irritability. A deficiency in calcium, common during periods of rapid growth, leads to irritability and emotional instability. Prolonged malnutrition, from insufficient diet or from poor choice of foods, invariably leads to emotional disturbances (16). Fatigue predisposes the individual to moodiness and gloominess. They are often accompanied by irritability and the tendency to fly off the handle in an emotional outburst (28).

Adjustment to New Environments Adjustment to a new environment is difficult at any age. For the adolescent the adjustment is especially difficult for two reasons: He is expected to adjust to several new environments in a short period of time; and his well-established habits of adjustment to a child's environment have accustomed him to thinking and behaving in a childish manner.

Owing to the fact that the adolescent looks like an adult, he is expected to adjust to these environments as an adult would and to behave accordingly. Furthermore, the child, more often than the adolescent, is prepared by his parents to meet new and stressful situations. The result is that the adolescent finds adjustments more difficult than the child. The more continuities there have been in child training, the easier the adjustment to new situations (52,169).

How the adolescent interprets a situation will affect his reaction to it. If he has not been prepared for it, he will likely interpret it as more threatening than it actually is and this will give rise to increased anxiety. The immature adolescent interprets situations in much the same manner as he did when he was a child. This leads to immature emotional reactions, especially temper outbursts reminiscent of his childhood days (61).

Situations in Which the Individual Feels Inadequate Many situations which confront the adolescent for the first time baffle and disturb him. In a coeducational college, for example, where social success is judged by dating and student activities, boys and girls who do not conform to the accepted pattern feel frustrated, and this leads to emotional disturbance. Girls who are unpopular suffer especially from emotional disturbances so long as they remain in this environment.

▷ **Social Expectations of More Mature Behavior** Many of the feelings of personal inadequacy which give rise to heightened emotionality stem from social expectations. Many adolescents set goals that are far beyond their capacities. When they fail to reach these goals, they frequently lower their goals, thus adding to their feelings of inadequacy (113, 122,143). Boys and girls, it has been found, who come from homes where the discipline is strict and expectations high become emotionally disturbed and go to pieces when they are confronted by unfamiliar tasks. Constant demands to live up to expectations are likely to lead to a generalized state of anxiety, and thus predispose the adolescent to heightened emotionality in all situations, not alone in those where social expectations are present. He comes to expect of himself what the social group expects of him; this leads to emotional tension (51,84).

Social Adjustments to the Other Sex One of the areas in which the social group expects the adolescent to achieve more mature behavior is in his relationships with members of the opposite sex. What to talk about, what is the correct social behavior, and many related problems are perplexing to an adolescent to whom all these problems are new. Like all new problems in which adjustment must be made, these result in nervous tension and general emotional excitement (39).

School Failure Many adolescents who have relatively little trouble in elementary school find adjustment to high school or college work very difficult. Whatever may be the cause of their failures, adolescents are keenly sensitive about them. The emotional disturbance may be so great that they will leave school, leave home, or even commit suicide.

Vocational Problems What to do after finishing school, where one's talents lie, how to avoid going into a vocation selected by the family but holding no interest for the adolescent, whether one will be able to get a job, and dread at the thought of giving up the carefree life of school for the more demanding life of the business world—these become problems for the adolescent as his school days come to an end. Many adolescents brood over their futures, and this predisposes them to emotional tension.

Religious Doubts To an adolescent whose childhood religious training has been along strict and orthodox lines, a period of doubt frequently comes when he finds that his school training or the religious beliefs of his friends disagree with the beliefs of his childhood. The more orthodox the early religious training, the more likely is the adolescent to have emotional disturbance.

Unfavorable Family Relationships The adolescent who feels secure in his parents' affection is prepared to meet the storm and strain of the adolescent years without too much disturbance. Unfortunately, many adolescents lack favorable relationships with their parents (56,84,138). Studies of adolescents admitted to mental hospitals have revealed that most had suffered from family troubles and that a high proportion of them had shown symptoms of emotional disturbance since early childhood (154, 158,166).

Many adolescents feel that they are misunderstood or unfairly treated by their families. They go around with chips on their shoulders and are ready to fly off the handle at the slightest provocation. Too strict parental discipline, too little independence for the adolescent, and a lack of understanding of adolescent interests are the chief troublemakers in the home. They lead to constant friction between parents and adolescents (64,68).

Obstacles That Prevent the Adolescent from Doing What He Desires Financial obstacles that make it impossible for the adolescent to have the clothes, school advantages, recreations, or spending money that his friends have are a source of great concern to him. He becomes emotionally upset whenever he is with his friends who have more than he. Parental restraints and financial dependence offer obstacles to prevent early marriage; this gives rise to emotional tension unless satisfactory substitute outlets are found (51).

common emotional patterns in adolescence

In adolescence, there are marked changes in the stimuli that give rise to emotions, just as there are changes in the form of emotional response. However, there is a similarity between childhood and adolescent emotions in that at both ages the dominant emotions tend to be unpleasant—mainly fear and anger in their different forms, jealousy, and envy. This, of course, does not mean that the adolescent does not experience the pleasant emotions—joy, affection, happiness, or curiosity. Like the child, he does. But, on the whole, they occur less frequently and with less intensity than the unpleasant emotions. This is especially true during the *early* years of adolescence.

Social factors are largely responsible for the dominance of the unpleasant emotions, for the form of expression each emotion takes, and for the type of stimulus that gives rise to the emotion. Thwarting of adolescent wishes and threats to the security and independence the adolescent is attempting to achieve come mainly from people and social situations rather than from the individual himself. Social pressures are largely responsible for the way in which the adolescent expresses his emotions.

Similarly, social factors are important in determining what the adolescent will respond to emotionally. If it is the "thing to do" to laugh at jokes related to members of minority groups, the adolescent will respond to such jokes with emotional reactions. Because of the high social value placed on personal appearance, the adolescent will be anxious if he feels that his ap-

pearance does not conform to social expectations. Furthermore, because different social classes have different values and different expectations, social-class differences in emotions are greater in adolescence than in childhood when the individual was less aware of and less influenced by social pressures than he is in adolescence (132,153). Figure 3–3 shows changes in emotional behavior from childhood into early adolescence. Note the marked drop in timidity and fighting both of which are socially unacceptable patterns of behavior in adolescence.

Research work related to the stimuli and responses in different emotions has been limited in scope for the adolescent years. Furthermore, the techniques used for the study of children's emotions are superior to those used in the study of adolescent emotions. In spite of these limitations, an attempt will be made to give as complete a picture as possible of the emotions commonly found among American adolescents today.

FEAR

By the time the child reaches adolescence, he has learned that many of the things he formerly was afraid of are neither dangerous nor harmful. As a result, he no longer fears them. This does not mean that fear vanishes with the onset of adolescence but rather that children's fears are replaced by more mature ones. The adolescent, for example, is far more likely to be afraid of social situations than of animals; the reverse is true of children. Furthermore, the adolescent is more likely to "borrow trouble" and imagine things that might happen to frighten him than the child, whose fears are more closely related to real experiences (74).

There are two important reasons for the changes that take place in fears in adolescence. The first is a *change in values.* The more important a thing is to a person, the more likely he is to be afraid if he feels that it is a threat to him. Speaking or acting in front of a group of teachers, parents, and peers is far less important to a child than to an adolescent who is anxious to create a good impression. As a result, audience sensitivity or stage fright is more common among adolescents than among children (132).

The second reason for change in fears is that the adolescent has many *more new experiences* to cope with than the child. Anything new and difficult is likely to give rise to fear in the adolescent, just as it is in the child. The adolescent is constantly confronted with the new and different as his social horizons broaden.

Types of Fears   The fears of adolescents may be subdivided, roughly, into four general classifications.

fears of natural phenomena and material objects   These include bugs, snakes, dogs, storms, strange noises, thunder and lightning, elevators, fire, water, trains, and airplanes.

fears of social relationship   These include (1) meeting people; (2) being with people who are clever, large, important, sly, sarcastic, cruel, overbearing, haughty, or humorous; (3) being alone; (4) being in a crowd; (5) reciting in class or making a speech; (6) being at parties with the other sex; (7) being in groups that are predominantly made up of adults. Shyness is often prolonged and intensified by adults' joking or forcing the adolescent into situations where he must display his weakness.

fears relating to self   These include poverty; death; serious illness of self or members of the family; being incapacitated by blindness, deafness, or paralysis; personal inadequacy with regard to sex, getting and holding a job, failure in school or business, popularity, examinations and grades, marriage, anything that would distress or annoy parents, and moral crises.

fears of the unknown   Anything unfamiliar to the adolescent is likely to give rise to fear. Among the common unknown experiences adolescents fear are staying alone in the house, being in the dark, going away

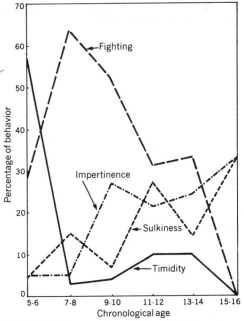

FIGURE 3–3 Changes in emotional behavior from childhood to adolescence. (Adapted from K. C. Garrison: *Growth and development.* 2d ed. New York: Longmans, Green, 1959. Used by permission.)

to a strange place, being with strange people, operations, and death (8,10,27,94,132, 153).

Variations in Fears   Adolescents vary in what they fear because their fears are closely related to what is important to them. There are, however, certain predictable variations in their fears. Girls' fears, on the whole, are different from those of boys of the same age. These *sex* differences are closely related to sex differences in values. Because girls put higher value on personal safety than boys, for example, they have more fears of animals and strangers than do boys (58, 94). *Social-class* differences in fears are likewise common. Adolescents of the lower social classes show more fear of threat from parents while those of the middle classes are more afraid of strangers and of social attitudes toward them (8).

What the adolescent fears will depend, to a certain extent, upon his *age*. The fears of senior high school students center around school activities and social relationships. Fears of the unknown, especially of the responsibilities they will be expected to assume as they grow older and of competency to earn a living, are likewise common at this age (8,10,128). By the time the adolescent reaches college age, he has fewer fears but shows a tendency to worry more than the younger adolescent does. The fears of the older adolescent are mainly social in nature (6,94). Figure 3–4 shows how fears decline as adolescence progresses. By the age of 16 years, most boys and girls claim that they have no fears. This may be a defense against being regarded as a "fraidy cat" (58).

Fear Responses Fear responses follow a fairly stereotyped pattern in adolescence. The two elements in the pattern of fear response are rigidity of the body and running away. Rigidity of the body is accompanied by paling, trembling, and perspiring. This is the dominant reaction in adolescence. The adolescent, to avoid the possibility of being looked upon by others as a "fraidy cat," learns to run before the fear situation arises. That is, he learns to avoid situations that might cause fear, worry, or anxiety. Whenever he has an examination for which he is unprepared, for example, he tries to get out of taking it by imagining he is not up to par physically and consequently cannot do justice to himself if he takes the examination at that time. In the same way, fear of social situations causes him to plan other activities for the times when the social situations will occur. He then rationalizes the avoidance to himself and to others by stressing the pressure of more important duties and responsibilities.

WORRY

As the number and intensity of fears decrease, worry is substituted for fear. Worry is a type of fear that comes mainly from imaginary causes. In all worry, there is an element of reality, but it is exaggerated out of all proportion. Thus, worry may be considered an emotional reaction to "borrowed trouble"; the trouble may come but it has not done so up to the present.

Like fear, worry is *specific* in the sense that it is related to a person, thing, or situation. An adolescent worries about an examination, about his adequacy to make a speech before a group, or about whether he will ever get a job. This differs from anxiety, which is a generalized state of fear not identified with any one specific cause. Worry is often more intense than fear, especially during adolescence when boys and girls realize that there is little for them to fear in our modern civilized life. Because it is the "thing to do" to worry during adolescence, social pressures tend to increase the frequency and intensity of worry. Many adolescents worry because their friends worry more than they (58).

Types of Worries Worries parallel fears in the sense that they are closely related to what is important to the individual. If, for example, it is important to the adolescent to create a good impression when he speaks before a group or participates in an athletic contest, he will worry about whether he will do so, even before he begins the activity (132). Because personal appearance is more important to girls than to boys, girls worry more about their looks and are more concerned when their looks do not come up to their expectations (153).

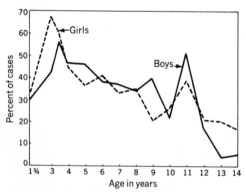

FIGURE 3–4 Frequency of specific fears of boys and girls at different ages. (Adapted from J. Macfarlane, K. Allen, and M. P. Honzik: *A developmental study of the behavior problems of normal children between twenty-one months and fourteen years.* Berkeley, Calif.: University of California Press, 1954. Used by permission.)

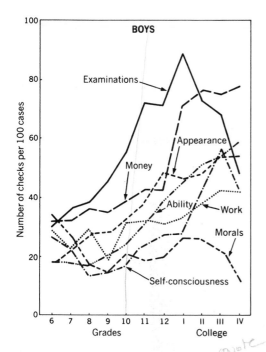

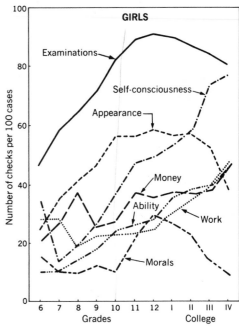

FIGURE 3–5 Age trends in worries and anxieties during the adolescent years. (Adapted from S. L. Pressey and R. G. Kuhlen: *Psychological development during the life span.* New York: Harper & Row, 1957. Used by permission.)

Worries, like fears, fall into four major categories: worries about material objects and natural phenomena, worries about social relationships, worries about self-adequacy, and worries about the unknown (141). Which of these is dominant for a given adolescent will depend mainly on what is important to him. And what is important to him will be influenced largely by the values of the social group with which he is identified. When an adolescent is identified with a high school group that is college-oriented, each adolescent in the group, regardless of his capacities, will worry about whether he will be accepted in the college of his choice (27,40,114,159).

Because high value is placed on social acceptance and early dating today, college students of this era have been reported to worry more about their looks, popularity, and marriage than was true of college students 20 years ago. While adolescents of today worry as much as did adolescents in the past, what they worry about has changed (139).

Variations in Worry Because worries are so markedly influenced by values, and be-

cause certain values are characteristically held by certain groups within a culture, there are worries that are predictable among the members of these subgroups. Among American adolescents of today, values change with *age*. Consequently, the worries of a young adolescent can be expected to be different from those of a child or an older adolescent. Because school demands are greater for high school students than for elementary school children, school worries play a dominant role in the young adolescent's emotional life. Worries about boy-girl relations, about quarrels with family members, and about popularity are dominant also at this age (40,46,58,114).

As adolescents grow older, their outlook on life becomes more mature. This influences the severity as well as the source of their worries. Changes in worries for boys and girls as they progress through adolescence is illustrated in Figure 3–5. If the adolescent remains in school or college throughout the adolescent years, many of the worries confronting him will be the same as those which concerned him when he was younger. If, on the other hand, the older adolescent goes to work, his worries will be more likely to center on getting and holding a job (75,139,141).

Because boys and girls have different interests and values, it is logical that there would be *sex* differences in worries. While boys may worry about many of the same things as girls, they are likely to worry about them a year or so later because of the normal lag in boys' sexual maturity (40,114). On the other hand, some of their most troublesome worries differ from those of girls. Boys, for example, worry more about their abilities and vocations. They also worry more about where and how to get the money they need for their social lives. As appearance and social acceptance are more important to girls, their worries center around these problems (9,45,75,139,140). Sex differences in worries are shown in Figure 3–5, page 85. Note that these differences become more pronounced as adolescents get older.

While there is relatively little difference in the amount of worrying adolescents of different *socioeconomic groups* do, what they worry about is different. One of the most pronounced socioeconomic differences in worries relates to school. Being admitted by a college of their choice, preparing for their future vocations, and meeting the "right" people in school and college are more highly valued by boys and girls of the middle and upper groups than by individuals of the lower socioeconomic groups. Lower-class adolescents' school worries tend to center around their adequacy to recite in class if called on by the teacher and their relationships with a teacher whom they regard as hostile to them because of their lower-class status (8). The school worries of boys and girls of high and low socioeconomic groups are shown in Figure 3–6.

Worry Responses The adolescent who is worried about something generally talks about his worries to his friends or teachers, or he may write to a newspaper or maga-

zine columnist. The major reason for verbalizing his worry is to gain sympathy, understanding, and help. The very fact that the adolescent shows little desire to avoid the things that worry him, as he does in the case of fear, and that he is willing to let others know of his emotional state would suggest that he is less concerned about an unfavorable social reaction than he is in the case of fear.

Another common response to worry is to have a harassed or worried look—a look of preoccupation with something not present and a tendency to disregard what is present. The worried adolescent who fails to respond to what is happening around him and appears to be looking off into space, sooner or later is asked what is the matter. This gives him the opportunity to verbalize his worries.

ANXIETY

Anxiety, like worry, is a form of fear. It is a (75):

> . . . *persisting distressful psychological state arising from an inner conflict. The distress may be experienced as a feeling of vague uneasiness or foreboding, a feeling of being on edge, or as any of a variety of other feelings, such as fear, anger, restlessness, irritability, depression, or other diffuse and nameless feelings.*

Because anxiety is an uncomfortable state, the individual tries to avoid it but often cannot do so (113).

As in worry, the threat that gives rise to this uncomfortable state is more often imaginary than real. The adolescent anticipates trouble more than being actually faced with it. However, anxiety differs from worry in one major aspect: it is a *generalized emotional state* rather than a specific one. In other words, the individual is not anxious about a specific thing; instead he is generally stirred up or in a state of jitters.

Anxiety takes two different forms: neurotic and socially oriented. *Neurotic anxiety* stems from feelings of generalized personal inadequacy, feelings of being incapable of competing with others in any or every situa-

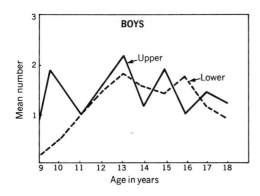

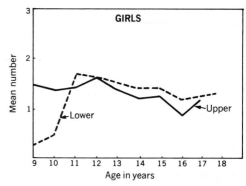

FIGURE 3–6 School worries of young adolescents from low and high socioeconomic groups. (Adapted from H. Angelino, J. Dollins, and E. V. Mech: Trends in the "fears and worries" of school children as related to socio-economic status and age. *J. genet. Psychol.*, 1956, **89**, 263–276. Used by permission.)

tion. It is accompanied by morbid fears, obsessional thoughts, and a tendency to build up defenses. *Socially oriented anxiety*, by contrast, stems from feelings of inadequacy in social situations. It is expressed in shyness, fear of being criticized, and low self-confidence. An individual who experiences socially oriented anxiety is more suggestible, more easily persuaded, and more gullible than the one who experiences the neurotic forms of anxiety (73). Socially oriented anxiety is normal in adolescence because few adolescents, especially in the early part of the period, escape it. As Jersild (75) has pointed out:

> From such evidence as is available it can be assumed that anxiety is widespread among adolescents. Probably all have what has been called "normal" anxiety, and a large proportion probably are burdened with mild or with severe forms of what has been called "neurotic" anxiety.

Origin of Anxiety   Anxiety normally develops from repeated and varied worries. The more often the adolescent worries and the more different worries he has, the more likely it is that his worries will develop into a generalized state of anxiety. What he is anxious about, as is true of what he worries about, is culturally determined (116). When, for example, the cultural group places high value on appearance, on popularity, on academic achievement, or on being like others of the same age group, anxiety develops when the adolescent feels that he has not measured up satisfactorily to cultural expectations. At first, his anxiety

may be socially oriented and show itself in shyness, lack of self-confidence, and fear of criticism. In time, if generalized feelings of inadequacy and inferiority develop, neurotic anxiety is likely to replace the socially oriented anxiety (9,95,113,118).

While anxiety may occur at any age, it is most likely to do so at times of rapid development and change. During adolescence, when the individual is "breaking the cocoon" that protected him throughout childhood and is emerging into a strange new world, he is most likely to suffer from feelings of inadequacy and to be anxious about his capacity to meet the new challenges that confront him (78,117). Most of the adolescent's anxiety is socially oriented; relatively little stems from feelings of guilt resulting from some inner conflict which, in time, gives rise to neurotic anxiety (146).

Expressions of Anxiety   In general, the expressions of anxiety fall into three major categories: behavior patterns, effects on achievements, and susceptibility to group influences.

behavior patterns   The characteristic behavior patterns of an anxious person are those of unhappiness, restlessness, unaccountable moodiness, mood swings, irritability, and dissatisfaction with self and others. Furthermore, as Jersild has pointed out, there is reason to believe that the adolescent is suffering from anxiety if he seems sullen and "ornery"; if he "overreacts," by being greatly upset by little things or bitterly angry at something that seems trivial to others; if he "underreacts," by being apathetic and unmoved in situations where normally a person would experience some emotion; if he is driven by compulsions to the point where he is in a constant "fever of activity"; if he acts distinctly "out of character" by behaving contrary to his normal patterns; if he is rigid, self-righteous, and dogmatic in his attitudes; or if he imposes impossible standards on himself (75). To cover up his self-dissatisfaction, the anxious adolescent may withdraw to a daydream world; he may use defense mechanisms; or he may project the blame for his self-dissatisfaction on others (41,75,107,117, 135,146). Figure 3–7 shows some of the common behavior patterns of anxious adolescents.

effects on achievement   How much effect anxiety has on either the quantity or the quality of work will depend not so much upon the intensity of the anxiety as upon the type of work the individual is doing. Anxiety may increase the speed of work but not necessarily the accuracy. It is especially detrimental in situations where preparation is impossible. When reasoning is involved, anxiety is far more detrimental than in situations where the activity can be carried out in a habitual manner. It is also more detrimental in situations in which the individual has experienced failure in the past (3,65,75,133,136,149,150,164).

susceptibilty to group influences   The more anxious the adolescent is, the more suggestible he is and the more influenced by the reactions of other people. This is especially true of persons who experience socially oriented anxiety (73). Anxiety makes the individual react as the group expects him to act and, in addition, it serves as a strong motivation to form social contacts. Social isolation for an anxious person is a source of concern that increases his anxiety and motivates him to act so that he can improve his social contacts (75,78,165).

Variations in Anxiety   How adolescents react to, handle, or defend themselves against anxiety-provoking situations will differ greatly. Their reactions will be determined, to a large extent, by how they interpret the situation that gives rise to their anxiety. If, for example, an adolescent is anxious about his future achievements or about getting a job, he is likely to be more anxious in a test situation than the adolescent who is less anxious about his future and, as a result, less concerned about how well he does (61). The more intelligent the adolescent, the more able he is to anticipate future problems and complications in the way of his plans. As a result, he is more likely to experience anxiety than is the less intelligent individual (3,147).

Because anxiety is considered sex inappropriate for boys, boys tend to withdraw from situations that might give rise to anxiety. If this is impossible, they build up defenses against such situations or try to hide any anxiety they may experience. When girls experience anxiety, they usually

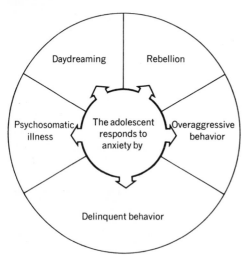

FIGURE 3–7 Typical responses to anxiety-producing stimuli during the adolescent years. (Adapted from L. D. Crow and A. Crow: *Adolescent development and adjustment*. 2d ed. New York: McGraw-Hill, 1965. Used by permission.)

react to it by withdrawing into daydreams; boys, by contrast, react to anxiety by rebelliousness and by acts that have a "nuisance value" (91,162). Adolescents of middle-class backgrounds and those whose parents are socially mobile experience more anxiety than do those of the lower or upper social classes or those who are socially more stable. American adolescents tend to experience more anxiety than those of England where social mobility is less widespread (122).

ANGER

Anger stimuli in adolescence are mostly social. While it is true that adolescents are angered by things and situations also, the greatest number and the most intense anger stimuli are related to people. The most common causes of anger among junior high school students are being teased, being unfairly treated by people, having a sibling take their property or impose on them, being lied to, being bossed, having sarcastic remarks made to them, or having things not go right (49,58,78). Much the same type of thing angers a high school student.

Among college students, people cause anger more frequently than do things. Anger is more violent in the former case than in the latter. Of the social causes, thwarted self-assertion, such as unjust accusations, insulting or sarcastic comments, unwelcome advice, contradictions, being teased, being bossed, and not being invited to a party are most common. Hostility toward others is more common among college students than nonhostility or self-hostility (63,138).

In addition to social causes, interruption of habitual activities, such as study and sleep, failure in activities undertaken, and thwarted plans give rise to anger. Thwarting of some course of action involving self-assertion invariably leads to anger (6,75, 119,138).

Boys, on the whole, are more often angered than girls by things that do not work as they want them to work and by situations. Girls, by contrast, are more often angered by people and social situations. This, unquestionably, is due in part at least to the fact that girls are given less freedom

and are more often thwarted in what they want to do by people than are boys.

Boys are more often thwarted by their own ineptitude. Throughout adolescence, the number and severity of anger experiences the individual has depend not so much upon the person's age and sex as upon the environment in which he is forced to live and work. The more environmental thwarting there is, the greater and the more frequent will be the anger experiences. Because girls at every age and in every social class are subjected to more thwarting from their environment than are boys, it is understandable that girls experience more anger (58,75,138).

Anger Responses Many young adolescents fly off the handle in temper tantrums not unlike those of young children. In his anger, the young adolescent will kick and throw things, stamp his feet, leave the room and slam the door behind him, refuse to speak, lock himself in his room and refuse to emerge until his anger subsides. Many girls, at puberty or during the early part of adolescence, burst into tears when they become angry. Because most adolescents were taught, as children, that "overt expressions of hostile feelings are usually kept out of sight by well-mannered people," the young adolescent is often embarrassed and ashamed when he expresses his anger in an outburst of temper (176). As a result, there is a decrease in fighting and other aggressive forms of behavior and a substitution of more mature patterns of anger response. (See Figures 3–8 and 3–9.) As may be seen in Figure 3–9, there is a slower decline in temper outbursts among boys than girls partly because of the greater energy of boys but mainly because of the greater cultural acceptance of aggressiveness in anger on the part of boys (107).

By the time they are 15 or 16 years old, most adolescents abandon aggressive responses as infantile. They then show their anger by stony glances at the person who angers them, by being sulky and disagreeable, by refusal to speak, by muttering under their breath, or by leaving the presence of those who have angered them. Except

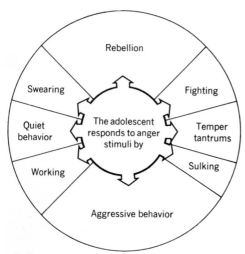

FIGURE 3–8 Typical responses to anger-producing stimuli during the adolescent years. (Adapted from L. D. Crow and A. Crow: *Adolescent development and adjustment.* 2d ed. New York: McGraw-Hill, 1965. Used by permission.)

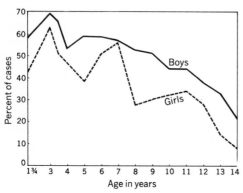

FIGURE 3–9 The frequency of temper tantrums among boys and girls at different ages. (Adapted from J. Macfarlane, K. Allen, and M. P. Honzik: *A developmental study of the behavior problems of normal children between twenty-one months and fourteen years.* Berkeley, Calif.: University of California Press, 1954. Used by permission.)

for crying by girls and kicking by boys, most of the overt expressions of anger characteristic of the temper outbursts of the younger adolescent have disappeared. However, the older adolescent substitutes verbal attacks for the physical attacks he used earlier. He calls people who annoy him names, he swears, and he lashes back with bitter sar-

casm. He tries to get his revenge by belittling and ridiculing. Whenever possible, and in whatever way possible, he humiliates his adversary.

As the adolescent grows older, the energy that might be used for attacks on others is spent in pacing the floor, in restlessness, in throwing or smashing things within his reach, or by engaging in some form of violent exercise to work off emotional steam. Instead of immediately releasing emotional tension through overt responses, the angry adolescent learns to hold back the overt responses until they will prove to be most effective (6,58,75). The adolescent is far less likely to blame himself for being responsible for the thing that angered him than he is to direct his hostility toward specific persons or toward no one in particular (63). Furthermore, the actual responses made by the angry adolescent are far less violent than what he said he felt like doing, thus showing an attempt to control the overt expressions of anger to conform to social expectations (119).

variations in anger responses There are marked variations in the ways in which adolescents express their anger. Boys, as a group, tend to express their anger more overtly than girls, both in physical and verbal attacks. This *sex difference* is not due to greater intensity of the boys' anger but to the fact that the social group will tolerate or even give its stamp of approval to more overt expressions of anger by boys than by girls. In boys, aggressive reactions in anger are regarded as a sign of masculinity; in girls, they are regarded as bad manners (58,107,176).

How the adolescent expresses his anger is greatly influenced by the type of *child-training methods* he has been subjected to. Those who have dominant or overprotective parents, for example, often have difficulty in expressing their anger overtly. Instead, they tend to displace it by finding an innocent victim for their pent-up anger (126). Or if they have been trained at home not to fight with their playmates when they are angry, it is not unusual for them to show hostility toward a parent, usually the mother, and to treat her as the scapegoat for pent-up anger (105).

The *religious training* the adolescent received in childhood has a marked influence on how he expresses anger as he grows older. If he has been brought up on the philosophy of turning the other cheek and loving his enemies, he will regard any aggressive response in anger as sinful. As a result, he becomes intropunitive—accepting the responsibility for the unpleasant situation that gave rise to his anger and showing marked feelings of guilt for any angry responses he makes. Those with less religious training, by contrast, blame others for the situation that aroused their anger, often allowing themselves free expression of anger with no feeling of guilt or shame (15).

Adolescents from the lower *socioeconomic* groups or from *minority* religious or racial backgrounds tend to be more aggressive when angry than those from higher socioeconomic groups or those with a majority-group background. This is especially true of boys. According to the values of the lower socioeconomic groups, aggressiveness when angry is a sign of masculinity (99,111). Adolescents of minority-group backgrounds show their aggressiveness more often, however, by displacing it than by direct attack on the people who have angered them (142,156).

Frequency of Anger   How frequently the adolescent is aroused to anger will depend partly upon the number and severity of environmental thwartings and partly upon his own levels of aspiration. Some adolescents live in homes and attend schools or colleges where a minimum of restrictions exists. Others are constantly thwarted by parental, school, or neighborhood restrictions. Likewise, some adolescents have a realistic concept of their abilities, while others do not. As a result, the latter will be aroused to anger more frequently than the former. Thus, there is evidence that the *number of anger experiences varies with the adolescent's environment, not with his age.* The

more thwartings there are, the more often he will become angry (6,58,79,119).

Duration of Anger   How long anger lasts depends partly on the adolescent's age and partly on how much he suppresses his angry outbursts. Among preschool children, for example, the average duration of an anger outburst has been found to be less than 5 minutes. Among college students, angry outbursts have been reported to vary in length from 1 minute to 2 days, with an average duration of 15 minutes. The reason for the greater duration is that the adolescent attempts to suppress his anger instead of expressing it directly and thus keeps it in his system longer. In general, the more severe the anger, the longer it lasts. However, most cases of anger in adolescence fall in the shorter time intervals (119).

ANNOYANCES

Annoyances are forms of anger but they are not so intense as anger. They are irritations or unpleasant feelings which have been built up as a result of conditioning; they come from unpleasant experiences with people, things, or even the individual's own acts. Annoyances are more common and more important in the life of the adolescent than is anger. Like anger, annoyances are unpleasant. They differ from anger in two major respects; first, the individual derives pleasure from talking about the things that annoy him, which is not true in the case of anger, and second, annoyances are more invigorating than anger, which tends to have a depressing effect (31,58,74,75).

Causes of Annoyances   Annoyances are mainly social in origin. The causes of adolescent annoyances may be classified, roughly, into five categories. They are:

1 Human behavior
2 Nonhuman things and activities, exclusive of clothes
3 Clothes and manner of dress
4 Alterable physical characteristcs of people
5 Persisting physical characteristics of people

Of these five categories, the annoyances arising from human behavior are most frequent; adolescents are more annoyed by the behavior of others than by any other single cause. Clothing and manner of dress are also sources of common annoyances (31).

It has been found that annoyances are relatively stable in the sense that what is annoying to an older child continues to be annoying to him during the adolescent years. Because social relationships provide the source of most annoyances, and because social relationships play an even more important role in the life of the adolescent than in the child's life, annoyances not only remain persistent but they tend to increase in intensity with age (36).

Responses to Annoyances The adolescent's response to annoying situations is very different from his response to anger-provoking situations. Instead of aggressively attacking the person or thing that annoys him, the adolescent shuns them whenever possible. Studies of social acceptance have revealed that adolescents who annoy their classmates are shunned by them. Even though they are in the same room, they are treated as if they were not present, and they are excluded from the activities of the group.

Similarly, adolescents shun places or things which annoy them. Instead of making aggressive attacks on situations that irritate him in an attempt to improve them, the adolescent withdraws and selects situations more to his liking. In addition to withdrawal from people or situations that give rise to annoyance, the adolescent, in his own behavior, tries to avoid the things that annoy him in the behavior of others. If, for example, he finds certain mannerisms annoying in others, he tries to avoid using them. However, adolescents sometimes do the very things that they have found to be annoying in others (32).

Variations in Annoyances Variations in annoyances result primarily from differences in environmental and social experiences. The adolescent whose *socioeconomic status*

is similar or even slightly superior to that of his classmates will have fewer situations to annoy him in the home than will the adolescent whose home background is inferior and who, as a result, is embarrassed and ashamed of his home, his parents, and his relatives. Similarly, a *popular* adolescent has fewer reasons to be annoyed with his classmates and teachers than has the adolescent whose social acceptance falls below the level he had hoped to achieve.

Annoyances likewise vary according to how *well adjusted* the adolescent is. Poorly adjusted adolescents tend, on the whole, to find more situations annoying to them. Furthermore, the intensity of these annoyances is greater (82).

FRUSTRATIONS

Frustrations are forms of anger which result from interference with the satisfaction of some need. They may result from deprivation arising from the environment or from the individual's inability to reach the goal he sets for himself because of some personal inadequacy. Frustrations are accompanied by feelings of helplessness; this gives rise to anger which may be minor or major in strength. While annoyances and frustrations are both forms of anger, they differ from one another in two major respects: First, annoyances arise mainly from social situations while many frustrations arise from the individual's ineptitudes, and second, annoyances generally give rise to withdrawal and avoidance reactions while frustrations lead to aggressive attacks on the obstacles that prevent the individual from doing what he wants to do.

Source of Frustration The higher the value the social group places on what the adolescent wants to do, the more frustrating it will be to him if he is unable to do it (89). When, for example, high value is placed on making a team in some prestigeful sport, it will be very frustrating to a boy not to make the team because he lacks the necessary skill. Similarly, when high value is placed on dating, a girl whose parents claim that she is too young to date or who is so unattractive that boys do not want to date her will be more frustrated than a girl whose friends regard dating as a waste of time.

Certain frustrations are more common than others. Among the most common are physique which is either not sex appropriate or attractive; poor health which is a handicap to participation in activities popular with the peer group; lack of money to do what members of the peer group do; personality traits that interfere with achieving social acceptance; and mental ability that is inadequate to reach the goals adolescents set for themselves. Most of these are obstacles in the path of successful achievement of their desires and have originated within themselves. Conflicts with parents, lack of social techniques, and conflicts with family standards—all of which are environmental in origin—are less frequent sources of frustration (26,62).

Reaction to Frustrations While not all frustrations are met with anger few are not accompanied by some degree of anger. Of the many forms of reaction to frustration, the following are the most common among adolescents:

Aggression toward others, "extrapunitive," or toward self, "intropunitive," is a common reaction. In the former, the reaction may be physically overt, sometimes violent, stemming from the adolescent's need to strike out at the offending person or object. In the latter, the reaction is generally less violent and more likely to be verbal than physical.

Displacement of anger, engendered by frustrations, is a common reaction among adolescents who have discovered that unfavorable social reactions result when they react aggressively. Consequently, they find an innocent victim, usually a parent, teacher, or law-enforcement officer and clear their systems of pent-up anger by verbal attacks, often behind the backs of their victims.

Passivity and withdrawal from the offending person or object are methods of reacting to frustration by adolescents who have discovered that there is little they can

do to change the frustrating situation. These may take the form of imaginary invalidism or daydreaming.

Regression to earlier situations that proved to be less frustrating is a common accompaniment of withdrawal. The adolescent who is unwilling to accept frustrations and yet who sees little opportunity to change them regresses to situations which have satisfied his needs in the past. The boy, for example, who is frustrated by not being chosen to play on the football team, may go back to bowling or some form of play where team membership is not essential.

Frustrations are sometimes met with *constructive behavior*. The adolescent may put forth more effort to overcome the block, use different ways to reach the same end, or work out substitute goals, if the obstacle is insurmountable. Of the different common forms of reaction to frustration, this method is most likely to lead to personal satisfaction and to good social adjustments (20,43,89,96,105,178).

Individual Differences Because the social group not only tolerates but even gives its stamp of approval to aggressiveness in *boys*, it is not surprising that adolescent boys react aggressively to frustrations more than do adolescent girls. *Northern* high school boys have been found to be more overtly aggressive, and Southern boys more passive, in their reactions to frustrations. Girls, in both areas, are more conforming and less aggressive than boys. *Negroes* tend to be more overtly aggressive than whites, especially boys. *Lower-class adolescents* are more aggressive in their reactions to frustration than are those of middle- and upper-class backgrounds whose training has emphasized the importance of avoiding aggressive behavior no matter what the situation is. Regardless of social-class background, adolescent girls tend to react more passively to frustrating situations than boys (43,105,111).

How the adolescent *perceives the situation* will have a marked influence on how he reacts to it. If, for example, he has found people in authority, whether parents or teachers, to be a source of frustration, he will perceive anyone in authority, even a member of the peer group who has been selected for a leadership role, as a source of possible threat to him. Consequently, he will react more aggressively than he would had his past experiences colored his present perceptions more favorably. Perception of the situation is markedly influenced by the *personality* of the individual. Persons who are well adjusted tend, on the whole, to perceive situations realistically and accurately; as a result, they do not regard them as sources of frustration. Neurotics tend to regard *any* obstacle as a frustration (151,170,178).

JEALOUSY

Jealousy occurs when a person feels insecure or when he is afraid that his status in the group or in the affections of a significant person has been threatened. The stimulus to jealousy is always social in origin. It can be aroused by any situation involving people for whom the individual has a deep feeling of affection or whose attention and acceptance he craves. Thus, in jealousy, two emotional elements are present, fear and anger. Which element plays a more important role will vary with the situation. In some cases of jealousy, fear of loss of status is stronger than anger, while in others, anger is stronger than fear.

As childhood draws to a close, jealousy is a relatively infrequent emotion. But it flares up again during puberty and often persists into the early part of adolescence. There are normally two peaks in the curve of jealous reactions, the first occurring during the preschool years, and the second, at puberty. Among girls, there is a tendency for jealousy to be stronger during the preschool years and, among boys, at puberty. The peaks of jealousy for boys and girls are shown in Figure 3–10. Note the relative absence of jealousy during the elementary school years, the time when boys and girls who are making reasonably good social adjustments experience greater feelings of security than they do at puberty or during the early years of adolescence.

Causes of Jealousy What gives rise to jealousy in adolescence will depend to a major extent on what makes the person feel insecure. And the degree of insecurity will depend on the values he places on relationships with certain people. As he grows older, the threat to security comes more in relationships outside the home than within the home. Thus, sibling jealousy is less common in late adolescence than it was earlier, and peer jealousy, more common.

This does not mean, however, that there is no sibling jealousy during adolescence. There is, but it comes mainly when younger siblings are given privileges at an earlier age than the adolescent was given the same privileges or when he feels that there is parental favoritism toward another sibling. If the independence that comes from privileges did not mean so much to him, he would have less reason to be jealous.

The high value placed on social acceptance is at the basis of much of the jealousy the adolescent experiences outside the home. He becomes jealous of classmates who are more popular than he. The less secure he feels in his social relationships with the peer group, the more likely he is to be jealous of those whose social acceptance seems assured. An adolescent who is college-oriented is often jealous of classmates whose academic work is superior to his and who are accepted in colleges which he aspires to attend.

Jealousy generally reaches a peak during the adolescent years when dating becomes important. Because this is a new experience for the adolescent, he feels insecure and unsure of his abilities to cope with the problems dating gives rise to. In addition, the high social value placed on popularity with members of the opposite sex makes the adolescent jealous of peers who achieve greater success in this area than he. A girl, for example, is likely to be extremely jealous of an age-mate who is asked for dates by boys who are regarded as the big wheels of the class, or who starts to go steady sooner than she.

Boys show less jealousy in dating situations than girls. On the other hand, the prestige value of achievement in sports and in making the "right" college is greater for boys. Consequently, when boys show jealousy of their peers it is generally in situations where girls are not involved—in strictly masculine areas of behavior.

Jealous Reactions Typically, the jealous reaction of the adolescent is verbal. Instead of a bodily attack on the individual who made him jealous, the adolescent will fight back with words. This substitute reaction takes many forms, the most common of which are sarcasm, ridicule, and talking about the individual in a derogatory manner when he is not present to defend himself. A more subtle form of verbal attack in jealousy is to make derogatory comments about the qualities, whether they be athletic ability, looks, or intelligence, which have made another a threat to the adolescent. Through these derogatory comments, he hopes to reduce the threat to his own status in the group.

ENVY

Envy is similar to jealousy in that it is an emotion directed toward an individual. It differs from jealousy in one major respect, however. It is not the individual who stimulates this emotion, but the *material possessions* of that individual. An adolescent girl, for example, may be very envious of one of her classmates whose clothes and home are far superior to hers. And because she envies this girl, she reacts to her in much the same way as if she were angry or jealous. Envy is, in reality, covetousness.

Even before childhood is over, it becomes apparent to the child that material possessions are an important asset and that they contribute to his social acceptance (5). Each year, as the child grows older, he is increasingly aware of how important material possessions are to social acceptance. To a young adolescent, they become a status symbol—an indication of his status in the social group. The adolescent realizes that material possessions not only give him prestige in the eyes of others but that they are essential to social acceptance. The better the material possessions, the greater will be

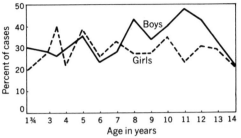

FIGURE 3–10 The frequency of jealousy among boys and girls at different ages. (Adapted from J. Macfarlane, K. Allen, and M. P. Honzik: *A developmental study of the behavior problems of normal children between twenty-one months and fourteen years.* Berkeley, Calif.: University of California Press, 1954. Used by permission.)

his prestige and, in turn, the greater his chances of acceptance (4).

Envy Responses The typical adolescent reaction to envy is *verbal* in form. The adolescent will tell those whose possessions he envies how "lucky" they are and will often hint or openly suggest that they share their possessions with him, claiming that his parents are too poor or "too tight" to give him the possessions he craves. Often the envious adolescent will try to minimize the value of the possessions of others or even ridicule them, thus compensating for his failure to have them. This sour-grapes attitude helps the adolescent to overcome to a certain extent the anger he feels when he realizes that others have more than he.

Some adolescents react to envy by trying to convince themselves that they are satisfied with what they have and that they are fortunate to have these things. This "Pollyanna" attitude is usually a product of their childhood training. It is closely related to home situations where the adolescent realizes that what he has is generally due to personal sacrifices his parents have made to give him things they can ill afford to give. Most adolescents, however, resent the fact that their fathers have not been more successful and, thus, able to give them the things their friends have.

Envy is not limited to verbal responses; it may lead to *action*. This action may take one of two common forms, *stealing* or *working* to be able to buy the material possessions the adolescent envies in others. Studies of juvenile delinquency have shown that stealing is one of the most common forms of misdemeanor among girls and that it ranks high among the misdemeanors of boys. Unlike the adult who steals to supply members of the family with food, clothing, or status symbols which they crave, the adolescent steals for his own benefit; he wants the material possessions or the money to buy them for himself. Typically, girls steal clothing, cosmetics, and costume jewelry while boys are more likely to steal cars (71, 90).

The envious adolescent may turn his energies into more socially acceptable behavior and work to earn the money to buy status symbols. Many adolescents take out-of-school jobs to buy the material possessions they envy in their classmates. Many, likewise, are motivated to study hard to get into prestige colleges and prepare for a prestige occupation which they believe will make it possible for them to have, in the future, the material possessions they envy in those who are economically more favored than they.

CURIOSITY

Curiosity in adolescence is weaker and more limited in scope than it is in childhood. Except when the adolescent goes to a completely new environment where there is little in common with his childhood days, there are few environmental stimuli to curiosity. This accounts for the limited scope of his curiosity as well as for the infrequency of its arousal.

For most adolescents the new interests arising from maturation of sex are the chief source of newness in their lives. Few boys and girls reach adolescence with so complete a knowledge of the physiology and psychology of sex that there is nothing new to stimulate their interest to explore and learn more. The typical adolescent, in the early years of this period, is so absorbed

with his changing body and changing interests that his attention is constantly attracted to the subject.

Aside from interest in sex as a source of new curiosity, the adolescent is also curious about scientific phenomena, world affairs, religion, and moral issues. These are far less universal in their appeal than sex. The motivating force back of most discussions about these matters, either with adults or with other adolescents, is to acquire further information or to clarify the adolescent's own point of view.

Responses in Curiosity When curious, the adolescent generally talks about the things that have aroused his curiosity and asks questions about them. He talks about sex to his friends or to any adults who are willing to discuss the matter with him. Books containing factual information about sex or a romantic treatment of sex in daily life are eagerly read by both boys and girls in the hope of supplementing the knowledge they had derived from talking about the matter. The adolescent gets firsthand information about the meaning of sex through stimulation of the sex organs and from contacts with members of the other sex with greater or less restraint. This matter will be discussed in detail in a later chapter dealing with sex problems.

Curiosity about matters other than sex is generally responded to in much the same way; the adolescent talks about them or asks questions about them. However, not all questioning is an indication of curiosity; it is sometimes for the purpose of showing off. The adolescent may want to trip the adult, show him that he is wrong, and thus display his own superiority. Usually, however, adolescents limit their questioning for this purpose to their peers, as they find the results more satisfactory.

HAPPINESS

Unlike most of the emotions already discussed, happiness is generalized rather than specific in form. It is a state of well-being, of pleasurable satisfaction—the opposite of anger, fear, jealousy or envy all of which lead to dissatisfaction. In its milder form, happiness results in a state of "euphoria"— a sense of well-being or of buoyancy; in its stronger form, it is known as "joy"—a state in which the individual is literally "walking on the clouds." Happiness is influenced to a large extent by the general physical condition of the individual, though good health alone is not enough to make the adolescent happy nor does it play as important a role in his happiness as it does in childhood (27).

Causes of Happiness There are four types of situations that can call forth happiness in varying degrees during the adolescent years. The first is one in which the individual "fits," or to which, by virtue of his capacities or abilities, he is *well adjusted*. A student whose IQ is high, whose academic preparation for college has been good, whose parents and teachers have encouraged his academic pursuits by their help and interest, and whose peers respect or even envy him for his academic achievements, will be happy in his college work because he fits—he is well adjusted to the college situation (27).

Feelings of superiority are the second common cause of happiness in adolescence. Because every adolescent at some time or other feels insecure and uncertain, any situation that gives rise to the opposite sort of feeling, no matter how short-lived it may be, produces at least a temporary state of happiness. Coming out at the head of the class in an examination, making the football team, being the belle of the ball, being elected to a class office, being invited to a dance by the best-looking boy in the crowd, or having an invitation accepted by the most popular girl are all situations that thrill and excite adolescents.

The third situation that calls forth joy in the adolescent is the *release of pent-up emotional energy*. When an adolescent has worried about a matter that never materializes (such as failing an examination for which he later discovers that he has received a high grade), or is angry at a remark that he later finds he has misinterpreted,

the release of the energy not used for overt action usually finds outlet in laughter and a general feeling of well-being.

The fourth type of situation that can give rise to happiness is one in which the adolescent *perceives a comic element*. The reason for his happiness is that he has a general feeling of well-being arising from a feeling of superiority; if he can laugh at others, he can feel superior to them. What the adolescent perceives as comic varies greatly. Most of the situations perceived as comic do not involve him personally. Instead, they involve others who are temporarily in a position of inferiority to him because of their stupidity, because they are the victims of ridicule, or because they are important people caught in an embarrassing or humiliating situation. This type of situation is known as the "objective comic" (29, 33,161).

It is a fairly universal rule, however, that the ability to perceive the comic elements in situations in which the individual himself is involved, the "subjective comic," is quite rare in adolescence. The reason for this is that the adolescent is far too sensitive to the opinions of others to want to put himself in a position in which he might be subjected to ridicule. When others laugh at him, it accentuates an already existing feeling of insecurity (38,100).

This has been well illustrated in a study of the attitudes of speech defectives toward humor based on speech defects. While it is true that all handicapped people are the butts of jokes at some time, they fail to find humor in such jokes. Stutterers, it has been found, resent jokes based on stuttering because they are highly sensitive about their defect. They feel that others do not understand that they are not trying to be funny when they speak. While they may cover up their resentment at jokes aimed at them by a façade of hardness and bravado, they still resent such jokes (70). Figure 3–11 shows the rating on humiliation for different jokes.

There are marked *variations* in perception of the comic, and hence in the personal satisfaction the adolescent derives

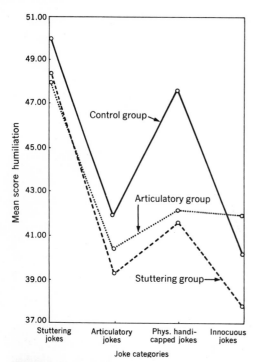

FIGURE 3–11 Humiliation ratings of three groups of subjects resulting from jokes of different types. (Adapted from L. S. Horowitz: Attitudes of speech defectives toward humor based on speech defects. *Speech Monogr.*, 1957, **24**, 46–55. Used by permission.)

from it (33,37,129). Boys, on the whole, have a better sense of humor than girls and derive more satisfaction from comic situations—provided they are not personally involved—than do girls. While there is no marked relationship between the adolescent's perception of the comic and the level of his intelligence, there is a definite relationship between intelligence and ability to empathize with, or put himself in the position of, the character depicted in the comic situation. Adolescents who are maladjusted derive more personal satisfaction from hostile humor than do those who are better adjusted. In the case of racial humor, for example, those with strong prejudices derive more satisfaction from such humor than do those who are better adjusted and who consequently feel embarrassed or guilty about inflating their egos at the expense of an innocent victim. And, finally, the per-

sonal satisfaction derived from comic situations will vary according to the number and strength of suppressed wishes that are given release in expressions of humor (120,121, 123,129,130,144).

Happy Reactions   The response in happiness varies little from one individual to another. The body is relaxed, and so is the face. The corners of the mouth turn upward in a smile. When the emotion is strong, smiling gives way to laughter. The individual produces sounds that vary in intensity according to the strength of the emotion. The characteristic laugh of boys is louder and lower in pitch than that of girls; sometimes the laughter of both is so uproarious that the whole body shakes and the sounds can be heard all over the house (58).

However, the adolescent soon discovers that uproarious laughter is not considered mature; if he wants to create the impression that he is grown up, he must control his laughter. If he laughs or even smiles just because he is happy, with no apparent reason, people are likely to regard him as "crazy." Should he smile or laugh in triumph over others, his response is regarded as gloating and he is considered a poor sport. Unless others laugh at a comic situation, he quickly discovers glances of disapproval from the other members of the group (25,37).

AFFECTION

Affection is a pleasant emotional state of relatively mild intensity; it is a *tender attachment* for a person, an animal, or an object. While commonly used interchangeably with "love," it differs from love in that, first, love is a stronger emotional state; second, love is normally directed toward a member of the opposite sex; and third, love has the components of sex desire. Affection may be directed toward members of the opposite sex, but it does not have the elements of sex desire nor does it have the same degree of intensity as love (60,85).

Affections are built up through pleasant associations; they are not innate. People tend to like those who like them and are friendly toward them. It is unlikely that a pleasant emotion would become associated with those who were indifferent, unfriendly, or rejectant in their behavior. Because a tender attachment for another comes from pleasant experiences, a reciprocal liking is developed; this leads to increasingly pleasant associations. As a result, affection literally grows with time; the more pleasant associations a person has with another, the more he likes him and shows it in his behavior (74,83).

Stimuli to Affection The stimuli that arouse affection in adolescence differ from those in childhood in a number of ways. First, in childhood, affection is aroused by people, objects (such as toys), and pets. In adolescence, by contrast, it is aroused primarily by people, rarely by inanimate objects, and only occasionally by animals, mainly family pets (23,87).

The second way in which stimuli that arouse affection among adolescents differ from those of children is in their intensity. Because the adolescent's affection is limited to a relatively few individuals and because adolescence is an age when all emotions are somewhat stronger than usual, the affections that the adolescent has for others are characteristically intense.

The third difference between the stimuli that arouse affection in adolescents and in children is in the type of people who are the major sources of stimulation. Among children, affection is mainly centered on family members, especially the mother. By adolescence, friction with different family members makes the adolescent's association with them less pleasurable. The result is that he shifts his affection to people outside the home with whom his relationships are, on the whole, less frictional. The adolescent who has few close friends is likely to center his affection on some hero, either real or fictional, whom he can shower with his affection without running the risk of being ignored or rebuffed (83).

Response in Affection Typically, a child reacts to the object of his affection by overt expressions. The adolescent is more restrained; he shows his affection by wanting to be with the person he is fond of, by doing little favors in the hope of making him happy, and by watching and listening in rapt attention to everything he does or says. In addition, he shows a tolerance toward the person for whom he has affection. This differs markedly from the intolerant, hypercritical attitude he shows toward those for whom he has little or no affection. He will, for example, defend a close friend against criticism for an act which he condemns in a person for whom he has little or no affection.

The usual response of affection by adolescents is a display of happiness in the presence of the person liked. This display takes the characteristic form—smiling, laughing, and relaxing the whole body. Unlike the child, the adolescent refrains from physical contact with the person, especially in public. The reason for this restraint is fear of social disapproval or ridicule. Even a conventional kiss in greeting causes the adolescent great embarrassment. In addition to fear of social disapproval is fear of rebuff; the adolescent "plays it safe" and avoids any behavior that might interfere with the friendly relationship he has already established. Fear of social disapproval is not the only reason for not showing affection. Some adolescents have personality patterns characterized by devaluation of self, dependency, anxiety, and conflict. These make the adolescent self-bound and prevent an affectionate interchange with others (75).

effects of the emotions

Any experience that is vivid and accompanied by intense emotions is likely to have a profound effect on a person's attitudes, values, and future behavior. This effect may be favorable or unfavorable depending on what emotion has been aroused, how intense it is, the person's previous experience involving this emotion, and the degree of preparation he has had for it. In general, the pleasant emotions have more favorable effects that the unpleasant ones (24,71,97).

Emotions have their good and bad features. The bad, however, so outweigh the good that control of the emotions becomes necessary. Continuous emotional strain makes the individual miserable and ineffectual. In time it can bring on physical ill health. Then, unless corrective measures are taken, the outcome is likely to be a mental breakdown. A brief survey of the good and bad features of the emotions will serve to highlight the important role emotions play in life.

GOOD FEATURES

On the good side of the emotional scale certain advantages can be listed. First, the emotions are a *source of motivation*. Fear, anger, love, curiosity—in fact, all emotions —drive the individual to action. Much of the striving for achievement comes from culturally engendered fears—fear of failure, of being looked down upon, of doing the wrong thing, of not being accepted, or of incurring the displeasure of others by violating cultural taboos. However, when emotions become strong, they often defeat their purpose by paralyzing action (3,164).

The second thing to be said in favor of the emotions is that they are a *source of enjoyment*. The emotions take the individual out of the rut of daily routine by adding excitement, which daily life so often lacks. Even though the emotion may not be pleasurable while it is taking place—and this is especially true of the unpleasant emotions—the aftermath, which usually takes the form of a letdown or a state of relaxation, is always pleasurable.

The third fact in favor of the emotions is that they *give strength* and endurance to the body. During an emotional state the individual is capable of feats that under unemotional conditions would be absolutely impossible. Even when the activity is completed, there is not the feeling of tiredness that invariably accompanies sustained action requiring a heavy expenditure of energy.

BAD EFFECTS

On the other side of the scale are the bad effects of the emotions, which, though only slightly more numerous, are far more important in their consequences than are the good effects.

Physical Effects Emotional tension upsets the homeostasis of the body; this is reflected in bodily as well as in behavioral changes. Sleep disturbances are the most common of the unfavorable physical effects of emotional tension. The individual is restless; his sleep is light and easily broken by periods of waking; he experiences many dreams, primarily nightmares; and insomnia soon develops. Chronic fatigue is the usual outcome. Emotional tension also causes headaches, loss of appetite, and digestive disturbances. In time, emotional tension leads to loss of weight, loss of energy, and a generally run-down condition (13,24,92,175).

Efficiency Emotional stress results in flightiness, instability, shifts of moods, unpredictability, and inconsistency of performance. As a result, the individual is inefficient in both motor and mental performances. The familiar example of the stagestruck amateur, whose mind becomes blank when he faces his audience and who so completely forgets well-learned lines that he requires constant prompting, tells the story of how emotions affect the ability to remember. Equally familiar is the stagestruck athlete who is so frightened by the crowds at a game that he plays far below his capacity and loses to a competitor of lesser ability but greater emotional control. Emotional tension likewise affects verbal performance. When an emotionally tense person speaks, the tone of his voice changes and he has difficulty in pronouncing his words. If the tension is great, he may stutter or slur, or he may choke over his words. Then the words come out with a rush, often so poorly articulated that no one can understand what he is trying to say (22,24,97).

Any strong emotion distracts the individual's attention from the task at hand. The result is that the individual finds it difficult or impossible to concentrate. If the task is a motor one, his performance will be variable and unpredictable. The more skill he has, however, the less the effect, even when the emotion is intense (56,167). Furthermore, he is more subject to accidents when his attention is distracted (49,127).

Emotional disturbances affect mental

performances even more seriously than motor performances (164). Rote memorizing, for example, is less affected than reasoning. The ability to see a problem from every angle is seriously affected by emotional tension. The stronger the emotion, the more irrational the person becomes. This is true even in the case of the pleasant emotions; it is a well-known fact that a person in love can see only what he wants to see.

Emotional stress affects learning unfavorably. When a student is under constant pressure to achieve high grades, he often becomes an underachiever and works below his capacity. If he persists in his studies, in spite of his discontent, he not only continues to work below his capacity but he develops marked feelings of inadequacy and guilt (3,48,160). This is especially true of students of average or slightly above average ability. For superior students, anxiety has been found to facilitate academic performance (3,12,112,141).

Personality Emotional strain, especially if prolonged, causes irritability and moodiness. Irritability may appear only in certain situations, or it may be general and show itself in a "chippy" attitude toward everyone and everything. Moodiness, by contrast, is usually not associated with its causes. Some people are chronically gloomy while others have their emotional ups and downs. Moodiness is usually accompanied by a timid, withdrawn type of behavior or by irritability and aggressiveness. The most common aftereffect of anger is a feeling of irritability or of being out of sorts. Almost as frequent is a tendency to feel disgusted with oneself, ashamed, or foolish (71,107). An adolescent who experiences highly developed anxiety is likely to blame himself for the cause of his anxiety. As a result, he develops a guilt complex which colors his personality unfavorably (11,44). Figure 3–12 shows how likes and dislikes affect the individual's adjustment.

Emotional Habits One of the most serious effects of the emotions is that, with repetition, they frequently develop into habits. Some individuals, for example, be-

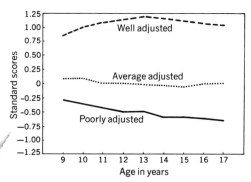

FIGURE 3–12 The affective index of adolescents and its relation to their adjustment. (Adapted from J. E. Anderson: The relation of attitude to adjustment. *Education*, 1952, **73**, 210–218. Used by permission.)

come so conditioned that they constantly anticipate difficulties. Worry thus keeps them in a state of apprehension. When emotional habits are established, the individual responds emotionally to new situations that are the same as, or similar to, situations to which he formerly responded in an emotional manner. Fortunately, during adolescence, emotional habits are still in an unstable state and are very transitory. Furthermore, they are easier to change then than they will be later.

emotional control

"Control" does not mean repression or elimination. Instead, it means learning to approach a situation with a rational attitude, to respond to it realistically instead of emotionally, and to avoid reading meanings into situations that could give rise to emotional reactions. This is control of the *mental* aspects of an emotional state. In addition, emotional control means control of the *overt expressions*, in motor or verbal form, of the emotions that are socially unacceptable. Achieving emotional control is one indication of emotional maturity (34, 74).

WHOLESOME VERSUS UNWHOLESOME CONTROL

Just keeping the overt expressions of the emotions under control is not an indication of emotional maturity. They must be kept under control in the right way—a way that wins social approval and, at the same time, does the least possible physical or psychological damage to the person. *Wholesome* emotional control involves behavior following emotional arousal "which will produce certain valued consequences. These consequences include the riddance of undesired tensions, or the attainment of desired ones, and the maintenance and enhancement of other values. These other values include such things as self-respect, one's job, friendships, etc." By contrast, *unwholesome* emotional control occurs when a person does not "respond emotionally as he is supposed or expected to, and when his emotionally-provoked behavior endangers his health, safety, his position, or anything else which he or society deems important" (79).

The two criteria that determine whether the control is wholesome or unwholesome are, first, *social reactions* to the individual's behavior, and second, the *aftereffects* of the emotional control on his physical and psychological well-being. If social reactions to his emotional control are satisfactory, the first criterion is fulfilled. But this alone is not enough. If the control is such that it makes the individual nervous, edgy, and irritable, it will damage his physical and psychological well-being and, in time, affect his social relationships. While the person may be judged more favorably by the social group when he controls the overt expressions of his anger than when he "blows his top," he is likely to experience fatigue, shame, guilt, disgust with himself, or to feel that he is a martyr because he has been picked on but not allowed to retaliate (75, 86,119).

INFLUENCE OF SOCIAL EXPECTATIONS

Society does not expect the adolescent to control his emotions at all times or in all places. Instead, it expects him to know when he may express and when he must control them. It also expects him to know what are the socially acceptable patterns of emotional expression. Too much expression, especially when in socially unacceptable forms of behavior, or too little expression

are both damaging. Just as too little control creates the impression that the adolescent is immature, so too much control, in addition to the damaging effects on his physical and psychological well-being, creates the impression that he is "less than human" (79).

In discussing the adolescent's ability to conform to these expectations and, at the same time, to protect himself from physical and psychological damage that too much or too prolonged emotional control inevitably brings, Jourard (79) has said:

The healthy personality displays neither immediate expression nor chronic suppression of emotion exclusively. Rather, he displays a capacity to choose between the alternatives of suppression and expression. When it will not jeopardize important values, he will express his feelings freely, in an almost unrestrained fashion: he may laugh with gusto, cry without restraint, express anger with intense verbal outpour. If other values would be endangered by such emotionality, he is capable of suppressing his feelings and carrying on whatever instrumental behavior is in process at the time of emotional arousal. . . . In the long run, this regime of selective suppression and release insures that the person will not suffer from the effects on his body and on his ability to perform produced by prolonged emotion-suppression; and he will not needlessly endanger his job, his reputation, his self-respect, and other important values, by heedless emotional explosions. In short, he can suppress when he chooses, and he can let go when he chooses—and it is he who does the choosing.

Variations in Social Expectations Emotional control is expected to increase with *age*. The older adolescent is expected to have better control over his emotions than the young adolescent who has more of the characteristics of a child than of an adult (49). Early maturers are subjected to more rigid social expectations than are their age-mates who continue to resemble children. Postmenarcheal girls, for example, are expected to show more emotional maturity in their behavior than are premenarcheal girls of the same age (42,125).

Boys, at all ages, are permitted to express their emotions more overtly than girls *except in the case of fear* which brands them as cowards. In defying authority, in swearing when angry, or in aggressive attacks on others in anger or jealousy, the boy wins far less social disapproval than the girl in similar situations. In fact, boys who express their emotions are likely to be envied and admired by the peer group. While some expression of anger in the form of tears may be tolerated in girls, most emotional expressions are frowned upon (54,103,152).

There is a socially approved way of expressing and of controlling the emotions for both sexes in every *social class*. The lower-class boy, for example, knows that aggressive attacks in anger are regarded as manly, while the lower-class girl knows that such behavior will win social disapproval. Middle-class adolescents know that only certain forms of expression, such as verbal attacks carefully camouflaged as wit, will be tolerated when they are angry or that laughing will be condoned only in certain situations and under certain conditions (59,129,176).

Parents who use authoritarian methods of discipline expect, on the whole, more emotional control from their children at all ages than do parents who use either democratic or permissive methods. Similarly, parents with a strong *religious* background have different expectations regarding emotional control, especially in the case of anger, than do parents with less interest in religion. Because *peer* values are, on the whole, homegrown, the social expectations of the peer group will be similar to those of the family group. This is true except in cases of social mobility, when the adolescent becomes identified with members of a peer group whose family backgrounds are superior (or inferior) to those of his own family (15,19,126,178).

Because *well-adjusted* adolescents show a maturity of behavior that is consistent in all areas, it is anticipated that they will show greater emotional control than will those whose behavior is immature (170). Thus, it is apparent that social expectations

vary not only according to the kind of group with which adolescents are identified but also according to the kind of people they are.

EFFECTS OF CONTROL

When an emotion is aroused but direct expression of it is suppressed, it does not die out at once. Like a dammed-up stream of water, the emotional energy will find some new outlet. This substitute form of expression, however, may be and often is physically or psychologically damaging. Of the many ways in which emotions whose overt expressions are controlled seek indirect outlets, the following are the most common.

Moods As was pointed out earlier in this chapter, adolescents frequently suppress emotional energy; this results in moodiness—a drawn-out state of emotionality of a less severe type than the emotion from which it originated. The angry adolescent, for example, is in a bad humor or an irritable mood; the frightened adolescent becomes nervous and jittery. If there are no further stimuli to reinforce the mood, the mood may die out in time. Body homeostasis will then be restored. But, because moods predispose the individual to react to a new stimulus with a mental set colored by his mood, the chances are that the mood will be reinforced by repeated stimuli from his environment.

In time, the dammed-up emotional energy may become too powerful for him to control, especially if he is tired or below par physically. As a result, he will blow up emotionally, reacting to a mild stimulus with a response proportionally too strong and too prolonged for the stimulus that gave rise to it. Knowing how others feel about emotional outbursts causes him to be embarrassed and ashamed. In addition, the impression of maturity he has tried so hard to create is jeopardized by this outburst (58,152,170,178).

Displacement Because emotional reactions aimed against others win social disapproval and are judged as immature or an indication of poor sportsmanship, the adolescent seeks outlets for his pent-up emotional energy which would not be so likely to be disapproved of by the social group. He thus displaces his emotional reaction from the stimulus that aroused it to a substitute—a person, an object, or even an animal—that was in no way involved in his emotional state. An adolescent brought up in an authoritarian home, for example, knows that he will be punished if he talks back to his parents when he is angry at them and that striking them would be even worse. He may, then, take it out on the family pet by kicking him, he may throw a book or a bottle of ink, or he may shove a younger sibling who is in his path. These are the scapegoats for his pent-up anger.

Prejudice against members of a minority group is a common form of displaced anger, just as contempt for women is often a displacement of the resentment aroused by an overprotective mother. However, because displacement is often recognized by others for what it is, the adolescent frequently tries to justify his act in his own eyes or in the eyes of others by *rationalization;* he gives a plausible and acceptable reason for his displacement even though it may not be the real reason.

Another common way of guarding against the social disapproval displacement may bring is camouflage in the form of wit. If the adolescent can make others laugh, he will divert their attention from him to the person against whom the wit is directed. Jokes based on minority religious or racial groups or on "feminine weaknesses" serve this purpose. They help to free the adolescent from fear of condemnation by the social group for his poor sportsmanship (29, 129,176,178).

Escape   Adolescents often find that if they can get away from the thoughts of the situation that gave rise to their emotional tension, they can forget about it. Should one, for example, find that an aggressive attack, even when well camouflaged, sooner or later leads to unfavorable social reactions, he may resort to daydreams in which he can let out his pent-up anger in fighting imaginary battles with those who anger him

without the unfavorable aftereffects he experiences in daily life.

Release of pent-up emotional energy through escape mechanisms may take forms other than daydreaming. The adolescent may, through identification with characters on the screen or in books, escape from unpleasant reality into a world where excitement is uninhibited, where wishes are unthwarted, and where frustrations are nonexistent. Pent-up fear may lead to escape through imaginary invalidism; the adolescent is not expected to do things that frighten him if he complains of not feeling well (59,176,178).

Sublimation   Pent-up emotional energy may be given outlet through channels that are highly socially acceptable. Instead of releasing pent-up anger in aggressive attacks on others, for example, adolescents may turn this energy into competition in athletics or studies. When lack of social acceptance is a constant source of anger to an adolescent, he can get rid of some of the pent-up anger by achievements beyond those of the peer group that has rejected him (79).

ACHIEVING WHOLESOME CONTROL

Because unwholesome control of the emotions plays havoc both physically and psychologically, the adolescent needs guidance in knowing how he can avoid some of this damage. Jourard has suggested two rules that can help the adolescent to cope with this problem successfully, provided *both* rules are followed. The first rule is to admit that one has the emotion that he has tried to control, and the second is to subject the cognitive aspects of the emotional response to reality testing (79). If, for example, the adolescent is jealous, he must admit to himself that he is jealous even though his jealousy has been so well hidden that others may not suspect its existence. Following the second rule means that he must submit his jealousy to reality testing to see if it is justified—if he has any reason to be jealous and if he could not achieve the attention and affection he craves by some means other than direct or indirect attacks on a person whom he believes has taken them away from him.

Because wholesome control of the emotions is possible only when the adolescent has "ego strength"—the ability to refrain from explosive, uncontrolled emotional outbursts if he wishes to do so and, at the same time, be able to let loose his feelings when he wants to—he must acquire the ability to decide which it will be and then carry out his decision. In discussing the factors that promote ego strength, Jourard (79) has pointed out:

> One such factor is autonomy, the possession of a high degree of skill and competence in many areas, so that the person is not obligated to be overly dependent on others. . . . Security is another factor, whether it is the by-product of diverse skill, or an assured source of income. Insecure persons are very prone to anxiety, and they may dread expressing their feelings because they believe that if they do so, they may lose status, their job, or friendships. Reality-contact can also promote healthy emotional behavior; the person can determine realistically what values are at stake in an emotional situation and what dangers are associated with suppression and expression of feelings. Autonomy, security, and reality-contact appear to make it possible for a person to choose how he will react under emotion, rather than reacting in a stereotyped manner with "explosions," with repression, or suppression.

emotional catharsis

The safest and surest way of minimizing the damaging effects of emotional control is by "emotional catharsis"—the purging of the mind and body of pent-up emotional energy. Catharsis has two aspects, both of which must be carried out if a return to physical and mental homeostasis is to be achieved. Mental catharsis alone will produce better results than physical catharsis alone. The reason for this is that clearing up the mental aspect of the emotion will, in time, eliminate further physical disturbances. But it is inadequate because it will not eliminate the bodily preparation for action that has already taken place (18,57).

The adolescent is anxious to control his emotions in the hope of creating the impression that he is grown up. The more control he exerts, the more damaging the effects will be. Furthermore, adolescence is a period in life when the most common and most intense emotions are the unpleasant ones—fear, anxiety, frustration, jealousy, and envy. Because they stir up the body more than the milder, pleasant emotions—happiness, affection, or curiosity—an adolescent needs the purging effects of catharsis. This is especially true during the early years of adolescence, the time generally regarded as a period of storm and stress (57).

PHYSICAL ASPECTS OF CATHARSIS

The physical aspects of catharsis consist of the elimination of pent-up physical preparation for action. When control over overt expressions of the emotion is exerted by the adolescent, this energy remains dammed-up, ready for use, until it is drained off. The common ways of purging the body of the physical harm this dammed-up energy will bring consist of giggling, laughing, crying, strenuous physical exertion in work or play, and in the case of older adolescents, sexual behavior—petting, necking, or intercourse (79).

Which form of purge will be used depends largely on what the adolescent has discovered from past experience will give him the greatest satisfaction and, at the same time, conform to socially approved patterns of behavior. An adolescent may, for example, get greater relief of the physical tensions of emotions through sexual activity than through other means. But unless he can use this outlet with the sanctions of the social group, he will be forced to make the decision between winning the disapproval of the group for his behavior or using a more acceptable outlet, such as sports, which gives him less personal satisfaction.

In spite of the fact that the common forms of physical catharsis all serve the purpose of purging the body of pent-up emotional energy, not all of them are possible or practical for every adolescent. To serve as a purge, strenuous activity in *sports* is excellent. But to be able to engage in sports, the adolescent must have enough skill to be an acceptable member of a team or he must have enough social acceptance to be included in the sports of the peer group (67).

Strenuous activity in *work* will serve the same purpose. But many adolescents have little time free from their studies for jobs and most regard home jobs as restrictions on their social and recreational plans. Furthermore, in the age of automation, strenuous work has been replaced by push-button techniques; the adolescent expends far too little energy when he works to drain off the energy pent up during the interval between work periods. Furthermore, many adolescents cannot get jobs even if they want them, and if they do, they usually avoid anything that carries the peer-group stigma of "menial."

Giggling is a common form of emotional catharsis among young adolescent girls; boys shy away from this behavior to avoid being called sissies (54,58). However, girls soon discover that giggling is frowned upon as childish. In their desire to create the impression that they are mature and sophisticated, they abandon its use. While *laughter*, if well controlled and subdued, wins social approval, uproarious laughter is regarded as gauche. Controlled laughter is inadequate as an outlet for pent-up energy, especially when the emotion from which this energy has come is intense or prolonged (37).

The least satisfactory way to purge the body of pent-up energy following an emotional state is by crying. Many adolescent girls who giggle uncontrollably alternate their giggling with crying and frequently end the giggling with crying as uncontrollable as the giggling. However, they quickly discover that it is considered not only immature but babyish. Boys who learned early in childhood that crying is regarded as a sign of being a sissy rarely indulge in this form of catharsis. Crying is also a poor catharsis because it leaves the adolescent with a feeling of exhaustion and an un-

happy outlook on life. The longer and harder the crying, the more energy will be used up. In addition, crying tends to arouse unhappy feelings about oneself and about life in general.

MENTAL ASPECTS OF CATHARSIS

The mental aspects of catharsis consist of ridding the mind of the attitudes that have given rise to the emotional state which the individual controls. To purge his mind of these attitudes, the adolescent must get an insight into and a perspective on them. By doing so, he can minimize their seriousness and then replace them with more wholesome attitudes. Unwholesome attitudes will not automatically disappear just because the overt expressions of the attitudes have been controlled. Instead, unwholesome attitudes must be replaced by wholesome ones (131).

In discussing the importance of mental catharsis, Jourard (79) has said:

> In most, if not all instances, a personality hygienist condemns repression of emotional tensions as unhealthy. The main reason for this condemnation lies in the fact that in spite of repression, the feelings exist—or at least the capacity to experience these feelings remains present and unchanged. When feelings have been provoked but are not recognized by the person, they produce effects both physical and psychological in nature. . . . When feelings have been repressed, more or less successfully, it is not only the person himself who is unaware of their presence. Other persons as well will not know how the person really feels. . . . One of the most important tasks in personality therapy . . . is that of aiding the patient to recognize his own feelings—to "unrepress" them, to experience and express them fully. This uncovering process generally is met with strong resistance on the part of the patient, however, since the experience of these feelings is quite threatening to security and to self-esteem.

Essentials in Mental Catharsis There are four things necessary to achieve satisfactory purging of the mind: recognition of the feelings that persist even after the overt expressions of the emotion associated with them have been controlled; ability to communicate feelings to others to get a more wholesome perspective on them; willingness to do so; and having people with whom one can or is willing to communicate. Only by bringing one's feelings out in the open and by seeing them through the eyes of another person who is not involved personally can one hope to get a perspective that will lead to wholesome feelings. As Worchel has pointed out, there is a therapeutic effect to mental catharsis "due to insight or new learning as the individual verbalizes his previous experiences" (172).

However, if new insight and new learning do not result, much of the therapeutic value is lost. Just blowing off emotional steam by getting it off one's chest or by letting down one's hair for the sake of talking about irritations or worries will have little value per se; they must result in a changed point of view, new attitudes, and a new perspective if they are to have a drive-reducing effect when a similar situation develops later. Merely expressing anxiety feelings concerning an anticipated failure will not eliminate the underlying threat. In fact, the more the adolescent thinks and talks about it, the more anxious he is likely to become (17,172).

Difficulties in Mental Catharsis Adolescents are faced with a number of difficulties in their attempts to free themselves from the pent-up mental states that will predispose them to future emotional reactions when similar situations arise. Of the many difficulties, the following are the most common.

difficulty in expressing feelings The child who was brought up with strict authoritarian training where emphasis was placed on the importance of covering up one's feelings reaches adolescence with a well-developed habit of keeping his feelings to himself. He finds it just as difficult to verbalize his pleasures as to verbalize his gripes (126,168). In a study of emotionally disturbed girls, for example, it was found that they had become so self-bound as a result

of unfavorable home environments that spontaneous verbalization with others was difficult and often impossible (148).

willingness to communicate How much the adolescent is willing to disclose about himself to another is greatly influenced by the closeness of his relationship with that person. This is one of the major stumbling blocks in clinical work with disturbed patients and in the attempts parents make to discuss problems with their adolescent sons and daughters (80).

An adolescent who has experienced years of conflict, criticism, punishment, and lack of overt expression of affection from his parents may wonder if his parents love him and will often conclude that they do not. He is then likely to refuse to disclose his troubles to them even though he feels in desperate need of help. Talking over problems, he has found, generally leads to parental criticism of his immaturity and the threat of taking away some of the independence he has fought to achieve (49,57, 126).

Under such conditions, the adolescent may be willing to turn to a member of the peer group, an understanding teacher, or a relative for help. However, how willing he is to do so will depend on how close his relationship with them is. If he feels insecure in his status in the peer group, he will hesitate to discuss his problems with anyone for fear of losing what status he has. He may hesitate to turn to an adult for fear that they will tell his parents, or he may be held back by the belief that adults are not interested in or sympathetic toward adolescents and their problems (50, 106).

lack of confidants Many adolescents are so on the fringe of social life that they literally have no real friends, though they may have a number of acquaintances (21, 109). This is well illustrated in a study of psychological breakdowns among college students. Breakdowns were found to be more common among students living at home than among those living in the residence halls. The explanation given was that students living in residence halls can drain off their anxieties by talking to their pals and thus get the emotional catharsis they need for wholesome attitudes. The off-campus students, by contrast, are deprived of the close friendships that make this draining off possible (47).

guidance in developing a perspective Even when an adolescent has people with whom he can discuss his problems, mental catharsis will not be successful unless the discussions lead to a change in the adolescent's attitudes. This can be done only by subjecting his attitudes to reality testing so that he can gain a better perspective on the situations that led to his attitudes. While it is true that he may gain some perspective from talking over his problems with friends, too often this is a case of the blind leading the blind; his friends are no more qualified to help him gain the needed perspective than he, himself, is.

What he needs is someone who can guide his reality testing in an objective, impersonal way. If his parents attempt to do this, he is likely to accuse them of "not understanding." While teachers and guidance counselors are equipped to help the adolescent gain insight into his problems, there is too little time available to deal with any but the problem cases and too much resistance on the part of the adolescent to go to them for help. The "uncovering process," which must precede any guidance from the counselor before changes in attitudes can be made, is regarded by the adolescent as a threat to his security or his self-esteem (79). As a result, he far too often rejects the help this guidance might give him (50,93,109).

Substitute Forms of Mental Catharsis Some adolescents are fortunate in discovering, more by trial and error than by guidance, ways of dealing with their negative attitudes successfully. In such cases, they purge their minds, to some extent at least, of their negative attitudes. The two common forms of substitute outlet are *wit* and *literary expression.* The adolescent who, through a witty joke or cartoon, can show his pent-up hostility toward a person or group may reduce his hostility, at least temporarily. However, there is the chance that social disapproval of his verbal attacks will outweigh the value he receives from this catharsis (29,129).

Literary expression, by contrast, is less in danger of arousing social disapproval. As a result, it proves to be a more satisfactory substitute than wit. Adolescents who find it difficult to express themselves verbally in face-to-face situations sometimes are able to do so in letter writing. Just writing down their feelings freely, however, does have a cathartic value (148). It was found that, immediately after the writing of aggressive Thematic Apperception Tests stories in a laboratory situation, subjects showed a decrease in aggressive behavior. Unless the writing of these stories helped the subjects to gain insight into their problems, however, it is safe to conclude that the cathartic effect was only temporary (17,102,104).

The diary is much more personal and is more of an outlet for feelings and emotions than any other form of literary expression. Girls, more than boys, use the diary as a confidant, recording in it their personal problems, aspirations, emotional reactions, and the events which brought them happiness or unhappiness (89,163). Sex differences in writing in diaries are shown in Figure 3–13.

Adolescents, especially during the junior and senior high school years, often use the social columns of the school paper to let off emotional steam about classmates they dislike. While it may give a temporary emotional relief to the writer to air his feelings in this way, it is not a wholesome form of cathartic, first, because it is not a pattern of emotional outlet he can continue to use after he leaves school, and second, because it does not lead to the learning experiences that will change his perspective— a requisite of wholesome mental cathartics (76).

Unquestionably, the most harmful of all forms of mental catharsis is *daydreaming.* Because the adolescent has no check on reality in his daydream, he is likely to allow himself to wallow, literally, in his distorted images of himself as a martyr until he has persuaded himself that he actually is a martyr. Then when he leaves the daydream world, he is confronted with situations that give rise to emotions. But instead of subjecting them to reality testing, he reacts to them with the distorted attitudes he developed in his daydream world (53,89).

SUCCESS OF CATHARSIS

The success of emotional catharsis may be judged from two frames of reference—the *immediate* and the *long term*. If the adolescent's physical and mental states are restored to normal, there is no question that the catharsis has been a success, for the time being at least. But temporary success is not enough; it is only a stopgap measure. Permanent relief can be achieved only when the cause of the condition is diagnosed and treated so that there will be no reoccurrence of the condition, or if so, only in a mild form.

The success of emotional catharsis can best be judged by using the three widely accepted criteria of emotional maturity. These criteria are:

1 *The emotionally mature person is able to control the overt expressions of his emotions until a convenient time and place to express them or to relieve himself of the pent-up energy, both physical and mental, in a socially acceptable manner.* Crying, for example, may give relief but it is not a socially acceptable form of behavior. Similarly, laughter will give relief if it is used in a place and at a time when it will not lead to social disapproval (172). Because of the high prestige value of sports and the social approval of work that leads to constructive ends, an emotionally mature person learns to use these forms of physical catharsis as soon after the emotions have been controlled as possible to avoid physical and mental damage.

2 *The emotionally mature person learns not only how to control his emotions but also how much control to use to satisfy his needs and to conform to social ex-*

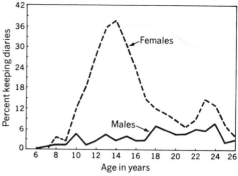

FIGURE 3–13 The ages at which boys and girls write in diaries. (Adapted from R. G. Kuhlen: *The psychology of adolescent development.* 2d ed. New York: Harper & Row, 1963. Used by permission.)

pectations. As Jourard has pointed out, "The chronic suppressor is often derogated as a 'stick,' or 'stone-face,' or an 'iceberg' " (79). The adolescent must learn when it is acceptable to express his emotions, how he may express them without winning social disapproval, and how much he may express them. He must learn that not all emotional expression is either bad or dangerous and that some expression is both acceptable and approved (79,172).

3 *The emotionally mature person assesses a situation critically before responding to it emotionally.* According to the traditional advice, one should count ten before speaking or acting when emotionally aroused. This is good advice if the time is spent wisely in assessing the situation critically. If it is merely spent in holding back the emotional expression until "ten" gives the go signal, it will do no good. It may result in even more unfavorable responses than would have occurred had the waiting period been omitted.

The long-term effects of not assessing the situation critically before acting or suppressing the emotional reactions have been explained by Jersild (75):

When an adolescent attaches old grievances to new persons and to new circumstances, he is likely to be suspicious, defensive, and unable to face the tasks of life in an effi-

cient way. He is endowing his present life with something unreal, something from within himself that distorts his view of things. The more his approach to his teachers or assignments at school, his employers, his companions, his parents, and the kind of discipline and support they are giving him is distorted by grievances from the past, the tougher the task of facing the problems of life will be. He will use energy to fight unnecessary battles. He may create an enemy where he might have found a friend. The one who is punished most severely by the adolescent who harbors unresolved attitudes of hostility is the adolescent himself.

By contrast, the emotionally mature person profits from the use of emotional catharsis by learning to analyze a situation for what is it worth and then deciding how to react to it (172). When an adolescent can ask, "Why should I worry and get ulcers?" about an examination, or can philosophically face a frustration or defeat by saying, "This won't affect the fate of the nation," there is positive evidence that he is well along on the road to emotional maturity.

BIBLIOGRAPHY

1 ALEXANDER, I. E., and A. M. ADLERSTEIN: Affective responses to the concept of death in a population of children and young adolescents. *J. genet. Psychol.*, 1958, **93**, 167–177.

2 ALEXANDER, T.: Certain characteristics of the self as related to affection. *Child Develpm.*, 1951, **22**, 285–290.

3 ALPERT, R., and R. N. HABER: Anxiety in academic achievement situations. *J. abnorm. soc. Psychol.*, 1960, **61**, 207–215.

4 AMATORA, SISTER M.: Free expression of adolescents' interests. *Genet. Psychol. Monogr.*, 1957, **55**, 173–219.

5 AMATORA, SISTER M.: Interests of preadolescent boys and girls. *Genet. Psychol. Monogr.*, 1960, **61**, 77–113.

6 ANASTASI, A., N. COHEN, and D. SPATZ: A study of fear and anger in college students through the controlled diary method. *J. genet. Psychol.*, 1948, **73**, 243–249.

7 ANDERSON, J. E.: The relation of attitude to adjustment. *Education*, 1952, **73**, 210–218.

8 ANGELINO, H., J. DOLLINS, and E. V. MECH: Trends in the "fears and worries" of school children as related to socio-economic status and age. *J. genet. Psychol.*, 1956, **89**, 263–276.

9 ANGELINO, H., and E. V. MECH: "Fears and worries" concerning physical changes: a preliminary survey of 32 females. *J. Psychol.*, 1955, **39**, 195-198.

10 ANGELINO, H., and C. L. SHEDD: Shifts in the content of fears and worries relative to chronological age. *Proc. Oklahoma Acad. Sci.*, 1953, **34**, 180–186.

11 ARNOLD, M. G.: *Emotion and personality.* New York: Columbia, 1960.

12 ATKINSON, J. W., and G. H. LITWIN: Achievement motive and test anxiety conceived as motive to approach success and motive to avoid failure. *J. abnorm. soc. Psychol.*, 1960, **60**, 52–63.

13 AX, A. F.: The physiological differentiation between fear and anger in humans. *Psychosom. Med.*, 1953, **15**, 433–442.

14 BARSCHAK, E.: A study of happiness and unhappiness in childhood and adolescence of girls of different cultures. *J. Psychol.*, 1951, **32**, 173–215.

15 BATEMAN, M. M., and J. S. JENSEN: The effect of religious background on modes of handling anger. *J. soc. Psychol.*, 1958, **47**, 133–141.

16 BELL, E. C.: Nutritional deficiencies and emotional disturbances. *J. Psychol.*, 1958, **45**, 47–74.

17 BERKOWITZ, L.: The expression and reduction of hostility. *Psychol. Bull.*, 1958, **55**, 257–284.

18 BERKOWITZ, L., J. A. GREEN, and J. R. MACAULAY: Hostility catharsis as the reduction of emotional tension. *Psychiatry*, 1962, **25**, 23–31.

19 BLAU, P. M.: Occupational bias and mobility. *Amer. sociol. Rev.*, 1957, **22**, 392–399.

20 BLOCK, J., and B. MARTIN: Predicting the behavior of children under frustration. *J. abnorm. soc. Psychol.*, 1955, **51**, 281–285.

21 BONNEY, M. E.: A sociometric study of the

peer acceptance of rural students in three consolidated high schools. *Educ. Admin. Supervis.*, 1951, **11**, 234–240.

22 BLOODSTEIN, O.: The development of stuttering. *J. speech hear. Disord.*, 1960, **25**, 219–237, 366–376; 1961, **26**, 67–82.

23 BOSSARD, J. H. S., and E. S. BOLL: *The sociology of child development.* 3d ed. New York: Harper & Row, 1960.

24 BRANSON, B. D.: Anxiety, discrimination and self-ideal discrepancy. *Personnel Guid. J.*, 1960, **38**, 373–377.

25 BRITT, S. H.: *Social psychology of modern life.* Rev. ed. New York: Holt, 1949.

26 BROWN, M., and V. MARTIN: The University High School study of adolescents: characteristics of high-school students. *Univ. high sch. J., Calif.* 1941, **19**, 177–219.

27 BROWN, N. L.: These high school fears and satisfactions. *Understanding the Child*, 1954, **23**, 74–76, 88.

28 BURCH, N. R., and T. H. GREINER: Drugs and human fatigue: GSR parameters. *J. Psychol.*, 1958, **45**, 3–10.

29 BYRNE, D.: The relationship between humor and the expression of hostility. *J. abnorm. soc. Psychol.*, 1956, **53**, 84–89.

30 CAPLAN, H.: The role of deviant maturation in the pathogenesis of anxiety. *Amer. J. Orthopsychiat.*, 1956, **26**, 94–107.

31 CASON, H.: Common annoyances. *Psychol. Monogr.*, 1930, **40**, no. 2.

32 CASON, H., and A. CHALK: Annoyance and behavior. *J. soc. Psychol.*, 1933, **4**, 143–155.

33 CATTELL, R. B., and L. B. LUBORSKY: Personality factors in response to humor. *J. abnorm. soc. Psychol.*, 1947, **42**, 402–421.

34 COLE, L., and I. N. HALL: *Psychology of adolescence.* 6th ed. New York: Holt, 1964.

35 COLEMAN, J. C., and J. E. MC CALLEY: Nail-biting among college students. *J. abnorm. soc. Psychol.*, 1948, **43**, 517–525.

36 CONRAD, H. S., and M. C. JONES: Some results from an "annoyance inventory" in a cumulative study of adolescents. *Psychol. Bull.*, 1942, **39**, 475–476.

37 COSER, R. L.: Some social functions of laughter. *Hum. Relat.*, 1959, **12**, 171–182.

38 COSER, R. L.: Laughter among colleagues. *Psychiatry*, 1960, **23**, 81–95.

39 CROW, A.: Parental attitudes toward boy-girl relations. *J. educ. Sociol.*, 1955, **29**, 126–133.

40 CROW, L. D.: Teen-age traits, interests, and worries. *Educ. Forum*, 1956, **20**, 423–428.

41 CROW, L. D., and A. CROW: *Adolescent development and adjustment.* 2d ed. New York: McGraw-Hill, 1965.

42 DAVIDSON, H. L., and L. S. GOTTLIEB: The emotional maturity of pre- and postmenarcheal girls. *J. genet. Psychol.*, 1955, **86**, 261–266.

43 DAVIS, J. M.: A reinterpretation of the Barker, Dembo, and Lewin study of frustration and aggression. *Child Develpm.*, 1958, **29**, 503–506.

44 DORIS, J., and S. SARASON: Test anxiety and blame assignment in a test situation. *J. abnorm. soc. Psychol.*, 1955, **50**, 335–338.

45 DOUVAN, E.: Independence and identity in adolescence. *Children*, 1957, **4**, 186–190.

46 DOUVAN, E.: Adolescent boys speak up. *Marriage fam. Living*, 1959, **21**, 74.

47 DRASGOW, J.: Problems of progeny related to parental education. *J. educ. Psychol.*, 1957, **48**, 521–524.

48 DRASGOW, J.: Underachievers. *J. counsel. Psychol.*, 1957, **4**, 210–211.

49 DUNBAR, F.: Homeostasis during puberty. *Amer. J. Psychiat.*, 1958, **114**, 673–682.

50 DUNLOP, K. W.: Some observations on acute difficulties at the college level. *Ment. Hyg., N.Y.*, 1959, **43**, 237–243.

51 ELKIN, F., and W. A. WESTLEY: The myth of adolescent culture. *Amer. sociol. Rev.*, 1955, **20**, 680–684.

52 FAW, V.: Learning to deal with stress situations. *J. educ. Psychol.*, 1957, **48**, 135–144.

53 FESHBACH, S.: The drive-reducing function of fantasy behavior. *J. abnorm. soc. Psychol.*, 1955, **50**, 3–11.

54 FRANK, L. K.: Personality development in adolescent girls. *Monogr. Soc. Res. Child Develpm.*, 1951, **16**, No. 53.

55 FRANK, L. K., and M. H. FRANK: *Your adolescent, at home and in school.* New York: Viking, 1956.

56 FRASER, D. C.: Environmental stress and its effect on performance. *Occup. Psychol.*, 1957, **31**, 248–255.

57 GALLAGHER, J. R., and H. I. HARRIS: *Emotional problems of adolescents.* Fair Lawn, N. J.: Oxford, 1962.

58 GESELL, A., F. L. ILG, and L. B. AMES:

Youth: the years from ten to sixteen. New York: Harper & Row, 1956.

59 GOLD, M.: Suicide, homicide, and the socialization of aggression. *Amer. J. Sociol.*, 1958, **63**, 651–661.

60 GOODE, W. J.: The theoretical importance of love. *Amer. sociol. Rev.*, 1959, **24**, 38–47.

61 GORDON, E. M., and S. B. SARASON: The relationship between "test anxiety" and "other anxieties." *J. Pers.*, 1954, **23**, 317–323.

62 GRACE, H. A.: Hostility: an educational paradox. *J. educ. Psychol.*, 1954, **45**, 432–435.

63 GRACE, H. A., and G. L. GRACE: Hostility, communication, and international tensions: III. The hostility factors. *J. educ. Psychol.*, 1951, **42**, 293–300.

64 GREGORY, I.: Studies of parental deprivation in psychiatric patients. *Amer. J. Psychiat.*, 1958, **115**, 432–442.

65 GROOMS, R. R., and N. S. ENDLER: The effect of anxiety on academic achievement. *J. educ. Psychol.*, 1960, **51**, 299–304.

66 HALL, G. S.: *Adolescence.* New York: Appleton-Century-Crofts, 1904.

67 HARTLEY, R. E.: Some safety valves in play. *Child Study*, 1957, **34**, 12–14.

68 HERBST, P. G.: The measurement of family relationships. *Hum. Relat.*, 1952, **5**, 3–35.

69 HILGARD, E. R.: *Introduction to psychology.* 3d ed. New York: Harcourt, Brace & World, 1962.

70 HOROWITZ, L. S.: Attitudes of speech defectives toward humor based on speech defects. *Speech Monogr.*, 1957, **24**, 46–55.

71 HORROCKS, J. E.: *The psychology of adolescence.* 2d ed. Boston: Houghton Mifflin, 1962.

72 JACOBSON, E.: Adolescent moods and the remodeling of psychic structures in adolescence. *Psychoanalytic Study of the Child*, 1961, **16**, 164–183.

73 JANIS, I. L.: Anxiety indices related to susceptibility to persuasion. *J. abnorm. soc. Psychol.*, 1955, **51**, 663–667.

74 JERSILD, A. T.: Emotional development. In L. Carmichael (ed.), *Manual of child psychology*, 2d ed. New York: Wiley, 1954, pp. 833–917.

75 JERSILD, A. T.: *The psychology of adolescence.* 2d ed. New York: Macmillan, 1963.

76 JONES, M. C.: A study of socialization patterns at the high school level. *J. genet. Psychol.*, 1958, **93**, 87–111.

77 JONES, M. C., and N. BAYLEY: Physical maturing among boys as related to behavior. *J. educ. Psychol.*, 1950, **41**, 129–148.

78 JOSSELYN, I. M.: Psychological changes in adolescence. *Children*, 1959, **6**, 43–47.

79 JOURARD, S. M.: *Personal adjustment.* New York: Macmillan, 1958.

80 JOURARD, S. M.: Self-disclosure and other-cathexis. *J. abnorm. soc. Psychol.*, 1959, **59**, 428–431.

81 KAPLAN, D. M., and W. GOODRICH: A formulation for interpersonal anger. *Amer. J. Orthopsychiat.*, 1957, **27**, 387–395.

82 KATES, S. L.: Subjects' evaluations of annoying situations after being described as being well adjusted or poorly adjusted. *J. consult. Psychol.*, 1952, **16**, 429–434.

83 KEISLAR, E. R.: Experimental development of "like" and "dislike" of others among adolescent girls. *Child Develpm.*, 1961, **32**, 59–69.

84 KENT, N., and D. R. DAVIS: Discipline in the home and intellectual development. *Brit. J. med. Psychol.*, 1957, **30**, 27–33.

85 KINSEY, A. C., W. B. POMEROY, C. E. MARTIN, and P. H. GEBHARD: *Sexual behavior in the human female.* Philadelphia: Saunders, 1953.

86 KIRKPATRICK, M. E.: The mental hygiene of adolescence in the Anglo-American culture. *Ment. Hyg., N.Y.*, 1952, **36**, 394–403.

87 KLINGBERG, G.: The distinction between living and not living among 7–10-year-old children, with some remarks concerning the so-called animism controversy. *J. genet. Psychol.*, 1957, **90**, 227–238.

88 KNOWLES, R. C.: Psychogenic illness and delinquency in children. *Marriage fam. Living*, 1957, **19**, 172–177.

89 KUHLEN, R. G.: *The psychology of adolescent development.* 2d ed. New York: Harper & Row, 1963.

90 KVARACEUS, W. C., and W. B. MILLER: *Delinquent behavior: culture and the individual.* Washington: National Education Association, 1959.

91 L'ABATE, L.: Personality correlates of manifest anxiety in children. *J. consult. Psychol.*, 1960, **24**, 342–348.

92 LACEY, J. I., and R. VAN LEHN: Differential

emphasis in somatic response to stress. *Psychosom. Med.*, 1952, **14**, 71–81.

93 LANDY, E., and E. SCANLANE: Relationship between school guidance and psychiatry for adolescents. *Amer. J. Orthopsychiat.*, 1962, **32**, 682–690.

94 LAPOUSE, R., and M. A. MONK: Fears and worries in a representative sample of children. *Amer. J. Orthopsychiat.*, 1959, **29**, 803–818.

95 LAWSON, E. D., and R. STAGNER: Group pressure, attitude change and autonomic involvement. *J. soc. Psychol.*, 1957, **45**, 299–312.

96 LAWSON, R., and M. H. MARX: Frustration: theory and experiment. *Genet. Psychol. Monogr.*, 1958, **57**, 393–464.

97 LAZARUS, R. S., J. DEESE, and S. FOSTER: The effects of psychological stress upon performance. *Psychol. Bull.*, 1952, **49**, 293–317.

98 LAZARUS, R. S., J. S. SPEISMAN, A. M. MORDKOFF, and L. A. DAVISON: A laboratory study of psychological stress produced by a motion picture film. *Psychol. Monogr.*, 1962, **76**, no. 34.

99 LESSER, G. S.: The relationship between overt and fantasy aggression as a function of maternal response to aggression. *J. abnorm. soc. Psychol.*, 1957, **55**, 218–221.

100 LEVINE, J.: Response to humor. *Scient. American*, 1956, **194**, 31–35.

101 LEVINE, J., and F. C. REDLICH: Failure to understand humor. *Psychoanal. Quart.*, 1955, **24**, 560–572.

102 LEWIN, K., R. LIPPITT, and R. K. WHITE: Patterns of aggressive behavior in experimentally-created social climates. *J. soc. Psychol.*, 1939, **10**, 271–299.

103 LIVSON, N., and W. C. BRONSON: An exploration of patterns of impulse control in early adolescence. *Child Develpm.*, 1961, **32**, 75–88.

104 LÖVAS, O. I.: Effect of exposure to symbolic aggression on aggressive behavior. *Child Develpm.*, 1961, **32**, 37–44.

105 LOWREY, L. G.: Adolescent frustrations and evasions. In P. H. Hoch and J. Zubin (eds.), *Psychopathology of childhood*. New York: Grune & Stratton, 1955, pp. 267–284.

106 LUCHINS, A. S.: On the theories and problems of adolescence. *J. genet. Psychol.*, 1954, **85**, 47–63.

107 MACFARLANE, J., L. ALLEN, and M. P. HONZIK: *A developmental study of the behavior problems of normal children between twenty-one months and fourteen years.* Berkeley, Calif.: University of California Press, 1954.

108 MALONE, K. J., and M. MASSLER: Index of nail biting in children. *J. abnorm. soc. Psychol.*, 1952, **47**, 193–202.

109 MASTERSON, J. F.: Psychotherapy of the adolescent: a comparison with psychotherapy of the adult. *J. nerv. ment. Dis.*, 1958, **127**, 511–517.

110 MAY, R.: *The meaning of anxiety.* New York: Ronald, 1950.

111 MC CARY, J. L.: Ethnic and cultural reactions to frustration. *J. Pers.*, 1950, **18**, 321–336.

112 MC KEACHIE, W. J.: Anxiety in the classroom. *J. educ. Res.*, 1951, **45**, 153–160.

113 MC KEACHIE, W. J., D. POLLIE, and J. SPEISMAN: Relieving anxiety in classroom examinations. *J. abnorm. soc. Psychol.*, 1955, **50**, 93–98.

114 MC NALLY, E.: The worries of the younger pupils in Scottish secondary schools. *Brit. J. educ. Psychol.*, 1951, **21**, 235–237.

115 MECHANIC, D.: *Students under stress: a study of the social psychology of adaptation.* New York: Free Press, 1962.

116 MEISSNER, W. W.: Comparison of anxiety patterns in adolescent boys: 1939–1959. *J. genet. Psychol.*, 1961, **99**, 323–329.

117 MEISSNER, W. W.: Some anxiety indications in the adolescent boy. *J. gen. Psychol.*, 1961, **64**, 251–257.

118 MEISSNER, W. W.: Some indications of sources of anxiety in adolescent boys. *J. genet. Psychol.*, 1961, **99**, 65–73.

119 MELTZER, H.: Students' adjustments in anger. *J. soc. Psychol.*, 1933, **4**, 285–308.

120 MIDDLETON, R.: Negro and white reactions to racial humor. *Sociometry*, 1959, **22**, 175–183.

121 MIDDLETON, R., and J. MOLAND: Humor in Negro and white subcultures: a study of jokes among university students. *Amer. sociol. Rev.*, 1959, **24**, 61–69.

122 MONTAGUE, J. B.: A study of anxiety among English and American boys. *Amer. sociol. Rev.*, 1955, **20**, 685–689.

123 MOORE, D. M., and A. F. ROBERTS: Societal variations in humor responses to cartoons. *J. soc. Psychol.*, 1957, **45**, 233–243.

124 MOULTON, R.: Oral and dental manifestations of anxiety. *Psychiatry*, 1955, **18**, 261–273.

125 MUSSEN, P. H., and M. C. JONES: Self-conceptions, motivations, and interpersonal attitudes of late- and early-maturing boys. *Child Develpm.*, 1957, **28**, 243–256.

126 NAKAMURA, C. Y.: The relationship between children's expressions of hostility and methods of discipline exercised by dominant overprotective parents. *Child Develpm.*, 1959, **30**, 109–117.

127 *New York Times* Report: Accident deaths high in men aged 15 to 24. *The New York Times*, Oct. 22, 1964.

128 NOBLE, G. V., and S. B. T. LUND: High-school pupils report their fears. *J. educ. Sociol.*, 1951, **25**, 97–101.

129 O'CONNELL, W. E.: The adaptive functions of wit and humor. *J. abnorm. soc. Psychol.*, 1960, **61**, 263–270.

130 OMWAKE, L.: Humor in the making. *J. soc. Psychol.*, 1942, **15**, 265–279.

131 OSGOOD, C. E.: *Method and theory of experimental psychology.* Fair Lawn, N. J.: Oxford, 1953.

132 PAIVIO, A., and W. E. LAMBERT: Measures and correlates of audience anxiety ("stage fright"). *J. Pers.*, 1959, **27**, 1–17.

133 PALERMO, D. S.: Relation between anxiety and two measures of speed in a reaction time task. *Child Develpm.*, 1961, **32**, 401–408.

134 PECKOS, P. S.: Nutrition during growth and development. *Child Develpm.*, 1957, **28**, 273–285.

135 PHILLIPS, B. N., E. HINDSMAN, and E. JENNINGS: Influence of intelligence on anxiety and perception of self and others. *Child Develpm.*, 1960, **31**, 41–46.

136 PICKREL, E. W.: The differential effect of manifest anxiety on test performance. *J. educ. Psychol.*, 1958, **49**, 43–46.

137 PLATT, H., G. JURGENSEN, and S. CHOROST: Comparisons of child-rearing attitudes of mothers and fathers of emotionally disturbed adolescents. *Child Develpm.*, 1962, **33**, 117–122.

138 POWELL, M.: Age and sex differences in degree of conflict within certain areas of psychological adjustment. *Psychol. Monogr.*, 1955, **69**, no. 2.

139 PRESSEY, S. L., and A. W. JONES: 1923–1953 and 20–60 age changes in moral codes, anxieties, and interests as shown by the "X-O Tests." *J. Psychol.*, 1955, **39**, 485–502.

140 PRESSEY, S. L., and R. G. KUHLEN: *Psychological development through the life span.* New York: Harper & Row, 1957.

141 PRESSEY, S. L., F. P. ROBINSON, and J. E. HORROCKS: *Psychology in education.* New York: Harper & Row, 1959.

142 RADKE-YARROW, M. J., and B. LANDE: Personality correlates of differential reactions to minority group belonging. *J. soc. Psychol.*, 1953, **38**, 253–272.

143 RAO, K. U., and R. W. RUSSELL: Effects of stress on goal setting behavior. *J. abnorm. soc. Psychol.*, 1960, **61**, 380–388.

144 ROBERTS, A. F., and D. M. JOHNSON: Some factors related to the perception of funniness in humor stimuli. *J. soc. Psychol.*, 1957, **46**, 57–63.

145 ROSENBAUM, M.: The role of psychological factors in delayed growth in adolescence: a case report. *Amer. J. Orthopsychiat.*, 1959, **29**, 762–771.

146 RUBÉ, P.: Adolescence. III. The outer world of adolescence. *Amer. J. Psychother.*, 1956, **10**, 87–96.

147 RUEBUSH, B. K.: Interfering and facilitating effects of test anxiety. *J. abnorm. soc. Psychol.*, 1960, **60**, 205–212.

148 SALZINGER, K.: A method of analysis of the process of verbal communication between a group of emotionally disturbed adolescents and their friends and relatives. *J. soc. Psychol.*, 1958, **47**, 39–53.

149 SARASON, I. G.: The effect of anxiety and two kinds of failure on serial learning. *J. Pers.*, 1957, **25**, 383–392.

150 SARASON, I. G.: Test anxiety, general anxiety, and intellectual performance. *J. consult. Psychol.*, 1957, **21**, 485–490.

151 SARGENT, S. S.: Reaction to frustration: a critique and hypothesis. *Psychol. Rev.*, 1948, **55**, 108–114.

152 SCHOEPPE, A.: Sex differences in adolescent socialization. *J. soc. Psychol.*, 1953, **38**, 175–185.

153 SECORD, P. F., and S. M. JOURARD: The appraisal of body-cathexis: body cathexis and the self. *J. consult. Psychol.*, 1953, **17**, 343–346.

154 SIEGEL, S. M.: The relationship of hostility to authoritarianism. *J. abnorm. soc. Psychol.*, 1956, **52**, 368–372.

155 SMITH, W., E. K. POWELL, and S. ROSS: Manifest anxiety and food aversions. *J. abnorm. soc. Psychol.*, 1955, **50**, 101–104.

156 SOMMER, R., and L. M. KILLIAN: Areas of value difference: Negro-white relations. *J. soc. Psychol.*, 1954, **39**, 237–244.

157 SPIELBERGER, C. D.: The effect of manifest anxiety on the academic achievement of college students. *Ment. Hyg., N.Y.*, 1962, **46**, 420–426.

158 SPIVACK, G.: Child rearing attitudes of emotionally disturbed adolescents. *J. consult. Psychol.*, 1957, **21**, 178.

159 STACEY, C. L.: Worries of subnormal adolescent girls. *Except. Children*, 1955, **21**, 184–186.

160 STRANG, R.: *The adolescent views himself.* New York: McGraw-Hill, 1957.

161 STRICKLAND, J. F.: The effect of motivation arousal on humor preferences. *J. abnorm. soc. Psychol.*, 1959, **59**, 278–281.

162 SUTTON-SMITH, B., and B. G. ROSENBERG: Manifest anxiety and game preferences in children. *Child Develpm.*, 1960, **31**, 307–311.

163 ULIN, C.: *Personlighetsbildningen hos unga flickor. Psychol. Abstr.*, 1946, **20**, no. 3224.

164 WALTER, D., L. S. DENZLER, and I. G. SARASON: Anxiety and the intellectual performance of high school students. *Child Develpm.*, 1964, **35**, 917–926.

165 WALTERS, R. H., W. E. MARSHALL, and J. R. SHOOTER: Anxiety, isolation, and suscepti-bility to social influence. *J. Pers.*, 1960, **28**, 518–529.

166 WARREN, W.: Abnormal behavior and mental breakdown in adolescence. *J. ment. Sci.*, 1949, **95**, 589–624.

167 WATERHOUSE, I. K., and I. L. CHILD: Frustration and the quality of performance. *J. Pers.*, 1953, **21**, 298–311.

168 WEST, B., and F. T. RAFFERTY: Initiating therapy with adolescents. *Amer. J. Orthopsychiat.*, 1958, **28**, 627–639.

169 WESTLEY, W. A., and F. ELKIN: The protective environment and adolescent socialization. *Soc. Forces*, 1957, **35**, 243–249.

170 WIRT, R. D.: Ideational expression of hostile impulses. *J. consult. Psychol.*, 1956, **20**, 185–189.

171 WORBOIS, G. M.: Effect of a guidance program on emotional development. *J. appl. Psychol.*, 1947, **31**, 169–187.

172 WORCHEL, P.: Catharsis and the relief of hostility. *J. abnorm. soc. Psychol.*, 1957, **55**, 238–243.

173 YOUNG, F. M.: The incidence of nervous habits observed in college students. *J. Pers.*, 1947, **15**, 309–320.

174 YOUNG, F. M.: A comparison of the nervous habits of preschool and college students. *J. Pers.*, 1949, **17**, 303–309.

175 ZAIDI, S. M. H.: Reactions to stress as a function of the level of intelligence. *Genet. Psychol. Monogr.*, 1960, **62**, 41–104.

176 ZANDER, A.: Group membership and individual security. *Hum. Relat.*, 1958, **11**, 99–111.

177 ZELIGS, R.: Social factors annoying to children. *J. appl. Psychol.*, 1945, **29**, 75–82.

178 ZUK, G. H.: The influence of social context on impulse and control tendencies in pre-adolescents. *Genet. Psychol. Monogr.*, 1956, **54**, 117–166.

CHAPTER 4
socialization

One of the most difficult problems the adolescent faces in his transition from childhood to adulthood is learning to be an adult in his relationships with other people. Although it is true that socialization began in babyhood, the adolescent still has much to learn. Furthermore, the patterns of social behavior he learned as a child are no more suited to his more mature relationships than

are the types of clothing he wore as a child suited to his adult body.

Even before childhood was over, the adolescent had discovered that his behavior and attitudes led more often to losing than to winning friends. Awareness of the need for changes in the pattern of his social behavior became increasingly strong when he emerged from puberty into adolescence and discovered that, at this time, he had lost more friends, affection, and respect than he had gained (302).

Adolescent girls, even more than boys, are concerned with how to improve their social adjustments. This is not because boys make better social adjustments than girls. Instead, the difference in concerns may be traced to two causes. First, the girl, age for age, is more mature in her attitudes than her male counterpart, and as a result, she views problems from the frame of reference of an adult earlier than a boy of her age. Second, the girl's social life is more dependent on the type of social adjustments she makes than is a boy's.

meaning of socialization

"Socialization" is the process of learning to conform to group standards, mores, and customs. It is the ability to behave in accordance with social expectations. As Child (46) has pointed out:

> Socialization . . . is a broad term for the whole process by which an individual, born with behavioral potentialities of enormously wide range, is led to develop actual behavior which is confined within a much narrower range—the range of what is customary and acceptable for him according to the standards of his group.

The process of socialization includes three distinct but interrelated learning experiences: *proper performance behavior,* or behavior in accordance with the approved standards of the group; *playing the social roles* the group prescribes for the individual; and *acquiring social attitudes* that lead to approved behavior (76,111,180). If the adolescent does not have the social attitudes that will lead to proper performance behavior or to playing the approved social roles, he must use "fronts" if he wants to avoid social disapproval. He must, for example, look interested even though bored, and he must show "proper" modesty when praised and "proper" sympathy when he defeats another in a game (76).

CRITERIA OF SOCIALIZATION

If judged *objectively,* the adolescent is said to be well socialized if he conforms to the three essentials outlined above. Because he behaves as the group expects its members to behave, he is acceptable to the group members and is regarded as a social person (85).

A nonsocial person is one who fails to conform in one or more respects to group expectations. This may be because he is ignorant of social expectations or because he does not wish, for one reason or another, to conform to them. In the former case, he is called "unsocial," and in the latter, "antisocial" (76). Because most adolescents are anxious to win social approval and acceptance, lack of conformity is generally due to ignorance of what the social group expects.

Because adolescents sometimes use fronts to cover up their real feelings and attitudes, the success of socialization must be judged *subjectively* as well as objectively. Just because the adolescent behaves in a social way is no guarantee that he feels social. Consequently, to judge the degree of socialization the adolescent has achieved, one must know what satisfaction he derives from playing the role the social group expects. Thus, to the three objective criteria of socialization, one must add a fourth, the subjective criterion of personal satisfaction. Only when all four have been fulfilled can the adolescent be said to be social (296).

Socialization is generally judged in terms of *social activity.* It is assumed that the better the socialization of the individual, the more active he will be socially. This, however, is not necessarily so. How active the individual is socially will depend upon many factors other than degree of socialization. An adolescent from a large family, for example, may have so many home duties and so little money for social activities that it is impossible for him to participate as he would like (295). Figure 4–1 shows the amount of social participation of high school students from families of five or more children. Married students in college have been found to show little interest in campus life, especially when they have children; but this

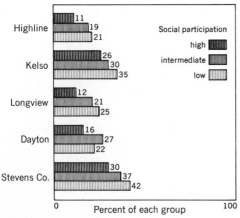

FIGURE 4-1 Social participation of adolescents from large families in five different high schools. (Adapted from C. L. Stone: Some family characteristics of socially active and inactive teenagers. *Family Life Coordinator,* 1960, **8,** 53–57. Used by permission.)

does not imply that they are poorly adjusted socially (101,326).

social expectations

Because learning to live up to social expectations is a difficult task, the adolescent is given guidelines to direct his learning. These guidelines can best be expressed in the form of developmental tasks. (See page 7 for a discussion of the meaning of developmental tasks.) Of the important developmental tasks for the adolescent years, the following relate to socialization: new relations with age-mates of both sexes; emotional independence of parents and other adults; developing intellectual skills and concepts necessary for civic competence; desiring and achieving socially responsible behavior; and acquiring a set of values and an ethical system as a guide to behavior (110).

REASONS FOR SOCIAL EXPECTATIONS

The social group has many reasons for expecting the adolescent to replace his childish social attitudes and behavior with those more suited to his new developmental status. It realizes that no adolescent or adult can be happy when he is friendless and that his needs for social contacts cannot be met un-

less he belongs to some social group. Furthermore, in a culture which places high prestige on popularity, the adolescent who lacks friends thinks of himself as a social failure. This soon becomes a generalized belief. He then regards himself as a failure (52,142).

From the long-term view, the value of socialization is not limited to happiness and favorable self-concepts; it influences the degree of success the person achieves in life. With the growing complexity of modern business and social life, the adolescent of today must be prepared to meet a wider variety of people and adjust to more different types of social situations as an adult than adolescents of past generations did. To get ahead in business today, one must be able to get along with all types of people, from "the castle to the gutter," instead of with a select few who have grown up together and exclude all who do not "belong." The same is true of social life (234).

Unquestionably the most important reason for expecting the adolescent to develop into a socially well-adjusted person is the knowledge that the pattern of socialization established during adolescence will determine what his pattern of later socialization will be. Studies of middle-aged people have revealed that lower-class people, who had not made good social adjustments in adolescence, regarded themselves as social failures or near failures as adults. Middle-class adults, on the other hand, were more satisfied with their social lives, just as they had been in their school days (111).

Adults referred to mental hygiene clinics for emotional difficulties were found to have had few friends when they were younger; in fact, many of them were social isolates (159). Follow-up studies of shy, retiring children have shown that, as adolescents, they made poor social adjustments. This pattern persisted into adulthood. By contrast, adolescents who are well adjusted socially are far more likely to be happy and successful as adults (207).

difficulties in making transition

While the adolescent was faced, once before, with the problem of revising his habitual patterns of behavior—at the time he entered school—he then had the help of parents and teachers to ease the emotional shock of the transition. By the time he has been in school for 6 or more years, it is assumed that he is equipped to handle the problems of transition alone, without the help he had when he entered school.

Adolescents are aware of the magnitude of the task that confronts them and often feel inadequate to cope with it (8,59,69, 77). Feeling that parents do not understand their problems and that teachers do not have time to help them with problems unrelated to academic work, they generally turn to their peers for advice and help. Frequently they supplement this with reading books that have a "how to win friends and influence people" theme or by writing to the lovelorn columns of newspapers and magazines for advice (84,243,288).

Recognizing the social as well as the academic problems that confront the young adolescent in the early stages of transition from elementary to high school, educators have established the junior high schools as "shock absorbers" or as a bridge to ease the transition from childish learning to mature studenthood (114). In spite of attempts to absorb the shock such a major transition inevitably causes in established patterns of behavior, the adolescent still experiences many worries, anxieties, and frustrations. Unless he is offered a helping hand, he may give up the struggle and revert to the patterns he found satisfactory when he was younger or he may withdraw almost completely from social contacts (68,196).

CAUSES OF DIFFICULTIES

There are many factors that contribute to the adolescent's difficulties in putting away childish social attitudes and behavior and replacing them with more mature forms. The most common and most serious obstacles are described in the following sections.

New Types of Groups The child has three "social worlds": the world of the family, the world of the school, and the world of the neighborhood. These are about equally important to him. With the ending of child-

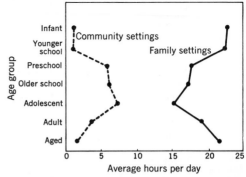

FIGURE 4–2 Time spent in family and community settings in childhood and adolescence. (Adapted from H. F. Wright: Psychological development in Midwest. *Child Develpm.*, 1956, **27**, 265–286. Used by permission.)

hood, these social worlds expand to include those of the different peer groups with which the adolescent is identified in school and in the community, the world of his out-of-school job, and the world of his community. Now the peer group becomes his dominant social world. He not only spends proportionately more time with the peer group than with any other group, but the influence of the peer group becomes the strongest social force in his life (33,52,184, 334). Figure 4–2 shows the proportion of time spent in the home and in the community settings at different ages.

For the adolescent, this shift results in a confusion between old and new values and a clash between the desire to be identified with the peer group and his parents' demand that he continue to regard the family as the major force in his social world. If he chooses the family, he will lose his chances for acceptance by the peer group. Choosing to follow the peer group will lead to constant friction in the home and, unless his status in the peer group is very secure, a feeling of not belonging anywhere (33,69,237, 243).

Added to this power struggle is the problem of adjusting to larger and more heterogeneous groups than the adolescent ever before encountered. Now he must adjust to both sexes, not to his own sex alone as he did in childhood; now he must adjust to peers of a wide range of backgrounds and values; now he must adjust to a new teacher for every subject as he enters the departmentalized world of the high school; and now he must adjust to different adults who direct his different recreational activities at school and in the community.

As the social worlds enlarge, it means constant adjustments to new people and situations as well as to old people in new situations. Henry and Warson have suggested that the number of interactional systems in any given social group can be determined by the use of the formula:

$$2^n - N - 1.$$

When the social group is composed of 4 members, there will be 11 interactional systems; when there are 5 members, there will be 26 interactional systems; and when there are 6 members, the number of interactional systems will jump to 57 (118).

Different Expectations Every cultural group and every subcultural group has its own standards of appropriate behavior by which it judges the socialization of every member. The adolescent discovers that if his family has moved up the social ladder, the interests and values he learned on a lower rung may not conform to those of the new group which he aspires to belong to. He also discovers that the differences in social expectations for members of the two sexes are much greater for an adolescent than for a child (19,40,155,163,272).

These variations add greatly to the problem the adolescent faces in conforming to social expectations. He often feels that he must be a chameleon, changing his colors constantly as he comes in contact with different people in different situations (33,76, 180). To complicate his problem still further, the adolescent finds that people judge him not as he is but in terms of their own values. The success-oriented person, for example, judges people by how successfully a person makes use of his abilities and skills, while the goodness-oriented person values affection, sympathy, tolerance, and forgiveness in interpersonal relationships (191).

Lack of Opportunities for Social Contacts
Socialization does not proceed in a vacuum,

nor is the adolescent born with the ability to get along with different people in different situations (106). Instead, he must have opportunities to learn to be a social person. Not all adolescents have opportunities to learn to be social, and some do not take advantage of the opportunities they have. The adolescent may not be acceptable to the group with which he would like to be identified because of the way he acts or because of prejudice against him, his religion, racial background, or the socioeconomic status of his family. He may not, on the other hand, have time or money to participate in social activities because of the necessity to work or to assume home responsibilities. Or he may be too isolated geographically to be able to spend enough time in social activities to belong to a group (12,30,101,226,252).

Some adolescents are deprived of opportunities to learn to be social by limitations in their environments. In suburban towns, for example, there is a tendency to protect adolescents from people and ways of life differing greatly from their own. As a result, they are permitted to learn only what their parents want them to learn about people and social activities (323).

Lack of Motivation Even when ample opportunities are offered to learn to be social, the adolescent will not take advantage of these opportunities unless social contacts and activities have proved to be satisfying to him in the past. The child whose social experiences have been enjoyable is motivated to learn to behave in the way the group expects him to behave. By the time such a child reaches adolescence, he will be so peer-oriented that he will have a strong motivation to live up to social expectations, or even beyond them, in the hope of increasing his acceptance (142).

Girls, on the whole, have a stronger motivation to take part in social activities and to be socially acceptable than boys. This may be, in part, because girls, who mature earlier than boys, find themselves faced with greater competition for social acceptance among boys than boys are, and, in part, because boys have regarded social activities as sissified ever since their childhood days (12,326). Very bright adolescents who, since early childhood, have found little personal satisfaction in social activities, have little motivation to learn to be social. As a result, they often fail to come up to social expectations for their age levels (124,165).

Lack of Guidance While most adolescents have a strong motivation to be popular, many do not know how to achieve this goal because of lack of guidance. This lack stems from two causes: first, parents' or teachers' belief that the adolescent will outgrow his unsocial behavior, and second, rejection of advice by the adolescent. When parents and teachers accept the belief that the child will automatically develop into a social person, they tend to sit back and let nature take its course.

Even when parents and teachers are not influenced by this traditional belief, they far too often meet resistance when they attempt to teach the young adolescent how to become a more social person because of the way the guidance is given. Adolescents often interpret the guidance to mean "bossing" or trying to "regiment their lives." As a result of the adolescents' rejectant attitudes, many adults give up in their attempts to guide the socialization of young people (33,73,84).

Lack of Suitable Models to Imitate Many adolescents learn more about how to behave in social situations by copying other people than by being told how to behave or by reading books of the social-improvement type. When with people who behave in a manner that leads to good social adjustments, they imitate such behavior. But they can equally as easily imitate the behavior of people who make poor social adjustments. Many juvenile delinquents, it has been found, grow up in environments where the only models of behavior they have to imitate are those of people who may conform to the expectations of a lawless group but who do not conform to the expectations of the majority of society (90,193).

In the modern American home where the father is away from home more than he is at home, adolescent boys are often deprived of a model of socially acceptable behavior because they feel that imitating mothers and female teachers will make them sissies. While girls have models more readily available, they often reject them because they regard them as old-fashioned (180,213, 266).

Turning outside the home for models, the adolescent generally selects popular members of the peer group or imitates characters in mass media. In the case of the former, he is learning how to conform to peer expectations but not to expectations of the broader social group. This may lead to better social adjustments at the moment, but it will not necessarily result in better social adjustments as he grows older (33,52, 77). Characters in mass media, especially movies, television, and stories, may provide a good model, but they are more likely to provide a poor one, even one whose behavior is antisocial. The reason for this is that the characters whose behavior is antisocial are generally colorful. Consequently, the adolescent, often unconsciously, imitates the patterns of social adjustment used by the characters that appeal to him because of their colorful behavior (181).

Poor Foundations Unquestionably one of the most serious difficulties the adolescent encounters in learning to be a socialized adult stems from the fact that he has a poor foundation on which to build (87,104,105, 134,154). Many poor foundations are the result of being identified with poorly adjusted people in the early, formative years of life. The child who imitated the social attitudes and behavior patterns of a poorly adjusted parent or teacher in the belief that this was the way to behave may find, as he reaches adolescence, that other people will not tolerate the way he acts (178,266,297).

Even good foundations are often weakened or distorted during the negative phase of puberty. The best-adjusted child may turn into a "glum, sober, self-imposed isolate" at this time. This temporary lapse is not usually serious. However, it does weaken the young adolescent's confidence in his ability to make good social adjustments. As a result, he enters adolescence with a poorer opinion of himself than he had when puberty began. Fortunately, the desire for social acceptance is generally strong enough to motivate him to revise his behavior (5,64,87,141,239).

The adolescent most likely to be seriously and permanently handicapped in his socialization by poor foundations is the deviant maturer. This is not only because he interprets being different from the group as being inferior, but also because he has a longer time to practice patterns of behavior that make social adjustments difficult for him. The late maturer of either sex, for example, is confronted with problems which are likely to make him antisocial. He resents the way his former friends drop him in favor of others who are more mature in appearance and behavior, and he rebels against being treated as a "kid" by them. He also resents not having the privileges his age-mates have and gets into the habit of fighting for his rights (42,63,140,206).

There are three chief reasons why poor foundations are a major, if not *the* major, difficulty the adolescent encounters in becoming socialized. The first is that attitudes and patterns of behavior, when repeated, become habitual. The second reason for the importance of foundations is that the individual acquires a reputation of being social or unsocial, of being a "good guy," an "odd ball," or a "smarty who thinks he knows it all." While it is true that a reputation can be lost if the individual changes his behavior radically or if he moves into a new area where his reputation cannot follow him, this is far less likely to happen than that the reputation will be persistent (141).

The third and most serious consequences of poor foundations is the effect they have on the individual's personality. Most children are aware, even before childhood ends, that they are not so popular as they would like to be. Adolescents are even more acutely aware of this problem. Awareness of their poor social adjustments is reflected in the deterioration of the self-concept between the ages of 9 and 13 years. This means that when they reach adolescence far too many boys and girls have a poor opinion of themselves. This interferes

with their socialization by making them doubt their ability to get along with people (5).

major areas of transition

If the individual is to live up to social expectations and achieve social acceptance, the whole social structure of his life must be changed when he reaches adolescence. This is a long and difficult task and one which he often fails to complete by the time he reaches legal maturity. The four major areas in which changes must occur include social groupings, friends, leaders, and social attitudes and behavior.

SOCIAL GROUPINGS
The gangs of late childhood gradually break up during the preadolescent period. At that time both boys and girls lose interest in strenuous activities. They withdraw from social groups and pass through a period when they prefer isolation. They show relatively little interest in their former friends and even less in adult companionship. For a time their behavior might justifiably be classed as antisocial. But this is only temporary. As they emerge from the physical transformation that accompanies puberty, they once again feel the need for social life. They then attempt to create a society for themselves that will meet their more mature needs and interests. The adolescent is more selective in the choice of his friends and he cultivates fewer friendships than he had as a child. This is especially true of girls, whose social groups are usually smaller and more sharply defined than those of boys (74,87).

How satisfactory the society of the peer group will be depends upon social distance in peer relationships. "Social distance" means the degree of intimacy that exists between friends. It depends partly on the frequency of contact and partly upon the degree of emotional warmth built up between two individuals. It is generally greatest where there is prejudice against an individual stemming from his religious, ethnic, racial, or socioeconomic background (27,74,96,306).

TYPES OF ADOLESCENT SOCIAL GROUPS

Most adolescents divide their friends into three types of groupings: their chums, their cliques, and their crowds. All the others whom they know in school, at work, or through social contacts are grouped together as acquaintances. Because they apparently have nothing in common other than the fact that their interests and activities bring them into the same environment, there is no basis of mutual attraction and hence no emotional warmth (52,199).

Typically, the groups of early adolescence are composed of individuals of the same sex. By mid-adolescence, friendships are with members of both sexes, and the social groupings thus become heterosexual. However, at every age within the adolescent span, there are marked individual differences in friendship groupings.

In addition to groups of friends, there are the formal groups, or clubs, sponsored by schools and churches. These offer opportunities for social activities to all individuals within a certain age range and are not based on friendship choice. Adolescents who do not find social acceptance among their peers may find a substitute in adolescent gangs, groups composed of individuals who, because of socioeconomic status, immaturity of behavior, personality defects, or some other cause, are socially unacceptable to their classmates in school.

These groups are more characteristic of the early than of the later adolescent years. An older adolescent who goes to college or some professional training school has opportunities to continue the group life of early adolescence because there are enough of his contemporaries available. The adolescent who goes to work after completing high school has contacts with people of all ages, few of whom are likely to be of his own age. As a result, the social groupings of the out-of-school older adolescent become similar to those of the adult (52,251).

Chums Chums, or pals, as boys prefer to call their best friends, are the adolescent's inseparable companions and his confidants. How many chums the adolescent has will vary from one individual to another. Best friends are often those who have known each other from childhood. They play the role of an ideal sibling to each other, with none of the rivalries and threats to status that real siblings so often present. They usually mirror each other in taste, in clothes, in choice of heterosexual partners, and in feelings about parents and siblings and people different from themselves. Best friends are together as much as possible. When it is impossible to be together, they spend much of their time on the telephone, talking about things that could readily wait until they saw each other again.

Chumming is not limited to young adolescents. However, older girls tend to spend more time with their chums than do older boys and they are more dependent on them. Of all types of adolescent friendships, chums are the most lasting. While it is true that chums do quarrel, sometimes very bitterly, there is generally a strong enough bond of mutual affection and interests to hold them together (52,74,191,331).

The adolescent who does not have a chum is likely to be out of line in social adjustments. Being deprived of a close social relationship with someone outside his own family is especially serious for an adolescent who feels that the relationship he formerly enjoyed with different members of his family has been strained to the point where he no longer wants to confide in them. Perhaps the most serious effect of not having a chum is that it deprives the adolescent of a chance of belonging to a clique, because cliques are usually formed from chum groups (198).

Cliques The clique is a small, exclusive, non-kin, informal, face-to-face social group. A "we" feeling causes the members of the clique to think and act alike. There is a strong emotional involvement, which expresses itself in two ways: As between members, it involves strong feelings of friendship and responsibility to render assistance in time of need, and in regard to other groups and outside demands, the clique is given preference, even over the families of its members (32,52,74,284).

A clique is usually made up of individuals who are brought together daily. There are the *school* cliques, made up of boys or girls who associate with each other around school. They are usually from the same class and from the same prestige group of the class. Second, there are the *recreational* cliques, which are generally made up of members of the school clique who come together outside the school for some form of recreation. The third type is the *institutional* clique, seen in specific, nonschool situations, such as Sunday school, Boy Scouts, or Camp Fire Girls. They may or may not be members of a school clique (123).

Adolescents begin to form cliques around the age of 14 years. At first they are made up of individuals of one sex. As heterosexual interests develop, there are more and more cliques composed of boys and girls in equal numbers. A boy with his pal will, for example, find satisfaction in the company of a girl with her chum. The four will go everywhere and do everything together (74,302).

Typically, a clique is composed of three or more individuals of similar interests. They may be close friends of childhood days, or they may be newly found friends. When the clique becomes large, it generally breaks up into several smaller cliques. There is a marked tendency to limit the membership of a clique when growth in numbers threatens the intimacy of the group (331). Like chums, cliques are far more lasting than are the friendships of childhood. That is because they are held together by strong ties of affection and common interests, both of which are weak in the friendships of children (74,229,284).

Girls' cliques are more closely knit than those of boys. There is a tendency for girls to be more resistant to the acceptance of new members in their cliques; they often "present an impregnable front to outsiders" (331). This presents a serious problem for girls who come to a school or neighborhood during the adolescent years. With boys, the problem is less serious. If a boy has anything to offer in the way of athletic or social skills, his chances of acceptance are fairly good (52, 331). In commenting on the importance

of athletic skills, Coleman has pointed out, "Athletics introduces an important democratizing factor in the status system for boys in high school by underrating social background as a basis for status" (51).

Clique Formation In general, commonalities of interest, background, intelligence, and socioeconomic status bind adolescents together into cliques. Cliques that enjoy activities away from home, who have automobiles to transport them to public places of amusement, for example, are more congenial than those whose interests are home-, community-, or school-centered. Similarly, adolescents whose parents put pressure on them to conform to social standards and do the "right things" feel more at home with friends with similar backgrounds than with adolescents who are more "emancipated" (239).

Socioeconomic similarity is an important factor in clique formation. There is little cutting across class lines. However, socioeconomic status is a more important factor in clique formation among girls than among boys. Also, members of the upper socioeconomic groups tend to form larger cliques than do persons in the lower socioeconomic classes (52,147,149,239).

Activities of Cliques Activities of the clique are likewise influenced by the age of its members, their degree of sexual maturity, the sex of the individuals, and many other factors. Hence, it is impossible to say what are the *typical* activities of adolescent cliques. It is possible, however, to list some of the *common* activities of cliques in present-day America. These cover a wide range. The most common are talking about clique matters; gossiping; exchanging confidences; criticizing members of the family and peers who do not belong to the clique; talking about members of the opposite sex; talking about, taking part in, or watching athletic contests; planning social functions; taking part in the activities of formal groups in the school or community, such as the Girl and Boy Scouts; visiting in homes of clique members; meeting and going to places of amusement together; eating either in the homes of clique members or at a local hangout of the clique; playing cards; going to the movies; dancing; or having double or triple dates with members of the opposite sex (52,74, 123,239). Some clique activities give rise to trouble, especially those connected with illegitimate violation of taboos, smoking, gambling, alcohol, driving fast automobiles, and sex (123).

The degree of emancipation from adult control is the most important single factor in determining the patterns of clique activities. Adolescents of the upper socioeconomic groups, especially girls, are given less freedom from adult supervision than are those of the lower groups. Adolescents of the upper socioeconomic groups spend more time with their clique members in activities centered in the school and home, while those of the lower groups spend more of their time away from school and home. Even when the activities are similar, the form they take will differ according to the socioeconomic status of the clique members. Getting together to talk, eat, gossip, and loaf, for example, occurs in the homes of adolescents of the upper socioeconomic groups, while adolescents of the lower socioeconomic groups generally meet on the street, in a corner store, or at a tavern (123,239).

Cliques of Out-of-school Adolescents When schooling is over, or when adolescents withdraw from school before graduating, they follow much the same pattern as school boys and girls. They spend almost all their leisure time with their clique mates or dates. However, owing to the fact that they have less leisure time if they are working and may be scattered in different areas of the community in their jobs, members of out-of-school cliques have less time to spend together.

In addition, the size of the clique is generally smaller when the adolescent is no longer in school. Hours of work and scattering are responsible for this. It is usual for clique relationships with former schoolmates to be retained for several months after the adolescent leaves school. Then, because of shifts of interest, the out-of-school adolescent usually joins a new clique made up of individuals whose interests are similar to his (123).

Influence of the Clique on the Adolescent's Behavior That the clique has a powerful influence on the attitudes, thoughts, and behavior of each member cannot be questioned. As Phelps and Horrocks have pointed out, "The informal group plays a much more important part in the life of the adolescent than do formally organized groups and may be thought of as a focal area of experience in the process of coming of age" (239).

wholesome influences The major contributions of the clique to the clique member are:

1 The clique offers the adolescent opportunities for companionship of a warm and friendly sort; this companionship gives him a feeling of security and acceptance.
2 The clique offers the adolescent opportunities for release of emotional tensions. Here he can let off pent-up emotional steam by expressing frankly and freely his antagonisms, his fears and worries, and his annoyances.
3 The clique offers the adolescent opportunities to develop social skills that will help him to make good social adjustments. In addition, it is of practical value to the adolescent by getting him invited to parties and assuring his acceptance at them.
4 The clique is valuable to the adolescent because it gives him a sense of personal importance.
5 The clique gives the adolescent prestige in the eyes of his peers. Once the adolescent is a member of a clique, the reputation of the clique is attached to him by individuals outside the clique.
6 The clique sets patterns and standards for the adolescent's behavior. At an age when the individual is rebelling against adult authority and demanding freedom to guide his behavior as he sees fit, the clique acts as a brake on the behavior of clique members.

7 The clique offers the adolescent a strong incentive to behave in a socially mature way.

8 The clique offers the adolescent an incentive to achieve independence. When there is a feeling of security from acceptance by the group, the adolescent is in a position where he will try to attain an independent status.

9 The clique promotes good social adjustments on the part of its members.

10 The clique helps the adolescent to adjust to school or to college. Having a small group of friends with him when he goes from junior to senior high school or from high school to college makes the transition easier for the adolescent (32,52,74, 123,147,239,284,302,320).

unwholesome influences There are many unwholesome effects of cliques, not only on members, but also on nonmembers. The effects on these two groups will be analyzed individually.

Effects on clique members The bad effects of the clique on its members may be as follows:

1 The clique encourages the development of snobbishness.

2 The clique stifles the individuality of its members. All cliques encourage considerable conformity on the part of members.

3 The clique stimulates envy on the part of members whose families cannot, or will not, give them what other members of the clique have.

4 The clique may and frequently does increase tensions between the adolescent and his parents.

Effects on nonmembers The bad effects of cliques on nonmembers are as follows:

1 The adolescent who is left out of cliques is made unhappy. An unhappy adolescent not only makes poor adjustments in the home and school, but works far below capacity.

2 The nonmember lacks status in society, whether it be in school, college, or community. He is not identified specifically with anyone and plays the role of the "lone wolf."

3 The adolescent who does not belong to a clique usually becomes very envious of those who have more money, more social position, and more cultural advantages than he.

4 The adolescent who does not belong to a clique may be badly hurt by being rejected. In time, this is likely to lead to feelings of inadequacy and inferiority, feelings that could easily develop into an inferiority complex.

5 The clique often proves to be a disrupting influence to school or campus unity, thus lowering the morale of individuals who are nonmembers.

6 Cliques, once formed, are tightly knit units that are hard to pierce. The newcomer, unless he or she has more than the average ability or personal attractiveness, is likely to find it impossible to make even a dent in the walls that surround the cliques (32,52,74,123,239,294, 302,331).

Crowds A crowd is the largest of the social units formed by adolescents. It is a "formed group" composed of individuals selected because of mutual interests, likes, dislikes, and social ideals. The members meet on the basis of *activities*, not because of mutual attraction as is true of chums and, to a lesser extent, of cliques. Nor is it a spontaneously formed group, made up of individuals who just happen to live near one another or attend the same school. The members of a crowd are selected because they fit. Not all members of the crowd are on equally intimate terms of friendship. This is especially true when the crowd becomes larger, as it generally does in late adolescence with the inclusion of the opposite sex (74,332).

Typically a crowd starts with a clique as a unit. Gradually new members are added. They may be single individuals, chums, or other cliques. The addition of new members is never, however, haphazard or chance. Before inviting newcomers to join the crowd, the members of the crowd discuss their qualifications and decide whether or not they will fit. In this respect the crowd is like the clique in that it is an "exclusive" social unit (74). The structural development of cliques and crowds is shown in Figure 4–3.

The crowd exists so long as the interests and activities meet the needs of the members. In a predominantly working-class high school, for example, the boys in the leading crowds generally break up into "college" and "noncollege" crowds after several years; they have too few interests in common to hold them together as one unit. Among girls, crowds generally divide during the sophomore year into "daters" and "nondaters" (50). However, after members reach the age of 17 years, most high school crowds begin to break up as the members go off to college, to jobs, to the armed services, or begin to go steady (74,123,302).

crowd activities The crowd may at first appear to be a loosely organized social unit. The different members just seem to drift together; there is no recognized leadership; and there are no planned activities. Most of the activities are carried out away from home, in a meeting place popular with all the members of the crowd. It may be a drugstore, a street corner, or the home of one of the crowd members where there is a game room set aside for the use of the crowd and where there will be a minimum of adult supervision or interference.

The typical activities of an adolescent crowd may be classed, roughly, in three major categories: playing, talking, and eating. Not one of these contains the excitement of adventure that appeals to the gang-age child. But to the adolescent, crowd activities fulfill a strong need for companionship and security that every adolescent craves.

Playing The usual play activities of crowds consist of games and sports, dancing, swimming, skating, skiing, picnicking, boating, going to the movies, listening to the radio, watching television, bowling, visiting in the homes of the crowd members, watching athletic contests, and driving in family cars. All these activities are social in character.

Talking Much of the time that the crowd spends together is devoted to talking and to discussing anything and everything from the most intimate personal matters to the most abstract sort of political or social problems. Sometimes the conversations are held in small groups; sometimes the discussion becomes general, with the entire crowd taking part and with each member free to express his or her opinion.

Eating A crowd meeting is never complete without eating. Once again, informality characterizes this activity. The members will eat wherever they happen to be, at the corner drugstore, in a member's home, in a community recreation hall, or in a movie. The important thing about eating, as far as the crowd members are concerned, is that they may be free to eat when and how they wish, without adult direction. Of almost equal importance, they want food that appeals to them, not food that is "good for them."

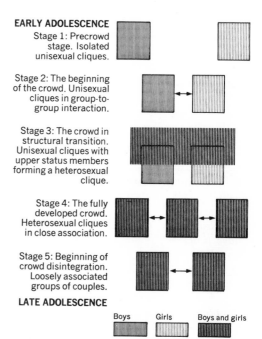

EARLY ADOLESCENCE

Stage 1: Precrowd stage. Isolated unisexual cliques.

Stage 2: The beginning of the crowd. Unisexual cliques in group-to-group interaction.

Stage 3: The crowd in structural transition. Unisexual cliques with upper status members forming a heterosexual clique.

Stage 4: The fully developed crowd. Heterosexual cliques in close association.

Stage 5: Beginning of crowd disintegration. Loosely associated groups of couples.

LATE ADOLESCENCE

Boys   Girls   Boys and girls

FIGURE 4–3 Stages in the development of cliques and crowds during the adolescent years. (Adapted from D. C. Dunphy: The social structure of the urban adolescent peer groups. *Sociometry*, 1963, **26**, 230–246. Used by permission.)

advantages of the crowd   The advantages of belonging to a crowd are so numerous that every adolescent should be a member of some crowd if he or she is to develop into a well-adjusted adult. Among its many advantages, the following may be listed as important for every adolescent.

Crowd life offers a feeling of security
This is especially important when home relationships are unsatisfactory to the adolescent.

Crowd life offers pleasurable pastimes
For the individual who is too old for toys and other childish amusements and yet too young to assume adult responsibilities during the leisure hours of the day, crowd life offers enjoyment.

Crowd life offers experience in getting along with people   The adolescent soon learns from the crowd what is socially acceptable and what is not. This knowledge will help him to make satisfactory social adjustments when he leaves behind him the sheltered life of childhood.

Crowd life helps the adolescent to develop tolerance and understanding   This development comes through discussions with individuals of different backgrounds and home training.

Crowd life offers an opportunity to acquire social skills   These social skills include dancing, conversational ability, good manners, tact, and skill in amusing others.

Crowd life offers an opportunity to judge people   The ability to size up a person quickly and accurately, which is so essential in adult life, develops through day-in, day-out contacts with the crowd.

Crowd life offers experience in courtship behavior   Courtship behavior is learned in socially approved circumstances and with protection against acquiring a reputation of being "fast."

Crowd life encourages the development

of loyalty   The adolescent learns loyalty not only to his intimate friends but to everyone who belongs to the crowd.

disadvantages of the crowd   In spite of the many advantages of adolescent crowds, they have their disadvantages. The most important disadvantages of the crowd are as follows:

Crowd behavior is so satisfying to an adolescent that it encourages him to neglect other responsibilities.

Crowd life encourages snobbishness.

Crowd life causes noncrowd members to be lonely.

Formally Organized Groups   In recent years, educators and church and community leaders have recognized the importance of youth groups as a means of keeping young people out of mischief, of offering opportunities for social life to those who have few such opportunities otherwise, and of encouraging a more democratic intermingling of adolescents who otherwise would form small cliques and deprive many of their classmates of opportunities for social life. The result has been the establishment of many such groups in the schools, churches, and community. Roughly, they can be divided into three categories: the *special-interest groups,* which pursue a single activity, such as basketball, dramatics, swimming, or handicrafts; *clubs,* which have some form of organization and a program that is inclusive of many types of activity; and *purpose groups,* which exist primarily to carry out some purpose of an idealistic or altruistic nature, such as the Hi-Y Club.

Formally organized groups are larger in number of members, as a rule, than are crowds. They are made up of many casual acquaintances and a few intimate friends. Members of a formal group are different from those of the clique or crowd in that they are not selected; they come together because of common interests and activities rather than because of emotional attachment. These groups are open to all and are not dependent on acceptance by the members (123,199).

Formal groups are most popular among adolescents between the ages of 13 and 17 years. After 17, there is a marked decline in interest and participation in such groups as the adolescent falls back on the informal groups, the clique or crowd, and devotes more of his time to a search for his lifework and his life mate (236,251,331).

For the most part, formally organized groups are made up of members of one sex, though many of their activities may include members of both sexes. A girls' club, for example, may spend more time in parties with boys than in the activities for which the club was organized (103,236,255). Unlike cliques and crowds, formal groups generally have an adult leader who plays a role of some imporance in determining the activities of the group and in planning ways to carry out the activities. In slum areas, the adult leader plays a more important role than in middle-class areas where the president of the club, chosen by the members to represent them, is more important. They want one of their members to be the leader though they will not rebel against an adult leader if he does not try to boss them and if he can provide for activities they enjoy (97,179).

advantages of formal groups   Formally organized groups offer many of the same opportunities for social participation offered by the more exclusive groups. They are generally more democratic, and hence have fewer disadvantages than the exclusive groups. The advantages they offer are as follows.

Emotional security   For the adolescent who does not belong to a clique, who is not really accepted at home, or who is dominated by his parents, there is refuge in the formal group; for him, the group has high significance.

Social skills   Because most of the activities of a formal group are controlled, in part at least, by adult leaders, every member of the group has an opportunity to participate and to learn different social skills. Even in special-interest groups, there are opportunities to learn to get along with members of the opposite sex informally by working with them.

Opportunities for fun   Every adolescent wants to have fun or at least wants to have the opportunity to have fun, should he wish to. When it is apparent that doors are closed to him, then the desire to have the opportunity to do the things his contemporaries are doing becomes almost an obsession with him.

Influence on personality   The formal group gives the individual who is not a member of a clique or a crowd some status; this, in turn, has a favorable effect on his personality. How much effect it has will depend, to a certain extent, upon the amount of his participation in club activities (103, 156,236,331).

disadvantages of formal groups   There are certain disadvantages of formal groups which, to date, have not been met satisfactorily. The most serious of these are described below.

Snobbishness   Within each group there is likely to be found a clique that runs the affairs of the group. Those who, because of socioeconomic status or national background, seem to be inferior to the others are left out of the cliques.

Lack of emotional warmth   There is less feeling of belonging when a group is open to all who come than when one is especially chosen to join. As a result, the formal club does not satisfy the members' need for close companionship.

Envy   Even though clubs and youth organizations offer social and other activities similar to, if not superior to, those offered by crowds and cliques, adolescents who do not belong to these exclusive groupings are envious of those who do. They feel that the inner circles have more than they, that their parties are more fun, and that they have a prestige based on exclusiveness that a club lacks.

Gangs From 12 to 14 years of age, children break away from the childhood gang. The gang loses both in quantity and quality. Persons of the higher IQ levels and better social adjustments leave the gangs and join official youth organizations. This is true of both boys and girls (332).

The main features of the gang change also. Now, they are usually made up of equal numbers of boys and girls, though some gangs are exclusively of one sex, as in childhood. Instead of being popular with their peers, most of the members have joined because of social problems arising in school life. Those who are poorly adjusted to school are likewise often antisocial in their attitudes. The brighter and better-adjusted adolescents are not attracted to gangs (57,167).

The need to find the security and ego satisfaction denied him in school is the basic reason the adolescent joins a gang. A number of studies have shown that adolescents who feel socially rejected join gangs of juvenile delinquents. Relatively few juvenile delinquents, on the other hand, are members of formally organized clubs or groups. They find little interest in the "socially good" groups where they feel rejected. Should the gang leader be especially revengeful in his attitude, he can quickly stir up the members to engage in acts of violence, thus satisfying his personal desire for revenge (90,217,273, 332).

Not all gangs are, of course, delinquent gangs. Loneliness and the urgent need to belong drive boys and girls to join some group. If the only group that will accept them is made up of delinquents, they too will become delinquents (27).

FRIENDS

The first major area of transition in socialization in adolescence is social groupings. The second major area of transition is in choice of friends. The friends of childhood days may satisfy the adolescent's social needs or they may not. Childhood friends are, in reality, playmates, not selected primarily for congeniality of interests and values. Only if they have qualities that fit into the more mature social needs of the adolescent will he find the playmates of his childrood adequate for friends. The young adolescent discovers that things he thought important in his playmates now seem less important, while things he regarded as of minor concern are now looked upon as essential qualities in the people he wants as friends. This is illustrated in Figure 4–4.

In the transition from childhood to adolescent friendships, there are certain marked changes in the individual's attitudes toward his friends, in his interest in selecting his friends, in his treatment of them, and in the number or type of friends he wants.

A brief survey of the changes that occur in this area of socialization during the adolescent years will illustrate how radical they are.

Choice of Own Friends The adolescent insists upon choosing his own friends. When parents try to persuade or force him to make friends with persons they consider "right" for him, whether they be of the same sex or of the opposite sex, the adolescent strengthens his determination to reject them as friends not because he finds them uncongenial but because he resents parental interference.

Because the adolescent insists upon choosing his own friends, he often makes mistakes. The individuals he selects frequently do not prove to be what he thought they were. A quarrel ensues, the friendship is broken, and the adolescent is then disillusioned. This is especially common in friendships with members of the opposite sex. As time goes by, the adolescent becomes more critical in the choice of friends. He discovers, for example, that judging an individual by looks alone is rarely a satisfactory basis for friendship; he learns that two individuals with different interests and abilities are not likely to have enough in common to form a lasting friendship.

Number of Friends The young adolescent looks upon a large number of friends as an indication of popularity. But, by the middle of adolescence, there is a change in attitude. Now the number of friends is not nearly so important as that the friends be of the right kind. What is meant by "right,"

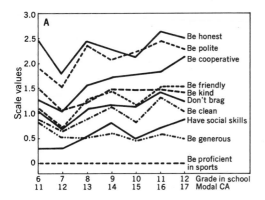

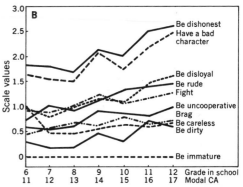

FIGURE 4–4 Patterns of behavior considered praiseworthy (A) and blameworthy (B) by girls at different ages in early adolescence. (Adapted from S. L. Pressey and R. G. Kuhlen: *Psychological development through the life span.* New York: Harper & Row, 1957. Used by permission.)

will, of course, depend upon the cultural pattern of the community. If wealth and social prestige are regarded as of primary importance, right friends will come from wealthy and socially prominent families. Several right friends are to be preferred to a large number who are not regarded as right by the peer standards.

As the adolescent's number of friends decreases, his circle of acquaintances widens. The adolescent will talk about classmates whom he knows only casually if he thinks this will impress others with his popularity with the right people. Like the adult, he learns the art of name-dropping and uses it as a prestige symbol. To be able to use it successfully, he must know enough about the peers he talks about to create the impression that they are his friends (233).

Friends of the Other Sex The third marked change that takes place in friendships is that the adolescent has a growing interest in friends of the opposite sex. As boys and girls become interested in members of the opposite sex and associate with them in cliques and crowds, they form definite opinions about the qualities they expect their friends to possess. Friends of the opposite sex, because their role is that of playmate rather than chum or confidant, are selected by different criteria than are friends of the same sex.

Having no values based on personal experiences of what they want in friends of the opposite sex, but many negative attitudes of what they do not want, both boys and girls in early adolescence tend to build

up values based on characters in the mass media and on adults for whom they have had romantic crushes. Most of these concepts are highly unrealistic and influenced by stereotypes of the "ideal" person. What the adolescent's ideal will be will depend on the cultural group. In the American teen-age culture of today, the ideal boy is an athletic hero, and the ideal girl is a person who is popular with members of the opposite sex (22,52,246).

Girls like a boy who is good-looking, masculine in build, neat, and clean. They dislike boys who are homely, sissified in build, and who have an unkempt appearance, such as shirttails out, trousers unpressed, hair cut so short that it is bristly, greasy hair, and pimply skin. They want a boy to be considerate, cooperative, a good sport, honest, and friendly. On the other hand, they do not like a boy who brags or talks incessantly about himself, or is so tongue-tied that they must do all the talking. In fact, they like a boy with the characteristics they admire in a hero on the screen or in stories.

Boys have their definite likes and dislikes for the girls they select as friends. Above all, they want them to be good-looking, feminine in appearance, and smartly dressed. They want their girl friends to have good manners, not to be gigglers, and to be natural, not show-offs. They like girls to have social skills, such as the ability to talk and dance well, to plan something to do when they are out on a date, and not to make undue demands on their pocketbooks. They regard a studious girl as a child—one who still conforms to parental demands. They do not like girls who are too forward and aggressive or who are hypercritical of the boys' appearance, behavior, and manners. And, above all else, they want girls to act their age, to be good sports when things do not go as they expected, and not to cry or make a scene in public. Thus, it is apparent that they too are thinking in terms of the ideal girl they have built up from mass media, not the typical girl (52,53,59,246, 253).

Friends of the Same Sex   In adolescence, there is a gradual shift from preference for friends of the same sex to preference for friends of the opposite sex. This shift begins around the middle of the high school period —at about 15 or 16 years of age for girls, and a year later for boys. By the latter part of adolescence it is usual and normal for an adolescent to have more friends of the opposite sex than of his own sex and to spend an increasingly large percentage of his time with them. In spite of this shift, there is no time in adolescence when the individual does not want friends of his own sex *as well as* friends of the opposite sex.

There are changes in the qualities the adolescent seeks in friends and in the type of person he selects as a friend. Changes begin around the junior high school age and continue into the latter part of adolescence. Boys' values change in terms of emphasis on certain traits rather than in terms of totally new traits. Girls' values, by contrast, change more radically.

The young adolescent girl who conforms to the pattern admired by adults—the quiet, sedate, nonaggressive individual who is friendly, likable, and has a good sense of humor—wins the admiration of other girls, just as she did in childhood. By the age of 15 years, girls admire a girl who is extroverted, active, a good sport, a good organizer, and a person who can keep

things lively for others. Similarly, boys admire different qualities in their friends as they grow older. The 12-year-old boy admires most a boy who is a leader in games. By the age of 15 years, he admires a boy who has athletic ability, who is aggressive and fearless, and who is personally attractive. Only in the area of attractiveness of appearance is there a marked change in values as boys grow older (52,246,253,304).

There are two major reasons for changes in values in the selection of friends: first, changes in *social needs*, and second, a desire to conform to *social expectations*. During the early part of adolescence, when feelings of insecurity are most pronounced, any individual who can give the adolescent a sense of security, who can understand his problems and can sympathize with him, will do much to help him overcome the insecurity that comes with sexual maturing. Need for security is best met by those who are similar to the adolescent in intelligence, age, level of maturity, abilities, socioeconomic status, interests, and values. This type of person fosters a sense of security in the adolescent—an "at-homeness"—because he speaks the same language as his friend and views life from a similar frame of reference. As a result, he can understand the adolescent's problems, advise him on their solution, and sympathize with him when he is in difficulties (81,199,229,244, 314).

That is why, during the early part of adolescence, girls feel more at home when they are with girls than with boys and why members of the same religious or racial groups find more in common with persons of their own groups (35,132,144).

As a sense of security is gradually attained and interest in members of the opposite sex develops, a new social need arises in the adolescent's life. With it come new standards in selecting friends. Now the adolescent needs friends who can help him make satisfactory adjustments to members of the opposite sex and meet the problems that heterosexual interests present. Friends must not only be congenial but they must also be acceptable to members of the opposite sex (267,314).

Because social needs vary from one adolescent to another, it is impossible to predict just what type of friend will meet the adolescent's social needs best. One adolescent, for example, may need a clinging-vine type as a friend while another needs a sparring partner. From those who are available, the adolescent selects as friends those who meet his needs best (133,267). As Anderson has said, "This sorting out process which begins in early childhood is one of the most striking features of the whole course of social development" (7).

If there are no peers available who meet his social needs, the adolescent often prefers to remain friendless. This does not mean that he is a social recluse; it means that he has no close personal friend or chum. As a result, he is cut off from much of the fun his age-mates have who belong to cliques or crowds. There may, on the other hand, be peers available who would satisfy his social needs but who, for one reason or another, do not wish to be his friend (132,150,229,261).

The second major reason for change in values in the selection of friends is the desire of the adolescent to conform to expectations of the peer group. A girl, for example, is not likely to select as a friend one who is unpopular or one whom the members of her clique or crowd disapprove (283,300).

Boys are also influenced in the choice of friends by the attitudes of members of their group, but less so than girls. As Horrocks (126) has pointed out:

> In so far as the group excludes or disapproves of an individual who has been accepted by one of its members, that member finds himself under considerable pressure to relinquish his acceptance. If the peer-group attachment of the adolescent is strong, it may be a powerful motivating force in the choice of his friends.

When a boy or girl has few or no friends among members of his own sex, there is definite evidence of maladjustment. Even if he is popular with members of the opposite sex, it still suggests that he has made poor social adjustments and has not conformed to peer expectations. Early-maturing girls, for example, are likely to be popular with boys but frowned upon by other girls who regard them as boy crazy and fast. This may be a temporary unpopularity with girls or it may be persistent (133, 142,223).

Adolescents who are personally and socially insecure are more choosy in the selection of friends than those who are more secure. They are afraid of group opinion about their choices. Furthermore, they want to have as friends members of their own sex who are popular enough to flatter their own egos and to increase their acceptance with the peer group. But because popular adolescents generally find greater congeniality among other popular adolescents, the boy or girl who is socially insecure is usually thwarted in his attempts to form friendships with popular members of his peer group (182).

Treatment of Friends In few areas is the need for transition in social behavior greater than in the way the adolescent treats his friends. Most adolescents treat their friends in a manner that would, at any other age, cause them to lose the very friends they want so much. This is especially true of young adolescents; it is more characteristic of girls than boys.

There are a number of reasons for the shabby way the adolescent treats his friends. Of these, the most important are, first, the fact that adolescent friendships are very intense and emotionally charged. Because the young adolescent concentrates on a few friends and is often on unfriendly terms with the members of his family, he tends to put all his "emotional eggs" in one basket and he wants to make sure that nothing happens to that basket (87,92).

The second reason for unfavorable treatment of friends is the tendency on the part of adolescents to idealize their friends. They put a halo on friends, and expect them to behave in a manner that is often beyond their capacities (79,228).

Third, the adolescent wants his friends to make a favorable impression on others, thus enhancing his own popularity. If his friends are popular, it helps to dispel some of the sensitivity he has about how the group reacts to him.

And, finally, the treatment of friends is greatly influenced by a habit carried over from childhood when it was the thing to do to fight, physically and verbally, to criticize, to engage in name-calling, to make derogatory comments, and to tell jokes at someone else's expense (87). Once the habit of treating people in this manner has developed, it will occur unconsciously in similar situations in the future. Adolescents are extremely critical of their friends of both sexes. While some adolescents take their friends' criticism in a good-natured manner, most resent it. Many quarrels are directly or indirectly brought about because of it. Girls are not so loyal to their friends as boys are to theirs. A girl frequently divulges secrets told to her in confidence, and she may even use this information to further her own interests. She will leave a girl friend in the lurch if, at the last minute, a boys calls and asks her for a date. Boys, by contrast, feel they can count on the loyalty of their friends, and they are sure their friends will support them if this support is needed. However, they are less willing to entrust their personal secrets to their friends than girls are.

Stability of Friendships   To satisfy his social needs, the adolescent must be able to count on having friends who are loyal and faithful, regardless of what happens. But the way he treats his friends does not encourage lasting friendships. At the time of puberty, many of the friendships of childhood are broken. This is due partly to changes of interests that accompany physical maturing and partly to the negative attitude and behavior characteristic of this age. Many boys and girls become hypercritical of their friends at this time, they lose interest in the things they formerly enjoyed, and they prefer seclusion to social activities (87,278,293).

After sexual maturing has taken place, the adolescent reestablishes many of the broken friendships of childhood. For both boys and girls, these friendships dating back to childhood days are frequently the most

satisfying because the persons involved have much in common. However, with changes in interests and values, adolescents establish new friendships with individuals with whom they have not previously associated.

Studies of friendships in adolescence have revealed that there is an increase in friendship fluctuations accompanying the onset of pubescence. This occurs in girls at an average age of 13 years, and in boys at 16 years. Following this, there is a downward trend in fluctuations to the age of 18 years (279). Figure 4–5 illustrates this temporary downward trend.

A rise in friendship fluctuations after 18 years is due to the fact that, after graduation from high school, many students go to college, into jobs, or into the armed services, they marry and move away, or they build up new friendships with the other "young marrieds" (322).

Rural adolescents have been found to be slightly more stable in their friendships than urban adolescents. The possible explanation for this is that rural adolescents, because of their more isolated lives, do not have opportunities to develop as varied friendships as urban adolescents (299). Girls' friendships are more stable than boys'; this is true throughout the major part of adolescence. The explanation for this is that boys are more democratic; girls tend to form cliques or to have a single friend as a chum (278,279). There is, however, little evidence of a drastic change in friendships among either boys or girls in adolescence (322). Likewise, there is little evidence that friendship fluctuations are greater among adolescents who are poorly accepted than among those who are well accepted by the peer group (127).

Broken friendships come from many causes. Some are due to environmental factors, such as shifts of families from one neighborhood to another, or to parental pressures. Others come from the formation of cliques where one friend is accepted while the other is not. With new values, especially relating to socioeconomic status, popularity with members of the opposite sex, or ethnic discrimination, former friends may be replaced by new ones.

Friendships with members of the individual's own sex stabilize slightly earlier than do friendships with members of the opposite sex. This is to be expected, in view of the fact that friendships with members of the opposite sex are formed for the first time during the adolescent years and the adolescent has had less time to establish values for the selection of friends of the opposite sex.

LEADERS 3.

The third major change the adolescent must make in the socialization patterns established during the childhood years is in the choice of leaders. As the childhood gang is replaced by more mature types of social groups, a new type of leader is needed. While the individual who fills the social needs of a group will vary according to the adolescents who make up the group, certain characteristics of the adolescent leader are fairly universal in our culture. This holds true for leaders among girls as well as among boys (289,292,310). The qualities adolescents want their leaders to have will be discussed in detail in the following chapter.

In childhood, social contacts are mainly for play. But in adolescence, the social group meets not just for play but for many other activities. This means that with different situations, it is essential to have different types of leaders. There is no such thing as a general leadership quality (17,72,74,79,87,92). A very bright adolescent, for example, may be chosen as leader in a group of other very bright individuals, but if placed in a group of those duller than he, he is a misfit and unlikely to be the leader. Only when the activity the group engages in requires the use of his superior intelligence will he be chosen as leader.

To the adolescent, the leader is his representative in the eyes of others. Consequently, adolescents want as leaders those who will represent them well and add prestige to the group members. A person who makes a good appearance, who has social know-how, and who impresses others with his abilities and self-confidence can be counted on to make a good impression on others (72,79,333).

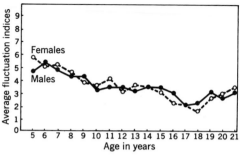

FIGURE 4–5 Friendship fluctuations throughout childhood and adolescence. (Adapted from C. A. Skorepa, J. E. Horrocks, and G. G. Thompson: A study of friendship fluctuations of college students. *J. genet. Psychol.*, 1963, **102**, 151–157. Used by permission.)

In childhood, the leader is always of the same sex as the members of the gang. In adolescence, this is also true in groups composed of individuals of one sex. When the group is composed of members of both sexes, on the other hand, boys are the leaders. Only minor leadership roles, such as secretary of the class or chairman of one of the minor committees, are entrusted to girls (58,185).

The final important change in leadership that occurs during adolescence is in the selection of leaders. Just as adolescents want to select their own friends and resent adult interference, so do they want to select their own leaders. Even if they make mistakes, as they do in the choice of their friends, they demand the right to make the choice and bitterly resent having a leader selected by others imposed on them (17,128,187,336).

4. SOCIAL ATTITUDES AND BEHAVIOR

The fourth major change in transition from childish to adult socialization is in the area of attitudes and behavior. Many of the attitudes of the child are unsocial or antisocial; the same is true of his behavior. These gradually change as the child becomes aware of the handicap they are to social acceptance. Back of much of the child's unsocial or antisocial behavior are unwholesome attitudes. They may be the result of unfavorable early social experiences or they may come from the acceptance of unwholesome attitudes prevalent in the peer group with which he is identified.

The age of sexual maturing is important in determining *when* changes in social attitudes and behavior will occur. Adolescents who mature earlier or later than the average also begin to show changes in attitudes and behavior earlier or later. An early-maturing girl, for example, is interested in boys sooner than her age-mates (60,138).

Not all changes in social attitudes and behavior stem from sexual maturing; some come from social pressures. At first, adolescents spend a great deal of their time, for example, lounging around and talking, often about trivia. As adolescence progresses, much of the lounging around is replaced by purposeful activities and the talking becomes more directed and meaningful (174, 277).

As a direct result of changed interests and attitudes that accompany sexual maturing, several important types of social behavior develop during the adolescent years. Most of this behavior appeared during late childhood, but in a less developed form. Of the different forms of behavior, the following are the most important.

Heterosexual Activities   The most marked change in social behavior in adolescence is in the area of heterosexual relationships. Throughout the latter part of childhood, heterosexual relationships are marked by antagonism between the sexes (87,105,144).

With sexual maturing, the adolescent develops a lively interest in members of the other sex. For girls, this comes early in adolescence. For boys, it appears a year or so later, owing to the later sexual maturing of boys. (See Figure 4–6.) Heterosexual relationships and behavior will be discussed at length in the chapter on sex interests.

Conformity to the Group   Conformity takes two different forms, acquiescence and conventionality. *Acquiescence* means agreement with expressed group opinions in situations involving pressure; the individual shifts to group opinion when his own is different. *Conventionality* means concurrence with the mores and social practices of the indi-

vidual's culture or subculture. Acquiescence and conventionality generally go hand in hand (58,166).

Conformity to the group does not begin in adolescence; children are highly sensitive to group opinions and try in both beliefs and behavior to conform to those of the peer group. But conformity becomes stronger when the child reaches adolescence. At that time, the opinions of others, but especially the opinions of one's own age group, are of immense importance. Regardless of how much the adolescent may depart from adult standards of dress, conduct, and accepted values, he is conservative where his age-mates are concerned (87,109,126).

In their desire to conform to the group, many adolescents go to extremes, often accepting opinions they do not agree with or doing things they do not approve of. In an art preference test, for example, students showed a tendency to shift their opinions when they differed from those of classmates (80,109). Similarly in judging ambiguous figures, they changed their judgments to conform to those of others (308). If the adolescent finds that good grades make him different, he may strive for mediocrity in the hope of being one of the crowd or a regular fellow (78).

Conformity to the group expresses itself more in behavior than in opinions. In manner of dress and in fads, the adolescent follows the crowd. The group ideals, standards, principles, and moral concepts become those of each member of the group. Loyalty to the group is shown in the use of language approved by the group, whether it be normal speech, slang, or swearing, and in show-off behavior used by other members of the group (48,87,152).

The adolescent does not conform to *all* members of the peer group. He conforms to those who have high power in the group and who, as a result, are looked upon as group leaders. The poorly accepted peer member, for example, does not stimulate others to conform to him. Similarly, in the home, the parent who has less power and authority does not stimulate emulation as does the parent with greater authority (21, 108,109,170).

Because of the willingness of adolescents to compromise in their values and standards, many adults regard the conformity of adolescents to the peer group with alarm; they feel that the adolescent will be led around by the nose to the point where he will get into trouble, if not actually become a juvenile delinquent. However, as Josselyn has stressed, adults should not be concerned if the adolescent is a conformist; it is good for him. She points out further, "What should be of concern is the type of peer group to which he is conforming" because this affects his solution to his social problems (143).

Conformity is greatest in the early part of adolescence. As the adolescent grows older, he shows greater stability and security. Consequently, the need for group approval is not so great as it was earlier (21,109,130, 308,317). In the case of adolescents whose sexual maturing deviates from that of the group, the pattern may be different. The child who is slow to reach sexual maturity, for example, is not motivated by the same strong drive to conform that affects his more mature age-mates. As a result, he will be considered different or "queer."

reasons for conformity There are many reasons for the adolescent's willingness to conform to standards set by the peer group. Of these, the following are the most important:

1 School or college life forces the adolescent into close contact with other adolescents.
2 As the adolescent breaks away from the dependence and security of the home, he seeks the security offered by social relationships with his peers.
3 The adolescent resents the lack of status in the family that he believes he should have when he reaches adolescence and finds that the group offers him this status.
4 The adolescent wants to have fun, and this requires companions.
5 To be able to make contacts with members of the opposite sex and enjoy activities with them, the adolescent must have status in some group.
6 The adolescent derives a feeling of se-

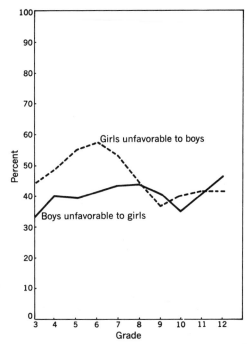

FIGURE 4–6 Attitude changes of boys and girls toward members of the opposite sex during the early adolescent years. (Adapted from D. B. Harris and S. C. Tseng: Children's attitudes toward peers and parents as revealed by sentence completions. *Child Develpm.*, 1957, **28**, 401–411. Used by permission.)

curity from conformity to the peer group and this gives him a source of strength, encouragement, and stability (43,108, 110,122,143,156,161,227).

variations in conformity There are marked variations in the degree to which adolescents conform to the group. Those who have a strong *motivation for group approval* are more likely to conform than those whose status is more secure or who see little opportunity to gain social approval (121,204). The more solidly a group is formed and the more secure the status of the adolescent within that group, the more the group will influence his behavior (270). This is illustrated in Figure 4–7.

The *type of individual* the adolescent is will also affect the degree to which he will conform. Authoritarian people are more influenced by group pressures than are non-

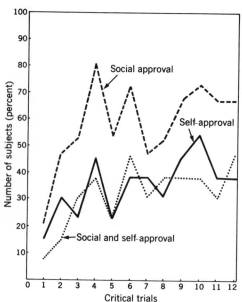

FIGURE 4-7 Conformity in test situations according to the amount of social and self approval the individual enjoys. (Adapted from G. Moeller and M. H. Applezweig: A motivational factor in conformity. *J. abnorm, soc. Psychol.*, 1957, **55**, 114–120. Used by permission.)

authoritarian. The reason for this is that authoritarian people have a "constant fear of not being like others" and, consequently, are "inclined to submit blindly to power and authority" (41,298). Adolescents who, as a result of overprotectiveness in childhood, have become overdependent, are more suggestible and more easily influenced by the group than those who are less dependent (43,61,134).

Anxiety predisposes the adolescent to conform to the group. The more anxious he is, the more suggestible and the more easily influenced (45,298,315). Anxiety leads to feelings of personal inadequacy; these feelings, in turn, lead to fear of being different (61,135). The adolescent who has a poor *evaluation of himself* is more conforming in his thinking and behavior than the one whose self-evaluation is more favorable (296). *Girls* tend to be more conforming than boys (43,62,235).

lack of conformity Adolescents often want to be different but hesitate to follow this desire. When they do, the difference generally takes the form of conformity to certain basic patterns of behavior of their peers. In the case of the leader, there may be deviations from the group pattern. These, in turn, will be followed by the other members of the group. Those who are not leaders must either conform or be excluded (126,151). The adolescent who is not wholeheartedly for the group generally loses status in it. As a result, most adolescents will conform to group expectations even when these conflict with their personal values and standards (110,123,257).

overconformity Overconformity can be just as bad as underconformity. Extreme conformists are more often found in the middle-social-class adolescents than in the lower- or upper-class groups. The reason for this is that middle-class parents, hoping for upward social mobility for their children, stress the importance of doing the right thing at the right time (215).

The adolescent who overconforms loses his identity as a person and, with it, the respect of the peer group. He soon acquires the reputation of being afraid of his own shadow, of being led around by the nose, or of being afraid to call his soul his own. Equally serious is the constant anxiety the overconformist experiences. He is so afraid of doing or saying the wrong thing that he is constantly on pins and needles when he is with others.

As a result of constant anxiety, the extreme conformist develops an authoritarian type of personality. He becomes outer-directed in the sense that he is dependent on external authority for the patterns of his behavior. Like most authoritarian people, the overconformist develops a punitive attitude toward anyone who shows individuality. He then condemns them when they show the independence he would like to show (166,215).

Self-assertiveness Like conformity, self-assertiveness springs from a desire to win the approval of the group. As the adolescent develops greater self-confidence, he can stand on his own feet. Toward the middle of adolescence he wants *both* approval and recognition. In his desire to become an individual and to achieve status with the group, the adolescent must call the attention of the group to himself.

To achieve this end the adolescent wears clothing of extreme styles or conspicuous colors; he tells off-color jokes; his laughter is boisterous; he speaks in an authoritative fashion about any and every subject, regardless of his ignorance of the subject; he uses big and unusual words to make others sit up and take notice; and he tries to change the tonal quality of his voice and his pronunciation of words, which generally results in affected speech. Boasting of his achievements, especially romantic conquests, accepting each new fad or fancy as it appears, putting on airs, engaging in daredevil stunts, and criticizing and trying to reform others are common forms of self-assertive behavior in the later part of adolescence (22, 32,52,87).

Early attempts at self-assertiveness are frequently characterized by crudeness and clownishness. In his zeal to attract attention, the adolescent frequently overdoes it. When he discovers that the social reaction is not favorable, he modifies his behavior. Gradually he learns through experimentation what is acceptable and what is not. In time crude showing off gives way to more subtle forms.

Resistance to Adult Authority   One of the most common ways adolescents assert themselves is through resistance to adult authority. This is not new in adolescence, but it is more pronounced than during childhood (13,110,123). While adolescents have an increasing tendency, with age, to challenge authority figures, this tendency generally reaches its peak between the tenth and twelfth grades. After that, it begins to wane, because adults' attitudes and restrictions become less stringent. When parents and teachers suddenly realize that the adolescent is approaching adulthood, they treat him more like an adult than they did earlier. Consequently, he has less need to challenge authority than he had previously. Not only do adolescents challenge home and school authority but they also challenge legal authority. This is more true of boys than of girls (330). The trends in challenging home, school, and legal authority are shown in Figure 4–8.

The adolescent girl in the home and school is surrounded by more restrictions than is the boy. Although girls rebel less than boys, they do not placidly accept adult authority (58,87,158,330).

Criticism and Attempts at Reform   During the gang age of childhood, it is common for boys and girls to criticize their siblings and friends openly and outspokenly. They also criticize parents, grandparents, teachers, and other adults, generally behind their backs (87). When physical maturity gives them the size and shape of adults, it also gives them the courage to criticize openly those whom they have formerly criticized behind their backs (317).

Their criticisms may be accompanied by suggestions for improvement, such as "Why don't you do it this way instead of the way you are doing it now?" or even by attempts on the adolescent's part to bring about the changes through his own efforts.

motivation in criticism   Back of criticism and attempts at reform may be one of three motives. The first is a sincere *desire to help others* by improving their ways of doing things (14). Criticism is generally directed toward those for whom the adolescent has the greatest regard (254).

The second motive that leads to criticism and reform is a *desire for retaliation*— to get even. The adolescent who is constantly criticized by others frequently turns around and gives them a taste of their own medicine. And, finally, criticism and attempts at reform are satisfying forms of *self-assertiveness*. The individual who feels that he can help others by showing where they are at fault and what they can do to correct their faults gets great ego satisfaction from doing so.

How strong and how persistent the hypercritical attitude of the adolescent will be depends upon many factors. Strict discipline in the home or school, repeated rebuffs from adults or from peers, or shifting of in-

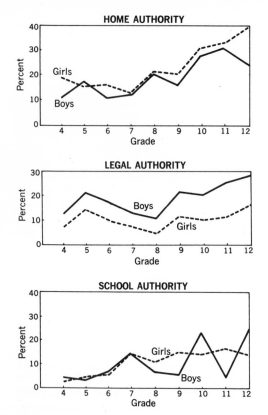

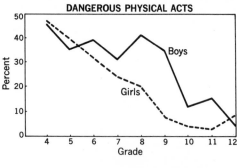

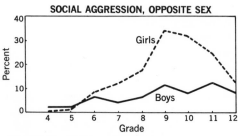

FIGURE 4-8 Forms of "daring" behavior of boys and girls in childhood and adolescence. (Adapted from S. L. Witryol and J. E. Calkins: Marginal social values of rural school children. *J. genet. Psychol.*, 1958, **92**, 81–93. Used by permission.)

terest to some new activity tend to lessen the tendency to criticize. Very bright adolescents are, on the whole, more critical than those of lower intellectual levels. Girls tend to be more critical of their mothers while boys tend to be more critical of their fathers (58,158).

Different forms of mass media of communication, especially movies, television, and advertisements in magazines and newspapers, contribute to the adolescent's dissatisfaction with life as it is. When the adolescent compares his own life with what is presented on the screen, for example, the comparison is apt to foster dissatisfaction. This contributes to his critical attitude toward what he has. As the adolescent develops a more mature outlook on life, some of the dissatisfaction wanes. With it, there is a waning in his desire to find fault and change things.

areas of criticism As his experiences broaden, the adolescent sees weaknesses in

his *parents*. He is somewhat disillusioned by the realization that his parents are not all he thought them to be (58). As a rule the adolescent picks out for criticism the traits of his parents that are markedly different from those of his friends' parents or from the standards set in the movies, magazines, books of etiquette, or other media.

To an adolescent girl her *home* is her background. She wants it to be as glamorous as possible to provide a fitting setting when she entertains her crowd, especially when members of the opposite sex are present. Even to an adolescent boy the home is important, not so much from the angle of the interior as of the exterior. When his friends see where he lives, he wants them to be impressed. The management of the home, the food selected, the way it is prepared, and the hours the meals are served are criticized if they do not please the adolescent.

Few *high schools, colleges,* or *universities* complete an academic year without one formal protest from the student body. The protest takes the form of criticism of the way things are done in the institution, whether it is a change in the faculty, a change in the athletics program, the dropping of courses, the food that is served, the banning of certain students from extracurricular activities because of poor grades, or the expulsion of a student because of misconduct. Occasionally, students go out on strike in an attempt to bring about the reforms they are demanding.

Both boys and girls are brutally frank in their condemnation of the appearance, dress, manners, points of view, in fact, everything about their *friends.* Nor do they limit themselves to friends of their own sex. It is not at all uncommon for girls to try to make over the boys they are interested in so that they will better conform to the girls' concepts of the ideal boy, or for boys to try to transform the girls into the pattern of their dream girls.

That the desire to criticize and attempts at reform are universal in adolescence and serve a useful purpose has been emphasized thus by Kirkpatrick (152):

> The adolescent has an uncanny capacity for seeing his elders for what they are and classifying by his figures of speech their pomposities, rigidities, and numerous other foibles. The pathway he is travelling should be more or less familiar to us because we once went the same way. Our concern about his hostilities should not be too great because his behavior is determined by mechanisms that are identifiable and understandable. His behavior pattern is, with some variation, almost universal and, our fears to the contrary, is not likely to be permanent. The worst thing that could happen to our society would be for our adolescent children to give up the struggle without a good fight and effect a truce or a compromise with life.

Liberalism and Radicalism Traditionally, youth is in rebellion against the older generation. It is not surprising, therefore, that adolescents tend to be more liberal in their views than their parents and teachers. These changes are due, in part, to intellectual maturation. They are mainly, however, the product of environmental influences, especially the school and college. A trend toward liberalism is generally apparent in late adolescence, especially among college students (192).

Girls, who at the beginning of college tend to be more conservative than boys, have been reported to show greater gains in liberalism. Social science majors tend to become more liberal in their attitudes than do natural science majors; students of the Catholic faith have been found to change least and those of the Jewish faith most. Students from large cities are more liberal than those from small towns. The better students, on the whole, are more liberal than those whose scholarship is of a lower order. The longer the student has been away from home, the more liberal he is likely to be. This suggests that place of residence is a more important factor in liberalism than age or intelligence (100,131,210,241,262,317).

Trends toward liberalism are illustrated in Figure 4–9, which shows changes in attitudes toward a number of different forms of behavior from the sixth grade through high school. Note the greater tolerance for being conceited, for immodesty, and for bribery among children than among adolescents and the more liberal attitudes of high school students toward divorce, smoking,

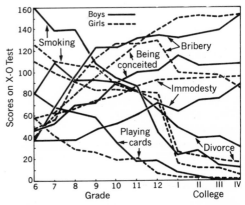

FIGURE 4–9 Changes in values used in judging other people with advancing age throughout the adolescent years. (Adapted from S. L. Pressey and R. G. Kuhlen: *Psychological development through the life span.* New York: Harper & Row, 1957. Used by permission.)

and playing cards. College seniors are more liberal in their views than high school students (192,245).

Liberalism often develops into "radicalism"—going to greater degrees of tolerance than anyone else. Among older adolescents, expressing radical points of view is a common way of asserting themselves and of attracting attention. As a general rule, the adolescent does not actually believe all he says. Frequently, he is spurred on to radical expression by the attention he attracts, even if it is not always favorable (44,116,263).

Radicalism does not limit itself to opinions or to expression of opinions; it is often expressed in behavior. Of the different forms of expression, the following are the most common: *evangelism*, in an attempt to recruit sympathizers and supporters to a radical belief or cause; *political action*, in the form of circulating petitions, speaking, or taking part in discussions on issues sponsored by radical organizations; and *Bohemianism*, or the pursuit of unconventional personal experiences and dress (188). Radicals among adolescents generally confine their nonconformist interests and activities to areas outside academic life (22).

variations in liberalism How liberal or how conservative an adolescent is depends to a certain extent upon the adolescent's past experiences, his concept of himself as a person, the degree of security he feels in social situations, and many other factors (62, 102,221). Among high school students, those whose *socioeconomic status* is inferior to that of their classmates are likely to have more radical attitudes than those of the higher levels. How radical they are, however, differs according to the *area of behavior*. Lower-class adolescents, for example, are more liberal about government control but more reactionary in regard to civil rights and race relations (22). College students are more liberal in their religious views than are most adults (248).

Once a more liberal attitude has been established, it tends to persist. In a follow-up study of attitudes of college students 14 years after the original rating, it was found that the radicals had become slightly more radical, and the reactionaries less reactionary. As adults, women shift toward liberalism but they are still more conservative than men (219). How liberal and how persistent liberalism will be depends, to a marked degree, upon the *cultural environment* in which the adolescent is and how long he remains in that environment (117,200).

Helping Others Children are, for the most part, self-bound; they expect others to do things with and for them and to gratify their every wish. By contrast, the young adolescent is actively, not passively, interested in the affairs of others. He wants to help them to solve their problems. Emotional outlets and feelings of superiority and security are the chief sources of satisfaction in helping others. These feelings are weak in emotionally insecure adolescents. Therefore, as a form of compensation, these adolescents direct their efforts to aiding others, receiving the emotional satisfaction and feeling of superiority that are lacking in other social relationships. In this way the emotionally insecure adolescent bolsters up his self-confidence. In addition, he is apt to gain the prestige and feeling of self-importance he craves. Because emotional insecurity is almost universal in early adolescence, few boys or girls of this age escape experiencing the desire to help others. As adolescence progresses and feelings of security and self-confidence replace those of inadequacy, the desire to help others decreases or takes the form of criticizing and making fun of others (172).

common forms of expression There are several forms of expression that are fairly universal in this tendency to help others. Perhaps the most common is *giving advice*. The young adolescent is very free in offering suggestions, solicited or unsolicited, not only to his family and friends but also to casual acquaintances. If his advice is not accepted, his usual reaction is to feel that the recipient is making a mistake by not mending his ways.

Many young adolescents take part in *school* or *community activities* in which they can be of service to others. They spend some of their leisure time in Scout work, Junior Red Cross, church work, social service work, or in community organizations designed to help others.

As the adolescent's horizon broadens he begins to think of himself as a member of society at large rather than of the school or neighborhood. His interest in *national and world affairs* is fostered by his studies in high school and college, as well as by listening to the radio, watching television, and reading newspapers and magazines. Toward the middle of adolescence this interest is strong enough to lead the adolescent not only to engage in much abstract thinking about government, politics, economics, and national and international affairs but also to discuss freely the problems related to these affairs (11).

The idealistic nature of the adolescent predisposes him to *disappointments, disillusionments,* and *cynicism.* When he discovers that his efforts to help, to bring about improvements, or to make some contribution to the group are unappreciated or even rebuffed, his attitude toward the group is likely to change to that of cynicism. When this happens, he develops an "I don't care" or "Let them do it themselves" attitude. This attitude colors his reactions to a marked degree and acts as a brake on his desire to help others. Older adolescents tend to be more cynical than younger because they have experienced more disillusionments. Boys, as a rule, are more cynical than girls (218).

Prejudice Social discrimination, snobbishness, or "prejudice," as it is generally called, is a social attitude organized and structured in a definable and consistent way; it is an attitude which causes, supports, or justifies discrimination. There are three elements in this attitude: first, beliefs, often based on stereotypes, that anyone who does not belong to the same group or who is different in any way, is inferior, while the members of one's own group are more important and, thus, superior (9,44). Second, there is an emotional accompaniment that ranges from indifference to bitter and violent hostility (2,55). And third, there are

beliefs about the appropriate treatment of those who are regarded as inferior (137). "Appropriate treatment" takes many forms, the most common of which are withdrawing from members of the group against which there is prejudice, using unfavorable terms to characterize them, or excluding them from groups and organizations made up of individuals against whom there is no prejudice (208).

Prejudice is directed against groups that hold a minority position in a given culture. A "minority group" is a subgroup in a larger society that is subjected to discrimination, segregation, or persecution at the hands of another subgroup, the "majority" (176). The terms "minority" and "majority" do not have numerical connotations but are differentiated by control of the economic, political, and ideological mechanisms of the social stratification, stemming from special cultural or physical features. The majority group, even though it may be numerically smaller than the minority, has the power to keep the minority group from achieving comparable status (107).

There is greater prejudice against certain racial or national groups and against certain religious groups than against others. In a study of university students from 23 nations, it was reported that they placed higher prestige on Americans, British, Swiss, and Canadians than on those from other nations. (See Figure 4–10.) Countries that have little prestige in the eyes of others are likely to incur prejudice (148). There is greater prejudice against Irish Catholics than against French, Italian, or Spanish Catholics, and greater prejudice against the Negro than against the Indian (31,195,303, 305).

Within the Negro group, prejudice against those from the West Indies or from Africa is less than against those from the United States. Even among the Negroes in this country, prejudice is greater toward those who are proud, persistent, forward, liberal, and independent than against those who are patient, good-natured, faithful, calm, obedient, and docile. There is discrimination against teen-age intelligentsia—the "brains" or "curve raisers"—and against

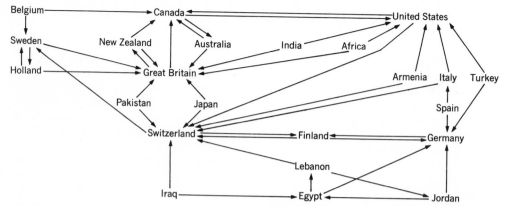

FIGURE 4-10 Sociogram showing the prestige of different nations as rated by university students from different nations. (Adapted from J. D. Keehn and E. T. Prothro: National preferences of university students from twenty-three nations. *J. Psychol.*, 1956, **42**, 283–294. Used by permission.)

nonconformists—the "kats." There is also prejudice against people in certain occupational groups, especially laborers, labor leaders, sailors, and artists (197,231,283).

origins of prejudice Most prejudice in adolescence is a carry-over from the early years of childhood (88,328). However, the early attitudes of prejudice are strengthened during the school years, especially between the ages of 12 and 16. It has been estimated that only about 25 percent of all prejudice develops for the first time after the person reaches 16 (2,194). At that age, prejudice developed earlier may start to wane but it often becomes stronger (9,137,197).

Prejudice is a product of learning (194). This is well illustrated in the words of a song in the musical comedy, "South Pacific," written by Oscar Hammerstein, II.

> You've got to be taught to hate and fear,
> You've got to be taught from year to year.
> It's got to be drummed in your dear little ear,
> You've got to be carefully taught.
>
> You've got to be taught to be afraid
> Of people whose eyes are oddly made,
> And people whose skin is a different shade,
> You've got to be carefully taught.
>
> You've got to be taught before it's too late,
> Before you are 6 or 7 or 8,
> To hate all the people your relatives hate,
> You've got to be carefully taught.

Psychological studies of prejudice show that the roots of prejudice go back to the early home experience of the adolescent; the foundations of prejudice are thus home grown. While parents *do not intentionally* build up prejudices against people of other groups, it is not uncommon for them to use hostile descriptions and stereotypes in explaining racial and religious differences to their children. Furthermore, parents often lack information about and understanding of cultural differences, with the result that, in their explanations, they are likely to build up unfavorable attitudes in the minds of their children (194,250).

Even without direct teaching, the individual will imitate the attitudes and behavior patterns of those whom he admires. Because the young child admires his parents, he will imitate them. Later, he will imitate members of the peer group, and still later, members of the larger social group with which he is identified. If it is "correct" to view and to treat those who do not belong to his group as inferior, he will learn to conform to social expectations and be prejudiced in his attitudes and behavior. *Social contagion* thus intensifies the prejudices already established in the home (9,186,216, 313).

factors influencing prejudice No one factor alone is responsible for the direction or the intensity of prejudice in adolescence. (See Figure 4–11.) Of the many factors, there is evidence that the following are the most important.

Parents Many prejudices, as was pointed out earlier, originate either directly or indirectly from parental attitudes and teachings. Clinging to parental patterns, therefore, is conducive to prejudice, while a critical attitude toward parental patterns is conducive to freedom from prejudice (2, 216,316). Adolescents from professional families are often idealistic and more liberal than their parents; they show far less prejudice than adolescents from families with the "businessman" outlook—an outlook which is more practical and conservative. The greatest prejudice is found among adolescents from the lower socioeconomic groups (47,171,225).

The *education* of the parents is closely related to their prejudice. College-trained parents tend to be less prejudiced than parents who have not had college training (98, 240,241,248,262). Parents with a favorable attitude toward one minority group generally encourage the development of favorable attitudes toward all minority groups (216,225,248).

Sex Girls *show* less prejudice against members of minority groups than do boys. This is true of high school as well as of college students (2,47,242,291). Their prejudices are expressed in ignoring members of minority groups rather than in making unfavorable comments about them or treating them as inferiors when they are present. Frequently, home pressure on girls to avoid members of minority groups is greater than on boys.

Social proximity In general, persons whose prejudice is strong have had few contacts with individual members of groups against which there is prejudice. Casual contacts do not diminish prejudice as markedly as does a more intimate type of contact (305). When contact is between those having similar economic or social status, there is likely to be less prejudice than when

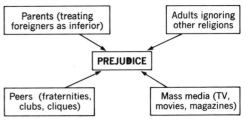

FIGURE 4–11 How prejudice develops.

economic and social status are divergent (2, 98,216,258).

On the other hand, social proximity may intensify rather than diminish prejudice (328). This is especially true when proximity is forced on members of the majority group or when there is social interaction. The more members of the majority group come in contact with members of the minority group and the more familiar they become with their attitudes and values, the less they may like them, and the greater their prejudice may be (216).

Religion Adolescents with strong religious interests tend to be less tolerant in their attitudes toward members of minority groups than those whose religious interests are weak (3,24,230,327). Anti-Semitic prejudice, for example, has been reported to be greater among adolescents who belong to religious groups than among those who do not (26). The strongest prejudice has been reported among adolescents of the Catholic faith, while the least prejudice has been found among those with no religious affiliation (2,216).

Personality In general, the personality pattern of a person showing prejudice is quite different from that of the unprejudiced individual (3). While on the surface the prejudiced individual may show traits that suggest good adjustment, there are generally repressed hostilities, repressed sexual wishes, anxiety concerning status, dependency needs, and guilt not consciously acknowledged (2,94,145,275,280). When prejudice is intense, the individual reveals an almost paranoid personality. In less intense forms, it is more characterized by withdrawal, depression, and antisocial personality trends (94,286). Adolescents who are better adjusted and show a more self-acceptant attitude tend to have more positive attitudes toward minority group members. Those who do not accept themselves as individuals of worth are likely to perceive others in a hostile and derogatory fashion (1,216,301,319).

Personality factors alone will not cause prejudice. However, the typical personality syndrome of the prejudiced person *predisposes* him to prejudice by making him more willing to accept the cultural stereotypes and attitudes that lead to prejudice (3,216). This is illustrated by the fact that adolescents in the same group differ in the degree of prejudice they experience (125,186,309). In Figure 4–12 are shown the personality characteristics of tolerant and prejudiced persons.

Cultural influences Much prejudice results from social contagion—it is the thing to do. It comes not from contacts with minority group members but from *contacts with the prevalent attitude toward them* (125,171,209,216). As Martin and Westie have pointed out, "Prejudice toward outgroups is part of the normative order of American society." This is shown by the fact that different social classes and subgroups *approve* the rejection of particular outgroups in varying degrees and what they believe to be the correct feelings and behavior toward the members of the outgroup. These authors further stress (186):

> *We find in our midst many Happy Bigots whose prejudices are born, not so much of personal psychological difficulties, but rather of the fact that their community and various groups inculcate, expect, and approve of their prejudices: personality factors probably serve primarily to predispose and to intensify or abate normative expectations.*

Stereotyping Reinforcement of prejudices developed in the cultural milieu comes more from culturally accepted stereotypes than from any one other factor (276). "Stereotyping" is a "tendency to attribute generalized and simplified characteristics to groups of people in the form of verbal labels" (312). Stereotypes are usually highly charged with emotions. They are evoked in the minds of the hearers by verbal labels which mobilize a complex of ideas and images plus strong feelings, attitudes, and personal values (38,75,224). The label, "nurse," for example, calls forth not only an image of a woman in white uniform but also the cultural values associated with nursing as a profession and the nurse as a person (65).

Stereotypes have three common characteristics: first, their content is mainly composed of the personality traits and physical features associated with persons of that group; second, they are generalized or "average" pictures of the personality traits and physical features common to a group of persons; and third, they are usually though not always uncomplimentary. Stereotyping, it must be stressed, is not inherently bad, though it tends to neglect individual differences (75,160,220,224). It is bad when the contents of the stereotype are incorrect or when it operates unfavorably against people or groups. As Vinacke has stressed, "It is probably not the fact of stereotyping, per se, which marks the prejudiced person so much as the content of the stereotypes and how they are used" (312).

Because most stereotypes are unfavorable, they intensify prejudice fostered through other media (220). Adolescents' stereotypes of Negroes and Jews illustrate this. To them are ascribed personal or group traits of a derogatory sort, highly colored by their own feelings toward members of these groups (23,89,249). Negroes are more often described in terms of "inferior" traits, while Jews are described in terms of "bad" traits (23,268,276). (See Figure 4–13.)

Stereotyping is not limited to members of the majority groups. Those who belong to the minority groups likewise have stereotypes of their own, of the majority, and of other minority groups. They use these stereo-

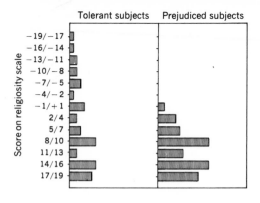

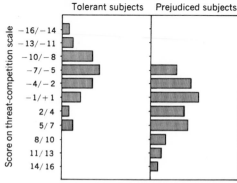

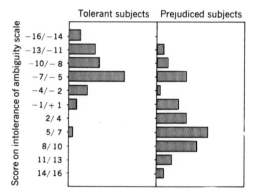

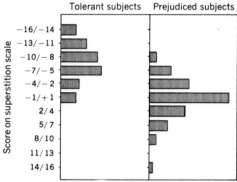

FIGURE 4–12 Scores of tolerant and prejudiced persons on a comparative attitude scale. (Adapted from J. G. Martin and F. R. Westie: The tolerant personality. *Amer. sociol. Rev.*, 1959, **24**, 521–528. Used by permission.)

types, as do members of the majority group, to judge individual members of these groups. The stereotypes of whites, as held by Negroes, for example, show them to be pleasure loving, grasping, deceitful, and cruel. Within their own group, they have stereotypes based on skin color and texture of hair (15,56,247).

effects of prejudice The psychological scars of prejudice are intensified in adolescence as prejudice becomes increasingly stronger. These scars are not limited to adolescents against whom prejudice is directed. They are to be found in the personality patterns of adolescents who are prejudiced as well; but here they are of a different type. *Adolescents who are prejudiced* show it in rudeness and ruthless denunciations of those whom they consider their "inferiors." They are *intentionally* rude because it gives them personal satisfaction and a feeling of superiority. In addition, they gain satisfaction

from being cruel to those they regard as inferior and they go out of their way to hurt the feelings of their victims by verbalizing their prejudices. Even though they may feel guilty about or ashamed of the way they treat members of minority groups, they generally use rationalizations and other defense mechanisms to protect themselves from recognition of the injustice of their behavior (2,9,94).

The prejudiced adolescent becomes suspicious of all who belong to minority groups and is afraid of fraud and trickery in any dealings he has with them. In addition, prejudice makes him sensitive to characteristics, whether physical, psychological, or names, that are part of his stereotype of the group against which he is prejudiced. As

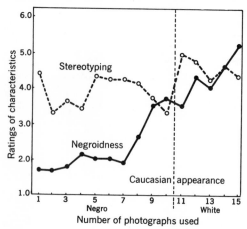

FIGURE 4–13 The relationship between personality stereotyping and physiognomic Negroidness in a study of photographs. (Adapted from P. F. Secord, W. Bevan, and B. Katz: The Negro stereotype and perceptual accentuation. *J. abnorm. soc. Psychol.*, 1956, **53**, 78–83. Used by permission.)

a result, he often intensifies his dislike for members of the group by intensifying the undesirable aspects of his stereotype of them (79,169,265,269). Perhaps the most serious psychological scar of being prejudiced is that the adolescent gains personal status in an unrealistic way and develops false feelings of personal superiority. This interferes with the development of healthy attitudes toward self and others and, in time, will result in personality maladjustments (9).

The effect of prejudice on the *adolescent against whom there is prejudice* is equally as serious, but in a different way (9). Having been the object of discrimination since early childhood, the adolescent has many unfavorable attitudes toward himself and toward members of the majority group when he reaches adolescence. How the foundations of unfavorable attitudes are established in childhood has been described thus by Allport (2):

> A child who finds himself rejected and attacked on all sides is not likely to develop dignity and poise as his outstanding traits. On the contrary, he develops defenses. Like a dwarf in a world of menacing giants, he cannot fight on equal terms. He is forced

to listen to their derision and laughter and submit to their abuse. There are a great many things such a dwarf-child may do, all of them serving his ego defenses.

On such foundations, the adolescent develops ways of expressing his resentments toward those who discriminate against him. He will show little interest in establishing friendly relationships with others, even when they do more than their share to make him feel that he is wanted. He will be suspicious of their motives just as the prejudiced adolescent is suspicious of the motives of those against whom he is prejudiced. When he is large enough to feel that he has an even chance to win in a fight, he may express his resentments by aggressive attacks on those who have discriminated against him. If he feels that his position is hopeless and that he is helpless in the face of the majority group, he is likely to submit but use passive sabotage to get even (10,212,249).

His rebellion, whether expressed or controlled, is usually accompanied by derogation of the group that has discriminated against him and by derogation of his own group as well. He feels ashamed of belonging to his group and may try to deny his membership by changing his name, his religion, or any feature, such as shape of nose or texture of hair, that identifies him with that group. Rejection of his group membership usually leads to self-rejection; he comes to dislike himself just as he dislikes the group with which he is identified (10, 321).

There are *individual differences* in the ways adolescents react to discrimination. The personality of the adolescent determines how he will react more than any other one factor. The adolescent subjected to authoritarian training methods in the home and school may react with marked aggressiveness or with submission, depending on how he habitually reacts to frustrations. Girls, who learn at home to be more submissive than boys, generally react to discrimination with submission, while boys are more likely to react with aggressiveness. Because lower-class adolescents are subject to more discrimination than those of other social classes, they tend to be more aggressive in their reactions (10,120,249).

combating prejudice Many attempts have been made to combat prejudice. Some have proved to be successful, but most, unfortunately, have met with failure or only partial success. Showing the *film,* "Gentleman's Agreement," to a group of university students led to an increased tolerance toward Jews (259). After a group of girls read two *books* about Negroes, they revealed a better attitude toward the Negro than they had previously or than did a control group (324).

Through *discussion,* it has been found, prejudiced attitudes can be changed more successfully than through mere exposure to persuasive forms of communication. From discussions with teachers and peers, the adolescent gets a new perspective on the group toward which he was prejudiced (202,324).

Figure 4–14 shows how a combination of film showing and discussion changed the ethnocentric attitudes of a group of high school students. While the group as a whole became more tolerant as a result of this experience, those who were high in ethnocentrism to begin with changed less than those who were lower. The value of discussion in changing attitudes was further emphasized in this experiment by the fact that those students who learned new attitudes through exposure to the film alone tended to regress to their former prejudiced attitudes more than did the students who learned new attitudes through *both* discussion and exposure to the film (203).

Even more effective in changing attitudes than discussion are *interpersonal relationships.* When Negro and white students work together in classes in high school, there is less prejudice than when they are separated. Girls have been found to be significantly less ethnocentric after 2 years in college than boys. Bright girls shift their attitudes away from prejudice more than do the less bright. This was not found to be true in the case of boys (91,241,242). *Visits to the homes* of adolescents against whom there is prejudice have been reported to result in more favorable attitudes (28,281).

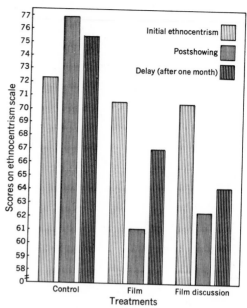

FIGURE 4–14 The influence of film showing and film showing and discussion on prejudiced adolescents. (Adapted from L. L. Mitnick and E. McGinnies: Influencing ethnocentrism in small discussion groups through a film communication. *J. abnorm. soc. Psychol.,* 1958, **56,** 82–90. Used by permission.)

Not all experiments in breaking down prejudices have produced such favorable results as those reported above. As Greenberg et al. have pointed out, the results of the studies to date indicate that "either proper techniques for attitude change have not as yet been developed, or . . . our techniques for measuring them have not been developed" (99).

Some attitudes are resistant to change, and some change for the worse, especially when contact is *involuntary.* Just being thrown together in the same classroom or on the same athletic team does not necessarily lead to social interaction. Whether there will be a decrease in prejudice and an increase in social interaction depends on the attitudes of the majority-group members toward the minority group (54, 157).

There is evidence that with increasing age in adolescence attitudes toward minority groups become stable and increasingly consistent. This suggests that, if prejudice is to be combated successfully, it must be done during the high school years or certainly during the early part of the adolescent's college career (328).

Because the roots of prejudice are in the home, it has been facetiously suggested that we "abolish the home" (89). This suggests how difficult the problem is. Even though adolescents rebel against their parents' attitudes and values, they are still influenced by them. Similarly, even though the adolescent becomes less subject to peer influences as he grows older, there is no time when he is not influenced by them to some degree. When, therefore, it is the thing to do to discriminate against members of a minority group, the adolescent will follow the pattern set by the peer group (3, 54). If prejudice is to be combated successfully, it is obvious then that prejudice must be made "unpopular" rather than "fashionable" (216). How this can be done is certainly an open question.

Without doubt the thorniest problem of all in combating prejudice is how to change the prejudiced attitudes of adolescents when these attitudes are closely interrelated with their personality patterns. Consequently, the first line of attack must center around helping the adolescent to gain greater *self-insight*, rather than insight into the objective nature of the problem (146). In addition, because perception of self precedes perception of others, this means that if the attitudes of prejudice are to be changed, the adolescent must *accept himself* before there is a chance that he will accept others (301).

This point of view was stressed by Bettelheim and Janowitz (23):

> It seems reasonable to assume that, as long as anxiety and insecurity persist as a root of tolerance, the effort to dispel stereotypes by rational propaganda is at best a half-measure. On an individual level only greater personal integration combined with social and economic security seems to offer hope for better inter-ethnic relations.

Not all adolescents enjoy social security, even though they may have economic security. Combating prejudice, then, becomes a problem closely associated with the problem of improving social acceptance. If the adolescent's social acceptance can be improved, his prejudices can be weakened and perhaps even replaced with tolerance toward and acceptance of members of minority groups.

Social Competency "Social competency" means a facility in dealing with people and social situations. To be socially competent, the adolescent must know what are the approved patterns of behavior in different social situations and how to carry out these patterns. A child can get along successfully in social situations of his peers without having a pattern of socially approved social skills and manners. As the social horizons broaden, new demands are made on the individual. In situations involving peers of both sexes, the adolescent discovers that social acceptance is dependent partly upon the possession of social skills and interests appropriate for his age and sex group. Adolescents who are superior to their age-mates in such social skills as dancing, carrying on a conversation, playing cards, or playing a musical instrument have a much better chance of social acceptance than those who lack these skills (34).

Most adolescent boys and girls are aware of their lack of social skills. This makes them ill at ease in social situations. Temporarily, they may withdraw from social situations in fear of the embarrassments that will come from doing the wrong thing. As Strang has observed, "Part of the unnecessary adolescent 'storm and stress' is doubtless due to a lack of the knowledge of the approved behavior in certain social situations" (297).

how social skills are learned Learning social skills is not an overnight experience; instead, these skills come gradually from experience in all types of social situations and from practice over a period of time. To develop social competency, the adolescent needs guidance in the home and school and opportunities to put into practice what he has learned. Individuals from the higher socioeconomic groups have opportunities in their homes to learn what is correct, while those who come from the lower socioeconomic groups generally grow up in a home environment where such knowledge is meager (102).

Just knowing what to do is not adequate. The adolescent must have *opportunities* to put into practice what he learns. Most junior and senior high schools today have extracurricular organizations that offer students opportunities to develop social skills. Unfortunately, many adolescents who lack social skills do not join these organizations. As a result they cut themselves off from the opportunities the organizations offer. This is especially true of adolescents from the lower socioeconomic groups who feel unwanted and rejected in the extracurricular activities of the school or in the social activities of community organizations (34).

As far back as the fourth grade, boys admit that they feel inadequate in social situations as compared with girls. This is corroborated by teachers and is commonly accepted as true by parents. The reason for this is primarily that boys regard anything relating to manners as indicative of a sissy. As a result, they rebel against learning *any* social skill for fear of being labeled sissies (87,293). By the time boys reach adolescence the gap between the sexes in social competency is wider than it was in childhood.

Even when the motivation to learn social skills is strong, the adolescent may run into difficulties when he discovers that there is no universally accepted pattern of such skills; he is then at a loss to know which to learn. While it is true that there are certain universally approved social skills in the American culture of today, such as being able to carry on a conversation with people of different ages and interests, there are others which vary from one community to another and from one subgroup to another in the same community. Ice skating may, for example, be an important social skill in one community while bowling may be equally important in another.

Among adolescents of the higher socioeconomic groups, knowing what to do at a formal party is essential to social acceptance.

In a lower socioeconomic group, this is unimportant, but knowing what to do in an informal teen-age party is very important. Similarly, knowing the approved way of responding when introduced to strangers may mean a formal "How do you do?" or "I am happy to meet you" in one subgroup, while in another, it may mean learning to say "Hi" with enthusiasm to age-mates, and "Pleased to meet you" to one's elders.

Even more complicated are the problems stemming from variations in age of sexual maturity. One of the advantages of early maturing is that the individual learns, ahead of his age-mates, the adult-approved social skills. Consequently, he seems more sophisticated, more poised, and more at ease than they. This is especially important for girls in their relationships with boys (141, 214).

contributions to socialization Social competency plays so important a role in the type of social adjustments the adolescent makes that it often compensates for unsocial or even antisocial behavior. A boy with charming manners, for example, will be popular with girls even if he is uncooperative, selfish, and egocentric. Similarly, a girl who is socially sophisticated will find ready acceptance among boys who, age for age, are less competent in social skills; they know that they can count on her to do the right thing at the right time and to keep the conversation rolling. Because popularity with members of the opposite sex leads to prestige with members of the same sex, the advantages of social competency are not limited to members of the opposite sex; they affect the type of social adjustments the adolescent makes with members of his own sex as well.

Then, too, social competency gives the adolescent poise and self-confidence—traits that are of great value in any social situation. These traits, added to the favorable impression he makes because of his social skills, will go a long way toward creating such a generally favorable impression that people will judge him favorably, irrespective of traits they may not like or approve.

It is apparent, then, that social competency is important enough in the socialization of an adolescent to devote more time and effort to its development than is usually done. Many adolescents recognize this and try to increase their proficiency by reading books on etiquette, by watching and listening to peers who have the reputation of being popular and sophisticated, and by studying the socially approved patterns of behavior as they are depicted on the screen. As their interest in girls awakens, boys are acutely aware of their deficiency in this area.

From a practical angle, knowledge of the role played by social competency leads to two positive suggestions: first, the earlier the child learns social skills and practices them until they become habitual, the more poised and self-confident he will be when he reaches adolescence; and second, if bad manners can be made unfashionable in childhood, especially among boys, one of the serious obstacles in the path of social acceptance can be removed. While it is true that social competency alone will not guarantee good social acceptance, it goes a long way toward doing so.

BIBLIOGRAPHY

1 ADORNO, T. W., E. FRENKEL-BRUNSWIK, D. J. LEVINSON, and R. N. SANFORD: *The authoritarian personality.* New York: Harper & Row, 1950.

2 ALLPORT, G. W.: *The nature of prejudice.* Reading, Mass.: Addison-Wesley, 1954.

3 ALLPORT, G. W.: Prejudice: is it societal or personal? *J. soc. Issues,* 1962, **18,** 120–134.

4 ALT, H.: Basic principles of child rearing in the Soviet Union: first hand impressions of an American observer. *Amer. J. Orthopsychiat.,* 1958, **28,** 223–240.

5 AMATORA, SISTER M.: Developmental trends in pre-adolescence and early adolescence in self-evaluation. *J. genet. Psychol.,* 1957, **91,** 89–97.

6 ANASTASI, A., and S. MILLER: Adolescent "prestige factors" in relation to scholastic and socioeconomic variables. *J. soc. Psychol.,* 1949, **29,** 43–50.

7 ANDERSON, J. E.: The development of social behavior. *Amer. J. Sociol.,* 1939, **44,** 839–857.

8 ANGELINO, H., J. DOLLINS, and E. V. MECH: Trends in the "fears and worries" of school children as related to socioeconomic status and age. *J. genet. Psychol.,* 1956, **89,** 263–276.

9 ARTER, R. M.: The effects of prejudice on children. *Children,* 1959, **6,** 185–189.

10 AUSUBEL, D. P.: Ego development among segregated Negro children. *Ment. Hyg., N.Y.,* 1958, **42,** 362–369.

11 AYER, F. L., and B. R. CORMAN: Laboratory practices develop citizenship concepts of high-school students. *Social Educ.,* 1952, **16,** 215–216.

12 BACH, M. L.: Factors related to student participation in campus social organizations. *J. soc. Psychol.,* 1961, **54,** 337–348.

13 BANHAM, K. M.: Obstinate children are adaptable. *Ment. Hyg., N.Y.,* 1952, **36,** 84–89.

14 BAXTER, B. N.: Vagaries of junior-high-schoolers. *Calif. J. second. Educ.,* 1946, **21,** 181–184.

15 BAYTON, J. A., L. B. MC ALLISTER, and J. HAMER: Race-class stereotypes. *J. Negro Educ.,* 1956, **25,** 75–78.

16 BECKER, M. G., and C. P. LOOMIS: Measuring rural, urban, and farm and nonfarm cleavages in a rural consolidated school. *Sociometry,* 1948, **11,** 246–261.

17 BELL, G. B., and H. E. HALL: The relationship between leadership and empathy. *J. abnorm. soc. Psychol.,* 1954, **49,** 156–157.

18 BELOFF, H.: Two forms of social conformity: acquiescence and conventionality. *J. abnorm. soc. Psychol.,* 1958, **56,** 99–104.

19 BENNETT, E. M., and L. R. COHEN: Men and women: personality patterns and contrasts. *Genet. Psychol. Monogr.,* 1959, **59,** 101–155.

20 BERKOWITZ, L.: Anti-Semitism and the displacement of aggression. *J. abnorm. soc. Psychol.,* 1959, **59,** 182–187.

21 BERKOWITZ, L., and R. M. LUNDY: Personality characteristics related to susceptibility to influence by peers or authority figures. *J. Pers.,* 1957, **25,** 306–316.

22 BERNARD, J.: Teen-age culture: an overview. *Ann. Amer. Acad. pol. soc. Sci.,* 1961, **338,** 1–12.

23 BETTELHEIM, B., and M. JANOWITZ: Ethnic tolerance: a function of social and personal control. *Amer. J. Sociol.*, 1949, **55**, 137–145.

24 BLAIR, G. M.: Personality and social development. *Rev. educ. Res.*, 1950, **20**, 375–389.

25 BLOS, P.: *On adolescence.* New York: Free Press, 1962.

26 BLUM, B. S., and J. H. MANN: The effect of religious membership on religious prejudice. *J. soc. Psychol.*, 1960, **52**, 97–101.

27 BOGARDUS, E. S.: The social distance differential. *Sociol. soc. Res.*, 1948, **32**, 882–887.

28 BOGARDUS, E. S.: Racial distance changes in the United States during the past thirty years. *Sociol. soc. Res.*, 1958, **43**, 127–134.

29 BONNEY, M. E.: A study of friendship choices in college in relation to church affiliation, in-church references, family size, and length of enrollment in college. *J. soc. Psychol.*, 1949, **29**, 153–156.

30 BONNEY, M. E.: A sociometric study of the peer acceptance of rural students in three consolidated high schools. *Educ. Admin. Supervis.*, 1951, **11**, 234–240.

31 BORING, E. G.: The woman problem. *Amer. Psychologist*, 1951, **6**, 679–692.

32 BOSSARD, J. H. S., and E. S. BOLL: *The sociology of child development.* 3d ed. New York: Harper & Row, 1960.

33 BOWERMAN, C. E., and J. W. KINCH: Changes in family and peer orientation of children between the fourth and tenth grades. *Soc. Forces*, 1959, **37**, 206–211.

34 BRETSCH, H. S.: Social skills and activities of socially accepted and unaccepted adolescents. *J. educ. Psychol.*, 1952, **43**, 449–458.

35 BRODERICK, C. B., and S. E. FOWLER: New patterns of relationships between the sexes among preadolescents. *Marriage fam. Living*, 1961, **23**, 27–30.

36 BROWN, D. G.: Sex-role development in a changing culture. *Psychol. Bull.*, 1958, **55**, 232–242.

37 BRUNER, J. S., and H. V. PERLMUTTER: Compatriot and foreigner: a study of impression formation in three countries. *J. abnorm. soc. Psychol.*, 1957, **55**, 253–260.

38 BUCHANAN, W.: How others see us. *Ann. Amer. Acad. pol. soc. Sci.*, 1954, **295**, 1–11.

39 BÜHLER, C.: School as a phase of human life. *Education*, 1952, **73**, 219–222.

40 BURCHINAL, L. G., G. R. HAWKES, and B. GARDNER: Adjustment characteristics of rural and urban children. *Amer. sociol. Rev.*, 1957, **22**, 81–87.

41 CANNING, R. R., and J. M. BAKER: Effect of the group on authoritarian and non-authoritarian persons. *Amer. J. Sociol.*, 1959, **64**, 579–581.

42 CAPLAN, H.: The role of deviant maturation in the pathogenesis of anxiety. *Amer. J. Orthopsychiat.*, 1956, **26**, 94–107.

43 CARRIER, N. A.: Need correlates of "gullibility." *J. abnorm. soc. Psychol.*, 1963, **66**, 84–86.

44 CENTERS, R.: Social class, occupation, and imputed belief. *Amer. J. Sociol.*, 1953, **58**, 543–555.

45 CENTERS, R., and M. HOROWITZ: Social character and conformity: a differential in susceptibility to social influence. *J. soc. Psychol.*, 1963, **60**, 343–349.

46 CHILD, I. L.: Socialization. In G. Lindzey (ed.), *Handbook of social psychology.* Reading, Mass.: Addison-Wesley, 1954, pp. 655–692.

47 CHYATTE, C., and D. F. SCHAEFER: Prejudice verbalization among children. *J. educ. Psychol.*, 1951, **42**, 421–431.

48 CLARK, W. H.: Sex differences and motivation in the urge to destroy. *J. soc. Psychol.*, 1952, **36**, 167–177.

49 COLEMAN, J. S.: The adolescent subculture and academic achievement. *Amer. J. Sociol.*, 1960, **65**, 337–347.

50 COLEMAN, J. S.: Analysis of social structures and simulation of social processes with electronic computers. *Educ. psychol. Measmt.*, 1961, **21**, 203–218.

51 COLEMAN, J. S.: Athletics in high school. *Ann. Amer. Acad. pol. soc. Sci.*, 1961, **338**, 33–43.

52 COLEMAN, J. S.: *The adolescent society.* New York: Free Press, 1961.

53 COLEMAN, J. S.: Teen-agers and their crowd. *PTA Magazine*, 1962, **56**, no. 7, 4–7.

54 COOK, S. W.: Desegregation: a psychological analysis. *Amer. Psychologist*, 1957, **12**, 1–13.

55 COOPER, J. B.: Emotion in prejudice. *Science*, 1959, **130**, 314–318.

56 COTHRAN, T. C.: Negro conceptions of white people. *Amer. J. Sociol.*, 1951, **56**, 458–467.

57 CRANE, A. R.: The development of moral values in children: IV. Pre-adolescent gangs

and the moral development of children. *Brit. J. educ. Psychol.*, 1958, **28**, 201–208.

58 CROW, A.: Parental attitudes toward boy-girl relations. *J. educ. Sociol.*, 1955, **29**, 126–133.

59 CROW, L. D.: Teen-age traits, interests and worries. *Educ. Forum*, 1956, **20**, 423–428.

60 CROW, L. A., and A. CROW: *Adolescent development and adjustment.* 2d ed. New York: McGraw-Hill, 1965.

61 CROWNE, D. P., and S. LIVERANT: Conformity under varying conditions of personal commitment. *J. abnorm. soc. Psychol.*, 1963, **66**, 547–555.

62 CRUTCHFIELD, R. S.: Conformity and character. *Amer. Psychologist*, 1955, **10**, 191–198.

63 DALE, R. J.: A method for measuring developmental tasks: scales for selected tasks at the beginning of adolescence. *Child Develpm.*, 1955, **26**, 111–112.

64 DAVIDSON, H. L., and L. S. GOTTLIEB: The emotional maturity of pre- and postmenarcheal girls. *J. genet. Psychol.*, 1955, **86**, 261–266.

65 DEUTSCHER, I.: The stereotype as a research tool. *Soc. Forces*, 1958, **37**, 55–60.

66 DE VAULT, M. V.: Classroom sociometric mutual pairs and residential proximity. *J. educ. Res.*, 1957, **50**, 605–610.

67 DICKENS, S. L., and C. HOBART: Parental dominance and offspring ethnocentrism. *J. soc. Psychol.*, 1959, **49**, 297–303.

68 DOUVAN, E.: Independence and identity in adolescence. *Children*, 1957, **4**, 186–190.

69 DOUVAN, E.: Adolescent boys speak up. *Marriage fam. Living*, 1959, **21**, 74.

70 DOWNIE, N. M., C. R. PACE, and M. E. TROYER: The opinions of Syracuse University students on some widely discussed current issues. *Educ. psychol. Measmt.*, 1950, **10**, 628–636.

71 DUDYCHA, G. J.: The religious beliefs of college freshmen in 1930 and 1949. *J. relig. Educ.*, 1950, **45**, 164–169.

72 DUFF, J. C.: Quest for leaders. *J. educ. Sociol.*, 1958, **32**, 90–95.

73 DUNBAR, F.: Homeostasis during puberty. *Amer. J. Psychiat.*, 1958, **114**, 673–683.

74 DUNPHY, D. C.: The social structure of the urban adolescent peer groups. *Sociometry*, 1963, **26**, 230–246.

75 EHRLICH, H. J.: Stereotyping and Negro-Jewish stereotypes. *Soc. Forces*, 1962, **41**, 171–176.

76 ELKIN, F.: Socialization and the presentation of self. *Marriage fam. Living*, 1958, **20**, 320–325.

77 ELKIN, F., and W. A. WESTLEY: The myth of adolescent culture. *Amer. sociol. Rev.*, 1955, **20**, 680–684.

78 EWALD, M. O.: The emotionally disturbed child in the classroom. *Education*, 1954, **76**, 69–72.

79 FENSTERHEIM, H., and M. E. TRESSELT: The influence of value systems on the perception of people. *J. abnorm. soc. Psychol.*, 1953, **48**, 93–98.

80 FESTINGER, L., J. TORREY, and B. WILLERMAN: Self-evaluation as a function of attractiveness in a group. *Hum. Relat.*, 1954, **7**, 161–174.

81 FIELDER, F. E., W. G. WARRINGTON, and F. J. BLAISDELL: Unconscious attitudes as correlates of sociometric choice in a social group. *J. abnorm. soc. Psychol.*, 1952, **47**, 790–796.

82 FISHMAN, J. A.: Negative stereotypes concerning Americans among American-born children receiving various types of minority-group education. *Genet. Psychol. Monogr.*, 1955, **51**, 107–182.

83 FORD, N. A.: Literature as an aid to social development. *Teach. Coll. Rec.*, 1957, **58**, 377–381.

84 FRANK, L. K., and M. H. FRANK: *Your adolescent, at home and in school.* New York: Viking, 1956.

85 FREEMAN, H. E., and M. SHOWELL: The role of the family in the socialization process. *J. soc. Psychol.*, 1953, **37**, 97–101.

86 GARRISON, K. C.: *Growth and development.* 2d ed. New York: Longmans, 1959.

87 GESELL, A., F. L. ILG, and L. B. AMES: *Youth: the years from ten to sixteen.* New York: Harper & Row, 1956.

88 GILES, H. H.: *The integrated classroom.* New York: Basic Books, 1959.

89 GLAD, J. B.: How children may be taught tolerance and cooperation. *Marriage fam. Living*, 1962, **24**, 183–185.

90 GLUECK, S.: *The problem of delinquency.* Boston: Houghton Mifflin, 1959.

91 GOFF, R. M.: Some educational implications of the influence of rejection on minority

group children. *J. exper. Educ.*, 1954, **23**, 179–183.

92 GOLD, M.: Power in the classroom. *Sociometry*, 1958, **21**, 50–60.

93 GOODNOW, R. E., and R. TAGUIRI: Religious ethnocentrism and its recognition among adolescent boys. *J. abnorm. soc. Psychol.*, 1952, **47**, 316–320.

94 GOUGH, H. G.: Studies of racial intolerance: I. Some psychological and sociological correlates of anti-Semitism. *J. soc. Psychol.*, 1951, **33**, 237–246.

95 GOUGH, H. G.: Studies of social intolerance: IV. Related social attitudes. *J. soc. Psychol.*, 1951, **33**, 263–269.

96 GRACE, H. A.: A note on the relationship of hostility and social distance. *J. educ. Psychol.*, 1952, **43**, 306–308.

97 GRAMBS, J. D.: The community and the self-governing adolescent group. *J. educ. Sociol.*, 1956, **30**, 94–105.

98 GRAY, J. S., and A. H. THOMPSON: The ethnic prejudices of white and Negro college students. *J. abnorm. soc. Psychol.*, 1953, **48**, 311–313.

99 GREENBERG, H., J. PIERSON, and S. SHERMAN: The effects of single-session education techniques on prejudice attitudes. *J. educ. Sociol.*, 1957, **31**, 82–86.

100 GUSTAD, J. W.: Changes in social attitudes and behavior: a review of the literature. *Educ. psychol. Measmt.*, 1951, **11**, 87–102.

101 GUSTAD, J. W.: A longitudinal study of social behavior variables in college students. *Educ. psychol. Measmt.*, 1952, **12**, 226–235.

102 HALL, W. E., and W. GAEDDERT: Social skills and their relationship to scholastic achievement. *J. genet. Psychol.*, 1960, **96**, 269–273.

103 HARMIN, M.: General characteristics of participating youth groups. *J. educ. Sociol.*, 1956, **30**, 49–57.

104 HARRIS, D. B., A. M. ROSE, K. E. CLARKE, and F. VALASEK: Personality differences between responsible and less responsible children. *J. genet. Psychol.*, 1955, **87**, 103–106.

105 HARRIS, D. B., and C. S. TSENG: Children's attitudes toward peers and parents as revealed by sentence completions. *Child Develpm.*, 1957, **28**, 401–411.

106 HARRIS, E. K.: The responsiveness of kindergarten children to their fellows. *Monogr. Soc. Res. Child Develpm.*, 1946, **11**, no. 2.

107 HARRIS, M.: Caste, class, and minority. *Soc. Forces*, 1959, **37**, 248–254.

108 HARVEY, O. J., H. H. KELLEY, and M. M. SHAPIRO: Reactions to unfavorable evaluations of the self made by other persons. *J. Pers.*, 1957, **25**, 393–411.

109 HARVEY, O. J., and J. RUTHERFORD: Status in the informal group: influence and influencibility at differing age levels. *Child Develpm.*, 1960, **31**, 377–385.

110 HAVIGHURST, R. J.: *Human development and education.* New York: Longmans, 1953.

111 HAVIGHURST, R. J.: The social competence of middle-aged people. *Genet. Psychol. Monogr.*, 1957, **56**, 297–375.

112 HAYES, M. L.: Attitudes of high-school students toward Negro problems. *J. educ. Res.*, 1953, **46**, 615–619.

113 HEATON, M. H.: Sororities and the school culture. *J. educ. Sociol.*, 1948, **21**, 527–535.

114 HECHINGER, F. M.: The junior blues. *The New York Times*, July 28, 1963.

115 HECHINGER, G., and F. M. HECHINGER: *Teen-age tyranny.* New York: Morrow, 1963.

116 HELFANT, K.: Parents' attitudes vs. adolescent hostility in the determination of adolescent sociopolitical attitudes. *Psychol. Monogr.*, 1952, **66**, no. 13.

117 HEMPHILL, J. K.: Relations between the size of the group and the behavior of the "superior" leader. *J. soc. Psychol.*, 1950, **32**, 11–22.

118 HENRY, J., and S. WARSON: Family structure and psychic development. *Amer. J. Orthopsychiat.*, 1951, **21**, 59–73.

119 HIMELHOCH, J.: Tolerance and personality needs: a study of liberalization of ethnic attitudes among minority group college students. *Amer. sociol. Rev.*, 1950, **15**, 79–88.

120 HINDMAN, B. M.: The emotional problems of the Negro high school youth which can be related to segregation and discrimination in a Southern urban community. *J. educ. Sociol.*, 1953, **27**, 115–127.

121 HOCHBAM, G. M.: The relation between group members' self confidence and their reactions to group pressures to conformity. *Amer. sociol. Rev.*, 1954, **19**, 678–687.

122 HOFFMAN, M. C.: Conformity as a defense mechanism and a form of resistance to genuine group influence. *J. Pers.*, 1957, **25**, 412–424.

123 HOLLINGSHEAD, A. DE B.: *Elmtown's youth.* New York: Wiley, 1949.

124 HOLLINGWORTH, L. S.: Personality and adjustment as determiners and correlates of intelligence. *39th Yearb. Nat. Soc. Stud. Educ.,* 1940, 271–275.

125 HOOD, W. R., and M. SHERIF: An appraisal of personality-oriented approaches to prejudice. *Sociol. soc. Res.,* 1955, **40,** 79–85.

126 HORROCKS, J. E.: *The psychology of adolescence.* 2d ed. Boston: Houghton Mifflin, 1962.

127 HORROCKS, J. E., and M. E. BUKER: A study of the friendship fluctuations of preadolescents. *J. genet. Psychol.,* 1951, **78,** 131–144.

128 HORROCKS, J. E., and B. A. WEAR: An analysis of interpersonal choice relationships of college students. *J. soc. Psychol.,* 1953, **38,** 87–98.

129 HOULT, T. H., and R. S. BOLIN: Some factors involved in high-school friendship choices. *Sociol. soc. Res.,* 1950, **34,** 273–279.

130 HUNT, R. G., and V. SYNNERDAHL: Social influence among children. *Sociol. soc. Res.,* 1959, **43,** 171–174.

131 IISAGER, H.: Factors contributing to happiness among Danish college students. *J. soc. Psychol.,* 1948, **28,** 237–246.

132 IZARD, C. E.: Personality similarity and friendship. *J. abnorm. soc. Psychol.,* 1960, **61,** 47–51.

133 IZARD, C. E.: Personality similarity and friendship: a follow-up study. *J. abnorm. soc. Psychol.,* 1963, **66,** 598–600.

134 JAKABCZAK, L. F., and R. H. WALTERS: Suggestibility as dependency behavior. *J. abnorm. soc. Psychol.,* 1959, **59,** 102–107.

135 JANIS, I. L.: Anxiety indices related to susceptibility to persuasion. *J. abnorm. soc. Psychol.,* 1955, **51,** 663–667.

136 JARECKY, R. K.: Identification of the socially gifted. *Except. Children,* 1959, **25,** 415–419.

137 JERSILD, A. T.: *The psychology of adolescence.* 2d ed. New York: Macmillan, 1963.

138 JOHNSTONE, J. W. C., and K. JOHASSON: *The social life of the teenager and its impact on education.* New York: Free Press, 1962.

139 JONES, H. E.: *Development in adolescence.* New York: Appleton-Century-Crofts, 1943.

140 JONES, M. C.: The later careers of boys who were early- or late-maturers. *Child Develpm.,* 1957, **28,** 113–128.

141 JONES, M. C.: A study of socialization patterns at the high school level. *J. genet. Psychol.,* 1958, **93,** 87–111.

142 JONES, M. C.: A comparison of the attitudes and interests of ninth-grade students over two decades. *J. educ. Psychol.,* 1960, **51,** 175–186.

143 JOSSELYN, I. M.: Psychological changes in adolescence. *Children,* 1959, **6,** 43–47.

144 KANOUS, R. A., L. E. DAUGHERTY, and T. S. COHN: Relation between heterosexual friendship choices and socioeconomic level. *Child Develpm.,* 1962, **33,** 251–255.

145 KASSOF, A.: The prejudiced personality: a cross-cultural test. *Soc. Probl.,* 1958, **6,** 59–67.

146 KATZ, D., I. SARNOFF, and C. MC CLINTOCK: Ego-defense and attitude change. *Hum. Relat.,* 1956, **9,** 27–45.

147 KEEDY, T. C.: Factors in the cohesiveness of small groups. *Sociol. soc. Res.,* 1956, **40,** 329–332.

148 KEEHN, J. D., and E. T. PROTHRO: National preferences of university students from twenty-three nations. *J. Psychol.,* 1956, **42,** 283–294.

149 KEISLAR, E. R.: Differences among adolescent social clubs in terms of members' characteristics. *J. educ. Res.,* 1954, **48,** 297–303.

150 KEISLAR, E. R.: Experimental development of "like" and "dislike" of others among adolescent girls. *Child Develpm.,* 1961, **32,** 59–66.

151 KELLEY, J. A.: Varying mores in school and college cultures. *J. educ. Sociol.,* 1958, **31,** 244–252.

152 KIRKPATRICK, M. E.: The mental hygiene of adolescence in the Anglo-American culture. *Ment. Hyg., N.Y.,* 1952, **36,** 394–403.

153 KLEINER, R. J., J. TUCKMAN, and M. LAVELL: Mental disorder and status based on religious affiliation. *Hum. Relat.,* 1959, **12,** 273–276.

154 KOCH, H. L.: The relation of certain formal attributes of siblings to attitudes held toward each other and toward their parents. *Monogr. Soc. Res. Child Develpm.,* 1960, **25,** no. 4.

155 KOHN, M. L.: Social class and parental values. *Amer. J. Sociol.,* 1959, **64,** 337–351.

156 KUHLEN, R. G.: *The psychology of adolescent development.* 2d ed. New York: Harper & Row, 1963.

157 LACEY, J. C.: Does teaching change students' attitudes? *J. educ. Res.,* 1956, **50,** 307–311.

158 LANSKY, L. M., V. J. CRANDALL, J. KAGAN, and C. T. BAKER: Sex differences in aggression and its correlates in middle-class adolescents. *Child Develpm.*, 1961, **32**, 45–58.

159 LANTZ, H. R.: Numbers of childhood friends as reported in the life histories of a psychiatrically diagnosed group of 1,600. *Marriage fam. Living*, 1956, **18**, 107–109.

160 LASSWELL, T. E.: Social class and stereotyping. *Sociol. soc. Res.*, 1958, **42**, 256–262.

161 LAWSON, E. D., and R. STAGNER: Group pressure, attitude change, and autonomic involvement. *J. soc. Psychol.*, 1957, **45**, 299–312.

162 LEEVY, J. R.: Social competence of high-school youth. *School Review*, 1943, **51**, 342–347.

163 LESSER, G.: The relationship between various forms of aggression and popularity among lower-class children. *J. educ. Psychol.*, 1959, **50**, 20–25.

164 LEVINE, G. N., and L. A. SUSSMANN: Social class and sociability in fraternity pledging. *Amer. J. Sociol.*, 1960, **65**, 391–399.

165 LEVINSON, B. M.: The inner life of the extremely gifted child, as seen from the clinical setting. *J. genet. Psychol.*, 1961, **99**, 83–88.

166 LEVINSON, D. J., and P. E. HUFFMAN: Traditional family ideology and its relation to personality. *J. Pers.*, 1954, **23**, 251–273.

167 LEWIS, E.: The function of group play during middle childhood in developing the ego complex. *Brit. J. med. Psychol.*, 1955, **27**, 15–29.

168 LIEF, H. I., and I. P. STEVENSON: Psychological aspects of prejudice with special reference to desegregation. *Amer. J. Psychiat.*, 1958, **114**, 816–823.

169 LINDZEY, G., and S. ROGOLSKY: Prejudice and identification of minority group membership. *J. abnorm. soc. Psychol.*, 1950, **45**, 37–53.

170 LIPPITT, R., N. POLANSKY, and S. ROSEN: The dynamics of power. *Hum. Relat.*, 1952, **5**, 37–64.

171 LIVSON, N., and T. F. NICHOLS: Social attitude configuration in an adolescent group. *J. genet. Psychol.*, 1957, **91**, 3–23.

172 LOBAN, W.: A study of social sensitivity (sympathy) among adolescents. *J. educ. Psychol.*, 1953, **44**, 102–112.

173 LOW, C. M.: The neglect of the personal-social needs of youth. *Progressive Educ.*, 1951, **28**, 52–56.

174 LUCK, J. M.: A study of peer relationships. *Group*, 1955, **17**, 13–20.

175 LUNDBERG, G. A., and V. BEAZLEY: "Consciousness of kind" in a college population. *Sociometry*, 1948, **11**, 59–74.

176 LUNDBERG, G. A., and L. DICKSON: Interethnic relations in a high-school population. *Amer. J. Sociol.*, 1952, **58**, 1–10.

177 LYLE, W. H., and E. E. LEVITT: Punitiveness, authoritarianism, and parental discipline of grade school children. *J. abnorm. soc. Psychol.*, 1955, **51**, 42–46.

178 LYNN, R.: Personality characteristics of the mothers of aggressive and unaggressive children. *J. genet. Psychol.*, 1961, **99**, 159–164.

179 MAAS, H. S.: The role of member in clubs of lower-class and middle-class adolescents. *Child Develpm.*, 1954, **25**, 241–251.

180 MACCOBY, E. E., and W. C. WILSON: Identification and observational learning from films. *J. abnorm. soc. Psychol.*, 1957, **55**, 76–87.

181 MACCOBY, E. E., W. C. WILSON, and R. V. BURTON: Differential movie-viewing behavior of male and female viewers. *J. Pers.*, 1958, **26**, 259–267.

182 MAISONNEUVE, J.: A contribution to the sociometry of mutual choice. *Sociometry*, 1954, **17**, 33–46.

183 MAJOR, C. L.: Measuring the effects of a semester of college work on the conservative-progressive tendencies of students. *Sch. Soc.*, 1946, **64**, 174–175.

184 MALM, M., and O. G. JAMISON: *Adolescence*. New York: McGraw-Hill, 1952.

185 MARKS, J. B.: Interests and leadership among adolescents. *J. genet. Psychol.*, 1957, **91**, 163–172.

186 MARTIN, J. G., and F. R. WESTIE: The tolerant personality. *Amer. sociol. Rev.*, 1959, **24**, 521–528.

187 MARTIN, W. E., N. GROSS, and J. G. DARLEY: Studies of group behavior: leaders, followers, and isolates in student organized groups. *J. abnorm. soc. Psychol.*, 1952, **47**, 838–842.

188 MATZA, D.: Subterranean traditions of youth. *Ann. Amer. Acad. pol. soc. Sci.*, 1961, **338**, 102–118.

189 MAYO, G. D., and J. R. KINZER: A comparison of white and Negro high-school students in 1940 and 1948. *J. Psychol.*, 1950, **29**, 397–405.

190 MC CANDLESS, B. R., and J. M. HOYT: Sex, ethnicity, and play preferences of preschool children. *J. abnorm. soc. Psychol.*, 1961, **62**, 683–685.

191 MC CANN, R. V.: Ambivalent images of man. *Relig. Educ.*, 1957, **52**, 436–438.

192 MC CLOSKY, H.: Conservatism and personality. *Amer. pol. sci. Rev.*, 1958, **52**, 27–45.

193 MC CORD, J., and W. MC CORD: The effects of parental role model on criminality. *J. soc. Issues*, 1958, **14**, no. 3, 66–74.

194 MC CORD, W., J. MC CORD, and A. HOWARD: Early familial experiences and bigotry. *Amer. sociol. Rev.*, 1960, **25**, 717–722.

195 MC DILL, E. L.: Anomie, authoritarianism, prejudice, and socioeconomic status: an attempt at clarification. *Soc. Forces*, 1961, **39**, 239–245.

196 MC NALLY, E.: The worries of the younger pupils in Scottish secondary schools. *Brit. J. educ. Psychol.*, 1951, **21**, 235–237.

197 MC NEIL, J. D.: Changes in ethnic reaction tendencies during high school. *J. educ. Res.*, 1960, **53**, 199–200.

198 MEEK, L. H.: *The personal-social adjustment of boys and girls with implications for secondary education.* New York: Progressive Education Association, 1940.

199 MEHLMAN, B.: Similarity in friendships. *J. soc. Psychol.*, 1962, **57**, 195–202.

200 MEREDITH, C. W.: Personality and social development during childhood and adolescence. *Rev. educ. Res.*, 1955, **25**, 469–476.

201 MILLER, H.: Conspectus for the study of socialization in the peer group. *J. educ. Sociol.*, 1960, **33**, 320–331.

202 MILLER, K. M., and J. B. BIGGS: Attitude change through undirected group discussion. *J. educ. Psychol.*, 1958, **49**, 224–228.

203 MITNICK, L. L., and E. MC GINNIES: Influencing ethnocentrism in small discussion groups through a film communication. *J. abnorm. soc. Psychol.*, 1958, **56**, 82–90.

204 MOELLER, G., and M. H. APPLEZWEIG: A motivational factor in conformity. *J. abnorm. soc. Psychol.*, 1957, **55**, 114–120.

205 MONTAGUE, J. B.: A study of anxiety among English and American boys. *Amer. sociol. Rev.*, 1955, **20**, 685–689.

206 MORE, D. M.: Developmental concordance and discordance during puberty and early adolescence. *Monogr. Soc. Res. Child Develpm.*, 1953, **18**, 1–128.

207 MORRIS, D. P., E. SOROKER, and G. BURRUSS: Follow-up studies of shy, withdrawn children: 1. Evaluation of later adjustment. *Amer. J. Orthopsychiat.*, 1954, **24**, 743–754.

208 MORSE, N. C., and F. H. ALLPORT: The causation of anti-Semitism: an investigation of seven hypotheses. *J. Psychol.*, 1952, **34**, 197–233.

209 MOSHER, D. L., and A. SCODEL: Relationships between ethnocentrism in children and the ethnocentrism and authoritarian rearing practices of their mothers. *Child Develpm.*, 1960, **31**, 369–376.

210 MULL, H. K., and A. SHELDON: A comparison of students of 1941 and 1951 in a liberal arts college in respect of their understanding of social issues. *J. soc. Psychol.*, 1953, **38**, 283–285.

211 MUSSEN, P. H.: Some personality and social factors related to changes in children's attitudes toward Negroes. *J. abnorm. soc. Psychol.*, 1950, **45**, 423–441.

212 MUSSEN, P. H.: Differences between the TAT responses of Negro and white boys. *J. consult. Psychol.*, 1953, **17**, 373–376.

213 MUSSEN, P. H., and L. DISTLER: Child-rearing antecedents of masculine identification in kindergarten boys. *Child Develpm.*, 1960, **31**, 89–100.

214 MUSSEN, P. H., and M. C. JONES: The behavior-inferred motivations of late- and early-maturing boys. *Child Develpm.*, 1958, **29**, 61–67.

215 MUSSEN, P. H., and J. KAGAN: Group conformity and perception of parents. *Child Develpm.*, 1958, **29**, 57–67.

216 MUUS, R., and C. B. STENDLER: Intergroup education in the public schools. *Educ. Forum*, 1956, **20**, 151–164.

217 MYERHOFF, B. L., and B. G. MYERHOFF: Field observations of "gangs." *Soc. Forces*, 1964, **42**, 328–336.

218 NEIDT, C. O., and M. F. FRITZ: Relation of cynicism to certain student characteristics. *Educ. psychol. Measmt.*, 1950, **10**, 712–718.

219 NELSON, E. N. P.: Persistence of attitudes of college students fourteen years later. *Psychol. Monogr.*, 1954, **68**, no. 2.

220 *New York Times* Report: *Der Spiegel* de-

cries German stereotype. *The New York Times,* July 24, 1964.

221 NEWCOMB, T. M.: *Social psychology.* New York: Dryden, 1950.

222 NEWCOMB, T. M.: The prediction of interpersonal attraction. *Amer. Psychologist,* 1956, **11,** 575–586.

223 NEWCOMB, T. M.: *The acquaintance process.* New York: Holt, 1961.

224 NIAB, L. N.: Factors determining group stereotypes. *J. soc. Psychol.,* 1963, **61,** 3–10.

225 NOEL, D. L., and A. PINKNEY: Correlates of prejudice: some racial differences and similarities. *Amer. J. Sociol.,* 1964, **29,** 609–622.

226 NOLAN, F. L.: Relationship of "status groupings" to differences in participation. *Rural Sociol.,* 1956, **21,** 298–302.

227 NORDBERG, H. O.: Social pressures influencing adolescent behavior. *Calif. J. second. Educ.,* 1954, **29,** 356–359.

228 NORTHWAY, M. E., and J. DETWEILER: Children's perception of friends and nonfriends. *Sociometry,* 1955, **18,** 527–531.

229 OPPENHEIM, A. N.: Social status and clique formation among grammar school boys. *Brit. J. Sociol.,* 1955, **6,** 228–245.

230 O'REILLY, C. T., and E. J. O'REILLY: Religious beliefs of Catholic students and their attitudes toward minorities. *J. abnorm. soc. Psychol.,* 1954, **49,** 378–380.

231 ORZACK, L. H.: Preference and prejudice patterns among rural and urban schoolmates. *Rural Sociol.,* 1956, **21,** 29–33.

232 OVESEY, L.: Masculine aspirations in women. *Psychiatry,* 1956, **19,** 341–351.

233 PACKARD, V.: *The status seekers.* New York: Pocket, 1961.

234 PACKARD, V.: *The pyramid climbers.* New York: McGraw-Hill, 1962.

235 PATEL, A. S., and J. E. GORDON: Some personal and situational determinants of yielding to influence. *J. abnorm. soc. Psychol.,* 1960, **61,** 411–418.

236 PATTERSON, F. K.: The youth community participation project. *J. educ. Sociol.,* 1956, **30,** 44–48.

237 PEASE, D., and L. V. SWANSON: Middle childhood and preadolescence deserve study too. *J. Home Econ.,* 1958, **50,** 33–35.

238 PECKOS, P. S.: Nutrition during growth and development. *Child Develpm.,* 1957, **28,** 273–285.

239 PHELPS, H. R., and J. E. HORROCKS: Factors influencing informal groups of adolescents. *Child Develpm.,* 1958, **29,** 69–86.

240 PHOTIADIS, J. D.: Education and personality variables related to prejudice. *J. soc. Psychol.,* 1962, **58,** 269–275.

241 PLAUT, W. T.: Changes in ethnocentrism associated with a four-year college education. *J. educ. Psychol.,* 1958, **49,** 162–165.

242 PLAUT, W. T.: Sex, intelligence, and sorority or fraternity membership and changes in ethnocentrism over a two-year period. *J. genet. Psychol.,* 1958, **93,** 55–57.

243 POWELL, M.: Age and sex differences in degree of conflict within certain areas of psychological adjustment. *Psychol. Monogr.,* 1955, **69,** no. 2.

244 PRECKER, J. A.: Similarity of valuing as a function in selection of peers and near authority figures. *J. abnorm. soc. Psychol.,* 1952, **47,** 406–414.

245 PRESSEY, S. L., and A. W. JONES: 1923–1953 and 20–60 age changes in moral codes, anxieties, and interests, as shown by the "X-O Tests." *J. Psychol.,* 1955, **39,** 485–502.

246 PRESSEY, S. L., F. P. ROBINSON, and J. E. HORROCKS: *Psychology in education.* New York: Harper & Row, 1959.

247 PROTHRO, E. T., and J. A. JENSEN: Comparison of some ethnic and religious attitudes of Negro and white college students in the deep south. *Soc. Forces,* 1952, **30,** 426–428.

248 PROTHRO, E. T., and O. K. MILES: A comparison of ethnic attitudes of college students and middle class adults from the same state. *J. soc. Psychol.,* 1952, **36,** 53–58.

249 RADKE-YARROW, M. J., and B. LANDE: Personality correlates of differential reactions to minority group belonging. *J. soc. Psychol.,* 1953, **38,** 253–272.

250 RADKE-YARROW, M. J., H. TRAGER, and J. MILLER: The role of parents in the development of children's ethnic attitudes. *Child Develpm.,* 1952, **23,** 13–53.

251 Recreation Survey: Recreational interests and needs of high-school youth: résumé of study conducted in Schenectady, N.Y. *Recreation,* 1954, **47,** 43–46.

252 REISSMAN, L.: Class, leisure, and social participation. *Amer. sociol. Rev.,* 1954, **19,** 76–84.

253 REMMERS, H. H., and D. H. RADLER: *The*

American teenager. Indianapolis: Bobbs-Merrill, 1957.

254 RESNICK, J.: Toward understanding adolescent behavior. *Peabody J. Educ.*, 1953, **30,** 205–208.

255 RICE, T. D., and C. REID: Group efforts toward self government and social responsibility. *J. educ. Sociol.*, 1956, **30,** 75–93.

256 RICHARDS, E. S.: Ethnic attitudes of college students. *Sociol. soc. Res.*, 1950, **35,** 22–30.

257 ROBBINS, F. G.: The impact of social climates upon a college class. *School Review*, 1952, **62,** 275–284.

258 ROBERTS, H. W.: The impact of military service upon the racial attitudes of Negro servicemen in World War II. *Sociol Psychol.*, 1953, **1,** 65–69.

259 ROSEN, T. C.: The effect of the motion picture, "Gentleman's Agreement," on attitudes toward Jews. *J. Psychol.*, 1948, **26,** 525–536.

260 ROSENBLUTH, J. F.: A "replication" of "some roots of prejudice." *J. abnorm. soc. Psychol.*, 1949, **44,** 470–489.

261 ROSENFELD, H., and J. JACKSON: Effect of similarity of personalities on interpersonal attraction. *Amer. Psychologist*, 1959, **16,** 366–367.

262 SANFORD, N.: Personality development during the college years. *J. soc. Issues*, 1956, **12,** 1–71.

263 SCHEFFLER, I., and C. N. WINSLOW: Group position and attitude toward authority. *J. soc. Psychol.*, 1950, **32,** 177–190.

264 SCHEIDLINGER, S.: Understanding the adolescent in a group setting. *J. educ. Sociol.*, 1949, **23,** 57–64.

265 SCODEL, A., and H. AUSTRIN: The perception of Jewish photographs by non-Jews and Jews. *J. abnorm. soc. Psychol.*, 1957, **54,** 278–280.

266 SEARS, R. R., E. E. MACCOBY, and H. LEVIN: *Patterns of child rearing.* New York: Harper & Row, 1957.

267 SECORD, P. F., and C. W. BACKMAN: Interpersonal congruency, perceived similarity, and friendship. *Sociometry*, 1964, **27,** 115–127.

268 SECORD, P. F., W. BEVAN, and B. KATZ: The Negro stereotype and perceptual accentuation. *J. abnorm. soc. Psychol.*, 1956, **53,** 78–83.

269 SECORD, P. F., and E. SAUMER: Identifying Jewish names: does prejudice increase accuracy? *J. abnorm. soc. Psychol.*, 1960, **61,** 144–145.

270 SEIDLER, M. B., and M. J. RAVITZ: A Jewish peer group. *Amer. J. Sociol.*, 1955, **61,** 11–15.

271 SHERIF, M., and H. CANTRIL: *The psychology of ego-involvements.* New York: Wiley, 1947.

272 SHERIFFS, A. C., and R. F. JARRETT: Sex differences in attitudes about sex differences. *J. Psychol.*, 1953, **35,** 161–168.

273 SHORT, J. F., and F. L. STRODTBECK: Why gangs fight. *Trans-Action*, September–October, 1964, pp. 25–29.

274 SIEGEL, A. E.: The influence of violence in the mass media upon children's role expectations. *Child Develpm.*, 1958, **29,** 35–56.

275 SIEGEL, S. M.: The relationship of hostility to authoritarianism. *J. abnorm. soc. Psychol.*, 1956, **52,** 368–372.

276 SIMMONS, D. C.: Protest humor: folkloristic reaction to prejudice. *Amer. J. Psychiat.*, 1963, **120,** 567–570.

277 SIMPSON, R. L., and I. H. SIMPSON: The school, the peer group, and adolescent development. *J. educ. Sociol.*, 1958, **32,** 37–41.

278 SINGER, A.: Certain aspects of personality and their relation to certain group modes and constancy of friendship choice. *J. educ. Res.*, 1951, **45,** 33–40.

279 SKOREPA, C. A., J. E. HORROCKS, and G. G. THOMPSON: A study of friendship fluctuations of college students. *J. genet. Psychol.*, 1963, **102,** 151–157.

280 SMITH, C. U., and J. W. PROTHRO: Ethnic differences in authoritarian personality. *Soc. Forces*, 1957, **35,** 334–338.

281 SMITH, F. H.: *An experiment in modifying attitudes toward the Negro.* New York: Teachers College, Columbia University, 1943.

282 SMUCKER, O.: The campus clique as an agency of socialization. *J. educ. Sociol.*, 1947, **21,** 163–168.

283 SOMMER, R., and L. M. KILLIAN: Areas of value difference: II. Negro-white relations. *J. soc. Psychol.*, 1954, **39,** 237–244.

284 SPAULDING, C. B.: Cliques, gangs, and networks. *Sociol. soc. Res.*, 1948, **32,** 928–937.

285 SPAULDING, C. B., and R. S. BOLIN: The

clique as a device for social adjustment among high school girls. *J. educ. Sociol.*, 1950, **24**, 147–153.

286 SPILKA, B., and E. L. STRUENING: A questionnaire study of personality and ethnocentrism. *J. soc. Psychol.*, 1956, **44**, 65–71.

287 SPINDLER, D. G., and L. S. SPINDLER: American Indian personality types and their sociocultural roots. *Ann. Amer. Acad. pol. soc. Sci.*, 1957, **311**, 147–157.

288 SPIVACK, G.: Child rearing attitudes of emotionally disturbed adolescents. *J. consult. Psychol.*, 1957, **21**, 178.

289 STAGNER, R.: *Psychology of personality.* 3d ed. New York: Mc Graw-Hill, 1961.

290 STEIN, A. B.: Adolescent participation in community co-ordinating councils. *J. educ. Sociol.*, 1948, **21**, 177–183.

291 STEPHENSON, C. M.: The relation between the attitude toward the Negroes of white college students and the college or school in which they are registered. *J. Psychol.*, 1952, **36**, 197–204.

292 STOGDILL, R. M.: Personal factors associated with leadership: a survey of the literature. *J. Psychol.*, 1948, **25**, 35–71.

293 STOLZ, H. R., and L. M. STOLZ: *Somatic development of adolescent boys.* New York: Macmillan, 1951.

294 STONE, C. L.: Sorority status and personality adjustment. *Amer. sociol. Rev.*, 1951, **16**, 538–541.

295 STONE, C. L.: Some family characteristics of socially active and inactive teenagers. *Family Life Coordinator*, 1960, **8**, 53–57.

296 STOTLAND, E., S. THORLEY, E. THOMAS, A. R. COHEN, and A. ZANDER: The effects of group expectations and self-esteem upon self-evaluation. *J. abnorm. soc. Psychol.*, 1957, **54**, 55–63.

297 STRANG, R.: *The adolescent views himself.* New York: McGraw-Hill, 1957.

298 STRICKLAND, B. R., and D. P. CROWNE: Conformity under conditions of simulated group pressure as a function of the need for social approval. *J. soc. Psychol.*, 1962, **58**, 171–181.

299 THOMPSON, G. G., and J. E. HORROCKS: A study of the friendship fluctuations of urban boys and girls. *J. genet. Psychol.*, 1947, **70**, 53–63.

300 THOMPSON, W. R., and R. NISHIMURA: Some determinants of friendship. *J. Pers.*, 1952, **20**, 305–315.

301 TRENT, R. D.: The relation between expressed self-acceptance and expressed attitudes toward Negroes and whites among Negro children. *J. genet. Psychol.*, 1957, **91**, 25–31.

302 TRESSELT, M. E.: The adolescent becomes a social person. *J. soc. Hyg.*, 1954, **40**, 130–134.

303 TRIANDIS, H. C., and L. M. TRIANDIS: Race, social class, religion, and nationality as determinants of social distance. *J. abnorm. soc. Psychol.*, 1960, **61**, 110–118.

304 TRYON, C. M.: The adolescent peer culture. *43rd Yearb. Nat. Soc. Stud. Educ.*, 1944, 217–239.

305 TUCKMAN, J., and I. LORGE: Attitude toward aging of individuals with experiences with the aged. *J. genet. Psychol.*, 1958, **92**, 199–204.

306 TURBEVILLE, G.: Social distance in Duluth. *Sociol. soc. Res.*, 1950, **34**, 415–423.

307 TURNER, R. H.: Preoccupation with competitiveness and social acceptance among American and English college students. *Sociometry*, 1960, **23**, 307–325.

308 VAN KREVELEN, A.: Stability of adolescents' judgments of an ambiguous figure after knowledge of others' judgments of same figure. *J. genet. Psychol.*, 1959, **94**, 23–27.

309 VAN KREVELEN, A.: Characteristics which "identify" the adolescent to his peers. *J. soc. Psychol.*, 1962, **56**, 285–289.

310 VAN ZELST, R. H.: Empathy test scores of union leaders. *J. appl. Psychol.*, 1952, **36**, 293–295.

311 VICKERY, F. E.: Adolescent interests in social problems. *J. educ. Res.*, 1946, **40**, 309–315.

312 VINACKE, W. E.: Stereotypes as social concepts. *J. soc. Psychol.*, 1957, **46**, 229–243.

313 VOSK, M.: Correlates of prejudice. *Rev. educ. Res.*, 1953, **23**, 353–364.

314 WALSTER, E., and B. WALSTER: Effect of expecting to be liked on choice of associates. *J. abnorm. soc. Psychol.*, 1963, **67**, 402–404.

315 WALTERS, W. H., W. E. MARSHALL, and J. R. SHOOTER: Anxiety, isolation, and susceptibility to social influence. *J. Pers.*, 1960, **28**, 518–529.

316 WEATHERLEY, D.: Maternal response to childhood aggression and subsequent anti-Semitism. *J. abnorm. soc. Psychol.*, 1963, **66**, 183–185.

317 WEBSTER, H.: Changes in attitudes during college. *J. educ. Psychol.*, 1958, **49**, 109–117.

318 WEISS, W.: An examination of attitude toward Negroes. *J. soc. Psychol.*, 1961, **55**, 3–21.

319 WELLER, L.: The relationship of personality and nonpersonality factors to prejudice. *J. soc. Psychol.*, 1964, **63**, 129–137.

320 WELLERMAN, B., and L. SWANSON: Group prestige in voluntary organizations: a study of college sororities. *Hum. Relat.*, 1953, **6**, 57–77.

321 WERTHAM, F.: Psychological effects of school segregation. *Amer. J. Psychother.*, 1952, **6**, 94–103.

322 WERTHHEIMER, R. R.: Consistency of sociometric position in male and female high school students. *J. educ. Psychol.*, 1957, **48**, 385–390.

323 WESTLEY, W. A., and F. ELKIN: The protective environment and adolescent socialization. *Soc. Forces*, 1957, **35**, 343–349.

324 WIEDER, G. S.: Group procedures modifying attitudes of prejudice in the college classroom. *J. educ. Psychol.*, 1954, **45**, 332–344.

325 WILLIAMSON, E. G., and D. HOYT: Measured personality characteristics of student leaders. *Educ. psychol. Measmt.*, 1952, **12**, 65–78.

326 WILLIAMSON, E. G., W. L. LAYTON, and M. L. SNOKE: *A study of participation in college activities.* Minneapolis: University of Minnesota Press, 1954.

327 WILSON, W. C.: Extrinsic religious values and prejudice. *J. abnorm. soc. Psychol.*, 1960, **60**, 286–288.

328 WILSON, W. C.: Development of ethnic attitudes in adolescence. *Child Develpm.*, 1963, **34**, 247–256.

329 WINGFIELD, R. G.: Bernreuter personality ratings of college students who recall having had imaginary playmates during childhood. *J. child Psychiat.*, 1948, **1**, 190–194.

330 WITRYOL, S. L., and J. E. CALKINS: Marginal social values of rural school children. *J. genet. Psychol.*, 1958, **92**, 81–93.

331 WITTENBERG, R. M., and J. BERG: The stranger in the group. *Amer. J. Orthopsychiat.*, 1952, **22**, 89–97.

332 WOLMAN, B.: Spontaneous groups of children and adolescents in Israel. *J. soc. Psychol.*, 1951, **34**, 171–182.

333 WOLMAN, B.: Leadership and group dynamics. *J. soc. Psychol.*, 1956, **42**, 11–25.

334 WRIGHT, H. F.: Psychological development in Midwest. *Child Develpm.*, 1956, **27**, 265–286.

335 YOSHINO, R. I.: The stereotype of the Negro and his "high priced car." *Sociol. soc. Res.*, 1959, **44**, 112–118.

336 ZELENY, L. D.: Social leadership. *Sociol. soc. Res.*, 1949, **33**, 431–436.

CHAPTER 5
social
status

"Social status," the position the individual holds in the group with which he is identified, comes from his acceptance by the members of that group. The number of friends he has, the prestigeful status of these friends, and whether his position in the group is that of leader or follower are generally regarded as foolproof evidence of the degree of social adjustment he has achieved. This means that an adolescent who can claim a large circle of friends and acquaintances, who is identified with the "right" crowd, and who is a leader more often than a follower is labeled as a "socially well-adjusted person."

An adolescent may conform to group expectations, he may have favorable attitudes toward people and social activities, but he may derive little personal satisfaction from the type of people who are available for him to associate with. This is especially true of very bright adolescents who, as a group, are well accepted by their age-mates though they show little interest in participating in the activities their age-mates enjoy. If one of the four major criteria of social adjustment were applied—satisfaction from social activities—one could not call such individuals "socially well adjusted." And yet, they enjoy a high degree of social acceptance (207).

An adolescent may be popular and have a wide circle of friends and acquaintances. But he would prefer to belong to a clique or crowd that is known to be composed of the "big wheels" of the school. He might hold a minor leadership role but would rather hold a more prestigeful leadership role. So long as the element of satisfaction is not present, he cannot be said to be well adjusted.

In most cases, however, there is a close relationship between social status and social adjustments. In fact, there is a close relationship between social acceptance, social status, *and* social activities. The adolescent who is socially well adjusted has high social status and this leads to more than average social activity. Conversely, the poorly adjusted adolescent gains little satisfaction from social activities and withdraws from them.

The status the adolescent has in the peer group can be determined by two criteria: first, the degree of his *acceptance* by the group and, second, the *role* he plays in that group, whether leader or follower. These two criteria will be discussed in detail in the following pages.

meaning of social acceptance

"Social acceptance," usually called "popularity," means the extent to which a person's company is regarded as rewarding to others in intimate, face-to-face relationships. "Popularity," in the strict sense of the word, emphasizes respect and admiration by others. It does not necessarily mean close, friendly relationships with people, as is true in social acceptance. As Naegele has pointed out, the respected are "chosen for office, rather than invited to parties" (243). They have prestige and are liked for qualities, whether of appearance or behavior, which are admired by others.

When a trait is associated with prestige, it is not necessarily associated with social acceptance. High marks and studiousness, for example, may be admired and respected but they will not necessarily make the person who possesses them fun to be with. They may be rewarding to the individual himself but not to the members of the social group. Consequently, not all adolescents who are popular in the sense that they are admired and respected by the group are socially accepted, nor, on the other hand, are all who are accepted popular in the sense that they have prestige in the eyes of the group (189,243).

In the American culture of today, great prestige is associated with a high level of social acceptance. Consequently, the adolescent judges himself, just as others judge him, by the quality and quantity of friends he has. To a girl, being popular is of even greater concern than to a boy because of the greater restrictions social convention places on the girl's initiative in making friends, especially among members of the opposite sex.

In many other cultures, where the prestige value of social acceptance is not so great, concern about popularity likewise is not so great. In France, the family plays a more important role in the adolescent's life than does the peer group; academic work is more important in the school than are extracurricular activities (298). Interest in social activities and obligations to the social group are less highly valued in Germany than in the United States (229). Social acceptance is far less of a preoccupation among university students in England than here (316). Peer acceptance is of only minor importance among both rural and urban adolescents in Egypt (110). Consequently, when little prestige is associated with social acceptance, the adolescent will not be greatly disturbed if he achieves relatively little acceptance (17,68).

Influence of Social Expectations Social acceptance can be achieved only when the adolescent conforms to the expectations of the members of the group with which he wants to be identified. These expectations are determined by what the group has found makes people easiest and pleasantest to be with (118,121,216,293). Furthermore, because the traits the adolescent likes best in himself are those which conform most closely to the ideals of his group, it is logical that he would most readily accept as a friend another adolescent who possessed these characteristics. On the other hand, the traits he dislikes most in himself are generally those he knows the group dislikes or disapproves of. Consequently, he is most likely to reject as a friend anyone who possesses such traits (215). Among older adolescents, for example, the popular image of a fraternity man is that of a "good fellow." If a young man wants to be accepted in a fraternity, he must avoid the appearance of studying too much and must create the impression that he is a good fellow (206).

If all adolescents within a given culture held the same values, it would not be too difficult for an individual to learn to conform to those values and, thus, guarantee his acceptance. This, however, is not the case. Different groups within the same culture have different expectations for those whom they are willing to accept as friends (35,80,211). A girl may realize that her chances of acceptance would be greatly increased if her family background were better. To achieve this, she may try to "reform" her parents, her home, and her siblings. But if the other girls feel her background is inferior to theirs, they will not accept her. On the other hand, in another group where most of the members have backgrounds similar to hers, she might win wide acceptance and have a large circle of friends (81, 289,294).

The values of various groups in a school are markedly influenced by the type of school it is (31,82). When the goals of the group are social in nature, high value is placed on personality, social skills, and socioeconomic status; when the goals are less social, more emphasis is placed on what the adolescent can contribute to the group (125).

DEGREES OF ACCEPTANCE

Social acceptance varies in degrees. There are some adolescents who are very popular. The "star" is an individual who is colorful, outgoing, and interesting to others; he is more involved with and interested in people than in things (68,219).

At the other extreme are the "social isolates"—those who have no close friends, who belong to no cliques or crowds, and who feel that no one cares for them or has any interest in them. There are two types of social isolates, the "involuntary isolates" and the "voluntary isolates." An involuntary isolate is one who wants to have friends but is forced into a state of social isolation against his will. He may be prevented from participating in social activities and having friends because of geographic isolation, necessity to work, or some condition over which he has no control. More often, however, it is because the members of the peer group do not want him as a friend. He may be actively disliked and, hence, *rejected* by the group. Or he may have so little to offer to the group that he attracts neither favorable nor unfavorable attention and, as a result, is *neglected*. He is regarded as a "neutral personality" who is overlooked rather than disliked and rejected. Both the rejectee and the neglectee want friends but the group does not want them as friends (42,150,243).

The second type of social isolates are the voluntary isolates—those who are not interested in group activities or in the people who are available as friends (128,146,172, 247). This is especially true of very bright or talented adolescents. They have so little in common with their contemporaries that they would rather be friendless than spend time with those who are available for friends (170,286). When adolescents have interests that are not sex appropriate, they find little in common with members of the peer group who conform more closely to peer standards of sex appropriateness. If a girl has a strong interest in scholastic and intellectual activities at the age when most adolescent girls are more interested in dat-ing, parties, and fun, she feels out of place with her peers and prefers isolation. Boys who are more interested in artistic or me-chanical activities than in sports prefer to spend their time doing what interests them, even if this means cutting themselves off from the group and its activities (219).

Between these two extremes, the star and the isolate, are varying degrees of popu-larity. Some adolescents are reasonably popu-lar in that they have a close friend, belong to a clique and a crowd, and are included in all or most of the social activities of their contemporaries. Most adolescents enjoy a moderate degree of popularity. Some are "fringers" in the sense that they are only tentatively accepted; their status is so pre-carious that one slight act or word may an-tagonize the group to the point where they will lose what status they have. Then there are the "climbers" who try to improve their status by winning acceptance among the members of a more prestigeful group than that with which they are identified (150).

Very few adolescents are unanimously popular and very few are completely isolated from the social group. Most fall between these two extremes of the continuum of so-cial acceptance, with the majority at average or near average. There is evidence that the curve for different levels of social acceptance is slightly skewed on the side of social isolates, suggesting that more adolescents fall below average in social acceptance than above average. The reason for this will be discussed later in the chapter.

awareness of acceptance

"Sociempathic ability," or the individual's "awareness of his own and others' socio-metric status in a given group of which he is a member," improves with age (11). It comes partly from psychological maturation and partly from learning in a given culture. While there is an increase in this ability with age, the greatest gain in ability to per-ceive the status of others comes between the seventh and eleventh grades. The greatest gain in ability to perceive one's own status, by contrast, comes between the eleventh

and twelfth grades (11,12,37,333). These differences are illustrated in Figure 5-1.

VARIATIONS IN AWARENESS

Awareness of status varies, according to the *degree of acceptance* the adolescent enjoys. The most popular—the stars—and the most isolated are, on the whole, the least aware of how others feel about them. In both cases, this is due to the fact that they have few close, personal contacts with their peers. As a result, they have no real way of know-ing how others feel about them (37,149). Reasonably popular adolescents, on the other hand, perceive accurately how others view them. There are two reasons for this: first, the popular are in a better position to know how others feel about them than are those who are unpopular, and second, they have little reason to be defensive about their status (10,11,49,113,142).

From his more frequent contacts with his peers, the popular adolescent can better estimate their opinions of him than can the less popular adolescent whose less fre-quent contacts makes his estimations of peer opinions less accurate (95). The relation-ship between accuracy of self-role perception and amount of time spent in peer activities is illustrated in Figure 5-2. Adolescents who are rejected are usually inaccurate in their perceptions of their status in the group. Those who underestimate their acceptance are, on the whole, more accurate than those who overestimate it. The latter fail to recog-nize how unpopular they are (142,174,279, 308). The neglectees, owing to the indiffer-ence of the peer group toward them, tend to have poor estimates of their status be-cause they have no frames of reference by which to judge it (310).

Girls, as a whole, are more accurate in judging the social acceptance others enjoy as well as their own status than are boys. Mem-bers of both sexes tend, however, to overesti-mate their popularity, though boys are greater offenders than girls in this (1,49, 212). Boys are more accurate in estimating how well they are accepted by members of the opposite sex while girls are more accu-rate in estimating their acceptance by mem-bers of their own sex (10,11). Sex differences in perception of sociometric status are shown in Figure 5–3.

Very *bright* adolescents tend to underestimate, and the dull tend to overestimate, their acceptance. This is due not to intellectual ability alone but to the fact that bright adolescents are better accepted than the dull (240). Adolescents of the lower *socioeconomic* groups tend to be less aware of the acceptance they have than those of the higher groups (55). Awareness of social acceptance is closely related to the adolescent's *need for affiliation* and his desire to be accepted. The more satisfaction the adolescent derives from social contacts, the more accurately he can judge how others feel about him (127,155). Awareness of degree of acceptance is better among *well-adjusted* than among poorly adjusted adolescents (11,174, 214,231).

Normally, there is a steady gain with *age* in the ability of both boys and girls to predict the status assigned to them in the group. This is true of their status with members of their own sex and with members of the opposite sex. As interest in socialization increases, following the puberty changes, there is an increase in the adolescent's awareness of how he rates with the peer group (11,55,107,307).

AIDS TO RECOGNITION OF STATUS

How the adolescent knows what others think of him is not a matter of chance or intuition. Instead, there are many indications from the behavior and speech of others to tell him how he rates with them. The most important of these indicators are discussed below.

Treatment by Others The popular adolescent is in demand. He is surrounded by his friends, he is telephoned by them, he is invited to do things with them, and his opinions are respected. When he gets into difficulties or is blamed for wrong doing, he can count on his friends to stand by him and help him out of his difficulties. He also finds that his friends applaud his efforts, even though his achievements may not be up to his or their expectations, and they excuse his mistakes (71).

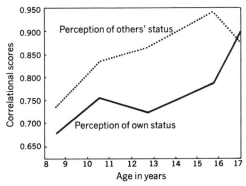

FIGURE 5–1 Perception of own and others' status. (Adapted from D. P. Ausubel, H. M. Schiff, and E. B. Gasser: A preliminary study of developmental trends in sociempathy: accuracy of perception of own and others' sociometric status. *Child Develpm.*, 1952, **23**, 111–128. Used by permission.)

The unpopular adolescent, on the other hand, is made to feel unwanted and unwelcome. He is not invited to parties or other group activities unless it is apparent that parental pressure was brought to bear to include him. Even in sports and other extracurricular activities open to all students, he is the last to be selected to play on a team or take an active part in the group work. Furthermore, the unaccepted adolescent quickly senses that his achievements are not applauded by the peer group. Any mistakes he makes are so openly criticized or condemned that he feels it necessary to rationalize or to project the blame for them onto someone else.

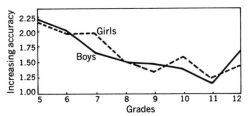

FIGURE 5–2 Relationship between self-role perception and amount of time spent in peer activities. (Adapted from J. E. DeJung and E. F. Gardner: The accuracy of self-role perception: a developmental study. *J. exp. Educ.*, 1962, **31**, 27–41. Used by permission.)

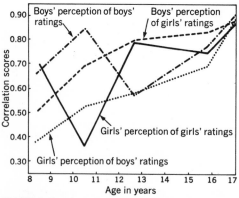

FIGURE 5–3 Sex differences in perception of sociometric status. (Adapted from D. P. Ausubel, H. M. Schiff, and E. B. Gasser: A preliminary study of developmental trends in sociempathy: accuracy of perception of own and others' sociometric status. *Child Develpm.*, 1952, **23**, 111–128. Used by permission.)

Names and Nicknames What his peers call him tells the adolescent very plainly what they think of him. Adolescents who are called by nicknames, most of which originated with their classmates, have been found to be more popular than those without nicknames. Adolescents called by their baptismal names, on the other hand, tend to be the least popular (97).

Designations of Levels of Acceptance By adolescence, most individuals are placed in categories by their contemporaries, with definite names attached to these categories. Teen-age boys, for example, use general terms to describe members of the peer group they accept or reject. Those whom they accept are labeled as "swell" or "wonderful guys," while those whom they reject are usually called "drips" or "squares" (115). Within these general categories, there are certain names commonly used by present-day American adolescents to indicate level of acceptance. These names are (232,233):

WHEELS—*"People who make the wheels go round," "run things wherever they are," "the active ones," "the top crowd"*

BRAINS—*"Students," "get most of their ideas from books," "tend to do what older people want," "good kids but they don't know the score"*

OUTSIDERS—*"Average kids," "they get around," "skaters," "not in the crowd"*

MICE—*"Quiet ones," "often left out or just not noticed," "inoffensive," "seldom heard"*

OUTCASTS—*"Left out of things," "you don't want to be with them."* There are three kinds of outcasts:

DRIPS—*Would-be wheels who make one uncomfortable*

DOPES—*Would-be brains who arouse antagonism*

WILD ONES—*"Could get into trouble,"often called "delinquent"*

Comments by Peers Typically, adolescents are brutally frank in their comments about their peers. When an adolescent is disliked, his peers literally go out of their way to let him hear their opinions of him, expressed within his earshot (6,133,262). Most high schools and colleges have newspapers or "house organs" which reflect the interests, activities, and values of the student group. In these, the gossip column plays an important role. *How often* a student is mentioned in the school or college paper is an indication of what role he plays in school life and what status he has with his classmates. *How* adolescents are mentioned likewise gives a clue as to whether or not they are the big wheels or of lesser importance (183).

factors influencing social acceptance

The relative importance of the different factors that contribute to social acceptance in adolescence varies according to the group involved. To be acceptable in one group, for example, a girl must be interested in dating and attractive enough to be popular with boys. In another group, these interests are far less important than being an outstanding athlete or a good student. A goody-goody who does not cheat, gamble, tell off-color jokes, swear, or neck would not be acceptable in one group but would be acceptable in another (81,256).

Similarly, some factors play a far more

important role in social acceptance among boys than among girls. This is illustrated in Figure 5–4. To be accepted by the leading crowd in high school, boys must, above everything else, be good athletes. In addition, they must be socially active, play a leadership role in some of them, and make good school grades. For girls, having nice clothes and coming from the "right" family top the list. Being an athlete or making good grades in school is far less important (80,81).

Lacking such qualities, the adolescent may and unquestionably will gain some acceptance. But it will be in crowds that are less prestigeful. If he is to make the leading crowd, he must conform to the values widely accepted as essential to social acceptance by such a group. As Coleman (81) has pointed out:

> The leading crowd seems to be defined primarily in terms of social success; their personality, clothes, desirability as dates, and —in communities where social success is tied closely to family background—their money and family.

A survey of some of the most important factors that contribute to social acceptance will show what role each plays. The following have been found to influence, to a greater or lesser degree, the social acceptability of American adolescents today.

FIRST IMPRESSIONS

The individual's status depends partly upon his actual behavior and partly on the picture people carry in their minds about him. It depends to a large extent upon the first impression he makes on them. If, for example, the adolescent creates the impression of being "cold" and "aloof," owing to shyness, he will be reacted to very differently than if he were judged by others to be "warm," "sympathetic," or "friendly" (193).

When older adolescents go away to college or professional training schools, to work, or into the armed services, they are often associated with complete strangers for the first time since they started school. Consequently, first impressions play an impor-

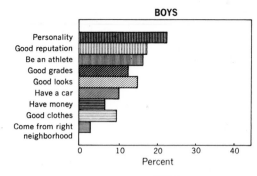

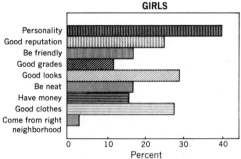

FIGURE 5–4 Qualities adolescents consider important for a boy's or girl's membership in the leading crowd. (Adapted from J. S. Coleman: *The adolescent society*. New York: The Free Press of Glencoe, 1961. Used by permission.)

tant role in determining how well they will be accepted in these new groups. If the first impression the new group gets of the adolescent is unfavorable, this will militate against their desire to try to know him better.

Making a favorable first impression, then, is extremely important to the adolescent's later acceptance. And knowing how the members of the group feel about him influences the adolescent's later behavior also (143,193). It has been found that adolescents most frequently accepted at a glance retain their position in the group as acquaintanceship progresses. This is less true of those who become isolated; they may or may not improve their status, depending on later impressions (20).

ATTRACTIVENESS OF APPEARANCE

Because people are judged by the impression they make on others, an attractive appearance is important to social acceptance (328). For boys as well as for girls, being attractive alone is not enough; they must also be sex appropriate in appearance. A masculine-looking boy, for example, has a better chance of acceptance by members of his own and of the opposite sex than an effeminate-looking boy who is better looking and better groomed. Similarly, a girl who creates the impression of being "masculine" will not be so acceptable to members of either sex as a more "feminine" girl (133, 301). While an attractive appearance is an important asset to social acceptance among adolescents of both sexes, it is especially important to girls (150). Popular girls, it has been found, spend more time on their clothes and grooming than do less well-accepted girls. By doing so, they improve their appearance and, hence, their chances of acceptance (109,328).

An unattractive appearance affects the attitudes and behavior of the individual himself. When adolescents are dissatisfied with their appearance, they worry about what effect it will have on social interactions (270). The adolescent becomes self-bound and tends to be preoccupied with self. In time, this leads to feelings of inadequacy which influence the individual's behavior unfavorably. Because girls are judged more by their appearance than boys, having an unattractive appearance is especially serious for them (62). In a study of the effects of grooming and clothing on the social acceptability of girls, it was found that the girls who made a poor appearance were more self-effacing, more negativistic in their attitudes, more withdrawn, and less interested in people and social activities than were the girls who made a better appearance and were better accepted by their contemporaries of both sexes (288).

REPUTATION

The reputation an adolescent acquires is due partly to his behavior and partly to the image he has created in the minds of others. In time, a person's reputation becomes a "halo" that is used to rate him (224). If favorable, it leads to prestige, respect, and a tendency to attribute to the individual *all* good qualities, though of different degrees of goodness (243,251). Once a reputation

has been established, it is difficult to change. An adolescent who acquires a bad reputation finds it difficult if not impossible to live it down. A good reputation, by contrast, enables an adolescent to do many things which, in those with less favorable reputations, would be severely criticized.

The reputation an adolescent acquires is often intensified by what others say about him. If the reputation is favorable, people will say favorable things: As a result, his halo grows. It is a case of nothing succeeds like success. By contrast, an unfavorable reputation is enhanced by the derogatory statements others make about him (183).

One of the most important reasons why adolescents want a large circle of friends and membership in a leading clique is that these enhance their reputations. If they acquire the reputation of being nice to everyone or of being "good guys," it will help to increase their chances of acceptance (192). Many boys try to improve their reputations by doing daring things or by defying the law because they found such behavior gave them prestige in childhood. But they quickly discover that peer values have changed when they reach adolescence. Instead of winning favor, such behavior is more likely to lead to the reputation of being "bad," "wild," or "delinquent" (233,248). By contrast, doing things that conform to peer values will result in a favorable reputation and, in turn, greater social acceptance. This is illustrated in Figure 5–5.

Behavior that contributes to a favorable reputation differs for members of the two sexes and for adolescents of different socioeconomic backgrounds. Girls, for example, cannot be "too free" with boys if they want to be accepted. By contrast, boys who "make conquests" gain prestige in the eyes of their peers (81). The upper-class boy who has the reputation of being a "gentleman" because of his social skills gains greater acceptance than a boy who has the reputation of being a "boor." A boy from the lower socioeconomic group, by contrast, would be rejected as a sissy if he had good manners while the boy who scorned all social skills would be accepted because he was masculine (50,53).

One of the problems associated with deviant sexual maturing is the likelihood of acquiring an unfavorable reputation among members of the peer group. This is especially likely to happen to early-maturing girls. The early maturer who acts in accordance with her physiological age rather than her chronological age often gets the reputation of being "fast" or "not nice" because she is socially and emotionally too immature to know how to control her behavior to conform to group expectations (183,186). Should she act in accordance with group expectations, on the other hand, she will acquire an envied reputation of being "sophisticated" or of "knowing her way around" (114).

SOCIAL PARTICIPATION

Other factors being equal, the more active the adolescent is socially, the better he is known to members of the peer group and the better his chances of being accepted. At both the high school and college levels, accepted adolescents play a much more active role in extracurricular activities of all sorts than do those whose acceptance is lower (109,115,243).

Popular adolescents are also active in the home and they frequently have part-time jobs after school and during vacations. Girls who are well accepted, it has been found, fulfill home responsibilities to a much greater extent than do those who are unaccepted (51,303). Figure 5–6 shows the relationship between social participation and high rank on the "chore score" for girls.

Poorly accepted adolescents do not play regularly on teams, they go to few school parties, they participate in few of the extracurricular activities of the school, and they participate little in the activities of their homes. Instead, their outside activities are usually hobbies, such as reading for pleasure, listening to the radio, watching television, or going to the movies, usually alone. They rarely serve on school or college committees, and they are never elected to school or college offices (50,115).

The reason that social participation and acceptance are so closely interrelated is that the adolescent not only makes himself

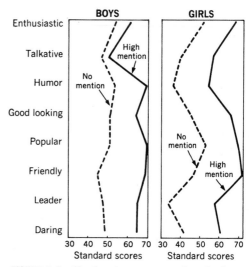

FIGURE 5–5 Conformity to peer values leads to favorable reputation and to social acceptance. (Adapted from M. C. Jones: A study of socialization patterns at the high school level. *J. genet. Psychol.*, 1958, **93**, 87–111. Used by permission.)

known by his activities but he becomes poised and confident. Thus, he feels free to contribute what he can to the group rather than withdrawing into himself as characteristically happens when an adolescent feels the "slap of rejection" (117,183). Figure 5–7 shows the behavior ratings of girls who are popular.

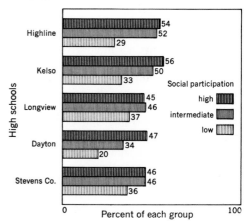

FIGURE 5–6 Relationship between social participation and home responsibilities. (Adapted from C. L. Stone: Some family characteristics of socially active and inactive teenagers. *Family Life Coordinator*, 1960, **8**, 53–57. Used by permission.)

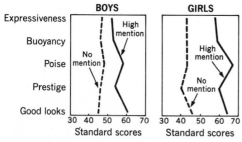

FIGURE 5–7 Ratings of boys and girls who are popular and unpopular with their peers. Those who are popular have high mention in their school publication while those who are unpopular have low or no mention. (Adapted from M. C. Jones: A study of socialization patterns at the high school level. *J. genet. Psychol.*, 1958, **93**, 87–111. Used by permission.)

Acceptance Syndromes Social participation, per se, will not lead to acceptance. The *quality* of the adolescent's behavior in a social situation is as important as the quantity. Adolescents who are popular offer something to the group and conform to group norms in their attitudes and behavior. There are two characteristic behavior syndromes found among adolescents who are well accepted: the *aggressive*, success-oriented type and the *less aggressive*, goodness-oriented type.

In the aggressive syndrome, the adolescent is out for what he can get for himself. In the less aggressive, goodness-oriented syndrome, the adolescent's interest is more directed toward the group and what he can do to bring satisfaction to its members. In both, adolescents are socially oriented; they do things for and with members of the peer group. They are friendly and outgoing in their actions, creating the impression that they are more interested in the welfare of the group than in their own welfare (151, 192). Early-maturing boys and girls tend to be more socially oriented than late maturers, though girls are characteristically more success-oriented, and boys, more goodness-oriented (183).

Alienation Syndromes Poorly accepted adolescents generally have unfavorable self-concepts. Such a concept is often caused by or the result of behavior that falls into three different types of alienation syndromes (109). The first type of alienation syndrome is the *recessive*, characterized by quiet, listless, reserved, withdrawn, and socially disinterested behavior. The second type, the socially *distinterested* syndrome, is characterized by self-bound, selfish behavior; the adolescent is concerned with his own interests and welfare, showing little interest in others or their activities. These two types of syndromes are found in the voluntary isolates and neglectees. The first is more characteristic of the neglectee, and the second of the voluntary isolate.

The third type of alienation syndrome, the socially *ineffective*, leads to social rejection. Socially ineffective behavior may take many different forms, such as being noisy and silly, causing trouble for others, being sneaky, cheating, resisting all adult authority, rejecting group mores about appearance and manners, showing off, trying to be sophisticated, and engaging in horse play.

Adolescents whose characteristic behavior in social situations conforms to the third type are generally looked upon as pests and nuisances by the peer group as well as by adults. If this socially ineffective behavior is mainly egocentric, such as trying to impress others or making unpleasant comments about others to boost one's own ego, it will be tolerated better than if it is mainly aggressive, such as annoying others, picking fights, or using bad words—the "delinquency-related behavior." However, both lead to social rejection, not just social neglect (109,117,138,196,306). Late maturers of both sexes are more likely than early maturers to show this third type of alienation syndrome. Girls concentrate on the egocentric forms of behavior, and boys on the aggressive forms (183).

CONVERSATIONAL SKILLS

Adolescents who are well accepted are almost universally described as "talkative" or as having a "sense of humor." In any social situation, they seem to be poised and at ease, never at a loss to know what to say or how to say it. Making a contribution to the group and helping to keep the conversational ball rolling adds to their acceptance. Recognizing this, they feel secure enough in their status to let themselves go verbally (41,115,117,183,259). Well-accepted adolescents like to laugh and joke, thus helping to create fun and adding to the enjoyment of others. By doing so, they increase their own acceptance (41,109). As Coser (84) has explained:

> Humor invites laughter, as a mark of its acceptance. If some group members refuse to respond, they indicate their rejection of the humorist, as well as of those who understand and feel with him.

Poorly accepted adolescents, by contrast, take little part in conversations. Thus they add little or nothing to the enjoyment of the group members. They are often judged as lacking a sense of humor because they do not joke; either they are not on intimate enough terms with the group members to understand the meaning of the jokes or they lack the security necessary to be able to enter into the situation and laugh with the group (109,117,259).

Socially unacceptable forms of speech contribute to social neglect or rejection. The adolescent who criticizes his peers, especially to their faces, who whines and complains about everything or anything, who makes derogatory statements to and about others, who boasts of his possessions and abilities, who is sarcastic, or who tells jokes that annoy or embarrass others, can quickly counteract any favorable impression he may have made by a good appearance or by participation in group activities (109,117,192).

In no area of speech is the difference between types that lead to acceptance or rejection more pronounced than in wit. Humorous stories and jokes, especially when focused on the teller—the subjective comic—increase the adolescent's chances of acceptance. Stories and jokes that ridicule others—the objective comic—that are told in a sarcastic or vindictive way or are salacious in content tend to antagonize the hearers. Clowning is almost universally regarded as an infantile form of behavior among adolescents. As such, it may win laughs from the group but not acceptance (83,133,140,217).

HEALTH

Most popular adolescents show the qualities that are associated either directly or indirectly with good health. Poor health, by contrast, makes a person pepless, unenthusiastic, and unwilling to do his share in cooperative activities. This is especially true during the puberty phase. At that time, the adolescent who is in poor health either shuns social activities completely or plays a passive role. Should poor health continue after the major part of the body transformation has been completed, the adolescent will feel like participating in peer activities to such a limited extent that he will achieve only marginal status in the group at best; he is more likely to be neglected or rejected (115,133,301).

Any physical handicap that makes social participation difficult or impossible, such as blindness or lameness, likewise militates against social acceptance. Even though members of the peer group may sympathize with their handicapped classmate, they are too preoccupied with having a good time to go out of their way to include in their activities one who cannot carry his share of the load. Furthermore, most handicapped adolescents develop unfavorable self-concepts. These are reflected in attitudes of self-pity or martyrdom, and are expressed in behavior which leads more often to neglect or rejection than to acceptance (57, 89).

PROXIMITY TO GROUP

Children tend to select their friends from their immediate neighborhoods. Adolescents, on the other hand, select friends who live successively further away with each passing year (96). This is illustrated in Figure 5–8. However, it is unquestionably true that adolescents who live close to the group will be able to participate in more activities than those who are socially isolated (246).

Studies of students in consolidated schools have shown that there are no more isolates among the transported than among the nontransported groups. While the town

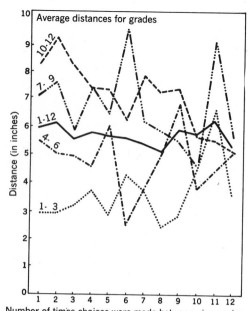

Average distances for grades

Distance (in inches)

Number of times choices were made between given pairs

FIGURE 5–8 Geographic proximity plays a less important role in sociometric status with increasing age. (Adapted from M. V. Duvault: Classroom sociometric mutual pairs and residential proximity. *J. educ. Res.*, 1957, **50**, 605–610. Used by permission.)

LENGTH OF ACQUAINTANCE

How long an adolescent knows his contemporaries may prove to be advantageous to acceptance, or it may prove to be the reverse. It depends on what sort of person he is (278). While length of acquaintance may increase the number of people the adolescent knows, it has little influence on his social status (148). Among college students, it has been found that time together has no real effect on degree of acceptance. When the adolescent enters a group, he establishes his social status in that group in a relatively short time. This status remains constant unless unusual circumstances occur to change it (39).

The two types of adolescents who have the greatest chances of not improving their acceptance with increased length of acquaintance are those who create unfavorable first impressions and those whose behavior is socially unacceptable to their peers. By contrast, social isolates have a good chance of increasing their acceptance as the group becomes better acquainted (148,291). Similarly, newcomers have a chance of improving their acceptance with time (257,258,304, 342).

Members of minority groups may improve their status with length of acquaintance or they may not. Improvement depends partly on the type of group the adolescents are seeking to enter and partly on how the minority-group members behave. When the group is tightly knit, it is difficult for *anyone* to pierce the barriers. It is especially difficult for minority-group members. Should the group, on the other hand, be less tightly knit, there is a greater chance that its members will be more tolerant in their attitudes toward members of minority groups. Under such conditions, the "generosity error" in rating as overcorrection for possible prejudice may open the doors to some members of minority groups (343). Length of acquaintance with members of minority groups is as likely to increase their rejection as to decrease it. The reason is that their behavior often becomes increasingly distasteful to members of the majority group with further contacts.

group, as a whole, is slightly better accepted than the students who come to school by bus, this is more likely to be due to differences in values and interests than to differences in proximity. Most schools try to schedule extracurricular activities at times when transported students can participate in them. Being transported, per se, therefore does not have much influence on degree of participation in school activities (38,40).

In a college dormitory, it was found that the distance upstairs, the position of the student's room on a large or small corridor, and living close to a popular person had little if any influence on the social acceptance of the student. *Acceptance depends mostly on the characteristics of the individual, not where he lives* (265). This point of view was stressed by Newcomb when he said that "propinquity is a facilitator but not a sufficient condition to develop a positive attraction" (246).

TYPE OF GROUP

How well accepted the adolescent is will depend on the *size* and nature of the group. When the group is small, the criteria used to judge the potential acceptance of a new member are mainly personal; he is judged by what he is, has, and can do. When the group is large, he is judged more by what he can contribute to the group, though personal qualities are never overlooked. Because small groups are generally more solidly formed than larger groups, it is harder to gain acceptance in a small group than in a large one (283).

The *nature* of the group plays an equally important role in whether the adolescent is accepted. If the group is primarily social in nature, acceptance can be gained only when the adolescent demonstrates his social skills and socioeconomic background to the satisfaction of the members. Should the group be less socially oriented, the adolescent's interests and contributions to the group are primary factors in determining his acceptance. A boy who shows marked athletic skills, for example, can gain acceptance in a group where the primary interests are centered around sports because of the contribution he can make to the prestige of the group (80). An open group—one which is in a continuous state of membership flux—is easy to gain acceptance in. By contrast, a closed group—one in which the membership is static—is harder to enter (343).

Successful groups are usually self-sufficient and self-contained. They do not want to accept new members because a newcomer might be a disruptive influence or might be a threat to some of the other members. By contrast, an unsuccessful group will be more receptive to new members. If they appear to have something of value to offer to the group, their degree of acceptance will depend on the dissatisfaction the group members have with the group as it is (80,133,341,342).

SOCIOECONOMIC STATUS

High socioeconomic status, in relation to the norm for the group, guarantees that the adolescent will be the center of attention in his group. He is judged not only by what he *has* but also by what he and the members of his family *are* in the community (52, 302,325). In judging people, one tends to attribute more favorable qualities to those of high income and less favorable qualities to those of low income. Income, thus, is a "significant variable in determining how one perceives persons" (213).

Adolescents who have poor social acceptance are often from a lower socioeconomic status than the majority of their classmates. It is true, however, that adolescents of low socioeconomic status may and sometimes do enjoy high peer acceptance (189, 209). Such individuals are known as "climbers" if they are operating easily among their peers; they are known as "strainers" if they are only tentatively accepted.

Handicaps from Low Socioeconomic Status

There are a number of reasons why adolescents of low socioeconomic status are handicapped in gaining peer acceptance. First, they are often handicapped by *lack of money* (109). Studies of accepted and unaccepted boys have shown that the latter start to work earlier and are dependent upon their earnings for most of their spending money. Having to work also cuts down the time they have available for peer activities (117). The high cost of participation in extracurricular activities at the junior and senior high school levels results in their being "principally a function of the accident of birth in an economic sense" (156). This results in the necessity for adolescents of the lower-income families to forego participation in many of the extracurricular activities and, in some cases, to withdraw from school (189). This is true also of college students. Many cannot afford to belong to fraternities, sororities, clubs, or to participate in the extracurricular activities of the campus (302).

The second reason for the poorer social acceptance of lower socioeconomic group adolescents is that they are, on the whole, *less well adjusted* than those from higher socioeconomic groups. Adolescents who come from the middle and upper groups are taught conformity as a means of achieving status. In addition, they learn to inhibit emotional expressions, to behave in a sophisticated way, and to feel loved and wanted. Even though adolescents from the lower groups may be more independent, they often feel unloved and unwanted in the home as well as among members of the peer group, and they feel inadequate in social situations. Consequently, they create the impression of being poorly adjusted and out of step with their peers (58).

The third cause of poor acceptance of adolescents from the lower socioeconomic groups is that they *feel out of place* in school. As a result, they often voluntarily withdraw from participation in social activities. In commenting on the school's attitudes toward such students, Coster (85) has pointed out that:

> American schools, consciously or unconsciously, have been prone to favor pupils from middle and upper socioeconomic strata which, generally, include a high proportion of academically competent youth.

The fourth way in which socioeconomic status influences the acceptability of an adolescent is in the *knowledge of correct social usages* and the *possession of social skills*. It is quite understandable that adolescents from better family backgrounds would be superior to those from poorer backgrounds in this area. Furthermore, when an adolescent is not acceptable to members of the peer group, he has little opportunity to learn social skills outside the home.

The fifth reason why socioeconomic status plays such an important role in social acceptance is that *values* accepted by members of one group may not be acceptable to members of another group. Boys from the lower socioeconomic groups, for example, are usually more aggressive than those from the upper groups. This leads to their rejection by members of both sexes (109,209, 213). And, finally, socioeconomic status influences the degree of *poise* and *self-confidence* the adolescent has in peer relationships. Adolescents who come from lower socioeconomic groups are concerned about their families' low status, about their lack of social skills and knowledge of social

usages, and they often discover that the attitudes and values they have learned at home are not acceptable to their upper-status peers. The more anxious they are to be accepted, the more anxious and ill at ease they are in social situations (284).

Sex Differences in Importance of Socioeconomic Status Socioeconomic status is more important to the social acceptance of girls than of boys. In one study, for example, it was reported that only 17 percent of the most popular girls came from the lowest socioeconomic groups while the majority of the most popular came from the highest groups (109). The role the adolescent girl plays in the extracurricular activities of high school illustrates how important the socioeconomic status of her family is. Cheer leaders are usually chosen from girls of upper-middle-class backgrounds—those who are conservative in dress and behavior and are college-oriented. The majorettes, by contrast, generally come from the lower-middle or the upper-lower classes. They are more flashy in dress and grooming and have little interest in academic work. Furthermore, they are seldom leaders in school activities. This is not true of boys to the same extent. Many of the school leaders among boys have a socioeconomic status inferior to that of the nonleaders (35,54,81,267).

Coleman (81) has explained the importance of socioeconomic status for acceptance among girls in the following way:

> Money, fancy clothes, good house, new cars, etc.—the "best." They express the fact that being born into the right family is a great help to a girl in getting into the leading crowd. They are not something a girl can change. . . . Her position in the system is ascribed according to her parents' social position and there is nothing she can do about it. . . . The leading crowd seems to be defined primarily in terms of social success: their personality, clothes, desirability as dates, and—in communities where social success is tied closely to family background—their money and family.

The reason that socioeconomic status of the family is less important for the boy than the girl during adolescence is that the boy can "escape" his socioeconomic background more than a girl can. The boy's social life is spent more away from home than in the home. Furthermore, because boys have more opportunities to earn money than girls, the low socioeconomic status of a boy's family is not so great a handicap to him in getting the clothes he wants and having money for extracurricular activities as it is for girls who must often depend on allowances from parents (81,109,201).

POSSESSION OF SKILLS

Skills will not, of course, guarantee social acceptance, though lack of skills may lead to social rejection. The adolescent who can do things with others and who has enough self-confidence to be willing to use his skills has an asset that contributes to his acceptance (73,185,221,305). Studies of the relationship between strength, skills, and popularity have revealed that strong boys are more popular than weak boys who experience generalized tensions due to feelings of masculine inadequacy. Strong boys have also been found to be superior in schoolwork, not because of higher IQs but because of better adjustment (36). One of the reasons why early-maturing boys gain greater peer acceptance than average or late maturers is that their superior physical strength makes superior athletic achievement possible (154, 199).

In a study of junior high school boys, it was found that one-half of the stars were outstanding athletes while three-fourths of the neglectees were low in athletic ability (230). This is true also of boys in senior high school. As Coleman has pointed out, "Athletic success seems the clearest and most direct path to membership in the leading crowd" (81). This is not true for girls. A girl who wins the reputation of being an outstanding athlete is likely to win the reputation also of being "masculine"—a reputation that will not enhance her chances for social acceptance (81,183).

Social skills, accompanied by social know-how, likewise contribute to popularity in adolescence. Knowing the correct thing to do and doing it aids social acceptance.

Lack of such knowledge leads to fear of social situations and a consequent withdrawal from such situations. Adolescents who feel incompetent to deal successfully with social situations belong to few of the school clubs and participate in few of the extracurricular activities where they would have an opportunity to improve their social skills and, as a result, their social acceptance (50,109, 175).

SOCIAL INSIGHT

To handle a social situation diplomatically, one must have social insight—the ability to size up social situations quickly and accurately. Adolescents who can tell, from facial expressions, speech, and general behavioral reactions, how others feel about different matters have a good chance of becoming the most popular members of the group (87, 129,240,307). As Kidd has pointed out, "Acceptability is likely to accrue in direct proportion to the extent to which one puts oneself in the other fellow's shoes" (196).

The adolescent who lacks social insight or whose social insight is below the level of that of his age-mates, is judged as tactless or as a boor. He constantly hurts other people's feelings and arouses antagonisms and resentments (67). Even worse, he is ignorant of the feelings he arouses in others and therefore continues to act in a gauche and ill-adapted manner. In time, he gets the reputation of being a boor. This militates against possible future acceptance even though he may improve his social insight (279,311).

Boys are generally less sensitive to the reactions of others than girls. This is one of the many reasons why girls are more popular than boys. Adolescents of the lower socioeconomic statuses often feel inadequate and inferior in social situations. They become so self-bound that they are less sensitive to the feelings of others than are adolescents of the higher socioeconomic statuses who, for the most part, feel more at home with members of the peer group (122,212).

INTELLIGENCE

The reason why high intelligence contributes to the adolescent's acceptability among his peers is that it enables him to take initiative in crowd activities, to plan for the successful carrying out of these activities, and to suggest substitute activities when group interest begins to lag. Even more important, above-average intelligence helps the adolescent to size up the group's interests and moods quickly and successfully so that he can adjust to them (130,154).

Too high intelligence in relation to other members of the group, however, is apt to make the adolescent out of step with his contemporaries. The reason for this is that very bright adolescents are often cocky and intolerant of their less bright classmates, they are uninterested in their activities, and they make little effort to contribute to them. By contrast, those whose intelligence is superior, but not too superior, rank above average in social acceptance. They can contribute something to the group but they are not so superior to the group that they feel out of place with the group members (16,117,146,183,322).

Adolescents who are markedly less intelligent than their peers gain little social acceptance. While they are generally not rejected, they are neglected and become social isolates even though they would like to participate in group activities. Their neglect comes in part from the fact they have little to contribute to the group and its activities and in part from the fact that their slowness in learning holds back the other members. Recognizing their inferiority, most dull adolescents become self-conscious and withdrawn, making little effort to participate in the activities of the group (117,170,208, 276).

ACADEMIC ACHIEVEMENT

Being a good student contributes to the social acceptance of an adolescent; but if he is too good a student, he is likely to get the reputation of being a brain or a curve raiser. Furthermore, an adolescent who has such good relations with his teachers that he acquires the reputation of being "teacher's pet" or of "polishing the apple" will find this a handicap to acceptance by the peer group (181). In a study of high school boys, it was found that the most accepted boys had school marks in the top 25 percent

of their classes. By contrast, the rejected boys had grades in the third 25 percent of their classes. In addition, the rejected boys disliked many of their teachers (117).

Adolescents who are well accepted generally have a better attitude toward school than do those who are poorly accepted (93). Very poor students generally dislike school and are disliked by both their classmates and teachers (170,208). They are "pests" in the classroom and tend to argue with their teachers about their grades. They take special delight in disturbing the good students and in making it difficult for them to study (109,117).

That academic achievement is of minor importance in social acceptance may be seen by the fact that adolescents claim they would like to be remembered as the years pass as the best athlete or the most popular, not as the best student. As Coleman has pointed out, for the "impressionable" freshman or even sophomore in high school, athletes stand out, not scholars. By junior or senior year, being a good student contributes more to social acceptance than it did earlier. However, brilliance has little effect in increasing acceptability; studiousness reduces it (80,81).

Variations in Effects For a *boy*, being both a scholar *and* an athlete leads to greater acceptance than being either alone (189, 190). But, of the two, being an athlete is far more important (81). *Girls* with high marks may be respected by members of their own sex and be influential in scholastic affairs. But respect does not necessarily lead to acceptance, especially when the respect is for academic rather than social achievements. In most schools, girls with high marks are rated as less popular than girls with lower marks (190). Only if a girl can be a successful student *and* popular with boys will she win social acceptance among girls. If a girl has *both* beauty and brains, it will contribute to her social acceptance. Of the two, beauty is far more important than brains (81).

In the first *year* of high school, academic achievement is less highly valued than it is later. Until the realization of the importance of grades dawns on them, adolescents put higher value on athletic than on scholastic achievement (80,81). At all ages, adolescents from the middle and upper *socioeconomic groups* look more favorably on a peer who is a good student than do those from the lower socioeconomic groups (27). Middle-class as well as lower-class boys prefer "activities" girls to studious girls; they like the "teen-age replica of the adult clubwoman" (81). This is true also, but to a lesser extent, of upper-class boys.

ACCEPTANCE OF GROUP INTERESTS AND VALUES

Adolescents feel more comfortable and at home with those whose interests and values are similar to theirs. A boy, for example, who is anxious to make a name for himself scholastically has little in common with one who places low value on academic achievement but high value on athletic achievement. To fit into a peer group, the adolescent must be similar to members of that group. The most acceptable adolescent, therefore, is the one who conforms most closely to the interests and values of his particular group (80,81,219).

Because the values of minority groups —whether religious, racial, or socioeconomic —are different from those of the majority group, it is difficult for adolescents of minority groups to win acceptance from members of the majority. A middle-class student in a predominantly working-class school, for example, would belong to a minority group. As such, he would enjoy little acceptance from his classmates, even though he were willing to accept their values (81). Rural students have a minority-group status in consolidated schools. Even when their economic status is similar to that of town students, their different values prove to be an obstacle to social acceptance by the town students. To them, they are "country hicks" (250).

Even when adolescents know the interests and values of the members of the group with which they want to be identified, they must be able or willing to accept them. Girls who do not like dating and who show little interest in parties and clothes have little chance of being accepted in a group where these interests and values dominate. Similarly, boys who do not have cars available for use, or whose time is limited by the necessity of working after school, will find themselves unacceptable in crowds of peers where high value is placed on having fun. Much as they would like to participate in this fun, their acceptance will depend on whether or not they *can* do so (79,219, 256).

FAMILY RELATIONSHIPS

Certain types of homes foster attitudes and behavior that contribute to social adjustment in adolescence, while others do much to make the adolescent unpopular. Parents of high school boys who are not satisfied with their sons' grades and are not interested in any social or athletic organization have sons who are below average in social acceptability (115). Parents who are neutral in their attitudes toward their children, but use harsh and autocratic disciplinary techniques, make adolescents either aggressive and rebellious or timid and overdependent, all of which contribute to poor social acceptance (187,329). When parents encourage their sons and daughters to do things with them rather than with members of the peer group, they contribute to the adolescent's social difficulties (48,109).

The adolescent who has been overprotected is unpopular because of the smugness and selfishness he has learned at home. This makes him aloof, convinced of his superiority, and unwilling to cooperate with others (77). By contrast, adolescents who are popular get along better at home, have more family responsibilities, and have parents who are better satisfied with them and their behavior (51,271). Parents who encourage their sons and daughters to visit in the homes of their peers, who are willing to permit their children to entertain at home and are hospitable to their children's guests, and who are satisfied with the popularity their children enjoy contribute to the social acceptability of adolescents (109). This is illustrated in Figure 5–9.

Some adolescents who are popular with their peers, however, have parents who ex-

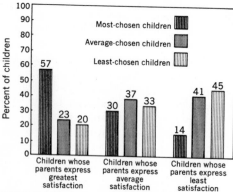

press little satisfaction with them. This is often due to the fact that their children spend so much time with the peer group and are so engrossed in out-of-the-home activities that the parents feel neglected. Adolescents who get along well with their peers generally get along reasonably well with their siblings; this contributes to their parents' satisfaction with them (109).

The adolescent who is well accepted generally has a favorable attitude toward his family and feels that his home life is both satisfactory and happy. As Warnath has pointed out, "The home thus appears indeed to be a seat of learning for the development of social skills and perhaps of the desire to participate in activities with other individuals" (323). Adolescents who are least satisfied with their homes and have unfriendly feelings toward their parents and siblings are found mostly in the low popularity groups (109).

Popular adolescents more often come from small than from large families. The only child is more often unpopular than the nononly child, both in childhood and adolescence. Furthermore, there is evidence that the youngest, and to a lesser extent, the oldest child in a family tend to be less popular than middle children. The best position, so far as social acceptance is concerned, is that between the youngest and the oldest (39,90,97,314).

PERSONALITY PATTERN

The personality pattern of the adolescent is of more importance than any other single factor in determining the degree of acceptance he will enjoy. This has been stressed by Coleman (81):

> The importance of having a good personality, or, what is a little different, "being friendly" or "being nice to the other kids" in these adolescent cultures is something that adults often fail to realize. Adults often forget how "personality-oriented" children are: they have not yet moved into the world of cold impersonality in which many adults live.

The personality pattern of a well-accepted adolescent is usually that of a group-centered individual—one whose behavior is directed toward the group—while that of the poorly accepted is self-centered or self-bound in that his behavior is directed toward satisfying his own desires, even when doing so is to the detriment of the group (4).

In the constellation of traits that lead to acceptance there are some disliked traits just as in the constellation that leads to rejection are to be found traits that are liked and admired. This means that a well-accepted adolescent is not a paragon of perfection so far as his personality traits are concerned. But the undesirable traits are outweighed by the desirable. Similarly, a poorly accepted adolescent has some traits which are a social asset, but they are outweighed by those which are a social liability (41,42,147,150).

Traits which contribute to acceptance have been labeled "bonanza" traits while those which lead to rejection have been called the "black-ball" traits. The adolescent whose personality pattern is characterized by a predominance of "bonanza" traits is described as "swell" or a "wonderful guy." When, on the other hand, there is a predominance of "black-ball" traits, the adolescent is labeled "no good" or a "real drip" (117).

Traits Leading to Acceptance The accepted adolescent is expansive, talkative, daring, sympathetic, sincere, generous, cooperative, willing to conform, trustworthy, objective, interested in and considerate of others, cheerful, good-natured, full of fun, has a good sense of humor, is well disciplined, tolerant of others, poised, self-confident, relaxed, builds up the egos of others, is optimistic, peppy, has a zest for life, a strong drive, and is flexible (42,109, 144,150,319). Just because these traits contribute to social acceptance does not mean that the more highly developed they are, the greater will be the adolescent's acceptance. Too much daring, for example, is more likely to lead to rejection than to acceptance; the peer group regards a too daring person as immature or a "fool" (183).

Well-accepted adolescents have favorable self-concepts. In general, they have a good opinion of themselves and of their abilities (115). Having a good opinion of themselves frees adolescents from anxiety. This enables them to turn outward, becoming group-oriented rather than self-oriented (42,239,255).

Traits Leading to Rejection The rejected adolescent has many of the same traits as the accepted, but they are overshadowed by "black-ball" traits. He may be timid, retiring, lethargic, in-grown, self-centered, stingy, stubborn, sullen, cold, and disinterested, or he may be restless, nervous, fidgety, conceited, bossy, cocky, tactless, sarcastic, argumentative, inconsiderate of others, immature in attitudes and behavior, and unwilling to conform to group mores in dress or actions (42,109,117,150,196,204). He often has a vulgar and disparaging attitude toward members of the opposite sex, engages in excessive drinking or sex behavior, and develops an adroitness in escaping responsibility for his antisocial acts (42,81,117,196). He likes to show off and demand attention by pranks and boisterousness. But the atten-

tion he gets is of an unfavorable sort and contributes to his rejection (42,150,196, 204).

Personality problems and disturbances contribute to the unacceptibility of the adolescent. These generally come from an unfavorable self-concept. Rejected boys have a generally poor opinion of themselves, their abilities, and their achievements, and they lack self-respect (42,115). Because of these poor opinions, they tend to reject themselves (234). Poor self-opinions sometimes lead to overacceptance which is expressed in intolerance of others and an exaggerated opinion of oneself and one's abilities (119).

Unfavorable self-opinions generally lead either to inferiority or superiority complexes. These in turn lead to different forms of compensation, none of which will increase the chances of acceptance. Adolescents may whine and complain about the way others treat them, they may paint a picture of themselves as martyrs, they may claim that others are constantly picking on them, they may become stubborn and negativistic in their attitudes and behavior, or they may retaliate for their rejection by expressing their resentments through devious measures, such as teasing, bullying, and disturbing others, or by verbal attacks on them and on innocent victims (91,196,284). In general, they make themselves into pests (109).

One of the most common accompaniments of poor self-opinions is anxiety. Unpopular adolescents show greater anxiety and trends toward schizoid and psychopathic deviant patterns than do those who are more popular (239). Frequently, anxiety is intensified when the adolescent feels that his lack of social acceptance springs from the low socioeconomic status of his family. This causes him to behave in a defensive way and to do things which antagonize his peers (284).

Traits Leading to Neglect The personality pattern of a neglected adolescent is that of a shy, retiring, introverted person. He is regarded as a neutral personality or colorless. Because the peer group overlooks him, he becomes a "social island" unto himself, participating little if any in the activities of the group and rarely talking unless spoken to. As he does or says nothing to antagonize others, he is rarely disliked. In fact, he is more likely to be liked than disliked. But he is not well enough liked to be accepted as a part of the peer group.

effects of acceptance on attitudes and behavior

How great and how lasting will be the effects of different degrees of social acceptance on the adolescent's attitudes and behavior will depend, to a marked extent, on how important social acceptance is to him. When an adolescent's other resources are too limited to meet his needs, when belonging to a given group represents to him the thing he wants above everything else, and when his home and family fail to give him emotional satisfaction, he will be more anxious to be popular than he would if these conditions were different (134,172).

For any adolescent, success in the "things that count" leads to self-satisfaction and happiness while failure leads to self-dissatisfaction and unhappiness. Because he sees himself as members of the peer group see him, his self-concept becomes a mirror image of their concept of him. Of all adolescents, stars and isolates are, without question, the most affected by the group. This is not alone because their status is most obvious to all but also because it is more pronounced. Knowing that everyone likes him and wants him as a friend cannot fail to bring ego satisfaction to the star. Realization that no one wants him as a friend could never give ego satisfaction and it inevitably makes the isolate question his own worth (81,277).

INFLUENCE OF POPULARITY

The popular adolescent is happy and secure. As a result, he can free his attention from himself and his problems to become interested in other people and things. He then becomes group-oriented rather than self-oriented or self-centered. He becomes a sympathetic, understanding friend, ready and willing to help his friends in trouble, to comfort them in distress, and to build up rather than tear down their egos by criticism and derogatory comments designed to inflate his own ego (42,109). Because he is secure in his status, he can afford to express his feelings toward others without fear of being rebuffed. Knowing that others accept him helps him to accept himself, to be satisfied with his status, and optimistic about his future (10,271,272,310,311).

The self-acceptant adolescent has an accepting attitude toward others (33,249). As a result, he becomes a cooperative member of the group, wanting to do his share or more to add to the satisfaction of the group members (41). He wants to conform to group expectations, and this increases his acceptance in the group (317,318). Because he is an accepted member of the group, he has opportunities to know how the different members of the group feel and act. This develops his social insight along with socially acceptable behavior (142,166,310).

Being an accepted member of a peer group is a powerful agency in socialization. This is shown by the fact that the behavior of well-accepted adolescents is more socially desirable and approved than is that of rejected adolescents (37,206). Furthermore, the well-accepted are willing to perform roles that satisfy the needs of others rather than their own needs (109). In spite of constant contact with members of the peer group, they maintain their individuality, conforming to the general values and accepted patterns of behavior of the group but varying them to suit their own needs. As a result of their individuality, they are better able to control the situation and to make a contribution than are those who conform more slavishly to the group stereotype (103, 132,157,219,237).

The adolescent's attitude toward and interest in social participation is greatly influenced by how satisfying social participation is to him. This, in turn, is largely determined by how well accepted he is. Popular adolescents, feeling wanted in different activities, become active participants in them. This provides them with opportunities to learn social skills, to develop greater social insight, and to internalize the values of the group (13,59,225,266,272).

The higher the acceptance of the adolescent, the more active he is in group affairs and the more prestigeful the role he plays. However, being a star has its disadvantages along with its advantages. It sets the individual off from the group, with the result that he has few close, warm friends. Furthermore, he does not reciprocate the affection and respect given him either because of indifference or because he does not want to show favoritism and thus alienate any of his friends (68). As a result, he is less happy and often finds less satisfaction from his social life than does the adolescent who is popular but not a star (210).

INFLUENCE OF UNPOPULARITY

Being rejected or neglected has just as devastating effects on the adolescent's attitudes and behavior as being accepted has favorable effects. It is difficult or impossible for a person to have a favorable opinion of himself when he realizes that others have an unfavorable opinion of him. And it is equally difficult for him to accept himself when others neglect him or refuse to accept him (42,249). The person who rejects himself becomes defensive in his attitudes. This leads to rigidity—a mental set that militates still further against good social adjustments and chances for acceptance (109).

The effects of lack of social acceptance on the adolescent's personality are more far-reaching and more lasting than is generally realized. No adolescent can escape developing feelings of inadequacy and inferiority when he sees how others feel about him. The adolescent most likely to be permanently injured by rebuffs from his contemporaries is the one who is very insecure (172).

The unpopular adolescent is unhappy, he is unsure of himself, and he frequently develops a pessimistic attitude toward life and a defeatist attitude toward himself (271). When this happens, it leads to the establishment of habits of timidity and resentfulness (132). Being unpopular cuts the adolescent off from social contacts, thus depriving him of the fun his contemporaries have, of opportunities to develop social skills, of opportunities to engage in the forms of recreation popular in adolescence, and of learning the meanings and values of the peer group. Without these opportunities, he is unable to develop social insight of a high enough level to understand the feelings and attitudes of his contemporaries. This makes him seem tactless and gauche, adding still further to his lack of acceptance (272,310, 311).

The more the adolescent is cut off from social contacts with the peer group, the more self-bound he becomes (128). Even when members of the peer group try to break the ice and reach him emotionally, he does not reciprocate either because he is suspicious of their motives or because he wants to protect himself from rebuffs which he fears will come as they have in the past. Inability to join members of the group emotionally causes the adolescent to become an "emotional outsider" (311). When barriers to interaction are established it makes later acceptance difficult if not impossible (195, 272). As a result of feelings of loneliness and rejection, the adolescent becomes dissatisfied with himself and his life. This leads to general maladjustment and unhappiness (37,126).

How lack of social acceptance influences the adolescent's behavior will vary from one individual to another. In general, however, it is likely to have any one of five common effects.

First, it may act as a *form of motivation* to win prestige through other channels, in the hope of thus winning acceptance in the group. More often, however, it leads to working below capacity, and to behavior of a disorganized sort that militates against an effective performance (30,45,279).

Second, lack of social acceptance makes the adolescent *aggressive* in his social relationships. The adolescent who is rejected by the peer group often boasts, bluffs, shows off, seeks the limelight, annoys others by horseplay or telling jokes at the expense of others; he is generally obnoxious in speech and behavior. He contributes little or nothing to the satisfaction of the members of the group, and he seems to go out of his way to spoil the fun the others are having (42,109, 195,337).

Third, lack of aceptance encourages the development of *substitute satisfactions* —excessive daydreaming and solitary forms of amusement, such as reading, watching television, going to the movies, or becoming so absorbed in studies or a job that there is little time left for social activities (59,81, 286).

Fourth, social isolation may produce anxiety and insecurity which lead to excessive *conformity*. Many adolescents feel that any status in the group is better than no status at all. Therefore, if conformity will provide them with some status, they will not only conform but overconform (103,157, 160,237,321).

And, finally, social isolation may make an adolescent *try to escape from an environment* in which he is forced to play the role of an isolate. He will shun the extracurricular activities of school or leave school because of lack of social acceptance (153,169, 231). School withdrawal, as Coleman has emphasized, is "*not* a consequence of doing well or poorly in school work; it is a consequence of being deprived of acceptance and status by his fellows" (81).

The adolescent will not "sit still while his self evaluation is being lowered by the social system of the school." Instead, he will "take his psychological self and energies elsewhere, leaving only a physical self in the school" (81). When he is old enough to take his "physical self" away from school, he will do so by dropping out. In this way he will keep his ego from being too greatly damaged to be repaired then or in the years to come.

INFLUENCE OF MARGINAL STATUS

The effects of being a fringer or a clinger are much the same as the effects of unpopularity. The adolescent is insecure and unhappy, living in constant fear of losing what status he has gained. This militates against the development of self-confidence and makes the adolescent hypersensitive. It also affects the way he treats others. In order to solidify his status, he is likely to try to undercut his competitors, either by actions or

by derogatory statements about them. This leads to a "peck order" which is resented by those whose status is more secure. In addition, attempts to improve his status will cause the adolescent to be easily influenced by anyone who will accept him (103,109, 132,310).

preponderance of socially isolated

Even in childhood, the curve of popularity is skewed toward the minus side, indicating that more children are below average in social acceptance than above average. This skew becomes greater in adolescence as the number of unaccepted boys and girls exceeds the accepted (51,242). (See Figure 5–10.) It has been estimated that only about 15 to 25 percent of all American adolescents have an acceptance status below the minimum needs for wholesome and satisfying personality development. However, there is evidence that many more enjoy less acceptance than they want or are striving to achieve (100).

Dissatisfaction with the acceptance they have achieved is not the only reason for the increase in number of adolescents who enjoy less than average social acceptance. The increase is due, in part, to the greater difficulty the individual has in achieving social acceptance in adolescence than in childhood. As was pointed out in the preceding chapter, adolescents are choosier about their friends than children are; they expect their friends to come up to an ideal they set. When they accept those who fall below this ideal, they often antagonize their friends by criticizing them and trying to reform the qualities they dislike. Furthermore, because adolescent social groups are more tightly knit structures than are children's gangs, gaining acceptance to these groups is more difficult, and retaining status, once accepted, more precarious (324).

One important aspect of the greater difficulty in achieving acceptance in adolescence is that the requirements for acceptance are stricter than they were earlier. Some of the qualities rated high in the requirements for acceptance, such as looks, socioeconomic status of the family, social

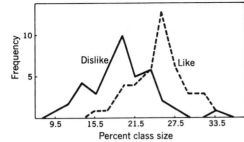

FIGURE 5–10 Percentages of students in one class who are liked and who are disliked by their classmates. (Adapted from J. F. Muldoon: The concentration of liked and disliked members in groups and the relationship of concentration to group cohesiveness. *Sociometry*, 1955, **18**, 73–81. Used by permission.)

skills, and social insight, were of relatively little importance in childhood. And yet many of these are beyond the adolescent's control (112,221,273).

persistence of acceptability

Studies of the relative statuses of adolescents in a group have shown that they remain more or less static. The stars remain the stars; the isolates, the isolates; and the neglectees, the neglectees. This is true for both boys and girls (116,327). The most stable are those who are best liked. It is most unusual for the popular to "fall from grace." By contrast, the least stable are the least liked. They may improve their status or they may be less liked with further acquaintance. This is especially true of the rejectees, who are likely to be more disliked with time than to be better liked. Those who are isolates tend, on the whole, to improve their status with further acquaintance (41,51,61,152,247).

Marked stability in sociometric status begins to appear in the last three years of high school (61,116,327). Persistence in sociometric status continues into late adolescence and early adulthood. College students who are popular with their classmates have, on the whole, been well accepted throughout their high school days. Those who are poorly accepted in high school tend to be poorly accepted in college (136). Among

young adults, those who have large circles of friends were, for the most part, well liked throughout their adolescent years (162, 220). As Jones has explained, the "pattern of social interaction represented by participating in extracurricular high-school activities provided many adolescents with social roles they found intrinsically congenial and likewise useful as a step toward other kinds of satisfying interpersonal relationships" (183).

REASONS FOR SHIFTS IN POPULARITY
Popularity at one age *will not guarantee popularity at another age*. There are three reasons for shifts in popularity: first, shifts in values; second, changes in groups; and third, changes in the adolescent's behavior (61,116). As Kuhlen and Lee (202) have pointed out:

> At one age a person may have those characteristics that make for popularity at that age and be very popular, but a year or more later may show a marked loss in popularity because new traits have assumed importance in the eyes of his agemates—traits which that person may not then possess.

While *values* change from age to age, the change is more often in the form of shift of emphasis than shift to completely new qualities. For example, boys in the seventh grade admire a boy who is ready to take daring chances. By ninth grade, they admire bravery, while by twelfth grade neither of these traits is greatly admired. Similarly, seventh-grade girls admire tidiness in a girl, while twelfth-grade girls emphasize good grooming and good taste in dress (133, 202,236,315,334).

In spite of the fact that values change from one age to another, there are certain values that remain static or nearly static. A popular person is one who is cheerful, enthusiastic, friendly, popular, cooperative, courteous and considerate of others, truthful and above board in conduct, controls his temper in annoying situations, loyal, a good sport, has high ideals, a sense of humor, frank, sincere, kindly, honest, truthworthy, and sympathetic. Similarly, there are certain qualities that will make a person unpopular at every age. They are: showing off, bluffing, seeking the limelight, bullying, arousing antagonisms in others, carrying a grudge, domineering, thinking he is misunderstood, using excuses or alibis, untidiness, sloppiness, snobbishness, silliness, flightiness, immaturity, insincerity, being demanding, inconsiderateness and thoughtlessness, unfriendliness, low moral standards, and a bad reputation (109,117,179,183,196).

The second reason for change in social acceptance status is change in *groups*. Going to a different type of group is likely to lead to change in popularity status. That is because different groups have different interests and values. A group that is interested in dating would not accept a girl whose interests are primarily centered on athletics or academic achievement. Similarly, a boys' group that is interested in sports would offer only low acceptance to a boy whose interests are academic (81,256).

And, finally, changes in social acceptance accompany changes in the adolescent's *behavior*. These changes may enhance or detract from his acceptance. It depends on what form the changes take in relation to the values of the group (61). A quiet, introverted adolescent will be overlooked and neglected until he becomes more extroverted in behavior and speech. Whether this change will lead to greater acceptance or greater social isolation will be determined by the quality of the change. Should he become aggressive and pushy, he will go from being neglected to being rejected; should he become cooperative and contribute something of worth to the group, he will go from being neglected to being accepted.

REASONS FOR PERSISTENCE IN POPULARITY

Even though social acceptance can and does change, it is more likely to be persistent (61, 116). There are a number of reasons for this persistence, the most important of which are:

The *personality traits* that lead to social acceptance are persistent, just as are those that lead to rejection or neglect. The leopard does not change his spots nor does the adolescent change his personality (47,117).

The *socioeconomic status* of the adolescent's family may change, but this does not guarantee that the adolescent will improve his acceptance status. As he tries to move up the social ladder, he will break off old friendships in the hope of improving his status only to find that the new group with which he wants to be identified will not accept him (32,101).

Opportunities to learn the interests and values of the group do not exist when an adolescent is unacceptable to it. The more he can participate in group activities, the sooner he can learn to conform; the less he participates, the less able he will be to conform (221,266,272).

The *reputation* the adolescent acquires in the group does more than any other factor to make his sociometric status persistent. Once the group gets an impression of an individual, it is difficult if not impossible to change that impression (41,136,181,191). As Singer has pointed out, the "picture of social friendship acceptance is molded and set in the early grades rather than at the adolescent level" (290).

improving social acceptability

Because the number of socially unacceptable adolescents is greater than the number of socially acceptable, because unacceptability tends to be persistent, and because unacceptability plays havoc with the adolescent's happiness and adjustments to life, one of the major problems American adolescents of today face is trying to improve their sociometric status. As Feinberg et al. have pointed out, "Unpopularity cannot be lightly dismissed as a 'passing phase'" (117). Instead, it should be changed when the individual is plastic and has a strong motivation to do so (293).

Far too often, unfortunately, lack of social acceptance is not recognized early enough by those whose responsibility it is to guide the child. Or, if it is recognized, there is a tendency to believe that the child will "outgrow" the characteristics which lead to lack of social acceptance when he reaches puberty. As a result, many children reach adolescence with well-established habits of behaving in ways that antagonize others, with reputations of being pests or squares, and with unfavorable self-concepts resulting from the rejection they have experienced over the years (109).

Some adolescents work out unaided the problem of improving their social acceptance. This they do by asking their friends why others do not like them, by observing the behavior of those who are better accepted than they, by trying to imitate them in the hope of improving their own acceptance, or by reading books on how to win friends. For most adolescents, however, aid is needed in the form of counseling (3).

AIDS IN IMPROVING ACCEPTANCE

Studies of attempts to improve the acceptability of adolescents have brought out three important fundamental principles. First, the adolescent is rejected or neglected for a reason. Before any headway can be made, this reason must be discovered and steps taken to correct the behavior that has led to unpopularity.

Second, emphasis should be placed on the development of strong positive assets rather than merely on the correction of negative assets (42). As Bonney has pointed out, "A socially good personality is a positive achievement: it is not simply the result of avoiding the bad" (41).

And, third, because boys are acceptable to their peers for different reasons than girls, emphasis must be placed on the development of strong positive social assets that are important to the acceptance of members of *that* sex, not necessarily of the other sex (81,109).

Many attempts have been made to help adolescents improve their acceptability. These have revealed some techniques which have proved to be successful. Of these, the following have brought the best results.

Removal or Modification of Traits That Cause Rejection or Neglect A girl who is untidy in appearance will be rejected even though she may have some outstandingly desirable characteristics. This is because very high value is placed on an attractive appearance by members of both sexes (109). The reason that it

is so important to remove or modify socially unacceptable characteristics is that they have a greater attention value than socially desirable ones. They can overshadow the desirable unless the latter are extremely strong (252).

Increased Participation in Socially Approved Group Activities This is especially important for adolescents who are overlooked and neglected because they have made no contribution to the group (42). Participation in sports, especially the prestigeful sports, is one way to improve a boy's social status (81, 230). Dating is equally as prestigeful among girls as sports are among boys (81). Through participation, the adolescent increases his acquaintanceship with his peers. This, in turn, increases his chances of being chosen as a friend, provided he has socially acceptable personality traits (278).

Improved Quality of Social Participation Being more active socially will not, per se, increase social acceptance. The quality of the activity is as important as the quantity; often quality is more important. An adolescent who is clumsy and awkward in his movements will not improve his acceptance by participating in sports; in fact, he will increase his rejection. Only when the quality of the activity conforms to social expectations can it be an aid to increased social acceptance (42).

Improvement in Social Skills With the beginning of social life with members of the opposite sex, the adolescent can no longer hope to be accepted if he is ignorant of socially approved patterns of behavior. As Bretsch has pointed out, "One avenue of promoting better adjustment on the part of school pupils is that of teaching them social skills which will enable them to function effectively in social situations" (50).

Improvement in Conversational Skills Because much of the time adolescents are with their peers is spent in talking, the ability to carry on a conversation is one of the most important social skills. Many adolescents are neglected because they fail to make a contribution to the conversation of the group. Just talking for the sake of talking, on the other hand, will not increase social acceptance. The *quality* of speech is equally as important as the quantity. The adolescent who talks endlessly about himself and his achievements is considered a bore; the one who talks in a derogatory way about others is labeled a snob (42,109,133).

Development of a Sense of Humor Almost every study of acceptance in adolescence has listed a sense of humor high in the traits that lead to social acceptance. A person with a sense of humor is regarded as fun to be with. One who lacks a sense of humor is often described as a bore, a square, or a party pooper (117). However, the wrong kind of humor is more damaging than helpful to social acceptance. Picking on others, horseplay, and jokes based on religion are almost universally regarded as wrong among adolescents. Sex jokes and sarcastic and clowning wit, on the other hand, will call forth different reactions—some favorable and some unfavorable (140).

Development of Social Insight There is a close relationship between popularity and ability to size up a social situation. The reason for this is that it provides a guide for action. If the adolescent perceives how people feel and what their reactions to him are, he will know how to react to them. If he fails to do so, he will react in an appropriate way (149).

Development of Self-insight It is just as important to see oneself accurately as to see social situations accurately. Poor self-insight leads to the formation of unrealistically high levels of aspiration. When these are not reached, the adolescent tries to compensate for his failure by the use of such defense mechanisms as blaming others for his failure or by withdrawing into the daydream world. This leads to poor adjustments; poor adjustments, in turn, lead to social rejection (42, 109,149).

Development of a Favorable Self-concept Almost unanimously, studies of social ac-

ceptability have stressed the fact that rejected and neglected adolescents have unfavorable self-concepts which are expressed in socially undesirable behavior. One important aid to social acceptance, then, is to help the adolescent improve his self-concept. This, in turn, is dependent on improving his social and self-insight. If he can judge other people and their reactions more accurately, he will then know how to act in social situations. Similarly, if he can be helped to narrow the gap between his real and ideal self-concepts, he can be more acceptant of himself and will have less need for defensive behavior. This will improve the quality of his behavior in social situations and his social acceptance (42,109,117,180).

Development of Self-confidence and Self-reliance The adolescent who can accept himself has confidence in his ability to carry out successfully what he undertakes and to get along reasonably well with his age-mates of both sexes. Furthermore, he is able to rely upon his own judgment instead of conforming blindly to the opinions and actions of others. When his peers realize that he has confidence in himself, they will have greater confidence in and respect for him (42,81, 212).

Improvement of Reputation Once a reputation is established, it tends to be persistent. It can be changed, but the only way to do so successfully is to behave in a socially approved manner so that one's peers will realize that their impressions were false. If an adolescent has the reputation of being a nonconformist, for example, he must learn to conform more closely to approved dress and patterns of behavior. The change in reputation cannot be expected to occur overnight or with one favorable impression; the adolescent must literally revise the pattern of speech and behavior that led to an unfavorable reputation (143,150,183).

Provide the Unaccepted with the Limelight Frequently, it is difficult or impossible for the adolescent to change his reputation because he lacks the opportunities to show his peers that he is not as they thought he was.

For that reason, a teacher can sometimes help by letting members of the peer group see the adolescent in a more favorable way. This is especially important for neglectees who may have created the impression that they have little of value to contribute to the group (123).

SEX DIFFERENCES IN AIDS

While it is unquestionably true that the aids listed above would help *any* adolescent to improve his social acceptance, some would be more helpful to girls while others would be more helpful to boys. Social skills, for example, are more important for girls, though boys find their social acceptance greater when they behave in a socially approved manner.

Even though boys emphasize positive qualities, and girls, negative qualities, in those whom they dislike, members of both sexes react more favorably to peers whose positive qualities outweigh their negative. Consequently, for both sexes, emphasis on the strengthening of positive qualities and attempts to remove or minimize traits that lead to rejection or neglect are certainly justified (147).

Social and self-insight are aids to social acceptance at any age and among members of both sexes. That boys tend, as a group to have poorer social and self-insight than girls of the same age levels (see pages 177 and 188), suggests that more emphasis should be placed on improving insight in the case of boys. Even more important, more emphasis should be placed on the development of a favorable self-concept and on self-acceptance among boys than among girls. This is especially true during the early years of adolescence when the desire for social acceptance is very strong (116).

DIFFICULTIES IN ACHIEVING IMPROVED SOCIAL ACCEPTANCE

Improving the adolescent's social acceptance is far from easy. This point of view has been stressed by a number of people who have worked in this area. Pastore, for example, has pointed out that it is more difficult to change a disliked into a liked person than vice versa (252). Elkins claims that it is "easier to adjust academic requirements to the needs of the youngster than it is to adjust the social needs of the child to the group in which he is a misfit or to attempt to adjust the social responses of the group to such a child" (109).

A more hopeful note was sounded by Brown when he stated that "a person is not born with the traits which make him most desired as a friend, but he can develop them if he so wills and if he has help from mature persons who are sensitive to the adolescent's need for social acceptance" (52). The first "if" in Brown's statement offers no real problem because almost every adolescent wants to have friends. As a result, he is anxious to do all he can to improve his acceptance.

The second "if," on the other hand, presents a major stumbling block for two reasons. First, the adolescent may not be fortunate enough to have a mature person who is sensitive to his need to help him to improve his acceptability. Many parents, for example, regard social activities as a waste of time—time that might better be spent on studies or some more productive activity. Such parents often regard the adolescent's desire for acceptability and popularity unsympathetically.

Second, even though the adolescent's parents may be both mature and sympathetic toward his needs, there is no guarantee that he will view them as such. More likely, especially during the early years of adolescence, he will regard any advice his parents give him as interference with his affairs or bossing, or he will label the advice they give him as old-fashioned and say it "won't work today because things are different" (48,81). He may turn to a member of the peer group for advice, but that advice will not come from a mature person even though he may be sensitive to the adolescent's need.

status of leader

Whether the adolescent plays the role of leader or follower is accepted by many as an indication of his social adjustment. Because the role of leader is more prestigeful than the role of follower, and because the number of leaders is far smaller than the number of followers, it is assumed that only those who are best adjusted socially will reach the pinnacle of the social ladder and be accepted as group leaders.

As has been stressed before, however, acceptance alone is not enough to guarantee good social adjustment. The subjective factor—personal satisfaction from playing a social role—must also be taken into consideration. There is no evidence that every leader derives satisfaction from his role nor is there evidence that every follower is dissatisfied with the role of follower. In fact, some leaders would rather be followers and some followers would rather be leaders. When personal satisfaction accompanies the leadership role, it is then possible to say that the leadership status is an indication of better social adjustment than the followership status (163).

In every social group, no matter how small it may be, there must be a leader. As Sherif et al. have pointed out, when interaction between members of a group becomes stabilized into a pattern, there is a hierarchy of statuses and roles for the individual members, each with its own expectations, responsibilities, and loyalties for the members occupying these statuses and roles (287). While these are generally consistent within the same group, the members may have different statuses and roles in other groups. That means that a leader may become a follower while a follower may become a leader in another group (107,244, 269).

WHAT IS A LEADER?

A leader is a person who has the potential ability to get others to act in a certain way (139). He can influence group opinion and bring it in line with his personal views (163, 309). Because he can satisfy the needs of the group members, the group crystallizes around him (336). This he can do for two reasons: first, he has demonstrated mastery of social relationships and has contributed more than the other members to the satisfaction of the needs of the group; and, second, he can arouse emotional reactions in group members, thus swaying them by

loyalty rather than by authority (74,111, 332,339).

The individual who is selected as a leader is different from the one chosen as a social companion (173). He also differs from his associates in the degree of influence he exercises. Even more important, he has such a strong motivation to be a leader that he is willing to make the personal sacrifices in time, energy, and other desires (such as doing things which give him greater personal satisfaction) that are essential if he is to satisfy the needs of the group well enough that they will be willing to follow him. Leadership is a working relationship among members of a group in which the leader acquires status through active participation and demonstration of his capacity for carrying cooperative tasks through to completion (74,135,176,300).

Contrary to popular opinion, leadership is not a specific attribute of a person. As DeHaan (94) has pointed out:

> Leadership is not a unitary trait or ability but, rather, it is made up of personal abilities and traits (which in some way make a person prominent and, thereby, eligible for the position as head of a group) plus consistent performance as a socioemotional specialist and a task specialist.

The "socioemotional specialist" is one who is most sensitive to the needs and feelings of others. He can give and receive affection, release tension, show agreement in a group, and facilitate a feeling of group solidarity. The "task specialist" is one who is outstanding in the task engaged in by the group (94).

There is little evidence of general leadership ability or of great men who inevitably emerge as leaders. Instead leadership depends on the situation. Thus, the distinctiveness of leaders does not depend on their attributes alone but rather on the relationship of their attributes to those of the other group members (188). That is why an adolescent may be a leader in one group in which his attributes surpass those of the other group members and a follower in a different group where his attributes are surpassed by those of another adolescent (74).

Function of the Leader The function of the leader is, fundamentally, to provide satisfaction from social activities for the group members. The more satisfaction the leader provides for the members of the group, the longer they will want him to maintain his status as leader (299). Providing satisfaction for the social life of the group members comes through different media, the most important of which are: first, holding the group together as a cohesive unit; second, maintaining the group in a state of moving equilibrium; third, achieving the purpose for which the group was formed; and, fourth, providing satisfaction for the more immediate needs of the group members (56,235, 292,332).

Types of Leaders Adolescents make a distinction between those who lead as a group and those who lead individually. Those who *lead as a group* are known as the big wheels—the top crowd or those who run things. They are the members of the leading crowd of any school or college class, and as a group, they set the patterns for the rest of the crowd to follow. This they can do because of their generalized prestige or prominence (81,232,233).

Those who *lead individually* are the headmen—the ones who play the role of a true leader by virtue of their activities in relation to the other members of the group. They may be the ones who lead in a small group—a clique or crowd—or they may lead in a large group, composed of the different cliques and crowds of a school or college class. The headmen are the real leaders, even in the leading cliques composed of the big wheels (74,107,219).

Adolescent leaders may be subdivided into various types, according to the criteria used in making the classification. When subdivided on the basis of *method by which they attain their leadership positions*, they are known as "appointed," "formal," or "informal." The appointed leader is selected for the role by an adult—a teacher or camp counselor—with or without the knowledge and consent of the peer group. The formal and informal leaders, by contrast, achieve their status through the wishes of their peers without adult interference. The formal leadership status comes from an election in which the individual receives more votes than his opponents; the informal leader is not voted on but is so regarded by at least one-third of the group members (66,223). When leaders are subdivided on the basis of their *attitudes* toward their role, they are "voluntary" or "involuntary." In the case of the former, the adolescent wants to be a leader; in the latter, he is elected, appointed, or designated as such though he would prefer to be a follower.

If leaders are subdivided according to the *method used to lead*, they are known as "authoritarian" or "democratic." The authoritarian leader is bossy, demanding, and inconsiderate of others; he ignores their wishes if these wishes do not coincide with his. By contrast, the democratic leader is sensitive to the wishes of the group, he is willing to comply with their wishes even when they do not agree with his, he is less likely to give direct orders than to give suggestions, he asks for opinions from others, and he shows concern for the feelings of others. Because the democratic leader's method of control is more rewarding to the followers, their loyalty to and affection for him is usually greater than for the authoritarian leader. The larger the group, the more authoritarian the leadership method tends to be (64,72,163,197,336).

Some leaders are "group-oriented," and some, "self-oriented." The group-oriented leader uses a participatory style of leadership, trying to size up the wants and needs of the group members. He then tries to plan activities that will fit their needs. Furthermore, he is willing to sacrifice personal wishes if they conflict with those of the group. By contrast, the self-oriented leader has more difficulty in leading. His followers quickly sense that he is more interested in his own welfare than in that of the group. Because he lacks the loyalty from the group that the group-oriented leader has, he is less likely to retain his status as leader, especially if his method of leading is characterized by aggressiveness (105,158,197,332). Such leaders are "power seekers" in the sense that they are determined to "control others lest others control them." In describing the technique used by such a leader, Barclay (19) has pointed out:

> Even at the nursery school stage he may have learned to do this with charm rather than temper tantrums. ("Jeff, you make pretend you're the captain this time and we'll let you be head of the scouting party in the next game.") As he grows older, if his circle holds values that require it, he may in addition take up a noble cause as justification for his efforts to control. If his principal purpose is to dominate, manage or maneuver others, however, he is still a power-seeker—"a prince with a hero's halo."

When subdivided according to the *activity engaged in*, there are athletic leaders, social leaders, intellectual leaders, or religious leaders. To satisfy the needs of the group, each leader must be a task specialist. This means that he has some distinguishing characteristic that enables him to meet the group's needs better than the other group members. The athletic leader, for example, is superior in athletic ability; the intellectual leader has higher scores on mental tests, better academic standing, and interests of a more intellectual nature; the social leader is superior in appearance, dress, manner, and social skills; and the religious leader has greater interest in religious activities than his followers (94,106,203,336).

And, finally, leaders may be subdivided on the basis of *sex*: there are typical girl leaders and typical boy leaders. The girl leader in adolescence is superior in appearance and social skills but somewhat cool and detached in her attitudes toward the group members: this makes her distant and a bit unattainable, the "cool" big wheel. Boy leaders, by contrast, are the "good guys," who are warm, friendly, and liked by everyone. The girl leader is followed because she has a flair for setting styles and has a generalized prestige in the school, though she is less wanted as a best friend than the boy leader. Because of their more friendly attitudes and because being led by a girl is not

considered sex appropriate for boys, boys are usually selected for leadership roles in activities involving members of both sexes. The one exception to this is social activities where it would be considered sex inappropriate for a boy to be a leader (53,60,74,219,244).

HOW LEADERS ARE MADE

Contrary to popular opinion, leaders are made, not born. There is no evidence to substantiate the belief that a person is a born leader who can step automatically into a leadership role without the training and practice such a role demands.

Case histories of leaders have shown that leadership is a status achieved over a relatively long period of time. Whether the individual's status will be that of a leader or follower depends to a large extent on the role he has played earlier, especially during his childhood (151). Of these roles, the most important are those played in the family group. Figure 5–11 shows the factors that make a leader.

Home Influences The adolescent's attitude toward himself and toward his abilities to be a leader are greatly influenced by *parental attitudes*. As Miles (238) has pointed out:

> Attitudes of parents appear to be crucial factors which are closely related to the social behavior of children. Parents of successful leaders show outstandingly different attitudes from the parents of other groups of children. The contrast is most marked when they are compared with parents of asocial children, especially parents of outcasts and overlooked children.

When the *adolescent's attitudes* toward his family and home are favorable, he will want to participate in family activities. This will give him training that will be of value in leadership roles. While leaders are often more critical of their parents than nonleaders, they are also more companionable with them. Consequently, the family relationships are more successful (109,223,264). *Sibling position* is of great importance in determining the leadership ability of adoles-

FIGURE 5-11 How leaders are made.

cents. Firstborn children are given more responsibility than children born later in the family. This helps the firstborn to learn to assume responsibilities—an essential for all leaders. Nonleaders most often are the youngest members of the family—those who have had to assume least responsibility (45, 159,264).

The most important home factor in the development of leadership is the type of *child-training method* used. The adolescent who has been subjected to strict, authoritarian training in the home learns to submit to authority rather than to exercise it; he learns to be a follower rather than a leader. If he submits meekly to parental authority, he will become a meek follower. Should he, on the other hand, rebel against parental authority, he will develop the habit of rebelling against *all* in authority. He thus becomes a disgruntled follower (163,281).

Adolescents who have been subjected to more democratic child training develop patterns of adjustment in the home which enable them to compete for leadership roles outside the home. A study of the home training of high school leaders led Miles (238) to conclude:

> *In general, parents of successful children are less inclined to protect children from the normal risks of life, to shield them from the normal responsibilities of life, and to prevent them from developing an adequate degree of independence which is so necessary for good mental health and normal functioning in the social group. Also, they tend to be less restrictive in the degree of control which they exercise over the child. Much more leeway is allowed children in making decisions, using judgment and experimenting with new situations. Also, the individual personality is given far more respect—his rights and his opinions are given consideration in the family group. In addition, parents of successful children*

appear to possess superior ability in evaluating forms of child behavior and characteristics of child personality which are desirable for the optimum development of the child himself.

An analysis of *home conditions* favoring the development of leadership has revealed that the following play important roles (22):

1 Work assignments in and out of the home.
2 Praise and reasoning as the preferred corrective measures.
3 Major responsibility for conducting the affairs of the home during some period prior to high school.
4 Outside jobs to supplement the allowance.
5 A home equipped with recreational facilities and frequently opened to the adolescent's friends.
6 Encouragement of interest in both sedentary and active activities.
7 Reasonable freedom of choice in issues involving moral standards.
8 A share in family planning and decisions.
9 The father at home in the evenings. This was especially important in the case of girl leaders.
10 Active in church affairs.

Peer-group Experiences Individuals who, in elementary school, were leaders in non-school groups are more likely to be leaders in adolescence than are those who played the follower role in childhood (22). By the time the child reaches the sixth grade, it is possible to predict with a fair degree of accuracy whether he will be a leader or follower in high school (151). Thus, it becomes apparent that "some of the stronger roots of leadership seem to lie in childhood experiences" (5).

Specific Training for Leadership A number of attempts have been made to train adolescents to play the role of leaders. When a group of high school students were given lectures on leadership qualities and techniques, combined with personal conferences dealing with leadership problems, it was found that the students showed improvement over a control group who had not received this instruction (108).

Other attempts to train adolescents to become leaders have included teaching in diplomacy, with emphasis on the fact that one can get more by requesting than by demanding; reinforcement of the leader's strong points; putting his intelligence to work; better understanding and acceptance of self through group counseling; and development of leadership values, especially personal integrity, consideration of others, and decision making. These studies have reported considerable growth in leadership and social insight (14,65,261).

Because making a leader is never easy, a cautious warning by Barclay (19) is well worth serious consideration:

> *In the final analysis, most of the qualities that are found in a good leader—by that we mean a leader for good—are qualities equally useful to the individual who wants nothing more than to manage his own life well, contributing to the welfare of others through his work but making no effort to hold power and having no compulsion to change society. Parents hopeful of developing a "leader," then, cannot be given a recipe for that product but they can be guided by what is conceded to be useful for rearing children as self-confident, self-aware, perceptive, socially responsible adults.*

DISTINGUISHING CHARACTERISTICS OF LEADERS

Whether an adolescent will have the role of leader or follower will depend upon his qualities *in relation to* similar qualities in the members of the group. If he has qualities that enable him to satisfy the social needs of the group better than the others, he will be selected as their leader (179). That is why leadership is not dependent upon the individual alone but on the situation in which he finds himself. That is why, also, a clique leader may not be a crowd leader or a leader in school affairs (23,188, 219,336).

In our culture, there is a stereotype of a leader that sets the pattern for what the group expects the leader to be (297). The adolescent who most closely conforms to this stereotype has the best chance of becoming a leader. He is the one whose attributes the members of the group desire but never hope to possess (235).

Studies of leadership traits have shown the following to play roles of greater or lesser importance.

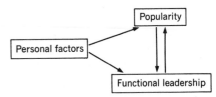

FIGURE 5–12 The interrelationship of personal factors, popularity, and leadership. (Adapted from G. Gardner: Functional leadership and popularity in small groups. *Hum. Relat.*, 1956, **9**, 491–509. Used by permission.)

Popularity A popular person is not necessarily a leader, though leaders are always popular. In fact, they are usually above average in popularity (74,131). Many popular adolescents are liked because of their easygoing ways but they lack other qualities essential to leadership (173). Being liked by others gives the adolescent an opportunity to be known and appreciated by his peers. As a result, he is foremost in their minds when the time comes to choose a leader. Popularity brings with it prestige. Equally important, popularity adds to self-confidence; this enables the adolescent to make use of what abilities he has for the benefit of the group (51,300,312).

Popularity enables the adolescent to influence the attitudes and behavior of others. The more popular he is, the more willing his peers are to follow (34). If he is a good leader, in the sense that he plays his role to the satisfaction of the group members, this will enhance his popularity and, with it, his leadership power. Leadership and popularity are, thus, not only interrelated but their relationship is a circular one (131). This is illustrated in Figure 5–12.

Prestige Popularity brings with it prestige and prestige is enhanced when the popular adolescent is selected as leader (23,81, 285). In a large group, the leader is generally one who has acquired prestige from past experiences. He is not only known to the majority of the group members but is liked and respected by them. A small group, by contrast, gives each member a chance to become known. This means that prestige is a less important factor in the small group than in the large (173). Prestige always en-

hances respect and respect enables the leader to influence his followers. As a result, he can bring better morale into the group, he can reduce tension among the members, he can bring about smoother functioning in the different activities, and he can increase the desire of each member to contribute his share. Good leaders make good groups in terms of group performance and satisfaction of the group members (43,45,183).

The successful leader acquires a halo which enhances his popularity, his prestige, and the respect others have for him (299). As a result, the members of the group attribute to him the qualities they admire; at the same time, they literally shut their eyes to any qualities he may have that they dislike. Furthermore, he is often chosen for leadership roles in activities for which he is not qualified because of the favorable reputation he has acquired. As Marak has pointed out, "A leader's authority extends to many areas not justified by his abilities, after the group members develop conceptions of him as a rewarding person" (218). Should the leader fall short of group expectations, his halo will be tarnished and there will be a decrease in his prestige (139).

Socioeconomic Status As Coleman has pointed out, adolescents "look upward" for their leaders to those whose backgrounds are superior to theirs (81). Consequently, upper-class adolescents dominate school activities (2). Whenever the socioeconomic status of leaders has been investigated, the findings point to the fact that leaders come from higher income brackets than non-leaders (15,76,194,223,274,326). In a study of college girls who belong to sororities, for example, it was found that 90 percent of the girls came from the "big business" group and 56 percent of the leaders from professional families (241). When fraternities and sororities exist, they generally take possession of the leadership positions of the major campus organizations (330).

Skills   A leader must have skills. Skills in one situation may give the individual prestige which, in turn, will facilitate his becoming a leader in situations where his particular skills are not needed (81,223, 305). In high school, for example, it was found in one study that 78 percent of the leaders had earned their letters in high school sports as compared with 64 percent of the nonleaders (80). Social life in adolescence demands new social skills. The adolescent leader must also know how to organize activities and conduct meetings. He must have good work habits and be efficient (51,285).

Of all the skills that play a role of importance in leadership during the adolescent years, skill in conversation stands out as one of the most important. Among older adolescents, especially, verbal facility and forcefulness of expression are essential to leadership. A leader has confidence in his ability to speak and has a pleasing voice. Leaders are generally more talkative than nonleaders (76,285,300).

Social Participation   In both high school and college, adolescents who participate in more than the average number of extracurricular activities are often found among the leaders. Not only do they participate in more activities but they spend more of their time in these activities. Furthermore, they are willing to assume responsibilities instead of merely enjoying themselves. They generally hold more than one position of responsibility, and they serve on committees as well as holding offices in many different groups (15,23,44,74,107,200,300). Transported high school students and off-campus college students are often unable to participate in extracurricular activities because these activities are scheduled at times when they are unable to attend. This adversely af-

fects their being elected to roles of leadership and it makes it impossible for them to accept leadership roles if asked to do so. This is not true, to such a marked extent, of part-time employment (253).

Social Insight   To be a leader, the adolescent must have social insight. This enables him to be keenly alive to situations, to evaluate situations, and to know what kind of action to take. He can then be perceptive of the group needs and be able to satisfy the greatest number or the most important of these needs (29,137,300,320).

The most effective leaders are those who are most familiar with the standards of the group and the degree to which these standards are shared by the group members. The longer the individual has been a member of a group, the more likely he will be to evaluate group opinion accurately (167). And the better he understands people, the better he can get along with them (129).

Ability to understand people and to size up social situations is of little importance in leadership if this ability is not used for the benefit of the group. The leader must be willing to take the group into his confidence and explain the whys and wherefores of his actions. His interest and understanding must be emotionally detached so that he will not act as his "brother's keeper," trying to solve other people's problems or direct their actions unless they ask for his help (331).

Intelligence   While social insight is not dependent upon intelligence alone, social insight accompanied by above-average intelligence is generally found in the adolescent leader. Intelligence is needed if the leader is to take the initiative in suggesting new activities, in directing associates, and in making decisions. How much above the average of the group the intelligence of the leader should be depends upon the activities of the group. A football captain, for example, does not need so high a level of intelligence as the captain of a debating team. Leaders, furthermore, have more mental energy than nonleaders, and they tend to be more liberal in their point of view. Intellectual ability is more important for leaders among boys than among girls (15,43,76,81,94,168,300, 340).

Leaders are, on the whole, superior in their *academic achievement,* though there are some leaders whose academic work falls below that of nonleaders. This is especially true of girls for whom academic achievement is less of an asset than it is for boys. And because leaders must be well accepted, the girl who stands too high academically has little chance of being popular enough to be in line for a leadership role (81,94,168, 300).

Interest Because of their interest in people, leaders extend this interest to politics, world affairs, and social organizations. They are less prejudiced in their attitudes, especially toward minority groups (214). In their recreational interests, leaders show a preference for recreations of the more mature type. For example, they attend movies less than nonleaders and show a preference for the more "sophisticated" type of movie. They are also more interested in art exhibits, ballet, and poetry than are nonleaders (168).

Values The leader must share the values most desired by the group as a whole *at that time.* Even more important, he must conform to these values and guide his behavior by them (223,340). However, because of his favorable status, the leader can be more socially bold in the sense that he deviates somewhat from the group values in his opinions and behavior, and thus brings something new to the group. As a result, he is more colorful and stimulating than followers who are too insecure in their status to deviate (23,145,183,219).

The leader conforms in interpersonal relationships but shows his individuality in his interests. If he is to retain the respect and loyalty of the group, he must know the right amount of conformity and not allow himself to overstep the limits. There are no "social rebels" among leaders except in adolescent groups made up of social rebels, as is true of delinquent gangs (15, 223). In discussing the importance of the

right amount of nonconformity to leadership, Barclay (19) has said:

The rule-breaker and value-creator—either child or adult—is a truly "superior person." He is self-respecting and self-directing. He is not swayed by desire or need for popular approval and sympathy and can survive personal hurt. He is proud but not vain. His really distinguishing feature, however, is his sensitivity in spheres where others are indifferent, his bravery, his willingness to sacrifice for uncommon ends and his self-sufficiency. Although such persons—when devoid of social sense—can act as powers for ill, the great movers and makers of our culture have had this "masterly" quality.

Physical Characteristics In general, leaders are taller than nonleaders. A leader generally has physical energy above that of nonleaders, above-average strength, and better health. Unquestionably health not only influences the individual's attitudes and predisposes him to more sociable behavior, but it also gives him an opportunity for more or less uninterrupted social contacts (94,179, 297,300).

Leaders in both high school and college are, on the average, 8 months younger than nonleaders. This suggests that early sexual maturing has given them an advantage from learning skills and developing self-confidence earlier than their peers (168,203).

Leaders are, on the whole, attractive looking though not necessarily beautiful or handsome. The adolescent who is attractive can feel confident that he is making a good impression on others and he knows that this is an aid to his acceptance by peers of both sexes (74,109,219). Because of the high value placed on sex appropriateness of looks as well as of behavior, the adolescent who conforms to the cultural stereotype for his sex group is more likely to be selected as a leader than the one whose appearance falls short of this stereotype (81). A study of the presidents of student bodies and student councils of men's colleges and universities revealed that there were no "physical monstrosities" among the leaders (46).

It is a generally accepted fact among

adolescents that their leaders must make a good appearance. The reason for this is that adolescents want to be represented by members of the peer group of whom they can be proud. To make a good impression on others, the leader must be nice looking, must wear becoming, stylish clothes, and must be well groomed. This is especially important for leaders of social activities (76, 81,94).

Personality Just as there is no one trait or combination of traits that makes a person popular, so there is no one trait or combination of traits that is always found in leaders. As Jennings (179) has stated:

> Leadership appears not explainable by any personality quality or constellation of traits. Some individuals are found who are as emotionally mature and as resourceful in ideas as the leader . . . yet are not "allowed" the role of leadership nor chosen more than the average citizen of the community. The why of leadership appears to reside in the interpersonal contribution of which the individual becomes capable in a specific setting eliciting such contributions from him.

Certain personality characteristics are invariably found in leaders. The *life goals* of leaders are more structured than are those of nonleaders; they know what they want out of life, now and in the future (168,194). Leaders are *sociable* and *extroverted*; they will bring satisfaction to others (182). They are, thus, *unselfish and outer-bound* rather than selfish and self-bound (43,44,74,141). Among members of both sexes, leaders show a tendency to be more *masculine* than feminine in their personality patterns. They have more traits that are highly valued in males than in females (76).

Leaders are *flexible*; they must be willing to make changes in the organizational structure if it is for the advantage of the group. Rigidity makes it impossible for them to meet the needs of the group (282). They must also be *liberal* and free from biases and prejudices which color their reactions to group members (168). The leader can be counted on to work for the best interests of the group. This *dependability* is one of the outstanding characteristics of the personality pattern of every leader (23,44,141). The leader is a *well-adjusted* individual. This leads to a favorable self-concept and self-confidence (94,182,244). With self-confidence comes a feeling of security and of personal worth which is expressed in the ability to be independent and to make decisions without being unduly swayed by the opinions of others. As a result, the leader can be *socially bold*—an essential to making a contribution to the group (26,171,268, 312).

One imporant aspect of good adjustment is *maturity*. The leader shows his psychological maturity in a number of ways, the most important of which are high frustration tolerance, ability to express hostility tactfully, ability to accept victory or defeat without too much emotion, ability to accept authority, and ability to set realistic goals (8,43,194,244). In addition, he has a reservoir of personal and social resources to provide tolerance in the event of misfortune (340). The leader rarely shows signs of excessive worry or anxiety; he seems basically *happy* (182). Just as there are no freaks in appearance among leaders, so there are no freaks of personality. Fewer *neurotic tendencies* are found among leaders than among nonleaders (66,268,340). Figure 5–13 shows the generally superior personality patterns of leaders.

Mere possession of the traits associated with leadership is not enough; the adolescent must *use* these traits in vital participation in the activities of the group. Using them for personal gain or satisfaction will not result in leadership status. Even the best-adjusted adolescent will not, for example, be selected to play the role of leader if his abilities are used for self-aggrandizement or if he is more concerned with the satisfaction he gets than the satisfaction he is able to provide for the members of the group.

PERSISTENCE OF LEADERSHIP

The popular belief is that "once a leader, always a leader." This is not universally true. Among children, leaders come and go. In adolescence, this is less true; in adulthood, even less true. This may be explained by the fact that traits that make for leadership do not develop early or that opportunities to engage in activities that develop leadership qualities are not found to any extent in the elementary school.

However, a marked relationship between leadership in junior and senior high school exists. Transfer of leadership from high school to college likewise occurs (44, 74,168,188,244,260).

How leadership in school and college is related to success in later life has also been investigated. All studies point to the conclusion that adult leaders held leadership posts in their school and college days far more often than adult nonleaders (44,88, 162). Adult women, for example, who hold many executive positions on boards of charitable institutions and serve on committees in leadership roles had leadership experience in their adolescent days. Business leaders among men, likewise, were usually leaders in their school and college days (274).

To understand why some adolescents who held leadership posts no longer do so while others who never or very rarely were leaders in school become leaders in college or adult life, one must look at the factors favoring persistence and those militating against it.

Factors Favoring Persistence There are many factors favoring persistence of leadership during the adolescent years, the most important of which are described below.

elected or acknowledged by at least one-third of the group Adolescents like to choose their own leaders without adult interference. If the person they choose is satisfactory they are very likely to give him a second, third, or fourth chance to lead them.

strong motivation to be a leader The adolescent who wants to be a leader will do all that he can to comply with the group's wishes to ensure continuation of the role.

flexibility As group interests change, the adolescent must be willing to change his

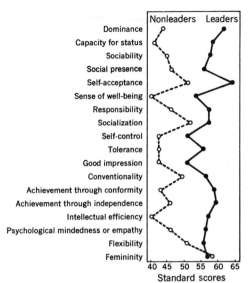

FIGURE 5–13 The personality patterns of leaders are generally superior to those of nonleaders. (Adapted from R. T. Johnson and A. N. Frandsen: The California Psychological Inventory profile of student leaders. *Personnel Guid. J.*, 1962, **41**, 343–345. Used by permission.)

interests and conform to those of the group. Should his abilities not be in line with the new activities favored by the group, he can retain his leadership status only if he can persuade the group to be interested in activities in which he can be a successful leader.

group-oriented attitude To be a successful leader, the adolescent must create the impression that he is selfless, thinking only of the welfare of the group.

conformity to group values As group values change, the adolescent must not only change his own values but he must also model his behavior to conform to the changed values.

competence in prestigeful activities Competence in athletic activities above that of the group members will put a boy in a prominent position that will facilitate selection for leadership roles; sophistication in social activities will do the same for girls.

confidence in ability to lead The adolescent must not only believe that he can succeed as a leader but he must convince others of this. Confidence is developed best by successful past achievements.

knowledge of leadership techniques There are tricks of the trade in leadership as in any other role. The "tricks" of leadership are best learned by participation in leadership activities over a period of time.

democratic family life Some of the most important tricks of leadership, such as assuming responsibilities or making decisions without reliance on others, are learned in a democratic home environment.

socially approved activities The group may derive temporary satisfaction from activities that are socially disapproved of, but if the leader gets them into trouble, they will not want a repetition of his leadership.

early maturing The early maturer has an advantage in that he changes his values and learns more mature patterns of behavior earlier than his peers.

halo effect of leadership If the leader makes good in his role, he wins the reputation of being a good leader. Instead of taking a chance on a "dark horse," his peers will play safe and consider him first when a new leadership role must be filled.

Factors Militating against Persistence The factors militating against persistence of leadership are, for the most part, the opposite of those which favor it. Of the many, the following are the most important.

appointed to lead Because adolescents resent adult interference, they will have a negative attitude toward anyone who is designated as their leader by an outsider. No matter how good a leader he may be, they will not elect him to future leadership roles. This is their way of asserting their independence.

elected or appointed to fill a gap Should a leader withdraw or lose his hold over the

group, the adolescent who is appointed or elected to replace him is usually regarded as a stopgap leader. If he makes good, or if his term of office is long enough to enable him to learn the role so that he can compare favorably with the leader he has replaced, his chances of being selected for future leadership roles will be increased.

weak motivation Some adolescents find the role of leader harder than they had anticipated. While they like the prestige associated with leadership, they would prefer to have fun and let others do the work.

rigidity A person who always feels that he is right and that his way is best will not have the loyalty and respect of the group which are needed if he is to be chosen as a leader again.

self-oriented attitude A leader who is out for personal glory soon discovers that the group resents his selfishness. As a result, he loses the loyalty of the group members. In addition, the morale of the group members becomes so low that they insist upon having a new leader.

individuality in values The adolescent who fails to comply with group standards and tries to become a law unto himself antagonizes the group. Furthermore, the group members may be ashamed to have him represent them because of the unfavorable impression his appearance and behavior create on others.

competence in nonprestigeful activities An outstanding student may be appointed or elected to a leadership role, but if he lacks competence in prestigeful activities, the halo from success in nonprestigeful activities will soon fade and, with it, his chances for future leadership roles.

lack of confidence to play leadership role Authoritarian training in the home or lack of previous experience in the leadership role makes an adolescent fearful of his ability to tackle the new role. If given this role, he is likely to be such a weak leader that the group will replace him with a leader in whom they can have confidence.

changes in group interests No matter how competent the leader, when group interests change to activities which are incompatible with the leader's talents, his chances of retaining the leadership role will depend upon his ability to persuade the group to be interested in activities in which he is competent. Failing to do this, he will be replaced by a leader who is competent in the preferred activities.

bad leadership The leader who cannot win the cooperation of the group or who suggests activities that lead the group into trouble with law-enforcing officers, parents, or teachers will not be selected again. One unfavorable experience is adequate to give him an unfavorable reputation.

late maturing One of the greatest disadvantages of being a late maturer is that the adolescent seems and looks younger than his peers. As they do not want to be represented by a "kid," even the most popular child leader will discover that late maturing will eliminate his chances of being selected as a leader in the adolescent years (19,22,44, 70,81,99,168,186,200,260,339).

status of follower

A follower is an accepted member of a social group whose activities are initiated, stimulated, and sometimes even determined or controlled by the leader. This is true of his interests and opinions as well as of his activities. The follower often does as much or even more for the group *quantitatively* than the leader. But, *qualitatively*, his contributions fall short of those of the leader. Many followers, for example, are willing workers who serve on committees *ad infinitum*. Occasionally, they are "middle leaders" who serve as heads of small committees delegated to carry out part of a larger project. Only occasionally are they elected to major leadership roles. When they are, it is likely to be

a leadership role of little prestige (43,56, 107,183,188).

An adolescent may be a follower because he is perceived by the group members to be less able to meet the needs of the group than the one who is selected as a leader. He either does not have the qualities the members want their leader to have or he has never demonstrated his ability to lead. He may not want to assume responsibilities or he may never have had an opportunity to do so (56,336).

TYPES OF FOLLOWERS

Just as there are different types of leaders, so there are different types of followers. When followers are subdivided according to their *attitudes* toward their role, they may be classed as "voluntary" or "involuntary." The voluntary follower is one who wants to be a follower; he is satisfied with the role he plays and is not anxious to change that role. In fact, he will withdraw his name from a nomination for a leadership role or will ask to be relieved of the responsibility of leadership if appointed. He is satisfied to be a follower either because he does not want to put in the time and effort needed to be a leader or because he has learned, from past experience, that he derives greater satisfaction from being a follower.

The involuntary follower, by contrast, is not satisfied with his role; he wants to be a leader but has not been given the opportunity to be one. This makes him angry and resentful toward members of the group who he feels are discriminating against him. This then leads to an uncooperative attitude toward group activities. In time, this often results in his rejection from the group by the other members. Or he may voluntarily withdraw from the group if he sees some possibility of becoming a leader in another group.

Followers may also be subdivided on the basis of their *contributions* to the group into "constructive" and "destructive" followers. The voluntary followers are usually constructive, and the involuntary, destructive. Constructive followers are imbued with the importance of contributing to the school's or college's social life and of participating in the different extracurricular activities. By dint of their efficiency and energetic participation, they create a demand for their services and are frequently appointed to committees. Because of their contributions, they are well liked and their status is reasonably secure. In fact, any change in status is generally in the direction of greater rather than lesser acceptance (28,163,183).

The destructive followers not only make few contributions to the group but they do much to impede the progress of the group toward its goals. For that reason, they are often called, "tear-downers." They refuse to serve on committees, or if they do serve, they contribute little except criticism of what the other committee members do. They are especially critical of the leader and go out of their way to negate any suggestions he may make. As a result of their critical, uncooperative attitudes, they make themselves disliked; this leads to their rejection. If they are less aggressive about their resentments and literally go on a "sit-down strike" whenever any work is to be done, they are neglected (244).

effects of status on attitudes and behavior

How the adolescent's status in the group affects his behavior, his attitudes, and his personality depends not upon whether he is a leader or a follower but on how satisfied he is with his status. If he is satisfied with the role he is playing, that role will have a very different effect on him than it would if he were dissatisfied with it. Going from a follower's role to a leader's role is a personality-strengthening experience; going from a leader's role to a follower's is a personality-weakening experience (305). Thus, it is apparent that the role the adolescent plays per se is not so important as his attitude toward it.

The leader who is satisfied with his role will be a more active participant in group affairs and more willing to adapt his interests to those of the group than he would be if he were less satisfied with his leadership status. Even though he may miss close friendships with his peers, he is willing to accept this as one of the prices he must pay for successful leadership (75,269,282).

Similarly, contented followers will contribute what they can to the satisfactions of the group, often doing more than their share voluntarily. Recognizing that they do not have the abilities or the motivation to be leaders, and being unwilling to make the sacrifices in terms of work, time, and close personal friendships that the role of leader demands, they are satisfied with their social lives as they are. Like the satisfied leader, they are *socially well-adjusted* people. They not only conform to social expectations but they derive personal satisfaction from the status they have in the group.

By contrast, those who are *socially poorly adjusted* are the dissatisfied leaders and followers. The adolescent who wants to be a follower but is appointed or elected to a leadership status against his will feels uncomfortable and unhappy in the role because he feels inadequate for it. While he may want to be a leader because of the prestige associated with it or because it will be a form of compensation for feelings of personal inadequacy, he is afraid to be a leader. It is a case of "uneasy lies the head that wears the crown." His anxiety is shown by hypersensitivity to the criticisms of disgruntled followers, by fear of introducing any innovations into the group activities, by mood swings from aggressive to affable—depending on the way the group members react to him and his suggestions—and by allowing himself to become emotionally involved in the personal affairs of some of the group members, thus creating the impression that he is playing favorites (75,105, 331).

Sensing that he is not playing his role to the satisfaction of the majority of the group members, such a leader becomes increasingly more anxious and unsure of his abilities. This intensifies the impression he creates in the minds of others that he is a poor leader and his own feeling of inadequacy for the role (75,120,244,269).

Unquestionably the most dissatisfied group member is the adolescent who wants to be a leader, who feels that he has the capacity to play the role better than the person who is a leader, and who resents having to be a follower. If he convinces himself that he is a martyr whose talents are buried by those who are jealous of him, he will become vindictive in his treatment of any group member who criticizes him or his actions (120,269,331).

From this brief survey of the attitudes of adolescents toward the roles they play in the peer group, it should be readily apparent that the popular belief that the higher the status of the adolescent in the peer group, the better his social adjustment, is not always true. A leader who is satisfied with his role does conform more closely to the criteria of good social adjustment than a satisfied follower. But a dissatisfied leader is certainly not as well adjusted socially as a satisfied follower. The most poorly adjusted of all is the dissatisfied follower. Only when the attitude of the adolescent toward the status he has in the group is taken into consideration can his social adjustment be assessed fairly and accurately.

BIBLIOGRAPHY

1 ABERNETHY, E. M:. The effect of sorority pressures on the results of a self-inventory. *J. soc. Psychol.*, 1954, **40**, 177–183.

2 ABRAHAMSON, S.: Our status system and scholastic rewards. *J. educ. Sociol.*, 1952, **25**, 441–450.

3 ALDRICH, M. G.: A follow-up study of social guidance at the college level. *J. appl. Psychol.*, 1949, **33**, 258–264.

4 ALEXANDER, T.: Certain characteristics of self as related to affection. *Child Develpm.*, 1951, **22**, 285–290.

5 ALLEN, P. J.: The leadership pattern. *Amer. sociol. Rev.*, 1952, **17**, 93–96.

6 ALLPORT, G. W.: Prejudice: is it societal or personal? *J. soc. Issues*, 1962, **18**, 120–134.

7 ANASTASI, A., and S. MILLER: Adolescent "prestige factors" in relation to scholastic and socioeconomic variables. *J. soc. Psychol.*, 1949, **29**, 43–50.

8 ARGYRIS, C.: Some characteristics of successful executives. *Personnel J.*, 1953, **32**, 50–55.

9 ARONSON, E., and J. MILLS: The effect of severity of initiation on liking for a group. *J. abnorm. soc. Psychol.*, 1959, **59**, 177–181.

10 AUSUBEL, D. P.: Sociempathy as a function of sociometric status in an adolescent group. *Hum. Relat.*, 1955, **8**, 75–84.

11 AUSUBEL, D. P., and H. M. SCHIFF: Some intrapersonal and interpersonal determinants of individual differences in sociempathic ability among adolescents. *J. soc. Psychol.*, 1955, **41**, 39–56.

12 AUSUBEL, D. P., H. M. SCHIFF, and E. B. GASSER: A preliminary study of developmental trends in sociempathy: accuracy of perception of own and others' sociometric status. *Child Develpm.*, 1952, **23**, 111–128.

13 BACH, M. L.: Factors related to student participation in campus social organizations. *J. soc. Psychol.*, 1961, **54**, 337–348.

14 BAILARD, V.: Developing leadership. *Personnel Guid. J.*, 1953, **32**, 135–138.

15 BAILEY, R. P.: College leaders remember high school. *Sch. Soc.*, 1956, **84**, 89–91.

16 BARBE, W. E.: Peer relationships of children of different intelligence levels. *Sch. Soc.*, 1954, **80**, 60–62.

17 BARCLAY, D.: Friendship's many faces. *The New York Times*, Aug. 13, 1961.

18 BARCLAY, D.: "No one will play with me." *The New York Times*, Oct. 29, 1961.

19 BARCLAY, D.: Leads in developing leadership. *The New York Times*, Feb. 4, 1962.

20 BARKER, R. G.: The social interrelations of strangers and acquaintances. *Sociometry*, 1942, **5**, 169–179.

21 BARNLUND, D. C.: Experiments in leadership training for decision-making discussion groups. *Speech Monogr.*, 1955, **22**, 1–14.

22 BARR, J. A., and K. H. HOOVER: Home conditions and influences associated with high school leaders. *Educ. Admin. Supervis.*, 1957, **43**, 271–279.

23 BASS, B. M., C. R. WURSTER, P. A. DOLL, and D. G. CLAIR: Situational and personality factors in leadership among sorority women. *Psychol. Monogr.*, 1953, **67**, no. 16.

24 BAVELAS, A., and K. LEWIN: Training in democratic leadership. *J. abnorm. soc. Psychol.*, 1943, **37**, 115–119.

25 BEDOIAN, V. H.: Social acceptability and social rejection of the underage, at-age, and overage pupils in the sixth grade. *J. educ. Res.*, 1954, **47**, 513–520.

26 BEER, M., R. BUCKHOUT, M. W. HOROWITZ, and S. LEVY: Some perceived properties of the difference between leaders and non-leaders. *J. Psychol.*, 1959, **47**, 49–56.

27 BEILIN, H.: The pattern of postponability and its relation to social class mobility. *J. soc. Psychol.*, 1956, **44**, 33–48.

28 BEILIN, H., and K. V. BERGIN: The social mobility of a limited urban group and some implications for counseling. *Personnel Guid. J.*, 1956, **34**, 544–552.

29 BELL, G. B., and H. E. HALL: The relationship between leadership and empathy. *J. abnorm. soc. Psychol.*, 1954, **49**, 156–157.

30 BELL, W.: Anomie, social isolation and the class structure. *Sociometry*, 1957, **20**, 105–116.

31 BENDER, I. E., and A. H. HASTORF: The perception of persons: forecasting another person's responses on three personality scales. *J. abnorm. soc. Psychol.*, 1950, **45**, 556–561.

32 BENDIX, R., and F. W. HOWTON: Social mobility and the American business elite. *Brit. J. Social.*, 1957, **8**, 357–369; 1958, **9**, 1–14.

33 BERGER, E. M.: The relation between expressed acceptance of self and expressed acceptance of others. *J. abnorm. soc. Psychol.*, 1952, **47**, 778–782.

34 BERKOWITZ, L.: Social desirability and frequency of influence attempts as factors in leadership choice. *J. Pers.*, 1956, **24**, 424–435.

35 BERNARD, J.: Teen-age culture: an overview. *Ann. Amer. Acad. pol. soc. Sci.*, 1961, **338**, 1–12.

36 BIDDULPH, L. G.: Athletic achievement and the personal and social adjustment of high school boys. *Res. Quart. Amer. Ass. Hlth. Phys. Educ. Recr.*, 1954, **25**, 1–7.

37 BJERSTEDT, A.: The interpretation of sociometric status scores in the classroom. *Acta psychol., Amsterdam*, 1956, **12**, 1–14.

38 BLANCHARD, B. E.: A social acceptance study of transported and non-transported pupils in a rural secondary school. *J. exp. Educ.*, 1947, **15**, 291–303.

39 BONNEY, M. E.: A study of friendship choices in college in relation to church affiliation, in-church preference, family size, and length of enrollment in college. *J. soc. Psychol.*, 1949, **29**, 153–166.

40 BONNEY, M. E.: A sociometric study of the peer acceptance of rural students in three consolidated high schools. *Educ. Admin. Supervis.*, 1951, **11**, 234–240.

41 BONNEY, M. E.: A study of constancy of sociometric ranks among college students over a two-year period. *Sociometry*, 1955, **18**, 531–542.

42 BONNEY, M. E., R. E. HOBLIT, and A. H. DREYER: A study of some factors related to sociometric status in a men's dormitory. *Sociometry*, 1953, **16**, 287–301.

43 BORDEAU, E., R. DALES, and R. CONNOR: Relationship of self-concept to 4-H Club leadership. *Rural Sociol.*, 1963, **28**, 413–418.

44 BORGATTA, E. F., R. F. BALES, and A. S. COUCH: Some findings relevant to the great man theory of leadership. *Amer. sociol. Rev.*, 1954, **19**, 755–759.

45 BOSSARD, J. H. S., and E. S. BOLL: *The sociology of child development.* 3d ed. New York: Harper & Row, 1960.

46 BOWDEN, A. O.: A study of the personality of student leaders in colleges in the United States. *J. abnorm. soc. Psychol.*, 1926, **21**, 149–160.

47 BOWER, E. M., T. A. SHELLHAMER, and J. M. DAILY: School characteristics of male adolescents who later became schizophrenic. *Amer. J. Orthopsychiat.*, 1960, **30**, 712–729.

48 BOWERMAN, C. E., and J. W. KINCH: Changes in family and peer orientation of children between the fourth and tenth grades. *Soc. Forces*, 1959, **37**, 206–211.

49 BRANDT, R. M.: The accuracy of self-estimate: a measure of self-concept reality. *Genet. Psychol. Monogr.*, 1958, **58**, 55–99.

50 BRETSCH, H. S.: Social skills and activities of socially accepted and unaccepted adolescents. *J. educ. Psychol.*, 1952, **43**, 449–458.

51 BRODY, D. S.: A genetic study of sociality patterns of college women. *Educ. psychol. Measmt.*, 1950, **10**, 513–520.

52 BROWN, D.: Factors affecting social acceptance of high-school students. *School Review*, 1954, **62**, 151–155.

53 BROWN, D. G.: Sex-role development in a changing culture. *Psychol. Bull.*, 1958, **55**, 232–242.

54 BROWN, W. H., and L. B. BOND: Social stratification in a sixth grade class. *J. educ. Res.*, 1955, **8**, 539–543.

55 BUCK, R. C.: Acquaintance positions in the

group. *Sociol. soc. Res.*, 1952, **37**, 33–36.

56 BUGENTAL, D. E., and G. F. J. LEHNER: Accuracy of self-perception and group perception as related to two leadership roles. *J. abnorm. soc. Psychol.*, 1958, **56**, 396–398.

57 BÜHLER, C.: School as a phase of human life. *Education*, 1952, **73**, 219–222.

58 BURCHINAL, L., B. GARDNER, and G. R. HAWKES: Children's personality adjustment and the socio-economic status of their families. *J. genet. Psychol.*, 1958, **92**, 149–159.

59 BURGESS, E. W.: Social relations, activities, and personal adjustment. *Amer. J. Sociol.*, 1954, **59**, 352–360.

60 CAMPBELL, W. J.: Preferences of children for others of the same or opposite sex. *Aust. J. Psychol.*, 1955, **7**, 45–51.

61 CANNON, K. L.: Stability of sociometric scores of high school students. *J. educ. Res.*, 1958, **52**, 43–48.

62 CANNON, K. L., R. STAPLES, and H. CARLSON: Personal appearance as a function in social acceptance. *J. Home Econ.*, 1952, **44**, 710–713.

63 CARTER, L., W. HAYTHORN, B. SCHRIVER, and J. LANZETTA: The behavior of leaders and other group members. *J. abnorm. soc. Psychol.*, 1951, **46**, 589–595.

64 CASSEL, R. N.: A constrict validity study of a leadership and a social insight test for 200 college freshmen students. *J. genet. Psychol.*, 1961, **99**, 165–170.

65 CASSEL, R. N., and A. E. SHAFER: An experiment in leadership training. *J. Psychol.*, 1961, **51**, 299–305.

66 CATTELL, R. B., and G. F. STICE: Four formulae for selecting leaders on the basis of personality. *Hum. Relat.*, 1954, **7**, 493–507.

67 CHAMBERS, F. M.: Empathy and scholastic success. *Personnel Guid. J.*, 1957, **36**, 282–284.

68 CHAPIN, P. S.: Sociometric stars as isolates. *Amer. J. Sociol.*, 1950, **56**, 263–267.

69 CHOWDHRY, K., and T. M. NEWCOMB: The relative abilities of leaders and nonleaders to estimate opinions of their own groups. *J. abnorm. soc. Psychol.*, 1952, **47**, 51–57.

70 CHRISTAL, R. E., and J. H. WARD: Predicting leadership ratings from high school activities. *J. educ. Psychol.*, 1959, **50**, 105–110.

71 CHRISTIANSON, J. R., and R. BLACK: Group participation and personality adjustment. *Rural Sociol.*, 1954, **19**, 183–185.

72 CHRISTNER, C. A., and J. K. HEMPHILL: Leader behavior of B-29 commanders and changes in crew members' attitudes toward the crew. *Sociometry*, 1955, **18**, 82–87.

73 CLARKE, H. H., and D. H. CLARKE: Social status and mental health of boys as related to their maturity, structural, and strength characteristics. *Res. Quart. Amer. Ass. Hlth. Phys. Educ. Recr.*, 1961, **32**, 326–334.

74 CLIFFORD, C., and T. S. COHN: The relationship between leadership and personality attributes perceived by followers. *J. soc. Psychol.*, 1964, **64**, 57–64.

75 COATES, C. H., and J. R. PELLEGRIN: Executives and supervisors: contrasting self-conceptions of each other. *Amer. sociol. Rev.*, 1957, **22**, 217–220.

76 COBB, K.: Measuring leadership in college women by free association. *J. abnorm. soc. Psychol.*, 1952, **47**, 126–128.

77 COLE, L., and I. N. HALL: *Psychology of adolescence.* 6th ed. New York: Holt, 1964.

78 COLEMAN, J. S.: The adolescent subculture and academic achievement. *Amer. J. Sociol.*, 1960, **65**, 337–347.

79 COLEMAN, J. S.: Analysis of social structures and simulation of social processes with electronic computers. *Educ. psychol. Measmt.*, 1961, **21**, 203–218.

80 COLEMAN, J. S.: Athletics in high school. *Ann. Amer. Acad. pol. soc. Sci.*, 1961, **338**, 33–43.

81 COLEMAN, J. S.: *The adolescent society.* New York: Free Press, 1961.

82 COLEMAN, J. S.: Teen-agers and their crowd. *PTA Magazine*, 1962, **56**, no. 7, 4–7.

83 COSER, R. L.: Some social functions of laughter. *Hum. Relat.*, 1959, **12**, 171–182.

84 COSER, R. L.: Laughter among colleagues. *Psychiatry*, 1960, **23**, 81–95.

85 COSTER, J. K.: Some characteristics of high school pupils from three income groups. *J. educ. Psychol.*, 1959, **50**, 55–62.

86 CROFT, I. J., and T. G. GRYGIER: Social relationships of truants and juvenile delinquents. *Hum. Relat.*, 1956, **9**, 439–466.

87 CRONBACH, L. J.: Processes affecting scores on "understanding of others" and "assumed similarity." *Psychol. Bull.*, 1955, **52**, 177–193.

88 CROWLEY, J. J.: High-school backgrounds of successful men and women graduates. *School Review*, 1940, **48**, 205–209.

89 CRUICKSHANK, W. M., and G. O. JOHNSON: *Education of exceptional children and youth*. Englewood Cliffs, N. J.: Prentice-Hall, 1958.

90 DAMRIN, D. E.: Family size and sibling age, sex and position as related to certain aspects of adjustment. *J. soc. Psychol.*, 1949, **29**, 98–102.

91 DAVIDS, A., and A. N. PARENTI: Personality, social choice, and adults' perception of these factors in groups of disturbed and normal children. *Sociometry*, 1958, **21**, 212–224.

92 DAVIDSON, H. H., and L. S. GOTTLIEB: The emotional maturity of pre- and postmenarcheal girls. *J. genet. Psychol.*, 1955, **86**, 261–266.

93 DAVIS, J. A.: Correlates of sociometric status among peers. *J. educ. Res.*, 1957, **50**, 561–569.

94 DE HAAN, R. F.: Social leadership. *57th Yearb. Nat. Soc. Stud. Educ.*, 1958, Part 2, 127–143.

95 DE JUNG, J. E., and E. F. GARDNER: The accuracy of self-role perception: a developmental study. *J. exp. Educ.*, 1962, **31**, 27–41.

96 DEVAULT, M. V.: Classroom sociometric mutual pairs and residential proximity. *J. educ. Res.*, 1957, **50**, 605–610.

97 DEXTER, E. S.: Three items related to personality: popularity, nicknames, and homesickness. *J. soc. Psychol.*, 1949, **30**, 155–158.

98 DEXTER, E. S., and B. STEIN: The measurement of leadership in white and Negro students. *J. abnorm. soc. Psychol.*, 1955, **51**, 219–221.

99 DIAMOND, S.: Sex stereotypes and acceptance of sex roles. *J. Psychol.*, 1955, **39**, 385–388.

100 DIMOCK, H. S.: *Rediscovering the adolescent*. New York: Association Press, 1937.

101 DINNEEN, M. A., and R. GARRY: Effect of sociometric seating on a classroom cleavage. *Elem. Sch. J.*, 1956, **56**, 358–362.

102 DITTES, J. E.: Attractiveness of group as function of self-esteem and acceptance by group. *J. abnorm. soc. Psychol.*, 1959, **59**, 77–82.

103 DITTES, J. E., and H. H. KELLEY: Effects of different conditions of acceptance upon conformity to group norms. *J. abnorm. soc. Psychol.*, 1956, **53**, 100–107.

104 DODSON, D. W.: Reassessing values in the present age. *J. educ. Sociol.*, 1958, **32**, 49–61.

105 DUFF, J. C.: Quest for leaders. *J. educ. Sociol.*, 1958, **32**, 91–95.

106 DUNKERLEY, M. D.: A statistical study of leadership among college women. *Stud. Psychol. Psychiat.*, *Catholic University of America*, 1940, **4**, no. 7.

107 DUNPHY, D. C.: The social structure of the urban adolescent peer groups. *Sociometry*, 1963, **26**, 230–246.

108 EICHLER, G. A., and R. R. MERRILL: Can social leadership be improved by instruction in its technique? *J. educ. Sociol.*, 1934, **7**, 233–236.

109 ELKINS, D.: Some factors related to the choice-status of ninety eighth grade children in a school society. *Genet. Psychol. Monogr.*, 1958, **58**, 207–272.

110 EL KOUSSY, A. H.: The characteristics of rural and urban adolescents in Egypt. *Vita hum, Basel*, 1960, **3**, 219–222.

111 ETZIONI, A.: Lower levels of leadership in industry. *Sociol. soc. Res.*, 1959, **43**, 209–212.

112 EXLINE, R. V.: Group climate as a factor in the relevance and accuracy of social perception. *J. abnorm. soc. Psychol.*, 1957, **55**, 382–388.

113 EXLINE, R. V.: Interrelations among two dimensions of sociometric status, group congeniality, and accuracy of social perception. *Sociometry*, 1960, **23**, 85–101.

114 FAUST, M. S.: Developmental maturity as a determinant in prestige of adolescent girls. *Child Develpm.*, 1960, **31**, 173–184.

115 FEINBERG, M. R.: Relation of background experience to social acceptance. *J. abnorm. soc. Psychol.*, 1953, **48**, 206–214.

116 FEINBERG, M. R.: Stability of sociometric status in two adolescent class groups. *J. genet. Psychol.*, 1964, **104**, 83–87.

117 FEINBERG, M. R., M. SMITH, and R. SCHMIDT: An analysis of expressions used by adolescents at varying economic levels to describe accepted and rejected peers. *J. genet. Psychol.*, 1958, **93**, 133–148.

118 FESTERHEIM, H., and M. E. TRESSELT: The influence of value systems on the perception of people. *J. abnorm. soc. Psychol.*, 1953, **48**, 93–98.

119 FEY, W. F.: Acceptance of others and its relation to acceptance of self and others. *J. abnorm. soc. Psychol.*, 1955, **50**, 274–276.

120 FIEDLER, F. E.: A note on leadership theory: the effect of social barriers between leaders and followers. *Sociometry*, 1957, **20**, 87–94.

121 FIEDLER, F. E., W. G. WARRINGTON, and F. J. BLAISDELL: Unconscious attitudes as correlates of sociometric choice in a social group. *J. abnorm. soc. Psychol.*, 1952, **47**, 790–796.

122 FIELDS, S. J.: Discrimination of facial expression and its relation to personal adjustment. *J. soc. Psychol.*, 1953, **38**, 63–71.

123 FLANDERS, N. A., and S. HAVUMAKI: The effect of teacher pupil contacts involving praise on the sociometric choices of students. *J. educ. Psychol.*, 1960, **51**, 65–68.

124 FORLANO, G.: Measuring the quality of social acceptability in some ninth grade core and noncore classes. *High School J.*, 1954, **38**, 12–16.

125 FRANKEL, G.: Acceptance and rejection in membership. *Group*, 1954, **16**, 11–16.

126 FREEDMAN, L., and A. B. HOLLINGSHEAD: Neurosis and social class. *Amer. J. Psychiat.*, 1957, **113**, 769–775.

127 FRENCH, E. G., and I. CHADWICK: Some characteristics of affiliation motivation. *J. abnorm. soc. Psychol.*, 1956, **52**, 296–300.

128 FROMM-REICHMANN, E.: Loneliness. *Psychiatry*, 1959, **22**, 1–15.

129 GAGE, N. L.: Accuracy of social perception and effectiveness in interpersonal relationships. *J. Pers.*, 1953, **22**, 128–141.

130 GALLAGHER, J. J.: Social status of children related to intelligence, propinquity and social perception. *Elem. Sch. J.*, 1958, **58**, 225–231.

131 GARDNER, G.: Functional leadership and popularity in small groups. *Hum. Relat.*, 1956, **9**, 491–509.

132 GERARD, H. B.: Some effects of status, role clarity, and group goal clarity upon the individual's reactions to group process. *J. Pers.*, 1957, **25**, 475–488.

133 GESELL, A., F. L. ILG, and L. B. AMES: *Youth: the years from ten to sixteen.* New York: Harper & Row, 1956.

134 GEWIRTZ, J. L., and D. M. BAER: The effect of brief social deprivation on behaviors for a social reinforcer. *J. abnorm. soc. Psychol.*, 1958, **56**, 49–56.

135 GIBB, C. A.: The principles and traits of leadership. *J. abnorm. soc. Psychol.*, 1947, **42**, 267–284.

136 GILBERT, G. M.: Stereotype persistence and change among college students. *J. abnorm. soc. Psychol.*, 1951, **46**, 245–254.

137 GILCHRIST, J. W.: Social psychology and group processes. *Annu. Rev. Psychol.*, 1959, **10**, 233–264.

138 GOERTZEN, S. M.: Factors relating to opinions of seventh grade children regarding the acceptability of certain behaviors in the peer group. *J. genet. Psychol.*, 1959, **94**, 29–34.

139 GOLD, M.: Power in the classroom. *Sociometry*, 1958, **21**, 50–60.

140 GOODCHILDS, J. D.: Effects of being witty on position in the social structure of a small group. *Sociometry*, 1959, **22**, 261–272.

141 GORDON, L. V.: Personal factors in leadership. *J. soc. Psychol.*, 1952, **36**, 245–248.

142 GOSLIN, D. A.: Accuracy of self perception and social acceptance. *Sociometry*, 1962, **25**, 283–296.

143 GOUGH, H. G.: On making a good impression. *J. educ. Res.*, 1952, **46**, 33–42.

144 GOUGH, H. G.: Predicting social participation. *J. soc. Psychol.*, 1952, **35**, 227–233.

145 GOWAN, J. C.: The interest patterns of student leaders. *Educ. psychol. Measmt.*, 1954, **14**, 151–155.

146 GRACE, H. A., and N. L. BOOTH: Is the "gifted" child a social isolate? *Peabody J. Educ.*, 1958, **35**, 195–196.

147 GREEN, T. C.: A comparison of status on two tests of social acceptability. *J. educ. Res.*, 1958, **51**, 493–503.

148 GRONLUND, N. E.: Acquaintance span and sociometric status. *Sociometry*, 1955, **18**, 62–68.

149 GRONLUND, N. E.: Sociometric status and sociometric perception. *Sociometry*, 1955, **18**, 122–128.

150 GRONLUND, N. E., and L. ANDERSON: Personality characteristics of socially accepted, socially neglected, and socially rejected junior high school pupils. *Educ. Admin. Supervis.*, 1957, **43**, 329–338.

151 GRONLUND, N. E., and W. S. HOLMLUND: The value of elementary school sociometric status scores for predicting pupils' adjustment in high school. *Educ. Admin. Supervis.*, 1958, **44**, 255–260.

152 GRONLUND, N. E., and A. P. WHITNEY: Relation between pupils' social acceptability in the classroom, in the school, and in the neighborhood. *School Review*, 1956, **64**, 267–271.

153 GUSTAD, J. W.: Changes in social attitudes and behavior: a review of the literature. *Educ. psychol. Measmt.*, 1951, **11**, 87–102.

154 HALE, C. J.: Physiological maturity of Little League baseball players. *Res. Quart. Amer. Ass. Hlth. Phys. Educ. Recr.*, 1956, **27**, 276–284.

155 HALPERN, H. M.: Empathy, similarity and self-satisfaction. *J. consult. Psychol.*, 1955, **19**, 449–452.

156 HAND, H. C.: Do school costs drive out the youth of the poor? *Progressive Educ.*, 1951, **28**, 89–93.

157 HARDY, K. R.: Determinants of conformity and attitude change. *J. abnorm. soc. Psychol.*, 1957, **54**, 289–294.

158 HARE, A. P.: Situation differences in leader behavior. *J. abnorm. soc. Psychol.*, 1957, **55**, 132–133.

159 HARRIS, D. B., A M. ROSE, K. E. CLARK, and F. VALASEK: Personality differences between responsible and less responsible children. *J. genet. Psychol.*, 1955, **87**, 103–106.

160 HARVEY, O. J., and C. CONSALVI: Status and conformity to pressure in informal groups. *J. abnorm. soc. Psychol.*, 1960, **60**, 182–187.

161 HARVEY, O. J., H. H. KELLEY, and M. M. SHAPIRO: Reactions to unfavorable evaluations of self made by other persons. *J. Pers.*, 1957, **25**, 393–411.

162 HAVIGHURST, R. J.: The social competence of middle-aged people. *Genet. Psychol. Monogr.* 1957, **56**, 297–375.

163 HAYTHORN, W., A. COUCH, D. HAEFNER, P. LANGHAM, and L. F. CARTER: The behavior of authoritarian and equalitarian personalities in groups. *Hum. Relat.*, 1956, **9**, 57–74.

164 HEATHERS, G: Acquiring dependence and independence: a theoretical orientation. *J. genet. Psychol.*, 1955, **87**, 277–291.

165 HIGGIN, G.: The effect of reference group functions on social status ratings. *Brit. J. Psychol.*, 1954, **45**, 88–93.

166 HIMMELWEIT, H. T., A. H. HALSEY, and A. N. OPPENHEIM: The views of adolescents on some aspects of the social class structure. *Brit. J. Sociol.* 1952, **3**, 148–172.

167 HITES, R. W., and D. T. CAMPBELL: A test of ability of fraternity leaders to estimate group opinion. *J. soc. Psychol.*, 1950, **32**, 95–100.

168 HODGES, H. M.: Campus leaders and non-leaders. *Sociol. soc. Res.*, 1953, **37**, 251–255.

169 HOLLINGSHEAD, A. DE B.: *Elmtown's youth.* New York: Wiley, 1949.

170 HOLLINGWORTH, L. S.: Personality and adjustment as determiners and correlates of intelligence. *39th Yearb. Nat. Soc. Stud. Educ.*, 1940, 271–275.

171 HOLTZMAN, W. H.: Adjustment and leadership: a study of the Rorschach Test. *J. soc. Psychol.*, 1952, **36**, 179–189.

172 HORROCKS, J. E.: *The psychology of adolescence.* 2d ed. Boston: Houghton Mifflin, 1962.

173 HORROCKS, J. E., and B. A. WEAR: An analysis of interpersonal choice relationships of college students. *J. soc. Psychol.*, 1953, **38**, 87–98.

174 HUREWITZ, P.: The neutral isolate: some personality, behavioral and role perception dynamics compared with a group of sociometric leaders. *Dissert. Abstr.*, 1961, **22**, Part 1, 6630.

175 HUTSON, P. W., and D. R. KOVAR: Some problems of senior high-school pupils in their recreation. *Educ. Admin. Supervis.*, 1942, **28**, 503–519.

176 JANDA, K. F.: Towards the explication of the concept of leadership in terms of the concept of power. *Hum. Relat.*, 1960, **13**, 345–363.

177 JARECKY, R. K.: Identification of the socially gifted. *Except. Children*, 1959, **25**, 415–419.

178 JENKINS, W. W.: An experimental study of the relationship of legitimate and illegitimate birth status to school and personal and social adjustment of Negro children. *Amer. J. Sociol.*, 1958, **64**, 169–173.

179 JENNINGS, H. H.: *Leadership and isolation: a study of personality in interpersonal relationships.* New York: Longmans, 1950.

180 JERSILD, A. T.: *The psychology of adolescence.* 2d ed. New York: Macmillan, 1963.

181 JOHNSON, E. E.: Student ratings of popularity and scholastic ability of their peers and actual scholastic performance of those peers. *J. soc. Psychol.*, 1958, **47**, 127–132.

182 JOHNSON, R. T., and A. N. FRANDSEN: The California Psychological Inventory profile of student leaders. *Personnel Guid. J.* 1962, **41**, 343–345.

183 JONES, M. C.: A study of socialization patterns at the high school level. *J. genet. Psychol.*, 1958, **93**, 87–111.

184 JONES, M. C.: A comparison of the attitudes and interests of ninth-grade students over two decades. *J. educ. Psychol.*, 1960, **51**, 175–186.

185 JONES, M. C., and H. E. JONES: Factors associated with prominence in extracurricular activities at the high-school level. *Amer. Psychologist*, 1949, **4**, 251.

186 JONES, M. C., and P. H. MUSSEN: Self-conceptions, motivations, and interpersonal attitudes of early- and late-maturing girls. *Child Develpm.*, 1958, **29**, 491–501.

187 KATES, S. L., and L. N. DIAB: Authoritarian ideology and attitudes on parent-child relationships. *J. abnorm. soc. Psychol.*, 1955, **51**, 13–16.

188 KATZ, E., P. M. BLAU, M. L. BROWN, and F. L. STRODTBECK: Leadership stability and social change: an experiment with small groups. *Sociometry*, 1957, **20**, 36–50.

189 KEISLAR, E. R.: A distinction between social acceptance and prestige among adolescents. *Child Develpm.*, 1953, **24**, 275–283.

190 KEISLAR, E. R.: Peer group ratings of high school pupils with high and low school marks. *J. exp. Educ.*, 1955, **23**, 375–378.

191 KEISLAR, E. R.: The generalization of prestige among adolescent boys. *Calif. J. educ. Res.*, 1959, **10**, 153–156.

192 KEISLAR, E. R.: Experimental development of "like" and "dislike" of others among adolescent girls. *Child Develpm.*, 1961, **32**, 59–66.

193 KELLEY, H. H.: The warm-cold variable in first impressions of persons. *J. Pers.*, 1950, **18**, 431–439.

194 KELLY, J. A.: Study of leadership in two contrasting groups. *Sociol. Rev.*, 1963, **11**, 323–335.

195 KIDD, J. W.: An analysis of social rejection in a college men's residence hall. *Sociometry*, 1951, **14**, 226–234.

196 KIDD, J. W.: Personality traits as barriers to acceptability in a college men's residence hall. *J. soc. Psychol.*, 1953, **38**, 127–130.

197 KIPNIS, D.: The effects of leadership style and leadership power upon the inducement

of an attitude change. *J. abnorm. soc. Psychol.*, 1958, **57**, 173–180.

198 KLAUSNER, S. Z.: Social class and self concept. *J. soc. Psychol.*, 1953, **38**, 201–208.

199 KROGMAN, W. M.: Maturation age of 55 boys in the Little League World Series. *Res. Quart. Amer. Ass. Hlth. Phys. Educ. Recr.*, 1959, **30**, 54–56.

200 KRUMBOLTZ, J. D.: The relation of extracurricular participation to leadership criteria. *Personnel Guid. J.*, 1957, **35**, 307–314.

201 KUHLEN, R. G.: *The psychology of adolescent development.* 2d ed. New York: Harper & Row, 1963.

202 KUHLEN, R. G., and B. J. LEE: Personality characteristics and social acceptability in adolescence. *J. educ. Psychol.*, 1943, **34**, 321–340.

203 LATHAM, A. J.: The relationship between pubertal status and leadership in junior high school boys. *J. genet. Psychol.*, 1951, **78**, 185–194.

204 LEHMANN, T. B., and R. L. SOLOMON: Group characteristics as revealed in sociometric patterns and personality ratings. *Sociometry*, 1952, **15**, 7–90.

205 LESSER, G. S.: The relationships between various forms of aggression and popularity among lower-class children. *J. educ. Res.*, 1959, **50**, 20–25.

206 LEVINE, G. N., and L. A. SUSSMANN: Social class and sociability in fraternity pledging. *Amer. J. Sociol.*, 1960, **65**, 391–399.

207 LEVINSON, B. M.: The inner life of the extremely gifted child, as seen from the clinical setting. *J. genet. Psychol.*, 1961, **99**, 83–88.

208 LIDDLE, G.: Overlap among desirable and undesirable characteristics in gifted children. *J. educ. Psychol.*, 1958, **49**, 219–228.

209 LIDDLE, G.: The California Psychological Inventory and certain social and personal factors. *J. educ. Psychol.*, 1958, **49**, 144–149.

210 LINDZEY, G., and J. A. URDAN: Personality and social choice. *Sociometry*, 1954, **17**, 47–63.

211 LIVSON, N., and W. C. BRONSON: An exploration of patterns of impulse control in early adolescence. *Child Develpm.*, 1961, **32**, 75–88.

212 LOBAN, W.: A study of social sensitivity (sympathy) among adolescents. *J. educ. Psychol.*, 1953, **44**, 102–112.

213 LUFT, J.: Monetary value and the perception of persons. *J. soc. Psychol.*, 1957, **46**, 245–251.

214 LUNDBERG, G. A., and L. DICKSON: Selective association among ethnic groups in a high-school population. *Amer. sociol. Rev.*, 1952, **17**, 23–35.

215 LUNDY, R. M.: Self perceptions and descriptions of opposite sex sociometric choices. *Sociometry*, 1956, **19**, 272–277.

216 LUNDY, R. M., W. KATKOUSKY, R. L. CROWELL, and D. J. SHOEMAKER: Self acceptability and descriptions of sociometric choices. *J. abnorm. soc. Psychol.*, 1955, **51**, 260–262.

217 MALPASS, L. F., and E. D. FITZPATRICK: Social facilitation as a factor in reaction to humor. *J. soc. Psychol.*, 1959, **50**, 295–303.

218 MARAK, G. E.: The evolution of leadership structure. *Sociometry*, 1964, **27**, 174–182.

219 MARKS, J. B.: Interests and leadership among adolescents. *J. genet. Psychol.*, 1957, **91**, 163–172.

220 MARSHALL, H. R.: Some factors associated with social acceptance in women's groups. *J. Home Econ.*, 1957, **49**, 173–176.

221 MARSHALL, H. R.: Prediction of social acceptance in community youth groups. *Child Develpm.*, 1958, **29**, 173–184.

222 MARSHALL, H. R., and B. R. MC CANDLESS: Relationships between dependence on adults and social acceptance by peers. *Child Develpm.*, 1957, **28**, 413–419.

223 MARTIN, W. E., N. GROSS, and J. G. DARLEY: Studies of group behavior: leaders, followers, and isolates in small organized groups. *J. abnorm. soc. Psychol.*, 1952, **47**, 838–842.

224 MAYO, D. G.: Peer ratings and halo. *Educ. psychol. Measmt.*, 1956, **16**, 317–323.

225 MAYO, S. C.: Age profiles of social participation in rural areas of Wake County, N.C. *Rural Sociol.*, 1950, **15**, 242–251.

226 MC ARTHUR, C.: Personalities of public and private school boys. *Harv. educ. Rev.*, 1954, **24**, 256–262.

227 MC CANDLESS, B. R., C. B. BILOUS, and H. L. BENNETT: Peer popularity and dependence on adults in preschool-age socialization. *Child Develpm.*, 1961, **32**, 511–518.

228 MC CARY, J. L.: Ethnic and cultural reactions to frustration. *J. Pers.*, 1950, **18**, 321–336.

229 MC CLELLAND, D. C., J. F. STURR, R. H. KNAPP, and W. H. WENDT: Obligations to self and society in the United States and Germany. *J. abnorm. soc. Psychol.*, 1958, **56**, 245–255.

230 MC CRAW, L. W., and J. W. TOLBERT: Sociometric status and athletic ability of junior-high-school boys. *Res. Quart. Amer. Ass. Hlth. Phys. Educ. Recr.*, 1953, **24**, 72–80.

231 MC GUIRE, C.: Family and age-mates in personality formation. *Marriage fam. Living*, 1953, **15**, 17–23.

232 MC GUIRE, C., and R. A. CLARK: Age-mate acceptance and indices of peer status. *Child Develpm.*, 1952, **23**, 141–154.

233 MC GUIRE, C., and G. D. WHITE: Social-class influences on discipline at school. *Educ. Leadership*, 1957, **12**, 229–231, 234–236.

234 MC INTYRE, C. J.: Acceptance by others and its relation to acceptance of self and others. *J. abnorm. soc. Psychol.*, 1952, **47**, 624–625.

235 MEDALIA, N. Z.: Authoritarianism, leader acceptance, and group cohesion. *J. abnorm. soc. Psychol.*, 1955, **51**, 207–213.

236 MEEK, L. H.: *The personal-social development of boys and girls with implications for secondary education.* New York: Progressive Education Association, 1940.

237 MENZEL, H.: Public and private conformity under different conditions of acceptance in the group. *J. abnorm. soc. Psychol.*, 1957, **55**, 398–402.

238 MILES, K. A.: Relationship between certain factors in the home background and the quality of leadership shown by children. Reported by J. E. Anderson: Parents' attitudes on child behavior: a report of three studies. *Child Develpm.*, 1946, **17**, 91–97.

239 MILL, C. R.: Personality patterns of sociometrically selected and sociometrically rejected male college students. *Sociometry*, 1953, **16**, 151–167.

240 MILLER, R. V.: Social status and sociempathic differences. *Except. Children*, 1956, **23**, 114–119.

241 MUELLER, J. H., and K. H. MUELLER: Socioeconomic background and campus success. *Educ. psychol. Measmt.*, 1945, **3**, 143–150.

242 MULDOON, J. F.: The concentration of liked and disliked members in groups and the relationship of concentration to group cohesiveness. *Sociometry*, 1955, **18**, 73–81.

243 NAEGELE, K. N.: Friendship and acquaint-

ances: an exploration of some social distinctions. *Harv. educ. Rev.*, 1958, **28**, 232–252.

244 NELSON, P. D.: Similarities and differences among leaders and followers. *J. soc. Psychol.*, 1964, **63**, 161–167.

245 NEUGARTEN, B. L.: Social class and friendship among school children. *Amer. J. Sociol.*, 1946, **51**, 305–313.

246 NEWCOMB, T. M.: The prediction of interpersonal attraction. *Amer. Psychologist*, 1956, **11**, 575–586.

247 NORTHWAY, M. L.: Sociometry and some challenging problems of social relationships. *Sociometry*, 1946, **9**, 187–198.

248 NYE, I., J. F. SHORT, and V. J. OLSON: Socioeconomic status and delinquent behavior. *Amer. J. Sociol.*, 1958, **63**, 381–389.

249 OMWAKE, K. T.: The relation between acceptance of self and acceptance of others shown by three personality inventories. *J. consult. Psychol.*, 1954, **18**, 443–446.

250 ORZACK, L. H.: Preference and prejudice patterns among rural and urban schoolmates. *Rural Sociol.*, 1956, **21**, 29–33.

251 PASTORE, N.: Attributed characteristics of liked and disliked persons. *J. soc. Psychol.*, 1960, **52**, 157–163.

252 PASTORE, N.: A note on changing toward liked and disliked persons. *J. soc. Psychol.*, 1960, **52**, 173–175.

253 PAULEY, B. G.: The effects of transportation and part-time employment upon participation in school activities, school offices held, acceptability for leadership positions and grade point average among high school seniors. *J. educ. Res.*, 1958, **52**, 3–9.

254 PECK, R. F., and C. GALLIANI: Intelligence, ethnicity, and social roles in adolescent society. *Sociometry*, 1962, **25**, 64–72.

255 PERKINS, H. V.: Teachers' and peers' perceptions of children's self-concepts. *Child Develpm.*, 1958, **29**, 203–220.

256 PHELPS, H. R., and J. E. HORROCKS: Factors influencing informal groups of adolescents. *Child Develpm.*, 1958, **29**, 69–86.

257 PHILLIPS, B. E.: Impact of pupil mobility on the schools. *Educ. Admin. Supervis.*, 1957, **43**, 101–107.

258 PHILLIPS, E. L., S. SHENKER, and P. REVITZ: The assimilation of the new child into the group. *Psychiatry*, 1951, **14**, 319–325.

259 POWELL, R. M.: The nature and extent of group organizations in a girls' dormitory: a sociometric investigation. *Sociometry*, 1951, **14**, 317–339.

260 PRYER, M. W., A. W. FLINT, and B. M. BASS: Group effectiveness and consistency of leadership. *Sociometry*, 1962, **25**, 391–397.

261 PTACEK, P. H.: A university's attempt to counsel student leaders. *J. higher Educ.*, 1957, **28**, 137–142.

262 RADKE-YARROW, M. J., and B. LANDE: Personality correlates of differential reactions to minority group belonging. *J. soc. Psychol.*, 1953, **38**, 253–272.

263 RAINWATER, L.: A study of personality differences between middle and lower class adolescents: the Sconzi Test in culture-personality research. *Genet. Psychol. Monogr.*, 1956, **54**, 3–86.

264 REALS, W. H.: Leadership in high school. *School Review*, 1938, **46**, 523–531.

265 REILLY, J. W., and F. P. ROBINSON: Studies of popularity in college: II: Do dormitory arrangements affect popularity? *Educ. psychol. Measmt.*, 1947, **7**, 327–330.

266 REISSMAN, L.: Class, leisure, and social participation. *Amer. sociol. Rev.*, 1954, **19**, 76–84.

267 REMMERS, H. H., and D. H. RADLER: *The American teenager*. Indianapolis: Bobbs-Merrill, 1957.

268 RICH, H. M., and N. G. HANAWALT: Leadership as related to the Bernreuter personality measures: V. Leadership among adult women in social activities. *J. soc. Psychol.*, 1952, **36**, 141–153.

269 ROCK, M. L., and E. N. HAY: Investigation of the use of tests as a predictor of leadership and group effectiveness in a job evaluation situation. *J. soc. Psychol.*, 1953, **38**, 109–119.

270 ROFF, M., and D. S. BRODY: Appearance and choice status during adolescence. *J. Psychol.*, 1953, **36**, 347–356.

271 ROSE, A. M.: Reference groups of rural high school youth. *Child Develpm.*, 1956, **27**, 351–363.

272 ROSE, A. M.: Attitudinal correlates of social participation. *Soc. Forces*, 1959, **37**, 202–206.

273 ROSE, G., N. FRANKEL, and W. KERR: Empathic and sociometric status among young

teen-agers. *J. genet. Psychol.*, 1956, **89**, 277–278.

274 ROSS, A. D.: Control and leadership in women's groups. *Soc. Forces*, 1958, **37**, 124–131.

275 ROSS, M. G., and C. E. HENDRY: *New understanding of leadership.* New York: Association Press, 1957.

276 SARASON, S. B., and T. T. GLADWIN: Psychological and cultural problems in mental subnormality: a review of research. *Genet. Psychol. Monogr.*, 1958, **57**, 3–284.

277 SATTERLEE, R. L.: Sociometric analysis and personality adjustment. *Calif. J. educ. Res.*, 1955, **6**, 181–184.

278 SCANDRETTE, O. C.: Social distance and degree of acquaintance. *J. educ. Res.*, 1958, **51**, 367–372.

279 SCHIFF, H.: Judgmental response sets in the perception of sociometric status. *Sociometry*, 1954, **17**, 207–227.

280 SCHOEPPE, A.: Sex differences in adolescent socialization. *J. soc. Psychol.*, 1953, **38**, 175–185.

281 SEARS, R. R., E. E. MACCOBY, and H. LEVIN: *Patterns of child rearing.* New York: Harper & Row, 1957.

282 SEEMAN, M.: Social mobility and administrative behavior. *Amer. sociol. Rev.*, 1958, **23**, 633–642.

283 SEIDLER, M. B., and M. J. RAVITZ: A Jewish peer group. *Amer. J. Sociol*, 1955, **61**, 11–15.

284 SEWELL, W. H., and A. O. HALLER: Factors in the relationship between social status and the personality adjustment of the child. *Amer. sociol. Rev.*, 1959, **24**, 511–520.

285 SHEARS, L. W.: The dynamics of leadership in adolescent school groups. *Brit. J. Psychol.*, 1953, **44**, 232–242.

286 SHELDON, P. M.: Isolation as a characteristic of highly gifted children. *J. educ. Sociol.*, 1958, **32**, 215–221.

287 SHERIF, M., B. J. WHITE, and O. J. HARVEY: Status in experimentally produced groups. *Amer. J. Sociol.*, 1955, **60**, 370–379.

288 SILVERMAN, S. S.: Clothing and appearance: their psychological implications for teen-age girls. *Teach. Coll. Contr. Educ.*, 1945 no. 912.

289 SIMPSON, R. L., and I. H. SIMPSON: The school, the peer group and adolescent development. *J. educ. Sociol.*, 1958, **32**, 37–41.

290 SINGER, A.: Certain aspects of personality and their relation to certain group modes, and consistency of friendship choice. *J. educ. Res.*, 1951, **45**, 33–42.

291 SKUBIC, S.: A study of acquaintanceship and social status in physical education classes. *Res. Quart. Amer. Ass. Hlth. Phys. Educ. Recr.*, 1949, **20**, 80–87.

292 SLATER, P. E.: Role differentiation in small groups. *Amer. sociol. Rev.*, 1955, **20**, 300–310.

293 SMITH, A. J.: Similarity of values and its relation to acceptance and the projection of similarity. *J. Psychol.*, 1957, **43**, 251–260.

294 SMITH, G. H.: Personality scores and the personal distance effect. *J. soc. Psychol.*, 1954, **39**, 57–62.

295 SMUCKER, O.: Prestige status stratification on a college campus. *Appl. Anthrop.*, 1947, **6**, 20–27.

296 SOMMER, R., and L. M. KILLIAN: Areas of value difference: Negro-white relations. *J. soc. Psychol.*, 1954, **39**, 237–244.

297 STAGNER, R.: Stereotypes of workers and executives among college men. *J. abnorm. soc. Psychol.*, 1950, **45**, 743–748.

298 STENDLER, C. B.: The learning of certain secondary drives by Parisian and American children. *Marriage fam. Living*, 1954, **16**, 195–200.

299 STEPHENSON, T. E.: The leader-follower relationship. *Sociol. Rev.*, 1959, **7**, 179–195.

300 STOGDILL, R. M.: Personal factors associated with leadership: a survey of the literature. *J. Psychol.*, 1948, **25**, 35–71.

301 STOLZ, H. R., and L. M. STOLZ: *Somatic development of adolescent boys.* New York: Macmillan, 1951.

302 STONE, C. L.: Sorority status and personality adjustment. *Amer. sociol. Rev.*, 1951, **16**, 538–541.

303 STONE, C. L.: Some family characteristics of socially active and inactive teenagers. *Family Life Coordinator*, 1960, **8**, 53–57.

304 STUBBLEFIELD, R. L.: Children's emotional problems aggravated by family moves. *Amer. J. Orthopsychiat.*, 1955, **25**, 120–126.

305 SUTTON-SMITH, B., and P. GUMP: Games and status experience. *Recreation*, 1955, **48**, 172–174.

306 SUTTON-SMITH, B., and B. G. ROSENBERG:

Peer perceptions of impulsive behavior. *Merrill-Palmer Quart.*, 1961, **7**, 233–238.

307 TAFT, R.: The ability to judge people. *Psychol. Bull.*, 1955, **52**, 1–23.

308 TAGIURI, R.: The perception of feelings among members of small groups. *J. soc. Psychol.*, 1957, **46**, 219–227.

309 TALLAND, G. A.: The assessment of group opinion by leaders, and their influence on its formation. *J. abnorm. soc. Psychol.*, 1954, **49**, 431–434.

310 TAYLOR, F. K.: Awareness of one's social appeal. *Hum. Relat.*, 1956, **9**, 47–56.

311 TAYLOR, F. K.: Display of dyadic emotions. *Hum. Relat.*, 1957, **10**, 257–262.

312 TERRELL, G., and J. SHREFFLER: A developmental study of leadership. *J. educ. Res.*, 1958, **52**, 69–72.

313 THEODORSON, G. A.: The relationship between leadership and popularity roles in small groups. *Amer. sociol. Rev.*, 1957, **22**, 58–67.

314 THORPE, J. G.: An investigation into some correlates of sociometric status within school classes. *Sociometry*, 1955, **18**, 49–61.

315 TRYON, C. M.: Evaluation of adolescent personality by adolescents. *Monogr. Soc. Res. Child Develpm.*, 1939, **4**, no. 4.

316 TURNER, R. H.: Preoccupation with competitiveness and social acceptance among American and English college students. *Sociometry*, 1960, **23**, 307–325.

317 TURNER, W. D.: Altruism and its measurement in children. *J. abnorm. soc. Psychol.*, 1948, **43**, 502–513.

318 UGUREL-SEMIN, R.: Moral behavior and moral judgments of children. *J. abnorm. soc. Psychol.*, 1952, **47**, 463–477.

319 VAN KREVELEN, A.: Characteristics which "identify" the adolescent to his peers. *J. soc. Psychol.*, 1962, **56**, 285–289.

320 VAN ZELST, R. H.: Empathy test scores of union leaders. *J. appl. Psychol.*, 1952, **36**, 293–295.

321 WALTERS, R. H., W. E. MARSHALL, and J. R. SHOOTER: Anxiety, isolation, and susceptibility to social influence. *J. Pers.*, 1960, **28**, 518–529.

322 WARDLOW, M. E., and J. E. GREENE: An exploratory sociometric study of peer status among adolescent girls. *Sociometry*, 1952, **15**, 311–318.

323 WARNATH, L. F.: The relation of family cohesiveness and adolescent independence to social effectiveness. *Marriage fam. Living*, 1955, **19**, 346–348.

324 WELLERMAN, B., and L. SWANSON: An ecological determinant of differential amounts of sociometric choices within college sororities. *Sociometry*, 1952, **15**, 326–329.

325 WELLERMAN, B., and L. SWANSON: Group prestige in voluntary organizations: a study of college sororities. *Hum. Relat.*, 1953, **6**, 57–77.

326 WERNER, E.: Milieu differences in social competence. *J. genet. Psychol.*, 1957, **91**, 239–249.

327 WERTHHEIMER, R. R.: Consistency of sociometric position in male and female high school students. *J. educ. Psychol.*, 1957, **48**, 385–390.

328 WHEELER, D. K.: Popularity among adolescents in Western Australia and in the United States. *School Review*, 1961, **69**, 67–81.

329 WILKINS, W. L.: Social peers and parents. *Education*, 1952, **73**, 234–237.

330 WILLIAMSON, E. G., and D. HOYT: Measured personality characteristics of student leaders. *Educ. psychol. Measmt.*, 1952, **12**, 65–78.

331 WILSON, V. W.: Some personality characteristics of industrial executives. *Occup. Psychol. London*, 1956, **30**, 228–231.

332 WISCHMEIER, R. H.: Group-centered and leader-centered leaders: an experimental study. *Speech Monogr.*, 1955, **22**, 43–48.

333 WITRYOL, S. L.: Age trends in children's evaluation of teacher-approved and teacher-disapproved behavior. *Genet. Psychol. Monogr.*, 1950, **41**, 271–326.

334 WITRYOL, S. L., and J. E. CALKINS: Marginal social values of rural school children. *J. genet. Psychol.*, 1958, **92**, 81–93.

335 WITRYOL, S. L., and G. G. THOMPSON: A critical review of the stability of social acceptability scores obtained with the partial-rank-order and the paired-comparison scales. *Genet. Psychol. Monogr.*, 1953, **48**, 221–260.

336 WOLMAN, B.: Leadership and group dynamics. *J. soc. Psychol.*, 1956, **42**, 11–25.

337 ZANDER, A.: Group membership and individual security. *Hum. Relat.*, 1958, **11**, 99–111.

338 ZELENY, L. D.: Experiments in leadership training. *J. educ. Sociol.*, 1941, **14**, 310–313.

339 ZELENY, L. D.: Social leadership. *Sociol. soc. Res.*, 1949, **33**, 431–436.

340 ZILLER, R. C.: Leader acceptance of responsibility for group action under conditions of uncertainty and risk. *J. Psychol.*, 1959, **47**, 57–66.

341 ZILLER, R. C., and R. D. BEHRINGER: Assimilation of the knowledgeable newcomer under conditions of group success and failure. *J. abnorm. soc. Psychol.*, 1960, **60**, 288–291.

342 ZILLER, R. C., and R. D. BEHRINGER: A longitudinal study of the assimilation of the new child in the group. *Hum. Relat.*, 1961, **14**, 121–133.

343 ZILLER, R. C., R. D. BEHRINGER, and J. D. GOODCHILDS: The minority newcomer in open and closed groups. *J. Psychol.*, 1960, **50**, 75–84.

CHAPTER 6
recreational
interests
and activities

The status of the adolescent in the peer group determines, to a large extent, what his recreational activities will be. If he is well accepted, he will have many more opportunities for recreations involving people than will the less well-accepted adolescent. The star, by contrast, will have fewer opportunities for recreations involving small numbers of the peer group as will the volun-

tary isolate. The star does not want to create the impression of playing favorites by selecting a few members of the peer group for recreations; the voluntary isolate simply does not have anyone to enjoy his leisure time with because he has isolated himself from the peer group.

The *type* of recreation the adolescent engages in is influenced by his social status just as is the amount. A leader who is secure in his status can usually persuade his followers to engage in recreations he enjoys. The less secure leader, by contrast, lets his followers decide what recreations the group will engage in; he hesitates to try to impose his own wishes on them for fear of jeopardizing his status. Clingers and climbers will spend their recreational time in activities everyone enjoys, regardless of their personal interests. Only the voluntary isolate can engage in the recreations he prefers without concern as to how this will affect his status in the group.

importance of recreations

To be well adjusted, the adolescent must have strong and satisfying recreational interests. "Recreations" are activities that bring "refreshment of strength and spirit after toil and activity." They are modes of diversion or play. Just as children differ in what play activities give them satisfaction, so do adolescents. Making something just for the enjoyment of doing so may be a recreation for one person and a source of tension and anxiety to another. Similarly, one person may get refreshment of strength and spirit from reading the classics while another can get similar benefits only from comics, tabloids, or scandal sheets.

BENEFITS OF RECREATIONS

In spite of individual variations, every adolescent needs recreations. The adolescent who lacks opportunities for recreations that fill his individual needs will be deprived of the important benefits recreation brings. Of the many important benefits of recreation to the adolescent, the following rank in top place.

Physical Health Recreations are essential to good health, especially those which involve exercise. During the growth years, this is important. It is even more important when the individual must spend time in inactivity. The young adolescent, who is still growing and whose school day necessitates long periods of inactivity, needs sports and outdoor recreations more than does the older adolescent whose growth has been completed or nearly completed.

Mental Health Recreations of different forms contribute to mental health by offering opportunities, first, to express aggressions that do not find an outlet because of restrictions of school or jobs; second, to be constructive or creative; and third, to relax and thus ease the tensions created by everyday living.

Improvement of Social Status Through recreations, the adolescent has an opportunity to get to know members of the peer group better, to be known to them, to develop social skills, and to improve his social insight. This leads to a more favorable social status.

Foundations for Adult Life The adolescent who develops a wide repertoire of recreational activities that bring him satisfaction will be able to select the ones that fit best into the pattern of his adult life (72, 80,113,163).

Recreation in adolescence is far more important today than it was in the past. The adolescent today experiences more stresses and tensions and has more free time than was formerly true. Social changes have also altered the pattern of recreation. The growth of large cities has made informal home entertaining difficult and has eliminated recreations that require considerable space. This has resulted in the growth of commercial recreations, such as movies, dance halls, and professional sports. Prolonged economic dependency, due to longer schooling in preparation for vocations, means that many adolescents do not have money for some of the recreations they would like to participate in.

Improved transportation enables adolescents to engage in recreations away from home and school, free from the supervision of parents and teachers. Social emancipation of women permits adolescent girls to engage in many forms of recreation formerly limited to boys. And by no means the least important social change, decline in cultural and religious opposition to many forms of recreation opens up a broader scope of recreational opportunities than was available to adolescents in past generations (38,118,183).

In spite of social and cultural changes in recreations, many people still regard taking time off to play or to enjoy oneself without any serious purpose as a sin or as a waste of time. As a result, far too little guidance is given to adolescents in how to use their recreational time to their greatest satisfaction (174). Only when a more wholesome social attitude toward recreation develops can the adolescent reap the benefits from his recreational activities. As Holton has stressed, "To play is no longer a sin but a necessary part of healthy living in a world of many stresses and much uneasiness" (80).

changes in recreational activities

With the onset of puberty, there are marked changes in the recreational activities of both boys and girls (45,67,84). However, at no time do recreational interests change suddenly and radically. The pace at which interests change appears to be determined by the pace of physical changes. When body changes occur at a fairly rapid rate, as is true of the changes at puberty, changes in recreational interests are speeded up. After puberty, body changes occur at a progressively slower rate. Accompanying this comes a slow and gradual change in recreational interests (125).

During the transition from childhood to more mature forms of recreation, the adolescent's interests are unstable and unpredictable at first as he tries out new recreations to see if they meet his needs or if they conform to the pattern approved by the group. This is accompanied by a shift in values in his interest in different recreations (5,55,104). The child's meager interest in parties, for example, shifts to a strong interest during adolescence.

Shifts in values of interests may result in difficult adjustment problems for the adolescent, unless his interests coincide with those of the peer group. A boy, for example, who becomes interested in social activities with girls before his friends do, may find himself temporarily out of step. This, in turn, may lead to loss of status in the peer group. As a general rule, stability in recreational interests begins to appear as the adolescent reaches the end of high school (45,67,104). Changes in recreational interests throughout adolescence are shown in Figure 6–1.

Several types of changes in the recreational interests of adolescents are described below.

CHANGES IN TIME SPENT IN RECREATION

When boys and girls reach adolescence, their leisure time decreases because of the increased responsibilities and duties imposed upon them by home and school. When leisure time is limited, the individual learns to be more selective in his choice of activities (23,39,156).

CHANGES IN NUMBER OF RECREATIONAL ACTIVITIES

With puberty, childish forms of leisure-time activity become more and more limited, as the physical energy needed for strenuous games and sports is spent in work of different kinds at home, in school, or on the job; as environmental opportunities or economic conditions further limit the adolescent in what he may enjoy during his leisure time, the number of activities contracts (67,80,125).

CHANGES IN COMPANIONS

Before adolescence, recreational activities are confined to like-sexed groups. By the middle of adolescence, interest in members of the opposite sex brings about a marked change in play companions. Boys now spend more of their leisure time with girls than with boys, and girls spend more time with boys. Because boys and girls enjoy their leisure time together, there is less difference in the recreational activities of the two sexes than at any time since early childhood, when boys and girls played together with the same toys (45,67).

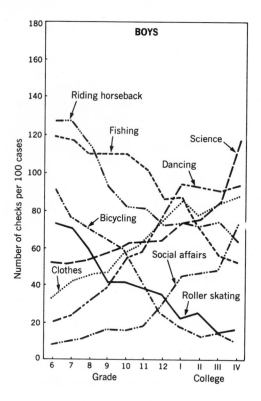

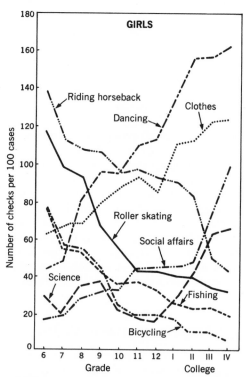

FIGURE 6–1 Changes in recreational interests throughout the adolescent years. (Adapted from S. L. Pressey and R. G. Kuhlen: *Psychological development through the life span*. New York: Harper & Row, 1957. Used by permission.)

CHANGES IN ENERGY EXPENDITURE IN RECREATION

By the age of 15 or 16 years, adolescents begin to show a preference for sitting around and talking, attending athletic contests as spectators, going to the movies, reading, playing card games, listening to the radio and hi-fi, watching television, and riding in automobiles. "Effortless" amusements gradually take the place of strenuous play (45, 156).

CHANGE FROM INFORMAL TO FORMAL ACTIVITIES

With the onset of adolescence, the trend toward formality becomes more and more marked. The adolescent makes appointments to meet in a specified place and to play at a definite time with his friends. He must be suitably dressed for the activity planned, and the equipment needed for the activity must be correct to the last detail.

This formality eliminates much of the enjoyment that spontaneity gives to the child. But of even more serious consequence, it places obstacles in the path of many adolescents whose environments and whose family incomes make it impossible to provide the equipment needed. A final obstacle to satisfactory recreation for the adolescent that is a direct result of formality is the difficulty of assembling an adequate group at a specified time and in an appointed place. Because of this, many adolescents are forced to limit themselves to forms of recreation that they can enjoy alone or with one or two companions (45, 110).

factors influencing adolescent recreations

The forms of recreation the adolescent engages in fill some need in his life *at that time* and, thus, give him satisfaction. The satisfaction the adolescent derives from the recreations may be from the pleasure of the activity itself; it may provide a welcome change from work; it may offer him new and different experiences; it may provide opportunities for contacts with old friends or the chance to make new friends; it may give him the chance to achieve something that is ego satisfying; or it may give him the opportunity to be creative (53).

Of the many factors that influence the form adolescent recreations take, the following are the most important.

PERSONAL INTERESTS

The adolescent has discovered, from past experiences, what recreations he finds interesting and what bore him. He then concentrates on those he finds interesting (6, 178). Many adolescents, for example, have interests that are individual in the sense that they prefer to do things alone or with a few intimate friends. As Strang has pointed out, "Many adolescents are not naturally 'group happy'; it is a strain for them to keep up with the more extrovert teen-agers" (151). Adolescents who are group happy will select recreations which involve members of the peer group (106).

OPPORTUNITIES

The adolescents most likely to be deprived of opportunities to enjoy recreations are those from rural areas, members of minority groups, girls, older adolescents, and those from very large families or from low-income families (36,120,153). Of these groups, it has been said that girls are the "largest group of recreationally underprivileged youth" (183). Coleman has said that "boys have far more to *do* than girls have"; that is why boys' recreational interests are more active (42).

The financial status of the family affects the recreations of girls more than it does those of boys. While all adolescents from large families or from families where the income is limited are prevented from engaging in many of the recreations they would prefer, boys are more fortunate in

this respect than girls (39). There are two reasons for this. First, schools and communities offer more *opportunities* for boys without cost than for girls, and second, boys are better able to earn *money* for recreations than girls who often are expected to devote their out-of-school time to home duties (6,24). Strang quoted a report of a 17-year-old girl who described her problem in this way (151):

> My one big problem is having no place to go at night so I can dance, meet boys, and also eat. Children here at Central don't come from people who have money. So they cannot be always giving partys. . . . I have a boy I wented with most all the time and he came over about three times a week. We either wented for a walk or to the movies—where else could we go? He went to school like me and couldn't pay to be going to dances all the time.

In addition to community-sponsored organizations for the recreation of adolescents, every community offers commercial recreation or loafing spots where adolescents may go to be with their friends. These include bowling alleys, poolrooms, roller- and ice-skating rinks, movies, and drugstores or snack bars where the adolescent and his friends can meet, eat, and talk. However, the adolescent of the lower socioeconomic groups often cannot afford to go to such places. As a result, he spends his time loafing on street corners with other adolescents who are in the same financial position as he. If the adolescent comes from a home where he feels he cannot have his friends, he often finds himself with no place to go but on the streets or to places of commercial entertainment (45,78,125,151).

PHYSICAL DEVELOPMENT

Adolescents with small physiques show less interest in sports than do those whose body builds make their success in sports possible. In the case of boys, the quality of their muscular tissue plays a role of importance in determining not only the type of activity they engage in but also the extent of their participation. Recreational interests are more influenced by physiological age than by chronological age. With sexual maturity comes a shift from childish recreations to more mature types. Sexually mature boys and girls shift from neighborhood games to social activities with members of the opposite sex (67,88,150).

INTELLIGENCE

Adolescents of the higher intellectual levels participate in a greater number of recreations of a diverse nature than do adolescents of lower intellectual levels. The bright adolescent spends more time in solitary activities and is more capable of finding satisfaction from his own resources than is the less bright individual. The type of radio program that appeals to the bright adolescent, for example, differs markedly from that appealing to the less bright. The reading interests of bright individuals are similar to those of individuals several years older than they (79,97).

SEX

Sex differences in interests are due partly to differences in physique and partly to cultural influences. In their recreational interests, girls show a preference for the more sedentary forms in which less vigorous activity is needed. By contrast, boys prefer competitive games requiring skill and muscular dexterity. The beginning of sex differences in recreation comes around the age of 6 years, reaches a peak in the early part of adolescence, and then begins to decline as the two sexes spend more time together in their recreations (178).

Differences in recreational activities on the part of boys and girls are due more to cultural influences than to innate differences. A boy, for example, might prefer drawing and painting as forms of recreation, but as these are not regarded as sex appropriate, he shies away from them and spends his time on activities considered appropriate for boys, such as sports or reading about sports and science. Girls are discouraged from participating in recreations that are considered inappropriate for them, because space and equipment for active sports and games are not provided by the school or community as they are for boys (42,45,67, 178).

ENVIRONMENT

Environment influences recreational activities in two ways. In the first place, the environment in which the adolescent lives determines what is *possible* for him to be interested in. The number of people present, the climatic conditions, and the facilities offered all play a role of importance in determining what interests it is possible for the adolescent to develop.

The second way in which environment influences interests is the effect of *cultural pressures*. In some areas, it is conventional and correct to be interested in music, art, and the theater. In other areas, an individual is considered peculiar if he is not interested in fishing, swimming, or sailing, which are popular forms of recreation in that community. Cultural pressures are placed on boys in high school to be interested in sports; girls are expected to spend much of their leisure time at parties or on dates, not in sports (28,44).

SOCIOECONOMIC STATUS

The socioeconomic status of the adolescent's family will influence not only what interests are possible for him to develop but also what form these interests will take. Adolescents of the upper socioeconomic groups can engage in more prestigeful recreations than can those of the lower groups (26,38, 72,74,126).

Differences in recreational interests among adolescents of different socioeconomic groups are not so marked in the early part of adolescence as they are later. They become very apparent when the cleavage occurs between students who are in the academic courses in high school, preparing for college, and those who are in the vocational training program, preparing for jobs after high school graduation. College-oriented adolescents have less time for recreations and they prefer those with higher prestige than do the adolescents who plan to go to work after finishing school. The college-oriented students, for example, spend more of their recreational time on sports, reading, clubs, and social activities with their peers; the work-oriented spend more time in movie attendance, dancing, and loafing (17,43,173).

PEER INTERESTS

Even though a boy may have little interest in sports, he must feign an interest if he wants to be accepted by boys to whom sports are important. Similarly, girls must feign an interest in boys and dating if they lack such interests when they want to belong to a clique or crowd of daters. Because interests developed to serve the purpose of social acceptance often do not fill a real need in the adolescent's life, they are not likely to be permanent (5,38).

PRESTIGE OF RECREATIONS

The prestige value of different recreations varies from one socioeconomic group to another. The adolescent whose family belongs to a given socioeconomic group will engage in the recreations approved by that group if he wishes to gain acceptance. Roller-skating and bowling, for example, have high prestige value among adolescents of the lower socioeconomic groups because they are recreations that can be engaged in for relatively small amounts of money. To upper-class adolescents, these recreations have little prestige; in fact, they are regarded as low-class or cheap sports. On the other hand, dances, club membership, and game attendance have high prestige among adolescents of the upper social classes (74,78, 118,123,142). One of the problems a socially mobile adolescent faces is acquiring an interest and proficiency in the recreations that have high prestige value in the social group with which he aspires to be associated (118).

POPULARITY

Movies and dancing, which give adolescents opportunities to meet and date members of the peer group, are more popular with well-accepted adolescents than are mass media which are solitary forms of recreation (26, 142). While all adolescents turn to mass media as a form of recreation, the *amount* of time devoted to mass-media recreations is determined by how well accepted the

adolescent is by the peer group. In discussing television watching, for example, Coleman contends that how long an adolescent "stays glued to a TV set" is an indication of his popularity. He goes on to explain why thus (45):

> Those who are in especially favored positions will not need to escape from the world in which they find themselves, and will turn to the world of mass media less often. Conversely, those in a particularly disadvantaged position will often use this way out of their unfavorable environment. . . . [When he is in a] system that fails to give him status and allow him a positive self-evaluation, the adolescent often escapes to a world where he need not have such a negative self-evaluation; the world of mass media.

common recreations of adolescence

In spite of variations in the ways in which adolescents spend their recreational time, some recreations may be regarded as typical of the American adolescents of today. In the following pages, brief descriptions will be given of the most typical.

conversations

Many boys and girls who as children were relatively inarticulate express themselves at length in speech during adolescence. The explanation of the temporary increase in desire to communicate with others may doubtless be traced to feelings of insecurity that characterize this age. Talking to others helps the insecure individual to establish himself through identification with another person (135).

The adolescent of today monopolizes the family telephone. No sooner has he left his friends than he must call them up. And unlike most adults, the adolescent will talk endlessly unless parental restraints are imposed. In spite of the fact that few home telephones are located in rooms offering complete privacy for the user, the adolescent is able to derive satisfaction from his telephone conversations by the use of secret language, abbreviations, or substitute names, in the hope that those who overhear will not understand what he is saying.

Boys, as a group, do less telephoning than girls. This is not because boys are more secure and have less need to keep in contact with their friends. It is because they have fewer restrictions on their activities than girls have. Therefore, they have more time for face-to-face talking. Much of the time spent in loafing around at street corners or in favorite teen-age hangouts is devoted to talking. Since girls are more restricted, talking over the telephone is a substitute for the face-to-face talking that is so popular with adolescent boys (17,42, 45).

In adolescence, playing games that require vigorous physical exertion gives way to sitting around and talking to friends. In fact, loafing with his friends is one of the most popular ways for an adolescent to spend his time. When asked to rank in order of preference their leisure-time activities, girls from 14 to 18 years placed "talking" in first place (125).

Few adolescent boys or girls are good listeners. Each individual is so anxious to talk that it is hard for him to be passive and listen to what others have to say. When the crowd gets together, it is almost impossible for one member to hold the rest of the group in silence for more than a few minutes. Everyone wants to have his say. At a party or an informal gathering, the general conversation may start with one or two of the most loquacious members of the group dominating it. Very soon, however, the group breaks up into smaller groups of two, three, or four members.

TYPES OF CONVERSATIONS

Types of adolescent conversations may be arbitrarily divided into three separate subdivisions, as follows.

Chitchat Chitchat is a light, trifling type of conversation suitable for occasions on which individuals of different degrees of social distance come together for social activities. In this type of conversation imper-sonal matters, such as weather, movies, books, social events in the community, or world affairs, are touched on lightly.

Wisecracking, or idle banter, poking fun at an individual, telling humorous stories or jokes, and punning, or play on words, are all forms of chitchat. They help to break down social barriers and compensate for shyness (49,57,68,105). This type of chitchat is frequently engaged in by young adolescents who are self-conscious and who lack social poise, especially with members of the opposite sex or with strange adults. It is often overdone and creates the impression that the individual is crude and ill-bred (67,68,170).

Discussions Discussions are types of conversation that have more content. Even though the same topics may feature in discussions as in chitchat, discussions are generally serious. Each individual who engages in the discussion contributes all that he knows about the subject.

Arguments Arguments frequently grow out of discussions. A conversation starts out to be a friendly exchange of views. When it becomes apparent that the points of view differ greatly, the discussion often turns into an argument, in which each individual champions his own point of view and tries to prove that the views of the others are incorrect. Frequently arguments become so heated that each individual loses his temper.

Arguments are more characteristic of middle and late adolescence than of early adolescence. The young adolescent does, however, engage in frequent arguments with his parents or relatives. Losing status with them means far less to him than losing status with his peers (24,67,79).

TOPICS OF CONVERSATION

Regardless of what form the conversation takes, certain topics are of fairly universal interest among adolescents.

Favorite Topics in Early Adolescence Comparisons of the topics most frequently talked about by boys in high school have revealed a greatly increased interest in talking about girls, dates, and matters relating to sex. There is also an increase in interest in current happenings and in vocational pursuits as boys go from freshman to senior year. Telling dirty jokes and talking about sexual relations appear in approximately 20 percent of the boys' conversations.

Among both boys and girls, references to academic, vocational, and world affairs increase with advance in high school, while references to clothes and social events decrease. By the senior year in high school, the favorite topics of conversation for boys are ball games, jokes, dates, movies, and politics, and for girls, parties, dates, jokes, books, the movies, movie stars, ball games, and teachers. They like to discuss the personal lives of their heroes—sports heroes for boys and heroes or heroines in movies and on the TV screen for girls (45,64,67, 71,87,88).

Characteristically, the topics discussed by the young adolescent are presented in two forms, boastful and critical. He talks about personal matters, such as clothes, material possessions, sex conquests, grades, or athletic achievement in a *boastful* manner, trying to impress his listeners and increase his prestige in their eyes. Impersonal matters, such as family members, the home, teachers, school, government, or world affairs, are discussed in a *critical* way. His criticisms are mainly destructive in nature, finding fault with anything and everything. He occasionally makes suggestions for reform, but these are most often impractical (50,67).

Favorite Topics in Late Adolescence   Dates, fraternities, sports, dancing, clothes, and drinking rank in first place in popularity for college men. College women talk mostly about dates, clothes, sororities, food, and dancing (148). Sex, even as late as the college years, is one of the most frequent topics of conversation of both boys and girls. Smutty jokes and stories are also popular (114,149,170).

VALUE OF ADOLESCENT CONVERSATIONS
Many adults consider adolescent conversations wasted time. This point of view was expressed by Stoke and West, who pointed out that "neither men nor women of college age seem to be burdened with seriousness in their conversations" (149). They granted that conversations may be "a form of indoor sport which ought to be continued for recreation's sake, but there is certainly no reason to recognize it as a major educational force" (148).

Conversations are a major educational force in the *socialization* of adolescents, because they help adolescents to understand themselves and their contemporaries. Even more important, conversations give them an opportunity to discuss their problems with their contemporaries in a free and uninhibited manner. This enables them to get a new perspective on their problems and to realize that the problems that have bothered them are similar to those faced by their friends.

Discussions and arguments enable the adolescent to present his views to others. Criticism of these views frequently results in their revision. Another advantage of adolescent conversations is that through trial and error the individual discovers what topics are interesting and socially acceptable to others and what topics are not.

NONTALKERS
Some boys and girls talk so little in group situations that they quickly get the reputation of being "dumb." In spite of their desire to talk, they are afraid to do so. Many times they are on the verge of saying something, only to be overcome by a feeling of panic that renders them speechless.

Experiences of this sort quickly build up such strong feelings of personal inadequacy that the shy adolescent shuns social situations. He then compensates by carrying on long, imaginary conversations. Another form of compensation is writing. Instead of expressing himself orally, he expresses his thoughts and feelings in voluminous writings, having little fear that anyone will see them. Still another form of compensation is to dominate the conversations at home. The adolescent who tries to do all the talking during the family dinner is likely to be compensating for not talking when he was with his friends.

To a certain extent much of the talking over the telephone may be explained as a form of compensation. The adolescent who hesitates to say what he thinks in a face-to-face social situation may find the courage to say it when he cannot see or be seen by another. There is good reason to believe that there is a close relationship between the use of the telephone as a means of communication and a feeling of personal inadequacy on the part of the user.

loafing

There is nothing that refreshes and revives the body and spirits of a young adolescent so much as loafing. Whether the loafing takes place in the home, in a milk bar or juke joint, or on street corners, it is a pleasurable recreation for him. However, it is made more pleasurable if the adolescent can loaf with his friends instead of alone. When he loafs, the adolescent relaxes his body by stretching out full length on the floor, on the family davenport, or on his bed. If he must sit up, he slouches in his chair, stretches out his legs to full length, drapes them over the side of the chair, or props them up on a nearby table. When loafing takes place on street corners, the adolescent slouches against a street light, or tree, or anything that is available to lean against or he sits on a doorstep or porch. Wherever he is, his body is in a relaxed position.

Even though the body is relaxed, the adolescent's mind is active. If he is with his friends, he will spend his time talking to them. If he is alone, he will be mentally active in daydreaming, reading, watching television, looking at pictures in magazines, or planning what he will do next. It is unusual for adolescents to be mentally as inactive as they are physically when they loaf.

The reason for enjoying loafing is that rapid physical growth during the early part of adolescence tends to deplete the adolescent's strength. He refreshes himself by be-coming physically inactive and by assuming postures that make relaxation possible. As growth comes to an end, there is less and less need for bodily relaxation. As a result, loafing is a less popular form of recreation among older adolescents than among younger.

LOAFING SPOTS

All boys and girls do some of their loafing at home, in any part of the house where they find conditions favorable to loafing in the way that gives them the greatest enjoyment. However, boys who are popular with their peers prefer to loaf away from home where they can be with their friends and talk as they wish without being overheard by adults. Girls, by contrast, do more of their loafing at home, even when they are with members of the peer group. Away from home, the loafing spots vary according to the sex and the socioeconomic status of the adolescent. Girls, for example, rarely loaf on street corners unless they belong to the lower socioeconomic groups. Boys of all socioeconomic groups like to loaf on street corners (121).

Near any junior or senior high school, there are favorite teen-age hangouts where adolescent cliques and crowds go after school. Here they can talk, drink Cokes, have a snack, and sprawl into as unconventional positions as they wish. These spots are regarded as off limits for adults. Some hangouts are considered respectable—suitable places for the "nice kids" to go; others are regarded as off limits for the nice kids, often because it is possible to smoke, drink, pet, or gamble as well as loaf there. Recognizing the need for loafing places in early adolescence, most schools provide student lounges, and most communities, youth canteens (17,67,183).

EVALUATION OF LOAFING

A reasonable amount of loafing meets the physical and mental needs of the adolescent. However, when too few opportunities are provided for recreations of a more stimulating type, there will, of necessity, be too much loafing. This will become boring for the adolescent. Under such conditions, there is a strong temptation to "stir up a little excitement" (45). In some instances, stirring up a little excitement may mean riding around in an automobile or finding a new place to eat and talk; in others, it may mean driving at forbidden speeds, finding a place that will serve liquor and permit sexual promiscuities. It may mean crashing a party to which the members of the group were not invited or it may merely mean hanging around the house or club where the party is given and watching what is going on.

The adolescent who has few friends and whose loafing is, as a result, done mainly in solitude, will often become bored with relaxation when he is rested. He will then want something more exciting to do. In search of this excitement, he will often ransack the family refrigerator or cake box, eating anything he finds available. Many overweight and obese adolescents are lonely loafers (29). The bored loafer will often turn on television to see if an exciting program is on the air. If so, he will get his excitement vicariously from television watching; if not, he is likely to turn to daydreaming and satisfy his need for excitement in that way.

Thus, it is apparent that while loafing may be pleasurable and needed, it must be controlled before it leads to harmful forms of recreation. Too little opportunity for loafing, due to a crowded schedule of school and home duties, is bad; too many opportunities for loafing are equally bad. How much time can be spent in healthy loafing will depend upon the individual adolescent and his environment. However, when it becomes apparent that the adolescent is showing boredom, it means that his need for this form of recreation has been met.

parties

Parties bring together members of both sexes for recreation which in many communities and schools is not possible under other circumstances. Being seen at parties is a status symbol for adolescents; it shows others that they have enough acceptance in the peer group to be invited (26,88). Because of this, many adolescents who are not invited to parties deeply resent the snub. Some react aggressively by party crashing.

Throughout adolescence, girls are more interested in parties than are boys. It is the girls who want the parties and who make most of the arrangements for them (45,63, 71,89,90).

High school students who drop out of school frequently are motivated to do so because the economic status of their parents makes it impossible for them to take part in school parties (26,70). Having no *place to entertain* is likewise a problem that interferes with giving and attending parties. Youth clubs offer the adolescent opportunities for parties, but many boys and girls are not members of these clubs, and hence are not included in the parties (26,35,67). Because of the small homes of today, few parents permit their sons and daughters to entertain at home. This tendency has grown stronger in recent years with the widespread publicity given to party crashing and vandalism.

Adolescents prefer informal gatherings, where it is not necessary to wear formal clothes or behave in an adult-approved fashion. A party that starts out to be formal generally becomes informal. The dancers dance as they like to dance; they sit in groups on the steps or porches to talk; and they push together the small tables so that they can all be together at one big table when they eat.

PARTY ACTIVITIES
The entertainment that is sure to be popular is *dancing* to the music of a piano, a radio, or a record player. Popular at every adolescent party are group singing to the accompaniment of a piano or some other musical instrument played by a member of the group; games in which an indefinite number of players can participate; listening to the radio; watching television; and talking.

Refreshments are an important part of the party. Simple food has a far greater appeal than "party" food. Everyday foods like hamburgers and frankfurters, plenty of soft drinks, cakes, pies, cookies, and candy are far more appealing to adolescents than dainty concoctions.

While *gambling* is primarily a male activity, girls sometimes engage in different forms of gambling, such as shooting crap or playing the slot machines when they are with boys. *Smoking* has come to be one of the popular activities of parties of junior and senior high school students. If the party is to be "fun," many adolescents feel that there must be liquor. *Drinking* begins in the high school age and is widespread among older adolescents, both in and out of college (45,152).

Where parties are held and what the activities are is greatly influenced by the cliques or crowds involved. Some adolescent crowds are composed of individuals who have automobiles so that they can go a considerable distance from home for their parties; some are limited to school or community parties. At some of the parties, gambling, drinking, telling off-color jokes and stories, petting, and necking are the favorite activities; at others, the entertainment consists mainly of talking, eating, dancing, listening to popular music, or playing games. Parties held away from home, school, or community centers are likely to be "wilder" in the sense that the activities are socially disapproved than is true of parties held where adults are within earshot (45,121,152).

dancing

With sexual maturing comes interest in dancing with members of the opposite sex. During the junior high school age, dancing is one of the favorite recreational interests of girls and, to a lesser extent, of boys. At first, dancing is limited mostly to girls while the boys form an interested audience (26, 45,67,76). In high school, dancing is one of the most popular of all recreations. From freshman to senior year, there is a gradual decrease in the proportion of students who do not attend dances. Girls in high school

show more interest in dancing than do boys, but, as it is the girls who usually give the parties or play a major role in organizing them in school or in community centers, dancing is one of the important party activities (18,123,124).

The older adolescent, whether in college or in a job, spends much of his leisure time in this form of recreation. For dates, going out to dance is one of the favorite forms of entertainment. There are relatively few girls in college who do not dance and who do not go to dances if they have the opportunity to do so. This is likewise true of college men (26,78,123). Increased interest in dancing throughout the adolescent years is shown in Figure 6–1, page 218. Note the greater interest shown by girls than by boys, even before adolescence begins.

DANCE PLACES

Where adolescents dance differs according to their socioeconomic status. In discussing the adolescents of "Elmtown," Hollingshead (78) has explained why this is so:

> The lower class boys and girls do not have access to the Country Club, and, in large part, they cannot attend lodge dances, because few of their parents belong. They could participate in the high school dances, but they are not "comfortable" there. This self-feeling is very important in the determination of where an adolescent goes and what he does. If his friends go to a certain place and do a given thing, he feels "comfortable." If his friends are not there and the activity is outside his action pattern, he feels "uncomfortable." The boys and girls . . . who attend the dances at Morrow's Hall or Scrugg's Tavern would be uncomfortable at the Country Club, because experience has not prepared them to go to the Country Club in any capacity other than as caddy, waitress, janitor, garbage collector, or workman. Conversely, the "Country Club crowd" would be morally outraged to be invited to dance at Scrugg's. The net effect is the segregation of the young people along class lines at the private, semipublic, and public dances.

NONDANCERS

Being a nondancer is more serious for girls than for boys. This is due to the high value placed on dating and parties by girls. A boy who gains prestige because of his athletic skills can be well accepted and invited to parties even though he does not dance. When there, he can talk to the boys and girls and not be conspicuous even if he does not dance. But he is likely to *feel* conspicuous and out of place because he lacks the social skills his age-mates possess. This will encourage him to stay away from parties, even though he is urged to attend. As a result, he will make poorer social adjustments than he otherwise would have made (26,45,121,142).

games and sports

The majority of high school boys claim that they would like to be remembered as athletic stars rather than as brilliant or popular students. This is less true for girls because of the lower prestige value of sports for girls and the higher value placed on popularity. During the impressionable freshman and sophomore years, boys discover that the athletes stand out as the heroes of the school. As a result, most boys want to be athletes (44,142,154).

The prestige associated with athletic competence is reinforced by the school, parents, and mass media. Success in sports is a *visible achievement* to members of the peer group; success in scholarship is not. Furthermore, success in scholarship brings prestige to the student, whereas success in sports brings prestige to the school, to the community, and to the athlete's class in school as well as to the athlete himself. As a result, most schools and colleges foster an interest in sports among the students (26, 45,46,61).

Parents encourage their sons to go out for sports. They are generally more pleased by their sons' athletic successes than by their scholastic achievements. This pleasure is increased when publicity in mass media, especially newspapers and radio, is given to athletic successes. While college sports have received wide publicity through newspapers, radio, and more recently, television, high school sports have only in the last decade or two been receiving the publicity that college sports have enjoyed. As Pressey and Crates have pointed out, "The hot breath of newspaper publicity on high-school events is largely a new thing, but it is growing, with high-school stadia, night games, bands, drum majorettes, and other paraphernalia of the athletic spectacle" (122). This publicity helps to reinforce the prestige value of sports for boys. Figure 6–2 shows the increase in newspaper space given to sports.

Few adolescent boys are uninterested in sports. Those who are unable to participate successfully show their interest by talking about sports, by reading the newspaper accounts of sports events, by listening to the radio or watching television recordings of sports events, and by attending the school or college games as spectators. Those who participate and win athletic honors are more likely to be selected as leaders and to be successful in adult vocations than are the nonparticipants. This is more true of boys than of girls (26,42,91).

FAVORITE SPORTS

The peak of popularity for sports comes between the ages of 12 and 17 years. During this period, sports of all types are popular among boys. (See Figure 6–3.) The favorite outdoor sports for boys are baseball, football, swimming, and track; the indoor favorites are basketball, bowling, swimming, and ping-pong. For girls, the outdoor favorites are swimming, tennis, baseball, and ice-skating: the favorite indoor sports are basketball, ping-pong, and roller-skating (132,140,179).

There is a close relationship between the type of sport the adolescent engages in and the amount of strength he has. In the case of boys, those who are stronger engage in a large number of games, and they prefer games requiring marked muscular strength and large-muscle coordination. Much the same is true of young adolescent girls. Girls of high levels of strength participate more

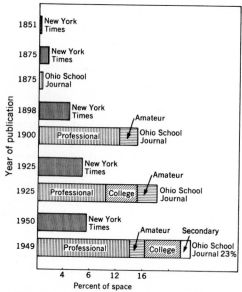

Year of publication		Percent of space
1851	New York Times	
1875	New York Times	
1875	Ohio School Journal	
1898	New York Times	
1900	Professional	Amateur / Ohio School Journal
1925	New York Times	
1925	Professional	College	Amateur / Ohio School Journal
1950	New York Times	
1949	Professional	College	Amateur Secondary / Ohio School Journal 23%

FIGURE 6–2 Increase in newspaper space given to sports news in New York City and Columbus, Ohio. (Adapted from S. L. Pressey and W. E. Crates: Sports and the public mind. *Sch. Soc.*, 1950, **72**, 373–374. Used by permission.)

in sports involving competition; those of low strength levels prefer games with little competition and of an individualistic type (161,162). Because early maturers acquire greater strength sooner than their age-mates,

Activity

Football	17
Basketball	14
Driving auto	11
Swimming	9
Collecting	6
Playing pool	5
Bicycling	5
Indoor ball	5
Reading books	4
Movies	4
Repairing	3
Gym work	2

FIGURE 6–3 Favorite sports for boys during the high school age. Each symbol stands for 1 point in the popularity index. (Adapted from H. S. Dimock: *Rediscovering the adolescent*. New York: Association Press, 1937. Used by permission.)

they develop competency in sports earlier; this gives them an advantage over their slower-maturing age-mates (95,108).

After the age of 16 or 17, there is a rapid decline in active participation in sports except for those adolescents whose skills enable them to play on high school or college teams or to engage in competitions (13, 128). Those who have the time and money to attend sports contests as spectators use this as a daytime opportunity for dating (78). Many girls are not interested in the sports contests, but they like the opportunity of being with the crowd or of going on a date (18,45,67,140,179).

GAMES OF INTELLECT AND GAMBLING

As interest in active sports declines, interest in games of intellect, such as puzzles, riddles, guessing games, card games, and games of chance, replaces it. These games offer the player much of the thrill and excitement that he formerly derived from participation in sports but without the necessity for expenditure of physical energy. Gambling often adds to the excitement and pleasure of these games. Gambling is not limited to games of intellect. Few adolescents find that being a spectator at an athletic contest is as exciting as being a participant. To increase the excitement, they bet on the game (67, 78,129,132).

hobbies

Hobbies are activities to which the individual gives his spare time because of the pleasure and satisfaction he gains. The two most common types of hobbies in adolescence are constructions, or making things, and collecting. If the adolescent derives enough enjoyment from them, they may and often do develop into lifelong hobbies.

CONSTRUCTIONS

Boys like to tinker around with cars, bicycles, musical instruments, radios, television sets, boats, or furniture which they remake or construct anew. Girls make clothing of all sorts, jewelry, and pottery. They also like to concoct new food combinations, though everyday family meals have little appeal for them. Because girls are expected to assume more responsibilities for their clothing and the home than are boys, they often regard making things as work. As a result, they generally have fewer constructive hobbies than boys (7,42,179).

Making things just for the fun of it wanes as the adolescent grows older. This is partly the result of a more critical attitude on the part of the adolescent toward his workmanship, partly because of limited leisure time, but mostly because of the growing interest in crowd life. Relatively few construction activities offer opportunities for being with a group. They are mostly solitary activities (125).

One of the few construction activities that retains its popularity throughout adolescence is *drawing*. The adolescent draws just for the fun of drawing, without any thought of displaying his achievements (82, 117).

In a study of the spontaneous drawings of adolescents, it was found that the most common subjects were words printed in a decorative fashion, drawings of both men and women, and caricatures. Over half of the caricatures were of men and only 5.6 percent of women. The caricatures of men emphasized peculiarities of physique, such as a too prominent Adam's apple, a receding chin, or a bald head; those of women emphasized badly kept hair or too prominent teeth (82). Figure 6–4 shows typical adolescent drawings.

COLLECTING

Interest in collecting reaches a peak between the ages of 9 and 13 years and then begins to wane. When at its peak, collecting is a "mania" in that children collect anything that takes their fancy. The adolescent shows more discrimination; as a result, he collects less. Only those things which are closely and intimately related to his life and interests in school or outside of school, or which have prestige in the eyes of the peer group are regarded by the adolescent as worthy of keeping (118,125).

To a child the chief source of enjoyment in collecting comes from the activity itself. This is not true of an adolescent. The objects he has collected have a real value for him. He enjoys looking at his collections and showing them to his friends. The adolescent's interest in orderliness in his collections is illustrated by his liking for scrapbooks, autograph books, memory books,

FIGURE 6–4 Typical drawings of adolescents.

photograph albums, and "character" books.

There are certain almost universally popular items that are collected regardless of the fads of the moment. Among the most popular items for boys are photographs of friends or of themselves at some memorable event; newspaper clippings about people they know, about people they have crushes on, or about themselves; phonograph records; letters received; badges and awards; old magazines; and programs of athletic events or plays at school. Girls make collections of sweaters, costume jewelry, photographs, letters, articles about their friends or themselves in the newspaper or the school paper, souvenirs of parties, beauty aids—especially different shades of lipstick and nail polish—and photographs of friends or of themselevs in some important dress or costume for a play. The college student, like the high school student, keeps souvenirs of the red-letter days of his college career, often saving these until he reaches middle or old age (92).

exploring

The adolescent derives little pleasure from exploring his immediate environment. He wants to go afield and explore unfamiliar places. Trips to the country, tramps through the woods, fishing, camping, living in a primitive fashion in the open, and travel to foreign lands are all fun for an adolescent (125). He likes to do his exploring in unconventional ways. He prefers hitchhiking, hopping freights, riding in busses, or traveling third class across the ocean to the more conventional methods of travel enjoyed by adults. Much of the pleasure the adolescent derives from this form of recreation comes from the fact that it is different, exciting, and free from adult supervision.

Exploring is popular only when the social interest predominates. Much of the enjoyment comes from being with the crowd or a small group of intimate friends who have much in common. Interest in exploring wanes toward the middle of adolescence, when interest in social activities with members of the opposite sex becomes prominent.

daydreaming

Daydreaming is one of the popular recreations of adolescence. In fact, almost all adolescents engage in this form of recreation at some time or other (93,141). With the withdrawal from the social group at the time of puberty, the adolescent has more time for daydreaming. Furthermore, the greater mental maturity of the pubescent makes daydreaming a more pleasurable experience than it was in childhood. It is not surprising, therefore, that daydreaming replaces, to some extent, the satisfactions the individual formerly derived from playing with his contemporaries (67,75,84).

The young adolescent is characteristically more introverted than the pubescent child and more concerned with his inner urges and subjective experiences. As a result, he retreats more and more from reality into the daydream world when life becomes too complicated for him. Throughout high school, daydreaming is a problem for the adolescent himself and for his teachers. Though there is normally a waning of interest in daydreaming as the adolescent grows older, there is still evidence that daydreaming is commonly engaged in by college students (92,141).

Because girls have less to do with their free time than boys, they tend to devote more time to daydreaming (93). The popular adolescent has less time and less need for daydreaming than does the less popular (144). The adolescent who enjoys his studies and has a strong motivation to achieve academic success spends less time daydreaming than does the bored student (144). The more time adolescents devote to different forms of mass media, the more likely they are to engage in excessive daydreaming. There are two reasons for this. First, mass media give them material for vivid visual images that make their daydreams enjoyable, and second, they are less physically tired than adolescents who engage in more active recreations (42,45,134,138,141,143).

SATISFACTION FROM DAYDREAMING

While all adolescents derive some satisfaction from daydreaming, what that satisfaction will be depends on the individual needs of the adolescent (93,141). The most common source of satisfaction, however, is that he can see himself and the world as he would like them to be (134). Jersild (84) has emphasized the role of wish fulfillment in daydreams thus:

> Through his imagination the adolescent, like the younger child, can leap over the barriers of time and space. He can transcend the limits of his own powers and vastly extend his reach. In fancy he can venture into many experiences that in actual life are not open to him. He can take risks he would fear to take in everyday life. He can be a great singer or actor, a soldier or a statesman. He can live in splendor even though his actual circumstances are drab, live a glamorous life even though his everyday existence is dull, find companions who respect and admire him while in everyday life he often feels lonely and unaccepted. In daydreams the boy can woo and win the most wonderful girl, and the girl loves and is loved by the ideal boy.

Daydreams are not always limited to the satisfaction of unfulfilled wishes of daily life. They serve other purposes too. One of the most valuable is release of pent-up emotional tension, especially that from anxieties and aggressions. In his daydream world, the frustrated adolescent can express his aggressions without fear of social disapproval or punishment; he can run away and hide from anxiety-producing situations without fear of being labeled a "fraidy cat." He can also find release for the strong surges of love that accompany sexual maturing without running the risk of social condemnation. Thus, daydreaming can be a useful form of emotional catharsis (48,93,141).

A more practical form of satisfaction comes from working out the solution of many of the problems that adolescence brings—solutions no longer handled by parents and teachers as they were in childhood (141). He may, for example, work out a solution to the money problem involved in buying the new car he regards as a must for social acceptance (48,93,141).

CONTENTS OF DAYDREAMS

The adolescent's daydream centers around interests that are dominant in his life at that time. These interests appear in a dramatized form, with the daydreamer the central character (84,93,103,134,144). Many of the daydreams of adolescents are woven around the themes of mass media. As Blazer (21) has explained:

> Modern civilization has provided us with "canned fantasies" in the form of movies, radio programs, and television shows. No longer do we have to develop our own daydreams: we can have them brought to us by a flick of the electric switch, or we can view them in technicolor at the neighborhood movie. Through the process of identification we are enabled to incorporate these manufactured dreams into our own repertory, where they serve as models for more dreams of the same type.

Daydreams are generally divided into two broad general categories: daydreams of superiority, which may take the form of love dreams, in which the desire for romance is satisfied, or achievement dreams, which satisfy the adolescent's desire for success; and daydreams of inferiority, in which the adolescent debases himself and gloats over his suffering. Some of these end pleasantly. In others, satisfaction from being a martyr at the hands of others persists until the end. At the time of puberty, there are likely to be more daydreams of the "suffering hero" or inferiority type than at any other time. Most of the daydreams of early and of late adolescence are of superiority (76,84,127,134,141).

Sometimes the themes are "psychological" in which what the dreamer does to another dominates; others are "environmental" and are centered around what another person does to the dreamer. A typical psychological theme of the inferiority type centers around the way the dreamer gets his revenge on another for the mistreatment he has received; a typical environmental theme of the superiority type shows the dreamer as the center of an admiring group, receiving praise and homage for his achievements (93,141,144,157).

EVALUATION OF DAYDREAMING

Without question daydreaming is a pleasant form of recreation. It may and often does serve as a stimulus to constructive life adaptations. From daydreaming the adolescent may get a better understanding of his difficulties. Furthermore, daydreams may stimulate expression in creative art, science, or other creative activities, which are based partly on daydreaming.

In the daydream the adolescent obtains satisfaction from the imagined success of some prestigeful achievement or from peer popularity (184). As Blazer has pointed out, "Fantasy serves as a substitute for the attainment of goals which would be satisfying, but which are either socially disapproved or are, in the estimation of the individual, beyond his reach" (21). More likely, however, daydreaming is a form of escape, especially at times of acute disappointment. It is a flight from reality that occurs when the individual finds that he cannot meet life's challenges to his satisfaction. Under such conditions, many adolescents resort "almost automatically to a favorite fantasy theme whenever they feel bored, insecure, frustrated, or neglected. They use phantasying as a child uses thumb-sucking to comfort and relax themselves" (21).

When daydreams lead to no appropriate action, they may develop into habits of retreat from the reality of life's rebuffs. Under such conditions, they become harmful (112). From a more practical angle, they often waste time which might be more profitably spent on studies or in some form of recreation that has a more socializing influence (112, 134).

One of the most damaging effects of daydreaming is that it tends to give the adolescent a distorted concept of himself and his abilities. In so doing, it militates against self-acceptance. The daydream of inferiority, for example, leads to the belief that one's capacities are below those of others. This causes self-dissatisfaction, a tendency to work below capacity, and withdrawal from social contacts. Daydreams of superiority, on the other hand, often result in concepts of an idealized self which are so remote from the real self-concept that they militate against both self-acceptance and social acceptance. The adolescent expects others to treat him in accordance with his idealized self-concept and then becomes angry and resentful when they fail to do so (141,144).

The daydreamer is often so completely satisfied with his imaginary life that he makes little effort to achieve success in real life. He then resorts more and more to daydreaming and withdraws from social participation. The result is that he is in danger of losing touch with reality (184). When daydreaming comes from failure or lack of interest in one's present environment, it is a retreat from reality to which the adolescent has little motivation to return (81).

So long as daydreaming remains a form of recreation that is indulged in with moderation and so long as the adolescent remains in touch with reality, it cannot be condemned as an unwholesome form of recreation. As Kuhlen has stressed, "It would be incorrect to assume that all daydreaming or fantasy is fraught with psychological dangers; again it is a matter of the extent to which engaged in" (92).

When, on the other hand, daydreaming affects the adolescent's life to the point where he uses it as a continual and habitual retreat from reality, there is indication of serious underlying maladjustment (81). As Jersild (84) has explained:

The more the adolescent's most compelling ideals, as embellished by his fancies, are removed from anything he can ever possibly be or achieve, the less likely he is to find something rewarding in the good things of life that lie within his reach. His fantasies take the place of reality and leave him empty-handed, except in his dreams. And where such a discrepancy between the real and the ideal exists, there is likely to be some sort of disorder in the emotional life, perhaps in the form of anxiety, perhaps in the form of many grievances against others, or oneself, perhaps in the form of discouragement and apathy.

reading

Reading serves two purposes for the adolescent: acquisition of knowledge and entertainment or relaxation. Not all the reading for knowledge is carried on in connection with school or college work; some is carried out voluntarily. Frequently it helps the adolescent to solve his problems or to gain a better insight into his problems so that he will be able to solve them better. It also helps the adolescent to gain more insight about people and his relationships with them. As a result, he forms more wholesome attitudes toward them (7,30,65).

In addition, much reading is purely for pleasure or relaxation. Mystery stories, romances, scandal sections of the newspapers, and comics are popular forms of reading for relaxation. The pleasure of such reading is increased if the reader can identify himself with the person he is reading about or with the setting. Frequently, such reading serves as the basis for the adolescent's daydreams.

Reading for fun is more limited in adolescence than in childhood. This can be explained by the fact that the adolescent has less leisure time than the child and more interest in social activities (179). Adolescents read for pleasure less in the summer than in the winter because summer offers more opportunities for outdoor activities with the peer group. Girls, at every age, read for pleasure more than boys. Adolescents who are unpopular read more than those who are popular (2,8,45,179).

CHANGES IN READING INTERESTS AT ADOLESCENCE

Between the ages of 12 and 14 years, when the "reading craze" reaches its climax, children are interested in almost any kind of reading. After that, reading interests change radically. First, no longer does the individual read anything and everything he can lay his hands on. He now reads what interests him most, whether it be mystery stories, autobiographies, romances, or poetry. The quality of the adolescent's reading is often questionable because there is less supervision and guidance of it than there is of children's reading (2,74). A second marked change in the reading of adolescents is the interest in reading newspapers, magazines, and short stories. This is due partly to the fact that

the adolescent has less time for reading for pleasure than the school child and partly to the fact that newspapers and magazines give him information relating to what is going on at the present (2,27,31,85). Books, in contrast, relate more to the past. And, third, adolescents want realism, not fairy-tale elements in their reading. While they may remember with nostalgia the fairy tales of their childhood, they no longer want to read them because they realize that they are only make-believe. They want to read about real people in real settings, about people who *might* be real, or about settings that *could* exist (25,47,48,139).

FAVORITE READING TOPICS

In spite of marked individual differences, there are certain topics that appeal to both boys and girls during the adolescent years. Sex differences in reading are shown in Figure 6–5. Adventure, mystery, humor, stories of athletics, of inventions, and of technical mechanics, biography, history, and travel begin to be popular. By the age of 15 years, boys begin to specialize in technical books along the lines of their hobbies. Between the tenth and eleven grades, there is a marked shift to a more mature type of reading material. After that, the reading interests of boys differ little from those of adult men.

When girls become sexually mature, they want emotional fiction and stories of a mature type. Girls prefer fiction to the informational reading that boys like, and, unlike boys, they enjoy poetry. Because girls become increasingly interested in romance as they grow older, much of their reading is of a trashy, unreal, and often sordid type (2, 10,27,45,48,67,116,179). Changes of interest in the reading of boys and girls during the high school age are shown in Figure 6–6.

FAVORITE READING MEDIA

Unlike the child who limits his reading almost exclusively to books, the adolescent reads from different media, a number of which are described below.

Books As the time available for reading decreases, the adolescent reads fewer

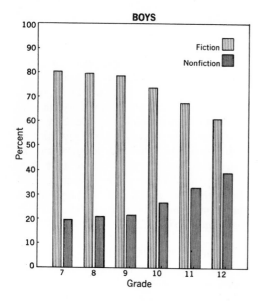

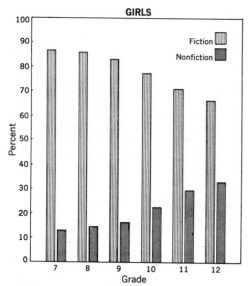

FIGURE 6–5 Sex differences in reading interests during early adolescence. (Adapted from P. S. McCarty: Reading interests shown by choices of books in public libraries. *School Review*, 1950, **58**, 90–96. Used by permission.)

books just for the fun of reading (10). Most adolescents say they would read more books if they had time to do so. When adolescents do read books, they are most often by well-known authors, preferably the modern authors (2,67,178).

Magazines During adolescence, proportionally more time is spent on magazine reading than on any other type of recreational reading. This becomes especially true by the time the adolescent reaches college age (116). At first, emphasis is on the "blood" and comic elements of magazines. Reading tastes, however, improve with age, especially among boys. Throughout the junior and senior high school years, the favorite magazines concentrate on the major positive (fun and popularity) and negative (overweight and academic failure) values of the readers. Except for the highly technical magazines meant mainly for boys, they all emphasize, in varying degrees, the theme, "How to be attractive in order to be popular in order to have fun" (17,179).

Because girls read more than boys and have different reading interests, there are a number of magazines written especially for them. They all include sections on clothes and fashions, self-improvement, health and weight problems, popularity, relations with boys and with parents, the new movies and records, intimate details about the personal lives of movie and television stars, "confessional columns" in which letters from teen-agers about their problems are answered, and pen-pal departments which encourage the reader to write to an unknown person (27,179).

Many older adolescents find the typical teen-age magazines too youthful; they then turn their attention to reading adult magazines, especially the sections that contain humor, short stories, and self-improvement articles, the scientific and travel sections, and the advertisements (2). The pictures—cartoons or advertisements—are one of the strongest appeals of the adult magazines (116).

The popularity of magazine reading in adolescence may be accounted for in a number of ways. Magazines are cheaper than books and more readily available. The wide variety of the content of magazines caters to the varying individual interests of adolescent readers. Furthermore, the great amount of space given to pictures in magazines adds to their appeal. Stories or articles in magazines can be read quickly; this is important when leisure time is limited. Finally, magazines give information in an up-to-date style and in language easy to read (2,116).

variations in magazine reading While all adolescents read magazines, the most marked differences are between the *sexes*. Boys show greater interest in magazines dealing with popular science, fiction, and humor; girls like magazines with romantic stories, stories of movie stars and their lives, the "true story" type of magazine, and articles about beauty, clothes and glamor. Adolescents of the higher *intellectual levels* and those who come from the upper *socioeconomic groups* read the "better" magazines. They show an earlier preference for adult magazines than do adolescents of lower intellectual and socioeconomic levels, who throughout adolescence show a preference for the cheap and sensational type of publication (2,8, 17,27,179).

Newspapers As the adolescent's horizons broaden, he becomes interested in community, national, and world affairs. No longer does he limit his reading of the newspaper almost exclusively to the comics and sports sections (86,136). He reads the serious parts of the paper, too. By the college years, this trend is more and more evident (2,8,31,85,86,100,116,136).

preferred sections of newspapers In general, adolescents prefer those sections of the newspaper related to the comics, sports, movies, crime news, society news, and advertisements. With increasing age, there is more interest in front page items, foreign and domestic news, editorials, letters to the editor, and items written by columnists (1, 31,119,136).

There are marked *sex* differences in the preferred sections of the newspaper. Girls show a greater interest in the society page, advertisements, woman's page, personals, fashions, general news items, and editorials than do boys. Boys, on the other hand, prefer the sections that deal with sports, comics, crime, radio, moving pictures, theater, and school news (2,18,31,116,136, 179).

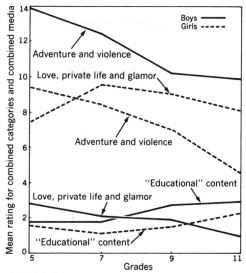

FIGURE 6-6 Changes of interest in different themes in mass media during the early adolescent years. (Adapted from P. I. Lyness: Patterns in the mass communications tastes of the young audience. *J. educ. Psychol.*, 1951, **42**, 449–467. Used by permission.)

Tabloids Tabloids, with their sensational presentation of the news and their emphasis on pictures, appeal to many adolescents of the junior and senior high school ages. Among high school students, "tabloids hold their own." The youngest students read them most avidly, as do those of limited intellectual abilities. Because a large number of high school students leave school before graduation, they presumably join the ranks of adult readers of tabloids. Center and Persons concluded their study of reading interests of high school students with a thought-provoking comment, "The level of book reading is higher than the level of newspaper and magazine reading" (37). Their explanation of this fact is that teachers give more direction to the reading of books than to the reading of newspapers and magazines. From 14 years of age on, there is a rising interest in the tabloids and in the amount of time spent on them (2, 31,116,136,165).

The Comics The comics may be comic strips in the daily newspaper, the Sunday funny paper, comic books, or comic sections in magazines. Wherever they appear, they rank high as favorites among adolescents. Interest declines more rapidly in comic books than in the comic strips in newspapers (2,20). Satirical magazines in a comics format, like *Mad*, are geared to adolescents and appeal to their desire to criticize. By identifying themselves with the characters in comics, adolescents are able to laugh at others (175). The comics are more popular in the early part of adolescence than in the latter part (98,116).

Girls show a slightly greater interest in reading comic strips during adolescence and continue to read them for a longer time than do boys. There is also a *sex difference* in the type of comic strip preferred. Girls prefer comics centering around feminine characters and pursuits that are typical of their own sex and that contain an element of romance and dating. Boys, on the other hand, prefer comics that emphasize sports, crime, adventure, and violence, and that have a predominantly masculine tone. Boys read more of the "objectionable" types of comics than do girls (8,20,34,98,179).

why comics appeal to adolescents The popularity of the comics can be explained largely by the fact that they present *"unhampered* human activity through which the reader vicariously satisfies his *thwarted* and *restrained* desires" (96). In the funnies the individual "may defy every law and he may do so with immunity" (96).

In addition, the comics present a vivid and realistic picture of almost every phase of American culture today. Bender and Lourie (16) have explained the appeal of the comics by saying:

> [The] subject matter in the comics deals with fundamental problems presented in caricature form. . . . Aggression is dealt with in most of the stories, but its purpose as carried out by the hero is to prevent hostile and noxious aggression by others. . . . A strikingly advanced concept of femininity and masculinity is displayed. Women in the stories are placed on an equal footing with men and indulge in the same type of activities.

The importance of realism in the comics is shown by the fact that the comics are "skewed toward reality." When the situation is real, the people will be unreal; if the situation is remote, the people will be real. The comics reflect the cultural patterns of acceptance and rejection regarding ethnic groups. Animals are especially important in producing humor (145). A number of words in the comics are either slang words or have slang meanings. Because the adolescent likes slang and uses it frequently, he likes to read material that is presented in the language he understands best and uses from choice (160).

There are other reasons for the adolescent's liking of the comics. He likes fast action, danger, plenty of conversation, and a hero or heroine who always wins by the slightest margin. Then, too, comics are easy to read and to understand, they appeal to more senses than other forms of reading, no imagination is necessary to understand them, the content of the comics is compatible with the adolescent's interests, especially his interest in suspense, mystery, adventure, and love, and last but by no means least, they are cheap to buy—cheaper than most magazines (15,32,34,98). Some of the popular appeals of comics are shown in Figure 6–7.

evaluation of comics There is little evidence that reading of the comics is helpful to the adolescent and much evidence that it is harmful. However, the harmful effects are less serious than they are during the childhood years; the adolescent understands that the comics are merely make-believe for his entertainment. Only when reading of the comics is excessive and prolonged beyond the age when this form of reading normally loses much of its appeal is there reason for concern. Furthermore, there is less reading of the comics at all ages today than in the past because of the greater appeal of television (19,20,98).

Because juvenile delinquents are often avid readers of comic books, many people blame comics for the increase in juvenile delinquency. But reading comics excessively is more likely to be a *symptom* than a cause of juvenile delinquency. However, the type of comics selected by juvenile delinquents or adolescents who are poorly adjusted tends to discourage learning self-control—especially in fighting and sex behavior—by glorifying excessive freedom. When frustrated, the adolescent often finds an outlet in comics that is more satisfying than daydreaming. When he must return to reality, however, he is likely to be more frustrated and unhappy than before (98,131,171).

Even more damaging is the effect of comics reading on the developing values of the adolescent (98,131). He learns to believe that to "reap the riches of the world one must be either a gang-lord or a muscle-man" because "magic and meanness" are glamorized (98). In addition, he learns methods of crime and a disrespect for law and law-enforcing agents. The "hideous is made glamorous," with the result that his values become distorted. Even though he may find an outlet for pent-up emotions in the activities of the characters in the comics, this is not a wholesome form of catharsis (171). However, it must be kept in mind that these damaging effects come only when reading the comics is *excessive* for the adolescent's age level (98,131).

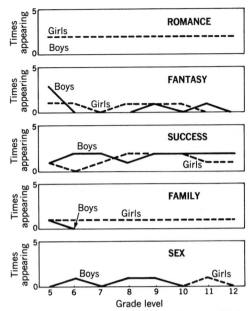

FIGURE 6–7 Relative importance of "appeals" in comic books. (Adapted from R. F. Butterworth and G. G. Thompson: Factors related to age-grade trends and sex differences in children's preferences for comic books. *J. genet. Psychol.*, 1951, **78**, 71–96. Used by permission.)

movies

Going to the movies is one of the favorite dating activities of the adolescent years, not only among high school and college students but also among those who are at work. Boys during childhood attend movies more than do girls; the reverse is true during adolescence. The reason for this is that boys in childhood like the numerous Western movies and comedies; for girls there are few movies that they like, such as movies of family life. The adolescent girl likes romances, of which there are many, more than does the adolescent boy, who has by this age outgrown his interest in Westerns and comedies (18,45,78,125).

Most junior and senior high school students attend the movies at least once a week; many attend twice or more; and approximately one-fifth see a feature through twice. High school seniors go to the movies less than do underclassmen, and college students go less than high school students. The older adolescent who is working usually attends more than the college student (45, 64,67,179).

The large number of adolescents who attend movies regularly suggests that the movies fill a real need in their lives. This they do by providing "vicarious satisfaction for those fundamental desires which life most often inhibits and suppresses" (96). The most common reasons adolescents go to movies are habit, personal satisfaction based on their interests, entertainment, and because it is the thing to do. Many go because they have nowhere else to go on dates, to help pass the time on dates without the necessity of talking, to give them a place to pet, or because they are bored with studies or other activities (74,81).

MOVIE PREFERENCES

The adolescent's preferences for different types of movies change with age. In general, there is a shift of interest from action and suspense, which the child likes, to movies that highlight conflicting emotions. There is greater and greater interest in romance with advancing age.

Interest in different types of pictures changes as the adolescent goes through high school. From the freshman to the senior year, there is an increase in preference for love pictures and melodrama and a decrease in preference for Western pictures. There is also an increasing interest in historical pictures (76,99,115,179).

The two sexes like the same types of films but rank them in a different order of preference. Girls are more likely to have a movie "hero" or "ideal" than are boys (66, 99,179). Cowboy and horror movies appeal to lower-class adolescent boys. They whistle, throw empty boxes, put their feet on the chairs, converse and laugh loudly during the showing of the film. Middle- and upper-class boys, by contrast, prefer "grade A" movies. They conduct themselves according to adult standards during the film showing. There are few socioeconomic-status differences either in movie preferences or in behavior at the movies on the part of adolescent girls, though girls from the lower socioeconomic groups concentrate more on romantic films with highly glamorized settings than do girls from the middle and upper classes (17).

INFLUENCE OF MOVIES

If a movie comes up to an adolescent's expectations and if it fills some need in his life, he will like it, and this, in turn, will result in some influence on his attitudes and behavior. Should the movie, on the other hand, fail to come up to his expectations or to fill some need in his life, he will be indifferent to it or actually dislike it. Under such conditions, it will have little or no influence on him.

What an individual gets from movies depends upon his background and his needs. He takes from the movie what is usable for him or what will function in his life. This may range all the way from juvenile delinquency to a woman's hair style. How much and what the individual remembers from a picture is also important in determining how much influence the picture will have on him. When the adolescent identifies with a character on the screen, the movie will have a far greater influence on him than when he views it critically. Generally the adolescent identifies with a character of the same sex, whose actions are most relevant to his needs or who is similar to him in major social characteristics, such as age, race, and socioeconomic status (60, 102,103,167).

There are a number of ways in which adolescents are influenced by the movies they see. Of these, the most important are discussed in the following sections.

Effects on Behavior Adolescents imitate widely the behavior patterns of movie actors and actresses. For girls, movies are one of the main sources of information on styles of clothing and makeup. Pictures dealing with society themes portray life in a vivid fashion from which adolescents derive models of conduct for similar life situations. From the movies, adolescents may copy the full span of one's relation to members of the opposite sex or merely small items of love techniques, such as kissing or use of the eyes in attracting attention (22).

Effect on Emotions Adolescents' principal response to the movies is that of amusement (166). Fear, horror, and agony are experienced to a less marked degree. The manifestations of these emotions vary from shielding the eyes at crucial scenes during the picture to nightmares and terrifying dreams. The effect of "danger" pictures decreases with the maturity of the individual (22,167,179).

Sentimental themes and touching scenes readily induce weeping on the part of many adolescents, especially girls, who sometimes experience "irresistible" weeping at sentimental movies. Erotic scenes, which have little effect before puberty, have their greatest effect between the ages of 16 and 18 years. Reactions to romantic scenes show marked individual differences, ranging from a sentimental feeling to a desire for a similar experience. Boys say that erotic films make them more loving to their girl friends. This is true also of girls. But the extent of their reactions is dependent upon the type of film seen (22,60,166).

Effects on Social Attitudes The reason why a movie can instill favorable or unfavorable attitudes toward national and religious groups, thus creating tolerance or prejudice, is that the characters and events are generally depicted in stereotypes. Thus attitudes are associated with these stereotypes. This is true also of attitudes toward certain groups of individuals, such as doctors. When, however, the adolescent is reasonably well adjusted, these effects are only minor and temporary (166). Even when the adolescent is a well-adjusted person, movies that are presented in an authoritative or highly emotionalized way can affect his social attitudes, especially if they deal with people and situations about which he has limited knowledge (173).

EVALUATION OF MOVIES

Many adolescents spend proportionally more time than they should in this sedentary form of recreation. From the point of view of physical well-being, some of this time could be spent more advantageously in more active forms of recreation. Furthermore, too, frequent movie attendance fails to develop self-sufficiency. The adolescent comes to rely upon outside sources for entertainment instead of depending upon his own initiative and efforts.

The movies may offer a powerful stimulus to fantasy life. This may be of a crude and erotic type, especially among boys. When a boy identifies with the male stars or heroes, where the principal determinants are either the prestige of the stars or what he could do if he were in their positions, then there are all the bad effects that accompany fantasy as an escape mechanism (167).

If, however, the adolescent is well adjusted, temporary retreat into the world of daydreams does not produce harmful effects. When, on the other hand, the adolescent is making poor social adjustments, this condition may be intensified by the movies.

But if he did not use the movies as a source of identification, he would unquestionably use some other source. As Kuhlen (92) has emphasized:

> Nor is it the fault of the movies that an occasional child is an avid attender who uses this means of escape from feelings of inferiority engendered elsewhere. If there were no movies this escape might be in reading or in sheer unsupported daydreaming.

radio listening

Many adolescents turn on the radio as soon as they reach home and keep it going while they study, read, eat, dress, or talk. They maintain that they can study better when the radio is going. They seem to enjoy the feeling that they are not alone in a room; the radio compensates for the absence of the crowd. It thus satisfies the adolescent's desire for companionship when no companionship is available. Most adolescents today own transistor sets; they can thus carry their radios wherever they go and listen to programs whenever they wish (45,67,115, 125).

The importance of the radio to the adolescent can be illustrated by the amount of time spent in radio listening. While radio listening does not rate as high as television watching during the junior high school age, its popularity increases as adolescence progresses (7,30,178,179). During the high school years, it has been reported that from one to three hours daily are spent in this form of recreation (67,115,125). For adolescents who like to listen to radio programs while they study, or for those who have transistor sets which they carry with them wherever they go, the time is even greater (17,111,147).

PROGRAM PREFERENCES

Adolescents will listen to almost anything, depending upon what is available when they can listen. But, given a choice of programs, they have definite preferences for certain types. For the most part, these preferences parallel their reading interests (42,45,67, 74).

Throughout the adolescent years, there is a marked increase in preference for programs that contain the latest popular music. While fads come and go in what is popular, from hillbilly, to rock and roll, to folk songs, the adolescent wants to hear the music that his friends are talking about or singing. There is an increase in liking for classical or semiclassical music as adolescence progresses; this is more true of adolescents of the upper socioeconomic groups than of those of the lower groups (12,111,130,179).

VARIATIONS IN RADIO LISTENING

More time is spent during the cold *months* of winter, when the adolescent can spend less time in sports or loafing with his friends, than during the months when the weather is warmer. Late afternoon and evening *hours* are the time of the day when the adolescent is most likely to be free to listen to the radio. With the freedom that comes over *weekends*, the adolescent has more time for radio listening than during the middle of the week when he is in classes or working.

Popular adolescents have less time to listen to the radio than do those who are less popular. If owning a large number of *records* is a status symbol, the adolescent will listen to records more than to the radio. The adolescent who owns a *hi-fi* radio is apt to spend more time on radio listening than is the adolescent whose radio set provides a greater variety of programs, but less music. As has been stressed before, adolescents who have *transistor* sets listen more than those who own larger sets which they cannot carry with them. If the adolescent's *car*, or the family car he is permitted to use, is equipped with a radio, he usually keeps it turned on while he is driving, either when alone or with friends.

While *boys* and *girls* spend approximately the same amount of time listening to the radio, girls have a broader range of program preferences than boys. When listening to specific radio programs, girls are likely to do more marginal listening than are boys (45,147,179). *Bright* adolescents prefer programs that make an intellectual appeal; adolescents of *average intelligence,*

on the other hand, like serial programs, popular dance music, sentimental stories, comedy and variety programs (45,67,179).

EFFECTS OF RADIO LISTENING

From kindergarten to high school age, there are signs of anxiety while listening to an exciting broadcast, fear after it is over, and reports of bad dreams and nightmares involving imagery from the programs. These, however, occur mostly in cases where fears and nightmares exist and are therefore incidental rather than primary (84,92).

The effects on the body are minor as compared with the effects on attitudes. Because the radio is listened to more hours a week than movies are seen, the effects on the adolescent's attitudes should be far greater. Furthermore, the adolescent is a suggestible individual who is influenced greatly by sources surrounded by prestige. To him a radio speaker is an important person; what he says is generally accepted without question. This is bound to have some effect on his attitudes (92).

To find out what influences certain types of programs have on the adolescent listener, one study analyzed 20 popular crime dramas. Instead of relieving frustration through identification, these programs were found to increase it. Furthermore, from these programs, the adolescent is likely to get an erroneous impression of the courts (133). An analysis of a daytime serial or "soap opera" showed that the principal appeal of a program of this sort is from identification with a character who represents the listener's desire for emotional satisfaction and social status. Because the characters and situations depicted in such programs are unreal and sometimes even fantastic, they tend to lead the listener away from reality instead of stimulating ambition and effort (169).

television watching

Television is the newest and most popular form of recreation for all age groups. Even though there are relatively few families in America today who do not have at least one television set, there is still some prestige to television watching—a prestige that comes from doing what everyone does. Furthermore, television programs are more humorous and of a better quality than they were in the early days; this has kept interest in television as a form of recreation alive and at a high level (7,30,40,115,177,182). In addition, television has (92):

> . . . all the dramatic appeal and impact of the movie, but this influence, like radio, is exerted within the intimacy of the home and is more readily accessible. Like radio, television conveys the drama of the immediate, on-the-scene experience. Thus its influence might well be expected to be greater than that of either movie or radio.

Because television sets are much more expensive than radios, it generally means that only one TV set is owned by a family. Since this must be shared by all family members, the adolescent frequently finds stiff competition with other family members for the use of the television at the time when he is free to watch his chosen programs (69,77,101,174,178,182). In spite of this, it has been found that young adolescents spend more time on television watching than they do on their studies (45,74). This is illustrated in Figure 6–8. They also spend as much time on television watching as on all other leisure-time activities combined (5,74).

VARIATIONS IN TELEVISION WATCHING

There are marked variations in the amount of time adolescents devote to television watching and in the type of program they watch (4,146,182). While *boys* and *girls* spend about equal amounts of time watching television during the junior high school age, there is a falling off of interest for boys in senior high school but a slight increase of interest for girls. The *brighter* the adolescent, the less time he is likely to spend watching television. In homes where there is little or no *parental control* over the amount of time devoted to television watching or over the type of programs viewed, more time is devoted to this form of recreation. The *popular* adolescent has less time for television watching than the unpopular

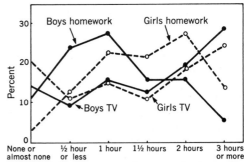

FIGURE 6–8 Hours per day spent by boys and girls in watching television and in studying. (Adapted from J. S. Coleman: *The adolescent society.* New York: The Free Press of Glencoe, 1961. Used by permission.)

because the former prefers to be out doing things with his friends (4,14,59,67,77,121, 137,146).

The most common cause of variations in time spent in watching television is the *personality pattern* of the viewer. The television "addict"—the viewer who spends more time on television watching than the average for his age level—shows less initiative than the occasional viewer. He prefers recreation of the escapist types. When there is no television to watch, he listens to the radio or goes to the movies (4,146,182). As Himmelweit et al. (77) have pointed out:

> With escape through television so readily available, the heavy viewer's outside contacts become more restricted still. Such contacts demand much effort and offer little promise of success; they therefore compare unfavorably with the certain, undemanding companionship of television. Within a given intelligence level, social class, and age group, the amount a child views gives an indication of the degree to which his life is satisfactory; heavy viewing is a symptom of unsatisfactory adjustment or of inadequate environmental facilities.

When several programs are presented simultaneously, the adolescent will choose the one that appeals most to him. These preferences follow along lines similar to those of radio and reading preferences (see pages 233 and 239–240). Just as there are marked individual differences in the amount of time spent in television viewing, so there are marked differences in program preferences (146,182). As Himmelweit et al. have emphasized, even the most popular programs are mentioned as favorites by only approximately one-third of the viewers they questioned. They further stressed that "within any given age and intelligence group there is thus a great deal of variation in taste, a fact which seems to be considerably underestimated in popular discussion" (77).

EFFECTS OF TELEVISION
Every possible type of harm to the viewer has been ascribed to television and all forms of behavior problems, ranging from thumb-sucking to juvenile delinquency, have been blamed on television watching. Today, however, there is a tendency to take a more moderate view than was taken at first. Furthermore, because children are more avid television watchers than adolescents and because they are more gullible in their reactions, they are more likely to be influenced, for good or bad, than adolescents (4,14,137,146,182).

Research in this area has been limited mostly to the effects of television watching on schoolwork and on different forms of recreation formerly engaged in by adolescents (94,137). In one study, 30 percent of the high school students questioned said that television helped them in their schoolwork because it provided educational programs that correlated with their studies. In addition, it opens up new interests, such as science, and encourages more and better quality of reading to supplement the knowledge gained from the educational programs. Seventy percent, however, said that television provided a strong temptation to take their time and attention from their homework as well as from their sports and games (77).

Television has brought about appreciable changes in the *family's pattern of leisure-time activity*. When families own television sets, they go to fewer movies, spend less time listening to the radio, read fewer books, magazines, and newspapers, converse and play less. While it brings the family into closer physical proximity, it restricts social interaction. Television families have more visitors in the home, but they, themselves, visit less and drive for pleasure less. There is also a tendency to disrupt meal patterns and to stay up later than is healthy for family members of all ages (9,40,109, 155,178,182).

Television watching affects the adolescent's *recreational activities*. Much of the time used for television watching is taken from the leisure time that would otherwise be devoted to different forms of recreation (4,14,40,101,179). However, it is the more casual, unstructured activities that are more likely to suffer. Television watching, for example, is more likely to cut into the time spent in loafing than into the time spent in playing with a team after school (77, 137,146,182).

Perhaps the most serious and most lasting influence of television watching is on the adolescent's *attitudes* and *values*. Because adolescents enjoy programs with excitement and thrills, there is a tendency to regard unsocial and destructive behavior as almost normal and to accept it as part of the pattern of daily living (58,182). In discussing the effects "violence" and "crime and filth" in television have on adolescents, Hechinger and Hechinger have pointed out that interest in such programs is a "form of slumming without getting one's feet dirty and one's mind too upset. Like everything else, the thrills come packaged" (73).

The effect on attitudes and values is not limited to programs dealing with crime, violence and "filth." Romance, for example, is shown in exaggerated forms; this sets a pattern that the adolescent expects to be duplicated in his or her own romance. Similarly, jobs of different types are depicted in such a manner as to make them seem more glamorous or more menial than they actually are. As a result, the adolescent's vocational aspirations are influenced to some extent by the attitudes and values he acquires from television (77,137,181).

In evaluating the effects of television

watching on the adolescent, one must always keep in mind that the effects will depend partly on the type of program the adolescent habitually watches and the amount of time he devotes to watching, but, more importantly, on the type of person he is and what he brings to his watching in the form of needs, attitudes, and values (77).

do recreations meet the adolescent's needs?

It is important, for two reasons, that recreations meet the adolescent's needs. In the first place, recreations contribute to the adolescent's *happiness* as well as to his *physical and mental health*. If the adolescent is to be a healthy, well-adjusted individual it is essential that his recreations meet his needs adequately. The second reason is that adolescent recreations *set the pattern for recreations in adult life*. With the trend toward shorter work hours and with increased affluence, adults need satisfying recreations if they are to maintain good physical and mental health.

Whether the adolescent's recreations will meet his needs or not is, unfortunately, not entirely in his hands. He may, for example, through no fault of his own be deprived of forms of recreation that would meet his needs and be forced into those which do not. Whether the recreational activities available will meet the needs of a particular adolescent depends to a large extent on whether he has a wholesome attitude toward them and how well accepted he is by the peer group that dominates the recreations.

Should there be strong pressures from members of the peer group and from parents and teachers to do well in a particular activity so as to be able to outstrip other members of the peer group, the pleasures and satisfactions that come from relaxation will be replaced by the stresses and anxieties that competition always brings. When boys, for example, are urged to compete with their peers in sports, these sports become a form of work rather than play. Similarly,

emphasis on popularity at parties makes party going a competitive form of work rather than a relaxing form of play for a girl. (See Figure 6–9.)

As Vincent and Mayers have pointed out, "Some work and play cannot be clearly separated: much play or part of it is work-like, and some work play-like" (164). Emphasis on competition with others in any recreation, whether it be sports, dancing, drawing, or collecting, robs it of its fundamental value as a means of bringing the adolescent the relaxation he needs from the stresses and strains of home, school, and peer-group life. In doing so, it encourages the adolescent to develop a competitive attitude which, in time, becomes a generalized attitude and affects all his recreations. When this happens, no recreation can be expected to meet his needs because his attitude toward it will be unhealthy.

Equally as important to meeting his needs is the degree of peer acceptance the adolescent enjoys. While it is true that lack

FIGURE 6–9 Party going may become a competitive form of work rather than a recreation.

of recreational facilities in the home, school, and community, and lack of money to engage in commercial forms of entertainment may be obstacles in the adolescent's path to satisfying recreations, they are less formidable and more subject to control than is the social acceptance obstacle.

If he lacks social acceptance, the adolescent is cut off from the majority of the different forms of recreation that have prestige value during the adolescent years—parties, movies, dancing, sports, games, and someone to talk to. While he could, for example, go to the movies alone or with a family member, he will not likely do so because this will advertise to others that he is not acceptable enough to his peers to be able to enjoy their companionship.

The adolescent with marginal social status will have opportunities for a wider variety of recreational activities than the unpopular adolescent. But he will be so anxious to retain what status he has that he will engage in many recreations because it is the thing to do, not because these recreations meet his needs. Consequently, he will derive little recreational benefit from them and will have little motivation to continue to participate in them as he grows older. Thus, the foundations for adult recreations will be so poor that they will have to be relaid later or he will pay the penalty in idleness and boredom during his adult life.

The voluntary isolate may claim that the popular recreations of adolescence bore him and that he prefers to do things alone—reading, watching television, listening to the radio, or working on a hobby. It is questionable whether a one-sided program of recreation can meet any adolescent's needs; too little variety inevitably leads to boredom. Furthermore, solitary recreations are largely those which lead to unhealthy attitudes toward self and others or to unrealistic levels of aspiration. This is especially true of daydreaming and escape types of reading, television, and radio—the types of recreation commonly engaged in by poorly accepted adolescents. While they may provide temporary satisfaction, they do so at a serious cost to the adolescent's personal and social adjustments.

It must be recognized, then, that satisfaction from recreations is closely related to the adolescent's social status. A wholesome and satisfactory recreational program for the adolescent years and as a foundation for wholesome recreations in adulthood depends upon a reasonably secure status in the peer group. As is true of children, also among adolescents recreational problems can be solved satisfactorily only when social-status problems are solved. This is never an easy problem, especially during the adolescent years when the social groups are tightly knit and difficult to penetrate and when previously won social acceptance can be lost through no fault on the adolescent's part as interests and values of the peer group change.

BIBLIOGRAPHY

1 ABRAHAM, W.: College students and their reading: a program for action. *Educ. Admin. Supervis.*, 1952, **38**, 111–114.

2 ABRAHAM, W.: The reading choices of college students. *J. educ. Res.*, 1952, **45**, 459–465.

3 Advertest Research: *The television audience today.* New Brunswick, N.J., 1949, vol. 1, no. 2.

4 ALBERT, R. S., and H. G. MELINE: The influence of social status on the uses of television. *Publ. Opin. Quart.*, 1958, **22**, 145–151.

5 ALLPORT, G. W.: Values and our youth. *Teach. Coll. Rec.*, 1961, **63**, 211–219.

6 AMATORA, SISTER M.: Analyses of certain recreational interests and activities and other variables in the large family. *J. soc. Psychol.*, 1959, **50**, 225–231.

7 AMATORA, SISTER M.: Home interests in early adolescence. *Genet. Psychol. Monogr.*, 1962, **65**, 137–174.

8 ANDERSON, E. M.: A study of the leisure-time reading of pupils in junior high school. *Elem. Sch. J.*, 1948, **48**, 258–267.

9 APPELL, C. T.: Television's impact upon middle class family life. *Teach. Coll. Rec.*, 1960, **61**, 265–274.

10 BARBE, W.: A study of the reading of gifted

high-school students. *Educ. Admin. Supervis.*, 1952, **36**, 148–154.

11 BATTORF, E. A.: A study comparing two methods of developing art appreciation with college students. *J. educ. Psychol.*, 1947, **38**, 17–44.

12 BAUMANN, V. H.: Teen-age music preferences. *J. Res. Music Educ.*, 1960, **8**, 75–84.

13 BELL, M., and C. E. WALTERS: Attitudes of women at the University of Michigan toward physical education. *Res. Quart. Amer. Ass. Hlth. Phys. Educ. Recr.*, 1953, **24**, 379–391.

14 BELSON, W. A.: Measuring the effects of television: a description of method. *Publ. Opin. Quart.*, 1958, **22**, 11–18.

15 BENDER, L.: The psychology of children's reading and the comics. *J. educ. Sociol.*, 1944, **18**, 223–231.

16 BENDER, L., and R. LOURIE: The effect of comic books on the ideology of children. *Amer. J. Orthopsychiat.*, 1941, **11**, 540–550.

17 BERNARD, J.: Teen-age culture: an overview. *Ann. Amer. Acad. pol. soc. Sci.*, 1961, **338**, 1–12.

18 BIBB, F. G.: A study of the 1,042 sophomores, juniors, and seniors of a mid-west high school. In M. Malm and O. G. Jamison, *Adolescence*. New York: McGraw-Hill, 1952, pp. 50–51.

19 BLAKELY, W. P.: A study of seventh grade children's reading of comic books as related to cerain other variables. *J. genet. Psychol.*, 1958, **93**, 291–301.

20 BLAKELY, W. P.: Reading of comic books by seventh grade children. *Elem. Sch. J.*, 1958, **58**, 326–330.

21 BLAZER, J. A.: Fantasy and its effects. *J. gen. Psychol.*, 1964, **70**, 163–182.

22 BLUMER, H.: *Movies and conduct*. New York: Macmillan, 1933.

23 BONNEY, M. E.: A sociometric study of the peer acceptance of rural students in three consolidated high schools. *Educ. Admin. Supervis.*, 1951, **11**, 234–240.

24 BOSSARD, J. H. S., and E. S. BOLL: *The sociology of child development*. 3d ed. New York: Harper & Row, 1960.

25 BOWEN, E.: Comeback for Goldilocks et al. *The New York Times*, Aug. 26, 1962.

26 BRETSCH, H. S.: Social skills and activities of socially accepted and unaccepted adolescents. *J. educ. Psychol.*, 1952, **43**, 449–458.

27 BROWN, C. H.: Self-portrait: the teen-age magazine. *Ann. Amer. Acad. pol. soc. Sci.*, 1961, **338**, 13–21.

28 BROWN, D. G.: Sex-role development in a changing culture. *Psychol. Bull.*, 1958, **55**, 232–242.

29 BRUCH, H.: Psychological aspects of obesity in adolescence. *Amer. J. pub. Hlth.*, 1958, **48**, 1349–1353.

30 BURGESS, E. W.: Social relations, activities, and personal adjustment. *Amer. J. Sociol.*, 1954, **59**, 352–360.

31 BURNS, D. G.: Newspaper reading in the secondary modern school. *Brit. J. educ. Psychol.*, 1955, **25**, 1–9.

32 BURTON, D. L.: Comic books: a teacher's analysis. *Elem. Sch. J.*, 1955, **56**, 73–77.

33 BURTON, P. W.: Newspaper reading behavior of high school students. *Sch. Soc.*, 1946, **63**, 86.

34 BUTTERWORTH, R. F., and G. G. THOMPSON: Factors related to age-grade trends and sex differences in children's preferences for comic books. *J. genet. Psychol.*, 1951, **78**, 71–96.

35 CAMERON, M. L.: An enquiry into the factors governing membership of youth clubs and juvenile organizations. *Brit. J. educ. Psychol.*, 1948, **18**, 48–52.

36 CANNON, K. L.: The relationship of social acceptance to socio-economic status and residence among high-school students. *Rural Sociol.*, 1957, **22**, 142–148.

37 CENTER, S. S., and J. L. PERSONS: The leisure reading of New York City high-school students. *English J.*, 1936, **25**, 717–726.

38 CLARKE, A. C.: The use of leisure and its relation to levels of occupational prestige. *Amer. sociol. Rev.*, 1956, **21**, 301–307.

39 CLIFT, V. A.: Recreational and leisure-time problems and needs of Negro children and youth. *J. Negro Educ.*, 1950, **19**, 333–340.

40 COFFIN, T. E.: Television's impact on society. *Amer. Psychologist*, 1955, **10**, 630–641.

41 COLE, L., and I. N. HALL: *Psychology of adolescence*. 6th ed. New York: Holt, 1964.

42 COLEMAN, J. S.: Academic achievement and the structure of competition. *Harv. educ. Rev.*, 1959, **29**, 330–351.

43 COLEMAN, J. S.: Analysis of social structures and simulation of social processes with elec-

tronic computers. *Educ. psychol. Measmt.*, 1961, **21**, 203–218.

44 COLEMAN, J. S.: Athletics in high school. *Ann. Amer. Acad. pol. soc. Sci.*, 1961, **338**, 33–43.

45 COLEMAN, J. S.: *The adolescent society.* New York: Free Press, 1961.

46 COLEMAN, J. S.: Teen-agers and their crowd. *PTA Magazine*, 1962, **56**, no. 7, 4–7.

47 COLLIER, M. J., and E. L. GAIER: Adult reactions to preferred childhood stories. *Child Develpm.*, 1958, **29**, 97–103.

48 COLLIER, M. J., and E. L. GAIER: The hero of the preferred childhood stories of college men. *Amer. Imago*, 1959, **16**, 177–194.

49 COSER, R. L.: Laughter among colleagues. *Psychiatry*, 1960, **23**, 81–95.

50 CROW, A.: Parental attitudes toward boy-girl relations. *J. educ. Sociol.*, 1955, **29**, 126–133.

51 CROW, L. D., and A. CROW: *Adolescent development and adjustment.* 2d ed. New York: McGraw-Hill, 1965.

52 DE BOER, J. J.: Radio and children's emotions. *Sch. Soc.*, 1939, **50**, 369–373.

53 DONALD, M. N., and R. J. HAVIGHURST: The meaning of leisure. *Soc. Forces*, 1959, **37**, 355–360.

54 DRIVER, H. L.: Learning self and social adjustment through small-group discussion. *Ment. Hyg., N.Y.*, 1952, **36**, 600–606.

55 DUNKELBERGER, C. J., and L. E. TYLER: Interest stability and personality traits. *J. counsel. Psychol.*, 1961, **8**, 70–74.

56 EDMAN, M.: Attendance of school pupils and adults at moving pictures. *School Review*, 1940, **48**, 753–763.

57 ELKINS, D.: Some factors related to the choice status of ninety eighth-grade children in a school society. *Genet. Psychol. Monogr.*, 1958, **58**, 207–272.

58 ELLISON, J.: Television: stimulant to violence. *Nation*, 1963, **197**, 433–436.

59 FAUST, M.: Televiewing habits of retarded and gifted pupils. *Education*, 1961, **81**, 300–302.

60 FEARING, F.: Influence of the movies on attitudes and behavior. *Ann. Amer. Acad. pol. soc. Sci.*, 1947, **254**, 70–79.

61 FEINBERG, M. R.: Relation of background experience to social acceptance. *J. abnorm. soc. Psychol.*, 1953, **48**, 206–214.

62 FEINBERG, M. R., M. SMITH, and R. SCHMIDT:

Analysis of expressions used by adolescents at varying economic levels to describe accepted and rejected peers. *J. genet. Psychol.*, 1958, **93**, 133–148.

63 FISHER, R. L.: Preferences of different age and socioeconomic groups in unstructured musical situations. *J. soc. Psychol.*, 1951, **33**, 147–152.

64 FLEEGE, U. H.: *Self-revelation of the adolescent boy.* Milwaukee: Bruce, 1945.

65 FORD, N. A.: Literature as an aid to social development. *Teach. Coll. Rec.*, 1957, **58**, 377–381.

66 GARRISON, K. C.: *Growth and development.* 2d ed. New York: Longmans, 1959.

67 GESELL, A., F. L. ILG, and L. B. AMES: *Youth: the years from ten to sixteen.* New York: Harper & Row, 1956.

68 GOODCHILDS, J. D.: Effects of being witty on position in the social structure of a small group. *Sociometry*, 1959, **22**, 261–272.

69 HAMILTON, R. V., R. H. LAWLESS, and R. W. MARSHALL: Television within the social matrix: II. Trends after 18 months of ownership. *J. soc. Psychol.*, 1960, **52**, 77–86.

70 HAND, H. C.: Do school costs drive out the youth of the poor? *Prog. Educ.*, 1951, **28**, 89–93.

71 HARRIS, D. B.: Sex differences in the life problems and interests of adolescents, 1935 and 1957. *Child Develpm.*, 1959, **30**, 453–459.

72 HAVIGHURST, R. J., and K. FEIGENBAUM: Leisure and life style. *Amer. J. Sociol.*, 1959, **64**, 396–404.

73 HECHINGER, G., and F. M. HECHINGER: *Teen-age tyranny.* New York: Morrow, 1963.

74 HEMMERLING, R. L., and H. HURST: The effects of leisure time activities on scholastic achievement. *Calif. J. educ. Res.*, 1961, **12**, 86–90.

75 HERTZ, M. R., and E. BAKER: Personality patterns in adolescence as portrayed by the Rorschach Ink Blot method: the color factors. *J. genet. Psychol.*, 1943, **28**, 3–61.

76 HICKS, H. A., and M. HAYES: Study of the characteristics of 250 junior-high-school children. *Child Develpm.*, 1938, **9**, 219–242.

77 HIMMELWEIT, H. T., A. N. OPPENHEIM, and P. VINCE: *Television and the child.* London: Oxford, 1958.

78 HOLLINGSHEAD, A. DE B.: *Elmtown's youth.* New York: Wiley, 1949.

79 HOLLINGWORTH, L. S.: Personality and adjustments as determiners and correlates of intelligence. *39th Yearb. Nat. Soc. Stud. Educ.*, 1940, 271–275.

80 HOLTON, S. M.: The pursuit of happiness. *High Sch. J.*, 1954, **37**, 165–168.

81 HORROCKS, J. E.: *The psychology of adolescence.* 2d ed. Boston: Houghton Mifflin, 1962.

82 HURLOCK, E. B.: The spontaneous drawings of adolescents. *J. genet. Psychol.*, 1943, **63**, 141–156.

83 HUTSON, P. W., and D. R. KOVAR: Some problems of senior high-school pupils in their social recreation. *Educ. Admin. Supervis.*, 1942, **28**, 503–519.

84 JERSILD, A. T.: *The psychology of adolescence.* 2d ed. New York: Macmillan, 1963.

85 JONES, H. D.: The extracurricular reading interests of students in a state college. *Sch. Soc.*, 1950, **72**, 40–43.

86 JONES, H. E.: *Development in adolescence.* New York: Appleton- Century-Crofts, 1943.

87 JONES, M. C.: A functional analysis of colloquial speech among adolescents. *Amer. Psychologist*, 1946, **1**, 252–253.

88 JONES, M. C.: A study of socialization patterns at the high school level. *J. genet. Psychol.*, 1958, **93**, 87–111.

89 JONES, M. C.: A comparison of the attitudes and interests of ninth-grade students over two decades. *J. educ. Psychol.*, 1960, **51**, 175–186.

90 JONES, M. C., and N. BAYLEY: Physical maturing among boys as related to behavior. *J. educ. Psychol.*, 1950, **41**, 129–148.

91 KRUMBOLTZ, J. D., R. E. CHRISTAL, and J. H. WARD: Predicting leadership ratings from high school activities. *J. educ. Psychol.*, 1959, **50**, 105–110.

92 KUHLEN, R. G.: *The psychology of adolescent development.* 2d ed. New York: Harper & Row, 1963.

93 LA GRONE, C. W.: Sex and personality differences in relation to fantasy. *J. consult. Psychol.*, 1963, **27**, 270–272.

94 LANG, K., and G. E. LANG: The unique perspective of television and its effect: a pilot study. *Amer. sociol. Rev.*, 1953, **18**, 3–12.

95 LATHAM, A. J.: The relationship between pubertal status and leadership in junior high school boys. *J. genet. Psychol.*, 1951, **78**, 185–194.

96 LEHMAN, H. C., and P. A. WITTY: The compensatory function of the Sunday "funny" paper. *J. appl. Psychol.*, 1927, **11**, 202–211.

97 LEVINSON, B. M.: The inner life of the extremely gifted child, as seen from the clinical setting. *J. genet. Psychol.*, 1961, **99**, 83–88.

98 LEWIN, H. S.: Facts and fears about the comics. *Nation's Schools*, 1953, **52**, 46–48.

99 LYNESS, P. I.: Patterns in the mass communications tastes of the young audience. *J. educ. Psychol.*, 1951, **42**, 449–467.

100 LYNESS, P. I.: The place of the mass media in the lives of boys and girls. *Journalism Quart.*, 1952, **29**, 43–54.

101 MACCOBY, E. E.: Television: its impact on school children. *Publ. Opin. Quart.*, 1951, **15**, 421–444.

102 MACCOBY, E. E., and W. C. WILSON: Identification and observational learning from films. *J. abnorm. soc. Psychol.*, 1957, **55**, 76–87.

103 MACCOBY, E. E., W. C. WILSON, and R. V. BURTON: Differential movie-viewing behavior of male and female viewers. *J. Pers.*, 1958, **26**, 259–267.

104 MALLINSON, G. G., and W. M. CRUMRINE: An investigation of the stability of interests of high school students. *J. educ. Res.*, 1952, **45**, 369–383.

105 MALPASS, L. F., and E. D. FITZPATRICK: Social facilitation as a factor in reaction to humor. *J. soc. Psychol.*, 1959, **50**, 295–303.

106 MARKS, J. B.: Interests and leadership among adolescents. *J. genet. Psychol.*, 1957, **91**, 163–172.

107 MC CARTY, P. S.: Reading interests shown by choices of books in public libraries. *School Review*, 1950, **58**, 90–96.

108 MC CRAW, L. W., and J. W. TOLBERT: Sociometric status and athletic ability of junior high school boys. *Res. Quart. Amer. Ass. Hlth. Phys. Educ. Recr.*, 1953, **24**, 72–80.

109 MC DONOUGH, E. C.: Television and the family. *Sociol. soc. Res.*, 1950, **35**, 113–122.

110 MC GHEE, M.: Schoolgirls' attitudes to films, youth clubs, homework, discipline, and sports. *Brit. J. educ. Psychol.*, 1950, **20**, 144–145.

111 MC KELLAR, P., and R. HARRIS: Radio preferences of adolescents and children. *Brit. J. educ. Psychol.*, 1952, **22**, 101–113.

112 MC KINNEY, F.: *Psychology of personal adjustment.* 3d ed. New York: Wiley, 1960.

113 MENNINGER, W. C.: Recreation and mental health. *Recreation*, 1948, **42**, 340–346.

114 MULL, H. K., and A. SHELDON: A comparison of students of 1941 and 1951 in a liberal arts college in respect of their understanding of social issues. *J. soc. Psychol.*, 1953, **38**, 283–285.

115 NEUBERT, R.: Recreation and the teen-ager. *Bull. Nat. Ass. Second. Sch. Principals*, 1955, **39**, 145–150.

116 NORVALL, G. W.: *What boys and girls like to read.* Morristown, N.J.: Silver Burdett, 1958.

117 OAKLEY, C. A.: Drawings of a man by adolescents. *Brit. J. Psychol.*, 1940, **31**, 37–60.

118 PACKARD, V.: *The status seekers.* New York: Pocket, 1961.

119 PATEL, A. S.: Newspaper reading interests of secondary school children. *J. educ. Psychol., Baroda.* 1953, **11**, 34–43.

120 PAULEY, B. G.: The effects of transportation and part-time employment upon participation in school activities, school offices held, acceptability for leadership positions, and grade point average among high school seniors. *J. educ. Res.*, 1958, **52**, 3–9.

121 PHELPS, H. R., and J. E. HORROCKS: Factors influencing informal groups of adolescents. *Child Develpm.*, 1958, **29**, 69–86.

122 PRESSEY, S. L., and W. E. CRATES: Sports and the public mind. *Sch. Soc.*, 1950, **72**, 373–374.

123 PRESSEY, S. L., and R. G. KUHLEN: *Psychological development through the life span.* New York: Harper & Row, 1957.

124 PUNKE, H. H.: Dating practices of high-school youth. *Bull. Nat. Ass. Second. Sch. Principals*, 1944, **28**, no. 119.

125 Recreation Survey: Recreational interests and needs of high-school youth: resumé of study conducted in Schenectady, N.Y. *Recreation*, 1954, **47**, 43–46.

126 REISSMAN, L.: Class, leisure, and social participation. *Amer. sociol. Rev.*, 1954, **19**, 76–84.

127 REMMERS, H. H., and D. H. RADLER: *The American teenager.* Indianapolis: Bobbs-Merrill, 1957.

128 RICHARDSON, C. E.: Thurstone Scale for measuring attitudes of college students toward physical fitness and exercise. *Res. Quart. Amer. Ass. Hlth. Phys. Educ. Recr.*, 1960, **31**, 638–643.

129 ROBERTS, J. M., M. J. ARTH, and R. R. BUSH: Games in culture. *Amer. Anthrop.*, 1959, **61**, 597–605.

130 ROGERS, V. R.: Children's musical preferences as related to grade level and other factors. *Elem. Sch. J.*, 1957, **57**, 433–435.

131 ROSE, A. M.: Mental health attitudes of youth as influenced by a comic strip. *Journalism Quart.*, 1958, **35**, 333–343.

132 ROSENBLATT, P. C.: Functions of games: an examination of individual difference hypotheses derived from a cross-cultural study. *J. soc. Psychol.*, 1962, **58**, 17–22.

133 ROWLAND, H.: Radio crime dramas. *Educ. Res. Bull., Ohio State University*, 1944, **23**, 210–217.

134 RUBÉ, P.: Adolescence: II. The inner world of adolescence. *Amer. J. Psychother.*, 1955, **9**, 673–691.

135 RUNNER, J. R.: Social distance in adolescent relationships. *Amer. J. Sociol.*, 1937, **43**, 428–439.

136 SCHRAMM, W.: Patterns in children's reading of newspapers. *Journalism Quart.*, 1960. **37**, 35–40.

137 SCHRAMM, W.: *The effects of television on children and adolescents.* New York: UNESCO Bulletin, 1965.

138 SCHRAMM, W., J. LYLE, and E. B. PARKER: *Television in the lives of our children.* Stanford, Calif.: Stanford, 1961.

139 SCHWARTZ, E. K.: A psychoanalytic study of the fairy tale. *Amer. J. Psychother.*, 1956, **10**, 740–762.

140 SESSOMS, H. D.: An analysis of selected variables affecting outdoor recreation patterns. *Sociol. Rev.*, 1963, **42**, 112–115.

141 SHAFFER, L. F., and E. J. SHOBEN: *The psychology of adjustment.* 2d ed. Boston: Houghton Mifflin, 1956.

142 SIMPSON, R. L., and I. H. SIMPSON: The school, the peer group, and adolescent development. *J. educ. Sociol.*, 1958, **32**, 37–41.

143 SINGER, J. L., and V. G. MC CRAVEN: Some characteristics of adult daydreaming. *J. Psychol.*, 1961, **51**, 151–164.

144 SINGER, J. L., and R. A. SCHONBAR: Correlates of daydreaming: a dimension of self-

awareness. *J. consult. Psychol.*, 1961, **25**, 1–6.

145 SPIEGELMAN, M., C. TERWILLIGER, and F. FEARING: The content of the comic strips: a study of a mass medium of communication. *J. soc. Psychol.*, 1952, **35**, 37–57.

146 STEINER, B. A.: *The people look at television: a study of audience attitudes.* New York: Knopf, 1963.

147 STERNER, A. P.: Radio, motion picture, and reading interests: a study of high-school students. *Teach. Coll. Contr. Educ.*, 1947, no. 932.

148 STOKE, S. M., and E. D. WEST: The conversational interests of college students. *Sch. Soc.*, 1930, **32**, 567–570.

149 STOKE, S. M., and E. D. WEST: Sex differences in conversaitonal interests. *J. soc. Psychol.*, 1931, **2**, 120–126.

150 STOLZ, H. R., and L. M. STOLZ: *Somatic development of adolescent boys.* New York: Macmillan, 1951.

151 STRANG, R.: *The adolescent views himself.* New York: McGraw-Hill, 1957.

152 STRAUS, R., and S. D. BACON: *Drinking in college.* New Haven, Conn.: Yale, 1953.

153 STRONG, E. K.: Interests of Negroes and whites. *J. soc. Psychol.*, 1952, **35**, 139–150.

154 SUTTON-SMITH, B., and P. GUMP: Games and status experiences. *Recreation*, 1955, **48**, 172–174.

155 SWANSON, C. E., and R. L. JONES: Television owning and its correlates. *J. appl. Psychol.*, 1951, **35**, 352–357.

156 SWENSEN, J., and J. RHULMAN: Leisure activities of a university sophomore class. *Educ. psychol. Measmt.*, 1952, **12**, 452–466.

157 SYMONDS, P. M.: *Adolescent fantasy.* New York: Columbia, 1949.

158 TANGNEY, H. F.: A study relating to the change in the newspaper reading interests of secondary school children since the entrance of the United States into World War II. *J. exp. Educ.*, 1942, **10**, 195–199.

159 THAYER, L. O., and N. H. PRONKO: Some psychological factors in the reading of fiction. *J. genet. Psychol.*, 1958, **93**, 113–117.

160 THORNDIKE, R. L.: Words and the comics. *J. exp. Educ.*, 1941, **10**, 110–113.

161 VAN DALEN, D. B.: A differential analysis of the play of adolescent boys. *J. educ. Res.*, 1947, **41**, 204–213.

162 VAN DALEN, D. B.: A differential analysis of the play of junior-high-school girls. *J. educ. Res.*, 1949, **48**, 22–31.

163 VINCENT, E. L., and P. C. MARTIN: *Human psychological development.* New York: Ronald, 1961.

164 VINCENT, M. J., and J. MAYERS: *New foundations for industrial sociology.* Princeton, N.J.: Van Nostrand, 1959.

165 WALL, W. D.: The newspaper reading interests of adolescents and adults. *Brit. J. educ. Psychol.*, 1948, **18**, 26–40, 87–104.

166 WALL, W. D., and W. A. SIMSON: The emotional responses of adolescent groups to certain films. *Brit. J. educ. Psychol.*, 1950, **20**, 153–163.

167 WALL, W. D., and W. A. SIMSON: The responses of adolescent groups to certain films. *Brit. J. educ. Psychol.*, 1951, **21**, 81–88.

168 WALL, W. D., and E. M. SMITH: The film choices of adolescents. *Brit. J. educ. Psychol.*, 1949, **19**, 121–136.

169 WARNER, W. L., and W. E. HENRY: The radio day time serial: a symbolic analysis. *Genet. Psychol. Monogr.*, 1948, **37**, 3–71.

170 WATSON, J., W. BREED, and H. POSMAN: A study in urban conversations: sample of 1,001 remarks overheard in Manhattan. *J. soc. Psychol.*, 1948, **28**, 121–133.

171 WERTHAM, F.: Are they cleaning up the comics? *New York State Educ.*, 1955, **43**, 176–180.

172 WHITE, R. C.: Social class differences in the use of leisure. *Amer. J. Sociol.*, 1955, **61**, 138–144.

173 WIESE, M. J., and S. G. COLE: A study of children's attitudes and the influence of a commercial motion picture. *J. Psychol.*, 1946, **21**, 151–171.

174 WILLIAMSON, E. G.: The extracurriculum and general education. *51st Yearb. Nat. Soc. Stud. Educ.*, 1952, part 1, 230–249.

175 WINICK, C.: Teenagers, satire, and *Mad. Merrill-Palmer Quart.*, 1962, **8**, 183–203.

176 WITTY, P. A.: Children's interest in comics, radio, motion pictures, and TV. *Educ. Admin. Superv.*, 1952, **38**, 138–147.

177 WITTY, P. A.: Comparative studies of interest in TV. *Educ. Admin. Superv.*, 1954, **40**, 321–335.

178 WITTY, P. A.: Studies of children's interests:

a brief summary. *Elem. English,* 1960, **37,** 469–475.

179 WITTY, P. A.: A study of pupils' interests, grades 9, 10, 11, 12. *Education,* 1961, **82,** 39–45, 100–110.

180 WITTY, P. A., and P. KINSELLA: Children and TV: a ninth report. *Elem. English,* 1958, **35,** 450–456.

181 WITTY, P. A., and P. KINSELLA: Children and the electronic Pied Piper. *Education,* 1959, **80,** 48–56.

182 WITTY, P. A., P. KINSELLA, and A. COOMER: A summary of yearly studies of televiewing: 1949–1963. *Elem. English,* 1963, **40,** 590–597.

183 WRENN, C. G., and D. L. HARLEY: *Time on their hands: a report on leisure, recreation, and young people.* Washington, D.C.: American Council on Education, 1941.

184 ZACHRY, C. B.: *Emotion and conduct in adolescence.* New York: Appleton-Century-Crofts, 1940.

CHAPTER 7
status
symbols

Long before childhood draws to a close, the child is well aware that people hold different statuses in the group, that some statuses are more prestigeful than others, and that statuses can be distinguished by signs or cues. The members of the different social classes, he discovers, are distinguished by the clothes they wear, the houses they live in, the material possessions they have, the

people they associate with, the community organizations they belong to, and the occupation of the family breadwinner (116, 180). As Guitar has pointed out, "The most fascinating aspect of our status-conscious society may well be the cool way the younger generation accepts the inevitability of status distinctions" (93).

By adolescence, the individual knows

that the image others have of him is greatly influenced by these cues. He knows that a favorable image goes a long way toward making his acceptance by the group possible. Furthermore, he discovers that once an image has been formed in the minds of others it is likely to persist relatively unchanged (90,91,205).

what are status symbols?

"Status symbols" are the cues or visible signs of something invisible; they *suggest* something to the observer because of their relationship with what can be observed. In the case of status symbols, the cues suggest the position, rank, or standing of the individual in the group with which he is identified. In order to do this, they must be visible. As Guitar (93) has stressed:

> Status symbols for the young fall chiefly into the display area. Food and drink labels, family tree, proper address—all so important to their parents—carry little weight with the younger generation. What counts is what you wear, drive, or play.

The association of symbols with status is the product of social learning. Among certain primitive tribes, for example, scarification is a sign of bravery—a trait highly valued by the group (161,206). The same is true of civilized peoples. Within a cultural group, each individual learns the meanings of the symbols by which the group members are judged (93):

> The status symbol is, above all, a means of communication. One guitar player meeting another guitar player needs no verbal contact. The sight of that peerless symbol serves the same purpose today as the aborigine's peace pipe did in times past. It suggests instantly that these two understand one another and can safely become friends. Or, as one boy put it, "Without your blanket, you are nothing. You have to carry your status symbol with you or fade."

The more anxious the adolescent is to be accepted by the peer group or the less secure his status in the group, the more concerned he is about the image he creates

in the minds of others. As a result, almost every adolescent becomes "status-symbol conscious" (217). This is a value he acquires from the adult group (93,181). Because status symbols contribute to the adolescent's "psychosocial welfare," they play a very important role in his life (55).

QUALITIES SYMBOLIZED

Almost all American adolescents of today use the status symbols discussed below to reveal qualities which they regard as especially important.

Identification with the Right Social Group
Through dress, speech, interests, and behavior, the adolescent tries to create an image of himself as a member of a social group that has prestige in the eyes of others (124).

Individuality
In major aspects of appearance and behavior, the adolescent wants to symbolize his identity with the right group. However, he wants to create an image of himself as an individual among those who belong to the right crowd.

Maturity
To an adolescent as to a child, there is a prestige associated with the adult status. Now that his body has reached adult size and proportions, the adolescent wants to create the image in the minds of all—parents, teachers, neighbors, and peers —that he is an adult (106,147,164). Davis and Havighurst (52) have shown how important it is to an individual, from childhood days, to be grown up:

> Age is the ladder by which the young child hopes to climb to his Arcadia. . . . Very early he discovers that other children . . . measure his prestige by his age. On the ladder of age, each step will lead him to higher privileges at home and at school, to sweeter triumphs over more and more "small fry," and to more dazzling signs of prestige. . . . Everything good, he is told by his parents, comes with age. More than anything else, therefore, the child yearns to become bigger and older. . . . To the young child, therefore, age seems to be the key which

unlocks all the forbidden doors of life. It is the magic gift of adults which brings power and social acceptance. It lifts the barriers to the most inviting and mysterious roads, opening toward freedom and adventure.

Furthermore, the adolescent discovers that different ages have different stereotypes associated with them—some favorable and some unfavorable. The most favorable of all, he knows, are associated with adulthood. Therefore, he wants to look and act as an adult so that he will be treated accordingly (145,200,201).

Autonomy Every adolescent knows that there is prestige attached to being independent. Therefore, he wants to impress upon others that he is autonomous—that he is capable of handling his own affairs and does not have to depend upon others (58,125). Being grown up means being autonomous. Therefore, he must indicate his autonomy if he is to create the image of being grown up. As Mead has emphasized, to an American boy of today, "Growing up means wearing long pants like his older brother, driving a car, earning money, having a job, being his own boss, and taking a girl to a movie" (161).

Sex Appropriateness Nothing is more of a stigma for a boy than to create the image of himself as a sissy. Similarly, no girl wants to create the image that she is a "crowing hen" or a tomboy. With the awakening of interest in members of the opposite sex, the desire to create an image of sex appropriateness is intensified (34,95,161).

VARIATIONS IN STATUS SYMBOLS
What status the adolescent wants to proclaim to others through the use of symbols will vary to some extent. There will also be variations in the type of symbol he uses to proclaim his status. *Age* differences are readily apparent in attitudes toward education. To a young child, education has no value. By first grade, on the other hand, going to school is a sign of growing up. Because this is important to the child, he

wants others to know what his new status is. By adolescence, the status of a high school or college student is an insignia of near adulthood; going to the "right" school or college is an insignia of belonging to a prestige group.

Adolescents of all *socioeconomic* groups want to be considered sex appropriate. But what constitutes sex appropriateness varies. To members of the lower socioeconomic groups, masculinity is synonymous with aggressiveness and domination of members of the female sex; to members of the middle and upper socioeconomic groups, it is synonymous with power through intellectual rather than physical force and equalitarian relationships with members of the female sex. Through their dress, speech, interests, and treatment of others, adolescents can show their masculinity in the form valued by their socioeconomic group (53,181,217).

Colors of clothing have different symbolic values among members of different *racial groups*. To many Europeans, for example, yellow is the color of cowardice. In Asia, by contrast, it symbolizes nobility and its use is limited to members of the imperial family. Black, to most Europeans and Americans is symbolic of mourning; among many Asian and African groups, it is symbolic of joy and is commonly used for wedding garments (244). Until recently, many Negroes in America realized that their occupational opportunities were limited to the unskilled and semiskilled categories. Education, therefore, had little status value for them. Now, with the trend toward equality in occupational opportunities, education is a status symbol for Negroes as it is for whites (88).

There are *sex differences* in values which the adolescent tries to symbolize in the image he creates of himself. Athletic achievement, for example, is highly valued by boys; academic achievement is not, unless it is accompanied by athletic successes (44). By their dress and speech, boys try to symbolize their status as athletes rather than as scholars. For girls, on the other hand, social success is more highly valued than athletic or academic achievement. Adolescent girls try to create the image of themselves as social successes; they avoid the use of any symbol that might suggest they are athletes or scholars. The wearing of glasses or tailored clothes, for example, suggests the scholar or the athlete; the wearing of frills and ruffles suggests the feminine girl whose interests are social.

evidence of importance of status symbols

It is important to know what status symbols are important to adolescents of both sexes and why. Several fruitful sources for information on this subject are discussed in the following paragraphs.

CONVERSATIONS

Adolescents talk about the things that are most important to them. A study of their conversations will, therefore, throw light on what status symbols they regard as most valuable, and which least. What a crowd discusses when it assembles for a social gathering, what a clique of intimate friends discuss at a midnight bull session, or what is talked over in confidence between an adolescent and his best friend give illuminating facts.

WRITINGS

From adolescents' writings in diaries, letters to friends, and the school "scandal sheets," their interest in different status symbols becomes readily apparent. The themes written for classroom assignments in school or college give a clue to what status symbols the adolescent considers important. Constant references to clothes, cars, and other material possessions or to family background and distinguished friends and relatives tell what the writer considers important (137, 222).

WISHES

Perhaps the best method of determining what status symbols the adolescent considers most important is to ask him what his wishes are. Studies of wishes at different ages have revealed that those relating to the acquisition of material possessions are dominant. Adolescents want things that are prestigeful to the group, even though they may not always be valuable (6,79,158,240, 245).

Because status symbols have different values for different adolescents, it is impossible to rank them in order of importance. Consequently, no attempt will be made to do so. Instead, the most common status symbols used by American adolescents of today will be selected from those in use in our culture.

appearance

The adolescent is well aware of the role first impressions play in the image others have of him. He knows equally well that first impressions are greatly influenced by appearance and that appearance plays a continuous role in the image he creates (198, 209,215). In discussing the symbolic value of a person's appearance, Jersild (118) has pointed out:

> Psychological attitudes can have an influence on his physical appearance. In everyday speech we note that a person has a "hang-dog look"; he "looks cranky," "harassed," "worried," "gay," "happy," "twinkling," etc. The relationship between an attitude and appearance is apparent when a person clearly is trying to falsify his or her appearance, as happens when a girl's dyed hair or false eyelashes give her an artificial look. . . . We see it also when a girl, seemingly unable to accept her own femaleness, selects the styles that are most likely to cover her from view, such as high-necked blouses, or loosely cut clothes that conceal the shapeliness of her body.

QUALITIES SYMBOLIZED

Appearance is used as a symbol of three qualities that are important to an adolescent. First, the adolescent tells others by his appearance that he is *attractive enough to be socially acceptable.* Every adolescent learns from experience that to be popular with both sexes, he must make a good appearance and conform to the pattern that is acceptable to the group. Furthermore, the adolescent knows that leaders are accepted not because of their abilities alone but because their appearance enables them to represent the group favorably (44,161).

Equally important, appearance helps to identify the individual with the social-class group with which he wants others to identify him. A casual if not an actually sloppy appearance distinguishes the adolescents of the "right" group from those who are less acceptable. Packard (180) emphasizes the use of casual appearance as a status symbol with the illustration of an adolescent boy:

> A *sixteen-year-old boy from a limited-success family was invited to attend a dance for young folks at a yacht club on the New England coast. His mother was thrilled and bought him a new blue serge suit for the occasion. The boy spent a miserable evening. Every boy at the dance except himself was wearing khakis and an old sports jacket. Among the yacht-club set this casual uniform was* de rigueur.

The second quality the adolescent wants to symbolize by his appearance is his *sex appropriateness.* The easiest and most successful way to tell others that he is sex appropriate is for the adolescent to look so. It is assumed that sex-appropriate behavior will accompany a sex-appropriate appearance (61,246).

Third, the adolescent uses his appearance to symbolize his grown-up status. Every adolescent has discovered that at every age people are treated in accordance with how old they appear to be rather than in accordance with their actual ages. The early maturer, for example, looks older than he is and is expected to assume duties and responsibilities usually associated with older ages. On the other hand, the late maturer finds that parents, teachers, and peers treat him "like a kid," giving privileges to his age-mates which they deny him (17,75,78, 169,232).

AREAS OF INTEREST

Every aspect of appearance and every item that plays even the smallest role in judgments by others becomes a source of concern for the adolescent. This concern is so pronounced that some adolescents are willing to withstand any amount of physical discomfort to correct defects or to beautify to the utmost the good features they possess. Girls, for example, are willing to wear uncomfortable shoes to make their feet look small and "feminine." Similarly, many adolescents are willing to go on starvation diets to become slim.

The areas of greatest interest in appearance are described below.

Body Size From movies, fashion magazines, pictures in newspapers, advertisements, television, and many other sources the adolescent learns what the prevailing standard is. He then compares himself with this standard. If his body size conforms, he is satisfied. With the realization that physical growth is completed or nearly completed, adolescents are faced with the fact that the discrepancy between their body size and the socially approved pattern is permanent.

Body Odors Interest in, and concern about, body odors is heightened by the advertisements for soaps, deodorants, chewing gum, toothpastes, and mouthwashes, which suggest that "you, too, may be suffering from B.O." and halitosis, or bad breath. The adolescent avoids foods that might affect his breath and conscientiously uses advertised products that stress their odor-removing advantages.

Hair Few adolescents are completely satisfied with the color of their hair. This motivates them to experiment with bleaches and dyes. Attempts along these lines are, of course, more common among girls than boys. Styling is far more important to an adolescent than are the color and texture of the hair. Both girls and boys spend a great deal of time in front of the mirror trying out different styles of hair arrangement. They copy styles worn by movie stars, girls and boys regarded as attractive, beautiful, or handsome, or those styles which are publicized in fashion magazines and newspapers as the latest or most fashionable.

Face Facial features are of less interest to an adolescent than the facial pattern. But should one feature be conspicuously homely, such as a too large nose, protruding teeth, or a receding chin, the adolescent is likely to focus his attention on this one feature and develop a concern out of all proportion to the homeliness of the feature. The complexion is even more important to the adolescent than the facial features. Interest in the complexion in many instances develops when skin eruptions and acne are common. Many girls, in their zeal to cover up a poor complexion, overdo it and use more cosmetics than are socially approved.

Nails The adolescent is interested not only in fingernails but also in toenails. To the girl fingernails are especially important. She realizes that they are a focal point of attention and keeps them clean and ornamented in the fashion of the day (22,33,86,215,237).

AIDS TO IMPROVED APPEARANCE

The pubescent child shows his interest in and concern about his appearance through worry; the adolescent takes a more constructive approach to the problem. From advice and suggestions from others, from ads in magazines, newspapers, on television or the radio, from "beauty aid" columns, and from trial and error, most adolescents discover that there are ways of improving their appearance so as to make it more to their liking (22,33,220).

Diets Adolescence is the "age of fad diets." Boys are primarily interested in diets that are claimed to build muscle tissue and, hence, to give them a more masculine look. Girls, on the other hand, are primarily interested in diets that will make them thinner and improve their complexions. Most adolescents are willing to try any diet that is claimed to make the changes in appearance they want to make. When improvement does not occur quickly, they often abandon that diet in favor of another which claims even better results (22,184).

Cosmetics The purpose of cosmetics is to "manipulate one's superficial physical structure so as to make a desired impression upon others" (237). In addition, cosmetics proclaim to others that the individual is sex appropriate (53). As Wax (237) has pointed out:

> Cosmetics help to identify a person as a female of our culture and, generally speaking, as a female who views herself and should be treated as socially and sexually mature. The girl who wears cosmetics is insisting on her right to be treated as a woman rather than a child.

To most young adolescent girls, the use of lipstick is the most important insignia of growing up. Girls of today do not want to look "natural"; they want people to know that they use lipstick because this, to them, is concrete evidence to all that they are near adults. Jones (123) has explained the early use of lipstick by adolescents of this era:

> Lipstick symbolizes as well as any one specific item could the sensitization in early adolescence toward a new sex role and toward being grown-up. While its use is confined to girls, opinions about it are not.

Techniques to Change Body Contour Boys and girls use many techniques to create the image of bodies that are both attractive and sex appropriate. A boy whose shoulders are too narrow to be "masculine" can have padding inserted in the shoulders of his coats to create the illusion that he has the sex-approved triangular body. If a girl's breasts are too small to be fashionably "feminine," she can quickly remedy this by wearing a padded brassiere—"falsies"—to give her the bust shape she wants. Controlling undergarments—corsets and girdles—can be used to produce the hourglass figure that is currently considered "typically feminine" (237).

Grooming Tidiness and cleanliness are associated with respectability and belonging to the "right" class of people; good grooming thus helps to create the image of "right" status (215). One of the newest status symbols of the adolescent girl in America today is a weekly trip to the hairdresser so that she can keep her hair well groomed and in the latest style (101).

The adolescent who is deliberately unkempt and sloppy in appearance is showing hostile feelings toward those in authority, mainly parents. It suggests that he is at odds with the peer group as well as with adults because he makes no attempt to conform to peer standards in his grooming (117).

Clothing Unquestionably, one of the greatest aids to improved appearance is clothing. Because of the important role clothing plays in the image the adolescent hopes to create, this topic is treated at length below.

VARIATIONS IN INTEREST IN APPEARANCE

According to tradition, girls are far more interested in appearance than boys. In fact, this difference is one that is usually emphasized as a distinguishing characteristic of the two *sexes*. Unquestionably this traditional belief is true about children (86). By adolescence, this is no longer true. According to Friedenberg, adolescent boys seem to "defy the male stereotype." He states further (76):

> Boys seem to me usually more concerned with their appearance than girls and also to have more idea what they actually look like and how other people will respond to the way they look. . . . Boys are often very vain. . . . They bask in physical regard like alligators on a log.

When the adolescent is dissatisfied with his status and anxious to improve it, he tries to change the image he *thinks* others have of him by using any status symbol he believes will serve this purpose. Thus, the adolescent's attitude toward and concern about his appearance give a clue to his satisfaction with his status. As Jersild (117) has stated:

> Clothing and grooming may reveal many nuances of attitude toward self. Sometimes directly, sometimes more subtly, a person's

> clothes and grooming are a projection of himself—his "real" or an idealized self which he is striving to live up to. We may suspect that a person does not accept himself wholeheartedly as he is if he feels a need to falsify his appearance to a considerable degree. . . . There are many ways of trying to look like the person one is not. One may strive to appear conspicuously older or younger. The young girl who disapproves of herself as she is attempts by make-up and hair-do to play up to an older part.

clothes

The adolescent's interest in clothes stems from the realization that clothes play an important—if not *the* most important—role in appearance. Appearance, in turn, determines what role the individual will play in the social group. Clothes are the "symbols by means of which group members judge one another" (112). In discussing the symbolic value of clothes, Jersild (117) has said:

> An article of clothing which seems thoroughly objective in character may have tremendous subjective meaning. It may be an important projection of self, a means of self-defiance, of self-vindication, or it may be a means of communicating with others.

Adolescents use clothes to improve their appearance in two ways: first, by *enhancing* their good physical traits, and second, by *camouflaging* their poor traits. A slightly overweight girl, for example, finds that she looks thinner in dark colors than in bright and that unadorned garments camouflage her figure (96,220).

QUALITIES SYMBOLIZED

Of the many qualities clothes can be used to symbolize, the following are the most important to the typical American adolescent of today.

Identification with the Peer Group Throughout history, clothes have been used to show the position of the wearer in the social group. As Hoult has pointed out,

"Clothes play an important role in structuring the nature of interpersonal relationships" (112). And because there are certain stereotypes of clothes commonly worn by different types of people, the wearer's status in the group is judged by the type of clothing he wears (140). Clothing, thus, is an "outward sign of a way of life" (9).

The adolescent learns early to make use of this outward sign to let others know that he belongs to the right group. Furthermore, when he looks like other members of the group, he feels that he belongs (93, 227). Unlike the adult who judges clothing by its becomingness and quality, the adolescent judges it in terms of what others are wearing. To him, this is the correct form of attire (41,202).

As the adolescent years progress and self-confidence replaces feelings of insecurity, the youth accepts eagerly the latest and most extreme of the prevailing styles. Extremes in style have great attention value. The adolescent girl who wears the very latest style arouses feelings of admiration and envy on the part of other girls. An adolescent who does not comply with fashion's dictates is considered stubborn, rebellious, conservative, "dated," highly individualistic, and to be pitied (36,41,202,203).

If there is a conflict between what the peer group considers stylish and parental standards, the adolescent will resist adult pressures and conform to peer standards. One of the major sources of parent-child conflict during adolescence centers around clothes. This is especially true of mother-daughter conflicts. In upper-class families, for example, conflicts generally center around overdressing, overornamentation, and acceptance of too extreme styles. Middle-class mothers object mainly to clothes their daughters wear for formal occasions, while those of the lower classes protest against their daughters' wearing of undergarments that reveal too much of their figures (8, 115).

While many adolescents dislike wearing a school uniform because they do not want to be "regimented," they like the uniform if it helps to identify them with a prestigeful school or college. In England,

for example, the traditional uniforms of the exclusive boys' schools, such as Eton and Harrow, are objected to on the grounds that they are "silly looking" and belong to eras long since passed (71). Just as the lab coat helps to identify the scientist in the professional world, so do school blazers, caps, or hats identify the high school or college student (233). Wearing an athletic uniform with the varsity insignia proclaims to all that the wearer not only belongs to a certain school or college but that his status is that of an outstanding athlete (15,36,44).

Socioeconomic Status It has been said that we "recognize the factory worker by his work clothes, the executive by his suit and the student by his slacks and sweater" (231). Among adolescents, the socioeconomic status of the wearer is likewise readily apparent in his characteristic style of dress (197). Girls of the upper social classes, for example, regard conservative styles and limited amounts of ornamentation as good taste; those of the lower-middle and lower classes look upon conservative dress as "frumpy" and favor flashy clothes with plenty of ornamentation (15,22,36,140).

There are three ways in which adolescents try to symbolize their socioeconomic status through their clothes. The first consists of wearing clothes that are made of superior materials by *prestige manufacturers* (180,197). In discussing the importance of prestige labels in adolescent girls' clothes, Bernard (22) has pointed out that if a girl is considered a good dresser, she wears labels:

> Her dresses are Lanz or Jonathan Logan. She wears shoes by Capezio for people who dare to be different. Her skirts are Pendleton and the right length and the sweaters to match are Garland. Her coat is a Lassie, and no good dresser uses any make-up but the current fad which usually alternates between Revlon and Coty. All these labels show (1) that she has money, (2) that she is allowed to spend it on her choices, and (3) that those choices are ones of quality.

The second way in which adolescents try to symbolize their socioeconomic status through their clothes is by the *number* of garments they have of each kind. The more evening dresses or sweaters a girl has, for example, the more money she is judged to have for clothing (227,230). Adolescents of the upper socioeconomic groups who do not have to tell others by their clothes what the family income is are far less concerned about having a large wardrobe and new garments for all important occasions than are adolescents whose socioeconomic status is less prestigeful (8,115).

The third symbol of socioeconomic status is *fashionableness* of clothing. Persons who are most anxious to impress others with their financial status are interested in "high fashion"—the latest and most extreme styles. By contrast, those whose socioeconomic status is known to be superior have a distaste for high style and prefer conservative styles. As Packard has said, "In clothing as in other matters, the really rich prize age, whereas men well below them in status prize newness. The New England aristocrat clings to his cracked shoes through many re-solings and his old hat" (180). The same values are held by adolescents. As Bernard (22) has pointed out;

> On first impression, a boy is rated by his appearance—either tweedy or cloddy, as the case may be. To rate well socially, a boy must look as tweedy as possible. . . . A girl may also be socially rated as to the clothes she wears. Girls dress to look tweedy or collegiate. . . . The goal is to look simple, the characteristic of tweediness.

Adolescents who are dissatisfied with the family socioeconomic status and who want to improve their lot in life, try to create the image of belonging to a higher socioeconomic group. In England, for example, boys of the working class are trying to "wipe out the old image of the working man—broken fingernails, frayed shirt, and cloth cap." They claim they do not want to "look like our fathers." Instead, they want to "look smart" like the adolescents of the middle- and upper-class groups (177).

Sex Appropriateness Every adolescent knows that members of the two sexes have different standards of what a good appearance means. However, both sexes emphasize that girls must look feminine as well as stylish and boys must look masculine and in style. When a girl deviates in appearance from the group, or from the stereotype of "feminine," the boy judges her unfavorably; this militates against any further interest in her (41,114,204,215).

Sex appropriateness is symbolized by clothes that are distinctly different for the two sexes. Even when boys and girls wear clothes that are very much alike—as in the case of blue jeans and shorts—boys want plain, unadorned shirts to proclaim their masculinity while girls prefer shirts of a slightly ornamented type to create a feminine appearance.

The more anxious the adolescent is to symbolize sex appropriateness, the more emphasis he places on clothes that are stereotypes of those of his own sex. Girls, for example, wear ruffles and highly ornamented clothes when they want to create the impression of being feminine, even when plainer clothes would be more becoming. Boys concentrate on sports clothes if they are anxious to proclaim their masculinity (113,215,231,237).

Individuality While adolescents conform to the prevailing style to show their identity with the group, they want to symbolize the fact that they are "special," not just like everyone else (202,203). As Bernard (22) has stated, "A girl should dress as the other girls do but with just a touch of individuality."

Maturity Just as older people wear clothes to make them look younger, so adolescents wear clothes to make them look older. They want to make sure that their clothes will be a true symbol of their near-adult status. Furthermore, they recognize, from childhood dramatic play, that dressing up does more to make one look older than anything one can do to change one's appearance.

To achieve an older look, the adolescent selects clothes that are associated with adults and rebels against wearing any garments associated with childhood. If snow caps that tie under the chin are in style for children, adolescent boys and girls wear hats, scarves over their heads, or go bareheaded.

The college student or young worker in the business world is just as anxious to distinguish himself from the high school student as the high school student is to distinguish himself from the elementary school child. One of the commonest ways adolescent girls of today try to achieve a more grown-up appearance when they go off to college is to substitute Bermuda stockings or nylons for bobby socks. The working girl shuns both bobby socks and Bermuda stockings as symbols of "teen-agers" (15). The adolescent boy who goes to college shuns blue jeans for army khakis—the "correct" collegiate style of today—while the boy who goes to work wears a tie to show that he has left behind him the high school or college years (93,177,227,230).

Independence Because neat grooming is important to an adult, sloppiness is a symbol of rebellion against adult domination (227). The sloppier the manner of dressing, the more evidence there is for others to see that the wearer is in control of his own affairs. Similarly, because adults favor conservatism in dress, the adolescent symbolizes his autonomy by bright colors and extreme styles. The more parents disapprove of the clothes their sons and daughters wear, the more determined they are to wear them (8,89,93). Should parents adopt the styles in vogue among their teen-age children's crowd, adolescents will resent their loss of an important symbol of independence. As one teen-ager moaned, "Is nothing sacred any more?" (227).

FOCAL POINTS OF INTEREST
There are certain features of clothing that have a strong appeal for adolescents and on which they concentrate their attention. The most important of these are as follows.

Color Bright colors, the child discovers, have great attention value. But the adolescent realizes that the attention is not always of a favorable sort. While the young adolescent likes his clothes to be brightly colored, there is a growing tendency with each passing year to prefer more and more subdued colors. Gaudy colors or color combinations are considered poor taste (24,25, 113,132,160,163,183,215,244).

Ornamentation The young adolescent, like the child and primitive man, loves to ornament his body. Costume jewelry, trimmings, flowers, laces, scarves, embroidery—in fact, any forms of ornamentation in style at the moment—are quickly accepted by the adolescent girl. These have attention value so far as members of the opposite sex are concerned. Ornamentation also makes the young adolescent appear older and more sophisticated. Older adolescent girls denounce ostentation in dress. They discover that an attractive appearance can be achieved better by lines and color than by ornamentation (149,183,202,203).

Becomingness To an adolescent, clothes serve as a means of improving his appearance. Therefore, he is interested in discovering what is becoming to him and what will make the most of his good features and at the same time cover up the bad features. Girls put special emphasis on the becomingness of the garment they contemplate buying. Not only color but line are considered in relation to the adolescent's own body physique and coloring.

Personal Likes and Dislikes Likes and dislikes in clothing are markedly influenced by what is in style at the moment, what is becoming to the wearer, and what the adolescent feels is appropriate for the occasion on which the clothes are to be worn. Because masculine clothes are so standardized, boys are given little opportunity to select their clothes on the basis of their likes or dislikes. Among high school and college girls, there is great interest in tailored suits and dresses, skirts and blouses, sweaters, shorts, slacks, and garments of conservative lines with little ornamentation. Clothes that are disliked are frilly or fussy, extreme or gaudy or too little-girlish (183,203,204).

Appropriateness The adolescent is keenly aware of the appropriateness of the garments he wears. Knowing that inappropriate garments will mark the individual as "ignorant," the adolescent is very careful to disregard personal feelings about clothing. No matter how much he or she may like a certain garment, the adolescent will not wear it unless it is "correct." Girls, even more than boys, are anxious to avoid criticism of their clothes (114,149).

Style Adolescents are style-conscious, perhaps more so than people of any other age. They know what is in style by reading the fashion magazines, the newspapers, and by watching movies and television. To them, what is in style is beautiful, while what is out of style is ugly. Interest in style appears at the beginning of adolescence and grows stronger with each passing year (93, 112,202,203,215,227).

Attention Value An adolescent is interested in the attention value of clothes, but in a more subtle way than children. He wants his clothes to attract attention to himself, especially the attention of members of the other sex. But the attention must be of a favorable sort (41,113,203).

VARIATIONS IN INTEREST

Interest in clothes varies. How great it will be depends, to a large extent, upon how important a role the adolescent believes clothes play in creating the impression he wants to create. His interest will also vary according to how satisfied or dissatisfied he is with the social status he already has. Because interest varies according to many different circumstances, it cannot be said that all adolescents are clothes-conscious and obsessed with fashion.

There is little variation with *age* in the degree of interest adolescents show in clothes, though the type of interest varies. Among young adolescents, the interest is mainly in experimenting with styles to discover which satisfies the wearer's needs best. Wax (237) explains the reason for this age difference in the adolescent girl:

Continually experimenting with new styles of dress and grooming, she is in effect trying on this or that role or personality to see what response it will bring to her. . . . The teen-ager follows fad and fashion . . . because she is experimenting with herself and has not yet developed a self-image with which she can be comfortable. An older, more stable woman, who knows herself and her roles and how she wishes to appear, can ignore fad and follow fashion at a distance.

In late adolescence, interest in clothes is more often concentrated on the status values of socioeconomic position and individuality than on trying to discover what clothes the wearer likes (177,203,220,227).

Boys are as interested in and concerned about their clothes as girls are. But their interest is of a different type. Girls put slightly more emphasis on clothes as a symbol of their social status, while boys stress individuality and autonomy symbols (22, 89,203).

Interest in clothes is closely related to the *personality* pattern of the adolescent. College women, it has been reported, who are traditional and conservative want to wear what their peers wear. Those who have a tendency to be economical in buying clothes have been found to be efficient, controlled, conscientious, and precise in their behavior (2).

Adolescents who are *well dressed* are more interested in clothes than those who are poorly dressed. Those who are *interested in social life* and have gained reasonably satisfactory acceptance are more interested in clothes than those to whom social life and social acceptance are less important. The *socially mobile* adolescent who is trying to come up in the social world is more interested in and aware of the symbolic value of clothes than one who is satisfied to remain in his present economic and social group (231). Adolescents who are permitted to *choose their own clothes* have greater interest in clothes than those who have little say in the choice (202,203,204). Adolescents who have grown up in families where *parents*, especially mothers, are interested in clothes generally have greater interest than those who come from homes where parents are unconcerned about and uninterested in clothes (204).

When interest in clothes is strong, many adolescents will make great personal sacrifices to have the type of clothes they consider essential as symbols of the status they wish to achieve (105,114,215). Many a girl, for example, will resort to questionable devices to obtain the clothing that her family's income cannot provide her with. She may deprive herself of movies, other forms of entertainment, and even food to buy such clothing. Many cases of juvenile delinquency are based on girls' petty thievery of clothing, costume jewelry, and other aids to personal adornment (85).

Excessive interest in clothes as compared with the amount normally found among adolescents of the same age and sex results from some kind of weakness or distortion in the self-structure. Excessive interest is shown in many ways, one of the most common of which is an unreasonable need to find out what others are wearing and where they buy their clothes. At the opposite end of the continuum of interest is the adolescent who scorns clothes in the sense that he shows no interest in styles and dresses poorly when he can afford better clothes. Like the individual who is deliberately sloppy and unkempt, such an adolescent is literally telling the world that he will do as he pleases regardless of social attitudes. Or he may feel that gaining acceptance by the social group is so hopeless that it is not worth his effort to try. Whatever his reason for excessive disinterest in clothes, it means poor personal and social adjustments (117).

speech

By the time the child reaches adolescence, he is well aware of the status value of speech. He then uses it as a means to an end—to create in the minds of others the image of himself that he wants them to have. As Lipsett has pointed out, the verbalizations people make of and about themselves—"self-talk," as he labels it—serve as symbols of themselves and the way they

evaluate themselves (146). A person who verbalizes inadequacy or inferiority, for example, literally tells others that he has a poor opinion of himself. Similarly, a person who uses words disapproved of by adults tells others that he is independent and not afraid of adult disapproval. Penny (185) has explained the value of speech as a status symbol:

> In our everyday communication relationships we constantly make inferences, perhaps not always consciously, about the communicator's motivation from both what he says and how he says it. We observe the fact that he repeatedly returns to particular topics, that he selects some aspects of a topic and disregards others, that he uses a particular tone of voice or style of speech, and so on. From such data we may infer that he has a "one track mind," that he is biased, that he is being sincere or insincere. Probably most inferences of this kind are made automatically, on the basis of very limited data together with rather broad assumptions about human nature. . . . In a sense, the communicative act is an experiment in which the communicator gets more or less immediate feedback concerning others' evaluation of him and his communication procedures. Such feedback must constitute an important aspect of the socialization process.

STATUS CLUES

Three aspects of speech are especially valuable as status symbols. They are how the person speaks, what he says, and the amount of talking he does. Each of these tells, either directly or indirectly, what every adolescent wants others to know about himself.

Quality of Speech How a person speaks, in terms of his pronunciation, the tonal quality of his voice, and the words he uses, serves to create impressions that tell others what his status is. For that reason, every adolescent becomes strongly interested in and concerned about these aspects of his speech.

tonal quality of voice With interest in appearance and clothes comes an interest in the quality of the voice. In childhood, when interest in appearance and dress is limited, the child is not interested in the tones he uses when speaking. In fact, he often has a contemptuous attitude toward a "pleasing voice." To a boy, a pleasing voice is an insignia of a sissy. To a lesser extent, girls have similar attitudes toward the tonal quality of their voices (34,86,111).

The adolescent boy's attention is first focused on his voice when puberty changes cause it to sound husky or to "crack." Boys at that time discover that harsh, coarse tones call forth unfavorable reactions, that voice cracks lead to amused reactions, and that a pleasant voice is a personality asset. Even among girls, where the change in tonal quality is far less pronounced than among boys, there is a strong interest in improving the voice during adolescence so that it will create a favorable impression.

Realization that they are judged by how they speak causes adolescent boys and girls to focus their attention on the improvement of the tonal quality of their voices. As is characteristic of adolescents, they go to extremes in this. The outcome is often an affected, unnatural tone which is a source of amusement to adults and of ridicule to other adolescents (22,86,182).

pronunciation Through his pronunciation of words, the adolescent tries to create the impression that he is a well-educated person who belongs to the right socioeconomic group. To create this impression, he often uses an affected style of pronunciation. Long before he reaches adolescence, the child discovers that members of different social classes pronounce the same word differently (23,42). As Packard (180) has pointed out:

> Upper-class members copy the British model, at least to the extent of striving for a cool, precise diction, and by pronouncing the "a" of tomato with an "ah." . . . The New England boarding schools nurturing future upper-class boys have long fostered the Harvard, or Proper Bostonian, accent.

If the adolescent has become accustomed, through childhood, to pronouncing

his words as members of his family, neighbors, and classmates do, he may discover that this identifies him with a social group he does not wish to be identified with. Consequently, he will try to change his pronunciation.

An adolescent from a *bilingual* family is often more concerned by his foreign accent than by the possibility of incorrect use of words. Getting rid of his foreign accent, developed as a result of using the mother tongue of his foreign-born parents in the home during the early, formative years of speech development, is a difficult task.

His concern about his foreign accent is intensified if it stems from the language of a country that has little prestige in the eyes of those with whom he is associated. Should he know, for example, that the people with whom he is associated look down upon the Irish, an Irish accent will identify him with that group (210,219). Regardless of the prestige of the nation, many adolescents prefer not to be different. This is especially true of boys. So long as they have a foreign accent, they feel that they are identified with a minority group (73,133).

words Because of the wide symbolic value of words, many adolescents become "linguistic snobs"; they try to impress others with their social superiority through the use of words that identify them with socially superior groups (42). The adolescent who is anxious to create the impression of being *identified with the right group* makes a point of using words he feels are "proper." Packard (180) has explained how members of different social classes use words to create an image of themselves:

> In general, both the upper classes and the lower classes in America tend to be more forthright and matter-of-fact in calling a spade a spade (for example: organs of the body, ·sexual terms, excretory functions, etc.) than people in between, members of the semiupper and limited success classes. . . . Persons who feel secure in their high status can display their self-assurance by using unpretentious language. Old Bostonians are notably blunt (often to the point of rudeness) in their language.

Studies of words used to convey the same meaning have revealed that certain words identify the speaker with the upper socioeconomic classes, and others, with the middle classes. A few samples, given below, will serve to illustrate this symbolic use of words (14,180):

UPPER CLASS	MIDDLE CLASS
Wash	Launder
Long dress	Formal gown
Rich	Wealthy
Hello	Pleased to meet you
What?	Pardon?
I feel sick	I feel ill
Sweat	Perspiration
Jobs	Positions
Legs	Limbs
Go to work	Go to business

To create the impression that he is *grown-up and sophisticated*, the adolescent builds up a vocabulary of long, technical, and unusual words. Instead of saying that he is "tired," he will claim that he is "fatigued"; he will talk about his "paraphernalia" instead of his "equipment." One of the advantages, from his point of view, of the courses he takes in high school and college is that he can learn new, technical words to use to impress others whose education is more limited than his (23,182). The study of psychology, for example, offers him unlimited opportunities to acquire new names for well-known patterns of human behavior. These he finds especially impressive if they have a Freudian flavor.

No words serve as status symbols for adolescents more effectively than do slang and swear words. "Slang" is a form of unauthorized speech. Slang words are not found in standard dictionaries nor is their use sanctioned by authorities (82). As Jersild (118) has pointed out:

Each generation of adolescents has a special lingo, a favored set of expressions with which they spice their conversation. This lingo constitutes only a small part of their total vocabulary. . . . This "tribal tongue" is imaginative and sometimes obscene. It changes frequently and is quickly out of date; and older adolescents abandon expressions when younger ones take them up.

When slang words prove to be offensive to the hearer, they are called "swearing." The personal reaction of the individual to the word thus determines whether it will be classed as slang or swearing. Slang and swearing play their most important roles as status symbols in adolescence. At this time, there are generally two peaks in the use of slang. The first occurs during the freshman and sophomore years of high school—at approximately the ages of 14 and 15 years—and the second at a similar period in college—from 17 to 19 years. At these ages, the speech of adolescents is "typically colorful (slangy, idiomatic) highly charged (vituperative, ecstatic) ostentatiously careless, and centered largely in personal and interpersonal relationships" (121).

The adolescent finds that when he speaks the language of the group he has a better chance of being accepted than when his speech creates the impression that he is a goody-goody tied to parental apron strings or that he disapproves of the careless speech of his contemporaries. As Bernard has pointed out, "The language of teen-agers serves to maintain barriers between them and the outside world" (22). The adolescent shows that he is an insider when he uses the words his contemporaries use and understand but which are foreign to members on the outside. Therefore, they serve as status symbols for the user (22). Slang words become more and more acceptable to the adolescent as he passes through high school (82,190). Figure 7–1 shows the rapid decline, during the adolescent years, in the number of adolescents who regard the use of slang as "wrong."

Because swearing is even more socially disapproved of than slang, the adolescent asserts his independence of adult control when he uses such forbidden words. Furthermore, since childhood, he has associated swearing with adults, especially adult males. Consequently, the adolescent boy who wants to show his sex appropriateness and his near-adult status uses swearing as a status symbol. In adult women, on the other hand, swearing is considered sex inappropriate. Therefore, adolescent girls use little swearing (82,86,92,118,121,144).

Content of Speech What the adolescent talks about and how he says it are even more important status cues than is how he speaks. Of the different aspects of the content of speech, the following help the adolescent to create in the minds of others the image of himself that he considers desirable.

critical and derogatory comments Being able to sit in judgment on others, to criticize and make derogatory comments about their speech and actions, and to suggest ways of reforming them implies superiority. A common form of derogatory comment is name-calling; it emphasizes the inferiority of the other person by the use of such labels as "nitwit," "idiot," or "sissy," or by saying, "He's nuts." Furthermore, criticizing others or making derogatory comments about them is associated in the mind of the adolescent with adulthood. Now that he has achieved near-adult size, he wants to impress people by speaking about others as adults do.

The more insecure the adolescent, the more likely he is to use these verbal attacks to inflate his ego and to help create a more favorable image of himself (60,86,236). A poor student, for example, gripes about anything and everything at school to make others think that his poor schoolwork is the fault of his teachers or the school. If he is a good student, he may gripe to identify himself with the "right" group who regard academic achievement as of minor importance (44,119).

name-dropping Talking about important people—"name-dropping"—is an indirect way of telling others that one knows and is associated with the right people. If the adolescent calls important people by their first names or, better still, by their nicknames, and can give details about their personal lives, this emphasizes that his relationship with them is on an intimate basis. Many adolescents exaggerate the degree of familiarity they have with prestigeful people.

bragging and boasting What the adolescent brags and boasts about will depend on what is highly valued by the group with

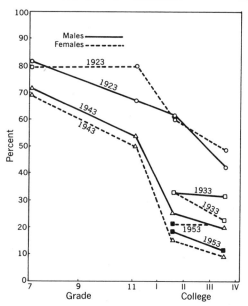

FIGURE 7–1 As adolescence progresses, there is a tendency to regard the use of slang more favorably than to think of it as "wrong." (Adapted from S. L. Pressey and A. W. Jones: 1923–1953 and 20–60 age changes in moral codes, anxieties, and interests, as shown by the "X-O Tests." *J. Psychol.*, 1955, **39**, 485–502. Used by permission.)

which he is identified. If the group places high value on autonomy, he will boast about his privileges; if the group feels that money, material possessions, and community position are essential to social acceptance, he will boast about his family, his ancestors, and the family heirlooms; and if the group places high value on success in heterosexual relationships, the adolescent will boast about his dates and "conquests." Most of the important things an adolescent wants to tell others about himself, whether they be his autonomy, his sex appropriateness, or his superior social status, he can do successfully by bragging and boasting, provided they are cloaked by a sense of modesty and a feigned reluctance to "talk about myself."

ex-cathedra approach The adolescent who wants to impress others with how grown up and sophisticated he is speaks with the "voice of authority"—in an "ex-cathedra" manner—about anything and everything. As a child, he discovered that "mother knows best" or was given to understand that one does not question what a teacher says. Consequently, he learned to associate speaking in an authoritative way with being grown up. As an adolescent, he now tries to create an image of himself as grown up by saying what he has to say in a manner that suggests he is completely sure of the accuracy of what he is saying. Often, to emphasize his sureness, he will preface his remarks with, "As X, the great authority on literature, claims," or "Freud found that. . . ."

radical ideas As was stressed earlier, (see pages 141–142) many adolescents express radical ideas, some of which they do not believe, to attract attention to themselves. The more radical the idea, the more attention value it has. In addition to attention value, the expression of radical ideas is a symbol of the adolescent's autonomy; it tells others that he is not dominated by others in his thinking. It also suggests that he feels secure enough in his status among members of the peer group to be able to be independent in what he says.

jokes and humor The adolescent who feels secure in his status can afford to tell jokes about himself—subjective comic. By contrast, the adolescent who feels less secure and who is anxious to show that he belongs to the group tells jokes about others —objective comic—especially members of minority groups. By doing so, he hopes that his ability to amuse others will increase his acceptance by them. Sex jokes and off-color stories are used in part by adolescents as a symbol of their autonomy. Because adult men tell more sex jokes than women, adolescent boys regard the telling of such jokes as a symbol of their sex appropriateness (28,247).

chitchat versus serious talk If adolescents talk about trivial matters, it implies that they feel somewhat insecure in their relationships with the people to whom they

are speaking; serious talk implies a close relationship and a well-accepted status. Furthermore, the light bantering talk of chitchat is regarded by adolescents as symbolic of a grown-up status. Girls engage in chitchat more often than boys; it is symbolic of femininity to avoid discussions of serious matters.

egocentric versus socialized speech The adolescent who talks mainly about himself and his affairs is trying to symbolize his importance. On the other hand, "socialized speech," in which the speaker concentrates on others and their affairs suggests that he feels less important than those about whom he is talking. Even though the adolescent may have learned, in childhood, that egocentric speech antagonized his listeners— especially when carried to extremes—he continues to use it in the hope of impressing others and of increasing his acceptance by them (23,42,60,185,236).

Quantity of Speech The amount of talking the adolescent does is a cue, of less significance than those just discussed, of his status. To an adolescent, dominating a conversation, from the point of view of determining both the amount of talking he does and what will be talked about, suggests an *adult status*. Therefore, talking in a poised, confident manner helps many adolescents to create the image of themselves as grown up.

The adolescent learned, as a child, that *popular* children do more talking than those who are less well accepted. Consequently, he uses this as a cue to tell others how popular he is. In addition, the adolescent associates amount of talking with *socioeconomic status*, with those of the upper-class groups talking more than those who come from linguistic environments of "relative deprivation." Finally, the adolescent associates amount of talking with *sex*. At every age from earliest childhood, he knows that girls talk more than boys and that they tend to dominate a conversation in heterosexual relationships. Girls, as a result, try to show their femininity by talking more than boys; boys attempt to show their masculinity by being the strong, silent types who say little and allow the girls to take over.

The adolescent who talks little may be trying to impress others with the fact that he is the deep-thinker type who says little and thinks much. But as adolescents put less value on intellectual than on social and athletic success, creating an image of oneself as an intellectual has little prestige value (23,44,86,182,185).

names and nicknames

Through the ages, among primitive as well as among civilized peoples, names have been used as symbols to identify people, their family connections, their racial and religious affiliations, their occupations, and their sex. Freud was the first to point out that names are "symbols of self"; as such, they are used to judge the individual. How important they are as symbols of the individual Freud further stressed when he pointed out that the forgetting of names, either consciously or unconsciously, is motivated by a desire to repress unpleasant associations with the person who bears the forgotten name (77). While this interpretation of forgetting may not be wholly accepted, it suggests that because many people know a person mainly by his name, his name serves as a symbol by which they judge him. As Murphy has pointed out, "One of the most important parts of a person is his name" (168).

Before a baby is a year old, he has learned to associate the name by which others call him with himself. Later, he learns that this label tells others certain things about himself, mainly his sex and the religious or racial background of his parents. When he begins to play with other children, the nickname they give him or how they react to the nickname bestowed upon him by members of his family tells him how they feel about him. As a result of these early learning experiences, the adolescent is well aware of the status value of his name and nickname. To him, they are as important as status symbols as are his clothes, his appearance, or his speech.

NUMBER OF NAME SYMBOLS

Every American adolescent today has at least two names, a "given" name—his first name—and his "last name," which is his family name or surname. In addition, many adolescents have a middle name or even two middle names. Then, too, he has one or more "kinship" names, and usually at least one "nickname." The kinship names identify his status in the family group— son, brother, grandson, cousin, or nephew. The nickname may be a term of endearment, usually given to him by his parents or some family member—Sonny, Junior, Dear or Pet (51,207). Or it may be a form of derogation—making fun of some physical or personality characteristic—Shorty, Fatso, Sissy, Smarty, or Dumbbell.

Sometimes a nickname shows a derogatory attitude toward the bearer's national or religious affiliation, such as Scotch or Yid. Other nicknames may have no real associations with the traits of the bearer; they originate from distortions of the individual's real name—Pat or Lizzie—or they may be made from the individual's initials —Cow or Jaw. With the exception of nicknames of endearment, most nicknames originate in the peer group (86,94,168).

Many adolescents regard the number of names a person has as symbolic of his status. The more he has, the more important he is. This symbol has come from foreign cultures, notably the British culture, where it is traditional to give children of the noble and royal families as many as six or eight names. Being named for someone in the family, especially if it is a prestigeful family member, is likewise a status symbol. Boys who add Jr., III, or IV, to their names are regarded as coming from more distinguished families than boys whose names are unrelated to any family member (165).

Because it is impossible to call a person by all his names, the name chosen to address him is looked upon as a symbol of his status among those who speak to him.

If he is called by his given name, for example, it denotes greater familiarity than if he is called by his surname. Being called by a nickname, on the other hand, signifies the greatest degree of familiarity (35,180).

Advantages and Disadvantages of Number of Names There are certain advantages to having a large number of names. In addition to creating the impression of being an important person, it enables the adolescent to select the name he wishes others to use. He thus can control to some degree the image they form of him. If, for example, he feels that "Francis" sounds like a girl's name, he can encourage people to call him by the nickname, "Frank," which he believes has a more masculine sound. Or if he has a middle name that is both masculine and distinctive, such as "Roger," he can tell people that his name is "F. Roger Smith," thus hiding the disliked first name.

In spite of the advantages to be derived from having a number of names, there is a disadvantage that cannot be overlooked —that of confusion of identity. When different "identity symbols" are used, it is difficult for the individual to know which is his real self. It is equally difficult for others to get a clear image of him if different names are applied to him. This confusion about one's name has been expressed in the old nursery rhyme (168):

> Mother calls me William
> Auntie calls me Will
> Sister calls me Willie
> But Dad calls me Bill

While the adolescent may be confused about which name is symbolic of his real self, the name used by a given individual gives him a clue as to what that person thinks of him. When, for example, his father calls him "Bill," it suggests that his father thinks of him as sex appropriate. When his sister calls him "Willie," it suggests that she regards him as a sissie (168, 207). The same is true of nicknames. When the mother refers to her adolescent son as "My darling," it signifies a favorable status; should his classmates call him "Mother's darling," it signifies a status in which he is the object of ridicule (59,104).

QUALITIES SYMBOLIZED

In every cultural group, names have physical or psychological characteristics associated with them. A person bearing the name of "John," for example, is thought of as trustworthy; "Robin" suggests a young, adventuresome male; "Percy," a sissy; and "Tony" a sociable good guy. The girl's name, "Agnes" suggests a person who is neither young nor good-looking; "Matilda" is associated with a homely girl (213). While few adolescents are aware of all the cultural associations with names, they are well aware of the fact that the names by which they are called serve as symbols of what others *think* they are (74). Figure 7–2 shows some common stereotypes associated with names.

Of the many qualities the adolescent believes his name symbolizes to others, the following are the most important.

| John | Throckmorton | Sue | Abigail |

FIGURE 7–2 Names are symbols in the minds of others.

Identification with the Right Group A common name, if it is associated with the type of people he wants to be identified with, appeals much more to an adolescent than does an unusual name. So long as a boy has the name of John or George, and a girl, the name of Mary or Anne, they feel secure in the fact that they are like others. A foreign name, especially if it is identified with a country that has little prestige in the eyes of Americans, or a name commonly identified with a minority religious group, is a source of concern (1,85,171).

Individuality Because all adolescents, after they have passed through the self-conscious stage of early adolescence, want to be recognized as individuals, they show a preference for names that are slightly different, though conforming in associations with the "right" groups. When, on the other hand, names are so individual that they are considered outlandish and are reacted to with amusement or scorn, they lead to feelings of inadequacy. The adolescent boy who has the given name of Romeo or Judge or the surname Hogg or Roach is sure it is creating an unfavorable image in all who hear the name. Similarly, a girl whose given name is Eldarema or Sophronia and whose family name is Christ—even though pronounced with a short i—feels that this is carrying individuality too far for the purpose of creating a favorable image (66,168,225).

One aspect of individuality that does not appeal to an adolescent is a surname different from that of his parents. When his mother remarries after the death or divorce of the father, his parents are known by one name, and he, by another. This embarrassment is intensified by the stigma associated with divorce and remarriage and by the fact that many of his friends feel sorry for him because he has a stepfather. Under such conditions, it is not unusual for an adolescent to want to be adopted by his stepfather, regardless of how he feels about him (218).

Sex Appropriateness A name or nickname that is sex appropriate goes a long way to create an image of the bearer as a sex-appropriate person. A boy named Percy, for example, is far more likely to be thought of as a sissy than a boy who is named John or Bob.

Sex appropriateness of names comes not from the names themselves so much as from the associations with these names. Certain names derive their associations from characters in the Bible or in literature; others become associated with characters in comics, on the screen, or in sports. "George," for example, is associated with the brave knight who slew the dragon; "Cleopatra" is associated with the "siren of the Nile." Names which in themselves are not symbolic of sex-inappropriate people may become so if associated with well-known characters in the different mass media who are caricatures of their sex. "Katinka" with its nickname, "Tinka," for example, suggests an obese female.

Some names and nicknames become symbolic of sex-inappropriate people because they are associated with both sexes. The name "Frances," for example, is associated with girls: "Francis," which is pronounced in the same way though spelled differently, is a boy's name. Any name that is a common symbol of members of the male sex, when changed slightly to make it a girl's name—a "hybrid name"—is usually symbolic of a masculine girl. A girl who is named Alberta or Paula, for example, is far more likely to be thought of as a masculine girl than is one who has a name that is never associated with members of the male sex. By contrast, a name that is never associated with members of the male sex, such as flower names like Violet and Rose will help to create an image of a feminine girl (85,168,225).

Degree of Acceptance What the adolescent's status in the group is and how well accepted he is by his peers is designated in two ways: first, by the name they use in speaking to or of him, and second, by the nickname they give him. In some high schools for boys, the students are addressed by their teachers by their surnames; in college, they are addressed by their surnames prefixed by "Mr." This, they know, means a greater social distance between them and their teachers than existed in elementary school.

In the home, as well, the adolescent knows that the degree of acceptance he enjoys *at the moment* is expressed in the name family members use in addressing him. If he is called by a pet name or his nickname, it means that he is in favor; if by his first name, it means that he is temporarily out of favor. Similarly, he knows how the peer group feels about him. If he is well accepted, he is far more likely to be called by a nickname than by his first name. When, on the other hand, the peer group gives him a nickname that is derogatory, he is aware, as are all who hear the name, that the group's acceptance of him is poor (54,59,85,168,207).

Even a favorable nickname, said with tones of ridicule or contempt, is a symbol of rejection: a nickname, not favorable in itself, said with tones of admiration and emotional warmth is symbolic of social acceptance (94). The same is true of a given or a surname. The adolescent knows, for example, that if a member of the group says his name with a tone of impatience, it means that the speaker has a poor opinion of him; a tone of admiration signifies good acceptance by that group member.

material possessions

In any culture where there is high value placed on wealth, material possessions are important status symbols. As Hechinger and Hechinger have pointed out, "In a society which judges prestige very largely by outward appearance, what an adolescent owns automatically turns into a yardstick of the entire family's place in the sun" (101).

The reason for the prestige value of material possessions is that they are "manifest." As such, they quickly and easily convey to others what the status of the individual is. Thus, material possessions may be regarded as objective correlates of status. This is especially important in a mobile society where family background and other status symbols lose, to some extent, their prestige value (53,56,112,180,191).

The adolescent knows that a favorable socioeconomic status is judged by the material possessions of the family, especially the size, type, furnishings, and location of the home, the make and number of cars the family has, the type and amount of clothing each family member has, the number and type of radios, record players, and television sets in the home, and the type and amount of jewelry the mother wears (116, 180).

Because material possessions are symbols of socioeconomic status, most Americans today are willing to put proportionally more of their income into them than they would, were their prestige value less. As Parsons (181) has pointed out:

Though the standard of living of any group must cover their intrinsically significant needs, such as food, shelter, and the like, there can be no doubt that an exceedingly large component of standards of living everywhere is to be found in the symbolic significance of many of its items in relation to status.

The affluence of the American culture today makes it possible for adolescents to spend money for status symbols which, in past generations, would have been unavailable (96,177,227,230). As Bernard has stated, our culture can afford a "large leisure class of youngsters who are consumers but not earners" (22). If they do work, they are usually free to spend what they earn as they wish. This means for material possessions that are prestigeful in the eyes of the peer group (22,93,227,230).

EXPRESSIONS OF INTEREST IN MATERIAL POSSESSIONS

There are a number of ways in which an adolescent shows how important material possessions are to him. As he visits in the homes of friends, reads newspapers and magazines, watches television and movies, the adolescent compares what he has with what others have. This makes him dissatisfied with his own possessions and envious of the possessions of others. His *envy* is expressed in many forms. He may, for example, *criticize* or *ridicule* the possessions of others in an unconscious attempt to convince himself and others that they are not worth having.

However, most adolescents know that they are worth having. Consequently, instead of criticizing the possessions of others, they are more likely to *complain* about the inferiority of their own possessions and to tell others how "lucky" they are to be able to have such possessions. Then they *blame their parents* for not providing them with the money needed for these posessions, as other parents do. They may even threaten to leave school and take a job so they may have the status symbols their friends have. Some adolescents take a more aggressive approach to the problem and *steal* what they would like to have (37).

Interest in material possessions as status symbols is shown by the constant *criticism* of the family's car, home, and furnishings and of the clothes the parents wear. The adolescent wants to make a good impression on members of the peer group and to be judged as favorably as possible by them. When he feels that his background falls below his standards, he tries to bring about reforms in it (86,143).

When the material possessions that an adolescent owns are so inferior to those of his classmates that he is convinced they are a serious handicap to social acceptance, it is not unusual for him to *drop out of school* and take a job so that he can have money for the possessions he believes will bring him greater acceptance (46). Many adolescents buy on the installment plan possessions they actually cannot afford but which they feel will give them greater prestige in the eyes of others (87,109,180,227,230).

Interest in material possessions is shown by what adolescents *collect*. Adolescents collect only those things which have prestige value in the eyes of members of the peer group. When it is prestigeful to have records, the adolescent will collect as many as he can afford to buy (22).

Perhaps the best indication of adolescent interest in material possessions comes from studies of wishes and daydreams during the adolescent years. When asked to express freely what he *wishes* he had, the adolescent shows his strong interest in material possessions by putting them at the top of his list. However, he does not wish for just anything; instead, his wishes are concentrated on material possessions that are prestigeful among the members of his group (5,6,40,227,230).

Interest in and importance of material possessions to an adolescent are well illustrated in his *daydreams*. If, for example, a daydream's locale is the home, it is the type of home he would like to live in. Similarly, his clothing, sports equipment, and, above all, his car in the daydream world are all so glamorized that they will win prestige for him among those who see them in his daydream world.

SEX DIFFERENCES IN SYMBOLIC VALUES

Adolescents of the two sexes are interested in different material possessions and for different reasons.

Girls A girl finds that clothing and various kinds of ornamentation are the best symbols of the socioeconomic status she wants to be identified with because they are readily manifest. If she can wear different dresses, sweaters, or costume jewelry to school every day of the week, if she can have a new dress and shoes for every party, and if she can have such a wide selection of cosmetics and perfume that she can vary her appearance and her "odor," it will tell others that her family is well-to-do.

If the home is on the "right" street or in the "right" neighborhood, if it conforms to the prevailing styles in architecture and furnishings as depicted in mazagines or on the screen, and if it has more rooms than are actually needed for family living—such as a TV room or a recreation room with built-in bar for entertaining—it symbolizes the family's affluence. When, in addition to the house, there are several garages with cars of the "right" make readily available for use by the different members of the family and a servant who is doing the housework instead of the mother, the symbolism of affluence is increased (53,136, 152,166,180).

Boys Because the social life of boys is primarily outside the home and because boys' clothing is so standardized in color and style that variations are limited, American boys symbolize their socioeconomic status by the cars they drive, preferably their own cars (63). Bernard (22) has stated:

> It is taken for granted that every teen-ager will learn to drive and that, if he does not have a car of his own, individually or as a member of a group, he will certainly have access to one. . . . In many cities it is an accepted pattern that in order to date a girl, a boy must be able to provide a car for transportation; she may not go in a cab or allow herself and her date to be driven by parents. Having acquired a car for transportation, socialization, and dating, a boy becomes so involved in its care and upkeep he has little time or interest left for other activities.

That car ownership is important to adolescent boys is shown by Figure 7–3 which indicates that there is an increase of 50 percent from freshman to senior year in high school (44).

"Automania" or an "overobsession with the automobile as a status symbol" is the boy's way of telling the world that he is *independent* and can come and go as he pleases, that he is *grown up* because the law permits him to own and drive a car, and that he is *sex appropriate* because a boy who owns his own car is a near man, not "mother's little darling." Then, in addition, by driving at speeds beyond the legal limit and by taking chances, he further impresses others with his masculinity, indicating that he is not "chicken" or a sissy (63).

If his car is an expensive model, preferably a convertible, and a new one rather than a second- or thirdhand jalopy, it implies that the family *socioeconomic status* is superior. When he is free to use his car to take members of the crowd for rides, it becomes a "clubhouse on wheels—a medium for holding a party." As adolescent boys explain it, "When you have your own car, you've got it made"—in the sense that the car, as a status symbol, establishes the boy in the eyes of others as the "right kind" (22,82,102,118,186).

While other material possessions, such as radios, television sets, records, sports equipment, and clothes are all-important status symbols, none can compare with a car. Not only is a boy's car manifest, but he can take it wherever he goes. In time, everyone associates it with him. This is not true of other material possessions; hence, their status value is limited as compared with that of a car (63,102,180).

money

In a culture that places high value on material possessions, money is an important status symbol. There are two reasons for this: First, money makes it possible to have the material possessions that help to establish the status of the individual in the eyes of others, and second, the individual is judged by others in terms of his money. There is a tendency to attribute more favorable qualities to a high-income person and less favorable qualities to one whose

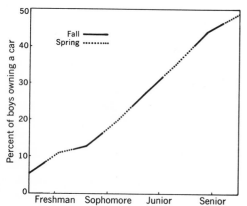

FIGURE 7–3 Car ownership becomes an increasingly important status symbol for boys as adolescence progresses. (Adapted from J. S. Coleman: *The adolescent society.* New York: The Free Press of Glencoe, 1961. Used by permission.)

income is low. While it is true that the income of the person who makes the judgments will influence his judgments of another person, there is always greater prestige associated with a person who has money than with one who literally lives on a hand-to-mouth basis (148,162,170).

Long before childhood is over, the child learns that his status in the group is influenced by how much money he has to spend. He discovers that teachers and other adults treat the children who come from big homes and whose families have big cars and important status in the community quite differently from those whose parents live on the "wrong side of the tracks." In spite of all people say, he is well aware that "money counts" (70,170).

The adolescent learned, during his childhood days, that to be able to serve as a status symbol, money must be manifest. This means that it must be spent or available for spending, not held as savings or investments. The only time the typical adolescent of today will save *voluntarily* is when saving makes it possible for him to buy some larger or expensive possession he would be unable to buy with his weekly allowance or earnings. A boy, for example, is willing to save to buy a car because of its high prestige value (105,120,167,227,230).

Because adolescents in the American culture of today think of money in terms of *spending*, and because spending helps them to achieve the status they crave, they do not feel guilty about spending all the money they have for status symbols, about borrowing when there is a status symbol they feel is a must, or about buying on an installment plan (227,230). Today, spending more than one has is approved by many adolescents because it serves as a status symbol; few regard it as "wrong" (190). Figure 7–4 shows the change in attitudes toward extravagance.

QUALITIES SYMBOLIZED

Because the adolescent's interest in money centers around spending, he wants to be sure that it will be used to symbolize qualities that are important in forming a favorable image of him. Of the qualities he

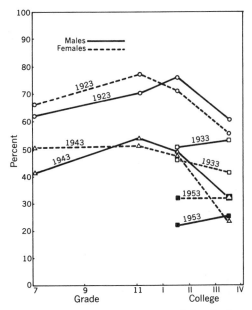

FIGURE 7–4 "Extravagance" is regarded as far less "wrong" by today's adolescents than by adolescents in past generations. (Adapted from S. L. Pressey and A. W. Jones: 1923–1953 and 20–60 age changes in moral codes, anxieties, and interests as shown by the "X-O Tests." *J. Psychol.*, 1955, **39**, 485–502. Used by permission.)

wants money to symbolize, the following are the most important.

Socioeconomic Status Having money readily available at all times implies that the adolescent has a sufficient supply to meet all needs. To create this impression, he demands an allowance as large as that of his friends, he takes money out of his savings if he begins to run short before the next allowance date, he borrows from his mother or a more prudent sibling, or he earns by part-time work enough to supplement his allowance. So long as he is never in a position where he must say, "I can't afford it" or "I have no money," he gives the impression that he is relatively affluent (162,170,188).

Being able to spend money for luxuries tells others even more emphatically that the family's socioeconomic status is favorable. Figure 7–5 shows how typical American high school students spend their money.

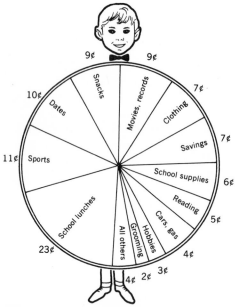
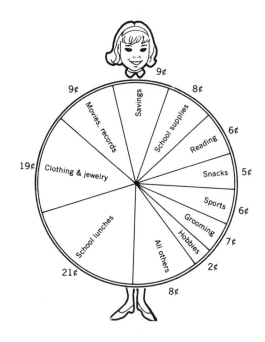

FIGURE 7–5 How adolescent boys and girls spend their money. (Based on data compiled for *Life Magazine* by Eugene Gilbert. May 13, 1957. Used by permission.)

A glance at these expenditures will show how many of them fall in the luxury category. When, for example, a girl can spend 10 cents out of every dollar for clothes and jewelry, 7 cents for grooming, and 9 cents for movies and recreations, while only 9 cents is put into savings, it suggests a relatively affluent state (62,161,188).

Nothing emphasizes the adolescent's favorable economic status better than being able to "treat" his friends. If he has a car at his disposal to take the crowd where it wants to go without asking everyone to chip in to pay for the gas, if he can set them up to drinks at some tavern away from the watchful eyes of parents, or if he has a plentiful supply of cigarettes to pass around, his peers will form an image of him as "rich." Many adolescents learn that popularity has a "price tag" attached to it (188).

Identification with the Right Crowd In every school and college, the leading crowds are composed mainly of adolescents whose families are affluent enough to have status symbols of all types, to entertain at home or in clubs, and they do not expect their children to work or to contribute, if they do work, to family expenses (44,177,180, 215,227,230). If they do work, they generally explain that it is for the "kicks" of it, that they are bored, or that "Dad has old-fashioned ideas about money" (162, 170).

One of the strong drives behind social mobility is the desire on the part of parents to live like the families whose sons and daughters "run everything" in high school and college. Many parents are so anxious to have their children accepted that they are willing to make sacrifices to provide their children with the money needed for the material possessions and the recreations associated with the "right crowds." Creating the impression of affluence helps to create the image of identification with people who are affluent (67,148).

Sex Appropriateness According to tradition, the male is the earner while the female is the recipient of money from the earner

Even if a boy's parents are willing to pay him for jobs done in the home, the boy prefers a job outside the home; this, he believes, has greater status value in the eyes of his peers. Girls, by contrast, feel that working for money in the home is more feminine than working outside the home. If they do take outside jobs, it is generally in some feminine line of work, such as baby-sitting (72,178).

The way adolescents spend their money is symbolic of their sex appropriateness. A glance at Figure 7–5, page 274, will show marked sex differences in the way young adolescents spend their money. Boys, for example, spend nearly twice as much for sports as do girls; girls spend nearly three times as much for clothing as boys.

Independence Even when the adolescent must rely upon an allowance from his parents, he wants to feel free to spend it as he wishes, without having to account to his parents for his expenditures (188,227). The most important way in which money symbolizes the adolescent's independence is in his ability to come and go as he wishes and where he wishes without parental interference. If the crowd suggests, on the spur of the moment, that it would be fun to take a car and go to some dance place, his ability to pay his share for the entertainment without telephoning his parents for permission or without going home to get money symbolizes an independent status he wants the peer group to associate with him (62,67,120,192).

Money goes a long way toward creating an image of a person who can demand what he wants and get it. The appearance of a flock of expensive cars in the school or college parking lots makes many educators feel that they must watch their step in their dealings with their affluent students and their even more affluent parents. Perhaps no group is more influenced by the image of the affluent adolescent of today than that composed of manufacturers, advertisers, and businessmen (227,230). The business world realizes that adolescents "have the money to call the tune: they are 'patrons' of the arts and must, therefore, be catered to" (22).

AMOUNT NEEDED AS STATUS SYMBOL

How much money the adolescent needs as a status symbol varies. If he is identified with a *group* whose members have more money to spend than he, what his family regards as an adequate allowance he will find inadequate for his needs. When, on the other hand, the adolescent has more money than the other members of the group, he may be envied by them; this focuses attention on him (67,170).

The *older* adolescent feels that he needs more money to spend than the younger. This is due to the fact that status symbols cost more as he grows older. He needs, for example, more sports equipment, more records, more clothes, and a more expensive car to impress his peers than he did when he was younger. Furthermore, the older adolescent needs more money for entertainment as less is supplied by parents, community centers, and schools than when he was a high school student (5,62,72,148, 167,192).

Many adolescents take part-time jobs while in high school and some drop out of school before graduation to be able to earn the money they feel so essential to achieving the status they aspire to hold in the peer group (62,120). Figure 7–6 shows the increase in number of students working part time from freshman to senior year in high school.

Boys, at all ages, need more money than girls. This is due, in part, to the fact that boys spend most of their time away from home, and as a result, must supply their own status symbols instead of relying on the family's symbols as girls do (6,22, 67,178).

privileges

When his body approximates that of an adult in size and shape, the adolescent wants the privilege of doing the things adults do. This, he feels, will identify him with adults and create an image of him as

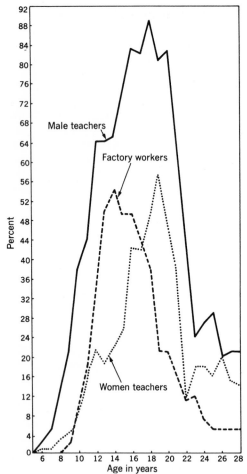

FIGURE 7–6 The number of adolescents working in part-time or summer jobs increases as the desire for status symbols increases. (Adapted from J. L. Norton: Patterns of vocational interest development and actual job choice. *J. genet. Psychol.*, 1953, **82**, 235–262. Used by permission.)

a near adult. Once this image has been created, he expects to be treated as an adult. Because most states permit adolescents to drive cars at some time between the ages of 14 and 18 years, the adolescent discovers the status value of being permitted to do what is usually associated with adults. This whets his appetite for more privileges. Today's adolescents look upon the right to smoke as an "American puberty rite" just as is the right to drive a car (179).

Modern adolescents hold the whip handle when it comes to getting what they want. In an affluent society where parents can afford to provide for their adolescent children without their financial help, and where adolescents can earn money while still in school or college, adolescents have a way of enforcing their demands for privileges that those in a less affluent society or in one where authoritarian child-rearing methods prevail do not have (227,230). As Bernard has said, American adolescents of today can demand that adults give them what they want or they will threaten to drop out of school, leave home, and become self-supporting (22).

Long before childhood came to a close, the adolescent discovered that some of his age-mates had more privileges than he. This led to friction with his parents, combined with demands for similar privileges. As a child, he could not use the threat of dropping out of school but he touched an equally sensitive parental spot—the parent's desire for his child to be popular (44). He learned that the phrase, "But *everyone* is allowed to do that," was the open sesame to the privileges he craved.

To enforce his demands for the privileges he feels are rightly his, the adolescent plays on parental sympathy when he lacks social acceptance by blaming them for his plight. He tries to look older and more sophisticated than he is and he talks with the voice of authority to impress upon adults his mature status.

If all else fails, he uses the tactics he has learned work effectively in business and industry—he goes on an "academic sit-down strike," working far below his intellectual capacities. Knowing that his parents are eager to have him go to college and preferably to a "name" college, he is in a favorable bargaining position and generally emerges the winner (214,238).

DIFFICULTIES IN GETTING PRIVILEGES
Adolescents whose parents have used *authoritarian methods of discipline* with their children are rarely willing to relax their control even as their children approach ma-

turity. This is especially true of foreign-born parents (19,131,226). *Firstborn children,* whether they be boys or girls, tend to be more overprotected than their siblings. As a result, when they reach adolescence, they find obstacles in the way to independence that their younger siblings are not likely to encounter. After a few years of conflict with their firstborn children, parents generally revise their attitudes and grant more privileges. Later children profit by this revision of parental attitudes. As a result, they find it easier to get the privileges they demand when they demand them (29,31,138,224).

Girls find it more difficult to get the privileges they feel they are entitled to than do boys. Parents fear that a girl with too much freedom will acquire an unfavorable reputation. While reluctant to give boys all the privileges they demand, parents sooner or later acquiesce because they do not want their sons to get the reputation of being sissies or of being tied to parental apron strings (58,99,125,186,214).

Of all adolescents, the ones who have the greatest difficulty in gaining privileges are the late maturers. By contrast, the early maturer has less difficulty; in fact, privileges are often given to him without his having to ask for them along with the responsibilities he is expected to assume (122,124, 169).

NUMBER OF PRIVILEGES

How many privileges an adolescent wants depends mainly on the *group* with which he is associated (186). *Boys,* as a group, expect to have more privileges than girls; and members of the lower socioeconomic groups expect more than those of the middle groups. Adolescents of the highest *socioeconomic* groups, like those of the lowest, generally have more privileges than middle-class adolescents. Adolescents who grow up in *large cities* or in *suburban* areas have, as a rule, more privileges than do those from small towns or rural districts. And, as would be expected, the adolescent who goes away to college or is working has more privileges than the younger adolescent who is still in high school (58,86,180,186,193).

LATCHKEY PROBLEMS

While adolescents want the privilege of running their own lives, the privileges that mean most to them are those which are most highly valued by the group with which they are identified. Only in those areas of behavior which are important to adolescents, as in social life and sports, are privileges important to any appreciable degree. The privilege of driving the grandparents to church on Sunday, for example, is not comparable to the privilege of driving one's peers to a party.

Because of the prestige associated with social life, most of the demands for privileges made by adolescents center around their new social lives. "Latchkey problems" include the hours of coming home after a party or other social function, the number of times a week the adolescent will be permitted to go out, the people with whom he associates, and the places where he goes.

Many of the arguments and frictions between adolescents and their parents center around the problems of independence in social affairs. The adolescent argues for more privileges than he is given, complains that he is being unfairly treated and that he misses out on the fun his friends have because his parents treat him "like a baby," is sullen, stubborn, refuses to speak, and is often disobedient (22,44,86,186).

QUALITIES SYMBOLIZED

Privileges that are manifest and are related to areas of behavior that are prestigeful in the eyes of the peer group symbolize many of the qualities the adolescent is anxious to have others ascribe to him. Of these, the following are most important to him.

Independence Being allowed to do what his age-mates do tells them that the adolescent is independent and no longer tied to parental apron strings. A few more privileges than they have, especially if given slightly sooner than they are given them, proclaims his greater independence. Too many privileges, on the other hand, may lead to an unfavorable reputation—a reputation of being "wild" or "fast." Too few suggest that he is afraid to "tell his parents off" and assert his independence (48,106, 189,238,243).

Socioeconomic Status Knowing that too many privileges suggest "wildness," most adolescents who want to create the image of belonging to an upper-class group are willing to accept some reasonable limitations on their demands for privileges. By doing so, they hope this will identify them with a better socioeconomic group than is generally associated with unlimited freedom (97,193,235,239).

Identification with the Right Crowd If the "nice kids" are restricted in the privileges they have, the adolescent who is restricted in what he can do gains the reputation of being a nice kid. If, on the other hand, he has few restrictions, he is identified with the "wild ones" and gains a reputation of being wild (69,159,186).

Sex Appropriateness Boys of all social classes symbolize their masculinity by their freedom to come and go as they please, where they please, and with whom they please.

The reverse is true of girls, especially during the early part of adolescence. At that time, the privileges girls are given are only slightly above those given a child. The more restricted a girl is, the more "feminine" she is judged to be; the more privileges she has, the more likely she is to be regarded as a "masculine" girl. The image of the sex-appropriate girl still is influenced by the stereotype of the well-protected person with limited privileges (81,106,135, 151,189,214). Both at home and in school, the adolescent who is given the privilege of deciding what he will do, where he will go, and with whom he will associate impresses others with his grown-up status. The adolescent who must ask permission or must consult an adult before he acts, creates the impression of being a child. That is why adolescents, when with members of the peer group, will break family rules about the time they return home from parties instead of calling up to ask permission to stay beyond the family curfew (58,80,83).

organizational affiliation

According to the old saying, "Birds of a feather flock together." The adolescent knows that he is judged by the people he associates with. Consequently, he wants to be associated with prestigeful organizations, whether they be school, church, or club.

PRESTIGE OF AFFILIATION

The prestige of affiliation with an organization depends on many conditions, of which the following are the most important.

Method of Joining There are two ways in which an adolescent may become affiliated with an organization: He may apply for membership or he may be invited by the members of the organization to join. Many of the school and community organizations are open to all adolescents of a given age range. Other clubs, especially the fraternities and sororities of high schools and colleges, are open only to those whom the members wish to have associated with them (142). Obviously, the prestige associated with joining by invitation is much greater than joining by application.

Exclusiveness of Organization There is far greater prestige in belonging to an organization that is "exclusive" than to one that is open to all. Belonging to an exclusive organization gives each member personal satisfaction; it also gives him prestige in the eyes of others (10).

How important exclusiveness is to the adolescent is well illustrated by how much of his free time he is willing to devote to different organizations (20,195). In Hollingshead's study of adolescents in "Elmtown," he found that students who belonged to school or community clubs devoted only a third of their free time to their activities as compared with nearly 70 percent by students who had their own exclusive clubs (108). Satisfaction from activities means less to adolescents than satisfaction from identification. Similarly, college girls who belong to low-prestige sororities gain less satisfaction from their affiliation than do girls who belong to high-prestige sororities (13,242).

Status in Organization The status the adolescent has in an organization influences the amount of prestige he derives from affiliation. Being a leader is more prestigeful than being a follower. An adolescent who is a leader in the organizations with which he is identified will create a more favorable image of himself than will the adolescent whose status is always that of a follower (12,13).

Activities of the Organization How much prestige the adolescent will derive from being affiliated with an organization is greatly influenced by the degree of prestige associated with the dominant activities of the organization. A special-interests club, in school or college, a history or science club, for example, is organized primarily to bring together individuals with strong interests in the dominant interest of the club. The club is identified in the minds of others with its dominant interest; that interest may have little prestige in the peer group. By contrast, a social club for girls or an athletic club for boys, especially if it is dominated by a prestigeful sport, such as tennis or swimming, will have great prestige. The adolescent who belongs will share some of the prestige through his affiliation (44,180,186).

How Affiliation Is Symbolized The adolescent who has a prestigeful affiliation is especially anxious to symbolize it. This he does by various methods. Many fraternities, sororities, and clubs, for example, have some distinguishing article of *clothing* which only members are permitted to wear. This may be a tie, a scarf, a cap, a blazer, a pin, or a ring. In addition to what he wears, the adolescent can show his affiliation by a *sticker* on his car or luggage, or by the use of *writing paper* with the organizational seal embossed on it. Without boasting or bragging, he can casually mention a person,

an event, or an activity related to the organization, and thus *talk* about his membership in it in this indirect fashion.

Most school and college *papers* report the activities of all organizations. To make sure that everyone knows he is identified with a particular organization, the adolescent who serves as an officer, a committee member, or a committee chairman makes reports of his activities which are published in the paper. The more active he is, the more often his name will be reported in connection with the organization; in turn, the more widely he will be associated with it in the minds of others (122).

QUALITIES SYMBOLIZED
Organizational affiliation tells others things about the individual which are incorporated in their image of him. Of these, the following are the most important.

Popularity The degree of social acceptance an adolescent enjoys is readily manifest by the type of organization with which he is affiliated and the status he occupies in that organization. If he belongs to an organization which admits members only by invitation, this symbolizes the fact that he is more popular than if he belongs to one which is open to all. When there are a number of organizations that admit by invitation in the same school or college, the more prestigeful the organization with which he is identified, the more popular he is judged to be. Because it is assumed that *everyone* would rather be a leader than a follower, the adolescent who is a follower in an organization is judged less popular than one who holds a leadership role.

When an adolescent belongs to a number of different organizations, he is regarded as more popular than when he belongs to only one, *unless* the one he is identified with is so prestigeful that it alone can symbolize his acceptance. It is a recognized fact that adolescents who enjoy little social acceptance in the organizations with which they are affiliated quickly drop out; those who enjoy acceptance often become "joiners."

Socioeconomic Status "Belonging" is a symbol of higher socioeconomic status not necessarily because members of the higher groups can afford the financial outlay for membership but mainly because they are better accepted by the other members. The adolescent who comes from a "right" family is accepted in the most exclusive organizations even though his financial status is poor; the adolescent whose financial status is superior but whose family background is inferior will be excluded from membership.

The higher on the socioeconomic ladder the adolescent's family is, the more organizations he is likely to be identified with. His socioeconomic status, thus, is symbolized by the *number* of his affiliations. It is also symbolized by his *status* in the organizations. It is a well-known fact among adolescents that the leaders are drawn mainly from those with higher socioeconomic status. The adolescent who holds the role of leader in one or more organizations is judged as coming from a higher-status family than is the adolescent whose role is always that of follower.

Sex Appropriateness Just as adult women belong to more organizations than men, so adolescent girls belong to more than do boys. In every school and college, there are more girls' clubs than boys' clubs. Furthermore, girls, like adult women, take more active parts in organizational affairs than do boys; they are willing to serve on more committees than are boys and willing to do more work on these committees.

Even more emphatically, the main activities of an organization symbolize sex appropriateness. The boy who belongs to a sports club is regarded as sex appropriate; he is thought of as a sissy if he belongs to a social club. The reverse is true of girls; belonging to a sports club suggests masculinity in girls, while belonging to a social club suggests femininity. In special-interest clubs, those which concentrate on science and world problems are regarded as masculine; those concentrating on languages, dramatics, and art are regarded as feminine.

A boy who belongs to an art club is thought of as effeminate; a girl in a similar position is thought of as feminine.

Adult Status Most children do not belong to organizations except those meant exclusively for children, such as dancing classes or the Scouts. Consequently, belonging to a grown-up organization, playing the role of grown-ups in that organization, and having minimum adult supervision over the activities of the organization suggests to others that the members are near adults. Many girls like to play the role of "junior club women" because it symbolizes to all that they are no longer children. Furthermore, because adult recreational activities are more often centered around organizations than around friendship groups, the adolescent who follows this pattern is symbolizing his near-adult status.

That organizational affiliation is recognized as a new and important status symbol to an adolescent who wants to create the impression that he is grown up is well illustrated by the fact that adolescents consciously try to identify themselves with their organizations to let others know of their affiliation. When, for example, they speak of their friends, they refer to them as "my fraternity brothers" or "my sorority sisters." Instead of talking about the members of a club as their "friends," they are "my clubmates." This, together with articles of clothing and other similar insignia of membership, leaves no doubt in the minds of others that the adolescent is following an adult pattern in his social life (4,39,44,50,57,98, 101,180,241,248).

tabooed pleasures

Just as Adam and Eve, in the Garden of Eden, were tempted to eat the only fruit they were forbidden to touch, so the adolescent is tempted to engage in activities that are forbidden. The very fact that they are forbidden gives them a halo of desirability. It is a case of the grass on the other side of the fence appearing greener than on the adolescent's side (11,212,228). In discussing the lure of tabooed pleasures, Hollingshead (108) has pointed out:

Law and the mores deny high-school students the right to enjoy the pleasures derived from tobacco, gambling, and alcohol. However, the system with which adults surround these areas of behavior lends them a special value which seems to act as a stimulus to many young people who desire to experience the supposed thrill of pleasures their elders deny them. The conspiracy of silence which is an essential part of the clandestine violation of the mores has already taught them how easy it is to avoid restrictions imposed by law and taboo if they are discreet about how, where, and under what circumstances it is done. Acquisition of knowledge of the means of transgressing against alcohol, tobacco, and gambling taboos without being caught and the thrill of violating these taboos take place for the most part in the clique.

The activities adolescents are forbidden to engage in are, for the most part, pleasures which adults enjoy. The reason for adults' depriving them of these pleasures is that they believe they are harmful to the adolescent, either physically or mentally, or they are harmful to society. In discussing the use of "pot"—the teen-agers' name for marijuana—by high school and college students, *Time* (228) has given the following explanation of why it is forbidden:

How perilous is pot? Medical authorities agree that it is not biochemically addictive, that it does not induce the physiological cravings or withdrawal symptoms of such drugs as heroin or cocaine. It affects the user's judgment, and if used daily, will dull a student's initiative and drive, but on the whole, "marijuana is probably less danger than alcohol.". . . What does concern parents, administrators and doctors is the possibility of psychological habituation. . . . "The emotionally susceptible person can get psychologically dependent on anything —caffeine and coffee, nicotine and cigarettes, alcohol or marijuana." And of these, pot leads to the worst possibility: that the student *may take to stronger, crippling drugs.*

Most adults try to calm adolescent resentments aroused by forbidding them to engage in these pleasures by telling them that they can engage in them when they are grown up. This merely serves to enhance the desirability of the forbidden pleasures and to increase the adolescent's motivation to show the world that he is old enough *now* to engage in adult activities (82,118).

In discussing cigarette smoking among adolescents, Lawton has pointed out that "initiation of smoking is seen largely as a social and psychological phenomenon, mediated by the mechanisms of curiosity, imitation, identification, status striving, and rebellion" (141). The "common way of using marijuana is the spur-of-the-moment party in a college student's apartment, a teen-ager's home when parents are away, or a car at a movie drive-in" (228).

The desirability of many of the forbidden pleasures is constantly called to the adolescent's attention by mass media of communication. Ads for different forms of liquor—whether beer, whisky, vodka, champagne, or wines—show adults enjoying these drinks in a gay party setting. The implication is that if you want to have fun at a party, you must drink. Ads for cigarettes show smartly dressed society women and successful business executives puffing away on cigarettes of their favorite brands. The adolescent girl who aspires to be a social success or the boy who dreams of himself as a business executive with the prestige and money that status will bring him comes to the conclusion that one asset to success is smoking in a sophisticated way.

Movies, television shows, pictorial sections of newspapers and magazines, and reports of the activities of men and women in newspapers or on radio add their share in glamorizing tabooed pleasures. The adult always drives, for example, he never uses public transportation. Making love is one of the everyday pleasures of men and women; it is what "makes the world go round" for them so why not for the adolescent also?

AREAS OF TABOOED PLEASURES

In the American culture of today, certain activities are forbidden to the adolescent until he reaches an age prescribed by law or by custom. He may not, for example, *drive* until the law of the state in which he lives says he may. He may not buy or be served *liquor* in any public place until the state in which he lives thinks it is safe for him to drink. At no age may he buy *narcotics* to make him forget his troubles, nor is he allowed to go to houses of prostitution to enjoy the pleasures of *sex* until he is legally an adult (11,65,157,228).

Pleasures that are regarded as less harmful are denied him by custom rather than by law. It is expected that his parents and teachers will enforce the customs. In spite of the recent publicity given to the supposed linkage between cancer and *cigarette smoking*, there are no laws saying that a person must wait until a given age to begin smoking or prescribing how much he may smoke. This is assumed to be a parental responsibility. In the same way, it is assumed that parents and teachers will chaperon social gatherings to ensure that the adolescents derive pleasure from activities other than *sex*. *Glue sniffing*, while harmful, is regarded more as a fad than as habit forming, as narcotics are. Therefore, its control is left in the hands of parents and teachers (16).

STATUS VALUES OF TABOOED PLEASURES

Frequently the forbidden activity is a far less pleasurable experience for the adolescent than he had anticipated. It is not uncommon, for example, for the first smoke or drink to make the adolescent slightly nauseated. If engaging in forbidden activities were motived by pleasurable results alone, many would be abandoned quickly. However, the adolescent soon discovers that they have great status value; for that reason, he continues to engage in them. In time, he may develop a liking for them, either because of the activity per se or because of its status value.

In the case of smoking, for example, both boys and girls report a greater liking as they go from high school into college. This is illustrated in Figure 7–7. Note that girls, in 1953, showed a greater liking for smoking than did girls in 1923 when smoking by girls was less socially approved than it is now. Note also that boys in 1923 showed a greater liking than in more recent years when smoking has become more common among girls and, hence, loses some of its value as a symbol of masculinity (153,155, 190,194,221).

The status value of some forbidden pleasures is so great that they are often engaged in to excess. This is especially true of adolescents who feel socially insecure and who are anxious to improve their status in the peer group. If, for example, the peer group regards drinking of hard liquor as a sign of true masculinity, a boy may become "high," "gay," or "buzzed" in his attempts to prove his masculinity (18,139,229). If group acceptance is influenced by strict adherence to the patterns of behavior approved by the group, excessive drinking may be the price the adolescent must pay to prove to the group that he will be an acceptable member (18,82,118,139,153,180,186).

Excessive smoking, like excessive drinking, more often results from a strong desire to establish a favorable status in the group than from the pleasure smoking gives (68, 110,208,221). This is true also of the use of narcotics. Smoking marijuana, injecting opium or heroin, or swallowing mescaline pills may start as a thrill promoter when an adolescent is bored or feels inadequate (11, 82,100,118,228). Not realizing the seriousness of what they do, many adolescent users become addicts before they reach the age of legal maturity (16,26,38,108,154).

The status value of forbidden pleasures takes five different forms, each of which tells others important things about the adolescent and influences the image they develop of him. These are discussed below.

Independence To show others that he is autonomous and able to decide what he wants to do, many an adolescent is willing to break family or school rules and even to break the laws. Most adolescent boys will, at some time or other, defy the law by driving at speeds beyond the legal limits

(102). Jersild (118) has commented on this:

> During the teens, speeding often seems to afflict youngsters as a contagious disease. Some boys even seem to be proud of getting a ticket for speeding, even though they thereby risk the loss of their driver's license, and many do have their licenses suspended or revoked.

In spite of the difficulties in obtaining *narcotics*, many adolescents try to show their independence by buying them on the black market and using them to show how independent of adult control they are (11, 65,154,173,174,175,176). This explanation has been given for the present trend toward using marijuana (228):

> Part of pot's attraction is "doing something illegal together.". . . To most psychiatrists, the increase in marijuana smoking represents not so much a search for new thrills as the traditional, exhibitionistic rebellion of youngsters against adult authority. Parents who are agreeable to students' drinking almost always boggle at drugs. "There is not much that students can do that is defiant," says a Boston psychiatrist. "They think with some degree of glee about what their parents would think if they knew they were smoking marijuana.

Because drinking and smoking are easier and safer ways to assert their independence than fast driving and the use of narcotics, they are more common methods of showing how independent the adolescent is. Many adolescents start to *drink* without parental knowledge and consent (139,212). They defy school rules about drinking on the premises just as college students do. Even more daringly, they may defy the law by falsifying their ages to be able to buy liquor or to drink in places that serve liquor to adults. Drinking as a symbol of independence is more often used by boys than by girls (3,82,118,139). Like drinking, *smoking* begins without parental knowledge and consent among most adolescents. It is done on school grounds and in off-limits areas of college buildings. By defying a strict rule, the adolescent can symbolize his independence more forcibly than by defying a lenient rule (44,68,108,110,153,179,211,221).

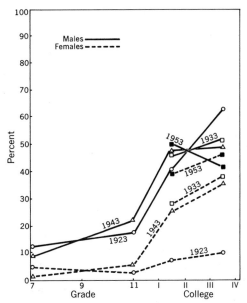

FIGURE 7-7   There is an increased "liking" for smoking as a status symbol among both boys and girls during adolescence. (Adapted from S. L. Pressey and A. W. Jones: 1923–1953 and 20–60 age changes in moral codes, anxieties, and interests as shown by the "X-O Tests." *J. Psychol.*, 1955, **39**, 485–502. Used by permission.)

Maturity   Drinking is more often associated with adults exclusively than is smoking. As a result, "Drinking precedes smoking as adolescents take up adult foibles" (223). Today, drinking often starts as early as junior high school (139). By the time adolescents reach senior high school, most have been able to convince their parents that "everyone does it" (3,108,139,172,187,223). Smoking usually starts as part of a "kind of defiant claim on adult status" (155). It soon becomes an accepted pattern of behavior which proclaims the adolescent's mature status (110,194,208,211,221).

Sex Appropriateness   Most of the tabooed pleasures are more closely identified with the stereotype of the male than of the female. A real man, according to the cultural stereotype, is bold and daring; he defies rules and even laws to assert his independence; and he does so openly, not behind adult backs.

Some of the forbidden pleasures that are commonly associated more with males than females are drinking, smoking, gambling, sex play, and fast driving. They are the ones the boy concentrates on to show how masculine he is. Excessive drinking, smoking, and speeding, and sexual excesses are especially common among boys who have feelings of masculine inadequacy and who want to prove to themselves and others that they are he-men.

Girls have less need than boys to go to excesses to prove their sex appropriateness. In fact, refraining from engaging in these forbidden pleasures, or doing so only when urged to do so by a boy, is symbolic of a girl's femininity (3,108,139,223).

When activities are engaged in by members of both sexes, adolescents can symbolize their sex appropriateness by the degree to which they engage in the activities and by what they do. In the case of drinking, for example, boys drink mostly beer and hard liquor; girls drink cocktails or other mixed drinks, such as spiked punch (3,18, 44,108,139,223). Boys try to symbolize their masculinity by smoking pipes or cigars which are rarely smoked by girls, or by smoking unfiltered cigarettes; filtered cigarettes are regarded by many boys as a sissy type of cigarette. Girls, on the other hand, more often use filter-tipped cigarettes, menthol-flavored cigarettes, or cigarettes smoked through a holder (68,110,153).

Identification   Like clothing and speech, doing what others do implies to others that one "belongs." When the group drinks, the adolescent who wants to be identified with the group drinks as much as the others, he drinks what they drink, and he goes where they do for his drinks (3,139). If drinking beer is the thing to do, he drinks beer; if drinking in a tavern or roadhouse is the thing to do, that is where he does his drinking; and if drinking with the clique is favored over drinking at mixed parties, he will do most of his drinking with the boys. A girl who wants to symbolize her identification with the "social" group of the school or college drinks when she is on dates with boys, she drinks cocktails rather than beer,

and she drinks at parties held in the "right" places—private homes, clubs, or hotels—not in taverns, cars, or roadhouses (18,103,108, 223).

To gain acceptance in some cliques, boys must prove their masculinity by having some sexual experience, while some girls' cliques regard loss of virginity as an "entrance requirement" (108,129,157,186,223). For adolescents who lack a feeling of identification with the group, use of drugs, such as smoking marijuana, gives them a feeling of belonging; "when they smoke there is a certain togetherness" (228).

One of the problems faced by a *socially mobile adolescent* is to give up forbidden pleasures, if they are frowned upon by the group with which he hopes to be identified, or to accept new ones, if he and his parents strongly disapprove of them. A socially mobile boy, for example, may discover that he must stop being a "hot-rod driver" if he wants to take "nice" girls out on dates. That can be a difficult problem for him if he has always associated reckless driving with true masculinity (82,118). Similarly, a socially mobile girl may discover that the "right" crowd serves cocktails or spiked punch at parties. If her family looks upon drinking as "wicked," it will complicate her upward climb very seriously (139,223,229).

Social Class   In the lower social classes, even today, smoking by girls, especially in public, is not so common as in the middle and upper classes. A girl gives a clue to her social-class identification by how much and where she smokes (110,153,208,221). The boy symbolizes his social-class background by the extent of his sex play and by the girls he selects as partners. Lower-class boys generally select lower-class girls for their sex-play partners while upper-class boys select girls from a lower social class than that with which they are identified (64,129,157).

Until recently, the use of narcotics was one of the best clues as to socioeconomic status. For the most part, in adolescence, the use of narcotics was limited to the "bad kids"—the juvenile delinquents or potential juvenile delinquents. It is becoming increasingly apparent today that many adolescents of the higher socioeconomic groups are using narcotics. Because narcotics are hard to get and expensive, they are one of the newest status symbols of the "affluent youth" in colleges and high schools (11,38, 65,82,100,173,175,176). Glue sniffing, as a cheaper and more readily accessible method of getting the "kicks" that narcotics give, is still limited mostly to the "bad kids." It too may, in time, be adopted by "affluent youth" as their new status symbol—should the getting of narcotics become too dangerous and too expensive (16).

BIBLIOGRAPHY

1 ADELSON, D.: Attitudes toward first names: an investigation of the relation between self-acceptance, self-identity and group and individual attitudes toward first names. *Disser. Abstr.*, 1957, **17**, 1831.

2 AIKEN, L. R.: The relationship of dress to selected measures of personality in undergraduate women. *J. soc. Psychol.*, 1963, **59**, 119–128.

3 ALEXANDER, C. N.: Consensus and mutual attraction in natural cliques: a study of adolescent drinkers. *Amer. J. Sociol.*, 1964, **69**, 395–403.

4 ALLPORT, G. W.: Values and our youth. *Teachers Coll. Rec.*, 1961, **63**, 211–219.

5 AMATORA, SISTER M.: Free expression of adolescent interests. *Genet. Psychol. Monogr.*, 1957, **55**, 173–219.

6 AMATORA, SISTER M.: Interests of preadolescent boys and girls. *Genet. Psychol. Monogr.*, 1960, **61**, 77–113.

7 AMATORA, SISTER M.: Home interests in early adolescence. *Genet. Psychol. Monogr.*, 1962, **65**, 137–174.

8 ANGELINO, H., L. A. BARNES, and C. L. SHEDD: Attitudes of mothers and adolescent daughters concerning clothing and grooming. *J. Home Econ.*, 1956, **48**, 779–782.

9 ANSPACH, K.: Clothing selection and the mobility concept. *J. Home Econ.*, 1961, **53**, 428–430.

10 ARONSON, E., and J. MILLS: The effect of severity of initiation on liking for a group. *J. abnorm. soc. Psychol.*, 1959, **59**, 177–181.

11 AUSUBEL, D. P.: An evaluation of recent adolescent drug addiction. *Ment. Hyg., N.Y.*, 1952, **36**, 373–382.

12 BABCHUK, N., R. MARSEY, and C. W. GORDON: Men and women in community agencies: a note on power and prestige. *Amer. sociol. Rev.*, 1960, **25**, 399–403.

13 BACH, M. L.: Factors related to student participation in campus social organizations. *J. soc. Psychol.*, 1961, **54**, 337–348.

14 BALTZELL, E. D.: *Philadelphia gentlemen*. New York: Free Press, 1958.

15 BARBER, B., and L. S. LOBEL: "Fashion" in women's clothes and the American social system. *Soc. Forces*, 1952, **31**, 124–131.

16 BARKER, G. H., and W. T. ADAMS: Glue sniffers. *Sociol. soc. Res.*, 1963, **47**, 298–310.

17 BARNES, M. W.: The nature and nurture of early adolescents. *Teach. Coll. Rec.*, 1956, **57**, 513–521.

18 BAUR, E. J., and M. M. MC CHUGGAGE: Drinking patterns of Kansas high school students. *Soc. Probl.*, 1958, **5**, 317–326.

19 BEHRENS, M. L.: Child-rearing and the character structure of the mother. *Child Develpm.*, 1954, **25**, 225–238.

20 BELL, W., and M. T. FORCE: Urban neighborhood types and participation in formal associations. *Amer. sociol. Rev.*, 1956, **21**, 25–34.

21 BEREZIN, F. C., and N. R. ROTH: Some factors affecting the drinking practices of 383 college women in a coeducational institution. *Quart. J. Stud. Alcohol*, 1950, **11**, 212–221.

22 BERNARD, J.: Teen-age culture: an overview. *Ann. Amer. Acad. pol. soc. Sci.*, 1961, **338**, 1–12.

23 BERNSTEIN, B.: Language and social class. *Brit. J. Sociol.*, 1960, **11**, 271–276.

24 BIRREN, F.: The effects of color on the human organism. *Amer. J. occup. Ther.*, 1959, **13**, 125–129.

25 BJERSTEDT, A.: Warm-cool color preferences as potential personality indicators: preliminary note. *Percept. mot. Skills*, 1960, **10**, 31–34.

26 BLAINE, G. B.: Moral questions stir campuses. *The New York Times*, Jan. 16, 1964.

27 BLOOD, R. O.: Uniformities and diversities in campus dating preferences. *Marriage fam. Living*, 1956, **18**, 37–45.

28 BOGART, L.: Adult talk about newspaper comics. *Amer. J. Sociol.*, 1955, **61**, 26–30.

29 BOSSARD, J. H. S.: *Parent and child.* Philadelphia: University of Pennsylvania Press, 1953.

30 BOSSARD, J. H. S., and E. S. BOLL: *The sociology of child development.* 3d ed. New York: Harper & Row, 1960.

31 BOWERMAN, C. E., and J. W. KINCH: Changes in family and peer orientation of children between fourth and tenth grades. *Soc. Forces,* 1959, **37,** 206–211.

32 BRETSCH, H. S.: Social skills and activities of socially accepted and unaccepted adolescents. *J. educ. Psychol.,* 1952, **43,** 449–458.

33 BROWN, C. H.: Self-portrait: the teen-type magazine. *Ann. Amer. Acad. pol. soc. Sci.,* 1961, **338,** 13–21.

34 BROWN, D. G.: Sex-role development in a changing culture. *Psychol. Bull.,* 1958, **55,** 232–242.

35 BROWN, R., and M. FORD: Address in American English. *J. abnorm. soc. Psychol.,* 1961, **62,** 375–385.

36 BUSH, G., and P. LONDON: On the disappearance of knickers: hypotheses for the functional analysis of the psychology of clothing. *J. soc. Psychol.,* 1960, **51,** 359–366.

37 CAVAN, R. S.: *Juvenile delinquency.* Philadelphia: Lippincott, 1962.

38 CHESSICK, R. D., D. H. LOOF, and H. G. PRICE: The alcohol-narcotic addict. *Quart. J. Stud. Alcohol,* 1961, **22,** 261–268.

39 CLARKE, A. C.: The use of leisure and its relation to levels of occupational prestige. *Amer. sociol. Rev.,* 1956, **21,** 301–307.

40 COBB, H. V.: Role-wishes and general wishes of children and adolescents. *Child Develpm.,* 1954, **25,** 161–171.

41 COBLINER, W. J.: Feminine fashion as an aspect of group psychology: analysis of written replies received by means of a questionnaire. *J. soc. Psychol.,* 1950, **31,** 283–289.

42 COHN, W.: On the language of lower-class children. *School Review,* 1959, **67,** 435–440.

43 COLE, L., and I. N. HALL: *Psychology of adolescence.* 6th ed. New York: Holt, 1964.

44 COLEMAN, J. S.: *The adolescent society.* New York: Free Press, 1961.

45 CONNOR, R. G.: The self-concepts of alcoholics. *Dissert. Abstr.,* 1961, **21,** 3871.

46 COOK, E. S.: An analysis of factors related to withdrawal from high school prior to graduation. *J. educ. Res.,* 1956, **50,** 191–196.

47 COOPER, L.: Predisposition toward parenthood: a comparison of male and female students. *Sociol. soc. Res.,* 1957, **42,** 31–36.

48 CROW, A.: Parental attitudes toward boy-girl relations. *J. educ. Sociol.,* 1955, **29,** 126–133.

49 CROW, L. D., and A. CROW: *Adolescent development and adjustment.* 2d ed. New York: McGraw-Hill, 1965.

50 CURTIS, R. F.: Occupational mobility and membership in formal voluntary associations: a note on research. *Amer. sociol. Rev.,* 1959, **24,** 846–848.

51 DANZIGER, K.: The child's understanding of kinship terms: a study in the development of rational concepts. *J. genet. Psychol.,* 1957, **91,** 213–232.

52 DAVIS, A., and R. J. HAVIGHURST: *Father of the man.* Boston: Houghton Mifflin, 1947.

53 DAVIS, J. A.: Status symbols and the measurement of status perception. *Sociometry,* 1956, **19,** 154–165.

54 DEXTER, E. S.: Three items related to personality: popularity, nicknames, and homesickness. *J. soc. Psychol.,* 1949, **30,** 155–158.

55 DICKINS, D.: Social participation as a criterion for determining minimum standards in clothing. *Rural Sociol.,* 1944, **9,** 341–349.

56 DODSON, D. W.: Reassessing values in the present age. *J. educ. Sociol.,* 1958, **32,** 49–61.

57 DONALD, M. N., and R. J. HAVIGHURST: The meaning of leisure. *Soc. Forces,* 1959, **37,** 355–360.

58 DOUVAN, E.: Independence and identity in adolescence. *Children,* 1957, **4,** 186–190.

59 DRAKE, D.: On pet names. *Amer. Imago,* 1957, **14,** 41–43.

60 DREGER, R. M.: Spontaneous conversations and story-telling of children in a naturalistic setting. *J. Psychol.,* 1955, **40,** 163–180.

61 DUNBAR, F.: Homeostasis during puberty. *Amer. J. Psychiat.,* 1958, **114,** 673–682.

62 DUNSING, M.: Spending money of adolescents. *J. Home Econ.,* 1956, **48,** 405–408.

63 DUVALL, E. M.: Teenagers and the automobile. *Marriage fam. Living,* 1961, **23,** 190–191.

64 EHRMANN, W.: *Premarital dating behavior.* New York: Holt, 1959.

65 ELDRIDGE, W. B.: *Narcotics and the law: a critique of the American experiment in nar-*

cotic drug control. New York: New York University Press, 1962.

66 ELLIS, A., and R. M. BEECHLEY: Emotional disturbance in children with peculiar given names. *J. genet. Psychol.*, 1954, **85**, 337–339.

67 ERIKSON, R. J.: The adolescent within the family. *J. child Psychol. Psychiat.*, 1956, **3**, 115–136.

68 EYSENCK, H. J., M. TARRANT, M. WOOLF, and L. ENGLAND: Smoking and personality. *Brit. med. J.*, 1960, **1**, 1456–1460.

69 FEINBERG, M. R., M. SMITH, and R. SCHMIDT: An analysis of expressions used by adolescents at varying economic levels to describe accepted and rejected peers. *J. genet. Psychol.*, 1958, **93**, 133–148.

70 FELDMAN, F. L.: Money: an index to personal problems in adolescents. *Marriage fam. Living*, 1963, **25**, 364–367.

71 FELLOWS, L.: Schoolboy dress scored in Britain. *The New York Times*, Aug. 11, 1963.

72 FINE, B.: Jobs that keep students in college. *The New York Times*, Feb. 21, 1954.

73 FISHMAN, J. A.: Degree of bilingualism in a Yiddish school and leisure-time activities. *J. soc. Psychol.*, 1952, **36**, 155–165.

74 FLUGEL, I.: On the significance of names. *Brit. J. med. Psychol.*, 1930, **10**, 208–213.

75 FOLKMAN, J. D.: Stressful and supportive interaction. *Marriage fam. Living*, 1956, **18**, 102–106.

76 FRIEDENBERG, E. Z.: *The vanishing adolescent.* New York: Dell, 1962.

77 FREUD, S.: *The standard edition of the complete works of Sigmund Freud.* London: Hogarth, 1953–1962.

78 FRICK, W. B.: The adolescent dilemma: an interpretation. *Peabody J. Educ.*, 1955, **32**, 206.

79 GAGE, N. L.: Accuracy of social perception and effectiveness in interpersonal relationships. *J. Pers.*, 1953, **22**, 128–141.

80 GALLAGHER, J. R.: Various aspects of adolescence. *Yale J. biol. Med.*, 1950, **22**, 595–602.

81 GALLAGHER, J. R., and C. D GALLAGHER: Some comments of growth and development in adolescents. *Yale J. biol. Med.*, 1953, **25**, 334–348.

82 GALLUP, G., and E. HILL: Youth: the cool generation. *Saturday Evening Post*, Dec. 22–30, 1961, pp. 63–80.

83 GARDNER, G. A.: The mental health of normal adolescents. *Ment. Hyg., N.Y.*, 1947, **31**, 529–540.

84 GARRISON, K. C.: *Psychology of adolescence.* 5th ed. Englewood Cliffs, N.J.: Prentice-Hall, 1956.

85 GARRISON, K. C.: *Growth and development.* 2d ed. New York: Longmans, 1959.

86 GESELL, A., F. L. ILG, and L. B. AMES: *Youth: the years from ten to sixteen.* New York: Harper & Row, 1956.

87 GILBERT, E.: How teenagers spend their money. *Life Magazine*, May 13, 1957.

88 GLENN, N. D.: Negro prestige criteria: a case study in the bases of prestige. *Amer. J. Sociol.*, 1963, **68**, 645–657.

89 GLICKMAN, A. S.: Clothing leadership among boys. *Dissert. Abstr.*, 1958, **18**, 682–684.

90 GOLLIN, E. S.: Organizational characteristics of social judgment: a developmental investigation. *J. Pers.*, 1958, **26**, 139–154.

91 GRONLUND, N. E.: Acquaintance span and sociometric status. *Sociometry*, 1955, **18**, 62–68.

92 GROSSER, G. S., and W. J. LACZEK: Prior parochial vs. secular secondary education and utterance latencies to taboo words. *J. Psychol.*, 1963, **55**, 263–277.

93 GUITAR, M. A.: Status seekers, junior grade. *The New York Times*, Aug. 16, 1964.

94 HABBE, S.: Nicknames of adolescent boys. *Amer. J. Orthopsychiat.*, 1937, **7**, 371–377.

95 HARRIS, D. B., and C. S. TSENG: Children's attitudes toward peers and parents as revealed by sentence completions. *Child Develpm.*, 1957, **28**, 401–411.

96 HARTMANN, G. W.: Clothing: personal problem and social issue. *J. Home Econ.*, 1949, **4**, 295–298.

97 HAVIGHURST, R. J.: *Developmental tasks and education.* New York: Longmans, 1953.

98 HAVIGHURST, R. J., and K. FEIGENBAUM: Leisure and life style. *Amer. J. Sociol.*, 1959, **64**, 396–404.

99 HEATHERS, G.: Acquiring dependence and independence: a theoretical orientation. *J. genet. Psychol.*, 1955, **87**, 277–291.

100 HECHINGER, F. M.: Education: drug issue. *The New York Times*, Feb. 28, 1965.

101 HECHINGER, G., and F. M. HECHINGER: *Teenage tyranny.* New York: Morrow, 1963.

102 HECHINGER, G., and F. M. HECHINGER: Seri-

ous epidemic of "automania." *The New York Times*, Aug. 11, 1963.

103 HECHT, C. A., R. J. GINE, and S. E. ROTHROCK: The drinking and dating habits of 336 college women in a coeducational institution. *Quart. J. Stud. Alcohol*, 1948, **9**, 252–258.

104 HELPER, M. M.: Learning theory and the self-concept. *J. abnorm. soc. Psychol.*, 1955, **51**, 184–194.

105 HEMMERLING, R. L., and H. HURST: The effects of leisure time activities on scholastic achievement. *Calif. J. educ. Res.*, 1961, **12**, 86–90.

106 HESS, R. D., and I. GOLDBLATT: The status of adolescents in American society: a problem in social identity. *Child Develpm.*, 1957, **28**, 459–468.

107 HESS, R. D., and G. HANDEL: The family as an emotional organization. *Marriage fam. Living*, 1956, **18**, 99–101.

108 HOLLINGSHEAD, A. DE B.: *Elmtown's youth.* New York: Wiley, 1949.

109 HOLMES, E.: Who uses consumer credit? *J. Home Econ.*, 1957, **49**, 340–342.

110 HORN, D., F. A. COURTS, R. M. TAYLOR, and E. S. SOLOMON: Cigarette smoking among high school students. *Amer. J. publ. Hlth.*, 1959, **49**, 1497–1511.

111 HORROCKS, J. E.: *The psychology of adolescence.* 2d ed. Boston: Houghton Mifflin, 1962.

112 HOULT, T. F.: Experimental measurement of clothing as a factor in some social ratings of selected American men. *Amer. sociol. Rev.*, 1954, **19**, 324–328.

113 HUNT, L. A.: A developmental study of factors related to children's clothing preferences. *Monogr. Soc. Res. Child Develpm.*, 1959, **24**, no. 1.

114 HURLOCK, E. B.: Motivation in fashion. *Arch. Psychol.*, N.Y., 1929, no. 111.

115 JACOBI, J. E., and S. G. WALTERS: Social status and consumer choice. *Soc. Forces*, 1958, **36**, 209–214.

116 JAHODA, G.: Development of the perception of social differences in children from 6 to 10. *Brit. J. Psychol.*, 1959, **50**, 159–175.

117 JERSILD, A. T.: *In search of self.* New York: Teachers College, Columbia University, 1952.

118 JERSILD, A. T.: *The psychology of adolescence.* 2d ed. New York: Macmillan, 1963.

119 JERSILD, A. T., and R. J. TASCH: *Children's interests and what they suggest for education.* New York: Teachers College, Columbia University, 1949.

120 JOHANNIS, T. B.: Participation by fathers, mothers, and teenage sons and daughters in selected family economic activity. *Family Life Coordinator*, 1957, **6**, 15–16.

121 JONES, M. C.: A functional analysis of colloquial speech among adolescents. *Amer. Psychologist*, 1946, **1**, 252–253.

122 JONES, M. C.: A study of socialization patterns at the high school level. *J. genet. Psychol.*, 1958, **93**, 87–111.

123 JONES, M. C.: Lipstick charts maturity. *The New York Times*, Mar. 21, 1959.

124 JONES, M. C.: A comparison of the attitudes and interests of ninth-grade students over two decades. *J. educ. Psychol.*, 1960., **51**, 175–186.

125 JOSSELYN, I. M.: Psychological changes in adolescence. *Children*, 1959, **6**, 43–47.

126 KASSER, E.: The growth and decline of a children's slang vocabulary, at Mooseheart, a self-contained community. *J. genet. Psychol.*, 1945, **66**, 129–137.

127 KATZ, L.: Monetary incentive and range of payoffs as determiners of risk taking. *J. exp. Psychol.*, 1962, **64**, 541–544.

128 KEISLAR, E. R.: A distinction between social acceptance and prestige among adolescents. *Child Develpm.*, 1953, **24**, 275–283.

129 KINSEY, A. C., W. B. POMEROY, C. E. MARTIN, and P. H. GEBHARD: *Sexual behavior in the human female.* Philadelphia: Saunders, 1953.

130 KIRKPATRICK, M. E.: The mental hygiene of adolescence in the Anglo-American culture. *Ment. Hyg.*, N.Y., 1952, **36**, 394–403.

131 KLATSKIN, E. A.: Shifts in child care practices in three classes under an infant care program of flexible methodology. *Amer. J. Orthopsychiat.*, 1952, **22**, 52–61.

132 KNAPP, R. H., J. BRIMNER, and M. WHITE: Educational level, class status, and aesthetic preference. *J. soc. Psychol.*, 1959, **50**, 277–284.

133 KOENIG, F. G.: Improving the language abilities of bilingual children. *Except. Children*, 1953, **14**, 183–186.

134 KOLKO, G.: Economic mobility and social

stratification. *Amer. J. Sociol.*, 1957, **63**, 30–36.

135 KOMAROVSKY, M.: Continuities in family research: a case study. *Amer. J. Sociol.*, 1956, **62**, 42–47.

136 KOPPE, W. A.: The psychological meanings of housing and furnishings. *Marriage fam. Living*, 1955, **17**, 129–132.

137 KUHLEN, R. G.: *The psychology of adolescent development*. 2d ed. New York: Harper & Row, 1963.

138 LANDIS, P. H.: The ordering and forbidding technique and teen-age adjustment. *Sch. Soc.*, 1954, **80**, 105–106.

139 LANG, B.: When teen-agers start to drink. *The New York Times*, July 19, 1964.

140 LASSWELL, T. E., and P. F. PARSHALL: The perception of social class from photographs. *Sociol. soc. Res.*, 1961, **45**, 407–414.

141 LAWTON, M. P.: Psychosocial aspects of cigarette smoking. *J. Hlth. hum. Behav.*, 1962, **3**, 163–170.

142 LEVINE, G. N., and L. A. SUSSMANN: Social class and sociability in fraternity pledging. *Amer. J. Sociol.*, 1960, **65**, 391–399.

143 LICCIONE, J. V.: The changing family relationships of adolescent girls. *J. abnorm. soc. Psychol.*, 1955, **51**, 421–426.

144 *Life* Magazine Report: High school fads: this year's jells and queens try hard to be different. *Life Magazine*, Nov. 17, 1949, pp. 185–189.

145 LINDEN, M. E., and D. COURTNEY: The human life cycle and its interruptions. *Amer. J. Psychiat.*, 1953, **109**, 905–915.

146 LIPSETT, L. P.: A self-concept scale for children and its relationship to the children's form of the manifest anxiety scale. *Child Develpm.*, 1958, **29**, 463–472.

147 LUCHINS, A. S.: On the theories and problems of adolescence. *J. genet. Psychol.*, 1954, **85**, 47–63.

148 LUFT, J.: Monetary value and the perception of persons. *J. soc. Psychol.*, 1957, **46**, 245–251.

149 MACAULAY, E.: Some notes on the attitude of children to dress. *Brit. J. med. Psychol.*, 1929, **9**, 150–158.

150 MARCUS, I. M., W. WILSON, I. KRAFT, D. SWANDER, F. SUTHERLAND, and E. SCHULHOFER: An interdisciplinary approach to accident patterns in children. *Monogr. Soc. Res. Child Develpm.*, 1960, **25**, no. 2.

151 MARTINSON, F. M.: Ego deficiency as a factor in marriage: a male sample. *Marriage fam. Living*, 1959, **21**, 48–52.

152 MASLOW, A. H., and N. L. MINTZ: Effects of esthetic surroundings: 1. Initial effects of three esthetic conditions upon perceiving "energy" and "well-being" in faces. *J. Psychol.*, 1956, **41**, 247–254.

153 MATARAZZO, J. D., and G. SASLOW: Psychological and related characteristics of smokers and nonsmokers. *Psychol. Bull.*, 1960, **57**, 493–513.

154 MAURER, D. W., and V. H. VOGEL: *Narcotics and narcotic addiction*. 2d ed. Springfield, Ill.: Charles C Thomas, 1962.

155 MC ARTHUR, C., E. WALDRON, and J. DICKINSON: The psychology of smoking. *J. abnorm. soc. Psychol.*, 1958, **56**, 267–275.

156 MC CARTHY, D.: Language development. *Monogr. Soc. Res. Child Develpm.*, 1960, **25**, no. 3, 5–14.

157 MC CORD, W., J. MC CORD, and P. VERDEN: Family relationships and sexual deviance in lower class adolescents. *Ind. J. soc. Psychiat.*, 1962, **8**, 165–179.

158 MC GUIRE, C.: Family and agemates in personality formation. *Marriage fam. Living*, 1953, **15**, 17–23.

159 MC GUIRE, C., and R. A. CLARKE: Age-mate acceptance and indices of peer status. *Child Develpm.*, 1952, **23**, 141–154.

160 MC INNES, J. H., and J. K. SHEARER: Relationship between color choice and selected preferences of the individual. *J. Home Econ.*, 1964, **56**, 181–187.

161 MEAD, M.: *Male and female*. New York: Morrow, 1952.

162 MEHLMAN, B., and R. G. WAREHIME: Social class and social desirability. *J. soc. Psychol.*, 1962, **58**, 167–170.

163 MENDELSOHN, A., and I. CRESPI: The effect of the autistic pressure and institutional structure on preferences in a choice situation. *J. soc. Psychol.*, 1952, **36**, 109–123.

164 MEYER, H. D.: The adult cycle. *Ann. Amer. Acad. pol. soc. Sci.*, 1957, **313**, 58–67.

165 MIDDLETON, D.: In Britain, names denote status and the more the better. *The New York Times*, July 5, 1960.

166 MINTZ, N. L.: Effects of esthetic surround-

ings: II. Prolonged and repeated experiences in a "beautiful" and ugly room. *J. Psychol.*, 1956, **41**, 459–466.

167 MOORE, D. F.: Sharing in family financial management by high-school students. *Marriage fam. Living*, 1953, **15**, 319–321.

168 MURPHY, W. F.: A note on the significance of names. *Psychoanal. Quart.*, 1957, **26**, 91–106.

169 MUSSEN, P. H., and M. C. JONES: Self-conceptions, motivations and interpersonal attitudes of late- and early-maturing boys. *Child Develpm.*, 1957, **28**, 243–256.

170 NEISSER, E. G.: Emotional and social values attached to money. *Marriage fam. Living*, 1960, **22**, 132–139.

171 *New York Times* Report: Trend is to Anthony in naming babies. *The New York Times*, July 15, 1962.

172 *New York Times* Report: Alcohol is called teenagers' trap. *The New York Times*, Aug. 17, 1963.

173 *New York Times* Report: Columbia finds marijuana users. *The New York Times*, Dec. 10, 1963.

174 *New York Times* Report: Yonkers assays its "Junkies Row." *The New York Times*, Aug. 21, 1964.

175 *New York Times* Report: Narcotics a growing problem of affluent youth. *The New York Times*, Jan. 4, 1965.

176 *New York Times* Report: No moral decay seen by Cornell. *The New York Times*, Feb. 21, 1965.

177 *New York Times* Report: Britain's best-dressed: the youthful mods. *The New York Times*, Feb. 24, 1965.

178 NORTON, J. L.: General motives and influences in vocational development. *J. genet. Psychol.*, 1953, **82**, 263–278.

179 NOSHPITZ, J.: A smoking episode in a residential treatment unit. *Amer. J. Orthopsychiat.*, 1962, **32**, 669–681.

180 PACKARD, V.: *The status seekers*. New York: Pocket, 1961.

181 PARSONS, T.: *Essays in sociological theory*. New York: Free Press, 1949.

182 PEAR, T. H.: *Personality, appearance, and speech*. London: G. Allen, 1957.

183 PEARSON, L. H.: Teen-agers' preferences in clothes. *J. Home Econ.*, 1950, **42**, 801–802.

184 PECKOS, P. S., and R. F. HEALD: Nutrition in adolescents. *Children*, 1964, **11**, 27–30.

185 PENNY, R.: Age and sex differences in motivational orientation to the communicative act. *Child Develpm.*, 1958, **29**, 163–171.

186 PHELPS, H. R., and J. E. HORROCKS: Factors influencing informal groups of adolescents. *Child Develpm.*, 1958, **29**, 69–86.

187 PITTMAN, D. J., and C. R. SNYDER: *Society, culture, and drinking patterns*. New York: Wiley, 1962.

188 POWELL, K. S., and D. A. GOVER: The adolescent as a consumer: facts and implications. *Marriage fam. Living*, 1963, **25**, 359–364.

189 POWELL, M.: Age and sex differences in the degree of conflict within certain areas of psychological adjustment. *Psychol. Monogr.*, 1955, **69**, no. 2.

190 PRESSEY, S. L., and A. W. JONES: 1923–1953 and 20–60 age changes in moral codes, anxieties, and interests as shown by the "X-O Tests." *J. Psychol.*, 1955, **39**, 485–502.

191 PRESSEY, S. L., and R. G. KUHLEN: *Psychological development through the life span*. New York: Harper & Row, 1957.

192 PREVEY, E. E.: Developing good habits in the use of money. *J. Home Econ.*, 1948, **38**, 79–81.

193 PSATHAS, G.: Ethnicity, social class and adolescent independence from parental control. *Amer. sociol. Rev.*, 1957, **22**, 415–423.

194 RAVEN, R. W.: Smoking habits of schoolboys. *The Lancet*, June, 1957, 1139–1141.

195 Recreation Survey: Recreational interests and needs of high-school youth: resumé of study conducted in Schenectady, N.Y. *Recreation*, 1954, **47**, 43–46.

196 REMMERS, H. H., and D. H. RADLER: *The American teenager*. Indianapolis: Bobbs-Merrill, 1957.

197 ROACH, M. E.: The influence of social class on clothing practices and orientation at early adolescence: a study of clothing-related behavior of seventh-grade girls. *Dissert. Abstr.*, 1962, **22**, 2897–2898.

198 ROFF, M., and D. S. BRODY: Appearance and choice status during adolescence. *J. Psychol.*, 1953, **36**, 347–356.

199 ROSANDER, A. C.: Age and sex patterns of social attitudes. *J. educ. Psychol.*, 1939, **30**, 481–496.

200 ROUCEK, J. S.: Age as a prestige factor. *Sociol. soc. Res.*, 1958, **42**, 349–352.

201 RUBÉ, P.: Adolescence: I. Is there a problem of adolescence? *Amer. J. Psychother.*, 1955, **9**, 503–509.

202 RYAN, M. S.: *Psychological effects of clothing: I. Survey of the opinions of college girls.* Ithaca, N.Y.: Cornell University Agricultural Experiment Station, 1952, Bulletin 882.

203 RYAN, M. S.: *Psychological effects of clothing: II. Comparison of college students with high-school students, rural and urban students, boys and girls.* Ithaca, N.Y.: Cornell University Agricultural Experiment Station, 1953, Bulletin 898.

204 RYAN, M. S.: *Psychological effects of clothing: III. Report of interviews with a selected sample of college women.* Ithaca, N.Y.: Cornell University Agricultural Experiment Station, 1953, Bulletin 900.

205 SAENGER, G., and S. FLOWERMAN: Stereotypes and prejudicial attitudes. *Hum. Relat.*, 1954, **7**, 217–238.

206 SCHEINFELD, A.: *The new you and heredity.* Philadelphia: Lippincott, 1961.

207 SCHNEIDER, D. M., and G. C. HOMANS: Kinship terminology and the American kinship system. *Amer. Anthropologist*, 1955, **57**, 1194–1208.

208 SCHUBERT, D. S. P.: Personality implications of cigarette smoking among college students. *J. consult. Psychol.*, 1959, **23**, 376.

209 SECORD, P. F., and S. M. JOURARD: The appraisal of body-cathexis: body-cathexis and the self. *J. consult. Psychol.*, 1953, **17**, 343–346.

210 SEEMAN, M.: The intellectual and the language of minorities. *Amer. J. Sociol.*, 1958, **64**, 25–35.

211 SELTZER, C. C.: Masculinity and smoking. *Science*, 1959, **130**, 1706–1707.

212 SHAW, D. M., and E. Q. CAMPBELL: Internalization of a moral norm and external support. *Sociol. Quart.*, 1962, **3**, 57–71.

213 SHEPPARD, D.: Characteristics associated with Christian names. *Brit. J. Psychol.*, 1963, **54**, 167–174.

214 SHERMAN, A. W.: Personality factors in the psychological weaning of college women. *Educ. psychol. Measmt.*, 1948, **8**, 249–256.

215 SILVERMAN, S. S.: Clothing and appearance: their psychological implications for teen-age girls. *Teach. Coll. Contr. Educ.*, 1945, no. 912.

216 SIMMEL, G.: Fashion. *Amer. J. Sociol.*, 1957, **62**, 541–558.

217 SIMS, V. M.: Relations between the social-class identification and personality adjustment of a group of high school and college students. *J. soc. Psychol.*, 1954, **40**, 323–327.

218 SMITH, W. C.: Remarriage and the stepchild. In M. Fishbein and R. J. R. Kennedy (eds.), *Modern marriage and family living.* Fair Lawn, N. J.: Oxford, 1957, pp. 457–475.

219 SOFFIETTI, J. P.: Bilingualism and biculturalism. *J. educ. Psychol.*, 1955, **46**, 222–227.

220 STOUT, D. R., and A. LATZKE: Values college women consider in clothing selection. *J. Home Econ.*, 1958, **50**, 43–44.

221 STRAITS, B. C., and L. SECHREST: Further support of some findings about the characteristics of smokers and nonsmokers. *J. consult. Psychol.*, 1963, **27**, 282.

222 STRANG, R.: *The adolescent views himself.* New York: McGraw-Hill, 1957.

223 STRAUS, R., and S. D. BACON: *Drinking in college.* New Haven, Conn.: Yale, 1953.

224 STRAUSS, B. V.: The dynamics of ordinal position effects. *Quart. J. Child Behav.*, 1951, **3**, 133–145.

225 STRUNK, O.: Attitudes toward one's name and one's self. *J. indiv. Psychol.*, 1958, **14**, 64–67.

226 TASCH, R. J.: Interpersonal perceptions of fathers and mothers. *J. genet. Psychol.*, 1955, **87**, 59–65.

227 *Time* Report: Students: "On the fringe of a golden era." *Time Magazine*, Jan. 29, 1965, pp. 56–59.

228 *Time* Report: The pot problem. *Time Magazine*, Mar. 12, 1965, p. 49.

229 ULLMAN, A. D.: Ethnic differences in the first drinking experience. *Soc. Probl.*, 1960, **8**, 45–56.

230 *U.S. News & World Report*: Will teen-agers make the sixties soar? *U.S. News & World Report*, Oct. 26, 1964, pp. 102–104.

231 VENER, A. M.: Clothes tell a story. *The New York Times*, Apr. 28, 1959.

232 WALTERS, J., F. I. STROMBERG, and G. LONIAN: Perceptions concerning develop-

ment of responsibility in young children. *Elem. Sch. J.,* 1957, **57,** 209–216.

233 WARBURTON, F. E.: The lab coat as a status symbol. *Science,* 1960, **131,** 895.

234 WARDEN, J. A.: Some desires or goals for clothing of college women. *J. Home Econ.,* 1957, **49,** 795.

235 WARNATH, C. F.: The relation of family cohesiveness and adolescent independence to social effectiveness. *Marriage fam. Living,* 1955, **19,** 346–348.

236 WATSON, J., W. BREED, and H. POSMAN: A study of adult conversations: sample of 1,001 remarks overheard in Manhattan. *J. soc. Psychol.,* 1948, **28,** 121–133.

237 WAX, M.: Themes in cosmetics and grooming. *Amer. J. Sociol.,* 1957, **62,** 588–593.

238 WEBSTER, H.: Changes in attitudes during college. *J. educ. Psychol.,* 1958, **49,** 109–117.

239 WERNER, E.: Milieu differences in social competence. *J. genet. Psychol.,* 1957, **91,** 239–249.

240 WHEELER, D. K.: Expressed wishes of students. *J. genet. Psychol.,* 1963, **102,** 75–81.

241 WHITE, R. C.: Social class differences in the use of leisure. *Amer. J. Sociol.,* 1955, **61,** 138–144.

242 WILLERMAN, B., and D. L. SWANSON: An ecological determinant of differential amounts of sociometric choices within college sororities. *Sociometry,* 1952, **15,** 326–329.

243 WILLIAMS, C. D.: College students' family problems. *J. Home Econ.,* 1950, **42,** 179–181.

244 WINICK, C.: Taboo and disapproved colors and symbols in various foreign countries. *J. soc. Psychol.,* 1963, **59,** 361–368.

245 WINKER, J. B.: Age trends and sex differences in the wishes, identifications, activities, and fears of children. *Child Develpm.,* 1949, **20,** 191–200.

246 WITRYOL, S. L., and J. E. CALKINS: Marginal social values of rural school children. *J. genet. Psychol.,* 1958, **92,** 81–93.

247 WOLFENSTEIN, M.: Children's understanding of jokes. *Psychoanalytic Study of the Child,* 1954, **8,** 162–176.

248 WRIGHT, C. R., and H. H. HYMAN: Voluntary association membership of American adults: evidence from national sample surveys. *Amer. sociol. Rev.,* 1958, **23,** 284–294.

249 ZIMMER, B. C., and A. H. HAWLEY: The significance of membership in associations. *Amer. J. Sociol.,* 1959, **65,** 196–201.

CHAPTER 8
levels
of
aspirations

Typically, adolescence is a time of idealism and romanticism. It is a time of dreaming of the future when the adolescent aspires to reach the moon and confidently expects to do so. He has fanciful ideas about his future, especially about marrying a person with whom he will live happily ever after, and about having a glamorous job which will provide him with the money he needs for the status symbols he regards as essential to happiness. Having these status symbols, he believes, will automatically open the doors which, up to now, have been closed to him. When he graduates from high school, he believes the world is at his feet and that he can have what he wants for the asking; when he graduates from college, he *knows* it is (74,170,181).

Adults laud adolescents who are ambitious and confidently predict that they will get ahead in the world. By contrast, the adolescent who is satisfied with things as they come is regarded as doomed to failure —the "drifter" who will turn into a ne'er-do-well. He is prodded to develop some ambition just as the ambitious youth is encouraged to aspire higher and higher with a helping hand from parents and teachers. Adolescents confidently believe that dreaming of the future combined with a helping hand from others is all that is needed to be a success in life.

america: the land of golden opportunity

Regardless of the culture in which he grows up, almost everyone would like to rise above his present status. Few prefer to remain where they are. Some may believe they are content and a few may say they are. However, in most cases this is due to a realization that improvement is impossible. The only way they can be happy, then, is to convince themselves that they are satisfied with things as they are. To ensure even greater satisfaction, some may develop a *Pollyanna attitude*—convincing themselves that they are glad things are no worse than they are. Others may adopt a *sour-grapes attitude*—convincing themselves that they do not want things above what they have because they are not worth having.

Traditionally, America is the land of "golden opportunity"—the place where those who are dissatisfied with their lot in life can achieve their ambitions to better it. America has not always been the land of "golden opportunity" that it is today. In the early colonial times, *sumptuary laws*—laws restricting the use of material possessions in accordance with the income of the family —made it impossible for citizens to "better themselves." Slavery limited the opportunities for many to follow any life except that prescribed by the slave owners. And low wages for all workers meant that a large portion of the population was doomed to live in the same status pattern as that of their parents and grandparents.

With the abolition of sumptuary laws and slavery and with the creation of labor unions to demand better wages and working conditions, the barriers to opportunity have been removed. As a result, America has become the land of opportunity *for all*. With this change has come the encouragement of youth to be ambitious—to aspire to better things than their parents had and certainly much better than their grandparents and more remote ancestors had (178, 182).

It is the desire to be able to provide for themselves the status symbols that will enable them to live the kind of lives they want to live that forms the fundamental basis of adolescent levels of aspiration (29). Figure 8–1 shows how Americans, as a nation, aspire to better themselves. In the ratings, 10 means the "best possible life," while 0 or 1 shows the worst possible life.

meaning of aspiration

In everyday usage, "ambition" and "aspiration" are synonymous and are used interchangeably. The definition of "ambition," as given by a standard dictionary, means an eagerness for honor, superiority, power, or attainment; it suggests a "personal uplifting." "Aspiration" means a longing for what is above one, with advancement as its end. The subtle distinction lies in the emphasis on "what is above one." Back of all motivation for achievement is the desire for something better—"what is above one," not just for "honor, superiority, power, or attainment." It also explains why achievement, per se, does not always bring satisfaction. An ambitious person will be satisfied with his attainment if it is satisfactory to others and lauded by them. A person who aspires to better himself will, by contrast, be satisfied only when his achievement is in line with the goal he sets for himself, regardless of how satisfying it may be to others (144, 161).

"Aspiration" means the goal the individual sets for himself in a task which has intense personal significance for him, or in which he is ego-involved. Because of this ego involvement, success leads to increased self-esteem while failure brings embarrassment, remorse, and feelings of inadequacy. Aspirations have three important aspects (3, 46).

1 *What performance or aspects of it the individual considers desirable and important—what he wants to do*
2 *How well he expects to perform, especially in the important aspects*
3 *How important the performance is to him, either as a whole or in its different aspects*

POSITIVE AND NEGATIVE ASPIRATIONS

Negative aspirations center around the desire to avoid failure; positive aspirations are oriented toward the goal of achieving success. In the case of the first, the adolescent will be satisfied if he passes an examination; in the second, he will be satisfied only if he does better than his classmates. Most adolescents aspire positively. Only if they have a history of failures are they likely to set goals centered around the avoidance of failure instead of around the achievement of success (110,112).

IMMEDIATE AND REMOTE ASPIRATIONS

Immediate aspirations are goals the individual sets for himself for the immediate future, such as the goal of passing the examination he is scheduled to take tomorrow or of winning the tennis tournament he is just entering. Remote aspirations are goals set for the future. The more immediate the goal, the more realistic it is likely to be. The adolescent who aspires to win the tournament he is just entering, for example, is more *realistic* in what he hopes to accomplish than the adolescent who aspires to be a doctor when he is still a high school student. The former is able to assess his opponents and to know, within limits, how his athletic skill compares with theirs. Being a doctor is so remote from the experience of the high school student that he has no yardstick by which to compare his potential medical skill with that of people in the profession or premedical students in college with whom he must compete for entrance to medical school (46,112).

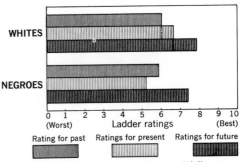

FIGURE 8–1 Aspirations for a "better life" among Americans. (Adapted from H. Cantril: A study of aspirations. *Scient. American*, 1963, **208**, no. 2, 41–45. Used by permission.)

HIERARCHY OF ASPIRATIONS

Remote goals may start out as separate and distinct aspirations. Sooner or later, they usually fit themselves into the individual's life plan. By adolescence, there is great pressure to formulate remote goals and to combine them into a hierarchy which will give the adolescent a path to follow to the pinnacle of the hierarchy. Even immediate aspirations serve as stepping-stones (35, 131).

If, for example, the adolescent aspires to be a doctor, there are many intermediate goals which must be reached before this remote goal is. He must aspire to graduate from high school and college with academic successes in line with the requirements for admission to medical school. Once he is admitted to medical school, his aspirations will concentrate on areas of medicine in which he aspires to specialize and on the more remote goals of internship and residency in hospitals where he can get the training he needs in the line of his special interest (77,110). In Figure 8–2 are shown the life plans of boys and girls in high school. Note the specific nature of the different aspirations in the lifetime hierarchy.

Once a hierarchy of remote goals has been established, it provides the adolescent with a path of action to direct his energies. But if his aspirations are unrealistic, the path may lead to failure and disappointment. If the student who aspires to be a doctor is unrealistic about his capacity for

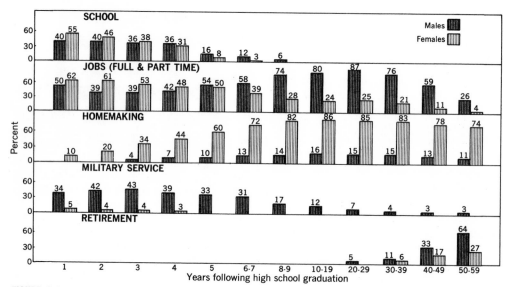

FIGURE 8–2 The lifetime plans of boys and girls during adolescence. (Adapted from H. T. Christensen: Lifetime family and occupational role projections of high school students. *Marriage fam. Liv.*, 1961, **23**, 181–183. Used by permission.)

this profession, he may upset the entire hierarchy of goals by failing a science course in college. Should his college achievement be only average, he may gain admission to a medical school with prestige far below his original aspiration.

Even though adolescents characteristically concentrate on the development of remote rather than immediate goals, there are some who cannot follow this pattern. They may lack the necessary intellectual maturity to develop the foresight essential to remote planning. Economic instability of his family may prevent the adolescent from planning for an education needed to achieve the goal he would like to reach. Because the choice of mate is at the basis of her remote goal of marriage, an adolescent girl cannot plan for where she will live, what her pattern of life after marriage will be, or whether she will combine marriage with a job or not. All this hinges on the choice of her future husband. The adolescent may be discouraged from developing remote aspirations on the grounds that by avoiding long-term

plans, "you will protect yourself from disappointment" (23).

STRENGTH OF ASPIRATIONS

The strength of aspirations depends not so much on whether they are immediate or remote as on how important the aspirations are to the individual. The value of an aspiration to the individual, in turn, is affected to some extent by how hard it is to reach. The more *difficult* it is to reach, the greater the halo in the eyes of the aspirant and the more strongly motivated he is to reach it (158). This was illustrated in the preceding chapter in the section dealing with organizational affiliation as a status symbol. (See pages 278–280.)

Even when a goal is important to an adolescent, the strength of his aspiration to achieve it will be influenced to some extent by *realism*. If he has reason to question his ability to achieve the goal, it will weaken his aspiration to succeed. An adolescent, for example, may know that he has little chance of being invited to join an exclusive fraternity in college because he knows few of the members of that fraternity and then only as casual acquaintances. Under such conditions, he will have a weaker aspiration than he would if he were confident that his chances of receiving an invitation to join were good.

In general, *remote* aspirations are stronger than immediate aspirations. The reason for this is to be found in the structure of the aspiration. Because of the hierarchial nature of remote aspirations, there is a strength to them which is not found in the simpler nature of immediate aspirations. The major exception to this general rule is to be found in the degree of realism of the aspirations. If an immediate aspiration is realistic while the remote aspiration is unrealistic, then the former will acquire a greater strength. It is a case of a "bird in the hand is worth two in the bush" (46, 77,112,158).

The strength of the aspiration will determine how it will affect the individual's behavior. If immediate aspirations are stronger than remote ones, the adolescent will satisfy the immediate, even if this interferes with the satisfaction of the remote. If, for example, being popular is more important to a high school student than a college degree, he will sacrifice his studies in favor of social activities. If, on the other hand, his remote goal is stronger than the immediate, he will be willing to sacrifice many of the social activities he would like to engage in and will postpone marriage until his education has been completed. The willingness to postpone immediate pleasures in favor of more remote rewards is a true measure of the strength of an aspiration (11,146).

Even more important, the strength of an aspiration influences the individual's willingness to do things he has little interest in doing. A boy who is anxious to become a doctor, for example, will be willing to work hard to master higher mathematics which he dislikes and finds difficult to understand because it is a requirement for entrance into medical school. Similarly, a girl who aspires to a home and family of her own will be willing to engage in petting or necking which she disapproves of or will drink at parties which she has been forbidden to do by her parents if she has reason to believe that such behavior will help her to achieve her ultimate goal (90,151).

meaning of level of aspiration

Level of aspiration is the standard a person expects and hopes to reach in a given performance. Because he has not yet reached this goal, his level of aspiration is the *discrepancy between his achieved and his stated goals* (46,156,181). The distance between his achieved and stated goals may be realistic in the sense that he has a good chance of success. On the other hand, the distance may be so great that his chances of reaching his stated goal are slim; therefore, his level of aspiration is unrealistic.

In the past, encouragement of realistic levels of aspiration on the part of children and adolescents was part of the child training of parents and teachers. While young people were not discouraged from being ambitious, they were encouraged to face facts realistically and to set goals that were possible to achieve. The purpose of this was not to thwart the young person's achievements but to safeguard him from failure with its accompaniment of disappointment and feelings of inadequacy.

Today, the tide has turned; unrealistic levels of aspiration are encouraged rather than discouraged. (See Figure 8–3.) The adolescent who claims he will make a million before he is 40 is not told that he is "too big for his britches." Instead, he is commended for his ambition and is promised any aid his parents can give him to achieve this goal (122,123).

If there are reasonable chances of reaching unrealistically high goals, setting high levels of aspiration should be both encouraged and commended. But when achieving the goal is less than a matter of chance because of inherent limitations within the adolescent himself or because of environmental obstacles over which there is little or no control, it is questionable whether such encouragement should be given. The reason for this is that unrealistically high levels of aspiration usually doom the adolescent to failure from the start. Failure, in turn, leads to psychological damage that can and does affect seriously the adolescent's personal and social adjustments.

"Choose your own career, Son. You can be a brain surgeon, banker, diplomat..."

FIGURE 8–3 Unrealistic levels of aspiration are often fostered by parents. (Adapted from "The Neighbors," by George Clark. *The Evening Bulletin*, Philadelphia, Penn., Apr. 1, 1965. Chicago Tribune–New York News Syndicate. 1965. Used by permission.)

When levels of aspiration are unrealistic, they are usually unrealistically high. Adolescents who aspire to levels of achievement above their present achievements are dissatisfied. How strong their motivation to improve is, on the other hand, will be the major determining factor in the degree of unrealism present in their levels of aspiration. As Strang (171) has explained:

Although level of aspiration is an individual matter, people tend to set their levels of aspiration relatively high when they are dissatisfied with their present status, or when they are confident and successful. They tend to set their levels of aspiration relatively low when their motivation is poor, when they fear failure, when they do not face failure frankly, or the situation realistically, when others think poorly of them, and when they feel insecure or have other personality problems.

METHODS OF STUDYING LEVELS OF ASPIRATION

Because the psychological damage from unrealistically high, or unrealistically low, levels of aspiration is great, a strong scientific interest in studying them has developed. This interest centers on finding out how levels of aspiration are developed, why they vary, when they develop, and what effects they have on the individual's behavior. Only when such knowledge is available will it be possible to guide and encourage the development of levels of aspiration that will lead to a healthy adjustment to life.

The logical way to find out about an adolescent's aspirations is to ask him. Most adolescents would resent this as intrusion into their private lives or they would be reticent to disclose their aspirations for fear of being thought presumptuous. Still others would not want to declare themselves and then face the embarrassment that would come should they fall short of their goals.

Even if a person is willing to tell his aspirations, there is the problem of whether they alone are responsible for his achievements. As Hilgard (77) has explained:

We must be cautious about assuming that because a person is able to announce his goal and to strive toward it we have then a complete picture of his motivation. Prestige-seeking, self-protection, and other goals inevitably enter to distort the clear picture of why a person is doing what he is doing.

Because of the difficulties involved, indirect methods have been used to get clues about the adolescent's levels of aspiration. Of these, the following have proved to be most fruitful.

Studies of Wishes Studies of wishes give clues about the adolescent's immediate as well as remote aspirations. If wishes concentrate mainly on material possessions, it shows that these are the goals the adolescent is most concerned with. Should his wishes, on the other hand, relate mainly to self-improvement, achievement, and social acceptance, it emphasizes that these are the goals that mean most to him (4,38,84,171,189,191).

Studies of Ideals If his ideal is an athletic hero, it suggests that the adolescent aspires to be a successful athlete; should his hero be an aviator, it is relatively safe to predict that his vocational aspirations are in the area of aviation (45,73,135,171).

Studies of Resolutions When a person resolves to change, it suggests that he is dissatisfied with himself. If, for example, he resolves to improve his conduct in school and to do better schoolwork, to be more cooperative and helpful, and to stop biting his nails, we get some idea of the aspirations that the individual considers important to him. Girls, on the whole, make more resolutions to improve themselves than boys. This suggests that girls may be aspiring unrealistically high (197).

Laboratory Experiments Laboratory experiments of levels of aspiration must, through necessity, be focused on a study of immediate aspirations. The subject in an experiment involving an exercise in arithmetic, for example, would be told how long it took him to do a page. He would then be asked to estimate how long he thought it would take him to do the next page. This estimate is used as his level of aspiration in that particular task (101).

While it is never possible to predict with complete accuracy what the individual's performance outside the laboratory will be on the basis of his performance in the laboratory, a laboratory experiment does give a clue to his characteristic pattern of aspiring. It is fairly safe to conclude that a person who consistently aspires unrealistically high or low, or is consistently realistic, in a laboratory situation has developed the habit of aspiring in that way in everyday life.

how levels of aspiration are developed

Long before the child reaches adolescence, he has developed many aspirations for what he will do when he is grown up. He has also learned to aspire in a way that is characteristically his—realistically or unrealistically (160). He may, for example, develop the habit of allowing himself to be swayed by others in setting his goals; or he may set his

goals with little outside influence, basing them mainly on an assessment of his abilities acquired from past successes and failures. While environmental pressures during the adolescent years, combined with the successes and failures met in the past unquestionably will modify, to some extent, the pattern of aspiring developed in childhood, the foundations of this pattern remain relatively unchanged (11,51,73,160).

Of the many factors that influence the form and intensity the adolescent's aspirations take, the following are the most important.

EARLY TRAINING

Many adolescents are subjected, from babyhood, to training which emphasizes the importance of achievement in whatever they do; they are praised for success and reproved for failure. Their parents set the goals they are expected to reach and then show them how to reach them. Their parents not only expect them to perform the tasks set for them, but to do it *independently*. This training is reinforced by rewards and punishment until the pattern of aspiring becomes internalized and parental guidance is no longer necessary.

Both parents participate in training for achievement, but in a slightly different way. Fathers beckon from the front while mothers push from behind. The mothers' approach to training is more emotionally involved in the sense that mothers place greater emphasis on warmth and approval for success and disapproval for failure than fathers do. Consciously or unconsciously, mothers arouse anxiety in their children as a source of motivation to achievement (55, 139,141).

PARENTAL AMBITIONS

Even before the child was born, his parents had a concept of what their dream child would be, and they use this as a model for their aspirations for him throughout his life. They, for example, have definite ideas about how much education they want their child to have, what vocation they want him to select, what social and academic achievements they expect of him, and what sports they want him to excel in (13,19,33,43,68, 89,156).

Many of the ambitions parents have for their children come from thwarted ambitions of their own which they believe were blocked by obstacles; these obstacles they now try to remove from their own children's path. Others come from parental competition with other parents. Parents want their child to do better than other parents' children, and thus, indirectly, put a feather in their cap. Still other parental ambitions come from parental experiences. Mothers who are career women, for example, expect their children to acquire early the traits that will make them successful in life (13,33, 88,105,138).

When parental ambitions are strong, they have a marked influence on the aspirations the adolescent sets for himself and the level of these aspirations. If parents feel that social acceptance by the "right" crowd is very important, they put pressure on the adolescent to participate in extracurricular activities in school or college, and they provide him with the status symbols to facilitate his acceptance. In doing this, they often ignore the adolescent's interests and abilities and even his own aspirations (68,89,127, 128,148,151).

EXPECTATIONS OF OTHERS

The adolescent's aspirations are greatly influenced by what other people expect of him. If, for example, his friends expect him to be a good athlete, his aspirations will center around athletic achievements. The stronger his desire to be accepted by the group, the higher will be his level of aspirations (53, 151,156). As Cronbach (46) has explained:

> The standard set by one's group affects his goals. A person who thinks of himself as a normal member of a group will strive for the attainments characteristic of that group. . . . He is most influenced by the individual with whom he identifies or the group to which he feels he "belongs.". . . Keeping up with one's group is necessary for self-respect.

The peer group is not the only social group that influences the aspirations set by the adolescent; he is influenced, to a lesser extent, by his teachers. If they expect him to achieve academic success, he comes to expect it of himself; if they expect him to fail, he lowers his level of aspiration to conform to theirs. How much influence teachers have on the students' aspirations depends to a great extent upon how prestigeful they are and how anxious the adolescent is to conform to their expectations for him (133, 142,168).

COMPETITION WITH OTHERS

In a highly competitive society, the individual learns early in life that he must not only keep up with the Joneses but must outstrip them if he wants to be an accepted member of the group (25,122). This he learns from his parents' competition with other parents before he is old enough to compete with his age-mates. As Child and Bacon (33) have pointed out:

> Mothers in the park compete over teething schedules, time of rolling over, sitting up, smiling, etc., and anxiously consult publications which give developmental norms. This competition between parents (often in the presence of the children) continues throughout the preschool years with regard to nearly every aspect of motor and verbal development.

At home, the child's older or younger sibling becomes a source of competition for him. The older child sets a pattern which he strives to imitate; the younger sibling's behavior sets a pattern he tries to excel to prove his superiority. If, as he grows older, the younger sibling surpasses him, he will aspire to live up to the standard set by the younger sibling (58,91,95,147).

The habit of competing with others, developed in the home, affects the child's characteristic method of forming his aspirations outside the home. When he goes to a child's party, for example, he aspires to win the prize for pinning the tail on the donkey because he has learned that prestige goes with success (33). By adolescence, the habit of competing with others plays an important role in determining what aspirations he will set for himself. If his friends aspire to be outstanding athletes, he will not only aspire to be an outstanding athlete but a more outstanding one than they are (2,93,190).

When satisfaction from success in competition with others is great, the adolescent will often develop aspirations in line with those with whom he can compete successfully, even if this means that his aspirations will ignore his interests, abilities, and needs (50). The satisfaction from success more than compensates for satisfaction from success in areas where there is little competition or in areas where competition is for success in unprestigeful activities (40).

CULTURAL TRADITIONS

In cultures where there is a class system and an authoritarian form of government, the belief grows up that the individual can aspire to reach a goal set for his class but can go no further. As a result of this belief, young people are discouraged from aspiring above their class limitations.

As class barriers have gradually been broken down and authoritarian rule replaced by democratic governments in many countries of the world, the traditional beliefs about aspiring above one's class have likewise started to give way to beliefs that one should aspire high because there is a good chance that these aspirations can be reached (164).

In a democracy, the traditional belief about equality of opportunities is so firmly established that children are brought up to believe that they can reach the top of the ladder if they will make the most of the opportunities their parents provide for them. This belief is fostered from earliest childhood by parental teachings, by stories of the Horatio Alger type, and by stories, movies, television shows, biographies, and autobiographies of successful men and women. These mass media, with their rags to riches theme, have been paralleled by those with the Cinderella theme—a young girl from a poor family marries the American counterpart of a prince, a handsome young man of wealth and assured social position (52,122, 123,164,186).

While it is unquestionably true that greater equality exists in America than in any other cultural group in the world today, there are still *limitations* to what one can do; this fact the traditional beliefs ignore. Some of those limitations exist in the individual himself. He may not have the physical or mental capacity to achieve what he wants to achieve. Other limitations are environmental. The individual may grow up in an environment where opportunities to develop his innate abilities do not exist. This is readily apparent in educational opportunities in some areas of the country and in opportunities to develop specialized skills in sports or the arts. Still other limitations are social. The individual may be prevented from doing what he is capable of doing because of prejudice against him. This is especially true of women and of members of minority religious or racial groups (123, 194).

The adolescent who has been encouraged to accept the belief about equality of opportunity since his childhood will often, understandably, aspire above his chances of success, even though his level of aspiration may be closely correlated with his abilities. If he fails to take into consideration obstacles which may stand in his way, his level of aspiration will be unrealistically high in spite of his ability and motivation.

Failure to take into consideration personal limitations even more often accounts for the adolescent's development of unrealistic levels of aspiration or aspirations in areas in which he lacks the ability to succeed. A conscientious student who aspires to go to college may be unrealistic in his level of aspiration because his grades reflect either his teachers' judgments of his abilities based more on his efforts than on his achievements or because he is in a school where other students have little interest in academic work or in a college education; by comparison, he impresses his teachers as being brighter than he is.

MASS MEDIA

The American traditional belief about equality of opportunity opening all doors to the individual has been reinforced by different forms of mass media of communication, especially books, radio, movies, newspapers, magazines, and television. Even school textbooks place emphasis on the importance of achievements; this stimulates the student to set levels of aspiration for his own achievements. While emphasis on achievement is not so pronounced today as it was in the past, it still plays an important role in many of the readers and other books the child is encouraged or expected to read (52). Figure 8–4 shows the trend in emphasis on achievement in school textbooks during recent years.

From childhood, the adolescent has not only been exposed to these mass media but he has learned to identify with the character that appeals most to him; that character is generally the hero for boys or the heroine for girls. Furthermore, as Americans like happy endings, the adolescent is accustomed to having the hero or heroine he has identified with reach his goal even if, in doing so, he may have had what appeared to be insuperable obstacles to overcome (18,31,41, 52,107,115).

One cannot be exposed to constant

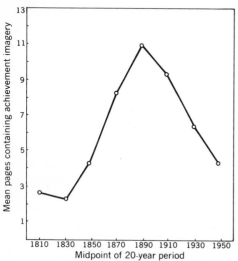

FIGURE 8–4 Trends in emphasis on achievement in school textbooks. (Adapted from R. deCharms and G. H. Moeller: Values expressed in children's readers: 1800–1950. *J. abnorm. soc. Psychol.*, 1962, **64**, 136–142. Used by permission.)

repetition of the theme that all ends well without believing that it holds true in real life also (41,42). This is illustrated by the expression of a teen-age girl's vocational aspiration, written after reading a biography of Madame Curie (171):

> *I should like to be a scientist like Madame Curie. I would like to practice medical science. I want to be a scientist because science is necessary to help our nation grow strong. Our nation must have strong and healthy people free from sickness. There must be scientists to find the necessary things to keep sickness away from our nation . . . to find new discoveries and to improve on the discoveries of others.*

The adolescent boy who finds his social acceptance in school or college below his expectations may set a level of vocational aspiration way above his potentialities in the belief that if he can acquire the status symbols others have. he will be as well accepted as they. This aspiration has been strengthened and perhaps even directed by the rags to riches theme of the mass media to which he has been exposed. In them, the successful hero in the business world becomes the social lion of the same social group that rejected him earlier (8,106,107).

Mass media have more influence on remote than on immediate goals. When it comes to the remote future, adolescents can aspire as high as they wish because there is always the possibility that something will happen to enable them to make a fortune. They may, for example, discover and patent a machine that will revolutionize the industrial world and make them into millionaires. As Stephenson (164) has pointed out, in his discussion of the effects of equality of opportunity on levels of aspiration:

> *Even though most British and American youth appear to aspire relatively high, their educational and occupational plans seem to more nearly approximate their class position.*

PAST EXPERIENCES

Much of the unrealistic aspiring of children can be traced to the fact that their limited experience makes it impossible for them to assess their capacities realistically. Not only do they set their goals unrealistically high, but their goals are more related to their wishes of the moment—whims—than to their real interests. Only in areas where children have had previous experience are their levels of aspiration related to their capacities.

Much the same is true of adolescents. In areas where they have had little or no experience they tend to aspire unrealistically high. In their vocational aspirations, for example, adolescents with some work experience are more realistic than those who have had no experience (115,155). Similarly, lack of experience in marriage plus the glamorized picture of marriage they get from popular media lead many adolescent girls to aspire to marriage as a solution to all their problems. Aspirations for large families are likewise based on lack of experience; few adolescent girls realize what it means in terms of work and expense to have a large number of children (20).

The *type* of aspiration the adolescent develops is likewise influenced by experience. Immediate aspirations are, on the whole, more influenced than remote aspirations. Success in a situation, for example, tends to encourage an individual to raise his aspiration while failure makes him lower it. But, if his aspirations relate to a remote experience, the present success or failure will have little influence. He will *expect* to do better in the future, even though he may have just recently experienced failure (103, 115).

Experience also determines whether the adolescent will aspire to achieve success or to avoid failure. After a failure, he is more likely to hope to avoid another failure than he is to aspire to achieve success. After failing an examination, for example, his aspiration for the makeup examination is to pass, not to pass with a brilliant grade (37).

If the adolescent is praised for his efforts, not for his achievements, or if his academic grades are based more on cooperativeness in the classroom, punctuality in getting his work done, and interest in trying to master the subject than on achievement, he is likely to believe that his capacity is greater than it is. Under such conditions, it is understandable that his level of aspiration in academic work may be unrealistically high (100,147).

INTERESTS AND VALUES

Adolescent interests influence aspirations in two ways. They determine, first, in what areas aspirations will be developed, and second, the level of these aspirations. An adolescent boy who has discovered the prestige value of sports will aspire to success in this area more than in the area of studies where prestige is lower.

Similarly, in the areas of mathematics and science, boys who have abilities in these areas are likely to develop aspirations for success; those whose abilities are limited will develop aspirations to avoid failure—or to pass. The more prestigeful these subjects are in the school, the higher the students' levels of aspiration are likely to be (114,129).

While interests and abilities are normally fairly closely related, interests may be stronger than abilities. This is true when there is high social prestige associated with an area of interest. On the other hand, they may be weaker than the individual's ability would justify if environmental conditions prevent his development of the interest (78). Negro students who are segregated from whites in schools have been found to set both academic and athletic aspirations above their capacities. Frustration has encouraged a stronger interest than their capacities justified and, with it, has encouraged a higher level of aspiration than was justified (5,174).

When interests are based on abilities, they tend to be stronger and more persistent than when based on group values with little relationship to the individual's own interests or abilities. When aspirations are developed from interests based on abilities, they are not only stronger but also more realistic than when they are influenced primarily by group values. An adolescent who aspires to be a scientist, for example, because of a sincere interest in science which springs from ability in this area will have a more realistic aspiration for a scientific career than will the adolescent whose aspiration is based mainly on the prestige associated with science and the realization that there are plenty of jobs with good pay available in this area (23,114, 173,183).

variations in aspirations

Among adolescents, goal-setting behavior varies in strength, in degree of realism, and in degree of remoteness of aspirations. For some, aspirations are a source of motivation to success; for others, they provide motivation to avoid failure. Some adolescents are satisfied, for example, only when they are as successful as they aspired to be; others are satisfied if they can avoid failure (110,112, 161). As Pressey and Kuhlen (131) have remarked:

> Some people are not satisfied unless their performance is of top quality, and they may even refuse to participate in an activity in which they cannot do better than most. Others are quite satisfied with a passable performance. Some people have a strong drive for vocational success: some are satisfied with "a living."

Some adolescents are "impractical idealists," aspiring way above their capacities. Others are "realists" whose levels of aspiration are well within their reach.

Normally, aspirations become more realistic with experience. What aspirations the adolescent has, as has been stressed earlier, will be influenced by the values of the group with which he is identified. These values change as adolescence progresses. Academic aspirations may, for example, increase in intensity as adolescents approach the college age, or they may weaken, if the adolescents have no plan to continue their education beyond high school.

Even in the same adolescent, aspirations vary in intensity in different areas of activities (66). In academic work, his aspirations are more likely to be high in subjects which he regards as a stepping-stone to vocational success—such as mathematics and sci-

ence—than in subjects which are required but from which he can see little practical benefit.

Variations in type of aspiration and in level of aspiration come from environmental factors as well as from characteristics of the adolescent. Of the many factors that play a role in variations in goal setting, the following are the most important.

CULTURAL IDEALS

Different cultures have different standards for what they expect of their members. These standards include levels of achievement and attitudes toward achievement. By the time a child reaches adolescence, he is expected to have learned what his cultural group expects of him and to assume the responsibility for guiding his behavior by these standards (32). Child and Bacon (33) have emphasized:

> There is a very wide variation among human societies in the extent to which children are trained to strive for achievement. . . . In some instances, the systematic training of children to orient themselves toward outstanding achievement has been seen as part of the way children are prepared to act effectively as adults in a society where earnest striving for personal advancement or competitive success is expected. Contrariwise, the absence of training in achievement orientation in certain other societies has been interpreted as preparation for a pattern of adult life in which competition and striving for personal advancement are not valued and indeed would be disruptive of a social system smoothly functioning under the guidance of other motives and goals.

That goal-setting patterns differ from one cultural group to another is not limited to civilized cultures: it is true also of cultures of lower civilization. The training of Jicarilla Apache Indian boys involves strong emphasis on achievement. Throughout childhood, boys are encouraged by their parents to compete with their age-mates. They are taught the skills needed for successful competition by their parents; they are urged on by their parents to higher accomplishments;

and they are ridiculed if they fall below the expected standards. By contrast, the Mountain Arapesh children have few demands for achievement placed on them. They are protected by their parents; they are not asked to perform tasks which are exacting or difficult; and there is little pressure on them to acquire skills (33,113).

As marked differences in cultural standards exist in civilized societies. In our present-day American society, children are subjected to constant pressures to achieve. According to Child and Bacon (33):

> As children progress through school, the emphasis on achievement becomes more elaborate and extensive, and even penetrates the area of recreation. There are real rewards for the child who shows athletic prowess. There is competition for the leading role in dramatic productions. Status in the Boy Scouts is definitely a function of various forms of achievement.

In other civilized groups, cultural ideals do not put emphasis on achievement or on the value of training children to compete with others for success. In the British West Indies, for example, the Negroes are impulsive, they indulge themselves, and then are willing to settle for almost nothing, if they can get it right away. They do not work or wait for bigger rewards, nor are they willing to sacrifice for them. By contrast, East Indians living side by side with them cling to their cultural ideals by training their children to strive for greater achievements through postponing immediate gains and pleasures for greater rewards (116).

SUBCULTURAL IDEALS

Within *socioeconomic* groups, adolescents from middle-class families have, as a group, been trained from early childhood to set goals for the future and to deprive themselves of immediate pleasures if these are likely to handicap them in reaching their ultimate goals. Lower-class adolescents, whose parents' philosophy of life is, characteristically, to eat, drink, and be merry while you have the opportunity and let the future take care of itself, are trained to be

more present- than future-oriented in their goal setting (11,33,137,146).

Racial subgroups within a culture likewise vary in their attitudes toward achievement and in the values they place on it. This is well illustrated in their attitudes toward striving for status through social mobility. Some groups are satisfied to remain static; others are more anxious to improve themselves and to move up the socioeconomic ladder. This is one of the factors that accounts for differences in social mobility rates among Americans today (93,122,123, 139). This matter will be discussed in more detail in the next chapter.

Negroes, as a group, tend to set immediate goals and to be more realistic about them than whites (116). In their vocational aspirations, for example, Negro adolescents are more realistic than whites; they realize that there are restrictions on job opportunities for them that do not exist in the case of whites (63,122,153). When, however, they are in nonsegregated schools and have a chance to compete with whites, Negroes often have unrealistically high levels of aspiration. This is partly a form of compensation for their status and partly in the hope of achieving a more desirable status (21,63).

There are *ethnic* group differences also. Italian parents put little pressure on their children to achieve high success; Greeks put strong pressure on theirs to achieve social-status improvement by educational and vocational mobility. Italian parents, it has been reported, are more lenient in their attitudes and are satisfied with lower occupational achievement in their children than are Greeks. They are, however, pleased when achievement is higher than they had expected. Greek parents, by contrast, are not only not satisfied when their children achieve less than they expected but they emphasize to them the importance of status improvement; they help them to shape their behavior to make this improvement possible (138,139,172).

Attitudes toward achievement vary according to the *religious* background of the adolescent. A high respect for scholarship, encouragement of children to take advantage of the learning opportunities their parents provide for them, and a desire to get ahead or better themselves, are closely associated with the Jewish cultural traditions (33). Jewish parents encourage their children to postpone immediate pleasures in favor of the greater rewards to come in the future (23,138,139,172).

Among Protestant and Catholic parents, by contrast, parental pressures for achievement are less powerful driving forces in the adolescent's life. While parents of these religious faiths want their children to better themselves, they put less pressure on their children to aspire high than do parents of the Jewish faith. Protestants, as a group, however, put more stress on achievement than Catholics (23,139).

TYPE OF FAMILY

Adolescents from an *economically* or *socially stable family* tend to concentrate on remote goals and to set higher levels of aspiration than do adolescents from economically or socially unstable families. When the economic condition of the family is unstable, owing to loss of job by the breadwinner, it is difficult for the adolescent to plan ahead. Because he cannot foresee what his future will be, he must live in the present unless he wants to face the frustrations that come when a more remote goal, such as going to college or a professional school, is upset by family financial hardships (13,23,93).

When a family is socially mobile, the adolescent does not know what lies ahead and, consequently, cannot plan for it. By contrast, a socially stable family allows him to know what lies ahead and this gives him a basis on which to plan and a knowledge of which goals are important to the members of the social group with which he is associated (13,93).

In *small* families, stronger pressure is brought to bear on the adolescent to aspire high and to work to achieve the goal he sets than in larger families. The reason for this is that adolescents from small families have a better chance of getting ahead than have those from larger families because of the greater opportunities their parents can give

them. When a family disaster strikes, such as loss of job by the breadwinner or death, adolescents from small families are less likely to be deprived of opportunities to move ahead than are those from larger families (20,140,180).

The *ordinal position* of the adolescent in the family affects the type and level of aspiration he sets. Children with older siblings begin, early in childhood, to aspire to do things like their older siblings and to do them as well. When the siblings are of the same sex, competition is keener and aspirations are more likely to be in the same areas of behavior than when the siblings are of two sexes. A boy with an older brother, for example, will usually compete with him to achieve success in sports. Having an older sister whose interests are more social than athletic will not encourage him to set similar aspirations; it will, however, encourage him to try to be as successful in his chosen sports as she is in her social activities (91). An adolescent characteristically regards his younger siblings as "kids." Hence, he has little desire to strive to surpass them (20, 91,110,180).

In middle- and upper-class families, parents expect more of the firstborn than of those born later and they give the firstborn more advantages to make these aspirations possible. This is especially true when the firstborn is a boy (145). In lower-class families, by contrast, the youngest child is more likely to receive pressures from parents and siblings to better himself than are the older siblings. By the time he is ready to strive to go ahead, parents are in a better financial position to help him. Also, older siblings often contribute their share. It is a feather in the cap of every family member to have one of its members move up the educational, vocational, and social ladders (20,140).

Strict, authoritarian *discipline* leads to unrealistically high levels of aspiration, democratic discipline to realistic levels, and permissive discipline to unrealistically low levels (13,43,91,110,140). In a home where the mother is the *dominant parent*, adolescents tend to set higher levels of aspiration than in homes where the father is dominant (63,93). This is because there is a closer emotional tie between mothers and adolescents than between fathers and adolescents, especially boys. Many boys will strive to succeed to "please Mother"; their father's proddings are more likely to fall on deaf ears or to lead to unrealistically low levels of aspiration (105,141).

Suburban parents, as a group, put greater pressure on their children for success —academically, socially, and vocationally— than do urban or rural parents. Rural parents put the least pressure on their children; they realize that educational opportunities are limited in rural areas and that without a good education, vocational opportunities will be limited. In urban areas, by contrast, where educational and vocational opportunities are far less limited, the aspirations of adolescents are influenced more by the subcultural backgrounds—socioeconomic, racial, and religious—of their families than by where they live (69,140,141).

Parents who have a *selfish attitude* want their children to aspire to goals they set for themselves in areas that were important to them but which, for reasons often beyond their control, they were unable to reach. Pressures on their children, thus, become a method of realizing their own unfulfilled wishes. Or they may want to create the impression of being good parents by having their children's achievements surpass those of their age-mates. They show their selfish motive by their reaction to their children's successes and failures; they react with warmth and approval to success and with disapproval or punishment to failure or success below their expectations (138,140,141).

Other parents believe that their children can be happy and successful in a highly competitive society only if they are trained to aspire to high achievement in areas which are valued by their group. In their zeal to make their children happy, they often encourage them to aspire beyond their capacities and willingly make sacrifices to enable them to reach these goals. In discussing the *unselfish motive* back of much unrealistic aspiring on the part of American adolescents

of today, Child and Bacon (33) have pointed out:

> It is likely that much of this training, as performed by parents and teachers, is quite consciously motivated by the intention of preparing children to take effective parts in the life of contemporary American society, in which motives for achievement in adults play so important a part. To be quite lacking in motive for achievement might be even more maladaptive in American society than to have an overly strong and compulsive need for achievement which is expressed in inappropriate ways.

GROUP STATUS

How much influence the group has on the adolescent's aspirations varies according to his status in the group and what the group expects of him. If, for example, the adolescent belongs or is anxious to belong to a group in school or college that puts high value on sports and relatively low value on academic achievement, the type of aspirations he sets and the level of his aspirations will follow the group pattern. If, on the other hand, his status is secure and he has no reason to try to impress the group members, his level of aspirations will be more realistic. The adolescent whose status is marginal and who sees an opportunity of improving it, will likely aspire unrealistically high in areas which will increase his prestige in the eyes of the group. In the case of the social isolate, the group exerts little influence on either the type or level of aspirations he develops (2,93).

When the adolescent *expresses* his aspirations, it increases his motivational level; this, in turn, increases his performance level. He knows that the group now expects him to do what he said he wanted to do and he does not want to appear as a failure in their eyes (87).

USE OF ESCAPE MECHANISMS

How much *time* an adolescent spends on different escape mechanisms, such as daydreaming, and on different forms of mass media is greatly influenced by how well accepted he is by the peer group. How much *influence* different escape mechanisms have on the adolescent's level of aspirations will be determined largely by what use he makes of them. To a lesser extent, his use of these devices determines the types of aspirations he develops. If he uses them merely as recreation in idle moments, they will have relatively little influence; if, on the other hand, he uses them as compensation for lack of social acceptance, they will have a profound influence.

Because compensation provides greater satisfaction when the adolescent identifies himself with characters in mass media than when he views them objectively, this also influences the effects they have on his aspirations. If a boy, for example, identifies himself with a sports hero, he will set higher levels of aspiration for himself in the same sport as his hero than he would if he viewed this athlete objectively (28,48,58,73,104, 149,165,171).

Excessive daydreaming — daydreaming more frequent and more fanciful than is characteristic of the individual's age level— encourages the adolescent to aspire far beyond his capacities. His aspirations are based more on a wishful estimate of his ability than on his real ability. By contrast, the adolescent who engages in daydreaming less frequently and less excessively, using it more as recreation than as a retreat from reality and more as a motivation to action than a retreat from action, will set more realistic goals (46,73,171).

The type of daydreaming engaged in is as important as the degree. When the daydream takes the "conquering hero" form, the adolescent will develop aspirations for success. The girl, for example, who daydreams of herself as a concert singer is likely to set aspirations in that area rather than in homemaking or in some other career. (See Figure 8-5.) If, on the other hand, daydreams take the "suffering hero" form, the adolescent may develop aspirations to avoid failure. Or he may develop aspirations unrealistically high and then explain to himself and others that his failure to reach his goals is not his fault but is due to the fact that others have blocked his path to success (28, 135).

PAST FAILURES AND SUCCESSES

Successes and failures in the past influence the level of the adolescent's aspirations more than the type of aspirations he sets. When the adolescent has been successful in the past, in the sense that his achievements came close to his aspirations, he usually raises his level of aspirations. If he has experienced failure, he may keep his level of aspirations constant, he may lower it, or he may raise it (103,115). What he does will be greatly influenced by how much below his expectations his achievement fell, what other people expect of him, and how he views his failure—either realistically or unrealistically (33,46,110,112,176).

The adolescent who experiences frequent success tends to develop a *generalized expectation* for future success. He thinks of himself as "good" and believes that he will succeed in everything he undertakes. Parents and teachers often reinforce this generalized expectation—maintaining that because he has been successful in *some* area, he can be equally successful in other areas in the future (13,26,43,72,93).

There is a tendency for people at all ages to aspire to have the things they have been prevented from having. This is a case of the grass on the other side of the fence looking greener. The adolescent who is frustrated and angry when obstacles are placed in his way may develop aspirations for something that would hold little interest for him if it were readily available. An adolescent whose late maturing prevents him from trying out for the football team because his body is too small will literally live for the day when his body becomes large enough to try out for the football squad (26).

The adolescent who has, from childhood, met obstacles in his path often develops the habit of aspiring unrealistically high or unrealistically low. This is well illustrated in the effect of segregation in schools on Negro students. Knowing that many job opportunities are closed to them and that many of the schools and colleges forced by law to enroll them as students do not accept them socially causes the adolescent to develop unrealistic levels of aspiration. If he resents the discrimination, he will aspire unrealistically high; if he accepts it, even though resentfully, he will aspire unrealistically low (63,65,72,135).

SEX

Not only do members of the two sexes develop different types of aspirations, influenced by interests that are sex appropriate and by group pressures, but they differ in the levels of their aspirations. As adolescence progresses, both boys and girls develop aspirations more in line with adult values (62, 65). Boys, for example, feel a need for greater attainment than do girls. As a result, the aspirations of boys are concentrated in areas, such as athletics, academic achievement, and vocations, where sex-appropriate achievements are possible. Girls, by contrast, put more emphasis on aspirations that relate to personal attractiveness and social acceptance—areas that are more highly valued among adult women than men (14). These sex differences are shown in Figure 8–6.

Another sex difference in type of aspiration is in immediate and remote aspirations. As was pointed out earlier, girls tend to have more immediate and fewer remote aspirations than boys. The reason for this sex differerence is that girls regard marriage as their major goal in adult life. Because they do not know, during adolescence, when they will marry, whom they will marry, or the socioeconomic status they will have after marriage, it is difficult for them to plan ahead. Even their educational aspirations are often on a month-to-month basis.

This is not true of boys. Regardless of marriage, they must plan ahead so that their education can serve as a foundation for their future vocational aspirations (23). Furthermore, because attainment of remote goals necessitates postponing many pleasures they might enjoy during their adolescent years, boys are more willing to make sacrifices at the present for greater future rewards than are girls, whose immediate aspirations do not require these sacrifices (11).

FIGURE 8–5 Conquering-hero daydreams often set the pattern for adolescent aspirations. (Adapted from R. Strang: *The adolescent views himself.* New York: McGraw-Hill, 1957. Used by permission.)

Both at home and in school, more pressure to achieve is put on adolescent boys than on girls. Parents expect more of their sons than of their daughters (141). This encourages boys to aspire unrealistically high. In academic work, sports, and vocational choices, boys' aspirations tend to be out of line with their capacities. Because parents

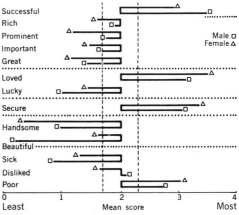

FIGURE 8–6 Sex differences in aspirations are based on adult values. (Adapted from E. M. Bennett and L. R. Cohen: Men and women: personality patterns and contrasts. *Genet. Psychol. Monogr.*, 1959, **59**, 101–155. Used by permission.)

expect girls to achieve more socially than boys, girls' social aspirations tend to be more out of line with their capacities (6,14,30, 45,94,185).

However, there is no clear-cut sex difference in levels of aspiration in every area; variations depend on many factors, especially previous experience. Boys, for example, who usually have more work experience outside the home and at an earlier age than girls, become more realistic about their vocational aspirations earlier than girls. When an adolescent girl enters the vocational world, she soon lowers the level of her vocational aspirations. This she does when she realizes that achievement in many work areas is blocked, or made especially difficult, for women and when she recognizes that she cannot hope to aspire to a high level of achievement in a vocation if she marries. Boys, by contrast, have less reason to lower their levels of vocational aspiration; they know that the obstacles that stand in the way of girls' achievements do not exist for them (36,57,82,123,152,188).

Experience likewise plays an important role in breaking down sex differences in levels of academic aspiration. Many boys, during the early years of high school, lower their levels of aspiration in academic achievement and raise them in athletic achievement because of the difference in prestige value associated with these activities. Later, when the boy aspires to enter a prestige college, he raises his level of academic aspiration, often unrealistically high.

Girls follow a pattern that is almost the reverse. At the beginning of high school, they often have unrealistically high levels of aspiration for academic and athletic achievement. When they discover the low prestige associated with these areas for girls, they lower their aspirations, sometimes unrealistically low. A bright girl, for example, in her attempts to counteract the impression that she is a brain, will aspire to do work little above passing—an unrealistically low level of aspiration for her abilities (16,39, 40). Thus, it is apparent that whether boys and girls differ in levels of aspiration is not dependent on their sex as much as on social pressures and previous experiences.

LEVEL OF INTELLIGENCE

There is a relationship between the level of the adolescent's intelligence and both the type of aspirations he sets for himself and the level of the aspirations. However, this relationship is not so high as one might expect; social pressures play an important role in distorting the relationship (17,177). When, for example, it is the thing to do to achieve high academic grades, many adolescents set unrealistically high levels of aspiration in the hope of winning peer approval. When being a good student is not the thing to do, many bright adolescents will set unrealistically low levels of aspiration in the hope of improving their status in the group.

On the whole, adolescents are well enough aware of their intellectual capacities by the time they reach high school to set realistic levels of aspiration. Also, recognition of obstacles which can prevent them from reaching a goal they want to set is more characteristic of bright than of less bright adolescents. This is taken into consideration as they form their levels of aspiration. The bright adolescent is likewise more aware of shortcomings within himself; this helps him to be more realistic (47).

On the whole, bright adolescents are better adjusted both personally and socially than are the less bright. This further contributes to a realistic approach to goal setting (177). Another difference between the bright and less bright that affects their levels of aspiration is the way in which they react to failure. When a very bright adolescent fails to reach a goal because it is unrealistically high, he lowers his goal. The less bright is far more likely to react to failure by developing feelings of personal inadequacy of by projecting the blame for his failure on others; he fails to realize that his capacities are not great enough to reach the high goal he set. As a result, he does not lower his aspirations to more realistic levels (17,47,73,177).

Pressures from parents, teachers, and peers and the influence of unrealism in the mass media have less effect on bright than on less bright adolescents. Because a bright adolescent can do good academic work with a minimum of effort, he is prodded less by teachers and parents than the one who has more difficulty in keeping his work up to standard. Peer-group pressures on the bright adolescent are likely to encourage him to lower the level of his aspirations—to avoid being a curve raiser. By contrast, peer pressures on the less bright are applied in an effort to avoid having the teacher hold back the class for the sake of the few who have learning difficulties.

The more intelligent the adolescent, the less pleasure he derives from romanticism and unrealism in mass media. As was pointed out earlier, the type of movies, television, and magazine and newspaper reading that appeals to bright adolescents is very different from the type that appeals to the less bright; the former are far less influenced by romanticism than are the latter. In the case of television, for example, not only do the bright spend less time watching TV, but they are far less likely to identify with the characters on the screen. As a result, they are less likely to develop an unrealistic approach to life or an unrealistic concept of their abilities which might lead to unrealistic levels of aspiration (107,192).

The difference between bright and less bright adolescents in the levels of aspiration they set for themselves is well illustrated in the area of vocational aspirations. Bright adolescents, as a group, set levels of aspiration in keeping with their intellectual abilities and the opportunities they have for training. The less bright, by contrast, are more influenced by what they would *like to do* or by what their parents want them to do than by what they are capable of doing. Furthermore, the less bright think less of how they are going to get the preparation they need for the vocations they choose or how they will meet the obstacles they may encounter in getting jobs in their chosen lines of work (47,49,175).

The *types* of aspiration set by adolescents of different intellectual levels also differ. Bright adolescents, as a group, set their aspirations more in line with their interests and capacities than by what is prestigeful in the eyes of the peer group. The less bright, by contrast, emphasize what others are aspiring to do or what they think

glamorous and prestigeful. The bright adolescent will not aspire to be a football player, for example, if he has little interest in sports and little capacity for football, even though he recognizes the prestige and glamour associated with a football hero. The less bright adolescent, on the other hand, will want to be a football hero because it is glamorous, not because he especially likes football or has the ability to play well enough to be outstanding.

PERSONALITY PATTERN

The adolescent who has a self-concept that makes him self-rejectant often aspires beyond his capacities; this is a form of compensation. The more dissatisfied he is with himself, the higher and more unrealistic his level of aspiration is likely to be. Many cases of excessive ambition are cloaks for self-dissatisfaction (46,110,112). The adolescent with an unstable self-concept sets goals relatively high in relation to his past performance and he is uncertain about how realistic his goal is. Like the adolescent with an unfavorable self-concept, the adolescent who has a favorable opinion of himself tends to set goals high in relation to his past performances. However, he differs from the adolescent with an unfavorable self-concept in that when his performance falls below his expectations he avoids the intropunitive explanations which the adolescent with a poor opinion of himself uses so freely (117,162, 168).

The confident, secure individual sets realistic goals for himself. When he realizes that his goal may be unrealistically high and that this was why he failed to reach it, he does not feel guilty, nor does it undermine his confidence about future achievements. By contrast, the adolescent who is insecure and lacks self-confidence is constantly striving to reach goals beyond his capacity; he is never satisfied unless he is "on top." Because these unrealistic aspirations cause him to fail, he becomes anxious, apprehensive, and even more insecure. He is upset emotionally by his failures, he is self-conscious about them because he is so anxious to make a good impression on others, and he feels guilty because he has fallen below others' expectations. To avoid a repetition of this emotion-producing experience, the poorly adjusted adolescent is likely to set his future levels of aspiration as unrealistically low as they formerly were unrealistically high. This enables him to succeed without undue pressure and to present a favorable picture in the eyes of others (110,115).

The adolescent who experiences relatively low anxiety tends to set higher goals than the one who is more anxious and more critical of his abilities and past performances. The more anxious the individual is, the more he overemphasizes his poor performances in the past and the less optimistic he is about his future achievements. This is in sharp contrast to the less anxious adolescent; he is more influenced by his successes than by his failures. As a result he sets his goals higher, often unrealistically higher, after he has achieved a success in some activity. Often, with repeated successes, the less anxious adolescent will develop an optimistic attitude about his abilities; with it will come a tendency to set *all* levels of aspiration high regardless of his abilities or past experiences (50,72,179).

The adolescent who has developed frustration tolerance sets more realistic goals than the one whose frustration tolerance is low. The former accepts frustrations when he realizes that they are beyond his control; the latter has a strong desire to "show others." This may lead to unrealistic levels of aspiration or it may take the form of retreat from reality and the setting of unrealistically low aspirations (56,154). Emotionally disturbed adolescents tend to set unrealistically high or low levels of aspiration; emotionally well-adjusted adolescents set aspirations within the limits of possible achievement. The former are influenced by exaggerated fears or wishes for success; the latter are able to maintain a good balance between their hopes and reality (50,190).

the achievement syndrome

Far too many adolescents, accustomed from childhood to having others—mainly parents and teachers—do what is necessary to give them what they want, feel that aspiring

alone will bring the desired results. While they no longer believe in fairies who wave wands and magically turn people and things into what the hero or heroine of the story wished for, they often fail to comprehend what role *they* must play in fulfilling their wishes and how complex this role is. This is not entirely their fault; they have not been given the training needed to achieve a goal they set for themselves, nor have they had to strive to reach this goal unaided.

Instead, they are constantly told that "you can do this if you really want to" and they are reminded that parents are only too eager to give them the opportunities they need to reach their goals. Mass media reinforce this principle. A girl, for example, who wants to improve her looks is told by innumerable ads for face creams, hair tints, and countless other beauty aids that all she has to do is to buy the foolproof product advertised.

It all sounds so easy. The same props the adolescent has been accustomed to rely on all his life are there; his role is only to pay the money required and the props will be his. He fails to realize that he must learn to direct his energies into the channels that will lead to success. Furthermore, he fails to realize that ability is an important factor in success. *Only when the adolescent is aware of what is needed to reach the goal he aspires to reach and is willing to learn how to do so can he hope to come up to his expectations and those of the significant people in his life.*

Aspirations are only the beginning of a chain of activities that lead to eventual success or failure. They may be satisfied in daydreams or in identification with some successful person. Or they may be the stimulus that arouses a motivation to fulfill these aspirations in real life. Which form of outlet the aspiration will take will depend to a large extent on the adolescent's past experiences and which of these provided him with greater satisfaction.

ACHIEVEMENT MOTIVATION
Back of all aspiration is the fundamental need for achievement. To fulfill this need, the individual is motivated to direct his be-

havior toward a goal he aspires to reach. This involves evaluation of his performance in terms of some standard of excellence (111). Adler, many years ago, recognized the importance of need for achievement when he emphasized that everyone has a "life plan"—a purpose or goal which determines his reactions. This life plan is developed early in life as a result of certain relationships between the individual and his physical-social environment. When the individual develops feelings of inferiority—whether they be physical, mental, or social in origin—he is motivated to compensate for these feelings by striving hard to reach the goal he set for himself and by aspiring to superiority in that goal. Thus, according to Adler, the will to power, which is in every individual, is stimulated to the goal of superiority by whatever inferiority complex he may have developed (1).

How the will to power will affect the individual's behavior will depend on how well adjusted he is. In a well-adjusted person, the drive to achievement is adjusted to reality and integrated with social drives. It then leads to reasonable satisfactions. By contrast, in a poorly adjusted person, this drive springs from unrealistic aspirations and is unrelated to social drives; it then leads to failure and maladjustive behavior. Furthermore, while the well-adjusted person tries to compensate for failure by excelling in activities in which he has greater ability, the poorly adjusted person overcompensates or tries to excel in the areas in which he has failed; this is a means of denying his weakness. The well-adjusted adolescent who fails in sports, for example, will try to excel in studies or in dramatics if he feels he has a chance for success in those areas; if he is poorly adjusted, he will bend all his energies to show others as well as himself that he has athletic ability.

In recent years, more emphasis has been placed on cultural pressures for achievement and less on the innate drive to achievement as stressed by Adler. There is also more emphasis on the role the social environment plays in determining what aspirations the adolescent will develop and less on some weakness which, according to Adler, is

the motivating force behind all aspirations (101). As McClelland has pointed out, the origin of achievement motivation is to be found in the different experiences children have (111). How strong or how weak this achievement drive is will depend on: first, the general energy level of the individual, caused by endocrine, metabolic, or other constitutional factors; second, cultural influences, especially family values regarding education and success; and third, child training to develop independence, self-reliance, self-confidence, and the desire to excel. If the child training is too permissive, it results in the development of a low achievement drive; if strict, in a high achievement drive (64).

Thus it is apparent that not one factor, but many, are responsible for the drive to achieve the goal the individual sets for himself. Furthermore, it is apparent that social and cultural forces play a more important role than innate factors both in goal-setting behavior and in achievement of the goal that has been set. To motivate the individual to reach the goal he sets, under social pressures from significant people in his life, he is promised special approval and rewards if he is successful and threats of disapproval and loss of affection if he fails (25,33,44, 179). When pressures are strong, he develops a *generalized* drive to success—an aspiration to be on top in everything he does. When pressures are weaker, the more realistic adolescent will realize that his aspirations must vary according to his abilities. As a result, his drive to achievement will *vary in strength* according to the strength of his aspirations in different areas (72).

The achievement drive is usually well established between the ages of 6 and 10 years—the first 5 years of the child's school experience. This is regarded as the critical period in achievement motivation. While there may be changes in the degree of achievement motivation as the child grows older and is influenced by social pressures outside the home, there is evidence that the changes are not significant. As Sontag and Kagan have pointed out, "High levels of achievement behavior at that age (the "critical age" between 6 and 10 years) are highly correlated with achievement behavior in adulthood" (160). In adolescence, the drive for achievement and recognition is so well developed that it is recognized by the adolescent's peers and is rated higher in popularity than in unpopularity or neglect. This is illustrated in Figure 8–7.

ELEMENTS IN THE ACHIEVEMENT SYNDROME

The complex process leading to achievement has been labeled the "achievement syndrome" (139,141). The three major elements that make up this syndrome are *aspiration* to act, *motivation* to act, and achievement *value*. Aspiration serves to direct the individual's energies, motivation drives him to use his energies to reach the goal he set, and value helps him to determine whether or not his energies are being used in activities which will conform to social expectations. All these elements in the achievement syndrome are the product of learning.

The adolescent has learned, from his training at home and in school, to aspire to goals which are prestigeful in the eyes of the group; he is trained to direct his energies into the channels that will lead to these goals and to do so independently so that when he is older he will be able to guide his energies without parental direction; and he is trained to assess his goals to see whether or not they are worthy of his energies before

he strives to reach them. To increase the adolescent's desire to reach the goals they consider valuable, parents reward the adolescent by their approval for success and punish him by their disapproval if he fails to come up to their expectations (139,141).

How strong or how weak the achievement syndrome will be depends mainly on the type of training the adolescent has received from his childhood days. Parents who have low aspirations for their children give them little training in reaching goals and provide little motivation for them to train themselves to do so. The result is that when an adolescent aspires to reach a goal, he often falls far short of it, even though he may have the necessary ability to reach it. He simply does not know how to mobilize his energies so that he can use them effectively. As a result, he often gains satisfaction in imaginary successes or blames himself and others for his shortcomings (33,36).

success or failure

Whether the achievement syndrome will lead to success or failure depends on the ability of the individual, what use he makes of his ability, and the presence or absence of obstacles in his way. As Child and Bacon (33) have pointed out:

If the child is gifted with natural competence and versatility he may completely internalize the achievement pressure and stand at the head of his class, eventually graduating from college magna cum laude, the captain of the football team and "most popular man in the class." A less-gifted child, of course, experiences failure to the degree of pressure on him to reach the very highest level of achievement.

Success and failure are also greatly influenced by the adolescent's personality pattern. If he feels inadequate, he will have "self-enhancing tendencies"; he will attempt to make himself seem more adequate and worthy as a way of improving his status or to gain recognition and approval. His interpretation of his achievement, whether as a success or a failure, will thus be greatly influenced by whether or not it fulfills his desire

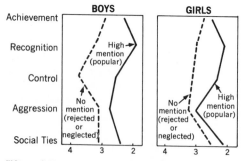

FIGURE 8–7 Aspirations for achievement and recognition are rated higher in boys and girls who are popular than in those who are unpopular. (Adapted from M. C. Jones: A study of socialization patterns at the high school level. *J. genet. Psychol.*, 1958, **93**, 87–111. Used by permission.)

for recognition and acceptance (54,125, 150). The relationship between personality, ability, and achievement is illustrated in Figure 8–8.

Objective versus Subjective Success and failure can be judged either objectively or subjectively, depending on the person's frame of reference (110,111). If the adolescent comes up to the expectations others have for him, he will be judged by them as a "success"; if he has done better than they expected him to, he will be considered a "real success." In spite of this, he may not be satisfied; he may even regard himself as a failure. The reason for this is that he has fallen below his own expectations; his achievements have not measured up to his level of aspiration. Should the expectations of others be unrealistically high in relation to his ability, he will likely accept their expectations as a standard and set his level of aspiration unrealistically high also. As a result, he will be both *objectively* and *subjectively* a failure when his achievements fall below both his own and others' expectations for him.

Should group expectations be below his capacity for achievement, his achievements will be successful in the eyes of the group members. They may, however, be failures in his own eyes, if his level of aspiration is higher than his ability. The closer group and personal expectations are to the adolescent's capacity, the greater the likelihood that his achievements will be regarded by *all* as successful. The greater the gap between group expectations or personal aspirations and capacity, the more certain it is that his achievements will fall below expectations and that the adolescent will be regarded by himself and by others as a failure (81,150,168,193). Because immediate goals are more likely to be realistic than remote goals, the chances of failure of a subjective type are greater in the case of the latter than of the former (36).

SUCCESS

In popular usage, "success" means a "favorable termination of a venture"; it means doing what you set out to do. Because differ-

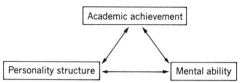

FIGURE 8–8 Personality and mental ability contribute to school achievements. (Adapted from A. D'Heule, J. C. Mellinger, and E. A. Haggard: Personality, intellectual, and achievement patterns in gifted children. *Psychol. Monogr.*, 1959, **73**, no. 13. Used by permission.)

ent people have different goals when they set out on a venture, it is understandable that success would have different meanings for each. As Strang (171) has stressed:

> "Success" has many different meanings, to young people and to adults. To a few it means having the highest marks in the class. To others it means reaching an individual goal or standard; anything below one's level of aspiration is failure. To many, success means passing in every subject. To some of these, barely "getting by" is enough. . . . To very mature adolescents, success means working up to their optimum capacity, realizing their intellectual potentialities.

Adolescents, like the adults with whom they come in contact in the home, school, neighborhood, community, and, indirectly, the nation through mass media, think of success mainly in terms of what is highly valued by the culture in which they live. This consists of *money and possessions* which serve as status symbols and *prestige* that comes from educational or occupational status. While the meaning of success varies, to some extent, every adolescent knows what is highly valued in the group with which he is identified; this then influences his interpretation of success (86).

Factors Contributing to Success Many people attribute success to luck or to influence. They believe that it comes from some outside source and that the person contributed little or nothing to the success he achieved (86). While it is unquestionably true that some people *seem* to have "all the luck," this is not true. The real difference between those who are lucky and those who are not is that the former take advantage of the opportunities they have and make the most of their potentials; those who are unlucky do not. A person may get ahead with influence for a time, but unless he does his share, his early success will turn into dismal failure.

All evidence points to the fact that success does not come automatically; *it must be won.* As has been stressed before, aspirations are not enough, nor is ability. The adolescent must have *training* and *guidance* to know how to use his abilities to the greatest advantage; he must have the *motivation* to use his abilities; he must be willing to *postpone immediate pleasures* for the sake of a larger goal; he must be *flexible* and willing to adjust to new roles and activities if they will contribute to his success, even though they may not be to his liking; he must have opportunities for *experience* to learn how to use his capacities and to assess his strengths and weaknesses; and, above all, he must be *willing to adjust* his levels of aspiration realistically to his abilities (11,15,24,80,86,96, 109,139).

Success in one area is often a stepping-stone to success in another, especially when the areas are related. This is due in part to the experience acquired in one situation that can be used to advantage in another and in part to the fact that the adolescent discovers what his capacities are; he then uses this knowledge to adjust his levels of aspiration for a new activity (15). Adolescents, for example, who are high achievers in academic work in school or college have been found to achieve more in occupational status than those whose academic achievements were low. The reason for this is that high academic achievement opens up doors to training which, in turn, will open up vocational doors that otherwise would be closed (10).

Obstacles to Success Even though the adolescent may have the major essentials needed for success, success may be blocked by obstacles over which he has little or no control. These obstacles may be *economic;* the adolescent may lack the money needed

to do what he wants to do and is capable of doing. They may be *social,* stemming from prejudice against the adolescent because of his race, religion, or sex.

Even when there are no obstacles, many adolescents achieve success below their potential. In speaking of the relationship between intelligence and academic achievement, Terman has pointed out that "Intellect and achievement are far from perfectly correlated" (177). This is equally true in other areas. There are many reasons for this. If the adolescent can satisfy his aspirations more easily and more successfully by *daydreaming* or by *identification* with a successful hero or heroine in some mass media, it will stifle his motivation to do what he is capable of doing in real life. Or he may have a strong motivation to reach the goal he set for himself but does not know how to do so because of *poor training and guidance* in making use of his capacities. Motivation may be weakened by the adolescent's unwillingness to admit or to accept his limitations. Unless he does so, he will aspire unrealistically high, meet repeated failures, and develop a "failure complex" (15).

Thus, it is apparent that the adolescent's achievements may fall below his potentials either because of obstacles in his environment or obstacles within himself. When he knows, or suspects, that he is capable of achievements above those he experiences, he feels guilty, ashamed and embarrassed. He blames himself for his shortcomings and often develops a feeling of personal inadequacy. When he knows or believes that the obstacles are environmental, he feels resentful and martyred. If he develops a martyr complex as a result of repeated failures, this is very likely to weaken his motivation to live up to his potentials in the future. Instead, he will develop an I-don't-care attitude (176).

Effects of Success While success affects different adolescents differently, there are certain effects that are fairly universal. Of these, the following are the most important.

level of aspiration There are two common reactions to success: first, to aspire higher, and second, to play safe. When the adolescent is confident that he can repeat his past successes, he is likely to raise his level of aspiration in the hope of winning greater group approval. If, on the other hand, he is not confident that he can succeed at a higher level he is more likely to hold his aspiration level constant or even to lower it to ensure continued success.

Even when guidance, training, opportunities, and encouragement are given, the adolescent may not reach the level of achievement he should because *they have come too late.* A student who has developed the habit of dawdling over his studies may find it difficult or impossible to improve his study habits later when he is shown how to study; the old dawdling habit takes precedence over the new, efficient habit. As Harris has pointed out, "It is possible, indeed likely, that a person who comes late to his training will never realize the full measure of his potential" (71).

Failure to reach the success one is capable of may be the result of *weak motivation.* An adolescent, accustomed since childhood to having help from parents and teachers in reaching his goals, may not be willing to reach these goals alone. Or he may feel inadequate to do so because he has lacked the necessary training in independence. By playing safe, he has a better chance of succeeding than he has if he aspired higher, even though reaching a higher level of achievement would give him greater satisfaction (27,34,102,133,147,156). Figure 8–9 shows the effect of success on level of aspiration.

development of success complex Success, when repeated, tends to build up the adolescent's self-confidence to the point where he expects to succeed in whatever he undertakes. This generalized expectation of success—the "success complex"—may be accompanied by raising higher and higher his levels of aspiration in any activities in which he has succeeded without too much effort. If he has had to work hard to succeed or if his successes are in less prestigeful areas, he is apt to hold his levels of aspiration constant or even to lower them (11,46,108).

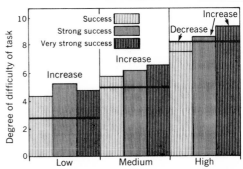

FIGURE 8–9 The effect of success on level of aspiration. (Adapted from K. Lewin: Behavior and development as a function of the total situation. In L. Carmichael (ed.), *Manual of child psychology.* 2d ed. New York: Wiley, 1954, pp. 918–970. Used by permission.)

liking for activity The adolescent develops a liking for activities in which he is successful. Students, it has been found, like school subjects in which they do well. However, because there is greater prestige associated with athletic success for boys and social success for girls, adolescent boys prefer sports, and girls, social activities over their studies (40,84).

increased motivation The adolescent who reaches the level of aspiration he set for himself derives enough satisfaction from his success and from the prestige it gives him to be willing to put forth greater effort in the future in the hope of winning further successes. In addition, he will try to improve his techniques to guarantee future successes. An adolescent who does well in a tennis tournament, for example, is motivated to practice harder, to read about how to play tennis better, and to take tennis lessons from a professional if he feels that his present success guarantees him a place on the varsity tennis team. The college student who makes the dean's list in his freshman year is motivated to study harder in the hope of winning a coveted Phi Beta Kappa key or of graduating *magna* or *summa cum laude.*

desire to publicize success Knowing that nothing succeeds like success, the adolescent wants others to know of his successes in the hope that this will increase his prestige in their eyes and, with it, his status. He, therefore, uses subtle methods of publicity. He tells others of his successes in a casual, or "Oh, by the way," approach. He also uses such status symbols as the wearing of athletic insignia to publicize his athletic successes, or a fraternity pin, blazer, or tie to publicize his social success (98,122).

satisfaction　Success does not always bring satisfaction; it may bring dissatisfaction if it falls below the adolescent's level of aspiration (7). Thus there are both "satisfied" and "dissatisfied" successes. Even if the adolescent reaches the goal he set for himself, there is no guarantee that he will be satisfied. He may feel that he set his goal too low or that he chose the wrong goal (157). The most dissatisfied adolescents are those whose successes fall below their expectations because they believe that some obstacle placed by others has blocked their paths to the successes they are capable of (159).

How much satisfaction the adolescent derives from his successes depends upon three important factors. The first of these is the *value* he attaches to the activity. A boy, for example, derives more satisfaction from a high grade in mathematics or science than from an equally high grade in English or a foreign language. To him, mathematics and science are stepping-stones to business success while English or a foreign language are "not salable."

The second factor that influences the adolescent's satisfaction is the *prestige* associated with the activity in which he is successful. In athletics, there is more prestige associated with football and baseball than with the "minor sports"—boxing, track, or tennis. Thus, success in a prestige sport is more satisfying than in a minor sport.

The third factor that influences the degree of satisfaction the adolescent derives from success is the *attitude of significant people* toward his success. Parents are prouder of their sons who achieve success in sports than in academic work: they are prouder of their daughters who achieve success in social activities than in either sports or academic work. These attitudes reinforce the adolescent's values and color his own attitudes (40). In discussing the attitude of members of the peer group toward academic achievement, Child and Bacon (33) have written:

> *The outstandingly successful achiever may earn the hostility of his less successful contemporaries. The taunting cry of "mother's boy," "teacher's pet," or the like, is on occasion a reflection of the fact that one person's achievement is not necessarily pleasing to everybody, and that the immediate social environment provides some realistic motivation which is in conflict with the desire for outstanding achievement.*

FAILURE

To fail means to "fall short"; it means an unfavorable termination of a venture. Failure may be *objective* or *subjective*, or both. When adults or members of the peer group expect more of the adolescent than he is capable of, his achievement is judged as a failure by them. If he has accepted their level of aspiration for him as his own, he will then judge himself as a failure. Or he may be objectively a success and subjectively a failure because his achievements have come up to the expectations of others but have fallen below his own expectations.

Failures in adolescence are most often subjective. The adolescent is not only unrealistic about what he thinks he can do but he has been so accustomed, throughout childhood, to have parents and teachers help him to achieve the goals he sets for himself that he continues to believe his abilities are greater than they actually are. This encourages the prolongation of unrealistically high levels of aspiration (33,46,59,81,161).

Failures can also be *acknowledged* or *grandiose*. In acknowledged failure, the adolescent recognizes that his abilities and the conditions confronting him will never permit him to reach the goals he has set for himself or that others expect him to reach. In grandiose failure, by contrast, the adolescent will not admit his limitations; instead, he convinces himself that he has been blocked in the achievement of his goal by someone or something over which he had no control. Figure 8–10 shows the different types of failure.

Which type of failure the adolescent experiences will influence his reactions to his failure. In the case of acknowledged failure, he may be disappointed but he will also become more realistic about his future goals. In the case of grandiose failure, he will not only be disappointed but he will also become embittered and develop paranoid beliefs which may eventually develop into a martyr complex (15,157).

Factors Contributing to Failure Most of the factors that contribute to failure are the opposite of those that lead to success. One of the most important is *lack of ability*— either mental or physical. If less were expected of the adolescent of limited ability, either by others or by himself, he would be a success for his level of ability. But, far too often, equal achievement is expected of all, regardless of individual differences in ability. The result is that some are doomed to failure; they simply have not the necessary ability to be successful at the level expected (33).

Failure may come from *lack of recognition of one's potentials*. An adolescent, deprived of opportunities for training or other learning experiences in sports when he was young, may be unaware of his potentials in this area. And, being unaware of his potentials, he will have little motivation to try to make successful use of them (166). On the other hand, he may be aware of his potentials but lack *opportunities for training*. A poor music teacher, for example, will lay such poor foundations that it will be difficult or even impossible for the adolescent to counteract them even when he is given better training.

More failures, however, come from *lack of motivation* than from lack of training or ability. While the adolescent wants to be a success, he either is unwilling to put forth the effort needed to reach the goal or he does not know how to use the effort he puts forth in a meaningful way.

This low motivation may also come from the low value he attaches to the activity. If a student, for example, sees little value to be derived from a school subject, he will be willing to put forth enough effort to pass the course but not enough to pass with a grade commensurate with his ability.

With the strongest motivation and the best use of his energies, on the other hand, the adolescent will inevitably fail if his *level of aspiration* is unrealistically high for his abilities. He is doomed to failure, even when he drives himself to do more than anyone thought he could do; he lacks the necessary ability to do what he is aspiring to do.

Effects of Failure The effects of failure are more variable and, therefore, harder to predict than are the effects of success (34, 46,168). This variation in response has been well illustrated by the way college students who fall below their expectations and those

Subjective   Objective   Acknowledged   Grandiose

FIGURE 8–10 There are different types of failure.

of their parents react. One student may pack his bags and leave college with the explanation, "Just say I'm a fish out of water. It's not the school. It's me. I don't fit." Another student, so "desperately afraid of losing out in the intense competition of college" will "build a psychological buffer for himself by not trying." Others will threaten, attempt, or actually commit suicide rather than face the psychological anguish that comes from guilt at falling below their own and their parents' expectations or from shame at letting down those who had pinned their hopes on them. How great the psychological anguish can be that makes a student think in terms of suicide is well illustrated in the following case (81):

> One freshman was the first from his village to go to Harvard. He was a straight-A student in high school, but went into a psychological tailspin when he got Cs on his first midterm examinations. He wasn't helped when the village band met him at the train station when he came home for Thanksgiving.

What effect failure will have on the adolescent depends on a number of factors. First, failures that are acknowledged by the adolescent are accepted more realistically than failures of the grandiose type in which the adolescent believes that he was prevented from succeeding by obstacles in his way (157). Second, whether he expects to fail or succeed will prepare him for his achievement; if he expects to fail, failure will have far less effect than if he expects to succeed and then fails (46). Third, when his status in the group is secure, failure will affect him very differently than it would, were his status marginal. It will also affect him very differently if he is a voluntary rather than an involuntary isolate (168). Fourth, if significant people in his life expect him to succeed, his reactions to his failure will be very different than if they were indifferent to his achievements or expected him to do approximately what he has done (12,33,195). Fifth, the adolescent's self-esteem affects his reaction to his failure. If his self-esteem is low, the adolescent will

be vulnerable to failure and will try to withdraw from situations in the future where he might fail. If, on the other hand, his self-esteem is high, he will not only be less vulnerable to failure but it will have the effect of challenge for the future.

Of the common effects of failure on adolescents, the following have been reported most frequently.

level of aspiration Some adolescents change their goals when they meet failure; they may raise or lower the goal. Others keep the same goal and persist in their attempts to reach it. Only when repeated failures convince them that the goal is too high will they lower it. Still others set no future level of aspiration after failure, thus protecting themselves from the embarrassment or resentment that stems from failure (27,34, 101). Figure 8–11 shows the effect of failure on level of aspiration.

If the failure is so pronounced that the adolescent realizes that he was aspiring too high, he is more likely to lower his level of aspiration than when the failure is slight; in the latter situation, he can hope for success the next time if he puts more effort into the performance (34). Immediate goals are more likely to be lowered following failure; remote goals will remain unchanged or may even be raised (27,102,156). Acknowledged failure is likely to lead to lowering levels of aspiration; grandiose failure encourages the adolescent to keep his goal constant or even to raise it. In the former he recognizes his limitations; in the latter he blames them on someone or something else (61,68,136).

When failure is known to others, the adolescent is more likely to lower his level of aspiration than when he alone is aware of it. This he can do better by lowering his level of aspiration to guarantee future success than by keeping it constant or raising it, thus running the risk of future failure (163, 169). If the adolescent expected to succeed, he will lower his level of aspiration for future performances less than he would had he expected to fail. Even when he lowers it, he usually does not lower it in proportion to his failure, because he expects to do better in the future. This expectancy usually stems from past successes in other areas (34,163).

Well-adjusted adolescents are, on the whole, more realistic about their abilities than are the poorly adjusted. Consequently, the former are more likely to lower their levels of aspiration following failure while the latter keep theirs constant or even raise them, explaining the past failure on circumstances over which they had no control (34, 67,102). When emotional stress due to frustrations caused by failure is strong, the adolescent usually lowers his level of aspiration, thus freeing himself of the possibility of future stress. If he can take his failures in a more stoic way, he is less likely to change his goals (132).

development of failure complex If failures come thick and fast, the adolescent will develop an expectation to fail in whatever he undertakes—a generalized feeling of inadequacy or a "failure complex." The result will be that he will have a defeatist attitude toward everything. Accompanying this will be a sense of futility which will be expressed in a what's-the-use approach to whatever he undertakes.

A failure complex is most likely to develop under four conditions: first, when the adolescent persists in setting unrealistic levels of aspiration and refuses to lower them even when he meets repeated failures; second, when his failures are of the grandiose type in which he believes that obstacles have been placed in his way by others and that he is helpless to remove them; third, when he expects success literally to knock at his door and fails to recognize how much time, effort, training, and planning are needed for success; and, fourth, when more is expected of him by others than he is capable of, regardless of how hard he may try (46,51,73,157).

effect on motivation In some adolescents, failure acts like a shot in the arm to jolt them out of a state of complacency. In others, it intensifies an already-existing belief that they are failures. Which effect it will have depends on a number of conditions, the most important of which are, first, whether the adolescent *expected* to fail or

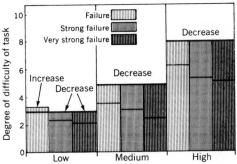

FIGURE 8–11 The effect of failure on level of aspiration. (Adapted from K. Lewin: Behavior and development as a function of the total situation. In L. Carmichael (ed.), *Manual of child psychology*. 2d ed. New York: Wiley, 1954, pp. 918–970. Used by permission.)

to succeed. If he expected to fail, his failure will intensify his belief that he is a failure; this will deaden the motivating power of failure. But if he succeeds after expecting to fail, the surprise will renew his self-confidence and motivate him to try harder (46).

Second, if the adolescent has a strong *need to gain status* in the eyes of others, he will react to failure by increased effort. If he still fails, in spite of increased effort, he will lower his goal to guarantee success (125). Third, the adolescent who acknowledges that his level of aspiration was too high or that he failed to do what he could to achieve his goal will be *motivated* by failure to try harder (157,193).

development of self-realism Failure can be a valuable learning experience in the sense that it teaches the adolescent his strengths and weaknesses. Owing to pressures from others and their own limited experience, many adolescents are unaware of what their capacities are. Failure can help them to discover them and thus encourage a more realistic concept of themselves.

Many adolescents, unfortunately, have been so indoctrinated with the belief that anyone can do whatever he wishes if he will only try hard enough, that they fail to benefit from their failures. Furthermore, it is ego deflating for a person to have to admit that he has limitations or that he cannot hope to achieve what others achieve. Still other adolescents have so convinced themselves that their failures stem from obstacles placed in their way by others that they refuse to recognize their own limitations. Under such conditions, failure intensifies the failure complex and defeatist attitudes (34,98,136).

development of failure tolerance Many adolescents have, since childhood, been protected against failure by parents and teachers who believe that failure is a destructive force in the development of a healthy personality. However, a time comes when such protection is no longer possible and when an occasional failure is inevitable. If the adolescent has not been prepared for it, this can be a crushing blow to his self-concept, his self-esteem, and his self-confidence. On the other hand, unless failures are too severe or too frequent, they can serve to develop "failure tolerance"—the ability to withstand the effects of failure and to profit by it.

Whether the adolescent will take advantage of this learning opportunity depends largely on how realistic he is about his abilities. If he is willing to see himself as he is, failure will help him to accept his defeats in a stoic way and to profit by them. If he refuses to see his limitations and blames others for them or tries to avoid situations where failure is probable, he will deprive himself of the opportunity to develop failure tolerance (46,110,112).

dislike for activity An occasional failure is ego deflating enough to condition the adolescent to dislike the activity in which the failure occurred. Frequent failures, especially when they are severe, lead to a strong dislike for the activity. In time, the dislike becomes *generalized* and spreads to related activities.

Many adolescents, for example, dislike school because they have failed to come up to their expectations in some area of the schoolwork. If they fail in a subject that they feel is important for their future vocational aspirations or in a subject in which they had expected to pass or to pass with a high grade, they not only develop a dislike for that subject but also for the teacher.

Several such experiences will result in a generalized dislike for school and everything connected with it. As a result, they will want to leave school as soon as possible and get jobs or they will become truants or school dropouts (84).

desire to hide failure Because failure is embarrassing and humiliating, the adolescent is motivated by pride to try to hide his failure from others, especially prestigeful people whose image of him he hopes will be favorable. He even tries to hide his failure from himself to avoid the feelings of shame that follow failure. This he may do by the use of ego defenses—such as blaming others for his failure or rationalizing its cause—or by lowering the level of his aspiration to guarantee success in the future.

When his failure is known to others, and it is too late to try to hide it, the adolescent will usually be motivated to try harder in the hope of counteracting the unfavorable image. More often than not this has a disruptive effect on his performance, owing to the emotional tension that accompanies failure. The result is that he not only fails again but his failure is likely to be more pronounced than before (9,98,169).

use of escape mechanisms Because all failure is ego deflating and a source of shame, many adolescents learn to use escape mechanisms to avoid future failures. Adolescents who have only moderate achievement needs are more oriented toward the avoidance of failure than toward the achievement of success. Others, in whom the achievement need is stronger, are oriented toward success; as a result, any failure they experience has a more damaging effect on their self-concepts than it would were they primarily concerned about avoiding failure (110,112).

Escape mechanisms take different forms. Which form the adolescent will use will depend upon which he discovers from experience spares him anxiety, embarrassment, and humiliation. He may *avoid setting any goal*; therefore, he cannot feel that he has failed, no matter how poor his achievement is. Or he can *avoid a situation where failure seems inevitable* (12,34,79). A boy who has limited athletic skill will avoid trying out for a team when he is sure he will not make it. Similarly many students drop out of school when they realize that their academic and social status is below what they had hoped to achieve (34,92, 126). In time, the adolescent will conclude that the easiest way to avoid the humiliation of failure is to avoid any situation where he might fail. As Child and Bacon (33) have pointed out:

> *In some people the avoidance of failure is highly generalized, so that a dominant motive may be that of protecting oneself against failure at the cost of withdrawing from a great variety of activities in which failure is a possible outcome.*

There are other less commonly used forms of escape mechanism which adolescents use. They may use *daydreaming* as an escape from real failure and as a place where they can achieve the success they crave in real life. They may escape from situations that offer a threat of failure by *imaginery invalidism*—by pretending or convincing themselves that they are ill and thus cannot face the situation. Or they may excuse their poor achievement on the grounds of illness. Still others may threaten to commit *suicide* or even attempt to do so. When an adolescent believes that he can never be anything but a failure because people place obstacles in his path which he is unable to remove, suicide seems to him to be the best solution to an intolerable problem (130).

Because escape from situations involving failure or threat of failure often seems cowardly to an adolescent, he may turn to the use of methods of self-defense, such as *rationalization* and *projection*, to explain his failures. If he uses rationalization, he will explain his failures as due to poor health, poor training, or some other plausible cause. He is more likely, however, to project the blame on someone else, thus focusing attention on the person or persons he claims are responsible for his failure (101,149).

dissatisfaction   How much self-dissatisfaction the adolescent experiences will depend not on the failure itself or on the severity of the failure but on other factors. One of these factors is the value he places on the activity in which he fails. If he fails a course in French, a boy is less likely to be upset than if he fails a course in mathematics. A second is the prestige of the activity in the eyes of significant people. Because sports are less prestigeful for girls than dating and social success, a girl will be far less disturbed if she fails to make a team than if she has no date for an important dance.

A third factor that colors the adolescent's attitude toward failure is the attitude of significant people toward it. When parents scold and nag about the failure and remind the adolescent of the many sacrifices they made to give him opportunities they never had, the adolescent is far more dissatisfied with his failure than he would be, had they said, "I can't blame you for failing math because I failed it too." Fourth, when people know of his failure, it is far more humiliating to the adolescent than when only he knows of it. The more important the people and the more significant they are to him, the more disturbing it is to him to have them know of his failure. And fifth, the degree of dissatisfaction the adolescent experiences from failure varies according to whether he expected to fail or not. If he expected to pass but failed, he will be far more dissatisfied with himself than if he expected to fail and his expectation was realized (68, 75,125,167,168,169).

Seriousness of Failure   Failure, no matter how major or minor it may be, has devastating effects on the adolescent. It can warp his whole outlook on life as well as his concept of himself as a person (176). At no other age in the entire life span is failure so serious and its effects so long-lasting and far-reaching as at adolescence. There are several reasons for this. In the first place, adolescence is the first time in the individual's life when he attempts to tackle problems alone. If his attempts are met with failure, he will conclude that he lacks the necessary ability to be successful without the aid of others. As a result, he will either revert to his former state of dependency or develop such a firmly established failure complex that it will deaden his future motivation for success.

The second reason for the seriousness of failure in adolescence is that the adolescent is unable to escape from situations that threaten him with failure as he will be able to do when he is older. He must, for example, stay in school whether he wants to or not and he must take prescribed courses, whether he is interested in the subjects or feels that they have any value for his future plans. As an adult, he can make his own choices, and as a child, he could rely on parental help if he ran into difficulties.

And, finally, the seriousness of failure in adolescence is greater than at other ages because this is the time when opinions of others have the most profound influence on the adolescent's opinion of himself. Furthermore, at no other time is the individual's personal life so open to so many people as in adolescence. This is due in part to the closely knit society of the adolescent cliques and in part to the fact that adolescents talk more freely about their hopes and fears than do either children or adults. The adolescent verbalizes his fears as a way of gaining sympathy, and expresses his hopes and aspirations as a way of improving his status in the eyes of significant people. Under such conditions, it is impossible for him to hide his failures as he could if he were less verbal.

BIBLIOGRAPHY

1 ADLER, A.: *Individual psychology.* New York: Harcourt, Brace & World, 1924.

2 ALEXANDER, C. N., and E. Q. CAMPBELL: Peer influences on adolescent educational aspirations and attainments. *Amer. sociol. Rev.,* 1964, **29**, 568–575.

3 ALLPORT, G. W.: Values and our youth. *Teach. Coll. Rec.,* 1961, **63**, 211–219.

4 AMATORA, SISTER M.: Free expression of adolescents' interests. *Genet. Psychol. Monogr.,* 1957, **55**, 173–219.

5 AUSUBEL, D. P.: Ego development among segregated Negro children. *Ment. Hyg., N.Y.,* 1958, **42**, 362–369.

6 AUSUBEL, D. P., H. M. SCHIFF, and M. P. ZELENY: "Real-life" measures of level of academic and vocational aspiration in adolescents: relation to laboratory measures and to adjustment. *Child Develpm.,* 1953, **24**, 115–168.

7 AUSUBEL, D. P., H. M. SCHIFF, and M. P. ZELENY: Validity of teachers' ratings of adolescents' adjustments and aspirations. *J. educ. Psychol.,* 1954, **45**, 394–406.

8 BAILYN, L.: Mass media and children: a study of exposure habits and cognitive effects. *Psychol. Monogr.,* 1959, **73**, no. 1.

9 BALDWIN, A. L., and H. LEVIN: Effects of public and private success or failure on children's repetitive motor behavior. *Child Develpm.,* 1958, **29**, 363–372.

10 BEILIN, H.: The mobility and achievement of a 1926 class of high school graduates. *J. counsel. Psychol.,* 1954, **1**, 144–148.

11 BEILIN, H.: The pattern of postponability and its relation to social class mobility. *J. soc. Psychol.,* 1956, **44**, 33–48.

12 BEILIN, H.: The utilization of high level talent in lower socioeconomic groups. *Personnel Guid. J.,* 1956, **35**, 175–178.

13 BELL, G. D.: Processes in the formation of adolescents' aspirations. *Soc. Forces,* 1963, **42**, 179–186.

14 BENNETT, E. M., and L. R. COHEN: Men and women: personality patterns and contrasts. *Genet. Psychol. Monogr.,* 1959, **59**, 101–155.

15 BERGER, E. M.: Willingness to accept limitations and college achievement: a replication. *J. counsel. Psychol.,* 1963, **10**, 176–178.

16 BERNARD, J.: Teen-age culture: an overview. *Ann. Amer. Acad. pol. soc. Sci.,* 1961, **338**, 1–12.

17 BLACKMAN, L. S., and H. KAHN: Success and failure as determinants of aspirational shifts in retardates and normals. *Amer. J. ment. Defic.,* 1963, **67**, 751–755.

18 BLAKELY, W. P.: A study of seventh grade children's reading of comic books as related to certain other variables. *J. genet. Psychol.,* 1958, **93**, 291–301.

19 BOEK, W. E., M. B. SUSSMAN, and A. YAN-

KAVER: Social class and child care practices. *Marriage fam. Living*, 1958, **20**, 326–333.

20 BOSSARD, J. H. S., and E. S. BOLL: *The sociology of child development*. 3d ed. New York: Harper & Row, 1960.

21 BOYD, G. F.: The levels of aspiration of white and Negro children in a nonsegregated elementary school. *J. soc. Psychol.*, 1952, **36**, 191–196.

22 BRETSCH, H. S.: Social skills and activities of socially accepted and unaccepted adolescents. *J. educ. Psychol.*, 1952, **43**, 449–458.

23 BRIM, O. G., and R. FORER: A note on the relation of values and social structure to life planning. *Sociometry*, 1956, **19**, 54–60.

24 BROMLEY, D. B.: Some experimental tests of the effect of age on creative intellectual output. *J. Gerontol.*, 1956, **11**, 74–82.

25 BUCHER, C. A.: The atomic age strikes youth. *Education*, 1955, **76**, 203–205.

26 BERNSTEIN, E.: Fear of failure, achievement motivation, and aspiring to prestigeful occupations. *J. abnorm. soc. Psychol.*, 1963, **67**, 189–193.

27 BYERS, J. E.: A study of the level of aspiration of academically successful and unsuccessful high school students. *Calif. J. educ. Res.*, 1962, **13**, 209–216.

28 CALOGERAS, R. C.: Some relationships between fantasy and self-report behavior. *Genet. Psychol. Monogr.*, 1958, **58**, 273–325.

29 CANTRIL, H.: A study of aspirations. *Scient. American*, 1963, **208**, no. 2, 41–45.

30 CAPLOW, T.: *The sociology of work*. Minneapolis: University of Minnesota Press, 1954.

31 CAPPA, D.: Types of story books enjoyed by kindergarten children. *J. educ. Res.*, 1956, **49**, 555–557.

32 CHILD, I. L.: Socialization. In G. Lindzey (ed.), *Handbook of social psychology*. Reading, Mass.: Addison-Wesley, 1954, pp. 655–692.

33 CHILD, I. L., and M. K. BACON: Cultural pressures and achievement motivation. In P. H. Hoch and J. Zubin (eds.), *Psychopathology of childhood*. New York: Grune & Stratton, 1955, pp. 166–176.

34 CHILD, I. L., and J. W. M. WHITING: Determinants of level of aspiration: evidence from every day life. In H. Brand (ed.), *The study of personality*. New York: Wiley, 1954, pp. 495–508.

35 CHRISTENSEN, H. T.: Lifetime family and occupational role projections of high school students. *Marriage fam. Living*, 1961, **23**, 181–183.

36 CHRISTENSEN, H. T., and M. M. SWIHART: Postgraduation role preferences of senior women in college. *Marriage fam. Living*, 1956, **18**, 52–57.

37 CLARKE, R. A., R. TEEVAN, and H. N. RICCIUTI: Hope of success and fear of failure as aspects of need for achievement. *J. abnorm. soc. Psychol.*, 1956, **53**, 182–186.

38 COBB, H. V.: Role-wishes and general wishes of children and adolescents. *Child Develpm.*, 1954, **25**, 161–171.

39 COLEMAN, J. S.: Athletics in high school. *Ann. Amer. Acad. pol. soc. Sci.*, 1961, **338**, 33–43.

40 COLEMAN, J. S.: *The adolescent society*. New York: Free Press, 1961.

41 COLLIER, M. J.: The psychological appeal in the Cinderella theme. *Amer. Imago*, 1961, **18**, 399–411.

42 COLLIER, M. J., and E. L. GAIER: Adult reactions to preferred childhood stories. *Child Develpm.*, 1958, **29**, 97–103.

43 CRANDALL, V. C., S. GOOD, and V. J. CRANDALL: Reinforcement effect of adult reactions and nonreactions on children's achievement expectations: a replication study. *Child Develpm.*, 1964, **35**, 485–497.

44 CRANDALL, V. J., W. KATKOVSKY, and A. PRESTON: A conceptual formulation for some research on children's achievement development. *Child Develpm.*, 1960, **31**, 787–797.

45 CRANE, A. R.: Stereotypes of the adult held by early adolescents. *J. educ. Res.*, 1956, **50**, 227–230.

46 CRONBACH, L. J.: *Educational psychology*. 2d ed. New York: Harcourt, Brace & World, 1963.

47 CROWLEY, F. J.: The goals of male high school seniors. *Personnel Guid. J.*, 1959, **37**, 488–492.

48 DAMERON, L. E.: Mother-child interaction in the development of self-restraint. *J. genet. Psychol.*, 1955, **86**, 289–308.

49 DARLEY, J. G., and J. A. HAGENAH: *Voca-*

tional interest measurement: theory and practice. Minneapolis: University of Minnesota Press, 1955.

50 DAVIDS, A., and A. A. WHITE: Effects of success, failure and social facilitation on level of aspiration in emotionally disturbed and normal children. *J. Pers.*, 1958, **26**, 77–93.

51 DAVIS, A., and R. J. HAVIGHURST: *Father of the man.* Boston: Houghton Mifflin, 1947.

52 DE CHARMS, R., and G. H. MOELLER: Values expressed in children's readers: 1800–1950. *J. abnorm. soc. Psychol.*, 1962, **64**, 136–142.

53 DEUTSCH, M.: Some factors affecting membership motivation and achievement motivation in a group. *Hum. Relat.*, 1959, **12**, 81–91.

54 D'HEURLE, A., J. C. MELLINGER, and E. A. HAGGARD: Personality, intellectual, and achievement patterns in gifted children. *Psychol. Monogr.*, 1959, **73**, no. 13.

55 DOUVAN, E.: Social status and success strivings. *J. abnorm. soc. Psychol.*, 1956, **52**, 219–223.

56 DYNES, R. R., A. C. CLARKE, and S. DINITZ: Levels of occupational aspiration: some aspects of family experience as a variable. *Amer. sociol. Rev.*, 1956, **21**, 212–215.

57 EMPEY, L. T.: Role expectations of young women regarding marriage and a career. *Marriage fam. Living*, 1958, **20**, 152–155.

58 FERGUSON, E. D.: The effect of sibling competition and alliance on level of aspiration, expectation and performance. *J. abnorm. soc. Psychol.*, 1958, **56**, 213–222.

59 FORD, L. H.: Reaction to failure as a function of expectancy for success. *J. abnorm. soc. Psychol.*, 1963, **67**, 340–348.

60 FORD, N. A.: Literature as an aid to social development. *Teach. Coll. Rec.*, 1957, **58**, 377–381.

61 FRANK, L. K.: Play in personality development. *Amer. J. Orthopsychiat.*, 1955, **25**, 576–590.

62 FRENCH, E. G., and G. S. LESSER: Some characteristics of the achievement motive in women. *J. abnorm. soc. Psychol.*, 1964, **68**, 119–128.

63 GIST, N. P., and W. S. BENNETT: Aspirations of Negro and white students. *Soc. Forces*, 1963, **42**, 40–48.

64 GOLDBERG, M. L.: Motivation of the gifted.

57th Yearb. Nat. Soc. Stud. Educ., 1958, part 2, 87–109.

65 GOTTLIEB, D.: Goal aspirations and goal fulfillments: differences between deprived and affluent American adolescents. *Amer. J. Orthopsychiat.*, 1964, **34**, 934–941.

66 GOULD, R., and H. B. LEWIS: Experimental investigation of factors governing changes in the meaning of the level of aspiration. *J. exp. Psychol.*, 1940, **27**, 422–439.

67 GRUEN, E. W.: Level of aspiration in relation to personality factors in adolescents. *Child Develpm.*, 1945, **16**, 181–188.

68 HAGGARD, E. A.: Socialization, personality, and academic achievement in gifted children. *School Review*, 1957, **65**, 388–414.

69 HALLER, A. O., and W. H. SEWELL: Farm residence and level of educational and occupational aspiration. *Amer. J. Sociol.*, 1957, **62**, 407–411.

70 HANSCHE, J., and J. C. GILCHRIST: Three determinants of the level of aspiration. *J. abnorm. soc. Psychol.*, 1956, **53**, 136–137.

71 HARRIS, D. B.: The development of potentiality. *Teach. Coll. Rec.*, 1960, **61**, 423–428.

72 HARSH, C. M., and H. G. SCHRICKEL: *Personality: development and assessment.* 2d ed. New York: Ronald, 1959.

73 HAVIGHURST, R. J.: *Human development and education.* New York: Longmans, 1953.

74 HAVIGHURST, R. J., and D. V. MAC DONALD: Development of the ideal self in New Zealand and American children. *J. educ. Res.*, 1955, **49**, 263–273.

75 HEBER, R. F., and M. E. HEBER: The effect of group failure and success on social status. *J. educ. Psychol.*, 1957, **48**, 129–134.

76 HERRIOTT, R. E.: Some social determinants of educational aspiration. *Harv. educ. Rev.*, 1963, **33**, 157–177.

77 HILGARD, E. R.: *Introduction to psychology*, 3d ed., New York: Harcourt, Brace & World, 1962.

78 HUGHES, J. H., and G. G. THOMPSON: A comparison of the value systems of Southern Negro and Northern white youth. *J. educ. Psychol.*, 1954, **45**, 300–309.

79 HUNT, D. E., and H. M. SCHRODER: Assimilation, failure-avoidance, and anxiety. *J. consult. Psychol.*, 1958, **22**, 39–44.

80 INLOW, J. M.: Job satisfaction of liberal arts

graduates. *J. appl. Psychol.*, 1951, **35**, 175–181.

81 JACKSON, D.: Crack-ups on campus. *Life Magazine*, Jan. 8, 1965, pp. 72–73.

82 JAHODA, G.: Social class attitudes and levels of occupational aspiration in secondary modern school leavers. *Brit. J. Psychol.*, 1953, **44**, 95–107.

83 JERSILD, A. T.: *The psychology of adolescence.* 2d ed. New York: Macmillan, 1963.

84 JERSILD, A. T., and R. J. TASCH: *Children's interests and what they suggest for education.* New York: Teachers College, Columbia University, 1949.

85 KAHL, J. A.: Educational and occupational aspirations of "common man" boys. *Harv. educ. Rev.*, 1953, **23**, 186–203.

86 KATZ, F. M.: The meaning of success: some differences in value systems of social classes. *J. soc. Psychol.*, 1964, **62**, 141–148.

87 KAUSLER, D. H.: Aspiration level as a determinant of performance. *J. Pers.*, 1959, **27**, 346–351.

88 KENT, N., and D. R. DAVIS: Discipline in the home and intellectual development. *Brit. J. med. Psychol.*, 1957, **30**, 27–33.

89 KINNANE, J. F., and M. W. PABLE: Family background and work value orientation. *J. counsel. Psychol.*, 1962, **9**, 320–325.

90 KINSEY, A. C., W. B. POMEROY, C. E. MARTIN, and P. H. GEBHARD: *Sexual development in the human female.* Philadelphia: Saunders, 1953.

91 KOCH, H. L.: The relation of certain formal attributes of siblings to attitudes held toward each other and toward their parents. *Monogr. Soc. Res. Child Develpm.*, 1960, **25**, no. 4.

92 KOELSCHE, C. L.: A study of the student drop-out problem at Indiana University. *J. educ. Res.*, 1955, **49**, 357–364.

93 KRAUSS, I.: Sources of educational aspirations among working-class youth. *Amer. sociol. Rev.*, 1964, **29**, 867–879.

94 KUHLEN, R. G., and G. H. JOHNSON: Changes in goals with adult increasing age. *J. consult. Psychol.*, 1952, **16**, 1–4.

95 LEES, G. P.: The social mobility of a group of eldest-born and intermediate adult males. *Brit. J. Psychol.*, 1952, **43**, 210–221.

96 LEHMAN, H. C.: *Age and achievement.* Princeton, N.J.: Princeton, 1953.

97 LESHAN, L. L.: Time orientation and social class. *J. abnorm. soc. Psychol.*, 1952, **47**, 589–596.

98 LEVIN, H., and A. L. BALDWIN: The choice to exhibit. *Child Develpm.*, 1958, **29**, 373–380.

99 LEVIN, M. M.: Status anxiety and occupational choice. *Educ. psychol. Measmt.*, 1949, **9**, 29–37.

100 LEWIN, K.: Behavior and development as a function of the total situation. In L. Carmichael (ed.), *Manual of child psychology.* 2d ed. New York: Wiley, 1954, pp. 918–970.

101 LEWIN, K., T. DEMBO, L. FESTINGER, and P. S. SEARS: Level of aspiration. In J. McV. Hunt (ed.), *Personality and the behavior disorders.* New York: Ronald, 1944, pp. 333–378.

102 LICHTENBERG, P.: Reactions to success and failure during individual and cooperative effort. *J. soc. Psychol.*, 1957, **46**, 31–34.

103 LOCKWOOD, W. V.: Realism of vocational preference. *Personnel Guid. J.*, 1958, **37**, 98–106.

104 LUCHINS, A. S.: On the theories and problems of adolescence. *J. genet. Psychol.*, 1954, **85**, 47–63.

105 MACCOBY, E. E.: Children and working mothers. *Children*, 1958, **5**, 83–89.

106 MACCOBY, E. E., and W. C. WILSON: Identification and observational learning from films. *J. abnorm. soc. Psychol.*, 1957, **55**, 76–87.

107 MACCOBY, E. E., W. C. WILSON, and R. V. BURTON: Differential movie-viewing behavior of male and female viewers. *J. Pers.*, 1958, **26**, 259–267.

108 MARTIRE, J. G.: Relationships between the self concept and differences in the strength and generality of achievement motivation. *J. Pers.*, 1956, **24**, 364–375.

109 MATTESON, R. W.: Self estimates of college freshmen. *Personnel Guid. J.*, 1956, **34**, 280–284.

110 MC CLELLAND, D. C.: *The achievement motive.* New York: Appleton-Century-Crofts, 1953.

111 MC CLELLAND, D. C.: Measuring motivation

in fantasy: the achievement motive. In D. C. McClelland (ed.), *Studies in motivation.* New York: Appleton-Century-Crofts, 1955, pp. 401–413.

112 MC CLELLAND, D. C., and G. A. FRIEDMAN: A cross-cultural study of the relationship between child-rearing practices and achievement motivation appearing in folk tales. In G. E. Swanson (ed.), *Readings in social psychology.* New York: Holt, 1953, pp. 243–248.

113 MEAD, M.: *Male and female.* New York: Morrow, 1952.

114 MEAD, M., and R. MÉTRAUX: Image of the scientist among high school students. *Science*, 1957, **126**, 384–390.

115 MINOR, C. A., and R. G. NEEL: The relationship between achievement motive and occupational preference. *J. counsel. Psychol.*, 1958, **5**, 39–43.

116 MISCHEL, W.: Preference for delayed reinforcement: an experimental study of a cultural observation. *J. abnorm. soc. Psychol.*, 1958, **56**, 57–61.

117 MITCHELL, J. V.: Goal-setting behavior as a function of self-acceptance, over- and underachievement, and related personality variables. *J. educ. Psychol.*, 1959, **50**, 93–104.

118 MORLAND, J. K.: Education and occupational aspirations of mill and town school children in a Southern community. *Soc. Forces*, 1960, **39**, 169–175.

119 MORSE, N. C., and R. S. WEISS: The function and meaning of work and the job. *Amer. sociol. Rev.*, 1955, **20**, 191–198.

120 NORTON, J. L.: Patterns of vocational interest development and adult job choice. *J. genet. Psychol.*, 1953, **83**, 235–262.

121 NUTALL, R. L.: Some correlates of high need for achievement among urban Northern Negroes. *J. abnorm. soc. Psychol.*, 1964, **68**, 593–600.

122 PACKARD, V.: *The status seekers.* New York: Pocket, 1961.

123 PACKARD, V.: *The pyramid climbers.* New York: McGraw-Hill, 1962.

124 PALMER, G. L.: Attitudes toward work in an industrial community. *Amer. J. Sociol.*, 1957, **36**, 17–26.

125 PARSONS, O. A.: Status needs and performance under failure. *J. Pers.*, 1958, **26**, 123–138.

126 PENTY, R. C.: *Reading ability and high school drop-outs.* New York: Teachers College, Columbia University, 1956.

127 PHILBAD, C. T., and C. L. GREGORY: Selective migration among Missouri high school graduates. *Amer. sociol. Rev.*, 1954, **19**, 314–322.

128 PHILBAD, C. T., and C. L. GREGORY: The role of test intelligence and occupational background as factors in occupational choice. *Sociometry*, 1956, **19**, 192–199.

129 POFFENBERGER, T., and D. NORTON: Factors in the formation of attitudes toward mathematics. *J. educ. Res.*, 1959, **52**, 171–176.

130 POWELL, E. H.: Occupation, status, and suicide: toward a redefinition of anomie. *Amer. sociol. Rev.*, 1958, **23**, 131–139.

131 PRESSEY, S. L., and R. G. KUHLEN: *Psychological development through the life span.* New York: Harper & Row, 1957.

132 RAO, K. U., and R. W. RUSSELL: Effects of stress on goal setting behavior. *J. abnorm. soc. Psychol.*, 1960, **61**, 380–388.

133 RASMUSSEN, G., and A. ZANDER: Group membership and self-evaluation. *Hum. Relat.*, 1954, **7**, 239–251.

134 REISSMAN, L.: Levels of aspiration and social class. *Amer. sociol. Rev.*, 1953, **18**, 233–242.

135 REMMERS, H. H., and D. H. RADLER: *The American teen-ager.* Indianapolis: Bobbs-Merrill, 1957.

136 RESNICK, J.: Toward understanding adolescent behavior. *Peabody J. Educ.*, 1953, **30**, 205–208.

137 ROSE, A. W., and M. C. WALL: Social factors in the prestige ranking of occupations. *Personnel Guid. J.*, 1957, **35**, 420–423.

138 ROSEN, B. C.: The achievement syndrome: a psychocultural dimension of social stratification. *Amer. sociol. Rev.*, 1956, **21**, 203–211.

139 ROSEN, B. C.: Race, ethnicity and the achievement syndrome. *Amer. sociol. Rev.*, 1959, **24**, 47–60.

140 ROSEN, B. C.: Family structure and achievement motivation. *Amer. sociol. Rev.*, 1961, **26**, 574–585.

141 ROSEN, B. C., and R. D'ANDRADE: The psychosocial origins of achievement motivation. *Sociometry*, 1959, **22**, 185–218.

142 ROSENFELD, H., and A. ZANDER: The influence of teachers on aspirations of students. *J. educ. Psychol.*, 1961, **52**, 1–11.

143 ROTHMAN, P.: Socioeconomic status and the values of junior high school students. *J. educ. Sociol.*, 1954, **28**, 126–130.

144 RUSSELL, D. H.: The development of thinking processes. *Rev. educ. Res.*, 1953, **23**, 137–145.

145 SCHACHTER, S.: Birth order, eminence and higher education. *Amer. sociol. Rev.*, 1963, **28**, 757–768.

146 SCHNEIDER, L., and S. LYSGAARD: The deferred gratification pattern: a preliminary study. *Amer. sociol. Rev.*, 1953, **18**, 142–149.

147 SEARS, P. S., and H. LEVIN: Levels of aspiration in preschool children. *Child Develpm.*, 1957, **28**, 317–326.

148 SEWELL, W. H., A. O. HALLER, and M. A. STRAUS: Social status and educational and occupational aspirations. *Amer. sociol. Rev.*, 1957, **22**, 67–73.

149 SHAFFER, L. F., and E. J. SHOBEN: *The psychology of adjustment.* 2d ed. Boston: Houghton Mifflin, 1956.

150 SILVERMAN, I.: Self-esteem and differential responsiveness to success and failure. *J. abnorm. soc. Psychol.*, 1964, **69**, 115–119.

151 SIMPSON, R. L.: Parental influence, anticipatory socialization, and social mobility. *Amer. sociol. Rev.*, 1962, **27**, 517–522.

152 SINGER, S. L., and B. STEFFLRE: Sex differences in job values and desires. *Personnel Guid. J.*, 1954, **32**, 483–484.

153 SINGER, S. L., and B. STEFFLRE: A note on racial differences in job values and desires. *J. soc. Psychol.*, 1956, **43**, 333–337.

154 SINHA, S.: Frustration as a determinant of level of aspiration. *J. educ. Psychol., Baroda*, 1954, **12**, 10–14.

155 SINNETT, E. R.: Some determinants of agreement between measured and expressed interests. *Educ. psychol. Measmt.*, 1956, **16**, 110–118.

156 SIVERTSEN, D.: Goal setting, the level of aspiration and social norms. *Acta psychol., Amsterdam*, 1957, **13**, 54–60.

157 SLOTKIN, J. S.: Life course in middle age. *Soc. Forces*, 1954, **33**, 171–177.

158 SMITH, D. C., and L. WING: Developmental changes in preference for goals difficult to attain. *Child Develpm.*, 1961, **32**, 29–36.

159 SOLLEY, C. M., and R. STAGNER: Effects of magnitude of temporal barriers, type of goal, and perception of self. *J. exp. Psychol.*, 1956, **51**, 62–70.

160 SONTAG, L. W., and J. KAGAN: The emergence of intellectual achievement motives. *Amer. J. Orthopsychiat.*, 1963, **33**, 532–534.

161 STAGNER, R.: *Psychology of personality.* 3d ed. New York: McGraw-Hill, 1961.

162 STEINER, I. D.: Self-perception and goal-setting behavior. *J. Pers.*, 1957, **25**, 344–355.

163 STEISEL, I. M., and B. D. COHEN: The effects of two degrees of failure on level of aspiration and performance. *J. abnorm. soc. Psychol.*, 1951, **46**, 79–82.

164 STEPHENSON, R. M.: Stratification, education, and occupational orientation: a parallel study and review. *Brit. J. Sociol.*, 1958, **9**, 42–52.

165 STEWART, B. R.: Developmental differences in the stability of object preferences and conflict behavior. *Child Develpm.*, 1958, **29**, 9–18.

166 STILL, J. W.: Man's potential—and his performance. *The New York Times*, Nov. 24, 1957.

167 STOTLAND, E.: Determinants of attraction to groups. *J. soc. Psychol.*, 1959, **49**, 71–80.

168 STOTLAND, E., S. THORLEY, E. THOMAS, and A. R. COHEN: The effects of group expectations and self-esteem upon self-evaluation. *J. abnorm. soc. Psychol.*, 1957, **54**, 55–63.

169 STOTLAND, E., and A. ZANDER: Effects of public and private failure on self-evaluation. *J. abnorm. soc. Psychol.*, 1958, **56**, 223–229.

170 STRANG, R.: How children and adolescents view their world. *Ment. Hyg., N.Y.*, 1954, **38**, 28–33.

171 STRANG, R.: *The adolescent views himself.* New York: McGraw-Hill, 1957.

172 STRODTBECK, F. L., M. R. MC DONALD, and B. C. ROSEN: Evaluation of occupations: a reflection of Jewish and Italian mobility differences. *Amer. sociol. Rev.*, 1957, **22**, 546–553.

173 STRONG, E. K.: Permanence of interest scores over 22 years. *J. appl. Psychol.*, 1951, **35**, 89–91.

174 STRONG, E. K.: Interests of Negroes and whites. *J. soc. Psychol.*, 1952, **35**, 139–150.

175 SUPER, D. E.: Dimensions and measurements of vocational maturity. *Teach. Coll. Rec.*, 1955, **57**, 151–163.

176 SYMONDS, P. M.: What education has to learn from psychology: VI. Emotion and learning. *Teach. Coll. Rec.*, 1958, **60**, 9–22.

177 TERMAN, L. M.: The discovery and encouragement of exceptional talent. *Amer. Psychologist*, 1954, **9**, 221–230.

178 *Time* Report: Students: "On the fringe of a golden era." *Time Magazine*, Jan. 29, 1965, pp. 56–59.

179 TRAPP, E. P., and D. H. KAUSLER: Test anxiety level and goal-setting behavior. *J. consult. Psychol.*, 1958, **22**, 31–34.

180 TURNER, R. H.: Some family determinants of ambition. *Sociol. soc. Res.*, 1962, **46**, 397–411.

181 URELL, C.: What do they want out of life? *Teach. Coll. Rec.*, 1960, **61**, 318–330.

182 *U.S. News & World Report:* Will teen-agers make the sixties roar? *U.S. News & World Report*, Oct. 26, 1964, pp. 102–104.

183 VEROFF, J., S. WILCOX, and J. W. ATKINSON: The achievement motive in high school and college women. *J. abnorm. soc. Psychol.*, 1953, **48**, 108–119.

184 WALLACE, W. L.: Institutional and life-cycle socialization of college freshmen. *Amer. J. Sociol.*, 1964, **70**, 303–318.

185 WALTER, L. M., and S. S. MARSOLF: The relation of sex, age and school achievement to levels of aspiration. *J. educ. Psychol.*, 1951, **42**, 285–292.

186 WARNER, W. L., and J. ABEGGLEN: *Big business leaders in America*. New York: Harper & Row, 1955.

187 WERTHEIM, J., and S. A. MEDNICK: The achievement motive and field independence. *J. consult. Psychol.*, 1958, **23**, 38.

188 WEST, L. J.: College and the years after. *J. Higher Educ.*, 1953, **24**, 415–419.

189 WHEELER, D. K.: Expressed wishes of students. *J. genet. Psychol.*, 1963, **102**, 75–81.

190 WILSON, A. B.: Residential segregation of social classes and aspirations of high school boys. *Amer. sociol. Rev.*, 1959, **24**, 836–845.

191 WINKER, J. B.: Age trends and sex differences in the wishes, identifications, activities, and fears of children. *Child Develpm.*, 1949, **20**, 191–200.

192 WITTY, P. A.: A study of pupils' interests, grades 9, 10, 11, 12. *Education*, 1961, **82**, 39–45, 100–110.

193 WORELL, L.: Level of aspiration and academic success. *J. educ. Psychol.*, 1959, **50**, 47–54.

194 YOUMANS, E. G.: Occupational expectations of twelfth grade Michigan boys. *J. exp. Educ.*, 1956, **24**, 259–271.

195 ZANDER, A.: Group membership and individual security. *Hum. Relat.*, 1958, **11**, 99–111.

196 ZELEN, S. L.: The effects of frustration and level of adjustment upon the reality of goal-attainment methods. *Dissert. Abstr.*, 1964, **24**, 3430–3431.

197 ZELIGS, R.: Trends in children's New Year's resolutions. *J. exp. Educ.*, 1957, **26**, 133–150.

CHAPTER 9
achievements
and
failures

The majority of American adolescents today want to better themselves—to rise above the status they now occupy in the social group. Relatively few parents are satisfied to have their children stand still; instead, they want them to "get ahead" (130,331,445). To achieve the American dream of success, many adolescents are given opportunities for advancement which their parents never had.

In addition, they are prodded by parents to make full use of these opportunities. Even more important, they are trained, from early childhood, to know how to reach their goals and to develop values which will guide their choices in areas where success is a stepping-stone to their ultimate goal—rising above their present status (75,191,329,330).

Since the Second World War, equal

opportunities have been opening up for all adolescents, regardless of race, religion, socioeconomic class, and sex. Because of the affluence of American families of all social classes, the American dream of success can be a reality for many more adolescents today than was ever before possible. As a result, the top of the ladder becomes more of a goal to aim for with every passing year and the competition for a place on the upper rung becomes keener (169,294,295,365).

THREE MAJOR STEPPING-STONES

The climb to the top of the socioeconomic ladder is made possible by three major stepping-stones: social mobility, schooling, and vocation. *Social mobility* is a stepping-stone that is largely under the control of the parents; whether the adolescent can have an opportunity to live in a better area of the community, go to a better school, and come in contact with the "right" type of people will depend upon the success of the breadwinner of the family. The adolescent's success or failure in *school* and the choice of a lifetime *vocation*, on the other hand, are stepping-stones over which he has more control. Even they are not free from parental influences.

Because of the strong desire the adolescent has to get ahead, his interest in these stepping-stones is centered around the areas where success will help him to get ahead rather than in areas where success leads to personal satisfaction. The adolescent is interested, for example, in the practical and work-oriented aspects of education, not in the cultural (75,158).

Because schooling and the choice of the right vocation will help the adolescent to move higher on the socioeconomic ladder, "academic and vocational aspirations constitute a highly significant aspect of adolescent goal structures and adjustment" (17). As Kosa et al. have emphasized, those who want to move up the ladder regard college as "an instrument for social mobility rather than an instrument of scholarship. . . . They accept the middle-class standards, conform to their peers from a higher class and try to ride the trend without much personal effort" (219). While the "school is the high

road to social status" for most adolescents, there are a few who can achieve status by other means. A successful athlete, for example, can become a success in life even with a limited education. The same is true of movie and television stars, artists, and others who have special talents (79). But, with the exception of the few who have special talents, the surest stepping-stone to success is schooling. It opens the doors to prestigeful and lucrative vocations; these, in turn, open the doors to upward social mobility.

I. INTEREST IN EDUCATION

Most educators are well aware that the typical American adolescent is not seriously interested in education except as a means to an end (75,131,185,195). On the surface, this statement seems to be contradictory to the increase in college enrollments and the overcrowding of high schools and colleges. Furthermore, adolescents are competing fiercely for admission to professional training schools—law, medicine, and engineering, especially—and to the graduate schools that grant master's and doctor's degrees (75, 369,427,445). As Hechinger and Hechinger have emphasized, "There has never been greater concern about getting into college, coupled with so little interest in actual learning" (161). Figure 9–1 shows the increase in level of education in the United States in the past years.

IMPORTANT ENDS IN EDUCATION

Education is a means to several ends. Each of these is of vital importance to adolescents as steps up the ladder to success. First, there is the *social* end—being identified with the "right" school or college (75,445).

That social goals are important to an adolescent is shown by the fact that the high school student identifies himself with his school by using its name when referring to himself and to others, as "I'm from ———— High," or "Those are the ———— High kids" (72). The college student does the same thing. In addition, students from many private schools, as well as those from colleges and universities, identify themselves with their educational institutions by using certain status symbols, especially blazers, ties, mufflers, pins, rings, and stickers on their book bags, cars, or book covers. Identifying themselves with a prestigeful educational institution helps to improve their status in the minds of others (46,53, 73,185,195,294).

Almost as important is the *vocational* end to be achieved from education. The more education the adolescent has, and the more insignia he has to show it—diplomas, degrees, honors, and membership in honor societies—the easier will be his climb to the top of the vocational pyramid. A college degree is now of not much greater value, vocationally, than a high school diploma was in past generations. Today's adolescents must get training in their chosen vocational fields by postgraduate studies if they wish to get to the top (185,195,294,295). Boroff (46) has explained why advanced education is vocationally valuable:

> *Personnel people, with an eye cocked at the old days when plain ability counted, insist that the college degree is only one feature considered and that the total individual is what counts. This statement overlooks one key factor; the degree is, in effect, a screening device. The way to break into executive life is through the college recruitment program. (To climb up from the ranks of plant workers is becoming increasingly difficult.)*

The third end is the *economic*; education is an investment that will pay big dividends. It is, as Boroff has pointed out, "part of the new folklore of our society that a degree is worth money—lots of money. Though the figure is unverifiable, its cash value has been pegged by common consent at $100,000 during an average lifetime. (This should be set against the moderate cost, ranging from $5,000 to $18,000 for the four years)" (46).

Furthermore, there is a progressive increase in average income with increase in education. Graduation at any level means about twice as much increase as when education is incomplete. The chances are that those who have the greatest amount of education will be the highest earners (136,447). In addition, those with the greatest amount

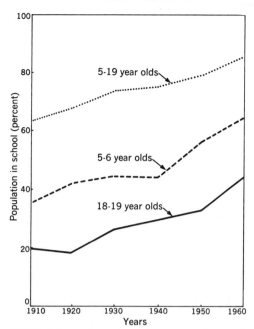

FIGURE 9–1 Today, education starts earlier and continues for a longer time for an increasing proportion of American children. (Adapted from P. N. Hauser: More from the census of 1960. *Scient. American*, 1962, **207**, no. 4, 30–37. Used by permission.)

of education will have more "fringe benefits" during their working lives, will retire later and have larger retirement benefits than those with more limited education (135, 185,195,294,315,409). Figure 9–2 shows the relationship between level of education and earning capacity.

areas of interest in education

When the child begins school, he is eager to learn (194). Changes in his attitudes toward school come with changes in his values. Before he reaches adolescence, he learns what is highly valued in school by parents, members of the peer group, and even teachers. These values he accepts as his own; he then develops interests and aspirations in line with them. While he would like to achieve success in *all* areas which are prestigeful, he becomes realistic enough to realize that he cannot hope to be equally successful in all. He, therefore, selects the areas

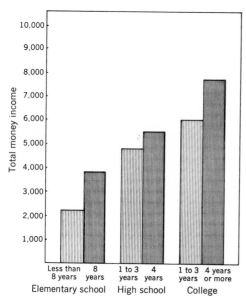

FIGURE 9–2 Lifetime income is markedly influenced by the amount of education the worker has had. (Adapted from President's Committee on Youth Employment Report: *The challenge of jobless youth.* Washington, D.C.: U.S. Department of Labor, April, 1963. Used by permission.)

in which his chances of success are greatest as the ones on which he will focus his interests and concentrate his efforts (259,448).

The areas of education in which most American adolescents are interested today are as follows.

ACADEMIC SUBJECTS

On the whole, students in both high school and college show greatest interest in subjects they believe will be of most value to them vocationally and in other areas of adult life. Furthermore, what is valuable to an adolescent in adult life will depend to some extent upon his sex and his aspirations for the future. The boy in high school or college, for example, who aspires to a career in business or industry would be interested in very different subjects from a girl whose aspirations centered around marriage, homemaking, and child rearing (4,7,183).

A lower-class girl whose aspirations are limited to marriage and a job that will sup-

plement the family income will be more interested in practical subjects than in theoretical and cultural studies. By contrast, the girl from a middle or upper socioeconomic group whose aspirations are likewise for marriage will concentrate her interest on cultural subjects—English, languages, the arts, and world history—which will contribute to her success in social life after marriage (6, 151,301,309,446).

Regardless of personal interest or ability, the adolescent's attitude toward school subjects is colored by what is considered *sex appropriate*. Science and mathematics, for example, are not regarded as a "woman's field." Even if girls do well in these subjects, it is believed that they will be of little value as the vocational doors will be closed to girls in these areas (269,413).

Many boys are conditioned, as children, to regard the study of literature, languages, and the arts, as "girls' stuff" and to believe that such subjects will do little to further their ambitions for success in the business world. In high school or college, then, boys take as few courses as possible in these areas and spend most of their time studying "useful" subjects. When a boy, because of a strong personal interest, takes courses in the arts, languages, or literature, he often feels called upon to rationalize his doing so to avoid being considered a sissy, or an impractical dreamer (211,302,310,338).

Because interest and motivation are closely correlated, the adolescent who has a strong interest in a subject, based on the belief that it will help him to achieve his vocational goal, will put more effort into mastering it than he would if he believed that it had no practical value. As a result, he generally does best in the subjects he regards as useful. Success leads to a liking for a subject; liking, in turn, leads to increased motivation, which normally leads to greater success (399,446).

GRADES

Adolescents are interested in grades not as an insignia of knowledge but as a means to an end—entrance into college, preferably a "name" college, into a professional training school, and into a prestigeful job in a prestigeful vocation. Why grades are important to an adolescent has been explained thus by Symonds (397):

> They indicate success or failure; they determine promotion; they indicate the probability of future success; they influence his parents' attitude toward him. Marks help to determine whether a pupil thinks of himself as successful, smart, or a failure, an outcast, stupid, a nitwit.

That grades play an important role in coloring the adolescent's attitude toward school or college has been illustrated by a study which showed a high correlation between grades received at the end of the semester and eighth-grade students' perception of school. When the student receives poor grades, it is often due to the fact that he has negative feelings about school, the teacher, or a specific subject. As a result of his poor grades, he dislikes school even more, does poorer and poorer work, and gets lower and lower grades. Thus, it becomes a circular situation. By contrast, the student who likes school gets better grades; this reinforces his positive attitudes toward school (255).

The importance adolescents attach to grades is readily apparent in their worry and anxiety about examinations and about courses in which they are not doing well. While it is true that able students suffer less from school anxieties and examination jitters than do less able students, few American students in high school or college today, who are anxious to get ahead in life, are free from worry about their academic work or unconcerned about their grades. Students whose vocational aspirations are directed toward work that requires little academic preparation are less anxious and concerned about their grades than are those whose aspirations require higher education as a stepping-stone (139,224,263,268,277,377).

Another common source of anxiety is how the peer group will react to grades. If the student does too good work, he will be labeled a curve raiser or a brain by his classmates. He knows that they resent his achievements, not because it makes the teacher expect more of them, but mainly because they believe he is conceited and regards them as stupid (70,400). The more anxious the adolescent is to be socially accepted the more likely he is to be concerned about how his peers will react to his grades. Figure 9–3 illustrates how one boy solved this problem.

The adolescent who aspires to high grades will use various methods to reach his goal. He may be willing to *sacrifice other activities*, especially sports and social activi-

FIGURE 9–3 The student's attitude toward academic achievement is greatly influenced by peer attitudes. (Adapted from Feifer's Fables. Hall Syndicate. *The Evening Bulletin*, Philadelphia, Penn., Mar. 7, 1965. Used by permission.)

ties, to give him enough time for his studies (416,446). He may select *easy courses*—those which have the reputation of being "gut courses." He will sacrifice interest and even future usefulness of subject matter to take courses that will guarantee him better grades (126). Perhaps the most common of all methods of getting good grades is *cheating*. This takes many forms but its aim is always to get a higher grade than is deserved for the work that has been done (160,378). Cheating will be discussed in detail in the chapter on adolescent morality.

The adolescent whose grades are below his aspirations may try to convince himself and his friends that good grades are not important, that if one gets a high school diploma or a college degree, that is all that matters (40). Others are satisfied with a "gentleman's C," because they spend their time in sports and social activities which they consider more important than grades (73,126,235). Some adolescents blame their teachers for being "against them" and for lowering their grades as a form of revenge (138,334). Others blame their lack of privacy, noise, and other distractions at home as responsible for their inability to study (385). A few are willing to lower their levels of aspiration as a way of relieving the anxiety that accompanies their drive for high grades (139,324,399).

ACADEMIC REWARDS

Most adolescents want a "reward" for the time and effort they put into acquiring an education. Some are satisfied with a high school diploma; some with a college degree; and a few, only when they have a higher degree. These rewards are important to students because they are "salable." When asked why they want a college diploma, many students answer, "Money." As Boroff has pointed out, "It is part of the new folklore of our society that a degree is worth money—lots of money" (46). Packard explains why this is so when he says, "Fascination with the diploma as a badge of eligibility apparently is becoming a permanent feature of life at the well-established corporations" (294).

Adolescents who do not get a diploma or a degree find their "sale's value" greatly diminished. In the case of the college diploma, lack of it "can tend to seal off opportunity from vast numbers of people and create a new kind of class society" (46). Because the type of education the adolescent gets and the symbols of it will determine what his vocation and social future will be, it is not surprising that interest in these status symbols is very strong (424). They are not symbols of knowledge, per se, but symbols of eligibility for jobs (46,294).

The "sale's value" of a student's education is increased if he is able to report honors of different types in addition to his diploma or degree. Being on the honor roll in high school, the dean's list in college, holding a scholarship or fellowship, and graduating with honors or with *cum laude* citations in different categories increase his "sale's value" in his competition with others (70). Knowing this serves as a motivation to many adolescents to achieve some academic award by hard study, by taking easy courses, or, if all else fails, by cheating (66, 405,426).

AUTONOMY

One of the major reasons for wanting to go to college, especially to a college away from home, is to be free from adult supervision and control (75,131,185). McDill and Coleman have pointed out, "College promises adult status but academic achievement carries the connotation of acquiescence and subordination to adults" (261). One of the common complaints of high school and college students is that they are too "regimented"—both in academic and extracurricular matters. In academic life, they complain about taking required courses in subjects they are not interested in or which they feel will never do them any good. They complain, in all but the largest high schools and colleges, about the narrow course offerings and about not being allowed to do creative intellectual work if one wants to get good grades (174). But, most of all, they complain about being regimented in their extracurricular lives—their sports, their special-interest clubs, and their social affairs.

Few adolescents want autonomy in

their studies. Most want to be *taught*—to have their teachers tell them what they are expected to know and drill them until they know it. When they fail to understand, they more often blame it on poor teaching than on their own lack of effort. Nothing is more rebelled against by the majority of students in both high school and college than "independent study"; they claim their teachers are "too lazy" to teach them (32,324).

By contrast, they want autonomy in the selection of courses of study and in extracurricular activities. They object to having to take courses prescribed for them if they are uninterested in the subject matter, if they feel they cannot do well in them, or if they can see no practical value to be gained. When it comes to extracurricular matters, their protests against regimentation by rules and requirements mount with each year. They want to be free to decide, for example, how much time they will devote to athletics and in what areas they will spend their time; they want to run their clubs and have the speakers they wish to hear; they want to be free to smoke, drink, and pet on school or college grounds without the policing of chaperons or threats of punishment for breaking the rules; and they want to be represented on the boards of faculty members that decide the school's or college's policies, whether these policies relate to academic or nonacademic matters (32,324, 405).

Many adolescents claim that their high schools and colleges are "child-centered" institutions—that they are treated as they were in elementary school. In their demands for autonomy, they often revolt by striking and refusing to attend classes unless the rules are changed. Others leave school or college before completing their education and get jobs so that they may have the autonomy they crave (4).

EXTRACURRICULAR ACTIVITIES
Interest in extracurricular activities, especially sports and social activities, is what makes education tolerable for many students (194). They are willing to accept the educational aspects of school to be able to have the athletic and social activities which high schools and colleges offer. Even adolescents who find the intellectual work of the school interesting and stimulating tend to look upon success in extracurricular activities as a more important end than what they get from their studies (7,72,238,362).

Extracurricular activities are a more important area of education to high school students than to those in college. There are two major reasons for this. First, the college student finds them a repetition of what he has already had in high school; as a result, he is somewhat bored with them. Second, as the college student approaches the time of getting a job, he realizes the importance to his future of making good marks; as a result, he becomes more serious about his studies (426).

factors influencing students' attitudes

There are many factors that influence the adolescent's attitudes toward school. Of these, the following are the most important.

CULTURAL VALUES
While America, as a nation, regards education as so important that it provides more free education for more students than any other nation in the world, it at the same time puts less value on scholarship than many of the nations that provide education for fewer of their children (72,276). Higher value, on the other hand, is placed on athletic achievements. The reason for this, Coleman points out, is to be found in the stress put on interschool and intercollegiate sports. According to Coleman (71):

It is a consequence of this that the athlete gains so much status: he is doing something for the school and for the community, not only for himself, in leading his team to victory, for it is a school victory. The outstanding student, by contrast, has little or no way to bring glory to his school. His victories are always purely personal, often at the expense of his classmates who are forced to work harder to keep up with him. It is no wonder that his accomplishments gain little reward and are often met by ridiculing remarks, such as "curve-raiser" or "grind," terms of disapprobation which have no analogies in athletics.

That different cultural groups have different attitudes about the values of education has been shown by studies of a number of subcultures in the United States. The training of the Jewish youth puts emphasis on the value of scholastic achievements and adjustment to schoolwork accompanied by a curtailment of social, recreational, and athletic activities (237,329). Mexican youth develop unfavorable attitudes toward education. These stem from the belief that they cannot get ahead in American life and from lack of parental aspirations and support of education (89,90). Similarly, many Negro youth develop unfavorable attitudes toward education because they believe that they will not be given an opportunity to use it, owing to discrimination against them in vocations (16).

SOCIAL-CLASS VALUES
What value the adolescent will place on education will depend, to some extent, upon the social-class background of his family. As Davie has pointed out, "his pattern of schooling is partially determined by the mere fact of his birth into a family of a particular social class status" (84). If members of his social class think higher education is important, he will also; if they feel that it is more important to concentrate on practical than on cultural subjects, he will accept this value and this will influence his attitude toward education (225,332,348,369).

In general, attitudes toward education become more favorable as one goes from the bottom to the top of the socioeconomic ladder. Those of the higher social classes believe that higher education is essential for success in life; those of the lower classes tend to devalue education. There is a difference, also, in the values placed on different aspects of education. Members of the lower social classes feel that practical subjects are more important than cultural; those of the higher classes feel that the reverse is true. Grades are more important to members of the middle than to those of the lower or

upper classes (77,78,158,348,424,440). Figure 9–4 shows the percentage of adolescents of different social classes in suburban and city high schools.

PARENTAL ATTITUDES
Parental attitudes toward education are influenced by the social class with which they are identified. These attitudes are then instilled into the adolescent from his earliest days in school (203). Middle-class parents, on the whole, are anxious to have their children rise in the world. They encourage their children to study hard, they show an interest in their academic and extracurricular activities, they are pleased when their children do well, and they show their displeasure when they fall below parental expectations (190, 424). By contrast, lower-class parents show little interest in their children's schooling, they are unconcerned about poor grades or deportment, and they permit adolescents to drop out of school if they want to go to work (43,68,117,432).

Middle-class parents train their children to be good students. Mothers, even more than fathers, demand that their children take their studies seriously, they set high standards for them, and they punish them if these standards are not reached (213). As Drews and Teahan have remarked, "The high achiever is a child who has a rigidly defined place in the home which he is expected to keep with docile acceptance" (98). The eldest children are especially subjected to this demanding training; as a result, they provide more than their share to the ranks of high achievers in school. The next in rank of high achievers are the only children who, like the eldest, are encouraged and helped by parents to become good students (233). Figure 9–5 shows the academic achievement of adolescents of different ordinal positions.

Parents who are discontented with their own status train their sons to take schooling seriously so that they will be able to climb the vocational and social ladders (190,204). Mothers tend to encourage their sons to aspire higher educationally than do fathers (56). Mothers who have a higher education are especially prone to encourage their children to aspire high educationally (68,202).

In addition to encouraging their children to do well in academic subjects, parents put pressure on them to take part in extracurricular activities and to achieve success in the ones that are prestigeful. These parental attitudes reinforce the cultural values and encourage the adolescent to devote more effort to being successful in extracurricular than in academic activities (73,190).

PEER-GROUP ATTITUDES

Peer attitudes toward school and toward academic achievement vary for the two sexes. For a *boy*, being a scholar *and* an athlete leads to greater social acceptance than either alone; of the two, being an athlete is more important to popularity than being a scholar (60,72,73,300). For a *girl*, beauty and brains combined lead to social acceptance, but beauty is much more important than brains. Good marks, on the other hand, contribute to respect from and liking by members of her own sex (210). But the girl who gets a reputation for being a good scholar finds that boys regard her as still a child—one who conforms to parental demands (73,74). These peer-group attitudes have a profound influence on the adolescent's attitudes toward the value of education (149).

As *boys* progress through high school, peer attitudes toward education become more favorable. This is because many of them are aspiring to enter "name" colleges. For *girls*, by contrast, the attitude of the peer group toward scholarly achievement becomes less favorable from the sophomore or junior year on (18,72,73,74,200).

Most of the students in college-preparatory schools value education as a stepping-stone to advancement. This is true also of colleges that emphasize training for professional schools or postgraduate work (74, 113,441). Because the adolescent's values are greatly influenced by those with whom he is most closely identified or whose acceptance he is most anxious to have, the group in school or college with which he is identified will have more influence on his attitudes toward education than the school or college

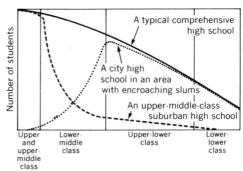

FIGURE 9–4 Percentages of adolescents of different social classes in city and suburban high schools. (Adapted from R. J. Havighurst: Social-class influences on American education. *60th Yearb. Nat. Soc. Stud. Educ.*, 1961, part 1, 120–143. Used by permission.)

group as a whole (280,336). Should a college student, for example, belong to a fraternity that puts high value on social or athletic achievements, he will accept the fraternity's relative low value on education as his and devalue academic achievement (149, 235).

SEX ROLES

When they reach adolescence, girls learn that their future roles will center around home and social activities; boys learn that theirs will be primarily vocational. As a result, boys put more emphasis on education as preparation for their vocational futures, and girls for their homemaking and social roles (18,74,117,200).

While boys are encouraged by parents to continue their education into college and graduate school, girls are encouraged to stop with graduation from high school or college. If they get a college degree, they are encouraged to specialize in studies that will give them a degree they can use—usually one in education or home economics. Boys are encouraged to concentrate on business subjects and get a degree that will prepare them for a business career (43,46,73).

VOCATIONAL PLANS

The adolescent's vocational aspirations and plans have a marked influence on his atti-

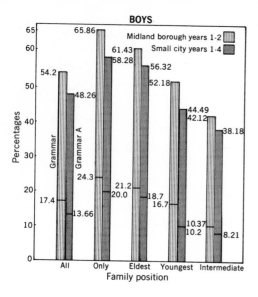

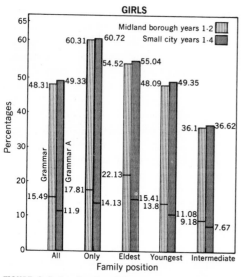

FIGURE 9–5 Academic achievement of adolescents of different ordinal positions in the family. (Adapted from J. P. Lees and A. H. Stewart: Family or sibship position and scholastic ability. *Sociol. Rev.*, 1957, **5**, 85–106. Used by permission.)

tude toward education. If he hopes and plans to go into a line of work that requires higher education and specialized training beyond college, he will not only aspire to get a college degree but to do good enough work

to enable him to enter a prestigeful school for professional and advanced training (46, 98,432).

By contrast, the adolescent who sees little hope of doing more than skilled laboring work will resign himself to getting as much education as the law requires and then will leave school for a job. If he has little or no encouragement at home to do well academically, he is likely to work below capacity. When parents devalue education, showing little or no interest in the school, in their children's achievements, or in their behavior in school, the adolescent's hopes to rise in the world are too weak for him to aspire to a vocation that requires more than a high school diploma (43,117).

The vocational aspirations of his friends affect the vocational plans of the adolescent, and his, in turn, affect his attitude toward education. If he is in a school where few of his classmates are planning to go into vocations requiring more than a high school education, he will be swayed by them to have a good time and forget about studying. He will then develop an attitude that education is of minor value *to him* (23,280, 441).

SOCIAL AND ACADEMIC SUCCESS

The adolescent who falls below his expectations in one or more school subjects usually develops a generalized dislike for school and for his teachers. Adolescents, by contrast, who do well academically like school and the subjects in which they do especially good work (8,20,255). However, peer attitudes toward academic success color the adolescent's attitudes toward success and, in turn, his attitude toward school. If the peer group considers academic achievement incompatible with being a regular guy or a "good Joe," it is hard for the good student to have a strong interest in school or to feel that education is important (444). How such attitudes affect the adolescent has been described by Pressey (314) thus:

The budding young scientist or scholar may be isolated or may associate only with a friend who is also considered "odd" or may belong only to an anemic subject club of no prestige in the community. . . . The teacher (perhaps made uncomfortable by keen questions) may even criticize his intense interest and the other youngsters may call him sissy or odd. For him there is frustration, not the furtherance of cumulative success.

Success or failure in extracurricular activities plays a more important role in determining the adolescent's attitude toward and interest in school than does success or failure in academic work. It is easy to like school if one is popular. On the other hand, it is difficult to be happy in a situation where there is discrimination and rejection, regardless of how much value one places on education (39). The adolescent who achieves both social and academic success will like school; social failure, especially when accompanied by peer discrimination, will reinforce the adolescent's dislike for school (229,266,356, 403).

ATTITUDE TOWARD TEACHERS

Long before the childhood days are over, many adolescents have developed either favorable or unfavorable attitudes toward teachers as people. These attitudes are partly the result of their own experiences, partly of the attitudes they have assimilated from parents and peers, and partly of the general cultural attitude toward teaching as a profession (10,63,231,266).

When a teacher likes her work and has good morale, this is reflected in good student morale. By contrast, teachers who do not like their work or who feel that the cultural attitude toward them is unfavorable produce an unhealthy emotional climate in the classroom which affects the attitudes of their students (11,40,373,398,401). Even when an adolescent likes a teacher as a person, his attitude toward her and toward school may be unfavorable if he has a strong dislike for the subject she teaches or if he feels that that subject has no practical value for him (5).

Without meaning to play favorites, most teachers are more interested in students who are eager to learn, who are conscientious about their work, and who make few problems for them in the classrooms.

Girls tend to be more conscientious students than boys and to present fewer disciplinary problems (123,156). Furthermore, teachers tend to be more interested in bright students than in dull. Other students sense this partiality on the part of their teachers and resent it (41,266,314,334,398).

Teachers tend to prefer the stars or near stars. The reason for this is that the behavior that makes others like or dislike them affects the teacher also (145). Having favorable treatment from the teacher reinforces the popular adolescent's favorable attitude toward school just as feeling that the teacher is against him reinforces the unpopular adolescent's unfavorable attitude. Because more unpopular adolescents come from lower-class backgrounds, the adolescent from the lower socioeconomic groups often feels that the teacher and the school are against him (78,145,156,398). This feeling is, to a large extent, justified. As Coster (78) has pointed out:

American schools, consciously or unconsciously, have been prone to favor pupils from middle and upper socioeconomic strata which, generally, include a high proportion of academically competent youth.

However, when a lower-class adolescent does show an interest in education, many teachers who have moved up the social scale by their vocational achievements, made possible by education, urge the student to do likewise by showing an interest in him and in his studies. As a result of teacher interest and encouragement, such a student has more favorable attitudes toward education than do most lower-class adolescents (158, 373).

TEACHING TECHNIQUES

Many adolescents, both in high school and college, regard the teaching techniques used in classes as boring, and the classroom work, dull. This is especially true of the very bright and the dull (184,401). Even for students of average ability, the typical attitude toward teaching techniques is unfavorable. There are a number of reasons for this. First, adolescents of today have grown up in an era of television and movies where the educational programs are presented with a glamour and *excitement* that would be impossible in the classroom. They have become so accustomed to sugarcoating that anything that lacks it seems dull (73,164). Second, the more rapid *pace* of high school and college teaching seems hard for them and requires more effort on their part than they have been accustomed to expend to learn. Third, because of their slower pace in the earlier grades, they have not learned *how to study* efficiently; as a result, they must spend more time on their lessons now than they feel is justified. Fourth, in the earlier grades they could rely on *help from parents*. Now, because their schoolwork is often too advanced for their parents, they must do their work unaided. And, finally, most adolescents have a well-developed *antiwork attitude*; they dislike anything that requires effort even when they can see the personal advantage to be derived from their efforts. When they can see little value from their studies, their antiwork attitude is intensified (300, 340,385,421,444).

effects of attitudes on performance

Adolescents bring to high school or college either favorable or unfavorable attitudes toward education (73,89). Even though their attitudes may change to some extent, the foundations are so well set by that time that the change will not be radical (184). Ruthven (335) maintains that there are three types of college students, each entering college with a characteristic attitude toward education which has been established long before he entered. The three types he described are as follows.

The Noisy Ones From the time they enter college they are "determined to be heard. Posing as authorities on almost everything at home and abroad, they insist they should run the university. . . . They usually claim to be liberals and boast of disrespect of authority."

The Playboys and Girls These are the "young people who go to college only on the insistence of their parents or because it is 'the thing to do'. . . and whose ambition is to get nothing more than to get a 'gentleman's grade' or to get married."

The Dedicated Ones These are the students who come to college "with their eyes firmly fixed on at least a general goal. They refuse to be discouraged by adversity or diverted from their course by college sideshows." Figure 9–6 shows some college "types."

In spite of the marked variations in attitudes, adolescents can be subdivided roughly into two major categories: those who are satisfied with education and those who are dissatisfied. The effect of these attitudes on their performance is markedly different.

satisfaction with education

The adolescent who likes school, enjoys his studies, feels reasonably well satisfied with his grades, and feels that his teachers treat him fairly will do good academic work. He may not work up to his capacity; this is more often because his interests and values are in extracurricular than in academic areas. While his academic achievements may not come up to his aspirations, he is satisfied with his grades. The discrepancy between what he hoped to do and what he did is small enough not to disturb him too much (114,385). Furthermore, his parents and teachers seem satisfied with his achievements (342). As Morrow and Wilson (281) have explained:

> *Family morale fosters academic achievement among bright high school boys via fostering positive attitudes toward teachers and toward school and interest in intellectual activities, as mediating variables.*

Many adolescents who are satisfied with school concentrate on their academic work because they feel this will help them to achieve their vocational goals. They concentrate their efforts on the subjects they know are important to future vocational success, even if this means depriving themselves of some of the extracurricular activities they would like to engage in (23,402). They do

"Noisy ones"   "Play boys" and "play girls"   "Dedicated ones"

FIGURE 9-6 College "types."

not feel that good academic work is incompatible with social acceptance. This may not mean membership in the "leading crowd," but in a crowd that is congenial to them (73,444).

Some adolescents find their major source of satisfaction in school in the extracurricular activities, especially sports and social affairs. If the students' satisfaction is reinforced by parental satisfaction, this will increase their liking for school or college (73,194). Furthermore, they will be proud to be identified with a school or college where extracurricular achievements are lauded and to receive recognition for their contributions to these achievements (72).

Satisfaction with education does not mean that the adolescent will not grumble or complain, criticize, or attempt to reform his school or college. He will do all of these but mainly because it is the thing to do. If he criticizes, he generally has a reason, and his suggestions for reform are usually realistic. If, for example, a class is poorly taught, he will criticize the teacher for poor instruction, not because he received a poor grade. If he feels that certain rules are unfair, he will suggest possible changes; he will not limit himself to grumbling and to accusing

the school of treating the students like "kids."

On the other hand, he may not vocalize his satisfaction with school. This is not because he is dissatisfied, but rather because it is not the thing to do. He does not want members of the peer group to feel that he is trying to polish the apple or become teacher's pet (73,116,194).

VARIATIONS IN SATISFACTION

Girls, more often than boys, are satisfied with what they are getting both in academic and extracurricular activities (121). Adolescents from the higher *socioeconomic* groups tend, as a whole, to be more favorable in their attitudes than those of the lower groups (88). *Bright* adolescents of all socioeconomic groups are better satisfied than those who are less bright. Being too bright for the group with which they are identified, on the other hand, leads to dissatisfaction (162,177).

Perhaps the greatest variations in satisfaction are related to differences in *personality.* Well-adjusted, mature adolescents tend, on the whole, to be better satisfied with their education than those who are poorly adjusted or immature (120,141,212,

279). Furthermore, the better-adjusted adolescent develops better study habits than the poorly adjusted who suffers from feelings of inadequacy and emotional stress. The result is that he does better academic work. This increases the satisfaction he derives from good social relationships in school (250, 444).

dissatisfaction with education

In adolescence, unfortunately, a majority of boys and girls are dissatisfied with their educational experiences. This attitude may be merely a way of following the crowd. Or it may be that dissatisfaction is more often vocalized than is satisfaction—partly because people at every age tend to be more vocal about things they dislike and partly because the adolescent who wants to be well accepted believes that this will enhance his popularity with the "right group" (73,89, 184).

Dissatisfaction with school is more often a result of social than of academic causes. It comes from feeling left out of things and not achieving the status in either athletics or social activities that had been hoped for. Being unpopular often makes an adolescent so dissatisfied with school that he does not try to do what he is capable of doing (198,320). Just as a favorable attitude, regardless of what causes it, leads to satisfaction with school so an unfavorable attitude, whether due to academic or social causes, leads to dissatisfaction (88,184).

Dissatisfaction varies in intensity from mild to strong. It also varies, in a predictable way, according to the type of adolescent. *Boys*, on the whole, are more dissatisfied with their educational experiences than are girls and they are more vocal about their dissatisfaction (184). Those who deviate markedly from the mean in *intelligence*, whether below or above the mean, are more dissatisfied than those whose intelligence is closer to the mean. Very bright adolescents are especially dissatisfied with their classroom work, the method of teaching, and their lack of autonomy in extracurricular activities. The less intelligent adolescents are dissatisfied with their lack of academic as well as

social success (3,107,198). Adolescents of the lower *socioeconomic* groups are, on the whole, more dissatisfied than those of the upper groups. Upper-class adolescents are less dissatisfied because schools and colleges literally cater to them both academically and socially (3,52,184,320).

EXPRESSIONS OF DISSATISFACTION

There are many ways in which adolescents show their dissatisfaction with school or college. Of these, the following are the most common.

Criticism and Attempts to Reform As was stressed earlier (see pages 139 to 141 for a more detailed discussion of criticism), adolescents are often hypercritical of their schools and colleges. This is not new in adolescence; older children are critical, too, but they do most of their grumbling to their parents and peers, because they are afraid to tell their teachers what they think is wrong with school. Adolescents do more of their grumbling to their teachers or to the administrators, though they, too, do their share at home and to their peers. While children complain most about the way the teacher treats them and the "unfairness" of their grades, adolescents complain about *everything* (184,194,320).

In junior and senior high school, the complaints are rarely given to the school authorities by individual students. They are more likely to be in the form of petitions, stating the complaints and requests or demands for changes. Rarely, also, do adolescents voice their complaints in the student publications. This may be because there is generally a faculty member on the publication board who would censor their complaints (200). If they have the backing of their parents, they sometimes go on strike, refusing to attend classes until the school "rights their wrongs."

College students are not only more vocal about the things they dislike but they are also bolder in their attacks. While they, too, usually hesitate to confront a teacher face to face with their complaints, for fear of flunking the course, they air their complaints in letters to student publications, usually anonymously written; they send representatives from the students to report to the faculty committees in charge of the areas in which their complaints lie; or they have mass walkouts, demonstrations, and picketing, similar to the methods used by labor unions. The most dissatisfied adolescents are the most critical and the most likely to try to lower the morale of the rest of the students by their complaints (52,97,102,184, 198,200).

Misbehavior It is not uncommon for a dissatisfied student to try to retaliate by causing trouble for those who have forced him to be in the situation against his will. This he does by disturbing the teacher or the other students by talking, by cutting up, by interrupting the teacher with questions that are mainly meant to disrupt her work, by disobeying rules and regulations, by showing disrespect for the teacher and all in authority, and by making it difficult for other students to study or to learn from classroom instruction. If the dissatisfaction is very great, adolescents may express their resentments at having to remain in school by arson, vandalism, and other forms of juvenile delinquency (214,320,455). This will be discussed in more detail in the chapter on moral development.

Underachievement "Underachievement" means achievement below the individual's tested capacity. The underachiever's achievements may be favorable in comparison with those of his classmates, but they are below what he is capable of doing. Torrence (412) has written:

> What is an underachiever made of? A scorned imagination, an unused memory, tabooed sensations, an interrupted thought, a rejected question, a forbidden daydream, an unexpressed idea, an unsought judgment, an unpainted picture, an unsung song, a safely hidden poem, unused talents. . . . These make an underachiever.

Some adolescents are *general* underachievers in the sense that their achievements are below their capacities in all or nearly all areas; others are *specific* under-

achievers, working below their capacities in only certain areas and up to their capacities in others. Underachievement is always an indication of dissatisfaction on the part of the adolescent (128,337,455).

Many adolescents are unaware that they are allowing their dissatisfaction to cause them to work below their capacities (408). In fact, some claim that they are doing the best they can. Other adolescents know that they can do better, but they blame their underachievement on others. Believing that some uncontrollable factor in their environment is responsible for their underachievement, they often become defensive in their attitudes, withdraw into the daydream world, or leave school (350,385, 429).

While underachievement may reach its peak in adolescence, it usually begins during childhood, often as early as the second or third grade. This is the time when the child's attitude toward school often changes from favorable to less favorable (142,194). As Shaw and Grubb have pointed out, the underachiever brings the tendency to work below his capacity with him, "at least in embryo form, when he enters high school" (354). A study of the pattern of development of underachievement has shown that for boys the predisposition to underachieve is present even when they enter school. This tendency increases up to the tenth grade and then decreases somewhat as boys begin to recognize the importance of education to their future vocations. In girls, underachievement is less pronounced up to the fifth grade; after that, it becomes increasingly greater as girls realize the social handicap good academic work can be for them (355). The pattern of development of underachievement is shown in Figure 9–7.

causes of underachievement Underachievement may be caused by dissatisfaction with circumstances in the school. It is more often generated outside the school and projected on the school (313,349). By adolescence, it has become a "symptom of deep-seated personality problems" (177). That school experiences alone are not responsible for underachievement was emphasized by

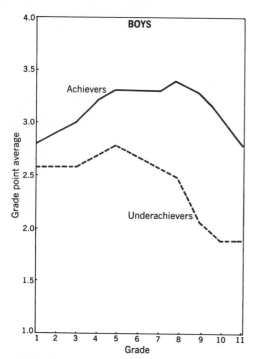

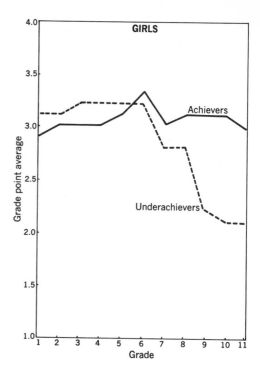

FIGURE 9–7 Patterns of development of under-achievement in boys and girls. (Adapted from M. C. Shaw and J. T. McCuen: The onset of academic underachievement in bright children. *J. educ. Psychol.*, 1960, **51**, 103–108. Used by permission.)

Wedemeyer when he said that the real cause for underachievement may be "found in the earlier emotional, educational, and personal history of the non-achieving youths, in their financial status, or in a combination of all these factors" (431).

Even though *school experiences* alone are not responsible for underachievement, they play a too important role to be over-looked or minimized. In general, the under-achiever does not like school, he has little academic drive, he doubts the value of higher education, he does not enjoy learning from books, he finds his subjects dull and the methods of teaching boring, and he is hypercritical of his teachers and of school in general (132,157,297,351,411). He has little encouragement from his parents to do well or has so much prodding that he re-volts and works below his capacity. He has poor study habits, is distracted and discour-aged easily, and has a tendency to pro-crastinate (248,444). He *pretends* not to be concerned about failures, especially in courses he feels are of little value to him (297). Furthermore, he has little interest in his future or concern about a job with high prestige (59,151,444).

The adolescent who is *anxious* to be well accepted by the social group but feels socially inadequate develops a feeling of per-sonal inadequacy. When he develops a poor opinion of himself, he is incapable of good academic work; this stifles what motivation he would otherwise have to do good work (117,120,274,313,353).

Hostility is at the basis of much under-achievement. This may come from parental pressures to achieve higher academic or so-cial success than the adolescent feels he is capable of or from rejection by the members of the peer group with which he wants to be identified. Only occasionally does hostility originate in the classroom, though situations in the classroom may intensify hostility that has developed elsewhere. The poorer the re-lationship with the parents, the more prone the adolescent is to underachievement (281,

354). Often hostility stems from the adolescent's belief that his parents have little interest in him or what he does at school, even when he is academically or socially successful (100,215,352).

Hostility resulting from peer rejection further increases dissatisfaction with school and the tendency to underachieve. If the adolescent cannot have what he wants in school—social acceptance—he finds that academic success gives him too little satisfaction to justify exerting himself to do what he is capable of doing (157,274,429,451).

variations in underachievement Underachievement is greater among *boys* than among girls. This is usually explained by the fact that girls conform more closely to adult expectations and that boys place a lower value on good academic work (81,99,353). *Very bright* adolescents tend to underachieve more than those of average ability; they feel that they must not be distinguished by academic success if they want to gain social acceptance (73,157). Among bright adolescents, there is less underachievement among those of the higher *socioeconomic* groups because they know that education is a necessary stepping-stone to success (264). Adolescents who have learned to *study effectively* tend to underachieve less than those who study ineffectually. Adolescents who are *immature* for their ages tend to underachieve more often than those whose maturity level matches that of their age-mates (59,248, 313,349,385).

Overachievement An "overachiever" is one whose performance is above his tested ability; he does better work than one would anticipate with his capacities (444). This he does by dint of hard work, by impressing his teachers with his seriousness and conscientiousness, or even by cheating (132, 385,408). On the surface, overachievement would suggest satisfaction rather than dissatisfaction with education. It may, at times, stem from a high level of intellectual curiosity or from the satisfaction the adolescent derives from his classroom work (238). More often, however, overachievement is associated with personality problems; it comes from conditions unrelated to the school or college situation (177).

Studies of overachievers have revealed that their dissatisfaction with education comes from two major sources. First, they are not satisfied with their achievements in academic work because their grades have not come up to their expectations or the expectations of their parents (98,274,408). Second, they are not satisfied with their social acceptance (59,279,325). As Coleman has pointed out, because academic achievement brings few social rewards, many of the best potential students do not go out for studies. Instead, they go out for sports and social life. As a result, the outstanding students— the "intellectuals"—in many American high schools and colleges are not those with the most intellectual ability. Instead, they are those who hope to improve their social status by achieving distinction in whatever area they can (71,73).

Dropouts Leaving a situation where one is dissatisfied is a common reaction. Some people leave *mentally*; they withdraw into a daydream world though physically they remain in the situation. Many more react to dissatisfaction by *physical* withdrawal. They drop out of school or college before they have received the reward for completion—a high school diploma or a college degree (165). It is possible, often in elementary school, to predict which students are most likely to drop out. Boys and girls who are socially isolated, who have few friends and belong to no gang, show a dislike for school that increases as they grow older. Those who are socially well accepted have more favorable attitudes toward school; as a result, they are far less likely to drop out before they complete their planned courses of study (51,146). In colleges, for example, students who join fraternities or sororities are less likely to drop out than those who have no such affiliation (15,106,440).

Dropping out of school is not an overnight decision in most cases; there are indications of the student's dissatisfaction in school phobias and truancy. A child who develops an abnormal fear of school—a "school phobia"—never completely overcomes his dislike for school. He literally lives for the day when he will no longer be forced against his will to go to school (64,205). Throughout his school years, the child's dislike for school will make him a truant, or he will stay away with parental consent if he is able to persuade his parents that he is not feeling well. Truancy and chronic absenteeism, due to imaginary invalidism, are usually forerunners of dropping out before finishing the level of schooling the student is engaged in (166,167,205,420).

causes of dropouts Some adolescents end their education *involuntarily* because of necessity. This necessity may be economic or familial. While girls are called upon for financial aid less frequently than boys, there are times when girls must end their schooling to help their families or to enable a young husband to complete his education (15,76,165,196,217).

Most dropouts are *voluntary*. The adolescent does not want to remain though he may try to camouflage his real reason by using sympathy-evoking excuses, such as "I was needed at home" or "I had to get a job to help out the family after Dad got sick." While it is possible to predict that certain children will never graduate from high school, or that those who go on to college or even a professional school will never complete their courses of study, there are many who drop out voluntarily without having shown such clear-cut evidences of dissatisfaction with education as truancy or imaginary illness (239).

Certain conditions encourage adolescents who have shown signs of dissatisfaction with their education to take the final step and drop out. Most often a constellation of related causes intensify the adolescent's dissatisfaction to the point where he sees no possible solution to his problem but to withdraw from an environment that has become intolerable to him (76,217). In the constellation of causes, certain conditions predispose the student to drop out while others serve as the driving force which motivates him to take the final step (15,106). As Livingston has emphasized, "Dropping out of school is the result of a complex se-

quence of events that is likely to be different for each individual" (246). Figure 9–8 shows some of the conditions which favor completion of college and those which favor withdrawal.

Of the many *predisposing* causes of voluntary dropouts, the most important fall into two major categories; those which make the adolescent feel inferior and those which make him feel that what he is doing is futile. Feelings of failure may develop in the classroom. The adolescent whose grades are poor or who is overage for his class is constantly reminded that he is an academic failure or near failure (143,360).

Feelings of failure more often originate from poor social acceptance than from poor academic achievement (106). And because social acceptance is the more highly valued, the adolescent who is neglected or rejected by his age-mates develops marked feelings of failure (15,106,410). Regardless of the cause, the adolescent who feels inferior to his classmates because of his poor acceptance will feel that his school life is a failure and that he is missing the most important things in education (86,240,284,285).

Feelings of futility about education are the second main type of predisposing cause of dropouts. The adolescent who can see little relationship between what he is getting in the classroom and his goals for adult life feels that he is wasting his time by remaining in school. Or he may feel that the period of training needed for his vocational goal is too long and that he is not only wasting his youth by remaining a student but also that

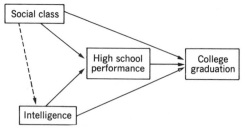

FIGURE 9–8 Conditions that favor the completion of college. (Adapted from B. K. Eckland: Social class and college graduation: some misconceptions corrected. *Amer. J. Sociol.*, 1964, **70**, 36–50. Used by permission.)

he must remain a dependent while his friends are earning good money (116,246, 284,285,333).

Feelings of failure and the futility of his experiences in education are often reinforced by parental attitudes. Many parents are critical and punitive of their children's academic achievement. Others reinforce the adolescent's feeling that the time he spends on education is wasted. When parents are unimpressed by the value of education, when they scorn book learning, or when they regard staying in school beyond the compulsory age as a financial burden on the family, they encourage the adolescent to feel that his education is futile (257,284).

Even though an adolescent is predisposed to drop out of school, he may not do so. There is usually some cause that makes him take the final step—the motivating cause. This may and often does cause the adolescent to make a sudden decision to drop out, though he may have been contemplating it for a long time. Of the many motivating causes of dropouts, the following are the most commonly reported. First, a student may need *money* for some special event or some important status symbol. A student who has had to sacrifice many extracurricular activities because he could not afford the cost may reach a breaking point when something he especially wants to do, such as taking a girl he is dating to a prom, is priced beyond his financial limits (285,360).

A second common motivating cause is *academic failure*. This may put the adolescent on probation so that he cannot participate in sports or other extracurricular activities; it may require the repetition of a course he has found difficult; or it may necessitate going back to a lower class which, in turn, means leaving his friends and making new ones (106,165). Many students drop out immediately after an examination period or over the summer vacation, when they learn that their failures will be a social as well as an academic handicap.

A third important motivating cause for dropping out is the *desire to do what one's friends are doing*. If an adolescent hears his friends talk about the big money they are earning, it is hard for him to continue to be a dependent, especially when he sees little personal gain from remaining in school. And, finally, he may be motivated to leave by *parental pressures* to go to work as his friends are doing or as his father did at his age (46,209,257,284,341).

age of dropping out It has been estimated that less than two-thirds of the ninth-grade students will remain in school long enough to complete their high school education and get a diploma (284,410). The usual age for boys and girls to drop out of school is 16 years—during the eighth, ninth, and tenth grades. Because they are older than their classmates, they feel that they are too old to be with such "kids." Furthermore, they realize that they will be 18 years old or older when they graduate, and this does not appeal to them. Students who are retarded in academic placement develop marked feelings of inferiority and futility about their education. As a result, it takes little in the way of a motivating cause to persuade them to drop out of school (76, 284,427).

At the college age, the vulnerable time for dropouts is during the first and second years, often after midyear or final examinations. As Boroff has pointed out, "The dropout rate approaches 60 percent, and casualties include the ne'er-do-wells, students whose funds have dried up and those who get bored, restless or married" (46). Leaving during Christmas or spring vacation often is a convenient way to avoid the embarrassment of poor grades for the term's work. When dropping out at such times, the student generally gives a plausible reason—poor health, economic reasons, or getting married (196,209).

temporary or permanent? Whether dropping out will be an end to the adolescent's education or merely an interruption will depend mainly on two factors: first, *when* he drops out, and second, *why* he drops out.

Students who drop out in high school are less likely to return to the classroom than are those who drop out in college. The reason for this is twofold: the college student discovers, when he tries to find a job, that the type open to him without a college education does not conform to his vocational aspirations. The second reason is that he can go to another college where, he hopes, conditions will be more to his liking (15, 46).

It is difficult for a high school student to transfer to another high school if conditions in his school are not to his liking. Furthermore, he often finds on-the-job training programs in the industries which pay high wages and which will prepare him for a job without a high school diploma. In the case of girls, going to business school for a few months to a year will give them the training they need for the type of job they want without taking time to finish high school (410).

The second factor that determines whether dropping out will be permanent or merely an interruption is the reason for doing so. If the adolescent is a voluntary dropout, the chances of his finishing his course of study are slim. Leaving a situation where one is dissatisfied does not provide a strong motivation to return, even when the rewards for finishing a course of study are high. Later, when the satisfaction from working is replaced by dissatisfaction from being in a dead-end job, family or other responsibilities may make it impossible for him to return to school or college (15,410).

The involuntary dropout, by contrast, regards dropping out as an interruption, not as an end to education. While some involuntary dropouts may never be able, for one reason or another, to complete their education, they want to and they live in the hope that some day it will be possible. The increase in night high schools for adults and in adult education classes on the college campus, correspondence courses for completion of high school or college work, and television courses for college credit—all show how eager some adults are to finish an interrupted education (15,196,209,410,427).

seriousness of dissatisfaction with education

Dissatisfaction lowers motivation. When this occurs, performance is quantitatively and qualitatively below the individual's capacity and below that of others of equal or even inferior ability whose motivation is stronger. Furthermore, when underachievement is recognized as such, the individual soon acquires the reputation of not trying or of doing just enough to get by.

When levels of aspiration are high in an area which is closely related to or influenced by achievements in another area, dissatisfaction can play havoc with the individual's chances of reaching the goal he has set for himself. The adolescent who aspires to a "name" college, for example, will meet such heavy competition for admission that his chances are slight. He will then have to settle for an education in a college of lower rank which he may previously have scorned (184).

Similarly, if the adolescent's vocational aspirations are focused on a highly competitive profession, such as law, medicine, or engineering, working below capacity in high school may jeopardize all chances of getting the training needed for one of these professions, first, because the adolescent is able, at best, to get into only a second-rate college, and second, because the habit of underachievement is likely to persist in college.

Another point well worth considering is the almost universal tendency to go into an academic slump at the time of the negative phase, during puberty. (See pages 59 and 60 for a more complete discussion of the effects of puberty on achievement.) For the average girl, this phase coincides with the junior high school age; for the average boy, with the end of junior high school and the beginning of senior high school. For late maturers, it may come during the critical high school years when the academic record of the student is carefully scrutinized by the admissions committees of colleges (184).

Even though the adolescent may develop into a "late bloomer," he still has an early record that is poor to pit against the records of early maturers or average maturers who were over the academic slump before their records counted seriously for college admission. If he has a carry-over of dissatisfaction with education from his elementary school days, his chances of changing his attitudes without help are slim (184,427).

The two most dissatisfied groups are made up of the adolescents at the two ends of the IQ continuum—the brightest and the dullest. Adolescents who are very bright are dissatisfied mainly because they are bored. Those who are dull, on the other hand, are dissatisfied because they feel that they are failures—both academically and socially (184). Students who are dull often drop out of school before completing their courses. Very bright students, as a result of boredom, work below their capacities and often drop out because they, too, find school or college intolerable (184). Both will become vocational misfits in time.

Adolescents whose dissatisfaction with their education is so great that they decide to drop out of school or college find getting jobs much harder than they had anticipated. It has been estimated that the rate of unemployment is three times as high among dropouts as among those who have completed their high school education (410,427,439). Idleness and general dissatisfaction lead many adolescents into delinquency. It has been reported, for example, that juvenile delinquency is ten times more frequent among dropouts than among adolescents who complete their high school education (138,284,341,410).

LONG-TERM EFFECTS OF DISSATISFACTION

Added to the immediate effects of dissatisfaction with school are several long-term effects which may far overshadow the consequences just discussed. One of these is the generalized negative attitude toward *any* book learning after leaving school. In the rapid transition into automation which is taking place now, the adolescent must be prepared to learn new vocational skills in the years to come if he is to keep up with the pace of change which will be inevitable in every area of work. An *antilearning attitude* makes many adults react negatively to reading anything except the news in tabloid form and to the possibility of taking refresher courses to learn new methods in their areas of work. If today's adolescents follow in their footsteps, they will be left far behind in their attempts to climb to the top of the vocational pyramid (295).

Another and equally serious long-term consequence of dissatisfaction with education is the effect it will have *on the children of today's adolescents.* In discussing dropouts, Schreiber has emphasized that "dropout parents breed drop-out sons" (341). This statement can be broadened to read, "Parents who are dissatisfied with education breed children who are likewise dissatisfied with education." As the children of today's adolescents grow up in an age where a life-time of education is essential to enable the worker to keep pace with the constant changes of business and industry, a negative attitude toward education will unfit them for what life holds in store.

Unless something can be done to make negative attitudes toward education unfashionable in the peer culture, our nation is in for trouble vocationally and psychologically. There will not be enough properly educated workers to do the work that must be done to meet the competition with nations where adolescents have more positive attitudes toward education. Even worse, there will be too many malcontents whose feelings of failure incapacitate them psychologically for doing the only kind of work they are trained to do (137,427).

A feeble but important beginning has been made by the "ivy league colleges" to make the scholar as prestigeful as the athlete or the fraternity man. However, traditions built up over generations cannot be eliminated overnight. Until the students in high school can be persuaded that a scholar is not a "square" who causes trouble for them by being a curve raiser, it will not be easy to transfer the halo from the head of the athlete or the "party girl" to the head of the scholar.

II. VOCATIONS

The American adolescent of today looks upon his future vocation as a stepping-stone to the better life he craves for himself and his future family. Thus, like education, a vocation is not looked upon as an end in itself. As Riesman (324) has pointed out:

College students today often act as if they believed that work in large corporations, and, beyond that, work in general, could not be basically or humanly satisfying (or at times even honest), but was primarily a way of earning a living, to find a place in the social order, and to meet nice or not-so-nice people.

Thus, the adolescent's attitude toward his future vocation is focused more on what the vocation can do for him than on the satisfaction he will derive from the work he does. Consequently, it determines his preference for the kind of work he will do and his degree of dedication to his job (22,173, 252,415).

The adolescent's level of aspiration in the vocational area is often unrealistically high (382). He wants to go into a line of work above that of his father, and in this desire he is encouraged by his parents, especially his mother. If members of his peer group are also aspiring to occupations above those of their parents, he gets encouragement from them as well as from his parents to raise his level of aspirations (56,179,236, 247,395). The older adolescent becomes more realistic as he makes his vocational plans (260,379). As Wilson has stated, the older adolescent shows a "healthy desire to climb to the top of the tree, but little yearning to move into another part of the forest, where there are taller trees" (442). Figure 9–9 shows the unrealistic vocational aspirations of the young adolescent and his tendency to plan more realistically for his future as he grows older.

concern about vocational choice

As the child approaches adolescence, his concern about his future vocation grows; he realizes that the time of going to work is literally just around the corner. The problem of vocational choice that seemed so remote and impersonal when he was a child becomes immediate, personal, and very important.

In addition, there are pressures from all sides to make a decision about his life career. At home, his *parents* press him to make up his mind. At school, his *teachers* press him to decide, in order to know how to prepare him for the type of work he wants to do. And, finally, his *friends* are talking and thinking about their future and they want him to state his position.

REASONS FOR CONCERN

There are many reasons why making a vocational choice is a source of great concern to the adolescent. First, with the trend toward specialization and the need for training for a specific job, changing from job to job if one is dissatisfied is difficult if not impossible. As Abramovitz has pointed out, "Religion apart, no aspect of human affairs has such pervasive and penetrating consequences as does the way a society makes its living—and how large a living it makes" (2). This is equally true of the individual. The adolescent knows that his whole future will be influenced by the decision he makes now. He further knows that this decision is for keeps (173,247,312).

Second, because work will be one of the chief activities of his adult life, the adolescent wants to be sure that his work will be to his liking and that it will fit into his other plans for the future (395). He does not, for example, want to sacrifice the good times he has been accustomed to since childhood to become a cog in a huge machine where neither the work itself nor the anxiety-producing competition with other workers will give him pleasure or time to enjoy his leisure (324).

A third factor that gives rise to concern is the knowledge, from reports in mass media of communication, that the number of prestige occupations is limited and that approximately one-half of all workers are in blue-collar or overall jobs (286). He does not know whether he has the ability or will be able to get the training needed for a prestige job (173).

Closely related to this is his fourth source of concern, that of his real ability. While he may have done reasonably good work in his local high school, he does not know how he compares with other adolescents in other areas of the country. Nor is he sure whether the abilities he has are those needed for the type of work that carries glamour and prestige (173,247,382).

The fifth source of concern stems from the fact that there is a very great variety of choice in occupations today in all categories. In the past, this problem was minor; the variety of job opportunities was much smaller and the educational opportunities to prepare for the high-prestige jobs were limited to the relatively few adolescents whose families could afford to give them the education needed for these jobs. Today, the situation is radically changed.

A sixth source of concern springs from the lack of security he feels about getting and keeping a job. No longer is it possible for an adolescent to feel secure in the thought that there is always his father's or uncle's business to fall back on if he does not like the line of work he selects or if he does not make a success of it. Furthermore, no longer is it possible for his father to place him so easily in a business of one of his friends (173,395).

Closely related to this is a seventh source of concern—what job opportunities will be available in the future as a result of the rapid changes accompanying the spread of automation. Will he, he wonders, find the training he is getting now so out of date in a few years that he will not be fitted for *any* job? As Crow and Crow (80) have expressed it:

> Many young people are much disturbed over the present vocational situation. . . . It can be understood easily that the youth's uncertainty regarding vocational planning is increased by the fact that it is difficult to determine with any degree of certainty what the occupational opportunities may be ten, or even five, years from now.

The final, and perhaps the most serious source of concern springs from the fact that adolescents have relatively limited opportunities to explore their vocational choices. Specialization makes it difficult or even impossible for the young person to go from job to job in different lines of work. Child-labor laws and parental opposition to the adolescent's working are additional barriers to trying out different jobs (83,119,317,395).

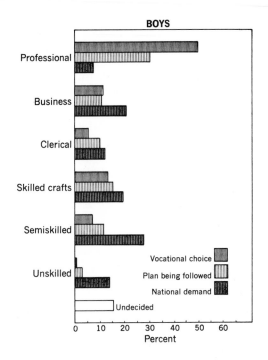

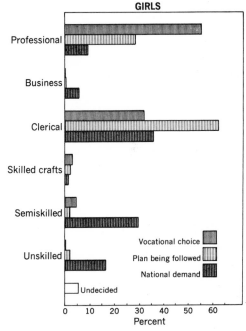

FIGURE 9–9 Occupational choice, plan followed, and national demand for different occupations. (Adapted from L. Cole and I. N. Hall: *Psychology of adolescence*. 6th ed. New York: Holt, Rinehart and Winston, 1964. Used by permission.)

age of vocational choice

The age at which adolescents choose their vocations varies greatly. Nor is the choice made rapidly or even finally when it is made. As Holden (172) has said, the individual's vocational choice is a:

> . . . *developmental process that spans many years, during which the ultimate decision is determined by a series of actions and occurrences, each one dependent at least in some measure on preceding ones. . . . There comes a time when the general direction followed cannot easily be reversed or changed.*

By the time boys and girls reach the seventh or eighth grade, their vocational choices are manifested in a "vocational choice level." They know what level of work they want to go into even though they may not yet have decided what type of job in that level they will aspire for (6,172,394,423).

The age at which vocational choices are made varies according to the type of work involved. Work that requires specific training, especially over a long period of time, is likely to be decided upon earlier than work that requires little in the way of specific training (172). In a comparison of age of vocational choices of teachers and factory workers, for example, it was found that teachers decided earlier on their careers than did factory workers. This is illustrated in Figure 9–10 which shows the peak ages of vocational choices for men and women teachers and for factory workers (289).

Even though vocational choices may not be made before adolescence draws to a close, *attitudes* toward different vocations are usually established before adolescence begins. In childhood, the individual has developed negative attitudes toward certain occupations; he definitely does *not* want to spend the rest of his life in these occupations. At the same time, he has positive attitudes toward other occupations; they appeal to him and he feels that he could be happy, or at least satisfied, if he selected any one of them as his life work.

Once established, these attitudes channel the person's interests into different voca-tional choice levels. In a study of high school seniors it was found that interest in teaching as a career was markedly influenced by attitudes formed earlier. Those who were interested in teaching as a career liked children and people, they wanted to help society, they felt that teaching offered them security and helped them to prepare for marriage. Those whose attitudes were unfavorable claimed that children got on their nerves, they disliked the work connected with teaching, especially the homework and discipline, and they felt that the cost of preparation for a teaching career was too high for the rewards teaching brings (197).

factors influencing vocational choice

Of the many factors that influence the vocational choices of adolescents, the following are the most important.

FAMILY

The family is, in most cases, the most important single factor in determining the adolescent's vocational choice. Parents exert the greatest influence, but older siblings and relatives play a role too important to be overlooked. Figure 9–11 shows how great the influence of the family is as compared with other influences in one group of adolescents. The influence of the family in shaping the adolescent's vocational aspirations begins early, often before the child enters school. Each year, as the child grows older, family pressures are increased. By adolescence, the individual's attitudes toward different vocations are well formed and serve as powerful forces in shaping his vocational interests and aspirations (183,288,298,326).

Positive and Negative Influences The type of influence the family has on an adolescent's vocational choice can be classed roughly as "positive" and "negative." The positive type consists mainly in giving advice that influences the adolescent's choice. This is done either by direct suggestions as to what the adolescent should choose or indirectly by putting emphasis of varying degrees on certain jobs that the parents consider desirable (12,62,192,216,361).

The negative type of family influence may be direct or indirect. Children and adolescents from both blue- and white-collar families are subjected to this type of influence, though it is more common in the former (104,428). Parents may tell their children to avoid certain types of work because of poor pay, long hours, the uncertainty of a steady job, low prestige, limited opportunities to get ahead, and many similar disadvantages. Or they may influence their children by incidental remarks they make about different jobs (188,369).

Indirectly, parents may influence their children's vocational choices through the type of work they themselves do. Many adolescents, it has been found, perceive their parents' jobs through parental eyes; if parents grumble about their work, adolescents will perceive these jobs unfavorably and will, as a result, develop a negative attitude toward them (104,371,428). On the whole, adolescents want jobs higher in the vocational scale than their fathers' jobs. In a nationwide survey of adolescents, it has been reported that 77 percent of the boys wanted to go into occupations different from their fathers' as compared with 23 percent who wanted to go into the same occupations (73).

Variations in Family Influence Young adolescents follow parental advice more readily in the choice of future vocations than do older adolescents; the influence of the family in vocational choice wanes after the age of 19 years (289). Of the different *family members*, the father's influence is usually the strongest, though this varies according to how the adolescent feels about his father. If the adolescent likes his father and identifies with him, he will be more influenced by his father than by his mother. When, on the other hand, the adolescent dislikes his father but identifies with his mother, he will try to meet his mother's expectations for him by selecting a vocation she wants him to enter and by rejecting the occupation his father prefers (375,383).

Parents put more pressures on their *daughters* to go into the occupations they consider suitable for them than they do on

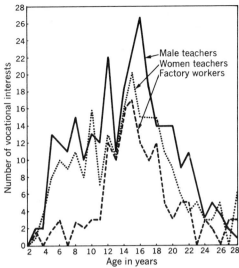

FIGURE 9–10 Peak ages of vocational choice for workers in two occupational areas. (Adapted from J. L. Norton: Patterns of vocational interest development and actual job choice. *J. genet. Psychol.*, 1953, **82,** 235–262. Used by permission.)

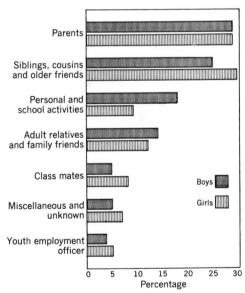

FIGURE 9–11 The importance of the family as compared with other factors in occupational choice. (Adapted from G. Jahoda: Job attitudes and job choice among secondary modern school leavers, II. *Occup. Psychol.*, London, 1952, **26,** 206–224. Used by permission.)

their sons (372). Parents of different *ethnic* groups exert different degrees of influence in their children's vocational choices. Italian parents, for example, are more lenient about their children's vocational aspirations and achievements than are Jewish parents (387).

The *socioeconomic status* of the family is an important factor in determining how much pressure parents put on their children to choose occupations they consider suitable for them (371). Adolescents from the higher socioeconomic groups are, as a whole, influenced more by their families than are those from the lower groups (104). When parents are college graduates, they are likely to urge their children to select occupations that require college education as a preparation and to select an occupation with high prestige (371).

When the father is dissatisfied with his work and the mother dissatisfied with the socioeconomic status it gives the family, parents are anxious to have their children select vocations that will make *social mobility* for them and the whole family possible. From earliest childhood, they instill in their children the desire to go into an occupation above the father's. As a result, the adolescent has a negative attitude toward all occupations in the parental level and a positive attitude toward those in a higher level (105, 110). This is illustrated in Figure 9–12.

SEX

Interest in occupations is quite different for members of the two sexes. To a boy, the vocation he selects will be a lifetime occupation. For that reason he wants to be sure that it will continue to be satisfying to him as he grows older. When he reaches adolescence, he has a general idea of what he wants to do but he defers making a final decision as long as possible in order to avoid making a choice he will later regret. Furthermore, because the vocation he selects will be his life career, he is willing to put more time and effort into preparation for it than he would if he regarded it as temporary (6, 67,94).

For the average girl, a job is merely a stopgap between school and marriage. Therefore, her attitude is less serious than is that of the typical boy. This is shown by the fact that she is unwilling to spend as much time and effort in preparation for a career as she would if this were to be a lifetime career. Furthermore, she is in no hurry to decide what she wants to do nor are there pressures placed on her to decide as is true of boys (94,258).

Because there are more openings available for boys than for girls, boys can afford to be more choosy about what line of work they want to enter. By contrast, the openings available to girls are more limited, stereotyped, and homogeneous. Furthermore, girls know that any job they have will be on a lower level, with less pay and less prestige, than that of boys of similar ability. This militates against their motivation to aspire to jobs that are more closely related to their abilities and interests; they settle for what they know they can get (45,289,295).

Boys want jobs that offer power, profit, independence, and prestige. They prefer to work with things and ideas; girls prefer to work with people (111,367,446). Furthermore, boys frequently aspire to careers that are above their abilities (188,430). Girls, by contrast, are less ambitious and more content to do what they can do. Likewise, they are aware of the difficulties they will encounter in rising to highly paid jobs and the keen competition they will have to meet. For that reason, many girls select careers in occupations where most of the workers are of their sex, thus eliminating the competition with men (295,357). Figure 9–13 shows the things considered important in jobs by boys and girls.

Long before they reach adolescence, boys and girls have "learned their sex stereotypes very well." As a result, their job choices are usually compatible with the cultural definition of "maleness" and "femaleness" (367). The more marked the tendency toward masculinity or femininity of interests, the more likely the individual is to select a sex-appropriate vocation and to retain his interest in it (414). Boys who decide to go into a traditionally feminine occupation, such as nursing or elementary school teaching, often find their self-esteem and prestige suffer because of the unfavorable social attitudes toward their choice of "feminine" occupaions (112,347).

SCHOOL

The influence of *teachers* in vocational selection is greatest up to 19 years of age and then wanes. Girls, at all ages, are more influenced in their vocational selections by their teachers than are boys (288,289,323). While *classmates* play some role in influencing the adolescent's choice of vocation, their influence is less than that of teachers or families in the early part of adolescence. Their influence increases, however, as the influence of parents and teachers decreases (150,329,441).

Course content of different school subjects becomes an increasingly important factor in determining the adolescent's interest in different vocations as he passes from high school into college. Students who do well in science courses and find science an interesting subject are far more likely to consider a career in science than are students who find science boring or who do poorly in this area of school work (220). *Grades* and academic success likewise influence the adolescent's vocational choice. Students who do well academically aspire to higher-level occupations than do those whose intellectual capacities or motivations are so limited that they fall in the lower percentiles of the class academically (289,304).

The *extracurricular activities* of the school are of no small importance in forming the adolescent's vocational aspirations. The adolescent who enjoys sports, for example, is often motivated to go into a line of work in which this interest can find expression, such as athletic director in a school or professional baseball, football, or basketball player. Similarly, adolescents who enjoy school or college dramatics often aspire to a career in which they can use this interest either directly, in acting, or indirectly, in the production of plays, movies, or television programs (65,73,94).

The last but by no means the least important way in which school helps to form the adolescent's vocational aspirations is by giving him a more *realistic concept* of his abilities and disabilities. From his studies

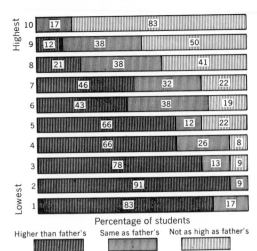

FIGURE 9–12 Adolescents characteristically develop negative attitudes toward occupations in the parental level and positive attitudes toward occupations in higher levels. (Adapted from L. T. Empey: Social class and occupational aspiration: a comparison of absolute and relative measurement. *Amer. sociol. Rev.*, 1956, **21**, 703–709. Used by permission.)

and extracurricular activities, the adolescent learns to evaluate himself in relation to his age-mates and to see how his abilities compare with theirs. That is why, by senior year in high school, many adolescents are willing to enter a vocation below the level they had originally aspired to (42,134,230,247).

DEGREE OF REALISM

Up to the age of 11 years, children are influenced in their choice of future occupation by fantasy. They are ignorant of their abilities and of what different vocations require in the way of ability and training. From 11 to 17 years, there is normally a gradual swing to reality. However, young adolescents are still ignorant of their capacities and they still have only limited job information. They may make tentative choices, changing to another job aspiration when they receive more information about it. Only after the age of 17 years do they base their choices on facts (134,393).

Lack of realism is shown in both *occupational choice* and *consideration of job opportunities*. Many adolescents become interested in preparing for an occupation in

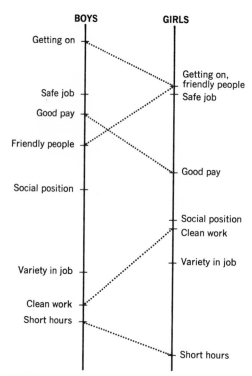

BOYS   **GIRLS**

Getting on

Getting on,
friendly people

Safe job — Safe job

Good pay

Friendly people

Good pay

Social position

Social position

Clean work

Variety in job — Variety in job

Clean work

Short hours

Short hours

FIGURE 9–13 Things considered important in jobs by boys and girls. A broken line indicates a sex difference significant at the 5 percent level. (Adapted from G. Jahoda: Job attitudes and job choice among secondary modern school leavers, I. *Occup. Psychol.*, London, 1952, **26**, 125–140. Used by permission.)

which they cannot possibly engage because of limited abilities (430). They choose on the basis of what they would like to do or what they think they would like to do. Their vocational aspirations are, thus, expressions of "illusory aspirations" (370,393,446).

Unrealism expresses itself also in lack of consideration of job opportunities. Many adolescents select a vocation because of its appeal to them; they do not take into consideration whether there will be an opening for them. Most adolescents, for example, want to be in white-collar jobs, but only about 50 percent of the jobs available in the entire country fall in this category; the rest are blue-collar or overall jobs.

While most unrealism takes the form of aspiring above one's capacities, it also takes the form of "undershooting"—of aspiring too low vocationally. This may happen among adolescents who are suffering from feelings of personal inadequacy or among those who are underachievers. It is also common among adolescents of the lower socioeconomic groups who have abilities but are discouraged from using them by their parents' negative attitudes toward education or by obstacles placed in their way, such as low socioeconomic status or minority-group identification (247,393,425).

Normally, unrealism in vocational choice wanes as adolescence progresses. This waning does not come of its own accord. Instead, it is the product of many factors, the most important of which are vocational counseling to acquaint the adolescent with the types of jobs available and the abilities needed for different jobs; a realistic assessment of his abilities; and an opportunity to get some work experience (452). By senior year in high school, most adolescents are ambitious, but not unrealistic (192,442). By the end of adolescence, many are vocationally mature in the sense that they show increasing wisdom in their vocational preferences and decreasing fantasy (247,382, 393,395).

VOCATIONAL INFORMATION

Too little information is likely to narrow the adolescent's range of interest. This encourages him to select from the few occupations he knows about, even if they are not well suited to his interests and abilities. Too much information may, on the other hand, confuse the adolescent, thus delaying his vocational choice. Or too much information about a given occupation, if the emphasis is on the undesirable aspects of it, may discourage him from selecting it, even though he has a strong preference for such work (47,147,197,247,425).

STEREOTYPES

Stereotypes of people in various occupations have a profound influence on the adolescent's attitudes toward these occupations. Such stereotypes are myriad. There are the stereotypes of the absentminded professor, the crafty politician, and the emotionally unstable artist. According to traditional beliefs, the country storekeeper has a friendly face, the bank president has a man-of-the-world look, and the surgeon has a confident expression (44,92,345).

When college students were asked to give their concepts of men of several professions, they claimed that the research scientist is high in intellectual but low in social dimensions; he is more intelligent, logical, orderly, persistent, precise, studious, and thorough but also less charming, friendly, humorous, poised, and self-confident than the businessman, engineer, or lawyer. Engineers, according to student concepts, are not so high in intelligence as research scientists, but equally lacking in social graces. Lawyers, by contrast, are equally high in intellectual and social dimensions; businessmen are low in intelligence but high in social dimensions (26).

Because of the present need for more scientists and teachers, the adolescent's stereotype of them is important in vocational selection. From science fiction and other sources, the adolescent has a composite image of the scientist which is anything but favorable. He is a man who wears a white coat, is elderly or middle-aged, small and stout or tall and thin, wears glasses, and has an absentminded expression. He is sometimes thought of as a villainous character with a "Frankenstein personality," sometimes as a "Savior of mankind," but more often as a person working in a bureaucratic society with pressures from all sides. He is a brain who is so engrossed in his work that he does not know what goes on in the world, he has few interests, he neglects his family, he is lonely, and he is a dedicated man who works for humanity, not for money or fame. The origin of many of the aspects of this stereotype can be traced to the days of black magic, during the Middle Ages, when the scientist was in the category of a sorcerer who was an enemy of the church (21,170,265,404). The stereotype of the scientist is shown in Figure 9–14.

The stereotype of teachers is equally as unfavorable as that of the scientist. This is markedly influenced by stereotyped portrayals of teachers in different forms of mass media, especially books, comics, movies,

FIGURE 9–14 Popular stereotype of the scientist.

and television. In literature, for example, the female teacher is usually unattractive looking, middle-aged, and dowdy in appearance. When she is young, she is portrayed as masculine; when middle-aged, as shrill and witchlike. The male teacher is portrayed as "stooped, gaunt, and grey with weariness. His suit has the shine of shabby gentility and hangs loosely from his undernourished frame." The stereotype of the teacher in movies is equally unfavorable. The teacher generally plays a comedy role; occasionally teachers appear as self-sacrificing, weak people who have devoted their lives to their pupils at the expense of their own happiness (342).

Stereotypes are widely held by members of a cultural group. Therefore, it is inevitable that these images would have a marked influence on the vocational selections of adolescents of that group. Many girls influence the boys they date to avoid selecting science as a career; they do not want to marry a person who, according to the cultural stereotype, will neglect his family, have few interests in social life, which girls value highly, and be unconcerned about financial rewards or fame—both of which girls value highly. Furthermore, many boys shy away from science as a career because they do not want their boy friends to think unfavorably of them (265,270). As Bendig and Hountras have emphasized, "If this stereotype continues to be transmitted from teacher to student, the problem of interesting high school students in scientific careers will remain with us" (26).

GLAMOUR AND PRESTIGE

Long before childhood is over, boys and girls are aware of the importance of *prestige* in jobs as a factor contributing to social acceptance; they know which jobs have prestige and which do not, and they are aware of the symbols by which job prestige is judged. They know that there is a hierarchy of occupations and that the "adult world is stratified along some principle of differentially evaluating occupations" (433).

In childhood, prestige of jobs was judged mainly in terms of the work done on the job and the type of clothing worn by the worker. Children, for example, associate more prestige with a job where the worker wears "dress-up clothes"—the white-collar job—than with the blue-collar or overall job (298,384,386). Adolescents, by contrast, judge the prestige of jobs more in terms of the degree of authority and autonomy the worker has, the financial rewards he receives, and the title he has on the job. Of these, the title is perhaps the most important because it is manifest: *everyone* knows what the worker's title is, but only a few know what salary he earns, how much authority he has over his subordinates, and how much independence the job permits him to have. That is why important sounding titles have such a strong

appeal for adolescents in making their vocational choices (251,253,291,417,433).

Prestige as a motivating factor in vocational choice is especially strong among those who are socially mobile. If their home environments offer few opportunities to gain social recognition, they hope to compensate for this by entering an occupation that will give them prestige among their peers and in the community. The stronger the achievement drive of the socially mobile, the more unrealistic their aspirations for prestigeful vocations will be (223,273, 304,365).

PERSONALITY

The personality pattern of the adolescent influences his vocational selection by predisposing him to select a work environment that offers opportunities to satisfy some of his basic personality needs. This influence is not necessarily conscious (370). If the adolescent chooses a vocation that fits his needs, he will be happy in his work and make good vocational adjustments; if he selects a vocation unsuited to his personality, he will be unhappy in his job, dissatisfied with his achievements, and anxious to change to another type of work that will suit his needs better (25,65,124,358).

An adolescent who suffers from feelings of inadequacy is not likely to consider an occupation where he would constantly be thrown with other people or where he would be expected to assume responsibility for major policy decisions. Girls, it has been found, who develop feminine inferiority complexes as a result of the way they are treated by boys at home and at school during childhood do not aspire to executive positions. They often turn them down when offered and prefer to work in jobs with less responsibility and, hence, less prestige (45, 295). The more marked the feelings of inadequacy, the more likely the adolescent is to try to find an occupation where he can play an inconspicuous role. In a study of chemists, for example, it was found that they preferred work which offered opportunities for solitary achievement and intellectual mastery to that which required close interpersonal relationships (358).

By contrast, the adolescent who likes interpersonal relationships, who feels confident of handling an authority role, who has the ability to cope with hostility and aggression, and who has a liking for and understanding of children will be interested in teaching as a career. One who lacks these qualities will have little interest in teaching (457). Similarly, an adolescent who is adventuresome finds office work boring; he wants a job that will permit him to travel around and be with people, such as salesmanship (65). Many adolescents, as they gain greater self-confidence, become interested in "adventurous" jobs. (See Figure 9–15.)

Because so many adolescents of today suffer from feelings of insecurity in their home lives, owing to family breakups, social mobility of the family, and the general insecurity of the world today, there is a widespread trend toward seeking work that will make a secure home life possible for them and their future families (37). From interviews with college students, Riesman (324) has made the following observation:

> It does not occur to them that they might be gifted and energetic enough to make a difference even in a big city. Rather, they want to be able to work through a face-to-face group—the postcollegiate fraternity of the small suburbs. Correspondingly, the very emphasis on family life which is one of the striking and in so many ways attractive qualities of young people today is an implicit rejection of large organizations. . . . The wish to build a nest, even a somewhat transient one, is a striking feature of the interviews, in contrast with the wish to build a fortune or a career which might have dominated some comparable interviews a generation earlier.

The desire to help others is often a strong motive in early vocational choices. The young adolescent feels insecure and inadequate; helping others increases his feelings of security and adequacy. That is why so many young adolescents think in terms of occupations which involve service to others, such as nursing, teaching, missionary work, or the ministry. By late adolescence,

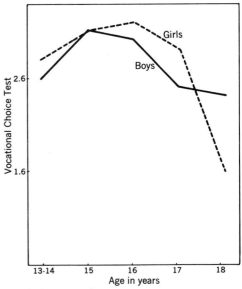

FIGURE 9–15 There is a decrease in interest in unadventurous jobs as adolescents gain more self-confidence and they show less interest in "safe" jobs. (Adapted from S. M. Chown: Personality factors in the formation of occupational choice. *Brit. J. educ. Psychol.*, 1959, **29**, 23–33. Used by permission.)

the individual normally feels more secure and adequate. Furthermore, he becomes more self-centered. As a result, he loses interest in helping others and becomes interested primarily in doing things that will be personally beneficial (65,358).

While personality plays a role of importance in vocational choice during adolescence, its role is less important in early than in late adolescence and less important in adolescence than in adulthood. The reason for this is that the adolescent has a limited knowledge of what work is involved in various vocations and what will be expected of him should he enter a vocation that appeals to him. Consequently, he is unable to know before he starts to work whether it will fit *his* needs or not. Only after he has had some work experience is he able to assess the situation more realistically and to discover whether he is in the right type of work for his individual personality makeup (25,124). This is one of the many reasons why vocational selection is less stable in early life than later. Figure 9–16 shows the relationship between personality traits and vocational choice.

stability of vocational interests

Vocational interests change frequently during adolescence. The most marked shifts come right after puberty, which occurs during the junior high school age and the early part of the senior high school period. By the sophomore year of high school, most

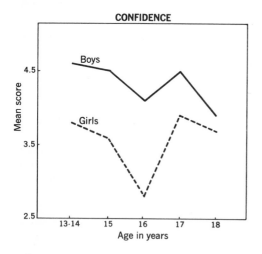

CONFIDENCE

Boys

Girls

Mean score

13-14   15   16   17   18
Age in years

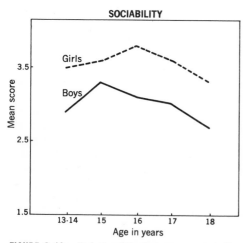

SOCIABILITY

Girls

Boys

Mean score

13-14   15   16   17   18
Age in years

FIGURE 9–16 Relationship between personality traits and occupational choice. (Adapted from S. M. Chown: Personality factors in the formation of occupational choice. *Brit. J. educ. Psychol.*, 1959, **29**, 23–33. Used by permission.)

students begin to show well-developed patterns of interest. This stability increases as they go into the junior and senior years (125,187). A comparison of freshmen and seniors in high school revealed that the highest area of interest remained the highest for 52 percent of the students, the second highest for 34 percent, and the third highest, for 28 percent (254). The greatest changes in interest have been reported in scientific and clerical work, with the greatest stability for accounting, law, and life insurance selling (187).

In late adolescence, there is even greater stability of interest. A comparison of choices made by sophomores in college with the choices they made in the freshman year showed that two-thirds did not change or, if they did, they shifted to a very closely related occupation. One-sixth shifted to a fairly closely related occupation, while the other one-sixth shifted to a different occupation (388,389). A comparison of the choices made in college with the occupations engaged in 19 years later revealed that approximately one-half of the group were in the occupations chosen during their early college years or in an occupation closely related to it. Those who did change were usually in occupations of lower prestige value, indicating a shift to a more realistic goal (390).

VARIATIONS IN STABILITY

How great and how frequent the shifts in vocational interest will be will vary. As has been pointed out earlier, shifts are more frequent during the *early* part of adolescence than during the later part. *Sex* differences in favor of the greater stability of girls' choices have been reported for the junior and senior high school ages and for college students. This may be due to one of three important causes: the earlier physical maturity of girls, which leads to earlier emotional and social maturity; the more restricted job opportunities for girls; and the less concern girls have about their vocations because they regard them primarily as stopgaps between education and marriage. The *personality* of the adolescent also influences the stability of his vocational interests. Self-sufficient, secure adolescents tend to be more persistent in their interests than those who suffer from feelings of insecurity and inadequacy. The more extroverted the adolescent, the more likely he is to be influenced in his vocational choice by members of the peer group (423).

Students who can make a vocational choice that is satisfactory to them in high school are usually brighter and more studious than those who are unable to make a choice and keep it. The reason for this is that more *intelligent* adolescents tend to make more realistic and more appropriate choices. Vocational interests that have developed through *school* influences show a higher survival value than those formed through outside influences. Adolescents who have received *vocational guidance* in school express interests that tend to be more persistent than those of adolescents whose interests have been influenced more by parental aspirations than by consideration of the adolescents' interests and abilities (127, 172,206,391).

CAUSES OF CHANGE

Adolescents have many reasons for changing their vocational aspirations. One, unquestionably, is *economic necessity*. A family crisis may necessitate the adolescent's leaving school or college. Or the adolescent may find that his family is unable to afford the long period of education necessary for preparation for the career he had hoped to have. More often, however, the change is due to a change in *interests*. What seemed to be an exciting, glamorous, or interesting occupation when he was younger may, as his values change, hold little interest for him. A boy who is intellectually competent may find too little challenge in sports to want to devote his life to being an athletic coach, as he had originally planned. As a result, he will decide on a nonathletic career while retaining his interest in sports as an avocation (25,391).

Intensive individual or group *vocational guidance* is often responsible for vocational changes. Guidance shows adolescents what is needed for different jobs and suggests lines of work they know little about but which may suit their needs better than the glamour jobs they have selected (127,391). Similarly, *work experience* can be an eye-opener for an adolescent whose knowledge of jobs is limited to what he has heard, read, or imagined about them (83,317). Through vocational guidance and work experience, it is inevitable that the adolescent will become more *realistic* about job possibilities and about his abilities for different jobs. With increased realism, change often occurs. However, change is more often in vocational level than in vocational category. The adolescent changes to a job on a lower level when he becomes aware of his limitations or of the jobs available in the category selected (125,391).

vocational satisfaction and dissatisfaction

If the job the adolescent has allows him to play the role he wants to play and if it fills certain needs that he had hoped it would fill, then he will be satisfied; if not, he will be dissatisfied. The extent of his dissatisfaction will depend on how far short of his expectations his job falls (273,393).

Job *dissatisfaction*, thus, is due to a number of causes. The adolescent may have had to take any job he could get when he applied, regardless of whether he wanted a job of that type or not (83). The more important it is to him to earn money, the more apt he is to accept what he can get instead of waiting for a job that is more to his liking. One of the reasons for the large percentage of unemployed adolescents today is that they can afford to be choosy about what jobs they take so long as their parents are able and willing to give them a home and spending money (425). Many adolescents are not subjected at home or in school to the discipline of the adult work world. They find the transition from the overprotective atmosphere of home and school to the impersonal, more demanding atmosphere of the work world hard to adjust to (153,395). The adolescent who, for example, has been accustomed to coming in late to school and being excused if he has a note from his parents resents being reprimanded by his employer or supervisor for coming to work late (30).

The adolescent who has looked forward eagerly to going to work may have a rude awakening when he finds that there is a large discrepancy between what he thought it would mean to work and what it actually is. If his work experience conforms to his expectations, he will be satisfied. But it rarely does; as a result, he is dissatisfied (430). He may, for example, discover that he has less autonomy in his job than he had at home or in school.

As the adolescent is forced, through his work experiences, to become more realistic, his dissatisfaction is likely to increase. This is especially true when he also has unrealistic concepts about his abilities and has aspired to a job too high for him. When he realizes that this is true, he will revise his aspirations downward and settle for a job that he can do. This type of resignation to the inevitable does not make for job satisfaction; instead, it makes the adolescent a psychological square peg in a round hole. As Latham has stated, "Although young people are perfectly capable of performing jobs they find they must take, some dissatisfaction accompanies this change in plans" (227).

The most dissatisfied adolescents are usually those who are school or college dropouts. Furthermore, employers are often more dissatisfied with the kind of work the adolescent dropout does than with that done by other adolescent workers. The very causes that led to dropping out of school— such as boredom, lack of interest and motivation, or unwillingness to work up to capacity—lead to employer dissatisfaction. Furthermore, the adolescent who expected his job to be more to his liking than school was often finds that this is not so. It is not surprising, under such conditions, that school dropouts contribute so heavily to the percentage of adolescents who are unemployed or who can get only occasional jobs. (83,178,425).

VARIATIONS IN SATISFACTION

Younger adolescents are generally less satisfied with their work than older adolescents.

This is due, in part, to the fact that it takes time for the adolescent to adjust to as radically different situations and expectations as he encounters in school and on the job. In part, it is due to the fact that the older adolescent can offer more of value to his employer; the result is that he is given a better job. The adolescent who can get a job that *suits him* and fills his needs will be far better satisfied than one who must take what he can get (27,368,393).

When the adolescent is forced into a job because of *parental pressure*, he will be far less satisfied than if the job is of his own choosing (110,364). The serious effects of parental pressures on job satisfaction have been explained thus by Jersild (193):

> It is, of course, the right of young persons to feel free to aspire to a vocational level above that of their parents, yet since such aspiration cannot always be achieved, unhappiness and a feeling of failure may be in store for those who persist in striving for goals beyond their reach. Overemphasis on occupational prestige can work a hardship on adolescents from families in the upper socioeconomic levels, as well as on other adolescents, for they may enter occupations corresponding to their family background even though they are not as satisfying personally as some other occupations might be.

Adolescents who are *career-oriented* put more value on the intrinsic features of the work than on the occupational rewards. Furthermore, they are willing to do work that will lead eventually to success, regardless of whether or not it is satisfying to them at the moment (193,273). How *significant people* in his life feel about his job has a marked influence on how the adolescent feels about it. If members of his family and friends are proud of his vocation and feel that he is in a prestigeful line of work, he will be far better satisfied with his job than if he knows or suspects that they disapprove of what he is doing. A boy who selects nursing or science as a career, for example, knows that the social attitude toward these vocations is unfavorable. This will predispose him to react unfavorably to his job, not because of the job itself but because he knows people react unfavorably to *any* jobs in these areas (103,163,168, 363).

Adolescents who have received *vocational counseling* generally are better satisfied with their jobs than are those who have received little or no counseling. To be effective in making the adolescent better satisfied with his work, the counseling should include more than casual on-the-job observation to enable the adolescent to know what are the bad as well as the good features of the job he is considering; an opportunity to talk to others who are doing work similar to what he is contemplating so that he can get a firsthand insight into what the job entails; recognition of the fact that working is not the same as going to school and that the worker is expected to assume responsibilities formerly assumed by teachers; realization that one must sacrifice certain personal wants and desires for the satisfaction of earning money; and awareness that job promotion and tenure are dependent upon the individual's achievements. Knowing what is in store for them when they enter the job will go a long way toward preparing adolescents psychologically for it (30,181,364).

EXPRESSIONS OF SATISFACTION AND DISSATISFACTION

The adolescent who likes his job is willing to put more effort into doing the work he is expected to do than is actually required. He is loyal to his employer and proud of his connection. While he may grumble about hours, poor pay, and countless other things, he generally is following the pattern set by his coworkers. Secretly, however, he feels that he has made a good deal for himself and that the experience he is getting will be invaluable as a stepping-stone to his life goal. If he does not win a promotion as soon as he expects, some of his enthusiasm may be temporarily dampened. Or he may accept his disappointment philosophically and hope for an advancement in the near future. This will increase his motivaton to try harder.

Unfortunately, relatively few adoles-

cents have such a favorable attitude toward their work. As is true of their attitudes toward school, their attitudes toward their jobs often deteriorate progressively as they remain on the job. And, as is true of their negative attitudes toward school, adolescents express negative attitudes toward their jobs in several common ways. The most usual way to show their dissatisfaction is to *walk off their jobs*, often without giving the customary notice. So long as there are plenty of jobs available, they can anticipate getting new jobs in a relatively short time. Until then, they can live off their savings or, if they are living at home, they can depend on their families to take care of them until they can get a new job.

A common accompaniment of walking off a job because of dissatisfaction with it is to be more *choosy* about accepting a new job. The adolescent whose experience has been a source of dissatisfaction is often conditioned to dislike *anything* resembling the job he has left. Therefore, he may refuse to consider any new job offer that resembles the old job either in the type of work or in the working conditions (425).

Just as dissatisfaction with school leads to *grumbling*, criticism, and faultfinding, so does dissatisfaction with jobs. This may be done openly, with and to coworkers, or it may be done away from the job, to family members and friends. How much grumbling there will be and how openly it will be expressed will depend in part on how important it is to the individual to have a job and what he thinks his prospects are of getting another one should his grumbling lead to loss of his job. Whether or not his dissatisfaction is verbalized, it inevitably leads to *underachievement*; the dissatisfied worker does less than he is capable of doing (410,425). In discussing the widespread trend among students to work below their capacities, Riesman (324) has emphasized how it affects their future:

> It has become fashionable to speak of one's work or other activities in deprecatory terms and to adopt a pose of relative indifference to the larger goals of an organization. . . . It is as if one had constantly to conduct

psychological warfare against an outside enemy. But, as in any such process, students become to some extent the victims of their own defenses. They come to believe that work cannot really be worth doing for its own sake, whether or not it is done on behalf of a large impersonal organization— a fear of overcommitment to one's work even while one is at the workplace. . . . We see the same attitudes, of course, among the junior echelons now engaged in work. One hears them talk of their benevolent company as a mink-lined rat-trap, or speak of the rat-race, or refer to fights over principle as ruckuses or blow-ups—if somebody cares, he is said to blow his top.

The adolescent who is dissatisfied with his job may not, for practical reasons, give it up or even work below his capacity; instead, he derives satisfaction from *outside activities* which compensate, in part, for the dissatisfaction his job gives him. He may, for example, derive more satisfaction from his home life than from his job. Or he may devote his free time to sports or some other hobby in which he excels (130). Or he may *glamorize some aspects of his work* and in that way compensate for the aspects that fail to give him satisfaction (324). In a study of psychiatric attendants, for example, it was found that many compensated for the dissatisfaction they experienced from the low prestige and status of their jobs by emphasizing the care of patients and the service to others who need help—qualities which are highly valued by the social group (363).

SERIOUSNESS OF DISSATISFACTION

Dissatisfaction is found almost universally among adolescents who work part or full time. It is also a mental set that is fairly well established among those adolescents with little or no work experience. From their friends, and often from their parents, they have acquired an *antiwork attitude* which predisposes them to enter any line of work with the feeling that working is one of the necessary evils of growing up. When predisposed to look upon work unfavorably, the adolescent will react with greater emo-

tional tension than he otherwise would to *anything* in his work that he finds not to his liking. This intensifies an already-existing antiwork attitude.

Furthermore, because dissatisfaction decreases the individual's motivation to do what he is capable of doing, the adolescent whose attitude toward his work is unfavorable will find himself outshadowed in a highly competitive work world by other workers of no greater ability than he. Of equal seriousness is the fact that unfavorable attitudes sooner or later are expressed in some form of *gripes*. The worker whose reactions to his company are consistently unfavorable will soon be spotted by his superiors as a troublemaker. The reputation of being a troublemaker, like the reputation of being a poor sport, is not something an adolescent can easily bury as he goes from one job to another.

The most serious aspect of dissatisfaction is that it is so universal that even those of superior ability feel that it is the thing to do to have a negative attitude toward work. The result is that adolescents who should, in adult life, supply vocational leadership will relinquish this role to those of lesser ability whose drive for achievement is strong enough to compensate for any dissatisfaction they may have. Emphasizing the seriousness of this, Riesman (324) has pointed out:

> *We are witnessing a silent revolution against work on the part even of those relatively privileged groups who have been free to choose their work and to exercise some freedom in the doing of it. This reflects, in part, the fact that much work is meaningless per se, save as a source of income, prestige, and sociability; but it also indicates . . . that people too readily accept their work as it comes, without hope of making it more meaningful.*

suggestions for improving attitudes toward work

The seriousness of unfavorable attitudes toward work emphasizes the importance of taking positive steps to improve them or to prevent them from developing. All attitudes are highly charged with emotions. Negative attitudes are colored by the unpleasant emotions, which are especially strong and very difficult to change. For that reason, it is best to try to *prevent* them. Most unfavorable attitudes trace their origin, either directly or indirectly, to unrealistic vocational aspirations. Therefore, the most positive approach to the problem is to introduce vocational guidance early enough in the adolescent's life that he will lay the foundations of realistic aspirations. Left to chance, the adolescent will develop strong negative and positive attitudes toward different levels of work early in his school life. If he is to be prevented from aspiring to unrealistic vocational goals, the adolescent must learn, while still a child, what his potentials are (454). Equally as important, he must be convinced that these potentials can be realized *only* if he is willing to put forth the effort needed to do so.

He must learn, before aspiring unrealistically high, that the *number of job opportunities decreases* as the prestige associated with jobs increases. This means that there will be stiff competition for jobs at the pinnacle of the vocational pyramid and that the prizes will go to those who are best prepared and have the best potentials for success.

The adolescent must learn to aspire to jobs within his potentials. Even more important, parents must learn not to try to fulfill their own aspirations through their children. Only when parents—and other significant people—can be convinced of the limitations of the adolescent can the problem of unrealistic vocational aspirations be met with any degree of success.

A second important attack on the problem of dissatisfaction with work must likewise come from vocational guidance. This attack should take the form of *painting a realistic picture* of what work means. If, for example, the adolescent is to develop a favorable attitude, he must know what the duties and responsibilities are as well as the pleasures and satisfactions. He must know that a factory job is routine work, that his associates will have limited education and

few cultural interests, that he will be expected to work at a pace set by his foreman to coincide with the pattern of work for the other workers, and that in the eyes of the world, this kind of job has low prestige value. On the positive side, he must become acquainted with the advantages in the form of high wages, fringe benefits, union membership which protects his rights and provides for support at times of unemployment, relatively short work hours, lack of homework, and minimum responsibility.

Far too often, the glamor side of a job is stressed and the realities of work are glossed over. Having an unrealistic picture of what working means inevitably leads to dissatisfaction. The only way to prevent this dissatisfaction from developing is to stress the unfavorable as well as the favorable aspects of a job and to show the adolescent that he must accept the good with the bad.

The third, but by no means least important attack on the problem of job dissatisfaction is to *combat the existing stereotypes* about various types of job. Because different adolescents have different abilities and interests, the satisfaction they derive from a job will depend on whether the vocational area they enter is suited to their abilities and interests. However, if they are prevented from doing so by unfavorable stereotypes of the kind of people who do the work they are best fitted to do or because the work they would like to do is considered sex inappropriate, they will turn their energies into lines of work where the cultural stereotypes are more favorable. Many girls, for example, go into teaching or nursing because this work is considered sex appropriate. Their talents and interests may fit them better for work in science or mathematics, but they are discouraged from entering these fields.

Because stereotypes are rooted in a cultural group, combating them is perhaps the most difficult of all hurdles to cross in vocational guidance. So long as the mass media continue to reinforce the cultural stereotypes the vocational counselor will have little success if he tries to convince an adolescent to go into a line of work suited to his interests and abilities, regardless of the traditional stereotype. Even if he can convince the adolescent to do so, he can be sure that the adolescent will become dissatisfied with his work when he becomes increasingly aware of the unfavorable social attitudes toward him for being in that work. This will counteract any satisfaction that the work itself would normally give him.

III. SOCIAL MOBILITY

The third essential stepping-stone to what almost every American adolescent wants—a better status in his world—is *social mobility*. By changing his geographic status, he hopes to be able to change his social status and become identified with the group he aspires to claim as his friends. No adolescent can change his residence at will; where he lives will depend on where his parents live. However, as most parents are anxious to have their children better themselves, they try to provide them with the opportunities to do so by moving from rural to urban areas, from urban to suburban, and from the poorer to the better neighborhoods in these areas.

In addition, to help their children to rise socially, parents provide them with the clothes, cars, and other status symbols that will identify them with the social groups they hope to become identified with; they encourage them to become active in the extracurricular affairs of their schools, especially those which have high prestige value; they join as many of the "right" community organizations as they can gain admission to; and they try to teach their children the approved mores of the group they aspire to be identified with, thus facilitating their acceptance by the group members (6,13,30, 93,95,201,303).

Motivation to rise above their present status is intensified among both adolescents and their parents by the realization that, regardless of how humble the origin of the family, it is possible to climb the social ladder and to become identified with the people at the top. This does not mean just geographic identification; it means, of even more importance, *social* identification

(243). Until recently, this was not possible. Consequently, the motivation to acquire a higher education and to select a prestigeful occupation was weaker than it is today (182,243). Even more important, the social attitude toward those who are mobile is far more favorable than it formerly was. As Lipset has pointed out, "In America the modest social origins of men of prominence are given widespread publicity, while comparable backgrounds in Europe are more likely to be conveniently forgotten" (242).

MEANING OF SOCIAL MOBILITY

To the layman, "social mobility" means moving upward in the social ladder. To the psychologist and sociologist, it means "changing one's social status" (85). Social and geographic mobility do not necessarily go hand in hand nor is social mobility dependent on geographic mobility, though it is greatly facilitated by it. Geographic mobility facilitates social mobility for the individual by burying the past for him and making it possible for him to start off with a clean slate (95).

There are two types of social mobility, horizontal and vertical. In "horizontal mobility," the individual moves to a similar group in the same social stratum as the one to which he originally belonged. "Vertical mobility" may be up or down, ascending or decending; the individual moves from one social stratum to another, either above or below the stratum with which he was originally identified. The individual who ascends the social ladder is known as a "climber"; the one who decends is known as a "skidder" or a "decliner" (95,262,435). Downward mobility is usually more rapid than upward. It takes several generations, as a rule, to become identified with a higher social-class group and to achieve a secure status in it; downward mobility can be achieved literally overnight (28,208).

Upward social mobility is made possible by a number of factors, the most important of which are occupational success and advancement; marriage to a higher-status person; inheritance of wealth; a fortunate investment of money earned or inherited; transfer of church membership to a higher-status church; purchase of a better home in a better residential district and the use of money to purchase status symbols; and association with people of higher status in community organizations (95,159,294). Fundamental to these factors is education which "provides a primary means by which a person becomes socially mobile in our society" (31). If the breadwinner of the family makes good in his vocation, he will climb the vocational ladder. In doing so, he will have the money to go to a better neighborhood (109). This is often in another community or in another area of the country. As the Hechingers have pointed out, "Large companies pick up their executives and their families like office furniture and ship them and their households across the country" (161). The ages when such moves are most common are shown in Figure 9–17.

Downward social mobility is likewise the result of many different factors, the most important of which are lack of education and training to hold a position equivalent to that of the father; marriage by women to men of lower occupational status than that of their fathers; incompetence in a chosen occupation; transfer of church membership to a lower-status church; immigration from a foreign culture, with loss of status due to acceptance of employment at a lower occupational level; prolonged unemployment; or loss of inherited money (159,294). Divorce or separation may also lead to downward mobility by dividing the family income so that the parent who keeps the children will have less to live on than he had when the family lived together as a unit (161).

VARIATIONS IN SOCIAL MOBILITY

In families where both parents are of the same social class, interest in having their children move up the social ladder is not so great as in families of *divergent* social classes. When the mother comes from a higher social class than the father, ambition to have the children improve their status is usually stronger than when the reverse is true (109,152,262).

Lower-status families are, on the whole,

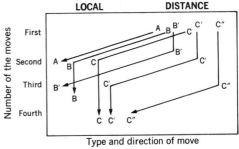

FIGURE 9–17 Patterns of family mobility. (Adapted from V. H. Whitney and C. M. Grigg: Patterns of mobility among a group of families of college students. *Amer. sociol. Rev.*, 1958, **23**, 643–652. Used by permission.)

less satisfied with their status than families of higher status. Therefore, they encourage their children to get ahead by providing them with opportunities for a better education than they themselves had (109,305, 327).

Social mobility varies according to the family's *philosophy of life*. When families feel that present pleasures should be sacrificed for greater future rewards, they instill this principle in their children from earliest childhood. As a result, families that are future-oriented are more interested in social mobility for their children than are present-oriented families (24,31,47,85).

Some adolescents are more *dissatisfied with their present status* than others; as a result, they are more anxious to get ahead. This dissatisfaction may originate either in the home or outside the home (109).

Dissatisfaction may originate in the school when the adolescent finds that the acceptance he is able to achieve is below the level he has aspired to. Popular adolescents are usually more mobile than less popular adolescents, and their families are more anxious and willing to help them (29, 152).

essentials in social mobility

Social mobility does not guarantee social *acceptance*. Because the social groups of adolescents are more tightly knit than children's gangs, gaining acceptance in an adolescent group is even more difficult than gaining acceptance in a children's gang. If the adolescent tries too hard, he will be regarded as pushy. If, on the other hand, he is too passive, he is likely to be overlooked and neglected. Using the *right* amount of aggressiveness may gain for him the acceptance he craves. But it is difficult to determine what is the right amount. This varies with the group and in the same group, according to the need for new members at that particular time. One thing, however, is certain; gaining acceptance in a new group is a slow process. It requires tact and social skill often greater than the average adolescent can be expected to have.

Certain essentials to gaining acceptance on the part of the socially mobile adolescent are described below.

DESIRE OF THE GROUP TO HAVE A NEW MEMBER

Because adolescent social groups are tightly knit units, the members are generally satisfied with one another's company and are not interested in having a stranger join them. A member of the group who feels insecure in his status is likely to look upon any newcomer as a possible threat. He will then oppose any suggestions on the part of the other members to include the newcomer in the group. It sometimes happens that a closely knit group feels the need for "new blood"—for someone who can contribute something new and interesting or prestigeful to the group. Under such conditions, a newcomer has a chance of gaining acceptance if he can create the impression that he can fill this need (1,24,85).

FAVORABLE IMPRESSIONS

The first and, to a lesser extent, the subsequent impressions the adolescent makes on the members of the group will have a marked influence on how seriously they consider him as a potential member. Even if the impression he makes is favorable, they may not be motivated to accept him if they are satisfied with the group membership as it exists. When, however, the group members feel the need for a new member, they will give him a chance to fill the vacancy if their favorable first impressions have convinced them that he might "fit." Under such conditions, he is accepted on a trial basis. Many adolescents who have enjoyed a reasonable degree of social acceptance in their former groups tend to feel that their new status is assured, once they have been invited to join a group for some particular activity. They then make the mistake of becoming too aggressive in their attempts to provide the group with something new. As a result, they lose the foothold they had gained (140,307,456).

DEMONSTRATION OF VALUED QUALITIES

To gain acceptance in an already-established group, the adolescent must demonstrate to the members his possession of some quality or ability they value highly. A boy who has demonstrated his ability in sports that are prestigeful will attract not only the attention but also the favorable attention of the group with which he hopes to become identified. Too marked ability in a prestigeful activity, on the other hand, may be more of a liability than an asset. An outstanding athlete may be regarded as a threat to the status of the leader of the group. To save his status, the leader may influence other members to reject the newcomer (72,73).

ACCEPTANCE OF SIMILAR INTERESTS AND VALUES

The interests and values of adolescent groups reflect those of the larger cultural groups with which their families are identified. Adolescent boys, for example, who have grown up in rural areas put high value on physical strength and being their own bosses; urban boys, by contrast, put higher value on athletic skills and on being associated with large corporations (57).

The socially mobile adolescent must learn and accept the interests and values of the members of the group with which he wants to be identified if he is to have any chance of winning acceptance. He must, for example, dress like the group members and show interest in the recreations they enjoy. And his moral values must conform to those of the group. In sex matters and cheating, for example, he must accept the moral standards of the group and live up to them, even if they are markedly divergent from those of the group with which he was formerly identified (69,87,267,436). When Jewish adolescents want to move in the best crowds, they must learn to achieve in valued areas, such as sports and social activities, not in academic work (73).

Unless the adolescent belongs to the group and has an opportunity to exchange views with group members, he will have no way of knowing what they value and what their interests are except by watching them or by listening to what they say when they are talking among themselves. A girl can, for example, learn what the approved style of dressing and grooming is by observing how the girls of the leading crowd are dressed and groomed (23,82).

WILLINGNESS TO TERMINATE OLD ASSOCIATIONS

If the adolescent has any chance of gaining acceptance in a new group, he must terminate his friendships with and loyalties to the members of the group with which he was formerly identified. He must even try to keep his parents in the background if they have not acquired the behavior patterns and appearance of the parents of the adolescents of the new group.

Breaking off old friendships is never easy and it is always a gamble. If there has been a warm attachment to former friends, it is never easy to terminate this pleasant relationship, especially when there is uncertainty about forming equally satisfying new relationships. Even with relatives, it is usually necessary to terminate relationships if acceptance is to be achieved by the socially mobile adolescent and his family. That is why geographic mobility aids in making social mobility possible (1,82,108, 343).

The adolescent must terminate *all* his old associations and form new ones. As Packard (294) has explained:

If we aspire to rise in the world but fail to take on the coloration of the group we aspire to—by failing to discard our old status symbols, friends, club memberships, values, behavior patterns, and acquiring new ones esteemed by the higher group—our chances of success are diminished. Sociologists have found that our home addresses, our friends, our clubs, our values, and even our church affiliations can prove to be "barriers" if we fail to change them with every attempted move up the ladder.

WILLINGNESS TO WAIT FOR ACCEPTANCE

In their eagerness to become a part of the group, adolescents often become too aggressive; they try to win acceptance by any means they can (346). One of the most common ways is by flaunting status symbols in the faces of the members of the group they want to be identified with. A girl, for example, may try to outdress the other girls; a boy may persuade his parents to give him a bigger and better car than the other boys have, thus hoping to impress them. Another common method by which adolescents try to gain acceptance quickly is by inviting the members of the group they want as friends to a party; they hope, in turn, to be invited to their parties.

Unless adolescents are aware that acceptance in a new group is difficult at any age, but especially so in adolescence, they are apt to judge themselves unfavorably and to develop feelings of personal inadequacy. If the adolescent has all the status symbols other adolescents in his class have and if he has learned the approved patterns of behavior for the group, it is logical that he will assume that lack of acceptance is due to some personal inadequacy (23,85,218). Should this lead to resentments or marked feelings of personal inadequacy, it will soon be shown in his behavior and even in his facial expressions. As a result, he will be less attractive to the group and have even less chance of gaining acceptance.

satisfactions and dissatisfactions of mobility

An analysis of the satisfactions and dissatisfactions reported in various studies of social mobility will show how they affect the adolescent and the effects they have on his personal and social adjustments.

SATISFACTIONS

If the adolescent can achieve the social acceptance he had hoped for in the group he wants to be identified with, he will be satisfied; he will feel that he has bettered himself (299). This satisfaction may, however, be short-lived. Unless his status in the new group is secure, he will experience the dissatisfactions which every fringer experiences. He will live in constant dread of saying or doing something that will weaken the acceptance he has gained. This constant feeling of insecurity about his social status, coming at a time when insecurity is a natural accompaniment of growing up, will counteract the satisfactions that came from moving into a new environment, from having new experiences, and from meeting new people. The downwardly mobile adolescent may, at first, welcome the opportunity to get away from the group to which he formerly belonged but in which he later felt like an outsider because he was unable to have and do what group members did. But his insecurity in the new group will be colored by shame, embarrassment, and resentments arising from conditions which have forced him into a situation he would never choose.

The adolescent, on the other hand, who gains acceptance in the new group will be satisfied with his new environment and his new social contacts. Unfortunately, few adolescents are so fortunate. They may feel that they have bettered themselves materially but they are aware of their deteriorating social relationships. Because material possessions are valueless except as status symbols, satisfaction with new material possessions decreases. The pride that a boy had in his new convertible, for example, disappears when he has no peers to ride with him.

Satisfactions will be greater if the adolescent is prepared for the problems he will encounter with social mobility and if he receives guidance in meeting them. If, for example, he knows that he has a better chance of winning acceptance with "con-genial and disarming aggression" than with pushiness, if he knows what constitutes congenial and disarming aggression, and if he is willing to substitute this for pushiness, he will be satisfied (85,115). Similarly, if he knows that *everyone* meets much the same problems in social mobility that he is facing, he will not develop feelings of personal inadequacy because he has failed to win social acceptance earlier (23,35,58).

DISSATISFACTIONS

The dissatisfactions outnumber the satisfactions of social mobility; they are more ego deflating than the satisfactions are ego inflating. Social mobility means uprooting the individual by breaking the ties he has with the past. The longer he has been a part of one environment, the deeper will be his roots and the stronger his emotional ties with the places and people in that environment. Because social relationships are particularly important to an adolescent, breaking his social roots will prove to be an especially traumatic experience (19,34,275, 339).

The degree of the trauma, however, will vary according to the type of mobility. If it is horizontal mobility, the adolescent can maintain his ties with his former friends by visits, by telephone calls, or by letter writing. In upward mobility, if he is to better himself, he must cut away from those who could be handicaps to him in his climb up the ladder of social success. The downwardly mobile adolescent will be too embarrassed and ashamed of his new status to try to keep alive his old friendships. For him, the uprooting will be traumatic because it will be colored by shame and humiliation (19).

Another common source of dissatisfaction comes from the anxiety which always accompanies "status-consciousness"—trying to keep up with the Joneses. The more anxious an adolescent is to win acceptance by a higher social group, the more status-conscious he becomes. Blalock (33) has pointed out that a highly status-conscious person is one who:

> . . . . adheres religiously to middle-class values. . . . Not only is he willing to sacri-

fice interesting work for a job that pays, but he is very much aware of the kinds of behavior required in playing the "social game." He is careful to learn the proper etiquette and to join the right organizations. In his interpersonal relations he associates with those persons who are in a position to help him advance toward the top, shunning those who are beneath him in status. . . . Unless he has obviously already "arrived," he is careful to engage in the proper amount of conspicuous consumption, trying to keep up appearances without being overly ostentatious. . . . He takes pride in knowing members of the elite, either personally or vicariously. In short, the extremely status-conscious person lives and acts as though status considerations are of the utmost importance. They are to him the essence of social interaction.

There are two groups of adolescents for whom social mobility is especially difficult. Adolescents from *minority groups* have a marginal status in any situation. Moving to a new group means another struggle to win acceptance and another situation in which they will experience prolonged rejection (35,73). For *girls*, social mobility is more difficult than for boys because girls' social groups are more tightly knit than boys'. Furthermore, because popularity has greater prestige value for girls than for boys, lack of social acceptance is apt to be more ego deflating for girls than for boys (73, 219).

Problems That Intensify Dissatisfaction For all adolescents, uprooting brings with it many problems, all of which are sources of dissatisfaction. First, there is the problem of *gaps in school or college work*. This may be due in part to gaps in knowledge stemming from changes in educational programs and in part to the emotional tension caused by adjustments to a new pattern of living. This may lead to *family* friction if parents feel that good academic work is essential to acceptance in the "right" crowd. It is certain to require more time for studying than formerly, thus cutting down on the time available for extracurricular activities—one

of the adolescent's major ways of gaining social acceptance (299,392,396).

The second problem encountered by the socially mobile adolescent is caused by ignorance of the *interests and values of the new peer group*. Because friendships can be established only when there are similarities in interests and values, the mobile adolescent must create the impression that he "speaks the same language" as those with whom he hopes to become identified (28, 85,283,435). A lower-class girl, for example, may overdress for school parties because her former friends regarded school parties as a time to dress up. In her new school, she may discover that informal clothes are considered correct (294). Similarly, an adolescent from a rural background may feel that a high school diploma is all that is important for success in life only to discover that the majority of students in an urban school regard anyone without a college education as inferior (226,287,303,321).

Feelings of uncertainty about what to do and how to do it lead to the third problem that enhances the dissatisfaction of mobile adolescents—a *suspicious attitude* about how their peers will treat them or what they will say to them or about them behind their backs. This leads to constant anxiety, which is expressed in overconformity and to a hypercritical attitude toward family members who, they believe, might disgrace them in the eyes of the peer group (85,95,392,418).

The fourth and most serious source of dissatisfaction is a period of *friendlessness* (359). If the adolescent has been cut off from the old friendships he enjoyed and has no substitutes to replace them, he is forced into a position where he must spend his leisure time alone, engaging in recreations which have never had much appeal for him (82,108,109). In addition to being cut off from social relationships with his peers, he may also be cut off from relationships with relatives. He, for example, had the pleasures of family gatherings at holiday times; these now have become a thing of the past (38, 244,245).

Almost as serious as friendlessness is the fifth source of dissatisfaction from social mobility—more or less constant *friction with members of the immediate family* (95). This friction may arise because the adolescent is ashamed of his parents and feels that they are a handicap to his social acceptance. It may arise because his parents are constantly prodding him to do the things they believe will bring him social acceptance. Or it may stem from a clash of values and interests between the adolescent and members of his family.

Even if the adolescent is able to gain some acceptance, it does not guarantee satisfaction. His position in the new group is too precarious to be comfortable and he feels too unlike his new associates to be at home with them. He hesitates, for example, to confide his problems to them as he did to his former chums, fearful that by doing so he will create an unfavorable impression which may jeopardize what acceptance he has achieved. He may be uncomfortable about doing things he formerly disapproved of, even though he has the permission or even the urging of his parents to do what the others do.

Thus, it is apparent that social mobility does not necessarily lead to satisfaction or happiness. Because many adolescents find that the doors are shut to them, they are far less contented than those who gain a marginal status in the group. They continue to hope that, in time, they will achieve the goal they have dreamed of and worked so hard to reach. If the doors are not opened, resentments added to anxiety may become so intense that the individual, as an adult, will wonder if it has been worth the sacrifices he made. Many suicides or attempts at suicide have been reported among upwardly mobile adults who have achieved the economic status they wanted in their communities but have failed to win the acceptance of others with similar status (50, 129,175,311).

Unquestionably, the most dissatisfied of all adolescents is the downwardly mobile one. While gaining acceptance may prove to be easier for him than for the upwardly mobile, he does not want acceptance by those whom he regards as his inferiors. If his downward slide has come about through

no fault of his but because of family circumstances over which he has no control, he will develop feelings of martyrdom which will distort his outlook on life and kill any motivation he may have had earlier to rise above his present status. For him, the discrepancy between his earlier aspirations and his present status will be so great that he will, in time, look for methods of escape, perhaps as a chronic alcoholic, a drug addict, or through suicide (50,95,129,438).

In conclusion, then, it is apparent that many adolescents do not find the pot of gold at the end of the rainbow they have been pursuing for so long and which they confidently had expected to find. While it is true that many will gain some acceptance in time, it is equally true that they may have a long wait for this. Even when they achieve it, they may not find it as rewarding as they had anticipated. The dissatisfactions and unhappiness stemming from social mobility, when added to the other sources of dissatisfaction and unhappiness that are inevitable accompaniments of the transition from childhood to adulthood in our culture, make adolescence one of the unhappy ages of growing up. Normally adolescents become happier as adolescence progresses and as they become adjusted to their new status in the social group. Whether this will hold true for adolescents who are socially mobile will depend largely on how realistically they have faced the problems that social mobility always gives rise to and on how willing they are to wait for the ultimate rewards.

BIBLIOGRAPHY

1 ABERGGLEN, J. C.: Personality factors in social mobility: a study of occupationally mobile businessmen. *Genet. Psychol. Monogr.*, 1958, **58**, 101–159.

2 ABRAMOVITZ, M.: Growing up in an affluent society. In E. Ginzberg (ed.), *The nation's children: I. The family and social change.* New York: Columbia, 1960, pp. 158–169.

3 ADAMS, A. A.: Identifying socially malad-

justed school children. *Genet. Psychol. Monogr.*, 1960, **61**, 3–36.

4 ALLEN, E. A.: Attitudes of children and adolescents in school. *Educ. Res.*, 1960, **3**, 65–80.

5 AMATORA, SISTER M.: Similarity in teacher and pupil personality. *J. Psychol.*, 1954, **37**, 45–50.

6 AMATORA, SISTER M.: Free expression of adolescents' interests. *Genet. Psychol. Monogr.*, 1957, **55**, 173–219.

7 AMATORA, SISTER M.: School interests of early adolescents. *J. genet. Psychol.*, 1961, **98**, 133–145.

8 ANASTASI, A.: Differentiating effect of intelligence and social status. *Eugen. Quart.*, 1959, **6**, 84–91.

9 ANDERSON, C. A.: A skeptical note on the relation of vertical mobility to education. *Amer. J. Sociol.*, 1961, **66**, 560–570.

10 ANDERSON, H. H., G. L. ANDERSON, I. H. COHEN, and F. D. NUTT: Image of the teacher by adolescents in four countries—Germany, England, Mexico, and the United States. *J. soc. Psychol.*, 1959, **50**, 47–55.

11 ANDERSON, L. W.: Teacher morale and student achievement. *J. educ. Res.*, 1953, **46**, 693–698.

12 ANDERSON, W. F.: The advantages and disadvantages of teaching as judged by parents of differing socioeconomic status. *J. educ. Sociol.*, 1955, **29**, 119–125.

13 ANSPACH, K.: Clothing selection and the mobility concept. *J. Home Econ.*, 1961, **53**, 428–430.

14 ARNHOLTER, E. G.: School persistence and personality factors. *Personnel Guid. J.*, 1956, **35**, 107–109.

15 ASTIN, A. W.: Personal and environmental factors associated with college dropouts among high aptitude students. *J. educ. Psychol.*, 1964, **55**, 219–227.

16 AUSUBEL, D. P.: Ego development among segregated Negro children. *Ment. Hyg., N.Y.*, 1958, **42**, 362–369.

17 AUSUBEL, D. P., H. M. SCHIFF, and M. F. ZELENY: "Real-life" measures of level of academic and vocational aspiration in adolescents: relation to laboratory measures and to adjustment. *Child Develpm.*, 1953, **24**, 155–168.

18 BACH, M. C.: Factors related to student participation in campus social organizations. *J. soc. Psychol.*, 1961, **54**, 337–348.

19 BACHELIS, W. D., and J. PIERCE-JONES: Adolescents' social mobility orientation in relation to F-Scale behavior. *Psychol. Rep.*, 1964, **14**, 75–79.

20 BATTLE, H. J.: Relations between personal values and scholastic achievement. *J. exp. Educ.*, 1957, **26**, 27–41.

21 BEARDSLEE, D. G., and D. D. O'DOWD: The college student's image of the scientist. *Science*, 1961, **133**, 997–1001.

22 BECKER, H. S., and J. CARPER: The elements of identification with an occupation. *Amer. sociol. Rev.*, 1956, **21**, 341–348.

23 BEILIN, H.: The pattern of postponability and its relation to social class mobility. *J. soc. Psychol.*, 1956, **44**, 33–48.

24 BEILIN, H., and K. V. BERGIN: The social mobility of a limited urban group and some implications for counseling. *Personnel Guid. J.*, 1956, **34**, 544–552.

25 BELL, H. M.: Ego-involvement in occupational decisions. *Personnel Guid. J.*, 1960, **38**, 732–736.

26 BENDIG, A. W., and P. H. HOUNTRAS: College student stereotypes of the personality traits of research scientists. *J. educ. Psychol.*, 1958, **49**, 309–314.

27 BENDIG, A. W., and E. L. STILLMAN: Dimensions of job incentives among college students. *J. appl. Psychol.*, 1958, **42**, 367–371.

28 BENDIX, R., and F. W. HOWTON: Social mobility and the American business elite. *Brit. J. Sociol.*, 1957, **8**, 357–369; 1958, **9**, 1–14.

29 BERKOWITZ, L., and J. R. MACAULAY: Some effects of differences in status level and status stability. *Hum. Relat.*, 1961, **14**, 135–148.

30 BERNARD, J.: Teen-age culture: an overview. *Ann. Amer. Acad. pol. soc. Sci.*, 1961, **338**, 1–12.

31 BIERI, J., R. LOBECK, and H. PLOTNICK: Psychosocial factors in differential social mobility. *J. soc. Psychol.*, 1962, **58**, 183–200.

32 BLAINE, G. B.: Moral questions stir campuses. *The New York Times*, Jan. 16, 1964.

33 BLALOCK, H. M.: Status consciousness: a dimensional analysis. *Soc. Forces*, 1959, **37**, 243–248.

34 BLAU, P. M.: Social mobility and interpersonal relationships. *Amer. sociol. Rev.*, 1956, **21**, 290–295.

35 BLAU, P. M.: Occupational bias and mobility. *Amer. Sociol. Rev.*, 1957, **22**, 392–399.

36 BLOOMGARDEN, L.: A current evaluation of the effect of discrimination and self-segregation on Jewish occupational choice. *J. Jewish communal Serv.*, 1962, **39**, 91–97.

37 BLUM, S. H.: The desire for security: an element in the vocational choice of college men. *J. educ. Psychol.*, 1961, **52**, 317–321.

38 BLUMBERG, L., and R. R. BELL: Urban migration and kinship ties. *Soc. Probl.*, 1959, **6**, 328–333.

39 BOGEN, I.: Pupil-teacher rapport and the teacher's awareness of status structure within the group. *J. educ. Sociol.*, 1954, **28**, 104–114.

40 BOND, J. A.: Analysis of factors affecting scholarship of high school pupils. *J. educ. Res.*, 1952, **46**, 1–16.

41 BONSALL, M., and B. STEFFLRE: The temperament of gifted children. *Calif. J. educ. Res.*, 1955, **6**, 162–164.

42 BORDIN, E. S., and E. H. WILSON: Change of interest as a function of shift in curriculum orientation. *Educ. psychol. Measmt.*, 1953, **13**, 297–307.

43 BORDUA, J. D.: Educational aspirations and parental stress on college. *Soc. Forces*, 1960, **38**, 262–269.

44 BORG, W. R.: The effect of personality and contact upon a personality stereotype. *J. educ. Res.*, 1955, **49**, 289–294.

45 BORING, E. G.: The woman problem. *Amer. Psychologist*, 1951, **6**, 679–692.

46 BOROFF, D.: American fetish—the college degree. *The New York Times*, Feb. 14, 1960.

47 BOROFF, D.: Portrait of a mobile nation. *The New York Times*, Aug. 26, 1962.

48 BOSSARD, J. H. S., and E. S. BOLL: *The sociology of child development*. 3d ed. New York: Harper & Row, 1960.

49 BOYER, W. H.: A survey of the attitudes, opinions, and objectives of high school students in the Milwaukee area. *J. educ. Sociol.*, 1959, **32**, 344–348.

50 BREED, W.: Occupational mobility and suicide among white males. *Amer. sociol. Rev.*, 1963, **28**, 179–188.

51 BROWN, F. G.: Identifying college dropouts with the Minnesota Counseling Inventory. *Personnel Guid. J.*, 1961, **39**, 280–282.

52 BUCHNER, L. J.: Personality repair through reading improvement. *Education*, 1957, **78**, 107–113.

53 BUDER, L.: Parents warned on "right" school. *The New York Times*, Sept. 25, 1962.

54 BÜHLER, C.: School as a phase of human life. *Education*, 1952, **73**, 219–222.

55 BURCHINAL, L. G.: Social status, measured intelligence, achievement, and personality adjustment of rural Iowa girls. *Sociometry*, 1959, **22**, 75–80.

56 BURCHINAL, L. G.: Differences in educational and occupational aspirations of farm, small-town, and city boys. *Rural Sociol.*, 1961, **26**, 107–121.

57 BURCHINAL, L. G., and J. D. COWHIG: Rural youth in an urban society. *Children*, 1963, **10**, 167–172.

58 BURCHINAL, L. G., B. GARDNER, and G. R. HAWKES: Children's personality adjustment and the socioeconomic status of their families. *J. genet. Psychol.*, 1958, **92**, 149–159.

59 BURGESS, E.: Personality factors of over- and underachievers in engineering. *J. educ. Psychol.*, 1956, **47**, 89–99.

60 CAREW, D. K.: A comparison of activities, social acceptance and scholastic achievements of men students. *Personnel Guid. J.*, 1957, **36**, 121–124.

61 CARLSON, R. O.: Variation and myth in the social status of teachers. *J. educ. Sociol.*, 1961, **35**, 104–118.

62 CARPER, J. W., and H. S. BECKER: Adjustments to conflicting expectations in the development of identification with an occupation. *Soc. Forces*, 1957, **36**, 51–56.

63 CHANSKY, N. M.: How students see their teacher. *Ment. Hyg.*, N.Y., 1958, **42**, 118–120.

64 CHOI, E. H.: Father-daughter relationships in school phobia. *Smith Coll. Stud. soc. Wk.*, 1961, **31**, 152–178.

65 CHOWN, S. M.: Personality factors in the formation of occupational choice. *Brit. J. educ. Psychol.*, 1959, **29**, 23–33.

66 CHRISTAL, R. E., and J. H. WARD: Predicting leadership ratings from high school activities. *J. educ. Psychol.*, 1959, **50**, 105–110.

67 CHRISTENSEN, H. T.: Lifetime family and occupational role projections of high school students. *Marriage fam. Living*, 1961, **23**, 181–183.

68 CHRISTIANSEN, J. R., J. W. PAYNE, and K. J. BROWN: Church participation and college desires of rural youth in Utah. *Rural Sociol.*, 1963, **28**, 176–185.

69 CLARKE, A. C.: The use of leisure and its relation to levels of occupational prestige. *Amer. sociol. Rev.*, 1956, **21**, 301–307.

70 COLEMAN, J. S.: Academic achievement and the structure of competition. *Harv. educ. Rev.*, 1959, **29**, 330–351.

71 COLEMAN, J. S.: The adolescent subculture and academic achievement. *Amer. J. Sociol.*, 1960, **65**, 337–347.

72 COLEMAN, J. S.: Athletics in high school. *Ann. Amer. Acad. pol. soc. Sci.*, 1961, **338**, 33–43.

73 COLEMAN, J. S.: *The adolescent society.* New York: Free Press, 1961.

74 COLEMAN, J. S.: Teen-agers and their crowd. *PTA Magazine*, 1962, **56**, no. 7, 4–7.

75 CONANT, J. B.: *The American high school today.* New York: McGraw-Hill, 1959.

76 COOK, E. S.: An analysis of factors related to withdrawal from high school prior to graduation. *J. educ. Res.*, 1956, **50**, 191–196.

77 COSTER, J. K.: Attitudes toward school of high school pupils from three income levels. *J. educ. Psychol.*, 1958, **49**, 61–66.

78 COSTER, J. K.: Some characteristics of high school pupils from three income groups. *J. educ. Psychol.*, 1959, **50**, 55–62.

79 CRONBACH, L. J.: *Educational psychology.* 2d ed. New York: Harcourt, Brace & World, 1963.

80 CROW, L. D., and A. CROW: *Adolescent development and adjustment.* 2d ed. New York: McGraw-Hill, 1965.

81 CURRY, R. L.: Certain characteristics of under-achievers and over-achievers. *Peabody J. Educ.*, 1961, **39**, 41–45.

82 CURTIS, R. F.: Occupational mobility and urban social life. *Amer. J. Sociol.*, 1959, **65**, 296–298.

83 DANSEREAU, H. K.: Work and the teen-ager. *Ann. Amer. Acad. pol. soc. Sci.*, 1961, **338**, 44–52.

84 DAVIE, J. S.: Social class factors and school attendance. *Harv. educ. Rev.*, 1953, **23**, 175–185.

85 DAVIS, A.: Personality and social mobility. *School Review*, 1957, **65**, 134–143.

86 DAVIS, D. A.: An experimental study of potential dropouts. *Personnel Guid. J.*, 1962, **40**, 799–802.

87 DAVIS, J. A.: Status symbols and the measurement of status perception. *Sociometry*, 1956, **19**, 154–165.

88 DAVIS, J. A.: Correlates of sociometric status among peers. *J. educ. Res.*, 1957, **50**, 561–569.

89 DEMOS, G. M.: Attitudes of student ethnic groups on issues related to education. *Calif. J. educ. Res.*, 1960, **11**, 204–206.

90 DEMOS, G. D.: Attitudes of Mexican-American and Anglo-American groups toward education. *J. soc. Psychol.*, 1962, **57**, 249–256.

91 DIENER, C. L.: Similarities and differences between over-achieving and under-achieving students. *Personnel Guid. J.*, 1959, **38**, 396–400.

92 DIENSTFREY, H.: Doctors, lawyers, and other TV heroes. *Commentary*, 1963, **35**, 519–524.

93 DODSON, D. W.: Reassessing values in the present age. *J. educ. Sociol.*, 1958, **32**, 49–61.

94 DOUVAN, E.: Independence and identity in adolescence. *Children*, 1957, **4**, 186–190.

95 DOUVAN, E., and J. ADELSON: The psychodynamics of social mobility in adolescent boys. *J. abnorm. soc. Psychol.*, 1958, **56**, 31–44.

96 DRESSEL, P. L.: Interests: stable or unstable. *J. educ. Res.*, 1954, **48**, 95–102.

97 DRESSEL, P. L., and J. M. GRABOW: The gifted evaluate their high school experience. *Except. Children*, 1958, **24**, 394–396.

98 DREWS, E. M., and J. E. TEAHAN: Parental attitudes and academic achievement. *J. clin. Psychol.*, 1957, **13**, 328–332.

99 DUFF, O. L., and L. SIEGEL: Biographical factors associated with academic over- and underachievement. *J. educ. Psychol.*, 1960, **51**, 43–46.

100 DULLES, R. J.: The myth of underachievement. *J. educ. Sociol.*, 1961, **35**, 121–122.

101 DUVALL, E. M.: *Family development.* Philadelphia: Lippincott, 1957.

102 DYE, M. G.: Attitudes of gifted children toward school. *Educ. Admin. Supervis.*, 1956, **42**, 301–308.

103 DYER, W. G.: A comparison of families of high and low job satisfaction. *Marriage fam. Living*, 1956, **18**, 58–60.

104 DYER, W. G.: Parental influence on the job attitudes of children from two occupational strata. *Sociol. soc. Res.*, 1958, **42**, 203–206.

105 DYNES, R. R., A. C. CLARKE, and S. DINITZ: Levels of occupational aspiration: some aspects of family experience as a variable. *Amer. sociol. Rev.*, 1956, **21**, 212–215.

106 ECKLAND, B. K.: Social class and college graduation: some misconceptions corrected. *Amer. J. Sociol.*, 1964, **70**, 36–50.

107 ELKINS, D.: Some factors related to the choice-status of ninety eighth-grade children in a school society. *Genet. Psychol. Monogr.*, 1958, **58**, 207–272.

108 ELLIS, E.: Some psychological correlates of upward social mobility among unmarried career women. *Amer. sociol. Rev.*, 1952, **17**, 558–563.

109 ELLIS, R. A., and W. C. LANE: Structural supports for upward mobility. *Amer. sociol. Rev.*, 1963, **28**, 743–756.

110 EMPEY, L. T.: Social class and occupational aspiration: a comparison of absolute and relative measurement. *Amer. sociol. Rev.*, 1956, **21**, 703–709.

111 EMPEY, L. T.: Role expectations of young women regarding marriage and a career. *Marriage fam. Living*, 1958, **20**, 152–155.

112 EVANS, K. M.: A study of attitude toward teaching as a career. *Brit. J. educ. Psychol.*, 1952, **22**, 63–69.

113 EWALD, M. O.: The emotionally disturbed child in the classroom. *Education*, 1954, **76**, 69–72.

114 FAIR, G.: A comprehensive high school studies learning. *Educ. Leadership*, 1959, **16**, 351–354.

115 FALK, G. J.: The role of social class differences and horizontal mobility in the etiology of aggression. *J. educ. Sociol.*, 1959, **33**, 1–10.

116 FARIES, M., and J. PERRY: Academic acceleration and the college student. *Personnel Guid. J.*, 1960, **38**, 563–566.

117 FEINBERG, M. R.: Relation of background experience to social acceptance. *J. abnorm. soc. Psychol.*, 1953, **48**, 206–214.

118 FERNBERGER, S. W.: Persistence of stereotype concerning sex differences. *J. abnorm. soc. Psychol.*, 1948, **43**, 97–101.

119 FINE, B.: Jobs that keep students in college. *The New York Times*, Feb. 21, 1954.

120 FINK, M. B.: Self concept as it relates to academic underachievement. *Calif. J. educ. Res.*, 1962, **13**, 57–62.

121 FITT, A. B.: An experimental study of children's attitude to school in Auckland, N.Z. *Brit. J. educ. Psychol.*, 1956, **26**, 25–30.

122 FOLKMAN, J. D.: Stressful and supportive interaction. *Marriage fam. Living*, 1956, **18**, 102–106.

123 FORD, T. R.: Social factors affecting academic performance: further evidence. *School Review*, 1957, **65**, 415–422.

124 FORER, B. R.: Personality factors in occupational choice. *Educ. psychol. Measmt.*, 1953, **13**, 361–366.

125 FORREST, A. L.: Persistence of vocational choice of the merit scholarship winners. *Personnel Guid. J.*, 1961, **39**, 466–471.

126 FOSMIRE, F. R.: The role of ego defense in academic reputation. *J. soc. Psychol.*, 1959, **49**, 41–45.

127 FOX, W. H.: The stability of measured interests. *J. educ. Res.*, 1947, **41**, 305–310.

128 FRANKEL, E.: A comparative study of achieving and underachieving high school boys of high intellectual ability. *J. educ. Res.*, 1960, **53**, 172–180.

129 FREEDMAN, L. Z., and A. DE B. HOLLINGSHEAD: Neurosis and social class. *Amer. J. Psychiat.*, 1957, **113**, 769–775.

130 FRIEDLANDER, F.: Underlying sources of job satisfaction. *J. appl. Psychol.*, 1963, **47**, 246–250.

131 GALLUP, G., and E. HILL: Youth: the cool generation. *Saturday Evening Post*, Dec. 22–30, 1961, pp. 146–148.

132 GEBHART, G. G., and D. P. HOYT: Personality needs of under- and overachieving freshmen. *J. appl. Psychol.*, 1958, **42**, 125–128.

133 GETZELS, J. W., and P. W. JACKSON: Occupational choice and cognitive functioning: career aspirations of highly intelligent and of highly creative adolescents. *J. abnorm. soc. Psychol.*, 1960, **61**, 119–123.

134 GINZBERG, E.: Toward a theory of occupational choice. *Occupations*, 1952, **30**, 490–494.

135 GLICK, P. C.: The life cycle of the family. *Marriage fam. Living*, 1955, **17**, 3–9.

136 GLICK, P. C., and H. P. MILLER: Educational level and potential income. *Amer. sociol. Rev.*, 1956, **21**, 307–312.

137 GOLBURGH, S. J., and J. F. PENNEY: A note on counseling underachieving college students. *J. counsel. Psychol.*, 1962, **9**, 133–138.

138 GOLDSMITH, J. M., H. KROHN, R. OCHROCH, and N. KAGAN: Changing the delinquent's concept of school. *Amer. J. Orthopsychiat.*, 1959, **29**, 249–265.

139 GORDON, E. M., and S. B. SARASON: The relationship between "test anxiety" and "other anxieties." *J. Pers.*, 1954, **23**, 317–323.

140 GOUGH, H. G.: On making a good impression. *J. educ. Res.*, 1952, **46**, 33–42.

141 GOUGH, H. G.: What determines the academic achievement of high school students. *J. educ. Res.*, 1953, **46**, 321–331.

142 GRACE, H. A., and N. L. BOOTH: Is the "gifted" child a social isolate? *Peabody J. Educ.*, 1958, **35**, 195–196.

143 GREEN, D. A.: A study of talented high-school drop-outs. *Voc. Guid. Quart.*, 1962, **10**, 171–172.

144 GRIGG, C. M., and R. MIDDLETON: Community of orientation and occupational aspirations of ninth grade students. *Soc. Forces*, 1960, **38**, 303–308.

145 GRONLUND, N. E.: Relationship between sociometric status of pupils and teachers' preferences for or against having them in class. *Sociometry*, 1953, **16**, 142–150.

146 GRONLUND, N. E., and W. S. HOLMLUND: The value of elementary school sociometric status scores for predicting pupils' adjustment in high school. *Educ. Admin. Supervis.*, 1958, **44**, 255–260.

147 GRUNES, W. F.: On perception of occupations. *Personnel Guid. J.*, 1956, **34**, 276–279.

148 HADLEY, S. T.: A school mark—fact or fancy? *Educ. Admin. Supervis.*, 1954, **40**, 305–312.

149 HALL, R. L., and B. WILLERMAN: The educational influence of dormitory roommates. *Sociometry*, 1963, **26**, 294–318.

150 HALLER, A. O., and C. E. BUTTERWORTH: Peer influences on levels of occupational and educational aspiration. *Soc. Forces*, 1960, **38**, 289–295.

151 HAND, H. C.: Girls' choices of high school subjects. *J. Home Econ.*, 1960, **52**, 659–661.

152 HANDEL, G., and R. D. HESS: The family as an emotional organization. *Marriage fam. Living*, 1956, **18**, 99–101.

153 HARRIS, D. B.: Work and the adolescent: transition to maturity. *Teach. Coll. Rec.*, 1961, **63**, 146–153.

154 HARTLEY, R. E.: Norm compatability, norm preference, and the acceptance of a new reference group. *J. soc. Psychol.*, 1960, **52**, 87–95.

155 HAUSER, P. M.: More from the census of 1960. *Scient. American*, 1962, **207**, no. 4, 30–37.

156 HAVIGHURST, R. J.: Social class and basic personality structure. *Sociol. soc. Res.*, 1952, **36**, 355–363.

157 HAVIGHURST, R. J.: Conditions productive of superior children. *Teach. Coll. Rec.*, 1961, **62**, 524–531.

158 HAVIGHURST, R. J.: Social-class influences on American education. *60th Yearb. Nat. Soc. Stud. Educ.*, 1961, part 2, 120–143.

159 HAVIGHURST, R. J., and R. ALBRECHT: *Older people.* New York: Longmans, 1953.

160 HECHINGER, F. M.: On cheating. *The New York Times*, Jan. 31, 1965.

161 HECHINGER, G., and F. M. HECHINGER: *Teen-age tyranny.* New York: Morrow, 1963.

162 HEIST, P., T. R. MC CONNELL, F. MALSTER, and P. WILLIAMS: Personality and scholarship. *Science*, 1961, **133**, 362–367.

163 HELPER, M. M., and L. L. MC QUITTY: Some relations of personality integration to occupational interests. *J. soc. Psychol.*, 1953, **38**, 219–231.

164 HEMMERLING, R. L., and H. HURST: The effects of leisure time activities on scholastic achievement. *Calif. J. educ. Res.*, 1961, **12**, 86–90.

165 HERRIOTT, R. E.: Some social determinants of educational aspiration. *Harv. educ. Rev.*, 1963, **33**, 157–177.

166 HERSOV, L. A.: Persistent non-attendance at school. *J. child Psychol. Psychiat.*, 1960, **1**, 130–136.

167 HERSOV, L. A.: Refusal to go to school. *J. child Psychol. Psychiat.*, 1960, **1**, 137–145.

168 HIGGIN, G.: The effect of reference group functions on social status ratings. *Brit. J. Psychol.*, 1954, **45**, 88–93.

169 HIMMELWEIT, H. T., A. H. HALSEY, and A. N. OPPENHEIM: The views of adolescence on some aspects of the social class structure. *Brit. J. Sociol.*, 1952, **3**, 148–172.

170 HIRSCH, W.: The image of the scientist in

science fiction: a content analysis. *Amer. J. Sociol.*, 1958, **63**, 506–512.

171 HODGE, R. W., P. M. SIEGEL, and P. H. ROSSI: Occupational prestige in the United States, 1925–1963. *Amer. J. Sociol.*, 1964, **70**, 286–302.

172 HOLDEN, G. S.: Scholastic aptitude and the relative persistence of vocational choice. *Personnel Guid. J.*, 1961, **40**, 36–41.

173 HOLLAND, J. L.: A theory of vocational choice. *J. counsel. Psychol.*, 1959, **6**, 35–44.

174 HOLLAND, J. C.: Creative and academic performance among talented adolescents. *J. educ. Psychol.*, 1961, **52**, 136–147.

175 HOLLINGSHEAD, A. DE B., R. ELLIS, and E. KIRBY: Social mobility and mental illness. *Amer. sociol. Rev.*, 1954, **19**, 577–584.

176 HOLMES, D.: An investigation of student attitudes which may be related to leaving college. *J. educ. Res.*, 1958, **52**, 17–21.

177 HORRALL, B. M.: Academic performance and personality adjustment of highly intelligent college students. *Genet. Psychol. Monogr.*, 1957, **55**, 3–83.

178 HUNTER, M.: War on poverty will focus on youth. *The New York Times*, Mar. 15, 1964.

179 HUTSON, P. W.: Vocational choices, 1930 and 1961. *Voc. Guid. Quart.*, 1962, **10**, 218–222.

180 INKELES, A., and P. H. ROSSI: National comparisons of occupational prestige. *Amer. J. Sociol.*, 1956, **61**, 329–339.

181 INLOW, G. M.: Job satisfaction of liberal arts graduates. *J. appl. Psychol.*, 1951, **35**, 175–181.

182 JACKSON, E. F., and H. J. CROCKETT: Occupational mobility in the United States: a point estimate and trend comparison. *Amer. sociol. Rev.*, 1964, **29**, 5–15.

183 JACKSON, J.: A statistical analysis of an alumni survey. *J. genet. Psychol.*, 1953, **82**, 215–234.

184 JACKSON, P. W., and P. W. GETZELS: Psychological health and classroom functioning: a study of dissatisfaction with school during adolescence. *J. educ. Psychol.*, 1959, **50**, 295–300.

185 JACOB, P. E.: *Changing values in college: an exploratory study of the impact of college teaching.* New York: Harper & Row, 1957.

186 JACOBI, J. E., and S. G. WALTERS: Social status and consumer choice. *Soc. Forces*, 1958, **36**, 209–214.

187 JACOBS, R.: Stability of interests at the secondary school level. *Educ. Res. Bull.*, 1949, **52**, 83–87.

188 JAHODA, G.: Job attitudes and job choice among secondary modern school leavers. *Occup. Psychol., London*, 1952, **26**, 125–140, 206–224.

189 JAHODA, G.: Social class attitudes and levels of occupational aspiration in secondary modern school leavers. *Brit. J. Psychol.*, 1953, **44**, 95–107.

190 JARRETT, W. H., and A. O. HALLER: Situational and personal antecedents of incipient alienation: an exploratory study. *Genet. Psychol. Monogr.*, 1964, **69**, 151–191.

191 JENNINGS, F. G.: Adolescents, aspirations, and the older generation. *Teach. Coll. Rec.*, 1964, **65**, 335–341.

192 JENSON, P. G., and W. K. KIRCHNER: A national answer to the question, "Do sons follow their fathers' occupations?" *J. appl. Psychol.*, 1955, **39**, 419–421.

193 JERSILD, A. T.: *The psychology of adolescence.* 2d ed. New York: Macmillan, 1963.

194 JERSILD, A. T., and R. J. TASCH: *Children's interests and what they suggest for education.* New York: Teachers College, Columbia University, 1949.

195 JERVIS, F. M., and R. G. CONDON: Student and faculty perceptions of educational values. *Amer. Psychologist*, 1958, **13**, 464–466.

196 JEX, F. B., and R. M. MERRILL: A study in persistence: withdrawal and graduation rates at the University of Utah. *Personnel Guid. J.*, 1962, **40**, 762–768.

197 JOHNSON, A. H.: The responses of high school seniors to a set of structured situations concerning teaching as a career. *J. exp. Educ.*, 1958, **26**, 263–314.

198 JOHNSON, E. E.: Student ratings of popularity and scholastic ability of their peers and actual scholastic performances of those peers. *J. soc. Psychol.*, 1958, **47**, 127–132.

199 JONES, E. S.: The probation student: what he is like and what can be done about it. *J. educ. Res.*, 1955, **49**, 93–102.

200 JONES, M. C.: A study of socialization patterns at the high school level. *J. genet. Psychol.*, 1958, **93**, 87–111.

201 JONES, M. C.: A comparison of the attitudes

and interests of ninth-grade students over two decades. *J. educ. Psychol.*, 1960, **51**, 175–186.

202 KAGAN, J., and H. A. MOSS: Parental correlates of child's I.Q. and height: a cross validation of the Berkeley Growth Study results. *Child Develpm.*, 1959, **30**, 325–332.

203 KAGAN, J., L. M. SONTAG, C. T. BAKER, and V. L. NELSON: Personality and I.Q. change. *J. abnorm. soc. Psychol.*, 1958, **56**, 261–266.

204 KAHL, J. A.: Educational and occupational aspirations of "common man" boys. *Harv. educ. Rev.*, 1953, **23**, 186–203.

205 KAHN, J. H., and J. P. NURSTEN: School refusal: a comprehensive view of school phobia and other failures of school attendance. *Amer. J. Orthopsychiat.*, 1962, **32**, 707–718.

206 KAPLAN, O. J.: Age and vocational choice. *J. genet. Psychol.*, 1946, **68**, 131–134.

207 KASDON, L. M.: Early reading background of some superior readers among college freshmen. *J. educ. Res.*, 1958, **52**, 151–153.

208 KAUFMAN, W. C.: Status, authoritarianism and anti-Semitism. *Amer. J. Sociol.*, 1957, **62**, 379–382.

209 KEATS, J.: The college majority—dropouts. *Life Magazine*, June 21, 1963, pp. 70–79.

210 KEISLAR, E. R.: Peer group ratings of high school pupils with high and low school marks. *J. exp. Educ.*, 1955, **23**, 375–378.

211 KELLY, P. J.: An investigation of the factors which influence grammar school pupils to prefer scientific subjects. *Brit. J. educ. Psychol.*, 1961, **31**, 43–44.

212 KENNEDY, W. A.: A multidimensional study of mathematically gifted adolescents. *Child Develpm.*, 1960, **31**, 655–666.

213 KENT, N., and D. R. DAVIS: Discipline in the home and intellectual development. *Brit. J. med. Psychol.*, 1957, **30**, 27–33.

214 KERCKHOFF, A. C., and T. C. MC CORMICK: Marginal status and marginal personality. *Soc. Forces*, 1955, **34**, 48–55.

215 KIMBALL, B.: Case studies in educational failure in adolescence. *Amer. J. Orthopsychiat.*, 1953, **23**, 406–415.

216 KINANE, J. F., and M. W. PABLE: Family background and work value orientation. *J. counsel. Psychol.*, 1962, **9**, 320–325.

217 KOELSCHE, C. L.: A study of the student drop-out problem at Indiana University. *J. educ. Res.*, 1955, **49**, 357–364.

218 KOLKO, G.: Economic mobility and social stratification. *Amer. J. Sociol.*, 1957, **63**, 30–38.

219 KOSA, J., L. D. RACHIELE, and C. O. SCHOMMER: The self-image and performance of socially mobile college students. *J. soc. Psychol.*, 1962, **56**, 301–316.

220 KRIPPNER, S.: Science as a vocational preference among junior high school pupils. *Voc. Guid. Quart.*, 1963, **11**, 129–134.

221 KROGER, R., and C. M. LOUTTIT: The influence of father's occupation on the vocational choices of high-school boys. *J. appl. Psychol.*, 1935, **19**, 203–212.

222 KUHLEN, R. G., and E. G. COLLISTER: Sociometric status of sixth- and ninth-graders who fail to finish high school. *Educ. psychol. Measmt.*, 1952, **12**, 632–637.

223 KUNDE, T. A., and R. V. DAWIS: Comparative study of occupational prestige in three western cultures. *Personnel Guid. J.*, 1959, **37**, 350–352.

224 LAPOUSE, R., and M. A. MONK: Fears and worries in a representative sample of children. *Amer. J. Orthopsychiat.*, 1959, **29**, 803–818.

225 LASSWELL, T. E.: Social class and stereotyping. *Sociol. soc. Res.*, 1958, **42**, 256–262.

226 LASSWELL, T. E.: Orientations toward social classes. *Amer. J. Sociol.*, 1960, **65**, 585–587.

227 LATHAM, A. J.: The relationship between pubertal status and leadership in junior-high-school boys. *J. genet. Psychol.*, 1951, **78**, 185–194.

228 LAWRENCE, P. F.: Vocational aspirations of Negro youth in California. *J. Negro Educ.*, 1950, **19**, 47–56.

229 LAYCOCK, S. R.: Counseling parents of gifted children. *Except. Children*, 1956, **23**, 108–119, 134.

230 LEACH, K. W.: Intelligence levels and corresponding interest area choices of ninth grade pupils in thirteen Michigan schools. *J. exp. Educ.*, 1954, **22**, 369–383.

231 LEEDS, C. H.: Teacher behavior liked and disliked by pupils. *Education*, 1954, **75**, 29–37.

232 LEES, J. P.: Social mobility of a group of eldest-born and intermediate adult males. *Brit. J. Psychol.*, 1952, **43**, 210–221.

233 LEES, J. P., and A. H. STEWART: Family or

sibship position and scholastic ability. *Sociol. Rev.*, 1957, **5**, 85–106.

234 LENSKI, G. E.: Trends in inter-generational occupational mobility in the United States. *Amer. sociol. Rev.*, 1958, **23**, 514–523.

235 LEVINE, G. N., and L. A. SUSSMANN: Social class and sociability in fraternity pledging. *Amer. J. Sociol.*, 1960, **65**, 391–399.

236 LEVINE, P. P., and R. WALLEN: Adolescent vocational interest and later occupation. *J. appl. Psychol.*, 1954, **38**, 428–431.

237 LEVINSON, B. M.: The problems of Jewish religious youth. *Genet. Psychol. Monogr.*, 1959, **60**, 309–348.

238 LEWIS, G. M.: Interpersonal relations and school achievement. *Children*, 1964, **11**, 235–236.

239 LICHTER, S. O., E. B. RAPIEN, F. M. SEIBERT, and M. A. SKLANSKY: *The drop-outs.* New York: Free Press, 1962.

240 LIDDLE, G.: The California Psychological Inventory and certain social and personal factors. *J. educ. Psychol.*, 1958, **49**, 144–149.

241 LINDENFELD, F.: A note on social mobility, religiosity, and students' attitudes toward premarital sexual relations. *Amer. sociol. Rev.*, 1960, **25**, 81–84.

242 LIPSET, S. M.: Constant values in American society. *Children*, 1959, **6**, 219–224.

243 LIPSET, S. M., and R. BENDIX: *Social mobility in industrial society.* Berkeley, Calif.: University of California Press, 1960.

244 LITWAK, E.: The use of extended family groups in the achievement of social goals: some policy implications. *Soc. Probl.*, 1959, **7**, 177–187.

245 LITWAK, E.: Occupational mobility and extended family cohesion. *Amer. sociol. Rev.*, 1960, **25**, 9–21.

246 LIVINGSTON, A. H.: High-school graduates and dropouts: a new look at a persistent problem. *School Review*, 1958, **66**, 195–203.

247 LOCKWOOD, W. V.: Realism of vocational preference. *Personnel Guid. J.*, 1958, **37**, 98–106.

248 LUM, M. K. M.: A comparison of under- and overachieving female college students. *J. educ. Psychol.*, 1960, **51**, 109–114.

249 LYMAN, E. L.: Occupational differences in the value attached to work. *Amer. J. Sociol.*, 1955, **61**, 138–144.

250 LYNN, R.: Two personality characteristics related to academic achievement. *Brit. J. educ. Psychol.*, 1959, **29**, 213–226.

251 MACCOBY, E. E.: Class differences in boys' choices of authority roles. *Sociometry*, 1962, **25**, 117–119.

252 MACK, R. W.: Occupational ideology and the determinate role. *Soc. Forces*, 1957, **36**, 37–44.

253 MAHLER, I.: Determinants of professional desirability. *J. soc. Psychol.*, 1961, **55**, 97–103.

254 MALLINSON, G. G., and W. M. CRUMRINE: An investigation of the stability of interests of high-school students. *J. educ. Res.*, 1952, **45**, 369–383.

255 MALPASS, L. F.: Some relationships between students' perceptions of school and their achievement. *J. educ. Psychol.*, 1953, **44**, 475–482.

256 MANN, H. M.: Some hypotheses on perceptual and learning process with their application to the process of reading: a preliminary note. *J. genet. Psychol.*, 1957, **90**, 167–202.

257 MANNINO, F. V.: Family factors related to school persistence. *J. educ. Sociol.*, 1962, **35**, 193–202.

258 MARKSBERRY, M. L.: Attitudes of college women toward selected roles in life. *Sch. Soc.*, 1952, **75**, 394–396.

259 MATTESON, R. W.: Self-estimates of college freshmen. *Personnel Guid. J.*, 1956, **34**, 280–284.

260 MC ARTHUR, C., and L. B. STEVENS: The validation of expressed interests as compared with inventoried interests: a fourteen-year follow-up. *J. appl. Psychol.*, 1955, **39**, 184–189.

261 MC DILL, E. L., and J. COLEMAN: High school social status, college plans, and academic achievement. *Amer. sociol. Rev.*, 1963, **28**, 905–918.

262 MC GUIRE, C.: Conforming, mobile, and divergent families. *Marriage fam. Living*, 1952, **14**, 109–115.

263 MC KEACHIE, W. J., D. POLLIE, and J. SPEISMAN: Relieving anxiety in classroom examinations. *J. abnorm. soc. Psychol.*, 1955, **50**, 93–98.

264 MC QUARY, J. P.: Some differences between under- and over-achievers in college. *Educ. Admin. Supervis.*, 1954, **40**, 117–120.

265 MEAD, M., and R. MÉTRAUX: Image of the scientist among high school students. *Science*, 1957, **126**, 384–390.

266 MEDLEY, D. M.: Teacher personality and teacher-pupil rapport. *J. teacher Educ.*, 1961, **12**, 152–156.

267 MEHLMAN, B., and R. G. WAREHIME: Social class and social desirability. *J. soc. Psychol.*, 1962, **58**, 167–170.

268 MEISSNER, W. W.: Some indications of sources of anxiety in adolescent boys. *J. genet. Psychol.*, 1961, **99**, 65–73.

269 MEYER, G. R., and D. M. PENFOLD: Factors associated with interest in science. *Brit. J. educ. Psychol.*, 1961, **31**, 33–37.

270 MICHAEL, D. M.: Scientists through adolescent eyes: what we need to know, why we need to know it. *Scient. Monthly*, 1957, **84**, 135–140.

271 MILLER, C. H.: Occupational choice and values. *Personnel Guid. J.*, 1956, **35**, 244–246.

272 MILLER, L. M.: *Guidance for the underachiever with superior ability*. Washington, D.C.: Department of Health, Education, and Welfare, 1961, Bulletin, 25, DE 25021.

273 MINOR, C. A., and R. G. NEEL: The relationship between achievement motive and occupational preference. *J. counsel. Psychol.*, 1958, **5**, 39–43.

274 MITCHELL, J. V.: Goal-setting behavior as a function of self-acceptance, over- and underachievement, and related personality variables. *J. educ. Psychol.*, 1959, **50**, 93–104.

275 MOGEY, J. M.: Changes in family life experienced by English workers moving from slums to housing estates. *Marriage fam. Living*, 1955, **17**, 123–128.

276 MOHANDRESSI, K., and P. J. RUNKEL: Some socioeconomic correlates of academic aptitude. *J. educ. Psychol.*, 1958, **49**, 47–52.

277 MONTAGUE, J. B.: A study of anxiety among English and American boys. *Amer. sociol. Rev.*, 1955, **20**, 685–689.

278 MONTAGUE, J. B., and B. PUSTILNIK: Prestige ranking of occupations in an American city with reference to Hall's and Jones' study. *Brit. J. Sociol.*, 1954, **5**, 154–160.

279 MORGAN, H. H.: A psychometric comparison of achieving and nonachieving college students of high ability. *J. consult. Psychol.*, 1952, **16**, 292–298.

280 MORRIS, J. F.: The development of adolescent value-judgments. *Brit. J. educ. Psychol.*, 1958, **28**, 1–14.

281 MORROW, W. R., and R. C. WILSON: Family relations of bright high-achieving and underachieving high school boys. *Child Develpm.*, 1961, **32**, 501–510.

282 MOSER, W. E.: The influence of certain cultural factors upon the selection of vocational preferences by high-school students. *J. educ. Res.*, 1952, **45**, 523–526.

283 NAM, C. B.: Nationality groups and social stratification in America. *Soc. Forces*, 1959, **37**, 328–333.

284 NEA *Research Bulletin*: High school dropouts. *NEA Research Bulletin*, 1960, **38**, 11–14.

285 *New York Times* Report: Costs held factor in school drop-outs. *The New York Times*, Mar. 5, 1962.

286 *New York Times* Report: 50% of working men in blue collar jobs. *The New York Times*, July 28, 1963.

287 *New York Times* Report: Freshmen rank social life first. *The New York Times*, Oct. 29, 1964.

288 NORTON, J. L.: General motives and influences in vocational development. *J. genet. Psychol.*, 1953, **82**, 263–278.

289 NORTON, J. L.: Patterns of vocational interest development and actual job choice. *J. genet. Psychol.*, 1953, **82**, 235–262.

290 ORZACK, L. H.: Preference and prejudice patterns among rural and urban school mates. *Rural Sociol.*, 1956, **21**, 29–33.

291 OSIPOW, S. H.: Perception of occupations as a function of titles and descriptions. *J. counsel. Psychol.*, 1962, **9**, 106–109.

292 OSTLUND, L. A.: Occupational choice patterns of Negro college women. *J. Negro Educ.*, 1957, **26**, 86–91.

293 OWENS, W. A., and W. C. JOHNSON: Some measured personality traits of collegiate underachievers. *J. educ. Psychol.*, 1949, **40**, 41–46.

294 PACKARD, V.: *The status seekers*. New York: Pocket, 1961.

295 PACKARD, V.: *The pyramid climbers*. New York: McGraw-Hill, 1962.

296 PARKER, H. J.: 29,000 seventh graders have made occupational choices. *Personnel Guid. J.*, 1963, **11**, 54–55.

297 PARRISH, J., and D. RETHLING: A study of the need to achieve in college achievers and non-achievers. *J. gen. Psychol.*, 1954, **50**, 209–226.

298 PAYNE, R.: Development of occupational and migration expectations and choices among urban, small town, and rural adolescent boys. *Rural Sociol.*, 1956, **21**, 117–125.

299 PAYNE, R.: Rural and urban adolescents' attitudes toward moving. *Rural Sociol.*, 1957, **22**, 59–61.

300 PECK, R. F., and C. GALLIANI: Intelligence, ethnicity, and social roles in adolescent society. *Sociometry*, 1962, **25**, 64–72.

301 PENTY, R. C.: *Reading ability and high school drop-outs*. New York: Teachers College, Columbia University, 1956.

302 PHEASANT, J. H.: The influence of the school on the choice of science careers. *Brit. J. educ. Psychol.*, 1961, **31**, 38–42.

303 PHELPS, H. R., and J. E. HORROCKS: Factors influencing informal groups of adolescents. *Child Develpm.*, 1958, **29**, 69–86.

304 PHILBAD, C. T., and C. L. GREGORY: Occupational selection and intelligence in rural communities and small towns in Missouri. *Amer. sociol. Rev.*, 1956, **21**, 63–71.

305 PHILBAD, C. T., and C. L. GREGORY: Occupational mobility in small communities in Missouri. *Rural Sociol.*, 1957, **22**, 40–49.

306 PHILLIPS, B. E.: Impact of pupil mobility on the schools. *Educ. Admin. Supervis.*, 1957, **43**, 101–107.

307 PHILLIPS, E. L., S. SHENKER, and P. REVITZ: The assimilation of the new child into the group. *Psychiatry*, 1951, **14**, 319–325.

308 PIERCE-JONES, J.: Vocational interest correlates of socio-economic status in adolescence. *Educ. psychol. Measmt.*, 1959, **19**, 65–71.

309 PIERCE-JONES, J.: Social mobility orientations and interests of adolescents. *J. counsel. Psychol.*, 1961, **8**, 75–78.

310 POFFENBERGER, T., and D. NORTON: Factors in the formation of attitudes toward mathematics. *J. educ. Res.*, 1959, **52**, 171–176.

311 PORTERFIELD, A. L., and J. P. GIBBS: Occupation prestige and social mobility of suicides in New Zealand. *Amer. J. Sociol.*, 1960, **64**, 147–152.

312 POWELL, M., and V. BLOOM: Development of and reasons for vocational choices of ado-lescents through the high school years. *J. educ. Res.*, 1962, **56**, 126–133.

313 POWELL, W. J., and S. M. JOURARD: Some objective evidence of immaturity in under-achieving college students. *J. counsel. Psychol.*, 1963, **10**, 276–282.

314 PRESSEY, S. L.: Concerning the nature and nurture of genius. *Scient. Monthly*, 1955, **81**, 123–129.

315 PRESSFY, S. L., and R. G. KUHLEN: *Psychological development through the life span*. New York: Harper & Row, 1957.

316 RATHS, J.: Underachievement and a search for values. *J. educ. Sociol.*, 1961, **34**, 422–424.

317 RAUNER, T. M.: Occupational information and occupational choice. *Personnel Guid. J.*, 1962, **41**, 311–317.

318 RAYGOR, A. L.: College reading improvement and personality change. *J. counsel. Psychol.*, 1959, **6**, 211–217.

319 REEVES, J. M., and L. GOLDMAN: Social class perceptions and school maladjustment. *Personnel Guid. J.*, 1957, **35**, 414–419.

320 REMMERS, H. H., and D. A. RADLER: *The American teenager*. Indianapolis: Bobbs-Merrill, 1957.

321 RENNIE, T. A. C., L. SROLE, M. K. OPLER, and T. S. LANGNER: Urban life and mental health. *Amer. J. Psychiat.*, 1957, **113**, 831–837.

322 RESNICK, J.: A study of some relationships between high-school grades and certain aspects of adjustment. *J. educ. Res.*, 1951, **44**, 321–333.

323 RICHEY, R. W., and W. H. FOX: *A study of some opinions of high-school students with regard to teachers and teaching*. Urbana, Ill.: Bulletin, School of Education, University of Illinois, 1951, no. 27.

324 RIESMAN, D.: The college student in an age of organization. *Chicago Rev.*, 1958, **12**, 50–68.

325 ROBINOWITZ, R.: Attitudes of pupils achieving beyond their level of expectancy. *J. Pers.*, 1956, **24**, 308–317.

326 ROE, A.: Early determinants of vocational choice. *J. counsel. Psychol.*, 1957, **4**, 212–217.

327 ROSE, A. M.: Distance of migration and socio-economic status of migrants. *Amer. sociol. Rev.*, 1958, **23**, 420–423.

328 ROSE, A. W., and M. C. WALL: Social factors in the prestige ranking of occupations. *Personnel Guid. J.*, 1957, **35**, 420–423.

329 ROSEN, B. C.: Race, ethnicity, and the achievement syndrome. *Amer. sociol. Rev.*, 1959, **24**, 47–60.

330 ROSEN, B. C., and R. D'ANDRADE: The psychosocial origins of achievement motivation. *Sociometry*, 1959, **22**, 185–218.

331 ROSENBERG, M.: *Occupations and values.* New York: Free Press, 1957.

332 ROTHMAN, P.: Socio-economic status and the values of junior high school students. *J. educ. Sociol.*, 1954, **28**, 126–130.

333 ROWLANDS, R. G.: Some differences between prospective scientists, non-scientists, and early leavers in a representative sample of English grammar school boys. *Brit. J. educ. Psychol.*, 1961, **31**, 21–32.

334 RUSSELL, I. L., and W. A. THALMAN: Personality: does it influence teachers' marks? *J. educ. Res.*, 1955, **48**, 561–564.

335 RUTHVEN, A. G.: *Naturalist in two worlds.* Ann Arbor, Mich.: University of Michigan Press, 1963.

336 RYAN, F. J., and J. S. DAVIE: Social acceptance, academic achievement and academic aptitude among high school students. *J. educ. Res.*, 1958, **52**, 101–106.

337 SALZINGER, K.: Academic achievement in a group of mentally disturbed adolescents in a residential treatment center. *J. genet. Psychol.*, 1957, **90**, 239–253.

338 SCHLESINGER, L. E.: Public attitudes toward science: I. Attitudes of secondary school female students. *J. soc. Psychol.*, 1954, **40**, 211–218.

339 SCHORR, A. L.: Mobile family living. *Soc. Casewk.*, 1956, **37**, 175–180.

340 SCHRAMM, W.: Mass media and educational policy. *60th Yearb. Nat. Soc. Stud. Educ.*, 1961, part. 2, 203–229.

341 SCHREIBER, D.: The dropout and the delinquent. *Phi Delta Kappan*, 1963, **44**, 215–221.

342 SCHWARTZ, J.: The portrayal of educators in motion pictures, 1950–1958. *J. educ. Sociol.*, 1960, **34**, 82–90.

343 SCUDDER, R., and C. A. ANDERSON: Migration and vertical occupational mobility. *Amer. sociol. Rev.*, 1954, **19**, 329–334.

344 SECORD, P. F., and C. W. BACKMAN: Interpersonal congruency, perceived similarity, and friendship. *Sociometry*, 1964, **27**, 115–127.

345 SECORD, P. F., W. BEVAN, and W. F. DUKES: Occupational and physiognomic stereotypes in the perception of photographs. *J. soc. Psychol.*, 1953, **37**, 261–270.

346 SEEMAN, M.: Social mobility and administrative behavior. *Amer. sociol. Rev.*, 1958, **23**, 633–642.

347 SEGAL, B. E.: Male nurses: a case study in status contradiction and prestige loss. *Soc. Forces*, 1962, **41**, 31–38.

348 SEWELL, W. H., A. O. HALLER, and M. A. STRAUS: Social status and educational and occupational aspiration. *Amer. sociol. Rev.*, 1957, **22**, 67–73.

349 SHAW, M. C.: Note on parent attitudes toward independence training and the academic achievement of their children. *J. educ. Psychol.*, 1964, **55**, 371–374.

350 SHAW, M. C., and M. D. BLACK: The reaction to frustration of bright high school underachievers. *Calif. J. educ. Res.*, 1960, **11**, 120–124.

351 SHAW, M. C., and D. J. BROWN: Scholastic underachievement of bright college students. *Personnel Guid. J.*, 1957, **36**, 195–199.

352 SHAW, M. C., and B. E. DULTON: The use of the parent attitude research inventory with parents of bright academic underachievers. *J. educ. Psychol.*, 1962, **53**, 203–208.

353 SHAW, M. C., K. EDSON, and H. M. BELL: The self-concept of bright underachieving high school students as revealed by an adjective check list. *Personnel Guid. J.*, 1960, **39**, 193–196.

354 SHAW, M. C., and J. GRUBB: Hostility and able high school underachievers. *J. counsel. Psychol.*, 1958, **5**, 263–266.

355 SHAW, M. C., and J. T. MC CUEN: The onset of academic underachievement in bright children. *J. educ. Psychol.*, 1960, **51**, 103–108.

356 SHELDON, P. M.: Isolation as a characteristic of highly gifted children. *J. educ. Sociol.*, 1959, **22**, 215–221.

357 SIEGEL, A. E., and E. A. CURTIS: Familial correlates of orientation toward future employment among college women. *J. educ. Psychol.*, 1963, **54**, 33–37.

358 SIEGELMAN, M., and R. F. PECK: Personality patterns related to occupational roles. *Genet. Psychol. Monogr.*, 1960, **61**, 291–349.

359 SILBERSTEIN, F. B., and M. SEEMAN: Social mobility and prejudice. *Amer. J. Sociol.*, 1959, **65**, 258–264.

360 SILVER, R. R.: Immaturity held key to dropouts. *The New York Times*, May 3, 1964.

361 SIMPSON, R. L.: Parental influence, anticipatory socialization, and social mobility. *Amer. sociol. Rev.*, 1962, **27**, 517–522.

362 SIMPSON, R. L., and I. H. SIMPSON: The school, the peer group, and adolescent development. *J. educ. Sociol.*, 1958, **32**, 37–41.

363 SIMPSON, R. L., and I. H. SIMPSON: The psychiatric attendant: development of an occupational self-image in a low-status occupation. *Amer. sociol. Rev.*, 1959, **24**, 389–392.

364 SIMPSON, R. L., and I. H. SIMPSON: Occupational choice among career-oriented college women. *Marriage fam. Living*, 1961, **23**, 377–383.

365 SIMS, V. M.: The relation of occupational tolerance to intelligence and social affiliation. *J. soc. Psychol.*, 1954, **40**, 17–21.

366 SINGER, S. L., and B. STEFFLRE: Age differences in job values and desires. *J. counsel. Psychol.*, 1954, **1**, 89–91.

367 SINGER, S. L., and B. STEFFLRE: Sex differences in job values and desires. *Personnel Guid. J.*, 1954, **32**, 483–484.

368 SINGER, S. L., and B. STEFFLRE: A note on racial differences in job values and desires. *J. soc. Psychol.*, 1956, **43**, 333–337.

369 SLOCUM, W. L.: Educational planning by high school seniors. *J. educ. Res.*, 1958, **51**, 583–590.

370 SMALL, L.: Personality determinants of vocational choice. *Psychol. Monogr.*, 1953, **67**, no. 1.

371 SMELSER, W. T.: Adolescent and adult occupational choice as a function of family socioeconomic history. *Sociometry*, 1963, **26**, 393–409.

372 SMITH, R. J., C. E. RAMSEY, and G. CASTELLO: Parental authority and job choice: sex differences in three cultures. *Amer. J. Sociol.*, 1963, **69**, 143–149.

373 SOLOMON, J. C.: Neuroses of school teachers: a colloquy. *Ment. Hyg., N.Y.*, 1960, **44**, 79–90.

374 SOMERVILLE, A. W., and F. C. SUMNER: The persistence of vocational preference in successful individuals. *J. Psychol.*, 1950, **30**, 77–80.

375 SOMMERS, V. S.: Vocational choice as an expression of conflict in identification. *Amer. J. Psychother.*, 1956, **10**, 520–535.

376 SPACHE, G.: Personality patterns of retarded readers. *J. educ. Res.*, 1957, **50**, 461–469.

377 SPIEGELBERGER, C. D., and W. G. KALZENMEYER: Manifest anxiety, intelligence, and college grades. *J. consult. Psychol.*, 1959, **23**, 78.

378 STEININGER, M., R. E. JOHNSON, and D. K. KIRTS: Cheating on college examinations as a function of situationally aroused anxiety and hostility. *J. educ. Psychol.*, 1964, **55**, 317–324.

379 STEPHENSON, R. M.: Occupational aspirations and plans of 443 ninth graders. *J. educ. Res.*, 1955, **49**, 27–35.

380 STEPHENSON, R. M.: Mobility orientation and stratification of 1,000 ninth graders. *Amer. sociol. Rev.*, 1957, **22**, 204–212.

381 STEPHENSON, R. M.: Realism of vocational choice. *Personnel Guid. J.*, 1957, **35**, 482–488.

382 STEPHENSON, R. M.: Occupational choice as a crystallized self concept. *J. counsel. Psychol.*, 1961, **8**, 211–216.

383 STEWART, L. H.: Mother-son identification and vocational interest. *Genet. Psychol. Monogr.*, 1959, **60**, 31–63.

384 STEWART, L. H.: Relationship of sociometric status to children's occupational attitudes and interests. *J. genet. Psychol.*, 1959, **95**, 111–136.

385 STRANG, R.: *The adolescent views himself*. New York: McGraw-Hill, 1957.

386 STRAUSS, A. L.: The learning of roles and concepts as twin processes. *J. genet. Psychol.*, 1956, **88**, 211–217.

387 STRODTBECK, F. L., M. R. MC DONALD, and B. C. ROSEN: Evaluation of occupations: a reflection of Jewish and Italian mobility differences. *Amer. sociol. Rev.*, 1957, **22**, 546–553.

388 STRONG, E. K.: Nineteen years follow-up of engineer interests. *J. appl. Psychol.*, 1952, **36**, 65–74.

389 STRONG, E. K.: Amount of change in occupational choice of college freshmen. *Educ. psychol. Measmt.*, 1952, **12**, 677–691.

390 STRONG, E. K.: Validity of occupational choice. *Educ. psychol. Measmt.*, 1953, **13**, 110–121.

391 STRONG, E. K.: Satisfactions and interests. *Amer. Psychologist*, 1958, **13**, 449–456.

392 STUBBLEFIELD, R. L.: Children's emotional problems aggravated by family moves. *Amer. J. Orthopsychiat.*, 1955, **25**, 120–126.

393 SUPER, D. E.: Dimensions and measurement of vocational maturity. *Teach. Coll. Rec.*, 1955, **57**, 151–163.

394 SUPER, D. E.: *The psychology of careers.* New York: Harper & Row, 1957.

395 SUPER, D. E., and P. L. OVERSTREET: *The vocational maturity of ninth grade boys.* New York: Teachers College, Columbia University, 1960.

396 SWITZER, R. E., J. C. HIRSCHBERG, L. MYERS, E. GRAY, N. H. EVERS, and R. FORMAN: The effect of family moves on children. *Ment. Hyg., N.Y.*, 1961, **45**, 528–536.

397 SYMONDS, P. M.: Pupil evaluation and self evaluation. *Teach. Coll. Rec.*, 1952, **54**, 138–149.

398 SYMONDS, P. M.: Characteristics of the effective teacher, based on pupil evaluation. *J. exp. Educ.*, 1955, **23**, 289–310.

399 SYMONDS, P. M.: What education has to learn from psychology: VI. Emotion and learning. *Teach. Coll. Rec.*, 1958, **60**, 9–22.

400 TANNENBAUM, A. J.: *Adolescent attitudes toward academic brilliance.* New York: Teachers College, Columbia University, 1962.

401 TAYLOR, P. H.: Children's evaluations of the characteristics of the good teacher. *Brit. J. educ. Psychol.*, 1962, **32**, 258–266.

402 TEAHAN, J. E.: Future time perspective, optimism, and academic achievement. *J. abnorm. soc. Psychol.*, 1958, **57**, 379–380.

403 TERMAN, L. M.: The discovery and encouragement of exceptional talent. *Amer. Psychologist*, 1954, **9**, 221–230.

404 TERMAN, L. M.: Are scientists different? *Scient. American*, 1955, **192**, no. 1, 25–29.

405 THISTLEWAITE, D. L.: Effects of social recognition upon the educational motivation of talented youth. *J. educ. Psychol.*, 1959, **50**, 111–116.

406 THOMAS, R. J.: An empirical study of high school drop-outs in regard to ten possibly related factors. *J. educ. Sociol.*, 1954, **28**, 11–18.

407 THOMPSON, M. L., and R. H. NELSON: Twelve approaches to remedy the dropout problem. *Clearing House*, 1963, **38**, 200–204.

408 THORNDIKE, R. L.: *The concepts of over- and underachievement.* New York: Teachers College, Columbia University, 1963.

409 TIBBITTS, C.: Retirement problems in American society. *Amer. J. Sociol.*, 1954, **59**, 301–308.

410 *Time* Report: Students: "On the fringe of a golden era." *Time Magazine*, Jan. 29, 1965, pp. 56–58.

411 TODD, F. J., G. TERRELL, and C. E. FRANK: Differences between normal and underachievers of superior ability. *J. appl. Psychol.*, 1962, **46**, 183–190.

412 TORRENCE, E. P.: Who is the underachiever? *NEA Journal*, 1962, **51**, no. 1, 15–17.

413 TORRENCE, E. P.: Changing reactions of preadolescent girls to tasks requiring creative scientific thinking. *J. genet. Psychol.*, 1963, **102**, 217–223.

414 TRAPHAGEN, A. L.: Interest patterns and retention and rejection of vocational choice. *J. appl. Psychol.*, 1952, **36**, 182–185.

415 TROW, D. B.: Autonomy and job satisfaction in task-oriented groups. *J. abnorm. soc. Psychol.*, 1957, **54**, 204–209.

416 TRUEBLOOD, D. L.: Effects of employment on academic achievement. *Personnel Guid. J.*, 1957, **36**, 112–115.

417 TUCKMAN, J.: Rigidity of social status rankings of occupations. *Personnel Guid. J.*, 1958, **36**, 534–537.

418 TUMIN, M. M.: Some unapplauded consequences of social mobility in a mass society. *Soc. Forces*, 1957, **36**, 32–37.

419 TUMIN, M. M., and A. S. FELDMAN: Theory and measurement of occupational mobility. *Amer. sociol. Rev.*, 1957, **22**, 281–288.

420 TYERMAN, M. J.: A research into truancy. *Brit. J. educ. Psychol.*, 1958, **28**, 217–225.

421 TYLER, L. E.: The development of "vocational interests": I. The organization of likes and dislikes in ten-year-old children. *J. genet. Psychol.*, 1955, **86**, 33–34.

422 TYLER, L. E.: Toward a workable psychology of individuality. *Amer. Psychologist*, 1959, **14**, 75–81.

423 TYLER, L. E.: The antecedents of two varieties of vocational interests. *Genet. Psychol. Monogr.*, 1964, **70**, 177–227.

424 UDRY, R. J.: The importance of social class in a suburban school. *J. educ. Sociol.*, 1960, **33**, 307–310.

425 *U.S. News & World Report:* Young people without jobs: how real is the problem? *U.S. News & World Report*, Aug. 19, 1963.

426 *U.S. News & World Report:* Changes in today's college students. *U.S. News & World Report*, Feb. 17, 1964.

427 *U.S. News & World Report:* Record rush for college: are entrance tests unfair? *U.S. News & World Report*, Mar. 9, 1964.

428 WAISANEN, F. B.: Self-attitudes and performance expectations. *Sociol. Quart.*, 1962, **3**, 208–219.

429 WALSH, A. M.: *Self-concepts of bright boys with learning difficulties.* New York: Teachers College, Columbia University, 1956.

430 WARREN, P. A.: Vocational interests and the occupational adjustment of college women. *J. counsel. Psychol.*, 1959, **6**, 140–147.

431 WEDEMEYER, C. A.: Gifted achievers and nonachievers. *J. higher Educ.*, 1953, **24**, 25–30.

432 WEIGAND, G.: Adaptiveness and the role of parents in academic success. *Personnel Guid. J.*, 1957, **35**, 518–522.

433 WEINSTEIN, E. A.: Children's conceptions of occupational stratification. *Amer. sociol. Rev.*, 1958, **42**, 278–284.

434 WEST, L. J.: College and the years after. *J. higher Educ.*, 1953, **24**, 415–419.

435 WESTOFF, C. F., M. BRESSLER, and P. C. SAGI: The concept of social mobility: an empirical inquiry. *Amer. sociol. Rev.*, 1960, **25**, 375–385.

436 WHITE, R. C.: Social class differences in the use of leisure. *Amer. J. Sociol.*, 1955, **61**, 138–144.

437 WHITNEY, V. H., and C. M. GRIGG: Patterns of mobility among a group of families of college students. *Amer. sociol. Rev.*, 1958, **24**, 643–652.

438 WILENSKY, H. L., and H. EDWARDS: The skidder: ideological adjustments of downward mobile workers. *Amer. sociol. Rev.*, 1959, **24**, 215–231.

439 WILLIAMS, P. V.: School dropouts. *NEA Jour.*, 1963, **52**, no. 2, 10–12.

440 WILLINGHAM, W. W.: College performance of fraternity members and independent students. *Personnel Guid. J.*, 1962, **41**, 29–31.

441 WILSON, A. B.: Residential segregation of social classes and aspirations of high school boys. *Amer. sociol. Rev.*, 1959, **24**, 836–845.

442 WILSON, M. D.: The vocational preferences of secondary modern school children. *Brit. J. educ. Psychol.*, 1953, **23**, 97–113, 163–179.

443 WILSON, P. B., and R. C. BUCK: The educational ladder. *Rural Sociol.*, 1960, **25**, 404–413.

444 WILSON, R. C., and W. R. MORROW: School and career adjustment of bright high-achieving and under-achieving high school boys. *J. genet. Psychol.*, 1962, **101**, 91–103.

445 WISE, W. M.: *They come for the best of reasons: college students today.* Washington, D.C.: American Council on Education, 1958.

446 WITTY, P. A.: A study of pupils' interests, grades 9, 10, 11, 12. *Education*, 1961, **82**, 169–174.

447 WOLFLE, D., and J. G. SMITH: The occupational value of education for superior high school graduates. *J. higher Educ.*, 1956, **27**, 201–212.

448 WORREL, L.: Level of aspiration and academic success. *J. educ. Psychol.*, 1959, **50**, 47–54.

449 WRIGHT, C. R., and H. H. HYMAN: Voluntary association membership of American adults: evidence from national sample surveys. *Amer. sociol. Rev.*, 1958, **23**, 284–294.

450 YASUDA, S.: A methodological inquiry into social mobility. *Amer. sociol. Rev.*, 1964, **29**, 16–23.

451 YEOMANS, W. N., and W. R. LUNDIN: The relationship between personality adjustment and scholarship achievement in male college students. *J. gen. Psychol.*, 1957, **57**, 213–218.

452 YOUMANS, E. G.: Occupational expectations of twelfth grade Michigan boys. *J. exp. Educ.*, 1956, **24**, 259–271.

453 YOUMANS, E. G.: Factors in educational attainment. *Rural Sociol.*, 1959, **24**, 21–28.

454 YONYEA, G. G.: Job perceptions in relation to vocational preference. *J. counsel. Psychol.*, 1963, **10**, 20–26.

455 ZEITLIN, H.: High school discipline. *Calif. J. educ. Res.*, 1962, **13**, 116–125.

456 ZILLER, R. C., and R. D. BEHRINGER: A longitudinal study of the assimilation of the new child in the group. *Hum. Relat.*, 1961, **14**, 121–133.

457 ZINILES, H., B. BIBER, W. RABINOWITZ, and L. HAY: Personality aspects of teaching: a predictive study. *Genet. Psychol. Monogr.*, 1964, **69**, 101–149.

CHAPTER 10
religious beliefs
and observances

Religion consists of two elements—a *faith* and *practices* in common with others of the same faith and centered around a place of worship. *Subjectively*, religion is important to an adolescent because it provides him with certainty and security not provided in other areas of life. *Objectively*, religion is important to an adolescent because it provides opportunities to enter into meaningful relationships with others in which he can share a common form of devotion. Of lesser importance, it helps to identify him with the people he wants to be identified with (32,44,82,122). For some adolescents, the subjective aspect of religion is far more important than the objective; for others, the reverse is true (17,35,64). As Crow and Crow (41) have said:

The term "religion" carries a variety of meanings. To some, it means assent to a theologically formulated system of beliefs. To others, it denotes a body of customary practices consisting of rites, mores, and private acts of devotion. To still others, it is an intimate personal experience of communion with God or of acute decision in which external values are at stake, or of standing under the judgment of the Ultimate. All of these are legitimate definitions, and these various aspects of religious life do not always appear in any one sequence.

are adolescents irreligious?

It is commonly said today that the modern generation of adolescents is "going to the dogs" and that this is mainly because religion plays such a minor role in their lives. Lack of religious instruction and observances in today's homes, lack of parental participation in church activities, and lack of religious instruction in today's schools are the most frequent arguments given for the minor role religion plays in the lives of modern adolescents (17,101). Many people blame higher education, especially the study of science, for lack of religious interest among today's adolescents (37,64). They maintain that adolescents have been "victimized by the idealizations of science at the expense of their souls." Furthermore, it is contended that adolescents are more concerned about germs, financial instability, and labor grievances than about "prayer and prophets" (42).

To back up the claim that our young people are irreligious are such arguments as the serious rise in juvenile delinquency, the increase in misdemeanors in the home and school, the increase in drinking, use of narcotics, premarital sexual behavior, illegitimacy, divorce, and venereal diseases, and the lack of respect for members of the older generations. Much of the instability and irresponsibility of modern youth is held to be the direct result of lack of religion in their lives (7,83,121). It has been claimed that if "parents practice partnership with God in their homes, their children's future is secure" (41).

Studies of adolescent religious interests have not shown these criticisms to be justified. Just because adolescents do not attend church regularly does not mean that they are irreligious. Nor does it mean that they are irreligious if they question some of the doctrines of the church or if they discard some of their own childhood religious beliefs. Lack of attendance at chapel services in college, for example, more often comes from the type of service than from lack of interest in religion itself (6,11,17,101,123).

EVIDENCE OF RELIGIOUS INTEREST

Interest in religion is shown more by the adolescent's attitudes than by his participation in religious observances (123,137,140). For example, in a nationwide poll of high school students, it was found that there is very little agnosticism and almost no atheism among high school students (135). In fact, most adolescents are better churchgoers than their parents (24,114). A comparison of ninth graders in 1959 with those in 1935 revealed that adolescents of this generation talk more about religion than did adolescents of the earlier generation (85). Refer to Figure 10–1 for a comparison.

Equally favorable attitudes toward religion have been found among older adolescents. There is little evidence that "among young intellectuals, religion is a thing of the past," as is so often claimed (6). In

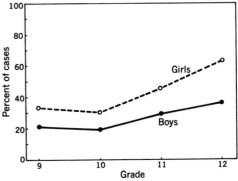

FIGURE 10–1 Talking about religion increases as adolescence progresses, especially for girls. (Adapted from M. C. Jones: A comparison of the attitudes and interests of ninth-grade students over two generations. *J. educ. Psychol.*, 1960, **51**, 175–186. Used by permission.)

one study of college students, for example, only one out of ten women and two out of ten men said that they regarded religion as playing no part in their lives (6). However, they tend to be religiously "moderate" rather than strong believers or nonbelievers (27). This is illustrated in Figure 10–2. The modern college student tends to be more serious than college students in past decades. One of the expressions of this greater seriousness is in religion, especially in church and in prayer (128).

While the religious interest of adolescents may express itself in forms that differ from adults' interests, there is much evidence that adolescents are not only interested in religion but that they also feel that religion meets a strong need in their lives. They show their interest in religion by discussing it in bull sessions, by taking courses offered in their colleges in comparative religion or in the philosophy of religion, and by participating in religious activities on the campus (63,123,124,140,146).

Most adolescents change their religious beliefs from those of their childhood days. No longer do they believe in the fairy-tale aspects of religion that appealed so strongly to them when they were young. However, change does not mean discarding of religious beliefs; it merely means that the beliefs of adolescents are more in keeping

with their mature outlook on life. It would be surprising and disturbing if an adolescent did not make revisions in his childish beliefs (26,82,132,151).

Unless the child grows up believing that wrongdoing will be punished after death, it is illogical to blame the rise in juvenile delinquency on lack of religion in the home or on lack of Sunday school attendance. For most children, moral and religious teaching are separate and distinct (111). When the adolescent breaks rules or laws and his behavior does not conform to social expectations, the blame can be traced to poor moral training rather than to lack of religion in his life (111,121).

The logical conclusion from the evidence presented above is that adolescents of today are not irreligious but rather that they are trying to find a religious faith that will fit their needs at this time. Remmers and Radler (135) have given the following picture of where today's adolescents stand in their religious attitudes and values:

The typical American teenager today retains a favorable attitude toward the church, attends services about once a week and says prayers once or twice a day. His religious beliefs usually agree with those of his parents. If there is disagreement between the parents, the adolescent is more likely to agree with his mother's religious values than with those of his father. This makes him more of a churchgoer, since the typical mother of a teenage child attends at least twice a month, while the father does not usually go to church that often. The average teenager thinks of God not as a person but as an omnipotent and omniscient bodiless spirit who exists everywhere. On the average, the teenager believes faith serves better than logic in solving life's important problems. He feels that his prayers are sometimes answered. He believes in the hereafter and expects his place there to be determined by his conduct here on earth. He believes that God guided or inspired the writing of the Bible, and that a good human society could not be built without such supernatural help.

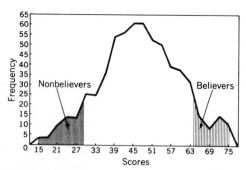

FIGURE 10–2 Distribution of scores on a religious inventory shows that most of the students are religiously "moderate." (Adapted from D. B. Brown and W. L. Lowe: Religious beliefs and personality characteristics of college students. *J. soc. Psychol.*, 1951, **33**, 103–129. Used by permission.)

need for religion

The adolescent needs religion but not theology (24). Among older adolescents, religion is the keystone to their philosophies of life in many cases (11,37,82,123). When Harvard men and Radcliffe women were asked, "Do you feel that you require some form of religious orientation or belief in order to achieve a fully mature philosophy of life?" 68 percent of the Harvard students and 82 percent of the Radcliffe students answered "Yes" (6). Because adolescence is a period of strain and insecurity, boys and girls need a religion that can give them faith in life and a feeling of security.

TYPE OF RELIGION NEEDED

Any religion that can give the adolescent faith in life and a feeling of security will meet his needs. A religion that is not continuous with life, that is set apart from the workaday world, does not furnish the adolescent with a faith to live by, nor does it help him to learn techniques of living (150). Instead, the adolescent should have the type of religious belief that can stand the strain of the conflicts and doubts so universal at this age. The religion he accepts must be such that he can understand its meaning and content. Furthermore, it must be personal rather than impersonal. As Strang (150) has pointed out:

> An adolescent who believes in God as a "very present help" not only in time of trouble but also as a daily source of guidance for his best development, has a certain resource of strength and courage. His concept of himself extends into infinity.

Above all, the adolescent's religion must be free from dogma. Adolescents of today incline toward a liberal point of view in all areas of their beliefs. Consequently, they will not tolerate dogmatic authority, whether in discipline, in teaching in schools or colleges, or in religion. When confronted with dogmatic authority, the adolescent tries to assert his independence by believing or acting in direct opposition to what he is supposed to believe or do. A religion that looks upon the pleasures of youth as immoral has little appeal for the adolescent of today (7,83,121).

Few religious beliefs acquired in childhood have the qualities that the adolescent needs. Now he wants a religion that can help him, not one that will mystify him or add excitement to his life as was true when he was a child. Instead of a "general religiosity," he now needs specific religious beliefs and attitudes (26). While an adolescent may not be able to define his religious beliefs or state exactly what his religious needs are, that does not mean that the need for religion is not present or that the adolescent is unaware of his need (11, 17,37,123). In discussing the emotional values of religion to adolescents which help to meet the needs of the age of "storm and stress," Cole and Hall (38) have emphasized three that are important for most adolescents:

> There is first the catharsis of guilt feelings through prayer, the confessional, or talks with ministers. The resulting feeling of being cleansed of sin, of being given another chance, and of reduced tension is of great value in adjustment. A second value is the increase of security, sometimes relatively superficial and sometimes profound, that may result from religious belief. A trust in God prevents the panic of despair, a belief in personal immortality with its promise of an everlasting perpetuation of the ego prevents the fear of death, the membership in a group gives a sense of belonging, and the chance to work with and help others leads to helpful identifications and attitudes. These values are not all of a religious nature, but they are of assistance in the search for happiness and adjustment. Religion may, therefore, be an important contributing factor to mental health. Finally, religion can become the basis for a sound philosophy of life, even though it does not always do so.

By late adolescence, most individuals feel that they have made a satisfactory orientation to religion (11,151). When religious adjustment is satisfactory, it gives the individual a feeling of security and belonging that contributes to his adjustments. It helps him to establish a set of values and goals that are essential to give meaning to his life. Without this, he will have little to live or work for (51,60,118). As Hanawalt (71) has pointed out:

> Religious belief is only one of the threads running through the fabric of security feeling and self-esteem. The pattern of the fabric depends upon the nature of the other threads and their interrelationships.

No one religion will necessarily meet the needs of all adolescents nor will it meet the needs of one adolescent. As Stone and Church (149) have emphasized:

> Different religions may appeal to the adolescent in different ways. He may be enthralled by the colorful pageantry of one, by the austere stringency of another, by the militantness of another, or by the castigations of another. In any event, his religion entails a projection of himself beyond mundane reality and into the absolute. His concern with religion is, of course, part and parcel of his concern with the nature of the world into which he is moving; and the nature and existence of God, and the need for and the possibility of faith, are among the topics endlessly debated in adolescent bull sessions.

VARIATIONS IN NEED FOR RELIGION

For some adolescents, the need for religion is best met by religious observances; for some, by a faith; and for others, by both a faith and observance (37,74,123). Adolescents who have, since childhood, been brought up in a *religious atmosphere* in the home and school generally have a greater need for religion than adolescents whose childhood environment has been devoid of religious experiences. On the other hand, a too religious environment, especially if it is characterized by an authoritarian approach to religion, is likely to foster such an unfavorable attitude on the part of the adolescent that it will militate against any need he might otherwise have had for religion (31,65,96,97,108). Adolescents who have

religious affiliations show greater interest in and need for religion than do those who lack such affiliations (44,100,152).

The attitude of the adolescent's *peers* toward religion has a strong influence on his own attitudes. If he is identified with a group whose members are active in church, who talk about religion, and who are influenced in their values and moral codes by their religions, he will feel a greater need for religion in his life than the adolescent who is identified with a group to whom religion is relatively unimportant (32,44, 101,136). *Girls* feel a greater need for religion in their lives than do boys. This is true late in adolescence just as it is in childhood and early adolescence; this is because from earliest childhood, girls are encouraged to be more interested in religion than boys (24,127,146).

Rural adolescents, on the whole, feel that religion plays a more important role in their lives than do adolescents from urban areas. In the suburbs, on the other hand, church affiliation is an important status symbol. The result is that suburban adolescents develop a greater feeling of dependency on religion than do urban adolescents (32, 44,101,106,122). Adolescents from lower *socioeconomic* groups tend, on the whole, to feel a greater dependency on religion than do those of higher socioeconomic status (106,122). Adolescents whose families belong to the Catholic *faith* or to small evangelical sects tend to feel a greater need for religion in their lives than do adolescents from Protestant or Jewish faiths (127). This may be explained in part by the fact that, in the former, religion has played a more important role in their lives since earliest childhood.

Of all factors influencing the adolescent's interest in and need for religion, *personality* is one of the most important. The adolescent whose personality pattern can be characterized as authoritarian, in that conformity, conservatism, rigidity, dogmatism, and inflexibility are dominant traits, shows a greater need for religion than the more liberal adolescent. In the former, dependency stemming from feelings of insecurity encourages him to turn to religion as a prop in situations in which he feels unable to cope with the problems he must face. The adolescent who is more secure and independent, on the other hand, feels less need for props; consequently, religion plays a less important role in his life (25,46,69,106).

While there are marked individual differences in adolescents' needs for religion and in the ways in which these needs are expressed, there are five developmental trends essential to making any religion fit the needs of every adolescent. These trends, closely correlated with the developmental status of the adolescent, occur in a predictable pattern and at predictable ages. They include religious awakening, doubt or indecision, changes in religious beliefs, increased tolerance toward the religious beliefs and practices of others, and changes in religious participation.

religious awakening

"Religious awakening" means an increased interest in religion which leads to a reconstruction of religious beliefs and attitudes. With age, there is increasing focusing of attention on matters that relate to the individual's life not only now but in the future and in life after death (83,98,124, 140). Figure 10–3 shows the increased interest shown during adolescence in the problem of what happens to people after death. After a period of religious apathy in late childhood, the adolescent experiences an interest in religion, which causes him to examine and reassess his childhood beliefs and practices. This frequently results in a change in religious attitudes and habits (151). When there are already pious habits, awakening is merely a more conscious acceptance of these habits and beliefs. On the other hand, the reevaluation of childhood beliefs may result in atheistic or agnostic tendencies. With the changes of interests that come at puberty, and the development of social consciousness that accompanies the new social horizons that open up at this age, it is logical that childish religious beliefs should be examined critically and evaluated (98,168).

In the past, this was the time in the

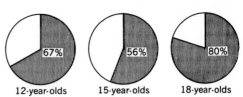

12-year-olds   15-year-olds   18-year-olds

FIGURE 10–3 There is an increase in interest in what becomes of people after death as adolescence progresses. (Adapted from P. H. Landis: *Adolescence and youth: the process of maturing.* 2d ed. New York: McGraw-Hill, 1952. Used by permission.)

individual's life when he was "converted." Much emphasis was placed on a confession of sin and guilt, a desire to lead a new life, and the acceptance of church membership (93).

Today, such emotionally toned experiences as the conversions of youth are relatively infrequent. This may be explained largely by the fact that religious values play a less important role in life today than they did in the past (98). Today, in the absence of such controls in the more liberal-minded American homes, the youth makes the readjustments of his religious beliefs without the emotional tensions that accompanied the conversions of past generations (11,17,97,151).

It was formerly believed that religious awakening was a function of pubescence and grew out of the sexual impulse. Both, it is true, come at approximately the same time. But there is no evidence to show that the relationship is one of cause and effect. Rather, increase in *intellectual development* is without doubt the cause of both religious awakening and sexual impulses that develop with pubescence.

TYPES OF RELIGIOUS AWAKENING
There are two general types of religious awakening, the *gradual* and the *catastrophic*. The gradual type takes a calm and continuous course that is characterized by a slow process of revision of religious beliefs and ideas only partially understood in childhood.

By contrast, the catastrophic type is

characterized by storm and stress, with vivid and sometimes morbid emotional experiences of fear, feelings of guilt, and shame. There is a sudden awakening of religious interest and an equally sudden revision of childish religious concepts. It is usually the result of an evangelistic type of teaching, which appeals more to the emotions than to the intelligence of the adolescent (41, 95).

Among adolescents of higher intellectual abilities, as is true of college students, gradual conversions are far more frequent than the catastrophic type (6,95,135,156). In the lower socioeconomic groups, more emphasis is placed on fervor in religious observances; in the higher socioeconomic groups, more emphasis is placed on formalized religion. As a result, gradual conversions are more common in the higher socioeconomic-status adolescents, and catastrophic, in the lower (47). In rural areas, where religion plays a more important role in the lives of adolescents and where religious beliefs are less challenged than in urban areas, the catastrophic type of awakening is very common (53). The cultural experiences the adolescent has and the practices of the religious denomination with which his family is identified will have a marked influence on what type of religious awakening he will experience (11,17,69,95, 101,123).

The *temperament* of the adolescent is also an important factor in determining the course of his religious awakening. An impetuous temperament or one characterized by melancholy predisposes the individual to an unsteady and highly emotionalized religious interest. By contrast, the calm, even-tempered, lighthearted individual who takes everything in his stride will follow a calm and peaceful course in his religious development. If he is plagued by feelings of guilt, he may, to allay these feelings, develop a strong religious fervor which will excite him to a sudden conversion of the catastrophic type (41).

AGE OF RELIGIOUS AWAKENING

It is difficult to tell just when religious awakening begins unless it shows a cata-strophic course. The child whose development has reached a level of 12 years or more M.A. shows a new interest in religion. Around this time the child begins to expect logically coherent answers to his questions about religion and to show an interest in religion that is not characteristic of those whose mental age falls below 12 years. There will, of course, be great individual differences in the chronological ages of the children when the mental age of 12 years has been reached (77).

FACTORS INFLUENCING RELIGIOUS AWAKENING

Awakened interest in religion during the early years of adolescence is brought about by a number of different causes. Increased *intelligence* with the accompanying ability to reason motivates the adolescent to ponder over the religious beliefs he accepted so unquestioningly during childhood. With increased *knowledge*, especially that derived from scientific studies in school, the adolescent views his childish beliefs in a new light. *Reasoning* has been found to be the most important single cause for changing religious attitudes and revising childish religious beliefs. Of less importance is *imitation*. When their friends are showing a new interest in religion and are reevaluating their childish religious faiths, many adolescents follow the crowd in this as in other matters (11,17,56,81,101).

Focusing attention on religion, in preparation for joining the church as a full-fledged member with the rights and privileges of the adult members, is certain to increase the adolescent's interest in religion. As he learns the doctrines and dogmas of his family's faith, and as the ceremonials of the church service are explained to him, he begins to see the religion of his childhood in a new light and with new meaning (85,129). If joining the family church is an important occasion in his family, and if it gives him status with his friends who are likewise taking this first step into adult status, the adolescent (41):

> . . . *may experience considerable emotional satisfaction during the period of prepara-*

tion and the ceremony itself; he may accept with great seriousness his "new" church status.

The emotional satisfaction from this experience will, unquestionably, lead to an increased interest in religion (32,44,97).

As a child, the individual was accustomed to go to his parents for advice, comfort, and aid. But with the onset of adolescence, boys and girls frequently lose touch with their parents. They then turn to friends and teachers, but they frequently find this an unsatisfactory substitute. As a result they turn to religion when they find themselves in need of *aid in meeting their personal problems.* Interest in religion is frequently aroused by *experiences of the beautiful,* such as nature and its phenomena, ecclesiastical forms and ceremonies, art, music, and poetry. *Blows of fate,* such as severe illness or death of a loved one, may likewise give rise to a heightened interest in religion. Dramatic incidents and traumatic experiences are less frequently the causes of religious awakening than is reasoning (5,6,81,129).

EFFECTS OF RELIGIOUS AWAKENING

Because of the emotional satisfaction the adolescent derives from his new status as a member of the church, he at first shows strong enthusiasm for religious activities. Not only does he accept his new status in the church with great seriousness, but he is eager to participate in religious conferences with other adolescents. This gives him an opportunity to discuss religious matters with his age-mates and to get their points of view. Many boys and girls, in the early years of adolescence, decide to dedicate their lives to service for their church. In addition, they often try to convert their age-mates to their faiths and persuade them to join their churches (11,85,101,123,150).

However, like most enthusiasms of youth, religious enthusiasm soon begins to wane. As the adolescent analyzes the beliefs he accepted when he joined his church, and when he compares the beliefs of his church with those of the churches of his friends, he begins to wonder if he can continue to be-

lieve what his church stands for. He even wonders if he would not find some other religion more to his liking. As doubt and indecision develop, enthusiasm wanes.

religious doubt

Religious doubt is the second common developmental trend in the transition from childish to adult religion. "Doubt" means to waver in opinion, to hesitate in belief, or to be undecided. It may be *active* or *passive.* Active doubt is a healthy characteristic of a person who is consciously seeking an answer to a troublesome question. In passive doubt, by contrast, there is little or no effort made by the doubter to settle the question one way or the other (140). It is an unhealthy type of doubt, sometimes referred to as "irrational doubt" because it is accompanied by an "attitude of indifference in which everything is possible, nothing is certain" (55). Active doubt is more heavily weighted with feelings of guilt and fear than is passive doubt. The adolescent who seeks to solve a problem about a religious belief may feel guilty because he is questioning his parents' beliefs; he may even fear the consequences to him either now or in later life if his answer leads him to reject a childhood belief (72,103,111).

Doubt in adolescence is stimulated mainly by focusing of the adolescent's attention on the doctrines of his church and on the beliefs he is expected to accept as his own when he is granted the status of a full-fledged member of his church. In preparation for this new status, he examines his childhood beliefs critically, and comes to doubt whether he can continue to accept them. As Ross has pointed out, focusing attention on religion tends to break through "a crust which had been years in the making" and unearths beliefs which had been "lying dormant since childhood." Relatively few adolescents are "in possession of religious concepts that could be called active in the sense that they (more or less consistently) were in the mind of the respondents" (140). Reading the Bible is one of the most common sources of doubt in the adolescent years (15).

AGE OF DOUBTING

While doubting begins in childhood, it normally reaches its peak in adolescence (75). By the time the child reaches the mental age of 12 years or more, he is no longer satisfied to accept religious teachings as they are given to him. He begins to question them unless his childhood instruction has been of the dogmatic sort. Doubt reaches a peak at the age of 17 years (77). It is then calmed, in one way or another, by the age of 20 years in the majority of cases (38). High school seniors, it has been found, are less willing to accept their religion unquestioningly than are freshmen, and college students, less than high school students (72,127,135).

Doubt is not an inevitable accompaniment of adolescent religious experiences. However, as Landis has pointed out, "about two-thirds of adolescents assume some definite negative attitudes toward parental teachings of all kinds, including religion" (95). When doubting is not present in adolescence, this suggests that the individual either has too little intelligence to question what was formerly believed or that he received a too dogmatic and too threatening type of teaching. Doubting is a good sign. It shows that the individual is growing up and is attempting to make the mental adjustments needed for maturity. Childish religious beliefs, like childish clothes, do not fit when the individual is mature.

A far greater cause for concern occurs when the adolescent makes a snap judgment about religion and decides to reject all religious beliefs because he cannot accept part of his religious teachings. Once the adolescent allows his doubts to lead to agnosticism, he is likely to maintain the stand he has taken, thus closing his mind to the possibility that there might be something of value for him in religion, even though it is not the religion of his parents. As Remmers and Radler (135) have stated:

> In our opinion doubts about religion, rather than causing parental concern, should evoke parental pride. The young man or woman who reaches the doubting stage does so only by thinking for himself *about the deep and meaningful sphere of religion.*

Strang emphasizes the importance of doubt when she says, "A person who does not have the courage to doubt may not acquire the wisdom to believe" (150).

CAUSES OF RELIGIOUS DOUBT

There are many causes of adolescent doubts concerning religious beliefs acquired during the years of childhood. The most common of these causes are described below.

Early Religious Training Disillusionment usually starts with the Santa Claus myth, which helps to destroy the faith the child has in every other aspect of his early teaching. Gradually, as his knowledge increases, he starts to question other teachings. The degree of skepticism present is closely related to the narrowness of the religious concepts learned in childhood and the dogmatism of the teachings. Doubts and antagonisms may also arise because of the established religious programs of the church. The adolescent fails to see how such formalized religion has any real meaning for him (72,103,111,150).

The most severe religious conflicts of adolescents generally occur in families of mixed marriages, especially if both parents are devout members of their own churches. The adolescent, under such conditions, has developed two sets of religious beliefs, often contradictory. Doubt arises as to which he will accept and which is the correct interpretation of religious teachings. Doubt, under such conditions, is intensified by emotional problems stemming from the acceptance of the religious beliefs of one parent and the rejection of the beliefs of the other (37,41,72,100,132).

Independent Thinking From early childhood, the typical American adolescent has been taught to think independently and to make decisions for himself. When he discovers that many of the things he had been taught and had accepted uncritically are not in harmony with facts presented in his schoolwork and reading, doubting begins (29). By the time he reaches high school, he is not only encouraged to think independently but also to make practical application of the theories he is studying to the problems of life. One of his problems is how religion can function in his life. Unfortunately, he finds little that he can apply to this problem in sermons that deal mainly with Biblical matters, dogmas, or concepts he is unable to understand. The result is a tendency to doubt the value of religion to him, to question many of the teachings of religion, and to develop a negative attitude toward the role of religion as a force in his life (37, 41,72). Consequently, "early faith, so firmly entrenched, thus receives a serious setback" (57).

Adolescents who come from authoritarian homes are discouraged from thinking independently; those who come from democratic homes are encouraged to be more independent in their thinking. In a study of high school seniors, those who tended to experience religious doubt were, for the most part, from homes of above average in social status where democratic methods of discipline prevailed (15).

How encouragement to think independently can result in doubts about earlier beliefs has been described thus by a high school girl (150):

> During adolescence, one's whole outlook on life changes. He sees things with his own eyes and not through the eyes of his parents. He must judge people and the world by his own standards. At this point he has two philosophies of life, we might say; that of his parents, and his own. These two philosophies are in constant conflict until the youth can get them straightened out in his mind.

Higher Education   The adolescent frequently finds contradictions between his childhood faith and the knowledge he acquires from courses in science and other studies in high school and college. Furthermore, critical analysis, which places emphasis on the fact that material must be proved to be believed, militates against accepting any doctrine on faith. An adolescent whose religion has taught him that prayer will bring rain, for example, may learn in his science classes that rain is caused by certain meteorological factors. Without intending to do so, his science teacher may arouse doubts not only about the effectiveness of prayer but also about many other concepts acquired from religious experiences (98,134). While college students, as a whole, show more religious doubt than high school students or older adolescents who do not go to college, the greatest doubt is generally found among those who major in science, especially those who later engage in research (127). Most students themselves recognize the influence of science on their doubts about religion. High school students admit that the study of certain sciences may alter their religious beliefs (134). College students who have had a number of courses in science before entering college find the influence of science less disturbing to their religious beliefs than occurred in the past (6,156).

Friends with Different Religious Beliefs
When the adolescent discovers that his intimate friends have religious beliefs different from his own, he begins to wonder which beliefs are correct. The more widely he discusses the matter with friends of different faiths, the more conflicting points of view he encounters. And, in turn, more and more serious doubts about his own faith arise. The really serious aspect of having friends of different religious faiths is that one's own religion may place taboos on certain forms of behavior that are permitted in the religions of one's friends (44,72,101). As Crow and Crow (41) have stated:

> A child reared in the home of strict adherents to certain specific denominational observances and taboos is likely to experience much mental confusion and emotional conflict when, as an adolescent, he is exposed to more liberal religious attitudes. For example, parents for religious reasons may disapprove of activities such as dancing, smok-

ing, card playing, engaging in recreational activities on the Sabbath, or attending theatrical performances or motion-picture programs. These taboos may not affect a child to any great extent, especially if his peer neighbors are similarly restricted. When he attends high school, however, his own changing interests and the less restricted behavior of his classmates may constitute for him an intolerable situation. He becomes even more disturbed if he has been taught to fear God's wrath and eternal damnation.

Dogmatic Teachings of the Church Dogmatic teachings, aloofness from everyday life, and the practice of scolding and condemning those who do not take an active part in church affairs or attend church regularly are all quickly recognized by the adolescent for what they are. He detects this insincerity, bigotry, and dogmatism and resents it (28,41,72,95,98,100). If the behavior of religious leaders and lay members who are regarded as pillars of the church does not conform to the church's teachings, attitudes of doubt and disillusionment will develop in adolescents who already are uncertain about the dogmatic teachings of the church (17,41,64,72).

PATTERN OF RELIGIOUS DOUBT

The majority of the religious doubts of adolescents fall into three categories: doubts concerned with the Bible; doubts about religious doctrines in general; and doubts concerning doctrines peculiar to a given denomination (38,71,94,150). Examples of *doubts relating to the Bible* concern the origin of man, the parting of the water, Noah and the ark, and Daniel in the lion's den. The *general religious doctrines* most often doubted may be expressed thus: "The coming of Jesus and the resurrection sound like a fairy tale" and "I don't believe you go to Heaven or Hell when you die. That's the end, there isn't any more." An example of doubting related to *doctrines peculiar to a given denomination* is the question about why it is wrong to dance, go to the movies, play cards, or engage in other worldly pleasures (15,72,97,153).

VARIATIONS IN DOUBTING

The more *intelligent* the adolescent, the earlier the doubting will begin and the more severe it is likely to be. The more formal, doctrinal, and dogmatic the *early religious training* has been, the more disturbance it will cause during the adolescent years. In denominations which give the most effective foundations in habits of religion, such as the Catholics and Lutherans, there is greater acceptance of the fundamental teachings and less doubting. Other churches demand less, get less belief, and consequently more doubting (15,94,97). Adolescents who are *affiliated with a religious denomination* doubt less than those who have no such affiliation (30). Students in *denominational colleges* move away from the traditional beliefs of their denominations to some extent as a result of doubting, but less so than students in secular colleges or universities (161).

Doubting is more common among adolescents with *college education* than among those who complete their education in high school (53,132). The more emphasis the adolescent places on *scientific studies* in high school or college, the more doubt he is likely to experience (72,127). Doubting is also influenced by members of the *peer group*. Adolescents whose friends are beginning to question their religious beliefs are far more likely to question their own beliefs than are adolescents whose friends discuss religion infrequently and who accept without question the faith of their parents (53, 85,132,140,153).

At all ages, *girls* doubt less than boys and their doubts are less intense. This may be explained in part by the fact that girls are more religious than boys and in part by the fact that they are more docile to adult demands (6,57,132,140). Doubt is more common among adolescents in *urban areas* than in rural, and more common in large cities than in small communities or suburban areas. In areas cut off from communication with the world, where life is difficult, or where one church usually serves the needs of all the people, religious beliefs are less challenged (53). Furthermore, because religion plays a more important role in family life in rural than in urban or suburban areas, there is a firmer religious foundation laid in childhood and less tolerance toward adolescent challenge of the family faith (34).

One of the most important factors influencing variations in doubting is the *personality* of the adolescent. Adolescents who are conservative are less likely to engage in doubting, and to be more guilt-ridden if they do, than are those who are liberal (37, 46,64,123). A comparison of extreme radicals and extreme conservatives has shown the latter to have come from conservative, churchgoing families where religious doubt would not be tolerated. Those who are radical, on the other hand, were found to be nonconforming in other areas of their behavior, not in religion alone (132). Adolescents who experience feelings of personality inadequacy have less confidence in their judgments than those who are more confident of their abilities to cope with problems. The former, as a result, are more likely to have religious doubts (6,90,140).

EFFECTS OF DOUBTING
Doubting in any area leaves its mark on later attitudes and beliefs. This is especially true when emotions are involved. The effects of doubting may be temporary or permanent, mild or severe, depending in part on how severe the doubting is and, in part, on the ways in which the doubting has been met by parents, teachers, or other adults. Of the many effects of doubting, the following have been found to be the most common and the most serious.

Confusion and Uncertainty When religious beliefs established in childhood are challenged by newly acquired knowledge or by conflicts with beliefs of other religious faiths, the adolescent is in a state of uncertainty; he does not know what to believe. As a result, he no longer feels certain about anything related to religion. He then develops a generalized skeptical attitude toward *all* his childhood beliefs and practices (97,150). Many adolescents say they would like to have more information than they

have about religion so they can find beliefs that "make sense to them" (95). Remmers and Radler report that 10 percent of the adolescents they questioned admitted to being confused about their religious beliefs (135).

Emotional Tension As is true of any mental conflict, doubt about religion is often accompanied by emotional tension. Brooding, depression, constant introspection, crying, and self-reproach are especially intense in the adolescent who is prone to introspection and who not only thinks but worries too much about religion. They are also severe if joining the church or a highly emotionalized type of conversion has occurred. The adolescent who suffers from feelings of inferiority will be more disturbed emotionally by religious doubt than will the adolescent who is more secure. Girls are more likely to be emotionally disturbed than boys; girls are more dominated by orthodox religious teachings which they usually accept more wholeheartedly than do boys (72,75, 95,140).

Acceptance of a Creed Doubt makes the adolescent hesitant about accepting a definite creed involving statements of belief. If, at the time he joined the church, he was expected to subscribe to certain creeds accepted by his church, feelings of guilt will rise if he now feels that he can no longer accept them as he had promised to do (95, 140,153,167).

Revision of Religious Beliefs For most adolescents, the period of doubt leads to a revision of religious beliefs to fit into their more mature intellectual status. The adolescent who is unable to reconcile his religious beliefs with his scientific knowledge is likely to discard the religious beliefs in favor of science (75,95,140). Which religious beliefs are most subject to revision and how they are revised will be discussed in the following section of this chapter.

Acceptance of Family Faith When the adolescent is able to reconcile his religious beliefs with his other knowledge, and when he finds that the church taboos on his social activities are "reasonable," he will cling to the family faith. However, he is usually less conventional and less orthodox than his parents in his beliefs and observances (72,97,132,153).

Decrease in Religious Observances Even though the adolescent is willing to accept the religious faith of his family, he shows little interest in religious observances, either in the home or at church. Until doubting leads to a clearer understanding of religion, the adolescent is confused about what to believe; this confusion is intensified by church attendance. As a junior high school girl put it (135):

> The reason most kids don't attend church as they used to is because they don't know what to believe. They go to one church and they tell you what is right or wrong and then go to another and hear entirely something different.

The social class to which the adolescent's family belongs has an influence on church attendance, even when there is doubting. Those who belong to the above-average classes tend to conform outwardly; they do not allow their personal disbeliefs to color their public behavior. Those of lower status, by contrast, tend to suit their church attendance to the degree of their religious belief. Adolescents who are more conservative will keep up appearances and continue their churchgoing and other religious observances either to avoid criticism or to try to reassure themselves (15,32,37,44,64,150).

Shift to Another Faith The adolescent whose doubt has caused him to be openly critical and cynical of his family's church and religious observances or whose religious faith has been identified with restrictive social taboos often finds his religion no longer useful to him; he then discards the family religion in favor of another that meets his needs better (95,97,98,100). This matter will be discussed in more detail later in the chapter.

MEETING RELIGIOUS DOUBT

The best way to meet religious doubt is through "active adaptation." Active adaptation may take one of three common forms:

1 *Rationalization of concepts and attitudes acquired earlier.* Common forms of rationalization consist of quoting the Bible or the teachings of famous ministers, seeking authorities who agree with one's own beliefs, and limiting friends and discussions of religion to individuals of one's own faith.
2 *Rejection of some or all religious concepts established in childhood because some of the concepts do not fit in with later scientific teachings.* Rejection is generally accompanied by emotional disturbance and comes usually after serious thought.
3 *Adjustment of childhood concepts to new situations.* The adolescent, after an evaluation of his concepts, adapts them to meet the needs of his widening experiences. This is the most common of the three forms of active adaptation.

The adolescent must be encouraged to talk freely and to seek help from religious advisers to clarify his ideas. Discussion groups with others who are experiencing similar doubts will go a long way toward helping the adolescent to realize that doubting is not unique with him. Then any feelings of guilt he might have had quickly disappear. Many churches today are gearing their teaching of youth groups to meet adolescent religious doubts. Questions about dogmas and practices are encouraged and answers are given by specially trained religious leaders. While it is true that some adolescents will meet their doubts without this help, most need outside help to give them insight into their problems and a perspective they would be unable to get alone because of their limited knowledge and experience (28,41,83,124,150).

Because doubting *always* leads to a weakening of beliefs, even when doubts are met sympathetically and with attempts to clarify them, it is evident that the best way to cope with the problem of religious doubt is to prevent it from occurring. If it does occur, it should be handled quickly and with understanding, before its harmful effects have had a chance to set in. The best preventive is to see to it that the "specific and concrete beliefs taught to children be beliefs compatible with the more abstract adult views, and not beliefs later to be discarded because of incompatibility" (94).

The adolescent whose religious doubts are met unsympathetically, who is made to feel guilty because of his doubts, or who is threatened with punishment after death for doubting his family's faith, has little motivation to adjust his childhood religious concepts as he grows older or to try to find a religious faith that will meet his more mature needs. A too intolerant attitude on the part of adults can readily turn him into an atheist or agnostic (7,121,124,140).

changes in religious beliefs

The third important developmental trend in religion during the adolescent years consists of changes in religious beliefs. Beliefs are based on concepts which change with increased knowledge and experience. It should not be surprising, therefore, that the religious beliefs that proved to be satisfactory no longer prove to be so to an adolescent (72). The child, for example, who represents God in a drawing by the back of a man's head because "God's face shone so brightly that one never saw it," cannot, as an adolescent, continue to have such a concept of God; he must revise it in keeping with his more mature intellectual capacity and experience (38).

It is popularly believed that changes in religious beliefs are a developmental trend that comes with the maturing of the body. In contradiction to this belief, Kuhlen and Arnold (94) have pointed out:

> . . . it would seem more reasonable to assume that they are the result of accumulated experience in combination with increasing intellectual maturity which makes the adolescent more capable of interpreting the environment of ideas and facts in which he is becoming increasingly immersed. . . . Also with greater maturity the adolescent is more capable of abstract generalizations which might result in discarding some specific beliefs in favor of more general ones.

In many cases, change in religious beliefs is part of the adolescent revolt against all authority. The child may question some of the concepts and beliefs as he grows older but he is not likely to change them; he will cling to them, even though there may be some doubt in his mind as to their correctness. Not so with the adolescent. Whether he verbalizes his changed concepts and beliefs or keeps them to himself, an adolescent with normal intelligence is bound to make revisions in all childhood concepts. The more authoritarian his training, the greater his revolt. This will affect his religious concepts as well as other concepts he has learned from authoritarian teaching (36,83,140).

The adolescent *should* revise his religious concepts so that the beliefs based on them will be meaningful and useful to him as he grows older (1). Adolescents who are afraid to change their religious beliefs, either because of threats from authoritarian parents or from supernatural powers, or because limited knowledge, intelligence, and experience make them incapable of making satisfactory changes, will find themselves as adults in possession of religious beliefs that are no more in keeping with their new status than clothing styled for a child (30, 34).

It is of practical importance to know *what* beliefs the adolescent is most likely to revise. Knowing this will give a better foundation on which to build a religious faith as he grows older. Furthermore, it will help to eliminate much of the doubt about religion that occurs during adolescence. Studies of changes in religious beliefs have shown, for example, that those most often subject to revision are the concepts that are specific in nature, such as the child's concept of God as a person or heaven as a place of eternal happiness and good times after death (140). Young children, for example, think of God as a "big man who watches you all the time." By adolescence, their concepts have become more generalized, as shown by the statement, "God is something we cannot see, something like love, but we know He is here" (166).

It is equally important, from a practical angle, to know *when* religious beliefs usually change. This enables parents or religious advisers to be prepared to help the adolescent make the changes and to be on the watch for the beginning of doubting. If, for example, it were known that most adolescents do not begin to change their childhood beliefs until they approach adulthood, a very different method would be needed than if it were found that changed beliefs occur shortly after the child reaches adolescence. In the former case, the responsibility for helping the adolescent to make the changes successfully would rest mainly with adults outside the home; in the latter, it would rest primarily with the parents (7, 121,124,140).

WHEN CHANGES OCCUR

Studies of groups of high school students show that changes in religious beliefs follow much the same pattern. In one study of the same group of boys from the ages of 12 to 16 years, it was found that changes in religious beliefs were most pronounced between the ages of 12 and 13 years (45). Among boys and girls of the Jewish faith, the discarding of the religious beliefs of their faith begins earlier than is usually believed and extends right through adolescence. Even those who attend religious schools do not retain their beliefs in the dogmas, though girls accept more beliefs than do boys and those of foreign-born parents who observe the traditional ceremonials in the home cling to the doctrines of their faith more than do those of more liberal home environments (54). Mathematically gifted high school students have been reported to discard their concrete religious beliefs at a much earlier age than the average high school students and to substitute more abstract beliefs for them at an earlier age (88).

College seniors, when questioned about the changes that had taken place since they entered college, reported that in many cases they had entered college with half-thought-out religious beliefs which they had accepted in an unquestioning fashion from parents, teachers, or religious leaders. Beliefs of a supernaturalistic sort disappeared when the students were stimulated to think about them. The more abstract the beliefs, the less likely they were to be changed. Furthermore, there is a trend toward unorthodox beliefs (5,70,87).

While seniors are more liberal, on the whole, in their religious beliefs than are freshmen, the difference is not so marked as is generally believed. This suggests that some changes in religious beliefs have taken place before the students entered college. In fact, many changes found at the end of college had already started in high school, but the students' doubts received no encouragement until they came in contact with professors and other students who did not hold the traditional beliefs. Women students in college change their religious beliefs less than do men students (5,6,27, 87).

A number of causes are responsible for changes in religious beliefs during late adolescence. The most important are the teaching in certain college courses, especially philosophy, biology, and psychology; contacts with fellow students; the general process of becoming more mature; reading outside of courses; the personal influence of professors in courses; and other influences outside the college life. Science courses, for example, have been reported to help to destroy beliefs in miracles; and history and literature courses, the idea that everything in the Bible is literally true. Experience with ineffectual praying was frequently the reason given for abandoning supernatural ideas in connection with prayer (6,70,112).

The general effect of college training is not to change religious beliefs that are firmly established but rather to lessen these beliefs. There is a turning away from orthodox beliefs toward "theological liberalism" (27,49,72). The more orthodox the religious faith, the more stable the beliefs (72). Courses in high school or college affect students of different faiths differently. Learning about science, for example, has been reported to have a greater effect on the religious beliefs of Jewish students than Protestant students. The least effect is on students of the Catholic faith (135).

CHANGES IN SPECIFIC BELIEFS

As time goes on, the adolescent's religious concepts become increasingly abstract, and his beliefs become general rather than specific. Some of the changes in religious concepts in adolescence are shown in Figure 10–4. Of the many religious concepts and beliefs adolescents have, the following have been found to undergo the most radical changes during the adolescent years.

God Adolescents who, as children, believed God to be the creator of the world, a powerful ruler, one who punishes for bad and rewards for good acts, and one who could be supplicated through prayer are most likely to change their concepts of God, and to the most pronounced degree. By the later part of adolescence, most adolescents have relinquished these Old Testament concepts and have adopted a concept of God as a friendly, intelligent Being who works in accordance with the laws of nature (28, 62,94,134). However, they still believe, as they did in childhood, that God is a person one should always obey, even though the fear of punishment for not doing so is less than it was in childhood (75,80,87,166).

While most adolescents believe in a Deity of some kind, their concepts vary greatly. Some think of God as an impersonal force, not concerned with individuals; others think of Him as a very personal Being (30, 132). Students in denominational colleges conceive of God as having a greater influence on their conduct than do students from nondenominational colleges (116). Adolescents of the Catholic faith have a greater tendency to conceive of God as an Omniscient Being who controls the destinies of man than do students of the Protestant and Jewish faiths (140).

However, in spite of the fact that most adolescents believe in a Deity of some kind, there is greater ambiguity of opinion about God than about other concepts and beliefs. This ambiguity was expressed by one high school graduate when he said (140):

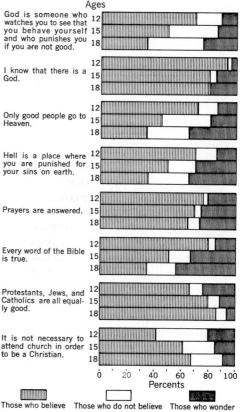

FIGURE 10–4 Changes in religious beliefs with age. (Adapted from L. Cole and I. N. Hall: *Psychology of adolescence.* 6th ed. New York: Holt, Rinehart and Winston, 1964. Used by permission.)

I believe in God but I don't really know what He's like. It's something that's more or less taken for granted. I guess He's some supernatural power. . . . I can't define it more than this. I believe in Him, yet there's uncertainty in it—it's sort of passed on from generation to generation—it becomes a more or less standard part of living. . . . To believe in God makes you feel better, makes you feel right with God. I feel that God's your conscience. If you do something and feel deep it's not right, it's God telling you it's wrong.

Jesus Most children have a concept of Jesus as a baby or as a child who behaved better than most children do. The adolescent's concept of Jesus is of a man, not a child. Some conceive of Him as divine, others as one of the great prophets and teachers of history who should be respected and revered as such (30). Adolescents of the Catholic faith have a greater tendency to conceive of Jesus as divine than do Protestants (140). There is less change in the concept of Jesus than in the concept of God; the major change consists of thinking of Jesus as a man rather than as a child (75).

Heaven and Hell   To a child, heaven is a place of eternal happiness where all the good things of life are to be found; hell is a place where there is eternal unhappiness and punishment, ranging all the way from fire to being deprived of all pleasures (75). As early as the sixth grade, there is a beginning of doubt about whether there is such a place as heaven; this doubt increases into adolescence (94). By freshman year in college, few adolescents believe in the "existence of angels" (48).

In the early part of adolescence, there is a marked decline in the belief that "hell is a place where you are punished for your sins on earth" (94). By freshman year in college, most adolescents no longer believe in the "existence of hell" or the "existence of the Devil" (48). Few adolescents believe in eternal punishment. Those who do, do not believe that this punishment is given in a place called "hell" (30).

Life after Death   Childish concepts of death as eternal sleep, and beliefs of what happens to people after they die are subject to much change and revision with advancing age. To a young child, death means departure (50,115). By adolescence, the concept of death changes; what form it takes depends upon the individual's concept of life (29). It may mean brutal destruction, liberation, transition, a painful separation, or loss to the family (19,43,107,154).

What happens to the individual after death is still a mystery in adolescence. While many adolescents refuse to think of it in relation to themselves, there are others for whom the problem is serious. It becomes increasingly serious as the adolescent

grows older (3,43,107,147,148). By senior year in high school, there is a growing skepticism about the possibility that "only our soul lives after death" (94). By the end of college, most students are skeptical about the possibility of any life after death (6,43, 50,107).

Catholics believe in a continued existence of the soul after death more than do Protestants—who are more ambiguous in their beliefs about the afterlife (86). This is well illustrated in the statement by an older adolescent Protestant boy (140):

I certainly believe in life after death—the soul passes on into the hands of a greater power than we can surmise. God is behind the formation of plans and God is within you. . . . I don't think that the soul enters a neutral state, but exactly what does happen, of course, nobody knows. But our lives must mean something more than just living on this earth, if we believe in this supreme power, so there must be some future after death.

Miracles   The childish belief in miracles usually gives way to skepticism when the adolescent studies science. By freshman year in college, few students believe that the "world was created in six solar days" or in "present-day miracles" (30,84,140).

The Bible   While high school students believe that God guided the writing of the Bible, there is a growing tendency as the student passes through high school to reject the childish belief that "every word of the Bible is true" and that it "is sinful to doubt the Bible" (30,94,134). Many older adolescents develop a skeptical attitude about whether the Bible is the written word of God or even inspired by Him when they learn that it was composed by a large number of men and modified from time to time throughout the ages (167).

The Sabbath   Different religious groups have their own concepts of the meaning of the Sabbath and what activities may be carried out on that day. Most children regard the Sabbath as a day of fairly strict religious observance (21). In a study of college students of different faiths, only 14.6 percent had not changed from their strict childhood training. A liberal attitude toward religious observance was developed by 44.8 percent of the group. Nearly half, 40.6 percent, did not observe the Sabbath but used it as a day for relaxation, recreation, or catching up on unfinished work of the week (28). One of the common reasons for loss of interest in church activities and for wanting to change from the family faith comes from the fact that the adolescent changes his concept of the meaning of the Sabbath from that of his parents or of the family church. This will be discussed in more detail in the following section.

Prayer The childish belief that prayers must be said daily by "good" people is revised markedly during adolescence. No longer does the adolescent believe that you must say prayers regularly, that prayers are "to make up for something you have done that is wrong," or that "prayers are answered." Instead, prayer is regarded as a "source of help in times of trouble" (6,74).

The Church There is a decline in the belief that "people who go to church are better than people who do not go to church" (6,74). Instead, adolescents regard church as a place where people can *learn how* to be good. Church teaches them how to resist temptation and helps them to shape their moral values and attitudes (75,111). In addition, adolescents think that the church is the "foundation of civilized life" and that it stands for the best in human life (140). Figure 10–5 shows some characteristic changes in religious concepts during adolescence.

REACTIONS TO CHANGED BELIEFS

As the adolescent disassociates himself from his childish religious beliefs, based on concepts he can no longer accept, it is inevitable that this would affect his attitudes and behavior. What effects changed religious beliefs will have and how long they will persist will depend, to a large extent, upon the type of religious instruction the

individual had in childhood and the reaction of his parents and friends to the changes that have taken place in his beliefs. The longer he has retained his childhood beliefs, the harder it will be for him to change and the more emotional tension there will be (12,37,38,64,72,140).

Changed beliefs and attitudes about religion may have any one of the following four effects on the adolescent.

Decreased Interest in Religion There is likely to be less interest in religion in late adolescence. The adolescent's attitude toward religion is also likely to be less strongly favorable to religion than it previously was (80,116). This changed attitude is accompanied by less interest in religious observances. It also makes him more tolerant toward people of other religious faiths. These effects will be discussed in the following two sections of this chapter.

Religious Reconstruction Changes in religious beliefs and attitudes generally result in a reconstruction or revision of beliefs that is adequate to meet the more mature intelligence of the adolescent. If this is to be true, however, it is essential that childhood concepts be carefully scrutinized and ample opportunity be given to change them without feelings of guilt on the adolescent's part. Frequently the changes are so radical that the final product does not harmonize with any accepted religious faith. It is, however, a philosophy of life, based on religion, that proves to be satisfactory to the individual himself (7,37,38,83,140).

Seashore (142) has described religious reconstruction thus:

> The ability to make revisions is one of the finest achievements of a balanced personality. If the educated person does not have that, he will be left holding a discredited doctrine, which he cannot possibly believe, and his religion will fade out or become stagnant.

Acceptance of Family Faith If the changes in religious belief have been minor, the adolescent is likely to retain the faith of his childhood. If, on the other hand, the

"Sunday" to a child   "Sunday" to an adolescent

FIGURE 10–5 Changes in religious concepts.

changes have been of major significance, he is likely to adopt another faith, different in most respects from that of his parents (12, 95,100,132,151).

In a study in which "orthodoxy" scores were determined on the basis of how closely high school students conformed to the religious beliefs of their families, it was found that the majority conformed either highly or moderately, with relatively few breaking away and developing "unorthodox" beliefs —beliefs that varied markedly from those held by their parents and families (113).

Among college students, the greatest reshuffling of faiths occurred among the Jewish students and the least among the Catholics (6). The more orthodox the church, the more likely it is to hold its members (7,64,72,83,151). When a shift is made, however, it is generally to a more liberal faith. Orthodox religions attract few converts (6,64,72,151,156). When parents, especially mothers, are devout, there is less likelihood of shifting to another faith than when parents are less interested in religion (40,137,151).

Agnosticism and Atheism While the adolescent is revising his religious beliefs, he may accept a religious philosophy of his own, he may accept the religion of his parents, he may accept a different religion, or he may drift into indifferent attitudes toward religion, feeling that religion has little of value to offer him (80,95,132). He may become an "agnostic"—one who withholds belief because he does not know or is unwilling to accept as proof what evidence there is available; or he may become an "atheist"—one who rejects some or all the essential doctrines of religion and who denies the existence of God (72,124,140).

Higher education is usually blamed for turning boys and girls into agnostics or atheists. However, there is little evidence to support the belief that the training the adolescent receives in college has had much influence on his religious beliefs (7,72,121).

religious observances

The fourth important developmental trend in religious interests and behavior during adolescence is a changed attitude toward religious observances (51,140,152,162). In an attempt to find out why adolescents engage in religious observances, Ross (140) questioned a number of adolescents of different ages, different religious backgrounds, and different socioeconomic statuses. He grouped his findings in three categories, as follows:

1 *A small group (perhaps 14 to 16 per cent) whose life is based on a God-man relationship find these practices meaningful and essential for clarity of purpose and morale reasons;*

2 *A group (perhaps 35 per cent) who are neither "converted" nor "weaned" but whose participation in these practices "eases their conscience," makes them "feel better," and has a "soothing effect" on a troubled mind—acting almost like a catharsis in alleviating anxiety; and*

3 *A third group (in which almost 50 per cent of those who carry on these practices may be classified) who are almost frankly superstitious and for whom such practices care for some of their fears by keeping them "in right with," and "protected by," the powers that be.*

While all religious observances decline as adolescence progresses, this decline is not always for the same reason. Consequently, the common religious observances of American adolescents today will be studied separately to show what decline in participation occurs, when it occurs, and why it occurs.

CHURCH ATTENDANCE

Studies of church and Sunday school attendance have shown that there is a gradual decrease in attendance as the adolescent years progress. Boys, as a rule, drop out sooner than girls, and their attendance is less regular. The peak of liking for church comes during the eleventh grade. After this there is a decline in interest in the church accompanied by a decline in church attendance. By the high school age, there is a marked decline in Sunday school attendance (38,132,133).

While most high school students claim

to have a favorable attitude toward the church, their attendance does not indicate this (15). There is a greater tendency to attend church irregularly than regularly, and for the number of regular attendants to decline as the adolescent passes through high school. Various statistics of attendance have been given for adolescents in different parts of the country, but they all point in the same direction (41,95,129,140). The older adolescent does not believe that church attendance is necessary to help him to lead a good life. As a result, church attendance among older adolescents is usually irregular (37,40,99,154).

Reasons for Nonattendance While there are many reasons for not attending church, the ones most often mentioned by adolescents are failure of the parents to attend, lack of interesting services, being forced to attend when they were younger, and the attitude of the church toward different forms of recreation, such as dancing and card playing (76,117,122,150).

Older adolescents have a number of gripes against the church, and these serve as a basis for their infrequent attendance. One complaint is that the church does little to make membership meaningful to young people (8). As one adolescent explained (140):

> I can't understand, for instance, why churches don't do a little role playing to solve some of the problems of the young people. Why do they stick to the same old-fashioned preaching when newer and more effective methods are known? Sunday school classes could be easily role played and lend themselves beautifully to it.

Many adolescents are sharply critical of institutionalized religion as they find it in so many of the churches. They complain that too much emphasis is placed on doctrinal and denominational differences and not enough on social and ethical aspects of religion (6,110). Adolescents maintain that they can become bored or even disgusted with long sermons that deal only with dogmatism or mysticism (41). As one adolescent put it (140):

Often the sermons are just a rehash of biblical jargon—they put old wheezes like "be kind to your fellow men," while I suspect that few people have tried it. I never doubted the sincerity of the preachers, but I have wondered if they had enough intellectual feeling for their work to be proficient at it.

Another pointed out his reason for not going to church when he said, "I dislike some of the formalism and meaningless traditionalism that clutter up some parts of the service" (140).

Many older adolescents center their complaints around the minister. While it is true that in the large urban churches the ministers are generally of high intellectual ability and have received extensive training for their work, in many of the smaller communities, this is not true. Far too often, as Landis has pointed out, they are "not the kind of men who are able to provide leadership for youth and inspire them with the ideals of religion as represented by the church" (98).

One of the major complaints adolescents have of the church is the church service itself. Figure 10–6 shows the gradual increase in adolescents who say they dislike the church service as they grow older.

Many adolescents do not attend church because of the attitude of the church, as expressed by the minister, toward various recreations engaged in by other young people in the community. A typical reaction to religious restrictions on social activities was made by an adolescent boy who said (140):

I think the churches are important, but they can't see the forest for the trees. . . .

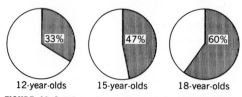

33%   47%   60%

12-year-olds   15-year-olds   18-year-olds

FIGURE 10–6 There is an increase in the number of adolescents who dislike the church services as adolescence progresses. (Adapted from P. H. Landis: *Adolescence and youth: the process of maturing.* 2d ed. New York: McGraw-Hill, 1952. Used by permission.)

Some churches frown on dancing, others on working on Sunday, and all of them are such little things that they can't concentrate on the big things that they are supposed to do.

The adolescent must make a choice about the restrictions of his church on his social activities. If he chooses to reject them, his decision will have one of three effects on his religious behavior. First, if the taboo is considered an inseparable symbol of piety, his religion goes with the taboo (98). Second, he may hide his activities from his parents and clergyman, pretending to conform to the church restrictions and continuing to pretend a deeply religious interest by attending church (95). Such adolescents "hide their activities from their ministers as they do from their teachers and parents, and happily go with the crowd" (76). Third, if caught in activities disapproved of by the ministers, adolescents usually withdraw from the church. This they do either by no longer attending the services of that church or any other church, or they join a church that is less restrictive in its attitude toward social activities.

The adolescent who comes to a new community frequently finds little welcome in the church. If his family is socially mobile, the difficulties of gaining acceptance in the youth organizations are as difficult as in the social organizations in school (122). As a result of social rejection, he is likely to withdraw from the church and no longer attend the services, as he does when he meets similar treatment in social situations (98).

Factors Influencing Church Attendance While there is unquestionably a decline in interest in church and church attendance as adolescence progresses, there are certain factors that contribute to variations in this decline. They are discussed below.

church affiliation Adolescents who are affiliated with a church attend church more regularly than do those who are not. This is true of the younger as well as of the older adolescent. The largest percentage of those who do not attend church is to be found among those with no church affiliation (58, 99,100,110,150,152,162).

religious faith There is a marked difference in amount and regularity of church attendance among adolescents of different faiths. Religious faiths which are strict and somewhat authoritarian in their dogmas, such as the Catholic and Lutheran, and those which have high social prestige value encourage more regular attendance than do faiths that are less authoritarian or less prestigeful (4,10,58,95,122,153). The more the church expects its members to attend, the more frequently and the more regularly the adolescent will attend (52,117). In Figure 10–7 are presented graphically the percentages of adolescents who attend church once a week, once a month, holidays only, and never, according to their faith.

age In high school, freshmen are more church-oriented than are seniors; the same holds true for college students (153). The older adolescent who lives at home with his family or in the neighborhood in which he has grown up attends church more than does the college student or the older adolescent whose work or military service takes him away from the pressures of family, friends, and neighbors to attend church regularly (34,58,95,99,117,122).

sex At every age in adolescence and among members of all denominations, girls attend church more than boys (32,56,58). Just as the social group expects adult women to attend church more than men and to take a more active part in the affairs of the church, so it does of adolescent girls (52,58,92,99,153).

home training Adolescents who have grown up in homes where authoritarian child-training methods are used, where the parents are devout in their religious beliefs and strict in their religious practices, and where such home rituals as grace at the table and evening prayers are part of daily life, are usually more conscientious about attending church than are adolescents who

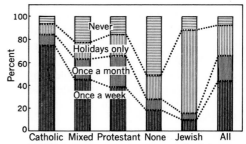

FIGURE 10–7 Church attendance of adolescents varies according to the religious affiliation of their parents. (Adapted from H. M. Bell: *Youth tell their story.* Washington, D.C.: American Council on Education, 1938. Used by permission).

have grown up in homes where child-training methods are more democratic and where less emphasis is placed on religious rituals (34,96). In homes of interfaith marriages, there is a tendency to place less emphasis on the religious training of the children and on religious observances in the home than in homes where both parents are of the same faith. Furthermore, there will usually be less parental pressure on the adolescent to attend church (22,41,99,132).

school Adolescents who have attended denominational schools since childhood and who later attend denominational colleges are more religion-oriented than are adolescents who have not had such religious influences in their school lives (10,58,78,91, 116).

personality The adolescent who feels insecure and inadequate, who has a tendency toward authoritarianism in his relationships with others, and who has a strong need for religion as a prop in his life will attend church more often and more regularly than one who has greater self-confidence and feelings of security. Adolescents who are prejudiced against members of other religious faiths tend to be better churchgoers than those with a more tolerant attitude toward other religions (5,20,56,89, 94,132,164).

environment Studies of urban and rural youth have shown that church membership becomes more general as the population of the area increases (16,39,91). In suburban areas, where it is "the thing to do" to go to church on Sundays and important religious holidays, churchgoing among adolescents is greater than in urban centers, and it usually outstrips attendance in the rural areas (21, 58,91,95,122).

socioeconomic status Church affiliation, as well as church attendance, is influenced by the socioeconomic status of the family to which the adolescent belongs (32,47,76, 99,169). Middle- and upper-class adolescents attend church more as members of a family group than do those of the lower classes. Furthermore, they dress especially for the occasion (47,58,99). Upper-class adolescents are conspicuous by their absence at all but the regular Sunday morning service. Figure 10–8 shows the relationship between the social class status of the adolescent's family and adolescent's church attendance.

Among the upper-class families, even among those who do not go to church regularly, it is a common practice to go as a family group on Thanksgiving, Christmas, Easter, and during Lent. As Bossard and Boll (21) have explained:

> These services are compulsory to the upper-class families as they are not to nonchurch-goers of the middle class. It seemed clear that these are occasions of high social, rather than of just religious, importance. Everybody who is anybody will be there.

One of the ways in which the socially mobile adolescent hopes to gain acceptance in the right group is by affiliation with the "right" church in the community and by attending the church services. This is especially true when the family move has been to the suburbs (95). As Packard (122) has pointed out, the adolescent discovers that:

> For the majority of American Christians, going to church is the nice thing that proper people do on Sundays. It advertises their respectability, gives them a warm feeling that they are behaving in a way their God-fearing ancestors would approve, and adds (they hope) a few cubits to their social stature by throwing them with a social group with which they wish to be identified. And even those who take their worshiping seriously often prefer to do it while surrounded by their own kind of people.

Because going to church is the thing to do, many adolescents who are anxious to be identified with the "right" social group continue their churchgoing and other religious observances even when their interest in religion has been weakened by doubts and their beliefs shaken by scientific and historical facts (150).

CHURCH RECREATIONS

Adolescents are interested in church clubs for social, not religious, reasons. As Hollingshead has pointed out, to them the church is "a community facility like the school, the drug store, the city government and the bowling alley" (76). The vital element in determining how much time they will devote to church recreations is whether they are accepted or rejected, not religious values. As Hollingshead (76) has stressed:

> If an adolescent derives pleasure from association with his clique mates in the church situation, he attends Sunday School, young people's meetings, and church parties without being more than nominally influenced by, or interested in, the religious aspects of the situation. Active participation and leadership in these clubs, as is true of school clubs, is in the hands of upper and upper-middle class adolescents. Those who do not belong to these classes are as uncomfortable in the church clubs as they are in the school clubs and, as a result, they attend infrequently or drop out.

To find out how much time adolescents of today devote to church recreations, such as socials, bazaars, picnics, clubs, and young people's societies, Bell asked boys and girls to report on how many had participated in their church recreational programs during the preceding year. Figure 10–9 presents this data graphically. Less than half of the young people in every religious group, it may be seen, participated (16).

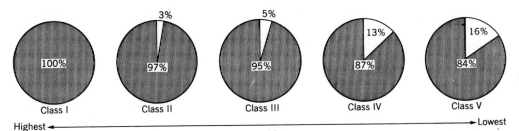

FIGURE 10–8 Relationship between social class of family and the adolescent's church attendance. (Adapted from P. H. Landis: *Adolescence and youth: the process of maturing.* 2d ed. New York: McGraw-Hill, 1952. Used by permission.)

Unquestionably one of the major reasons for the lack of interest in church recreations today is that there are so many competing social organizations in the schools and communities which satisfy the recreational and social needs formerly satisfied through the church (21,98). This is especially true of older adolescents, whether they are in college or at work.

Church social clubs appeal more to girls than to boys at all ages, but especially at the high school age (133). The social attitude toward boys who attend such clubs is that they are sissies, old-fashioned, "a bunch of Christers," or "panty waists." Among girls, on the other hand, it is considered socially correct for a girl to be a "church girl" and to take an active part in the social life connected with the church. More adolescents from the upper social

groups belong to church clubs than from the lower groups; those of the lower social groups are looked down upon by the other girls and made to feel unwelcome (76,169). Socially mobile adolescents often use church recreational groups as a means of trying to gain acceptance in the social groups with which they would like to be identified. If they join the "right" groups in the "right" churches, they hope that this will facilitate their acceptance by the "right" people (47, 95,122).

CHURCH ACTIVITIES

Activities other than worship and social functions are a part of the life of every church. These activities are for the most part regarded by adolescents as the responsibility of the adult members. Relatively few girls and even fewer boys are interested enough in them to take an active part (120). This is especially true of adolescents of the lower socioeconomic groups who are inactive in *all* community organizations (76,95,169).

The reasons why adolescents participate so little in church activities, Weaver (159) reported, are as follows:

1 *Personal quarrels always enter into anything the group undertakes.*
2 *Lack of activity.*
3 *Leader is a "dictator."*
4 *Meetings are "dead."*
5 *Not enough friendliness.*

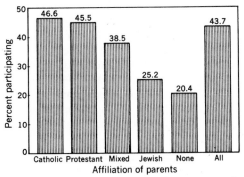

FIGURE 10–9 Participation of adolescents in church recreational activities varies according to the faith of their parents. (Adapted from H. M. Bell: *Youth tell their story.* Washington, D.C.: American Council on Education, 1938. Used by permission.)

Most adolescents find that other community organizations provide better opportunities for them to serve others than the church does (98).

HOME RELIGIOUS OBSERVANCES

Family religious observances are far less common in America today than in the past. On the basis of results obtained from a representative group of adolescents and young adult males, Ross concluded that "Bible reading, family worship, and grace at meals are historic religious practices which, to judge by this group, are fast disappearing" (140). For the most part, these observances are limited to holiday celebrations, such as Christmas, Easter, or Passover. They are generally family gatherings of a social nature, with little emphasis on religion (21, 23,140).

In some families, grace is said before meals and the adolescent son or daughter may be asked to say the grace. Occasionally, there are family prayers, usually on Saturday or Sunday night, and occasionally the Bible is read by the father to the assembled family group. In most families, saying prayers before going to bed is an individual ritual, supervised by a parent when the children are small, but unsupervised after that. Some families permit no work, no sewing or cooking, and no recreations of any type on Sunday (21,23,140).

Family rituals are more common in middle- than in upper- and lower-class families and slightly more characteristic of Protestant and Jewish families than those of the Catholic faith; the latter do their worshiping in church (21,23,65,140). In Orthodox Jewish families, parents put strong pressures on their adolescent sons and daughters to follow the religious observances of their faith, such as eating Kosher meat and serving it in their future homes (137, 138). In urban and suburban families, home religious rituals are far less common than in rural areas. However, there is a tendency for rural families of today to have fewer home religious observances than was true in the past (34,68).

PRAYER

While the adolescent may pray once or twice daily, through force of habit, his prayers are likely to be merely a ritual, not a personally gratifying experience (120,

134). Occasional prayers are said by all but agnostics during the high school age. Under unusual circumstances, the adolescent will pray at any time or place (15).

Older adolescents say prayers less frequently than do younger (6,27). In one study of older adolescents, it was reported that 42.5 percent prayed daily or oftener, 26.6 percent once or several times a week, while 30.8 percent prayed infrequently, if at all (140).

Like church attendance, the frequency of praying is related to the religious faith of the adolescent. Those of the Catholic faith pray regularly and regard prayer as part of their daily experience. Protestants pray less and more irregularly than Catholics. Adolescents of the Jewish faith pray least of all and a larger percentage of them say they never pray. Within each faith, boys pray less than girls; persons with a college education pray less than high school graduates. Adolescents with the least education pray the least and the most infrequently (140,150).

Reasons for Praying In childhood, prayers are generally requests for personal favors. Typically prayer in childhood has "degenerated into a begging ritual" (105). Because many of the things a child asks for in his prayers are not given him, the child is likely to become skeptical of the value of prayer.

Most children change their concepts of prayer as they grow older. Those who do not revise their concepts may continue to pray because it is expected of them by their parents and by the church, but it serves little purpose in their lives (104).

The reasons given by a group of high school students for prayer, in order of frequency, were as follows (126):

To ask for personal benefits
To express thanks
To talk to God
To ask for guidance
To comply with habit
To seek comfort
To ask for help for others
To ask for forgiveness

A few comments by high-school students will reveal how they feel about prayer and their reasons for praying. One student commented (126):

> I can talk to God when I can talk to nobody else. He is a friend who will always be with me in the darkness of my room. I often say prayers that are memorized but I get more satisfaction from making up my own—I feel that I am talking to God and that he is listening.

According to another high school student (126):

> Like all humans, I only call upon God's help when everything else seems to fail. It is not right to do this; I think there should be time for prayer in every day. But to be truthful, I only give prayer when I need help, when a situation arises which is too large for me to untangle.

The reasons older adolescents give for prayer have been classified in four categories, as follows (140):

1 *Those for whom prayer seems to be a meaningful way of communication with God. Of the group questioned, 17 per cent gave this reason.*
2 *Those for whom prayer approximates a period of self-analysis or meditation—26 per cent.*
3 *Those for whom prayer is a kind of technique—a magical gesture not unlike the proverbial rabbit's foot which is used to bring good luck—which can be used in time of crisis or need. For 42 per cent, prayer served this purpose.*
4 *Those who never pray and have no comment to make about it—15 per cent.*

Because many of the reasons given for prayer suggest that it is used mainly as an emergency measure, it is not surprising to find that adolescents pray mostly in unusual situations, rather than every day (160). The truth of this statement is illustrated by the following comments (140):

> When I was depressed I often wanted to get drunk, just to lie in the gutter. I didn't care what happened to me, but I always

> prayed and this helped me. It helped me more than anything else. Prayer helps the self more than anything.

> Well, usually before a test I pray to the Lord if He couldn't help me in some way. It gives me courage in myself. I think it helps.

> I pray in church on Sundays. I'd pray, too, if I'd get into trouble or if I thought I might die.

Reasons for Not Praying Adolescents have many reasons for not praying. For the most part, their reasons are related to doubts and skepticism about the value of religion. Having been taught, as children, that prayer was a way of getting God's help or of having God give them something they wanted, adolescents are often disillusioned when they discover, from their own experiences, that their prayers do not always bring the results they want. As one high school student explained (126):

> I don't believe in prayers. When I was ten years old I wanted a bicycle very much, so I prayed in order to get it. I would pray every morning, and at night before I would go to bed; sometimes when I had time during the day I prayed too. I didn't get the bike, so I could never again see any sense in praying. Since that time on I never prayed again.

Form of Prayer The form the adolescent's prayer takes is influenced largely by his reason for praying. The prayers used by adolescents in the senior year of high school were analyzed and classified in five different categories. They are (15):

1 Memorized or habitual prayers, *such as the Lord's Prayer.*
2 Prayers for something definite and personal. *The adolescent calls for help in his prayers when he is in a tight spot or when he is frightened.*
3 Prayers for forgiveness.
4 Prayers for some altruistic good, *said mostly in times of emergency.*
5 Prayers for the well-being of loved ones *who are sick, hurt, or in danger.*

The form of prayer the adolescent prefers will, unquestionably, be influenced by his childhood experience with prayer, by the faith to which he belongs, and by his own personality. While the adolescent does say prayers that have been memorized, there is a growing tendency to abandon the use of such stereotyped prayers and to say his prayers spontaneously as if he were talking to God (160).

increase in religious tolerance

The fifth, and perhaps the most significant developmental change in religion during the adolescent years is increase in religious tolerance. Not only is there a growing tendency to believe that "Catholics, Jews, and Protestants are equally good," but there is less tendency to wonder about this question as the adolescent reaches the end of his high school course (94).

The change toward religious tolerance is gradual; it accompanies the pattern of religious doubt. The more the adolescent doubts the religious beliefs he acquired during his childhood, the more open-minded he is toward the beliefs of members of other religious faiths. As his social horizons broaden and as he comes in contact with more members of the peer group of different religious faiths in school and in the community, he sees religions in a more mature and more understanding way. How contacts with members of the peer group help to bring about religious tolerance has been explained by Crow and Crow (41):

> Because of his association with other young people whose respective church affiliations demand that they adhere to specific religious observances that differ from those of his own church, the adolescent considers any such obligations superficial, insignificant, and unrelated to fundamental religious truth. The adolescent's attitude is strengthened by the fact that he admires and respects the other teen-agers.

VARIATIONS IN TOLERANCE
The more religious the adolescent is, the less he has doubted his early religious be-

liefs; and the more dogmatic the religion of his family, the less increase there will be in a tolerant attitude toward members of other faiths (20,72,125,131,145,164).

The acceptance of a conventional, externalized religion makes for less tolerance than a personal and internalized religion (103,111,123,164). Among Catholics, for example, the daily communicants are more intolerant of persons of other faiths than are the occasional communicants (144). Adolescents who shift from one social group to another have an opportunity to sample the doctrines and teachings of various denominations. As a result, these adolescents are likely to become more tolerant in their attitudes toward other religions than are adolescents who are more socially static (37,72,98).

EFFECTS OF INCREASED TOLERANCE
Increase in liberality of religious beliefs has a profound effect on the adolescent's behavior. Of the many effects, the following are the most important.

Decrease in Prejudice Increase in tolerance leads to decrease in prejudice against members of minority-group faiths. This is especially true of persons of the Jewish faith (6,20,54,141,164). Decreased prejudice, in turn, breaks down the barriers between members of the peer group, with the result that many adolescents form friendships with members of other religious faiths. These friendships tend to be less close than friendships with members of the same faith. The reason for this is the difference in values which are associated with members of other religious faiths (102). Refer to pages 131 to 133 for a more complete discussion of the role of values in friendships.

The social and aspirational values of Jewish adolescents, for example, differ markedly in some respects from those of the Protestant and Catholic faiths. To an adolescent boy of the Jewish faith, academic achievement is regarded as very important because it is a stepping-stone to vocational and social mobility. Protestant and Catholic boys, by contrast, put more value on athletic and social success. As a result, they regard the Jewish boy as a grind, an eager beaver, a curve raiser or an apple polisher, and find little in common with him (39,66,139).

Change of Religious Faith The adolescent whose church has an intolerant attitude toward social activities, whose minister preaches sermons that are primarily doctrinal and authoritarian, and who finds the ritualistic services meaningless and boring, is likely to consider joining a church of another faith where conditions are more to his liking. His increased tolerance toward other religions enables him to see the good in them. Whether he will carry out his desire to change church membership will depend largely on the emotional reactions of his parents; if they put up too great a protest, to please them he may abandon his desire to change. Parents who are devoutly religious strongly object to their children's desire to change faiths, even when they marry a person from another faith (10,40,137, 138,151).

Clinging to a faith that does not meet his needs will not increase the adolescent's satisfaction with his own church. In fact it will be more likely to increase his antagonism and to encourage him to be even more tolerant toward other religions. Some adolescents who are dissatisfied with their religions change, even when this causes family friction. The adolescents who are most likely to change are those who marry a member of another faith or first-generation Americans of minority groups who find the family religion an obstacle to achieving their social or vocational aspirations. Boys, more often than girls, change their religions for these reasons (100,151).

Interfaith Dating and Marriage Until recently, interfaith marriages were relatively infrequent. They occurred more often in urban centers than rural, and most often in the large cities (13). Such marriages are frowned upon by members of the clergy of *all* denominations who regard them as risky in the sense that the divorce rate in interfaith marriages has always been high in comparison with intrafaith marriages (22,96). The highest rate is in mixed Catholic and

Protestant marriages (155). This is illustrated in Figure 10–10.

Parents have also opposed their children's dating members of other faiths in the belief that such dating might lead to marriage. This has been the source of friction between parents and their adolescent sons and daughters for a number of years; it is growing in extent as interfaith dating becomes more common.

In spite of the hazards involved in interfaith marriages, the chances are that they will become more frequent in the years to come. As more and more adolescents go to college where they come in contact with people from many different faiths, and where they will, unquestionably, not only be encouraged to think independently but will learn facts that contradict their childhood religious concepts, they will become increasingly tolerant in their attitudes toward members of other religious faiths. Furthermore, as interfaith marriages are more common in adolescence than in adulthood, so long as the trend toward early marriages continues, so will the trend toward interfaith marriages continue.

reasons for interfaith marriages There are many reasons for the increase in interfaith marriages among today's adolescents. Unquestionably one of the most important contributing factors is the increase in *religious tolerance* which comes from opportunities for broader social contacts (13). In

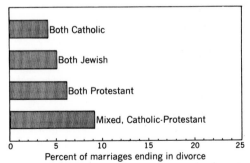

FIGURE 10–10 The high divorce rate of mixed marriages is one line of evidence of how "risky" such marriages are. (Adapted from G. M. Vernon: Interfaith marriages. *Relig. Educ.*, 1960, **55**, 261–264. Used by permission.)

addition, *decreased interest in religion due to doubts* makes many adolescents regard religion as of too minor importance to be an obstacle to happiness in a marriage with a person they find congenial because of common interests. When both young people feel that religion is a relatively unimportant force in their lives and when their religious tolerance leads them to believe that interfaith marriages have as good a chance of success as any other marriages, they are willing to take the chance by doing what parents and clergy have warned is a serious risk (13).

To minimize the risk of having an interfaith marriage go on the rocks, one partner, usually the boy, is often willing to give up his faith and accept the faith of the other (97). To break down parental opposition of the girl's family to their proposed marriage, many a boy is willing to accept the faith of the girl's family on the ground that one religion is as good as another. This usually leads to friction with his own parents and a strained relationship between them, the girl, and her parents (22, 151).

Another contributing factor to interfaith marriages during adolescence is a *limited number of members of the opposite sex* of the same religion to choose from in the school or community (13,14,122,163). As Bossard and Boll (22) have pointed out:

> A great deal depends on the religious make-up of the population in any particular area, and the relative number of persons of marriageable age in any religious group. We are tempted to make a generalization here and say that the smaller the number of unmarried persons of marriageable age in any religious group the higher will be the percentage of persons in that group who make mixed marriages.

Even when there is a limited number of members of the opposite sex of marriageable age, whose religion is the same as his, the adolescent will not marry outside his faith if he has a strong interest in religion. But with increased tolerance toward other religions, factors other than religion play important roles in mate selection.

factors influencing interfaith marriages

There are certain factors that contribute to the frequency of interfaith marriages. The *younger* the adolescent, the greater the chance of his marrying a person of a different faith. There are two reasons for this. First, his immaturity and inexperience do not permit him to see the potential pitfalls ahead which older adolescents and young adults are more clearly aware of. And, second, early adolescence is, typically, the age of religious doubt when the adolescent is ready to abandon his religion and all religion because he sees little value to be gained from it. As early marriages continue to rise, so will interfaith marriages (13,22, 33).

College students are more likely to marry outside the family faith than are persons who go to work after high school. The democratic atmosphere of a college campus or of the armed services leads the adolescent to look for congeniality of interests in the people he meets. Pressures he would have been subjected to at home to select friends of the same religious faith are missing (13). Mixed marriages are more common in *nondenominational* than in denominational colleges (102). Regardless of where he is, the older adolescent who has come from a home where a *religious atmosphere* prevails is far less likely to marry outside his faith than is the one whose home environment has not encouraged him to be too serious about religion (13,96,97, 134,143).

An adolescent who, regardless of his early religious training, has become *emancipated* from the traditions of his family and the social group with which they are identified, is very likely to marry someone of another faith. This frequently leads to friction with his family and to partial if not total rejection by his former friends (13,73,97, 143). *Parents* most likely to oppose interfaith dating and marriage are those who married within their own faith. By contrast, parents whose own marriage was an interfaith one are more liberal (13). This is illustrated in Figure 10–11. As may be seen from these data, fathers are more liberal in their attitudes toward interfaith marriages for their children than are mothers (130). *Interdenominational* marriages are even more common than interfaith marriages in families where the parents are of different faiths (130).

Adolescents who come from families *disorganized* by death, separation, or divorce, are especially prone to marry outside the family faith (13). Adolescents whose families are *socially mobile* are often encouraged by their parents to marry outside their faiths if they come from a minority religious group. Marrying into a family of a socially approved religious faith, they believe, will aid their climb up the social ladder. By contrast, adolescents from static families are more likely to be encouraged to marry within their faiths, even if this means identification with a minority religious group (13,22,33,122). Families that are very religious regard education as a better stepping-stone to upward mobility than religion; families that are less religious look upon the "right" religion as a necessary stepping-stone in their upward climb (143).

long-term effects of transitional changes

The important changes in religious beliefs, attitudes, and observances, as discussed in this chapter, may have a temporary or permanent effect on the adolescent's religious interests and activities. For most adolescents, the effects follow a fairly predictable pattern. In this pattern, there is evidence that the late teens are less religious years than the early teens, especially for boys. This relatively low interest in religion extends into the early twenties, which have been called the "least religious period of life" (129,140). However, as the adolescent marries and assumes the responsibilities of parenthood, there is generally a return to religion. Parents of young children feel that it is their responsibility to teach their children the fundamentals of their own faith and to see that they receive proper religious instruction in Sunday school. In addition, they feel it is their responsibility to set a good example by church attendance. Re-

ligious practices and rituals connected with holiday observances that prevailed in their own homes are now revived (6,15,21).

During late adolescence, when religious interests and activities are at a low point, religion lacks the "compulsive quality" that is needed to make it a force in the adolescent's life (95). As Ross has pointed out, "It is fairly clear that religion is not now an active, ever present, and compelling force in the lives of most respondents." Instead, it is more often placed on the "periphery of life" where its influence is indirect and of secondary importance (140).

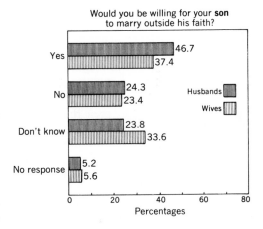

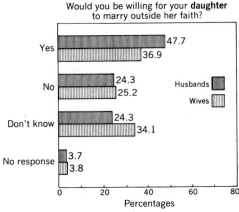

FIGURE 10–11 Attitudes of parents toward interfaith marriages for their children. (Adapted from A. J. Prince: A study of 194 cross-religious marriages. *Family Life Coordinator*, 1962, **11**, 3–7. Used by permission.)

Adolescents who are able to solve their religious doubts and find a faith that meets their needs gain a feeling of security and a meaning in their lives (18). Catholic adolescents, whose doubts about religion are less frequent and less severe than are those of Protestants or Jews, generally reach adulthood with a happy, or at least a satisfied, attitude toward religion. The least happy are generally those of the Jewish faith. This is not because they have more doubts and a greater tendency to push religion into the periphery of their lives, but rather because of the social reaction to members of their faith (135).

How important it is for adolescents to resolve their religious doubts becomes apparent when one realizes that doubts can and do become persistent. The adolescent can develop the habit of doubting, of being skeptical, and of feeling that religion has nothing of value for him. On the other hand, if he can resolve his doubts and come to the conclusion that religion can play an important role in his life, even though his religion is less conventional and orthodox than that of his parents, he will develop an attitude that will predispose him to seek the help that religion can give. As Hyde has pointed out, adolescence is a critical period in the religious development of the individual because it is a "period of choice, in which children are taking sides and making up their minds either to accept a religious philosophy or else to ignore it" (80).

What decision the adolescent makes will set the pattern for his mature faith or lack of faith. As Nelson has stressed, "What a student believes in college can hardly be ignored or considered as of mere transient importance" (117). If he decides then that religion is of little value to him, he may continue to believe this to be true for the major part of his adult life. A deep interest in religion in adolescence is usually reflected in an equally deep interest during old age; an attitude of skepticism in adolescence is reflected in disinterest during old age (18, 68).

Consequently, for those who believe that the young people of today are going to the dogs because of their lessened interest in religion, it becomes apparent that society must take positive steps to help young people to resolve the doubts they experience in adolescence. Even more important, it should be the responsibility of those who lay the child's religious foundations—his parents, grandparents, and Sunday school teachers—to see that these foundations are of a type that will not lead to doubts and disbeliefs as the child grows older. Healthy religious foundations laid in childhood will go a long way toward producing a healthy attitude toward religion throughout life.

BIBLIOGRAPHY

1 ADINARAYAN, S. P., and M. RAJAMANICKAM: A study of student attitudes toward religion, and the spiritual and the supernatural. *J. soc. Psychol.*, 1962, **57**, 105–111.

2 ALEXANDER, I. E., and A. M. ADLERSTEIN: Affective responses to the concept of death in a population of children and early adolescents. *J. genet. Psychol.*, 1958, **93**, 167–177.

3 ALEXANDER, I. E., R. S. COLLEY, and A. M. ADLERSTEIN: Is death a matter of indifference? *J. Psychol.*, 1957, **43**, 277–283.

4 ALLEN, E. E., and R. W. HITES: Factors in religious attitudes of older adolescents. *J. soc. Psychol.*, 1961, **55**, 265–273.

5 ALLPORT, G. W.: *The individual and his religion.* New York: Macmillan, 1950.

6 ALLPORT, G. W., J. M. GILLESPIE, and J. YOUNG: The religion of the postwar college student. *J. Psychol.*, 1948, **25**, 3–33.

7 AMATORA, SISTER M.: Needed research on religious development during adolescence. *Catholic psychol. Rec.*, 1963, **1**, 1–9.

8 ANDERSON, L.: The attitude of young rural people toward the church. *Relig. Educ.*, 1942, **37**, 34–40.

9 ANTHONY, S.: *The child's discovery of death.* New York: Harcourt, Brace & World, 1940.

10 APPLEBY, L.: The relation between rigidity and religious participation. *J. pastoral Care*, 1957, **11**, 73–83.

11 ARGYLE, M.: *Religious behavior.* London: Routledge, 1958.

12 BABIN, P.: The faith of adolescents toward

the end of school. *Relig. Educ.*, 1962, **57**, 128–131.

13 BARNETT, L. D.: Research into interreligious dating and marriage. *Marriage fam. Living*, 1962, **24**, 191–194.

14 BEALER, R. C., F. K. WILLITS, and G. W. BENDER: Religious exogamy: a study of social distance. *Sociol. soc. Res.*, 1963, **48**, 69–79.

15 BEEKMAN, E.: What high-school seniors think of religion. *Relig. Educ.*, 1947, **42**, 333–337.

16 BELL, H. M.: *Youth tell their story.* Washington, D.C.: American Council on Education, 1938.

17 BELLAH, R. N.: Religious evolution. *Amer. sociol. Rev.*, 1964, **29**, 358–374.

18 BENDER, I. E.: Changes in religious interest: a retest after 15 years. *J. abnorm. soc. Psychol.*, 1958, **57**, 41–46.

19 BERNARDA, M.: Wat denken jonge mensen over den dood? *Vlaam. Opeodk. Tijdschr.*, 1949, **30**, 32–40.

20 BLUM, B. S., and J. H. MANN: The effect of religious membership on religious prejudice. *J. soc. Psychol.*, 1960, **52**, 97–101.

21 BOSSARD, J. H. S., and E. S. BOLL: *Ritual in family living.* Philadelphia: University of Pennsylvania Press, 1950.

22 BOSSARD, J. H. S., and E. S. BOLL: *One marriage, two faiths.* New York: Ronald, 1957.

23 BOSSARD, J. H. S., and E. S. BOLL: *The sociology of child development.* 3d ed. New York: Harper & Row, 1960.

24 BOYER, W. H.: A survey of the attitudes, opinions and objectives of high school students in the Milwaukee area. *J. educ. Sociol.*, 1959, **32**, 344–348.

25 BROEN, W. E.: Personality correlates of certain religious attitudes. *J. consult. Psychol.*, 1955, **19**, 64.

26 BROEN, W. E.: A factor-analytic study of religious attitudes. *J. abnorm. soc. Psychol.*, 1957, **54**, 176–179.

27 BROWN, D. G., and W. L. LOWE: Religious beliefs and personality characteristics of college students. *J. soc. Psychol.*, 1951, **33**, 103–129.

28 BROWN, F. J.: *Educational sociology.* 2nd ed. Englewood Cliffs, N.J.: Prentice-Hall, 1954.

29 BROWN, L. B.: A study of religious beliefs. *Brit. J. Psychol.*, 1962, **53**, 259–272.

30 BROWN, L. B.: Religious beliefs and reports of childhood experiences. *Psychol. Rep.*, 1962, **10**, 269–270.

31 BROWN, L. B., and D. J. PALLANT: Religious belief and social pressure. *Psychol. Rep.*, 1962, **10**, 813–814.

32 BURCHINAL, L. M.: Some social status criteria and church membership and church attendance. *J. soc. Psychol.*, 1959, **49**, 53–64.

33 BURCHINAL, L. G.: Membership groups and attitudes toward cross-religious dating and marriage. *Marriage fam. Living*, 1960, **22**, 248–253.

34 BURCHINAL, L. G.: Farm-nonfarm differences in religious beliefs and practices. *Rural Sociol.*, 1961, **26**, 414–418.

35 CLARKE, W. H.: How do social scientists define religion? *J. soc. Psychol.*, 1958, **47**, 143–147.

36 CLARKE, W. H.: *The psychology of religion.* New York: Macmillan, 1958.

37 CLARKE, W. H.: Religion as a response to the search for meaning: its relation to skepticism and creativity. *J. soc. Psychol.*, 1963, **60**, 127–137.

38 COLE, L., and I. N. HALL: *Psychology of adolescence.* 6th ed. New York: Holt, 1964.

39 COLEMAN, J. S.: *The adolescent society.* New York: Free Press, 1961.

40 COOKE, T. F.: Interpersonal correlates of religious beliefs. *Dissert. Abstr.*, 1962, **23**, 1103.

41 CROW, L. D., and A. CROW: *Adolescent development and adjustment.* 2d ed. New York: McGraw-Hill, 1965.

42 DAVIES, R.: Are students losing their religion? *Christian Century*, 1939, **56**, 767–769.

43 DIGGORY, J. C., and D. Z. ROTHMAN: Values destroyed by death. *J. abnorm. soc. Psychol.*, 1961, **63**, 205–210.

44 DILLINGHAM, H. C.: Protestant religion and social status. *Amer. J. Sociol.*, 1965, **70**, 416–422.

45 DIMOCK, H. S.: Some new light on adolescent religion. *Relig. Educ.*, 1936, **31**, 273–279.

46 DREGER, M. S.: Some personality correlates of religious attitudes, as determined by projective techniques. *Psychol. Monogr.*, 1952, **66**, no. 3.

47 DYNES, R. R.: Church-sect typology and socioeconomic status. *Amer. sociol. Rev.*, 1955, **20**, 555–560.

48 DUDYCHA, G. J.: The religious beliefs of college students. *J. appl. Psychol.*, 1933, **17**, 585–603.

49 DUDYCHA, G. J.: The religious beliefs of college freshmen in 1930 and 1949. *J. relig. Educ.*, 1950, **45**, 164–169.

50 FEIFEL, H. (ed.): *The meaning of death.* New York: McGraw-Hill, 1959.

51 FEIN, L. G.: Religious observances and mental health. *J. pastoral Care*, 1958, **12**, 99–101.

52 FICHTER, J. H.: The profile of Catholic religious life. *Amer. J. Sociol.*, 1952, **58**, 145–149.

53 FORD, T. R.: Status, residence, and fundamentalist religious beliefs in the Southern Appalachians. *Soc. Forces*, 1960, **39**, 41–49.

54 FRANZBLAU, A. N.: Religious beliefs and character among Jewish adolescents. *Teach. Coll. Contrib. Educ.*, 1934, no. 634.

55 FROMM, E.: *Man for himself.* New York: Holt, 1947.

56 FRYMIER, J. R.: Relationship between church attendance and authoritarianism. *Relig. Educ.*, 1959, **54**, 369–371.

57 GARRISON, K. C.: *Psychology of adolescence.* 5th ed. Englewood Cliffs, N.J.: Prentice-Hall, 1956.

58 GARRISON, K. C.: The relationship of certain variables to church-sect typology among college students. *J. soc. Psychol.*, 1962, **56**, 29–32.

59 GARRITY, F. D.: A study of the attitude of some secondary modern school pupils toward religious education. *Relig. Educ.*, 1961, **56**, 141–143.

60 GAYL, R. F.: Conflict and cooperation between psychiatry and religion. *Pastoral Psychol.*, 1956, **7**, 29–36.

61 GESELL, A., F. L. ILG, and L. B. AMES: *Youth: the years from ten to sixteen.* New York: Harper & Row, 1956.

62 GILLILAND, A. R.: The attitudes of college students toward God and the church. *J. soc. Psychol.*, 1940, **11**, 11–18.

63 GILLILAND, A. R.: Changes in religious beliefs of college students. *J. soc. Psychol.*, 1953, **37**, 113–116.

64 GLADSTONE, R., and G. C. GUPTA: A cross cultural study of the behavioral aspects of the concept of religion. *J. soc. Psychol.*, 1963, **60**, 203–211.

65 GLASNER, RABBI S.: Family religion as a matrix of personal growth. *Marriage fam. Living*, 1961, **23**, 291–293.

66 GOODNOW, R. E., and R. TAGIURI: Religious ethnocentrism and its recognition among adolescent boys. *J. abnorm. soc. Psychol.*, 1952, **47**, 316–320.

67 GOTTLIEB, D., and C. RAMSEY: *The American adolescent.* Homewood, Ill.: Dorsey, 1964.

68 GRAY, R. M.: The personal adjustment of the older person in the church. *Sociol. soc. Res.*, 1957, **41**, 175–180.

69 GREGORY, W. E.: The orthodoxy of the authoritarian personality. *J. soc. Psychol.*, 1957, **45**, 217–232.

70 GRIFFIN, H. C.: Changes in the religious attitudes of college students. *Relig. Educ.*, 1929, **24**, 159–164.

71 HANAWALT, N. G.: Feelings of security and of self-esteem in relation to religious belief. *J. soc. Psychol.*, 1963, **59**, 347–353.

72 HAVENS, J.: A study of religious conflict in college students. *J. soc. Psychol.*, 1964, **64**, 77–87.

73 HEISS, J. S.: Interfaith marriage and marital outcome. *Marriage fam. Living*, 1961, **23**, 228–233.

74 HICKS, H. A., and M. HAYES: Study of the characteristics of 250 junior-high-school children. *Child Develpm.*, 1938, **9**, 219–242.

75 HILLIARD, F. H.: The influence of religious education upon the development of children's moral ideas. *Brit. J. educ. Psychol.*, 1959, **29**, 50–59.

76 HOLLINGSHEAD, A. DE B.: *Elmtown's youth.* New York: Wiley, 1949.

77 HOLLINGWORTH, L. S.: The adolescent child. In C. Murchison (ed.), *A handbook of child psychology.* 2d ed. Worcester, Mass.: Clark University Press, 1933, pp. 882–908.

78 HORNE, E. P., and W. H. STENDER: Student attitudes toward religious practices. *J. soc. Psychol.*, 1945, **22**, 215–217.

79 HOWELLS, T. H.: A comparative study of those who accept as against those who reject religious authority. *Univ. Ia. Stud. Charact.*, 1928, **2**, no. 2.

80 HYDE, K. E.: The religious concepts of adolescents. *Relig. Educ.*, 1961, **56**, 329–334.

81 IISAGER, H.: Factors influencing the formation and change of political and religious attitudes. *J. soc. Psychol.*, 1949, **29**, 253–265.

82 JERSILD, A. T.: *The psychology of adolescence.* 2d ed. New York: Macmillan, 1963.

83 JOHNSON, P. E.: *Psychology of religion.* Rev. ed. Nashville, Tenn.: Abingdon, 1959.

84 JONES, H. E.: *Development in adolescence.* New York: Appleton-Century-Crofts, 1943.

85 JONES, M. C.: A comparison of the attitudes and interests of ninth-grade students over two generations. *J. educ. Psychol.*, 1960, **51**, 175–186.

86 KALISH, R. A.: Some variables in death attitudes. *J. soc. Psychol.*, 1963, **59**, 137–145.

87 KATZ, D., and F. H. ALLPORT: *Students' attitudes.* Syracuse, N.Y.: Craftsmen, 1931.

88 KENNEDY, W. A.: A multidimensional study of mathematically gifted adolescents. *Child Develpm.*, 1960, **31**, 655–666.

89 KIRSCHNER, R., J. L. MC CARY, and C. W. MOORE: A comparison of differences among religious groups of children on various measures of the Rosenzweig Picture-Frustration Study. *J. clin. Psychol.*, 1962, **18**, 352–353.

90 KITAY, P. M.: Radicalism and conservatism toward conventional religion: a psychological study based on a group of Jewish college students. *Teach. Coll. Contr. Educ.*, 1947, no. 919.

91 KOSA, J., and C. O. SCHOMMER: Religious participation, religious knowledge, and scholastic aptitude: an empirical study. *J. scient. Stud. Relig.*, 1961, **1**, 88–97.

92 KOSA, J., and C. O. SCHOMMER: Sex differences in the religious attitudes of Catholic college students. *Psychol. Rep.*, 1962, **10**, 285–286.

93 KUHLEN, R. G.: *The psychology of adolescent development.* 2d ed. New York: Harper & Row, 1963.

94 KUHLEN, R. G., and M. ARNOLD: Age differences in religious beliefs and problems during adolescence. *J. genet. Psychol.*, 1944, **65**, 291–300.

95 LANDIS, B. Y.: Religion and youth. In E. Ginzberg (ed.), *The nation's children.* New York: Columbia, vol. 2, *Development and education*, pp. 186–206, 1960.

96 LANDIS, J. T.: Marriages of mixed and non-mixed religious faiths. *Amer. sociol. Rev.*, 1949, **14**, 401–407.

97 LANDIS, J. T.: Religiousness, family relationships, and family values in Protestant, Catholic, and Jewish families. *Marriage fam. Living*, 1960, **22**, 341–347.

98 LANDIS, P. H.: *Adolescence and youth: the process of maturing.* 2d ed. New York: McGraw-Hill, 1952.

99 LAZERWITZ, B.: Variations in church attendance. *Soc. Forces*, 1963, **39**, 301–309.

100 LAZERWITZ, B., and L. ROWITZ: The three-generations hypotheses. *Amer. J. Sociol.*, 1964, **69**, 529–538.

101 LENSKI, G. E.: Social correlates of religious interest. *Amer. sociol. Rev.*, 1953, **18**, 533–544.

102 LESLIE, G. R., and A. H. RICHARDSON: Family versus campus influences in relation to mate selection. *Soc. Probl.*, 1956, **4**, 117–121.

103 LONDON, P., R. E. SCHULMAN, and M. S. BLACK: Religion, guilt, and ethical standards. *J. soc. Psychol.*, 1964, **63**, 145–159.

104 MAC LEAN, A. H.: The idea of God in Protestant religious education. *Teach. Coll. Contr. Educ.*, 1930, no. 410.

105 MANWELL, E. M., and S. L. FAHS: *Consider the children—how they grow.* Boston: Beacon Press, 1940.

106 MARTIN, C., and R. C. NICHOLS: Personality and religious belief. *J. soc. Psychol.*, 1962, **56**, 3–8.

107 MAURER, A.: Adolescent attitudes toward death. *J. genet. Psychol.*, 1964, **105**, 75–90.

108 MC KENNA, SISTER H. V.: Religious attitudes and personality traits. *J. soc. Psychol.*, 1961, **54**, 379–388.

109 MEAD, M.: *Male and female.* New York: Morrow, 1952.

110 MERRY, F. K., and R. V. MERRY: *The first two decades of life.* 2d ed. New York: Harper & Row, 1958.

111 MIDDLETON, R., and S. PUTNEY: Religion, normative standards and behavior. *Sociometry*, 1962, **25**, 141–152.

112 MULL, H. K.: A comparison of religious thinking of freshmen and seniors in a liberal arts college. *J. soc. Psychol.*, 1947, **26**, 121–123.

113 MYERS, M. S.: Latent role of religious orienta-

tion. *Stud. higher Educ., Purdue Univ.*, 1951, **78**, 61–94.

114 MYERS, M. S.: The role of certain religious values for high-school pupils. *Stud. higher Educ., Purdue Univ.*, 1951, **79**, 79–85.

115 NAGY, M.: The child's theories concerning death. *J. genet. Psychol.*, 1948, **73**, 3–27.

116 NELSON, E.: Student attitudes toward religion. *Genet. Psychol. Monogr.*, 1940, **20**, 323–423.

117 NELSON, E. N. P.: Patterns of religious attitude shifts from college to fourteen years later. *Psychol. Monogr.*, 1956, **60**, no. 17.

118 OATES, W.: *Religious factors in mental illness.* New York: Association Press, 1955.

119 O'REILLY, C. T., and E. J. O'REILLY: Religious beliefs of Catholic college students and their attitudes toward minorities. *J. abnorm. soc. Psychol.*, 1954, **49**, 378–380.

120 ORR, A. E., and F. J. BROWN: A study of out-of-school activities of high-school girls. *J. educ. Sociol.*, 1932, **5**, 266–273.

121 OSTOW, M.: The nature of religious controls. *Amer. Psychologist*, 1958, **13**, 571–574.

122 PACKARD, V.: *The status seekers.* New York: Pocket, 1961.

123 PARSONS, H. L.: Religious beliefs of students at six colleges and universities. *Relig. Educ.*, 1963, **58**, 538–544.

124 PHENIX, P. H.: *Religious concerns in contemporary education.* New York: Teachers College, Columbia, 1959.

125 PHOTIADIS, J. D., and J. BIGGAR: Religiosity, education and ethnic distance. *Amer. J. Sociol.*, 1962, **67**, 666–672.

126 PIXLEY, E., and E. BEEKMAN: The faith of youth as shown by a survey in public schools of Los Angeles. *Relig. Educ.*, 1949, **44**, 336–342.

127 POPPLETON, P. K., and G. W. PILKINGTON: The measurement of religious attitudes in a university population. *Brit. J. soc. clin. Psychol.*, 1963, **2**, 20–36.

128 PRESSEY, S. L., and A. W. JONES: 1923–1953 and 20–60 age changes in moral codes, anxieties, and interests, as shown by the "X-O Tests." *J. Psychol.*, 1955, **38**, 485–502.

129 PRESSEY, S. L., and R. G. KUHLEN: *Psychological development through the life span.* New York: Harper & Row, 1957.

130 PRINCE, A. J.: A study of 194 cross-religious marriages. *Family Life Coordinator*, 1962, **11**, 3–7.

131 PROTHRO, E. T., and J. A. JENSEN: Interrelations of religious and ethnic attitudes in selected Southern populations. *J. soc. Psychol.*, 1950, **32**, 44–49.

132 PUTNEY, S., and R. MIDDLETON: Rebellion, conformity, and parental religious ideologies. *Sociometry*, 1961, **24**, 125–135.

133 Recreation Survey: Recreational interests and needs of high-school youth: resumé of study conducted in Schenectady, N.Y. *Recreation*, 1954, **47**, 43–46.

134 REMMERS, H. H., M. S. MYERS, and E. M. BENNETT: Purdue survey. *Purdue Opin. Panel*, 1951, **10**, no. 3.

135 REMMERS, H. H., and D. H. RADLER: *The American teenager.* Indianapolis: Bobbs-Merrill, 1957.

136 ROKEACH, M.: Political and religious dogmatism: an alternative to the authoritarian personality. *Psychol. Monogr.*, 1956, **70**, no. 18.

137 ROSEN, B. C.: Conflicting group membership: a study of parent-peer group cross-pressures. *Amer. sociol. Rev.*, 1955, **20**, 155–161.

138 ROSEN, B. C.: The reference group approach to the parental factor in attitude and behavior formation. *Soc. Forces*, 1955, **34**, 137–144.

139 ROSENBERG, M.: The dissident religious context and emotional disturbance. *Amer. J. Sociol.*, 1962, **68**, 1–10.

140 ROSS, M. G.: *Religious beliefs of youth.* New York: Association Press, 1950.

141 SAPPENFIELD, B. R.: The responses of Catholic, Protestant, and Jewish students to the menace check list. *J. soc. Psychol.*, 1944, **20**, 295–299.

142 SEASHORE, C. E.: The religion of the educated person. *J. higher Educ.*, 1947, **18**, 71–76.

143 SELFORS, S. A., R. K. LEIK, and E. KING: Values in mate selection: education versus religion. *Marriage fam. Living*, 1962, **24**, 399–401.

144 SHINERT, G., and C. E. FORD: The relation of ethnocentric attitudes to intensity of religious practice. *J. educ. Sociol.*, 1958, **32**, 157–162.

145 SIEGMAN, A. W.: A cross-cultural investigation of the relationship between religiosity, ethnic prejudice and authoritarianism. *Psychol. Rep.*, 1962, **11**, 419–424.

146 SPOERL, D. T.: The values of post-war college students. *J. soc. Psychol.*, 1952, **35**, 217–225.

147 STACEY, C. L., and K. MARKIN: The attitudes of college students and penitentiary inmates toward death and a future life. *Psychiat. Quart. Supple.*, 1952, **26**, part 1, 27–32.

148 STACEY, C. L., and M. L. REICHEN: Attitudes toward death and future life among normal and subnormal adolescent girls. *Except. Children*, 1954, **20**, 259–262.

149 STONE, L. J., and J. CHURCH: *Childhood and adolescence.* New York: Random House, 1957.

150 STRANG, R.: *The adolescent views himself.* New York: McGraw-Hill, 1957.

151 TAMNEY, J. B.: An exploratory study of religious conversion. *Dissert. Abstr.*, 1962, **23**, 2237.

152 TELFORD, C. W.: A study of religious attitudes. *J. soc. Psychol.*, 1950, **31**, 217–230.

153 THOMPSON, O. E.: High school students' values: emergent or traditional? *Calif. J. educ. Res.*, 1961, **12**, 132–144.

154 VAN DYKE, P., and J. PIERCE-JONES: The psychology of religion of middle and late adolescence: a review of empirical research, 1950–1960. *Relig. Educ.*, 1963, **58**, 529–537.

155 VERNON, G. M.: Interfaith marriages. *Relig. Educ.*, 1960, **55**, 261–264.

156 VINACKE, W. E., J. EINDHOVEN, and J. ENGLE: Religious attitudes of students at the University of Hawaii. *J. Psychol.*, 1949, **28**, 161–179.

157 WATSON, G. B.: An approach to the study of worship. *Relig. Educ.*, 1929, **24**, 849–858.

158 WEAVER, P.: Using psychological insights in the religious education of adolescents and young adults. *Relig. Educ.*, 1946, **41**, 276–283.

159 WEAVER, P.: Youth and religion. *Ann. Amer. Acad. pol. soc. Sci.*, 1949, **236**, 152–160.

160 WELFORD, A. T.: Is religious behavior dependent upon affect or frustration? *J. abnorm. soc. Psychol.*, 1947, **42**, 310–319.

161 WELLS, H. K.: Religious attitudes at a small denominational college as compared with Harvard and Radcliffe. *J. Psychol.*, 1962, **53**, 349–382.

162 WILEY, M. L.: Religion in higher education. *J. higher Educ.*, 1952, **23**, 350–371.

163 WILLITS, F. C., R. C. BEALER, and G. W. BENDER: Interreligious marriage among Pennsylvania rural youth. *Marriage fam. Living*, 1963, **25**, 433–438.

164 WILSON, W. C.: Extrinsic religious values and prejudice. *J. abnorm. soc. Psychol.*, 1960, **60**, 286–288.

165 WITHEY, R. A.: The role of religion in higher education. *Sch. Soc.*, 1952, **76**, 257–261.

166 WRIGHT, H. D., and W. A. KOPPE: Children's potential religious concepts. *Character Potential*, 1964, **2**, 83–87.

167 YOUNG, J. R.: The changing attitudes of adolescents toward religion and the church. *J. relig. Educ.*, 1929, **24**, 775–778.

168 ZETTERBERG, H. L.: The religious conversion as a change of social roles. *Sociol. soc. Res.*, 1952, **36**, 159–166.

169 ZIMMER, B. G., and A. H. HAWLEY: Suburbanization and church participation. *Soc. Forces*, 1959, **37**, 348–354.

CHAPTER 11
moral
development

One of the important developmental tasks of adolescence is replacing childish morality with a morality that will serve as a guide to conduct throughout adult life (59,76). The adolescent, for example, is expected to learn that honesty does not merely mean refraining from taking things that belong to others or from telling lies; it includes *all situations* in which there is freedom from fraud. It means that taking the printed thoughts or words of another and using them without due credit is called "plagiarism"; that copying the work of another, with or without his consent, is called "cheating." Pretending to be friendly with a person he dislikes or saying pleasant things to his face and unpleasant things behind his back are also forms of dishonesty (20,24,41,54,80).

In addition to replacing the specific moral concepts of childhood with general moral principles, the adolescent is expected to assume responsibility for the control of his behavior. Now, morality based on external control is expected to be replaced by morality based on internal controls. The adolescent is expected to make a decision about what to do in a given situation and stick to his decision without having someone threaten him with punishment if he fails to do so. In this transition from childish to mature morality, the adolescent's behavior is characterized by increasing self-control, self-decision, and self-determination (24,28,66,104,111).

meaning of morality

"Morality" comes from the Latin word *moralis*; it means "customs, manners, or patterns of behavior that conform to the standards of the group." At every age, the individual is judged by how he conforms to the standards of the group. These judgments lead society to label him as "moral," or "immoral," depending on the degree of his conformity. What the social group expects is defined in terms of rules and laws; both are based on the prevailing customs of the social group. If the adolescent conforms to society's rules and laws, he is considered a "moral" person. While he may not always agree with the rules and laws, he conforms because he realizes that it is the smart thing to do (24,28,41,102,104,111). As Wiggam has pointed out, moral people "choose the right conduct simply because they see it is the course of action that promises the best consequences" (161).

If doing what is expected by the social group is regulated by controls from *within*, the individual is known as a "morally mature" person; he is a "well disciplined person who has thorough control of himself, who takes care of the situation within himself and without outer regulation" (165). This does not mean that he becomes a law unto himself (24,41,80,102). As Chave (17) has emphasized:

One cannot be moral until one recognizes the social consequences of one's acts, and one is moral to the degree that one controls one's conduct with concern for these consequences.

The "immoral" person is one who fails to conform to group expectations, as defined by customs, rules, and laws. He does so not because of ignorance of these expectations, but rather because he feels no obligations to the group or does not approve of the standards of behavior expected by the group. In most cases, it is the former. His behavior is directed *against* the group with the intention of retaliating for what he considers unfair treatment. Most misdemeanors and delinquent acts of adolescents stem from this cause rather than from ignorance (28,41,76,80,111).

By contrast, an "unmoral" or "nonmoral" person violates social expectations because of ignorance. By adolescence, there is some unmoral behavior but relatively little except in situations so unrelated to what has been experienced in the past that the adolescent has had no opportunity to learn what is expected of him. Thus, one can say that adolescents who fail to behave as the social group expects more often do so through *intent* than through ignorance; they are more often immoral than unmoral (41,80,111,149).

difficulties in making transition to adult morality

As social horizons broaden, the moral values of childhood are no longer adequate to meet all the needs of the adolescent. He must now learn new moral values to meet new needs, especially those arising from new social relationships with members of the opposite sex, drinking and smoking, honesty, and obeying the law. One of the major developmental tasks of the adolescent is to learn what the group expects of him and then be willing to mold his behavior in conformity to these expectations, without the constant guidance, supervision, and proddings he experienced as a child.

CAUSES OF DIFFICULTIES

Because the adolescent is anxious to win social approval and to avoid social disapproval, it would be logical to conclude that the replacement of childish morality with a more mature type would be a relatively simple task for him. While the motivation is strong, there are many obstacles which make this transition far from easy. Of the many obstacles, the following are the most common.

Foundations in Making Moral Decisions

How well prepared the adolescent is to make moral decisions when confronted by alternatives will depend upon the type of training he received during childhood. As Peck and Havighurst (117) have emphasized:

> To an almost startling degree, each child learns to feel and act, psychologically and morally, as just the kind of person his father and mother have been in their relationship with him.

If the adolescent has been brought up in a home where democratic forms of discipline prevail, he will be far better prepared to cope with the problem of making moral decisions in conformity with group expectations than if his childhood training has been authoritarian or so lax that he has had little motivation to learn to conform to group expectations (54,80,111,149).

How important a role early training plays in preparing the adolescent to make moral decisions when faced by a complexity of alternatives has been emphasized by Landis (96) thus:

> In every crucial situation the child from the democratic home has a big advantage over his brow-beaten counterpart in the authoritarian family. . . . The iron hand of the authoritarian home is not conducive to the development of such traits (quick thinking and self-assurance): the child from such a home has two strikes on him from the start.

Number of Moral Alternatives

As life becomes more complex, there are more mores, more rules, and more laws to govern the lives of the members of the social group. When the adolescent leaves childhood behind, he is faced with the complexities of adult society and is expected to meet the challenges they present. He will come in contact with people of different social, economic, racial, and religious backgrounds, each with its own set of mores which may differ in marked degree from the mores that governed his life during childhood days (95). Furthermore, he will have less guidance by adults in meeting moral challenges than he had as a child; it is now his responsibility to make his own decisions when moral alternatives arise (3,28,41,76,80). For adolescents today there are many more moral alternatives than in the past and many more moral decisions to make. As Landis (96) has pointed out:

> In our day of a self-sufficient teen-age society and unchaperoned paired relationships, teen-agers are called upon to make more moral decisions before they are 20 years of age than their great grandparents made in a lifetime.

Conflict in Type of Moral Values

The adolescent discovers that there are different moral values for the two sexes, for individuals of different socioeconomic groups, for those of different racial and religious backgrounds, and for those of urban and rural environments. These conflicting values make it difficult for him to decide which to accept (28,41,73). Mentally alert adolescents and those with broader social experiences are able to adapt their behavior to group standards more successfully than are adolescents who are less mentally alert or less experienced in social relationships (11, 29,111).

The *community* in which the adolescent grows up frequently adds confusion to the problem of what moral values to accept. In the case of drinking, for example, the adolescent learns that it is wrong for a high school student to drink in public places, such as taverns and bars (24). And yet many taverns will serve liquor to adolescents under the legal age. He is told that one should show respect for one's elders, but he soon discovers that society disparages age (15).

While the moral standards of the community will be influenced by the majority cultural group, other groups will not abandon their own mores and accept those of the majority group. As a result, the adolescent, in high school, in college, or at work, will be faced with conflicting moral values and the necessity of making a decision when different alternatives are present (14,64).

Within a cultural group, standards of conduct not only differ in the various *social classes* but they are often contradictory (153). The adolescent finds, for example, that in one group an act is considered smart, while in another the same act will mark him as a sucker (20,25,53,131).

Similarly, there are differences in social-class attitudes toward honesty and sex behavior. Middle-class adolescents feel that honesty is sometimes a handicap to popularity; members of the lower class feel that it is an asset (20,28,69,91). Members of the lower class not only condone but approve premarital intercourse for adolescent boys because they regard it as a sign of true masculinity. Middle-class adolescent boys, on the other hand, are severely criticized for such behavior just as are girls of all social classes (84).

Within the American culture, rapid changes in moral values cause conflicts between the moral standards of the *peer group* and those of *parents* and *other adults*. Frequently, adults refuse to accept these new moral values. The result is that there is constant friction between adolescents as to which values to accept as guides to their behavior (62,89,93,105).

Conflict in Severity of Moral Judgments Because moral values are a reflection of the prevailing social values, when the social values change, so do the moral (64,80,102). Since the First World War, the changes have been away from the puritanical morality of the Victorian era to greater liberality (84,129). In one study, gambling was ranked in seventh place among 16 "worst practices" in 1919; during the late 1950s, it

was not even ranked among the 16. Swearing and vulgar talk, likewise, are viewed far more leniently by today's adolescents than they were by the 1919 group (125).

Members of the older generations tend, as a rule, to be more severe in their judgments of right and wrong than do adolescents (62,89,131). Shifts toward more liberal attitudes toward smoking, the use of slang, flirting, immodesty, and extravagance have been reported by Pressey and Jones from 1923 to 1953 (119). These shifts are shown in Figure 7-1, page 265, for slang; Figure 7-7, page 283, for smoking; and Figure 7-4, page 273, for extravagance.

Shifts in attitudes toward behavior formerly condemned as wrong are not due to immorality on the part of the young people, as so many older people claim, but rather to shifts in social values (25,62,102). Today's adolescents, for example, are more liberal toward cheating than their parents and grandparents were when they were adolescents. The reason for this is that it is a widespread practice today, stemming from pressures on students to get good grades to qualify for college admission. The result is that it has become the thing to do; obviously, then, it is not condemned as wrong (69,143). Similarly, the leniency in attitudes toward promiscuous sex behavior stems from the prevalance of such behavior. Boys of today are under pressure to prove their masculinity, and girls, by boys, to keep their steadies (6,102).

The moral values of adults, learned when they were adolescents, are as out of date today as are the clothes they wore then. Unless parents revise their moral values to conform to those prevailing today, they will judge behavior from a radically different frame of reference than their adolescent sons and daughters do. While there is evidence that most parents make some slight revision in their attitudes, they are still less liberal in their point of view than their children are. This increases the difficulty the adolescent has in learning adult moral behavior (25,62,119).

Double Standards A common source of conflict in moral values comes from the double standards which prevail in almost all cultures, including the American culture. These relate to socially approved behavior for members of the two sexes: what is considered right for girls is considered wrong for boys and vice versa. In childhood, certain patterns of behavior are considered more *appropriate* for boys than for girls. But they are not condemned as wrong for girls. However, in adolescence, girls become acquainted with the double standards of morality that hold for the adult members of the social group (84). While different standards of accepted behavior for the two sexes are gradually breaking down, so long as they prevail they will make the transition to adult morality difficult for both boys and girls (25,41,89,119).

Conflict with Standards in Mass Media Because adolescence is an age of hero worship, the adolescent models his moral behavior according to the pattern set by the *person he admires*. If his model is one whose behavior conforms to prevailing standards, making the transition to adult morality will be facilitated. Far too often, however, the model is one who has received popular attention, not for socially approved behavior as often as for socially disapproved. So long as the adolescent admires and hopes to be like that individual, his moral values will suffer because he will be basing them on a model that will not win him respect or acceptance in his own group either then or as he grows older (100,105).

Pressures from Peer Group When peer standards differ from adult standards, the adolescent must choose between the two. The more anxious he is to win social approval and the more insecure his status in the peer group, the more likely he is to ignore adult standards in favor of those of his peers (28,111,153). Many instances of discrepancy between the adolescent's moral code and his behavior can be traced to peer pressures (28,66).

In an opinion poll of young adolescents, 52 percent of the boys said they smoked; only 26 percent said they approved of smoking. With regard to drinking, 45 percent said they sometimes drank, but only 14 percent approved of drinking. Among the girls 27 percent claimed they sometimes drank but only 8 percent said they approved of drinking (126). These facts are illustrated in Figure 11–1. The conclusion one is justified in drawing is that the difference between what they do and what they approve "reflects peer-group pressures to smoke and drink under certain circumstances" (96).

EFFECTS OF DIFFICULTIES

There are a number of ways in which the difficulties, just discussed, of making the transition from childish to adult morality affect the transition. These effects trace their origin to the adolescent's confusion about what is right and what wrong, what should be done and what should not be. The first effect is to *slow down the learning process* and, thus, delay the transition. When an adolescent is not sure of just what code of standards to accept, or if he must learn several contradictory codes, he cannot be expected to learn the adult code and use it as a guide to his behavior as quickly as he could, were there just one code that everyone followed (41,80,102,111).

The second effect follows closely the first—*weakening of motivation to conform* to one or several moral codes. In the case of religion, doubt about the right doctrine to accept weakens the adolescent's motivation to participate in religious observances. In the same way, doubt about the right moral code weakens his motivation to act in a morally approved way. If what he does, for example, wins adult approval but is regarded by members of the peer group as sissy or "chicken," he will have little desire to act in a manner that will win him adult approval (62,102).

The third effect of the difficulties the adolescent encounters in making the transition to adult morality stems from a question in his mind about the *fairness of adult standards*. When they differ markedly from those of the peer group, he begins to wonder if they are not carry-overs of another era, as out of date today as are the fashions of the era when adults were governed by these moral codes. In the case of cheating, for example, today's adolescent could argue that when his parents were preparing to enter college, competition for entrance into a name college was not what it is today nor was a college education so essential for getting a job as it now is. Furthermore, because everyone does it, he argues that this gives cheating the stamp of approval. Therefore, he concludes, branding cheating as dishonest is unfair (54,69,143).

The fourth and most serious consequence of the confusion resulting from the many difficulties the adolescent faces in making the transition to adult morality is the difficulty he encounters in *making a decision where two or more moral alternatives are present*. Making a decision that could lead to social disapproval as easily as it could lead to approval, to punishment as easily as to praise and reward, places the adolescent in a predicament.

He knows that he cannot rely on parents and teachers to get him out of a scrape as he could when he was a child. He further knows that society's judgments will be directed toward him, not toward his parents who failed in their duties as guardians of his morals. Making a decision that can affect his future status in the social group becomes a problem of major concern. To avoid this, he will withhold judgment as long as possible in the hope that some decisive factor may appear to help him come to a conclusion. When this becomes his characteristic pattern of reaction to moral alternatives, he will begin to doubt his ability to decide moral issues. He will then develop a hesitancy which will create the impression that he lacks moral courage (41, 54,76).

VARIATIONS IN MAKING TRANSITION

Girls, on the whole, have less difficulty in making the transition than do boys, primarily because their early training has been stricter and because rules of conduct are more important to girls. They know that adhering to cultural values enhances their prestige. For boys, by contrast, violation of rules and even of laws gives them greater prestige, especially in the eyes of the peer

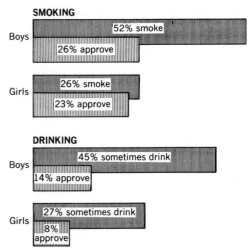

FIGURE 11–1 Adolescents often do things they disapprove of because they are influenced by peer pressures. (Adapted from P. H. Landis: *Adolescence and youth: the process of maturing.* 2d ed. New York: McGraw-Hill, 1952. Used by permission.)

group, than they could get by being law-abiding citizens (34,41,76,80,149).

The *personality pattern* of the adolescent, however, is a more important factor in determining the ease or difficulty of making the transition than any other factor. Peck and Havighurst (117) have classified moral character according to five "types," varying in the difficulty involved in reaching a mature moral status. These five types are:

1 The amoral type *lacks internalized principles and has little regard for the consequences of his behavior. This is the most infantile, impulsive, and irresponsible kind of personality.*

2 The expedient type *is one who is primarily self-centered in that he considers other people's welfare only to gain his own ends; he behaves according to the moral standards of the group only so long as it suits his purpose, primarily to get what he wants and to avoid social disapproval.*

3 The conforming type *is one whose main moral principle is to do what others do*

and what they say he should do. *This type follows rules and laws specific for each occasion instead of having generalized moral principles.*

4 The rational conscientious type *has his own internal standards of right and wrong by which he judges his acts, but he is rigid in applying his moral principles. To him, an act is "good" or "bad" because he defines it as such, not because of the good or ill effects it may have on others.*

5 The rational altruistic type *represents the highest level of moral maturity. Such a person has a stable set of moral principles by which he guides his behavior. In addition, he tries realistically to appraise the results of a given act and to assess it in terms of whether or not it serves others as well as himself. He is, thus, "rational" in his assessment of his conduct, in the light of his principles and "altruistic" in showing a concern for the welfare of others as well as of himself.*

In a follow-up study of a small group of boys and girls from the ages of 10 to 17 years, Peck and Havighurst reported that there was a marked tendency for them to show the same level of morality at ages 13 and 16 as they had shown when at 10. The adolescent's "character type," they concluded, has been established by the age of 10 years, owing to the early moral training received at home. As a result, many adolescents find the transition to adult morality difficult or impossible; they are handicapped by the early personality foundations they have laid (117).

The adolescent, for example, who is the expedient type, is in the habit of thinking of what he wants and of conforming to social expectations only so long as it suits his purpose; considering the welfare of others would be foreign to his usual pattern of behavior. Similarly, an adolescent of the amoral type is accustomed to being held back only by fear or threat of punishment; internalizing a control over his behavior would be a major revision in his usual pattern of behavior.

morality is learned

There is no evidence to confirm the popular belief that a person is born good or bad in the sense that he conforms or fails to conform to the mores of the group with which he is associated. On the other hand, there is ample evidence that morality is learned. Like all learning, it can be controlled and directed so that the individual will acquire the ability to conform to the expectations of his group. As Hemming has emphasized, "Moral development is the process by which the community seeks to transform the egocentricity of the baby into the social behavior of the mature adult" (66).

The process of becoming a moral person, begun early in childhood, continues through the adolescent years. There are six aspects or phases of learning "true morality" —moral behavior that is controlled from within rather than by forces from the outside. These six phases are (60):

1 *Learning to inhibit impulses.*
2 *Learning moral rules and principles.*
3 *Learning motives and attitudes from people, especially the significant people in the individual's life.*
4 *Acquiring an ideal self, as early as 5 or 6 years of age, as a model to imitate. This may change as the individual grows older but its value as a guide persists.*
5 *Formation of a scale of values.*
6 *Application of moral principles to new situations.*

Attitudes and values learned in childhood are subject to change and revision as the adolescent comes in contact with people of different attitudes and values. Changes occur, but the foundations laid earlier persist, modified to some extent (3,4,28,80, 98). This suggests that the most important learning in the development of morality is the "under-the-roof culture"—the learning that takes place when the social group is limited to that of the family (18,62,73).

Far too often the learning that takes place in the home emphasizes the negative side of moral codes. This means that children and adolescents are usually more certain of what they should not do than of what they should do. This leaves the "path to goodness undefined for them" (42). To avoid the perplexity that comes from too much emphasis on the negative side of moral codes, Landis (96) has suggested that:

> *The ideal situation . . . is for youth . . . to have sufficient inflexibility in the family and primary-group pattern so that certain definite values and standards are well marked, and yet to acquire sufficient experience in other groups so that he develops the power of discernment; and a variety of experience which will help him to reflect as an adult those phases of life in which he feels that he should participate in order to realize what for him are the most desirable objectives.*

In the early days of American education, schools and colleges were church-sponsored and the teachers were often ministers of the churches. Gradually, with the growth of secular schools, less emphasis has been placed on teaching morality except those moral codes specifically related to school or college behavior. A study of textbooks used in schools from 1810 to 1950, for example, revealed the marked decline that has taken place in the stress put on morality (32). (See Figure 11–2.) While Sunday schools and churches still combine the teaching of morality with the teaching of religion, decline in interest in religious observances from childhood into adolescence means that many older children and adolescents do not profit from the instruction given in morality (89,102).

Moral training consists not only of teaching the individual the moral codes of the group but also of instilling in him a *high regard* for these codes, so that he will be willing to accept them and guide his behavior accordingly. Many adolescents *know* what is considered right. They may, for one reason or another, refuse to accept this standard as their own. When, therefore, there is the possibility of escaping punishment or loss of social approval, they act in

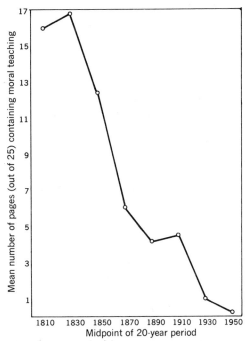

FIGURE 11–2 There has been a marked decrease in emphasis placed on moral teaching in school textbooks since the early nineteenth century. (Adapted from R. deCharms and G. H. Moeller: Values expressed in children's readers: 1800–1950. *J. abnorm. soc. Psychol.*, 1962, **64**, 136–142. Used by permission.)

accordance with their own standards, disregarding the standards of the group (28, 62,73,76).

It is essential that the adolescent learn to control his behavior so that external controls will not be necessary. This is for his own benefit as well as for the good of the social group. As he reaches adulthood, the adolescent will be held responsible for his acts; no longer can he rely on parents and teachers to tell him what to do and what not to do. He must decide for himself and then act in accordance with his decision (3, 41,80,111). In addition, it is essential that he do so for the benefit of others. As Poffenberger (118) has pointed out:

> *If a society is to survive, it must enforce its mores, folkways, and laws. These codes are most effective when the moral logic behind*

them is understood and accepted. This understanding and acceptance can best be gained through identification with sympathetic and understanding adults whose own values are made clear to the child and adolescent.

role of conscience in morality

The adolescent's conscience is the controlling force that makes external restraints unnecessary. "Conscience" is a term conveniently used to refer to a sense of rightness or wrongness of one's acts (2,96). As Finney has defined it, "Conscience is self-control by inner standards, learned by identification with others' ideals, and maintained by a remorseful or unworthy feeling when one violates it" (48). Eysenck refers to conscience as an "interiorized policeman" or "inner light" (47). Members of the Freudian school of psychologists sometimes refer to it as the "super ego" (48). Gesell (52) has explained "conscience" in terms of the concept of self:

> The self has the strange capacity to commune with itself both as a spectator and as a mentor with a small voice. This most mysterious of all self-phenomena proves to be a profound reality for the growing adolescent. This is his conscience.

Those who believe that a person is born moral or immoral usually believe that conscience is a part of the hereditary endowment. Many people, even today, refer to conscience as the "voice of God" telling the person what to do or what not to do. As Eysenck (47) has explained, to them conscience is:

> . . . some kind of deus ex machina implanted in the human being in some mysterious way, which ceaselessly keeps an eye on his activities, and gives him a sharp tweak whenever he deviates from the straight and narrow path of duty.

Just as there is ample evidence that people are not born moral or immoral but become so through learning, so is there ample evidence that the individual's conscience is likewise a product of learning.

It is often referred to as the "voice of the herd" because the control of the individual's behavior comes from his knowledge of what the cultural group with which he is identified expects of him (28,76,102).

The major task in moral training is "conscience building." Only when the individual knows what is expected of him and is willing to accept the mores of the group as a guide to his own behavior is he controlled by his conscience (80,95,149). That early experiences in the home play an important role in conscience building has been emphasized by Sears et al. (136):

> Mothers who love and accept their children and who use love-oriented techniques of discipline rather than material or physical techniques, produce relatively more children with high conscience.

CONSCIENCE BUILDING

Conscience building is the result of conditioning. Early in childhood, the child learns to associate pleasant emotional reactions with behavior the group approves and unpleasant emotions, especially fear and anxiety, with acts that are disapproved. From these unpleasant emotions develop guilt and shame, both of which play important roles in checking behavior that would win the disapproval of the group. Conscience is thus "conditioned anxiety responses to certain types of situations and actions" (47).

Guilt and shame, developed from fear and anxiety, act as deterrents to behavior. They are thus internalized controls over behavior. "Guilt" is a (5):

> . . . special kind of negative self-evaluation which occurs when an individual acknowledges that his behavior is at variance with a given moral value to which he feels obligated to conform. . . . It is one of the most important psychological mechanisms through which an individual becomes socialized in the ways of his culture. It is also an important instrument for cultural survival since it constitutes a most efficient watchdog within each individual, serving to keep his behavior compatible with the moral values of the society in which he lives.

If a person felt no guilt, he would have little motivation to conform to social expectations (76,102). Guilt, therefore, becomes an "internalized watchdog." However, before guilt can develop, a person must, first, accept certain standards of right and wrong or of good and bad as his own; second, accept the obligation of regulating his behavior to conform to whatever standards he has adopted and feel accountable for lapses from them; and, third, possess sufficient self-critical ability to recognize when a discrepancy between behavior and internalized values occurs (5).

"Shame" differs from guilt in that it is aroused in the individual by an "actual or presumed negative judgment of himself by others resulting in self-depreciation vis-a-vis the group" (5). Shame can be *non-moral*, as occurs in embarrassment when a person commits a breach of propriety or it can be *moral*, as when it is aroused by negative moral judgments of others. Shame, thus, relies on external sanctions alone; guilt relies on *both* internal and external sanctions. Shame may accompany guilt or it may be experienced alone (76,102,127). In the development of conscience, shame plays no role; guilt is the motivating factor that determines the course of the person's behavior (5). Behavior controlled by shame is "other-directed" while behavior controlled by guilt is "inner-directed" (2). Both are the product of learning.

When the adolescent realizes that his behavior is falling below the standards he has set or the expectations of the social group, guilt or shame may lead to a greater leniency in attitude toward the behavior in which he has fallen short (2). If an adolescent is tempted to cheat, for example, and does so, his attitude toward cheating is more lenient than it previously was. If, on the other hand, he resists the temptation either because of fear or guilt, his attitude toward cheating becomes more severe and intolerant (69,109,143).

TYPES OF CONSCIENCE

Peck and Havighurst (117) have distinguished four qualitatively different kinds of conscience. The first and least effective consists of a:

> . . . collection of harsh, crude "don'ts." At best, these act in an unthinkingly repressive way. At worst, they are so internally inconsistent or so excessively frustrating that they are impossible to follow.

The second kind of conscience is:

> . . . largely a matter of rule conformity, with the main weight of authority still residing in the people around one. Its one central principle is a willing, sometimes anxious desire to do whatever the "respected others" require.

Adolescents who have this kind of conscience:

> . . . possess a body of internalized rules for actions which they could not easily discard nor dramatically alter without feelings of guilt. The preponderant element in their moral control system, nonetheless, seems to be the desire to do "what people I respect want me to do." They find a good deal of needed reassurance in their acceptance by the "respected other," and experience shame when found wanting.

The third kind of conscience described by Peck and Havighurst:

> . . . consists of a firmly organized body of internalized moral rules which maintain their own autonomy. They are not so much affected by what other people may say; but neither do they permit themselves to be questioned or tested by rational inquiry.

The fourth kind of conscience is a:

> . . . firm set of internalized moral principles which are accessible to rational questioning and testing. . . . This most mature form of conscience is not a discrete entity, functioning in isolation from day-to-day experience. Instead, it changes and deepens in wisdom as new experiences are encountered.

VARIATIONS IN INFLUENCE OF CONSCIENCE

Adolescents who are bright or who come from upper middle-class backgrounds learn to control their behavior by feelings of guilt sooner than those who are less bright or who come from lower-class backgrounds (9, 11,76,80). Because adolescents of the Catholic faith have more emphasis placed on moral training in the home than do those of other faiths, they develop a conscience as a guide to their behavior earlier than adolescents of other faiths with similar mental abilities and socioeconomic backgrounds (9, 102). Throughout adolescence, the role of conscience in moral behavior is more important for girls than for boys (10,80,127). Adolescents who are extroverted in their behavior are more susceptible to social attitudes than are introverts; as a result, they are more easily conditioned to experience guilt and shame when their behavior falls below social standards (47,111).

Regardless of these variations, every adolescent whose behavior falls short of his standards has a strong sense of personal inadequacy. Even in the absence of social disapproval, he will have a guilty conscience of greater or lesser severity. This leads to marked emotional tension. Unquestionably some of the unhappiness that every adolescent experiences traces its origin to a guilty conscience for real or imagined wrongdoing (3,41,73,80,102,111).

changes in moral concepts

From his parents, teachers, and other adults in authority, the child learns what is right and what is wrong. Adults interpret for him the moral codes of the community and punish him when he violates these codes. However, the moral codes of childhood are not adequate to meet his more mature needs when he reaches adolescence. They must be revised to conform to the codes that guide the lives of the adult members of the community. This is especially true of moral codes that have a religious foundation. If, for example, the child has learned that God watches him, telling him what to do or what not to do, and then rewards him if he obeys or punishes him if he disobeys, he will no longer accept this concept when he begins to doubt his childish religious beliefs (28,71,102,111).

Lax moral training in childhood, or failure to punish the child when he intentionally violates the accepted codes of the group, results in the establishment of faulty codes, which may prove to be a source of trouble later on (28,73,76,80,104).

Whether the adolescent will reach a higher level of moral behavior, where his conduct is regulated by moral principles and moral choice, or a lower "popular" level, where conduct is controlled by praise and reward from his immediate social environment will depend to a large extent upon how much he revises his moral concepts as he goes through adolescence (61). A follow-up study of a group of seventh- and eighth-grade children 12 years later showed that 75 percent of those who had rated in the upper third of the group in honesty as children continued to be honest in adulthood. This suggests that once moral concepts are formulated into a moral code during the adolescent years, they will persist almost unchanged throughout life (80).

TIME OF CHANGE

It is generally assumed that changes in moral concepts will accompany the process of sexual maturing. Studies of moral concepts have not shown this to be true. Furthermore, there is no evidence of a sudden change in moral concepts with age. Instead, there is a gradual but steady increase in moral discrimination from the ages of 12 to 16 years (41,77,111,149). Even at 16 years, the ability to apply moral beliefs to an increasing range of conflicting life situations is still quite undeveloped and the adolescent finds conflicts hard to face (61). Thus, there is no evidence of a parallel between maturity in moral thinking and physical maturing (28,36,41,54,80).

As the adolescent passes from the narrower environment of his childhood to the broader environment of the community at large, it is necessary for him to broaden and revise some of his codes of behavior (43). This adjustment is frequently difficult for him, especially when he is placed in larger groups where he is unknown, as in a large college or university, or in a new community. In his attempt to adjust his moral codes to his new environment, he may go too far and for a time "sow wild oats." It unquestionably will, however, bring about changes in moral concepts. This is seen by the fact that the most marked change in moral concepts generally comes between high school and college (80,111,119,149). During late adolescence, the "oughts" of custom and law are well understood; they come to be more and more accepted as the adolescent progresses through college or enters the adult world of work. Students who work their way through college or older adolescents who are working in business or industry are likely to be superior to other adolescents of the same age in the maturity of their moral concepts (28,41,80,113).

TYPES OF CHANGE

There are a number of ways in which the moral concepts, learned in childhood, must be changed to meet the needs of the adolescent. For one thing, the adolescent is expected to *generalize* his childish moral concepts. Generalizing specific moral concepts and incorporating them into a workable code to use in any situation is a gradual process that continues throughout the adolescent years (43,61,80).

As the adolescent evaluates different forms of behavior in terms of moral concepts, he is likely to find some behavior less desirable than others. No longer are "wrong" things wrong to the same degree as they were when he was a child. He now ascribes *degrees of seriousness* to different acts; some of the things that he learned were wrong as a child he now views in a more liberal manner. When students of grades 6 through 12 were asked to write down behaviors that would be praised or blamed by their contemporaries, it was found that they became more liberal toward certain forms of behavior than toward others as they grew older. For example, twelfth graders rated being dishonest more serious, as compared with being careless, than they had during the sixth grade (152).

In Figure 11–3 are shown changes in moral values regarding different forms of behavior, from the sixth grade through college. From this it is apparent that there is a marked drop in the seriousness attached

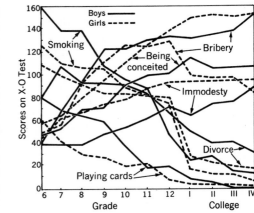

FIGURE 11–3   Moral values regarding different forms of behavior change from childhood into adolescence. (Adapted from S. L. Pressey and R. G. Kuhlen: *Psychological development through the life span.* New York: Harper & Row, 1957. Used by permission.)

to smoking, card playing, and divorce as the adolescent becomes older, just as there is a marked increase in the seriousness associated with conceit and bribery. Smoking and divorce, which are often strongly condemned by children and even by some young adolescents, were found to be only mildly condemned by older adolescents. On the other hand, bribery and immodesty, which are regarded as relatively minor offenses by children, are more strongly condemned by older adolescents (119,120). In behavior relating to sex, there are even more marked changes in moral values with age. This is especially true of attitudes toward masturbation, flirting, petting, necking, and premarital intercourse. Many adolescents regard masturbation as wrong, just as they did in childhood; others have a more tolerant attitude toward it. While they may not regard it as wrong, they usually think of it as a socially disapproved form of behavior (84,145). Many adolescents likewise show a greater leniency in their attitudes toward flirting, petting, and premarital intercourse. In the case of the latter, they regard it as permissible if the couple is engaged and if it is an expression of deep affection on the part of both (88,124).

When college students were asked

whether they consider all immoral acts, or only certain ones, intrinsically worse for a woman than for a man, 56 percent of the group said that there are no acts that are worse for a woman than for a man. On the other hand, 61 percent of the others thought that telling obscene stories was worse for women, and 71 percent, that illicit sexual behavior was more a moral responsibility for women. The acts that women can do and be judged no more severely than men are cheating, lying, stealing, and flirting (81). In the area of sexual behavior, on the other hand, the *double standard* persists. Women, for example, disapprove of premarital relations of engaged couples more than men do (78,124). A prostitute is more condemned than are married men who have relations with prostitutes (116).

The final important type of change in moral concepts in adolescence is a gradual increase in concern for the *motives* behind an act. Children tend to condemn an act as right or wrong on its face value without considering the reason for the act. For example, if they believe that telling a lie is wrong, they condemn all lying; they are unwilling to concede that there *might* be times when a lie is justified. By contrast, from 12 years of age on, there is a gradual increase in the tendency to liberalize moral concepts and to believe that certain acts that are usually labeled as wrong may be right under certain circumstances. Adolescents also recognize that punishment may be just and fair under some circumstances and unfair under others (42,77,80).

SPECIFIC MORAL CONCEPTS

With advancing age, the individual changes his concepts of right and wrong. In this change, some concepts become more liberal, others more conservative, and a few, more rigid. A brief survey of some of the most important moral concepts will serve to illustrate the changes that occur during adolescence.

Honesty Moral values relating to honesty are well established by adolescence; little change occurs as the individual be-

comes older. There is, however, a greater consistency in behavior where honesty and dishonesty are involved than is found during the childhood years. This is, unquestionably, due at least in part to the adolescent's ability to generalize moral concepts so that they may be applied to a wide variety of related situations (57,80).

Studies of honesty in different areas of behavior, such as telling the truth or the use of property, show that concepts are widely and unquestionably accepted by high school students. They strongly disapprove of *borrowing things without permission* or of using even small sums of family money without gaining permission to do so. In judging the honesty of others, the young adolescent uses rigorous and even extreme standards. However, as he grows older, he becomes more liberal in his attitudes (69, 80,119,143).

Cheating Honesty in school situations shows how marked are the changes in moral values with advancing age. Studies of cheating in junior and senior high schools as well as in colleges suggest that about one-third of the students cheat; under specific circumstances, the number may be as high as two-thirds. There are certain social pressures placed on the adolescent to maintain his status in school to guarantee his status in the social group. The greater emphasis the parents and the school place on grades, the more lenient will be the adolescent's attitude toward cheating (6,20,63,69,112,133, 143).

When a student feels that cheating is justified because of the pressures placed on him to get high grades and when most of his friends are under similar pressures and resort to cheating, he will cheat and not feel guilty about it or ashamed if caught. Among college students, even when an honor system prevails, there is a fairly universal belief that cheating is justified and that the major problem is to work out a system of cheating that will be so foolproof there will be no chance of being caught (4,16,63,69,92). That pressure to get good grades is an important factor in changing the adolescent's concept of cheating has been emphasized thus by Rogosin (132):

> *Putting a premium on acquiring high marks, and then assuming that resistance to temptation will automatically take place because of a generalized trait of honesty, is to fly in the face of all the available scientific information and evidence. Honor systems of one kind or another cannot be said to exist in a social vacuum.*

Girls are less tolerant in their attitudes toward cheating than are boys at every age, but especially so in late adolescence. Poor students regard cheating as a "must" to maintain their status in school; as a result, they have a more tolerant attitude toward it than good students. Students who were formerly satisfied with a gentleman's C because they could get into the college of their choice with such grades are today more lenient in their attitudes than are students whose educational aspirations are to get a high school diploma and then a job (4,16, 63,69,111,143).

Lying Lying is a form of dishonesty that has been found to follow a pattern similar to that of cheating. Before adolescence, there is a strong tendency to condemn it as wrong under all circumstances. This is especially true when children have learned moral concepts in relation to their religion and have associated lying with displeasing God and the possibility of punishment in hell after death (20,71,102). If a child has had his mouth washed out with soap for telling lies, he develops a strong belief that lying is wicked and that, under no circumstances, should a person lie (141).

As children grow older and spend more time with members of the peer group, their attitude toward lying becomes more lenient. They recognize that there are times when lies are not only necessary but are permitted. The most common of such circumstances is when telling the truth might be construed as tattling on a friend (52). By adolescence, condemnation of lies on moral grounds declines as the age of the individual increases (80). However, most adolescents believe

that one should tell the truth *except* in circumstances where others will be harmed by doing so. Like the older child, the adolescent has a strong feeling of resentment toward anyone who tattles and believes that telling the truth about others may be interpreted as tattling (61,80,133).

If, for example, an adolescent is asked by a parent what a sibling did or said, out of loyalty to his sibling he would feel justified in lying if the truth might lead to trouble for the sibling. Similarly, at school, he feels justified in lying to protect a classmate from punishment if he knows the classmate's behavior, if he is caught, will lead to punishment. At all ages, boys have a more lenient attitude toward lying than do girls. This is illustrated in Figure 11–4.

Stealing Adolescents regard stealing as one of the worst offenses—even more serious than cheating and lying. As the older child comes in contact with members of the peer group he learns that different kinds of stealing are differently interpreted. The result is that, when he enters adolescence, he has a more lenient attitude toward stealing than he had as a child (20,61,80,162).

When high school boys were asked to rate different forms of stealing on the basis of their seriousness, they considered such acts as the following more serious: snitching

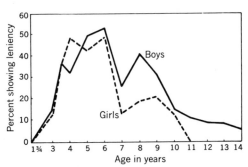

FIGURE 11–4 Boys at all ages have a more lenient attitude toward lying than girls. (Adapted from J. Macfarlane, L. Allen, and M. P. Honzik: *A developmental study of the behavior problems of normal children between twenty-one months and fourteen years.* Berkeley, Calif.: University of California Press, 1954. Used by permission.)

fruit from a peddler's stand, swiping flowers from a park, swiping your mother's wrist watch and pawning it, and lifting a dollar from your father's pants pocket when taking the pants to the tailor. The forms of stealing they considered less serious consisted of keeping a dollar you find on the street without trying to find the owner, keeping a candy package you find after it has fallen from a truck, helping yourself to chocolates from a box in your sister's room, and sneaking by an "El" cashier without paying. The most frequent reason given for their judgments of the relative seriousness of different forms of stealing was their unwillingness to injure others (44).

Destructiveness Destroying the possessions of others is recognized as morally wrong before childhood ends. Very few boys, except those who are delinquent, engage in this form of excitement after they are 10 years old, and few girls even as late as 10 years. Destroying things, just for excitement and fun, is regarded by adolescents as so wrong that few can imagine themselves engaging in such activities (21). However, some adolescents persist in destructiveness to prove to themselves and to members of the peer group that they are unafraid to flaunt the law or to defy those in authority (23,163). This is especially true of boys. Sex differences in destructiveness are shown in Figure 11–5.

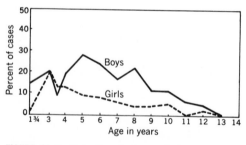

FIGURE 11–5 Intentional destructiveness reaches its lowest point at the time of puberty. (Adapted from J. Macfarlane, L. Allen, and M. P. Honzik: *A developmental study of the behavior problems of normal children between twenty-one months and fourteen years.* Berkeley, Calif.: University of California Press, 1954. Used by permission.)

Drinking There are marked changes in the moral values assigned to drinking from childhood to adolescence. To a child, drinking under any circumstances is likely to be regarded as wrong. Early in adolescence, boys not only begin to drink but they no longer condemn those who drink. This is true of girls also, though the change of attitude generally comes later, when the girl starts to drink occasionally as part of the accepted social pattern for parties and dates. Among boys, drinking to excess is not considered wrong but rather as a way of proving to the group that one is a good sport and not effeminate. Refer to pages 282 to 284 for a more complete discussion of drinking during adolescence.

Responsibility Standards of responsibility are highly developed in adolescence, especially those related to work outside the school. Punctuality in attending meetings, completing accepted jobs, and aiding the family financially all stand high in moral values among high school students (3,41,56, 73,111). However, accepting responsibility for one's acts when they violate rules and laws is less well developed. This will be discussed more fully in the following chapter.

morality building through discipline

The term "discipline" comes from the Latin word *disciplina*, which means "teaching" or "instruction." In modern times, as in the past, the main purpose of discipline is to teach the individual a reasonable degree of social conformity. In addition, discipline teaches him that the world responds in an orderly way to his actions, that certain behaviors will always be followed by punishment and others by praise (28,41,110). And finally, discipline helps the individual to develop self-control and self-direction so that he can make wise decisions on his own responsibility. He thus develops a conscience to motivate him to carry out his decisions (50,58).

The modern concept of discipline, thus, puts emphasis on learning what the social group expects, self-control, and self-direction, all of which are motivated by social sensitivity to the welfare of others (28, 41). In discipline, an attempt is made to correct behavior that is at variance with the standards set by authority (147). However, not everyone today accepts this concept of discipline. In a study of home training, Peck and Havighurst (117) found that:

> . . . a remarkable diversity of parental behavior went by the name of "discipline." Anything from a brutal beating, to ineffectual verbal nagging unbacked by action, to rigorously enforced conformity to every parental dictate (and lots of them), to a clearly reasoned, left-handed guidance of a child along a well-explained path, with allowance for non-dangerous, experimental side excursions—all these were called "discipline" by somebody. They were not equal, needless to say, in their effect on character.

ESSENTIALS OF DISCIPLINE

If the adolescent is to learn what society expects of him and be motivated to control his behavior to conform to these expectations, discipline must include four essential elements: education in moral concepts, reward for socially approved behavior, punishment for intentional wrongdoing, and consistency in social expectations. Not one of these can be neglected if the adolescent is to achieve the desired goal of self-controlled behavior.

Education in Moral Concepts Many adults go on the assumption that, when the child reaches adolescence, he has learned what is right or wrong and that no further training is necessary. This is far from true. As the social horizons broaden in adolescence, boys and girls must know what boundaries society places in many new situations and what society will tolerate. The function of rules and laws is to teach the individual what these boundaries are, not alone to restrain undesirable behavior.

If, for example, the adolescent learns that smoking is not permitted on the school premises, that he is not permitted to stay out after 11 o'clock on school nights, and that the legal limit for driving in the city is 30 miles an hour, he knows what is ex-

pected of him. While he may not agree with these rules and laws and he may attempt to break them, he still knows that he must face the consequences if he does so (61,137). In general, the learning of moral concepts should be completed, or nearly so, when the adolescent reaches legal maturity. After that, he will be held responsible for his acts without the constant guidance and supervision he formerly had from parents and teachers.

Reward for Socially Approved Behavior Rewards serve two purposes: first, they are *educational* in that they tell the adolescent that his behavior has won social approval and, therefore, is "good" behavior; second, they are *ego bolstering*, and this stimulates him to continue to act in that way (51, 155). Because many adolescents, as a defense against feelings of insecurity, build up a cocky attitude which suggests that they are conceited and self-satisfied, many adults shy away from using rewards on the ground that they will add to an adolescent's conceit and encourage him in his smugness. Others argue that it will kill any motivation the adolescent might have to do what is expected of him. They claim that it is better to use threats of punishment as a club over the adolescent's head than to reward him for good behavior (107).

There is evidence, however, that rewards do not have bad effects; on the contrary, they are strong motivating forces to conform to society's expectations. As such, they are a "potent instrument in discipline" (155). To motivate, however, rewards must be developmentally appropriate. While a child might respond favorably to a reward for good behavior, such as being allowed to stay up late to watch television if he is "nice to Grandmother," the adolescent would scoff at such a reward.

Material rewards are always acceptable to an adolescent, provided they are things that have prestige value in the eyes of the peer group, such as a new article of clothing, new sports equipment, or money for a dance, a trip, or a new transistor radio. Unquestionably, the greatest reward for an adolescent is praise. Far too often, the comments made to him by parents and teachers are in the form of criticism; a kind word is a pleasant relief from constant nagging. Not only is praise ego bolstering but it has great educational value. It tells the adolescent that his act was so acceptable that it was worthy of commendation. However, to be a "potent instrument in discipline," praise must be used judiciously, not just when a parent or teacher happens to be in a good mood. And the strength of the praise must be regulated according to the goodness of the act. Indiscriminate use of lavish praise takes away its educational value because the adolescent has no way of judging the relative goodness of an act (76,80,107,155).

Punishment for Intentional Wrongdoing
Punishment is not pleasant at any age. In adolescence, it is likely to be humiliating as well. This is especially true when the punishment used is similar to that applied to children, such as spankings, slaps, or being sent to bed without anything to eat. When parents use poor judgment about the type of punishment they use, when there is disagreement between the parents about whether the adolescent should be punished and how he should be punished, and when the severity of the punishment is out of proportion to what the adolescent has done, it is likely to have an unfavorable effect. Indiscriminate use of punishment causes it to lose its value as a guidepost for mature behavioral control (107).

Like reward, punishment serves two major functions in discipline. First, it *deters the repetition* of socially undesirable acts, and second, it shows the adolescent *what the social group considers wrong.* If punishment is to motivate the adolescent to avoid behaving in a socially unacceptable way, he must view the punishment as fair and deserved. Otherwise, his resentment will kill any motivation he might otherwise have developed to avoid such acts in the future. Equally as important, punishment must be given only when it is evident that the adolescent knew what was expected of him but intentionally violated this expectation. If punishment is to show the adolescent what the social group considers wrong, its severity

must be in keeping with the severity of the wrongness of his act. He should not, for example, be as severely punished for coming into class late as for cheating; nor must he be as severely punished for coming home late at night as for going to forbidden places where liquor is served or where he will be associating with adults of questionable reputation (137,155).

Far too often, the adolescent is punished by an adult who is angry because of what the adolescent has done. The severity of punishment, under such conditions, reflects the adult's anger more than the seriousness of the misbehavior. Furthermore, adults judge the seriousness of misbehavior in terms of their values, not in terms of the values of the peer group, and punish accordingly. If, then, adults punish according to their values, the severity of the punishment may seem out of proportion to the seriousness of the act, as the adolescent judges it (90). As a result, the second major function of discipline—to show the adolescent what the group considers wrong and the seriousness of his wrongdoing—will not be fulfilled.

If, then, punishment is to serve the purpose of aiding in self-control, it must have the following characteristics (139):

1 It should be related in form to the misbehavior.
2 It must be certain and consistent.
3 It must be fair and just.
4 It must be impersonal.
5 It must be constructive and conducive to better self-control.
6 It should be withheld until the adolescent's motive is understood.
7 It should avoid the arousal of fear.
8 It should not involve the assignment of extra work that is unrelated to the act for which the adolescent is being punished.

Spankings and whippings, so common in childhood, are relatively infrequent forms of punishment for adolescents living in cities and small towns; they are quite frequent for those living in rural areas. By far the most common form of punishment reported by junior and senior high school boys and girls is being "talked to" or scolded.

Other commonly used forms of punishment are "being made to stay at home," being slapped, and being deprived of pleasures and privileges (70,146,147).

While fathers do punish adolescents, especially boys, mothers are more often the ones who punish. The reason for this is that the modern father is away from home for the major part of the day, thus leaving the mother to discipline the children (146). Among juvenile delinquents, on the other hand, the father more often administers the punishment. This will be discussed in more detail in the next chapter.

An adolescent is likely to receive punishment whenever he breaks a rule, at home or in school, or when he does things he has been told not to do. In one study, the conditions that led to punishment were reported to be wild play, fighting with a sib, really losing one's temper, refusing to do what parents tell one to do, using "bad" language, smoking cigarettes, and swearing (90). The use of punishment is increasingly less frequent as the adolescent approaches legal maturity. Whether this is because older adolescents do not need punishment as much or because parents and teachers feel they are too old to be punished has not been determined. Boys at every age are punished more than girls; boys tend to be more rebellious against rules and laws than girls. Adolescents from small towns and cities are punished more than those who come from farm homes (26,146).

Consistency in Social Expectations If discipline is to serve its purpose of teaching the adolescent a reasonable degree of social conformity, it must be consistent (50,137). The importance of consistency is that it gives the adolescent a feeling of security in knowing where his boundaries, limits, and freedoms are; this eliminates confusion (51). It helps him to know that there is moral orderliness in the world. Even more important, it teaches him that rewards and punishments are predictable, not haphazard.

Variations between extremes of leniency and severity lead to confusion. This, in turn, leads to lack of security and self-confidence. Of even greater seriousness, in-

consistency in discipline slows down the learning process. In addition, inconsistent discipline causes friction between parents and children; adolescents consider it unfair to be punished one day for an act which previously has gone unpunished. In time, this causes the adolescent to lose respect for his disciplinarians. When this happens, it weakens his motivation to obey their rules (1,22,134). In commenting on adolescents' reactions to inconsistent discipline, Strang (148) has written:

> The inconsistencies of adults are vexatious to adolescents. . . . Adolescents, as well as younger children, want the security that comes from knowing exactly what they can do and what they cannot do. They do not like to live in an uncertain world, in which the same act is punished one day and ignored the next.

There are a number of reasons for inconsistencies in discipline. Parents and teachers who are inexperienced in their roles are often uncertain of what they should expect of an adolescent, especially when they are constantly told by the adolescent that everybody is allowed to do something different. Inconsistency may and often does stem from an ambivalent attitude toward the adolescent on the part of his parents; they swing from love to bitter resentment, depending on how he treats them and what he says to them. More often, however, it traces its origin to conflicts in parental attitudes toward discipline. When this occurs, the lenient parent is likely to be stricter in the presence of the stricter parent than he or she is when alone with the adolescent; the strict parent vacillates from his usual strictness to greater leniency in the presence of the other parent (12,121,142,150,156).

Mothers tend to be more inconsistent in their discipline of both children and adolescents than do fathers. Mothers may have strict rules but they often fail to impose them; they threaten to punish and then allow the offender to go scot free; and they give both rewards and punishments more in relation to their feelings toward the adolescent at the moment than in relation to the goodness or badness of the act (134).

Middle-class mothers tend to be the most inconsistent of all disciplinarians, mainly because they impose strict rules and then fail to follow through on them (159). The most lenient and most severe disciplinarians tend to be the most consistent (12,87). However, they too are inconsistent at times (142).

need for discipline

To play its role successfully, discipline must be adjusted to the developmental status of the individual. Vincent and Martin (155) have explained why people need discipline at every age:

> Everyone needs discipline (rules of conduct) in order to adjust his needs and desires to those of others, and in order to keep the affection and approval of people around him.

Without discipline, the adolescent will not develop the ego controls needed to help him adjust to the reality demands of life; with discipline, he will develop these controls and, as a result, make good adjustments to life's demands (38).

Some parents assume that an adolescent is capable of guiding his own conduct, and therefore they abandon all attempts at discipline. But the problem of learning to fit into the adult world is very great for the adolescent. Often an adolescent does the wrong thing just because he does not know how to deal with the situation in the right way. He needs guidance in acquiring techniques of meeting difficult and perplexing problems. Furthermore, the adolescent's values change from week to week, thus adding to his feelings of insecurity. From discipline, he derives a steadying influence provided by the people in his environment who remain the same in values and attitudes (27,55,107,147).

Adolescents feel the need of discipline but not of the type they had in childhood. What adolescents rebel against is the authoritarian rule that they resented in childhood and which they resent even more now that they are near adults. Their rebellion, as Hechinger and Hechinger have pointed out, stems from the fact that they are "testing their power at least as much as they are rebelling, and they fully expect and want to have a limit set for their actions" (65).

Older adolescents feel that their parents and teachers should not use the same authoritarian approach used earlier; they want a more mature type of discipline, one that puts more stress on guidance than on prohibitions and punishments. Boys regard rules as external controls to keep them out of trouble and to restrain any negative behavior they might be tempted to engage in. Girls, on the other hand, look upon rules as a means of teaching them how to behave and as standards to direct and channel their energies (37). Adolescents frankly state that they feel the need of discipline, especially when its emphasis is on guidance. As one girl put it (148):

> I want adults to help me make my decisions, show me where I am wrong, teach me the good things of life, distinguish good from bad, and prevent me from taking the wrong road.

Another high school student (148) expressed concern for guidance by saying, "The help I want from my parents is to raise me the right way so I won't get mixed up with the wrong people." Still another voiced this opinion (148):

> I think we respect our elders more if they show concern about our affairs, even if we don't think so at the time. I, for one, would hate to be able to go wherever I wanted and come home as late as I wished. I think we need certain restrictions.

Adolescents feel a special need for discipline in areas of behavior which are new and for which they have no childhood experiences as guides. This is especially true in behavior related to members of the opposite sex. Because of the complexity of the sex problem for adolescents today, they want guidance even more than was true of adolescents in the past when chaperonage served as a guide for behavior in this new area of experiences (88).

Most important of all, they want consistency in the discipline that is used to guide their behavior. Many adolescents complain more about inconsistencies than about too great strictness or leniency in discipline. They even go so far as to say that parents and teachers should not make exceptions to rules, no matter what the circumstances are (39).

VARIATIONS IN NEED

The *younger* the adolescent, the greater his need for the security discipline can give him. However, within any age group, this will vary according to the *degree of adjustment* of the individual. Boys and girls who are well adjusted need less discipline than do those who are poorly adjusted. When poor adjustment stems from too much discipline, the need is for more freedom of choice and fewer restraints imposed by those in authority. Freedom and responsibility under guidance generally produce better results than too much or too little discipline (128). Because *girls,* from earliest childhood, conform to authority more than do boys, girls need less discipline than boys (154). Figure 11–6 shows the difference between boys and girls in their attitudes toward authority.

methods of control

Methods of controlling the behavior of adolescents can be divided roughly into three systems: the authoritarian, the democratic, and the permissive. They differ markedly in the way in which they attempt to control the behavior of the individual and in the effects they have on him.

AUTHORITARIAN CONTROL

Authoritarian control is based on the belief that parents know best and that the adolescent must submit to their commands or be punished. It is further believed that this type of control helps to give the child a "proper" conception of parental authority and of his relationship to that authority (41,99).

There are three characteristics of the authoritarian method: first, little or no attempt is made to explain to the adolescent the reason for the rules he is expected to

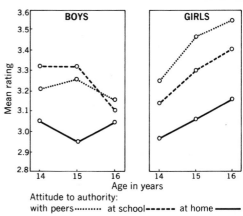

Attitude to authority:
with peers ·········· at school ------ at home ————

FIGURE 11–6 Differences between boys and girls in their attitudes toward authority during early adolescence. (Adapted from E. Tuma and N. Livson: Family socioeconomic status and adolescent attitudes to authority. *Child Developm.,* 1960, **31,** 386–399. Used by permission.)

submit to; second, it is assumed that his breaking of rules is intentional and he is not given an opportunity to explain his reason for doing so; and third, punishment is almost always corporal and of a harsh and sometimes cruel nature. The authoritarian parent regards punishment as a reinforcer; consequently, the harsher it is, the better it will teach the individual that he must conform to adult commands (101).

In homes where authoritarian control is used, parents set high standards for their children and punish them when they fail to live up to these standards. In such homes, parents set themselves above their children and establish formal dictatorial relations with them (72,83,117,155). Authoritarian parents commonly use one of two different types of control: they either use "blanket warnings" that leave the adolescent insecure and afraid to engage in any new behavior, or they set certain limits, at the same time encouraging the adolescent to engage in accepted forms of activity. The second type of control produces better results and fewer resentments (38,41,80).

DEMOCRATIC CONTROL

The democratic method of control is a more flexible type in which the person in authority explains why certain behavior is expected and why the offender will be punished if he violates these expectations. Its four outstanding characteristics are: first, the belief that the person involved has a right to know what is expected of him and to understand why; second, a willingness to hear his reasons for violating these expectations before administering punishment; third, inflicting punishment only when it is evident that the adolescent knew he was disobeying and, then, to punish him in accordance with the seriousness of his act; and fourth, the use of punishment more closely related to the act rather than corporal punishment which is both humiliating and anger producing to the adolescent (45,99).

While many people regard the democratic method of control as a sign of parental softness, it is far from that (83,138, 155). In discussing families who use democratic methods of control, Peck and Havighurst (117) have emphasized:

> The most democratic of these families, relative to the entire population, were by no means "child-centered" in the manner caricatured as "progressive." The parents unmistakably and firmly reserved the right to make final decisions, whenever they felt it necessary. They had an attitude, though, of expecting and encouraging the child to learn to make an increasing number of decisions each year, on more issues, as his judgment became competent on such issues.

PERMISSIVE CONTROL

Permissive control is, in reality, little or no control. Instead of rules formulated by parents or by parents in cooperation with their children, the adolescent is allowed to do what he thinks is right, even if this is not in accordance with what the parents think is right. Because this does not mean that the adolescent will be breaking rules—as there are few rules to break—punishment is rarely given by the permissive disciplinarian. The belief is that the wrongdoer will learn from the consequences of his act that it was wrong. This, they believe, will teach him not to repeat the act.

While permissive control may come

from indifference on the part of parents and teachers, more often it is the result of the belief that the adolescent is now old enough and experienced enough to manage his affairs alone without the control needed in childhood. It may come from the belief that some of the friction in the home or school could be eliminated if the adolescent were given more freedom. It may be based on the belief that he is capable of making his own decisions as he claims he is. It sometimes comes from the belief that too many thwartings damage the adolescent's personality by weakening his self-confidence and building up resentments. Parents who believe this feel that unless the adolescent is given more freedom to handle his affairs, he will become overly dependent and "weak" (22,68,134,137). Figure 11–7 shows the characteristics of different types of discipline.

VARIATIONS IN CHOICE OF METHOD

Which of the three common methods of control will be used depends largely on which was used when the adolescent was a *child*. If his parents believed that authoritarian control was the best method of bringing up children, or if he went to a school where authoritarian control was used, the chances are that he will be subjected to similar control as an adolescent (13,19, 164). The type of disciplinary method will vary according to where the family lives, its socioeconomic status, and many other factors. In *urban* areas, home discipline is less autocratic than in farm areas, where young people must be controlled as a means of aid in the work of the farm. The modern urban family, by contrast, tries to prepare its young people to control their own behavior so that they may live independently as early as possible (41,62,158).

As the *social status* of the family improves, there is greater flexibility of disciplinary methods and a more democratic approach. On the other hand, the lower the socioeconomic status of the family, the stronger the authoritarian control. Working-class parents want to assure that there will be "respectable" behavior; to do so, they rely on corporal punishment as a means to

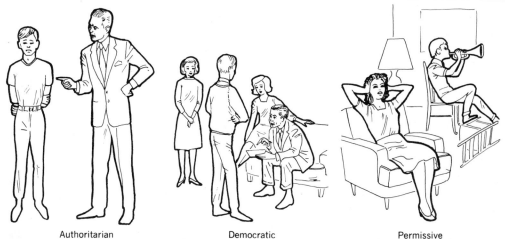

Authoritarian   Democratic   Permissive

FIGURE 11-7 Types of discipline.

an end. As a result, many lower-class adolescents concentrate on avoiding punishment, while asserting their independence of parental domination. Middle-class parents are more anxious to train their children to control their own behavior so that they can win social approval. This they try to do by stimulating feelings of guilt and shame and by threats of loss of parental love (74,90, 122).

Within the middle class, parents who are *better educated* are more democratic in their methods of control than are less well-educated parents (30). Regardless of the social class of the family, *foreign-born parents* are more authoritarian than are native-born parents (123). The same is true of families with strong *religious interests*; the more religious the family, the more authoritarian the discipline usually is. Jewish parents tend to be less authoritarian in their training methods than do Catholic parents; Mormon and Latter-day Saints are extremely strict (94,160). Within families, parents tend to be more authoritarian in their control of their *daughters* than of their sons. This is true in adolescence just as it is throughout the childhood years (82,136).

evaluation of methods of control

How successful the method of control is must be assessed not only in terms of what

effects it has on the adolescent's behavior but also what effect it has on his attitude toward the person in authority, toward people in authority in general, and on his motivation to try to conform to social expectations. As Landis (96) has pointed out:

> The ultimate test of a disciplinary pattern is the extent to which it helps the individual reach a place of maturity wherein he can make all decisions for himself and face the responsibilities for his own choices, whether good or bad.

An evaluation of the three commonly used patterns of control will enable one to see which comes closest to producing "moral maturity"—the goal of moral development as the individual goes from childhood into maturity.

AUTHORITARIAN CONTROL

Adolescents brought up by authoritarian control "receive their morality ready-made from domineering parents" (96). As a result, they are unprepared to cope with the problems adolescence brings. If they are given more freedom then than they had earlier, it comes too suddenly for them to handle; this makes them unsure of themselves. If, as is more often the case, there is a continuation of the authoritarian control that existed throughout their childhood years, they become either shy and insecure or their insecurity makes them compensate by overboldness and rebellion. Much as they want to be independent, they lack confidence in their ability to make decisions and carry them out successfully (38,45,96).

Overstrictness causes the adolescent to believe that the whole world is hostile. He may, then, become submissive and toe the mark in a blind, unthinking way, even if he does not allow himself to act in an openly antagonistic manner (55,117). As a result, he may and often does become a high achiever in whatever he undertakes. He rarely causes trouble for his parents, teachers, or others in authority (38). Such adolescents develop a "priggish self-justification" for their submissiveness and have an attitude of contempt for those who cause trouble for others or whose behavior falls below social expectations (49). This "Pecksniffian attitude" of moral superiority makes them thoroughly disliked by members of the peer group who regard them as goody-goodies (162).

More often, however, overstrictness which leads to feelings that the world is hostile causes the adolescent to reject authority and to try to assert his independence. As Frank has pointed out, "The stricter the parents, the stronger may be the revolt and the more outrageous the 'hell-raising'" (49). Many adolescents, when they find that they cannot change the authoritarian control in the home or school, leave home or drop out of school or both. Among girls, one of the reasons for early marriage is to escape the parental domination of their homes. However, few adolescents brought up in authoritarian homes change to more democratic methods of control when they become parents. The long-term effects of authoritarian training have been found to leave their mark on the individual to the point where he, too, becomes authoritarian in his treatment of others. As Peck and Havighurst (117) have explained:

> Harshly autocratic but consistent parents create a child who is overtly submissive during youth and apt to take over the role of a rigid rule-transmitter upon embarking on parenthood himself. . . . During childhood and youth, the child's overt compliance and submissiveness may seem the opposite of the parents' dominating assertiveness; but even by late adolescence, most such children show a restless urge to break free and set up their own families where they can be "boss." This replication of the parental style does not obtain in all cases; but the replication of the authoritarian, conforming value system does seem to apply in all such cases.

PERMISSIVE CONTROL

Unlimited freedom adds to the adolescent's already present feeling of insecurity. There are few things that will precipitate panic behavior so readily as the lifting of all adult control. Furthermore, adolescents resent lack of adult guidance, they are enraged when they do something wrong and have to pay the penalty for it just because no one warned them that it was wrong, and they look upon excessive permissiveness as an indication of weakness on the part of the disciplinarian or as due to lack of interest in them and their welfare. In general, adolescents do not welcome freedom to guide their own behavior. Instead, they resent it (55,86).

Adolescents who have grown up in permissive homes or whose parents relax discipline when the child reaches adolescence tend to become "spoiled brats" or "little monsters" whom others dislike and reject (157). They are disliked by members of the peer group as well as by adults because of their lack of consideration for the welfare of others and because they are uncooperative and selfish. Whenever they meet an obstacle in their path, they are unequipped to cope with it. They also lack the ability to persist in whatever they undertake because they have never learned to persist in situations where the odds were against them.

Perhaps the most serious effect of overly permissive control is that it fails to develop in the adolescent a sense of shame or guilt as a motivating force to conform to social expectations. Because he was never reproved or punished except when he did something seriously wrong and, even then, in too mild a manner to make much impression on him, the adolescent has no internal control over his behavior. Should he find himself in a situation where permissiveness is not an accepted form of control, as in college or in the world of business, he will feel that he is being mistreated and misunderstood if demands are made on him to conform to rules and regulations (5,47, 68,157). In discussing overly permissive control, Peck and Havighurst (117) have stressed the serious effects it has on the child and, later, on the adolescent and adult:

> Parents who are lazy and uncritically glad to let their child run loose to rear himself betray a childish self-centeredness that is mirrored in a child who is selfishly expedient. He is anxious enough for further approval to make him responsive to social expectations, but his capacities for self-discipline and self-restraint are too weak to generate very dependable moral behavior. Such parental "indulgence" may be obvious or subtle, but it is discernible and its effect is predictably poor character.

DEMOCRATIC CONTROL

Family relationships and the relationships the adolescent has with his teachers are far more wholesome when democratic control is used than when the control is either authoritarian or too permissive. When rules are explained and warnings are given about the punishment that will follow if the rules are broken, the adolescent feels that he is being fairly treated. While he may not always agree with the disciplinarian and he may argue that no one else has to abide by such rules, he at least knows that the rules are not laid down as an arbitrary whim of the disciplinarian. As a result, he is likely to conform, even though he puts up a protest first (45).

Democratic disciplinarians have a greater influence over the adolescent than any other type, and, in the long run, get more loyalty and respect from them. As a result, they can guide the adolescent in situations where he feels inadequate. This eliminates many of the failures and misbehaviors adolescents experience who rebel against all guidance because they feel the person in control is unfair or mean. This leads to a more wholesome attitude on the part of the adolescent, which is reflected in better relationships with members of the peer group as well as with those in authority (33,45,99,114,144,157).

The advantage of having democratic control, Peck and Havighurst have emphasized, is that it "produces mature, genuinely self-disciplined moral behavior." Furthermore, they emphasize, "This, in short, appears to be the best kind of discipline, and appears to be the only effective way to produce children of wholly mature, rational, self-disciplined morality" (117).

EVALUATION OF PUNISHMENT

Because punishment plays an important role in all forms of control—authoritarian, permissive, and democratic—the adolescent's reaction to the punishment he receives is a factor of no small significance in his reactions to the control over his behavior exercised by those in authority. An adolescent views the punishments he receives in a more critical manner than does the child, who invariably becomes angry and resentful when he is punished, no matter how much he may have deserved the punishment. When the adolescent feels that the punishment was fair and deserved, and that the motives of the person who administered the punishment were not at fault, he then accepts the punishment in a spirit of good sportsmanship. He does not harbor a grudge as a child does; he does not interpret this to mean that the person who punished him no longer loves him; nor does he seek means of revenge, especially by being disobedient in the same way in the near future.

While most adolescents consider their parents' punishments fair and sensible and realize that the parents punish, not in anger or dislike, but rather because they believe that it is necessary to their development, they nevertheless resent being punished (85,97). Adolescents are very critical of certain types of punishment, such as corporal punishment; they are very sensitive to the opinions of their peers, which makes them resent being embarrassed before the group at home or in school; and they resent anything that seems unfair. This is especially true when punishment is a disguised hostility on the part of the parent or teacher who administers it (117,147).

Adolescents have their own opinions about how they should be punished and for what reasons. In one study of adolescents between the ages of 12 and 16 years, the opinion expressed was that the best way of dealing with a dishonesty situation was by explaining to the individual why he was wrong. In dealing with lying, they felt that a confidential talk was better than punishment. While, to most of the group, punishment was regarded as retributive and to some extent reformative, only a few regarded it as a deterrent (75).

Girls, because of a feeling of loyalty or obligation to their parents, have difficulty in expressing negative and critical feelings toward their parents after they have been punished; instead, they often displace their negative feelings on others. When severely punished, they feel justified in expressing negative feelings. Boys, on the other hand, do not hesitate to express negative feelings toward those who punish them (67,115).

Corporal punishment is closely associated with personality disorders and often leads to marital difficulties (151). It leads to dislike for parents, rude answering, being irritated at and being ashamed of parents, infantile dependence, lack of self-control, being finicky about food, being curious about sex matters, having a tendency to homesickness, being less apt to decide on a vocation while in high school or college, being uncomfortable when with other people, having a tendency to worry, and having feelings of guilt. Those who are punished less severely and subjected to less corporal punishment are better adjusted (136).

In commenting on severe punishment, especially that which involves the use of corporal punishment, Peck and Havighurst (117) have remarked:

> The whole idea of penal "treatment" flies in the face of human nature. Severe punish-

ment breeds hatred; hatred breeds either antisocial behavior or a grudging, resentful conformity to convention which has no real ethical intent in it. It is a matter of record that the "punishment" theory of crime prevention simply does not work.

Davitz (31) has gone further in his explanation of why the "punishment theory of crime prevention simply does not work":

> Punishment and rejection give rise to fear; fear promotes defensive reactions; and the defensive reactions elicit further punishment. This is the vicious circle of maladjustment. The child lives in an interpersonal world of constant threat. The consequence is unhappiness and fear.

EVALUATION OF REWARD

The use of rewards motivates action in accordance with social expectations and a wholesome attitude toward those in authority. When rewards are given for good behavior, punishment for intentional wrongdoing loses much of its sting (115). Because adolescents are subjected to more criticism and faultfinding by adults in authority than praise or any other form of reward, these positive types of discipline are a welcome relief to them and affect their attitudes favorably. As has been stressed earlier, too few disciplinarians use rewards in any form and far too many are hesitant to use praise for fear of making the adolescent conceited or lazy about trying to do what he is capable of doing. As a result, one of the most important aspects of discipline is neglected in favor of the more harmful effects of punishment.

EVALUATION OF CONSISTENCY

An important aspect of discipline that is too often neglected is consistency. Severity or laxity of discipline, per se, has been found to be less damaging than inconsistency. Not only does inconsistency cause confusion so that the adolescent does not know what is expected of him, but, of more serious consequences, it causes the adolescent to lose respect for the disciplinarian. This, in time, often spreads to all in authority. Firm authority, which is characteristic of consistent discipline, "represents the relatively unbudging reality with which the adolescent has to cope in the present and in later life" (55).

Studies of adult criminals have revealed that, as children, they had been subjected to inconsistent discipline. Persons who, by contrast, were subjected to strict discipline that was consistent rarely developed into criminals (106). If severe discipline is consistent and administered by parents or teachers who are fair and show a respect for the individual's rights as a person, he will become "insulated" against delinquency as an adolescent and against criminality as an adult (67,135). This will be discussed in more detail in relation to juvenile delinquency.

LONG-TERM EFFECTS OF CONTROL

In an evaluation of different methods of control, the long-term effects must be taken into consideration. The adolescent who rebels against discipline, especially if it is overstrict or inconsistent, is likely to develop unfavorable attitudes that will carry over into adult life. A study of married men and women revealed that men's reactions to authority during their youth had no effect upon their marital roles. In the case of the wives, however, dislike for their childhood discipline was associated with a dominant role in their marital relationships. This was true also of those wives whose childhood training was indulgent or who rebelled against authority (103). In evaluating different methods of discipline, Peck and Havighurst (117) have pointed out that:

> The only method that works in favor of mature, dependable character is first to give people—whether children or adults—reason to feel an incentive to behave ethically; and then guide them intelligently, patiently, and with growing freedom to make and test their own decisions. This way works; none of the other methods of child rearing, or of reformation, breeds more than unthinking, rigid compliance at best—and many methods breed savagely hostile revenge behavior.

After a period of rebellion against discipline, most adolescents realize that discipline is essential, since they are not adequately prepared to meet the challenges of life alone. Furthermore, they come to realize that the mores and laws of society are made not to interfere with their pleasures but to allow people to live together harmoniously and happily. As Hacker and Geleerd (55) have said:

> The final acceptance of the restrictions within the limits of renewed ego activity marks the end of the adolescent period, as shown by the general calming down of the violent vacillation between the extremes of the elation of the superman and the depressions of deep despair.

BIBLIOGRAPHY

1 ABBE, A. E.: Maternal attitudes toward child behavior and their relationship to the diagnostic category of the child. *J. genet. Psychol.*, 1958, **92**, 167–173.

2 ALLINSMITH, W.: Conscience and conflict: the moral force in personality. *Child Develpm.*, 1957, **28**, 469–476.

3 ANDERSON, H. H., and G. L. ANDERSON: Social development. In L. Carmichael (ed.), *Manual of child psychology*. 2d ed. New York: Wiley, 1954, pp. 1162–1215.

4 ANDERSON, W. F.: Attitudes of university students toward cheating. *J. educ. Res.*, 1957, **50**, 581–588.

5 AUSUBEL, D. P.: Relationships between shame and guilt in the socialization process. *Psychol. Rev.*, 1955, **62**, 378–390.

6 BECKER, L. J.: The changing moral values of students. *J. Home Econ.*, 1963, **55**, 646–648.

7 BECKER, W. C., D. R. PETERSON, L. A. HELLER, B. J. SHOEMAKER, and H. C. QUARY: Factors in parental behavior and personality as related to problem behavior in children. *J. consult. Psychol.*, 1959, **23**, 107–118.

8 BELLER, E. K.: Two attitude components in younger boys. *J. soc. Psychol.*, 1949, **29**, 139–151.

9 BOEHM, L.: The development of conscience: a comparison of American children of different mental and socioeconomic levels. *Child Develpm.*, 1962, **33**, 575–590.

10 BOEHM, L., and M. C. NASS: Social class differences in conscience development. *Child Develpm.*, 1962, **33**, 565–574.

11 BONSALL, M. R., and B. STELLFRE: The temperament of gifted children. *Calif. J. educ. Res.*, 1955, **6**, 162–165.

12 BRIM, O. C.: The acceptance of new behavior in child-rearing. *Hum. Relat.*, 1954, **7**, 473–491.

13 BRODBECK, A. J., P. NOGEE, and A. DI MARCIO: Two kinds of conformity: a study of the Riesman typology applied to standards of parental discipline. *J. Psychol.*, 1956, **41**, 23–45.

14 BRONFENBRENNER, U.: The role of age, sex, class and culture in studies of moral development. *Relig. Educ.*, 1962, **57**, S-3–S-17.

15 BROWER, D.: Child psychology: a look at tomorrow. *J. genet. Psychol.*, 1963, **102**, 45–50.

16 CANNING, R. C.: Does an honor system reduce classroom cheating? An experimental answer. *J. exp. Educ.*, 1956, **24**, 291–296.

17 CHAVE, E. J.: *Personality development in children.* Chicago: University of Chicago Press, 1937.

18 CHWAST, J.: Value conflicts in treating delinquents. *Children*, 1959, **6**, 95–100.

19 CLARK, E. J.: Teacher reactions toward objectionable pupil behavior. *Elem. Sch. J.*, 1951, **51**, 446–449.

20 CLARK, T. B.: *What is honesty?* Chicago: Science Research, 1952.

21 CLARK, W. H.: Sex differences and motivation in the urge to destroy. *J. soc. Psychol.*, 1952, **36**, 167–177.

22 CLIFFORD, E.: Discipline in the home: a controlled observational study of parental practices. *J. genet. Psychol.*, 1959, **95**, 45–82.

23 COHEN, A. K.: *Deliquent boys: the culture of the gang.* New York: Free Press, 1955.

24 COLE, L., and I. N. HALL: *Psychology of adolescence.* 6th ed. New York: Holt, 1964.

25 COLE, M., F. M. FLETCHER, and S. L. PRESSEY: Forty-year changes in college student attitudes. *J. counsel. Psychol.*, 1963, **10**, 53–55.

26 COLEMAN, J. S.: *The adolescent society.* New York: Free Press, 1961.

27 COLM, H.: Help and guidance as discipline for pre-adolescents. *Nerv. Child*, 1951, **9**, 131–138.

28 CRANE, A. R.: The development of moral values in children: IV. Preadolescent gangs and the moral development of children. *Brit. J. educ. Psychol.*, 1958, **28**, 201–208.

29 CROW, L. D., and A. CROW: *Adolescent development and adjustment.* 2d ed. New York: McGraw-Hill, 1965.

30 DAMERON, L. E.: Mother-child interaction in the development of self-restraint. *J. genet. Psychol.*, 1955, **86**, 289–308.

31 DAVITZ, J. R.: Contributions of research with children to a theory of maladjustment. *Child Develpm.*, 1958, **29**, 3–7.

32 DE CHARMS, R., and G. H. MOELLER: Values expressed in children's readers: 1800–1950. *J. abnorm. soc. Psychol.*, 1962, **64**, 136–142.

33 DENTLER, R. A., and L. J. MONROE: *Problem behavior of junior high school youth in Kansas.* Bureau of Child Research, University of Kansas: Child Research Series, no. 8, 1961.

34 DIGGORY, J. C.: Sex differences in judging the acceptability of actions. *J. soc. Psychol.*, 1962, **56**, 107–114.

35 DIMOCK, H. S.: Some new light on adolescent religion. *Relig. Educ.*, 1936, **31**, 273–279.

36 DIMOCK, H. S.: *Rediscovering the adolescent.* New York: Association Press, 1937.

37 DOUVAN, E.: Independence and identity in adolescence. *Children*, 1957, **4**, 186–190.

38 DREWS, E. M., and J. E. TEAHAN: Parental attitudes and academic achievement. *J. clin. Psychol.*, 1957, **13**, 328–332.

39 DRUCKER, D.: Authority for our children. *Harper's Magazine*, 1941, **182**, 276–282.

40 DU BOIS, F. S.: The security of discipline. *Ment. Hyg., N.Y.*, 1952, **36**, 353–372.

41 DURKHEIM, E. (ed.): *Moral education.* New York: Free Press, 1961.

42 DURKIN, D.: Children's concepts of justice: a comparison with the Piaget data. *Child Develpm.*, 1959, **30**, 59–67.

43 DURKIN, D.: The specificity of children's moral judgments. *J. genet. Psychol.*, 1961, **98**, 3–13.

44 EBERHART, H. C.: Attitude toward property: a genetic study by the paired comparison rating of offenses. *J. genet. Psychol.*, 1942, **60**, 3–35.

45 ELDER, G. H.: Parental power legitimation and its effect on the adolescent. *Sociometry,* 1963, **26**, 50–65.

46 ELIAS, L. J.: *High school youth look at their problems.* Pullman, Wash.: State College of Washington, 1949.

47 EYSENCK, H. J.: The development of moral values in children: VII. The contribution of learning theory. *Brit. J. educ. Psychol.,* 1960, **30**, 11–21.

48 FINNEY, J. C.: Some maternal influences on children's personality and character. *Genet. Psychol. Monogr.,* 1961, **63**, 199–278.

49 FRANK, L. K.: This is the adolescent. *Understanding the Child,* 1949, **18**, 65–69.

50 GARRISON, K. C.: A study of student disciplinarian practices in two Georgia high schools. *J. educ. Res.,* 1959, **53**, 153–156.

51 GEISEL, J. B.: Discipline viewed as a developmental need of the child. *Nerv. Child,* 1951, **9**, 115–121.

52 GESELL, A., E. L. ILG, and L. B. AMES: *Youth: the years from ten to sixteen.* New York: Harper & Row, 1956.

53 GORDON, R. A., J. F. SHORT, D. S. CARTWRIGHT, and F. L. STRODTBECK: Values and gang delinquency: a study of street-corner groups. *Amer. J. Sociol.,* 1963, **69**, 109–128.

54 GRACE, G. L., and H. A. GRACE: The relationship between verbal and behavioral measures of values. *J. educ. Res.,* 1952, **46**, 123–131.

55 HACKER, F. J., and E. R. GELEERD: Freedom and authority in adolescence. *Amer. J. Orthopsychiat.,* 1945, **15**, 621–630.

56 HARRIS, D. B.: Parental judgment of responsibility in children and children's adjustment. *J. genet. Psychol.,* 1958, **92**, 161–166.

57 HARTSHORNE, H., and M. MAY: *Studies in deceit.* New York: Macmillan, 1928.

58 HAVIGHURST, R. J.: The functions of successful discipline. *Understanding the Child,* 1952, **21**, 35–38.

59 HAVIGHURST, R. J.: *Human development and education.* New York: Longmans, 1953.

60 HAVIGHURST, R. J.: Moral character and religious education. *Religious Educ.,* 1956, **51**, 163–169.

61 HAVIGHURST, R. J., and H. TABA: *Adolescent character and personality.* New York: Wiley, 1949.

62 HECHINGER, F. M.: Adults vs. teen-agers. *The New York Times,* Dec. 12, 1964.

63 HECHINGER, F. M.: On cheating. *The New York Times,* Jan. 31, 1965.

64 HECHINGER, G., and F. M. HECHINGER: College morals mirror our society. *The New York Times,* Apr. 14, 1963.

65 HECHINGER, G., and F. M. HECHINGER: *Teenage tyranny.* New York: Morrow, 1963.

66 HEMMING, J.: Some aspects of moral development in a changing society. *Brit. J. educ. Psychol.,* 1957, **27**, 77–88.

67 HENRY, A. F.: Sibling structure and perception of disciplinary roles of parents. *Sociometry,* 1957, **20**, 67–74.

68 HENRY, J.: Permissiveness and morality. *Ment. Hyg., N.Y.,* 1961, **45**, 282–287.

69 HETHERINGTON, E. M., and S. E. FELDMAN: College cheating as a function of subject and situational variables. *J. educ. Psychol.,* 1964, **55**, 212–218.

70 HICKS, H. A., and M. HAYES: Study of the characteristics of 250 junior-high-school children. *Child Develpm.,* 1938, **9**, 219–242.

71 HILLIARD, F. H.: The influence of religious education upon the development of children's moral ideas. *Brit. J. educ. Psychol.,* 1959, **29**, 50–59.

72 HOEFLIN, R.: Child rearing practices and child care resources used by Ohio farm families with preschool children. *J. genet. Psychol.,* 1954, **84**, 271–297.

73 HOFFMAN, M. L.: Power assertion by the parents and its impact on the child. *Child Develpm.,* 1960, **31**, 129–143.

74 HOLLINGSHEAD, A. DE B.: *Elmtown's youth.* New York: Wiley, 1949.

75 HOPKINS, K. D.: Punishment in schools. *Brit. J. educ. Psychol.,* 1939, **9**, 8–28.

76 JERSILD, A. T.: *The psychology of adolescence.* 2d ed. New York: Macmillan, 1963.

77 JOHNSON, R. C.: Early studies of children's moral judgments. *Child Develpm.,* 1962, **33**, 603–605.

78 JONES, A. H.: Sex, educational, and religious influences on moral judgments relative to the family. *Sociol. soc. Res.,* 1943, **8**, 405–411.

79 JONES, L. V., and C. MORRIS: Relations of temperament to the choice of values. *J. abnorm. soc. Psychol.,* 1956, **53**, 345–349.

80 JONES, V.: Character development in children: an objective approach. In L. Carmichael (ed.), *Manual of child psychology.* 2d ed. New York: Wiley, 1954, pp. 781–832.

81 KATZ, D., and F. H. ALLPORT: *Students' attitudes.* Syracuse, N.Y.: Craftsman, 1931.

82 KELL, L., and J. ALDOUS: The relation between mothers' child-rearing ideologies and their children's perceptions of maternal control. *Child Develpm.*, 1960, **31**, 145–156.

83 KENT, N., and D. R. DAVIS: Discipline in the home and intellectual development. *Brit. J. med. Psychol.*, 1957, **30**, 27–33.

84 KINSEY, A. C., W. B. POMEROY, C. E. MARTIN, and P. H. GEBHARD: *Sexual behavior in the human female.* Philadelphia: Saunders, 1953.

85 KIRKENDALL, L. A.: The influence of certain incentives in the motivation of children. *Elem. Sch. J.*, 1938, **38**, 417–424.

86 KIRKPATRICK, M. E.: The mental hygiene of adolescence in the Anglo-American culture. *Ment. Hyg., N.Y.*, 1952, **36**, 394–403.

87 KLATSKIN, E. H.: Shifts in child care practices in three classes under an infant care program of flexible methodology. *Amer. J. Orthopsychiat.*, 1952, **22**, 201–205.

88 KLEMER, R. H.: Student attitudes toward guidance in sexual morality. *Marriage fam. Living*, 1962, **24**, 260–264.

89 KLINGER, E., A. ALBAUM, and M. HETHERING: Factors influencing the severity of moral judgments. *J. soc. Psychol.*, 1964, **63**, 319–326.

90 KOHN, M. L.: Social class and the exercise of parental authority. *Amer. sociol. Rev.*, 1959, **24**, 352–366.

91 KOHN, M. L.: Social class and parental values. *Amer. J. Sociol.*, 1959, **64**, 337–351.

92 KRUEGER, W. C. F.: Students' honesty in correcting grading errors. *J. appl. Psychol.*, 1947, **31**, 533–535.

93 KUHLEN, R. G.: *The psychology of adolescent development.* 2d ed. New York: Harper & Row, 1963.

94 KUNZ, P. R.: Religious influences on parental discipline and achievement demands. *Marriage fam. Living*, 1963, **25**, 224–225.

95 LANDIS, P. H.: *Adolescence and youth: the process of maturing.* 2d ed. New York: McGraw-Hill, 1952.

96 LANDIS, P. H.: The ordering and forbidding technique and teen-age adjustment. *Sch. Soc.*, 1954, **80**, 105–106.

97 LEDERER, M.: We're telling you. *Ladies Home Journal*, 1944, **61**, 20–21.

98 LEHMANN, I. J.: Learning: III. Attitudes and values. *Rev. educ. Res.*, 1958, **28**, 468–474.

99 LEVINSON, D. J., and P. E. HUFFMAN: Traditional family ideology and its relation to personality. *J. Pers.*, 1954, **23**, 251–273.

100 LODGE, H. C.: The influence of the study of biography on the moral ideology of the adolescent at the eighth grade level. *J. educ. Res.*, 1956, **50**, 241–255.

101 LOEVINGER, J.: Patterns of parenthood as theories of learning. *J. abnorm. soc. Psychol.*, 1959, **59**, 148–150.

102 LONDON, P., R. E. SCHULMAN, and M. S. BLACK: Religion, guilt, and ethical standards. *J. soc. Psychol.*, 1964, **63**, 145–149.

103 LU, Y. C.: Home discipline and reaction to authority in relation to marital roles. *Marriage fam. Living*, 1953, **15**, 223–225.

104 MAC RAE, D.: A test of Piaget's theories of moral development. *J. abnorm. soc. Psychol.*, 1954, **49**, 14–18.

105 MARTIN, W. E.: Learning theory and identification: III. The development of values in children. *J. genet. Psychol.*, 1954, **84**, 211–217.

106 MC CORD, J., and W. MC CORD: The effects of parental role model on criminality. *J. soc. Issues*, 1958, **14**, no. 3, 66–74.

107 MC DAVID, J., and H. M. SCHRODER: The interpretation of approval and disapproval by delinquent and nondelinquent adolescents. *J. Pers.*, 1957, **25**, 539–549.

108 MC GHEE, M.: School girl's attitudes to films, youth clubs, home work, discipline and sport. *Brit. J. educ. Psychol.*, 1950, **20**, 144–145.

109 MILLS, J.: Changes in moral attitudes following temptation. *J. Pers.*, 1958, **26**, 517–531.

110 MORRIS, C., and L. V. JONES: Value scales and dimensions. *J. soc. Psychol.*, 1955, **51**, 523–535.

111 MORRIS, J. F.: The development of adolescent value-judgments. *Brit. J. educ. Psychol.*, 1958, **28**, 1–14.

112 MUELLER, K. H.: Can cheating be killed? *Personnel Guid. J.*, 1953, **31**, 465–468.

113 MULL, H. K.: The ethical discrimination of various groups of college women. *J. soc. Psychol.*, 1952, **35**, 69–72.

114 MUSSEN, P. H., and J. KAGAN: Group conformity and perceptions of parents. *Child Develpm.*, 1958, **29**, 57–67.

115 NAKAMURA, C. Y.: The relationship between children's expressions of hostility and methods of discipline exercised by dominant overprotective parents. *Child Develpm.*, 1959, **30**, 109–117.

116 NEEDHAM, M. A., and E. M. SCHUR: Student punitiveness toward sexual deviation. *Marriage fam. Living*, 1963, **25**, 227–229.

117 PECK, R. F., and R. J. HAVIGHURST: *The psychology of character development*. New York: Wiley, 1962.

118 POFFENBERGER, T.: The control of adolescent premarital coitus. *Marriage fam. Living*, 1962, **24**, 254–260.

119 PRESSEY, S. L., and A. W. JONES: 1923–1953 and 20–60 age changes in moral codes, anxieties, and interests, as shown by the "X-O Tests." *J. Psychol.*, 1955, **39**, 485–502.

120 PRESSEY, S. L., and R. G. KUHLEN: *Psychological development through the life span*. New York: Harper & Row, 1957.

121 PUTNEY, S., and R. MIDDLETON: Effect of husband-wife interaction on the strictness of attitudes toward child rearing. *Marriage fam. Living*, 1960, **22**, 171–173.

122 RAINWATER, L.: A study of personality differences between middle and lower class adolescents: the Szondi test in culture-personality research. *Genet. Psychol. Monogr.*, 1956, **54**, 3–86.

123 RAPP, D. W.: Child rearing attitudes of mothers in Germany and the United States. *Child Develpm.*, 1961, **32**, 669–678.

124 REISS, I. L.: Consistency and sexual ethics. *Marriage fam. Living*, 1962, **24**, 264–269.

125 REMMERS, H. H., and D. H. RADLER: *The American teenager*. Indianapolis: Bobbs-Merrill, 1957.

126 REMMERS, H. H., and B. SHIMBERG: *Purdue opinion poll for young people*. Lafayette, Ind.: Purdue University Press, 1949.

127 REMPEL, H., and I. SIGNORI: Sex differences in self-rating of conscience as a determinant of behavior. *Psychol. Rep.*, 1964, **15**, 277–278.

128 RESNICK, J.: Towards understanding adolescent behavior. *Peabody J. Educ.*, 1953, **30**, 205–208.

129 RETTIG, S., and B. PASAMANICK: Changes in moral values among college students: a factorial study. *Amer. sociol. Rev.*, 1959, **24**, 856–863.

130 RETTIG, S., and B. PASAMANICK: Moral value structure and social class. *Sociometry*, 1961, **24**, 21–35.

131 RETTIG, S., and B. PASAMANICK: Invariance in factor structure of moral value judgments from American and Korean college students. *Sociometry*, 1962, **25**, 73–84.

132 ROGOSIN, H.: What about "cheating" on examinations and honesty? *Sch. Soc.*, 1951, **74**, 402–403.

133 ROSEN, B.: *The development of moral judgment*. Worcester, Mass.: Clark University Press, 1948.

134 ROSENTHAL, M. J.: The syndrome of the inconsistent mother. *Amer. J. Orthopsychiat.*, 1962, **32**, 637–644.

135 SCARPITTI, F. R., E. MURRAY, S. DINITZ, and W. C. RECKLESS: The "good" boy in a high delinquency area: four years later. *Amer. sociol. Rev.*, 1960, **25**, 555–558.

136 SEARS, R. R., E. E. MACCOBY, and H. LEVIN: *Patterns of child rearing*. New York: Harper & Row, 1957.

137 SETTLAGE, C. F.: The values of limits in child rearing. *Children*, 1958, **5**, 175–178.

138 SEWELL, W. H., P. H. MUSSEN, and C. W. HARRIS: Relationships among child training practices. *Amer. sociol. Rev.*, 1955, **20**, 137–148.

139 SHEVIAKOW, G. V., and F. REDL: Discipline. *Yearb. Dept. Superv. Curric. Dev.*, 1944, 7–8.

140 SIEGEL, L., H. L. COON, H. B. PEPINSKY, and S. RUBIN: Expressed standards of behavior of high school students, teachers, and parents. *Personnel Guid. J.*, 1956, **34**, 261–266.

141 STAINS, K. B.: The beginnings of dishonesty. *Understanding the Child*, 1954, **23**, 55.

142 STAPLES, R., and G. W. SMITH: Attitudes of grandmothers and mothers toward child-rearing practices. *Child Develpm.*, 1954, **25**, 91–97.

143 STEININGER, M., R. E. JOHNSON, and D. K. KIRTS: Cheating on college examinations as a function of situationally aroused anxiety and hostility. *J. educ. Psychol.*, 1964, **55**, 317–324.

144 STENDLER, C. B.: A study of some socio-moral judgments of junior-high-school children. *Child Develpm.*, 1949, **20**, 15–28.

145 STOKES, W. R.: Our changing sex ethics. *Marriage fam. Living*, 1962, **24**, 269–272.

146 STOTT, L. H.: Home punishments of adolescents. *J. genet. Psychol.*, 1940, **57**, 415–428.

147 STRANG, R.: What discipline means to adolescents. *Nerv. Child*, 1951, **9**, 139–146.

148 STRANG, R.: *The adolescent views himself.* New York: McGraw-Hill, 1957.

149 TABA, H.: The moral beliefs of sixteen-year-olds. In J. M. Seidman (ed.), *The adolescent: a book of readings.* Rev. ed. New York, Holt, 1960, pp. 592–596.

150 TASCH, R. J.: Interpersonal perceptions of fathers and mothers. *J. genet. Psychol.*, 1955, **87**, 59–65.

151 TERMAN, L. M., P. BUTTENWIESER, L. W. FERGUSON, and W. B. JOHNSON: *Psychological factors in marital happiness.* New York: McGraw-Hill, 1938.

152 THOMPSON, G. G.: Age trends in social values during the adolescent years. *Amer. Psychologist*, 1949, **4**, 250.

153 TRENT, R. D.: The expressed values of institutionalized delinquent boys. *J. genet. Psychol.*, 1958, **92**, 133–148.

154 TUMA, E., and N. LIVSON: Family socioeconomic status and adolescent attitudes to authority. *Child Develpm.*, 1960, **31**, 387–399.

155 VINCENT, E. L., and P. C. MARTIN: *Human psychological development.* New York: Ronald, 1961.

156 VON MERING, F. H.: Professional and non-professional women as mothers. *J. soc. Psychol.* 1955, **42**, 21–34.

157 WATSON, G.: Some personality differences in children related to strict or permissive parental discipline. *J. Psychol.*, 1957, **44**, 227–249.

158 WERNER, E.: Milieu differences in social competence. *J. genet. Psychol.*, 1957, **91**, 239–249.

159 WHITE, M. S.: Social class in child rearing practices and child behavior. *Amer. sociol. Rev.*, 1957, **22**, 704–712.

160 WHITEMAN, P. H.: The relation of religious affiliation to parents' opinions concerning child rearing and children's problems and parents' evaluation of their own personalities. *Dissert. Abstr.*, 1959, **20**, 2149–2150.

161 WIGGAM, E. A.: Do brains and character go together? *Sch. Soc.*, 1941, **54**, 261–265.

162 WITHERS, S.: Putting the label on stealing. *The New York Times*, July 21, 1963.

163 WITRYOL, S. L., and J. E. CALKINS: Marginal social values of rural school children. *J. genet. Psychol.*, 1958, **92**, 81–93.

164 WOODS, P. J., K. B. GLAVIN, and C. M. KETTLE: A mother-daughter comparison on selected aspects of child rearing in a higher socioeconomic group. *Child Develpm.*, 1960, **31**, 121–128.

165 WRENN, C. G.: Student discipline in a college. *Educ. psychol. Measmt.*, 1949, **9**, 625–633.

CHAPTER 12
moral knowledge
and
moral behavior

Knowledge of right and wrong does not necessarily guarantee behavior consistent with this knowledge. As Crow and Crow (44) have pointed out:

> Many adolescents are able to answer correctly all or most of the items on a test designed to discover extent of recognition of generally accepted moral concepts. Yet, in their behavior, at least some of these same young people fail to apply one or more of the conduct standards which, in the form of test items, were answered correctly.

Abstract knowledge that it is wrong to cheat does not necessarily keep an adolescent from cheating when it will be to his personal advantage to do so either to improve his own grade or to help a friend (87,121). In a study of honesty, a correlation of .25 between moral knowledge and conduct was reported. This suggests a marked discrepancy between knowledge of right and wrong and the individual's behavior (87).

Few adolescents are consistently moral in the sense that they conform to standards of right and wrong *at all times.* As Pressey and Kuhlen (195) have put it:

> There are no separate groups of saints and sinners. Some people are sometimes honest, sometimes not, sometimes helpful, sometimes not—average in virtue as in other traits.

explanations of discrepancies

If discrepancies between moral knowledge and behavior are not due to ignorance, then what is responsible for them? Several explanations have been offered. The first is *peer-group pressures.* Because the adolescent is anxious to be popular, he has a strong motivation to act in accordance with what the group thinks right, even when this is contrary to his own moral values.

In discussing the laxity of sexual morals on some college campuses today, Hechinger and Hechinger (96) have emphasized the role played by peer-group pressures when permissiveness by college authorities exists:

> In the absence of . . . guidance, the exploiters of permissiveness exert the strongest group pressure. This is especially important in the domain of sex morality among young adults. Unless the authorities strongly condemn immoral behavior, pressure by the "fast-living" set becomes irresistible.

Many adolescents who withstand peer-group pressures express the opinion that they "sometimes wonder if it pays to behave myself." While some of their contemporaries may admire them, many do not. In fact, many will regard them as goody-goodies or "chicken." A boy who refuses to drive faster than the speed limit when he is with a group that wants to race or a girl whose friends regard virginity as a sign of a "kid," must do what the group expects or run the risk of losing status in the group. Only an adolescent who has very strong moral convictions could be expected to jeopardize his social life to adhere to moral values that are not accepted by the members of the group with which he is identified (144,256).

The second explanation commonly given for discrepancies between moral knowledge and moral behavior is *confusion* about what moral values are the right ones. This is especially true when moral concepts learned at home differ from those of the peer group (194). While adolescents may agree in a general way with adults about desirable behavior, they often disagree about specific aspects of behavior (224). Confusion may arise when the adolescent is uncertain about how abstract concepts, such as honesty, can be applied to specific situations. This is intensified when he sees some adults—especially parents, people in public life, and religious leaders—doing things he has been told are wrong. As he sees it, if it is all right for them to preach one thing and practice another, it is for him too (21, 91,214).

Confusion is intensified by the way the mass media present certain forms of behavior and the way people in the entertainment world win popular acclaim, even though their behavior may fall far short of the standards society expects others to conform to. In speaking about television and its effects on moral standards of children and adolescents, Barclay (15) has pointed out that:

> Television makes plain that The Law is clear and inexorable on such matters as premeditated murder, horse-stealing, bank hold-ups and the robbing of stagecoaches. But just what this dramatic and powerful force has to do with what they consider the mere pranks and shenanigans of youth—prying off hubcaps, altering road signs, worming into empty houses, "borrowing" automobiles—is not so easily understood. In fact, books and movies and TV shows may even confuse their understanding by pre-

senting such actions as harmless fun or high adventure.

Perhaps the greatest confusion comes in behavior where a double standard rules. As was stressed earlier (see pages 429 and 430), girls go through childhood learning that behavior that is right for boys is right for them and that what boys should not do, they, too, should not do. It is understandable, then, that both boys and girls in adolescence will be somewhat confused about right and wrong when they discover that the moral principles of childhood no longer hold for both sexes and that new standards must be learned and adhered to (172,203, 230).

A third common explanation for the discrepancies between moral knowledge and moral behavior in adolescence is *immature control of strong urges to engage in self-satisfying but socially disapproved acts,* such as sexual indulgence (44). Many adolescents simply do not know what are the acceptable methods to use to attain their goals. But, because the goals are so important to them, they will strive to reach them by any method they can (240). Adolescents, for example, who want to win the acceptance of the group will try to do so by engaging in attention-getting acts even though these acts may get them into trouble with teachers, parents, or law-enforcing officers. Accepting a dare to do something that is forbidden or disapproved of will, they hope, increase their chance of winning favorable attention and, with it, acceptance (224,256).

A fourth possible explanation for discrepancies is closely related to the third— *immature control of strong urges to reach a goal which is important but inability to see how this can be done in an acceptable way.* A student who has set a high level of aspiration for academic success may see no way of reaching this goal by his own efforts. He therefore cheats in important examinations (44,214). A girl may shoplift clothes and personal ornaments so that she can make as good an appearance as the girls with whom she wants to be identified (44).

A fifth explanation for the discrepancy

between beliefs and behavior was suggested by Havighurst and Taba when they emphasized the role played by *expediency and emotional factors* in making decisions and forcing individuals to sacrifice some of their abstract beliefs. The juvenile delinquent, for example, lacks the emotionalized desire to adhere to what he knows is right. Then, when he gets into trouble, he is frequently genuinely sorry for it. This exists in nondelinquents, but to a lesser degree (92).

And, finally, the discrepancy between knowledge of right and wrong and the behavior the adolescent engages in has been explained as closely related to *striving for independence* (98). An adolescent, for example, who rebels against what he regards as an unreasonably strict law may drive at 70 or 80 miles an hour on a road where he knows the speed limit is 45 miles (44). Much of the criticized sexual morals on college campuses today can be explained in terms of rebellion against authority. As Hechinger and Hechinger (96) have explained:

> *The recent rash of stories of rebellion against moral codes on the campus can only be understood in the light of the fact that many girls and most boys who enter college have had greater social "freedom" in high school than they are given, at least officially, in their freshman year. Add to this the physical distance from the home community and the heady relief that comes with relative anonymity, and rebellion seems almost a natural step.*

variations in discrepancies

All adolescents, as is true of all people at all ages, occasionally engage in behavior which they know is wrong. Some, however, do so more frequently than others. Because girls conform more to authority and rebel less than boys, there are fewer discrepancies between moral knowledge and behavior among *girls* than among boys (144,243, 256). However, in both sex groups, *late maturers* are more rebellious against authority than are early or average maturers. Consequently, there are more discrepancies between moral knowledge and behavior in the former than in the latter groups (120,170). Normally, there are more discrepancies between knowledge and behavior in early than in late adolescence, not because the *older adolescent* necessarily has more moral knowledge but, rather, because he is less rebellious in his attitudes toward those in authority (224).

Very strict *authoritarian discipline* encourages discrepancies between moral knowledge and behavior. A study of honesty in different cultures, including Germany, England, Mexico, Sweden, and the United States, revealed that children and adolescents from societies where more democratic child-training methods prevail tend to be more honest and less defensive than those from more authoritarian societies (178). When the adolescent is *punished* by the mother, he is more likely to turn his anger inward than outward, against others, as he does when punished by the father. As a result, the adolescent who is punished most by the father is likely to break more rules and laws, out of spite and revenge, than is the adolescent who is punished by the mother. However, if the adolescent *feels loved*, he will be far less likely to do what he knows is wrong, regardless of severity of discipline and regardless of who punishes him for wrongdoing, than is true of the adolescent who feels rejected by family members (196,243).

effects of discrepancies

How discrepancies between moral knowledge and behavior will affect the adolescent's attitudes toward self and his behavior will depend greatly on whether or not his misbehavior is *known to others*. If he is caught cheating, for example, he will try to clear himself of blame to avoid having feelings of shame. This he may do by lies in which he intentionally tries to deceive others by claiming innocence. Or he may project the blame on someone else, thus focusing attention on another person instead of on himself. He may, in the case of cheating, say that the other student looked over his shoulder or copied the an-

swers without his knowledge or consent. If he can convince his accuser of his innocence, he will have no reason to be ashamed.

If the adolescent breaks a law and is caught, as in the case of speeding, he is more likely to plead innocence than to use any other excuse. He may, for example, say that he did not know what the speed limit was in that area. More likely, he will try to look innocent and say he had no idea that the car was going so fast because he did not look at the speedometer. Having used innocence as a way of escaping punishment when he was a child, he tries to use it as an adolescent. If it works, he will continue to use it; if it does not work, he will try other tactics. Of these, the most effective, he discovers, is to say that he is sorry and will never do it again. Knowing that most adults are lenient with adolescents, he hopes to play on their sympathies. If he is successful, he will not experience shame; instead, he will have a feeling of personal triumph.

When misbehavior is *not detected by others*, adolescents react very differently. They may feel guilty, and this lowers their self-esteem. To avoid this, they are likely to try to convince themselves that the rules or laws are unreasonable, that everyone else does it, or that there are times when violating moral values is justified (95,207). He may rationalize a lie by saying that he did not want to tell the truth because the person's feelings would be hurt; therefore, lying was a "kindness" on his part. If he breaks a law, he will explain to himself that "laws are meant to be broken" or that the law is unreasonable and should be changed.

While guilt does act as an internalized policeman to keep the adolescent from repeating an act for which he experienced feelings of guilt, the use of rationalization tends to weaken its restraining value. Only when the adolescent feels that he has had a narrow escape from being caught is he likely to be restrained to any marked extent by feelings of guilt. On the other hand, guilt that has been weakened by rationalization is more likely to change his moral values from strict to lenient. As was pointed out earlier, an adolescent who cheats is more likely to develop a more lenient attitude toward cheating than to hold to his former concept of its wrongness. Similarly, a lawbreaker who is not caught and who rationalizes his act weakens his formerly strict moral concept of lawbreakers and develops a more tolerant attitude (8,63,87, 121,214).

types of discrepancies

Behavior that is not in strict accordance with the standards of the group falls into two general categories: misdemeanors and juvenile delinquencies. When the divergence from the accepted pattern is slight, the misbehavior is generally referred to as a "misdemeanor." A misdemeanor is willful badness, mischievousness, or disobedience of a minor sort. More serious divergences, on the other hand, are labeled as "juvenile delinquency." In many instances it is difficult to draw a sharp line of distinction. However, a fairly good criterion is the effect the individual's misbehavior has on the group. When misbehavior inconveniences or harms others, it is classed as delinquency. Should the effect be limited to the individual and be merely a source of irritation to the group, it is generally referred to as a misdemeanor. The term "misdemeanor" is generally applied to behavior which is in defiance of *rules*—precepts for conduct set by parents, teachers, or other adults in authority. By contrast, the term "delinquency" is generally applied to misbehavior in defiance of laws—precepts for conduct set by the governing authorities of the community, the state, or the nation.

The important point to note in making this distinction is that misdemeanors are often the forerunners of delinquency. The satisfaction the adolescent derives from misdemeanors will, in time, diminish. Then, more serious misbehavior must be engaged in to provide the satisfaction formerly derived from less serious misbehavior (37,75). Studies of juvenile delinquents have stressed, almost universally, that delinquency does not "come out of the blue." Instead, the histories of juvenile delinquents stress that

they have misbehaved since earliest childhood, becoming progressively more troublesome with each passing year.

MISDEMEANORS

Many young children discover, unfortunately, that they get more attention when they are naughty than when they are good. When they feel that they are being neglected or ignored, it is not surprising that they *intentionally* try to focus attention on themselves. Even though they are reproved or punished for their naughtiness, they feel that the satisfaction derived from being in the limelight more than compensates for the temporary dissatisfaction or even pain that comes with punishment. This is especially true when siblings or members of the peer group side with them against the parent or teacher who has punished them.

If the child learns when he is young to use misbehavior as an adjustive technique to satisfy his need and desire for attention and approval from the peer group, he must increase the intensity of his misbehavior with each passing year if he is to continue to derive satisfaction from it. As a result, by the time he reaches adolescence, much of his misbehavior is more annoying to others and more closely related to antisocial acts than it was when he was younger (13,83,177).

AGE OF MISDEMEANORS

The peak of misdemeanors generally comes between the ages of 13 and 14 years (146). This is illustrated in Figure 12–1. Gradually, during late childhood, there is an increase in the desire to achieve independence from adult control and to win the esteem of members of the peer group. This, added to the normal disequilibrium that accompanies the physical changes of puberty, is responsible for the increase in misdemeanors at this age. If the young adolescent is able to achieve greater freedom from adult authority as he develops an adult appearance, his troublesome behavior begins to subside. If, on the other hand, adult authority is intensified, troublesome behavior will continue (41,69,177,190).

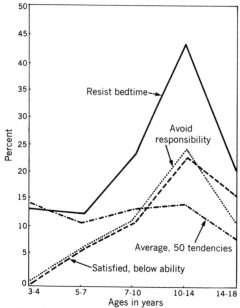

FIGURE 12–1 Misdemeanors reach a peak in frequency during the period of puberty and then wane rapidly. (Adapted from A. Lang: Parents' reports of undesirable behavior in children. *Child Develpm.*, 1941, **12**, 43–62. Used by permission.)

Among older adolescents who are still in college or professional training school, there is often a second peak of misdemeanors just before adulthood is reached. Much of the blowing off of steam in pantie raids, party crashing, and other troublesome behavior during the spring months stems from a flaunting of authority and an attempt to achieve independence while still economically dependent. Older adolescents who achieve independence by entering the work world do not experience this second period of misdemeanors (13,86,96).

causes of misdemeanors

Sometimes the trouble can be traced to *ignorance* of what is right or wrong. Faulty home training or lack of training in the home or school may be the basis of trouble, particularly in the early part of adolescence. Or it may stem from *frustrations* in the home or school that are being expressed in this manner as a form of release (38).

Studies of boys who misbehave in school have revealed that there is a close relationship between their sociometric status and their behavior. Boys whom teachers judge as behaving badly in school tend to be rejected by their classmates. It is not always possible to determine whether peer rejection is a cause or an effect of misbehavior. In both cases, however, the boys are suffering from frustrations; this motivates them to misbehave (43). The relationship between sociometric status and classroom behavior is shown in Figure 12–2.

More often misdemeanors result from the individual's *desire for attention.* The adolescent willfully breaks rules and ignores regulations in the hope of gaining admiration from others for his audacity. He even goes so far as to boast about what he has done, frequently exaggerating the wrongness of his acts. Drinking among young adolescent boys, as has been pointed out previously, is more often a bid for attention than anything else. A boy wants to convince his friends that he is a regular fellow, not effeminate, that he can "hold it like a man" without being affected by it (108).

The desire for *excitement and thrill*, especially if it is strong, may lead the adolescent into trouble. In discussing the spring outbursts which are common on many college campuses, Harrison (86) has pointed out:

Youngsters who explode in spring are doing what has come naturally for years, but, like their elders, they are using more potent ammunition these days. . . . These springtime outbreaks are among the growing pains. . . . Our culture subjects these youngsters to many conflicting tendencies and pressures. It rushes them on toward adulthood by dress, hair-do's, social activity, early drinking, dating and sexual activity. But, on the other hand, our technological progress puts the damper on jobs and prolongs dependence and education. Youngsters looking for a pigeonhole become beatniks, let off steam in headline-making parties or join social causes, such as the civil rights movement, to find their answers. . . . These things generally happen around spring examination time. The students are frustrated in their work and "have to explode somewhere."

Among the tabooed "pleasures"— smoking, drinking, use of narcotics, and sex—the adolescent finds excitement not from the activities themselves so much as from attempts to defy adult authority and get away with it. Using drugs, for example, stems primarily from an exaggerated amount of adolescent thrill seeking and bravado, combined with the temptation offered in neighborhoods where drug peddlers make it easy for them to satisfy their desire for thrills in this manner (7). Refer to pages 281 to 285 for a more complete discussion of the relationship between thrill seeking and tabooed pleasures.

Among boys, the desire to assert their *independence* of adult authority becomes increasingly strong not only in the home but in the school and community (44). In their flaunting of authority, they often do things they know are wrong to prove to themselves and their peers that they are brave and masculine. Many of these flauntings of authority are in response to dares by members of the peer group. The adolescent's "attraction to dare situations appears to reflect strivings for social esteem" even when his behavior may bring reproof or punishment from the adult group. A gain in peer prestige, he feels, is worth the price he may have to pay in punishment (256). Figure 4–8 on page 140 shows the increase in flauntings of authority in the home and school at different ages.

common forms of misdemeanors

Because home rules are markedly different from school rules and community expectations, the common misdemeanors of adolescence can be divided into three general categories: home, school, and community.

HOME MISDEMEANORS
Home misdemeanors are myriad. They include willful disobedience and defiance of parental authority, especially in relation to social activities—where the adolescents go, what they do, with whom they go, and

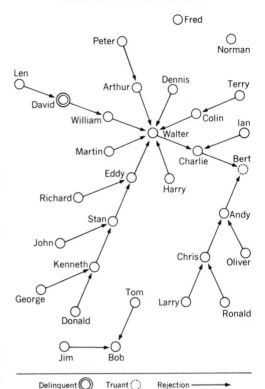

WHICH BOYS DO YOU LIKE LEAST?

Delinquent ◎ Truant ⬚ Rejection ⟶

FIGURE 12–2 Relationship between sociometric status and classroom behavior. (Adapted from I. J. Crofts and T. G. Grygier: Social relations of truants and delinquents. *Hum. Relat.*, 1956, **9**, 439–466. Used by permission.)

when they return home. These are the common latchkey problems of almost every home where there are adolescent boys and girls. (See pages 277 to 278 for a more complete discussion of latchkey problems.) In addition, other home misdemeanors include aggressive verbal attacks on siblings, temper outbursts, breaking and spilling things intentionally, rudeness to family friends and relatives, lying, minor pilfering from parents and siblings, dawdling over routine activities, shirking responsibilities, and contradiction of parents (13,69,146,190,224).

SCHOOL MISDEMEANORS
In most schools and, to a lesser extent, in colleges, rules are more numerous and stricter than in many homes. The reason for this is that, to enable the teacher to con-

centrate on teaching, the behavior of the students must be controlled so that the teacher's role of disciplinarian can be reduced to a minimum. Furthermore, there must be rules to guarantee a certain amount of orderliness in the school buildings during times when the students are not in classrooms.

Because school authorities are concerned about pupil achievement, they regard any behavior that interferes with the school routine as a misdemeanor. A student who makes trouble for the teacher or for the school authorities is regarded as a problem. Furthermore, because adolescents like school and their studies less than do children, and because they are more rebellious against authority, it is not surprising that school misdemeanors increase in adolescence. Even in colleges, there are more misdemeanors than one would expect for individuals who regard education as an important stepping stone to their vocational and social future (58,168,231).

Among *high school students,* the most commonly reported misdemeanors include cutting classes, tardiness, talking and cutting up in class, cheating, bullying other students—especially those who are small, members of minority groups, or good students— failure to prepare assignments, interrupting, rudeness, insubordination, smoking, drinking, forging a parent's signature on an excuse note, laughing and giggling in class to distract the attention of other students from their studies, fighting, throwing things, inattention, swearing, carelessness in work, minor vandalism, lying, and illicit sex acts (58,67,80,95,207). There are more misdemeanors when teachers are young and inexperienced than when they are older and more experienced (59).

When adolescents dislike a particular teacher or teachers in general, they are more troublesome than usual (133). They are also more troublesome in classes where they find the subject matter dull or of little practical value. If they find class discussions dull or if they feel unprepared to participate in them, they often cut up to kill time in the hope that they will not be called on (58, 69,132). Adolescents who perceive the teacher as hostile to them engage in more misdemeanors than do those who perceive the teacher as more favorable to them (4, 45,111,133,147). Adolescents who are popular with their peers generally behave better in school than do those who are unpopular; the unpopular try to win peer attention and approval by cutting up (43,217,256).

An extensive study of misdemeanors in one high school has shown the relative frequency of different misdemeanors *in that school.* In order of frequency, they were:

DISTURBANCE *(creating noise, too much talking, disorderly conduct, interruption of procedure, and interfering with instruction)* —39.6 *percent*

DISOBEDIENCE *(ignoring teacher's requests, ignoring school regulations, refusing to comply with rules, loitering, parking off campus, and leaving class without permission)—37.9 percent*

DISRESPECT *(discourteous to teacher, lack of respect, rude, answering teacher back, and insubordination)—5.0 percent*

MISREPRESENTATION *(signing a false name or forging name to pass or excuse, using someone else's identity card, lying)—4.7 percent*

IGNORING HEALTH AND SAFETY FACTORS *(throwing things, littering campus, stealing paper clips or paper pads, thumbtacks on chairs, and running in halls)—4.1 percent*

SMOKING *(carrying or smoking lighted cigarettes or cigars on or near campus)—2.4 percent*

FIGHTING *(hand-to-hand conflict with exchange of blows)—1.7 percent*

PROPERTY DAMAGE *(writing on or cutting into furniture, breaking Coke bottles, breaking windows, and flooding urinals or fountains)—1.6 percent*

PROFANITY AND OBSCENITY *(cursing, drawing or displaying lewd pictures, masturbation, and accentuation of sex organs)—1.1 percent*

GAMBLING *(dice games, matching coins, pitching pennies, and card games)—.7 percent*

THEFT *(stealing of personal or school property)—.7 percent*

CHEATING *(copying during examinations or*

securing assistance, allowing others to copy, and using notes or other material during examinations)—.6 percent

In this school, it was found that 41 percent of the students had been reported one or more times for misdemeanors with an average of three each. The pattern was the same for members of both sexes and for students of different socioeconomic statuses. The greatest frequency of misdemeanors occurred during the last three months of the school year, with the peak in April. During the school day, the greatest number of misdemeanors occurred during the first and last periods. In classes having a high number of disciplinary problems, nine times as many students failed as in classes with a low number of disciplinary problems (262). The relative frequency of school misdemeanors is illustrated in Figure 12–3.

College misdemeanors are similar to those in high school. The most commonly reported include cheating, drinking, smoking in forbidden areas, going to off-limits places, destruction of college property, breaking the "quiet" rules in dormitories, cutting classes without excuses, inattentiveness and attempts to disrupt classroom work, especially when there is a young and inexperienced instructor in charge, talking in the libraries, taking books from the library without signing them out, cutting pages out of library books or writing in them, entertaining members of the opposite sex in dormitory rooms at forbidden times, and making pantie raids on the women's dormitories. As is true in high school, these misdemeanors are more frequent among men than among women students; they are more frequent during the spring months than at other times of the year (86,95,96, 207).

COMMUNITY MISDEMEANORS

Community misdemeanors are, for the most part, carried out in connection with recreational activities, usually when adolescents are not in the home or the school. Unless adolescents have home responsibilities or jobs that keep them busy after school, over

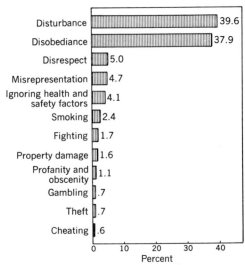

FIGURE 12–3 Frequency of school misdemeanors as reported by teachers in one school. (Adapted from H. Zeitlin: High school discipline. *Calif. J. educ. Res.*, 1962, **13**, 116–125. Used by permission.)

weekends, and during vacations, they have plenty of leisure time to get into mischief. In many suburban communities, for example, adolescents complain that there is nothing to do and that they are bored. In their attempt to stir up some excitement, they often engage in activities that are annoying to and troublesome for others.

Many of the recreations engaged in by *younger* adolescents, especially boys, are mischievous and annoying, though not actually in conflict with the law. Such activities as hopping freight trains, playing hooky from school, smoking, drinking, hitching rides on autos, and socially aggressive behavior toward members of the opposite sex or members of their own sex of a different clique (such as putting snow down a person's back or pulling a girl's hair) stem more from the desire for excitement than from a desire to do anything intentionally wrong (84,246). When a boy is dared to do these annoying things, he feels that his masculinity has been challenged. Therefore, he must prove his bravery or lose the respect of his peers (256).

Among *older* adolescents, in the junior and senior years of high school and in college, community misdemeanors are more serious. In the desire to stir up some excitement, many adolescents engage in the "suicidal game of 'chicken' on the highways" or in shoplifting (118). Just as reckless driving gives them a thrill and brings the admiration of their less daring peers, so shoplifting becomes a game where the winner has stirred up the excitement he craved and, at the same time, won the admiration of his peers. For some adolescents, shoplifting is an "entrance requirement" for the social clique they aspire to join. That factors other than need are at the basis of shoplifting may be seen by the fact that it is a popular game among affluent adolescents and that they usually steal small, inexpensive items, many of which they have no use for (255).

Another common form of community misdemeanor is party crashing. The adolescent who is not invited to a party given by one of his classmates in high school or by a fraternity in college of which he is not a member may resent this so deeply that he will decide to crash the party. Because there are usually others who have likewise not been invited, it is easy to get together enough to avoid the risk of being turned away at the door. Some party crashers behave like invited guests, once they are inside the door, but many do not. As Wallace (246) has pointed out:

> Even teenagers who are seemingly supplied with all the necessities and most of the luxuries of life, commit acts both infuriating and catastrophic. The troublesome party-crasher expresses hostility (whatever its source may be) in the most direct manner available. At the lower level of misbehavior is petty theft: packages of cigarets, bottles of liquor, cigaret lighters, books, records and other small, easily concealed items. Minor vandalism is also common—the grinding out of cigaret butts on rugs, the deliberate breaking of glassware or windows, or intentional "accidents" in which lamps and tables are tipped over or mailboxes demolished by cars. . . . The violence of the suburban teenager often exceeds that of his delinquent cousin in the slums.

variations in misdemeanors

Boys engage in more misdemeanors than do girls partly because they want to show their independence and partly to show how masculine they are (13,69,190). Many of their misdemeanors are in response to dares by their peers (256). The adolescent who is making poor adjustments at home, in school, or with his peers usually engages in more misdemeanors than does the adolescent who is well adjusted. This is seen in the case of truancy. As was pointed out earlier (see pages 347 and 348), truants are usually boys and girls who are making poor academic and social adjustments. This is equally true of other forms of school and home misdemeanors (43,58,217,262).

Misdemeanors are more common among adolescents of the lower socioeconomic groups than of the higher. This is due, in part, to the fact that adolescents of the lower groups are often subjected to harsh, punitive, and inconsistent discipline which makes them revengeful and, in part, to the fact that they have learned moral values which are not always in harmony with the moral values of society as a whole (90,101, 169,188). While adolescents of middle and upper socioeconomic groups engage in misdemeanors also, they are usually not so frequent or so serious. For them, misdemeanors are often a substitute for boredom which comes from too much leisure time and too few responsibilities (246).

Misdemeanors vary according to the degree of social acceptance the adolescent enjoys (43,262). When an adolescent belongs to a clique, he must do as his friends do to maintain his status in the clique. A girl, for example, may not like to smoke or drink, and she knows that she will be breaking a strict family rule if she does so. But if her friends smoke and drink, she feels that she must also to avoid having them feel that she is not one of them. How great the social pressures of the clique are has been emphasized by Hollingshead (108):

> To be in a clique in which socially tabooed activities are a part of its action pattern, one has to participate in them. The reason

is that one's membership is dependent first upon the conformity to the values held by the majority of the group and, second, upon how congenial the activities participated in by the group are to him.

While many adolescents do not find such activities pleasurable, they find the companionship of intimate friends pleasurable enough to compensate for doing some things they do not want to do or which they feel are wrong. Only when the adolescent sees little or no chance of gaining social acceptance is he free from peer-group pressures to engage in activities he feels are wrong.

Misdemeanors vary markedly according to the *environment* in which the adolescent lives. If the adolescent finds the *home* environment congenial and if he is happy there, he will engage in fewer misdemeanors than will adolescents who are unhappy. As Dentler and Monroe (48) have stated:

The better the quality of interpersonal relations between youth and parents, and the better the participation of youth in home-centered activities, the less likely the occurrence of serious misconduct, namely theft, vandalism, truancy, gang fighting, and the like.

Community environments that offer young people opportunities for wholesome recreations have fewer disturbances than do those which offer little to do (40,97,246,262).

effects of misdemeanors

Even though misdemeanors lead to some form of punishment, most adolescents feel that the price they pay is worth it if they have been able to win peer attention and esteem. Unfortunately, attention and esteem are often only momentary; the peer group that laughed at the adolescent's antics in class may regard him as a pest if he repeats his antics and disturbs their study time. Soon he acquires the reputation of being a nuisance or of acting "like a kid"—a reputation that does not bring him the acceptance he was trying to win (234). Similarly, the adolescent who wins a place for himself in a clique that admits only those who have the "nerve" to shoplift may discover that this is not the clique he really wants to be identified with. As a result of his shoplifting, the peers he had hoped to win as friends reject him (49).

Sensing the disapproval of his peers and knowing that he has won the disapproval of adults lead to feelings of guilt and shame which, if too strong and too continuous, can readily lead to poor mental health. In time, a guilt complex will develop. The adolescent who, at first, derived satisfaction from doing things his peers thought daring now finds himself in a situation in which he experiences more shame than pride, more guilt than self-satisfaction. In time, this can lead to schizoid tendencies which will warp his personality (98,238).

An even more serious aspect of misdemeanors is that they encourage the adolescent to develop a pattern of adjustment to life which will not be acceptable as he grows older. Adults, for example, will not find cutting up and bullying others amusing; on the contrary, they will find it childish and a sign of poor sportsmanship and warped values. Similarly, if his characteristic method of adjusting to boredom is to stir up some excitement by dangerous driving, party crashing, or shoplifting, the adolescent will discover that adult society will not be so lenient as it was when he was a teen-ager.

Like any stimulant, misdemeanors as ego boosters must be increased in frequency and intensity as time goes on. By mid-adolescence, misdemeanors may have to be of such a serious nature to do the tricks they did successfully earlier that the adolescent will now be labeled a juvenile delinquent. He may have to be isolated from society to prevent his harming others by his unsocial and morally irresponsible acts.

However, so long as the individual remains in an environment where his misbehavior is admired, applauded, or required for acceptance, he will have little motivation to learn new adjustive techniques. That is why too close and too constant contact with members of the peer group can be harmful in the sense that it gives the adolescent a concept of peer morality which may not be the concept adults hold. Contact with adults in the home, the school, and the community, either in work or in social life, will go a long way toward showing the adolescent what the adult members of society expect. It will impress upon him the fact that adulthood is just around the corner when he, too, will be judged by the standards of adults and will stand or fall according to their judgments of him.

JUVENILE DELINQUENCY

A delinquent is a "minor who has committed an unlawful act for which he would be sent to prison if he were an adult" (206). As Perlman has pointed out, "Legally speaking, a juvenile delinquent is one who commits a delinquent act as defined by law and who is adjudicated as such by an appropriate court" (189). Although state laws vary, most states regard an adolescent as a "juvenile" if he is under 16 or 18 years of age; adolescents over these ages are usually tried as adults if they commit crimes (151). Furthermore, an adolescent might be considered a delinquent in one state but not in another (189).

In most states, a delinquent is an adolescent who is "deemed to be in need of care or protection, or who is proved to be beyond the control of his parents as well as [one who has] been found guilty of committing an offense" (100). The difference between delinquent and nondelinquent behavior is one of *degree*. The delinquent, like the nondelinquent, is attempting to adjust to the social group with which he is identified. The difference is that the delinquent belongs to a group whose behavior is socially unacceptable; he, therefore, is learning socially unacceptable patterns of behavior. The nondelinquent, by contrast, is learning patterns of behavior that are socially approved (22,31,35,141). Thus, delinquent behavior comes from the "failure of social controls to produce behavior in conformity with the norms of the social system" (201).

Because delinquency comes from the individual's method of adjusting to society, the chances are that delinquency, unless the methods of adjustment are corrected, will persist into the adult years. As a result, the delinquent will become an adult criminal. As Healy and Bronner have explained, "Delinquency very frequently is the beginning of a criminal career and crime is the continuance into manhood of conduct tendencies which started in childhood or early youth" (93). Glueck and Glueck, in their study of 1,000 delinquents, found that two-thirds to three-fourths of the group first showed delinquent behavior in childhood, with the onset of misbehavior occurring between 9 and 10 years of age (75,77).

Today, there is overwhelming evidence that delinquency doesn't "just happen," nor is it an overnight development (206). Delinquents have carried out many acts of misconduct, often serious misdemeanors, during their preadolescent years and many have shown signs of poor personal and social adjustment from their preschool years (19, 167,239,254,257,258). In a study of adults who had been categorized as problem children thirty years earlier, Robins and O'Neal point out that they all showed signs of having had a "disturbed life pattern." This, they maintain, suggests that "childhood behavior problems signal a high probability of adult difficulties" (212).

There are many forewarnings that the child is on the path that may in time lead to delinquency. Of these, the most important are the way he feels about his family, his school, and the peer group (184). There are certain "spotting symptoms" that can be used to determine whether the individual is making such poor adjustments that he *may* be headed for delinquency. If he shows behavior problems not characteristic of his age, such as enuresis or temper tantrums; if he does unsatisfactory work at school and often engages in truancy; if he makes poor social adjustments not only to the peer group but to adults and older people; and if he has a poor self-concept, characterized by feelings of inadequacy, of inferiority, and of rejection, there is ample evidence that he is headed for trouble unless remedial steps are taken to correct his patterns of poor adjustment (103,137,155, 159,180,206,233).

extent of juvenile delinquency

Authoritative reports from courts and other law-enforcing agencies indicate that juvenile delinquency is on the increase in America. This is also true of many other countries throughout the world (78,204,244). In 1952, there was a 10 percent increase in the nation over the preceding year, while in 1962, it was reported that 12 percent of all crimes were committed by juveniles (175, 246). In 1964, the number of arrests of boys and girls under 18 years of age rose 11 percent over 1962, the fifteenth consecutive year in which an increase had occurred (179). Figure 12–4 shows the increase in juvenile crimes since 1940. This increase is serious not only because of its effects upon society but also because it is symptomatic of maladjustment on the part of the offenders. Unless remedial steps are taken, the maladjustment will increase; this then will lead to adult criminality. The increasing number of juvenile delinquents indicates that society is not meeting the needs of its young people. If it were, they would develop into law-abiding citizens (10,42,140, 235,236).

There is evidence that juvenile delinquency is even more widespread than has been officially reported. The statistics on which the data showing the rate of juvenile delinquency are based refer *only* to cases that came in formal conflict with the law. Many adolescents who commit crimes that would put them in the category of juvenile delinquents are not caught (221,261). Furthermore, many who are caught are not fingerprinted, nor are public records of the offenses made. The purpose of this is to avoid branding young people as criminals (64). Many cases of juvenile delinquency are dealt with by the police and parents, not by the courts. This is especially true of delinquents from the more affluent strata of society (149,189,222).

Piliavin and Briar have explained how police decide which adolescents will be arrested and thus suffer from the stigma arrest

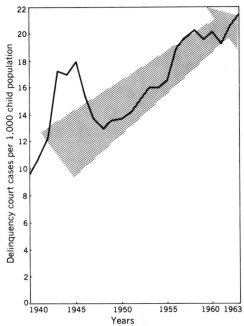

FIGURE 12–4 The rise in juvenile delinquency has been alarmingly rapid in recent years. (Adapted from B. M. Beck: Innovations in combating juvenile delinquency. *Children*, 1965, **12**, 69–74. Used by permission.)

brings. They use such cues as group affiliations of the adolescent, his age, race, grooming, dress, and demeanor. For example, an adolescent with well-oiled hair, wearing a black jacket and dirty jeans, and showing lack of respect for the police officer will be arrested. The adolescent who is contrite, respectful, and fearful of sanctions is regarded as "Basically law-abiding." As a result, he is not arrested but is given an informal or formal reprimand. By contrast, the "would-be tough guys" or "punks" are usually arrested. This suggests that in using their discretion about whom to arrest and whom not to arrest, the police give "more weight to the juvenile's character and life situation than to actual offending behavior." Piliavin and Briar conclude their study thus (192):

> The official delinquent, as distinguished from the juvenile who simply commits a delinquent act, is the product of a social judgment, in this case a judgment made by the police. He is a delinquent because someone

in authority has defined him as one, often on the basis of the public face he has presented to officials rather than of the kind of offense he has committed.

Furthermore, the police have no opportunity to make "social judgments" about an adolescent unless his unsocial acts are reported. Many adults do not report cases of delinquency to the police. In the case of party crashing, for example, parents of the adolescent who gave the party hesitate to report damage done to their homes because they do not want to jeopardize their son's or daughter's popularity by subjecting the invited guests to police questioning (246). Many shopkeepers fail to report shoplifting because they do not want to incur the ill will of their adult patrons by accusing their children of shoplifting or by reporting them to the police (255).

AREAS OF INCREASE IN DELINQUENCY

Some segments of the juvenile population are contributing more to the increase in delinquency than others. Since the mid-thirties, and noticeably so since the Second World War, the percentage of *girl* delinquents has increased more markedly than that of boys. Not only are there more girl delinquents now, but the number is increasing at a more rapid rate than for boys. Furthermore, the delinquent acts of girls today are more serious than they were in the past; today they more closely approximate those of boys in degree of seriousness (131,176,179,218,241,253).

Delinquency in *urban areas* is greater than in rural, and the rate of increase is greater. This is especially true of slum areas and areas close to transportation and industry (42,159,163). The explanation given for the greater increase in urban areas is that in the smaller communities, the system of social control is integrated and more certain than in the larger communities. Through neighbors, the delinquencies of adolescents are brought to the attention of the parents. Divergent behavior is then stamped out before it has time to take root. In cities, by contrast, such behavior is reported to the police, even though the of-

fense is no greater than that committed by an adolescent in a rural district (78,143, 175,176,179).

The adolescent in a large city often feels lost and isolated, with no real sense of belonging. This gives him a feeling of insecurity that makes him an easy prey to the influences of a delinquent gang (42,107, 149). In rural areas, the delinquent usually belongs to a delinquent family—a family that lacks acceptance in the community because its moral behavior does not conform to that of the standards of the community as a whole (143).

Delinquency, in past generations, was limited mainly to adolescents of the lower *socioeconomic* groups. No longer is delinquency "class-bound," however; today it permeates every stratum of society, with a rapid increase in the upper strata. Even though many cases are not brought to court, the delinquent acts of adolescents of the upper classes often rival or surpass those of the lower classes in seriousness. While the motive back of affluent delinquency is mainly to "stir up some excitement," the acts used to do so are similar to those of members of the lower socioeconomic groups (42,94,97,149,159,183,211,235).

Increase in delinquency is greater among the *minority groups* than among the majority. This is especially true of the Negroes and Puerto Ricans (12,34,105). Because *school dropouts* find it difficult to get jobs, there has been, in recent years, a greater increase in delinquency among adolescents who have not finished high school than among those who graduate. The greater the *unemployment* among adolescents, the greater the increase in juvenile delinquency (10,42,126,155,253).

age of juvenile delinquency

While delinquent behavior begins in childhood, the peak is generally reached during late adolescence. Statistics from different areas in the country show that the largest number of arrests are made of youth between the ages of 17 and 19 years (31,175, 244). As Hollingworth has pointed out, "The majority of criminals lose their way socially while they are still in adolescence" (109).

Under the age of 11 years, delinquent boys outnumber delinquent girls 10 to 1. By middle adolescence, the rapid increase in girl delinquents and the relatively stable rate of increase for boys cuts down the ratio between the two sexes to 3.5 to 1 (174). This situation may be explained at least in part by the fact that young girls are more closely supervised and not given as much or as early freedom as boys. Only as girls approach the end of adolescence is there less supervision and, hence, an increase in delinquency (10,131,137,149,253).

The reason that delinquency reaches its peak in middle to late adolescence is that at that age many adolescents must make social adjustments without the aid of parents or teachers. The adolescent may fall by the wayside if his training in childhood has not been adequate.

There are other reasons why middle to late adolescence is a peak age in juvenile delinquency. These are: (1) The adolescent is a more "vulnerable" individual than his younger or older brother, and as a result he is more easily affected by problems and stimuli; (2) for the first time, he strikes back because he is now strong enough or well enough integrated against a problem that has been pressing for a number of years; (3) he is now aware of a whole new set of problems and adjustments, those related to his awakened sex drive; and (4) juvenile delinquency serves as a form of compensation for feelings of inadequacy (22,31,35,140,193,239,257).

As Lowrey (151) has pointed out, the period from 16 to 19 years is a time when conflict over differences, such as patterns of family living and child rearing, is sharply accentuated; this often causes delinquency. He goes on to explain:

A great deal of delinquency in this period, however, in so far as it is an expression of personality as opposed to social factors, is a matter of compensation for the conflict over difference. . . . It is within this area that intellectual inferiority, with inadequate provision for educational potential, is espe-cially important. Pressures for success and conformity in standard educational proce-dures, derived from the family, the school, and class competitions, frequently operate to force the inadequate individual toward delinquent behavior as a means of compen-sation for his own feelings of inadequacy and as proof to the group of his adequacy.

traditional beliefs about delinquency

From the earliest of civilized times, attempts have been made to explain why it is that the individual is a delinquent. There have been three general types of explanation of delinquency; the "prescientific mystical" ex-planation, which ascribed delinquent be-havior to some force outside of or beyond the individual, such as evil spirits; the early "modern particularistic" explanation, which attempted to explain a specific behavior act on the basis of some particular factor, such as heredity, religion, broken homes, en-docrine glands, or some physical abnormal-ity; and the "modern quasi-scientific empiri-cal" explanation, which emphasizes the interrelationship existing between all the forces or conditions that affect the be-havior of the individual (10,140,159,186, 236,257).

There was a time, for example, when it was believed that delinquency was a he-reditary trait. The saying, "Like father, like son," illustrates this belief. Similarly, many adolescents were said to have "bad blood," thus implying that they would unquestion-ably inherit criminal tendencies from a family member (157). There has also been a widely accepted belief that there is a "delinquent type"—an individual who is predisposed to delinquency. Today, it is rec-ognized that there is no such thing as a delinquent type. As Lowrey (151) has pointed out:

There are no such entities as "delinquent" or "criminal" personalities. To be sure, there are delinquents and criminals and, naturally, each has a personality, normal or abnormal, but all attempts to establish a distinctive delinquent or criminal type have come to naught.

Studies of personality have shown that not a single trait is more characteristic of delinquents than of nondelinquents (245). Instead, a delinquent is an ordinary boy or girl who is a product of his environment, including his family relationships and his training at home, his neighborhood, school, and associates, and some peculiarity in himself, such as poor intelligence or unhappiness. The patterns, attitudes, and practices of the delinquent are transmitted from person to person or from group to group through the influence of the leaders. The adolescent accepts the patterns of delinquent behavior either because of some inadequacy in himself or in his relationship to his environment or because his immediate environment presents predominantly deviant behavior patterns (100,137,151,167, 186).

There is evidence, however, that some boys and girls are more *predisposed to delinquency* than others. A boy, for example, who is influenced by peers whose behavior falls below social expectations, thinks of himself as his group expects—as tough and aggressive or as cool and calculating. If he molds himself into such patterns to conform to group expectations, he is likely to develop into a delinquent (232). In a comparison of 500 delinquents with 500 nondelinquents, Glueck and Glueck reported that the mesomorphic body build (muscular, strong, and active) predominates in delinquents as compared with ectomorphs (tall, slender, and relatively weak-muscled) or endomorphs (tall, round, and weak-muscled) (76). The reason that mesomorphs are more prone to delinquency is that they have an excess of energy, a liking for vigorous activity, and a strong response to frustration. Because they are active, they encounter many frustrations. And because they are vigorous, they react to frustrations in an aggressive manner which often leads to fighting and property damage—behavior which society classes as delinquent (229).

Critical analyses of delinquents of different body types have revealed that body type per se is not responsible for delinquent behavior. Instead, there are many factors other than body structure which contribute to delinquency though these factors may play a differential role among body types (76,186). As Sheldon (220) has noted:

> To try and predict such a thing as criminality from the somatotype alone would be like trying to predict where a bullet will strike by describing only the gun and the bullet and powder charge. You still have to deal with such variables as how the gun was aimed.

When an adolescent has a predisposition to behave in a nonmoral way, either through ignorance or intent, the pressures to grow up and to assume the status of an adult before the individual has learned how to do so may become a threat which will turn a predisposition into a reality (125).

That not all adolescents will respond in the same way has been shown by the fact that there are different types of juvenile delinquents, categorized on the basis of some dominant characteristic. There are the "organic" delinquents, whose delinquency is caused by some brain damage; the "neurotic" delinquents whose delinquent behavior is strongly influenced by a home where the parents are "problem" parents; the "asocial" delinquents whose delinquency stems from factors other than the social environment, mainly feelings of rejection in the home and school; and the "social" delinquents whose delinquency is influenced by the type of people they are associated with (17).

causes of juvenile delinquency

While the causes of juvenile delinquency are many and varied, they may be divided roughly into two categories, the "predisposing" causes and the "motivating" causes. The predisposing causes are those which set the stage or pave the way for delinquent behavior. They are the factors that heighten the likelihood of delinquency (26). The motivating causes, on the other hand, drive the adolescent into immoral behavior. These causes occur in the lives of all adolescents. Whether or not they will lead to delinquent behavior will depend upon the presence or absence of the predisposing causes and their relative strengths.

PREDISPOSING CAUSES

Some predisposing causes would be adequate, *alone*, to set the stage for delinquent behavior; most would not (31,35,186,254, 257). As Resnick has pointed out, "Many factors operate to produce an antisocial individual" (206). Furthermore, some of the predisposing causes are more important for girls, and some, for boys. Boys, for example, are more group-oriented than girls. Consequently, identity with a delinquent gang and pressures from gang members are more important predispositions to delinquency in boys than in girls. Unfavorable home conditions, by contrast, play a more important role in predisposing girls to delinquency (167,235,249,253). Among the most important of the predisposing causes of juvenile delinquency are the following.

Low-grade Intelligence Delinquents as a group are slightly below average in intelligence as compared with the population as a whole. (See Figure 12–5.) There are more mentally defective individuals among delinquents than among adolescents as a whole; at the same time, there are some who are above normal, even in the superior groups. Many bright adolescents come in conflict with the law; many dull ones do not (30, 73,74). In many cases, delinquents are not so much deficient in intellectual ability as in *the utilization of their ability* in school tasks. Hence, they create the impression that they are dull (210).

When intellectual ability is lower than that of their peers, adolescents develop a feeling of inadequacy. If this is combined with inability to cope with problems which their peers are able to cope with successfully, they may turn to delinquency as a form of compensation. The lower level of intelligence characteristic of many delinquents makes it difficult for them to profit from experience and to learn intelligently. Furthermore, low intelligence is generally accompanied by lack of foresight and plan-

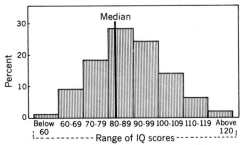

FIGURE 12–5 Distribution of IQ scores in a delinquent group. (Adapted from L. Cole and I. N. Hall: *Psychology of adolescence.* 6th ed. New York: Holt, Rinehart and Winston, 1964. Used by permission.)

ning ability. When combined with impulsiveness, this leads to unsocial behavior. Delinquents generally do better on motor than on verbal tasks; they prefer to act rather than to think carefully and to verbalize. They show unreflective thinking, poor judgment, and poor planning ability (21).

Unfavorable Attitudes toward School For the average adolescent, school is a pleasant, or at least a tolerable, experience. For the student who has difficulties with learning, there are so many frustrations and humiliations that school is often an intolerable experience (154).

When the school puts emphasis on traditional school subjects, the individual with a low IQ or a dislike for school may find it impossible to do the work required. Many delinquents, it has been reported, have difficulties in learning, especially in the areas of reading and arithmetic; they do such poor work that they often are forced to repeat one or two grades (5,60,139,173, 239). In one study of delinquents, it was found that more than half the members of the group had repeated two or more grades, while less than 10 percent had repeated no school grades. Many who did not repeat were pushed through school faster than their achievements warranted (5). Constant failure and retardation add to the adolescent's dislike for school (79).

Not only is the general attitude of delinquents toward school unfavorable, but their behavior is also. They engage in more misdemeanors and are more often truants than are nondelinquents. They have poorer citizenship ratings in school and get along less well with their teachers and fellow pupils (43,58,173). They spend more time with out-of-school friends than with their peers in school; they participate in few extracurricular activities; and they lack a sense of belonging to school. Because they are academic and social failures or near failures in school, they often drop out before completing their high school education (31,54, 74,126,139,217,239). Should the teacher regard the misbehavior which often springs from boredom and dislike for school as a reflection on her ability as a disciplinarian, she may intensify the adolescent's dislike for school by her rejective, punitive attitude (65,173).

Idle Time There is an old saying that "idle hands get into mischief." This holds true today just as it did in the past. But, today, there is more opportunity for idleness than in the past when workdays were longer and when the wealth was centered in the hands of only a small proportion of the population. In a period of affluence, and at a time when chores formerly done by adolescents are done by automation, adolescents have both the time and money to get into mischief if they are bored. This is especially likely to happen in communities which provide little in the way of "thrills" and excitement for their young people (36,82,94,97,115,149,255). (See Figure 12–6.)

When idleness is combined with frustrations caused by conditions in the school, the predisposition toward delinquency increases (36,115,173,227). In a study in which an attempt was made to determine at what months and at what times of the day delinquencies are most frequent, it was reported that there is an increase in delinquencies during the summer vacation months, especially in the latter part. The longer the school year, the fewer the number of juvenile delinquencies (247).

Adolescents who drop out of school in the hope of getting a job that will be less frustrating and more tolerable than school has been often find the doors of business and industry closed to them because of their limited training and experience. This means increased idle time and little money available to do what they had hoped to do. Only when families are able to provide their teen-age sons and daughters with spending money during their idleness will the temptation to get money by whatever means they can be reduced. Frequent and severe delinquencies are much less common among adolescents who continue their education until they complete high school or college. School attendance eliminates much of the idleness that predisposes adolescents to delinquency and at the same time provides them with training to help them secure jobs and incomes to satisfy many of their needs (36,42,82,89,115,149,239).

Physical Condition A comparison of delinquents and nondelinquents revealed that the delinquents had slightly more defects, such as defective vision, dental caries, diseased tonsils, and endocrine disorders, than their siblings had and that the state of their general health was slightly poorer (76). Delinquents, as a group, grow up more slowly than nondelinquents up to the age of 14 years, after which they surpass the nondelinquents. In fact, approximately one-half of all delinquents are early maturers and are sexually precocious in their interests and behavior (56). There is some evidence that there are more cases of epilepsy and brain injury among delinquents than among nondelinquents (76,220,229).

Confused Moral Values Conflict in values, competing cultural values, vaguely defined values, and adherence to amoral values are at the basis of much juvenile delinquency (240). Adolescents who reject adult values in favor of those of their peers do so because they have a stronger emotional attachment for their peers (131,219). In cases where more emphasis in discipline is placed on *what not to do* rather than on what to do, adolescents are at a loss to know what society expects of them (15,22, 159,177). For example, they may be per-

FIGURE 12–6 Idle hands often get into mischief.

plexed about what constitutes rightful self-defense and what constitutes unlawful aggression (57).

Moral values differ in different social groups, and adolescents who fail to achieve status in one group must accept the values of the group that will accept them if they want companionship. If, for example, their companions have a hostile attitude toward police and all in authority, they must too (32). Or if their companions have values based on a pattern of life that gives thrills, kicks, and excitement, they, too, will get most of their fun from acts that are tabooed by "squares." They, too, will scorn "getting on" in jobs. Instead, they will prefer quick success to steady jobs, and they will show disdain for hard work (10,141,156,173, 254).

Thus, while there is little evidence to show that delinquents are lacking in knowledge of right and wrong, confusion causes their ideals to remain intellectual so that they are never emotionally absorbed. The adolescent takes over the ideals and values of people he is fond of. If the attachment is for peers of the wrong sort, delinquency is the usual outcome. Because the delinquent's emotional attachments are for individuals of low moral values, he accepts these values as his, even though he may know that they are not the moral values widely accepted by society (37,56,122,149,163, 173).

Degree of Socialization While a delinquent may be disliked by his teachers because of his troublesome behavior in school, he generally gets along well with his age-mates. He participates in athletics and other recreational activities and often shows qualities of leadership. Few delinquents are "loners"; most are peer-oriented (202,260). They have friends but their friends are of an unacceptable type (54). Many of them are gang-oriented but they are identified with unruly gangs and have a reputation for mischief (36,142,249,253,257). As Harris has emphasized, most juvenile delinquents are not socially maladjusted in the sense that they get along poorly with people. On the contrary, they are usually well adjusted to the group to which they belong, but the standards of this group are too deviant to be acceptable to the larger social group (85). Some show social instability, but this is not characteristic of juvenile delinquents alone (23).

The juvenile delinquent's activities indicate an early identification with ways of behavior that are forbidden to young people—drinking, for example, smoking, gambling, and the use of profanity—even though they may be tolerated among adults. When an adolescent uses profane language, he is likely to be shunned by many of his peers; this throws him into the delinquent group (18). As a result, he is out of touch with the activities of his peers and he finds the activities that are socially acceptable too lacking in excitement to be satisfying to him (35,74,137).

When there are many adolescents of a poor socioeconomic background in a school, they have few places to meet and do things with their friends, other than in the street, in poolrooms, cellars, or similar areas of the community that encourage delinquent behavior. As a result of this deprivation, they gang together and seek adventure by stealing rides, destroying property, gambling, drinking, and staying away from school and home in the search of fun and adventure (36,74,82,137,160). Furthermore, because many delinquent groups are not well integrated, it is not unusual for their leaders to use aggressive attacks on others to deal with the internal disharmony of their group and the consequent threat to their leadership status (223).

Even in areas of the community where more wholesome forms of recreation are provided, those who are made to feel unwelcome shun such recreations and seek fun with others who make them feel welcome. Working-class boys, for example, face "status-frustration" and are handicapped in their socialization in a middle-class status system. Their gangs become a solution to this problem. Once they join a gang, they make a clean break with the middle-class groups, including their moral values, and

engage in aggression against the source of their frustration (10,36,128). As Bossard and Boll have pointed out, "Delinquent gangs are a natural product of the social education process in areas where the prevailing patterns are antisocial" (24).

Adolescents who have the greatest difficulty in becoming socialized through identification with some social group are those who are sex inappropriate in appearance and behavior. Boys who have feminine interests are more predisposed to becoming delinquents than are those whose interests are mainly masculine. Appropriately identified girls are less aggressive and less prone to delinquency than are those who are not appropriately identified (31,99,241).

That *socialization of the wrong type*, rather than lack of socialization, is a predisposing cause to juvenile delinquency has been emphasized thus by Dresher (54):

> The seeds of delinquency grow in the soil of poor social relationships, unsolved personal problems, and frustration, and root in social inadequacy, social disorganization, and moral and social deprivation, that results in social abandonment and delinquency.

While the delinquent can make friends, he "cannot make friends with society at large." Furthermore, it is possible to be antisocial and still not be a delinquent (2). This further emphasizes the role played by *type* of socialization rather than degree of socialization as a predisposing cause of delinquency.

When an adolescent is identified with a peer group that is delinquent, he may find when he tries to withdraw from the group and become a member of another group whose behavior conforms more to social expectations and to parental demands, that the other group will not accept him because he has acquired a reputation for being "wild." As one boy who tried to get out of a group that had begun to buy and use narcotics explained it, "I can't get into another crowd because they think I am dirty and a bad influence" (204).

Unfavorable Environmental Conditions In a poor environment, the moral values will be low, and the individual, from earliest childhood, will be surrounded by patterns of behavior that present crimes more as commendable than reprehensible acts. He will see the easy money, good clothes, and cars that are the fruit of crime, and he will see crime as an opportunity to improve his own lot in life (74,82,156,163).

Studies of the areas of cities where the rate of delinquency is highest have shown that they are characterized by poor housing, congestion, lack of recreational facilities, and general poverty. As the distance from the slum centers increases, there is a decrease in the delinquency rates. The lowest rates of delinquency are found in the better residential areas of the cities and in high-class suburban areas, which provide better recreational facilities for young people, a better pattern of living, and a higher standard of moral values (22,42,77,141, 163,179,202).

However, even in the better residential areas, there is more delinquency than is reported to the public. Some of the contributors to this are members of well-to-do and socially favored families. Their delinquency stems from boredom and a desire to have some excitement and thrill in life. Others become delinquent because they feel inadequate as compared with more affluent members of the community. This is especially true of suburban areas, where many adolescents suffer from "relative deprivation." As Wallace (246) has stated:

> The suburbs, no matter how great their accumulation of wealth, are by no means economically homogeneous. In a large high school the range of parents' incomes may extend from $7,000 or less, to $50,000 or more. By slum standards, a yearly income of $7,000 is more than adequate, but in the suburbs it is not. A suburban teen-ager whose family is in a relatively low income bracket, even though he may be supplied with all his requirements in the way of food, clothing, and shelter, may feel keenly, resentfully deprived in relation to his wealthier classmates. To the truly deprived youngster in an urban ghetto, the "predicament" of the poor suburban teen-ager may be laughable, but the suburbanite feels it none the less bitterly. . . . Material goals are so prominent that it may be unbearable to have less income than one's neighbor. That is the explanation of a seeming paradox: if poverty causes crime, how can the U.S. be the richest country in the world and have the highest rate of crime? Poverty causes crime in the U.S. because the American emphasis on material goals threatens the self-conceptions of persons who are relatively unsuccessful in terms of wealth and income.

When adolescents suffering from "relative deprivation" realize that the culturally approved goals of wealth, prestige, and status cannot be reached by approved means, there is a pressure from the peer group to engage in deviant behavior to achieve them. If an adolescent, for example, cannot reach the socially approved goals of success, prestige, and status by approved means, such as a high-prestige job, then he will try to reach them by unapproved methods which sooner or later will lead to delinquency (37,77,173,242,257).

Mass Media of Communication The environment in which the individual grows up influences him indirectly through the various forms of mass communication. Studies of the effects of mass communication media have all stressed that they are not directly responsible for delinquency. But, when there are other predisposing factors present, such as emotional instability, poverty, or unfavorable family relationships, the different forms of communication may and sometimes do intensify the unfavorable condition already present (187).

For the normal, well-adjusted individual, the comics act as a mental catharsis for emotional tensions, even those which glorify the more vicious forms of crime. However, studies have revealed that delinquents read many more of the "harmful" and "questionable" comics than do nondelinquents; they read the "harmless" type in about equal numbers. This may keep the spirit of crime alive in the delinquent group, though there is no evidence of a cause-and-effect relationship between delinquency and reading of the comics. (See pages 236 and 237 for a more detailed account of the relationship of the reading of comics to behavior, especially to delinquent behavior.)

Unfavorable Home Conditions The behavior and attitudes of parents are important in the making of a juvenile delinquent just as they are in the making of a law-abiding citizen. When close family ties exist, as one finds in devoutly religious families or in families where strong traditional ties hold the family members together, delinquency is uncommon. By contrast, in families where there is little affectional relationship between the members and where the children have little respect for their parents, delinquency is common (157,198,237).

However, unfavorable family relationships per se will not necessarily predispose the adolescent to delinquency. Nor will a good home, when other conditions are unfavorable, immunize him against delinquency. As MacIver has pointed out, the "family is not an island apart from the group and the neighborhood" (152). Any abnormal home in which disease or tragedy leaves permanent scars heightens the likelihood of delinquency (26,78,181).

There are many deviant conditions in the home of an adolescent which may predispose him to delinquent behavior. One of the most serious of these is a home broken by death, divorce, separation, or desertion (50,56,77,165,221,226,254). While a broken home is serious at any time, it is especially serious for the younger child if it means that his mother will have to go out to work or place him in a foster home. If, on the other hand, the child is not deprived of his mother's care during the early years of life, he is not likely to develop into a delinquent as he grows older *unless* there are other unfavorable conditions in his environment (81,167,171). A "structurally unbroken" home where there is tension between parents is as serious as a broken home (35,50,77,167).

Adolescents differ in their reactions to broken homes; some are far more affected by them than are others (167). It is more serious for girls to have a disorganized home than it is for boys because girls have closer ties with their homes in adolescence than do boys. When the home environment is frictional, the girl's relationships with the family members are of the type that predispose her to become a delinquent (10, 37,72,237,253). Older adolescents are less affected by broken homes than are younger, because they have members of the peer group for the companionship and affection they formerly received at home. However, if they are socially isolated from the peer group, they feel lonely and rejected when their homes are broken (50,131,167). A majority of sex delinquencies among girls are to be found among those who come from broken homes; this is a form of compensation for the affection they crave but do not get at home. Truancy, ungovernable behavior, and running away from home are also common ways in which the adolescent shows his feeling of deprivation when his home is broken (29,74,77,162,221,234).

Studies of the parents of delinquents have revealed that they provide a very poor model for their children to imitate (151, 157,254). Frequent arrests, lack of respect for the law, drinking, sexual irregularities, dishonesty, emotional instability, irresponsibility, and low moral standards are common among the parents of delinquents (77,79, 235).

Equally as serious as identification with a parent who provides a socially unacceptable model to imitate is *lack of identification* with a parent. This causes the adolescent to reject the values and goals of a parent, even when they are socially approved values and goals (131). If harsh and punitive discipline in adolescence causes the identification established in childhood to break down, the adolescent will often reject a model of behavior that would have led to socially approved behavior in favor of one that leads to delinquency (77,124,257). Many delinquent boys, coming from broken homes, have no father to identify with. If they identified with their mothers when they were younger, they later attempt to become "masculine" by rejecting "goodness" —which they associate with females—in favor of the "bad boy role"—which they associate with masculinity (9).

Delinquents report that they are *dissatisfied with their homes*, they are highly critical of their parents and siblings, and they feel that their parents show favoritism toward their siblings (54). They perceive the mother as the more punitive parent who requires more work and study than the father (259). It is not uncommon for a delinquent girl to say that she hates her mother (250). Delinquents, because they feel rejected and unloved by their parents, find it hard to communicate with them or to turn to them for advice and help (56, 131). They feel that their parents require too many chores at home and show little appreciation for what they do (77,226). Because delinquent boys feel rejected by their fathers, they spend little time and engage in few activities with them (158).

The delinquents who are most influenced by unfavorable family relationships are those who are illegitimate or adopted children; those who grow up in homes where the marital relationship between the parents is frictional; and those who have a stepparent who has a hostile attitude toward the stepchildren (6,50,185). Often they are neglected by their parents and receive little supervision or guidance. This is not because their mothers work, as is so often claimed, but because of an unfavorable attitude toward the child on the part of the mother (77,100,161,181,235).

In homes where parents are foreign-born, there are constant clashes between parent and adolescent regarding standards of behavior. Parents are either strict in trying to enforce the old world standards on their children or are bewildered about what to do. This results in overly strict, overly lenient, or inconsistent discipline. In his strivings to be acceptable to his peers, the adolescent frequently disobeys parental authority and behaves in a manner that leads him into trouble with the law (148).

The *discipline* in the homes of delinquents is usually poor. In some families, parents are excessively permissive (100,158, 251). In others, discipline is overstrict and allows for little freedom. This leads to re-

sentments on the part of the adolescents and to friction between them and their parents about standards of conduct (14,226). Even more serious is the fact that the disciplinary methods used by parents of delinquents are often inconsistent. As a result, the adolescent does not know what to expect and he loses respect for the disciplinarian (158). Inconsistency in discipline predisposes the adolescent to delinquency more than the type of discipline used (35, 37,157,235).

The *attitude of the disciplinarian* toward the adolescent is likewise more important than the type of discipline used. Parents of delinquents have been found to be less kindly in their disciplinary practices than parents of nondelinquents. The mothers, for example, show little approval of or pleasure in their children; instead, they have punitive, controlling, and authoritarian attitudes (153,158). Fathers often openly display dislike for their offspring. They are frequently weak, inexperienced, and vacillating in their methods of controlling their children (77,251). Furthermore, parents of delinquents often show a disregard for the mores and ethics of society and a derogatory attitude toward those in authority. This gives the adolescent a poor model to imitate and weakens his motivation to conform to social expectations (35,150).

Unjust or *overstrict* punishment builds up a resentful attitude toward the punisher and toward society in general (46,200). Parents of delinquents rely mainly on physical punishment as a means of control and show poor judgment regarding the type and severity of punishment they use (74,157). In homes where the father whips his children for misbehavior, the delinquency rate is found to be higher than in homes where less corporal punishment is used (77,158, 235). Studies of juvenile delinquents have revealed that they receive less *religious training* in the home and attend Sunday school and church less than do nondelinquents (31,77,158). As J. Edgar Hoover (110) has pointed out:

> In practically every home where juvenile delinquency is bred, there is an absence of

religious training for children. . . . Most of them have never been inside a church.

In families where religion plays an important role, there are usually close family ties which help to insulate the adolescent against delinquency (152,197,215). Regarding this Peck and Havighurst (188) have observed:

> *While no single religious denomination stands out as closely related to high or low moral maturity, it is nevertheless true that the children who rank high come from families that are actively religious and the boys and girls themselves have attended Sunday school and church services fairly regularly.*

Studies of *size of family* in relation to delinquency have shown that, proportionately, there are fewer delinquents among only children than among those who come from large families. The majority of delinquents come from large families (6). This may be explained partly by the impossibility of providing individualized training when the number of children is large and the family income small and partly by the fact that in large families adolescents often feel that they are imposed upon when they are expected to do more chores around the house and assume more responsibilities for the care of younger siblings than their friends do. If this interferes with their social lives, it increases their resentments and feelings of martyrdom—feelings which may predispose them to delinquency (24,77,187, 235,250).

While *poverty* is not in and of itself a cause of juvenile delinquency, it produces causes. It causes parents to neglect their children, especially when mothers must go out to work, and it produces tension in the home (10,37,161,181,257). Poverty makes it impossible for youth to have the things their peers have. This creates envy and motivation to get them by any means possible. Furthermore, poverty produces undernourishment and poor physical health, both of which mean low mental resistance to temptations (100). Figure 12–7 shows some of the conditions within the home which have been found to predispose a group of boys to delinquent behavior.

Personality It must be recognized that "not all delinquents are maladjusted and not all maladjusted are delinquents" (6). Delinquency is only one expression of a disturbed *personality pattern* (106). On the other hand, studies of the personality characteristics of adolescents have shown that the delinquent is a different type of person from the nondelinquent. As Lowrey (151) has stated:

> [The] *delinquent personality is, in general, characterized by immaturity, egocentricity, and inability to establish emotional relationships with others, primarily because of lack of ability to identify or because of actual hostility.*

Lowrey goes on to explain that no one of these characteristics is peculiar to the delinquent. But they are often more pronounced than in normal individuals owing "to the subtle effects of interaction between individual and environment, leading to the establishment of particular personality sets" (151). A comparison of the personality traits of delinquents and nondelinquents is shown in Figure 12–8.

There are certain personality patterns commonly found among juvenile delinquents (117). The *unsocialized, aggressive* delinquent feels deprived, rejected, misunderstood, and insecure. This results in hostile, cruel, violent, destructive behavior (115,173,216).

The *socialized* delinquent, by contrast, is better accepted by his peers and by society in general. He has strong loyalties to his friends and is anxious to win their favor. Because of lax discipline and unfavorable home conditions, he is generally without decisiveness and persistence (19,20,114,117, 259).

The *emotionally disturbed* delinquent suffers from feelings of rejection and deprivation of love. He blames others for his own shortcomings and is suspicious and jealous (20,68,74,79). In recent years, there has been a marked increase in emotionally disturbed adolescents, especially in the case of girls (42,115,179).

Regardless of the personality pattern of the delinquent, every delinquent has an *unfavorable self-concept.* He likes himself much less than does the nondelinquent (204). This may be due to school or social failures, physical inadequacies, or any number of other causes. When inadequacies in one area become general and when the adolescent develops an inferiority complex, it breaks down his resistance to pressures from a delinquent peer group and a delinquent subculture. He is then predisposed to behave in a socially unacceptable manner (3, 19,51,52,115). When feelings of inadequacy and inferiority cause the adolescent to perceive himself as lonely, rejected, and persecuted, and to have negative attitudes toward his future goals, he often defends himself against these attitudes by hitting back or stealing (62).

Constellation of Predisposing Causes   From the analysis of the many different factors that are known to predispose adolescents to delinquent behavior, it should be apparent that not one factor alone is responsible. Instead, "many factors operate to produce an antisocial individual." Because many of his personality needs are unsatisfied at home, at school, or in the community, the delinquent is an "emotional cripple," showing behavior patterns that are mainly the result of emotional difficulties (206). As has been stressed before, delinquency is only one of many possible forms of expression of a disturbed life pattern; some emotional cripples become psychopaths while others become juvenile delinquents (6).

To indicate how many factors may operate to predispose a boy or girl to delinquent behavior, Kvaraceus has suggested the following "delinquency-producing equation," composed of three complex factors working together and each contributing to the end result—juvenile delinquency. This equation is: *factors under the skin* (personality makeup) × *factors in the culture and subculture* × *factors in community attitude.*

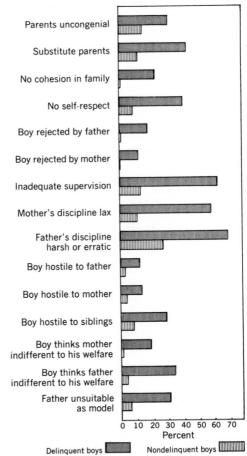

FIGURE 12–7 Conditions within the home that predispose boys to delinquent behavior. (Adapted from L. Cole and I. N. Hall: *Psychology of adolescence.* 6th ed. New York: Holt, Rinehart and Winston, 1964. Used by permission.)

When certain conditions and variables are "right," the probability is juvenile delinquency (138,141).

MOTIVATING CAUSES

One or more of the predisposing causes of juvenile delinquency listed above are present in the lives of the majority of adolescents. The motivating cause, working in collaboration with the predisposing cause or causes, produces a driving force that is too strong for the individual to resist. The result is behavior contradictory to the standards of con-

Delinquents ▨▨▨ Nondelinquents ▨▨▨

FIGURE 12–8 Comparison of personality traits of delinquent and nondelinquent boys. Note the more forceful traits of the delinquents. (Adapted from L. J. Cronbach, *Educational psychology.* 2d ed. New York: Harcourt, Brace & World, 1963. Used by permission.)

duct approved by the group to which he belongs (22,37,141,238).

In the absence of a motivating cause, the predisposing causes would not lead to delinquent behavior even though the adolescent were in a state of readiness to act; the stimulus to release the energy must be applied before the act will take place (254). Idle time, for example, will not lead to acts of vandalism, reckless driving, or shoplifting unless the adolescent is motivated to engage in these unsocial acts by boredom. If he is enjoying his idleness, he will behave in a socially approved way—by engaging in recreations that satisfy him. By contrast, the bored adolescent will gain satisfaction only when he engages in acts that are socially disapproved of (35,82,159,257).

Delinquent behavior, thus, is a response to the thwarting of *some* desire. If the only motive that will give the individual personal satisfaction is some form of socially disapproved behavior which he can do well, he will then turn to delinquency. If, for example, a girl finds that the only way she

can achieve the satisfaction she craves from popularity with members of the opposite sex is by promiscuous sex behavior, she will become a sex delinquent. Should she, on the other hand, be able to satisfy her desire for popularity by more socially approved dating behavior, she will not turn to sex delinquencies (60).

Studies of the motives of juvenile delinquents have revealed that they are the motives of normal but immature young people, rather than of criminals. All normal, well-adjusted adolescents, for example, want material possessions as status symbols; they want adventure and excitement; and they want to create the impression that they are important members of the peer group. In their desire to satisfy these motives, they may use behavior patterns which they found acceptable when they were younger but are no longer acceptable as they approach adulthood. The adolescent who discovered when he was younger that he could impress others by exaggeration may develop into a pathological liar as he grows older. Or, he may be motivated to steal prestigeful possessions, such as a car or clothing, to satisfy his desire to be a "big shot" in the eyes of the peer group (9,11,104). Vandalism and other forms of destructiveness in adolescence may be carry-overs of behavior patterns that the adolescent learned as a child satisfied his desire to "get even" with those whom he felt had treated him unfairly (36,115, 258).

Types of Motivating Causes   Motivating causes in juvenile delinquency can be divided, roughly, into two major categories: planned and impulsive. Sometimes the motive is thought out, *planned* in every detail, and carefully executed. Delinquent acts of this type are "goal-motivated" in the sense that the adolescent carries out the act to achieve a goal which is important to him. Stealing a car, for example, is motivated by a desire to win approval and acceptance by members of a peer group who place high value on material possessions. Goal-motivated acts of delinquency occur mainly in adolescents who have been exposed to schooling in delinquent techniques, either in the home or as a member of a delinquent gang (35,37,115,159,257).

The second major category of motives to delinquent behavior consists of *impulsive* acts which the adolescent carries out in response to a frustration. The delinquent acts impulsively in a fit of anger, jealousy, or envy; he then bitterly regrets his act after it has been completed. An adolescent may, for example, impulsively steal a car he finds unlocked to impress members of a peer group that have rejected him. Or an adolescent who "hates" school and is angry because he received a poor grade may impulsively throw a stone and break a window of the school. Impulsive acts are common among delinquents whose lives are full of frustrations. And as most delinquents experience many frustrations, their acts of delinquency are more often impulsive than planned (31,36,115,141,159).

Common Motivating Causes Whether planned or impulsive, the motivating causes of juvenile delinquency are many. Of these, the following are the most common.

dissatisfaction with present conditions and a desire for better things This is often intensified by mass media of communication, especially movies, ads in magazines and papers, and romantic stories. Stealing, whether impulsive or planned, is a quick and easy way to get status symbols. Many burglaries of homes where the owners are away and holdups of cashiers in banks, of housewives alone in their homes, or of people in cars or walking on the street who "look as if they have money" are motivated by the desire for easy money for the better things of life (11,115,257).

strong emotions Emotions, especially anger, jealousy, fear, or envy, which the adolescent has not learned to control, are motivating causes in delinquency. Many of the race riots that have been plaguing America since the passage of the Civil Rights Act of 1964 stem from what members of a minority group regard as "unfair treatment" of a member of their race by the police or members of the majority group. These are usually touched off by some relatively minor incident that angers teen-agers of the minority group. Anger then leads to street fighting and attacks on innocent by-standers. Adolescents from affluent families, angered if not invited to a party, may gang together and crash the party, often wrecking furniture and carrying off "souvenirs" of their triumph as a form of retaliation.

boredom Adolescents with too few responsibilities, too few opportunities for satisfying achievements, or too few opportunities for recreation of a wholesome type are often bored. Breaking the law by driving faster than the speed limit, falsifying his age to buy liquor, shoplifting to see if he can "get away with it," or destroying personal or public property in a spring riot to ease the boredom of studying for final examinations are all ways of getting "kicks" which the bored adolescent feels he cannot get from a more socially approved pattern of behavior (22,31,35,82,257).

feelings of inferiority These feelings are often accompanied by doubts about sex appropriateness. The adolescent who feels inferior to others—whether his feeling relates to physical, mental, or social inferiority—is motivated to compensate by behavior which will prove to others as well as to himself that he is not inferior. Should it spring from doubts about sex appropriateness, a feeling of inferiority will be compensated for by behavior associated with members of that sex. A boy, for example, will compensate by flaunting the law and showing his daring by doing things that are illegal because boys are expected to be brave and daring (36,82,96,149).

assertion of independence If breaking home and school rules will not satisfy the desire for independence and freedom, the adolescent will break laws. Falsifying his age to be able to buy liquor, buying drugs from a drug "peddler," shoplifting, speeding, and sexual delinquencies are all more common among adolescents from authoritarian homes and schools than from democratic. Furthermore, they often follow a punishment which the adolescent regards as unfair because he has been "treated like a kid" (37,115,257,258).

desire for social acceptance The desire to be accepted, especially by the "right" crowd, motivates many adolescents to "follow the crowd." Affluent teen-agers who engage in shoplifting explain, when caught, that "everyone does it" just as do those who are caught buying liquor or drugs (11, 82,255). Similarly, if the members of their crowd want to crash a party or take part in a spring riot on the college campus, the desire for popularity will motivate them to follow suit (31,159,258).

desire for sexual gratification This desire is especially strong in adolescents who feel unloved at home, who have doubts about their sex appropriateness, and who have highly romanticized concepts of sex based on identification with characters in mass media. An adolescent boy with a strong desire for sexual gratification may be motivated to rape girls or to visit in the red-light district of the community which he knows is illegal at his age. Sexual promiscuity, resulting in illegitimate babies or the contraction of venereal disease, is a common expression of a strong desire for sexual gratification among adolescent girls (30,73, 94,97,210,246,259).

insulation against delinquency

From the survey of predisposing and motivating causes of juvenile delinquency, given above, it should be apparent that *every* adolescent *might* become a delinquent. Why, then, do relatively few turn to delinquency as a way of life while the majority accept the socially approved values of their communities and obey the rules and laws that have been established as guides to their behavior? The answer is that some adolescents are "insulated" against delinquency and others are not.

An adolescent who is insulated against delinquency is "thought by others to be good and conceives of self as a law-abiding

and conventional individual" (198). He has developed internalized law-abiding norms of behavior and concepts of self which will protect him from possible delinquencies in the future (215). Even though he experiences many of the conditions that would predispose him to delinquency and even though the different motives to react in a delinquent manner are present, the adolescent will not succumb to them, no matter how great the temptation. Insulation against delinquency is, thus (197):

> . . . an ongoing process reflecting an internalization of non-delinquent values and conformity to the expectations of significant others. . . . It may be an outgrowth of discovery in social experience that playing the part of the good boy and remaining a good boy bring maximum satisfactions (of acceptance) to the boy himself.

By contrast, the adolescent who has not acquired an insulation against delinquency may readily succumb to temptations from his environment or from strong personal drives. As Toby has explained, "Crime arises when the temptation to violate a rule is stronger than the individual's guilt feelings and fear of social disapproval" (238). The reason that "socially disorganized" communities have a higher rate of crime than "socially organized" is that in the former, the individual lacks motivation to conform to rules (238).

HOW INSULATION IS ACQUIRED
No adolescent is born with an insulation against delinquency. Instead, it must be acquired by learning, either through trial-and-error experiences or through guidance. What, then, insulates some adolescents against the pressures of delinquency while others succumb to them? The most obvious answer is "fear—fear of social disapproval and rejection or fear of punishment." While unquestionably fear is an insulator against juvenile delinquency, its value as such is limited. If the adolescent has reason to believe that his misdeed will go undetected, fear will not act as a deterrent. However, even though most adolescents are afraid of being caught and punished, their fear may

be outweighed by a desire to satisfy a strong need which has been unsatisfied in everyday life (238).

The only satisfactory form of insulation comes from the satisfaction of basic needs in socially acceptable ways. The adolescent whose basic needs have been met at home, at school, or in the peer group is insulated against delinquent behavior (198). In this insulation, the mother plays a dominant role. The adolescent who feels loved, accepted, and respected as an individual by his mother, even though he may be rejected or neglected by his father, is usually insulated against delinquency. On the other hand, if he feels rejected by his mother, even though accepted by his father, he is likely to channel his energies into delinquent acts (157).

While the mother plays a dominant role in the insulation process, the whole atmosphere of the home contributes its share. The adolescent who grows up in a family where there are strong emotional ties between the members, where parents teach their children socially acceptable values and patterns of behavior, where they set a good example for their children to imitate, and where attempts are made to encourage the children to achieve success in school and to avoid social groups whose behavior patterns are socially unacceptable is provided with a bulwark against antisocial influences in the peer group and in the neighborhood (152,215,237).

When insulated adolescents live in a high-delinquency area of the community, they show their insulation against delinquent influences by a high level of social responsibility, by strict concepts of right and wrong, by conforming to the expectations of their parents, teachers, and others in authority, and by working hard to come up to the expectations of significant people in their lives in school and in whatever they undertake (215,254).

Knowing that their parents are interested in them, in their activities, and in their friends, and that their teachers are willing to help them in whatever way they can, insulated adolescents have a strong motivation to live up to what the significant people in their lives expect of them (197). Because they feel that they have been fairly treated, that they are loved and respected as individuals, and that they have good homes—even though poor in material possessions—they develop favorable self-concepts. Such concepts are the product of good socialization (19,196,215). By contrast, the adolescent who has a poor self-concept has no resistance to deviancy, delinquent companions, and a delinquent environment; he is not insulated against potential delinquency. As a result, he falls prey to delinquent influences. The adolescent who has been insulated veers away from the street corner and its delinquent pressures (52,254).

Just as a favorable self-concept insulates an adolescent against delinquency, so does a realistic one. If he sees himself as he is, not as he would like to be, there is little chance that he will try to compensate for feelings of inadequacy that come from falling short of an unrealistic self-image by behavior that deviates from the socially accepted pattern (3,19,196,197). Figure 12–9 shows some of the environmental conditions that will help to insulate adolescents against delinquency.

LONG-TERM EFFECTS OF INSULATION

How long the adolescent will remain insulated against delinquent behavior will depend mainly on his ability to maintain a favorable self-concept in the face of mounting situational pressures (215). If, for example, he is in a stable family in a good neighborhood, it will be easier to do so than if he is in an unstable family in a poor neighborhood (197). If the insulation is strong enough to protect him from situational pressures to become a member of a delinquent group up to the age of 16 years—the "critical age" of institutionalized delinquents—his chances of remaining insulated are good (215).

By contrast, the adolescent not so insulated will be susceptible to environmental pressures. Even when caught in delinquent acts, he will not be restrained from future delinquencies by feelings of guilt or shame or by fear of punishment. Instead, he will

FIGURE 12–9 Environmental conditions that help to insulate adolescents against delinquency. (Adapted from L. D. Crow and A. Crow: *Adolescent development and adjustment.* 2d ed. New York: McGraw-Hill, 1965. Used by permission.)

more likely develop into a "repeater," with each delinquent act becoming more serious than the previous one. This will be the starting point of an adulthood of criminality (197,215,250).

forms of delinquent behavior

Delinquent acts take any number of possible forms. However, they can be grouped roughly into four general categories (49,57, 71,78,94,97,148,164,179,182,199,208,254).

1 *Harm to self or others directly or indirectly involved in social situations.* These include such acts as assaults on people, muggings, crowd disturbances, and attempts at self-destruction by stabbing, shooting, and drowning. The victims of delinquent assaults may be children, adolescents, or adults; they may be members of rival gangs, of minority groups, or of innocent bystanders.

2 *Damage to or misappropriation of property.* Delinquencies in this category include vandalism, burglaries, larcenies, arson, shoplifting, and thefts of all types, especially clothes, costume jewelry, and cars.

3 *Ungovernability, or refusal to obey parental, academic, or legal authorities.* This may range from strong defiance to "slick" surface conformity. It includes such behavior as truancy, running away from home, driving without a license, buying and drinking liquor, or buying narcotics.

4 *Acts leading to possible danger to self or others.* This includes speeding, use of narcotics, glue sniffing, party crashing, unauthorized use of weapons, sexual misconduct, juvenile prostitution, etc.

INCREASE IN SERIOUSNESS

Since the Second World War, there has been a marked increase in the seriousness of juvenile crime. Boys of 10 years of age, for example, are now committing the types of burglaries and holdups that boys of 15 and 16 used to do; boys of 15 and 16 are being arrested for the kinds of crimes that used to be committed by young men of 20 or 21 years of age. The three most vicious types of crime committed in recent years are assault, rape, and criminal homicide, though burglary, larceny, and auto thefts have likewise increased greatly (244).

Sexual delinquencies not only are more common among younger adolescent girls today, but they are of a more serious type. Approximately 50 percent of the delinquent girls who are institutionalized are either suffering from venereal diseases or they are pregnant (78,94,176,246,250).

VARIATIONS IN DELINQUENCIES

Most cases of delinquency among adolescents under the *age* of 14 or 15 years involve offenses against property, such as robbery, burglary, larceny, auto thefts, forgery, fraud, receiving stolen property, and arson. To the young adolescent, it is fun and exciting to annoy others and to see if one can break the laws without being caught. In late adolescence, by contrast, the common forms of delinquency are offenses against persons in the form of rape, sexual irregularities, intoxication, and attempts at homicide or suicide (74,94,246,255). There are *racial* differences in delinquencies. White boys, for example, steal cars more often than do Negro boys, not because the Negroes do not want cars, but rather because they are afraid they will be accused of theft by the police if they are seen driving cars (252). Among Negro girls, sexual delinquencies are more common than among white girls of the same ages (127).

Among *boys*, delinquencies consist mostly of stealing, disorderly conduct, burglary, destruction of property, acts of mischief and carelessness, traffic violations, drug addiction, and injuries to persons. For girls, by contrast, the most common offenses are sexual irregularities, running away, petty stealing, ungovernability, and incorrigibility. Boys engage in a wider variety of delinquent behavior than do girls. On the whole, their behavior is of a more serious nature in that it is harmful to others while that of girls is more harmful to themselves (72, 250,255). Almost three times as many boys as girls are brought into juvenile courts (78).

Rural offenses are, for the most part, individual acts, such as trespassing on the property of others, threatening to beat up people, hanging around taverns, and being with "bad" associates. On the whole, they are relatively unsophisticated acts as compared with those of urban and suburban youth. Urban delinquencies depend mainly on supportive peer-group relationships and include such acts as thefts, gambling, truancy, and drinking. There is a growing tendency to drug addiction among adolescents in urban centers where it is relatively easy to obtain narcotics. The more serious delinquent acts predominate in the *lower-class groups*; those with "nuisance value" predominate in the middle- and upper-class groups. Therefore, the type of delinquent acts that are most common in urban and suburban areas will be determined by the predominant social class in that area (33, 42,78,94,107,246).

corrective measures

Early methods of dealing with juvenile delinquency made use of severe corporal punishment. The belief behind these methods was that the only way to "drive out the devil" was through the use of physical force. As the belief in the presence of the devil in

the culprit gave way to the realization that environmental causes in one form or another were primarily responsible for producing juvenile delinquency, corporal punishment became less severe and other forms of punishment replaced it.

Furthermore, investigations of the effect of corporal punishment on the attitude of the individual punished revealed that more harm than good resulted. The development of a revengeful attitude toward the punisher, toward all in authority, and toward rules and regulations merely served as a motivation to further delinquent behavior. Follow-up studies of juvenile delinquents who had been institutionalized as punishment for their offenses showed that many were repeaters when they were released from the institutions (53,74,75,119,250).

That institutionalization does not correct the cause or causes of delinquency has been emphasized by a study of adolescent boys' attitudes when released from institutions. Some changes in self-concepts did result; fewer of the boys, for example, perceived themselves as criminals than they had earlier. There were also some changes in their values, with more emphasis on ambition, responsibility, and willingness to consider the interests of others in interpersonal relationships than there had previously been. However, few felt that the institutional experience had been a benefit to them (225). Furthermore, after being released from an institution, many delinquents find that the social group rejects them as jailbirds; therefore, it is difficult to get jobs. This does not encourage the continuation of any favorable attitude that might have been fostered by institutionalization (197,215,250).

Present trends in dealing with juvenile delinquency place emphasis on rehabilitation and prevention rather than on punishment and vengeance (152). Of the two, prevention offers more hope for cutting down the increasingly serious growth of this social evil than does rehabilitation.

REHABILITATION

"Rehabilitation" means "curing" delinquency once it has become an established pattern of life for the adolescent. Because there is no one cause of juvenile delinquency, there can be no one method of treatment to cure it. Furthermore, it has been recognized for a long time that rehabilitation must be adjusted to the conditions that led to delinquency. Adolescents whose delinquency results from personal maladjustment, for example, are usually sent to clinics for psychiatric treatment. Those who show few signs of personality maladjustment but who are products of poor environmental conditions are usually sent to approved training schools where environmental conditions are better than those in which the delinquents have grown up (1,6, 102).

However, no matter what method of rehabilitation is used, it will not cure delinquency if the adolescent does not *want* to be reformed and if he has found the pattern of his delinquent life satisfactory. As Cole and Hall (39) have pointed out, for a delinquent, there is *"no other life* that is so rewarding."* They go on to elaborate on why this is so:

> *The typical delinquent does not want to be reformed; he wants only not to get caught. He can rarely be reclaimed through love, because he is no longer capable of giving or receiving affection. His deep hatred of schools and teachers prevents a rescue through education. And it is of little use to talk about "congenial work," because no work could be as congenial to him as delinquency. What the would-be reformer often overlooks is that the delinquent likes to steal from adults, because the act pays back in small measure the multiple rejections he has received from the adult world. He likes to "gang up" on a "good" boy, because the attack will do something to cancel the hurt of rejection of other "good" children. He likes random vandalism, because it gives him a chance to work off a bit of his long score against society. He likes to feel callous toward people, because this attitude prevents him from getting hurt. Moreover, success in such activities as those just mentioned brings him prestige among other delinquents. Their approval he wants; that of the world he can do without.*

PREVENTION

Attempts are being made to prevent the occurrence of delinquency by stressing the necessity for improving living conditions among the underprivileged, for more recreational opportunities, and for better parental supervision (1,44,102,246,255). As Papanek has pointed out, we offer our children poor homes, inadequate community facilities, and an excess of crime in mass media, we give them no status, and then we get juvenile delinquency (187). It is now recognized that the delinquent "presents a psychological deficit. He is a less adequate personality" (260). If he is to be prevented from reaching this state, measures must be taken to deal with the situations in his life that give rise to the type of child who later becomes a delinquent. A follow-up study of antisocial young children who were given psychiatric treatment revealed, for example, that many showed improvement in their peer relationships and school work. Others were not so improved; as a result, they were more predisposed toward delinquency (209).

That prevention is more important than rehabilitation has been emphasized by Peck and Havighurst (188) from the results of a follow-up study of children from 10 years of age into middle adolescence. According to their findings, there is:

> . . . *a characteristic personality and character pattern which was largely laid down by age ten and changed little thereafter. . . . This suggests that the child of each character type starts very early and develops along that type path, and that growth simply makes him more and more that kind of person. Since the family influence is usually continuously the same, whether in a stable or confused pattern, this is understandable. . . . It has been found that most individuals tend to maintain* the same attitudes and motives *through the years, in major aspects of morality.*

Identification by Danger Signals Because delinquency is only a step away from nondelinquency and because adolescence is the period when behavior problems of childhood "mature into full-fledged delinquency," the present trend is to try to identify the potential delinquent and socialize him so that he will fit into the group (85). The age of 8 years has been found to be the "key age" when delinquent behavior begins (130,180). Through the use of questionnaires, tests, and observations of behavior, potential delinquents can now be identified and remedial steps taken to socialize them by correcting the conditions that give rise to later delinquency. While the major offenses of girls, sex delinquencies, do not show up as early as stealing and other common forms of delinquency in boys, it is nevertheless possible to identify those who may, at a later age, become delinquents (74,77,112,130,180).

There are certain patterns of behavior indicative of an adolescent who is particularly vulnerable to delinquency. He feels dissatisfied with school because of poor schoolwork, little scholastic aptitude, or repetition of grades; he plays truant or is a dropout; he belongs to no recognized or supervised peer group; he has low values and ideals; he has unsatisfactory home conditions; he lives in a high-delinquency neighborhood; he feels rejected in the home, school, or neighborhood; he experiences greater resentments, suspicions, destructiveness, and hostility than other adolescents of the same age; he has poor social insight and shows little sensitivity to conventions and mores; he has difficulties in interpersonal relationships; he solves problems by withdrawal or aggressiveness; he uses more ego defenses than other adolescents of the same age; he has unrealistic levels of aspiration; and he is more emotionally unstable than is usual for that age, as shown in general irritability, low tolerance level, lack of responsibility, and vacillating emotions (103, 113,116,136,139,180).

While these are danger signals, Kvaraceus (136) has stressed:

Not every child who shows one or more of these signs will become a delinquent. However, from the evidence at hand, it is safe to say that a major portion of these unfortunate children who will appear in the juvenile courts of tomorrow will be drawn from the reservoir of children who show several of these characteristics.

Of all the danger signals of delinquency, the most important one is unfavorable home conditions. In the investigation of potential delinquency, special emphasis should be placed on the discipline used by the father, the supervision by the mother, the affection of the mother and the father for the child, and the cohesiveness of the family (1,102,103,112,197,215).

Control of Predisposing Causes Most of the factors contributing to potential delinquency are controllable, provided they are recognized and dealt with in time. Dealing with one alone is not enough. If the potential delinquent is to be socialized so that he will learn to fit into the larger social group, consideration must be given to his home life, his adjustments to his family, his school, his peers, and to the acceptance of a socially approved moral code (53,85,130, 155). Work-camp programs or well-organized and supervised boys' or girls' clubs have been shown to be effective ways of dealing with youngsters who are behaving in a manner to suggest that they may, in time, become delinquent (28,66,85).

Certainly it is not enough to blame *parents* for the delinquent behavior of their children. Nor is it fair, as has been done in some communities, to punish the parents when their children are brought to the juvenile courts. Parents do not *intentionally* train their children to be delinquent. It may be ignorance on their part as to how to bring up their children so that they will develop more wholesome attitudes toward their responsibilities to society; it may be unfavorable conditions beyond their control; or it may be mistaken kindness on the part of affluent parents to give their children a happy, carefree time to enjoy life before they settle down to the problems and responsibilities of adult living.

In their idleness, adolescents become bored and want some excitement. They expect society to do things for them because they have been accustomed to that kind of treatment in the home (53,94,213,228,

255). Recently, the chief of police of a fashionable suburban community published an open letter to the young people of his community in answer to the questions they so often ask, "Where can we go?" "What can we do?" The letter goes as follows:

> Your parents do not owe you entertainment. Your village does not owe you recreational facilities. The world does not owe you a living. You owe the world something. You owe it your time and energy and your talents so that no one will be at war or in poverty or sick or lonely again. In plain, simple words: grow up; quit being a crybaby; get out of your dream world—start acting like a man or a lady.

In the *schools*, much can be done to prevent juvenile delinquency by controlling the causes that predispose the child to delinquent behavior. Specific suggestions as to how this can be done consist of (1) hiring teachers who "understand children"; (2) community study and utilization of community resources; (3) planning a curriculum that meets the "imperative needs of youth" and putting it into operation; (4) providing child guidance services for the study and treatment of personality disorders; and (5) providing classes for slow learners so that they will not be made to feel inferior by a constant comparison of their work with that of more rapid learners (1,25,102,123,155).

One of the most important ways of preventing delinquency is to *treat all offenders fairly and equally*, regardless of the socioeconomic status of their parents (119, 155,236). No adolescent from a slum home can be expected not to be resentful when he is taken to court and punished for an act for which an adolescent from an affluent home receives no punishment and often is never taken to court at all (53). When, for example, an affluent adolescent is caught shoplifting, he may say, "My parents are good customers of yours," thus threatening the shopkeeper with loss of business if the matter is reported to the police. Then, if the embarrassed parents offer to pay the bills for what has been taken, it is assumed that the matter will be dropped and for-

gotten as a prank of youth. And it usually is (255).

Even older adolescents from affluent families when caught in an act of vandalism will (94):

> . . . shrug off the damage, saying that they would pay for it. Generally, parents are ready to pay for teen-age destruction. Teen-agers know that, in an age of easy affluence, money will take care of all consequences.

However, the impact on other adolescents whose parents cannot or will not pay for their vandalism is even more serious than the effect on affluent adolescents who develop the belief that they can be a "law unto themselves." As Hechinger (94) has pointed out:

> The rise in this type of delinquency (vandalism) threatens to turn into hostility the resentment of underprivileged youths in slums who face arrest and reform school for transgressions far less destructive to property.

Equally as serious as the hostility engendered by treatment that suggests that laws may be broken if you are fortunate enough to have parents to pay to keep you out of juvenile courts and reform schools is the implication that lawbreaking is all right if you belong to the "right" group and that this is the way the "right" people behave. In explaining why this belief develops, Hechinger has stated, in his discussion of the effects of vandalism by affluent youth (94):

> The impact of society vandalism on adolescent mores is far-reaching. Teen-agers and even pre-teeners, from 11 to 17, shape their behavior largely in the image of models or idols. For serious-minded youngsters, the image to live up to may be the adult scientist or artist or astronaut; but in the adolescent mass-culture it is more likely to be the rock 'n' roll singer, with his immature dating and mating habits, or the glamour of the social set. The activities of society— ranging from the established elite to the pseudo-social jet set—unofficially substitute

an outside view of high life in America for that provided by nobility and royalty in older societies.

A careful analysis of all the suggestions given for coping with the problem of juvenile delinquency shows that major emphasis is placed on providing activities in the home, school, and community in which the adolescent can feel successful and accepted and which provide socially approved outlets for his energies. In addition, emphasis is placed on the importance of the adolescent's feeling that he is loved not only by his parents but admired and liked by his teachers and peers. As Cole and Hall (39), have pointed out:

> The attack upon the problem is indirect and consists essentially in substituting acceptance for rejection by means of activities that are within the established social norms but are more satisfying to the adolescent than his delinquency.

BIBLIOGRAPHY

1 AARONS, Z. A.: Some problems of delinquency and their treatment by a casework agency. *Soc. Casewk.*, 1959, **40**, 254–262.

2 ADLER, A.: *What life should mean to you.* Boston: Little, Brown, 1931.

3 AMOS, W. E.: A study of self-concept: delinquent boys' accuracy in selected self-evaluations. *Genet. Psychol. Monogr.*, 1963, **67**, 45–81.

4 ANDERSON, H. H., G. L. ANDERSON, L. H. COHEN, and F. D. NUTT: Image of the teacher by adolescent children in four countries—Germany, England, Mexico, and the United States. *J. soc. Psychol.*, 1959, **50**, 47–55.

5 ASH, P.: The discrepancy between reported schooling and tested scholastic ability among adolescent delinquents. *J. appl. Psychol.*, 1947, **31**, 323–328.

6 ASUNI, T.: Maladjustment and delinquency: a comparison of two samples. *J. child Psychol. Psychiat.*, 1963, **4**, 219–228.

7 AUSUBEL, D. P.: An evaluation of recent adolescent drug addiction. *Ment. Hyg., N.Y.*, 1952, **36**, 373–382.

8 AUSUBEL, D. P.: Relationships between shame and guilt in the socialization process. *Psychol. Rev.*, 1955, **62**, 378–390.

9 BACON, M. K., I. L. CHILD, and H. BARRY: A cross-cultural study of correlates of crime. *J. abnorm. soc. Psychol.*, 1963, **66**, 291–300.

10 BAKWIN, H.: Causes of juvenile delinquency. *Amer. J. Dis. Children*, 1955, **89**, 368–373.

11 BALL, J. C.: Delinquent and nondelinquent attitudes toward the prevalence of stealing. *J. crim. Law Criminol. police Sci.*, 1957, **48**, 259–274.

12 BALOGH, J. K., and P. FINN: Juvenile delinquency proneness among Negroes. *Except. Children*, 1961, **27**, 397–399.

13 BANDURA, A., and R. H. WALTERS: Dependency conflicts in aggressive adolescents. *Soc. Forces*, 1958, **14**, 52–65.

14 BANDURA, A., and R. H. WALTERS: *Adolescent aggression: a study of the influence of child-training practices and family interrelationships.* New York: Ronald, 1959.

15 BARCLAY, D.: "Law course" for the young. *The New York Times*, Apr. 16, 1961.

16 BAUGH, V. S., and B. L. CARPENTER: A comparison of delinquents and nondelinquents. *J. soc. Psychol.*, 1962, **56**, 73–78.

17 BECK, B. M.: Delinquents in the classroom. *NEA J.*, 1956, **45**, 485–487.

18 BENNETT, L. A.: Perpetuation of delinquency through language usage. *J. crim. Law Criminol. police Sci.*, 1959, **50**, 34–37.

19 BERNABEU, E. P.: Underlying ego mechanisms in delinquency. *Psychoanal. Quart.*, 1958, **27**, 383–396.

20 BIRKENESS, V., and H. C. JOHNSON: A comparative study of delinquent and nondelinquent adolescents. *J. educ. Res.*, 1949, **42**, 561–572.

21 BLANK, L.: The intellectual functioning of delinquents. *J. soc. Psychol.*, 1958, **47**, 9–14.

22 BLOCK, H. A., and F. T. FLYNN: *Delinquency: the juvenile offender in America today.* New York: Random House, 1956.

23 BORDUA, D. J.: Juvenile delinquency and "anomie": an attempt at replication. *Soc. Probl.*, 1959, **6**, 230–237.

24 BOSSARD, J. H. S., and E. S. BOLL: *The sociology of child development*. 3d ed. New York: Harper & Row, 1960.

25 BOWMAN, P. H.: Effects of a revised school program on potential delinquents. *Ann. Amer. Acad. pol. soc. Sci.*, 1959, **322**, 53–61.

26 BRIGGS, P. F., R. D. WIRT, and R. JOHNSON: An application of prediction tables to the study of delinquency. *J. consult. Psychol.*, 1961, **25**, 46–50.

27 BRODBECK, A. J., P. NOGEE, and A. DI MARCIO: Two kinds of conformity: a study of the Riesman typology applied to standards of parental discipline. *J. Psychol.*, 1956, **41**, 23–45.

28 BROWN, R. C., and D. W. DODSON: The effectiveness of a boys' club in reducing delinquency. *Ann. Amer. Acad. pol. soc. Sci.*, 1959, **322**, 47–52.

29 BROWNING, C. J.: Differential impact of family disorganization on male adolescents. *Soc. Probl.*, 1960, **8**, 37–44.

30 BURT, C.: *The subnormal mind*. 3d ed. Fair Lawn, N.J.: Oxford, 1955.

31 CAVAN, R. S.: *Juvenile delinquency*. Philadelphia: Lippincott, 1962.

32 CHAPMAN, A. W.: Attitudes toward legal authorities by juveniles. *Sociol. soc. Res.*, 1955, **40**, 170–175.

33 CLARK, J. P., and E. P. WENNINGER: Socioeconomic class and area as correlates of illegal behavior among juveniles. *Amer. sociol. Rev.*, 1962, **27**, 826–834.

34 CLARK, K. B.: Color, class, personality and juvenile delinquency. *J. Negro Educ.*, 1959, **28**, 240–251.

35 CLINARD, M. B.: *Sociology of deviant behavior*. Rev. ed. New York: Holt, 1963.

36 CLOWARD, R. A., and L. E. OHLIN: *Delinquency and opportunity: a theory of delinquent gangs*. New York: Free Press, 1960.

37 COHEN, A. K.: *Delinquent boys: the culture of the gang*. New York: Free Press, 1955.

38 COHLER, M. J.: A new look at the old problem of discipline. *Sch. Rev.*, 1948, **56**, 468–475.

39 COLE, L., and I. N. HALL: *Psychology of adolescence*. 6th ed. New York: Holt, 1964.

40 COLEMAN, J. S.: *The adolescent society*. New York: Free Press, 1961.

41 COLM, H.: Help and guidance as discipline for preadolescents. *Nerv. Child*, 1951, **9**, 131–138.

42 CONANT, J. B.: Social dynamite in our large cities. *Crime & Delinquency*, 1962, **18**, 102–115.

43 CROFTS, I. J., and T. G. GRYGIER: Social relations of truants and juvenile delinquents. *Hum. Relat.*, 1956, **9**, 439–466.

44 CROW, L. D., and A. CROW: *Adolescent development and adjustment*. 2d ed. New York: McGraw-Hill, 1965.

45 DAVIDSON, H. H., and G. LANG: Children's perceptions of their teachers' feeling toward them related to self-perception, school achievement, and behavior. *J. exp. Educ.*, 1960, **29**, 107–118.

46 DAVIS, A., and R. J. HAVIGHURST: *Father of the man*. Boston: Houghton Mifflin, 1947.

47 DENTLER, R. A., and L. J. MONROE: The family and early adolescent conformity and deviance. *Marriage fam. Living*, 1961, **23**, 241–247.

48 DENTLER, R. A., and L. J. MONROE: *Problem behavior of junior high school youth in Kansas*. Lawrence, Kan.: Bureau of Child Research, University of Kansas, Child Research Series, no. 8, 1961.

49 DENTLER, R. A., and L. J. MONROE: Social correlates of early adolescent theft. *Amer. sociol. Rev.*, 1961, **26**, 733–743.

50 DESPERT, J. L.: *Children of divorce*. Garden City, N.Y.: Doubleday, 1962.

51 DINITZ, S., W. C. RECKLESS, and B. KAY: A self gradient among potential delinquents. *J. crim. Law Criminol. Police Sci.*, 1958, **49**, 230–233.

52 DINITZ, S., F. R. SCARPITTI, and W. C. RECKLESS: Delinquency vulnerability: a cross group and longitudinal analysis. *Amer. sociol. Rev.*, 1962, **27**, 515–517.

53 DOWNS, W. T.: Order in the court. *Children*, 1962, **9**, 139–143.

54 DRESHER, R. H.: Seeds of delinquency. *Personnel Guid. J.*, 1957, **35**, 595–598.

55 DU BOIS, F. S.: The security of discipline. *Ment. Hyg., N.Y.*, 1952, **36**, 353–372.

56 DUNBAR, F.: Homeostasis during puberty. *Amer. J. Psychiat.*, 1958, **114**, 673–682.

57 DURKIN, D.: Children's concepts of justice: a

comparison with the Piaget data. *Child Develpm.*, 1959, **30**, 59–67.

58 EASTON, M. T., L. A. D'AMICO, and B. N. PHILLIPS: Problem behavior in school. *J. educ. Psychol.*, 1956, **47**, 50–57.

59 EATON, M. T., G. WEATHERS, and B. N. PHILLIPS: Some reactions of classroom teachers to problem behavior in school. *Educ. Admin. Superv.*, 1957, **43**, 129–139.

60 ECKENRODE, C. J.: Their achievement is delinquency. *J. educ. Res.*, 1950, **43**, 554–560.

61 EHRMANN, W.: *Premarital dating behavior.* New York: Holt, 1959.

62 EPSTEIN, E. M.: The self-concept of the delinquent female. *Smith Coll. Stud. soc. Wk.*, 1962, **32**, 220–234.

63 EYSENCK, H. J.: The development of moral values in children: VII. The contribution of learning theory. *Brit. J. educ. Psychol.*, 1960, **30**, 11–21.

64 F. B. I. Report: Uniform crime reports for the United States and its possessions. *Annu. Bull.*, 1950, **21**, 106–109.

65 FENTON, N.: The delinquent in the classroom. *47th Yearb. nat. Soc. Stud. Educ.*, 1948, part 1, 48–65.

66 FRIED, A.: A work camp program for potential delinquents. *Ann. Amer. Acad. pol. soc. Sci.*, 1959, **322**, 38–46.

67 GARRISON, K. C.: A study of student disciplinarian practices in two Georgia high schools. *J. educ. Res.*, 1959, **53**, 153–156.

68 GATLING, F. T.: Frustration reactions of delinquents, using Rosenzweig's classification system. *J. abnorm. soc. Psychol.*, 1950, **45**, 749–752.

69 GESELL, A., F. L. ILG, and L. B. AMES: *Youth: the years from ten to sixteen.* New York: Harper & Row, 1956.

70 GIBBENS, T. C. N.: Juvenile prostitution. *Brit. J. Delinquency*, 1957, **8**, 3–12.

71 GIBBENS, T. C. N.: Car thieves. *Brit. J. Delinquency*, 1957, **8**, 257–265.

72 GIBBONS, D. C., and M. J. GRISWOLD: Sex differences among juvenile court referrals. *Sociol. soc. Res.*, 1957, **42**, 106–110.

73 GIBSON, R.: Incidence and pattern of crime among mental defectives. *Ment. Hyg., N.Y.*, 1957, **41**, 404–407.

74 GLUECK, S. (ed.): *The problem of delinquency.* Boston: Houghton Mifflin, 1959.

75 GLUECK, S., and E. T. GLUECK: *Unravelling juvenile delinquency.* New York: Commonwealth Fund, 1950.

76 GLUECK, S., and E. T. GLUECK: *Physique and delinquency.* New York: Harper & Row, 1956.

77 GLUECK, S., and E. T. GLUECK: *Family environment and delinquency.* Boston: Houghton Mifflin, 1962.

78 GOTTLIEB, D., and C. RAMSEY: *The American adolescent.* Homewood, Ill.: Dorsey, 1964.

79 GOUGH, H. G., and D. R. PETERSON: The identification and measurement of predispositional factors in crime and delinquency. *J. consult. Psychol.*, 1952, **16**, 207–212.

80 GREENE, J. E.: Alleged "misbehaviors" among senior high school students. *J. soc. Psychol.*, 1962, **58**, 371–382.

81 GREGORY, I.: Studies of parental deprivation in psychiatric patients. *Amer. J. Psychiat.*, 1958, **115**, 432–442.

82 GRYGIER, T.: Leisure pursuits of juvenile delinquents. *Brit. J. juv. Delinquency*, 1955, **5**, 210–228.

83 GUMP, P. V., and J. S. KOUNIN: Milieu influences in children's concepts of misconduct. *Child Develpm.*, 1961, **32**, 711–720.

84 HARRIS, D. B.: Relationships among play interests and delinquency in boys. *Amer. J. Orthopsychiat.*, 1943, **13**, 631–637.

85 HARRIS, D. B.: The socialization of the delinquent. *Child Develpm.*, 1948, **19**, 143–153.

86 HARRISON, E.: Youth and spring equal explosion. *The New York Times*, May 3, 1964.

87 HARTSHORNE, H., and M. MAY: *Studies in deceit.* New York: Macmillan, 1928.

88 HATHAWAY, S. R., and E. C. MONACHESI: The personalities of predelinquent boys. *J. crim. Law Criminol. Police Sci.*, 1957, **48**, 149–163.

89 HATHAWAY, S. R., O. M. MONACHESI, and M. L. ERICKSON: Relationship of college attendance to personality characteristics and earlier delinquent behavior. *Sociol. Quart.*, 1960, **1**, 97–106.

90 HAVIGHURST, R. J.: *Human development and education.* New York: Longmans, 1953.

91 HAVIGHURST, R. J.: Moral character and religious education. *Relig. Educ.*, 1956, **51**, 163–169.

92 HAVIGHURST, R. J., and H. TABA: *Adolescent*

character and personality. New York: Wiley, 1949.

93 HEALY, W., and A. F. BRONNER: What makes a child delinquent? 47th Yearb. Nat. Soc. Stud. Educ., 1948, part 1, 30–47.

94 HECHINGER, F. M.: Affluent delinquency. The New York Times, Sept. 5, 1963.

95 HECHINGER, F. M.: On cheating. The New York Times, Jan. 31, 1965.

96 HECHINGER, G., and F. M. HECHINGER: College morals mirror our society. The New York Times, Apr. 14, 1963.

97 HECHINGER, G., and F. M. HECHINGER: Teenage tyranny. New York: Morrow, 1963.

98 HEILBRUN, A. B.: Social value: social behavior inconsistency and early signs of psychopathology in adolescence. Child Develpm., 1963, **34**, 187–194.

99 HEILBRUN, A. B.: Social value: social behavior consistency, parental identification and aggression in late adolescence. J. genet. Psychol., 1964, **104**, 135–146.

100 HENRIQUES, B. L. G.: The adolescent delinquent boy. Practitioner, 1940, **162**, 299–304.

101 HENRY, J.: Permissiveness and morality. Ment. Hyg., N.Y., 1961, **45**, 282–287.

102 HERBERT, W. L., and F. V. JARVIS: Dealing with delinquents. New York: Emerson, 1962.

103 HERZOG, E.: Identifying potential delinquents. Washington, D.C.: U.S. Department of Health, Education, and Welfare, 1960.

104 HIGHTOWER, H. K.: School problems of pupils who steal. Educ. Admin. Superv., 1947, **33**, 229–234.

105 HILL, M.: The metropolis and juvenile delinquency among Negroes. J. Negro Educ., 1959, **28**, 277–285.

106 HINKELMAN, E. A.: A comparative investigation of differences in personality adjustment of delinquents and nondelinquents. J. educ. Res., 1953, **46**, 595–601.

107 HOFFMAN, H. R., I. C. SHERMAN, F. KREVITSKY, and F. WILLIAMS: Teen-age drug addicts arraigned in the narcotic court of Chicago. J. Amer. med. Ass., 1952, **149**, 655–659.

108 HOLLINGSHEAD, A. DE B.: Elmtown's youth. New York: Wiley, 1949.

109 HOLLINGWORTH, L. S.: The psychology of the adolescent. New York: Appleton-Century-Crofts, 1928.

110 HOOVER, J. E.: The youth problem today. Chicago Schools, 1948, **30**, 33–35.

111 HYMES, J. L.: Behavior and misbehavior: a teacher's guide to action. Englewood Cliffs, N.J.: Prentice-Hall, 1957.

112 ILLSON, M.: Child study seeks delinquency signs. The New York Times, Feb. 8, 1954.

113 JACQUES, O. M.: Predicting juvenile delinquency proneness by group tests. Personnel Guid. J., 1958, **36**, 489–492.

114 JASTAK, J., and L. G. GILLILAND: Personality problems of juvenile delinquents as revealed by psychological tests. Delaware State med. J., 1950, **22**, 225–228.

115 JENKINS, R. L.: Motivation and frustration in delinquency. Amer. J. Orthopsychiat., 1957, **27**, 528–537.

116 JENKINS, R. L., and E. BLODGETT: Prediction of success or failure of delinquent boys from sentence completion. Amer. J. Orthopsychiat., 1960, **30**, 741–756.

117 JENKINS, R. L., and S. GLICKMAN: Patterns of personality organization among delinquents. Nerv. Child, 1947, **6**, 319–329.

118 JERSILD, A. T.: The psychology of adolescence. 2d ed. New York: Macmillan, 1963.

119 JOHNSTON, N.: The sociology of punishment and correction. New York: Wiley, 1962.

120 JONES, M. C., and P. H. MUSSEN: Self-conceptions, motivations, and interpersonal attitudes of early- and late-maturing girls. Child Develpm., 1958, **29**, 491–501.

121 JONES, V.: Character development in children: an objective approach. In L. Carmichael (ed.), Manual of child psychology. 2d ed. New York: Wiley, 1954, pp. 781–832.

122 JOSSELYN, I. M.: Psychological changes in adolescence. Children, 1959, **6**, 43–47.

123 KAMINKOW, H. B.: Basic school approaches in preventing juvenile delinquency. Understanding the Child, 1953, **22**, 73–78.

124 KATES, S. L., and R. W. HARRINGTON: Authority-figure perspective and aggression in delinquents. J. genet. Psychol., 1952, **80**, 195–210.

125 KAUFMAN, I., E. S. MAKKAY, and J. ZILBACH: The impact of adolescence on girls with delinquent character formation. Amer. J. Orthopsychiat., 1959, **29**, 130–143.

126 KELLY, F. J., and D. J. VELDMAN: Delinquency and school dropout behavior as a function of impulsivity and nondominant values. *J. abnorm. soc. Psychol.*, 1964, **69**, 190–194.

127 KINSEY, A. C., W. B. POMEROY, C. E. MARTIN, and P. H. GEBHARD: *Sexual behavior of the human female.* Philadelphia: Saunders, 1953.

128 KITSUSE, J. I., and D. C. DIETRICK: Delinquent boys: a critique. *Amer. sociol. Rev.*, 1959, **24**, 208–215.

129 KOBRIN, S.: The conflict of values in delinquency areas. *Amer. sociol. Rev.*, 1951, **16**, 653–661.

130 KONOPKA, G.: Co-ordination of services as a means of delinquency prevention. *Ann. Amer. Acad. pol. soc. Sci.*, 1959, **322**, 30–37.

131 KONOPKA, G.: Adolescent delinquent girls. *Children*, 1964, **11**, 21–26.

132 KOWATRAKUL, S.: Some behaviors of elementary school children related to classroom activities and subject areas. *J. educ. Psychol.*, 1959, **50**, 121–128.

133 KRAFT, A. H.: Personality correlates of rebellion-behavior in school. *Dissert. Abstr.*, 1962, **23**, 1074–1075.

134 KRAMER, D., and M. KARR: *Teen-age gangs.* New York: Holt, 1953.

135 KVARACEUS, W. C.: Delinquent behavior and church attendance. *Sociol. soc. Res.*, 1944, **28**, 284–289.

136 KVARACEUS, W. C.: The role of the administrator in relation to juvenile delinquency. *47th Yearb. Nat. Soc. Stud. Educ.*, 1948, part 1, 136–137.

137 KVARACEUS, W. C.: The delinquent. *Rev. educ. Res.*, 1959, **29**, 545–552.

138 KVARACEUS, W. C.: The nature of the problem of delinquency in the United States. *J. Negro Educ.*, 1959, **28**, 191–199.

139 KVARACEUS, W. C.: Forecasting delinquency: a three-year experiment. *Except. Children*, 1961, **27**, 429–435.

140 KVARACEUS, W. C., and I. M. MC INNIS: Selected references from the literature on exceptional children: juvenile delinquency. *Elem. Sch. J.*, 1963, **31**, 353–355.

141 KVARACEUS, W. C., and W. B. MILLER (eds.): *Delinquent behavior: culture and the individual.* Washington, D.C.: National Education Association, 1959.

142 KVARACEUS, W. C., and W. E. ULRICH: *Delinquent behavior: principles and practices.* Washington, D.C.: National Education Association, 1959.

143 LACEY, J. C.: The ecology of juvenile delinquency in the small city and the rural hinterland. *Rural Sociol.*, 1957, **22**, 230–234.

144 LANDIS, P. H.: Points of stress in adolescent morality. *Sch. Soc.*, 1940, **51**, 612–616.

145 LANDIS, P. H.: *Adolescence and youth: the process of maturing.* 2d ed. New York: McGraw-Hill, 1952.

146 LANG, A.: Parents' reports of undesirable behavior in children. *Child Develpm.*, 1941, **12**, 43–62.

147 LEAVITT, J.: Teacher-pupil relationships. *J. educ. Res.*, 1959, **29**, 210–217.

148 LEE, R. H.: Delinquent, neglected, and dependent Chinese children of the San Francisco Bay region. *J. soc. Psychol.*, 1952, **36**, 15–34.

149 LELYVELD, J.: The paradoxical case of the affluent delinquent. *The New York Times*, Oct. 4, 1964.

150 LINDEN, M. E.: Relationship between social attitudes toward aging and the delinquencies of youth. *Amer. J. Psychiat.*, 1957, **114**, 444–448.

151 LOWREY, L. G.: Delinquent and criminal personalities. In J. McV. Hunt (ed.), *Personality and the behavior disorders.* New York: Ronald, vol. 2, pp. 794–821, 1944.

152 MAC IVER, R. M.: Juvenile delinquency. In E. Ginzberg (ed.), *The nation's children.* New York: Columbia, vol. 3, pp. 103–123, 1960.

153 MADOFF, J. M.: The attitudes of mothers of juvenile delinquents toward child rearing. *J. consult. Psychol.*, 1959, **23**, 518–520.

154 MALM, M., and O. G. JAMISON: *Adolescence.* New York: McGraw-Hill, 1952.

155 MARTIN, L. M.: Three approaches to delinquency prevention. *Crime & Delinquency*, 1961, **7**, 16–24.

156 MATZA, D., and G. M. SYKES: Juvenile delinquency and subterranean values. *Amer. sociol. Rev.*, 1961, **26**, 712–719.

157 MC CORD, J., and W. MC CORD: The effects of parental role model on criminality. *J. soc. Issues*, 1958, **14**, no. 3, 66–75.

158 MC CORD, J., W. MC CORD, and A. HOWARD: Family interaction as antecedent to the direction of male aggressiveness. *J. abnorm. soc. Psychol.*, 1963, **66**, 239–242.

159 MC CORD, W., and J. MC CORD: *Origin of crime*. New York: Columbia, 1959.

160 MC KAY, H. D.: The neighborhood and child conduct. *Ann. Amer. Acad. pol. soc. Sci.*, 1949, **261**, 32–41.

161 MEEK, L. S.: Effects of maternal employment on children: evidence from research. *Child Develpm.*, 1960, **31**, 749–782.

162 MEIER, E. G.: Girls involved in sex offenses. In G. Meyer (ed.), *Studies of children*. New York: King's Crown, 1948, pp. 157–167.

163 MILLER, W. B.: Lower class culture as a generating milieu of gang delinquency. *J. soc. Issues*, 1958, **14**, no. 3, 5–19.

164 MILLER, W. B., H. GEERTZ, and H. S. G. CUTTER: Aggression in a boys' street corner group. *Psychiatry*, 1961, **24**, 283–298.

165 MONAHAN, T. P.: Family status and the delinquent child. *Soc. Forces*, 1957, **35**, 250–258.

166 MONAHAN, T. P.: The trend in broken homes among delinquent children. *Marriage fam. Living*, 1957, **19**, 362–365.

167 MONAHAN, T. P.: Broken homes by age of delinquent children. *J. soc. Psychol.*, 1960, **51**, 387–397.

168 MOUSTAKAS, C. E.: *The teacher and the child: personal interaction in the classroom*. New York: McGraw-Hill, 1956.

169 MULL, M. K.: The ethical discrimination of various groups of college women. *J. soc. Psychol.*, 1952, **35**, 69–72.

170 MUSSEN, P. H., and M. C. JONES: The behavior-inferred motivations of late- and early-maturing boys. *Child Develpm.*, 1958, **29**, 61–67.

171 NAESS, S.: Mother-separation and delinquency. *Brit. J. Criminol.*, 1962, **2**, 361–374.

172 NEEDHAM, M. A., and E. M. SCHUR: Student punitiveness toward sexual deviation. *Marriage fam. Living*, 1963, **25**, 227–229.

173 NETTLER, G.: Antisocial sentiment and criminality. *Amer. sociol. rev.*, 1959, **24**, 202–208.

174 *New York Times* Report: Youth has big part in 1950 crime rise. *The New York Times*, Apr. 12, 1950.

175 *New York Times* Report: Youth delinquency growing rapidly over the country. *The New York Times*, Apr. 20, 1952.

176 *New York Times* Report: New trends seen in juvenile crime. *The New York Times*, Nov. 18, 1952.

177 *New York Times* Report: Pupils told how to avoid crimes. *The New York Times*, Feb. 20, 1961.

178 *New York Times* Report: U.S. children top list for honesty. *The New York Times*, Sept. 3, 1961.

179 *New York Times* Report: Major crime rose 10% in U.S. during 1963. *The New York Times*, July 21, 1964.

180 *New York Times* Report: Way of predicting delinquency found accurate in 10-year test. *The New York Times*, Nov. 18, 1964.

181 NYE, F. I.: *Family relationships and delinquent behavior*. New York: Wiley, 1958.

182 NYE, F. I., and J. F. SHORT: Scaling delinquent behavior. *Amer. sociol. Rev.*, 1957, **22**, 326–331.

183 NYE, F. I., J. F. SHORT, and V. J. OLSON: Socioeconomic status and delinquent behavior. *Amer. J. Sociol.*, 1958, **63**, 381–389.

184 OJEMANN, R. H.: Forewarnings of delinquency. *National Parent-Teacher*, 1955, **49**, no. 7, 20–22.

185 O'KELLY, E.: Some observations on relationships between delinquent girls and their parents. *Brit. J. med. Psychol.*, 1955, **28**, 59–66.

186 PALMORE, E. B., and P. E. HAMMOND: Interacting factors in juvenile delinquency. *Amer. sociol. Rev.*, 1964, **29**, 848–854.

187 PAPANEK, E.: Re-education and treatment of juvenile delinquents. *Amer. J. Psychother.*, 1958, **12**, 269–296.

188 PECK, R. F., and R. J. HAVIGHURST: *The psychology of character development*. New York: Wiley, 1962.

189 PERLMAN, I. R.: Delinquency prevention: the size of the problem. *Ann. Amer. Acad. pol. soc. Sci.*, 1959, **322**, 1–9.

190 PETERSON, D. R.: Behavior problems of middle childhood. *J. consult. Psychol.*, 1961, **25**, 205–209.

191 PETERSON, D. R., H. C. QUAY, and T. L. TIFFANY: Personality factors related to juvenile delinquency. *Child Develpm.*, 1961, **32**, 355–372.

192 PILIAVIN, I., and S. BRIAR: Police encounters with juveniles. *Amer. J. Sociol.*, 1964, **70**, 206–214.

193 PLAUT, J. S.: Who is the delinquent? 47*th*

Yearb. Nat. Soc. Stud. Educ., 1948, part 1, chap. 19.

194 PRESSEY, S. L., and A. W. JONES: 1923–1953 and 20–60 age changes in moral codes, anxieties, and interests, as shown by the "X-O Tests." *J. Psychol.*, 1955, **39**, 485–502.

195 PRESSEY, S. L., and R. G. KUHLEN: *Psychological development through the life span.* New York: Harper & Row, 1957.

196 RECKLESS, W. C., S. DINITZ, and B. KAY: The self-component in potential delinquency and potential non-delinquency. *Amer. sociol. Rev.*, 1957, **22**, 566–570.

197 RECKLESS, W. C., S. DINITZ, and E. MURRAY: Self-concept as an insulator against delinquency. *Amer. sociol. Rev.*, 1956, **21**, 744–748.

198 RECKLESS, W. C., S. DINITZ, and E. MURRAY: The "good" boy in a high delinquency area. *J. crim. Law Criminol. Police Sci.*, 1957, **48**, 18–25.

199 REDL, F.: Our trouble with defiant youth. *Children*, 1955, **2**, 5–9.

200 REINHARDT, J. M., and V. H. FOWLER: Social and ethical judgments of two groups of boys —delinquent and non-delinquent. *Amer. J. crim. Law Criminol.*, 1930, **21**, 364–378.

201 REISS, A. J.: Delinquency as the failure of personal and social controls. *Amer. sociol. Rev.*, 1951, **16**, 196–207.

202 REISS, A. J., and A. L. RHODES: The distribution of juvenile delinquency in the social class structure. *Amer. sociol. Rev.*, 1961, **26**, 720–732.

203 REISS, I. L.: Consistency and sexual ethics. *Marriage fam. Living*, 1962, **24**, 264–269.

204 REMMERS, H. H., and D. H. RADLER: *The American teenager.* Indianapolis: Bobbs-Merrill, 1957.

205 REMMERS, H. H., and B. SHIMBERG: *Purdue opinion poll for young people.* Lafayette, Ind.: Purdue University Press, 1949.

206 RESNICK, J.: The juvenile delinquent: an explanation. *Educ. Admin. Superv.*, 1955, **41**, 218–223.

207 RETTIG, S., and B. PASAMANICK: Differential judgment of ethical risk by cheaters and noncheaters. *J. abnorm. soc. Psychol.*, 1964, **69**, 109–113.

208 REXFORD, E. N.: Some meanings of aggressive behavior in children. *Ann. Amer. Acad. pol. soc. Sci.*, 1959, **322**, 10–18.

209 REXFORD, E. N., M. SCHLEFER, and S. T. VAN AMERONGEN: A follow-up of a psychiatric study of 57 antisocial young children. *Ment. Hyg., N.Y.*, 1956, **40**, 196–214.

210 RICHARDSON, H. M., and E. F. SURKO: WISC scores and status in reading and arithmetic of delinquent children. *J. genet. Psychol.*, 1956, **89**, 251–262.

211 ROBINS, L. N., H. GYMAN, and P. O'NEIL: The interaction of social class and deviant behavior. *Amer. sociol. Rev.*, 1962, **27**, 480–492.

212 ROBINS, L. N., and P. O'NEIL: Mortality, mobility, and crime: problem children thirty years later. *Amer. sociol. Rev.*, 1958, **23**, 162–171.

213 ROBINSON, M.: Mental health for child and delinquent. *Survey*, 1950, **86**, 293–297.

214 ROGOSIN, H.: What about "cheating" on examinations and honesty? *Sch. Soc.*, 1951, **74**, 402–403.

215 SCARPITTI, F. R., E. MURRAY, S. DINITZ, and W. C. RECKLESS: The "good" boy in a high delinquency area: four years later. *Amer. sociol. Rev.*, 1960, **25**, 555–558.

216 SCHARR, J. H.: Violence in juvenile gangs: some notes and a few analogies. *Amer. J. Orthopsychiat.*, 1963, **33**, 29–37.

217 SCHREIBER, D.: Dropout and the delinquent: promising practices gleaned from a year of study. *Phi Delta Kappan*, 1963, **44**, 215–221.

218 SCHWARTZ, E. E.: Statistics of juvenile delinquency in the United States. *Ann. Amer. Acad. pol. soc. Sci.*, 1949, **261**, 9–20.

219 SCOTT, J. F.: Two dimensions of delinquent behavior. *Amer. sociol. Rev.*, 1959, **24**, 240–243.

220 SHELDON, W. H.: *Varieties of delinquent youth.* New York: Harper & Row, 1949.

221 SHORT, J. F., and F. I. NYE: Reported behavior as a criterion of deviant behavior. *Soc. Probl.*, 1957, **5**, 207–213.

222 SHORT, J. F., and F. I. NYE: Extent of unrecorded juvenile delinquency. *J. crim. Law Criminol. police Sci.*, 1958, **49**, 296–302.

223 SHORT, J. F., and F. L. STRODTBECK: The response of gang leaders to status threat: an observation on group process and delinquent behavior. *Amer. J. Sociol.*, 1963, **48**, 571–579.

224 SIEGEL, L., H. L. COON, H. B. PEPINSKY, and S. RUBIN: Expressed standards of behavior of high school students, teachers, and parents. *Personnel Guid. J.*, 1956, **34**, 261–266.

225 SIMPSON, J. E., T. G. EYNON, and W. C. RECKLESS: Institutionalization as perceived by the juvenile offender. *Sociol. soc. Res.*, 1963, **48**, 13–23.

226 SLOCUM, W. L., and C. L. STONE: Family culture patterns and delinquent-type behavior. *Marriage fam. Living*, 1963, **25**, 202–208.

227 SMITH, P. M.: The schools and juvenile delinquency. *Sociol. soc. Res.*, 1952, **37**, 159–180.

228 SOLOMON, B.: Preventive recreation. *Recreation*, 1951, **44**, 562–566.

229 STAGNER, R.: *Psychology of personality.* 3d ed. New York: McGraw-Hill, 1961.

230 STOKES, W. R.: Our changing sex ethics. *Marriage fam. Living*, 1962, **24**, 269–272.

231 STOUFFER, G. A. W., and J. OWENS: Behavior problems identified by today's teachers and compared with those reported by E. K. Wickman. *J. educ. Res.*, 1955, **48**, 321–331.

232 STRODTBECK, F. L., J. F. SHORT, and E. KOLEGAR: An analysis of self-descriptions by members of delinquent gangs. *Sociol. Quart.*, 1962, **3**, 331–356.

233 STULLKEN, E. H.: Danger signs of delinquency. *National Parent-Teacher*, 1953, **47**, no. 7, 4–6.

234 SUTTON-SMITH, B., and B. G. ROSENBERG: Peer perceptions of impulsive behavior. *Merrill-Palmer Quart.*, 1961, **7**, 233–238.

235 TAIT, C. D.: *Delinquents: their families and the community.* Springfield, Ill.: Charles C Thomas, 1962.

236 TAPPAN, P. W.: *Crime, justice, and correction.* New York: McGraw-Hill, 1960.

237 TOBY, J.: The differential effect of family disorganization. *Amer. sociol. Rev.*, 1957, **22**, 505–512.

238 TOBY, J.: Criminal motivation: a sociocultural analysis. *Brit. J. Criminol.*, 1962, **2**, 317–336.

239 TRAVERS, J. F.: Critical problems of the school: delinquency. *Clearing House*, 1962, **36**, 337–342.

240 TRENT, R. D.: The expressed values of institutionalized delinquent boys. *J. genet. Psychol.*, 1958, **92**, 133–148.

241 TRESE, L. J.: *Delinquent girls.* New York: Fides, 1962.

242 TRIPPE, M. J.: The social psychology of exceptional children: factors in society. *Except. Children*, 1959, **26**, 171–175, 188.

243 TUMA, E., and N. LIVSON: Family socioeconomic status and adolescent attitudes to authority. *Child Develpm.*, 1960, **31**, 387–399.

244 *U.S. News & World Report:* Is crime in U.S. out of hand? *U.S. News & World Report*, Mar. 22, 1965, pp. 38–43.

245 VOLKMAN, A. P.: A matched-group personality comparison of delinquent and nondelinquent juveniles. *Soc. Probl.*, 1959, **6**, 238–245.

246 WALLACE, R.: "Where's the party—let's crash it!" *Life Magazine*, July 5, 1963, pp. 63–67.

247 WATTENBERG, W. W.: Delinquency during summer months. *J. educ. Res.*, 1948, **42**, 253–267.

248 WATTENBERG, W. W.: Church attendance and juvenile misconduct. *Sociol. soc. Res.*, 1950, **34**, 195–202.

249 WATTENBERG, W. W.: Factors associated with repeating among preadolescent "delinquents." *J. genet. Psychol.*, 1954, **84**, 189–195.

250 WATTENBERG, W. W.: Differences between girl and boy "repeaters." *J. educ. Psychol.*, 1956, **47**, 137–146.

251 WATTENBERG, W. W., and J. J. BALISTRIERI: Gang membership and juvenile misconduct. *Amer. sociol. Rev.*, 1950, **15**, 744–752.

252 WATTENBERG, W. W., and J. J. BALISTRIERI: Automobile theft: a "favored-group" delinquency. *Amer. J. Sociol.*, 1952, **57**, 575–579.

253 WATTENBERG, W. W., and F. SAUNDERS: Sex differences among juvenile offenders. *Sociol. soc. Res.*, 1954, **39**, 24–31.

254 WIRT, R. D., and P. F. BRIGGS: Personality and environmental factors in the development of delinquency. *Psychol. Monogr.*, 1959, **73**, no. 15.

255 WITHERS, S.: Putting the label on stealing. *The New York Times*, July 21, 1963.

256 WITRYOL, S. L., and J. E. CALKINS: Marginal social values of rural school children. *J. genet. Psychol.*, 1958, **92**, 81–93.

257 WOLFGANG, M. E. (ed.): *The sociology of crime and delinquency.* New York: Wiley, 1962.

258 YABLONSKY, L.: *The violent gang*. New York: Macmillan, 1962.

259 YOUNG, F. M.: Responses of juvenile delinquents to the Thematic Apperception Test. *J. genet. Psychol.*, 1956, **88**, 251–259.

260 ZAKOLSKI, F. C.: Studies in delinquency: I and II. Personality structure of delinquent boys. *J. genet. Psychol.*, 1949, **74**, 109–117, 119–123.

261 ZAKOLSKI, F. C.: Studies in delinquency: III. An individual test. *J. genet. Psychol.*, 1953, **83**, 279–292.

262 ZEITLIN, H.: High school discipline. *Calif. J. educ. Res.*, 1962, **13**, 116–125.

CHAPTER 13
sex interests
and behavior

Transition from childish sexual behavior to adult involves more than the physical changes that occur at puberty; it involves the development of new interests and attitudes and the learning of new patterns of behavior. In cultures where emphasis is placed on the development of foundations in these areas during the childhood years, the transition is made with relative ease and speed. In cultural groups, such as that of present-day America, where the segregation of the sexes is encouraged throughout childhood, where knowledge about sex is taboo and often faulty, and where the roles of the two sexes are similar, the transition is far more difficult and requires the major part of the adolescent years.

At first, sexual feelings and drives are

diffuse and can be fixed on anyone or anything. What form these feelings and drives will take depends largely on learning and the influence of social pressures (187). As Josselyn has pointed out, "The typical young adolescent is not a heterosexual person psychologically, no matter how heterosexual he may be acting" (119). Not until the diffuse sexual feelings and drives are focused on members of the opposite sex and lead to patterns of behavior normally associated with these feelings and drives can the adolescent be considered a "heterosexual person."

meaning of heterosexuality

"Heterosexuality" means the focus of interest on members of the opposite sex. There is, to be sure, some heterosexual behavior in the childhood years. Interest in members of the opposite sex in childhood places major emphasis on competition. In adolescence, by contrast, the interest is romantic and is accompanied by a strong desire to win the approval of members of the opposite sex.

In the early part of adolescence, this romantic interest in members of the opposite sex is very different from later. It frequently takes the form of erotic daydreams, talking about sex and members of the opposite sex, interest in appearance, and crude forms of showing off to attract the attention of members of the opposite sex (189). As Crow and Crow (47) have explained:

> Girls may become shy in the presence of their former boy pals. They may "moon" over the pictures of popular motion-picture actors or television stars. Little cliques of preadolescent girls may display silly, giggling attitudes in the presence of boys, or may seem to evince an attitude of superiority to boys of their own age.

Later this interest becomes more mature; it shows itself in a desire to dance, to have dates, and to engage in other sociosexual activities (189).

Heterosexual interests depend largely upon the maturing of the sex organs (119,122, 196,198). Sexual responsiveness *does not depend upon physical or emotional stimuli*. It is influenced by the *glandular condition* of the individual. Gonadal insufficiency delays the development of sexual responsiveness, as may be seen in the case of castration. Testosterone stimulates sexual responsiveness in both males and females. Pituitary and thyroid deficiencies affect sexual responsiveness unfavorably (123,124, 177,198).

Social factors play an important role in determining *what form* heterosexuality will take (48,198). Because a strong sex drive is commonly regarded as a sign of masculinity, adolescent boys are motivated to engage in sexual behavior of all types (124). Girls who look upon marriage as a way of establishing themselves as women are predisposed to engage in dating and different forms of expression of love at an earlier age than are girls who find other avenues of self-expression rewarding (57). As Duvall has explained, "Being in love as a teenager appears, in some cases, to be an escape hatch for those who feel that other doors to the future are closed" (58).

Furthermore, because our culture "sells love on every hand," it helps to channel the erotic drive into patterns of behavior that win cultural approval (58). Mass media focus the adolescent's attention on the importance of heterosexual relationships. The majority of popular songs, for example, have a love theme. They help the adolescent to identify with the role of lover or loved one and to learn the approved patterns of behavior in romance. This is true also of movies, television, and literature (108,114). Because the sex drive is influenced by psychological factors, sexual behavior in adolescence often becomes "primarily a psychological rather than a physical matter" (124).

Even though the physical changes that occur at puberty predispose the adolescent to respond to members of the opposite sex in a manner that differs markedly from the behavior of children, *direct stimuli* are needed to call forth heterosexual behavior. Whether these stimuli come from contact with members of the opposite sex or from other sources, they release the sex drive that has developed from the physical and glandular changes occurring at puberty. Of the many stimuli producing erotic responses in adolescents, the following have been reported to be the most frequent: conversations about sex, daydreams involving sexual behavior, obscene pictures, nude art, dancing, nudity of the opposite sex, songs and music with a romantic theme, movies, stories, and television programs that deal with sex, viewing the sexual parts of a member of the opposite sex, and exhibitionistic sexual activities (58,108,114,122,123,188, 189).

It is a well-known fact that boys respond to more stimuli and are more easily aroused sexually than are girls. While the reasons for these differences have never been fully determined, the following speculations are most commonly given: boys differ from girls in innate sex drive, the sensory capacity to stimulation of boys differs from that of girls, and the sociosexual acculturation of boys and girls is different. Of the three speculations, the third is most widely accepted (123,189).

INFLUENCE OF AGE OF SEXUAL MATURING
The age at which sexual maturing occurs and the speed with which it takes place influence the onset and intensity of heterosexual interests. Persons who mature early not only show an early interest in members of the opposite sex, but they may settle down into a mature relationship of engagement and marriage before they are out of their teens. Those who mature late, on the other hand, show no interest in heterosexual relationships until after their earlier-maturing peers have already surpassed them in social experiences with members of the opposite sex (116,189,207,213). While delay in sex interest is not apt to have serious permanent consequences, it may mean a relatively unhappy adolescence (88).

OPPORTUNITIES FOR DEVELOPMENT
Adolescence is the golden age for learning to get along with members of the opposite sex. However, learning to be a heterosexual person will not take place in a vacuum; opportunities must be provided for learning and the adolescent must have the motivation necessary to take advantage of the opportunities given. As Cole and Hall have pointed out, "The boy-and-girl friendships are essential to normal adjustment. Nothing that results from them could possibly be as serious as their failure to develop" (41).

Two environmental conditions are essential to the successful establishment of heterosexual relationships. First, the adolescent must be in an environment in which there is a *sufficient number of members of the opposite sex* of appropriate age, intellectual status, and personality adjustment to give him an opportunity to select congenial companions and to have pleasurable social contacts with them. Because most adolescents are in junior or senior high school, in college, or in some professional training school, they have ample opportunities to meet and associate with members of the other sex in their work and play (155).

The second requisite for successful adjustment is an encouraging, sympathetic, and helpful *attitude on the part of parents and other adults*. With the realization that he has someone to turn to for help, advice, and encouragement, the adolescent is better able to tackle the problems that heterosexual adjustment give rise to. Unfortunately, too often parents encourage unhealthy attitudes toward heterosexual problems as a means of protecting their children. Even worse, they laugh at the shyness, self-consciousness, and crudeness that characteristically accompany early heterosexual relationships (132).

An environment in which the sexes are segregated not only increases the difficulty the adolescent experiences in social contacts with members of the opposite sex, but, even more seriously, it tends to develop in the adolescent a feeling of self-inadequacy in situations where there are members of the opposite sex (57,142,189).

problems resulting from sexual maturity

There are three important developmental tasks which the adolescent is expected to master in our culture before he reaches the age of legal maturity. They are: first, the development of new patterns of relationships with age-mates of both sexes; second, preparation for marriage and family living; and, third, acquiring a masculine or feminine sex role (88). Because of these social expectations, the adolescent is faced with problems that never occurred during the sexually immature years of childhood. These problems are accentuated by the lag between the sex maturing and the social maturing of the individual that delays the age of marrying. Each year that marriage is delayed beyond the age of sexual maturity, these problems become more numerous and more serious (30).

TYPES OF PROBLEMS

"Love problems" include all those perplexities and conflicts that young people encounter in making satisfactory adjustments in boy-girl relationships. They include sex problems but are not limited to such problems. The following are the most common.

Boy-Girl Problems   Studies of the sex problems of adolescents have revealed that "boy-girl" problems are the most serious of all. Problems facing the young adolescent consist of "not having a boy or girl friend," wanting more dates, not knowing what to do on a date; being bashful; not knowing what to talk about on a date; not knowing how to keep a member of the other sex interested; how much petting to permit; how to break off with a boy or girl when one wants to change; how to avoid activities they do not enjoy or approve of, such as drinking or going to big parties, and yet be popular; how to get the "right" boy or girl to notice them; how aggressive can a girl be when boys are scarce and avoid antagonizing her friends; and how to convince parents that they are too overprotective about what their sons and daughters do when they

date. In general, the younger adolescent's boy-girl problems center mainly around establishing heterosexual relationships (47, 181,192,214,223). For the older adolescent, boy-girl problems include going steady, petting, necking, premarital intercourse, selection of a future mate, obstacles in the way of marriage, knowing what makes a successful marriage, wondering how to prepare for marriage and family life, long engagements, marrying a person of a different race or religion, how to control a boy when he gets out of line during petting, how to control one's self during petting, blind dates, and how to avoid contracting a venereal disease if one "plays the field." Even older adolescents are sometimes faced with the problems of not knowing where and how to meet individuals of the other sex and of how to get dates. This is especially true of intellectually gifted adolescents. They find the boys or girls of their own age too immature, while those who are their intellectual equals regard them as "kids" (41,47,48,51,57,181,214).

Social-Sex Problems   A second group of sex problems facing the adolescent relates to social behavior with members of the other sex. The young adolescent is often embarrassed, ill-at-ease, and self-conscious. This makes him awkward and tongue-tied. In addition, there is the problem of social skills, such as dancing, playing games, and carrying on a conversation. There are also problems of etiquette, of knowing what is the socially correct thing to do on a date or at a party with members of the two sexes (110,181,192).

Moral-Sex Problems   The moral aspects of sex behavior give rise to many problems because of the conflict with adult standards, the double standard, and the different standards for different socioeconomic and racial groups (123,226). Many adolescents are faced with a conflict between popularity and standards of behavior. A girl may, for example, want to be liked by the popular boys in her class, but they have the reputation of being "fast" while the more conservative boys have the reputation of being "squares" (181). When a girl behaves in a "proper way," she may suffer from unpopularity; when she behaves in a more "normal way," she suffers from feelings of guilt. According to peer standards, "first she did wrong and felt rejected, then she did right and felt wrong" (192). Because the world is black and white with no compromising shades of gray for many teen-agers, it complicates the moral aspects of their sex problems (192).

Specifically, the moral aspects of sex problems relate to petting and necking, premarital intercourse when going steady or engaged, sexual promiscuity, discussions of sex with one's own or the other sex, thinking about or daydreaming about sex, and what is considered the proper behavior when with members of the other sex. Because girls are more harshly judged for any deviation from the culturally approved pattern of sex behavior than are boys, problems arising from the moral aspects of sex are more numerous and more serious for girls (41,129,181,184,192,219).

Sex-role Problems   For young adolescents, achieving an appropriate sex role is sometimes a major problem. Boys learn to be "regular boys" in late childhood, just as girls learn to be "real girls," not tomboys. However, with the beginning of heterosexual relationships, the role of members of the two sexes becomes more clearly defined. The girl wants to act in a socially approved feminine manner, just as the boy wants to act like a man. Accepting the restraints society places on a girl's behavior and being willing to meet the problems these restraints bring is one of the developmental tasks of adolescent girls. For the boy, problems relating to aggressiveness in heterosexual relationships are difficult, especially for the young adolescent who feels insecure and uncertain of how to act (30,41,88,181, 223).

Problems of Abnormal Sexuality   The final group of sex problems in adolescence centers around sexually abnormal behavior. Even though many young adolescents engage in masturbation, in homosexual forms of behavior, and in homoerotism, they know such behavior is disapproved of and they have feelings of guilt about it. How to satisfy the normal sex urges and, at the same time, behave in a morally approved manner presents problems for both boys and girls (122, 123). Closely related to this is the problem of how to avoid contracting a venereal disease and what to do about it, should it be contracted. This problem is of special concern to boys, who are more promiscuous in their sexual behavior during adolescence than are girls (51,189).

tasks in achieving heterosexuality

From the survey of the problems resulting from sexual maturing given above, it should be apparent that achieving heterosexuality is a long and difficult process for many adolescents in the American culture of today. In fact, many do not achieve complete heterosexuality before they reach legal maturity; some never achieve it. The reason for the difficulties the adolescent encounters, as was stressed earlier, is that little preparation is given in childhood for the developmental tasks the individual is expected to master in this area of his behavior. What preparation he is given often proves to be more of a handicap than a help. This is especially true in the case of attitudes toward sex and toward socially approved roles for members of the two sexes.

In achieving heterosexuality, the adolescent must master six major tasks: acquisition of knowledge about sex and about the approved sex roles, developing a wholesome attitude toward sex and sex roles as a source of motivation to behave in a socially approved manner, learning the approved patterns of sex behavior, achieving wholesome values as a guide to the selection of a life mate, learning to express "love" for another, and learning to play the approved role for members of the individual's sex. Each of these major tasks will be discussed in detail in the remainder of this chapter and in the following chapter.

knowledge about sex and sex roles

Before the adolescent can make good adjustments to members of the other sex, before he can be prepared for marriage with its duties and responsibilities as well as its pleasures and satisfactions, and before he can play the sex role society expects him to play, he must have information about these matters. While most boys and girls have considerable information about sex before they reach adolescence, this information is limited and some of it is false.

Throughout childhood, curiosity about sex has led the child to ask questions; to explore his own body and those of playmates of his own or of the other sex; to pick up bits of information from comics, movies, television, stories, smutty jokes, salacious pictures, or the peer "grapevine"; and to read books or to see educational films designed to give children the "facts of life." Most of this information is concentrated on reproduction; to a lesser extent, it is concentrated on the relationship between the sexes in marriage. Unfortunately, emphasis is too often placed on avoidance of relationships with members of the opposite sex to prevent the child from "getting into trouble" as he grows older and to avoid contracting a venereal disease (5, 48,51,139,190,197).

How much and how accurate information the child has when he reaches adolescence will depend to a certain extent upon the *knowledge his parents* have and how willing or able they are to give him the information he is seeking. For the most part, the child who has well-informed parents will have more sex knowledge than the child whose parents have meagre knowledge (121, 178). Children from professional families, for example, usually have more information than those from clerical, skilled, or semi-skilled families. Children of employed mothers, especially when the mothers are in professional or executive work, have more information than children whose mothers are housewives (140,144). *Boys*, as a rule, have more information about sex than girls, but their information is more about male

than about female sexual physiology. Girls with one or two *foreign-born parents* maintain that they get more wholesome information about sex and feel more adequately prepared for marriage than do girls whose parents are American-born (60,122,123, 130).

AREAS OF ADOLESCENT INTEREST

The pubescent is preoccupied with sex to the extent that he thinks about sex, daydreams about sexual matters, discusses sex with his intimate friends, trades information with his clique mates and other associates, reads anything and everything he can get about sex, and spends much of his time when alone exploring and stimulating different areas of his body to see what sensations he can elicit. At this time, many boys and girls claim that "sex really gets on your mind" (79,234). At first, interest is concentrated on the physiological changes occurring in the individual's own body or in the bodies of his friends. Later, as interest in members of the opposite sex begins to develop, curiosity about how sex maturing is affecting them and what changes are taking place in their bodies is aroused.

When the puberty changes have been completed, the adolescent wants to know about *love*, not the physical aspects alone but the emotional and social as well. What does it feel like to fall in love? How can you tell when love is the real thing, not merely infatuation? What is the sex relationship of marriage? What are the "safe" and "sure" methods of birth control? How safe is premarital intercourse? How frequently can intercourse be engaged in? How can a girl control a boy who tries to go too far? Will too much control of sex behavior make a girl lose a steady? What causes venereal diseases and how can one be protected against them? And how can the strong urge of sex be expressed to give the individual satisfaction safely? (20,28,32,54, 57,143,181,189).

Some adolescents do show an interest in the problems and responsibilities that come with marriage, such as economic and in-law problems, child care, and a wife's career after marriage; most are primarily interested in problems that focus on boy-girl relationships. While adolescents show an interest in knowing about the socially approved sex roles for members of the two sexes, their interest, once again, is centered more on the roles of the two sexes in dating than in marriage and parenthood (47,96, 180,214).

SOURCES OF INFORMATION

Studies have revealed that the common sources of information are parents, relatives, companions, books, magazines, pamphlets, the school, and movies. (See Figure 13-1.) Much information, however, comes from the grapevine and dirty stories. Most adolescents claim that their first information came from unwholesome sources. Those who receive their information from wholesome and reliable sources, such as parents, teachers, doctors, and books, have information that is superior in quality and quantity and they are more satisfied with the information they have (4,5,32,46,91,144).

Girls get most of their first information about sex from their mothers and girl friends; the major sources of boys' first information are their friends, dirty stories, and the school grapevine. However, this first information is generally limited to the origin of babies and menstruation for girls; boys are told about the origin of babies and the dangers of venereal diseases. When instruction is given in the home, it comes more often from the mothers than the fathers for girls; in the case of boys, the reverse is true. Even among older adolescents, parents and the school play a relatively unimportant role in sex instruction; more information comes from mass media of communication, from their friends, and from the grapevine than from more wholesome sources (4,28,32,144).

In a comparison of girls from two generations, it was found that the girls of today are receiving more of their first sex information from parents and relatives and less from their playmates and friends than their mothers did (140). This is illustrated in Figure 13-2. Furthermore, schools are taking over more responsibility for sex education, either in specialized instruction, aided by films and group discussion or by incorporating the material into courses in science (130,156,180,204).

When adolescents attempt to get information about sex and discover that they are blocked or that the information is inadequate, they take the matter into their own hands and try to satisfy their curiosity by experimentation. Early in adolescence, experimentation takes the form of manual manipulation accompanied by direct observation of the female anatomy, exhibitionistic sex play, attempts at intercourse, and oral contacts. Boys and girls engage in petting of the milder types—kissing, manual exploration, and manipulation by the boy of the girl's breasts and reproductive organs. The boy may attempt intercourse, especially if he is dating a younger girl or one who comes from a lower-class family. Kissing games, as a means of satisfying curiosity, are likewise common, as is masturbation. Figure 13-3 shows common forms of exploration used by boys. Among older adolescents, petting in the more advanced forms and attempts at intercourse are more

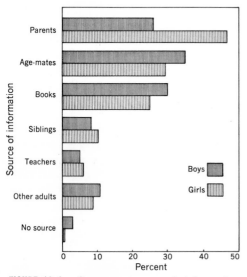

FIGURE 13-1   Common sources of information about sex. (Adapted from L. Cole and I. N. Hall: *Psychology of adolescence*. 6th ed. New York: Holt, Rinehart and Winston, 1964. Used by permission.)

common ways of satisfying curiosity (62, 122,123,124,189,198). Different forms of experimentation are discussed in more detail on pages 555 to 561.

Among older boys, in high school and college, experimentation often includes visits to houses of prostitution or an evening affair with a pickup. They usually go out with other boys in search of excitement and knowledge about sex which they are afraid to get with girls of their own age group. Prostitution, thus, is a "male-group" activity. Sexually inexperienced boys are especially anxious to test their ability to perform and function normally, while, at the same time, proving to themselves and others that they are grown up, daredevils, and sophisticated. Being able to experiment without fear of consequences adds to their desire to supplement what knowledge about sex they have been able to acquire through experimenting with girls of their own groups (125).

EVALUATION OF SOURCES *Summary?*

The adolescent of today needs more and better sex education than was needed in the past, when chaperonage and other safeguards protected adolescents in their heterosexual relationships. Furthermore, sex education is needed not only to give the adolescent the facts of life but also to help him understand and accept the social-sex role society expects him to play and to acquaint him with sex techniques, ways of handling the sex drive, and other facts needed to make healthy adjustments to marriage (122, 123,140).

There are marked differences of opinions about who should assume the responsibility for the sex instruction of the adolescent. An evaluation of agencies of instruction will throw light on their relative merits.

Parents Many adolescents feel that their parents should assume the responsibility for their sex instruction. Some claim that this can and should be supplemented by the school. However, many adolescents feel that the information they get from their parents is inadequate or faulty (57, 143,192,214). In the case of masturbation,

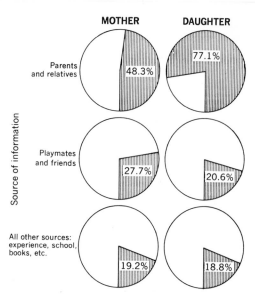

FIGURE 13–2 Girls of today are receiving more of their first sex information from parents and relatives than was true when their mothers were young. (Adapted from P. H. Landis: *Adolescence and youth: the process of maturing.* 2d ed. New York: McGraw-Hill, 1952. Used by permission.)

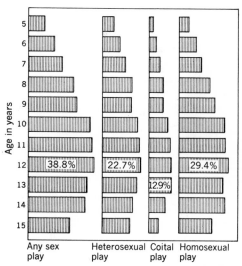

FIGURE 13–3 Common forms of sex exploration used by boys at different ages. (Adapted from A. C. Kinsey, W. B. Pomeroy, and C. E. Martin: *Sexual behavior in the human male.* Philadelphia: Saunders, 1948. Used by permission.)

for example, adolescent boys are often told that this will cause insanity, feeblemindedness, acne, loss of virility, and a host of other physical ills. This misinformation, it is important to note, is not given intentionally by parents. Rather, it is based on information the parents received in their own youth which came from literature—purporting to be scientific—which supported such beliefs (189).

Furthermore, parents are apt to give information about sex in an embarrassed, half-ashamed way that both upsets and embarrasses the adolescent. Then, too, there is often a lack of intimacy between the adolescent and his parents; this makes communication difficult on both sides, especially in the case of boys (119). Parents may be unable to break their own inhibitions and reserves concerning the subject of sex; they may lack adequate vocabulary to discuss sex so that the adolescent can understand; or their religious background may inhibit the imparting of sex information (32,86,140).

How good home instruction is depends not only upon the knowledge the parents have but, even more importantly, on their willingness and ability to impart this information. Because far too many parents believe that they have fulfilled their parental duty when they tell their children about procreation, when they prepare their daughters for menstruation and their sons for nocturnal emissions, and when they warn them against the dangers of sexual activities, it means that the adolescent has large gaps in the knowledge he would like to have (74).

Schools Adolescents who feel that their parents are not adequate to give sex instruction favor the schools as the best agency. They claim that the best instruction comes through class discussions, lectures, and suggested readings. There are differences of opinion regarding when the schools should give the instruction. Some adolescents claim that it should begin in elementary school; most believe it should be given in the junior or senior high schools, or both (181,192, 214).

Educators are becoming more and more aware of the important role they must play in the sex education of children and adolescents. They adhere to the belief that "schools should include in some required course all facts concerning sex that pupils are likely to need, otherwise many will not learn them" (41). In discussing the responsibility of the school in this area, Remmers and Radler (192) have pointed out:

> The physical and emotional changes that typify the turbulent period of adolescence and the tricky social relationships that accompany them are entirely too important to be neglected by modern education. . . . The young people themselves, their children and society at large all pay the price of continued ignorance and misinformation.

Rubin (173) has emphasized even more strongly the necessity for the schools to do more in the area of sex education than they have done to date:

> In Mid-Victorian days, "a conspiracy of silence" by schools on the sex question was not too damaging because the conspiracy was enforced by virtually all the official and unofficial agencies of society. Today, when sex is used to sell everything from newspapers to new cars and when easily available paper-backs and magazine articles pour off the press, silence on the part of the school means abdication of the community's most responsible sector, leaving the field wide open for the huckster and the quack.

Most educators believe that sex education should not be just "reproductive education." Instead, it should be all-inclusive, covering the psychological and emotional aspects of sex as well as the physical. In addition, it should include information about intersex associations, sex roles, pregnancy and its possible complications, childbirth with its potential hazards, the use of contraceptives, the prevention and treatment of venereal disease, the causes and control of deviant sex behavior, especially masturbation and homosexuality, the dangers of abortion, and a host of other related problems (4,32,48,51,130,143,204). It is further believed that more stress should be placed on the development of values in selecting a mate and on preparation for meeting the problems of marriage and parenthood (100,135).

Mass Media There is no question about the fact that books, educational films, and magazine articles written by specialists in sex education will give both correct and adequate information about the areas of sex interest that are important to the adolescent. However, to romantic idealistic adolescents, these sources may seem cold and impersonal and the facts too "scientific." Any information they glean from romantic stories, movies, television, or the comics will have more appeal. But because the information is dependent upon the adolescent's *interpretation* of what is said or done, it can readily be distorted—and it often is.

Some of the sex information adolescents get from the peer "grapevine" is based on facts learned from reliable books and magazine articles; much of it comes from other forms of mass media or from their own experimentation. Not only is such information likely to be distorted by misinterpretations, but, even worse, it is usually colored by the teller's own attitudes toward sex. And because the type of adolescent who gets personal satisfaction from being in the limelight of attention through his ability to impart such information may not have his facts straight, it is understandable that much of that information will be exaggerated and distorted (4,48,57,79,115).

Experimentation Information about sex gained from experimentation is usually correct but it is often badly distorted by the unfavorable attitudes of the experimenter. Knowing that social attitudes toward premarital sex behavior are unfavorable leads the adolescent to have marked feelings of guilt; should he be caught in his experimentation, shame will be added to his guilt. Furthermore, he will be afraid that experimentation will lead to "trouble"—either premarital pregnancy for the girl or the contraction of a venereal disease for the boy (48,51,57,79,115). In commenting on the

dangers involved in experimentation and the effects these have on the adolescent's attitudes, Remmers and Radler (192) have pointed out:

> *Sheer curiosity leads little children to investigate their bodies and those of their playmates. . . . The same experimentation after puberty is another matter. To discourage it completely might prevent teenage boys and girls from ever developing healthy relationships with the other sex. On the other hand, to allow it to go to its logical extreme can cause tragedy, since adolescents are no longer children. Boys can become fathers and girls can become pregnant. The two striking things about sex before marriage are these: (1) it's fun, and (2) it's dangerous. The real solution to the sex problem of the teenage boy or girl is to avoid the dangers but not to miss out on all the fun.*

ADOLESCENTS' REACTIONS TO SEX INSTRUCTION

Few adolescents feel that the sex information they have is adequate to meet their needs; they have many questions they would like to ask but find neither their parents nor the school willing or able to answer them (25,121,180). As a result, they display "an abysmal ignorance of simple sex facts." The blame for this may be "laid directly at the door of American sex education in general," either in the home or the school, or both (65). When sexual curiosity is not satisfied or is squashed, it may set up learning blocks that affect *all* learning (136). However, because sexual curiosity is normally strong, it is far less likely to be squashed than to be turned into channels that will provide the adolescent with the information he craves (48,189).

A common way in which adolescents try to get the information they want but have not been able to get is by writing to newspaper and magazine columnists for advice on all sorts of love problems. The peak age for doing so is 18 years. Surprisingly, almost three times as many boys, it has been reported, write for advice as girls. The most common sex problems they seek information about relate to birth control and approved forms of sexual behavior. Boys are mainly concerned about their own sexual behavior and genital adequacy; girls ask questions mainly about reproduction, their own responsiveness, and their anatomy, such as the size of their breasts (91,105, 183,216,227).

attitudes toward sex

If sex is to be fun for the adolescent and lead to wholesome heterosexuality, he must have a favorable attitude toward sex. This attitude must include not only the adolescent's feelings toward sex per se but also toward members of the opposite sex and toward the socially approved roles each sex is expected to play in the culture. Obviously a favorable attitude would be impossible if major emphasis in sex education were placed on the negative aspects of sex, if the members of one sex were conditioned to have unfavorable attitudes toward members of the opposite sex, or if the role society expects the members of one sex to play were regarded as inferior to that which society expects members of the other sex to play.

Attitudes that are favorable will lead to good heterosexual adjustments, just as unfavorable attitudes will lead to poor adjustments. Even more important, once an attitude has been learned, it is very difficult to change. As Mussen et al. (168) have stated:

> No amount of information or reassurance in preadolescence or adolescence will enable the child to adopt a healthy attitude toward sexuality if in the preceding years he has been taught to fear sexual responses. . . . Clinicians have found that when unfavorable sexual attitudes have been built up . . . it is extremely difficult, and sometimes impossible, to shift them through the use of rational advice given in adolescence. Even extensive psychotherapy may fail to change attitudes which have become too deeply ingrained.

CONDITIONS AFFECTING ATTITUDES

The adolescent's attitude toward sex is influenced by three conditions: the type of sex instruction he has had since earliest childhood, the attitudes of significant people in his life toward sex, and the type of earlier associations he has had with members of the opposite sex. Because each of these conditions plays a role of great importance in shaping the adolescent's attitudes, each will be discussed in detail.

Type of Sex Information Attitudes about sex are established during the early years of life. Whether these attitudes are healthy or not will be determined largely by the people from whom the child derives his information. The "conspiracy of silence" in the home and the emphasis on "don'ts" lead to unfavorable attitudes, especially when the arousal of fear plays an important role in sex education (51,52,115,129). Furthermore, when much of the adolescent's knowledge about sex matters has come from smutty stories and jokes or sexy literature, unfavorable attitudes already present are intensified (4,48,79,143).

Studies of different sources of sex information have revealed that adolescents who receive their first information from parents or from the school have far more favorable attitudes than those who receive their first information or the major part of it elsewhere. Parents who are better educated and come from the better socioeconomic groups help their children to establish more wholesome attitudes than parents who are less well educated and belong to the lower socioeconomic groups.

Adolescents who receive most of their sex instruction from the clergy, as in the case of Catholic youth, are least liberal in their attitudes; the most liberal are those who receive their instruction from doctors, nurses, adult friends of the family, or from reading (30,55,144).

Attitudes of Significant People Because the closest associations during the early, formative years of life are with one's parents, it is not surprising that the adolescent's attitude toward sex is a reflection of his parents' attitudes. Even as social contacts broaden and the adolescent is influenced by teachers, peers of his own sex, and, later, peers of the opposite sex, this basic attitude continues to be dominant. Remmers and Radler (192) have emphasized the persistence of early attitudes:

The young man or woman's feelings about his sexual urges and behavior depend almost entirely on the feelings of his parents. This makes their responsibility greater than mere talk. Mother must set a good example for daughter and father must for son. At the same time, every boy must have a pleasant relationship with his mother and every girl must feel the same kind of warmth between her and her father. Granted such happy patterns of growth up to and through the teen years, children usually grow into happily married people without unwholesome or disgraceful experiences along the way.

Earlier Associations   In the preschool years, the child experiences pleasant associations with members of the opposite sex. In fact, he often finds them more congenial as playmates than members of his own sex (223). By kindergarten, or certainly by first grade, boys begin to show a preference for playmates of their own sex. Strong pressures are put on boys by parents—especially fathers—by older male siblings, and by peers of their own sex, to play with boys. They soon learn that if they do not comply with these expectations they will be regarded as sissies (53,133,208).

By middle childhood, there is not only a strong preference for playmates of the same sex but an indifference to or active antagonism toward members of the opposite sex. From then until puberty, boys have a strong dislike for playing with girls. What few contacts they have with them are characterized by teasing, bullying, criticizing, and interfering with the girls' play. If invited to a party for members of the two sexes, boys will either ignore the girls or do all they can to spoil the fun girls are trying to have alone. In school or in camp, when

boys are assigned a task to be carried out with girls, they will try to avoid it. If forced to work with girls, they will let the girls do most of the work or actually hinder it in the hope of being assigned to a task with boys. At this time, boys avoid talking to girls whenever possible; when they are forced to do so, they go out of their way to make rude and derogatory comments about them. They make fun of romance in real life, on the screen, and over the air, and they make derisive comments about "love" (34,70,79,134,158).

By the time boys and girls reach puberty, antagonism between the sexes reaches its peak. Now it becomes an actual dislike or aversion rather than an antipathy toward members of the opposite sex. This coincides with the negative phase: it is just another expression of the pubescent's unsocial attitude toward life. Usually this phase lasts for six months to a year and a half. It is less intense in boys than in girls and is of shorter duration (79,118,169,211).

While unquestionably sex aversion comes partly from the physical upheaval that occurs at puberty, social causes play a far more important role than physical. A girl may resent bitterly the physical discomforts of menstruation which boys are spared. This alone is not enough to be responsible for the strong aversion there is for members of the opposite sex at this age. A resentment at the more favored position of boys in society, the preferential treatment boys usually receive in the home and at school, the greater leniency in attitudes toward boys' misdemeanors, and the attitude of smug superiority boys assume—all have contributed their share to an attitude of resentment on the part of girls.

This is intensified by family friction, intolerance of the father toward the mother, quarreling between parents, and the constant reminder of friction between the sexes in divorces, stories, and movies about unhappy marriages. Because members of the male sex are usually more favored than members of the female sex in such situations and because the physiological changes at puberty have fewer unfavorable effects on boys, boys' aversion to girls at this age is usually less severe than girls' aversion to boys (70,85,133,158).

Antagonism between the sexes is bound to affect the attitudes of both boys and girls toward sex, toward their own sex, and toward members of the other sex in an unfavorable way. It makes them extremely modest and self-conscious about the physical aspects of sex. This is especially true of girls who have developed a feeling of feminine inadequacy because of the way they have been treated by boys. They will not, for example, undress or go to the toilet before girls or women, except their mothers. Both boys and girls are so antagonistic toward members of the opposite sex that they will not deliberately touch a member of the opposite sex except under conventional circumstances, as in games or dancing. Even then, they show their antagonism by trying to make the member of the other sex uncomfortable by pinching, deliberately stepping on his or her feet, or tripping the partner.

Girls think of themselves as they have been accustomed to be treated—as inferior to boys. Boys, on the other hand, think of their own sex as superior. Many girls intensify their feelings of inferiority by developing feelings of martyrdom and resentment. Because boys feel superior to girls, they expect to assume leadership roles in any situation—either at school or in social life—in which their activities include girls. Their attitude of smug superiority has little of the resentment and antagonism characteristic of the girls' attitude; instead, it is more neutral while that of girls is more emotionally toned (34,70,85). It can be characterized by the expression, "Nuts to girls" (214).

While antagonistic attitudes toward members of the opposite sex are almost universal in the American culture of today, the intensity of the antagonism varies. A girl whose childhood pal was her father, who got along peacefully with her brothers and their friends, and who was liked by the boys in her neighborhood or class at school will have a far less unfavorable attitude toward members of the male sex when she reaches

adolescence than will the girl whose childhood has included a series of annoying and embarrassing episodes initiated by boys and by male relatives.

If a girl has grown up in a family where there is an older male sibling who has treated her well and who has been a hero in her childish eyes, she is less likely to have a resentful attitude toward boys than is the girl whose childhood was plagued by teasings and bullyings of an older brother and his friends. A boy with an older sister who has treated him well will have a more favorable attitude toward girls than a boy whose older sister has played the role of mother substitute in a harsh and punitive manner (133,134). In suburban areas or neighborhoods of cities where pressures are put on children in the fifth and sixth grades to associate with members of the opposite sex—even to the point of having dates—there is far less antagonism than in communities where pressure is put on children to avoid all dating and "grown-up" social activities (23).

IMPROVEMENT IN ATTITUDES

Heterosexuality could never be achieved successfully with the typical attitudes most boys and girls have at the time they become sexually mature. A radical change must, therefore, take place. How favorable this shift is will depend "far more upon what has happened long previously than upon any special measures or special training [adopted] when the event itself takes place" (167). A strongly antagonistic attitude toward members of the opposite sex and an unfavorable attitude toward sex matters or toward one's own sex are not easy to reverse.

Because girls reach puberty sooner than boys, the attitude of girls improves sooner than that of boys. Girls of today show signs of an improved attitude toward boys generally during their thirteenth year. However, they still prefer girls to boys at this age. Not until a year or two later does their attitude improve to the point where they prefer boys to girls.

Boys begin to show a change in their attitude a year or two later than girls. However, this change is primarily in the direction of indifference to girls rather than toward interest and liking. When boys do show an interest in girls, they are likely to be interested in a *particular* girl, not girls in general (34,49,85,161,214). Figure 4–6, page 137, shows the shift in boys' and girls' attitudes toward members of the opposite sex.

Causes of Improvement While the sex drive, which strengthens with the maturing of the sex organs, is, in part, responsible for changes in attitudes, social pressures and social expectations are likewise very important forces. If maturation of the sex drive alone were responsible, the lag between the development of interest in members of the opposite sex would not be so long as it is nor would the change on the part of girls be greater than that of boys (122,123).

The difference in changes in attitudes is largely the result of social pressures. Being popular with members of the opposite sex is more prestigeful for girls than for boys. As was stressed earlier (see pages 185 and 186), popularity in girls depends on the social success a girl has with members of the opposite sex; for boys, athletic success is the major source of prestige (42,91).

Parents—but especially mothers—put pressure on their daughters to date early and to marry early. In the case of boys, pressures to date and to marry early are weak or absent. Mothers do not want to lose their sons, and fathers do not want their sons to "ruin their chances of success" in the business world by "wasting their time" on dates or by marrying early and assuming responsibilities that are likely to interfere with their chances of getting ahead. Consequently, they are likely to discourage their sons' interest in girls (1,42, 133).

Furthermore, members of the peer group put pressures on the young adolescent boy to avoid girls. Having taken the stand for many years that girls are silly and a waste of time, they find it hard to change their attitudes. Were there more prestige associated with dating, these peer pressures

might be less severe. And, finally, change in attitude on the boy's part is more difficult because he has verbalized his negative feelings about girls over the years; it is now ego deflating to have to admit that he was wrong. Parental and peer comments about his former negative verbalizations may delay even further the time when he will *show* his changed attitude and get up the courage to appear in public with a girl or even to talk to a girl (42,79,85,91,214).

EFFECTS OF IMPROVED ATTITUDES
Without question, the attitudes of the typical adolescent toward sex are more wholesome than they were during childhood. However, there are individual differences in how much improvement takes place; boys, as a group, show less improvement than girls. Girls are subjected to stronger pressures from parents and members of the peer group to change their attitudes, and girls gain more prestige for behavior associated with changed attitudes.

Girls become "boy-conscious" and "boy-crazy" earlier and more intensely than boys become "girl-crazy." Boys continue to prefer masculine companionship throughout adolescence, though they may prefer the companionship of a *particular* girl to that of boys (34,85,161,214). Throughout adolescence, boys show a progressively better opinion of themselves, of members of the male sex, and of the masculine role; girls, by contrast, have less favorable attitudes toward their own sex, toward the feminine role, and toward themselves as individuals. While their attitudes toward their own sex are deteriorating, their attitudes toward the opposite sex are improving. Even though boys' attitudes toward girls and the feminine role improve, there is little evidence that they change radically for the better as adolescence progresses. Boys may *behave* in a socially approved manner when they are with girls but this more often than not is a "veneer of equalitarianism overlying their more firmly established beliefs" (158).

IMPORTANCE OF IMPROVED ATTITUDES
How important a role improved attitudes play in achieving good heterosexual devel-

opment can best be shown by what happens when the unfavorable childhood attitudes are *not* replaced by favorable ones. The *lag in change* in attitudes toward members of the opposite sex leads to many social problems at an age when high prestige is put on dating and popularity with members of the opposite sex. Were this lag limited to the year or slightly more of difference in age of sexual maturing of the two sexes, it would be of little consequence. However, as boys cling tenaciously to their childhood dislike of girls, they force girls to play a more aggressive role in heterosexual relationships than is approved in our culture. The result is that girls often acquire the reputation of "chasing the boys"—a reputation that dims much of the prestige the girl would otherwise acquire from her social successes (41, 91,159).

The effect on boys of this lag is to give them the upper hand in their relationships with girls; they are in a position to strike a hard bargain with the girls they date. Much of the petting, necking, and premarital intercourse that occurs during dating is the price the boy expects the girl to pay for the time and money he spends to entertain her. This matter will be discussed in detail in the next chapter.

The neutral attitude boys have toward girls leads to *keen* competition among girls to win the attention and interest of boys. As a result, girls form less close and less permanent friendships with members of their own sex than boys do. Even more seriously, they often break friendships with girls who are congenial because they are afraid boys will judge them unfavorably if seen with a person the boys do not like or label as a "drip" (41,85,214). See pages 132 and 133 for a more complete discussion of this matter.

Some of the loneliness and maladjustment characteristic of adult women may be traced to the keen competitiveness of adolescent girls with one another for masculine attention. Not only does it become a habitual pattern of adjustment for many girls but it leads to the breaking of friendships at a crucial age in friendship formation. If girls carry over into adulthood the atti-

tude of suspicion toward members of their own sex which is an accompaniment of competitiveness, they will form few friendships with other women. This is in direct contrast to the more favorable attitude boys have toward their pals during adolescence and to the stronger and more stable friendships boys form during the adolescent years.

Unquestionably the most serious effects of inadequate change of attitudes are on the *personalities* of boys and girls in adolescence and on their *life adjustments*. Because boys continue to regard members of their own sex more favorably than members of the female sex, they treat girls in much the same way as members of minority groups are treated. This leads to a "female inferiority complex" and a "male superiority complex." As a result of these complexes, boys tend to overvalue themselves and their abilities; girls tend to undervalue themselves and their abilities.

These complexes also affect the *relationships* of members of *the two sexes* in social, business, and family life—the three most important areas of life for American adults. As is true of all minority-group members, women often have a derogatory attitude toward members of their own sex. Because men regard women as the "inferior sex," they give them few opportunities to engage in activities with them on an equalitarian basis. Like members of a minority group, women resent this treatment. The resentment, in turn, plays havoc with their loyalty to their employers in the business world and to their happiness in marriage (17,83,176).

Because of the seriousness of the long-term effects of inadequate change in attitude toward members of the opposite sex, attempts are being made today to segregate the sexes as little as possible in childhood and to make the roles of the two sexes similar. It is hoped that this will eliminate the tendency for sex antagonism to get a firm foothold. Time alone will tell how successful this will be. Like prejudice against racial and religious groups, prejudice against members of the female sex has become traditional. Only time and reeducation can eliminate prejudice, whatever its form.

Improved attitudes toward sex as a *bio-logical function* have been reported since the first appearance of the Kinsey reports and the radical changes that have taken place in sex education of children in the home and school. The result has been less frigidity and better sexual adjustments to marriage. (Frigidity will be discussed later.) At first glance, this may seem contradictory in face of the alarming rise in divorce in the years since the First World War, accelerated after the Second. There is evidence today that divorce is usually due to maladjustments *other than sex*. (Divorce will be discussed later in relation to early marriages.) Marital unhappiness stems more from sex-role maladjustments than from sexual maladjustments. This problem, likewise, will be discussed later.

One of the most important effects of improved attitudes toward sex as a biological function is on excessive modesty. The mid-Victorian belief that a "lady" was excessively modest and that girls who deviated from the prevailing standards were not nice has been replaced by a more wholesome attitude toward modesty. Many things which, in the past, were regarded as indications of immodesty are, today, accepted in a matter-of-fact way (184). No longer, for example, does an adolescent girl experience a trauma when she is subjected to a physical examination by a doctor, especially a male doctor, nor does she blush when she mentions her menstrual period to her intimate friends. Changes in attitudes toward immodesty are shown in Figure 13–4.

pattern of approved heterosexual behavior

In the development of heterosexual behavior, adolescents pass through phases or stages that are fairly definite and predictable. Today there is a tendency for parents to put pressure on adolescents to pass through these stages rapidly and to reach adult heterosexuality at an earlier age than was true in the past. Because each stage offers the adolescent learning opportunities that prepare him for the following stage, telescoping the stages deprives him of the

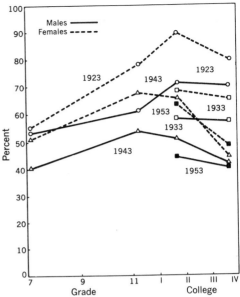

FIGURE 13–4 Changes in attitudes toward immodesty as "wrong" have been marked in recent years. (Adapted from S. L. Pressey and A. W. Jones: 1923–1953 and 20–60 age changes in moral codes, anxieties, and interests, as shown by the "X-O Tests." *J. Psychol.*, 1955, **39**, 485–502. Used by permission.)

learning opportunities he needs. The result is that he is ill prepared to cope with the problems the next stage gives rise to.

Because the adolescent in the American culture of today has had little experience in heterosexual relationships, he has much to learn about the approved patterns of behavior. Even with the best possible guidance and help, the transition is never easy. As Strang has pointed out, "Like the course of true love, interest in heterosexual relations does not run smooth" (214).

The pattern of heterosexual relationships with the characteristic behavior at each age level is illustrated in Figure 13–5. Note the gradual transition to more mature forms of behavior and the fact that, when boys and girls reach adolescence, they must literally learn altogether new patterns of heterosexual behavior. The different phases through which boys and girls pass in the development of approved heterosexual behavior, are discussed below.

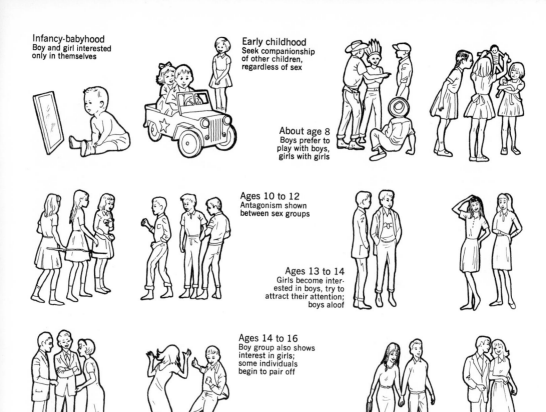

Infancy-babyhood
Boy and girl interested
only in themselves

Early childhood
Seek companionship
of other children,
regardless of sex

About age 8
Boys prefer to
play with boys,
girls with girls

Ages 10 to 12
Antagonism shown
between sex groups

Ages 13 to 14
Girls become inter-
ested in boys, try to
attract their attention;
boys aloof

Ages 14 to 16
Boy group also shows
interest in girls;
some individuals
begin to pair off

Ages 16 to 17 on
"Going out in couples"
becomes general

FIGURE 13–5 The seven stages in boy-girl relationships. (Adapted from A. Scheinfeld: *The
new you and heredity*. Philadelphia: Lippincott,
1961. Used by permission.)

CRUSHES AND HERO WORSHIP

In the transition from sex aversion to falling in love with a member of the opposite
sex, it is quite usual for the young adolescent to develop a strong emotional attachment for an older individual of the same or
of the opposite sex. When the attachment
is directed toward a member of the same
sex who is known to the individual or with
whom he has personal contacts, it is usually
referred to as a "crush." A strong emotional
attachment for an older member of the
same or of his opposite sex, whom the adolescent admires from afar, is called "hero
worship."

Crushes   A crush is a "species of ab-
sorbing affection which involves jealousies

and demands the exclusive response of the
object to which it becomes attached" (107).
The usual time for crushes is during the sex-
aversion phase. This generally falls between
the ages of 12 and 15 years. At this time
there is a need for some outlet for affection.
Because adolescents feel too old to show
affection for parents or other relatives, they
seek new sources of attachment outside of
the home.

   The object of a crush is frequently a
teacher or an older schoolmate who has
won distinction in scholastic or extracurricular activities. The basis for attraction is
some quality or ability that the adolescent
admires but that he lacks. The person on
whom a boy has a crush thus serves as a
source of "projection of the boy's ideal because he possesses a few traits the boy admires greatly. He therefore puts him on a
pedestal and invests him with a halo" (73).

   Because girls develop sexually sooner

than boys and thus have an earlier need for some outlet for the expression of the newly developed sex drive, girls have more crushes than do boys. Their crushes are likely to last until the boys catch up to them in physical development and are interested in heterosexual relationships. It is also possible that boys will not admit they have crushes because they think it silly (41,73,79). The frequency of crushes varies according to whether or not it is the expected thing to do. The more isolated girls are from contacts with members of the opposite sex, the more likelihood there is that the fad of having crushes will develop (109,195).

Even when having a crush is not the thing to do, there are certain adolescents who compensate for feelings of inadequacy by identifying themselves with a love object. The young adolescent needs an older guide to inspire and lead him. When the crushee shows a personal interest in the adolescent, he feels understood, safe, and secure. This in turn leads him to respond with love and affection. The crush for many a young adolescent unquestionably fills a real need (73, 76,79).

Crushes are intense and all-absorbing while they last, but they are quickly forgotten when interest in members of the other sex is aroused. Generally a crush will last from 1 to 6 months, and may be replaced by another crush of equally short duration. Both girls and boys may continue to have crushes up to the age of 16 years, but with decreasing frequency and intensity as they reach the middle of adolescence (76,79,109).

crush behavior Crush behavior has certain characteristics that are similar to those of romantic love. The adolescent wants to be in the presence of the loved one constantly and is unhappy when the loved one is out of sight. Feelings toward the loved ones are openly shown by the writing of notes and the giving of presents to the loved ones; by making personal sacrifices; by using excessive terms of endearment; by imitating the clothes, speech, mannerisms, and activities of the beloved; and by encouraging others to tease the crushee about his or her

crush. Sometimes the adolescent's vocational choice is markedly influenced by the vocation of the individual on whom he has a crush.

evaluation of crushes Family friction is often created when the adolescent fixes his affection on someone outside the home and talks constantly about that person's good qualities, while making hypercritical remarks about the parents and other family members. A girl who has a crush on a teacher, for example, lauds the teacher to the sky but depreciates or belittles the mother's qualities and shows little interest in or love for the mother (189). Much the same is true when a boy idolizes an athletic coach or camp counselor, while belittling his father's business success as of minor importance as compared with the athletic success of his coach or counselor (76,79).

Crushes have been found to offer no barrier to successful heterosexual attachments, even when they persist up to 16 years of age. There is no evidence that, for the normal, well-adjusted adolescent boy or girl, crushes will lead to homosexual behavior. Only when they persist into late maturity, and are *preferred* to other types of sex behavior, may they be regarded as abnormal (71,79,122,123).

Having a crush helps the young adolescent in two processes which are going on at this time: (1) the gaining of independence, and (2) the formation of his identity by deciding what sort of person he is or wants to be. Too much influence by parents may cause the young adolescent to lose his identity and to follow the pattern they have set for him. Or it may cause him to "burst out in unhappy rebellion," doing just the opposite of what they want him to do. The influence of someone outside the home, on the other hand, prevents this from taking place. In discussing the value of having a crush, Gallagher (76) has pointed out:

Many—perhaps most—adolescent boys and girls, though they are perfectly normal and are not being overwhelmed by the changes in their emotions which are part of growing up, would benefit considerably in their emo-

tional development were they to have feelings of admiration and respect for some stable adult outside their family circle. They need such a person because they are uncertain and lack confidence in themselves. At this time the confidence of this person, to whom they have not had close ties, can give, will enable them to achieve greater independence more smoothly and gain the knowledge of where they are going that we wish for them.

Hero Worship Hero worship differs from a crush in that the affection is directed toward a person the adolescent does not come in personal contact with or whom he knows only slightly. The young adolescent is typically a hero-worshiper; he needs someone he can look up to, admire, imitate, and follow. As G. Stanley Hall pointed out many years ago, "Every youth is always profoundly influenced by someone a little older, and is more or less plastic to his or her will" (84). Hero worship is more common in boys, just as crushes are more common among girls.

Hero worship does not begin in adolescence, but is more common and has a more profound influence on the individual's life then. Children usually hero-worship a member of the family—a parent, an older sibling, or a relative. The 11- to 12-year-old wants to be like persons with certain roles, such as athletes, movie and TV stars, or national heroes, rather than like family members (88,232). Today moving-picture and TV stars are the most common objects of adolescent hero worship.

hero-worship behavior The characteristic behavior of the hero-worshiper consists of admiring and adoring the loved one from afar. The adolescent watches attentively and approvingly every movement made by the adored one; he hangs breathlessly on his every word; he makes a point of collecting information about the activities and interests of the object of his adoration; he attempts to imitate the clothes, mannerisms, and behavior of the loved one and to act in a manner that he believes the loved one

would approve; he assumes a sophisticated grown-up appearance and manner to avoid having the loved one regard him as a "kid" (41,71,79).

evaluation of hero worship Hero worship may encourage the adolescent to strive for success; it helps him to formulate values and set goals to guide his life; it furnishes the motives to transform desires into action; it lifts him up when his spirit bogs; it bolsters his vascillating conduct and thus makes for steadiness and consistency of aim (73). Equally as important, hero worship is an attempt by a younger person to grasp a concrete picture of the personality he dreams of for himself.

For many young adolescents who are unsure of themselves and who suffer from feelings of inadequacy, hero worship serves as a form of identification. As Cole and Hall (41) have pointed out, the girl who engages in hero worship of those more successful than she:

gives admiration so thoroughly that the successes of others become hers just as truly as if she had had a hand in them. In this manner, she avoids failure and tension and escapes even comparisons with others, while she finds happiness and freedom from what could easily have become a chronic sense of her own inadequacy or inferiority.

If, however, the adolescent's heroes are ill-chosen, and if the ideals are not the right type for him to copy, the effects of hero worship will be harmful. Furthermore, it is likely to establish ideals of conduct that, when applied to the adolescent's peers, will show them up to be crude, callow, and unsophisticated. This often leads to a hypercritical attitude toward the person the adolescent is dating and to attempts to bring about reforms to make that person conform more closely to his ideal. Many budding romances are broken as a result.

PUPPY LOVE

Hero worship gives way to "puppy love," in which the adolescent transfers his affection to persons of approximately his own age.

As interest in this new type of love object increases, interest in older individuals wanes. This phase of heterosexual development is frequently referred to as the puppy-love stage, because the behavior characteristic of this phase is awkward, playful, and reminiscent of young puppies. What to an adult appears to be silly is, in reality, an attempt on the adolescent's part to adjust himself to new situations (41,214).

In the case of girls, interest in boys may be seen as early as 13 and 14 years of age, while among boys, interest in girls is not common before 15 or 16 years. Boys *seem* to be absorbed in sports, radio, and other activities with boys. On the surface, boys before 15 or 16 retain much of their childhood antagonism to girls (47,79).

Puppy love is complicated for girls by the fact that they attain sexual maturity earlier than boys. They therefore find the boys of their own age callow, unsophisticated, and completely uninterested in heterosexual relationships. As a result they seek out the more mature boys of their own age or boys who are slightly older than they. They are interested in boys in general, not in any one boy in particular. Any boy who shows the slightest interest in them will be their target. After a few months or a year, girls become more discriminating and more selective (118,169).

Adjustment Problems   The puppy-love stage presents many adjustment problems for the young adolescent girl and many more for the boy. Even though the first heterosexual experiences with real people on an *equal* footing are new and exciting, they are frequently terrifying also. The young adolescents do not know just what to say or do. Whatever they do, they are apt to do clumsily. Even with members of the opposite sex whom they have known from early childhood days, they are apt to be ill at ease.

Other adjustment problems that cause feelings of insecurity on the adolescent's part are the emphasis placed on manners, which during childhood assumed a very minor role; the development of new social skills, such as dancing; the acquisition of new conversational topics and new techniques of presentation that will prove to be interesting to members of the opposite sex; uncertainty about socially approved behavior with members of the opposite sex; and, finally, new knowledge about sex matters as they pertain to members of the opposite sex (9,47,79,85,159,214).

Characteristic Behavior   Typically, puppy love takes the form of wise-cracking or mental fencing, teasing, roughhousing, and hauling each other about. These are backhanded ways of showing mutual interest, resorted to most frequently if observers are present. In place of the shy behavior characteristic of crushes and hero worship, the behavior of the adolescent who has reached the girl-crazy, boy-crazy stage is bold and aggressive. This is a compensation for feelings of insecurity; it serves to cover up embarrassment and self-consciousness.

Both boys and girls at this age are anxious to attract the attention of the other sex. Owing to their ignorance of social conventions, the methods they use are frequently silly, crude, and in bad taste. They wear loud-colored, extreme styles of clothing. The girls make themselves conspicuous by adopting eccentric styles of hairdress and by using too much makeup.

Girls on the whole are sillier and more aggressive than boys at this stage, owing to their earlier sex maturing. When they discover that boys of their own age show little or no interest in them, they try to arouse their interest by aggressive, show-off behavior, which is frequently extreme. Should this not produce the desired results, girls then turn their attention to older boys.

At this age boys and girls go around in crowds in which the different members pair off. It gives the adolescent a feeling of security to be with others and to realize that he has friends to fall back on in case of a social emergency. Both boys and girls are frank and unashamed of their interest in members of the opposite sex. They do not hesitate to hold hands or to engage in a certain amount of petting in the presence of the other members of the crowd (47,79, 85,159,202,214).

Evaluation of Puppy Love Puppy love is very time-, energy-, and attention-consuming. For a short time the adolescent is so engrossed in his romance that his *school-work suffers*. Characteristically, early concentration of affection on a member of the opposite sex of the same age is short-lived. Constant shifting of affection from one individual of the opposite sex to another so distracts the adolescent's attention that schoolwork and home responsibilities are neglected. This neglect of responsibilities, in turn, leads to parental criticism and *strained parent-child relationships*.

Through short-lived intense affairs and through conversations with others, adolescents learn how to *appraise members of the opposite sex*. After a few affairs that end disastrously, both boys and girls discover what qualities they like in members of the opposite sex and how to look for these qualities. The result is that they become more selective.

Boys and girls learn *social skills* that they had no need for when their relationships were limited to members of their own sex. They learn to dance well, to carry on a lively, interesting conversation, and to be a passable player in the different sports favored by the crowd.

Puppy-love affairs enable young adolescents to learn what is *socially acceptable in their group*. They then have a better pattern to follow and are able to model their own behavior in accordance with this pattern. Finally, early experiences with peers of the opposite sex build up feelings of *self-confidence and security*. If all goes well and the adolescents find that they are reasonably popular, self-confidence is established. As this occurs, much of the crudeness that characterized early behavior disappears and is replaced by a more restrained, more mature form of behavior.

DATING

"Dating" is not a colloquialism for the "courtship" of past generations because its main purpose is to provide a pleasant social experience for a boy and a girl with no commitment beyond that expectation. Unlike in courtship, the serious purpose of marriage is not involved. Thus, dating is *an end in itself*. It not only serves the function of giving the adolescent pleasurable social experiences, but it lays the foundations for a wise, intelligent, and objective choice of a mate (149,164).

Dating differs from courtship in other respects also. Chaperonage is no longer considered necessary, as it was in the past, and the young couple is thus free from the ever-present guardian of the girl's "name." While the *role* played by members of each sex in courtship was prescribed by tradition, with dating beginning earlier than courtship did in past generations, the roles of the sexes are changing radically. Girls are, today, playing a more aggressive role; boys play a more defensive role. This not only affects dating but it also is responsible, in part, for going steady, pinning, short engagements, and early marriages (135,140,164,170).

Unquestionably one of the most pronounced differences between dating and courtship centers around the approved *activities* of the relationships. Courtship was carried out mainly in the home; in some public place of entertainment, such as theaters, concerts, and dance halls; or at parties in the school, in the college, at a club, or at the home of a friend. Dating, by contrast, is usually away from home, more often in cars or at public places of entertainment—such as dance halls, juke joints, or athletic contests.

There are marked changes in social sanctions regarding what young people can do on dates as well as where they can go. The favorite activities for dates are dancing; going to the movies; engaging in some athletic activity, such as swimming, bowling, or tennis; riding in cars; attending school or college parties and athletic contests; stopping off at a teen-age hangout for something to eat or drink; petting; necking; and drinking. Boys of today expect a certain amount of petting to accompany their dating; this was impossible in the days when courtship took place under the watchful eye of a chaperone (117,135,142,159,164,202, 217,218).

Age of Dating Shortly after the First World War, the median age for beginning to date was 16 years. Today, it is 14 years, though many boys and girls have their first dates several years before that (23,203). Furthermore, early dating in the past was limited mainly to adolescents of working-class families; today, it is even more prevalent in middle- and upper-class families (193). By the time boys and girls reach the sophomore year in high school, the majority have not only had their first dates but many are dating regularly (7,33,36,150,186).

Early dating occurs mainly because of parental pressures and peer-group expectations. Mothers are more likely to put pressure on their daughters than on their sons to date early. It is not unusual, in some communities, for mothers to give parties for 10- and 11-year-olds to which "couples only" are invited (90). Even fathers take pride in the social successes of their preteen daughters. They encourage them to date as soon as they can find a boy who will accept their invitations to go to a party with them when transported in father's car with father at the wheel (217).

Peer pressures are equally as strong as parental pressures. It is the "thing to do" and "everyone dates." Furthermore, as social life in adolescence is organized around pairing, an adolescent who does not date is left out of most of the social activities of the peer group and is considered a "square." A girl who does not start to date early is even more seriously handicapped socially than a boy (33,41,45,91,150,217).

By the time boys and girls are 16 years old, they show a social sophistication and maturity in dating behavior equal or superior to that of 18-year-olds several decades ago (15,117,142). Because of greater social sophistication at an earlier age, adolescent dating today is following a different pattern from that in the past. This results in going steady at an earlier age, earlier engagements and marriages, and earlier indulgence in

petting, necking, and premarital intercourse (7,48,57,142,202).

Dating Patterns Dating begins as a part of clique behavior. Girls of a clique combine with a boys' clique and go out together on double or triple dates. The first dates are usually to a movie, a party, or some athletic contest. Early dates are mainly with members of the same school class. By the tenth or eleventh grade, only about half of the dates are with individuals of the same class at school. Boys tend to date girls in classes below them; girls, on the other hand, date boys who are ahead of them in school or who have finished school (23,45,164).

Early dates are likewise with members of the same clique. If the adolescent dated is from another clique, he must be approved by the members of the clique in which he is being included. There is less restraint on the dating patterns as the cliques break up. As a result, there is more crossing of social and economic class lines in dating than there was earlier. Boys more often than girls cross class lines and date girls of a lower socioeconomic status. By contrast, when girls cross class lines, it is usually to date a boy of a higher socioeconomic status. This crossing of class lines, however, usually does not occur until single dating begins. Then it is more characteristic of both boys and girls of the middle-class groups than those of the lower or upper (7,61,62,106, 142,154). Figure 13–6 shows the characteristic pattern of dating today.

Variations in Dating As a general rule, *older* adolescents date more than younger and their activities are less supervised (135, 151). In the early part of adolescence, *girls* date more than boys. This is especially true in the junior and senior years of high school when girls date older boys in college and at work as well as boys in their classes at school. The reason is that girls are less seriously concerned about their academic work than boys are (15,22,106,202).

Adolescents who are *popular* get more satisfaction from dating and give their dating partners more satisfaction than those

| Double or triple dates | Single dates | Going steady |

FIGURE 13–6 Dating usually follows a predictable pattern.

who are less popular. *Empathy*—the ability to put oneself in the psychological shoes of another—adds to the adolescent's popularity and the satisfaction he derives from his dating experiences. As a result, the better the adolescent is able to experience empathy, the more dating he is likely to do (7,202, 210,220).

The adolescent who wants to *marry* early and have children begins to date sooner and dates more frequently than the adolescent who is more interested in a career. An adolescent who has a strong *career drive* will not only date less than one whose career drive is weaker but he will date more different girls and start to go steady later than the adolescent who is less interested in preparing himself for a career (58,140,151,192,228). Figure 13–7 shows the ages at which interest in love, courtship, and marriage are especially strong and serious for boys and girls. Note the marked sex differences.

Fathers, as was pointed out earlier, tend to resist their children's dating more than mothers, especially in the case of sons (8). On the other hand, mothers encourage their daughters to start to date early. *Mothers* are anxious to have their daughters

marry young, but they discourage early marriages for their sons (8,41,106,217). Foreign-born parents are stricter about ages of dating and the amount of dating their sons and daughters do than are American-born parents (59,152,233).

When the family's *socioeconomic status* is favorable, both boys and girls begin to date earlier and more frequently than when the family status is less favorable. However, the former have fewer steady dates because they expect to go to college and marry later. Adolescents of the lower socioeconomic groups generally date more with people outside of school than with their classmates; the reverse is true of adolescents of the middle and upper socioeconomic groups (16,22,98,228). Adolescents in *cities* start to date earlier and date more than those in rural districts. This pattern is not determined by socioeconomic status as much as by ease of contact with other young people (206).

The *religious background* of the family influences the age of dating, the amount of dating, and the pattern of dating of adolescents, especially girls. Adolescents of the Jewish faith start dating earlier than those of other faiths, they play the field more

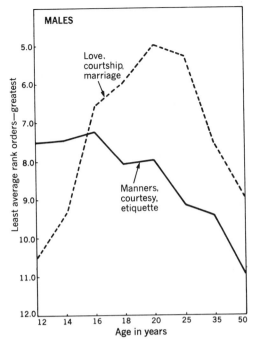

FIGURE 13–7 Ages at which interest in love, courtship, marriage, and etiquette are especially strong and serious. (Adapted from unpublished data of P. M. Symonds in F. K. Shuttleworth: The adolescent period: a graphic atlas. *Monogr. Soc. Res. Child Develpm.*, 1949, **14**, no. 1. Used by permission.)

extensively, and they begin to go steady at an earlier age. Adolescents of the different Protestant faiths, by contrast, start dating later and date less frequently at first than do Jewish adolescents. However, among the Protestants there is a shorter lag between beginning to date and going steady. The latest dating and going steady occur among Catholic adolescents. However, Catholics of Italian and Puerto Rican ancestry have been found to be more promiscuous in their dating activities than Protestant or Jewish adolescents or Catholic adolescents of other ancestry (11).

Adolescents from *happy homes* start dating earlier and are more active in dating than are those from unhappy homes. Poor family relationships result in poorer relationships with members of the opposite sex. This is especially true for girls. Some adolescents from unhappy homes reject their parents and try to find a substitute source of satisfaction through dating. When, on the other hand, the parents' marriage is happy, it not only establishes a more favorable pattern of love and marriage for the adolescent to imitate but it also affects

the degree of emotional weaning of the adolescent from his parents (58,138,228).

The relationship of the adolescent with the *parent of the same sex* is a more important factor in dating than the relationship with the parent of the opposite sex; it influences boys' dating more than girls'. If a son loves his father and is submissive to his mother, he will be encouraged in his dating behavior. Should the mother disapprove of his dating, he is likely to regard her as domineering and rebel, thus dating more than she would like (58,138, 228).

If the adolescent feels a strong *obligation to his parents*, either financially or emotionally, he is likely to date less than he otherwise would. When the father is missing from the home, because of divorce or death, both boys and girls begin to date earlier, go steady earlier, and become engaged earlier; they are also more often involved in broken engagements than adolescents whose parents are both in the home. Broken engagements are often due to haste in trying to find the father substitute (3).

Boys and girls who have an attractive *appearance* and are dressed well date earlier and more than those who are less attractive. This is more true for girls than for boys (41,91). The adolescent who worries about his physical appearance, who is less sex appropriate or less mature than his age-mates, or who feels that he is less attractive looking than they, becomes shy, sensitive, and timid; this affects his dating unfavorably (79,117). The *emotional maturity* of the adolescent influences the type of affection he is capable of experiencing. If he is emotionally immature, he will have many infatuations which will result in frequent dating accompanied by much petting and necking. However, he will shift from one dating partner to another more often than the more mature adolescent whose affections for the dating partner are more stable (10,67,68). Emotionally mature adolescents tend to be more popular than immature ones; this contributes to their dating frequency (41,62,79).

Evaluation of Dating Critics of dating point out the following arguments as the basis for their objections: that boys and girls "waste" valuable time that might better be spent on their studies and preparation for adult life; that their academic work suffers and this affects their future vocational opportunities; that boys and girls become so preoccupied with looks, pleasure seeking, and other activities that they neglect their home, community, and other responsibilities; that dating encourages the development of a highly competitive spirit which militates against good social adjustments, especially in the case of girls; that adolescents are too young and inexperienced to be able to cope with the mature relationships involved in dating without the danger of getting into trouble in these days when chaperonage is a thing of the past; that dating is an expensive form of amusement which few adolescents or their parents can

afford and this encourages adolescents to drop out of school or college before completing their studies; and that dating breaks down family solidarity because adolescents who date have little time to devote to activities with their families (40,90,91,117, 164,212). The effect of dating on family recreations is shown in Figure 13–8.

Whether dating is a *good preparation for marriage*, as most adolescents believe it to be, has been questioned by some. The contention is that dating is a competitive form of association between the sexes in the "period of dalliance" between puberty and marriage (48,57). It is largely dominated by a quest for thrills and excitement in which each tries to deceive the other by pretense of love and devotion. While it unquestionably provides thrills and fun, the exploitative element of dating is likely to be harmful and the capacity to love is permanently injured (62,164,230). Mead emphasizes that dating can be a barrier to happiness in marriage because the girl must learn to protect herself against the boy's sexual advances. This affects her attitude toward the male sex, which, in turn, affects her later adjustment to marriage (159).

The critics of dating are especially vocal in their arguments against *early* dating. Strang (214) has listed a number of reasons why dating is undesirable for boys and girls in the sixth and seventh grades—ages which are even today considered early for dating. According to Strang, the major arguments are:

1 *Youngsters of this age are already faced with all the problems of adjustment which they can handle.*
2 *The difference in maturity between boys and girls of this age is especially wide.*
3 *The initiative for early dating seems to come chiefly from a few socially aggressive girls and from adults who think it is "cute"; most of the children of this age do not have the "emotional readiness" for it.*
4 *Many children of this age prefer other activities such as games, taffy pulls, square dancing, eating, talking together.*

Other critics of early dating argue that

starting to date before socially or emotionally ready leads to early marriage or premarital pregnancies, that it causes adolescents to be bored and jaded with activities suitable for their ages because they have been engaging in them for so long, and that it encourages girls to develop an aggressive attitude in heterosexual relationships which will prove to be a serious handicap to good adjustment as they grow older (22,33,90, 217). On the other hand, Lowrie maintains that early daters delay going steady for a longer time than those who start to date later; this gives them more experience in relationships with members of the opposite sex before going steady. Late daters, he maintains, often rush into going steady too soon; they experience greater emotional involvement; and they often marry with too little experience to select a mate wisely (152).

In spite of these criticisms, there are many advantages to dating: these, on the whole, outweigh the disadvantages. Of the many advantages, the following are the ones most often given (38,41,45,91,123,138,159, 215):

1 Dating gives the adolescent experience in evaluating different personality types and behavior patterns of members of the opposite sex.
2 Dating tempers the highly romantic and unrealistic ideas of love and of members of the opposite sex.
3 Dating gives experience in adjusting to others in different types of situations.
4 Dating offers opportunities for broader experiences and experiences that would be imposible with members of the same sex.
5 Dating helps to develop poise, self-confidence, and emotional balance.
6 Dating reduces emotional excitement on meeting and associating with a member of the opposite sex.
7 Dating is a means of having a good time socially.
8 Dating gives a kind of sexual release and reduces sexual tension.
9 Dating provides a wider acquaintance from which a mate may eventually be selected.

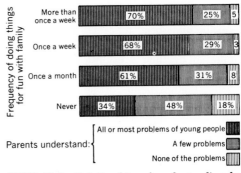

FIGURE 13–8 Relationship of understanding by parents of young people's problems and the frequency of the adolescent's doing things for fun and entertainment with the family. (Adapted from C. L. Stone: Family recreation: a parental dilemma. *Family Life Coordinator*, 1963, **12**, 85–87. Used by permission.)

10 Dating defines the roles of members of the two sexes and the relationship between the two sexes.
11 Dating helps boys and girls to control their own behavior, choose their own friends, and build up concepts of right and wrong in this area of behavior without adult help or supervision.
12 Dating gives the adolescent recognition and prestige in his own group. In this way, it helps to establish the status of the individual in his group.

Nondaters In spite of the advantages dating gives, a number of adolescents do not date or they date only infrequently. This is more true of boys than girls (33). There are a number of reasons why boys and girls do not date. They may be so absorbed in some activity, such as sports or studies, that they have little or no time for social life. Through their own chosen activities, they gain the recognition from the group whose esteem they value highly. They feel that the social life of their peers is trivial and irrelevant to their interests. Or, they may be so physically immature that they feel disqualified for the dating game, in which physical readiness for sex is expected. They may lack the clothes and money needed to date. The personality patterns of adolescents who do not date are those of shyness, slight maladjustment emotionally, and social reticence. As success in dating depends upon accepting the roles approved by their peers, those adolescents who disapprove of dancing, card-playing, kissing, holding hands, or moderate necking are outside the peer culture and find themselves with few dates (41,45,48,57,159, 186).

Nondaters are at a disadvantage in the American culture of today. Because the social life of adolescence is organized about paired groups, adolescents must pair in order to participate. Those who do not date in their high school days lack the experiences that come from dating. They are thus deprived of learning how to behave in social situations with members of the opposite sex. By late adolescence, when they go to college or to work, they feel inadequate to meet the demands of a near-adult social life. As a result, they feel frustrated and turn to more introverted forms of recreation. They often doubt their normality and often gain the reputation of being "squares." Self-doubts and an unfavorable reputation can and often do play havoc with their future personal and social adjustments (15,42,142, 186,202).

GOING STEADY

After a period of "playing the field," the boy selects one girl whose attractions for him are greater than those of other girls with whom he associates. Gradually, he spends more and more time with her, and his dates with other girls are reduced to a minimum. Then he is expected to have dates with no other girls, and the girl of his choice, in turn, is expected to refrain from having dates with other boys. It soon becomes known in the peer group that the young couple is going steady and the girl is known as the boy's "girl" while the boy becomes identified as the girl's "boy friend." This means "hands off" for everyone else (95,194,201).

A small number of boys and girls begin to go steady as early as junior high school. The number increases with each grade in high school. However, even by senior year, going steady is far from universal. Studies have revealed that by junior or senior year, 20 to 30 percent of the girls have never gone steady and that 30 to 40 percent of the boys are still playing the field or are dating only infrequently (7,33,42,142,182,202, 225).

By the time the adolescent has finished high school and gone to work or to college, steady dating becomes increasingly more frequent. Some adolescents go steady only once; others, two, three, or more times. Some steady dating arrangements last for only a few months; others last for a year or more. Sometimes going steady leads to marriage; often it does not. As a general rule, going steady is more likely to last longer and to lead to marriage in late adolescence than in early adolescence (33,95,160,182).

Even though girls as a whole begin to date earlier than boys, they begin to go steady at about the same age as boys. The reason for this is that parental restrictions on girls are greater than on boys (150). Adolescents who begin to date later than the average age tend to go steady sooner than the early daters. The result is that they start to go steady at about the same age as those who started their dating careers earlier (152). In the past, going steady at an early age was found mainly among adolescents from working-class families; today, it is common among adolescents of all classes (182,193). In large cities, going steady generally comes later than in small towns or rural areas where the number of eligible boys is more limited than in the cities (106,146,206). Adolescents who are emotionally maladjusted find it difficult to remain interested in one person for any length of time. As a result, they have one steady after another. Better-adjusted adolescents, by contrast, start to go steady later and go steady with the same person for a longer time (174).

Factors Influencing Going Steady A number of factors encourage adolescents to go steady and a number discourage it. Those which *encourage* going steady are: "everyone does it" or it is "the thing to do"; the boy and girl believe that they are in love and that dating others is meaningless when they prefer each other's company; it is a social asset in that it is a symbol of status, it gives adolescents prestige in the eyes of their peers, and it assures participation in the peer social life; it serves as a form of protection for adolescents who enjoy only marginal popularity, by providing them with a partner for different social activities (45, 159,169,182).

In early going steady, there is little evidence that the thought of marriage plays an important role. Instead, the reasons for going steady are almost entirely social. Later, going steady is more serious; many adolescents, especially girls, regard it as a preliminary step to marriage. This has a marked influence on the type of boy they are willing to go steady with. So long as going steady is for social reasons, the personal attractiveness of the individual selected is of paramount importance. Later, when going steady is regarded as a serious step toward marriage, girls become more choosy about the boys they allow themselves to fall in love with (45,64,95,160). This is less true of boys for reasons that will be discussed in more detail later.

Many adolescents *do not go steady* for a number of reasons. Of these, the most important are lack of opportunity due to other responsibilities, unpopularity with members of the opposite sex, parental disapproval and home restrictions on dating activities, and choice. Adolescents who are career-oriented feel that they have too little time for dating or they do not want to become involved in a situation that may jeopardize their plans for the future. Popular adolescents may choose not to go steady in preference to playing the field. If they are extremely popular, they have dating security without a steady (15,42,186,202). This suggests that the steady dater is often "drawn from the middle social group: those who rate high enough on the dating scale to be desirable as a steady but not so high that dating security is no problem" (182). As Poffenberger (182) has suggested, from a survey of reasons adolescents of high school age give for and against going steady:

There are enough limiting factors in the "going steady" *relationship to make it unlikely that this form of dating behavior will ever involve a majority of high school students at any one time.*

Advantages and Disadvantages of Going Steady

Girls feel that going steady is more important than do boys because of the "feeling of approbation which the steady attention of one boy gives them" (14). In one study, the advantages and disadvantages of going steady given by boys and girls were as follows (235):

ADVANTAGES

Gives security (dates assured).
Gives more likelihood of having nice dates.
Don't have to sit at home.
Makes the girl feel more popular.
Gives a chance to know each other well.
May help to determine whether you want to make it a still longer period.
Costs less money.
May make family feel more secure because they know this boy or girl.

DISADVANTAGES

It is easier to get started than to stop.
Boys may have to work; so girl has to stay home.
Makes it hard to make up your mind to a change.
May shut you off from other friends.
May cause unpleasant arguments in the family.
Family may think it too serious.
Family may want you to go with their choice. This produces discord.
One may be more serious than the other and he or she may want to carry on too long.
May not leave you free to make new friends in college or in work.
One person may not satisfy all needs.
Costs more money.
It is hard to get in circulation again after you stop going steady. This is especially true for girls.

Many adolescents find that steady dating presents problems that are difficult for them to cope with. They often find it difficult to adjust to the expectations and intimate associations that are inevitable parts of the pattern of going steady. Also, because of the desire for security in their social lives, they frequently find it difficult to dissolve a relationship that has guaranteed them social security. Furthermore, it is difficult for them to explain to their peers why they have broken off their relationships, especially when it is expected that one go steady to have status in the group (42,45, 95,186,202).

Of even greater seriousness is the fact that going steady often forces an adolescent into a marriage he does not want or which he is not ready for either emotionally or economically. This is primarily the result of the type of activity that characterizes going steady. When boys and girls go steady, it is customary for the boy to spend much time in the girl's home, coming regularly for meals and joining her family for many of the holiday celebrations. The girl goes to the boy's home for meals or family celebrations and is treated as a potential daughter-in-law. The families soon take it for granted that the young people will be married, as do relatives and friends of the family (31). It takes more social sophistication than most adolescents have to cope with the embarrassment and explanations that would result should they wish to break off.

Going steady gives license to adolescents to engage in sexual behavior of an advanced type. As Ehrmann (62) has pointed out:

> Going steady added respectability to petting and for some even sexual intercourse. Many made it quite clear that they engaged in extensive physical lovemaking activities "only with a steady, not just with any boy that came along."

Because adolescents who go steady have dates almost every evening of the week, it is inevitable that extensive physical lovemaking would play an important role in their evening activities. Should this lead to premarital pregnancy, many adolescents are forced into a marriage they had not planned, or had not planned so soon (14,95,128,182, 202).

Attitudes toward Going Steady   While members of the *peer* group often put pressures on their friends to go steady and regard them as "squares" if they do not follow the prevailing pattern of dating, there are even today some adolescents who regard those who go steady as "sappy" or "dopey." They accuse them of being "roped in" by a girl and her mother. This, of course, is much more true of boys than of girls, who regard going steady as "romantic" and look upon it as a prestige symbol of social success (41,91,106). By late adolescence, relatively few members of the peer group have an unfavorable attitude toward their age-mates who are going steady (14,42,186, 202).

Parental attitudes are far more likely to be unfavorable than favorable. A few parents, mainly mothers, may regard early going steady as "cute." Or they may feel that it is a feather in the maternal cap to have a daughter so attractive and socially precocious that a boy would want to go steady with her. Most mothers, however, are more concerned than pleased when their children start to go steady during the high school years (90,217,218). They interfere and, whenever possible, break up the attachment (126,127,166,179,182).

Because going steady often does lead to marriage eventually, parents are especially concerned about the individual with whom their child is going steady. Should the adolescents cross class lines, the concern is intensified. As West has pointed out, "Parents are very careful, regarding their children, of the 'company they keep.' Class lines may not be crossed in approved dating, courtship, or marriage" (224).

End of Going Steady   A majority of young adolescents, and even those in college, find that the individuals they go steady with do not measure up satisfactorily. As a result, there are conflicts over becoming too involved, friction, and tension. A quarrel or loss of interest on the part of one or both leads to the end of the romance. While going steady has proved to be a good security measure for the young adolescent when he or she first starts dating, many prefer to play the field, once they feel more comfortable with members of the opposite sex. They find it more fun to date different people. Hence, it is usually a relief to end a relationship that has lost its appeal (59, 106,164,182).

Some romances end less happily; there may be an abrupt and highly emotionalized ending. How many breakups the adolescent will experience before he finds the right person to be his life mate varies. On the whole, it has been reported that girls have from two to five romances with boys with whom they have gone steady for varying lengths of time before they find the one they want to marry; boys, on the average, have fewer broken romances (45,95,145).

Following the break, there is usually a period of readjustment. It means that the girl must get back into circulation again, a more difficult task for her than for a boy. For most, there is little readjustment. Others may take several weeks or even several months to readjust themselves; very few take a year. In a short time, the cycle begins again; dating, going steady, and breaking up (38,95).

Not all cases of going steady end in a breakup; some end in marriage. In one study of high school students who were going steady, 40 percent of the boys and slightly over 50 percent of the girls said they were planning to marry their steadies (182). When adolescents go steady with the same individual for a year or more, they are likely to progress to the next stage in the romance pattern—pinning and engagement.

PINNING AND ENGAGEMENT

In the traditional American courtship pattern, going steady with one person for a period of time is followed by a formal announcement of their intention to marry. How this announcement will be made will vary according to the socioeconomic status of the girl's family. If the family is prominent in the community, the announcement will be made on the society page of the local newspaper; if less prominent, in a less

formal way. The groom-to-be traditionally gives the girl an engagement ring which she wears in public for the first time when the engagement is announced. Thus, an engagement is an open declaration of the intention of two people to marry (48,72,141,149, 164,182,228).

In recent years, a preliminary step to the engagement has been introduced into the American culture. This is known as "pinning." It is a method adolescents use of announcing to others that they are thinking seriously of marriage, but it lacks the finality of an engagement. Instead, it corresponds to the "understanding to be married" of past generations. As a token of this understanding, the boy gives the girl his pin—a fraternity, dormitory, or service pin. This is regarded as a temporary gift to be returned if they later decide that they do not want to marry. No public announcement is made by the girl's parents; the only announcement that is made is by the young people themselves. The pin, worn traditionally near the girl's heart, on the left side of her dress, is her way of telling others that she is "engaged to be engaged" (149,164, 194).

The period of pinning is usually longer than that of the engagement. The tendency today is to follow up the formal announcement of the engagement with a wedding in a few weeks or months. During the period of pinning, the young people try to discover if they are really in love and if they want to marry. They use this time to visit in the homes of both, to discuss matters that will affect their marriage, such as economic problems, whether the girl will work after marriage or remain at home, how many children they want and how they will be spaced, and their sexual relationships. These matters, in past generations, were not discussed until after marriage (135,140).

Characteristics of Periods There are three outstanding characteristics of the periods of pinning and engagement which are almost universal in the American culture of today. Unfortunately, each of these characteristics is more likely to be a preparation for disillusionment and unhappiness than for happiness in marriage. These characteristics are described below.

romanticism The tendency to see the loved one and the marital state through rose-tinted glasses is characteristic of love in all cultures. In the American culture this tendency has been heightened by the influence of mass media of communication. This "romantic complex" is so all-pervasive that it characterizes the adolescent's whole outlook on his relationships with the loved one (50). The popular songs "fit neatly into the drama of courtship" and provide the young person with the patterns of behavior as well as the words of love (13,108).

While most girls, when they reach adolescence, outgrow fairy tales, the impact of these wish-fulfilling stories on their attitudes toward love still persists (43). It is further enhanced by the romantic theme in novels and magazine fiction which gives a highly glamorized image of courtship with emphasis on a romantic chance encounter between two young people who fall in love at first sight, who have a short but highly emotional courtship, and then marry and live happily ever after (66). Boys as well as girls are influenced by this romantic complex (58,66,72,186,202).

The amount of romanticism present *differs* at different stages during the courtship pattern. It is usually at its lowest point in the beginning and end, and at its peak during the going-steady and pinning stages. As the adolescent approaches marriage and is faced with the problems marriage brings, some of the romanticism is replaced by realism. This usually occurs when the pinning stage is over and the formal announcement of the engagement is made. Because the period of the engagement is relatively short today, the young people are faced with the serious business of preparing for a home and a life of their own, where responsibilities formerly assumed by parents will now have to be assumed by them (57,102,104, 141).

Girls tend to be more romantic than boys about courtship and marriage; they are not expected to assume the responsi-bilities that marriage brings, as boys are (103). Girls in college or in a professional training school are especially romantic during the later stages of courtship because they are unaware of the practical problems of living; these are all taken care of for them by the people who run the student residences in which they live (104). Because of their greater romanticism, girls are likely to face greater disillusionment and disappointment when they make the transition from engagement to marriage than boys are. As a young bride explained, "It is a big step from the bridal veil to the garbage pail."

Because disillusionment and disappointment are such common accompaniments of marriage—especially marriages during the adolescent years—romanticism makes the transition into adult heterosexual relationships in marriage even more difficult than it otherwise would be. This accounts, in part, for the alarming increase in unhappy marriages and divorces among those who are married early. In discussing the disillusionment that so frequently comes with marriage, especially an early marriage, Hobart (101) has stated:

Such prevalent disillusionment suggests the existence of important unrealism generating influences in the courtship process. The widespread emphasis on romanticism in the American culture—the so-called romantic cult—which appears to be particularly associated with advanced courtship may in effect be preparing engaged couples for inevitable disillusionment in marriage.

role playing There are stereotypes of the "perfect" wife and the "perfect" husband. Through the mass media, adolescent boys and girls become thoroughly familiar with these stereotypes. They then expect the person they marry to conform to them (13,66,108). A boy may not, for example, be like the Nordic stereotype of the perfect lover in looks but, in behavior, he wants to be like Romeo. He writes poetry or romantic love letters to his girl; he composes music or sings to her the most romantic of the popular songs; he brings her gifts and waits on her hand and foot, trying to satisfy her every wish or whim as a page in a court in the Middle Ages would have done. He thus plays the role of the perfect lover. The girl, in turn, plays the role of the perfect housewife, preparing the boy's favorite foods when he comes to her parents' home for a meal, knitting socks or sweaters for him, and purring over every baby she sees on the street or on the screen.

Because the male is supposed to be the more aggressive, the boys poses as a typical male who can dominate any situation, whether it be in the way he speaks to a waiter in a restaurant, to the gas-station attendant, or to the girl he has pinned. He wants her to see him as the "dominant type," the kind of person that the cultural stereotype depicts as the perfect male. She, in turn, poses as the clinging vine of the female cultural stereotype—the nonaggressive person who feels secure only when she has a strong masculine arm to support her.

When courtship has reached the pinning stage, it can easily be upset by disillusionment. And, as there has been no public announcement of the intention to marry, the ending of a pinning relationship is not accompanied by the embarrassment to all that occurs when an engagement is broken. However, once the engagement has been announced and the date for the wedding set, posing as the romantic lover or the ideal wife is no longer as important as it was in the more precarious period of pinning. As a result, role playing decreases. In its place comes the characteristic behavior of the individual, not the behavior of the stereotype (93).

Boys, for example, who have been pampered at home become less thoughtful of their future wives. They expect them to be the "thoughtful ones," as has been true in their parents' home. Similarly, girls who have literally put "their brains in mothballs" during the pinning stage, for fear of losing a boy who does not want a wife who is a "brain," now remove the mothballs and show their intellectual capacities. The girl who has played the traditional clinging-vine role shows, as the day of her wedding approaches, an efficiency and ability to control any situation that may make her fiance look like the clinging vine.

If role playing were permanent, it would not endanger a marriage. But as it is generally only temporary, ending when the critical periods of pinning and of the early part of the engagement are safely passed, it can be and often is the source of disillusionment that jeopardizes a marriage. This can happen to a marriage at any age. It is especially serious in the case of a marriage during the adolescent years—the time when romanticism is at its peak. This disillusionment occurs in both boys and girls, thus doubling the chances that their marriage will end in the divorce courts.

sexual intimacies According to tradition, the approved forms of sexual intimacy vary according to the stage of courtship. Kissing, for example, is approved for dating, necking while going steady, petting for pinning and the engagement, and sexual intercourse is reserved for marriage (12). Today, this pattern is speeded up with the general relaxation of standards of approved sex behavior and with the absence of chaperonage (62,120,191,218,219).

Cross-cultural studies have revealed that sexual intimacies during the pinning and engagement stages are as great in America today as in some of the countries that have been regarded as "too liberal." In a comparison of Norwegian and American university students, for example, it was reported that American students do not, as a whole, approve of full sexual relations during the engagement period to the same extent that the Norwegians do. However, approval and actions are not always highly correlated (128,191,200,218,219). This was found to be true also of Americans as compared with Danish. American students, however, approved of necking after one month of dating; of petting about one month before announcing the engagement, during the pinning stage; and of starting coitus about one-half month before the wedding (39). Boys approve of premarital coitus more than girls (12,39,218). Attitudes toward different degrees of sexual intimacy at different stages in the courtship pattern are illustrated in Figure 13–9.

Whether sexual intimacies are a good foundation for marriage is a highly debated question today. This matter will be discussed in more detail in the following chapter. However, there is evidence that many marriages during the adolescent years are the result of suspected or diagnosed pregnancies (69,82,199). Even though the American culture is more permissive in its attitudes today than in the past, it has not yet reached the point where premarital pregnancies are not frowned upon, with the possible exception of members of the lower social classes (38,62,69,120,219). This results in hurried marriages—shotgun marriages—with their accompaniments of marked feelings of guilt on the part of the girl and resentments at being forced into a marriage he was not emotionally or economically ready for on the part of the boy (12,38,218). This explains, to some extent at least, the high divorce rate in teen-age marriages.

ADOLESCENT MARRIAGES

Since the Second World War, there has been a gradual but steady decrease in the median age at marriage. Now, according to the latest census figures, the median age for girls is between 18 and 19 years, and for boys, 21 years. This trend toward early marriages is following more closely the pattern in Asian than in European countries. The common time for girls to marry in the American culture today is during the first year after high school; for boys, it comes several years after they graduate from high school and have had time to get established in some occupation (6,89,171).

Early Marriages Any marriage before the median age for that *particular population* is, statistically speaking, an "early marriage." However, as popularly used, the term relates more to the *individual's status in society than to his chronological age*. An adolescent who marries while he is still dependent on others for support is thought of as marrying early; an adolescent of the same chronologi-

cal age who is working and is financially able to support himself and a family is not nearly so likely to be thought of as marrying early. Early marriages in the American culture of today are, actually, "student marriages" (27,35,40,82,89,186,202).

Among the lower socioeconomic groups, adolescent marriages have been common for generations. Boys are at their physical peak in late adolescence and are able to get jobs that make use of their physical skills. Because the girls of their neighborhoods do not plan education beyond the compulsory age limit, they are eager to marry as soon as they finish school. By doing so, they avoid domestic or factory work which would be their lot had they remained under the parental roof. Thus, while they marry at an early age chronologically, they are not economically or sociologically married early (27,35,37,89,202). For girls who do not go to high school, the ages of 14 to 16 are the most frequent for marriage (171).

Before the early 1940s, college marriages were rare. Marriage meant the automatic end of the young person's education. However, following the Second World War and the Korean War, many married veterans returned to the college campuses to complete their education. As a result, most colleges relaxed their rules against married students. Even today, fewer students marry while in high school or college than in postgraduate professional training school. The average age for college girls to marry is 22 years—usually the year they graduate from college (40,163,171,218).

When girls marry in their teens, they are likely to marry boys several years older than they, who are out of school and self-supporting. Marriage between two adolescents of the same age is more common in the college group than in the high school group. It is also more common than among adolescents who have completed their education at junior or senior high school and are working (26,27,35,82,135,139,202). Early marriages are more common among Catholic than among Protestant or Jewish adolescents of the same socioeconomic groups (29).

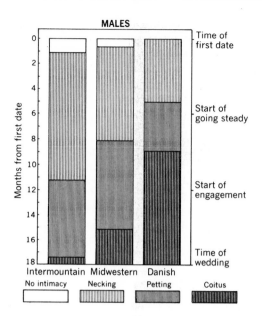

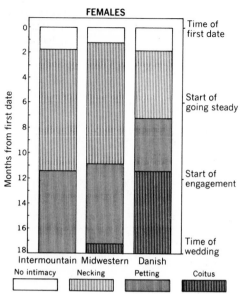

FIGURE 13–9 Cultural differences in attitudes toward degrees of sexual intimacy at different stages in the courtship pattern. (Adapted from H. T. Christensen and G. R. Carpenter: Timing patterns in the development of sexual intimacy: an attitudinal report on three modern Western societies. *Marriage fam. Living*, 1962, **24**, 30–35. Used by permission.)

Reasons for Early Marriage There are many reasons for marriage among adolescents who are still in school or college. Of these, the most common is suspected or diagnosed *pregnancy* (35,37,77,78,87,120, 153,221). In one study it was reported that nearly one-half of the high school girls who married while they were still in school were pregnant. When high school girls marry high school boys, it has been found that 87 percent of them are pregnant (27). In other studies, it has been found that 65 to 70 percent of the girls who marry while still in high school have their first babies in nine months or less time, suggesting that the reason for their marriage was real or suspected pregnancy (82,199). Among college students, marriage during a semester usually suggests pregnancy. However, premarital pregnancy is a less common cause for college students to marry than it is for high school students (120,218,221).

There are other reasons than pregnancy for marriage while in high school or college. Of these, the most common is a *desire to escape* from a situation the adolescent has not been able to adjust to satisfactorily. Poor adjustments generally come from the fact that the adolescent has unrealistic as-

pirations. Failing to reach the goals he has set for himself, he looks for a means of escape from a situation in which he feels inadequate and is unhappy. Girls are especially anxious to escape from their homes, which they often find too restrictive, and from school or college where they find little interest in studies. In some cases, the desire to escape from school may be motivated by poor social acceptance or lack of acceptance by the group the girl aspires to be identified with. Because boys are less restricted at home than girls and because they realize the necessity of education for occupational success, the desire for escape is a less common motive for early marriage among boys than among girls (26,42,58,157,165).

Adolescents with unrealistic aspirations tend to be poorly adjusted. This predisposes them to dash into marriage before they are ready for the responsibilities of marriage in the belief that marriage will give them the *status in the group* they crave. For girls, this is the status of an adult; for boys, it is a status of security and emotional satisfaction which they feel they have been deprived of. Poor adjustments and emotional instability likewise make the adolescent highly suggestible and easily influenced by those with whom he is associated. If getting married is the "thing to do," the poorly adjusted adolescent will follow in the footsteps of the group (10,14,26,157,231).

Adolescents who are poorly adjusted tend to be more influenced by mass media of communication than those who are better adjusted. (See pages 238 and 239 for a more complete discussion of this matter.) Consequently, they have a highly *romanticized concept of marriage* and of the status marriage gives. The more dissatisfied the adolescent is with his present status, the stronger the motivating influence of this glamorized concept of marriage (10,217).

Adult pressures on adolescent girls to start to date early and to go steady early as symbols of their popularity *imply adult approval of early marriage.* The adolescent frequently uses this as the real or the rationalized reason for marrying before finishing school or college. Because parental pressure to date early is greater on girls, many girls want to marry early to show others how popular they are. Many adolescents are, literally, forced into early dating, early going steady, and early marriage by mothers who look upon this as a prestige symbol for their daughters (35,42,186,217,218).

Peer presures are often stronger than maternal pressures and adult approval. A married girl in a high school class can and often does literally start a fad for marriage. This is especially true if she has a "glamour wedding" and marries an older person who can afford to give her the status symbols that her classmates crave. Much the same thing happens in college or in graduate school. Many girls are so influenced by the marriage of a classmate that they want to follow in her footsteps (35,42,94,202).

Conditions Contributing to Early Marriage
The analysis of the reasons for early mar-

riage, given above, will show that early marriages are not characteristic of the present era alone. In fact, in the past, many of the same reasons for marrying early existed as exist today. Why, then, are there many more early marriages now than in the past? There is no one answer to this question but several. Unquestionably, the greater *affluence* of our culture today makes early marriage possible. Parents can afford to contribute to the support of a home for their married sons and daughters while they continue their education. Furthermore, because there are many *job opportunities for girls* today, a girl can earn enough to support her husband while he completes his education.

Then, too, modern *contraceptive methods* make family planning possible so that it is not essential for a young couple to have a "nest egg" for the expenses of a baby within a year after marriage. When adolescents marry because of pregnancy, the parents on both sides generally assume the financial responsibilities of the baby's birth as a means of making marriage possible as a "face-saver" for the young couple.

Unquestionably the most important reason for the greater number of early marriages today as compared with the past is the greater *permissiveness* on the part of adults, especially parents and high school and college authorities. The adolescent of today knows that his parents put such high value on education as a stepping-stone to future success that they will help him to continue his education in spite of his marriage.

There is an equally permissive attitude toward premarital pregnancy among many parents of today. True, while the shotgun technique used by the irate father of the girl is still in use, the parents of today's bride try to make a good bargain with the boy who is the father of their daughter's child in the hope that this will lead to a happy marriage for their daughter and a minimum of social stigma for the whole family.

The permissive attitude of colleges toward early marriage and the growing trend of equally permissive attitudes on the part of public high schools have unquestionably added great weight to the increase in marriages among students. While high schools and colleges do not, as a whole, approve of early marriage any more than parents do, they make it possible for adolescents to continue their education after marriage. Many colleges even provide living quarters for married students (27,35,37,40,56,87,111, 128,218).

Evaluation of Early Marriage   There is ample evidence that "early marriages are risky as compared with later marriages" (147). Short engagements and early marriages are proving to be responsible, in part at least, for the alarming rise in divorce that has taken place since the Second World War, and for other indications of failure in marriage, such as desertions, separations, problem children, juvenile delinquency, and unhappiness on the part of all members of the family (6,42,140).

There are ample reasons for the greater incidence of failure than of success in early marriages. The *kind of person* who marries early is, as a general rule, not psychologically ready for marriage; he may suffer from emotional instability and feelings of personal inadequacy. Each new challenge adds strain to an already weak personality pattern which sooner or later breaks under the burden (26,56,111). Because the early years of adolescence are years of *idealism, romanticism, and unrealism,* most adolescents who marry while they are still students have such a faulty concept of marriage that disillusionment is inevitable (56,66). As Beigel has pointed out, in reference to the stereotypes of marriage presented in the mass media, "There is no doubt that such pressure-cooker recipes for happiness do not presage well for marriage" (10).

Early marriages are, inevitably, accompanied by *financial problems.* Not only does the adolescent have too little money for the pleasures and status symbols he enjoyed before marriage, but he may be forced back into the state of dependency on his family which he had hoped to escape. While dependency at any time in adolescence is the source of frustration, in marriage it is so serious that it threatens the success or even the existence of the marriage (111,112).

This status of dependency is especially difficult for adolescents who had romanticized concepts of their dream home, the car, and other material possessions they hoped to have. Some adolescents go hopelessly into debt to have them; most are forced to abandon their dreams and face a reality of dependency on parents. How seriously this can affect the adolescent's adjustment to marriage has been explained thus by Herrmann (97):

> *The optimistic expectations of teenagers about their first home after marriage and the high priority assigned to car ownership both appear to be potential sources of financial problems for teenagers entering marriage . . . these expectations and attitudes are almost certain to be carried over into marriage and are almost equally certain to become stumbling blocks for young couples.*

Persons who marry early often find themselves misfits in adolescent *social activities* and out of touch with members of the *peer group* with which they were formerly identified. The more popular an adolescent has been before marriage, and the higher the value he has placed on social acceptance, the harder is the adjustment to social isolation (42,111,202).

The greatest risk in early marriage comes from the necessity to marry to establish the paternity of a child conceived out of wedlock (69,162). The traditional shotgun marriage is far more likely to be an unhappy one than a marriage based on a strong desire on the part of both young people to marry. Added to the resentments aroused by a forced marriage are the feelings of guilt and shame that both young people are bound to experience when they realize that people suspect or know the reason for their marriage (38,87).

Very often, a forced marriage is accompanied by the necessity of *dropping out of school or college* before completing the studies necessary for a chosen vocation.

Some boys find that they must make radical changes in their vocational aspirations because the financial support they had planned on from the working of the wife is no longer available after the birth of a child. A *change in vocational plans* can be a serious threat to marital happiness (27, 40,218).

In spite of the risks involved, some early marriages are happy and are never threatened by separation or divorce. While the conditions that contribute to the success of early marriages vary, five are especially important. These are: first, approval and encouragement from parents of both young people; second, freedom from serious financial difficulties due either to the ability of one or both of the marriage partners to earn money or to the willingness of parents to aid in the support of the young people *without* imposing a state of dependency on them as the price for this aid; third, a sincere desire to marry early in the belief that growing up with one's children is essential to happiness in marriage; fourth, absence of compulsion to marry because of suspected or diagnosed pregnancy; and, fifth, a realistic understanding and acceptance of the realities of marriage and parenthood— a willingness to accept the bad with the good or, as the marriage vow says, "for better or for worse" (172).

BIBLIOGRAPHY

1 ABERLE, D. F., and K. D. NAEGELE: Middle class fathers' occupational role and attitudes toward children. *Amer. J. Orthopsychiat.*, 1952, **22**, 366–378.

2 ALEXANDER, T.: Certain characteristics of the self as related to affection. *Child Develpm.*, 1951, **22**, 285–290.

3 ANDREWS, R. O., and H. T. CHRISTENSEN: Relationship of absence of a parent to courtship status: a repeat study. *Amer. sociol. Rev.*, 1951, **16**, 541–544.

4 ANGELINO, H., E. R. EDMONDS, and E. V. MECH: Self-expressed "first" sources of sex information. *Psychol. Newsletter*, 1958, **9**, 234–237.

5 ANGELINO, H., and E. V. MECH: Some "first" sources of sex information as reported by sixty-seven college women. *J. Psychol.*, 1955, **39**, 321–324.

6 BABER, R. E.: *Marriage and the family.* 2d ed. New York: McGraw-Hill, 1953.

7 BARDIS, P. D.: Attitudes toward dating among the students of a Michigan high school. *Sociol. soc. Res.*, 1958, **42**, 274–277.

8 BARDIS, P. D.: Attitudes toward the family among college students and their parents. *Sociol, soc. Res.*, 1959, **43**, 352–358.

9 BAXTER, B. N.: Vagaries of junior-high-schoolers. *Calif. J. second. Educ.*, 1946, **21**, 181–184.

10 BEIGEL, H. G.: Romantic love. *Amer. sociol. Rev.*, 1951, **16**, 326–334.

11 BELL, R. R., and L. BLUMBERG: Courtship intimacy and religious background. *Marriage fam. Living*, 1959, **21**, 356–360.

12 BELL, R. R., and L. BLUMBERG: Courtship stages and intimacy attitudes. *Family Life Coordinator*, 1960, **8**, 61–63.

13 BERNARD, J.: Teen-age culture: an overview. *Ann. Amer. Acad. pol. soc. Sci.*, 1961, **338**, 1–12.

14 BINGER, C.: The pressures on college girls today. *Atlantic Monthly*, 1961, **207**, no. 2, 40–44.

15 BLOOD, R. O.: A retest of Waller's rating complex. *Marriage fam. Living*, 1955, **18**, 41–47.

16 BOCK, E. W., and L. G. BURCHINAL: Social status, heterosexual relations, and expected ages of marriage. *J. genet. Psychol.*, 1962, **101**, 43–51.

17 BORING, E. G.: The woman problem. *Amer. Psychologist*, 1951, **6**, 679–692.

18 BOSSARD, J. H. S., and E. S. BOLL: *The sociology of child development.* 3d ed. New York: Harper & Row, 1960.

19 BOWMAN, H. A.: *Marriage for moderns.* 4th ed. New York: McGraw-Hill, 1960.

20 BOYDSTON, D. N.: Sex hygiene problems of university freshmen. *J. counsel. Psychol.*, 1958, **5**, 148–149.

21 BRECKENRIDGE, M. E., and E. L. VINCENT: *Child development.* 5th ed. Philadelphia: Saunders, 1965.

22 BREED, W.: Sex, class, and socialization in dating. *Marriage fam. Living*, 1956, **18**, 137–144.

23 BRODERICK, C. B., and S. E. FOWLER: New patterns of relationships between the sexes among preadolescents. *Marriage fam. Living*, 1961, **23**, 27–30.

24 BROWN, D. G.: Sex-role development in a changing culture. *Psychol. Bull.*, 1958, **55**, 232–242.

25 BROWN, F.: What American men want to know about sex. *J. soc. Psychol.*, 1948, **27**, 119–125.

26 BURCHINAL, L. G.: Adolescent role deprivation and high school age marriage. *Marriage fam. Living*, 1959, **21**, 378–384.

27 BURCHINAL, L. G.: School policies and school age marriages. *Family Life Coordinator*, 1960, **8**, 43–48.

28 BURCHINAL, L. G.: Sources and adequacy of sex knowledge among Iowa high school girls. *Marriage fam. Living*, 1960, **22**, 268–269.

29 BURCHINAL, L. G., and L. E. CHANCELLOR: Social status, religious affiliation, and ages at marriage. *Marriage fam. Living*, 1963, **25**, 219–221.

30 BURNHAM, A.: Changes sought in sex attitudes. *The New York Times*, Aug. 11, 1963.

31 BUTLER, R. M.: Mothers' attitudes toward the social development of their adolescents. *Soc. Casewk*, 1956, **37**, 219–226, 280–288.

32 CALDERWOOD, D.: Differences in the sex questions of adolescent boys and girls. *Marriage fam. Living*, 1963, **25**, 492–495.

33 CAMERON, W. J., and W. F. KENKEL: High school dating: a study in variation. *Marriage fam. Living*, 1960, **22**, 74–76.

34 CAMPBELL, W. J.: Preferences of children for others of the same or opposite sex. *Aust. J. Psychol.*, 1955, **7**, 45–51.

35 CAVAN, R. S., and G. BEILING: A study of high school marriages. *Marriage fam. Living*, 1958, **20**, 293–295.

36 CHRISTENSEN, H. T.: Dating behavior as evaluated by high-school students. *Amer. J. Sociol.*, 1952, **57**, 580–586.

37 CHRISTENSEN, H. T.: Why all these young marriages? *National Parent-Teacher*, 1958, **52**, 4–7.

38 CHRISTENSEN, H. T.: Cultural relativism and premarital sex norms. *Amer. sociol. Rev.*, 1960, **25**, 31–39.

39 CHRISTENSEN, H. T., and G. R. CARPENTER: Timing patterns in the development of sexual intimacy: an attitudinal report on three modern Western societies. *Marriage fam. Living*, 1962, **24**, 30–35.

40 CHRISTOPHERSON, V. A.: College marriage in public and private institutions of higher education, 1943–1958. *Family Life Coordinator*, 1960, **8**, 49–52.

41 COLE, L., and I. N. HALL: *Psychology of adolescence.* 6th ed. New York: Holt, 1964.

42 COLEMAN, J. S.: *The adolescent society.* New York: Free Press, 1961.

43 COLLIER, M. J.: The psychological appeal in the Cinderella theme. *Amer. Imago*, 1961, **18**, 399–411.

44 CRESPI, L. P., and E. A. STANLEY: Youth looks at the Kinsey report. *Publ. Opin. Quart.*, 1948, **12**, 687–696.

45 CRIST, J. R.: High school dating as a behavior system. *Marriage fam. Living*, 1953, **15**, 23–28.

46 CROW, A.: Parental attitudes toward boy-girl relations. *J. educ. Sociol.*, 1955, **29**, 126–133.

47 CROW, L. D., and A. CROW: *Adolescent development and adjustment.* 2d ed. New York: McGraw-Hill, 1965.

48 DAVIS, M.: *Sex and the adolescent.* New York: Dial Press, 1958.

49 DAVIS, O. L.: The effect of a school camp experience on friendship choices. *J. educ. Sociol.*, 1960, **33**, 305–313.

50 DEAN, D. G.: Romanticism and emotional maturing: a preliminary study. *Marriage fam. Living*, 1961, **23**, 44–45.

51 DESCHIN, C. S.: *Teen-agers and venereal disease.* Washington: D.C.: U.S. Department of Health, Welfare, and Education, 1961.

52 DESENBERG, B. N.: Home sex education and monogamy. *Marriage fam. Living*, 1947, **9**, 89–92.

53 DINITZ, S., R. R. DYNES, and A. C. CLARKE: Preference for male or female children: traditional or affectional? *Marriage fam. Living*, 1954, **16**, 128–130.

54 DIXON, M. M.: Adolescent girls talk about themselves. *Marriage fam. Living*, 1958, **20**, 400–401.

55 DRUCKER, A. J., H. T. CHRISTENSEN, and H. H. REMMERS: Some background factors in sociosexual modernism. *Marriage fam. Living*, 1952, **14**, 334–337.

56 DUVALL, E. M.: Student marriages. *Marriage fam. Living*, 1960, **22**, 76–77.

57 DUVALL, E. M.: *Love and the facts of life.* New York: Association Press, 1963.

58 DUVALL, E. M.: Adolescent love as a reflection of teen-agers' search for identity. *J. Marriage Fam.*, 1964, **26**, 226–229.

59 DUVALL, E. M.: Identifying potential conflict areas in high school dating. *J. Marriage Fam.*, 1964, **26**, 103–106.

60 DUVALL, E. M., and A. B. MOTZ: Age and education as factors in school experience and personal-family adjustments. *School Review*, 1945, **53**, 413–421.

61 EHRMANN, W. W.: Student cooperation in a study of dating behavior. *Marriage fam. Living*, 1952, **14**, 322–326.

62 EHRMANN, W. W.: *Premarital dating behavior.* New York: Holt, 1959.

63 ELLIS, A.: A study of human love relationships. *J. genet. Psychol.*, 1949, **75**, 61–71.

64 ELLIS, A.: Love and family relationships of American college girls. *Amer. J. Sociol.*, 1950, **55**, 550–558.

65 ELLIS, A., and E. W. FULLER: The sex, love, and marriage questions of senior nursing students. *J. soc. Psychol.*, 1950, **31**, 209–216.

66 ENGLAND, R. W.: Images of love and courtship in family-magazine fiction. *Marriage fam. Living*, 1960, **22**, 162–165.

67 ENGLISH, O. S.: Sexual love—man toward woman. In M. F. Ashley-Montagu (ed.), *The meaning of love.* New York: Julian Press, 1953, pp. 165–175.

68 EVANS, W. N.: Two kinds of romantic love. *Psychoanal. Quart.*, 1953, **22**, 75–85.

69 FALK, U. A., and G. J. FALK: The unmarried mother: a sociological profile. *Family Life Coordinator*, 1965, **14**, 17–19.

70 FINE, B.: Battle of the sexes begins at start of grammar school. *The New York Times*, May 27, 1962.

71 FINGER, F. W.: Sex beliefs and practices among male college students. *J. abnorm. soc. Psychol.*, 1947, **42**, 57–67.

72 FISHBEIN, M., and R. J. R. KENNEDY (eds.): *Modern marriage and family living.* Fair Lawn, N.J.: Oxford, 1957.

73 FLEEGE, U. H.: *Self-revelation of the adolescent boy.* Milwaukee: Bruce, 1945.

74 FRANK, L. K.: Adolescence as a period of transition. *43rd Yearb. Nat. Soc. Stud. Educ.*, 1944, chap. 1.

75 FRAZIER, E. F.: Sociologic factors in the formation of sex attitudes. In P. H. Hoch and J. Zubin (eds.), *Psychosexual development in health and disease.* New York: Grune & Stratton, 1949, chap. 13.

76 GALLAGHER, J. R.: That favorite teacher: a parent's enemy or ally? *Marriage fam. Living*, 1961, **23**, 400–402.

77 GENNÉ, E., and W. GENNÉ: *Christians and the crisis in sex morality.* New York: Association Press, 1962.

78 GENNÉ, W.: Early marriage and the modern family. *Family Life Coordinator*, 1962, **11**, 66–68.

79 GESELL, A., F. L. ILG, and L. B. AMES: *Youth: the years from ten to sixteen.* New York: Harper & Row, 1956.

80 GIEDT, F. H.: Changes in sexual behavior and attitudes following class study of the Kinsey report. *J. soc. Psychol.*, 1951, **33**, 131–141.

81 GOTTLIEB, D., and C. RAMSEY: *The American adolescent.* Homewood, Ill.: Dorsey, 1964.

82 GRAY, H.: Marriage and premarital conception. *J. Psychol.*, 1960, **50**, 383–397.

83 HACKER, H. M.: Women as a minority group. *Soc. Forces*, 1951, **30**, 60–69.

84 HALL, G. S.: *Adolescence.* New York: Appleton-Century-Crofts, 1904.

85 HARRIS, D. B., and S. C. TSENG: Children's attitudes toward peers and parents as revealed by sentence completions. *Child Develpm.*, 1957, **28**, 401–411.

86 HARRIS, M., B. LEMON, and L. F. BECK: Sex instruction in the classroom. *Educ. Leadership*, 1949, **6**, 519–524.

87 HAUSER, S., and C. HOBART: Premarital pregnancy and anxiety. *J. soc. Psychol.*, 1964, **63**, 255–263.

88 HAVIGHURST, R. J.: *Human development and education.* New York: Longmans, 1953.

89 HAVIGHURST, R. J.: Early marriage and the schools. *School Review*, 1961, **69**, 36–47.

90 HECHINGER, G.: Slowing down the social pace. *The New York Times*, Apr. 14, 1963.

91 HECHINGER, G., and F. M. HECHINGER: *Teen-age tyranny.* New York: Morrow, 1963.

92 HEISS, J. S.: Variations in courtship progress among high school students. *Marriage fam. Living*, 1960, **22**, 165–170.

93 HEISS, J. S.: Degree of intimacy and male-

female interaction. *Sociometry*, 1962, **25**, 197–208.

94 HENTON, J. M.: The effects of married high-school students on their unmarried classmates. *J. Marriage Fam.*, 1964, **26**, 87–88.

95 HERMAN, R. D.: The "going steady" complex: a re-examination. *Marriage fam. Living*, 1955, **17**, 36–40.

96 HERON, A.: Adolescents and preparation for parenthood. *Brit. J. educ. Psychol.*, 1952, **22**, 173–179.

97 HERRMANN, R. O.: Expectations and attitudes as a source of financial problems in teen-age marriages. *J. Marriage Fam.*, 1965, **27**, 89–91.

98 HILL, T. J.: Dating patterns and family position. *Clearing House*, 1955, **29**, 552–554.

99 HILLMAN, C. H.: An advice column's challenge for family-life education. *Marriage fam. Living*, 1954, **16**, 51–54.

100 HIMES, J. S.: Value concensus in mate selection among Negroes. *Marriage fam. Living*, 1952, **14**, 317–321.

101 HOBART, C. W.: Disillusionment in marriage and romanticism. *Marriage fam. Living*, 1958, **20**, 156–162.

102 HOBART, C. W.: Romanticism and marriage role opinions. *Sociol. soc. Res.*, 1958, **42**, 336–343.

103 HOBART, C. W.: The incidence of romanticism during courtship. *Soc. Forces*, 1958, **36**, 262–267.

104 HOBART, C. W.: Attitude changes during courtship and marriage. *Marriage fam. Living*, 1960, **22**, 352–359.

105 HOHMAN, M.: Adolescent attitudes toward seeking help with personal problems. *Smith Coll. Stud. soc. Wk.*, 1955, **25**, 1–31.

106 HOLLINGSHEAD, A. DE B.: *Elmtown's youth.* New York: Wiley, 1949.

107 HOLLINGWORTH, L. S.: *The psychology of the adolescent.* New York: Appleton-Century-Crofts, 1928.

108 HORTON, D.: The dialogue of courtship in popular songs. *Amer. J. Sociol.*, 1957, **62**, 567–578.

109 HURLOCK, E. B., and S. SENDER: The "negative phase" in relation to the behavior of pubescent girls. *Child Develpm.*, 1939, **6**, 325–340.

110 HUTSON, P. W., and D. R. KOVAR: Some problems of senior high-school pupils in their social recreation. *Educ. Admin. Superv.*, 1942, **28**, 503–519.

111 INSELBERG, R. M.: Social and psychological factors associated with high school marriages. *J. Home Econ.*, 1961, **53**, 766–772.

112 INSELBERG, R. M.: Marital problems and satisfactions in high school marriages. *Marriage fam. Living*, 1962, **24**, 74–77.

113 JERSILD, A. T.: *The psychology of adolescence.* 2d ed. New York: Macmillan, 1963.

114 JOHNSTONE, J., and E. KATZ: Youth and popular music: a study in the sociology of taste. *Amer. J. Sociol.*, 1957, **62**, 563–568.

115 JONES, A.: Sexual symbolic response in prepubescent and pubescent children. *J. consult. Psychol.*, 1961, **25**, 383–387.

116 JONES, M. C.: The later careers of boys who were early- or late-maturers. *Child Develpm.*, 1957, **28**, 113–128.

117 JONES, M. C.: A comparison of the attitudes and interests of ninth grade students over two decades. *J. educ. Psychol.*, 1960, **51**, 175–186.

118 JONES, M. C., and P. H. MUSSEN: Self-conceptions, motivations, and interpersonal attitudes of early- and late-maturing girls. *Child Develpm.*, 1958, **29**, 491–501.

119 JOSSELYN, I. M.: Psychological changes in adolescence. *Children*, 1959, **6**, 43–47.

120 KANIN, E. J.: Premarital sex adjustments, social class, and associated behaviors. *Marriage fam. Living*, 1960, **22**, 258–259.

121 KARIEL, P. E.: Social class, age, and educational group differences in childbirth information. *Marriage fam. Living*, 1963, **25**, 353–355.

122 KINSEY, A. C., W. B. POMEROY, and C. E. MARTIN: *Sexual behavior in the human male.* Philadelphia: Saunders, 1948.

123 KINSEY, A. C., W. B. POMEROY, C. E. MARTIN, and P. H. GEBHARD: *Sexual behavior in the human female.* Philadelphia: Saunders, 1953.

124 KIRKENDALL, L. A.: Toward a clarification of the concept of male sex drive. *Marriage fam. Living*, 1958, **20**, 367–372.

125 KIRKENDALL, L. A.: Circumstances associated with teenage boys' use of prostitution. *Marriage fam. Living*, 1960, **22**, 145–149.

126 KIRKENDALL, L. A.: Reply to Mowrer and

Poffenberger. *Marriage fam. Living*, 1960, **22**, 330–333.

127 KIRKENDALL, L. A.: Values and premarital intercourse. *Marriage fam. Living*, 1960, **22**, 317–322.

128 KIRKENDALL, L. A.: Evaded problem: sex on the campus. *Family Life Coordinator*, 1965, **14**, 20–24.

129 KIRKENDALL, D. A., and D. S. BRODY: The arousal of fear: does it have a place in sex education? *Family Life Coordinator*, 1964, **13**, 14–16.

130 KIRKENDALL, L. A., and A. HAMILTON: Current thinking and practices in sex education. *High Sch. J.*, 1954, **37**, 143–148.

131 KIRKPATRICK, C., S. STRYKER, and P. BUELL: An experimental study of attitudes towards male sex behavior with reference to Kinsey's findings. *Amer. sociol. Rev.*, 1952, **17**, 580–587.

132 KLEMER, R. H.: Factors of personality and experience which differentiate single from married women. *Marriage fam. Living*, 1954, **16**, 41–44.

133 KOCH, H. L.: The relation in young children between characteristics in their playmates and certain attributes of their siblings. *Child Develpm.*, 1957, **28**, 175–202.

134 KOCH, H. L.: The relation of certain formal attributes of siblings and attitudes held toward each other and toward their parents. *Monogr. Soc. Res. Child Develpm.*, 1960, **25**, no. 4.

135 KOLLER, M. R.: Some changes in courtship behavior in three generations of Ohio women. *Amer. sociol. Rev.*, 1951, **16**, 366–370.

136 KRONHAUSEN, P., and E. KRONHAUSEN: Sex education—more avoided than neglected? *Teach. Coll. Rec.*, 1963, **64**, 321–330.

137 LANDIS, J. T.: Attitudes and policies concerning marriage among high school students. *Marriage fam. Living*, 1956, **18**, 128–136.

138 LANDIS, J. T.: Dating maturation and children from happy and unhappy marriages. *Marriage fam. Living*, 1963, **25**, 351–353.

139 LANDIS, P. H.: Marriage preparation in two generations. *Marriage fam. Living*, 1951, **13**, 155–156.

140 LANDIS, P. H.: Adolescence and youth: the process of maturing. 2d ed. New York: McGraw-Hill, 1952.

141 LANDIS, P. H.: *Your marriage and family living.* 2d ed. New York: McGraw-Hill, 1954.

142 LANDIS, P. H.: Research on teen-age dating. *Marriage fam. Living*, 1960, **22**, 266–267.

143 LANTAGNE, J. E.: Interests of 4,000 high school pupils in problems of marriage and parenthood. *Res. Quart. Amer. Ass. Hlth. Phys. Educ. Recr.*, 1958, **29**, 407–416.

144 LEE, M. R.: Background factors related to sex information and attitudes. *J. educ. Psychol.*, 1952, **43**, 467–485.

145 LE MASTERS, E. E.: *Modern courtship and marriage.* New York: Macmillan, 1957.

146 LERNER, M.: *America as a civilization.* New York: Simon & Schuster, 1957.

147 LOCKE, H. J.: *Predicting adjustment in marriage.* New York: Holt, 1951.

148 LOCKE, H. J., and G. KARLSSEN: Marital adjustment and prediction in Sweden and the United States. *Sociol. soc. Res.*, 1952, **17**, 10–17.

149 LOWRIE, S. H.: Dating theories and student responses. *Amer. sociol. Rev.*, 1951, **16**, 334–340.

150 LOWRIE, S. H.: Sex differences and age of initial dating. *Soc. Forces*, 1952, **30**, 456–461.

151 LOWRIE, S. H.: Factors involved in the frequency of dating. *Marriage fam. Living*, 1956, **18**, 46–51.

152 LOWRIE, S. H.: Early and late dating: some conditions associated with them. *Marriage fam. Living*, 1961, **23**, 284–291.

153 LOWRIE, S. H.: Early marriage: premarital pregnancy and associated factors. *Marriage fam. Living*, 1965, **27**, 48–56.

154 LUNDBERG, G. A., and L. DICKSON: Selective association among ethnic groups in a high-school population. *Amer. soc. Rev.*, 1952, **17**, 23–35.

155 MALM, M., and O. G. JAMISON: *Adolescence.* New York: McGraw-Hill, 1952.

156 MARTIN, P. C.: Objectives in teaching high school youth about pregnancy and childbearing. *Marriage fam. Living*, 1962, **24**, 403–406.

157 MARTINSON, F. M.: Ego deficiency as a factor in marriage: a male sample. *Marriage fam. Living*, 1959, **21**, 48–52.

158 MC KEE, J. P., and A. C. SHERRIFFS: The dif-

ferential evaluation of males and females. *J. Pers.*, 1957, **25**, 356–371.

159 MEAD, M.: *Male and female.* New York: Morrow, 1952.

160 MERRILL, F. E.: *Courtship and marriage.* New York: Holt, 1959.

161 MEYER, W. J.: Relationships between social need strivings and the development of heterosexual affiliations. *J. abnorm. soc. Psychol.*, 1959, **59**, 51–57.

162 MONAHAN, T. S.: Does age at marriage matter in divorce? *Soc. Forces*, 1953, **32**, 81–87.

163 MORGAN, C.: Social background and high school student marriages before and after World War II. *Marriage fam. Living*, 1963, **25**, 481–483.

164 MORGENSTERN, J. J.: What schools can do about teen-age dating patterns. *NEA J.*, 1961, **50**, 8–11.

165 MOSS, J. J., and R. GINGLES: The relationship of personality to the incidence of early marriage. *Marriage fam. Living*, 1959, **21**, 373–377.

166 MOWRER, O. H.: Critique. *Marriage fam. Living*, 1960, **22**, 322–324.

167 MURSELL, J. L.: *Education for American democracy.* New York: Norton, 1943.

168 MUSSEN, P. H., J. J. CONGER, and J. KAGAN: *Child development and personality.* 2d ed. New York: Harper & Row, 1963.

169 MUSSEN, P. H., and M. C. JONES: Self-conceptions, motivations, and interpersonal attitudes of late- and early-maturing boys. *Child Develpm.*, 1957, **28**, 243–256.

170 *New York Times* Report: U.S., British teens differ on worries. *The New York Times*, Feb. 26, 1953.

171 *New York Times* Report: Study finds college girl weds later. *The New York Times*, June 1, 1964.

172 *New York Times* Report: Matrimony for young weighed. *The New York Times*, July 23, 1964.

173 *New York Times* Report: U.S. sex attitudes called Victorian. *The New York Times*, Apr. 12, 1965.

174 NIMKOFF, M. F., and A. L. WOOD: Courtship and personality. *Amer. J. Sociol.*, 1947, **53**, 263–269.

175 PACKARD, V.: *The status seekers.* New York: Pocket, 1961.

176 PACKARD, V.: *The pyramid climbers.* New York: McGraw-Hill, 1962.

177 PARKER, E.: *The seven ages of woman.* Baltimore: Johns Hopkins, 1960.

178 PHIPPS, M. J.: Some factors influencing what children know about human growth. *Amer. Psychologist*, 1949, **4**, 391–392.

179 POFFENBERGER, T.: Individual choice in adolescent premarital sex behavior. *Marriage fam. Living*, 1960, **22**, 324–330.

180 POFFENBERGER, T.: Responses of eighth grade girls to a talk on sex. *Marriage fam. Living*, 1960, **22**, 38–44.

181 POFFENBERGER, T.: Sex-courting concerns of a class of twelfth grade girls. *Family Life Coordinator*, 1961, **10**, 75–81.

182 POFFENBERGER, T.: Three papers on going steady. *Family Life Coordinator*, 1964, **13**, 7–13.

183 POMEROY, W. B.: An analysis of questions on sex. *Psychol. Rec.*, 1960, **10**, 191–201.

184 PRESSEY, S. L., and A. W. JONES: 1923–1953 and 20–60 age changes in moral codes, anxieties, and interests, as shown by the "X-O Tests." *J. Psychol.*, 1955, **39**, 485–502.

185 PRESSEY, S. L., and R. G. KUHLEN: *Psychological development through the life span.* New York: Harper & Row, 1957.

186 Purdue Opinion Panel: *Youth's attitudes toward courtship and marriage.* Lafayette, Ind.: Purdue University Press, 1961, no. 62.

187 RAFFERTY, F. I., and E. S. STEIN: A study of the relationship of early menarche to ego development. *Amer. J. Orthopsychiat.*, 1958, **28**, 170–179.

188 RAMSEY, G. V.: The sexual development of boys. *Amer. J. Psychol.*, 1943, **56**, 217–233.

189 REEVY, W. R.: Adolescent sexuality. In A. Ellis and A. Abarbanel (eds.), *The encyclopedia of sexual behavior.* Englewood Cliffs, N.J.: Hawthorn, 1961, pp. 52–67.

190 REEVY, W. R.: Child sexuality. In A. Ellis and A. Abarbanel (eds.), *The encyclopedia of sexual behavior.* Englewood Cliffs, N.J.: Hawthorn, 1961, pp. 258–267.

191 REISS, I. L.: The scaling of premarital permissiveness. *J. Marriage Fam.*, 1964, **26**, 188–189.

192 REMMERS, H. H., and D. H. RADLER: *The American teen-ager.* Indianapolis: Bobbs-Merrill, 1957.

193 RIESMAN, D.: Permissiveness and sex roles. *Marriage fam. Living*, 1959, **21**, 211–217.

194 ROGERS, E. M., and A. E. HAVENS: Prestige rating and mate selection on a college campus. *Marriage fam. Living*, 1960, **22**, 55–59.

195 ROSE, A. A.: Insecurity feelings in adolescent girls. *Nerv. Child*, 1944, **4**, 46–59.

196 SCHEINFELD, A.: *The new you and heredity.* Philadelphia: Lippincott, 1961.

197 SEARS, R. R., E. E. MACCOBY, and H. LEVIN: *Patterns of child rearing.* New York: Harper & Row, 1957.

198 SHUTTLEWORTH, F. K.: A biosocial and developmental theory of male and female sexuality. *Marriage fam. Living*, 1959, **21**, 163–170.

199 SIEGEL, E.: The medical problems of the teen-age mother. *Marriage fam. Living*, 1963, **25**, 488–491.

200 SIMENSON, W., and G. GEIS: Courtship patterns of Norwegian and American university students. *Marriage fam. Living*, 1956, **18**, 334–338.

201 SMITH, E. A.: Dating and courtship at Pioneer College. *Sociol. soc. Res.*, 1955, **40**, 92–98.

202 SMITH, E. A.: *American youth culture.* New York: Free Press, 1962.

203 SMITH, G. F.: Certain aspects of the sex life of the adolescent girl. *J. appl. Psychol.*, 1924, **8**, 347–349.

204 SMITH, H. A.: An approach to the problem of sex education. *Clearing House*, 1955, **30**, 38–40.

205 SMITH, H. E.: Dating and courtship patterns: some explorations. *J. educ. Sociol.*, 1961, **35**, 49–58.

206 SMITH, W. M.: Rating and dating: a re-study. *Marriage fam. Living*, 1952, **14**, 312–317.

207 SOLLENBERGER, R. T.: Some relationships between the urinary excretion of male hormone by maturing boys and their expressed interests and attitudes. *J. Psychol.*, 1940, **9**, 179–189.

208 SPEROFF, B. J.: The stability of sociometric choice among kindergarten children. *Sociometry*, 1955, **10**, 129–131.

209 STAUDT, V. M.: Attitudes of college students toward marriage and related problems: II. Age, educational, familial, and economic factors in marriage. *J. Psychol.*, 1952, **34**, 95–106.

210 STEWART, R. L., and G. M. VERNON: Four correlates of empathy in the dating situation. *Sociol. soc. Res.*, 1959, **43**, 279–285.

211 STOLZ, H. R., and L. M. STOLZ: *Somatic development of adolescent boys.* New York: Macmillan, 1951.

212 STONE, C. L.: Family recreation: a parental dilemma. *Family Life Coordinator*, 1963, **12**, 85–87.

213 STONE, C. P., and R. G. BARKER: The attitudes and interests of premenarcheal and postmenarcheal girls. *J. genet. Psychol.*, 1939, **54**, 27–71.

214 STRANG, R.: *The adolescent views himself.* New York: McGraw-Hill, 1957.

215 TEMPLETON, J. E.: The influence of family size on some aspects of teenagers' attitudes, behavior, and perceptions of family life. *Family Life Coordinator*, 1962, **11**, 51–57.

216 THOMPSON, A.: How to be a woman. *Seventeen Magazine*, July, 1951, pp. 71, 106.

217 *Time* Report: The pre-teens. *Time Magazine*, Apr. 20, 1962, p. 68.

218 *Time* Report: The second sexual revolution. *Time Magazine*, Jan. 24, 1964, pp. 54–59.

219 *Time* Report: Students: little sex without love. *Time Magazine*, Apr. 9, 1965, p. 46.

220 VERNON, G. V., and R. L. STEWART: Empathy as a process in the dating situation. *Amer. sociol. Rev.*, 1957, **22**, 48–52.

221 VINCENT, C. E.: *Unmarried mothers.* New York: Free Press, 1961.

222 WALTERS, J., D. PEARCE, and L. DAHMS: Affectional and aggressive behavior of pre-school children. *Child Develpm.*, 1957, **28**, 15–26.

223 WARNATH, C. F.: What college students think. *Family Life Coordinator*, 1961, **10**, 85–86.

224 WEST, J.: *Plainville, U.S.A.* New York: Columbia, 1945.

225 WHITEHEAD, J.: The case for going steady. *The New York Times*, July 14, 1957.

226 WHYTE, W. F.: A slum sex code. *Amer. J. Sociol.*, 1943, **49**, 24–31.

227 WILLIAMS, E.: *Tips for teens.* New York: McNaught Syndicate, 1948.

228 WINCH, R. F.: Courtship in college women. *Amer. J. Sociol.*, 1949, **55**, 269–278.

229 WINCH, R. F.: The relation between loss of a parent and progress in courtship. *J. soc. Psychol.*, 1949, **29**, 51–56.

230 WINCH, R. F.: Further data and observations on the Oedipus hypothesis: the consequence of an inadequate hypothesis. *Amer. sociol. Rev.*, 1951, **16**, 784–795.

231 WINCH, R. F.: *The modern family.* New York: Holt, 1952.

232 WINKER, J. B.: Age trends and sex differences in the wishes, identifications, activities, and fears of children. *Child Develpm.*, 1949, **20**, 191–200.

233 WOLFORD, O. P.: How early background affects dating behavior. *J. Home Econ.*, 1948, **40**, 505–506.

234 WOLMAN, B.: Sexual development in Israeli adolescents. *Amer. J. Psychother.*, 1951, **5**, 531–559.

235 WOOD, M. W.: *Living together in the family.* Washington, D.C.: American Home Economics Society, 1946.

CHAPTER 14
sex values and
sex roles

If a marriage is to survive the many strains life will put on it, the selection of a marriage partner is of vital importance. In many civilized and primitive cultures, today as in the past, it is believed that young people are too inexperienced to be able to make a wise choice. Therefore, for the good of the young people as well as for that of society, the choice should be made by adults. Adolescents in the American culture of today feel that the choice of a life mate is their prerogative. As is true in the choice of their friends, they strongly reject adult advice and bitterly resent adult interference (88).

Adolescents who are away from home —at school, college, in the armed services, or on a job—become more democratic in their attitudes toward people than do those who remain under the parental roof. In addition, they have more chances to meet people who are different from them in background. Frequently they find these people more interesting and congenial than those they have grown up with. The result is that they often prefer them as possible marriage partners. When this happens, they are likely to choose a mate their parents disapprove of (152). Foreign students in American universities come in contact with the prevailing American pattern of choosing one's life mate without parental interference. Many then break away from the traditions of their own culture of having adults make the choice for them. There is, for example, a trend for Japanese students in American universities to choose their own mates, even to the extent of choosing an American rather than a Japanese—a trend which their parents often strongly disapprove of (3).

establishing wholesome values in mate selection

The fourth important task the adolescent must face in making the transition to adult sexuality is establishing values that will enable him to make a wise choice in selecting his life mate. He must establish values regarding what is important and what is relatively unimportant not only for the present but also for a lifetime relationship. Because the trend is toward earlier marriages, the foundation values must be established by the time the adolescent begins to date. With dating experiences, these values may undergo some change. But they are not likely to undergo radical changes because they are too heavily weighted emotionally. Nor is it possible for the adolescent to use the values he has established for the selection of friends of the same sex, or even for friends of the opposite sex, as a basis for these new values. A life mate fills different needs in the individual's life than does a friend (54).

OBSTACLES TO WISE MATE SELECTION

Lack of experience with members of the opposite sex is by no means the only obstacle to the adolescent's making a wise selection of a life mate. Even those who have had considerable dating experience do not always make a wise choice. The obstacles to a wise selection may be attitudes that are unfounded and, hence, unwholesome, or they may be environmental factors.

Attitudes The four attitudes discussed below are serious obstacles to wise mate selection.

the idea that there is only one person one could possibly marry According to tradition, everyone has a "soul mate"—a person who is destined to be his life mate and who is the ideal person for him. Acceptance of this traditional belief leads the adolescent to search for his "ideal." Adolescents who hold this belief also believe that in some mysterious way they will instantly recognize their ideal, once they meet (203,230).

the idea that falling in love is a sudden and violent process The concepts of "love at first sight" and of "falling head over heels in love" are fostered by different forms of mass media from the fairy-tale days of the adolescent's childhood. Acceptance of these beliefs makes the adolescent skeptical about considering as a life mate a person who does not arouse his emotions suddenly and violently (203).

undue emphasis on one characteristic Many adolescents believe that the right person for them must have some specific characteristic which they admire and consider essential. It is not unusual, for example, for a girl who has always been financially handicapped to believe that the only man she would consider marrying is one who is rich or has prospects for wealth either through inheritance or successful achievement.

narrowing the field of selection too soon When the adolescent believes that the right person for him must have one particular characteristic which he considers vital in his future mate, he is likely to jump to the conclusion that he has found the right person when he meets someone with the characteristic he is seeking. As a result, he decides then and there to marry that person without stopping to consider that other qualities may be present that will militate against a happy relationship with that person (6,197,222,230).

Environmental Obstacles There are certain environmental obstacles that prove to be barriers to wise mate selection. These are especially serious for girls. The following are the most serious: the conservative attitude of people regarding the proper method of meeting young men; the unbalanced sex ratio, especially in areas where work takes young men away from the community; the cultural emphasis on the importance of beauty and sex; social stratification and segmentation, which excludes members of the outgroup as ineligible; urbanization with its few opportunities for young people to meet after they have completed school; the highly competitive courtship system which is controlled by the young people rather than by adults; and the social pressures on girls to behave in a more conservative manner than boys (25,153,222,230,263).

HOW VALUES ARE ESTABLISHED

In spite of the fact that adolescents have had, since early childhood, relatively few contacts with peers of the opposite sex, they have definite concepts of the type of person they want to date and later to marry. These concepts are based partly on *practical experiences* in the home and in the homes of their friends and partly on mass media. If, for example, a girl's father is inconsiderate of her mother and shows little appreciation of what the mother does for him, the girl is likely to build up a concept of the type of boy she wants to date or marry in which consideration for others is an outstanding characteristic. Traditionally, boys want a wife who cooks as "Mother does."

Mass media add glamour and unrealism to the more practical concepts established earlier (23,118). The young adolescent girl, for example, develops a concept of the ideal lover as close to the Nordic stereotype of a tall, muscular, and solidly built masculine body and a handsome face

that is reminiscent of a Greek god. In addition, he has a high socioeconomic status; he is "adored" by women; he has a technique of lovemaking that sweeps women off their feet; and he puts women on a pedestal where they are protected from the chores of daily living (72).

What the *social group* considers important the adolescent accepts as a value by which he judges members of the opposite sex (25). These become the "prestige ratings" which he uses in selecting dates and a future mate (53,197). If, for example, he is in a college where there are fraternities and sororities, he discovers that girls who belong to sororities have a higher prestige rating than those who do not and that membership in certain sororities is rated higher (208). Similarly, because athletic ability ranks higher in the prestige scale than academic achievements, girls want to date boys who are athletes rather than those who are scholars (49).

In spite of these influences, adolescents of today are establishing values for marriage beyond the point of an "ideal mate." In part, this is due to the *marriage courses* given in many schools and colleges. In part, it is due to popular concern about the failure of marriage and suggestions offered in newspapers, magazines, and over the air for remedying this situation (6,112,142,251). As a result, adolescents are showing an "alertness and a realistic attitude toward most of the vital problems of marriage" (231).

Shifts in Values From dating and going steady, the adolescent discovers that certain qualities he considered important in a date are not so important as other qualities needed in a potential mate. These values are illustrated in Figure 14–1. At the age of 14 years, for example, girls want boys who are good looking; at 17, they put intelligence ahead of looks. Boys like "cuties" when they are 14 years old; at 17, they regard common sense and social skills as of greater importance. Both boys and girls learn that looks are only superficial; though looks are important, other qualities, they believe, are more important (52). Similarly, love and sex are of paramount importance in early dating. As boys and girls begin to think seriously of marriage, they recognize that other qualities, such as emotional maturity, agreeable personality, similar interests, intelligence, financial responsibility, and family background are also important (153,197,222,230,272).

This shift in values with dating experience is the outcome of a "filtering process" in which the adolescent eliminates many of the qualities he thought important at first and keeps those which, in the beginning of his heterosexual experiences, seemed less important. This is well illustrated in the case of similarity of religious background. As was pointed out earlier (see pages 417 and 418), during the phase of religious doubt and skepticism, adolescents regard religious differences as of minor importance in dating and mate selection. Later, as they resolve their doubts, they discover that religious differences can be a source of serious disharmony in marriage (222,230).

In spite of shifts in values, there are certain qualities that contribute to "dating prestige." These are regarded as critically important to popularity with members of the opposite sex for either casual or serious dating. Adolescents of both sexes feel that a date should be good-looking, well-groomed, considerate, polite, friendly, cheerful, an intelligent conversationalist, emotionally mature, sensible about money, intellectually stimulating, a good dancer, a good sport, natural and unaffected, popular with both sexes, prominent in activities, healthy, and full of pep. All these qualities make for relaxed, pleasant, and satisfying human relationships. In brief, they are qualities characteristic of a person who is "fun to be with" (27,53,111,116,197,229).

When considering the qualities of a potential mate, adolescents mention many of the qualities mentioned above. In addition, they emphasize similarity of background and interests, ambition, industriousness, good financial prospects, a desire for home life and children, being able to cook

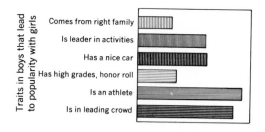

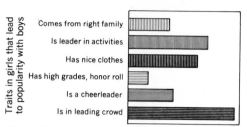

FIGURE 14–1 Values considered important by boys and girls in selecting "dates." (Adapted from J. S. Coleman: *The adolescent society.* New York: The Free Press of Glencoe, 1961. Used by permission.)

and being a good housekeeper, being able to get along harmoniously with one's in-laws, being thrifty. Less importance is attached to such qualities as rating socially, having a car and a good income, and being serious about religion (45,111,231,251). In Figure 14–2 are shown the ratings of some of the qualities considered important in a potential mate.

Sex Differences in Values There are marked sex differences in values adolescents develop regarding dates and potential mates. Among high school students, boys put more stress on physical attractiveness, being a good cook and housekeeper, and nonuse of tobacco; girls emphasize the importance of the man's being a good provider, being considerate of others, and having parental approval. Among college students, women emphasize more than men good financial prospects, similarity of backgrounds, general intelligence, ambition and industriousness, education, congenial in-laws, freedom from hereditary blights, sexual purity, nonuse of liquor, and capacity and desire for children. Men put more emphasis than women on attractiveness, popularity, being

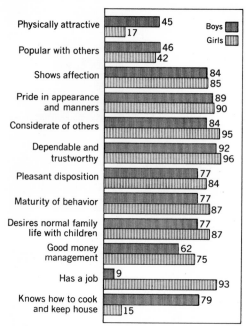

Trait	Boys	Girls
Physically attractive	45	17
Popular with others	46	42
Shows affection	84	85
Pride in appearance and manners	89	90
Considerate of others	84	95
Dependable and trustworthy	92	96
Pleasant disposition	77	84
Maturity of behavior	77	87
Desires normal family life with children	77	87
Good money management	62	75
Has a job	9	93
Knows how to cook and keep house	79	15

FIGURE 14–2 Some traits considered important by boys and girls in a future mate. (Adapted from Purdue Opinion Poll, 1961, No. 62. Used by permission.)

a good cook and housekeeper, being a non-smoker, emotional stability and agreeableness, good health, and a desire for home and children. Boys want much the same type of girl for a date as for a future mate; girls, on the other hand, want more glamour in a boy who is a date than in one who is considered as a possible life mate. In a life mate, girls consider practical qualities of major importance (7,27,45,53,116,165,197).

CHARACTERISTICS WITH HIGH VALUE

There are many factors that contribute to the attractiveness of an adolescent to a member of the opposite sex. These are greatly influenced by the values he has developed. The characteristics most often mentioned in studies of what adolescents claim they want in a date or in a life mate are discussed below.

Physical Beauty What the group considers beautiful is accepted by the adolescent as his standard; it is this standard that determines, in large measure, his choice

(53,69,197). Good health is important, not only because of its relationship to looks but also because it influences what the adolescent can do (231,251).

Physical characteristics that have become associated with one sex and are, thus, regarded as sex appropriate play an important role in the attractiveness of the adolescent. Because height is associated with sex appropriateness, boys prefer girls who are slightly shorter than they. This is especially true of boys who feel socially or personally inferior (16).

Manner of Dressing Style of clothing, grooming, and personal adornment are important factors in attracting members of the opposite sex. No matter how pretty the girl or how attractive the boy, their appeal to members of the opposite sex diminishes in proportion to the out-of-date quality of their clothes. Grooming is a powerful factor in sexual attractiveness. Boys are keenly aware and highly critical of the grooming of girls, though girls as a rule are somewhat more tolerant of boys in this respect (49, 103,130,215).

Novelty A new person or an old person who has changed markedly during the growing-up process is sure to command attention, at least temporarily, from members of the opposite sex. How long the attention will be held and how appealing it will be will depend upon such factors as personal attractiveness, style of dress, grooming, and personality (23,53,72,118).

Age Adolescent boys and girls are attracted mostly by individuals of approximately their own age. If the mate is selected while the adolescents are still in high school or college, there is likely to be little difference in their ages. If, however, the selection is made when their education has been completed, both boys and girls prefer a marriage in which the man is the older (33,49, 53,116,142,176,197,231).

Intelligence and Education Whether the individual is selected as a date or a potential mate, both boys and girls prefer those whose intelligence is similar to theirs. However, there is a slight tendency for girls to prefer boys who are superior to them in intelligence as future husbands. In addition, they want them to *use* their intellectual abilities and education to make a success in life (45,53,130,230,251). Boys regard intelligence in girls as of less importance than in men (197,222). Most want the girls they date or marry to be of equal intelligence but not superior to them. This is especially true of boys who suffer from feelings of inadequacy (17,49).

In the selection of a life mate, high school students generally select those with a high school education; those who are college graduates select college graduates. Few want a mate with less education than they. College women, more than men, feel that a college man should marry a college woman (81,82,222,230,231,251).

Personality Today's adolescents are attracted, as dates, to individuals who have pleasant, agreeable personalities. In the selection of a life mate, personality and disposition are rated high. Most adolescents say they would not marry a person with an unattractive personality or disposition (53, 111,112,130,197,250).

The more an adolescent is dissatisfied with his own personality deficiencies, the stronger will be the attraction of a member of the opposite sex who possesses the characteristics he lacks. An adolescent who is an introvert, for example, is more likely to be attracted to one who is extroverted, as he would like to be, than to an introvert, who is as he is and wishes he were not. This holds true for dating as well as for marriage selection (35,91,146,153,194,195,222,270).

Similarity of Interests Similarity of interests is not only responsible for bringing together two people in friendship, but it is frequently a factor of importance in developing the friendship into romance and marriage. Similarity of interests comes from similarity in body build, intelligence, social and cultural backgrounds, socioeconomic status, religion, education, and many other factors (6,49,116,148,222,224,230).

Religious Faith The more strongly devoted the youth is to his own faith, the more likely he is to be attracted to a girl of the same faith. When, however, religious faith plays a relatively unimportant role in the individual's life, it also plays an unimportant role in romantic love (222,229, 231). How much dating there will be between adolescents of different faiths will depend to a large extent upon how many adolescents of the same faith are available for them to date; the fewer there are, the greater the likelihood of dating outside the family faith and the less the family opposition (15,53,160,197,222,230).

In the selection of a mate, religion plays a more important role than it does in dating. Even though nationality differences are breaking down, there is still a strong cleavage between religious groups (117). While college students are more liberal in their attitudes toward mixed marriages than high school students, they are likely to be influenced by family and church pressures (246). There is a tendency to believe that marriages between different Protestant faiths have a better chance for success than any other form of mixed marriage. Even such marriages are hazardous, especially if members of the family and social group with which the adolescent is associated disapprove. When one partner is willing to adopt the faith of the other, there are still many problems that make such a marriage hazardous (34,105,106,222,230, 252,268). See pages 417 to 419 for a further discussion of interfaith marriages.

Racial Background In the past, dating among individuals of different racial backgrounds was infrequent, as was marriage. Today, this has changed. With exchange of students from foreign countries both in high school and in college, with the overseas duty of older adolescents in the armed services, and with the increase in student tours to foreign countries during summer vacations, young people of different racial backgrounds are coming in contact with one another in ways that would have been impossible before. Furthermore, pressures on adolescents to be "democratic" and "hospitable" to foreigners has led to dating and, less frequently, to marriage. These pressures have motivated interracial dating, especially among those adolescents who have difficulties in getting other dates or who find the members of their own racial group who are available "dull" as compared with the fascination of foreign manners (10,11,29,156).

However, most adolescents do not find as much satisfaction in such dating as in dating individuals more similar to themselves. Foreigners are ignorant of American dating customs and, as a result, they do not fit into a group. In addition, there is a language barrier which makes communication difficult. Should dating lead to marriage, the chances of divorce are high (156). This is partly because such radically dissimilar backgrounds give the two young people relatively little in common and partly because there is still discrimination on the part of the older generation against mixed marriages (12,13,28,30).

Family Background As has been pointed out (see page 521), there is some crossing of class lines in dating. Boys date persons of an inferior social class more often than do girls. In the selection of a mate, much the same principle holds true. While "Cinderella marriages" do occur, they are infrequent (59). The individual is most likely to select a mate from a family background similar to his (6,59,65,66,116,197,213).

Parent Image According to the Freudian theory, the Oedipus complex plays a role of great importance in mate selection. The kind of person an individual will love as he grows older is determined largely by the kinds of people he learned to love as a child. Thus, the person chosen as a mate will resemble a parent in the important physical or personality traits the person likes; he will be different from the parent in traits the individual dislikes in his parents (26,195,238).

Sex Appropriateness At no age is sex appropriateness in appearance and behavior

more important than in adolescence. Consequently, it is a factor of importance in the adolescent boy's selection of the girls he dates. Young boys may, for example, prefer tomboys, but adolescent boys prefer feminine girls. Similarly, a girl does not want to be seen on a date with a boy whom her friends regard as a sissy (49,172,207, 226).

In the selection of a life mate, sex appropriateness plays an even more important role than it does in dating. Not only do boys and girls expect those whom they plan to marry to be sex appropriate in appearance and behavior but they now expect sex appropriateness in their values as well. Boys, for example, are strongly influenced by the traditional views of the role of a wife—more so than girls are of the traditional role of a husband. Girls tend to have more modern values regarding the role of women both in the home and outside of it (32,178, 228). This matter will be discussed later in this chapter.

Residential Propinquity As place of residence and social class are closely interrelated, and as dating is mainly with members of the same school class and clique within a school, dating in early adolescence is generally with individuals who live in the same neighborhood (23,42,49,129,167). The younger the individual marries, the more likely he is to marry close to home. This, however, is more true of persons of the lower than of the higher socioeconomic groups (47). In general, as distance increases, there is a decrease in percentage of marriages (42,47,129,167,217).

CHARACTERISTICS WITH LOW VALUE
In establishing the values which they use as the basis for selecting dates and, later, marriage partners, adolescents include characteristics they dislike as well as those they like. For the most part, the disliked characteristics are personal traits. When a disliked trait is especially strong, it may readily outweigh a constellation of favorable traits. A girl who is bossy, for example, may be physically attractive, well dressed, a good

sport, come from a sigh socioeconomic status, and have a number of other outstanding qualities. But, as is true in friendships with members of her own sex, one outstandingly unfavorable trait can overshadow the desirable ones.

Most studies of traits that play an important role in dating and mate selection have placed emphasis on the traits adolescents like; relatively few have put emphasis on those they dislike. While it might be assumed that if a trait were not mentioned as liked, one could automatically assume that it was disliked, this assumption is not valid. The trait may not have been mentioned because the adolescent felt it played too minor a role to be worthy of mention. For that reason, it is essential to ask adolescents what they dislike about members of the opposite sex as well as what they like.

In one study, *high school students* were asked specifically, "What traits do you dislike in girls (boys)?" A listing was then made for both sexes in order of frequency of their responses. The listings for the two sexes were as follows (53):

TRAITS OF GIRLS DISLIKED BY BOYS	TRAITS OF BOYS DISLIKED BY GIRLS
Sloppiness of appearance	*Sloppiness of appearance*
Overweight or underweight	*Boastfulness*
Tendency to flirt or "two-time"	*Act like big shots*
Talk too much	*Display poor manners*
Extremes of dress	*Stinginess*
Little regard for money	*Being conceited*
Too much interest in self	*Poorly groomed*
Lack of punctuality	*Laziness*
Snobbishness	*Foolish behavior at parties*
Talk about other dates	*Exhibit fresh behavior*
Too much make-up	*Shyness*
Sulking and pouting	*Smoking excessively*
Being conceited	*Using bad language*
	Discourtesy to elders
	Talks too much
	Wants to be center of attention

Bites nails	*Moodiness*
Smokes and drinks	*Sponging off other boys*
Giggling or talebearer	*Asking for date at last minute*
Inability to dance	
Immature behavior	
Mingling with a fast crowd	

When *college students* were asked what they disliked or what traits they considered undesirable in dating, the males were found to be critical of females who flirted with or bragged about others during a date; who preferred popular "numbers"; who were egotistical on a date, poor sports, lacking in a sense of humor; or who were too talkative or loud. Girls, on the other hand, were critical of males who wanted too much necking or petting, who used profanity or vulgarity, who preferred popular "numbers"; who were egotistical on a date; who indulged in drinking or smoking; or who stayed too late on dates (44).

In addition to these major complaints, a number of minor complaints have been revealed in another study of college students. Among girls, complaints centered on the annoying personal habits of the young men they dated, such as biting fingernails and having a laugh like a "hyena," being too talkative or not talkative enough, and being too old, too young, or too short. The minor complaints the young men had against the girls emphasized such traits as their attitude toward money, being insincere, having no sense of humor, and being too "masculine" (6).

EVALUATION OF SEX VALUES

When values carried over from childhood are strongly romanticized, the change will have to be greater and more drastic than it would, had the values established in childhood been more realistic. The more frequently the adolescent dates and the longer he delays going steady, the greater the possibility that he will establish wholesome, realistic values.

When an adolescent gets along well with his parents and feels that he can communicate with them, he is more influenced by them than when there are psychological barriers between them. Even when family relationships are far from harmonious, and communication between the different members is limited, parents *indirectly* play an important role in determining what selections will be made. This is done, first, by providing a *social milieu* for "proper" dating and courtship through residence in class-typed neighborhoods and identification with people of similar backgrounds; second, by planning *social and recreational activities* for the young people to make sure that only the ones they approve of will be included; and third, by *threats* to remove economic support if they marry out of their class (241). However, when adolescents go away to school or college, to work, or into the armed services, they often develop new values that are different from the parental values. They then marry outside the parents' value systems (50).

Adolescents who are well accepted by the peer group or who are anxious to be well accepted are more likely to be influenced by peer value system than by parental values. This prolongs the tendency to cling to unrealistic values. Because peer influences tend to be strong in the early years of adolescence when family relationships are often frictional, there is a serious hazard in selecting a life mate at this time. The choice will not be a satisfactory one for the adolescent as his values change and as he becomes more mature (107).

The unrealistic values which served as the basis for the development of a concept of an ideal mate can be the source of psychological trouble even after the value change has taken place. Either consciously or unconsciously, the adolescent boy will judge the person he dates or the person he selects as a mate by his concept of the dream girl, just as a girl will compare the boy with her dream man. If they want to date and if they later want to marry, they will have to take what they can get or what is available in the areas where they live. Few adolescents are in a position to roam over the face of the globe in search of a person who conforms to their ideal.

The longer the adolescent plays the field and the longer he postpones going steady, pinning, or marrying, the better will be his chances of developing realistic values. Consequently, the better will be his chances of finding as a life mate a person who conforms closely to his more mature values. Just as work experience helps an adolescent to establish realistic values about a vocation, so does a reasonably long period of dating help him to establish realistic values in heterosexual relationships (76,153,230).

learning to express love

The fifth important task in achieving a mature level of heterosexuality is learning how to express the feelings and emotions aroused by the loved one. Children are self-bound; they want to be loved and to have others do things to make them happy. When they are very young, they occasionally show their affection for adults or playmates by hugging, patting, fondling, or kissing. However, there is little demonstration of affection by doing things to make others happy. When the child reaches school age, he regards all demonstration of affection as babyish. True, he may show others that he likes them by slapping them on the back or by saying they are "good guys," but that is his limit. Girls, like boys, are embarrassed by all demonstrations of affection during the closing years of childhood (53,83,102,144, 265).

In making the transition to heterosexuality, the adolescent has the major tasks of learning to be *outer-bound* instead of self-bound, of learning to show affection for others as well as receiving it, and of learning to show appreciation for the affectionate demonstrations of others. Because this is such a radical change in the individual's habitual pattern of reacting to others, it takes the adolescent time to learn to express the love he has for a member of the opposite sex. It is even more difficult and takes longer for boys than for girls, because boys have less of a foundation on which to build (83,250).

ESSENTIALS IN DEMONSTRATIONS
OF AFFECTION

In learning to be outer-bound, there are two essentials the adolescent must learn: how to show his affection and how much affection to show. These take time, guidance, and experience.

Method of Expression The childish ways of showing affection for others are no longer socially acceptable when the individual reaches adolescence. He must, therefore, learn to show his affection in a socially approved way. Before he can do this, he must know what forms of expression are socially approved and what are regarded as in poor taste. He learns by observing other people, both members of the peer group and adults, and by observing the patterns of lovemaking as portrayed in the mass media. From reading love stories, from watching movies and television, from listening to popular songs, and from reading the classics in school, he learns how people make love and and how they express their love in words and actions. These he uses as patterns for his own behavior (23,118).

Degree of Permissiveness Regardless of how much affection the adolescent has for another, he learns that he must control some of the overt expressions of his affection, just as he must control the overt expressions of anger, fear, jealousy, and other emotions. How much control he must exert will depend on the stage of dating. In the later stages of dating, affection is stronger than in the early stages when the adolescent is playing the field or is going from one steady to another. Too great permissiveness in these early stages wins the girl the reputation of being "loose," and the boy that of being a "wolf." However, as they progress to the later stages of dating, boys and girls can be increasingly more permissive in their expressions of affection for each other without incurring social disapproval (65,88,203,204).

Regardless of the stage of dating, girls are more restrained in their expressions of affection than are boys. They set limits on their sex play for different stages in dating and try to keep the boys from overstepping these limits. Girls know that they cannot be too free if they want to maintain a favorable reputation. Boys, by contrast, who make conquests gain prestige in the eyes of their peers. A girl can tease a boy to keep him interested, but she must control the expression of her affection for him to retain this interest. Only when she has the social guarantee inherent in going steady, pinning, or engagement is she willing to express her affection as completely as a boy does. Even then, she often suffers from feelings of guilt at having violated the socially approved standards of behavior for her sex (9,49,101, 128,202,203).

Permissiveness in the expression of affection has been increasing among girls since the Second World War. This is more true of *college* than of noncollege* girls, of girls of the middle and upper *socioeconomic groups* than of the lower, and of the pinning and engagement stages than of the early, playing-the-field type of dating (20, 202,248,249). Permissiveness also varies according to the *religious background* of the adolescent. Protestant adolescents, for example, have been found to go steady longer than Jewish adolescents; this encourages permissiveness in sex play. Among Catholics, those of Italian ancestry tend to be more sexually aggressive than those of Irish ancestry, who are strongly puritanical in their sex behavior (19,55,202).

COMMON FORMS OF EXPRESSION
OF AFFECTION

In the early stages of heterosexual relationships, especially in the crush and hero-worship stages, expressions of affection are mainly nonphysical. Gradually, with the increase in the sex drive with the completion of the puberty changes, affection is replaced by love—"a strong emotional attachment, a cathexis, between adolescents or adults of opposite sexes with at least the components of sex desire and tenderness" (88). With this come physical expressions in addition to the nonphysical. In the later stages of dating, all of the common forms of expression of affection, both physical and nonphysical, are used to let the loved one know how great the love is. Of the common forms of expression of affection, the following are most often used.

Services for the Loved One Adolescents are especially desirous of making sacrifices for those whom they love. This gives them a feeling of self-importance. Whether the service takes the form of gifts, entertainment, or services that will assist the loved one is of little importance. So long as the loved one seems appreciative and happy, the adolescent feels amply rewarded.

Keepsakes Anything that has belonged to the loved one or, better still, has been used by the loved one, is especially highly prized. The value of keepsakes is not their true worth but their association with and symbolism of the person to whom they belonged or by whom they were selected or used.

Constant Association The adolescent in love is unhappy when away from the loved one. For that reason the couple make every possible effort to study together, to play games together, to walk to and from school together, to attend the same social functions, and, whenever possible, to eat together.

Confidences The adolescent is not satisfied with being with the loved one. He wants to share his joys and sorrows, his hopes and ambitions, his beliefs and feelings with the individual for whom he has a strong romantic attachment. But this is not adequate. The adolescent also wants to tell his confidants of his own sex how he feels about the loved one and what his hopes are for success in this romantic adventure.

Creative Expression When it is impossible to be with the loved one, the adolescent feels the need for some outlet for his pent-up love. Frequently he turns to some creative activity. Writing poetry or love letters; writing in a diary; composing music; knitting articles that the loved one can use; making things of wood, leather, clay, or

metals; painting pictures; and daydreaming are all activities that may be motivated by love.

Jealousy All love is accompanied by jealousy. The stronger the love, the greater the jealousy. Anyone who shows an interest in the loved one or who attempts to arouse the interest or affection of the loved one will be able to arouse the jealousy of an adolescent in love. The adolescent displays his jealousy by trying to get rid of the threat of danger that the interloper presents. Instead of fighting and inflicting physical pain, as the child does, the adolescent fights mostly through the use of words. He is sarcastic and hypercritical in his comments to the person whom he regards as a "love thief." Furthermore, to show the loved one how inferior the interloper is and how superior he himself is, the adolescent takes advantage of every possible opportunity to make derogatory comments about his rival.

Necking "Necking" is a form of physical intimacy characterized by casual kissing and fondling. It is confined to latitudes not lower than the neck (134,135). In the early stages of heterosexual relationships, the shy, self-conscious adolescent may have a craving for physical contact with a member of the opposite sex who has attracted his attention, but he is hesitant to try to effect it for fear of being rebuffed. To break down the barriers between the sexes, kissing games are a common activity at teen-age parties. In addition, they satisfy the young adolescent's curiosity about what kissing "feels like" and "what it does to you" (200,247).

Once the ice has been broken and it is apparent to a boy that the girl he likes will not rebuff his kisses, kissing increases in frequency and in intensity from simple lip kissing to "soul kissing" accompanied by stroking the hair or face of the loved one. Kissing begins with the first dating experiences, even though it may have started earlier in party situations. As dating progresses, kissing and other forms of necking increase to the point where they are a common accompaniment of every date, even the first date when a boy today expects at least a "good-night kiss" as a reward for the entertainment he has provided for the girl (139,202).

With changed social attitudes toward necking, and especially toward kissing, girls lose any feeling of guilt they may have experienced in the past when they allowed boys to kiss them, and now like it (192). Figure 14–3 shows the increase in liking for kissing throughout the early years of adolescence among girls today as compared with girls of a past generation.

Petting Petting is "any sort of physical contact which does not involve union of the genitalia but in which there is a deliberate attempt to effect erotic arousal." It includes "all conceivable forms of physical contact except actual union of the genitalia" (135). One of its purposes is to give sexual release (136). Petting may be one of two types, passive or participant. In *passive* petting, the female is the object of the sexual advances of the male; in *participant* petting, the female is active, reciprocates, and stimulates the male by various techniques (198). Some petting is carried out as a way of releasing sexual tension; most is a way of expressing affection for another. According to the adolescent moral code, the former is not approved, but the latter is (202,203,249).

Adolescents of today begin to pet at a much earlier age than did adolescents of past generations. While very few boys and girls have any petting experience before puberty, there is a sharp rise in the number who pet after they are 13 years old. From then until late adolescence, petting is almost universal (65,101,134,135,199,204). This is illustrated in Figure 14–4. As Reevy has pointed out, "Truly, petting can be called a phenomenon of present-day youth, as almost all of today's youth is experiencing it" (199). At first, young adolescents pet openly, when they are with members of their crowd. Later, as petting becomes more intimate, adolescents pet mainly in private. By junior or certainly by senior year in high school, "petting parties" are common on all dates, with the possible exception of a first date (49,62,103,138,216,248).

Adolescents pet more frequently today

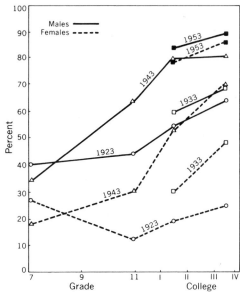

FIGURE 14–3 There is an increase in liking for kissing among both boys and girls during adolescence. This is more pronounced now than it was several decades ago. (Adapted from S. L. Pressey and A. W. Jones: 1923–1953 and 20–60 age changes in moral codes, anxieties, and interests, as shown by the "X-O Tests." *J. Psychol.*, 1955, **39**, 485–502. Used by permission.)

than formerly. This can be explained by the fact that they date more frequently and have less chaperonage than adolescents of the past. How frequently adolescents pet is greatly influenced by the type of dating they are engaging in. If they are going steady, for example, they will not only date

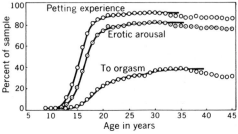

FIGURE 14–4 Petting experiences among girls increase rapidly during the adolescent years. (Adapted from A. C. Kinsey, W. B. Pomeroy, C. E. Martin, and P. H. Gebhard: *Sexual behavior in the human female.* Philadelphia: Saunders, 1953. Used by permission.)

more frequently but will engage in more advanced forms of petting. The petting of girls is more sporadic than that of boys and is more influenced by the type of dating they are engaging in. Boys, on the other hand, expect to pet on *every* date, regardless of the circumstances (65,139,198,199, 203,204).

petting techniques Petting techniques today are elaborate and go to great lengths, compared with the past (139,199). This is especially true as dating involvement increases and adolescents reach the stages of going steady and pinning (127,128). Present-day petting techniques expand in a more or less standard sequence. At first, there is generally bodily contact accompanied by lip kissing. This is followed by deep kissing, or soul kissing. The next steps are deliberate manipulation of the female breast by the male, mouth contacts with the breast, manual manipulation of the female genitalia, but less often of the male genitalia, then an apposition of the naked genitalia, oral stimulation of the male genitalia, and finally oral stimulation of the female genitalia. Petting to a climax occurs occasionally but not very frequently. Most of the action in petting originates with the male and is designed to stimulate the female (64,65,134,135,199,203,204).

reasons for petting Today's adolescents (199):

> . . . have learned to employ petting as an end in itself, and for many adolescents it is the method of achieving heterosexual orgasm or heterosexual satisfaction in a sociosexual context where, frequently, coitus can be avoided.

In addition to the sexual satisfaction petting gives, adolescents have other reasons for petting. Among girls, the reasons most commonly given are infatuation, liking it, curiosity, that "others do it," lack of courage to resist, desire to please the man, fear of being unpopular, to gain and hold on to popularity. A girl who does not pet will have fewer dates than the girl who pets. Those who permit petting are in more demand for dates (62,87,103,135,199,216, 219).

Toward the later part of adolescence many girls take a firm stand against petting, except when they are going steady. The promiscuous petting they formerly engaged in is now regarded as "childish" or "cheap." As they begin to think seriously of marriage, they do not want to ruin their chances of making a good match because they have acquired a reputation for indiscriminate petting. Their desire to please all members of the opposite sex has given way to a desire to please one individual whom they regard as a potential husband (62,128,135, 207,249).

While boys have many of the same reasons for engaging in petting that girls have, one of their major reasons is to convince themselves and others that they are truly masculine. Petting is one way of testing their sexual capacity. This is especially true in the case of boys whose physique is not sex appropriate and who do not have the athletic prowess that is commonly associated with masculine boys in our culture (49,136,207). Boys who are sexually "wild" in the sense that they try to pet on every date and to pet to extremes that are offensive to girls are generally those who suffer from feelings of masculine inadequacy rather than from an abnormally strong sex drive (62,66,67,202).

variations in petting Contrary to popular opinion, petting is more frequent among adolescents of the middle and upper *socioeconomic* groups and of the higher *educational statuses* than it is of the lower (65, 87,138,203,216,249). Among adolescents of the lower socioeconomic levels and among those who leave school at the end of the compulsory school age, petting is less frequent than coitus (49,65,103,203). By contrast, petting is "pre-eminently an occupation of the high school and college levels" (134). Among high school and college students, it is quite usual for a boy to expect at least a kiss on his first date and for those who are going steady to engage in extreme forms of petting or in sexual intercourse (67,135,248).

Adolescents who are active churchgoers and are from devoutly *religious* families are far less likely to engage in the extreme forms of petting, especially to the point of orgasm, than are those who come from families where religion has played a minor role (157,199,202). Adolescents whose families are *socially* mobile adopt the codes of the group they aspire to become identified with and engage in petting of the type approved by that group (157).

Because of the double standard that still prevails, *girls* are at every age and in every socioeconomic group more conservative in their petting than boys. While they may tease a boy to "keep him interested," they put limits to petting more often than boys do (101,202,203,204). This is true not only during the early stages of dating but also during the later stages. Even though they may not conform to their ideal limits, girls are more consistent and less willing to gamble with the serious type of sex play than are boys (128).

Boys, by contrast, are more liberal in their attitudes toward petting and more aggressive. This holds true for all stages of petting from the first date to the engagement period (128,138,203,204). Aggressive petting is very common, especially when the couple is in an automobile or has been drinking. Boys who date younger girls or girls from lower socioeconomic groups tend to be especially aggressive even to the point where they offend or frighten the girls they are dating. With girls of their own age and socioeconomic status, higher-status boys usually limit their aggressive petting to the later, more advanced stages of dating (64, 65,66,127,202). Figure 14–5 shows the relationship between aggressive petting and social status among boys.

evaluation of petting One of the arguments commonly raised against petting is that it will lead to greater sexual liberties, which in turn may lead to pregnancies or venereal diseases (135,174,198,199). Unsuccessful experiences with petting and necking may condition the adolescent unfavorably not only toward a repetition of these experiences but also toward marriage. Some

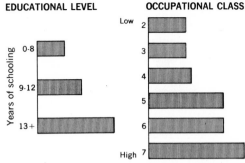

EDUCATIONAL LEVEL   **OCCUPATIONAL CLASS**

FIGURE 14–5 Petting to a climax is more common among boys of the upper educational and occupational levels than among those of the lower levels. (Adapted from A. C. Kinsey, W. B. Pomeroy, and C. E. Martin: *Sexual behavior in the human male.* Philadelphia: Saunders, 1948. Used by permission.)

adolescents are seriously disturbed by petting and are left more or less nervously exhausted by it, unless an orgasm is reached. If an orgasm is reached, there will be no bad physical effects though there may be bad psychological effects (101,135,204).

When boys are especially aggressive in their petting and when girls are literally trapped in a car with a boy who has been drinking, there will not only be disgust and anger on the girls' part but also fear, guilt, and disillusionment. The more helpless the girl is when the boy's petting reaches offensive forms, the more traumatic the experience for the girl and the more likely it is to condition her unfavorably toward physical expressions of affection (65,101, 127,139,202,203).

On the other hand, there are arguments given in favor of petting. For girls, petting has three values. They are as follows (135):

1 *Petting provides most girls with their first real understanding of a heterosexual experience, and, therefore, is a healthy preparation for marriage.*

2 *Petting introduces the girl to the physical, psychologic, and social problems involved in making emotional adjustments to other individuals, thus allowing her to adjust to various types of males.*

3 *Petting prepares the girl for orgasm in marriage.*

Kinsey et al. (134) have expressed the following opinion about the value of petting to marital adjustment:

The girl who, as a result of premarital petting relations, has learned something about the significance of tactile stimulation and response, has less of a problem in resolving her inhibitions after marriage. . . . There is, then, considerable evidence that premarital petting experience contributes definitely to the effectiveness of the sexual relations after marriage.

How much petting will contribute to marital happiness will depend, to a certain extent, upon the type of petting and the reason for it (174). Petting "with affection" leads to a more satisfactory relationship before and after marriage than does petting without affection which is motivated more by curiosity or a desire for sexual release (202,249). Passive petting has been found to be more predictive of marital happiness than participant petting. Regardless of the type of petting and the motivation for it, too much petting and petting of too advanced types is more likely to be predictive of unhappy than of happy marriages (76, 101,136,198,203,204).

Premarital Intercourse In the past, it was an accepted fact that only "loose girls" engaged in intercourse before marriage, though there was a rather general acceptance of the fact that adolescent boys must "sow their wild oats" before marriage. Today, there is widespread concern about the fact that girls, as well as boys, are "sowing their wild oats" and that, as a result, there has been an alarming increase in illegitimate babies and shotgun marriages among girls of the upper socioeconomic groups and of the higher educational statuses (101,162, 202,216,248). Not only do girls of these groups frankly say that they have had intercourse with one or more boys, but many talk or even boast about their sexual experiences as boys do (20,87,216,248,249). Because sexual intercourse during the engagement period is so widespread today, virginity is no longer considered as important as it was in the past (41,196,245).

For most adolescents, their first experience with premarital intercourse comes between the ages of 16 and 18 years, though some have their first experience earlier. Most adolescent premarital intercourse occurs between 16 and 20 years of age though the incidence in adolescence is not so great as during the early twenties. (See Figure 14-6.) Intercourse on a first date is relatively rare except when a boy makes an aggressive sexual attack on the girl after he has been drinking. In the later stages of dating, on the other hand, intercourse is likely to occur on every date. This is especially true of the engagement period (41,66, 196,248).

During the high school years, boys more often engage in intercourse with girls younger than they or of a lower socioeconomic status whom they date primarily because they find them more willing to engage in intercourse (65,66,138,203,216). Among older adolescent boys, especially those in college, the girls with whom they have intercourse are mainly girls of their own age and socioeconomic status whom they date seriously enough to be considering as future mates. It is not usual today for adolescent boys at any age to have intercourse with professional prostitutes, except perhaps as their first experience (135,196,248).

In commenting on intercourse in early adolescence and the places where it usually takes place, Reevy (199) has stressed:

Apparently the patterns of sexual motoric behavior of adolescents are developed before young people leave home (as for example, to go to college) and these patterns develop under their parents' "watchful eyes." Fears that their offspring will behave in markedly different ways sexually, once they leave home, are largely irrational.

reasons for engaging in intercourse Not all premarital intercourse is motivated by a reason; sometimes it is impulsive and unplanned. When adolescents engage in extensive petting, especially after drinking, they sometimes go further than they had intended or wanted to. Under such conditions, they will experience greater feelings of guilt and remorse than satisfaction; this is often accompanied by fear of pregnancy as a result of failure to use contraceptives (62,101,138,203,204).

When boys *intentionally* engage in intercourse, they do so for many reasons, the most important of which are curiosity about an experience that is regarded as forbidden fruit; a desire to prove to themselves and others that they are grown up and sophisticated; a desire to test their potency and eliminate any fears they may have of impotency; to be one of the crowd and do what their friends do; to avoid being teased, razzed, or called "lily-pure"; to avoid being on the defensive about their virginity when their friends talk about their experiences and conquests; to satisfy a strong sexual desire which they formerly satisfied by masturbation; and the belief that because they are in love and will be married soon, there is no reason to wait (69,87,137,138,166, 196,202,245,249).

According to studies made, girls give the following reasons: love for the boy and a wish to satisfy his requests, plans to marry in the near future and willingness to start sexual relations before marriage to please the boy, fear of losing the boy if she fails to comply with his requests, heavy petting that went too far to put a stop to it, a way of gaining popularity with boys, a means of forcing a boy into marriage if he is reluctant, and a feeling that it is all right if both want it and if they are planning to marry in the near future (20,41,62,87,101, 138,196,202,203).

Not only do boys and girls have reasons for engaging in premarital intercourse but they also have valid reasons for *refraining* from doing so. Among these reasons, the ones most frequently given are strong moral standards engendered in the home, fear of disapproval of parents and friends and of social ostracism if discovered, fear of pregnancy, fear that it will prevent marriage because of loss of respect for each other, fear of gaining the reputation of being promiscuous, wanting to wait until marriage, and fear of consequences that might interfere with educational and vocational plans (20,128,196,202,245). Figure 14–7

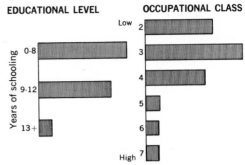

FIGURE 14–6 Premarital intercourse occurs more frequently among boys of the lower educational and occupational levels than among those of the higher levels. (Adapted from A. C. Kinsey, W. B. Pomeroy, and C. E. Martin: *Sexual behavior in the human male.* Philadelphia: Saunders, 1948. Used by permission.)

shows some of the reasons girls give for not engaging in premarital intercourse.

variations in premarital experiences Premarital intercourse is far more common among *older* adolescents than among younger. It is more common among both boys and girls of the lower *socioeconomic* groups than among those of the higher, though recent publicity given to the "promiscuous sex behavior" of college students may suggest that this is not so, especially for *boys* (138,216,249). As Reevy (199) has pointed out:

> Social level is a factor affecting incidence of coitus so markedly that by late adolescence almost all of the boys of the lower social levels but not nearly so many of the higher social classes have experienced intercourse. Approximately one-half of the college-destined, three-fourths of those who have reached the high-school level, and eight-tenths of those who have stopped at the grade-school level have experienced heterosexual coitus by the end of adolescence.

The *socioeconomic* status of girls has less influence on their sexual behavior in this respect than is true of boys. While premarital intercourse is more frequently engaged in by girls of the lower social classes in early and mid-adolescence, the gap be-

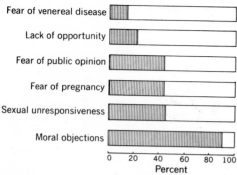

Fear of venereal disease

Lack of opportunity

Fear of public opinion

Fear of pregnancy

Sexual unresponsiveness

Moral objections

0   20   40   60   80   100
Percent

FIGURE 14–7 Reasons girls give for not engaging in premarital intercourse. (Adapted from A. C. Kinsey, W. B. Pomeroy, C. E. Martin, and P. H. Gebhard: *Sexual behavior in the human female.* Philadelphia: Saunders, 1953. Used by permission.)

tween the social classes gradually narrows as they approach adulthood (20,196,199, 212,248,249). Girls of all social classes generally limit this type of sexual behavior to the later *stages* of *dating* except in the cases of lower-class girls who date upper-class boys. Boys, by contrast, will engage in intercourse at *any* stage in dating, even on the first date, if they can persuade or force the girl to do so (65,67,127,135,139). Girls whose parents are *socially mobile* tend to be more cautious about engaging in behavior that might interfere with their acceptance by the group they hope to be identified with than girls whose family status is more static. This is less true of boys (157).

Boys who *mature early* not only engage in intercourse earlier than those who mature late but they engage more frequently during the adolescent years and even up to middle age. This has not been found to be true of girls (134,135). The incidence of premarital intercourse is higher for adolescents of all ages and both sexes who attend church infrequently, regardless of their religious affiliation, than for those whose *religious training* has been stricter and who are more devout (55,196,199,202).

psychological effects of engaging in premarital intercourse What effects premarital intercourse will have on adolescents will depend to a large extent upon the moral values

they have established and upon their belief as to its "safety." Girls of all social classes have been brought up to believe that such behavior is wrong. Many boys disapprove of engaging in premarital intercourse. They may, however, show an inconsistency between their beliefs and actions, owing primarily to pressures from their peers. Girls, to a lesser extent, are influenced by peer pressures to engage in behavior they consider wrong (62,75,134,135,196,199).

When a person does something he believes is wrong, feelings of guilt and shame are inevitable. To ease these feelings, many boys and girls rationalize their behavior by saying that they will be married in a few weeks or months. However, if they know their parents disapprove of premarital intercourse, and if they have a close relationship with their parents, even this rationalization is not adequate to reduce their feelings of guilt (20,65,196,202).

In addition to feelings of guilt, many adolescents experience fear of being ostracized by the social group if their behavior becomes known and fear of pregnancy which might lead to a shotgun marriage and seriously interfere with their educational and vocational plans. In girls, there is the added fear that pregnancy will cause her to lose the boy she loves and force her to face the social stigma of having an illegitimate child alone. In addition, many girls experience the fear that, by refusing to engage in premarital intercourse with the boy they love, they will lose him (66,196,249). In commenting on the exploitative aspect of premarital intercourse, Gottlieb and Ramsey have stressed that "there appears to be a system of mutual exploitation with males seeking the sexual exploitation of females and females seeking the socio-economic exploitation of males" (90).

Ehrmann (66) is even more emphatic in his comments:

In more ways than one it is a sorry picture, where both boys and girls are offered exploitative roles, the boys playing on each girl's hope of permanence and early marriage to get cheap and immediate and unsatisfactory sexual compliance, the girl playing on the vulnerability of the boy who begins to court her by entangling him in sexual intimacy which will propel him toward marriage.

Regrets at having started sexual relationships before marriage often plague both boys and girls. However, once they have started, they find it difficult to stop. This often leads to an earlier marriage than either had planned for. The result is a feeling of being trapped, which is shown in resentments against the marriage partner (63,162, 249). Boys are far more likely than girls to regret *not* having experienced intercourse before marriage. Few girls have such regrets (134,135,196,245). (See Figure 14-8.)

learning to play approved sex roles

Learning to play approved sex roles, the sixth task in achieving mature heterosexuality, is one of the most difficult and most resisted, especially by girls. Long before childhood is over, both boys and girls are well aware of the fact that there is a culturally approved sex role for members of the two sexes. They are also well aware that they are expected to play these roles and that failure to do so will be a handicap to them in their acceptance by members of the peer group (96,98,110,175,209,210,211, 243).

Furthermore, both boys and girls discover that the role boys are expected to play is more favorable and more prestigeful in the eyes of the cultural group than is the approved role for girls (74,140). As a result, girls become increasingly more dissatisfied with the feminine role. Boys, by contrast, become increasingly satisfied with the role society expects them to play; they show no desire to change to the girls' role (24, 95,99,100,163,175,190,211).

Uncertainty about Approved Adult Roles
Even though children know that members of the two sexes are expected to play different roles, they have somewhat blurred concepts of them and they often believe that the role of women in adult life is superior to that of men. The reason for this is that in their own homes, in the homes of their

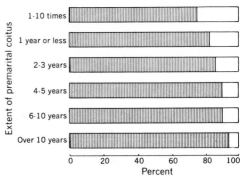

FIGURE 14-8 Regrets girls have for engaging in premarital intercourse vary according to the extent with which they engage in it. (Adapted from A. C. Kinsey, W. B. Pomeroy, C. E. Martin, and P. H. Gebhard: *Sexual behavior in the human female.* Philadelphia: Saunders, 1953. Used by permission.)

friends, and in school, women are in control (14,70,171,232). As children approach adolescence, the approved roles for men and women gradually become more distinctly defined. In addition, it becomes increasingly apparent to them that the female role is not more powerful than the male role (123,164, 190,191). As a result, both boys and girls show a greater preference for the masculine role. Figure 14-9 shows sex differences in sex-role preferences.

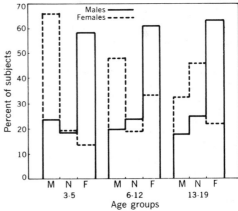

M=Masculine role   N=No preference   F=Female role

FIGURE 14-9 Sex-role preferences for males and females at different ages. (Adapted from V. Piskin: Psychosexual development in terms of object and role preferences. *J. clin Psychol.,* 1960, **16**, 238-240. Used by permission.)

There are reasons for these blurred and often erroneous concepts of adult sex roles during childhood. When children see the mother working outside the home and the father helping with the home responsibilities, it is hard for children to realize that their roles are supposed to be different (8, 114,143,185). When the father is away from home during the major part of the child's day and the mother is in control of the home, it is natural for the child to assume that the mother's role is superior to that of the father. They then interpret this to mean that the role of adult women is superior to that of adult men (2,80,181, 189). If, in addition, an older sister plays the role of mother substitute, this further reinforces the child's concept of the superiority of the adult female role (36,85, 140). In school, children of the two sexes receive the same training: girls are given advantages similar to those of boys. This suggests to them that they will be playing similar roles when they become adults because the school constantly reminds them that their schooling is a preparation for adult life (85,158).

The seriousness of blurred concepts is that both boys and girls approach adolescence without a clear understanding of what society will expect of them. It is especially serious for girls who will be forced to accept a role they have not been prepared for and which they soon discover is considered inferior to the role boys are supposed to play. In addition, they discover that there is a double standard of conduct which permits boys to do things for which girls are seriously condemned (85,92,218,219).

STEREOTYPES OF ADULT SEX ROLES

In adolescence, the vague and poorly defined concepts of sex roles learned in childhood are gradually replaced by clearly defined ones based on cultural stereotypes. In every culture, there are certain ways of behaving that are regarded as "typically masculine" and others that are looked upon as "typically feminine." These form the sex stereotypes of the culture (58,80,143,173, 177).

Stereotype of Male Role The cultural stereotype of the adult male is that of a man who is physically large and powerful; this physical superiority is reflected in his characteristic manner of behavior in all situations. He is frank, straightforward, and dominant in his social relationships; he is intellectually rational and competent, thinks clearly, and is broad-minded; he is bold, vigorous, and effective in dealing with his environment; and he is ambitious, courageous, daring, adventuresome, and self-confident in whatever he does. The stereotype of the male contains some vices as well, but these are limited to mild exaggerations of the desirable characteristics. For example, the typical adult male is thought of as somewhat boastful, stubborn, or reckless, but these qualities are an outgrowth of his strength and superiority (1,49,173,225).

The stereotype of the adult male contains elements relating to his behavior. At home, he is the head of the household, making decisions about all matters of importance and determining the pattern of the life for every member of the family. He contributes financially and through his leadership to the welfare of the family but not through work except that which is "too heavy" for a woman (122,125,161,240). In society, he plays a leadership role in any situation where women as well as men are involved, and in work, he has more power and prestige than the women workers. His work is typically masculine, involving physical or mental prowess, and is never in occupations which are regarded as "women's work," such as nursing or beauty culture (89,225,266).

Stereotype of Female Role The stereotype of the adult woman is that of the typical "lady"—a female with a petite, delicate body build, whose behavior fits her appearance. She is graceful and has well-developed social skills, is poised, well mannered, tactful, sophisticated, but modest; she has emotional warmth and shows concern for the affairs of others, is little interested in material success, but is artistic, religious, and sensitive. Her weak qualities, like those of the stereotyped male, are exaggerations of her desirable qualities; she may be too submissive, emotional, snobbish, or frivolous (49,173,225).

The traditional role of the adult woman, according to the cultural stereotype, is other-oriented in the sense that she achieves fulfillment by proxy (235). This fulfillment comes from serving others in the home, whether husband, children, or elderly parents, or from serving others in a job oriented toward helping others, such as nursing, teaching, or domestic service. Because service to others is traditionally most satisfying to a woman if it is for her own family, the stereotype of an adult woman is of a married woman, not a single woman or widow (56,206,233). Whether in the home or outside, the "typical" woman of the American culture plays a subordinate role, leaving all decision making and other matters of importance to the male (89,122,161, 264).

Relative Importance of Roles Adolescents soon discover that the cultural stereotype of the adult male contains more favorable and more prestigeful characteristics than that of the adult female. Furthermore, adolescents discover, long before they reach adulthood, that society expects them to use the cultural stereotypes as models. Girls are aware that they must be typically feminine if they are to be popular with boys; boys know that their social acceptance will be enhanced by conformity to the stereotype of the typical male (89,178,233,235).

ACCEPTANCE OF STEREOTYPES OF SEX ROLES

Knowing what is the approved role for one's sex does not necessarily guarantee acceptance of this role, nor does it guarantee motivation to pattern one's behavior in accordance with it. Acceptance will depend primarily on how closely such a role conforms to the individual's concept of what he would like to be and how much prestige in the eyes of the group the role has. It is difficult, for example, for a boy whose interests and abilities are primarily intellectual

or artistic to play the role of an athlete or to prepare for a vocation in business or industry that is far removed from his interests.

Similarly, a girl who has derived personal satisfaction from intellectual activities in high school or college or from playing a leadership role in extracurricular activities will find it far from easy to accept the traditional role of wife and mother if, by doing so, she must give up her intellectual activities and play a subordinate role in the home. However, when a role is prestigeful, it is easier to accept than when it lacks prestige. This is especially true when the role, per se, does not fit into the individual's interests and abilities. A boy with artistic interests, for example, finds it easier to turn his talents into advertising or some similar area in the business world when he is rewarded by financial success and prestige than does the girl who finds playing the role of wife and mother is neither as prestigeful nor as economically rewarding as the role she formerly played which made use of her intellectual abilities and interests (31,58,85,186,235).

Acceptance by Boys Boys, at all times and in all socioeconomic groups, find acceptance of the stereotyped adult masculine role easier and more satisfying than girls find the adult female role (3,104,173,273). There are definite reasons for this. Boys, since earliest childhood, have been trained to play the masculine role; strong pressures at home and in the peer group have been put on them to do so (43,97). As a result, there is little ambiguity in their minds about what the approved role is. They have known, since childhood, that the male role is more prestigeful than the female role and they have discovered the ego satisfaction of playing it.

Even more important, boys know that the more sex appropriate they are, the greater their acceptance by the peer group. This adds to their motivation to conform to the male-role stereotype (1,89,94,95,104, 159,180,183). Because it is to a boy's personal advantage to accept the stereotype of the adult male role, there is little likelihood that many adolescent boys would prefer the female role. As Ausubel has commented, "The male counterpart of a 'tomboy' who relishes sewing and reads girls' books is indeed a rarity" (4).

Because it is also to a boy's personal advantage to accept the cultural stereotype of the adult female role, it is not surprising that most adolescent boys expect the girls they date and the one they will eventually marry to play a role subordinate to theirs and to acquire the physical and personality characteristics that are unquestionably feminine (3,85,264). It is especially important for boys who find it difficult, for one reason or another, to conform to the stereotype of the adult male to expect the girls they date to be feminine (60,125,178).

Acceptance by Girls Girls of the lower *socioeconomic groups* find acceptance of the traditional concepts of sex roles easier than do girls from the middle and upper groups; girls of the lower groups have grown up in homes and neighborhoods where they constantly see adults playing these roles and they have been trained from childhood to play the traditional role prescribed for adult women (104,173,222). Negro girls are accustomed to a matriarchal family when the fathers desert the mothers. They become accustomed to a pattern of female authority in the home and tend to depreciate the male role (4).

Girls of the middle and upper socioeconomic groups, by contrast, have been permitted and even encouraged since earliest childhood to play a role similar to that of boys; they have been accustomed to seeing their parents and the parents of their friends play more equalitarian than traditional roles; they have been educated in high school and college in a manner similar to boys; many of them have been trained for careers in fields that are traditionally thought of as masculine; and many have played leadership roles which gave them a taste of the ego satisfaction of having authority. As a result, acceptance of the traditional concepts of male and female sex roles is difficult for them (104,132,173).

This difficulty is intensified by, first, the fact that accepting the traditional concepts of sex roles will necessitate *learning new skills*, new patterns of behavior, and new attitudes toward their own and the opposite sex, and second, by the fact that the traditional adult female role is far *less prestigeful* than the role they have been playing. Furthermore, the girl who has been educated along the same lines as boys and has more often than not outstripped the boys in grades resists accepting a role which she knows can be played by a person of less intelligence and education than she. She further resists playing a role which requires training and learning of skills which she is not interested in acquiring and which she knows have little prestige (31,37,85,125, 132,173,182).

CONCEPTS OF EQUALITARIAN ROLES

As a result of this resistance toward the acceptance of the traditional concepts of sex roles, many girls would like to substitute concepts of more equalitarian roles. They confidently expect that playing such roles in their adult lives will be possible, just as it has been throughout their childhood years (3,58,186,233).

Role of Men The concept of the equalitarian role for men is that of a man who shares equally with his wife in the care of the home and children, in decision making, and in the financial support of the family. Because the wife is the intellectual and educational equal of her husband, this concept holds that husband and wife should share equally in all family planning—whether it relates to spending or investing the family income—in decisions about training the children, about the kind of work the husband and wife should do in the home, and about their jobs in the business world (119, 161,264).

The equalitarian concept holds that the role of the father is more than that of supporter and disciplinarian of his children; he wants to be a "good father" in the sense that he shares in the care and training of his children (40,125). This concept holds that a man does not have delusions of grandeur about himself just because he is a male. Rather, he regards differences between

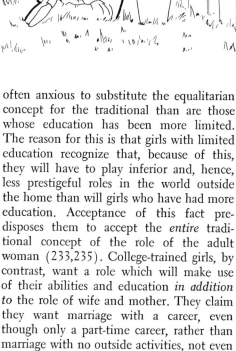

FIGURE 14–10 Concepts of equalitarian roles.

the sexes as "differences," not as superiorities or inferiorities. Most important of all, this concept includes the belief that a male who is equalitarian in his attitudes and behavior would not be regarded as a henpecked husband but as a good husband and father (8,85,240). (See Figure 14–10.)

Role of Women   The equalitarian concept of the adult female role is that in which a woman gains self-fulfillment in life through actualizing her own potentials rather than by proxy through helping others to achieve their potentials (235,273). This does not mean giving up the roles of wife and mother, but rather adding to them roles which make use of her training and abilities, either in jobs or in community activities (71,151). In the home, her role is on a par with her husband's, sharing in all matters relating to the management of the home and the training and care of the children (51,60,61). Figure 14–11 shows some of the important components of the equalitarian concept of sex roles in adult life.

Variations in Acceptance of Concepts   Girls who have had a college education are more

often anxious to substitute the equalitarian concept for the traditional than are those whose education has been more limited. The reason for this is that girls with limited education recognize that, because of this, they will have to play inferior and, hence, less prestigeful roles in the world outside the home than will girls who have had more education. Acceptance of this fact predisposes them to accept the *entire* traditional concept of the role of the adult woman (233,235). College-trained girls, by contrast, want a role which will make use of their abilities and education *in addition to* the role of wife and mother. They claim they want marriage with a career, even though only a part-time career, rather than marriage with no outside activities, not even volunteer community services (46,168,178). Figure 14–12 shows the postgraduate role expectations of a group of college seniors.

EFFECTS OF SEX-ROLE CONCEPTS
The adolescent's concept of himself as a person will be affected by which concept of sex role—traditional, equalitarian, or a combination of both—he accepts and whether he accepts the concept voluntarily or involuntarily. This effect comes partly from

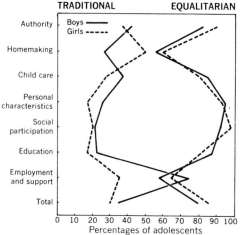

FIGURE 14–11 Important components of the traditional and equalitarian concepts of sex roles as identified by adolescents. (Adapted from M. S. Dunn: Marriage role expectations of adolescents. *Marriage fam. Living*, 1960, **22**, 99–111. Used by permission.)

the way the adolescent perceives the reactions of others to him and partly from how he feels about the patterns of behavior and attitudes that are associated with the role with which he is identified (97,104,267).

Traditional Role Acceptance of the concept of traditional roles will affect the members of the two sexes differently. A brief analysis of the effects that have been reported will serve to substantiate this statement.

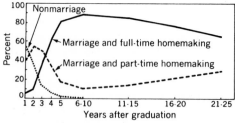

FIGURE 14–12 Postgraduation role expectations of a group of senior college women. (Adapted from H. T. Christensen and M. M. Swihart: Post graduate role preferences of senior women in college. *Marriage fam. Living*, 1956, **18**, 52–57. Used by permission.)

effects on boys Boys who accept the concept of the traditional role of males in our culture experience a feeling of superiority and ego satisfaction from being identified with a role that is prestigeful in the eyes of the cultural group. In addition, acceptance of the traditional male role increases the boy's social acceptance with members of both sexes; this leads to better social and personal adjustment and to greater emotional stability (40,173,179,225, 266).

Feelings of personal superiority—a common accompaniment of identification with the traditional male role—lead to intolerance of any indication of femininity in other boys and to admiration for typically masculine boys (1,149,183,264). In addition, the boy who has identified himself with the traditional masculine role scorns all activities that are not considered sex appropriate and tries to identify himself with those which are regarded as sex appropriate. He regards any occupation that is traditionally associated with girls—teaching or nursing, for example—as inferior to those traditionally associated with men—law and medicine, say—and he resents any girl who aspires to enter one of the occupations that "belong to men" (89,273).

Acceptance of the traditional masculine role leads to the development of a personality pattern characteristic of men (14). The traits characteristic of this pattern will be discussed in more detail in the chapter on personality. Outstanding among these are self-confidence, egocentrism, authoritarianism, strong drive for achievement, fearlessness, and adventuresomeness (18, 22). Even boys who find acceptance of the traditional male role difficult derive enough personal and social satisfaction from doing so to justify the sacrifice in personal interests. Consequently, they conform, at least outwardly, to the approved patterns of behavior and attitudes of the traditional male (43,170,266,267,273).

effects on girls When a girl identifies herself with the traditional female role and tries to conform to the socially approved attitudes and behavior patterns of the ideal woman, she will win the approval of the social group and, with it, acceptance by the group (61,173,264). However, to do this she must devote her study time to "feminine" subjects; she must read feminine books and magazines; she must be interested in social activities and service to others; she must plan to enter a feminine line of work until marriage and then give up her career to devote her time to her home and family; and she must develop typically feminine personality characteristics, such as graciousness, submissiveness, and sympathy for the weak and oppressed (18,22,31,104,186,266).

Social approval and acceptance, however, do not guarantee *self-acceptance*—an essential to good self-adjustment. On the contrary, there is ample evidence that girls who accept the traditional sex role more often develop unfavorable than favorable self-concepts. This is true even when a girl *voluntarily* accepts this role because of earlier training, her own desire to be a wife and mother, parental and peer pressures and expectations, her religion, or a model of maternal happiness in her own home (126,233,234,235,273). The reason for her poor self-concept is partly that she finds the role she accepts boring and frustrating and partly that she discovers the role is even less prestigeful than the role she played as a child and far less prestigeful than the adult male role.

If the girl finds the role she voluntarily accepted far short of what she had anticipated, that it does not tax her abilities or make use of her training, that it is little appreciated by those for whom she has sacrificed her personal interests, that the work is dull, that it is lonely and too confining, and that the romanticism she had associated with the traditional female role does not exist, her attitude toward it will be far from favorable. However, having accepted this role, she realizes that she is "trapped"; there is no way for her to escape (132,267).

Discovery of the unfavorable social attitude toward her role further intensifies her discontent and frustration. She soon learns (145):

> Our present age does not emphasize the value "housewife" either in education or in school. To the contrary, there is a thorough indoctrination that being a housewife is a fate not a call.

In time, the girl accepts the prevailing view of her inferiority. This then undermines her respect for herself as a member of the female sex and derogates the feminine role. As a result, she develops a minority-group complex (4,40,93,104,126,186).

When this happens, it plays havoc with her personal and social adjustments. Like any minority-group member, she not only loses respect for herself and her abilities, but she develops deep resentments against those who treat her as an inferior. As a result, she loses many of the qualities that make a girl or woman happy and well adjusted. Instead, she becomes bitter, often complaining about her lot and wishing that she had been born a member of the male sex. In addition, she develops many of the characteristics of a member of a minority group: she becomes hypercritical of her own sex; she takes delight in trying to put members of the male sex "in their place"; and she refuses to do many of the things society expects of members of her sex, such as being "social" and gracious in her relationships with others (18,93,145,186).

The greatest damage to good personal and social adjustment comes when a girl *involuntarily* accepts the traditional female role and poses as being truly feminine while, inwardly, rebelling against it. She accepts this role against her better judgment to please her father or, more often, to please the boy she wants to marry (104,126). Many girls start to pose as more feminine than they are when they discover that this adds to their popularity with members of the opposite sex (49,233,235). The type of adolescent girl most likely to pose as being more acceptant of the traditional female role than she actually is is one who is intelligent, highly educated, and interested in a career that is traditionally masculine (71, 126).

Such girls fall in the category of "marginal women"; they are not truly feminine nor have they rejected the female role completely. They want to be popular with the boys, to marry, and to have children. But, at the same time, they want to have a career in addition to marriage. When they discover that this is rarely possible, they are dissatisfied and disillusioned. Even worse, they are articulate about their dissastisfaction and complaining about their unfortunate lot in life (71,80,93,126,186).

Their dissastisfaction and disillusionment comes from many sources. The most important of these are the necessity for value change, low prestige of their role, and feelings of being trapped. As Korner has pointed out, "Becoming a housewife requires considerable value adjustments from many women" (145). The girl who has put high value on creativity and intellectual achievement, for example, finds it difficult to put equally high value on activities that can be carried out by a person of limited intelligence and education—activities which she has always regarded as drudgery (71, 145).

The girl who has been educated along the same lines as boys, who has planned to enter a prestigeful occupation, and who has been accustomed to playing a leadership role in school or college finds the acceptance of a role with little prestige even more difficult than the girl who voluntarily accepts it. The girl who posed as feminine, but who confidently expected to combine career with marriage, is especially disillusioned with marriage when she discovers that she must abandon, at least temporarily, a prestigeful role and devote her entire time and efforts to a role the social group regards as unprestigeful (18,71,132).

The most serious cause of disillusionment and dissatisfaction for the girl comes from feeling *trapped* in a situation not to her liking and not prestigeful in the eyes of the world. As Kiell and Friedman have pointed out, the college girl feels that she is entering a world where the horizons are unlimited. If she has had "glimpses and perhaps a taste of unlimited horizons and aspirations" which are then closed to her and replaced by a role which she has always regarded as drudgery, it is not surprising that "active discontent results from her ability to conceive of a better alternative to her present condition and from her inability to realize such a better alternative" (132). In her attempt to reconcile herself to the role she had not anticipated playing as her *only* role she may try socially approved female activities, such as community work, only to find that they are poor substitutes for the role she abandoned. Should she consider returning to the career she abandoned, she will feel guilty because society will criticize her for neglecting her family (81,126,132).

Because of the disillusionment and dissatisfaction a girl sooner or later experiences if she tries to convince herself and others that she wants to play the traditional female role when, in reality, she does not, the damage to her personal and social adjustment is even more serious than that to the girl who voluntarily accepts the traditional role. For the former, the "rewards of housewifemanship are frustration and lowered self-esteem. Plowed under is the healthy self-concept she had before marriage" (132). Not only will she become embittered and resentful, but she is likely to verbalize her attitudes to her family, her friends, and her acquaintances. The result is the development of a deeply disturbed personality and rejection by the social group because of her unfeminine attitudes (18,93,145).

Equalitarian Role Because the equalitarian roles for the two sexes are relatively new in our culture and because they exist in few other cultures in the world, it is difficult for the social group to accept them. This is especially true among members of the older generation. It is even more so among men who resist the acceptance of a role that is less prestigeful and less ego satisfying than the traditional role. Because of this social resistance to the acceptance of equalitarian roles, the effects on those who do accept them are greatly influenced by the prevailing cultural attitudes.

effects on boys A boy who rejects the socially approved traditional role for men in favor of the equalitarian role is usually regarded by the social group as effeminate, a sissy, or henpecked (18,240). As Koch (141) has pointed out:

> There is evidence that it is more serious in our culture for the boy to deviate from the male type than for the girl to deviate from the female type. In other words, a sissy is more frowned upon than a tomboy.

A boy who feels incapable of playing the traditional male role, either because of lack of masculine physique or because of too long identification with adult women in childhood, which has resulted in the development of feminine attitudes, interests, and patterns of behavior, quickly senses the unfavorable attitude of the social group toward him (43,104,170,173). Should he, for example, show more interest in female recreations than in sports, should he prefer "feminine" subjects, such as art, literature, and languages in school or college to the "masculine" subjects of mathematics and science, should he prepare for a "feminine" occupation, such as teaching or nursing, or should he verbalize his belief in the equalitarian status of the two sexes in business or the home, he must be prepared for the taunts of sissy and henpecked (94,154,173, 180,221,266,273).

Knowing how the social group feels about a male who rejects the traditional male role in favor of an equalitarian role, the boy who does so generally feels the necessity of justifying his choice by using defense mechanisms. He may, for example, rationalize his interest in "sissy subjects" by explaining that they will be an asset to him in the line of business he has selected for his future vocation. He soon discovers, however, that rationalization is not so effective as a defense mechanism as is compensation. Much of the wild sex behavior of boys, their preoccupation with sex jokes, pictures, literature, and movies, their aggressive patterns of petting, and their authoritarian, dogmatic approach to all members of the female sex are ways of defining themselves as typically masculine and of covering up characteristics that fall short of the virile ideal (1,136,180,183,207).

effects on girls The rejection of the traditional sex roles and substitution of equalitarian roles is even more damaging to the personal and social adjustments of girls than the outward acceptance but inward rejection of the traditional female role. Like boys, they are faced with unfavorable social attitudes and poor social acceptance. They know that they are disapproved of by members of their own sex as well as by members of the opposite sex; they suspect that they are regarded as "squares"; they sense that they are pitied because they are not popular with members of the opposite sex; and they believe that people accuse them of preferring the equalitarian role because they cannot play the traditional role successfully (14,104,173,233,235,266). A girl who prefers not to marry because she does not like the traditional role of wife and mother knows that society has a derogatory attitude toward an unmarried woman (56). The girl who aspires to an equalitarian role in the business world knows that she will not only be faced with social disapproval because she has rejected the traditional female role, but that she will find barriers to the achievement of the role she aspires to (31,126,186,188).

Furthermore, the girl knows that society is often highly critical of and punitive in its attitude toward women who substitute the equalitarian role for the traditional (21,173,264). If she works after marriage, she realizes that she will be criticized for "neglecting her family for selfish reasons" (86). If she, in addition, expects her children and husband to share some of the home responsibilities, she will be accused of henpecking her husband and of spoiling her children's youth (76,80). Should her children do poorly in school or get into trouble with the law, she will be blamed and criticized for putting selfish interests ahead of her maternal responsibilities (260).

To eliminate the damaging effects of social disapproval and rejection on her self-concept, the girl who accepts the equalitarian role may try to erect defenses against her "masculine" behavior. In doing so, she will suffer from inner conflicts and strains (126,154). Even worse, she will soon discover that the defenses she uses increase rather than decrease social disapproval; this is not true in the case of boys. For example, if she uses rationalization to explain that she prefers being single to the role of wife and mother, she knows she will be accused of having a sour-grapes attitude. If she tries to compensate by promiscuous sex behavior to show that she is sex appropriate in her interests and drives, she will be accused of being fast or loose. As a result, many girls who prefer the equalitarian role succumb to the pressures of the social group—against their better judgment—and accept the traditional feminine role (273). By doing so, they more often than not increase the psychological damage that was already done by their acceptance of the equalitarian role.

EFFECTS OF ROLE CONFLICTS

The seriousness of conflict between traditional and equalitarian roles for the adolescent is increased when this conflict is between the role the adolescent *wants* to play and the role significant people in his life think he *should* play. Girls, as has been pointed out before, often believe that their fathers and male peers expect them to play the traditional female role. Girls likewise know that their mothers, even though they may be dissatisfied with their own roles as wives and mothers, expect them to be feminine as a means of increasing their popularity with boys (49,80,126). Furthermore, mothers are realistic enough to know that in our culture today, with its shortage of domestic help, a girl has no alternative but to play the traditional female role if she marries. To many American mothers, having a daughter who does not marry is a stigma on the whole family. Nor are girls spared pressures from their female peers to be feminine. A girl may be a tomboy while she is a young child, but being a tomboy when she is older is one of the quickest ways of winning social rejection (49,80,104, 126).

Boys also know that their fathers, older brothers, and peers expect them to play the traditional male role (49,83). They know only too well that trying to play an equalitarian role or, even worse, a role identified in any way with the female sex is sure to bring social scorn and, with it, rejection (43,49,104).

Whenever a person experiences a conflict between what he wants to do and what he knows others expect him to do, there is bound to be anxiety, guilt, and resentment. Furthermore, until the conflict is settled— and settled to the satisfaction of all concerned—there will be friction. A girl who insists, for example, upon playing an equalitarian role when she is dating a boy whose concept of the ideal woman conforms to the traditional stereotype, will have a frictional courtship that is likely to lead to a breakup. Should she give in and accept the traditional role, she will be unhappy and dissatisfied. Later, if she reverts to the equalitarian role, this will lead to friction in her marriage (60,80,84,126,178).

When she finds housework and child care far less interesting and rewarding than work outside the home and then decides to take a job, she will find herself in constant conflict with her husband, her family, her friends, and her neighbors, who maintain that her place is in the home. To reduce friction, she may resort to rationalization to explain that she is working to save money for the children's education. Or she may project the blame on her husband, accusing him of not earning enough to support the family. A girl who has an equalitarian concept of the male's role in marriage will bitterly resent his traditional concept of his role when he refuses to help with the housework and care of the children on the ground that they are "woman's work" (80,104, 126).

When a conflict arising over differences in sex-role concepts is settled by one individual's acceptance of the role others think he should play, it will not make the role any more attractive and appealing than it previously was. In fact, the reverse is more likely to be true; involuntary acceptance is usually colored by strong resentments. Should the conflict be settled by the individual's acceptance of the role he *wants* to play and by rejection of the role others think he should play, he will suffer from feelings of guilt, shame, and inferiority stemming from unfavorable attitudes of others because of his sex inappropriateness. If, on the other hand, the conflict is settled by compromise, each giving in to the other to a certain extent, neither is satisfied; each blames the other whenever anything goes wrong (80,84,126).

Because conflict is inevitable when two people in close heterosexual relationships have different concepts of the roles they should play and because conflict is an inevitable cause of poor family relationships, the only wise solution to the problem is for adolescents to limit their dating to individuals whose concepts of sex roles are similar to theirs and who, as a result, see eye to eye on this important matter. Even more important, in the selection of a mate, this principle should be followed to the letter. Posing as masculine or feminine is rarely a solution. Sooner or later the individual reverts to the role he prefers. When this is impossible, he feels frustrated, resentful, and unhappy.

Unfortunately, adolescents tend to be romantic and unrealistic; they believe that love and marriage will solve *all* their problems, including the problem of their differences in sex-role concepts. This is one of the many reasons why early marriages are hazardous. The adolescent who is aware of the scientifically proved fact that attitudes are difficult to change and that the longer they have existed, the more resistant to change they become, will recognize that it is folly to believe that marriage is the solution to this problem.

An interesting sidelight on this matter comes from a study of the attitudes of Japanese-American and Caucasian-American students toward marriage roles. In this study it was found that the attitudes of the male students were more traditional while those of the female students tended to be more democratic and equalitarian. Knowledge of this led many female students to select as husbands men who held concepts more similar to those than members of their own cultural group did (3). Perhaps American

adolescents of today could learn a meaningful lesson from this study.

success in making transition to heterosexuality

There is strong evidence that the sex drive is influenced by psychological factors, especially the individual's *attitudes toward sex*. As such, it can be controlled by culturally approved attitudes or distorted by unfavorable attitudes. As Kirkendall has pointed out, "Sexual behavior is primarily a psychological rather than a physical matter" (136). While it is true that the sex drive is a "physical urgency rooted in the biochemical nature of the individual," the physiological sex tensions that accompany this drive are accentuated by psychological factors. Because these psychological factors differ according to the cultural group, there are individual differences in the ways in which adolescents strive for sexual release and in the form this release takes (136).

Some adolescents find the sex drive hard to manage; they experience many sex tensions and they use outlets for these tensions that are not approved by the social group. Other adolescents whose interests are in matters other than sex are less affected by sex in mass media. Furthermore, their training helps them to develop more wholesome attitudes which lead to more wholesome and socially approved patterns of sexual behavior.

If, for example, an adolescent has learned to think of sex behavior as horrible and dangerous or to think that childbearing is the inevitable price one must pay for sexual relationships, these beliefs will foster an attitude that will lead to very different behavior than would occur, had his early training put more emphasis on the self-fulfillment that comes from heterosexual experiences and on the joys of parenthood (33). Adolescents who have learned to think of normal expressions of the sex drive as signs of masculinity or femininity show a greater interest in members of the opposite sex and in sexual behavior (21,134,136).

If *environmental conditions* are unfavorable to the normal development of heterosexuality, the result is usually a warped attitude toward sex. When the adolescent whose physical development is normal claims to have no interest in members of the other sex or in activities involving members of the other sex, he is left out of most of the social activities of his contemporaries, because these activities are planned for members of the two sexes. As a result of this, he loses the opportunity to learn the social skills his contemporaries are learning. Of equally serious importance is the fact that with sexual maturing comes the awakening of sex drives and desires that must be satisfied in some way.

UNSATISFACTORY ADJUSTMENTS

When unhealthy attitudes toward sex have developed or when environmental conditions prevent a normal pattern of sexuality from developing, the result is a turning of the sex drive into channels that lead to unwholesome and socially disapproved forms of sexual behavior. Few adolescents fail to make the transition into normal heterosexuality. Failure is most likely to occur when unsatisfactory adjustments have continued over a period of time without corrective measures to improve the adolescent's attitudes toward sex or his environment or both.

When this happens, the result is usually the development of one or more forms of sex aberrations, combined with heightened interest in sex. Among the forms of unsatisfactory adjustment made by the adolescent, the following are the most common.

Masturbation Masturbation is stimulation of the genital organs by stroking, fondling, or playing with them to produce pleasurable sensations (135). Some cases of masturbation have developed accidentally. Owing to local irritations, pressure of too tight clothing, or curiosity, the child manipulates his genital organs. Other cases of masturbation are learned through tuition. Boys are generally introduced to masturbation as a "new sport" by older boys. Most girls learn to masturbate as a result of the

exploration of their own genitals (115,134, 135,147,199).

The peak of masturbation comes in adolescence. Masturbation generally begins as a form of outlet for sexual tension during the years immediately preceding or very soon after puberty. This means around the age of 13 or 14 years for boys and a year or two earlier for girls. When the adolescent is making good, or relatively good, heterosexual adjustments, there is a decline in masturbation in late adolescence. (See Figure 14–13.) As sex outlets in the form of necking, petting, and intercourse appear, masturbation decreases. Frequent masturbators are those who have not made good heterosexual adjustments or who are emotionally and socially immature (134,135, 136,199,271).

Thus, masturbation in adolescence, if it is practiced more frequently than is usual for a given age level and when it is the preferred form of sexual outlet, can be regarded as a danger signal. It indicates that the adolescent is not making the transition into heterosexual maturity as satisfactorily as one should expect for his age level. As Strang (236) has explained, masturbation:

> . . . represents an infantile stage of sexual development and an attempt to satisfy the sex drive without incurring the risk involved in heterosexual relations. . . . When the practice persists into the teens, it should be regarded as representing retarded rather than abnormal sexual development. . . . The occasional practice should be accepted at the time, with the knowledge that it can be overcome, and with the expectation that it will be replaced by more mature sex interests. If, however, masturbation is used as the exclusive method by which an adolescent expresses the sex drive, he may never achieve intimacy with the opposite sex. Thus he fails to achieve his most important adolescent task.

variations in masturbation At all ages in childhood and adolescence, masturbation is more frequent for *boys* than for girls. It is more common in boys' or girls' *schools* and *camps* than in coeducational institutions. It occurs more often among adolescents who feel *insecure* than among those who are popular and secure in their relationships with their families. Adolescents of the higher *socioeconomic* levels and those who continue their education into college masturbate more during the early years of adolescence than do those of the lower socioeconomic groups who usually end their education earlier. (See Figure 14–14.) However, by the later part of adolescence, boys and girls of the lower socioeconomic groups use coitus more than masturbation as a sexual outlet; those of the higher socioeconomic groups concentrate on petting. Girls, who often limit their petting to avoid having it lead to intercourse, consider masturbation more desirable than coitus. They continue to practice it if they have not achieved adequate satisfaction from petting (75,134, 135,199,212).

In spite of these variations, masturbation is the most common indication of difficulty in making the transition into adult heterosexuality. As Reevy has stressed, "For all adolescents considered together, however, masturbation still leads all other forms of sexual behavior as a source of orgasm" (199).

psychological effects of masturbation Many traditions from early medicine, from religious teachings, and from folklore emphasize the harmful physical and mental effects of masturbation. According to these traditions, masturbation may produce excessive nervousness, feeblemindedness, or insanity. Some traditions go so far as to say that masturbation will affect the individual's appearance and will cause acne, so that even casual observers can detect the fact that he engages in this harmful practice. There is no scientific evidence to show that masturbation is the cause of any of these conditions.

Actually, acceptance of these old wives' tales about masturbation causes worry and anxiety that have far greater and far more damaging effects than the physical causes. The physical effects, except for temporary

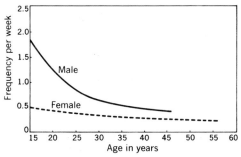

FIGURE 14–13 Boys and girls differ in the amount of masturbation they engage in and in the age of starting. (Adapted from A. C. Kinsey, W. B. Pomeroy, C. E. Martin, and P. H. Gebhard: *Sexual behavior in the human female.* Philadelphia: Lippincott, 1953. Used by permission.)

fatigue, sleepiness, and release of physical tension, are almost negligible. In many cases masturbation serves a good purpose by relieving sex tension. There is no evidence that masturbation in adolescence causes frigidity (75,134,135,199,236).

Homoerotism Homoerotism is the "tendency for persons of one sex to have strong libidinal attachments to members of their own sex." Hero worship and crushes are forms of erotic attachment that occur before or during puberty. Should this attachment persist after sexual maturity has been completed or should it be the *preferred* form of sex behavior, it is regarded as a

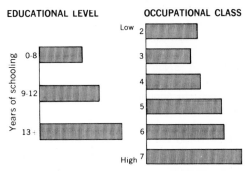

FIGURE 14–14 Masturbation among boys varies according to their educational and occupational levels. (Adapted from A. C. Kinsey, W. B. Pomeroy, and C. E. Martin: *Sexual behavior in the human male.* Philadelphia: Saunders, 1948. Used by permission.)

form of maladjustment (236,250). Those who, in adolescence or adult life, show homoerotic tendencies, have been found, most often, to be girls who have a strong resentment of being female, based on the feeling that women have an inferior status in our culture, and, in the case of both sexes, to have been frequent and excessive masturbators (147).

Crushes and hero worship are normal stages in the transition from childish to mature sexual development. However, a prolongation of this form of immature sexual behavior is a danger signal of sexual maladjustment. As Strang (236) has pointed out, if crushes and hero worship are:

> . . . unwisely handled by a person who is frightened by the relation and breaks if off suddenly or by a person who has a neurotic need for the adolescent's devotion, the experience may result in . . . [the adolescent's] withdrawal from any close relationship in the future, or in a permanent homosexual orientation.

See pages 516 to 518 for a more complete discussion of crushes and hero worship.

Homosexuality Homosexuality consists of experiencing sexual pleasures from physical associations between members of the same sex (134,135,199). Adolescents who are in reformatories, in noncoeducational schools or colleges, or whose environments make association with members of the opposite sex difficult and infrequent sometimes use this form of outlet for their sexual drives. Homosexuality is more frequent in early than in late adolescence (53,134,135, 212).

Certain adolescents are more likely to become homosexuals than others. Studies of adult women who had had homosexual experiences have revealed that many of the women had a somewhat masculine appearance, such as masculine hair distribution, heavy shoulders, and deep voice. There is a tendency for men who have had homosexual experience to be somewhat more effeminate in appearance than those who have had no such experience (135,147). Among early-maturing boys, twice as many have homosexual experiences in early adolescence as compared with those who mature at the average age (75,134).

Boys who, as children, were physically weak and who preferred feminine play to masculine, or who preferred the feminine role to the masculine, have been found to contribute to the number of male homosexuals (38,39,40). If the boy's identification with his mother is exaggerated in childhood, he may become a homosexual and find it easier to become excited and stimulated by men than by women as he grows older. As Symonds has pointed out, "It is believed that homosexuality can be understood, in part, in terms of identification in early childhood" (244).

Most adolescents, especially older adolescents, know that the social attitude toward homosexuality is very punitive. This causes them to experience marked feelings of guilt—should they engage in it—and shame—should their acts become known to others (75,134,135). While there is little evidence that homosexuality is damaging physically, it is damaging psychologically because of the (199):

> . . . social and moral indignation and the psychological turmoil that is aroused when people are identified as having been involved in such behaviors. Further, most states have laws that prohibit such sexual contact and in some cases the penalties are most severe.

Sex-role Inversion Sex-role inversion means identification with and adoption of the psychological identity of the opposite sex. The invert is an individual of either sex whose thoughts, perceptions, attitudes, fantasies, feelings, preferences, interests, and behavioral tendencies are typical of the opposite sex. Because the inversion encompasses his entire psychological makeup, it affects the individual's total personality structure (38,39). Thus, as Brown (38) has explained:

> In a very real sense the typical invert may be described as a psychosomatic misfit in that his body is characteristic of one sex (e.g., anatomically male) but his personality

is characteristic of the other sex (e.g., psychologically female).

While there is evidence that sex-role inverts are often homosexuals, this is not always the case. There is a difference between these two types of psychosexual maladjustment (39). The homosexual is psychologically a member of his own sex in the sense that he prefers the role of his own sex to that of the other sex and he plays this role. However, sexually he prefers to gain his satisfaction either predominantly or exclusively with members of his own sex. Thus, homosexuality is (38):

> . . . quite restricted in meaning, referring simply to an individual's aim and object in sexual activity per se, while inversion is a much broader phenomenon, referring to the composition of the individual's total personality structure and not merely his preferred form or mode of sexual activity.

There is evidence that sex-role inversion is more common among boys than among girls. The explanation given for this is that boys grow up in a culture in present-day America where their major contacts are with women, both at home and in school. As a result, they become accustomed to identifying with female rather than with male models. Later, when they have more opportunity for identification with male models, they may not want to do so because they find the males available to identify with—the father, a male relative, a teacher, or a camp counselor—less warm and acceptant in their attitudes, more harsh and punitive in their behavior, weak and ineffectual, or "psychological nonentities" who do not win their respect, admiration, or desire to imitate (39,170,180).

Furthermore, if the boy's earlier identification with his mother or some other female has been pleasanter and more ego satisfying, he *prefers* to continue to identify with that person. In addition, some boys, as was pointed out earlier, have neither the physical build nor the psychological abilities to play the male role as successfully as they can play the female role (38,40,49).

While girls may prefer the masculine role to the feminine, they are far less likely to experience sex-role inversion than are boys. The reason for this is that they have not, except in unusual conditions, learned through identification with a male model to play the male role. As Brown has emphasized, "The development of inversion in females would seem to depend on *both* a basic and predominant identification with and preference for the masculine role" (38).

psychological effects of inversion The psychological damage of sex-role inversion is serious for both boys and girls because of the unfavorable social attitudes toward members of both sexes when they do not pattern their behavior along lines approved by the social group. However, as being a sissy is more strongly condemned in our society than being a tomboy or a "crowing-hen" type of woman, and because the approved role for females is less clearly defined than that for males, the psychological damage of sex-role inversion is greater for males than for females (38,39).

Frigidity Frigidity means lack of emotional warmth in heterosexual relationships. As a rule girls are more frigid than boys. And for generations this was a socially approved pattern of behavior for well-brought-up girls.

Popular beliefs have stressed the fact that the sex drive is weaker in girls of higher socioeconomic status than in girls of lower status. Attempts have even been made to explain frigidity by looking for a glandular defect. These beliefs are not substantiated by scientific evidence. Rather, psychiatric investigations reveal that frigidity is the result of conditioning. It develops because unfavorable attitudes have been established by the way in which sex education has been given. Similarly, emphasizing the fact that sex expressions are base and animallike may condition in the girl feelings of guilt and disgust. These in turn will check her desire for normal overt expressions of love (135,199,223,253).

When frigidity accompanied by impotency appears in boys, it is likewise more often caused by conditioning than by glandular deficiencies. Only when the sex organs and secondary sex characteristics are undeveloped or diseased can the cause of frigidity be traced to glandular trouble. In boys, as in girls, frigidity usually comes from unfavorable attitudes toward sex that have developed from misinformation about sex matters or from the way in which sex instruction has been given (134,223,253).

psychological effects of frigidity The psychological damage of frigidity is far greater today than it was in the past when suppression of the expression of the sex drive was regarded as a sign of a "thoroughbred" —whether male or female. Since the publication of the Kinsey reports and the popularization of the Freudian theories about the damage caused by suppression of a strong drive, such as the sex drive, there has been a marked change in the cultural attitude toward sexual restraints.

Because petting has become an accepted part of dating, just as intercourse is an accepted part of marriage, the adolescent who wants to win and hold the affection of a member of the opposite sex must show his affection by actions, not by words alone. It is ego deflating to a boy to have his advances to a girl rebuffed just as it is ego deflating to a girl not to have a boy want to engage in petting with her. This generally leads to the breakup of dating. In the later stages of courtship, it usually leads to the end of pinning or of the engagement. Because a girl's prestige in the social group is dependent on her popularity with boys, a girl who cannot win and hold the attention of boys is unfavorably judged by the social group. This, in turn, leads her to judge herself unfavorably (21,33,49,115,147).

Sexual Promiscuity Some adolescents find the sex drive hard to manage; they experience many sexual tensions which must find an outlet. If they have not learned how to channel this energy into approved patterns of behavior, they develop into what the social group labels as "promiscuous" people. As Kirkendall has explained, a "sexually promiscuous person is often a conflict-ridden or psychologically maladjusted person" (136).

There is little evidence that sexual promiscuity is the product of a stronger-than-normal sex drive. On the contrary, some boys and girls who are promiscuous in their heterosexual relationships are compensating for feelings of inadequacy stemming from a weaker-than-normal sex drive. On the other hand, boys and girls who spend much of their recreational time on different forms of mass media—especially those which concentrate on romantic themes —are erotically aroused more often and more intensely than those whose interests are in other areas. The less popular an adolescent is, the more time he is likely to devote to daydreaming which, during adolescence, often concentrates on a romantic theme. Lack of popularity eliminates many of the opportunities for healthy heterosexual activities enjoyed by adolescents who are better accepted socially.

While it is unquestionably true that boys and girls of the lower intellectual levels devote more time to mass media of communication that stress sex and romance than do those of higher intelligence, there are too many boys and girls of the higher intellectual levels who are sexually promiscuous to justify the belief that intellectual inferiority, per se, is responsible for it. Instead, evidence points to social maladjustment which predisposes the adolescent to unwholesome forms of recreation (109,134, 135,199).

Poor social adjustments do not explain the greater incidence of sexual promiscuity among boys than among girls, nor is there evidence that the sex drive in boys is so much stronger that they are less able to manage it than are girls. The difference between the sexes, on the contrary, can be traced to differences in *fear of consequences*. Knowing that a double standard of sex behavior is still widely accepted in our culture and knowing that the social group will admire, if not applaud, the boy's sexual behavior as a sign of masculinity while, at the same time, condemning girls and labeling them as loose for similar behavior, the boy who finds sexual promiscuity a quick and easy way to manage his sex drive has little to hold him back.

Furthermore, unlike the girl, he will not have to pay a penalty for his promiscuity in the form of the social stigma that comes with having an illegitimate child; he can deny his role of paternity, he can refuse to marry the girl who has become the mother of his child, or he can project the blame on the girl for trying to "trap him into marriage" by allowing herself to become pregnant. This encourages many boys to ignore attempting to handle their sex drives in a more socially approved manner (57,73,134, 135,136,256).

Even though girls are more restrained by fear of consequences than boys, there are many girls who are sexually promiscuous. Some of them are rebelling against the double standard and the socially inferior status of women. They are trying to prove their equality with boys. Other girls are promiscuous in their sex behavior in the hope of increasing their popularity with boys or of forcing a boy into marriage. Girls who date boys of a higher socioeconomic status are especially influenced by this. Still others who suffer from feelings of rejection in their homes find compensation in promiscuous sex behavior (77,79,120,255).

In more extreme forms, sexual promiscuity leads to *sexual delinquencies*. In boys, this may take the form of aggressive sexual attacks on girls or women of all ages, of rape, or of physical disfigurement of a female after rape. In girls, the most common form of sexual delinquency is prostitution. This is often accompanied by the bearing of illegitimate children which some girls keep as a method of obtaining state aid for the support of their children. They thus free themselves of the necessity of getting a job (73,124,155,184,254,257,259).

psychological effects of promiscuity The psychological effects of sexual promiscuity are the most serious of all forms of sexual maladjustment. Knowing how unfavorably the social group looks upon promiscuous sex behavior adds to the already-existing feeling

of social rejection that has been largely responsible for the behavior. Furthermore, because extreme forms of sexual promiscuity often become delinquencies, the adolescent experiences the social stigma associated with any form of juvenile delinquency. Because society expects girls to control their sex drives more than boys, the psychological damage sexual promiscuity brings to girls is unquestionably greater than boys experience. However, neither sex is spared.

SATISFACTORY ADJUSTMENTS

In spite of widespread publicity in the mass media about sexual maladjustments, there is evidence that most adolescents make the transition from childish to adult sexuality successfully. This transition may not be completed when the adolescent reaches legal maturity, owing mainly to environmental obstacles resulting from the necessity for longer education with its accompaniment of a dependency state. However, delay in transition means only that progress is being made at a slower-than-normal rate, not maladjustment in the sense that the adolescent *prefers* an immature form of sexuality to a more mature one.

Today, the conditions that predisposed adolescents of past generations to prefer sexual immaturity to sexual maturity are better understood and better controlled. Recognition of the important role of attitudes toward sex has led to more complete and more wholesome sex education in the home and in the school. Even more important, it has led to emphasis on the positive values of sex rather than the negative, which formerly were stressed.

In addition, encouragement of heterosexual activities as soon as young adolescents show an interest in them, provision for such activities under less formal conditions than in the past, and removal of the watchful eye and attentive ear of the chaperon have all eliminated some of the major obstacles to transition to adult sexuality. Knowing that longer periods of dependency are obstacles to achieving adult sexuality for an increasing number of adolescents, many colleges and universities today are providing living quarters for married students and work opportunities to eliminate the prolongation of a state of dependency on parents.

Even with the fostering of wholesome attitudes by better sex education and the removal of obstacles in the path of transition, the achievement of adult heterosexuality will not occur in the absence of motivation on the adolescent's part. This motivation is supplied mainly by the adolescent's need for love and acceptance by a person whom he loves, respects, and finds to be a congenial companion. While all children and adolescents throughout the ages and in all cultures have needed love and acceptance, today's adolescents in the American culture need them even more than in the past because of the breakdown of the large family system and the deterioration of family relationships.

As a result of these home conditions, being in love with a member of the opposite sex not only satisfies the adolescent's sex drive, but also his need for affection which is not fully or adequately met in the home. It is this need which supplies today's adolescents with the motivation to make the transition into adult sexuality.

Characteristics of Satisfactory Adjustment

An adolescent who is making satisfactory adjustments in heterosexuality shows the following characteristics at *approximately* the same time as other adolescents:

1 He is learning to manage his sex drive so that he can turn its energy into socially approved patterns of heterosexual behavior. If the drive is too strong and the environmental obstacles temporarily in his way too great to do this, he learns to *sublimate* this drive. This he does by developing patterns of behavior that will siphon off the energy engendered by this drive and turn it into socially accepted behavior not related to sex—such as sports and recreations with members of his own sex—until these temporary obstacles are removed.

2 He is abandoning childish forms of sexuality, such as masturbation, sex play with members of his own sex, crushes and hero worship, in favor of more mature patterns of behavior involving members of the opposite sex.

3 He is anticipating and planning for marriage and parenthood by developing wholesome values to use in the selection of a life mate and by learning the practical aspects of the roles he will play in marriage rather than by concentrating on the romantic aspects of these roles as he did when he was younger.

4 He is learning to express his affection for others not by words alone but by acts that contribute to the happiness and security of the loved one. This love is not limited to a physical attraction for the loved one. Instead, it includes respect. Thus, it has a psychological and moral aspect as well as a physical.

5 He is learning to play the approved sex role for his sex. Even though the adolescent may prefer another role, he will accept the culturally approved role *if* he feels that he can do so without resentments and feelings of martyrdom. If, on the other hand, he feels that he cannot accept this role, he will be honest enough not to pose as doing so. Instead, he will accept the role he feels he can fulfill satisfactorily without the use of defense mechanisms to explain and justify it.

6 He is learning to respect the role society expects members of the opposite sex to play. He recognizes that this role makes as important a contribution to the welfare of society as his own. Furthermore, he will recognize that every role has its advantages as well as its disadvantages. He will then be willing to accept the good with the bad instead of wishing that he could play the role of the opposite sex.

When the adolescent has mastered these learning experiences successfully and has patterned his behavior according to their standards, he will be considered a "psychosexually mature" person. As Brown has pointed out, in discussing the characteristics of a psychosexually mature male, "A normal male is one who has identified with, incorporated, and prefers the masculine role: his sexual desire for the female is one aspect of this role" (40). The same characteristics are found in a psychosexually mature female.

BIBLIOGRAPHY

1 ALLEN, D. A.: Anti-femininity in men. *Amer. sociol. Rev.*, 1954, **19**, 591–593.

2 ANGRILLI, A. F.: The psychosexual identification of pre-school boys. *J. genet. Psychol.*, 1960, **97**, 329–340.

3 ARKOFF, A., G. MEREDITH, and J. DONG: Attitudes of Japanese-American and Caucasian-American students toward marriage roles. *J. soc. Psychol.*, 1963, **59**, 11–15.

4 AUSUBEL, D. P.: Ego development among segregated Negro children. *Ment. Hyg., N.Y.*, 1958, **42**, 362–369.

5 AVERY, C. E.: Toward understanding the problems of early marriage. *Family Life Coordinator*, 1961, **23**, 27–34.

6 BABER, R. E.: *Marriage and the family.* 2d ed. New York: McGraw-Hill, 1953.

7 BANTA, T. J., and M. HETHERINGTON: Relations between needs of friends and fiances. *J. abnorm. soc. Psychol.*, 1963, **66**, 401–404.

8 BARCLAY, D.: Trousered mothers and dishwashing dads. *The New York Times*, Apr. 28, 1957.

9 BARDIS, P. D.: Attitudes toward dating. *Sociol. soc. Res.*, 1958, **42**, 274–277.

10 BARNETT, L. D.: Attitudes toward interracial dating. *Family Life Coordinator*, 1963, **12**, 88–90.

11 BARNETT, L. D.: Research on international and interracial marriages. *Marriage fam. Living*, 1963, **25**, 105–107.

12 BARNETT, L. D.: Students' anticipations of persons and arguments opposing interracial dating. *Marriage fam. Living*, 1963, **25**, 355–357.

13 BARNETT, L. D.: The influence of arguments encouraging interracial dating. *Family Life Coordinator*, 1963, **12**, 91–92.

14 BARRY, H., M. K. BACON, and I. L. CHILD: A cross-cultural study of some sex differences in socialization. *J. abnorm. soc. Psychol.*, 1957, **55**, 327–332.

15 BEALER, R. C., F. K. WILLITS, and G. W.

BENDER: Religious exogamy: a study of social distance. *Sociol. soc. Res.*, 1963, **48**, 69–79.

16 BEIGEL, H. G.: Body height in mate selection. *J. soc. Psychol.*, 1954, **39**, 257–268.

17 BEIGEL, H. G.: The value of intelligence in the heterosexual relationship. *J. soc. Psychol.*, 1957, **46**, 65–80.

18 BEILIN, H., and E. WERNER: Sex role expectations and criteria of social adjustment for young adults. *J. clin. Psychol.*, 1957, **13**, 341–343.

19 BELL, R. R., and L. BLUMBERG: Courtship intimacy and religious background. *Marriage fam. Living*, 1959, **21**, 356–360.

20 BELL, R. R., and J. V. BUERKLE: Mother and daughter attitudes to premarital sexual behavior. *Marriage fam. Living*, 1961, **23**, 390–392.

21 BENE, E.: Suppression of hetero-sexual interest and of aggression by middle class and working class grammar school boys. *Brit. J. educ. Psychol.*, 1958, **28**, 226–231.

22 BENNETT, E. M., and L. R. COHEN: Men and women: personality patterns and contrasts. *Genet. Psychol. Monogr.*, 1959, **59**, 101–155.

23 BERNARD, J.: Teen-age culture: an overview. *Ann. Amer. Acad. pol. soc. Sci.*, 1961, **338**, 1–12.

24 BIELIAUSKAS, V. J.: Sexual identification in children's drawings of human figures. *J. clin. Psychol.*, 1960, **16**, 42–44.

25 BINGER, C.: The pressures on college girls today. *Atlantic Monthly*, vol. 207, no. 2, pp. 40–44, 1961.

26 BLOCK, J.: Personality characteristics associated with fathers' attitudes toward child rearing. *Child Develpm.*, 1955, **26**, 41–48.

27 BLOOD, R. O.: Uniformities and diversities in campus dating preferences. *Marriage fam. Living*, 1956, **18**, 37–45.

28 BLOOD, R. O., and S. O. NICHOLSON: International dating experience of American women students. *Marriage fam. Living*, 1962, **24**, 129–136.

29 BLOOD, R. O., and S. O. NICHOLSON: The attitudes of American men and women students toward international dating. *Marriage fam. Living*, 1962, **24**, 35–41.

30 BLOOD, R. O., and S. O. NICHOLSON: The experiences of foreign students in dating American women. *Marriage fam. Living*, 1962, **24**, 241–248.

31 BORING, E. G.: The woman problem. *Amer. Psychologist,* 1951, **6**, 679–692.

32 BORKE, H., and M. B. MC FARLAND: Effect of tradition on husband choice and role as wife: a case report. *J. clin. Psychol.,* 1959, **15**, 128–132.

33 BOSSARD, J. H. S., and E. S. BOLL: *The sociology of child development.* 3d ed. New York: Harper & Row, 1960.

34 BOUMA, D. H.: Religiously mixed marriages: denominational consequences in the Christian Reformed church. *Marriage fam. Living,* 1963, **25**, 428–432.

35 BOWERMAN, C. E., and B. R. DAY: A test of the theory of complementary needs as applied to couples during courtship. *Amer. sociol. Rev.,* 1956, **21**, 602–605.

36 BRIM, O. G.: Family structure and sex role learning: a further analysis of Helen Koch's data. *Sociometry,* 1958, **21**, 1–16.

37 BROWN, D. G.: Masculinity-femininity development in children. *J. consult. Psychol.,* 1957, **21**, 197–205.

38 BROWN, D. G.: The development of sex-role inversion and homosexuality. *J. Pediat.,* 1957, **50**, 613–619.

39 BROWN, D. G.: Inversion and homosexuality. *Amer. J. Orthopsychiat.,* 1958, **28**, 424–429.

40 BROWN, D. G.: Sex-role development in a changing culture. *Psychol. Bull.,* 1958, **55**, 232–242.

41 BURGESS, E. W., and P. WALLIN: *Engagement and marriage.* Philadelphia: Lippincott, 1953.

42 CATTON, W. R., and R. J. SMIRCICK: A comparison of mathematical models for the effect of residential propinquity in mate selection. *Amer. sociol. Rev.,* 1964, **29**, 522–529.

43 CAVA, E. L., and H. L. RAUSCH: Identification and the adolescent boy's perception of his father. *J. abnorm. soc. Psychol.,* 1952, **47**, 855–856.

44 CHRISTENSEN, H. T.: Factors in the size and sex composition of families: a survey of student opinion. *Proc. Utah Acad. Sci.,* 1948, **23**, 107–113.

45 CHRISTENSEN, H. T.: Dating behavior as evaluated by high-school students. *Amer. J. Sociol.,* 1952, **57**, 580–586.

46 CHRISTENSEN, H. T., and M. M. SWIHART: Post graduate role preferences of senior women in college. *Marriage fam. Living,* 1956, **18**, 52–57.

47 CLARKE, A. C.: An examination of the operation of residential propinquity as a factor in mate selection. *Amer. sociol. Rev.,* 1952, **17**, 17–22.

48 COLE, L., and I. N. HALL: *Psychology of adolescence.* 6th ed. New York: Holt, 1964.

49 COLEMAN, J. S.: *The adolescent society.* New York: Free Press, 1961.

50 COMBS, R. H.: Reinforcement of values in the parental home as a factor in mate selection. *Marriage fam. Living,* 1962, **24**, 155–157.

51 COOPER, L.: Predisposition toward parenthood: a comparison of male and female students. *Sociol. soc. Res.,* 1957, **42**, 31–36.

52 CROW, L. D.: Personality traits admired by adolescents. *Clearing House,* 1954, **29**, 23–28.

53 CROW, L. D., and A. CROW: *Adolescent development and adjustment.* 2d ed. New York: McGraw-Hill, 1965.

54 DAY, B. R.: A comparison of personality needs of courtship couples and same-sex friendships. *Sociol. soc. Res.,* 1961, **45**, 435–440.

55 DEDMAN, J.: The relationship between religious attitude and attitude toward premarital sex relations. *Marriage fam. Living,* 1959, **21**, 171–176.

56 DEEGAN, D. Y.: *The stereotype of the single woman in American novels: a social study with implications for the education of women.* New York: King's Crown, 1951.

57 DESCHIN, C. S.: Teenagers and venereal disease. *Children,* 1962, **9**, 144–148.

58 DIAMOND, S.: Sex stereotypes and acceptance of sex role. *J. Psychol.,* 1955, **39**, 385–388.

59 DINITZ, S., F. BANKS, and B. PASAMANICK: Mate selection and social class: changes during the past quarter century. *Marriage fam. Living,* 1960, **22**, 348–351.

60 DUNN, M. S.: Marriage role expectations of adolescents. *Marriage fam. Living,* 1960, **22**, 99–111.

61 DUVALL, E. M.: What kind of husbands and wives do teenagers expect to be? *Marriage fam. Living,* 1960, **22**, 183–185.

62 DUVALL, E. M.: Adolescent love as a reflection of teen-agers' search for identity. *J. Marriage Fam.,* 1964, **26**, 226–231.

63 DUVALL, E. M.: Identifying potential conflict

areas in high-school dating. *J. Marriage Fam.*, 1964, **26**, 103–106.

64 EHRMANN, W. W.: Student cooperation in a study of dating behavior. *Marriage fam. Living*, 1952, **14**, 322–326.

65 EHRMANN, W. W.: Influence of comparative social class of companion upon premarital heterosexual behavior. *Marriage fam. Living*, 1955, **17**, 48–53.

66 EHRMANN, W. W.: *Premarital dating behavior*. New York: Holt, 1959.

67 EHRMANN, W. W.: Premarital sexual behavior and sex codes of conduct with acquaintances, friends, and lovers. *Soc. Forces*, 1959, **38**, 158–164.

68 ELLIS, A.: A study of human love relationships. *J. genet. Psychol.*, 1949, **75**, 61–71.

69 ELLIS, A.: *The folklore of sex*. New York: Boni, 1951.

70 EMMERICH, W.: Parental identification in young children. *Genet. Psychol. Monogr.*, 1959, **60**, 257–308.

71 EMPEY, L. T.: Role expectations of young women regarding marriage and a career. *Marriage fam. Living*, 1958, **20**, 152–155.

72 ENGLAND, R. W.: Images of love and courtship in family-magazine fiction. *Marriage fam. Living*, 1960, **22**, 162–165.

73 FALK, U. A., and G. J. FALK: The unmarried mother: a sociological profile. *Family Life Coordinator*, 1965, **14**, 17–19.

74 FAULS, L. B., and W. D. SMITH: Sex-role learning of five-year-olds. *J. genet. Psychol.*, 1956, **89**, 105–117.

75 FINGER, F. W.: Sex beliefs and practices among male college students. *J. abnorm. soc. Psychol.*, 1947, **42**, 57–67.

76 FISHBEIN, M., and R. J. R. KENNEDY (eds.): *Modern marriage and family living*. Fair Lawn, N.J.: Oxford, 1957.

77 FLECK, S.: Pregnancy as a symptom of adolescent maladjustment. *Int. J. soc. Psychiat.*, 1956, **2**, 118–131.

78 FRIED, E. G., and M. F. LISSANCE: The dilemmas of German youth. *J. abnorm. soc. Psychol.*, 1949, **44**, 50–60.

79 FRUMKIN, R. M.: The unwed mother. *Sexology*, 1955, **21**, 548–551, 656–659.

80 GEIKEN, K. F.: Expectations concerning husband-wife responsibilities in the home. *J. Marriage Fam.*, 1964, **26**, 349–352.

81 GENNÉ, E., and W. GENNÉ: *Christians and the crisis in sex morality*. New York: Association Press, 1962.

82 GENNÉ, W.: Early marriage and the modern family. *Family Life Coordinator*, 1962, **11**, 66–68.

83 GESELL, A., F. L. ILG, and L. B. AMES: *Youth: the years from ten to sixteen*. New York: Harper & Row, 1956.

84 GIANOPULOS, A., and H. E. MITCHELL: Marital disagreement in working wife marriages as a function of husband's attitude toward wife's employment. *Marriage fam. Living*, 1957, **19**, 373–381.

85 GINZBERG, E.: The changing pattern of women's work: some psychological correlates. *Amer. J. Orthopsychiat.*, 1958, **28**, 313–321.

86 GLENN, H. M.: Attitudes of women regarding gainful employment of married women. *J. Home Econ.*, 1959, **51**, 247–252.

87 GOLDSEN, R. K.: *What college students think*. Princeton, N.J.: Van Nostrand, 1960.

88 GOODE, W. J.: The theoretical importance of love. *Amer. sociol. Rev.*, 1959, **24**, 38–47.

89 GOODENOUGH, E. W.: Interest in persons as an aspect of sex difference in the early years. *Genet. Psychol. Monogr.*, 1957, **55**, 287–323.

90 GOTTLIEB, D., and C. RAMSEY: *The American adolescent*. Homewood, Ill.: Dorsey, 1964.

91 GRAY, H.: Psychological types in married people. *J. soc. Psychol.*, 1949, **29**, 189–200.

92 GRAY, S. W.: Masculinity-femininity in relation to anxiety and social acceptance. *Child Develpm.*, 1957, **28**, 203–214.

93 HACKER, H. M.: Women as a minority group. *Soc. Forces*, 1951, **30**, 60–69.

94 HACKER, H. M.: The new burdens of masculinity. *Marriage fam. Living*, 1957, **17**, 227–233.

95 HALL, M., and R. A. KEITH: Sex-role preference among children of upper and lower social class. *J. soc. Psychol.*, 1964, **62**, 101–110.

96 HARTLEY, R. E.: Children's concepts of male and female roles. *Merrill-Palmer Quart.*, 1959, **6**, 83–91.

97 HARTLEY, R. E.: Sex-role pressure and the socialization of the male child. *Psychol. Rep.*, 1959, **5**, 457–468.

98 HARTLEY, R. E., and F. P. HARDESTY: Children's perceptions of sex roles in childhood. *J. genet. Psychol.*, 1964, **105**, 43–57.

99 HARTLEY, R. E., and A. KLEIN: Sex-role con-

cepts among elementary-school-age girls. *Marriage fam. Living*, 1959, **21**, 59–64.

100 HARTRUP, W. W., and E. A. ZOOK: Sex-role preferences in three- and four-year-old children. *J. consult. Psychol.*, 1960, **24**, 420–426.

101 HAUSER, S., and C. HOBART: Premarital pregnancy and anxiety. *J. soc. Psychol.*, 1964, **63**, 255–263.

102 HEATHERS, G.: Acquiring dependence and independence: a theoretical orientation. 1955, **87**, 277–291.

103 HECHINGER, G., and F. M. HECHINGER: *Teenage tyranny*. New York: Morrow, 1963.

104 HEILBRUN, A. B.: Conformity to masculinity-femininity stereotypes and ego identity in adolescents. *Psychol. Rep.*, 1964, **14**, 351–357.

105 HEISS, J. S.: Premarital characteristics of the religiously intermarried in an urban area. *Amer. sociol. Rev.*, 1960, **25**, 47–55.

106 HEISS, J. S.: Interfaith marriage and marital outcome. *Marriage fam. Living*, 1961, **23**, 228–233.

107 HENTON, J. M.: The effects of married high-school students on their unmarried classmates. *J. Marriage Fam.*, 1964, **26**, 87–88.

108 HERRMANN, R. O.: Expectations and attitudes as a source of financial problems in teen-age marriage. *J. Marriage Fam.*, 1965, **27**, 89–91.

109 HERZOG, E.: Who are the unmarried mothers? *Children*, 1962, **9**, 157–159.

110 HESS, R. D., and G. HANDEL: Problems of aggression in parents and their children. *J. genet. Psychol.*, 1956, **89**, 199–212.

111 HEWITT, L. E.: Student perceptions of traits desired in themselves as dating and marriage partners. *Marriage fam. Living*, 1958, **20**, 344–349.

112 HIMES, J. S.: Value consensus in mate selection among Negroes. *Marriage fam. Living*, 1952, **14**, 317–321.

113 HOBART, C. W.: Some effects of romanticism during courtship on marriage role opinions. *Sociol. soc. Res.*, 1958, **42**, 336–343.

114 HOFFMAN, L. W.: Effects of the employment of mothers on parental power relations and the division of household tasks. *Marriage fam. Living*, 1960, **22**, 27–35.

115 HOLLINGSHEAD, A. DE B.: *Elmtown's youth*. New York: Wiley, 1949.

116 HOLLINGSHEAD, A. DE B.: Cultural factors in the selection of marriage mates. *Amer. J. Sociol.*, 1950, **15**, 619–627.

117 HOOVER, H. F.: *Attitudes of high-school students toward mixed marriages*. Washington, D.C.: Catholic, 1950.

118 HORTON, D.: The dialogue of courtship in popular songs. *Amer. J. Sociol.*, 1957, **62**, 567–578.

119 JACOBSON, A. H.: Conflict of attitudes toward roles of the wife and husband in marriage. *Amer. sociol. Rev.*, 1952, **17**, 146–158.

120 JAHODA, M., and J. HAVEL: Psychological problems of women in different social roles. *Educ. Rec.*, 1955, **36**, 325–335.

121 JERSILD, A. T.: *The psychology of adolescence*. 2d ed. New York: Macmillan, 1963.

122 JOHANNIS, T. B., and J. M. ROLLINS: Teenager perception of family decision-making. *Family Life Coordinator*, 1959, **4**, 70–74.

123 JOHNSON, M. M.: Sex-role learning in the nuclear family. *Child Develpm.*, 1963, **34**, 319–333.

124 JONES, W. C., H. J. MEYER, and E. F. BORGATTA: Social and psychological factors in status decisions of unmarried mothers. *Marriage fam. Living*, 1962, **24**, 224–230.

125 JOSSELYN, I. M.: Cultural forces, motherliness and fatherliness. *Amer. J. Orthopsychiat.*, 1956, **26**, 264–271.

126 KAMMEYER, K.: The feminine role: an analysis of attitude consistency. *J. Marriage Fam.*, 1964, **26**, 295–305.

127 KANIN, E. J.: Male aggressiveness in dating-courtship relations. *Amer. J. Sociol.*, 1957, **63**, 197–204.

128 KAREN, R. L.: Some variables affecting sexual attitudes, behavior and inconsistency. *Marriage fam. Living*, 1959, **21**, 235–239.

129 KATZ, A. M., and R. HILL: Residential propinquity and marital selection. *Marriage fam. Living*, 1958, **20**, 27–35.

130 KENT, D. P.: Subjective factors in mate selection: an exploratory study. *Sociol. soc. Res.*, 1951, **35**, 391–398.

131 KERCKHOFF, A. C., and K. E. DAVIS: Value consensus and need complementarity in mate selection. *Amer. sociol. Rev.*, 1962, **27**, 295–303.

132 KIELL, N., and B. FRIEDMAN: Culture lag and housewifemanship: the role of the married

female college graduate. *J. educ. Sociol.*, 1957, **31**, 87–95.

133 KING, E. V.: Personality characteristics—ideal and perceived in relation to mate selection. *Dissert. Abstr.*, 1961, **21**, 3882.

134 KINSEY, A. C., W. B. POMEROY, and C. E. MARTIN: *Sexual behavior in the human male.* Philadelphia: Saunders, 1948.

135 KINSEY, A. C., W. B. POMEROY, C. E. MARTIN, and P. H. GEBHARD: *Sexual behavior in the human female.* Philadelphia: Saunders, 1953.

136 KIRKENDALL, L. A.: Toward a clarification of the concept of male sex drive. *Marriage fam. Living*, 1958, **20**, 367–372.

137 KIRKENDALL, L. A.: Circumstances associated with teenage boys' use of prostitution. *Marriage fam. Living*, 1960, **22**, 145–149.

138 KIRKENDALL, L. A.: Evaded problem: sex on the campus. *Family Life Coordinator*, 1965, **14**, 20–24.

139 KIRKPATRICK, C., and E. J. KANIN: Male sex aggressiveness on a university campus. *Amer. sociol. Rev.*, 1957, **22**, 52–58.

140 KOCH, H. L.: Sissiness and tomboyishness in relation to sibling characteristics. *J. genet. Psychol.*, 1956, **88**, 231–244.

141 KOCH, H. L.: The relation of young children between characteristics of their playmates and certain attributes of their siblings. *Child Develpm.*, 1957, **28**, 175–202.

142 KOLLER, M. R.: Some changes in courtship behavior in three generations of Ohio women. *Amer. sociol. Rev.*, 1951, **16**, 366–370.

143 KOMAROVSKY, M.: Functional analysis of sex roles. *Amer. sociol. Rev.*, 1950, **15**, 508–516.

144 KOPPITZ, E. M.: Relationships between some background factors and children's interpersonal attitudes. *J. genet. Psychol.*, 1957, **91**, 119–129.

145 KORNER, I. N.: Of values, value lag, and mental health. *Amer. Psychologist*, 1956, **11**, 543–546.

146 KTSANES, T.: Mate selection on the basis of personality type: a study utilizing an empirical typology of personality. *Amer. sociol. Rev.*, 1956, **21**, 602–605.

147 LANDIS, C., et al.: *Sex in development.* New York: Hoeber-Harper, 1940.

148 LANDIS, P. H.: *Adolescence and youth: the process of maturing.* 2d ed. New York: McGraw-Hill, 1952.

149 LANSKY, L. M., V. J. CRANDALL, J. KAGAN, and C. T. BAKER: Sex differences in aggression and its correlates in middle-class adolescents. *Child Develpm.*, 1961, **32**, 45–58.

150 LARSEN, V. L.: Sources of menstrual information: a comparison of age groups. *Family Life Coordinator*, 1961, **23**, 41–43.

151 LEOPOLD, A. K.: The family woman's expanding role. *Marriage fam. Living*, 1958, **20**, 278–282.

152 LESLIE, G. R., and A. H. RICHARDSON: Family versus campus influences in relation to mate selection. *Soc. Probl.*, 1956, **4**, 117–121.

153 LEVINGER, G.: Note on need complementarity in marriage. *Psychol. Bull.*, 1964, **61**, 153–157.

154 LEVINSON, D. J., and P. E. HUFFMAN: Traditional family ideology and its relation to personality. *J. Pers.*, 1954, **23**, 251–273.

155 LEVY, D.: A follow-up study of unmarried mothers. *Soc. Casewk*, 1955, **36**, 27–33.

156 LIND, A. W.: Interracial marriage as affecting divorce in Hawaii. *Sociol. soc., Res.*, 1964, **49**, 17–25.

157 LINDENFELD, F.: A note on social mobility, religiosity, and students' attitudes towards premarital sexual relations. *Amer. sociol. Rev.*, 1960, **25**, 81–84.

158 LIPMAN, A.: Educational preparation for the female role. *J. educ. Sociol.*, 1959, **33**, 40–43.

159 LIPMAN, A.: Cultural lag and masculinity. *J. educ. Sociol.*, 1962, **35**, 216–220.

160 LOCKE, H. J., G. SABAGH, and M. M. THOMAS: Interfaith marriages. *Soc. Probl.*, 1957, **4**, 329–333.

161 LOVEJOY, D. D.: College student perceptions of the roles of the husband and wife in family decision-making. *Family Life Coordinator*, 1961, **9**, 43–46.

162 LOWRIE, S. H.: Early marriage, premarital pregnancy and associated factors. *J. Marriage Fam.*, 1965, **27**, 48–56.

163 LYNN, D. B.: A note on sex differences in the development of masculine and feminine identification. *Psychol. Rev.*, 1959, **66**, 126–135.

164 LYNN, D. B.: Learning masculine and feminine roles. *Marriage fam. Living*, 1963, **25**, 103–105.

165 MAC BRAYER, C. T.: Differences in perception of the opposite sex by males and females. *J. soc. Psychol.*, 1960, **52**, 309–314.

166 MACE, D. R.: Is chastity outmoded? *Woman's Home Companion*, Sept., 1959, pp. 36–38.

167 MARCHES, J. R., and G. TURBEVILLE: The effect of residential propinquity on marriage selection. *Amer. J. Sociol.*, 1953, **58**, 592–595.

168 MARKSBERRY, M. L.: Attitudes of college women toward selected roles in life. *Sch. Soc.*, 1952, **75**, 394–396.

169 MARTIN, J. G.: Racial ethnocentrism and judgment of beauty. *J. soc. Psychol.*, 1964, **63**, 59–63.

170 MC CORD, W., J. MC CORD, and P. VERDEN: Family relationships and sexual deviance in lower class adolescents. *Int. J. soc. Psychiat.*, 1962, **8**, 165–179.

171 MC GUIRE, C.: Sex role and community variability in test performances. *J. educ. Psychol.*, 1961, **52**, 61–73.

172 MC KEE, J. P., and A. C. SHERRIFFS: The differential evaluation of males and females. *J. Pers.*, 1957, **25**, 356–371.

173 MC KEE, J. P., and A. C. SHERRIFFS: Men's and women's beliefs, ideals and self-concepts. *Amer. J. Sociol.*, 1959, **64**, 356–363.

174 MEAD, M.: *Male and female.* New York: Morrow, 1952.

175 MILNER, E.: Effects of sex role and social status on the early adolescent personality. *Genet. Psychol. Monogr.*, 1949, **40**, 231–325.

176 MORGENSTERN, J. J.: What schools can do about teen-age dating patterns. *NEA J.*, 1961, **50**, 8–11.

177 MORRIS, W. W.: Ontogenetic changes in adolescence reflected by the drawing-human-figures technique. *Amer. J. Orthopsychiat.*, 1955, **25**, 720–728.

178 MOSER, A. J.: Marriage role expectations of high school students. *Marriage fam. Living*, 1961, **23**, 42–43.

179 MUSSEN, P. H.: Some antecedents and consequences of masculine sex-typing in adolescent boys. *Psychol. Monogr.*, 1961, **75**, no. 2.

180 MUSSEN, P. H.: Long-term consequents of masculinity of interests in adolescence. *J. consult. Psychol.*, 1962, **26**, 435–440.

181 MUSSEN, P. H., and L. DISTLER: Masculinity, identification and father-son relationships. *J. abnorm. soc. Psychol.*, 1959, **59**, 350–356.

182 MUSSEN, P. H., and E. RUTHERFORD: Parent-child relations and parental personality in relation to young children's sex-role preferences. *Child Develpm.*, 1963, **34**, 589–607.

183 NEIMAN, L. J.: The influence of peer groups upon attitudes toward the feminine role. *Soc. Probl.*, 1954, **2**, 104–111.

184 *New York Times* Report: Major crimes rose 10% in U.S. in 1963. *The New York Times*, July 21, 1964.

185 OLSEN, M. E.: Distribution of family responsibilities and social stratification. *Marriage fam. Living*, 1960, **22**, 60–65.

186 OVESEY, L.: Masculine aspirations in women. *Psychiatry*, 1956, **19**, 341–351.

187 PACKARD, V.: *The status seekers.* New York: Pocket, 1961.

188 PACKARD, V.: *The pyramid climbers.* New York: McGraw-Hill, 1962.

189 PAYNE, D. E., and P. H. MUSSEN: Parent-child relationships and father identification among adolescent boys. *J. abnorm. soc. Psychol.*, 1956, **52**, 358–362.

190 PISKIN, V.: Psychosexual development in terms of object and role preferences. *J. clin. Psychol.*, 1960, **16**, 238–240.

191 PORTER, L. G., and C. L. STACEY: A study of the relationships between self-ratings and parent-ratings for a group of college students. *J. clin. Psychol.*, 1956, **12**, 243–248.

192 PRESSEY, S. L., and A. W. JONES: 1923–1953 and 20–60 age changes in moral codes, anxieties, and interests, as shown by the "X-O Tests." *J. Psychol.*, 1955, **39**, 485–502.

193 PRESSEY, S. L., and R. G. KUHLEN: *Psychological development through the life span.* New York: Harper & Row, 1957.

194 PRINCE, A. J.: Factors in mate selection. *Family Life Coordinator*, 1961, **10**, 55–56.

195 PRINCE, A. J., and A. R. RAGGALEY: Personality variables and the ideal mate. *Family Life Coordinator*, 1963, **12**, 93–96.

196 PRINCE, A. J., and G. SHIPMAN: Attitudes of college students toward premarital sex experience. *Family Life Coordinator*, 1958, **6**, 57–60.

197 Purdue Opinion Panel: *Youth's attitudes toward courtship and marriage.* Lafayette, Ind.: Purdue University Press, 1961, no. 62.

198 REEVY, W. R.: Premarital petting behavior and marital happiness prediction. *Marriage fam. Living*, 1959, **21**, 349–355.

199 REEVY, W. R.: Adolescent sexuality. In A. Ellis and A. Abarbanel (eds.), *The encyclopedia of sexual behavior*. Englewood Cliffs, N.J.: Hawthorn, 1961, pp. 52–67.

200 REEVY, W. R.: Child sexuality. In A. Ellis and A. Abarbanel (eds.), *The encyclopedia of sexual behavior*. Englewood Cliffs, N.J.: Hawthorn, 1961, pp. 258–267.

201 REISS, I. L.: Toward a sociology of the heterosexual love relationship. *Marriage fam. Living*, 1960, **22**, 139–145.

202 REISS, I. L.: Sexual codes in teen-age culture. *Ann. Amer. Acad. pol. soc. Sci.*, 1961, **338**, 53–62.

203 REISS, I. L.: Premarital sexual permissiveness among Negroes and whites. *Amer. sociol. Rev.*, 1964, **29**, 688–698.

204 REISS, I. L.: The scaling of premarital sexual permissiveness. *J. Marriage Fam.*, 1964, **26**, 188–198.

205 REMMERS, H. H., and D. H. RADLER: *The American teen-ager*. Indianapolis: Bobbs-Merrill, 1957.

206 RENNE, R. R.: Woman power and the American economy. *J. Home Econ.*, 1957, **49**, 83–86.

207 RIESMAN, D.: Permissiveness and sex roles. *Marriage fam. Living*, 1959, **21**, 211–217.

208 ROGERS, E. M., and A. E. HAVENS: Prestige rating and mate selection on a college campus. *Marriage fam. Living*, 1960, **22**, 55–59.

209 ROSENBERG, B. G., and B. SUTTON-SMITH: The measurement of masculinity and femininity in children. *Child Develpm.*, 1959, **30**, 374–380.

210 ROSENBERG, B. G., and B. SUTTON-SMITH: A revised conception of masculine-feminine differences in play activities. *J. genet. Psychol.*, 1960, **96**, 165–170.

211 ROSENBERG, B. G., and B. SUTTON-SMITH: The measurement of masculinity-femininity in children: an extension and revalidation. *J. genet. Psychol.*, 1964, **104**, 259–264.

212 ROSS, R. T.: Measures of the sex behavior of college males, compared with Kinsey's results. *J. abnorm. soc. Psychol.*, 1950, **45**, 753–755.

213 ROTH, J., and R. F. PECK: Social class and social mobility factors related to marital adjustment. *Amer. sociol. Rev.*, 1951, **16**, 478–487.

214 ROTHSTEIN, R.: Authoritarianism and men's reactions to sexuality and affection in women. *J. abnorm. soc. Psychol.*, 1960, **61**, 329–334.

215 RYAŃ, M. S.: *Psychological effects of clothing*: I. *Survey of opinions of college girls*. Ithaca, N.Y.: Cornell University Agricultural Experiment Station, 1952, Bulletin 882.

216 SANFORD, N.: *The American college*. New York: Wiley, 1962.

217 SCHNEPP, G. J., and L. A. ROBERTS: Residential propinquity and mate selection on a parish basis. *Amer. J. Sociol.*, 1952, **58**, 45–50.

218 SCHOEPPE, A.: Sex differences in adolescent socialization. *J. soc. Psychol.*, 1953, **38**, 175–185.

219 SCHOEPPE, A., and R. J. HAVIGHURST: A validation of development and adjustment hypotheses of adolescence. *J. educ. Psychol.*, 1952, **43**, 339–353.

220 SEARS, R. R., E. E. MACCOBY, and H. LEVIN: *Patterns of child rearing*. New York: Harper & Row, 1957.

221 SEBALD, H.: Parent-peer control and masculine-marital role: perceptions of adolescent boys. *Dissert. Abstr.*, 1964, **24**, 3003.

222 SELFORS, S. A., R. K. LEIK, and E. KING: Values in mate selection: education versus religion. *Marriage fam. Living*, 1962, **24**, 399–401.

223 SENOUSSI, A. E., A. L. COMREY, D. R. COLEMAN, and J. S. DRUCKMAN: Factors in marital discord. *J. Psychol.*, 1957, **44**, 193–222.

224 SHELLENBERG, J. A., and L. S. BEE: A reexamination of the theory of complementary needs in mate selection. *Marriage fam. Living*, 1960, **22**, 227–232.

225 SHERRIFFS, A. C., and J. P. MC KEE: Qualitative aspects of beliefs about men and women. *J. Pers.*, 1957, **25**, 451–464.

226 SHUTTLEWORTH, F. K.: A biosocial and developmental theory of male and female sexuality. *Marriage fam. Living*, 1959, **21**, 163–170.

227 SMITH, E. A.: *American youth culture*. New York: Free Press, 1962.

228 SMITH, E., and J. H. G. MONANE: Courtship values in a youth sample. *Amer. sociol. Rev.*, 1953, **18**, 635–640.

229 SMITH, W. M.: Rating and dating: a re-study. *Marriage fam. Living*, 1952, **14**, 312–317.

230 SNYDER, E. C.: Attitudes: a study of homogamy and marital selectivity. *J. Marriage Fam.*, 1964, **26**, 332–336.

231 STAUDT, V. M.: Attitudes of college students toward marriage and related problems: II. Age, educational, familial, and economic factors in marriage. *J. Psychol.*, 1952, **34**, 95–106.

232 STEIMEL, R. J.: Childhood experiences and masculinity-femininity scores. *J. counsel. Psychol.*, 1960, **7**, 212–217.

233 STEINMANN, A.: Lack of communication between men and women. *Marriage fam. Living*, 1958, **20**, 350–352.

234 STEINMANN, A.: The concept of the feminine role in the American family: a study of the concept of the feminine role of 51 middle-class American families. *Dissert. Abstr.*, 1958, **19**, part 2, 899–900.

235 STEINMANN, A.: A study of the concept of the feminine role of 51 middle-class American families. *Genet. Psychol. Monogr.*, 1963, **67**, 275–352.

236 STRANG, R.: *The adolescent views himself.* New York: McGraw-Hill, 1957.

237 STRAUSS, A.: The ideal and the chosen mate. *Amer. J. Sociol.*, 1946, **52**, 204–208.

238 STRAUSS, A.: The influence of parent-images upon marital choice. *Amer. sociol. Rev.*, 1946, **11**, 554–559.

239 STRAUSS, B. V.: The dynamics of ordinal position effects. *Quart. J. child Behav.*, 1951, **3**, 133–145.

240 STRODTBECK, F. L.: The interaction of a "henpecked" husband with his wife. *Marriage fam. Living*, 1952, **14**, 305–308.

241 SUSSMAN, M. B.: Parental participation in mate selection and its effect upon family continuity. *Soc. Forces*, 1953, **32**, 76–81.

242 SUSSMAN, M. B., and H. C. YEAGER: Mate selection among Negro and white college students. *Sociol. soc. Res.*, 1950, **35**, 46–49.

243 SWENSEN, C. H., and K. R. NEWTON: The development of sexual differentiation on the draw-a-person test. *J. clin. Psychol.*, 1955, **11**, 417–418.

244 SYMONDS, P. M.: *The dynamics of human adjustment.* New York: Appleton-Century-Crofts, 1946.

245 TEBOR, I. B.: Male virgins: conflicts and group support in American culture. *Family Life Coordinator*, 1961, **9**, 40–42.

246 THOMAS, J. L.: The factor of religion in the selection of marriage mates. *Amer. sociol. Rev.*, 1951, **16**, 487–491.

247 *Time* Report: The pre-teens. *Time Magazine*, Apr. 20, 1962, p. 68.

248 *Time* Report: The second sexual revolution. *Time Magazine*, Jan. 24, 1964, pp. 54–59.

249 *Time* Report: Students: little sex without love. *Time Magazine*, Apr. 9, 1965, p. 46.

250 TRESSELT, M. E.: The adolescent becomes a social person. *J. soc. Hyg.*, 1954, **40**, 130–134.

251 VAIL, J. P., and V. M. STAUDT: Attitudes of college students toward marriage and selected problems: I. Dating and mate selection. *J. Psychol.*, 1950, **30**, 171–182.

252 VERNON, G. M.: Interfaith marriages. *Relig. Educ.*, 1960, **55**, 261–264.

253 VINCENT, C. E.: Social and interpersonal sources of symptomatic frigidity. *Marriage fam. Living*, 1956, **18**, 355–360.

254 VINCENT, C. E.: The adoption market and the unwed mother's baby. *Marriage fam. Living*, 1956, **18**, 124–127.

255 VINCENT, C. E.: Ego involvement in sexual relations: implications for research on illegitimacy. *Amer. J. Sociol.*, 1959, **65**, 287–295.

256 VINCENT, C. E.: Unmarried fathers and the mores: "sexual exploiter" as an ex post facto label. *Amer. sociol. Rev.*, 1960, **25**, 40–46.

257 VINCENT, C. E.: Unwed mothers and the adoption market: psychological and familial factors. *Marriage fam. Living*, 1960, **22**, 112–118.

258 VINCENT, C. E.: *Unmarried mothers.* New York: Free Press, 1961.

259 VINCENT, C. E.: Teen-age illegitimacy: a Pisgah perspective. *Marriage fam. Living*, 1962, **24**, 290–293.

260 VON MERING, F. H.: Professional and nonprofessional women as mothers. *J. soc. Psychol.*, 1955, **42**, 21–34.

261 VON SELLE, M.: Mother-daughter classes in family living. *J. soc. Hyg.*, 1954, **40**, 54–59.

262 WALKER, K.: The celibate male. *Practitioner*, 1954, **172**, 412–413.

263 WALLACE, K.: Factors hindering mate selection. *Sociol. soc. Res.*, 1960, **44**, 317–325.

264 WALTERS, J., and R. H. OJEMANN: A study of the components of adolescent attitudes con-

cerning the role of women. *J. soc. Psychol.*, 1952, **35**, 101–110.

265 WALTERS, J., D. PEARCE, and L. DAHMS: Affectional and aggressive behavior of preschool children. *Child Develpm.*, 1957, **28**, 518–529.

266 WEBB, A. P.: Sex-role preferences and adjustment in early adolescents. *Child Develpm.*, 1963, **34**, 609–618.

267 WEISS, R. S., and N. M. SAMUELSON: Social roles of American women: their contribution to a sense of usefulness and importance. *Marriage fam. Living*, 1958, **20**, 358–366.

268 WILLITS, F. C., R. C. BEALER, and G. W. BENDER: Interreligious marriages among Pennsylvania rural youth. *Marriage fam. Living*, 1963, **25**, 433–438.

269 WINCH, R. F.: Further data and observations on the Oedipus hypothesis: the consequences of an inadequate hypothesis. *Amer. sociol. Rev.*, 1951, **16**, 784–795.

270 WINCH, R. F., and T. KTSANES, and V. KTSANES: The theory of complementary needs in mate-selection: an analytic and descriptive study. *Amer. sociol. Rev.*, 1954, **19**, 241–249.

271 WOLMAN, B.: Sexual development in Israeli adolescents. *Amer. J. Psychother.*, 1951, **5**, 531–559.

272 ZUBRACK, F.: Adolescent values in marital choice. *Marriage fam. Living*, 1959, **21**, 77–78.

273 ZUK, G. H.: Sex-appropriate behavior in adolescence. *J. genet. Psychol.*, 1958, **93**, 15–32.

CHAPTER 15
family
relationships

Relationships between people rarely remain static. This is true of relationships with members of the family just as it is of relationships with personal friends, social acquaintances, or business associates. The change may be for the better or for the worse. This depends partly on the changes that are taking place in the people involved and partly on their expectations of one another. A person who is ill, for example, will be less pleasant to be with than one who is well. When a person expects others to think and act as he wants them to, and criticizes them when they do not, his relationships will be less harmonious than if he hesitated to criticize or suggest ways for them to reform.

pattern of family relationships

There is a predictable pattern of relationships among family members which varies quantitatively more than it varies qualitatively. Typically, the relationship of a baby with his family is favorable; he is the center of love and attention. Any disturbing behavior on his part is forgiven on the ground that he is too young to know better. Even before the baby reaches his first birthday, his relationships with the different members of his family begin to worsen. This deterioration is shown in a decrease in parental warmth and intellectual stimulation, in greater parental restrictiveness and punitiveness, and in impatience and intolerance on the part of siblings that often spring from jealousy (50,52,327).

While family relationships may improve later when the child spends more time outside the home, the deterioration continues and increases as childhood draws to a close. At that time, friction with *all* members of the family is usual. Difficulties in getting along with different members of the family usually start around the age of 12 years and reach their maximum between 15 and 17 years (299). Puberty, as was stressed earlier, brings physical changes that make the pubescent child moody, irritable, secretive, uncooperative, and quarrelsome (112,139,203). Unless parents recognize the relationship between the changes taking place in the child's body and his behavior, they are likely to be critical and punitive in their treatment of him. This increases the child's feeling that no one loves him; it widens the gap between parents and the child still further (139,343).

As the growth spurt of puberty slows down and as body homeostasis is gradually restored, the young adolescent begins to feel better; this is reflected in the quality of his behavior. As a result, there is a gradual improvement in family relationships, beginning sometime between the ages of 15 and 16 years for girls and a year or two later for boys. How soon this improvement occurs will depend partly on the age of sexual maturing of the adolescent and partly on how soon his family, especially his parents, recognize that he is no longer a child and then revise their habitual way of treating him (50,139,299).

In late adolescence, family relationships are normally on a better basis. The improvement that takes place as adolescents grow older is well illustrated by a study of conflicts girls had with their parents at different times in adolescence. This study revealed that 69.7 percent of girls had one or more conflicts with their fathers during their high school days, but only 39.6 percent had conflicts when they were in college; 81.5 percent had conflicts with their mothers during high school days, whereas 58.7 percent continued to have conflicts when they were in college (81).

effects of family friction on home climate

The home climate—the "psychological atmosphere" of the home—varies markedly from home to home. Some homes have a good climate, some a poor climate, and some a changeable climate. Even within the same home, the climate may vary from time to time for the same individual; it is certain to vary for the different children of the family. In general, however, the home climate is more likely to be poor than good during the early years of adolescence, when friction with different family members is at its peak. Then it normally improves as adolescence progresses.

Because it is the parents who are primarily responsible for establishing the home and for control over it, it is they who are largely responsible for the type of climate that exists. Furthermore, parents are largely responsible for setting the tone of relationships between the different members of the family. In one study, it was found that when parents are happy with each other the home climate is far happier than when parental relationships are unfavorable (334). This is illustrated in Figure 15-1.

Unfortunately, most adolescents do not

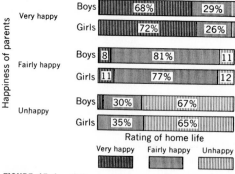

Happiness of parents

Very happy — Boys 68% | 29%
Very happy — Girls 72% | 26%

Fairly happy — Boys 8 | 81% | 11
Fairly happy — Girls 11 | 77% | 12

Unhappy — Boys 30% | 67%
Unhappy — Girls 35% | 65%

Rating of home life

Very happy | Fairly happy | Unhappy

FIGURE 15–1 When parents are happy, adolescents perceive the home climate as happy. (Adapted from W. L. Slocum: Some factors associated with happiness in unbroken homes. *Family Life Coordinator*, 1958, **6**, 35–39. Used by permission.)

feel that their homes have a climate that is favorable to wholesome relationships between the different members. As a result, they are unhappy, critical, and faultfinding. This attitude affects their relationships with their parents as well as with their siblings and other relatives. Other family members, perceiving the adolescents' behavior as unsocial, unfriendly and unappreciative, retaliate by criticisms, faultfinding, and derogatory statements. As a result, a vicious circle is set into motion. Each member's relationship with every other member goes from bad to worse as frictional relationships reinforce each other (173). When this happens, more and more members of the family are drawn into the deteriorating relationships until the home climate is so frictional for all members that everyone is made unhappy (153). See Figure 15–2 for a graphic illustration of the vicious circle of parent-child relationships.

The reason for the spread of tension in a family is that there is a delicate interplay of psychological forces in the relationships of the home. It is possible to upset this interplay should one member of the family be out of step with another or with family expectations. As Berman has pointed out, "Any emotional experience that disturbs the psychic equilibrium of one member of the family will bring about a dis-

turbance in the psychological equilibrium of all members of the family" (40).

When, for example, conflict exists between a parent and an adolescent or between an adolescent and his sibling, the parent becomes annoyed and punitive in his attitude. This, in turn, leads him to become more restrictive of the adolescent's activities as a form of punishment. If the adolescent resents this and interprets his parent's restrictiveness to mean the parent's rejection of him, it will increase the friction that already exists (25). Should his siblings or the other parent feel that he has been treated unfairly, they may side with him and accuse the restrictive parent of being unfair. In time, the whole family may be taking sides (25,50,153,173).

Once a vicious circle of this sort has been set into motion, the only way to stop it from gaining further momentum is for one of the family members to change his attitude and, in turn, his behavior toward the other members who are involved. Perhaps the quickest and surest way of doing this is for one or more of the family members to absent themselves from the others until all have had time to gain perspective on the problems that gave rise to the friction.

When an adolescent is out of the home for the major part of the day—at school or with his peers—he is less likely to have a frictional relationship with his family than is the adolescent who is at home most of the time. Similarly, when a mother works outside the home, family relationships are less frictional than when she is around the major part of the day, *provided* her working does not give rise to other sources of friction. If it does, the therapeutic effect of separation will be counteracted by new sources of friction (152,186,273,303).

overt expressions of friction

In the past, when authoritarian control of the family by the parents was the accepted pattern, overt expressions of annoyance and hostility were limited to parents and grandparents. On the surface, then, the emotional climate of the home *appeared* to be calm and peaceful, even though there may have been hidden smoldering resentments.

With today's emphasis on democracy in child training and freedom of expression, hostilities between family members are openly expressed, even by the youngest children. During the childhood years, physical attacks are common. Gradually, however, verbal attacks begin to predominate as the child discovers that his parents, his peers, and the social group will not tolerate physical aggressions. The more democratic the home, the more outspoken each member is when things are not to his liking (50,52, 139,299,359).

When *parents* object to what their adolescent sons and daughters do, they find fault with it, criticize, make derogatory comments, compare them and their achievements with those of their siblings, and nag. When the adolescent, for example, is forgetful of household chores, he is nagged about it until the task is finally done. If he makes what his parents consider unrealistic demands for material possessions, he is apt to receive an ego-deflating denial (67,73, 115).

The parents' expressions of annoyance and hostility provide the *adolescent* with a model for his own expressions. Adolescents make derogatory comparisons of their parents and the parents of their friends, they make unrealistic suggestions about how their parents could improve themselves or their activities, they nag about being "overprotected" or being made "different" from their peers, they complain that their parents expect too much of them, and they find fault with things that are done for them as well as with things that their parents expect them to do for themselves (50,67,73,139).

Most of the verbal attacks adolescents make on grandparents and other relatives are made behind their backs—in the presence of friends, parents, or siblings. *Grandparents*, on the other hand, have been accustomed to more authoritarian control in the home; they do not hesitate to criticize and find fault overtly with the adolescent.

Boys do not hesitate to tell their brothers or sisters what they think of them

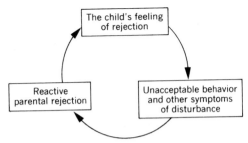

FIGURE 15–2 The vicious circle of parent-child relationships. (Adapted from D. Hallowitz and B. Stulberg: The vicious cycle of parent-child relationship breakdown. *Soc. Casewk.*, 1959, **40**, 269–275. Used by permission.)

and why; girls then follow suit. As Bossard and Boll have pointed out, sibling relationships are characterized by "stark frankness" in which each sees the other "with their hair down" (52). That there is plenty of bickering, name-calling, criticizing, faultfinding, and ego-deflating comparisons with others among siblings in most homes is a truism that requires little further emphasis (50,67,139,184).

EFFECTS OF OVERT EXPRESSIONS

There is no question about the fact that it is better for the *individual* to be able to express highly charged emotional attitudes openly. But, from the point of view of *family relationships*, overt expressions are damaging. The reason for this is that the person who is the target of the verbal attack is emotionally aroused and may not have an opportunity to express his resentments at the attack made on him adequately to clear his system. This results in the development of an unfavorable mood which predisposes him to react unfavorably to other family members (37).

No member of the family is spared the damaging effects of overt expressions of hostilities within a family. However, different members are affected differently. The characteristic effects are discussed below.

On Parents Parents who have sincerely tried to be "good" parents are deeply hurt by the constant criticisms made by their adolescent sons and daughters. Mothers, more often than fathers, are psychologically damaged by their children's outspoken resentments, annoyances, and antagonisms, partly because it is they who have devoted many years to doing things for the children and partly because the verbal attacks generally reach their peak at about the time the mother reaches the menopause, a time in her life when she is physically and psychologically less able to tolerate friction than she normally can (67).

On Adolescents   The effect on adolescents of overt expressions of hostility is even more damaging than on their parents. The younger the adolescent, the more insecure he is and the more ego deflating any criticism from *any* source. Furthermore, expressions of hostility exaggerate the already-existing feelings the adolescent has that his *parents* do not "understand" him. Friction with *siblings*, when overtly expressed, has much the same effect as overt expressions of friction with parents—it undermines a healthy ego concept the adolescent is trying so hard to build up and it adds to the feeling of insecurity and not belonging (184).

The least damaging effect on the adolescent comes from overt expression of friction from *grandparents* and *elderly relatives*. Even if grandparents or relatives are living with the adolescent's family, the adolescent is less disturbed by their criticism and fault-finding than by that of other family members. The reason for this is that adolescents of today regard these relatives as "has-beens" who are too out of step with modern times to be concerned about.

On Elderly Relatives   Even though the adolescent is not markedly affected by frictional relationships with grandparents and other elderly relatives, the elderly relatives are hypersensitive to any suggestion that they are old and out of step with the times. Furthermore, they feel that a young person should show respect for his elders. They are, as a result, angered at the "impertinence" of a young person who dares to say derogatory things to their face. Instead of

being hurt, as parents are, grandparents are both hurt and indignant (16,149).

EFFECTS OF NAGGING

Unquestionably the most damaging effects of overt expressions of hostility come from nagging. This is true of *all* family members. Studies of nagging have revealed that it is a pattern of overt expression of hostility that is rarely limited to one member of the family. As Ellis and Nye (115) have pointed out:

> *Nagging shows a strong tendency to run in families. If the father nags, one may predict with good accuracy that the mother will nag also. . . . This lends support to the idea that nagging may be a family cultural trait—an approved and expected technique for controlling adolescents.*

When the adolescent is told time after time that he is neglecting his duties and responsibilities; that he is wasting time on social activities that could better be spent in studying; or that he is rude and impertinent, the cumulative effect that comes with nagging makes each verbal attack seem harsher and more difficult to accept than a single attack would be. When a mother, for example, is constantly criticized for being inefficient and for not using "modern methods" in the running of the home, each repetition reinforces the previous criticisms. The result is that the psychological damage to her ego is intensified.

EFFECTS OF NONEXPRESSION

Nonexpression of hostility is also damaging. It may be said that words left unspoken cannot harm a person nor can physical attacks that are curbed. However, the person who refrains from saying or doing things that would give vent to his hostility is damaged directly, and the persons against whom he has feelings of hostility are indirectly damaged through strained family relationships. Even more important, a controlled emotion predisposes the individual to think about and to exaggerate the cause of the hostility, thus keeping the mood alive and intensifying it. Sooner or later, it will be too strong to be controlled. It will then burst forth in a physical attack or a verbal tirade of an intensity out of all proportion to the situation that gave rise to it. This nullifies all the benefits derived from controlling the hostility, both from the point of view of family relationships and the effect it has on the individual's attitude toward himself.

In conclusion, then, it becomes apparent that because both expression and nonexpression of hostility worsen family relationships, some other approach to the problem must be taken if the relationships are to be favorable. To date, the only remedy that seems to solve this dilemma is *communication* which brings about an emotional catharsis for all who are involved in the friction. This was discussed earlier (see pages 106 to 108) and it will be discussed later in this chapter.

conditions affecting the home climate

While it is true that in every country and in every cultural group conflicts in the home are more common when the children of the family reach adolescence, they are more frequent and more serious in the United States than elsewhere (149).

Many reasons have been given to explain the extent of conflicts in the American home today. A survey of some of the many factors that affect the home climate in American families will help to show who is responsible for its condition. Furthermore, such a survey helps one to see which factors are controllable and, thus, to see how the home climate can be improved.

UNDERSTANDING OF OTHERS

Just as better social relationships outside the home are achieved when an individual is able to understand the feelings, thoughts, emotions, and motives of others, so it is in the home. The individual who is capable of *empathy*—of putting himself in the psychological shoes of another and of viewing a situation from his frame of reference—makes far better social adjustments than does the individual who lacks empathic

ability. (See pages 166 to 168 for a more complete discussion of empathy and its relationship to social adjustments.)

Aids to Understanding   There are two aids to understanding: communication and shared experiences. Through *communication*, an individual is able to understand the other person's point of view and to give his own point of view so that the other person can understand him. Without communication, misunderstanding is common (398). Parents, for example, who feel that it is sufficient to lay down the law to their children get poorer cooperation than parents who feel that their children are entitled to know the reasons for the restrictions (75).

In the homes of adolescents, there is rarely an absence of talking, but there is a shortage of communication. Adolescents talk to their parents and siblings while their parents and siblings talk to them. But the talking consists mainly of criticism, faultfinding, nagging, and derogatory remarks; it is less often an attempt to understand or make others understand each family member's point of view.

The second aid to understanding is *sharing experiences* with others by doing things with them. A teen-age daughter, for example, who is critical of her mother's "inefficiency" in preparing a family meal will get a new perspective on the matter if she helps with the preparation and has an opportunity to learn how much time and effort are needed for preparing even the simplest meal.

How important a role communication and shared experiences play has been demonstrated by a study of families where parents made a practice of discussing family problems with their children. The children of these families, regardless of their age or sex, reported that family life was happier than was true in families where such discussions did not take place (334). This is illustrated in Figure 15–3.

Equally as important as willingness to communicate with their children is *parental respect* for the child's opinions. When parents respect the opinions of their children,

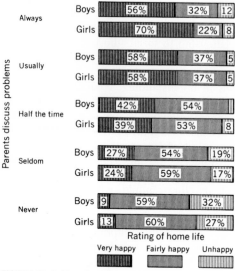

Parents discuss problems		Boys	56%	32%	12
Always		Girls	70%	22%	8
Usually		Boys	58%	37%	5
		Girls	58%	37%	5
Half the time		Boys	42%	54%	
		Girls	39%	53%	8
Seldom		Boys	27%	54%	19%
		Girls	24%	59%	17%
Never		Boys	9	59%	32%
		Girls	13	60%	27%

Rating of home life

Very happy   Fairly happy   Unhappy

FIGURE 15–3 Family life is perceived as happier by adolescents when parents discuss family problems with them than when they fail to do so. (Adapted from W. L. Slocum: Some factors associated with happiness in unbroken homes. *Family Life Coordinator*, 1958, **6**, 35–39. Used by permission.)

even though they may not agree with them, the home climate is regarded as happier by the children than when parents seldom or never show such respect (334). This is illustrated in Figure 15–4. Adolescents who communicate most with their siblings have better relationships with them than those who limit their speech to verbal attacks. The siblings with whom they communicate most are the ones with whom they have the best relationships (334). This is illustrated in Figure 15–11, page 612.

Adolescents who do things with their families just "for fun" get along better with them than do adolescents who spend most of their leisure time with their peers, using the home primarily as a place to eat, sleep, and study (55). Spending leisure time together fosters a feeling of mutual understanding. There is thus evidence that "understanding and togetherness seem to go hand in hand" (252,348).

Breakdown in Understanding Friction is inevitable when *both* communication and sharing of experiences are absent; misunder-

standing is almost a certainty. This is most likely to happen during the period of puberty. However, after the puberty growth spurt has ended, the adolescent does not necessarily return to his former relationships with family members; in fact, the deterioration that set in earlier is accelerated and lack of communication becomes a habit (50, 104,139,299). To make matters worse, the adolescent is likely to turn to someone outside the home—a teacher, recreational leader, or camp counselor—whom he has temporarily put on a pedestal and hero-worships; this antagonizes his family (194).

There are many reasons for the *breakdown in communication* between the adolescent and his family. First, rapid *social and cultural changes* give the adolescent of today many experiences which his parents did not have. Thus parents are often unable to understand them or cope with them. While the gap between parents' and adolescents' youth may not be long in years, the gap between them may be very great in mores (65,201,300,393,395). One of the most common complaints of adolescents is that older people don't understand them; the older people feel much the same way (200,273,300,398).

The second cause of breakdown in communication between the adolescent and his parents is his belief that they *do not try to understand him* or sympathize with his problems. Many adolescents feel that their parents are so old-fashioned, rigid, and set in their ways that they automatically condemn anything that differs from the way it was when they were young. They complain that their parents are not trying to keep up to date (300,308,351).

Breakdown in communication may come, third, from the adolescent's belief that his parents have *unrealistically high levels of aspiration* for him and do not understand his reasons for falling short of their goals. Hence, he feels that there is little to be gained by talking over his problems with them (101). Fourth, breakdown in communication is often the result of *generally poor relationships with people*. The adolescent who does not want to talk to his parents, his siblings, or his grandparents almost always has an antagonistic attitude toward them (104,351). And, finally, breakdown in communication may result from *lack of shared experiences*. The adolescent who spends most of his waking time with his peers has little time to talk to the family and little desire to do so; his interests are so remote from theirs that he feels they have nothing in common (55,194,348).

Effects of Misunderstanding Breakdown of communication and absence of shared experiences often lead to misunderstandings. When a person misunderstands another, there is a less friendly relationship between them than when understanding exists. Even though there may not be an actual misunderstanding, there is usually a tendency to "read meanings" into what a person has said (212,330). Adolescents *assume* that parents feel about them as all other adults do. This, they then interpret, means that their parents have little love or respect for them (153,176).

Parents, on the other hand, anticipate that their sons and daughters will have a tendency to undervalue them as they do all adults. They also believe that adolescents have an unrealistically high opinion of themselves and their capacities. As a result, they believe that adolescents will repudiate any suggestions or advice given to them by adults (176). As Hess and Goldblatt (176) have explained:

> One of the central problems of parent–teen-ager relations lies not so much in disparity between their respective evaluations of adolescents as in the fact that each group mistrusts or misunderstands the opinions of the other. Parents and adolescents thus interpret teen-age behavior and problems in different and often contradictory terms.

INDEPENDENCE

All through childhood, the adolescent has been fighting against parental overprotectiveness. If his fight produces no results, or results below his expectations, he becomes resentful. When he gains the stature of an adult at puberty, his demands for indepen-

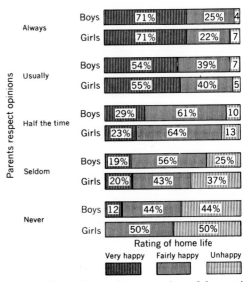

FIGURE 15–4 Parental respect for adolescents' opinions contributes to the happiness of the home climate. (Adapted from W. L. Slocum: Some factors associated with happiness in unbroken homes. *Family Life Coordinator*, 1958, **6**, 35–39. Used by permission.)

dence are intensified. Late maturers, who are more often treated in accordance with their size than their age, are especially demanding in their fight for independence.

Few parents feel that an adolescent should not have independence; they disagree with the adolescent on how much and how soon independence should be given (25,232). As Bealer et al. (29) have pointed out:

> The adolescent seeking to establish his identity in adult society may disagree with his parents regarding when recognition of his maturity should occur. He may wish to engage in activities which symbolize his adulthood while his parents feel that he is still too young. . . . Once the youth is accepted as a member of the adult society, this type of conflict ceases.

Gaining independence is important to an adolescent both personally and socially. If he is given as much independence as his friends have, this increases his self-confidence. If he has less independence than they, he feels that his family believes he is not capable of handling independence as successfully as his peers do. This not only brings resentments and feelings of inadequacy, but it makes him doubt his own abilities. To others, independence is a status symbol—it tells his peers that he is no longer a child but has been granted the status of a near adult. See pages 275 to 278 for a more complete discussion of this.

Reasons for Not Granting Independence Most adults, including parents, feel that the adolescent must learn to be an independent person, but they often fail to provide him with opportunities to learn to be one. They may even place blocks in his way when opportunities are available. They have many reasons, either conscious or unconscious, for this. Of all the reasons, perhaps the most important and most common is *habit* (15,88,248). Studies of the way mothers treat their children from babyhood into adolescence have revealed a marked consistency in the type of treatment the mother uses from year to year. If she is overprotective when the child is young, she tends to be overprotective and restrictive of the child's freedom as he grows older and reaches adolescence (27,323). In commenting on the failure of parents to change their treatment of the child to adjust to his changed needs as he grows older, Bowerman and Kinch (55) have written:

> There would appear to be something like a law of perseveration in human relations, according to which we tend to react to another person in the same manner until there is some force operating, such as a status change imposed on the relationship which modifies our perception of the other and the way in which we shall react to him. We would expect, for this reason, that parents tend to hold the same demands and expectations of their children until a change in external circumstances forces them to look at their children from a new perspective. These changes are increase in growth and puberty changes and starting high school or junior high school.

Parents, but especially mothers, who have derived satisfaction from the dependency of their children, far too often, for selfish reasons, try to prolong their children's dependency. While their *selfishness* is, unquestionably, usually unconscious, the effect on the adolescent is the same; they cannot or will not release their hold on him and cut the parental apron strings (26,52, 139,274). Because adolescents of today need a long *period of training* for their life careers and because parents must, for the most part, be financially responsible for this training, they tend to expect dependency of their children as a reward (295).

Parents are often not sure that the adolescent is experienced enough to handle successfully the independence he demands. They are afraid of what the world may do to their inexperienced, innocent, and dependent child; they do not want him to be hurt. Many adolescents who demand independence are also unsure of their ability to handle it successfully. They are afraid of making wrong decisions and then regretting them later. However, adolescents will not admit this, even to themselves (134, 137, 158).

Effect on Family Relationships If the adolescent is denied the independence his friends have, he will be resentful of his parents (154). One of the common ways he shows this resentment is by devaluation of his parents—"parent belittlement." He is negative in his attitude toward his parents and everything they have or do; he turns to outsiders for help and advice, criticizes his parents, and repudiates their companionship and plans for his future (137).

Even more seriously, adolescents who are denied the independence their friends have experience a severe blow to the self-confidence and self-esteem they are trying so hard to build up. When given some independence, but not so much as their friends have, many adolescents misuse it in an attempt to convince their friends that they are equally as independent as they. As a result, parents are likely to reimpose restraints. This only serves to increase the adolescents' rebellion (134,154).

The adolescent who is given the freedom he has demanded and then fails to use it successfully blames his parents because they "babied" him too long and did not teach him how to make his own decisions. Resentment against his parents, combined with the ego-deflating experience of failure, has a devastating effect on his relationships with his parents and upon his attitude toward his home and family (220).

CONFLICT OF VALUES

With social and cultural changes come changes in interests; with changes in interests, changes in values and the problems they entail are inevitable (97,305). As Symonds has pointed out, "Change the social and economic structure of society and you immediately change the relative emphasis of these problems and interests" (360). Since the turn of the century, change has not only been rapid but it has been toward a greater leniency in all values. The result is that values learned during the childhood and youth of today's parents are completely out of date in many respects with the values held by today's adolescents (156).

Changes in values from cultural and social changes are further complicated in many homes when parents are foreign-born, when they come from different areas of the country in which they now live, and when they are socially mobile. The most serious conflict of values comes in families where parents are foreign-born and bring with them the values they learned in their own countries—values which are often very different from those of present-day America (28,38,125,182,211,249,306,398).

Parents of today, as a result of these radically changed values, are literally "strangers in today's world while adolescents are at home in it" (254). As a result, as Mead has pointed out, "We cannot guess their needs by remembering our own, we cannot find the answers to their questions by looking into our own hearts" (252).

When people view the same situation from different frames of reference, it is difficult for them to see eye to eye. Each tends to think the other is wrong in his values while he is right. This leads to friction (242). Because parents are the people in authority in the home, they expect their children to accept their values. Friction is intensified when adolescents complain that their parents are old-fashioned and when they make derogatory comparisons of their parents with the parents of their friends (387).

Friction is most serious in areas which are important to either parents or adolescents. To parents, for example, thrift, hard work, and a good reputation are goals for which every young person should strive; to adolescents of today, having fun, being popular, and having status symbols equal or superior to those of their friends are the goals they strive to reach (142,223,271, 354). Similarly, to a mother, virginity is a highly valued asset to making a good marriage. Many daughters, however, disagree and contend that intercourse during the engagement period is the expected thing by men today (34).

Effects of Clash in Values   Whether the adolescent accepts or rejects parental values, there will be friction in the family. As Ellis and Nye (115) have explained:

> The underlying bases for parent-child conflicts are usually dependent on either an opposition of activity or an opposition of attitudes. Sometimes these conflicts arise from disputes in a single complex of values, such as religion, and grow until they color all value decisions of the parent.

When the adolescent accepts the parents' values, he will be out of step with his peers. This will lead to partial or total social rejection (79,387,389). He will then blame his parents for his lack of social acceptance. Many adolescents try to conform, in part at least, to parental standards to maintain peace and harmony in the home. To do this, they accept parental values but interpret them more liberally than their parents do (150).

When the adolescent accepts peer values in favor of parental values, he increases his social acceptance. But, by doing so, he will increase family friction (389). Added to the annoyance and punitiveness of parents when adolescents refuse to conform to their standards is the feeling of embarrassment the adolescent experiences when his parents are different from the parents of his friends.

Only when parents are able and willing to revise the values they learned in their youth to be more in step with the values that prevail today can the friction resulting from value clashes be reduced. If parents feel that today's values are inferior to those of their own youth, they will refuse to make a revision. Sometimes parents' refusal to change their values comes from ignorance of what the new values are. The parent who has limited communication and few shared experiences with his adolescent son or daughter cannot know what the world of today's youth is like any more than he can know what a foreign land is like if his travels have been limited to his own country.

PARENTAL AGE

As a general rule, the home climate is more frictional when parents are overage than when they are younger (31,299,302,318, 387). In a large family, some of the children arrive when their parents are in the late twenties or even the mid-thirties. In late marriages, even the firstborn may arrive when his parents are in the thirties or early forties. Should one parent be decidedly older than the other, as in "May-December marriages," the child will have one young and one overage parent (49,52,145).

Causes of Conflict There are many reasons for the effect parental age has on the home climate. Of these, the following have been found to be the most important.

First, the wider the gap between the ages of the parent and the adolescent, the less able they are to see eye to eye on matters of importance to each. Age, per se, does not cause mental rigidity. However, many older parents do not want to change or they are too isolated from the cultural patterns of young people to be able to understand their points of view. Younger parents, by contrast, are more in step with the times. As a result, they understand their adolescent sons and daughters better (145,159, 160,299).

Second, older parents are less inter-

ested in or less able to participate in young people's activities than are younger parents. An older father, for example, may not be physically able to engage in sports as he did when he was younger (79,348).

Third, older parents often have less energy for activities adolescents enjoy. Their health may be poor and this makes them nervous, irritable, and nagging in their relationships with their adolescent children. A mother who is experiencing the menopause when her children reach their teen years is more often than not suffering from the physical and psychological problems the menopause brings. The noise and friction among the children in the family, the confusion in the household when young people gather for recreations, and the characteristic untidiness, preoccupation with looks, and neglect of home chores get on her nerves. A younger mother, in better health, takes these matters more in stride (52,160).

Fourth, young parents are more interested in having fun with their contemporaries than are older parents. Being out of the house more, younger parents are not with their children so much that they get in each other's hair. If adolescents welcome this freedom from parental supervision, their relationships with their parents will be good. If, on the other hand, they regard this as parental neglect, it will lead to resentments that will cause friction with their parents (50,52).

Fifth, the age of the parents has a marked influence on their attitudes toward the parental role. Young parents tend, as a group, to be more casual about their parental responsibilities. Older parents, by contrast, are likely to be overprotective, strict in discipline, and demanding of greater responsibility and achievement on the part of their children (50,52,376).

Sixth, the age of the parents influences their feelings of adequacy for the parental role. Young parents generally feel inadequate to handle the responsibilities parenthood brings. This feeling of inadequacy is expressed in nervous, tense, and inconsistent treatment of their children. By contrast, older parents are more relaxed and consistent in their treatment (31,33,309,376).

FIGURE 15-5 Parents who try to appear "young" are often embarrassing to an adolescent because they do not "act their age"; overage parents are embarrassing because they "look like grandparents."

Seventh, older parents, owing to their greater experience, tend to have higher aspirations for their children than do younger parents. They are, as a result, more likely to nag and complain about the adolescent's behavior which they regard as a waste of time and to prod him to study and to take advantage of the opportunities they provide for him. Younger parents, who are more inclined to have fun themselves, encourage their children to follow the pattern set by their peers and to enjoy themselves while they are still young (1,115,376).

An eighth cause of friction in the home stemming from parental age is that adolescents are often embarrassed and ashamed of parents who look and act much older than the parents of their friends. Much of the criticism of looks and the attempts to reform their parents' looks stem from their embarrassment about their parents' ages. Adolescents are embarrassed and ashamed of parents who do not "act their ages." This leads to a critical, faultfinding attack on the parent which annoys the parent (50,52). (See Figure 15-5.)

The final way in which parental age affects the home climate is the disparity between the ages of the two parents. Should one of the parents be overage and the other approximately average in age, there is likely to be a clash of interests and values between the parents, especially as far as the child's behavior is concerned. Fortunately, for the welfare of the adolescent, it is usually the father who is older than the mother. As the mother is with the adolescent more than the father, the damaging effects of age are not as marked as they would be if the difference were reversed (49,50,52,160).

TOGETHERNESS

In recent years, "togetherness" has been extolled as one of the major ideals of American family living. Young men have been urged to share home duties and child-care responsibilities with their wives; wives have been advised to learn about their husbands' jobs so they can be real helpmates to them; and both parents have been told that if the children share in the planning, decision making, chores, and recreations with their parents the home will be a utopia.

While togetherness as a philosophy of home life may produce a good home climate when children are young, this does not necessarily mean that it always will. A situation that satisfied their needs when the children were younger may not do so as they become more mature, both physically and psychologically. One of the things most important to an adolescent is changing from a status of dependency to one of independence.

An important expression of independence in adolescence is turning away from family togetherness to more and more interests in and activities with the peer group. (See Figure 15–6.) Doing things with the family appeals less and less to adolescents, while doing things with their peers appeals more and more (55,67). As Coleman has pointed out, as the adolescent "lives more and more in a society of his own, he finds the family a less and less satisfying psychological home" (79).

Furthermore, the adolescent is under pressure by parents, teachers, and peers to be socially active in the school and community. He knows that social prestige goes with popularity in the peer group, not with activities with the family. To win this prestige, boys and girls cannot adhere to the philosophy of family togetherness. Furthermore, they are well aware of the greater parental pride associated with success in athletic and social activities among their peers than with activities carried out with family members. This adds to their motivation to turn their time, energies, and interests away from family and toward peer activities (79,340).

Variations in Togetherness Normally, *young* adolescents spend more time in the home, doing things with and for the members of their families, than do older adolescents (190,348). At every age, from earliest childhood, *boys* spend more time with their peers and less time with their families than do girls (28,55). Adolescents whose families are *socially mobile* are more home-oriented than peer-oriented. This difference in togetherness is not through choice; it comes from lack of acceptance by the new group (55). Adolescents from *large families* break away from togetherness sooner than do those from small families; this is because in large families parents put less pressure on children to be at home (9,55).

The more *popular* the adolescent is with peers of both sexes, the more socially active he will be and the less time he will have to do things with his family. A study of the relationship between dating and participation in family recreations has shown that adolescents who frequently participate in activities with their families date less than adolescents who spend less time in family recreational activities (348). This relationship is shown in Figure 15–7.

Effects of Breakdown of Togetherness As the adolescent turns more and more to outsiders, it is not surprising that they have more influence on his *values* and *decision making* than do parents (28,55). (See Figure 15–6.) How much the adolescent will be influenced by outsiders' values will depend mainly on how great a gap there is between parental values and those of members of the peer group (28,142). This is well illustrated in the case of clothing. Both boys and girls wear what their peers consider right, regardless of parental attitudes (147).

This does not mean that adolescents reject *all* parental values or turn to outsiders for advice in making *all* decisions. Instead, where they turn for advice will be influenced by the decision to be made (337). In a study of high school girls, it was reported that the girls turned to parents for advice in situations which have a long-time consequence, such as the choice of a career, but to their peers in situations where the choice is of immediate consequence, as what dress to wear to a party (59). As the adolescent turns more and more to outsiders for advice

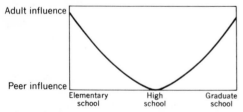

FIGURE 15–6 Young adolescents turn more to the peer group and are more influenced by their peers than by their parents. (Adapted from D. Gottlieb and C. Ramsey: *The American adolescent.* Homewood, Ill.: Dorsey Press, 1964. Used by permission.)

and values, it is apparent that the "home has less and less ability to mold him" (79).

The second effect of breakdown of togetherness is the feeling, by the adolescent, that he no longer *needs his parents* as he did when he was younger. The growing realization of his ability to be independent, economically as well as socially, makes him feel less and less need for his parents. As a result, the adolescent is often casual in his treatment of his parents, showing them less consideration, respect, and affection than he previously did. While most parents want and expect their adolescent children to become increasingly independent as they grow older, they cannot help resenting the new treatment they receive from their independence-conscious sons and daughters (50, 139,274,294).

While many parents, especially those who believe in democratic home training, assign relatively few *home* chores to children when they are young, they expect the children to assume more and more of these chores as they grow older. The adolescent who is away from home a good part of the day simply does not have time for these added chores, nor does he want to make time for them. Adolescents even slight the chores related to their own personal possessions, claiming that they don't care how disorderly their rooms or clothes are (142, 189,190).

Effects on Home Climate How parents feel about the adolescent's preoccupation with activities outside the home, what values they place on these activities, and how competent they feel to advise their children will determine how great the effect of breakdown of togetherness is on the home climate. If, for example, parents feel that they can give better advice than outsiders can because they know their children better and are more interested in their welfare, they will resent the willingness of their children to follow outside advice (55,194).

The adolescent who is away from the family members more than he is with them and whose family relationships are quite equalitarian has fewer frictions than does the adolescent who is constantly with his

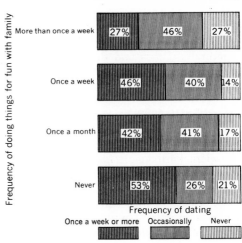

FIGURE 15–7 Adolescents who date frequently participate in family recreational activities less than do those who date less. (Adapted from C. L. Stone: Family recreation: a parental dilemma. *Family Life Coordinator*, 1963, **12**, 85–87. Used by permission.)

family and whose relationship with the family is still submissive. The reason is partly that each family member develops his own interests and thus has something to contribute to the others and partly that with limited contacts each family member learns to treat the others as individuals in their own right, just as he does his friends and acquaintances. The parent-child dependency relationship is then replaced by a relationship similar to friendship (192,383).

Adolescents who are popular with their peers get along better with their families than do those who are less popular. The adolescent who lacks social acceptance is moody and unhappy. This predisposes him to have frictional attitudes toward everyone, both in the home and outside. Even more important, many adolescents project the blame for their poor social adjustments on their families (52,78,112,351). Adolescents who are very popular spend so much time away from home that there are few opportunities for them to engage in frictional relationships with their families. Those who are less popular than they would like to be tend to have greater friction with their families. The reason for this is that they are so anxious to be accepted that they are willing to accept peer values if there is a conflict with home values and to break home rules if they find these rules conflict with the rules their peers are governed by (55,340).

PARENTAL CONTROL

Few adolescents question the fact that there must be some parental control over their behavior. Furthermore, few question the fact that they deserve punishment when they willfully violate family rules established as guidelines for their behavior. What they do question is the type of control they are subjected to and the fairness of the punishment meted out to them when they violate a rule. This is what leads to friction.

To produce a healthy home climate, parents must be able and willing to adapt the culturally defined role of parent as one in *complete* control over his child, regardless of his age, to meet the needs of a changing younger generation (81,169). One of the fundamental causes of parent-child friction is parental failure to do so (115).

Effects of Different Types of Control Because there is a marked difference in the way major types of discipline control the adolescent's behavior, it is logical that the effects they would have on family relationships would be different (25). A hasty survey of the effects of different types of discipline on family relationships will serve to show how they affect the home climate.

authoritarian control In the authoritarian home, the adolescent becomes submissive and is afraid to take responsibility. This leads to friction with his parents who expect him to take more responsibility as he grows older (155,169). While he obeys the parental dictates, he develops a dislike for his parents. Because the adolescent brought up in an authoritarian home is constantly thwarted in achieving the independence he craves, he develops such a strong resentment against his parents that he will not communicate with them or turn to them for advice and help in meeting his problems. This results in a deepening of the cleavage between him and his parents (81,139,203, 327).

How seriously authoritarian control affects the adolescent's attitude toward his parents and, in turn, his treatment of them, has been emphasized by Landis (222):

> *Those who demand obedience, respect, and honor, in line with the Fourth Commandment, actually receive much less honor and respect than the democratic parent who employs more subtle means of winning favor and respect from his children.*

democratic control The adolescent whose parents use democratic control has more harmonious relationships with his parents. Because he likes and respects them, he is willing to go to them for advice and help with his problems. Furthermore, he has a less critical attitude toward them than has the adolescent from an authoritarian home, he is more appreciative of his home life and what his parents do for him, and he does not hesitate to show his respect and appreciation. As a result, the climate of the home is warm and acceptant (60,220,222,236).

permissiveness Permissiveness is literally no control. As a result, the adolescent has little respect for his parents, little appreciation for what they do for him, and little motivation to carry his load in the home. Instead, he selfishly expects his parents to wait on him while he, in turn, does little or nothing for them. The adolescent who is permitted to do as he pleases feels insecure and unsure. When things go wrong, he carries a resentment against his parents, claiming that it was their fault because they did not warn or guide him (50,52,350,374).

Inconsistent Control Inconsistency in discipline produces more friction than consistency, regardless of whether the control used is lenient or harsh (25). When an adolescent feels that his parents are unfair because of their inconsistency, his siblings usually gang up with him against his parents and defend him as a martyr. This does not help to produce a happy home climate or to foster an affectional bond between the adolescent and his parents (99,109,369).

Source of Control Because mothers in today's homes have so much authority, it is not surprising that both boys and girls have a more frictional relationship with their mothers than with their fathers (25, 98,109,168,214). When there is a strong emotional attachment on the part of the adolescent for the dominant parent, friction subsides. Unquestionably the most severe friction comes from methods of control that differ from those used in the homes of the adolescent's friends. A mother who is much stricter than other mothers will stir up a seriously frictional relationship with the adolescents in the family. This will involve the father, who, in a desire to be fair and not harm the children's chances for social acceptance, will champion their cause and plead for greater leniency on the part of the mother (208).

MARITAL RELATIONSHIPS

Adolescents who say that their parents' marriage is happy likewise say that their homes are happy places in which to live. The reason for this is that there is less friction between their parents, between parents and children, and between siblings (191, 334). When parents are not happily married, their relationship with one another tends to be frictional. Furthermore, a parent who is emotionally disturbed because of a frictional relationship with a spouse is likely to project the emotionally disturbed attitude into a parent-child relationship. This causes friction with the child even though he was in no way responsible for the friction (212,227,296).

Marital happiness has a tendency to decline as parents reach middle age. This may be the result of many factors, such as unsatisfactory sexual adjustments; disenchantment with marriage and parenthood; personal, social, and economic restrictions resulting from the strains of parenthood; a frictional home climate, resulting partly from parental friction and partly from parent-child and sibling friction; and changes in interests which cause parents to have less in common as they grow older. For the mother, dissatisfaction usually reaches its peak at the menopause, the time when her

children reach the adolescent years (72,83, 122,227,230,397).

While many fathers become increasingly disenchanted with their roles as husbands and fathers, especially when they realize that their children show a preference for the mother and treat them as the proverbial fifth wheel to a wagon, this is by no means the only cause for deterioration in marital adjustments. For many men, this is the beginning of the "dangerous age"— the time when they recognize that their youth is rapidly passing, that they are becoming middle-aged, and that there is little time left to have fun before old age strikes them. They would like to have the freedom to take advantage of their opportunities for fun before it is too late (39,199,385).

Effects of Deterioration in Marital Relationships Since deterioration in marital relationships affects the whole family, it can be and often is catastrophic. When the home climate is emotionally charged to the point where every member is at odds with every other member, it becomes so unpleasant for the adolescent that he wants to be out of the house as much as possible.

When parents are preoccupied with their own problems, they give the adolescent the impression that they are disinterested in him, in his affairs, and in his friends. As a result, the adolescent is hesitant about bringing his friends to his home, not knowing what kind of atmosphere will be prevailing at the time or what sort of reception his friends will get. Parents who are unhappily married may try to compensate for the unhappiness of the home by indulging the adolescent's every wish as a way of winning his favor. Or they may talk against the other parent as a way of justifying the role they play in family quarrels (129,216,227,296).

The most serious effect of marital friction is that, once it starts, it is constantly reinforced by the reactions of other family members who are affected by it. The adolescent who is unhappy and disturbed by the emotionally charged atmosphere of his home reacts unfavorably to his parents, his siblings, and his relatives; this establishes a frictional relationship with them. One parent, then, is likely to blame the other for not controlling the adolescent better. As a result, marital friction is intensified. Thus, the circle of bad family relationships moves at an increasingly rapid rate.

BROKEN HOMES

When family friction reaches a peak of intensity which makes every member unhappy and frictional in his relationship with every other member, a break in the family is likely to occur. Sometimes adolescents run away from home; sometimes they join the Army or marry; and sometimes the parents separate or divorce. If the root of the trouble is marital discontent, it would be logical to assume that family friction will cease as soon as the parents separate. Studies have shown that while the home climate is improved after a break, the broken home is far less happy than an unbroken home in which there is no more than the usual amount of family friction. In fact, sometimes a break in the family merely serves to intensify friction (95,148,216,275). From studies of adolescents from broken and unbroken frictional homes, Slocum has concluded, "Evidently broken homes were much more often unhappy than unbroken ones" (334).

Effect of Home Breaks on Home Climate While it is true that homes that have an unhappy climate are improved when the source of the unhappiness has been removed by the separation or divorce of the parents, this does not by any means bring a permanent solution to the problem. The reason for this is that any home, broken by death, separation, or divorce, has problems that are potential sources of friction. Of the many possible sources of friction in a "solo" home—a home where there is only one parent—the following are the most common and most serious.

economic condition of the home Frequently a break in the family means a complete change in the pattern of family living. In divorce, the children will probably be living with their mother. To make ends meet on the money the father provides for support, she may have to go to work or to live with her parents or relatives. If the home is broken by death of the father, the source of earned income is gone; if it is broken by death of the mother, there will be the expense of hiring someone to take charge of the home.

downward mobility Economic changes in the broken home almost always lead to downward social mobility. To the status-symbol-conscious adolescent, not having money to spend for the things his friends have will, in time, mean changing to another social group. Downward social mobility (see pages 371 to 374 for a more complete discussion of the effects on the adolescent) inevitably makes the adolescent unhappy and discontented. This is then reflected in a frictional attitude toward parents, whom the adolescent blames for "ruining his social life."

added home responsibilities As the economic condition of the home deteriorates, every family member is called upon to do more than was formerly necessary to keep the home running. Because social life is important to an adolescent, and because adolescents have been accustomed to have relatively few home duties, many feel martyred when called on to do this unaccustomed work.

preoccupation of remaining parent The parent with whom adolescents live in a solo home is preoccupied with his or her own problems. Adolescents who have been accustomed to turning to their parents for help and advice will feel that the parent is no longer interested in their problems. Furthermore, a home where one member is so preoccupied with personal problems that the interests and concerns of the other members are ignored is likely to be characterized by coolness and lack of empathy. These contribute their share to making the home climate unpleasant for the adolescent.

overprotectiveness Sooner or later, even the parent who is most preoccupied with his own problems will realize that the responsibility for the care and guidance of the children rests on his shoulders alone. As a result, he tries to do what *both* parents formerly did; this often leads to overprotectiveness. The independence-conscious adolescent bitterly resents this.

increased emotional tension Should the break in the home be caused by death, there will be an increase in emotional tension on the part of all family members caused by grief and by worry about financial and other adjustment problems. When the break results from desertion, separation, or divorce, there is a period of bitter resentments, quarrels, and heightened emotional tension before the break comes. Even though a period of calm may follow the actual break, it is likely to be broken by a resumption of emotional tension resulting from the adjustment problems the break brings.

troublesome behavior Adolescents from broken homes get into more trouble both at home and outside the home and are more often predisposed to delinquency than are adolescents from intact homes. (See pages 478 and 479 for a more complete discussion of this matter.)

If the mother is in control of the solo home, she is likely to be overly strict with her son when he gets into trouble in the belief that she must play the role of the father as well as of the mother. Should the daughter behave in such a way that her father thinks she is headed for trouble, he will be far more punitive in his treatment than he would have been had the mother been in the home also to supervise her behavior.

attachment to one parent The adolescent almost always is more emotionally attached to one parent than to the other. If the father divorces the mother so he can marry another woman, the children of the family are likely to side with the mother, feeling that she has been mistreated. Parents quickly sense their children's attitudes toward them. A critical attitude will be resented by the parent and will lead to friction.

When the adolescent visits in the home of the missing parent and returns to his own home with glowing accounts of the good times he has had, this will intensify the resentment of the parent with whom he lives against the missing parent. This situation is made even worse if the adolescent praises the new spouse of the missing parent.

Even a dead parent can be the source of trouble in a family. If the remaining parent paints a picture of the dead parent in glowing colors to the children, hoping to give them happy and respectful memories of that parent, it may in time lead to such a glamorized image of the dead parent that the living parent, by comparison, will seem less desirable. When the broken home has been reconstructed by bringing in a stepparent, the comparison of the dead parent with the stepparent is inevitably more favorable to the former.

being different Even though divorce is more common today than it was in the past, it is still far from accepted by the majority of Americans. The adolescent is well aware of this. As a result, he is highly sensitive to the unfavorable social attitude he believes people have toward his family because his parents have been divorced. Anything that makes an adolescent different, especially if being different is associated with social disapproval, is likely to arouse in him resentments toward his parents. He feels that they have been responsible for putting barriers in the way to the social acceptance and approval he craves.

A home broken by death is not subject to social disapproval as is the home broken by divorce. However, it, too, makes the adolescent feel that he is different, and thus, inferior. A girl, for example, who is often called upon for extra help at home feels that she is different from other girls who do not have these responsibilities.

stepparent Many homes, broken by death or divorce, are reconstructed by remarriage. Some adolescents, after experiencing the problems that come with a break in their homes, urge their parents to remarry for their own selfish reasons. A girl who has the responsibility of running the home after her mother's death may urge her father to remarry, believing that this will free her from home responsibilities so that she can do the things her friends do.

While remarriage may solve many of the problems that come when a home is broken, it often brings new problems that are as serious as the problems it solves, if not more so. This subject will be discussed at length in the section on "invaded" homes.

Broken versus Unbroken Homes Which is more damaging to the home climate, a home that is broken because the parents are unhappily mated or one that remains unbroken in spite of parental unhappiness and friction? This is a question that has been answered both ways. There is no question about the fact that an adolescent is "very disturbed when the relationship between the parents is very disturbed" (95). "Almost every serious researcher in American family behavior has suggested that the effects of continued home conflict might be more serious for the children than the divorce itself" (148).

However, before a decision can be made as to which is less damaging, one must consider certain variables that influence the effects of breaking an unhappy home and of holding it together. How *unhappy* the home was before the break and how much discord prevailed are important factors. If one parent wants a divorce to be free to marry someone else, the effect on the home climate is not so great as when the break comes because the discord has become intolerable. How much the break takes the children of the family *by surprise* also plays a role in the effects a break has. If they had no suspicion that things were not going well between their parents, the break will be more of a shock and a greater source of resentment than if they knew that the break was imminent or had even urged it.

When an unhappy home is broken by a *separation*, usually on a trial basis, every member of the family has a motivation to clear up the problems that led to the separation in the hope of ending the break. A broken home is more damaging to *adolescents* than to young or grown children. Provisions are usually made for the care of the younger children; grown children have their own interests and often their own homes. It is the adolescent who bears the brunt of the problems a break in the home brings. A break in a *large family* intensifies the problems every break brings; as a consequence, it is more damaging than a break in a small family. If the parents can meet the socioeconomic and other *needs* of the children, regardless of their ages, the break is less serious than when it results in privations.

Perhaps the most serious variable is the extent to which the children of the family are *involved* in the disputes that lead to the break and how much each parent tries to play on the sympathies of the children to win their loyalty away from the other parent. If the adolescent is used as a go-between in the frictional situation, he will be more emotionally disturbed by resentments against one parent and strong loyalties and sympathies toward the other than he would be if the friction took place out of his hearing. Figure 15–8 shows the effects of broken as contrasted with unbroken homes on parent-adolescent adjustments.

In spite of these variables, evidence shows that a home broken by divorce or separation is more damaging to the home climate than one broken by death. Evidence likewise points in the direction of the solo home being less damaging than the reconstructed home. Whether the break is caused by death or divorce, adolescents make better adjustments to their families if the parents do not remarry. Perhaps the most damaging of all situations is an unhappy home that is broken by divorce and then reconstructed, so that the adolescent has four rather than two parents (24,56,62,63,95,135,138,148, 215,216,218,275,286,288,320). More about this in the section on invaded homes.

FAMILY SIZE

Two of the major changes that have taken place in the American family since the turn of the century have been the decrease in the size of the family in the middle and upper socioeconomic groups and the shift from the elongated to the nuclear family—terms which will be discussed in the section below entitled "Composition of Family" (149, 242,254,393,395).

One of the many commonly mentioned advantages of the smaller families of today is that they are less frictional than large families. There is no question about the fact that the smaller the family, the fewer interpersonal relationships there will be and, hence, the fewer possibilities for friction. Refer to page 120 for a description of the formula used to determine the number of interpersonal relationships in groups of different sizes. According to this formula, a family of two parents and two children would have 11 interactions: a family of two parents and eight children, on the other hand, would have 1,013 interactions (52, 172).

Size determines the *number* of relationships that will exist in a family but not the *type*. It is the type of relationship that exists between two people in the family that is largely responsible for the home climate. This is well illustrated by the fact that American homes of today are more frictional than in the past. There are a number of reasons for this. In the first place, there has been a widespread trend away from authoritarian control and toward *democratic control*. Democratic control encourages family members to do and say what they wish. This gives rise to more friction than when such desires are curbed. Second, modern life encourages the development of *different interests, activities, and values*. The closer these are, the more harmony there will be; the more divergent, the greater the chance of friction.

Finally, the *attitudes* of parents toward children, toward their role as parents, and toward the size of the family, have all changed radically. Parents, for example, who accept the parental role willingly, who recognize and accept the restrictions, work, and privations parenthood brings and who feel that the molding of a child into a well-adjusted person is one of their most important contributions in life will have a very

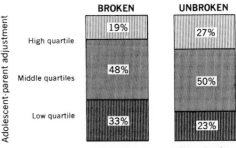

FIGURE 15-8 Effects of broken and unbroken homes on parent-adolescent relationships. (Adapted from F. I. Nye: Adolescent-parent adjustment: age, sex, sibling number, broken homes, and employed mothers as variables. *Marriage fam. Living*, 1952, **14**, 327–332. Used by permission.)

different influence on the home climate than will those who are more concerned with their own interests and satisfactions (15,181,313,315).

Effects on Home Climate Because it is inevitable that families of different sizes will have different patterns of living, the effects family size has on the home climate are, of necessity, also different. A brief summary of the effects will serve to illustrate this point.

one-child families The adolescent who grows up as the only child in the family may suffer from overprotectiveness and from high parental aspirations, both of which are potential sources of friction with his parents. On the other hand, his parents are more likely to treat him in a democratic than in an authoritarian way. Parents of only children tend to be more indulgent about both privileges and material possessions (322).

Because the only child is usually the pride of both his parents and grandparents, he has a happy, relaxed, nonfrictional home environment. Having no siblings to rival or to fight with, his home is spared the sibling friction of homes with several children of different ages, both sexes, and different levels of maturity (12,50,52,163,251,322).

small families A family of two or three children—average today, but small as compared with families of past generations—tends to be a very frictional one. The small family is usually democratically controlled, encouraging every member to express his thoughts and feelings freely. It is democratic also in the emphasis parents place on the development of each child's individuality. The result is that there may be many clashes of interests, attitudes, and values among the different members.

Because a small family is usually economically in a better position than a large one, parents are able to be ambitious for their children, providing them with the advantages that will enable them to get ahead in life. Parental pressure for better achievement and disappointment when the children fail to reach the levels of aspiration set for them are a constant source of friction in small families.

Small families are usually planned, not only as to the timing of the children's arrival but also as to sex. A home with members of both sexes among the children has far greater potential for friction than a home with all children of one sex (184). Unquestionably one of the chief causes of poor home climate in a small family is its vulnerability to parental separation or divorce. The child who grows up in a small family may, by the time he reaches adolescence, be forced to face friction-arousing conditions that come with a break in the family in *addition* to all the others that are inevitably associated with small families (25,88,95,114,148,191).

large families Some of the most common and most serious potential causes of friction in homes are to be found where there are six or more children. Through necessity, the control must be authoritarian. While adolescents brought up in a large family are less overprotected than in small families, they are usually too restricted by economic conditions to use their independence. Furthermore, they are not encouraged to develop independent interests, attitudes, or values, because these would lead to too great friction with other family members.

Financial strain limits the status sym-

bols, the recreations with peers, and the educational advantages an adolescent from a large family can have. These limitations, in turn, lower his opportunities for social acceptance in the group he would like to be identified with. Often, through necessity, older siblings are deprived of social activities with their peers because they must take care of younger siblings. With any family crisis, such as unemployment of the father, death, or divorce, economic problems are added to the problems which normally give rise to friction under such conditions (8,25, 50,51,52,191,273,305,342).

In spite of these potential sources of friction in a large family, the home climate is often less frictional than in a small family. The reason for this is that friction is quickly controlled by authoritarian methods to prevent a state of anarchy and chaos from developing. That the home climate is more damaging to the individual, even though it it may *seem* more advantageous to the group, has been explained in this way by Templeton (364):

> The number of relationships and experiences which may occur within the family setting multiply rapidly as family size increases. It is thus likely that conflicting demands, conflicting loyalties, conflicting interests, and conflicting goals will also increase. With the greater likelihood of such conflict, parents are apt to turn to more inflexible, authoritarian forms of control to maintain some order. Such conflict and inflexible rules make adjustment more difficult for the children. . . . In a society where the smaller family is the norm, larger families attract attention, and this may add to the discomfort of the children. They may feel that the real or imagined shortcomings of their families are on display.

How family size affects adolescent-parent adjustment is illustrated in Figure 15–9. Note that the best adjustment is made in families where there is only one child or only one sibling; the poorest adjustments of all are in families of five or more children.

Variations in Effects Small families, it has been found, are more disadvantageous to boys than to girls; the reverse is true for large families. In a small family, a boy is more likely to be overprotected; in a large family, he is given more independence and at an earlier age. In a large family, a girl may be given more independence than in a small family. But at the same time, she is given more home responsibilities. This interferes with her social activities and is a constant source of resentment against her family. In addition, in a large family there is less money for the status symbols which are so important to adolescent girls. This is a further barrier to her social success and a further cause for resentments toward her family (50,51,52,221,305).

Studies of marital tension have revealed that families with four or five children have much greater tension between the husbands and wives than do smaller families. In a small family, the wife can manage the home and children with minimum help from the husband. In a large family, by contrast, the husband is called on to do work which he regards as "woman's work" (122). Because financial problems are greater in a large family, and because many mothers take jobs to relieve the tensions these problems bring, only to increase them when the family members are opposed to her working, it is logical to find that family relationships are poorer among *all* family members in a large than in a small family (52,239,273,303).

COMPOSITION OF FAMILY

A small or a large family may be either a "nuclear" family—made up of the parents and their children—or an "elongated" family—made up of members of three or more generations. Nuclear families are more common today than in the past and more common in urban than in rural areas (254). Figure 15–10 shows a diagram of an elongated family.

Causes of Friction   Elongated families tend to be more frictional than nuclear. There are three major factors that influence the climate of these two types of homes and each exerts a different influence.

age variations   When age differences

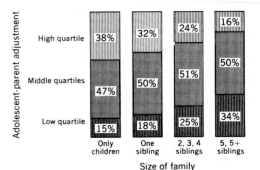

FIGURE 15–9   Adolescent-parent adjustment in different-sized families. (Adapted from F. I. Nye: Adolescent-parent adjustment: age, sex, sibling number, broken homes, and employed mothers as variables. *Marriage fam. Living*, 1952, **14**, 327–332. Used by permission.)

are large, the greatest impact on the home climate comes from the effect on parent-adolescent relationships; when small, from sibling relationships (184). In a large nuclear family, the difference in age between parent and adolescent will be greater for the last-born than for the firstborn child; the difference in sibling ages will be less for middle-born than for first- and last-born children. In an elongated family, age gaps increase in both number and length, thus providing a setting for potentially serious frictional relationships.

The wider the gap in ages, the less harmonious the interests, needs, values, and aspirations and the greater the potentiality of friction. In an elongated family, the age difference between the adolescent and his grandparents or other elderly relatives makes it impossible for them to see eye to eye on many matters that are important to each. While pressure to show respect for their elders may keep adolescents from engaging overtly in frictional relationships with them, the antagonisms are there and smolder under the surface, often breaking out in a frictional relationship with their parents (3,74, 211,355).

Age differences between siblings are equally as important as potential causes of friction (184). The adolescent who has started to date steadily and is thinking seriously of marriage resents the ridicule of siblings who are still in the sex-antagonism

FATHER'S FAMILY   MOTHER'S FAMILY

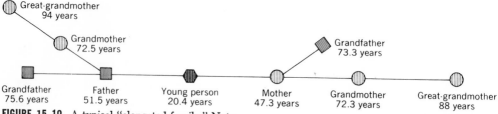

Great-grandmother
94 years

Grandmother
72.5 years

Grandfather   Grandfather
75.6 years   73.3 years

Father
51.5 years

Young person
20.4 years

Mother
47.3 years

Grandmother
72.3 years

Great-grandmother
88 years

FIGURE 15–10 A typical "elongated family." Note the preponderance of females. (Adapted from R. Albrecht: Intergeneration parent patterns. *J. Home Econ.*, 1954, **46**, 29–32. Used by permission.)

stage; the young adolescent who is just becoming interested in dating resents the big-sister or big-brother advice and patronizing attitude of the older sibling.

The greater the age difference between siblings, the less their paths meet in the home and the fewer opportunities there are for frictional relationships. Also, with age, the adolescent has a more tolerant and understanding attitude than does the child or young adolescent. This helps to reduce friction, though not to eliminate it (50,52,139, 184,203,226,327).

status variations In any family, each member has a status peculiar to him and he is expected to play a given role. The roles of the parents are prescribed by tradition, with the *father* playing the role of provider, and the *mother*, the role of manager of the home and the controlling agent of the children. The role each child plays is likewise influenced by tradition. The *first-born*—whether male or female—is usually the center of attention; he is permitted greater freedom of action in some respects and less in other respects than later children. He is encouraged to fulfill aspirations that have gone unfulfilled in his parents' lives or to rise above the family. This encourages the development of attitudes of superiority on the part of the firstborn and the feeling that he is the parental favorite. In addition, the oldest child is expected to set a good model for younger siblings and, in large families, to assume responsibility for some of their care (17,52,321,322,327,353).

The status of the *second* child or of the *middle* children in a large family is less affected by parental aspirations. Parents tend to treat them more casually and to expect less of them than of the firstborn. In fact, they are often somewhat neglected as compared with oldest and youngest children. This they quickly sense (7,77,122, 126,141,203,226).

In many respects, the status of the *last-born* child is the most favorable in the entire family. Because he is the baby, the family expects less of him than of his older siblings; they are expected to do things for him rather than the reverse. He is protected against their physical and verbal aggressions on the ground that he is "just a baby." But he is not reproved or punished for aggressive attacks on his older siblings. Even when he reaches adolescence, this status remains relatively unchanged (7,50,203,273,353).

Tradition prescribes the role of *grandparents* in the elongated home. Today, it is far more usual for an elderly relative to live in the home of a married child than the reverse. Whether the elderly relative is a grandmother, grandfather, uncle, or aunt, it is usual for that relative to make demands on the mother, to interfere with the training of the children, and to expect to be waited on more than is necessary on the basis of health. While the relative may assume some of the financial and work load, he expects to have a status similar to the status held in his own home when the married child was young (3,16,74,106,211,305, 355).

How the individual perceives his status and how he feels about it will determine the quality of his relationships with other family members. If a grandmother feels that her son-in-law and grandchildren resent her presence in the home, her resentments toward them will be reflected in a frictional relationship (52,327).

Adolescents resent having things imposed upon them without any choice or any opportunity to express their preferences; therefore being expected to play an assigned role will lead to friction. The firstborn daughter, for example, is expected to be the mother's helper just as the firstborn boy is expected to be the father surrogate in the father's absence from home. Because the role has been assigned rather than voluntarily selected, the adolescent is likely to rebel against it (16,106,153,211,322).

sex variations Some families are predominantly female, and others, predominantly male (96,130). In an elongated family, the elderly relative is most likely to be female, thus adding weight to the female side. This is illustrated in Figure 15–10 on page 610.

In a family with two children, a girl-girl combination will foster more jealousy and, hence, more friction than a girl-boy or boy-boy combination (184). An older sister, for example, is more likely to play an aggressive role in her relationship with a younger sister than with a younger brother (203,240,353). Friction during early adolescence is likely to be worse between siblings of the same sex than between siblings of the two sexes; relationships improve as adolescence progresses (37,98,113,273,353, 396). Figure 15–11 shows the relationships of older adolescent boys and girls with their siblings of both sexes.

Friction between adolescents and their *parents* increases as the number of daughters increases (122). Girls with sisters tend to be more defiant of parental authority than girls with brothers (324). Firstborn daughters tend to conform more to parental expectations and to have, as a result, a less frictional relationship with them than do later daughters. This stems from the jealousy of the eldest toward her siblings and her desire to regain parental affection which she believes the younger siblings have usurped (321).

While parents have some friction with their older sons, the friction is not likely to be so severe or so frequent as the friction with their daughters who, even though older, are given less independence than boys (81,273,299).

Girls at every age feel that their mothers prefer their brothers, just as boys feel that their fathers prefer the girls of the family. This results in greater friction between the adolescent and his parent of the same sex (324,391).

Furthermore, quarrels with mothers and fathers are about different matters. Girls have more quarrels with their fathers about dating and mate selection and more with their mothers about other standards and values outside the family, about parental behavior, and about independence (35,81, 232). Boys have more conflicts with their fathers about matters that are of great personal importance to them, such as their choice of vocation, spending money, and heterosexual relationships; with their mothers, about matters of less personal concern, such as religion, church attendance, and household chores (81,98).

In an elongated family, there is greater friction when there is a preponderance of female members. When there is a maternal grandmother living in the home, for example, she is likely to make many demands on her daughter, just as she did when the daughter was a child. The husband and children usually resent the time the mother devotes to doing things for the grandmother. Should the elderly relative in the home be a grandfather, there is likely to be a more harmonious relationship with the family, partly because the husband finds him more congenial, partly because he is out of the home more and hence makes fewer demands on the mother's time, and partly because he does not try to interfere with the management of the home or the discipline of the children as grandmothers often do (3,74,133,211).

INVASION BY OUTSIDERS
Because the typical American family of today is a nuclear one, adolescents have become accustomed to a small, closely knit family unit. In this family unit, they be-

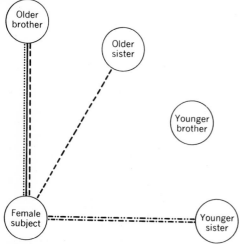

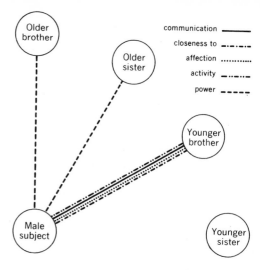

FIGURE 15–11 Relations of older adolescents with siblings of both sexes. (Adapted from A. Yourglich: Explorations in sociological study of sibling systems. *Family Life Coordinator*, 1964, **13**, 91–94. Used by permission.)

come accustomed to a pattern of life developed to meet the needs of all family members (91). Anything that upsets the homeostasis of family life is disturbing to them.

Invasion by outsiders is always a complicating factor in any home; it is especially so during adolescence when adjustment to parents and siblings is difficult enough without the added complication of outsiders (128). Furthermore, when the homeostasis of family life is upset, adjustments must be made by *all* family members if homeostasis is to be restored.

Types of Invaders Some people who come into the home upset the homeostasis of the family more than others. Of the invaders in any American home today, the following are the most common.

boarders or paying guests How much the "paying guest" will upset the family will depend on whether or not the individual will be in the home the major part of the time, whether he will take his meals with the family or share kitchen privileges, what parts of the house will be available for his use, and what his age and sex are. A young teacher, for example, who is in

school most of the day and who spends weekends in social activities will be less upsetting to a home than an unemployed middle-aged woman. Because men spend more time outside the home than women and because they are less likely to interfere with the accustomed pattern of life in the home, men, normally, are less upsetting to the homeostasis of the family.

servants Most adolescents who have been accustomed to having the mother do the housework regard the part-time domestic worker as an intruder. They are critical of the looks, behavior, work habits, and speech of these intruders; they especially resent any authority the intruder may have over them during the mother's absence.

When the servant is present, there may be a restraint placed on the adolescent not to "interfere." Although a servant may free the adolescent from household chores he would otherwise have to do, the presence of a servant, or any outsider, is often a source of friction (52,239,287).

guests Each family member is likely to be influenced by the presence in the home of guests, and the home climate will be changed. The effect may be to increase family solidarity or to increase friction. Only children, who might be expected to welcome the arrival of guests, frequently resent them because they regard them as "intruders" who absorb the time and interest of their parents. Children in large families likewise often resent guests because of the extra work it means for each family member, because it may mean sharing their rooms with outsiders, or because it proves to be a strain on the family budget.

Because early adolescence is a self-conscious, hypercritical age, guests are likely to be more unfavorable to the home climate then than as adolescence progresses. The young adolescent resents comments about how much he has grown or questions about his interest in members of the opposite sex. He is likely to be critical of the looks of the guests, their behavior, or the rigidity of their attitudes, and even of their speech and table manners. The older adolescent, who is more tolerant of older people and more poised in social situations, accepts family guests more graciously and may even welcome their presence in the home (50,52).

relatives The nuclear family of today tries to isolate itself from the extended kinship group that characterized families of past generations. However, families with traditional values are more likely to open their doors voluntarily to relatives for short or extended visits than are those which emphasize the value to children of having fewer conflicting elements in their lives (91, 213). The mother's relatives are more likely to visit than are the father's. This is especially true in families with strongly traditional religious values, as is true of families of the Catholic or Jewish faith (36).

When relatives live many miles away, their visits are usually less frequent but longer in duration. A small nuclear family is more likely to have relatives visit for special occasions than is a large family and to have the entire family of the relative rather than just one or two members (307). This is because of space and economic strain in the large family rather than because of weak kinship ties (311).

A child may look forward eagerly to the visit of a relative. The adolescent, by contrast, regards the visit as an intrusion, especially when living quarters are cramped and the relative intrudes upon his private property, even to the point of taking over his room. This resentment is intensified if the relative feels that he has the right to criticize the adolescent, order him around, or have authority over him.

Although the adolescent may not be directly involved, he is greatly affected by any friction that may develop between his parents and visiting relatives. Such friction is likely to develop when the mother's and father's relatives are incompatible or antagonistic toward one another. It is also to be expected in a socially mobile family when the adolescent and his family have acquired a pattern of life, interests, and values that differ markedly from those of the relatives. The result is a frictional home environment as long as the relatives remain in the home or even when a visit from the relatives is proposed (36,50,52,91).

grandparents In past generations, when families lived closer together than they do today, children learned to regard their grandparents as a part of the family unit. Today, there is less opportunity for children to get to know their grandparents intimately. The result is that, by the time they reach adolescence, they regard their grandparents more as outsiders than as family members. Should circumstances require their parents to bring a grandparent into the home as a permanent member of the family, or should the grandparents come only for occasional visits, there is likely to be disharmony among the family members (3,106,211).

There are many reasons why a three-generation household is hazardous. In the first place, when the grandparent is in the home of a grown child, there is a role reversal which few older people can or will make; the elderly parent resents being in a subordinate position. In addition, the elderly parent is often made to feel unwanted and useless in his child's home (143,233). Second, as the elderly parent is more often the mother than the father, she is in the home more, has a more emotional relationship with her married child, and is more likely to make demands than the father does. This takes the daughter's time away from her own family, which both her husband and children resent (74,133).

Third, the prevailing attitude toward old people today is negative; the elderly person is well aware of this (16). As a result, the grandparent develops many of the characteristics of a minority-group member. This makes him difficult to live with (16, 23,100,205,206,207,316).

Finally, when grandparents try to inflict the rigid standards and harsh discipline that prevailed in their own youth on their grandchildren, there is friction not only with the adolescent but with his parents who side with him against the grandparent (3,106,305,355).

Grandparents generally have a more favorable attitude toward their grandchildren than grandchildren have toward them. If the grandparents are not financially dependent on the family and if they are not expected to play the role of parent surrogate when the mother is at work, they may enjoy their role in the family more than the family enjoys having them. Furthermore, the presence of a grandparent in the home may free the adolescent children of many home responsibilities, which then permits them to be more active socially with their peers (266,347). When this happens, the home climate is improved and the hazards of a three-generation household are reduced.

Because grandmothers generally favor their grandsons, and grandfathers, their granddaughters, there is normally less friction between grandmothers and grandsons than between grandmothers and granddaughters. But there is more friction between grandfathers and grandsons than between grandfathers and granddaughters (61,98). However, the grandfather is a less disturbing influence in the family than the grandmother because he is more remote from the grandchildren (61,375).

stepparents Of all "invaders" in the home, stepparents are unquestionably the ones who can upset the homeostasis most and for the longest time. There are a number of factors in the stepparent situation that are likely to prove detrimental to a healthy home climate. The conditions leading to trouble are discussed below.

The stereotype of the wicked stepparent From earliest childhood, the adolescent has read or heard about "wicked" stepmothers. As a result, he develops a concept of a stepparent that he applies to the person who replaces his real parent (50,52, 293,336). This "hangs a millstone about the neck of the stepmother and makes her role an exceedingly difficult one" (336).

Attitude of peers If the adolescent feels that having a stepparent makes him "different," the effects are serious because the adolescent wants to be like his peers. Should his friends feel sorry for him, reacting to him as if he were a "martyr," having a stepparent may increase his social acceptance, but at the same time increase his antagonism toward the stepparent (52,197, 336,373).

Individualized attitudes on the part of both the stepparent and the stepchild During the interval between losing a real parent and acquiring a stepparent, the *adolescent* may have been subjected to conditions in the home that were seriously damaging to his personality. If, for example, the break in his home gave him more freedom and more attention from the solo parent, he may have acquired an attitude of independence which will make him resentful toward anyone who might take away this independence (52,336,373).

The reason the *stepparent* has for marriage will have a marked influence on his attitudes. If a woman, for example, wants to resolve her own neurotic conflicts, if she has fantasies about helping a "poor motherless child," or if she has a strong need to express her maternal impulses, these factors will affect the way she treats the stepchild (197).

The stepparent may resent the stepchild because he is a constant reminder that the mate's love formerly belonged to someone else. Or the stepparent's attitude may be colored by a feeling of inadequacy for the role. Many stepmothers feel adequate to handle young children. But because of inexperience in dealing with adolescents, they feel inadequate. A stepmother may, for example, ask an adolescent boy to help with the home chores, not realizing that he will resent being treated like a "sissy" (50,293, 336).

Age and sex of the stepchild These are important factors in determining the type of effect a stepparent has on the home climate. As a general rule, very young children and adults can assimilate a stepparent more easily and more successfully than an adolescent can (52,54,197,293,317).

Girls, who spend more of their time at home than boys do, resent a stepparent more when they are adolescents than they do as young children, and more than boys do. Because adolescent girls tend to have a more frictional relationship with their own mothers than boys and a less frictional relationship with their fathers (see pages 610 and 611 for a discussion of the reasons for this), it is not surprising that girls get along better with stepfathers than with stepmothers. Boys, by contrast, get along better with their own mothers than with their own fathers. The same is true of stepparents (41,54,148,336).

Sex of stepparent Adjusting to a stepfather is in any situation easier than adjusting to a stepmother. If the stepparent is a father, and if he is not too authoritarian in his attitude toward the adolescent, there may be an improvement in the home climate with his arrival, especially if the financial status of the family is improved (41,54, 197,317).

Operational factors, or circumstances involved in the establishment of new relationships If the adolescent knows ahead of time that there is the possibility of having a stepparent and if he has an opportunity to become acquainted with the stepparent before he "invades" the home, his attitude will be more favorable than if he has no warning of the change. What ideas the stepparent has about discipline, how quickly these ideas are put into practice, the possible presence of children belonging to the stepparent, and the arrival of stepsiblings into the home shortly after the new family has been established are all complicating factors that damage the home climate (41,52,148,336).

Adjustment to own parents Remarriage always results in a changed relationship between the parent and the adolescent son or daughter. This change is very marked at first when the parent is preoccupied with the new spouse. The adolescent not only resents this preoccupation but he also resents the influence of the stepparent on his own parent. A mother who, before remarriage, devoted her time and attention exclusively to her children may now devote more time and attention to her new husband than to her children (41,54,148, 293).

In conclusion, then, there is evidence that in a home where there is a stepparent, there is "more stress, ambivalence, and low cohesiveness" than in normal homes (54). The disruptive "intruder" is more likely to be a stepmother than a stepfather. Not only does she have more influence on the children of the family, regardless of their age, than does the stepfather but the influence she has is of a far less favorable type. That many more juvenile delinquents come from homes where there are stepmothers than stepfathers would suggest that more often than not the home climate is not improved by the "invasion" of a stepmother (371).

SOCIOECONOMIC STATUS

There are many reasons for the influence socioeconomic status has on family relationships and, in turn, on the home climate (52,334). First, the type of relationship the adolescent has with his parents differs markedly in families of different statuses. In lower-class families, parents' relationships with their children tend to be rigid and hierarchical. In middle-class families, by contrast, open, flexible, and equalitarian relationships are more common. Lower-class parents communicate little with their children; the adolescent fears the parents' authority and explosive anger and feels that he is rejected by his parents. Middle-class adolescents, on the other hand, have more freedom to express their opinions to and about their parents, they have little fear of parental authority, and they feel loved and accepted (238). The higher the socioeconomic status of the family, the greater the feeling on the adolescent's part that he is loved and secure (272,273,334).

Second, the attitude of parents toward their children has a marked influence on family relationships. The attitude of parents of upper-class families is one of "possessive pride and hope." Their children are important to them; they give them every possible educational and cultural advantage. Adolescents from upper-class families know that they are loved and wanted by their parents. Adolescents in the lower-class families learn that their parents regard them as the "inevitable payments for sex relations." As a result, the adolescent often feels unloved, unwanted, and rejected. Adolescents from middle-class families are "wanted chiefly as marriage fulfillment" (52). While treated kindly by his parents, the adolescent from the middle-class family is under constant pressure to take advantage of the opportunities his parents give him to "better himself" (1,27,52,250,376).

Third, there is less friction between lower-class parents and their adolescent children resulting from discipline than in middle-class families. It is the frustrations that middle-class adolescents experience that is primarily responsible for friction with their parents. Upper-class adolescents, who have relatively few restrictions on their activities and who see little of their parents because they are preoccupied with business or social activities, have few conflicts with them (38, 52,238,280,327).

Fourth, families differ markedly in the material possessions they are able to afford. The type of home, the location of the home in the community, the clothing, the spending money, and the other status symbols the adolescent has are all influential in determining his social status in the peer group.

When the adolescent finds that his lack of social acceptance by his peers is due to lack of money, it frequently brings strong resentments toward his parents (8,249,334).

Fifth, social mobility influences home climate. Families that are anxious to improve their status put pressure on their children to conform rigidly to the patterns of behavior and values of the class they aspire to belong to. These pressures are thwarting to the adolescent's desire for independence and cause a frictional relationship to develop. Furthermore, shifting of social classes tends to disrupt family relationships, especially with relatives. This encourages an emotionally toned climate in the home (249,250,398).

Finally, insecurity in either social or economic status leads to emotional insecurity; it, in turn, is damaging to the home climate. The adolescent whose family's social and economic status is relatively secure knows where he stands economically and can plan for expenditures for status symbols similar to those of his friends. This increases the security of his social status, and with better acceptance by the peer group, he will have a more favorable attitude toward his family (66,388).

PARENTAL OCCUPATIONS

In a democracy, the social status of a family is determined largely by the occupation of the family breadwinner. The higher the prestige rating of the occupation, the higher the social status of the family. In recent years, there has been a growing tendency for married women to work after their children reach school age and need less maternal supervision and care (120). However, in judging the social status of the family, the father's occupation is used as the criterion, not the mother's.

In spite of the fact that the father's occupation is more important than the mother's in the eyes of society, in the home the mother's occupation often plays a more important role than the father's in determining what the home climate will be. The effect her occupation has on the home climate, unlike that of the father, comes mainly from the problems it gives rise to in the home and the disruption of the traditional pattern of family living. Because the effects of the father's and mother's occupations on the home climate are very different, each will be discussed separately.

Father's Occupation The father's occupation affects the type of relationships the different family members have in a number of ways, four of which are very common and very important. First, the prestige associated with the father's occupation has a marked influence on the adolescent's attitude toward the father. Indirectly, it affects the adolescent's attitude toward himself (42,52,108,292).

The second way in which the father's occupation affects the adolescent's relationships with the family is through the economic rewards the occupation brings. In a study in which adolescents were asked to evaluate the adequacy of the family income in terms of "very satisfactory," "good," "reasonably sufficient," "not quite sufficient," and "definitely insufficient," it was found that there was a marked relationship between their evaluations of the adequacy of the family income and the degree of happiness in the home (334).

Third, the father's occupation affects his relationships with his adolescent sons and, to a lesser extent, with his daughters through the influence it has on his aspirations for them (45,229). It also influences the standards he sets for them. From his experiences in the work world, the father knows what attitudes, skills, and personal qualities are essential for success. In his attempt to foster them in his sons, the standards of the occupational world "infect" the home and influence the relationship the father has with them (1).

The fourth effect of the father's occupation is that, if his job takes him away from home for varying lengths of time, there will be a temporary break in the family and a change in the home environment. How this affects the home climate was discussed in relationship to solo homes, pages 604 and 605. When the father returns, there must be readjustments which are often stressful for all family members (345,394).

effects on home climate When the adolescent and his mother are satisfied with the father's occupation, not only in terms of what it does *to* the family but also in terms of what it does *for* the family, it will have a favorable effect on the home climate. A father who is successful is less resented when he expects his children to do good work at school than a father whose occupation is unprestigeful, whose income is low, and who puts pressures on his children as a form of compensation for his own vocational dissatisfaction (1,66). In a study of how adolescents rate the happiness of their homes, it was found that the proportion of happy homes rose with the rise in the occupational status level (334).

When the man's family is dissatisfied with his job and puts pressures on him to change, his resentment at their unfavorable attitudes is usually increased by a realistic awareness of his limited capacities and training for other jobs and of the difficulties involved in getting a new job as the worker approaches middle age. Dissatisfaction on the part of the family is increased if the worker is shifted to a job in another community unless this shift brings with it monetary and prestige rewards adequate to compensate for the dissatisfactions the family experiences when moving to another community (30,66,107,317,357,388).

Mother's Occupation Important as the father's occupation is in its influence on the home climate, it is usually far surpassed by the influence of the mother's occupation. The reason for this is that the mother's occupation *always* disturbs the homeostasis of the family more than the father's does. In addition, every family member is affected more by the mother's working outside the home and more seriously so than by the father's work (48,331).

variations in effects There are a number of conditions related to the mother's occupation which affect, in varying degrees, the home climate. Of these, the following are the most important.

Age of children There is no question

about the fact that the younger the child, the more serious will be the effect on him and on the home climate when the mother goes to work. The adolescent does not need a person to take care of him as a young child; he spends the major part of the day at school or with the peer group.

On the other hand, if the adolescent has been accustomed to having the mother at home during his childhood, there is a marked upset in the homeostasis of family living when she suddenly leaves the home to work outside. This necessitates readjustments on the part of every family member; with these adjustments will come the stress that is inevitable in any change (48,239, 287,303,331).

Reason for working A woman may find her home duties greatly lessened when her children reach the adolescent years; she may then take a job to relieve her boredom; she may feel that home duties are not adequate to satisfy her needs or to give her the intellectual stimulation she craves; she may dislike housework and prefer to earn money to pay someone to do the housework for her; she may want to give her children social, educational, and other advantages which her husband's income is not adequate to provide; she may have to work to support her children after the death or divorce of her husband; or she may work to be able to contribute to the support of an elderly parent (11,179,268,277,303,312, 331).

Whatever the reason, other family members either know or suspect what it is. This is bound to affect their attitudes toward her and the way they react to her working. The reason the mother has for working outside the home also affects her attitude toward herself and toward her work. If she is working for selfish reasons— reasons other than to help her family—she will feel guilty because she is not conforming to the cultural stereotype of the good mother. If, on the other hand, her reasons are unselfish—to help her family—she will try to compensate in every way for any inconvenience and privation her working gives the different members of her family. Women who work for selfish reasons are more likely to put their work before their families, except in cases of serious emergency (48,144, 151,290,330,331).

Husband's attitude How a working mother's husband feels about her working will affect their marital relationship; this, in turn, will affect the home climate. If the husband suspects or knows that his wife is working because she finds the traditional role of homemaker boring, he will resent her dissatisfaction with the role she voluntarily selected when she married him. If it is because she feels that her husband does not earn enough to supply the family's needs and wants, he will resent her constant reminder of this by her work and by her buying things for the family (18,48,166, 179,239,331).

Children's attitudes Adolescents resent their mothers' working for many reasons: for example, the working mother does not fit into the cultural stereotype they have learned of the good mother; if the mother is away from home, this interferes with their social lives because they are not able to entertain their friends in their homes and they have to assume home responsibilities when their friends are having fun; the working mother tends to introduce the efficiency methods of the business world into the home and this often leads to criticisms of the way the adolescent does the tasks assigned to him; the working mother usually has high aspirations for her children and puts greater pressure on them than the nonworking mothers of their friends; because the mother is often tired and irritable after a day of work outside the home, she does less for her children than their friends' mothers do; and she is less available to discuss their problems or give advice (48,180, 298,303,317,331,376).

While both boys and girls object to their mothers' working, they do so for different reasons. Boys object to having their mothers work because they feel it will be looked upon unfavorably among their peers (283). Adolescent girls, on the other hand, are often lonely and uhappy when their mothers are out of the home. They then stay out of the home, often associating with an antisocial group whose mothers also give them little care or supervision. They resent the home responsibilities they must assume when the mother works. This, plus the fact that the mother has little time after work to help them to entertain—which they regard as a handicap to their social lives—adds to their resentments (48,151,290,298). Both boys and girls claim that "there is no home life when Mother has to be away all day, coming home all tired out at night" (128).

Attitude of the social group Because the attitudes of the adolescent toward himself and toward his family are greatly influenced by the attitudes of his peers, how he feels about his mother's working outside the home will be greatly influenced by how his peers feel about it. In small towns, the attitude toward working mothers is less favorable than in urban and suburban areas (180,268,283,298,331).

The adult members of the social group tend to disapprove of working mothers more than do members of the adolescent peer group. Men look upon working wives as a threat to masculine domination in the home and many regard a man whose wife is working as a "failure" (18,166,179). Women are well aware of the disapproval other women have of a working mother unless there is a need for her to work. Awareness of this not only affects the mother's attitude but also the attitude of her children. This is a common source of friction in the home (144,239). Figure 15–12 shows the attitudes of other women toward the working mother with children of different ages.

Provisions for home chores When children are young, the working mother must make provision for the care of her children while she is out of the home. Because adolescents do not need such care, it is usual for the working mother to expect her husband and the adolescent children in the family to assume these responsibilities during her absence and to help her when she is at home (287,376).

How much responsibility for the run-

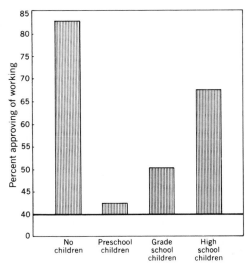

FIGURE 15–12 Attitudes of women toward working mothers with children of different ages. (Adapted from H. M. Glenn: Attitudes of women regarding gainful employment of married women. *J. Home Econ.*, 1959, **51**, 247–252. Used by permission.)

ning of the home working mothers expect the different family members to assume varies greatly (179,298). The higher the education of the mother, the less will she expect in the way of help from her family. This is due in part to the fact that with a higher education she can earn more and, hence, pay for some outside help and in part to her realization that her guidance and association with her adolescent sons and daughters are important to their development. She, then, tries to compensate for her time away from the home by more planned and shared interests and by imposing fewer duties on them (303,319).

Type of work When a mother's work is prestigeful, the pride her family feels in her achievements counteracts some of the unfavorable effects of her being away from home. The adolescent's adjustments to the parents and the home climate in general are better when the mother works part time than when she works full time or not at all. Figure 15–13 illustrates the effects on mother-adolescent adjustments of full- and part-time work and of unemployment.

Even more damaging to the home climate than full-time work is *sporadic* work. Occasional or sporadic work entails constant adjustments and readjustments on the part of all family members.

effects of mother's work How the mother's work is *viewed* by different family members determines what its influence will be. If the employment, for example, is viewed by the adolescent as a rejection of the maternal role or by the husband as an indication of the family's feeling that he is a failure as a breadwinner, it will have a markedly different effect on the home climate than it would if family attitudes were more favorable (247).

The employment status of the mother will affect the different members of the family differently. As Blood (48) has pointed out, the employment and status of the mother:

> . . . reflect a lower status for the masculine side of the family. The father has less status—the sons see it and slump too. By contrast, daughters of working mothers are more independent, more self-reliant, more aggressive, more dominant, and more disobedient. Such girls are no longer meek, mild, submissive and feminine like "little ladies" ought to be.

Within any family, the effects of the mother's employment may range from quiet

submission to bitter resentment. It may cause conflicts that lead to divorce or it may solve the economic problems of the family that threatened divorce (277,278). The effect of the mother's employment on the adolescent may be favorable or it may be so unfavorable that it will lead to problem behavior or even juvenile delinquency. However, there is little evidence that the mother's employment leads to juvenile delinquency per se; other conditions set the stage for this unsocial behavior (48,256,276,331). Instead, there is evidence that "Maternal employment *per se* is not the overwhelming influential factor in children's lives that some have thought it to be" (332).

The effect of maternal employment on the mother's relationships with her sons and daughters is different. When the mother works, the son has more free time for social life because it is less necessary for him to take an afterschool job to earn spending money or to contribute to the family income. The daughter, by contrast, is expected to assume more responsibilities in the home; this interferes with her social life. Furthermore, because a mother is more important to a girl's socialization than to a boy's, the girl whose mother works often feels that she is handicapped socially (256, 290,331).

Maternal employment seems to have little or no effect on father-son relationships. If there is any effect, it is more likely to strengthen the relationship because the father and son agree that the mother's place is in the home. In the case of father-daughter relationships, the effect is very different. As Maccoby (239) has pointed out:

> Curiously enough the girls with working mothers seemed to have more disturbance in their relationships with their fathers than with their mothers. Possibly the mother's working in some way weakens the father's role in the family so that the daughter does not respect him as she might otherwise. An equally possible explanation, however, is that a number of the mothers are working because their husbands are unstable, a quality which might produce nega-

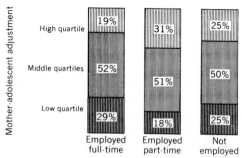

FIGURE 15–13 Effects of full- and part-time employment of mothers on mother-adolescent adjustments. (Adapted from F. I. Nye: Adolescent-parent adjustment: age, sex, sibling number, broken homes, and employed mothers as variables. *Marriage fam. Living*, 1952, **14**, 327–332. Used by permission.)

tive feelings toward a man on the part of both wife and daughter.

In conclusion, then, it is apparent that maternal occupation is only one of many factors that influence the quality of the home climate. When the home climate of a family where the mother works is unfavorable, this may be due more to other conditions in the home, such as a poor marital relationship, unrealistically high aspirations on the part of either or both parents for their children, poor economic conditions of the home or the mother's rejection of her role as homemaker (332,344,384). Thus, as Maccoby has stated, "Clearly no single way of organizing family life is best for all. Some mothers should work while others should not" (239).

PARENTAL ASPIRATIONS

Even before a child is born, his parents have aspirations for him. By the time the child reaches adolescence, parental aspirations are intensified. They then become even more damaging to the adolescent's happiness and to family relationships than they were before (181,313). See pages 299 and 300 for a more complete discussion of the influence of parental pressures on the aspirations of adolescents.

Effects on Home Climate   When the adolescent comes up to parental expectations, his parents are pleased, satisfied, and acceptant in their attitudes. This has a favorable influence on the home climate. Unfortunately, most adolescents fall below their parents' expectations. This is not because the adolescent does not try to achieve the success his parents hope for, but because the expectations are unrealistically high. His parents then remind him of the personal sacrifices they have made to provide opportunities for him and accuse him of not taking advantage of them.

This attitude on the part of parents arouses bitter resentments in the adolescent and brings about a strained parent-adolescent relationship. His parents resent his "not trying" and blame him for "wasting his time" on social or other activities, thus putting further strain on the parent-adolescent relationship. This not only proves to be extremely damaging to the home climate but it plays havoc with the adolescent's personal adjustments. His relationships with other family members are affected as well as his relationships with his parents (101,154, 203).

The greatest damage to family relationships comes when the behavior of one of the members is perceived as a disgrace by the rest of the family. When family members have high aspirations and expectations for the other members, they tend to perceive the failure to come up to expectations as bringing disgrace to the family. If, for example, an adolescent fails in school—a failure his teachers anticipated on the basis of his ability—his parents react to it as if it were a disgrace to the entire family (52).

More serious than the "subjective disgraces"—disgraces based on failure to come up to unrealistically high levels of aspiration—are the "objective disgraces"—disgraces so viewed by the social group. When an adolescent girl has an illegitimate child, how disgraced the family feels will be influenced by the attitudes of the social group with which the family is identified. If the group does not regard illegitimacy as serious, especially if the illegitimate child's parents are married before or after the child's birth, the family members will have a more tolerant attitude toward the girl than they would if the social group labeled this a disgrace (188).

Whether disgrace is subjective or objective, it gives rise to friction in the family and to deep resentments against the offender because of the damage his behavior has done to their image in the eyes of the social group. While the family, through loyalty, may rally to the support of the disgraced member, this does not eliminate their resentments or the friction such resentments give rise to (52).

CONCEPTS OF FAMILY ROLES

Long before the child reaches adolescence, he has built up a concept of his role in the family as well as concepts of the roles of other family members. Parents and siblings likewise have concepts of the roles various family members should play (174,339).

In these concepts, as in all concepts, there is an "emotional weighting" that ranges from strong to weak. This weighting determines the degree of liking the individual has for the family member and, even more important, it determines how easy or difficult it is to change the concept. An adolescent's concept of "mother" as an "ideal" woman, for example, will contribute heavily to his preference for the mother as compared with the father (328).

Children of today grow up in a culture much more permeated by the influence of mass media than their parents and grandparents did. As a result, today's adolescents have much more stereotyped concepts of family roles (231). If a husband has come from a cultural background or social class that is different from his wife's, his concepts of family roles will be different from hers (21,61,127,243,362).

Concepts of family roles, as is true of all concepts, change with changed experiences. Adolescents who have concepts of parents based on their childhood experiences and mass media have been found to change their concepts as a result of a course in child psychology. This change was from concepts of parents as harsh, punitive, and demanding, to concepts of a more tolerant type (85). A mother's concept of an equalitarian role for the father in the home will change when she realizes how unrealistic it is for her to expect her husband to share equally in the care of the children when his work takes him out of the home for the major part of the day (71,250).

Concepts of Specific Roles Owing to similar cultural influences and pressures, certain concepts are widely held by the majority of Americans. Because of age and cultural-experience differences, however, today's adolescents have concepts that differ markedly from those of their parents in some respects.

role of parents Unlike the child who thinks of parents as people who do things for him, the independence-conscious *adolescent* has a concept of a "good parent" as one who guides his behavior to help him avoid mistakes; who is interested in his activities and friends; who is readily available to give advice when the adolescent needs it; who enjoys doing things with and talking to his children; who is fair in his discipline; who tries to see things from the point of view of his children and their friends; and who gives his children a voice in the family plans and a chance to express their opinions (4,52,85,86,175,195,308).

The concept of the role parents should play also covers patterns of behavior adolescents dislike and which they feel their parents should avoid. The most common peeves adolescents have against their parents are unfair and inconsistent discipline; overprotectiveness; not trusting them; treating them as children; interfering in their friendships; trying to influence their decisions without considering their interests or needs adequately; nagging and complaining about their behavior; boasting about them to outsiders; not dressing or acting "their ages"; having favorites among the children of the family; complaining about homemaking duties; arguing or bickering with each other; and doing or saying things that embarrass them when their friends are present (4,21,52,175,192,228,308). Boys are more concerned about the personal habits and conduct of their parents while girls are more critical of their parents' temperamental traits and characteristics, especially those which affect interpersonal relationships (20,308).

To *parents*, the concept of the role they should play is to equip their children for happy, useful lives (244,361). If they are "good" parents, they are "thoroughly committed to the idea that the primary business of parents is to make their children as completely independent of the parents at as early an age as possible" (19). Parents have different concepts of how this can best be done. Some believe that the best way is the traditional way; some that it is the modern, developmental way. According to the *traditional* way, the parents play an authoritarian role, with the father playing a role superior to that of the mother in the training of the children. This concept emphasizes the molding of the child into a pattern approved by the parents and making him conform to this pattern (105,166, 209).

By contrast, the *developmental* concept of the parents' role emphasizes respect for the child as an individual, satisfaction in personal interaction, pride in growth and development, and a permissive, growth-promoting type of guidance (80,362,378, 379). In short, "good" parents are those who "give to the world children who are happy as they look back to their homes, and eager and adequate as they look forward to the assumption of their responsibilities" (361).

role of father In recent years, the concept of the father's role in the home has changed radically. The result is that adolescents today have very different concepts of the father's role than their fathers have. The adolescents' concept of the father's role is usually more like the mother's concept of that role than like the father's (166,244,308, 362).

As he grows up, the adolescent has become accustomed to seeing in the movies, in comics, and on television a stereotype of "father" as an overly permissive person, an "amiable boob of the situation comedies —the ineffectual but lovable bungler" (129, 231). In these mass media, there is (165):

> . . . an overt and cheerful acceptance of Dad's decline. . . . But while a hasty glimpse might lead the viewer to believe that Mom is wearing the pants, she is merely the caretaker and spokesman for the real power behind the throne—the children.

The *adolescent* of today, influenced by mass media as well as by his own experiences, thinks of a good father as permissive in his attitudes and treatment of his children; as just, controlling his children by love rather than by fear or harsh punishments; lots of fun to be with, mild, and reasonable in his demands; industrious; interested in his children and willing to do things with and for them; a good example for them to imitate; interested in his child's future and willing to plan and even make sacrifices for it; and deriving satisfaction from his parental role (80,102,111,192,244,362).

Lower-class adolescents tend to think of the father as the "boss," because it is he who earns the money, who punishes, who makes important decisions, and who dominates the mother as well as the children. Middle- and upper-class adolescents, by contrast, perceive the mother as having greater authority than the father. The adolescent's concept of the father, regardless of his social class, is more heavily weighted with respect and fear than is his concept of the mother (61,116,166,195,244,349,362). Figure 15–14 shows how adult men and women remember their mothers and fathers at different stages in growing up.

Boys and girls, during adolescence, perceive their fathers differently. *Boys* tend to think of the father as more irritable and nagging than the mother, stricter, more hostile and negative in his treatment of his son than of his daughter, and as more likely to ignore and neglect his son than his daughter. *Girls*, on the other hand, generally have more favorable concepts of their fathers. Girls more than boys perceive their fathers as affectionate and attentive (103, 253).

Parents often have markedly different concepts of the father's role in the family. Men, as a whole, but especially those of the

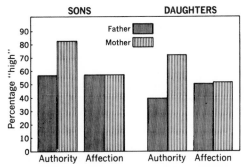

FIGURE 15–14 How adult men and women remember their parents at different stages during their youth. (Adapted from W. C. Bronson, E. S. Katten, and N. Livson: Patterns of authority and affection in two generations. *J. abnorm. soc. Psychol.*, 1959, **58**, 143–152. Used by permission.)

lower socioeconomic groups, cling to the traditional concept of the father's role which puts major emphasis on providing for his children and family, on disciplining and advising his children, and on setting a good example for them to follow. Mothers, on the other hand, tend to favor the developmental concept which emphasizes the role of the father as fostering the growth and development of his children, of understanding and being companionable with them, and of doing things for and with them (193,209,279,363).

role of mother The concept of the role the mother plays is radically changed as the adolescent goes from childhood into adolescence. He is greatly influenced in making this change by the stereotype of "mother" he becomes accustomed to in the mass media (228,231). How detrimental this influence is on the adolescent's concept of the role the mother plays in the family has been described thus by Crowther (90):

> Something amazing is happening to the conventional image of Mom (short for American mother) in recent films. It is being severely "dumped on," to use a contemporary phrase. Mother is being presented as a boy's (or a girl's) worst friend. . . . Suddenly he is confronted by the accumulating idea that mothers are without infallible wisdom and, indeed, can be bad for a kid. And fathers have not come off much better in all the films, though they have usually been subordinate to the mothers and sometimes even victimized by them—all of which makes for further implication of the nefariousness of Mom.

By the time the child reaches adolescence, his concept of the importance of mother's role has almost been reversed. Instead of being the "boss," she is now seen as a subservient member of the family (20, 83,116,117,190,244,262). (Refer to Figure 15–14, page 623.) Stoodley (349) has explained the reasons for this change in concept of the mother's role thus:

> As children grow up they naturally pick up ideas as to who is the "big wheel" in their family. More often than not it isn't Mother. Perhaps they go to a school where the teachers are women, but the principal is a man. Perhaps they see that the jobs they consider important are occupied mostly by men. Or perhaps they absorb the sentiment of their social milieu which associates prestige with some specific kind of expertness, whether it be that of the certified accountant, the skilled mechanic, or the physician. Society does not associate this expertness with the mother's role.

Girls' concepts of the mother's role tend to change more than boys'. More important, however, is the fact that the emotional weighting of the *boys'* concepts of the mother's role is more favorable than girls'. Boys, for example, claim that their mothers nag and punish them less than their fathers do, that they are more interested in them and their affairs, more loving and nurturant in their behavior, and more permissive. Girls find their mothers' treatment to be just the opposite (44,80,103).

Both *parents* have their own concepts of what role the mother should play in the home. If they accept the traditional concept, they emphasize that the mother should guide her children with understanding; that she should keep the house and be readily available to do things with and for her children, regardless of their ages; that she should teach them moral and religious values; and that she should set a good example for them to follow. Parents who accept the developmental concept of the mother's role emphasize her influence in the growth and development of the child more than physical care, the importance of her having interests outside the home and sharing many interests and experiences with her children as they reach the adolescent years (44,80,363). Fathers, regardless of their social class, more often accept the traditional than the developmental concept; mothers, on the other hand, tend to favor the developmental and often feel frustrated when circumstances force them to play the traditional role (57,105,304).

role of child The *adolescent's* concept of his role in the family is largely a product of his parents' concept of that role and of the way adolescents are portrayed in the mass media. During childhood, the former influence is more important in the development of his concept than the latter; by the time the child reaches adolescence, the reverse is true.

If *parents* have the traditional concept of a "good" child, they will expect their adolescent sons and daughters to respect their elders, whether they be parents, grandparents, or outsiders; to obey and try to please them; to be ambitious and eager to learn as a preparation for their future roles in life; and to honor their parents for their unselfish love and devotion. In addition, the "good" child is never a troublemaker in the home. Instead, he is cooperative and eager to share in the work and responsibilities of the home (85,105,155,363).

Adolescents who have been brought up in a home where the parents have developmental concepts of the child's role learn to think of their role as equalitarian rather than inferior. According to the developmental concept, parents do not try to mold their children according to their own wishes. Instead, they try to foster development along the lines of their children's abilities and interests. Because of family loyalty and affection, adolescents think of the "good" child as one who *wants* to participate in family activities and to make his contribution to the running of the home in any way he can (80,105,155,171,189).

Typically, the role of the adolescent in the American family, as portrayed by the mass media, is that of the "boss." The home is centered around the children, and their parents are willing servants whose strongest desire is to give their children a "happy, carefree youth" with all the status symbols and money needed to achieve this goal. The teen-ager brought up in the affluence of today's home is not curbed by "old-fashioned" moral training but is free to do what his peers do, regardless of parental disapproval. He is depicted as having few if any home responsibilities, other than to lend his presence occasionally to family gatherings. And, above all, he is depicted as the pride, joy, and hope of his ambitious, self-sacrificing parents (90,129,165,349). With constant exposure to such a stereotyped picture, it would be incredible if the concept the adolescent learned from his parents would not be revised to a greater or lesser extent.

roles of relatives For many adolescents of today, concepts of the roles relatives play in the family put major emphasis on such unfavorable characteristics as "unwelcome guest," "intruder," and "troublemaker" (16, 74,100,336,347,367). While concepts of the role of relatives tend, on the whole, to be unfavorable, the most unfavorable relate to *female* relatives. The grandmother, for example, is perceived by both boys and girls as playing a role of greater authority in their lives than the grandfather. Even as adults, men remember their grandmothers as more affectionate and permissive to them; for adult women, the memories are of a grandmother who played a less affectionate and more authoritarian role (61). This is illustrated in Figure 15–15. Concepts of the role of the stepfather are more favorable than those of the stepmother. This is due, in part, to the fact that a stepfather plays a less important role in the home than a stepmother and, in part, to the fact than the stereotype of "stepfather" in mass media is usually far more favorable than that of "stepmother" (293,327,336).

Effects of Concepts on Home Climate In primitive and many civilized cultures throughout the world, the role of each family member is rigidly prescribed by convention, custom, and even law. Each child growing up in a given culture learns what these prescribed roles are and accepts them without question. As a result, family life is not affected by frictions arising from conflicting concepts (243,253,362). Today, there is a gradual change taking place in middle-class American families in the ideology of the "good" father, mother, and child (171,217,378).

Because of this change, there is less *psychological distance* between parent and child than there is in cultures where the parent is in a position of absolute authority

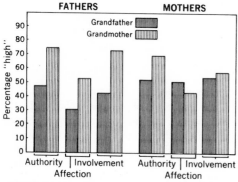

FIGURE 15-15 Adult memories of youthful attitudes toward grandparents. (Adapted from W. C. Bronson, E. S. Katten, and N. Livson: Patterns of authority and affection in two generations. *J. abnorm. soc. Psychol.*, 1959, **58**, 143–152. Used by permission.)

over the child, and the husband, over the wife. As psychological distance decreases, there is a tendency for friction to increase.

If changes in family concepts were all in the same direction and in the same amount, frictions would not develop. But changes tend to be in different directions and in varying amounts. A husband may, for example, change his concept of the wife's role from traditional to partially equalitarian while the wife's concept of her role has changed to the wholly equalitarian role she finds prevails among her friends. This disparity in concepts will unquestionably lead to friction (61,243).

When one parent does not play the role the other parent thinks he or she should play, there will be criticism and friction. If the father thinks he is a "good" father but his adolescent son does not, there will be friction between father and son. The father who holds the traditional concept of the "good" child will find it hard to accept the "impertinence" and "lack of respect" his child, brought up by a mother with strongly developmental concepts of her role, shows in his relationships with him (5,187, 228,329).

Thus, it is not the relationship of the parent with the adolescent son or daughter or between the husband and wife, per se, that is important. Rather, it is *how each individual involved in this relationship perceives it.* When mothers and their adolescent sons and daughters *both* perceive their relationship as favorable, there will be less friction between them than if either the mother or the daughter perceived it as less favorable than the other. The same is true of fathers' and adolescents' perceptions (244). This is illustrated in Figure 15–16.

The most detrimental effect on the home climate comes when a family member has an unrealistic, idealized concept of the role another member of the family should play. If, for example, a younger sibling idealizes an older, or if the son has a highly unrealistic concept of "mother," each will judge the individual who plays that role by the concept he has. Few family members, unfortunately, can live up to an idealized concept. In time, the critical attitude, engendered by a specific situation in which the individual's behavior fell short of the idealized concept, may become general, spreading to everything that individual says or does (58,87,102,129,198,244,328).

Lazar and Klein (228) have explained the critical attitude of adolescents toward their parents as stemming from a revision of childhood concepts of their parents:

> *By criticizing his parents, the teen-ager is trying to bring them down to life size and helping himself to feel as competent as they are. He is trying to convince himself that "They're not so perfect after all.". . . This effort to accept that his parents are less than perfect is behind much of the teen-ager's arrogance and hostility. Few parents, of course, have ever claimed to be perfect and it is often difficult for them to understand that their child finds it necessary to prove that they are not. But it is useful to keep in mind that, when the teen-ager lashes out, he is not angry because his mother or father tried to fool him with a false picture of perfection: he is simply rebelling against his own childish fantasy of their perfection.*

Almost as detrimental as romanticized concepts is a situation in which a member of the family who has strongly developed concepts of the role he should play in the family is forced, through circumstances, to play a role which he feels belongs to another family member. An adolescent daughter, for example, whose concept of a "good" mother is one who does things for her children, will understandably be resentful when she is expected to assume some of the care of younger siblings (52). The husband who conceives of the father's role as the one traditionally associated with men will resent being a "partial mother" or a "mother's helper." As Josselyn has emphasized, in explaining this resentment, "It is not what he does that is so important but how he feels when he does it" (193).

Changes in the father role, necessitated by circumstances associated with modern living, affect the adolescent's concept of what the father should be. As Levin (231) has pointed out, adolescents want their father:

> . . . to be ideal, God-like, and when we find he is not, we are disappointed. Yet circumstances conspire to undermine the ideal. Social change insists that father share his free time with his wife. The widespread disappearance of domestic help propels him into the nursery and kitchen. . . . Suburbia . . . relegates him to ungodlike tasks such as emptying the garbage pail.

Even though concepts of family roles do change, and often markedly, as time passes, this does not automatically guarantee an improvement in family relationships. There are two important reasons for this. First, patterns of behavior, once established, tend to be persistent. The individual literally gets into the habit of behaving in a frictional manner with an individual whose behavior is contrary to his concept of what it should be.

The second reason for persistence of poor family relationships, in spite of changes in concepts of family roles, is that relationships with one family member rarely remain static; instead, they spread to other family members. Once a specific frictional relationship spreads to include all or most of the family members, there is little chance of its improving even when one family member

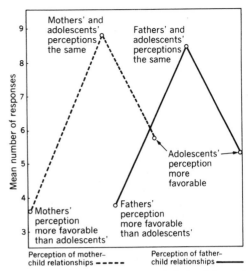

FIGURE 15–16 How parents and their adolescent sons and daughters perceive their relationships with one another. (Adapted from P. H. Maxwell, R. Connor, and J. Walters: Family member perception of parent role performance. Merrill-Palmer Quart., 1961, **7**, 31–37. Used by permission.)

changes his concept of family roles. All members, as has been pointed out earlier, must change their concepts in the same direction and to the same degree if improvement in family relationships is to take place.

FAVORITISM

In any human relationship, whether it be in the home or outside, it is natural and normal for a person to prefer one individual to another and to feel more comfortable and "at home" with that individual. Certain family members fill the adolescent's needs better than others, just as they do the needs of his parents or grandparents. This results in a warm, affectionate bond between them which is recognized or sensed by other family members and is usually resented.

At every age level, the individual's needs change somewhat as his pattern of life changes. An adolescent, for example, needs someone to whom he can turn for advice and help. If the mother is not only readily available to help him with his problems but is understanding and sympathetic in her attitudes, it is logical that the adolescent would prefer her to his father who is rarely available when he is needed most and, if he is available, is too tired or preoccupied with his own problems to take time to discuss those of the adolescent (70,92).

Preferences are also greatly influenced by the individual's perception of the emotional reactions of others toward him. When an adolescent is aware of the hero-worshiping attitude of a younger sibling, it is logical that he would prefer this young sibling to another who goes out of his way to criticize and ridicule everything he says or does. Because fathers often feel that showing their affection is "unmasculine" when directed toward their sons, but "masculine" when shown to their daughters, boys interpret this to mean that the father prefers the girls of the family (52,105,198,244).

Common Preferences There are certain preferences that are commonly found, though far from universal. These are discussed below.

preference for children Parental favoritism is usually centered on the firstborn or the last-born child of a large family. Boys are more often the favorites than are girls, though fathers tend to favor their daughters, and mothers, their sons. The child of the family who is bright, who achieves academic or athletic success, who is popular, or who is ambitious is usually a favorite of both parents because of the prestige he vicariously brings to the family. The child who is physically or mentally handicapped often *seems* to be the parents' favorite because of the time and attention parents must give him as a result of his handicap.

The emotional reaction of the child toward his parents likewise influences their reactions to him. Because sons idealize their mothers more often than daughters do, the mother turns her affections more to her sons than to her daughters. One of the reasons for the father's favoritism for his daughters is that they do not hesitate to show him their affection, while boys, in their attempts to show how "masculine" they are, do (52, 108,198,253,323,349,397).

preference for parent *Girls* who, in childhood, tended to regard the mother as the "favorite" parent often shift their preference to their father. This is partly because they resent the mother's favoritism for a brother; partly because the role of the mother seems less prestigeful and glamorous than it did when the adolescent was a child and the father's role now seems more glamorous and prestigeful; and partly because the father shows a preference for the girls of the family and a more permissive attitude toward them and their activities than the mother does.

When *boys* shift their preferences, it is more likely to be toward an equal liking for both parents than toward a preference for either parent. Most boys recognize that the father is less to be feared and more to be respected than they realized when they were younger. As a result, the father's value, in their eyes, rises while the mother's may rise or it may remain stationary (15,33,52, 198,274,289,306,349,363). In the case of both boys and girls, the shift is away from an "uncritical fondness" for the mother to a more neutral, "take-for-granted" attitude toward both parents (157).

preference for siblings Most girls, in early adolescence, prefer their sisters to their brothers. Then, as adolescence progresses, they usually shift their preference to their brothers. An adolescent girl generally prefers an older brother to a younger because the older brother has less of a derogatory attitude toward her, because of her sex, than has a younger. When there are several siblings of both sexes, the girl selects as her favorite the one of each sex whose interests are in common with hers and who shows a more affectional attitude toward her.

Boys, throughout adolescence, tend to prefer their brothers to their sisters. If they have any preference among their sisters, it is generally for a younger rather than for an older sister. Among their brothers, they usually prefer a younger brother who hero-worships them to an older brother whose attitude is one of superiority. As is true of girls, boys show a preference for a brother whose interests are similar to theirs and with whom, as a result, they have more in common (52,91,93,184,307,358,366). Figure 15–11, page 612, shows the attitude of adolescents toward siblings of both sexes.

Regardless of the sex of the sibling, adolescent boys and girls show a preference for a sibling who is handicapped physically or mentally, or who is "picked on" by one or both parents. By contrast, the sibling who is a parent's favorite is rarely ever a favorite among the other siblings. Boys and girls resent the special attention and privileges given to the parent's pet and they show it by rejecting that sibling (68,76,121, 123,157,281).

preference for relatives   Which relatives the adolescent prefers will depend largely upon how they treat him. There is a tendency for the paternal grandmother to be preferred to the maternal and the aunts on the father's side of the family to those on the mother's. Because male relatives rarely assume positions of authority over the adolescent, his preference will be conditioned partly by the way they treat him and partly by how prestigeful their occupations are (76,281,307,366).

Effects on Home Climate   There are two types of favoritism that are especially damaging to the home climate. The first is favoritism that has been shifted from one family member to another. When the adolescent girl shifts from regarding the mother as her favorite parent, as she did in childhood, to the father, it is inevitable that the mother will be hurt and annoyed. Two sisters who, as children, were very close because of similar interests, may develop a frictional relationship when the older shifts her affection to an older brother.

The second type of favoritism that is especially damaging to the home climate is favoritism concentrated on one family member. If the firstborn son is the favorite of both parents and grandparents and may even be a hero to the baby of the family, the other members will resent the attention and affection lavished on him. Similarly, if the children of the family side with the mother against the father, it certainly will not improve the relationship between the parents. Nor will parent-child relationships be improved if the children gang up against the parent whom they perceive as having treated one of them unfairly.

Any split in family relationships, no matter how slight it may be, always leads to friction. Nothing will produce a split more quickly and more permanently than favoritism. When this happens, the family unit is divided into warring camps, each accusing the other of mistreating its members. When, by contrast, the family lives, works, and plays as a unit, held together by mutual respect and affection and by loyalty to the family as a whole, friction will be reduced to a minimum (191,217,334).

effects of home climate on the adolescent

The psychological climate of the home in which the adolescent grows up has a marked influence on his personal and social adjustments. This influence may be direct or indirect. *Directly*, it influences his characteristic patterns of behavior. If the home climate is happy, he will react to people and things in a happy, philosophical manner. If it is frictional, he will carry the frictional patterns of behavior learned in the home to situations outside the home and react to them as he habitually reacts to similar situations in the home (167,237,284).

Indirectly, the home climate influences the adolescent by the effect it has on his attitudes. If he learns to resent the authority of his parents because he perceives it as tyrannical and unfair, he will develop attitudes of resentment against *all* in authority. This often leads to radical, nonconforming behavior. A happy home climate will encourage a favorable attitude toward people in authority.

While the home climate may not have as great effects, either directly or indirectly, on the adolescent as it does on the child, nevertheless the effects are too great to be overlooked. Furthermore, the home climate of childhood is likely to persist, thus reinforcing the effects it had earlier in the adolescent's life (82,94,263,274). This point of view has been emphasized by Peck and Havighurst (285):

> The most powerful, most persistent attitudes, perceptual sets, and reaction patterns of adolescents appear to be those they have learned in the first ten years of life through their emotionally paramount, moment-by-moment interactions with their fathers and mothers. "There is no place like home" is sheer unsentimental fact in a child's world.

Which of the many conditions within the family has the greatest influence on the adolescent will depend to a large extent upon what *type of individual* he is. A quiet, reserved, introspective adolescent, for example, will react quite differently to friction between his parents than will a more extroverted adolescent whose interests are centered in activities outside the home. As a general rule, however, the parent-child relationship is the most important single influence in determining what the psychological climate of the home will be and the effect the home climate has on the adolescent (6,32,152,282,285). Peck and Havighurst (285) have explained this thus:

> Each adolescent is just about the kind of person that would be predicted from a knowledge of the way his parents treated him. Indeed, it seems reasonable to say that, to an almost startling degree, each child learns to feel and act, psychologically and morally, as just the kind of person his father and mother have been in their relationships with him.

AREAS OF INFLUENCE

The areas in which the home climate has the greatest influence on the adolescent's attitudes and behavior are described below.

Personal Adjustment When the home climate is characterized by affection, respect, and tolerance for all by all family members, by cooperation and collaboration, by little or no destructive competition among the family members, and by little or no conflict, the adolescent will develop a wholesome self-concept; this will be reflected in good adjustments to life. When, on the other

hand, the home climate is characterized by friction, stemming from unfavorable relationships between the different family members, it will militate against the development of a wholesome self-concept, especially if the adolescent is directly involved in the conflicts with different members of the family (118,210,234,273).

A study of the effects of parent-child conflicts has shown how they affect the personal adjustments of the young adolescent. This is illustrated in Figure 15–17. As Schaefer and Bayley (323) have emphasized, on the basis of these findings:

> The data reported here . . . support hypotheses about maternal influence upon the development of the child. An analysis of progressive changes in parent-child correlations suggests that the child's social, emotional, and task-oriented behaviors are, to some extent, a reaction to the parental behaviors he has received throughout the period of childhood.

The mental health of the adolescent, whether good or bad, is influenced more by the organization of the family and the role the adolescent plays in that organization than by the mental health of significant family members, especially the mother (386). This is well illustrated in studies of the effects of ordinal position on the adolescent's adjustments (364). The firstborn, for example, who has been displaced by the arrival of a new sibling (353):

> . . . will walk constantly as if with a chip on his shoulder. . . . He has learned from bitter experience that he may be displaced. In line with this, a general attitude of pessimism is common among the first-born.

By contrast, the youngest, who will never be dethroned as older siblings were, is likely to be cheerful and happy, to have an optimistic outlook on life, and to make good personal adjustments (353). Thus, the child's "position in the sequence of brothers and sisters is of very great significance for the course of his later life" (132).

Social Adjustment Adolescents who are poorly adjusted socially in school or with their classmates frequently come from a home climate characterized by family frictions and resentments. If, on the other hand, the home climate is pleasant and the adolescent enjoys doing things with and for the members of the family, he learns to behave in a socially mature way. This makes him popular with his peers as well as with adults (69,212,325,334,372). As Warnath has explained, "The home thus appears indeed to be a seat of learning for the development of social skills, and perhaps of the desire to participate in activities with other individuals" (381).

The influence of the home climate on the socialization of the adolescent extends to areas that include learning to conform to group mores, to communicate with others, and to express a liking for others. If the individual comes from a happy home, he will have developed the habit of conformity to home standards and will, voluntarily, do so when with outsiders. If, on the other hand, he comes from a frictional home, he has doubtless developed the habit of rebelling against home standards—a habit which he will carry into his social relationships outside the home (52,131,390).

A poor home climate discourages communication between family members; a favorable home climate encourages it (334). Ability to communicate is a quality essential to popularity and even more so to leadership. Equally important in social acceptance is the ability to express affection for others. The adolescent who comes from a home with a frictional climate finds it difficult to establish affectional relationships with outsiders just as he does with family members. As a result, he gives the impression of being cold, indifferent toward social life, and uninterested in people. Adolescents who come from happy homes are able to transfer some of the affection formerly directed toward their family members to their peers (164,381).

Maturity of Behavior An unhappy home life has a marked influence on the adolescent's emotional stability, making him moody, depressed, irritable, and unstable. A happy home climate, by contrast, has been

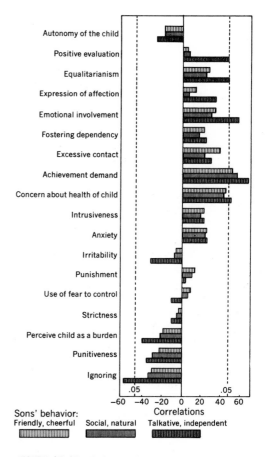

FIGURE 15–17 Relation between early maternal behavior and the boy's adolescent behavior. (Adapted from N. Bayley: Research in child development: a longitudinal perspective. *Merrill-Palmer Quart.*, 1965, **11**, 183–208. Used by permission.)

found to be associated with emotional stability and maturity of emotional control (22,202,323,338,352). Similarly, moral maturity, characterized by inner control of behavior, is more characteristic of adolescents who come from happy homes; moral immaturity, characterized by intentional misbehavior, misdemeanors, and delinquencies, is more characteristic of adolescents from homes where the psychological climate is poor (22,245).

Work Attitudes In a happy home, adolescents want to be cooperative and do their share to help in the running of the home.

As a result, they develop wholesome work attitudes—attitudes which are characterized by cooperativeness and a desire to work up to their capacities (190,334). These wholesome attitudes are carried out of the home and result in good academic achievement through the fostering of positive attitudes toward teachers and intellectual interests. They also lead to better adjustment to the school routine and to a desire to participate in the extracurricular activities of the school or college (52,82,235,261).

An unwholesome home climate, by contrast, plays havoc with the development of favorable attitudes toward work. The adolescent who perceives his home as frictional grumbles about the chores assigned to him and does them only under pressure; rarely does he work up to his capacity. The same unfavorable attitude is responsible for underachievement in school and a critical, faultfinding reaction to the school and teachers (241,352).

Unfavorable work attitudes likewise play havoc with the adolescent's adjustments in the business or industrial world as he grows older. On the other hand, adolescents who have grown up in a wholesome home climate are more likely to be achievers than underachievers in their adult vocations (370). A small amount of friction in the home climate may increase achievement motivation and lead to better work and greater success. However, this is not likely to happen if friction is persistent or intense (352).

Dating Adolescents who get along well with their families and regard their homes as happy start to date earlier and date more frequently than do adolescents from unhappy homes (13,22,334). Because large families tend to have a more frictional home climate than smaller families, adolescents from large families date less than do those from smaller families (364). The home climate affects the dating behavior of boys and girls differently. Girls who do not get along well with their mothers, it has been found, are especially eager to date and go steady. This is a form of compensation for the lack of happiness they experience at home. When boys get along well with their mothers, they date less than boys who get along less well. They start to go steady later than girls who come from homes where the climate is favorable. This sex difference may be explained by differences in maternal pressures on boys and girls (13,113,310,379,390). Girls from unhappy homes are far more likely to engage in premarital sex relationships and to have illegitimate babies than are girls who come from happy homes. Refer to pages 558 to 560 for a more complete discussion of this problem.

Marriage The happier the parents' marriage and the happier the home climate, the more favorable will be the adolescent's attitude toward marriage. When, on the other hand, adolescents come from homes where the climate is frictional, their attitudes toward marriage may be favorable or unfavorable, depending partly on what caused the frictional home climate and partly on their sex. Adolescent boys, it has been found, have a less favorable attitude toward marriage when their parents are divorced than do girls. Girls, by contrast, often feel that they have learned much from their parents' marital failure and that this will enable them to have a happier marriage (236,365,379). When a girl constantly hears her mother belittle her father, the mother is "doing her best to ensure misery for her daughter" (258).

Adolescents from large families, subjected to the frictional relationships that frequently accompany living in such families, often decide to have no children or certainly only small families. Adolescents from happy homes are so convinced that the more children in the home the "merrier" it will be decide that they want to have large families (83,185,273).

Happiness An adolescent growing up in a happy home climate will, unquestionably, be a happier person than one whose home is unpleasant, even though the former may have more unpleasant experiences outside the home than the latter. What determines the degree of happiness the adolescent experiences will be primarily the type of relationship he has with his parents.

Although adolescents spend more time outside the home than in the home and although they often create the impression that their affections are concentrated more on their peers than on their families, most adolescents feel that the fundamental basis of their happiness is to be found in their homes. And, within the home, the attitude of their parents toward them is more important to their happiness than any other factor. When asked, for example, to state the "hardest things for you to take," both boys and girls ranked their parents' disapproval even higher than a break with their friends (79).

When boys and girls feel, during their adolescent years, that they receive too little parental affection to meet their needs, they are unhappy and feel rejected (183,264). While poor relationships with their siblings and relatives may lead to an unhappy home climate, the relationships are less important in making the adolescent unhappy than is the general atmosphere in the home that comes from these poor relationships (270).

An unhappy home climate during the adolescent years can and often does cause a rift in the family structure which persists for the remainder of the lives of the different family members (22,261,310). By contrast, a happy home climate encourages all members of the family to develop a loyalty toward the other members; this results in family solidarity. In times of crisis as well as in times of happiness, the members of a happy family flock together. They enjoy doing things together and being together, even though each may have his own family and his own adult pattern of life.

It is a widely recognized fact that the American family of today is a less stable and less loyal unit than families in the past. There is a tendency to blame the change on vocational and social mobility which encourages geographic distance between members of a family. While this explanation unquestionably is, in part, correct, a more fundamental cause for the change in cohesiveness of the family can be found in the degree of happiness each family member experiences when he is with other family members. And this, in turn, is dependent mainly upon the type of psychological climate that prevails in the home.

BIBLIOGRAPHY

1 ABERLE, D. T., and K. D. NAEGLE: Middle-class fathers' occupational roles and attitudes toward children. *Amer. J. Orthopsychiat.*, 1952, **22**, 366–378.

2 ADAMS, E. B., and I. G. SARASON: Relation between anxiety in children and their parents. *Child Develpm.*, 1963, **34**, 237–246.

3 ALBRECHT, R.: Intergeneration parent patterns. *J. Home Econ.*, 1954, **46**, 29–32.

4 ALDOUS, J.: A study of parental role functions. *Family Life Coordinator*, 1961, **10**, 43–44.

5 ALDOUS, J., and L. KELL: Child-rearing values of mothers in relation to their children's perceptions of their mother's control: an exploratory study. *Marriage fam. Living*, 1956, **18**, 72–74.

6 ALDOUS, J., and L. KELL: A partial list of some theories of identification. *Marriage fam. Living*, 1961, **23**, 15–19.

7 ALTUS, W. D.: Birth order, intelligence, and adjustment. *Psychol. Rep.*, 1959, **5**, 502.

8 AMATORA, SISTER M.: An investigation of certain economic factors in large families. *J. soc. Psychol.*, 1959, **49**, 207–214.

9 AMATORA, SISTER M.: Analyses of certain recreational interests and activities and other variables in the large family. *J. soc. Psychol.*, 1959, **50**, 225–231.

10 AMATORA, SISTER M.: Home interests in early adolescence. *Genet. Psychol. Monogr.*, 1962, **65**, 137–174.

11 ANDERSON, E. S., and C. FITZSIMMONS: Use of time and money by employed homemakers. *J. Home Econ.*, 1960, **52**, 452–455.

12 ANDERSON, J. E.: The relation of attitude to adjustment. *Education*, 1952, **73**, 210–218.

13 ANDREWS, R. O., and H. T. CHRISTENSEN: Relationship of absence of a parent to courtship status: a repeat study. *Amer. sociol. Rev.*, 1951, **16**, 541–544.

14 ANGELINO, H., L. A. BARNES, and C. L. SHEDD: Attitudes of mothers and adolescent daugh-

ters concerning clothing and grooming. *J. Home Econ.*, 1956, **48**, 779–782.

15 ANTONVSKY, H. A.: A contribution to research in the area of the mother-child relationship. *Child Develpm.*, 1959, **30**, 37–57.

16 ARNHOFF, F. N., H. V. LEON, and I. LORGE: Cross-cultural acceptances of stereotypes toward aging. *J. soc. Psychol.*, 1964, **63**, 41–58.

17 ASHLEY-MONTAGU, M. F.: Sex order of birth and personality. *Amer. J. Orthopsychiat.*, 1948, **18**, 351–353.

18 AXELSON, L. J.: The marital adjustment and marital role definitions of husbands of working and nonworking wives. *Marriage fam. Living*, 1963, **25**, 189–195.

19 BAIN, R.: Making normal people. *Marriage fam. Living*, 1954, **16**, 27–31.

20 BARCLAY, D.: How girls judge mother's role. *The New York Times*, June 21, 1953.

21 BARCLAY, D.: Family business in brief. *The New York Times*, Feb. 18, 1962.

22 BARDIS, P. D.: Attitudes toward the family among college students and their parents. *Sociol. soc. Res.*, 1959, **43**, 352–358.

23 BARRON, M. L.: Minority group characteristics of the aged in American society. *J. Geront.*, 1953, **8**, 477–482.

24 BARTLETT, C. J., and J. E. HORROCKS: A study of the needs status of adolescents from broken homes. *J. genet. Psychol.*, 1958, **93**, 153–159.

25 BATH, J. A., and E. C. LEWIS: Attitudes of young females toward some areas of parent-adolescent conflict. *J. genet. Psychol.*, 1962, **100**, 241–253.

26 BAUER, F. C.: Mother shouldn't smother. *The New York Times*, July 28, 1963.

27 BAYLEY, N., and E. S. SCHAEFER: Relationships between socioeconomic variables and the behavior of mothers toward young children. *J. genet. Psychol.*, 1960, **96**, 61–77.

28 BEALER, R. C., and F. K. WILLITS: Rural youth: a case study in the rebelliousness of adolescents. *Ann. Amer. Acad. pol. soc. Sci.*, 1961, **338**, 63–69.

29 BEALER, R. C., F. K. WILLITS, and P. R. MAIDA: The rebellious youth subculture. *Children*, 1964, **11**, 43–48.

30 BECKER, H. S., and J. CARPER: The elements of identification with an occupation. *Amer. sociol. Rev.*, 1956, **21**, 341–348.

31 BEHRENS, M. L.: Child-rearing and the character structure of the mother. *Child Develpm.*, 1954, **25**, 225–238.

32 BEIER, E. G., and F. RATZEBURG: The parental identification of male and female college students. *J. abnorm. soc. Psychol.*, 1953, **48**, 569–572.

33 BELL, R. Q.: Retrospective attitude studies of parent-child relations. *Child Develpm.*, 1958, **29**, 323–338.

34 BELL, R. R., and J. V. BUERKLE: Mother and daughter attitudes to premarital sexual behavior. *Marriage fam. Living*, 1961, **23**, 390–392.

35 BELL, R. R., and J. V. BUERKLE: The daughter's role during the "launching stage." *Marriage fam. Living*, 1962, **24**, 384–388.

36 BELL, R. R., and J. V. BUERKLE: Mothers and mothers-in-law as role models in relation to religious background. *Marriage fam. Living.*, 1963, **25**, 485–486.

37 BENE, E.: Family relations as experienced by psychologically disturbed children. *Brit. J. med. Psychol.*, 1959, **32**, 226–231.

38 BENEDICT, R.: Child rearing in certain European countries. *Amer. J. Orthopsychiat.*, 1949, **19**, 342–350.

39 BERGLER, E.: *The revolt of the middle-aged man.* New York: Wyn, 1954.

40 BERMAN, S.: Adjustments of parents to children in the home. *J. Pediat.*, 1948, **32**, 66–77.

41 BERNARD, J.: *Remarriage: a study of marriage.* New York: Holt, 1956.

42 BETTLEHEIM, B., and E. SYLVESTER: Notes on the impact of parental occupation: some cultural determinants of symptom choice in emotionally disturbed children. *Amer. J. Orthopsychiat.*, 1950, **20**, 785–795.

43 BIERI, J.: Parental identification, acceptance of authority, and within-sex differences in cognitive behavior. *J. abnorm. soc. Psychol.*, 1960, **60**, 76–79.

44 BIERI, J., and R. LOBECK: Acceptance of authority and parental identification. *J. Pers.*, 1959, **27**, 74–86.

45 BLAU, P. M.: Occupational bias and mobility. *Amer. sociol. Rev.*, 1957, **22**, 392–399.

46 BLOOD, R. O.: Consequences of permissiveness for parents of young children. *Marriage fam. Living*, 1953, **15**, 209–212.

47 BLOOD, R. O.: Impact of urbanization on

American family structure and functioning. *Sociol. soc. Res.*, 1964, **49**, 5–16.

48 BLOOD, R. O.: Long-range causes and consequences of the employment of married women. *J. Marriage Fam.*, 1965, **27**, 43–47.

49 BOSSARD, J. H. S.: Marrying late in life. *Soc. Forces*, 1951, **29**, 405–408.

50 BOSSARD, J. H. S.: *Parent and child.* Philadelphia: University of Pennsylvania Press, 1953.

51 BOSSARD, J. H. S., and E. S. BOLL: Adjustment of siblings in large families. *Amer. J. Psychiat.*, 1956, **112**, 889–892.

52 BOSSARD, J. H. S., and E. S. BOLL: *The sociology of child development.* 3d ed. New York: Harper & Row, 1960.

53 BOWERMAN, C. E., and G. H. ELDER: Variations in adolescent perception of family power structure. *Amer. sociol. Rev.*, 1964, **29**, 551–567.

54 BOWERMAN, C. E., and D. P. IRISH: Some relationships of stepchildren to their parents. *Marriage fam. Living*, 1962, **24**, 113–121.

55 BOWERMAN, C. E., and J. W. KINCH: Changes in family and peer orientation of children between the fourth and tenth grades. *Soc. Forces*, 1959, **37**, 206–211.

56 BOWLBY, J.: Childhood mourning and its implications for psychiatry. *Amer. J. Psychiat.*, 1961, **118**, 481–498.

57 BRIGGS, V., and L. R. SCHULZ: Parental response to concepts of parent-adolescent relationships. *Child Develpm.*, 1955, **26**, 279–284.

58 BRIM, O. G., R. W. FAIRCHILD, and E. F. BORGATTA: Relations between family problems. *Marriage fam. Living*, 1961, **23**, 219–226.

59 BRITTAIN, C. V.: Adolescent choices and parent-peer cross-pressures. *Amer. sociol. Rev.*, 1963, **28**, 385–391.

60 BRONFENBRENNER, U.: The changing American child: a speculative analysis. *J. soc. Issues*, 1961, **17**, no. 1, 6–18.

61 BRONSON, W. C., E. S. KATTEN, and N. LIVSON: Patterns of authority and affection in two generations. *J. abnorm. soc. Psychol.*, 1959, **58**, 143–152.

62 BROWN, F.: Depression and childhood bereavement. *J. ment. Sci.*, 1961, **107**, 754–777.

63 BURCHINAL, L. G.: Characteristics of adolescents from unbroken homes and reconstituted families. *J. Marriage Fam.*, 1964, **26**, 44–51.

64 BURCHINAL, L. G., and P. E. JACOBSON: Migration and adjustments of farm and urban families and adolescents in Cedar Rapids, Iowa. *Rural Sociol.*, 1963, **28**, 364–378.

65 BURGESS, E. W.: The family in a changing society. *Amer. J. Sociol.*, 1948, **53**, 417–422.

66 BURGESS, E. W.: Economic, cultural, and social factors in family breakdown. *Amer. J. Orthopsychiat.*, 1954, **24**, 462–470.

67 BUTLER, R. M.: Mothers' attitudes toward the social development of their adolescents. *Soc. Casewk*, 1956, **37**, 219–226, 280–288.

68 CAHN, P.: Sociometric experiments on groups of siblings, *Sociometry*, 1957, **15**, 306–310.

69 CASS, L. K.: Parent-child relationships and delinquency. *J. abnorm. soc. Psychol.*, 1952, **47**, 101–104.

70 CAVA, E. L., and H. L. RAUSH: Identification and the adolescent boy's perception of his father. *J. abnorm. soc. Psychol.*, 1952, **47**, 855–856.

71 CAVAN, R. S.: *The American family.* New York: Crowell, 1953.

72 CENTERS, R., and G. H. BLUMBERG: Social and psychological factors in human procreation: a survey approach. *J. soc. Psychol.*, 1954, **40**, 245–257.

73 CHOROST, S. B.: Parental child-rearing attitudes and their correlates in adolescent hostility. *Genet. Psychol. Monogr.*, 1962, **66**, 49–90.

74 CLARK, A. W., and P. VON SOMMERS: Contradictory demands in family relations and adjustment to school and home. *Hum. Relat.*, 1961, **14**, 97–111.

75 CLIFFORD, E.: Discipline in the home: a controlled observational study of parental practices. *J. genet. Psychol.*, 1959, **95**, 45–82.

76 CODERE, H.: A genealogical study of kinship in the United States. *Psychiatry*, 1955, **18**, 65–79.

77 COHEN, F.: Psychological characteristics of the second child as compared with the first. *Indian J. Psychol.*, 1951, **26**, 79–84.

78 COLE, N. J., O. M. SHAW, J. STENECK, and L. H. TABOROFF: A survey assessment of current parental attitudes and practices in child rearing. *Amer. J. Orthopsychiat.*, 1957, **27**, 815–822.

79 COLEMAN, J. S.: *The adolescent society*. New York: Free Press, 1961.

80 CONNOR, R., T. B. JOHANNIS, and J. WALTERS: Intra-familial conceptions of the good father, good mother, and good child. *J. Home Econ.*, 1954, **46**, 187–191.

81 CONNOR, R., B. J. JOHANNIS, and J. WALTERS: Parent-adolescent relationships. *J. Home Econ.*, 1954, **46**, 183–187.

82 COOPER, J. B., and J. H. LEWIS: Parent evaluation as related to social ideology and academic achievement. *J. genet. Psychol.*, 1962, **101**, 135–143.

83 COOPER, L.: Predisposition toward parenthood: a comparison of male and female students. *Sociol. soc. Res.*, 1957, **42**, 31–36.

84 COSTIN, F.: The effects of child psychology on attitudes toward parent-child relationships. *J. educ. Psychol.*, 1958, **49**, 37–42.

85 COSTIN, F.: Effects of child psychology on students' perceptions of their parents' attitudes toward parent-child relationships. *Child Develpm.*, 1963, **34**, 227–236.

86 COX, F. N.: An assessment of children's attitudes toward parent figures. *Child Develpm.*, 1962, **33**, 821–830.

87 CRANDALL, V. J., and A. PRESTON: Verbally expressed needs and overt maternal behavior. *Child Develpm.*, 1961, **32**, 261–270.

88 CRANDALL, V. J., A. PRESTON, and A. RABSON: Maternal reactions and the development of independence and achievement behavior in young children. *Child Develpm.*, 1960, **31**, 243–251.

89 CRIST, J. R.: High school dating as a behavior system. *Marriage fam. Living*, 1953, **15**, 23–28.

90 CROWTHER, B.: Poor mom. *The New York Times*, Apr. 22, 1962.

91 CUMMINGS, E., and D. M. SCHNEIDER: Sibling solidarity: a property of American kinship. *Amer. Anthropologist*, 1961, **63**, 498–505.

92 CURRIE, E. M.: Family interaction. *Smith Coll. Stud. soc. Wk.*, 1961, **32**, 61–62.

93 DAVIS, C., and M. L. NORTHWAY: Siblings: rivalry or relationships. *Institute for Child Study, University of Toronto*, 1957, **19**, no. 3, 10–13.

94 DENTLER, R. A., and J. G. HUTCHINSON: Socioeconomic versus family membership status as a source of family attitude consensus. *Child Develpm.*, 1961, **32**, 249–254.

95 DESPERT, J. L.: *Children of divorce*. Garden City, N. Y.: Doubleday, 1953.

96 DINITZ, S., R. R. DYNES, and A. C. CLARKE: Preferences for male or female children: traditional or affectional? *Marriage fam. Living*, 1954, **16**, 128–134.

97 DIXON, J. P.: Our changing society: impact on families. *J. Home Econ.*, 1963, **55**, 495–500.

98 DOLAN, C. R.: An investigation of the authoritarian figures in the lives of adolescents as measured by a forced-choice instrument. *Dissert. Abstr.*, 1961, **21**, 2811–2812.

99 DOUVAN, E.: Independence and identity in adolescence. *Children*, 1957, **4**, 186–190.

100 DRAKE, J. T.: Some factors influencing students' attitudes toward older people. *Soc. Forces*, 1957, **35**, 266–271.

101 DRASGOW, J.: Problems of progeny related to paternal education. *J. educ. Psychol.*, 1957, **48**, 521–524.

102 DREGER, R. M., and A. SWEETLAND: Traits of fatherhood as revealed by the factor-analysis of a parent attitude scale. *J. genet. Psychol.*, 1960, **96**, 115–122.

103 DROPPLEMAN, L. F., and E. S. SCHAEFER: Boys' and girls' reports of maternal and paternal behavior. *J. abnorm. soc. Psychol.*, 1963, **67**, 648–654.

104 DUNBAR, F.: Homeostasis during puberty. *Amer. J. Psychiat.*, 1958, **114**, 673–682.

105 DUVALL, E. M.: Conceptions of parenthood. *Amer. J. Sociol.*, 1946, **52**, 193–203.

106 DUVALL, E. M.: *In-laws: pro and con*. New York: Association Press, 1954.

107 DYER, W. G.: A comparison of families of high and low job satisfaction. *Marriage fam. Living*, 1956, **18**, 58–60.

108 ECKHOFF, E., J. GAUSLAR, and A. L. BALDWIN: Parental behavior toward boys and girls. *Acta psychol.*, Amsterdam, 1961, **18**, 85–99.

109 ELDER, G. H.: Structural variations in the child rearing relationship. *Sociometry*, 1962, **25**, 241–262.

110 ELDER, G. H., and C. E. BOWERMAN: Family structure and child-rearing patterns: the effect of family size and family composition. *Amer. sociol. Rev.*, 1963, **28**, 891–905.

111 ELDER, R. A.: Traditional and developmental conceptions of fatherhood. *Marriage fam. Living*, 1949, **11**, 98–100, 106.

112 ELKINS, D.: Some factors related to the

choice-status of ninety eighth-grade children in a school society. *Genet. Psychol. Monogr.,* 1958, **58,** 207–272.

113 ELLIS, A.: Love and family relationships of American college girls. *Amer. J. Sociol.,* 1950, **55,** 550–558.

114 ELLIS, A., and R. M. BEECHLEY: A comparison of child guidance clinic patients coming from large, medium, and small families. *J. genet. Psychol.,* 1951, **79,** 131–144.

115 ELLIS, D., and F. I. NYE: The nagging parent. *Family Life Coordinator,* 1959, **8,** 8–10.

116 EMMERICH, W.: Family role concepts of children ages six to ten. *Child Develpm.,* 1961, **32,** 609–624.

117 EMMERICH, W.: Variations in the parent role as a function of the parent's sex and the child's sex and age. *Merrill-Palmer Quart.,* 1962, **8,** 3–11.

118 EPSTEIN, N. B., and W. A. WESTLEY: Parental interaction as related to the emotional health of children. *Soc. Probl.,* 1960, **8,** 87–92.

119 ESSERT, P. L., I. LORGE, and J. TUCKMAN: Preparation for a constructive approach to later maturity. *Teachers Coll. Rec.,* 1951, **53,** 70–76.

120 *Family Life Coordinator* Report: More married women in the labor force. *Family Life Coordinator,* 1965, **14,** 19.

121 FARBER, B.: Family organization and crisis: maintenance of integration in families with a severely mentally retarded child. *Monogr. Soc. Res. Child Develpm.,* 1960, **25,** no. 1.

122 FARBER, B., and L. S. BLACKMAN: Marital role tensions and number and sex of children. *Amer. sociol. Rev.,* 1956, **21,** 596–601.

123 FARBER, B., and W. C. JENNÉ: Interaction with retarded siblings and life goals of children. *Marriage fam. Living.,* 1963, **25,** 96–98.

124 FARBER, B., and J. C. MC HALE: Marital integration and parents' agreement on satisfaction with their child's behavior. *Marriage fam. Living,* 1959, **21,** 65–69.

125 FERNANDEZ-MARINA, R., E. D. MALDONADO-SIERRA, and R. D. TRENT: Three basic themes in Mexican and Puerto Rican family values. *J. soc. Psychol.,* 1958, **48,** 167–181.

126 FISCHER, A. E.: Sibling relationships with special reference to the problems of the second-born. *J. Pediat.,* 1952, **40,** 254–259.

127 FISHER, H. H.: Family life in children's literature. *Elem. Sch. J.,* 1950, **50,** 516–520.

128 FLEEGE, U. H.: *Self-revelation of the adolescent boy.* Milwaukee: Bruce, 1945.

129 FOSTER, J. E.: Father images: television and ideal. *J. Marriage Fam.,* 1964, **26,** 353–355.

130 FREEDMAN, D. S., R. FREEDMAN, and P. R. WHELPTON: Size of family and preference for children of each sex. *Amer. J. Sociol.,* 1960, **66,** 141–146.

131 FREEMAN, H. E., and M. SHOWELL: The role of the family in the socialization process. *J. soc. Psychol.,* 1953, **37,** 97–101.

132 FREUD, S.: *The standard edition of the complete psychological works of Sigmund Freud.* London: Hogarth, 1953–1962.

133 FRIED, E. G., and K. STERN: The situation of the aged within the family. *Amer. J. Orthopsychiat.,* 1948, **17,** 142–181.

134 GALLAGHER, J. R., and C. D. GALLAGHER: Some comments on growth and development in adolescents. *Yale J. biol. Med.,* 1953, **25,** 334–348.

135 GARDNER, D. B., G. R. HAWKES, and L. G. BURCHINAL: Noncontinuous mothering in infancy and development in later childhood. *Child Develpm.,* 1961, **32,** 225–234.

136 GARDNER, G. E.: Separation of the parents and the emotional life of the child. *Ment. Hyg., N.Y.,* 1956, **40,** 55–64.

137 GARDNER, L. P.: An analysis of children's attitudes toward fathers. *J. genet. Psychol.,* 1947, **70,** 3–28.

138 GEISMAR, L. L., and M. A. LA SORTE: Factors associated with family disorganization. *Marriage fam. Living,* 1963, **25,** 479–481.

139 GESELL, A., F. L. ILG, and L. B. AMES: *Youth: the years from ten to sixteen.* New York: Harper & Row, 1956.

140 GETZELS, J. W., and P. W. JACKSON: Family environment and cognitive style: a study of the sources of highly intelligent and of highly creative adolescents. *Amer. sociol. Rev.,* 1961, **26,** 351–359.

141 GEWIRTZ, J. L.: A factor analysis of some attention-seeking behaviors of young children. *Child Develpm.,* 1956, **27,** 17–36.

142 GILBERT, E.: Allowance, chores, cars, dates are rated high on conflict list. *The New York Times,* Mar. 1, 1963.

143 GLASSER, P. H., and L. N. GLASSER: Role reversal and conflict between aged parents and

their children. *Marriage fam. Living*, 1962, **24**, 46–51.

144 GLENN, H. M.: Attitudes of women regarding gainful employment of married women. *J. Home Econ.*, 1959, **51**, 247–252.

145 GLICK, P. C.: The life cycle of the family. *Marriage fam. Living*, 1955, **17**, 3–9.

146 GLICK, P. C., and E. LANDAU: Age as a factor in marriage. *Amer. sociol. Rev.*, 1950, **15**, 517–529.

147 GLICKMAN, A. S.: Clothing leadership among boys. *Dissert. Abstr.*, 1958, **18**, 682–684.

148 GOODE, W. J.: *After divorce.* New York: Free Press, 1956.

149 GOODE, W. J.: *The family.* Englewood Cliffs, N.J.: Prentice-Hall, 1964.

150 GRATER, H. A.: Behavior standards held by university females and their mothers. *Personnel Guid. J.*, 1960, **38**, 369–372.

151 GRAY, R. M., and T. C. SMITH: Effect of employment on sex differences in attitudes toward the parental family. *Marriage fam. Living*, 1960, **22**, 36–38.

152 GRAY, S. W., and R. KLAUS: The assessment of parental identification. *Genet. Psychol. Monogr.*, 1956, **54**, 87–114.

153 HALLOWITZ, D., and B. STULBERG: The vicious cycle of parent-child relationship breakdown. *Soc. Casewk*, 1959, **40**, 268–275.

154 HANDFORD, N. P.: Mothers of adolescent girls. *Smith Coll. Stud. soc. Wk.*, 1954, **24**, 9–34.

155 HARRIS, D. B.: Parental judgment of responsibility in children and children's adjustment. *J. genet. Psychol.*, 1958, **92**, 161–166.

156 HARRIS, D. B.: Sex differences in the life problems and interests of adolescents, 1935 and 1957. *Child Develpm.*, 1959, **30**, 453–459.

157 HARRIS, D. B., and S. C. TSENG: Children's attitudes toward peers and parents as revealed by sentence completions. *Child Develpm.*, 1957, **28**, 401–411.

158 HAVIGHURST, R. J.: *Human development and education.* New York: Longmans, 1953.

159 HAVIGHURST, R. J.: The leisure activities of the middle-aged. *Amer. J. Sociol.*, 1957, **63**, 152–162.

160 HAVIGHURST, R. J., and R. ALBRECHT: *Older people.* New York: Longmans, 1953.

161 HAVIGHURST, R. J., and A. DAVIS: A comparison of the Chicago and Harvard studies of social class differences in child rearing. *Amer. sociol. Rev.*, 1955, **20**, 438–442.

162 HAWKES, G. R., L. G. BURCHINAL, and B. GARDNER: Size of family and adjustment of children. *Marriage fam. Living*, 1958, **20**, 65–68.

163 HAYES, D. H.: Freedom and fears in the family today. *Understanding the Child*, 1952, **21**, 39–44.

164 HEATHERS, G.: Acquiring dependence and independence: a theoretical orientation. *J. genet. Psychol.*, 1955, **87**, 277–291.

165 HECHINGER, G., and F. M. HECHINGER: *Teenage tyranny.* New York: Morrow, 1963.

166 HEER, D. M.: Husband and wife perceptions of family power structure. *Marriage fam. Living*, 1962, **24**, 65–67.

167 HEILBRUN, A. B.: Social value: social behavior inconsistency and early signs of psychopathology in adolescence. *Child Develpm.*, 1963, **34**, 187–194.

168 HEILBRUN, A. B.: Perceived maternal attitudes, masculinity-femininity of the maternal model and identification as related to incipient psychopathology in adolescent girls. *J. gen. Psychol.*, 1964, **70**, 33–40.

169 HELLERSBERG, E. F.: Food habits of adolescents in relation to family training and present adjustment. *Amer. J. Orthopsychiat.*, 1946, **16**, 34–51.

170 HENRY, A. F.: Family role structure and self blame. *Soc. Forces*, 1956, **35**, 34–38.

171 HENRY, J.: Permissiveness and morality. *Ment. Hyg., N.Y.*, 1961, **45**, 282–287.

172 HENRY, J., and S. WARSON: Family structure and psychic development. *Amer. J. Orthopsychiat.*, 1951, **21**, 59–73.

173 HERBST, P. G.: The measurement of family relationships. *Hum. Relat.*, 1952, **5**, 3–35.

174 HERON, A.: Adolescents and preparation for parenthood. *Brit. J. educ. Psychol.*, 1952, **22**, 173–179.

175 HERTZ, R. F.: 100,000 children tell how children should behave. *This Week Magazine*, July 24, 1955.

176 HESS, R. D., and I. GOLDBLATT: The status of adolescents in American society: a problem in social identity. *Child Develpm.*, 1957, **28**, 459–468.

177 HICKS, H. A., and M. HAYES: Study of the characteristics of 250 junior-high-school children. *Child Develpm.*, 1938, **9**, 219–242.

178 HODGES, A., and B. BALOW: Learning disability in relation to family constellation. *J. educ. Res.*, 1961, **55**, 41–42.

179 HOFFMAN, L. W.: Effects of the employment of mothers on parental power relations and the division of household tasks. *Marriage fam. Living*, 1960, **22**, 27–35.

180 HOFFMAN, L. W.: Effects of maternal employment on the child. *Child Develpm.*, 1961, **32**, 187–197.

181 HOFFMAN, L. W., S. ROSEN, and R. LIPPITT: Parental coerciveness, child autonomy, and child's role at school. *Sociometry*, 1960, **23**, 15–22.

182 IANNI, F. A. J.: The Italo-American teenager. *Ann. Amer. Acad. pol. soc. Sci.*, 1961, **338**, 70–78.

183 IAZZETTA, V. B.: Perceptions of mothers and daughters as they pertain to certain aspects of the self concept. *Dissert. Abstr.*, 1961, **21**, 3360–3361.

184 IRISH, D. P.: Sibling interaction: a neglected aspect in family life research. *Soc. Forces*, 1964, **42**, 279–288.

185 ITKIN, W.: Some relationships between intrafamily attitudes and preparental attitudes toward children. *J. genet. Psychol.*, 1952, **80**, 221–252.

186 ITKIN, W.: Relationships between attitudes toward parents and parents' attitudes toward children. *J. genet. Psychol.*, 1955, **86**, 339–352.

187 JACOBSON, A. H.: Conflict of attitudes toward the roles of the husband and wife in marriage. *Amer. sociol. Rev.*, 1952, **17**, 146–150.

188 JENKINS, W. W.: An experimental study of the relationship of legitimate and illegitimate birth status to school and personal and social adjustment of Negro children. *Amer. J. Sociol.*, 1958, **64**, 169–173.

189 JOHANNIS, T. B.: Participation by fathers, mothers, and teenage sons and daughters in selected child care and control activities. *Family Life Coordinator*, 1957, **6**, 31–32.

190 JOHANNIS, T. B.: Participation by fathers, mothers, and teenage sons and daughters in selected household tasks. *Family Life Coordinator*, 1958, **6**, 61–62.

191 JOHANNIS, T. B., and J. ROLLINS: Attitudes of teen-agers toward family relationships and homogamy of social characteristics in their parents. *Sociol. soc. Res.*, 1959, **43**, 415–420.

192 JOHNSON, P. P.: Conceptions of parenthood held by adolescents. *J. abnorm. soc. Psychol.*, 1952, **47**, 783–789.

193 JOSSELYN, I. M.: Psychology of fatherliness. *Smith Coll. Stud. soc. Wk.*, 1956, **26**, 1–13.

194 JOSSELYN, I. M.: Psychological changes in adolescence. *Children*, 1959, **6**, 43–47.

195 KAGAN, J., B. HOSKEN, and S. WATSON: Child's symbolic conceptualization of parents. *Child Develpm.*, 1961, **32**, 625–636.

196 KAGAN, J., and J. LEMKIN: The child's differential perception of parental attributes. *J. abnorm. soc. Psychol.*, 1960, **61**, 440–447.

197 KAVANAGH, G.: The influence of a stepmother's motivation in marriage upon her stepchild's symptom formation. *Smith Coll. Stud. soc. Wk.*, 1961, **32**, 65–66.

198 KENT, D. P.: Subjective factors in mate selection: an exploratory study. *Sociol. soc. Res.*, 1951, **35**, 391–398.

199 KINSEY, A. C., W. B. POMEROY, and C. E. MARTIN: *Sexual behavior in the human male.* Philadelphia: Saunders, 1948.

200 KITANO, H. H. L.: Inter- and intragenerational differences in maternal attitudes towards child rearing. *J. soc. Psychol.*, 1964, **63**, 215–220.

201 KLAPP, O. E.: Ritual and family solidarity. *Soc. Forces*, 1959, **37**, 212–214.

202 KNOWLES, R. C.: Psychogenic illness and delinquency in children. *Marriage fam. Living*, 1957, **19**, 172–177.

203 KOCH, H. L.: The relations of certain formal attributes of siblings to attitudes held toward each other and toward their parents. *Monogr. Soc. Res. Child Develpm.*, 1960, **25**, no. 4.

204 KOGAN, K. L., and J. K. JACKSON: Conventional sex role stereotypes and actual perception. *Psychol. Rep.*, 1963, **13**, 27–30.

205 KOGAN, N.: Attitudes toward older people: the development of a scale and an examination of correlates. *J. abnorm. soc. Psychol.*, 1961, **62**, 44–54.

206 KOGAN, N., and F. C. SHELTON: Beliefs about "old people": a comparative study of older and younger samples. *J. genet. Psychol.*, 1962, **100**, 93–111.

207 KOGAN, N., and F. C. SHELTON: Images of "old people" and "people in general" in an older sample. *J. genet. Psychol.*, 1962, **100**, 3–21.

208 KOHN, M. L.: Social class and parent-child

relationships: an interpretation. *Amer. J. Sociol.*, 1963, **68,** 471–480.

209 KOHN, M. L., and E. E. CARROLL: Social class and the allocation of parental responsibilities. *Sociometry,* 1960, **23,** 372–392.

210 KOHN, M. L., and J. A. CLAUSEN: Parental authority behavior and schizophrenia. *Amer. J. Orthopsychiat.,* 1956, **26,** 297–313.

211 KOLLER, M. R.: Studies of three-generation households. *Marriage fam. Living,* 1954, **16,** 203–206.

212 KOPPITZ, E. M.: Relationships between some background factors and children's interpersonal attitudes. *J. genet. Psychol.,* 1957, **91,** 119–129.

213 KOSA, J., L. D. RACHIELE, and C. O. SCHOMMER: Sharing the home with relatives. *Marriage fam. Living,* 1960, **22,** 129–131.

214 LAMBERT, W. W., L. M. TRIANDIS, and M. WOLF: Some correlates of beliefs in the malevolence and benevolence of supernatural beings: a cross societal study. *J. abnorm. soc. Psychol.,* 1959, **58,** 162–169.

215 LANDIS, J. T.: The trauma of children when parents divorce. *Marriage fam. Living,* 1960, **22,** 7–13.

216 LANDIS, J. T.: A comparison of children from divorced and non-divorced unhappy marriages. *Family Life Coordinator,* 1962, **11,** 61–65.

217 LANDIS, J. T.: A re-examination of the role of the father as an index of family integration. *Marriage fam. Living,* 1962, **24,** 122–128.

218 LANDIS, J. T.: Social correlates of divorce and nondivorce among the unhappy married. *Marriage fam. Living,* 1963, **25,** 178–180.

219 LANDIS, P. H.: *Adolescence and youth: the process of maturing.* 2d ed. New York: McGraw-Hill, 1952.

220 LANDIS, P. H.: The ordering and forbidding technique and teen-age adjustment. *Sch. Soc.,* 1954, **80,** 105–106.

221 LANDIS, P. H.: Teenage adjustments in large and small families. *J. nat. Ass. Women Deans and Counselors,* 1955, **18,** 60–63.

222 LANDIS, P. H.: The families that produce adjusted adolescents. *Clearing House,* 1955, **29,** 537–540.

223 LANDIS, P. H.: Research on teen-age dating. *Marriage fam. Living,* 1960, **22,** 266–269.

224 LANE, B.: Attitudes of youth toward the aged. *J. Marriage Fam.,* 1964, **26,** 229–231.

225 LASKO, J. K.: Parent-child relationships: report from the Fels Research Institute. *Amer. J. Orthopsychiat.,* 1952, **22,** 300–304.

226 LASKO, J. K.: Parent behavior toward first and second children. *Genet. Psychol. Monogr.,* 1954, **49,** 97–137.

227 LAW, S.: The mother of the happy child. *Smith Coll. Stud. soc. Wk.,* 1954, **25,** 1–27.

228 LAZAR, E. A., and C. KLEIN: What makes parents repulsive? *The New York Times,* Feb. 7, 1965.

229 LE MASTERS, E. E.: Social class mobility and family integration. *Marriage fam. Living,* 1954, **16,** 226–232.

230 LE MASTERS, E. E.: Parenthood as a crisis. *Marriage fam. Living,* 1957, **19,** 352–355.

231 LEVIN, P. L.: Putting down father. *The New York Times,* Mar. 21, 1965.

232 LICCIONE, J. V.: The changing family relationships of adolescent girls. *J. abnorm. soc. Psychol.,* 1955, **51,** 421–426.

233 LINDEN, M. E.: The older person in the family. *Soc. Casewk,* 1956, **37,** 75–81.

234 LLOYD, R. G.: Parent-youth conflicts of college students. *Sociol. soc. Res.,* 1952, **36,** 227–230.

235 LONGSTRETH, L. E., and R. E. RICE: Perceptions of parental behavior and identification with parents by three groups of boys differing in school adjustment. *J. educ. Psychol.,* 1964, **55,** 144–151.

236 LU, Y-C.: Parent-child relationships and marital roles. *Amer. sociol. Rev.,* 1952, **17,** 357–361.

237 LUCAS, C. M., and J. E. HORROCKS: An experimental approach to the analysis of adolescent needs. *Child Develpm.,* 1960, **31,** 479–487.

238 MAAS, H. S.: Some social class differences in the family systems and group relations of pre- and early adolescents. *Child Develpm.,* 1951, **22,** 145–152.

239 MACCOBY, E. E.: Children and working mothers. *Children,* 1958, **5,** 83–89.

240 MACFARLANE, J., L. ALLEN, and M. P. HONZIK: *A developmental study of the behavior problems of normal children between twenty-one months and fourteen years.* Berkeley, Calif.: University of California Press, 1954.

241 MAGARY, L.: Severe disturbances in young women reflecting damaging mother-daughter relationships. *Soc. Casewk*, 1959, **40**, 202–207.

242 MARMOR, J.: Psychological trends in American family relationships. *Marriage fam. Living*, 1951, **13**, 145–147.

243 MATSUMOTO, M., and H. T. SMITH: Japanese and American children's perceptions of parents. *J. genet. Psychol.*, 1961, **98**, 83–88.

244 MAXWELL, P. H., R. CONNOR, and J. WALTERS: Family member perception of parent role performance. *Merrill-Palmer Quart.*, 1961, **7**, 31–37.

245 MC ARTHUR, A.: Developmental tasks and parent-adolescent conflict. *Marriage fam. Living*, 1962, **24**, 189–191.

246 MC CORD, J., W. MC CORD, and E. THURBER: Some effects of paternal absence on male children. *J. abnorm. soc. Psychol.*, 1962, **64**, 361–369.

247 MC CORD, J., W. MC CORD, and E. THURBER: Effects of maternal employment on lower-class boys. *J. abnorm. soc. Psychol.*, 1963, **67**, 177–182.

248 MC FARLAND, M. B., and J. B. REINHART: The development of motherliness. *Children*, 1959, **6**, 48–52.

249 MC GUIRE, C.: Family life in lower and middle class homes. *Marriage fam. Living*, 1952, **14**, 1–6.

250 MC GUIRE, C.: Conforming, mobile, and divergent families. *Marriage fam. Living*, 1954, **16**, 109–115.

251 MC GUIRE, C., and G. D. WHITE: Social-class influences on discipline at school. *Educ. Leadership*, 1957, **14**, 229–231, 234–236.

252 MEAD, M.: The impact of culture on personality development in the United States today. *Understanding the Child*, 1951, **20**, 17–18.

253 MEAD, M.: *Male and female*. New York: Morrow, 1952.

254 MEAD, M.: The changing American family. *Children*, 1963, **10**, 173–174.

255 MEDINNUS, G. R.: The relation between several parent measures and the child's early adjustment to school. *J. educ. Psychol.*, 1961, **52**, 153–156.

256 MEEK, L. S.: Effects of maternal employment on children: evidence from research. *Child Develpm.*, 1960, **31**, 749–782.

257 MERRY, F. K., and R. V. MERRY: *The first two decades of life*. 2d ed. New York: Harper & Row, 1958.

258 MEYERS, C. E.: Emancipation of adolescents from parental control. *Nerv. Child*, 1946, **5**, 251–262.

259 MOGEY, J. M.: A century of declining parental authority. *Marriage fam. Living*, 1957, **19**, 234–239.

260 MONAHAN, T. P.: Broken homes by age of delinquent children. *J. soc. Psychol.*, 1960, **51**, 387–397.

261 MORROW, W. R., and R. C. WILSON: Family relations of bright high-achieving and underachieving high school boys. *Child Develpm.*, 1961, **32**, 501–510.

262 MOTT, S. M.: Concept of mother: study of four- and five-year-old children. *Child Develpm.*, 1954, **25**, 99–106.

263 MUSSEN, P. H., and J. KAGAN: Group conformity and perceptions of parents. *Child Develpm.*, 1958, **29**, 57–60.

264 MUSSEN, P. H., H. B. YOUNG, R. GADDINI, and L. MORANTE: The influence of the father-son relationships on adolescent personality and attitudes. *J. child Psychol. Psychiat.*, 1963, **4**, 3–16.

265 NAKAMURA, C. Y.: The relationship between children's expressions of hostility and methods of discipline exercised by dominant overprotective parents. *Child Develpm.*, 1959, **30**, 109–117.

266 NEUGARTEN, B. L., and K. K. WEINSTEIN: The changing American grandparent. *J. Marriage Fam.*, 1964, **26**, 199–204.

267 *New York Times* Report: New version urged for Mother Goose. *The New York Times*, Apr. 30, 1954.

268 *New York Times* Report: Suburban wives join job hunters. *The New York Times*, Apr. 3, 1960.

269 *New York Times* Report: Autonomy found to be chief goal of bright students. *The New York Times*, Oct. 19, 1964.

270 *New York Times* Report: Few teen-age marriages turn out well, survey says. *The New York Times*, Apr. 14, 1965.

271 NYE, F. I.: Adolescent-parent adjustment: rurality as a variable. *Rur. Sociol.*, 1950, **15**, 334–339.

272 NYE, F. I.: Adolescent-parent adjustment:

socio-economic level as a variable. *Amer. sociol. Rev.*, 1951, **16**, 341–349.

273 NYE, F. I.: Adolescent-parent adjustment: age, sex, sibling number, broken homes, and employed mothers as variables. *Marriage fam. Living*, 1952, **14**, 327–332.

274 NYE, F. I.: The rejected parent and delinquency. *Marriage fam. Living*, 1956, **18**, 291–300.

275 NYE, F. I.: Child adjustment in broken and unhappy unbroken homes. *Marriage fam. Living*, 1957, **19**, 356–361.

276 NYE, F. I.: Employment status of mothers and adjustment of adolescent children. *Marriage fam. Living*, 1959, **21**, 240–244.

277 NYE, F. I.: Employment status of mothers and marital conflict, permanence, and happiness. *Soc. Probl.*, 1959, **6**, 260–267.

278 NYE, F. I.: Maternal employment and marital interaction: some contingent conditions. *Soc. Forces*, 1961, **40**, 113–119.

279 OLSEN, M. E.: Distribution of family responsibilities and social stratification. *Marriage fam. Living*, 1960, **22**, 60–65.

280 ORT, R. S.: A study of role-conflict as related to class levels. *J. abnorm. soc. Psychol.*, 1952, **47**, 425–432.

281 PARSONS, T.: The kinship system in the contemporary United States. *Amer. Anthropologist*, 1943, **45**, 22–28.

282 PAYNE, D. E., and P. H. MUSSEN: Parent-child relations and father identification among adolescent boys. *J. abnorm. soc. Psychol.*, 1956, **52**, 358–362.

283 PAYNE, R.: Adolescents' attitudes toward the working wife. *Marriage fam. Living*, 1956, **18**, 345–348.

284 PECK, R. F.: Family patterns correlated with adolescent personality structure. *J. abnorm. soc. Psychol.*, 1958, **57**, 347–350.

285 PECK, R. F., and R. J. HAVIGHURST: *The psychology of character development.* New York: Wiley, 1960.

286 PENISTON, D. H.: The importance of "death education" in family life. *Family Life Coordinator*, 1962, **11**, 15–18.

287 PERRY, J. B.: The mother substitutes of employed mothers: an exploratory inquiry. *Marriage fam. Living*, 1961, **23**, 362–367.

288 PERRY, J. B., and E. H. PFUHL: Adjustment of children in "solo" and "remarriage"

homes. *Marriage fam. Living*, 1963, **25**, 221–223.

289 PETERSON, D. R., W. C. BECKER, D. J. SHOEMAKER, Z. LURIA, and L. A. HELLMER: Child behavior problems and parental attitudes. *Child Develpm.*, 1961, **32**, 151–162.

290 PETERSON, E. T.: The impact of maternal employment on the mother-daughter relationship. *Marriage fam. Living*, 1961, **23**, 355–361.

291 PLATT, H., G. JURGENSEN, and S. B. CHOROST: Comparison of child-bearing attitudes of mothers and fathers of emotionally disturbed adolescents. *Child Develpm.*, 1962, **23**, 117–122.

292 PODOLSKY, E.: The father's occupation and the child's emotions. *Understanding the Child*, 1954, **23**, 22–25.

293 PODOLSKY, E.: The emotional problems of the stepchild. *Ment. Hyg.*, N.Y., 1955, **39**, 49–53.

294 POFFENBERGER, T.: A research note on father-child relations and father viewed as a negative figure. *Child Develpm.*, 1959, **30**, 489–492.

295 POLLOCK, O.: Some challenges to the American family. *Children*, 1964, **11**, 19–20.

296 PORTER, B. M.: The relationship between marital adjustment and parental acceptance of children. *J. Home Econ.*, 1955, **47**, 157–164.

297 PORTER, L. G., and C. L. STACEY: A study of the relationships between self-ratings and parent-ratings for a group of college students. *J. clin. Psychol.*, 1956, **12**, 243–248.

298 POWELL, K. S.: Maternal employment in relation to family life. *Marriage fam. Living*, 1961, **23**, 350–355.

299 POWELL, M.: Age and sex differences in degree of conflict within certain areas of psychological adjustment. *Psychol. Monogr.*, 1955, **69**, no. 2.

300 PRESSEY, S. L., and A. W. JONES: 1923–1953 and 20–60 age changes in moral codes, anxieties, and interests, as shown by the "X-O Tests." *J. Psychol.*, 1955, **39**, 485–502.

301 PSATHAS, G.: Ethnicity, social class, and adolescent independence from parental control. *Amer. sociol. Rev.*, 1957, **22**, 415–423.

302 PUNKE, H. H.: High-school youth and family quarrels. *Sch. Soc.*, 1943, **58**, 507–511.

303 RADKE-YARROW, M., P. SCOTT, L. DE LEEUW,

and c. heinig: Child-rearing in families of working and nonworking mothers. *Sociometry*, 1962, **25**, 122–140.

304 rainwater, l.: Social status differences in the family relationships of German men. *Marriage fam. Living*, 1962, **24**, 12–17.

305 ramsey, c. e., and l. nelson: Changes in values and attitudes toward the family. *Amer. sociol. Rev.*, 1956, **21**, 605–609.

306 rapp, d. w.: Child-rearing attitudes of mothers in Germany and the United States. *Child Develpm.*, 1961, **32**, 669–678.

307 reiss, p. j.: The extended kinship system: correlates of and attitudes on frequency of interaction. *Marriage fam. Living*, 1962, **24**, 333–339.

308 remmers, h. h., and d. h. radler: *The American teenager.* Indianapolis: Bobbs-Merrill, 1957.

309 robertson, w. o.: An investigation of maternal concerns by mail survey. *Child Develpm.*, 1961, **32**, 423–436.

310 robey, a., r. j. rosenwald, j. e. snell, and r. e. lee: The runaway girl: a reaction to family stress. *Amer. J. Orthopsychiat.*, 1964, **34**, 762–767.

311 robins, l. n., and m. tomanec: Closeness of blood relatives outside the immediate family. *Marriage fam. Living*, 1962, **24**, 340–346.

312 rollins, m. a.: Monetary contributions of wives to family income in 1920 and 1960. *Marriage fam. Living*, 1963, **25**, 226–227.

313 rosen, b. c.: Race, ethnicity, and achievement syndrome. *Amer. sociol. Rev.*, 1959, **24**, 47–60.

314 rosenbaum, m.: Psychological effects on the child raised by an older sibling. *Amer. J. Orthopsychiat.*, 1963, **33**, 515–520.

315 rosenthal, m. j., m. finkelstein, i. ni, and r. e. robertson: A study of mother-child relationships in the emotional disorders of children. *Genet. Psychol. Monogr.*, 1959, **60**, 65–116.

316 roucek, j. s.: Age as a prestige factor. *Sociol. soc. Res.*, 1958, **42**, 349–352.

317 rouman, j.: School children's problems as related to parental factors. *J. educ. Psychol.*, 1956, **50**, 105–112.

318 roy, k.: Parents' attitudes toward their children. *J. Home Econ.*, 1950, **42**, 652–653.

319 roy, p.: Maternal employment and adolescent roles: rural and urban differentials. *Marriage fam. Living*, 1961, **23**, 340–349.

320 russell, i. l.: Behavior problems of children from broken and intact homes. *J. educ. Psychol.*, 1957, **31**, 124–129.

321 sampson, e. e.: Birth order, need achievement and conformity. *J. abnorm. soc. Psychol.*, 1962, **64**, 155–159.

322 schacter, s.: Birth order and sociometric choice. *J. abnorm. soc. Psychol.*, 1964, **68**, 453–456.

323 schaefer, e. s., and n. bayley: Consistency of maternal behavior from infancy to preadolescence. *J. abnorm. soc. Psychol.*, 1960, **61**, 1–6.

324 schmuck, r.: Sex of sibling, birth order position and female dispositions to conform in two-child families. *Child Develpm.*, 1963, **34**, 913–918.

325 schoeppe, a., e. a. haggard, and r. j. havighurst: Some factors affecting sixteen-year-olds' success in five developmental tasks. *J. abnorm. soc. Psychol.*, 1953, **48**, 42–52.

326 schwartz, e. k.: A psychoanalytic study of the fairy tale. *Amer. J. Psychother.*, 1956, **10**, 740–762.

327 sears, r. r., e. e. maccoby, and h. levin: *Patterns of child rearing.* New York: Harper & Row, 1957.

328 secord, p. f., and s. m. jourard: Mother-concepts and judgment of young women's faces. *J. abnorm. soc. Psychol.*, 1956, **52**, 246–250.

329 serot, n. m., and r. c. teevan: Perception of the parent-child relationship and its relation to child adjustment. *Child Develpm.*, 1961, **32**, 373–378.

330 sharp, l. j.: Employment status of mothers and some aspects of mental illness. *Amer. sociol. Rev.*, 1960, **25**, 714–717.

331 siegel, a. e., and m. b. haas: The working mother: a review of research. *Child Develpm.*, 1963, **34**, 513–542.

332 siegel, a. e., l. m. stolz, e. a. hitchcock, and j. adamson: Dependence and independence in children of working mothers. *Child Develpm.*, 1959, **30**, 533–546.

333 sklarew, b. h.: The relationship of early separation from parents to differences in adjustment in adolescent boys and girls. *Psychiatry*, 1959, **22**, 399–405.

334 slocum, w. l.: Some factors associated

with happiness in unbroken homes. *Family Life Coordinator*, 1958, **6**, 35–39.

335 SLOMAN, S. S.: Emotional problems in "planned for" children. *Amer. J. Orthopsychiat.*, 1948, **18**, 523–528.

336 SMITH, W. C.: Remarriage and the stepchild. In M. Fishbein and R. J. R. Kennedy (eds.), *Modern marriage and family living*. Fair Lawn, N.J.: Oxford, 1957, pp. 457–475.

337 SOLOMON, D.: Adolescents' decisions: a comparison of influence from parents with that from other sources. *Marriage fam. Living*, 1961, **23**, 393–395.

338 STAGNER, R.: *Psychology of personality*. 3d ed. New York: McGraw-Hill, 1961.

339 STAUDT, V. M.: Attitudes of college students toward marriage and related problems: II. Age, educational, familial, and economic factors in marriage. *J. Psychol.*, 1952, **34**, 95–106.

340 STENDLER, C. B.: The learning of certain secondary drives by Parisian and American children. *Marriage fam. Living*, 1954, **16**, 195–200.

341 STEPHENS, W. N.: Judgments by social workers on boys and mothers in fatherless families. *J. genet. Psychol.*, 1961, **99**, 59–64.

342 STÖCKLE, O.: The family with many children and its significance for social education. *Heilpädag. Werkbl.*, 1954, **23**, 144–149.

343 STOLZ, H. R., and L. M. STOLZ: *Somatic development in adolescent boys*. New York: Macmillan, 1951.

344 STOLZ, L. M.: Effects of maternal employment on children: evidence from research. *Child Develpm.*, 1960, **31**, 749–782.

345 STOLZ, L. M., et al.: *Father relations with war-born children*. Stanford, Calif.: Stanford, 1954.

346 STONE, C., and P. H. LANDIS: An approach to authority pattern in parent-teenage relationships. *Rural Sociol.*, 1953, **18**, 233–242.

347 STONE, C. L.: Three-generation influences on teen-agers' conceptions of family culture patterns and parent-child relationships. *Marriage fam. Living*, 1962, **24**, 287–288.

348 STONE, C. L.: Family recreation: a parental dilemma. *Family Life Coordinator*, 1963, **12**, 85–87.

349 STOODLEY, B. H.: Mother role as a focus for some family problems. *Marriage fam. Living*, 1952, **14**, 13–16.

350 STOUT, I. W., and G. LANGDON: A report on follow-up interviews with parents of well-adjusted children. *J. educ. Sociol.*, 1953, **26**, 434–442.

351 STRANG, R.: *The adolescent views himself*. New York: McGraw-Hill, 1957.

352 STRAUS, M. A.: Conjugal power structure and adolescent personality. *Marriage fam. Living*, 1962, **24**, 17–25.

353 STRAUSS, B. V.: The dynamics of ordinal position effects. *Quart. J. child Behav.*, 1951, **3**, 133–145.

354 STRONG, L.: Family living—can it be taught? *The New York Times*, Oct. 20, 1963.

355 STRYKER, S.: Relationships of married offspring and parent. *Amer. J. Sociol.*, 1956, **62**, 308–319.

356 STUBBEFIELD, R. L.: Children's emotional problems aggravated by family moves. *Amer. J. Orthopsychiat.*, 1955, **25**, 120–126.

357 SUPER, D. E.: A theory of vocational development. *Amer. Psychologist*, 1953, **8**, 185–190.

358 SUSSMAN, M. B.: The isolated nuclear family: fact or fiction. *Soc. Probl.*, 1959, **6**, 333–340.

359 SUTTON-SMITH, B., B. G. ROSENBERG, and E. F. MORAN: Historical changes in the freedom with which children express themselves on personality inventories. *J. genet. Psychol.*, 1961, **99**, 309–315.

360 SYMONDS, P. M.: Sex differences in the life problems and interests of adolescents. *Sch. Soc.*, 1936, **43**, 751–752.

361 SYMONDS, P. M.: *The dynamics of parent-child relationships*. New York: Teachers College, Columbia, 1949.

362 TASCH, R. J.: The role of the father in the family. *J. exp. Educ.*, 1952, **20**, 319–361.

363 TASCH, R. J.: Interpersonal perceptions of fathers and mothers. *J. genet. Psychol.*, 1957, **87**, 59–65.

364 TEMPLETON, J. A.: The influence of family size on some aspects of teen-agers' attitudes, behavior and perceptions of home life. *Family Life Coordinator*, 1962, **11**, 51–57.

365 TERMAN, L. M.: Correlates of orgasm adequacy in a group of 556 wives. *J. Psychol.*, 1951, **32**, 115–172.

366 TOMAN, W.: *Family constellation*. New York: Springer Publishing Co., 1961.

367 TUCKMAN, J., and I. LORGE: Attitude toward aging of individuals with experience with the aged. *J. genet. Psychol.*, 1958, **92**, 199–204.

368 TUCKMAN, J., I. LORGE, and G. A. SPOONER: The effect of family environment on attitudes toward old people and the older worker. *J. soc. Psychol.*, 1953, **38**, 207–218.

369 TUMA, E., and N. LIVSON: Family socioeconomic status and adolescent attitudes to authority. *Child Develpm.*, 1960, **31**, 387–399.

370 TYLER, L. E.: The development of "vocational interests": I. The organization of likes and dislikes in ten-year-old children. *J. genet. Psychol.*, 1955, **86**, 33–34.

371 *U.S. News & World Report:* Why young people "go bad." *U.S. News & World Report*, Apr. 26, 1965, pp. 56–62.

372 VAN EGMOND, E.: Socialization process and education. *Rev. educ. Res.*, 1961, **31**, 80–90.

373 VINCENT, C. E.: The loss of parents and psychosomatic illness. *Sociol. soc. Res.*, 1955, **39**, 404–408.

374 VINCENT, E. L., and P. C. MARTIN: *Human psychological development.* New York: Ronald, 1961.

375 VOLLMER, H.: The grandmother: a problem in child rearing. *Amer. J. Orthopsychiat.*, 1937, **7**, 378–382.

376 VON MEHRING, F. H.: Professional and nonprofessional women as mothers. *J. soc. Psychol.*, 1955, **42**, 21–34.

377 WALLACH, M. A., D. N. ULRICH, and M. B. GRUNEBAUM: Relationship of family disturbance to cognitive difficulties in a learning-problem child. *J. consult. Psychol.*, 1960, **24**, 355–360.

378 WALLER, W., and R. HILL: *The family: a dynamic interpretation.* New York: Holt, 1951.

379 WALLIN, P.: Marital happiness of parents and their children's attitudes to marriage. *Amer. sociol. Rev.*, 1954, **19**, 20–23.

380 WALSH, A. M.: *Self-concepts of bright boys with learning difficulties.* New York: Teachers College, Columbia, 1956.

381 WARNATH, C. F.: The relation of family cohesiveness and adolescent independence to social effectiveness. *Marriage fam. Living*, 1955, **17**, 346–348.

382 WATSON, G.: Some personality differences in children related to strict or permissive parental discipline. *J. Psychol.*, 1957, **44**, 227–249.

383 WEBSTER, H.: Changes in attitude during college. *J. educ. Psychol.*, 1958, **49**, 109–117.

384 WEIL, M. W.: An analysis of the factors influencing married women's actual or planned work participation. *Amer. sociol. Rev.*, 1961, **26**, 91–96.

385 WERNER, A. A.: Sex behavior and problems of the climacteric. In M. Fishbein and E. W. Burgess (eds.), *Successful marriage.* Rev. ed. Garden City, N.Y.: Doubleday, 1955, pp. 475–490.

386 WESTLEY, W. A., and N. B. EPSTEIN: Family structure and emotional health: a case study approach. *Marriage fam. Living*, 1960, **22**, 25–27.

387 WILLIAMS, E. I., and C. D. WILLIAMS: Relationships between authoritarian attitudes of college students, estimates of parents' attitudes, and actual parental attitudes. *J. soc. Psychol.*, 1963, **61**, 43–48.

388 WILLIAMSON, R. C.: Socio-economic factors and marital adjustments in an urban setting. *Amer. sociol. Rev.*, 1954, **19**, 213–216.

389 WILSON, M. S.: Do college girls conform to the standards of their parents? *Marriage fam. Living*, 1953, **15**, 207–208.

390 WINCH, R. F.: The study of personality in the family setting. *Soc. Forces*, 1950, **28**, 310–316.

391 WINCH, R. F.: Further data and observations on the Oedipus hypothesis: the consequences of an inadequate hypothesis. *Amer. sociol. Rev.*, 1951, **16**, 784–795.

392 WOOLF, D. M.: A study of some relationships between home adjustment and the behavior of junior-college students. *J. soc. Psychol.*, 1943, **17**, 275–288.

393 WRIGHT, H. F.: Psychological development in Midwest. *Child Develpm.*, 1956, **27**, 265–286.

394 WYLIE, H. L., and R. A. DELGADO: A pattern of mother-son relationship involving the absence of the father. *Amer. J. Orthopsychiat.*, 1959, **29**, 644–649.

395 YOUNG, K.: What strong family ties mean to our society. *Soc. Casewk*, 1953, **34**, 323–329.

396 YOURGLICH, A.: Explorations in sociological study of sibling systems. *Family Life Coordinator*, 1964, **13**, 91–94.

397 ZUNICH, M.: Relationship between maternal behavior and attitudes toward children. *J. genet. Psychol.*, 1962, **100**, 155–165.

398 ZUNICH, M.: Attitudes of lower-class families. *J. soc. Psychol.*, 1964, **63**, 367–371.

CHAPTER 16
personality changes
in adolescence

The adolescent has two important reasons for wanting to improve his personality. First, he has discovered from childhood experiences how important a role personality plays in social adjustments. As Coleman (92) has pointed out:

> The importance of having a good personality, or, what is a little different, "being

friendly" or "being nice to the other kids" in their adolescent cultures is something that adults often fail to realize. Adults often forget how "personality-oriented" children are: they have not yet moved into the world of cold impersonality in which many adults live.

The adolescent's second reason for wanting

to improve his personality is his dissatisfaction with his personality as it is. During the months of withdrawal from the social group, the pubescent becomes self-centered and introverted. As he takes stock of himself, of his changing body and feelings, and of the successes and failures he has made up to date, he is often dissatisfied with himself. This is more true of boys than of girls (10,11,12,145,389,440).

The more aware adolescents are of the "marketable value" of personality, the stronger is their motivation to bring about improvements (280). Dissatisfaction generally reaches its peak between the ages of 15 and 16 years. After that both boys and girls become increasingly more satisfied with the improvements they have been able to effect in their personalities (108,310). This trend in increased self-satisfaction is illustrated in Figure 16–1. However, there is evidence that adolescents from the higher socioeconomic groups show greater self-satisfaction than do those from the lower socioeconomic groups (213).

The improvement is more often in the form of *quantitative* than of *qualitative* changes. Traits that are undesirable improve and become less undesirable; those that are desirable become more so. A radical change, resulting from replacing one trait by another—qualitative change— is far less likely to occur. This is true in spite of strong mo-

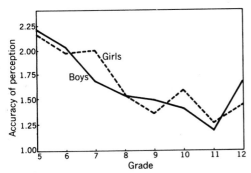

FIGURE 16–1 There is a trend toward increased accuracy of perception by the adolescent with improvements made in his personality. (Adapted from J. E. deJung and E. F. Gardner: The accuracy of self-role perception: a developmental study. *J. exp. Educ.*, 1962, **31**, 27–41. Used by permission.)

tivation on the adolescent's part to get rid of socially undesirable characteristics and to replace them with traits that everyone admires (257,438,459).

obstacles to personality improvement

In spite of strong motivation to improve personality during adolescence, many obstacles stand in the way. Some of these obstacles are of the adolescent's own making; others are beyond his control. Of the many obstacles to improvement, the following are the most common and most troublesome.

TRADITIONAL BELIEFS ABOUT PERSONALITY

There is a widely held traditional belief that the individual *inherits* his personality from his parents and other ancestors, just as he does his eye color or other physical features. This belief is expressed in the saying, "He is a chip off the old block." Popular justification for this belief is that children resemble their parents in many of their personality characteristics, just as their parents resemble the grandparents. Because of this similarity, it is taken for granted that heredity has been responsible. The possibility that the similarity is due to learning is often overlooked (15,81,171).

It is a well-established scientific fact that children learn many of their behavior patterns through imitation of those with whom they are constantly associated. A boy, for example, who regards a father or older brother as his hero, will imitate his aggressiveness or shyness or stinginess, regardless of whether or not these are socially approved traits. They are characteristics of *his hero* and that is all that is important to the child (5,350,407).

That personality characteristics are a product of learning more than of inheritance has been emphasized by Carlson and Stieglitz (76):

> We are what we are today, to a great degree, because of what happened to us in our yesterdays, and no two people have had identical sequences of yesterdays. Fur-

thermore, the effect of all these experiences increases with age, because they accumulate.

The serious obstacle to improvement that comes from the belief that personality is inherited is that it stifles motivation. Believing that what one is born with is there for life encourages the adolescent who wants to improve his personality to feel that there is nothing he can do about it.

Contradictory as it may sound, there is another widespread traditional belief that personality undergoes changes, often radical in nature, at the times in life when the body undergoes radical changes. These times are at puberty and the climacteric. Unquestionably there are changes in personality at these times. But all evidence points to the fact that the changes are the result of environmental and social factors rather than of hereditary trends. The way in which the pubescent child is treated by parents, teachers, and peers is responsible for his personality changes. This is emphasized by studies of deviant maturers who are treated in accordance with their physical age rather than their chronological age. Refer to pages 62 to 67 for a more complete discussion of the effect of deviant maturing on personality.

It is commonly believed that changes in personality accompanying physical changes will always be in the direction of improvement. This belief is expressed in the common saying, "He will *outgrow* that when he is older." The seriousness of accepting this traditional belief is that it weakens the adolescent's motivation to try to make changes. Similarly, parents and teachers who hold this belief will literally fold their hands and do nothing. This allows undesirable personality traits to become reinforced with repetition.

PERSONALITY STEREOTYPES

In every cultural group, there are widely held beliefs that certain personality characteristics are associated with certain racial, religious, and occupational groups, with members of the two sexes, and with certain physical features. These stereotypes may associate desirable or undesirable personality characteristics with certain "types" of peo-

ple. When these beliefs are accepted, there is a tendency to believe that *all* people belonging to a particular group are "typical" in that they all have the same traits (390).

English people, for example, are believed to be typically cool and reserved; Latins, excitable; Irish, pugnacious; and Swedes, stolid (68,402). As has already been mentioned (see pages 358 to 360), personality stereotypes are also associated with people in certain occupational groups. The personality syndrome believed to be characteristic of the artist contains such qualities as creativity, sensitivity to the feelings of others, a tendency toward depression and cycloid disposition, introversion accompanied by a tendency to harbor intense feelings of guilt, and emphasis on aesthetic values (51, 122,327).

Within the family, there are stereotypes of the personalities of different family members. The firstborn child is characterized as uncertain, mistrustful, shrewd, stingy, and wealthy; the youngest is believed to have a personality syndrome which includes such traits as feelings of security, spontaneity, a good-natured and confiding disposition, generosity, stupidity, naïvité, softness, and a fondness for animals. Because of his stupidity and generosity, he is thought of as the "poor" member of the family (189,411).

Unquestionably the most widely held stereotypes of personality are those associated with physical features—"physiognomy." For centuries, it has been believed that certain physical features are so universally associated with certain personality characteristics that you can judge a person's personality accurately by a careful observation of his physical features. However, some physical features are believed to be more important than others in judging personality traits. The skin texture, height of forehead, fullness of lips, quality of voice, and facial tension, for example, are used more in judging personality than are the width of the face, eyelid visibility, or height of eyebrows (35,291,402,414,416,417). Figure 16–2 shows some of the widely held personality types associated with certain physical features.

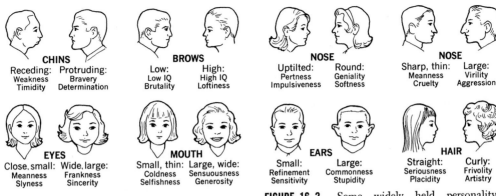

All of these notions are wrong!

CHINS
Receding: Protruding:
Weakness | Bravery
Timidity | Determination

BROWS
Low: | High:
Low IQ | High IQ
Brutality | Loftiness

NOSE
Uptilted: | Round:
Pertness | Geniality
Impulsiveness | Softness

NOSE
Sharp, thin: | Large:
Meanness | Virility
Cruelty | Aggression

EYES
Close, small: | Wide, large:
Meanness | Frankness
Slyness | Sincerity

MOUTH
Small, thin: | Large, wide:
Coldness | Sensuousness
Selfishness | Generosity

EARS
Small: | Large:
Refinement | Commonness
Sensitivity | Stupidity

HAIR
Straight: | Curly:
Seriousness | Frivolity
Placidity | Artistry

FIGURE 16–2 Some widely held personality "types" associated with certain physical features. (Adapted from A. Scheinfeld: *The human heredity handbook*. Philadelphia: Lippincott, 1956. Used by permission.)

Effects on Personality Improvement An adolescent who accepts these cultural stereotypes comes to think of himself in terms of the stereotype associated with his identity. If he has a sloping chin, for example, he thinks of himself as having a "weak will," according to the stereotype. Or if one or both of his parents are from Ireland, he will believe that he is the "pugnacious type." While not specifically claimed, it is *assumed* that the personality traits associated with a stereotype are hereditary. As such, they are a part of the endowment the adolescent receives from his parents and other ancestors.

Consequently, with the acceptance of stereotypes about personality comes the acceptance of the belief that it is difficult if not impossible to change a trait that belongs to the stereotyped syndrome. This weakens the motivation to try to improve the personality regardless of how dissatisfied the adolescent may be. If he likes the traits associated with the stereotype, no real harm will come from accepting it. But if he dislikes the traits, he will be dissatisfied with himself and with the thought that he cannot change his hereditary endowment.

PERSONALITY IDEAL

Just as every *child* has a concept of what he wants to look like when he grows up, so he has a concept of his grown-up personality. The child's concept of his personality is likely to be highly romanticized and unrealistic. Always the person the child idealizes is a person who plays an important role in his childish world, whether that person be a parent, teacher, camp counselor, or

hero in a movie or television program (24, 61,294,396,458,461).

By *early adolescence*, the crush or hero-worship stage, boys and girls form a concept of their ideal personalities on the basis of real people who play certain roles that are prestigeful and who have a well-recognized place in our society. These are mainly adults other than parents or teachers. Some of them are known to the adolescent; most are people he has read or heard about or has seen on the screen (113,163,198,201,202, 515). Unlike adolescents of past generations, today's adolescents draw their ideals mainly from entertainment personalities; at the turn of the century, it was more common to draw ideals from political figures (514). Furthermore, they are almost always people from the adolescent's own culture; American adolescents select American heroes for their ideals (198,201,458).

The *older adolescent* has a more realistic concept of his ideal. He also is more influenced by class consciousness (1,92,163, 353). Furthermore, members of both sexes, as they grow older, put great emphasis, in the selection of their ideals, on the qualities that are highly valued in the social group with which they are identified (61,96,100, 308).

The older adolescent usually has a *stereotype* of the ideal person rather than a specific person whom he regards as an ideal. This stereotype is composed of traits from different people he has idealized and each is highly valued by the social group. Because the adolescent learns, as he grows older, that certain traits are more valued than others, his stereotype changes with age (92,163,198,201,277,511). Reading plays an important role in the development of his stereotype of an ideal person. As Strang (461) has explained:

> Although fewer adolescents than might be expected report conscious identification with specific characters in fiction, it is possible that many youngsters draw upon various fictional sources for qualities which they may incorporate into their ideal selves. For example, they may get clues for solving their own problems of adjustment from characters who know how to get along with others (e.g., Antonia in Cather's My Antonia), or those who have a good set of values (e.g., Kristin in Undset's Kristin Lavransdatter), or those who can transcend major tragedies in their lives (e.g., Jane Eyre in Brontë's Jane Eyre).

Effects on Personality Improvement The adolescent uses this ideal for the patterning of his own personality. He imitates the person he idealized not only in such externals as dress and speech but, often unconsciously, in his values, his likes and dislikes, and his interests (198). This provides him with the motivation necessary to change his patterns of behavior and to learn to behave in a manner that is more approved by the social group (198,354).

Should the adolescent cling to an unrealistic ideal because of his intense admiration for some glamorized person, he may be in for trouble. By the end of high school, if his aim should be to "be a very great person and do great things that people will talk about," he is likely to be doomed to great disappointment (491,516). More often than not, those who do cling to unrealistic ideals become maladjusted people because they are "frustrated and distraught idealists" (230).

Another source of difficulty in having an ideal comes when the adolescent ideal-izes a person not approved or admired by the group. Under such conditions, in his attempt to model the pattern of his behavior after that of his ideal, the adolescent will develop characteristics that will cause a cleavage between him and his contemporaries. When this happens, the adolescent becomes a "social misfit in his or her immediate adolescent surroundings" (422).

COMPLEXITY OF PERSONALITY PATTERN

Few adolescents realize what the term "personality" really means or how complex the personality pattern is. They feel that if they can change some handicapping trait, such as shyness, aggressiveness, or lack of self-confidence, that is all that must be done. To understand how inadequate such an approach is one must know what the term means and realize how complex the personality pattern is.

Meaning of Personality The word "personality" is derived from the Latin word *persona*, meaning a mask worn by the actor while speaking or performing on the stage. The actor revealed the character he was depicting through his speech and actions. Present-day definitions of "personality" stress much the same meaning. Personality is not one definite, specific attribute. Instead, it is the "quality of the individual's total behavior" as revealed in the individual's "habits of thought and expression, his attitudes, and interests, his manner of acting, and his personal philosophy of life" (517). These have their physical basis in the individual's neural, glandular, and general bodily states which provide the hereditary foundations for personality. They are, also, the motivating forces which determine what type of adjustments to life the individual will make (8).

Meaning of Personality Pattern The personality pattern is not made up of many separate and distinct attributes which are loosely organized and totally unrelated. Instead, as the term "pattern" would suggest, there is a definite organization of the many attributes which combine to make up the personality. This organized unity is composed of traits or specific qualities of behavior built up around a "core" or "center of gravity." Like the hub of a wheel, the core not only serves to integrate and interrelate the different traits but it also influences the form they will take. (See Figure 16–3.) In a healthy, normal personality, the organization of these different parts of the pattern is well integrated and fairly stable over a period of time; the abnormal personality pattern, however, shows disorganization in varying degrees (8,58,257,420,446).

The *core* of the personality pattern contains the concept the individual has of himself as a person; it is a "composite of the thoughts and feelings which constitute a person's awareness of his individual existence, his conception of who and what he is" (227). It is the "organization of qualities that the individual attributes to himself" (249). These qualities may be physical or psychological; one thus has a *physical* as well as a *psychological* self-image. The physical self-image consists of such qualities as tallness, fatness, sex-appropriate features, and blondness. The psychological self-image consists of such traits as timidity, honesty, and aggressiveness. While these two aspects of the self-image are usually distinct in childhood, by the time the child reaches adolescence they have fused and become his concept of himself as a physical

and psychological individual (18,55,114).

The concept of self may be real or ideal. The *real* concept of self is a "mirror image" of what the adolescent believes significant people in his life—his parents, teachers, and peers—think of him both physically and psychologically. How they treat him and how they appraise him will determine, to a large extent, how he will appraise himself. These "reflected appraisals," if favorable, will lead the adolescent to approve of himself; if unfavorable, they tend to make him devalue himself (111,138,236). If he consistently perceives these appraisals to be unfavorable—either correctly or incorrectly—he will develop a distorted self-concept. This will play havoc with the type of adjustment he makes (2, 319). Usually, the mirror image is not based on what one person is perceived to think of him but rather on his perception or misperception of the appraisals of the group as a whole; it is thus derived from "generalized others" (368).

By contrast, the *ideal* self-concept is what the adolescent *would like to be*. This ideal self-concept, as has been stressed earlier, is made up of the adolescent's hopes and aspirations for himself—what he would like to be and what he knows the social group holds in high esteem. Sometimes the real and ideal self-concepts, both physical and psychological, are similar; more often they are very dissimilar. Only a few adolescents are able to improve their personalities so that their real self-concepts will approximate the ideal. The significance of this will be discussed in detail later in the chapter.

The second component of the personality pattern consists of *traits* or a group of related and consistent reactions which are characteristic of the individual's typical pattern of adjustment. They are integrated into the personality pattern and are influenced by its core—the self-concept. If, for example, the adolescent thinks of himself as superior to others, he will develop a characteristic pattern of adjustment which his peers will describe as "having a swelled head." If, on the other hand, he feels that he is slighted at home because of parental favoritism toward a sibling, he will behave

"I AM A BIG WHEEL"

Makes derogatory comments

Rationalizes weaknesses

Dominates conversation

Demands attention

Criticizes others

Stinginess

Selfishness

Projects blame

Snobbishness

FIGURE 16–3 The personality pattern is like a wheel. The hub is the "core" of the pattern—the concept of self—which serves to integrate and interrelate the different "traits"—the spokes of the wheel.

both at home and away from home in a manner that will lead others to say that he "feels sorry for himself" or "suffers from a martyr complex" (8,420,446).

how the pattern is developed The pattern of personality becomes "organized around nodal points or experiences which have received particular emphasis and much reiteration" (18). It is (363):

> . . . formed from the interaction of significant figures (first the mother, later the father, and siblings, later extra-familial figures) with the child. The child brings to this interaction a certain biological constitution, certain needs and drives, and certain intellectual capacities which determine his reactions to the way in which he is acted upon by these significant figures.

Once the pattern has been established, it does not change unless steps are taken to produce a change. In young children, the core of the pattern is not well established; it can still be changed without disturbing the total personality balance. By adolescence, however, the personality pattern is less flexible because of the larger and more fixed core of habits and attitudes (58).

While the hereditary endowment of the individual provides the potentials for the personality pattern, what form these potentials will take will be determined by environmental influences (5,18,363). At an early age, the child learns to think of himself in a characteristic manner and to develop characteristic patterns of response closely related to his self-concept. This learning may be guided and directed or it may be haphazard and influenced by chance. As Jersild (226) has pointed out:

> From an early age, without being deliberate about it, he (the child) acquires ideas and attitudes about himself and others. These are woven into the pattern of his life. They may be true or false, healthy or morbid. Their development is left largely to chance.

Because the personality pattern begins to develop from the moment of birth, early experiences have a basic and continuing effect on the form the pattern takes (162, 295). While the child, as he grows older, will not necessarily remember specific childhood experiences, the effect on his concept of self of favorable or unfavorable experiences will be on the attitudes established through these experiences (25,151,418). His "affective index," or outlook on life, will be set early, as will his likes and dislikes. These are the result of learning and of experiences with related stimuli in the past that have become tied together in more generalized attitudes. Before childhood is over, the child's outlook on life, based on his personal experiences, is a part of the core of his personality pattern. As such, it has an influence of importance in determining his adjustments to life (18).

In the development of the personality pattern, how others treat him and how they appraise him determine how he will appraise himself. His concept of himself, as was stressed earlier, is a mirror image—a reflection of what he *believes* significant people in his life think of him. This he often judges by the interest they show in him and in his activities. Middle- and upper-class parents, for example, usually show a greater interest in their children and in their children's activities than do parents from the lower classes. This is one of the factors that contribute to more favorable self-concepts among upper- and middle-class children (268). When boys, for example, feel that their fathers are interested in them, they develop more favorable self-concepts than when they believe their fathers are uninterested. As Rosenberg (384) has pointed out:

> Adolescents who report close relationships with their fathers are more likely to have high-esteem and stable self-images than those who describe their relationship as more distant.

By the time the child reaches adolescence, the self-image is essentially completed. However, it may be revised and changed as new experiences cause the adolescent to see himself differently through the eyes of others than he did when he was a child (55,79,99,185,363). As Strang (461) has said:

If the adolescent has the impression that others think he is "dumb," retarded in reading, socially unacceptable, he tends to see himself in these negative ways. . . . If, on the other hand, his parents, teachers, and friends have realistically accentuated the positive in his personality, he will take a more hopeful attitude toward himself.

While the *traits* that constitute a part of the personality pattern are based on a hereditary foundation, they, like the concept of self, are a product of learning. They are learned partly through *molding* by training methods used in the home and school and partly by *imitation* of the person with whom the adolescent identified himself during the early, formative years of life (61,267,281, 489). Some traits are learned by *chance*. If, through trial and error, the adolescent learned, when he was a child, that aggressiveness won him prestige in the eyes of the peer group, he will repeat the aggressive behavior in any situation where it is likely to bring him prestige. In time, it will develop into a habitual pattern of behavior (152,159).

Throughout childhood, the adolescent discovered that certain personality traits were admired and others scorned. He tried, therefore, to develop those which would increase his chance for social acceptance. While admired traits change with age, to some extent, the adolescent who craved social approval consciously tried to conform to the approved pattern and to develop the traits that were admired *at that age*. These traits, through constant repetition, in time develop into his characteristic way of adjusting to life; they become increasingly difficult to change as he grows older (64,132, 434,448,489).

characteristics of personality pattern There are four characteristics of all personality patterns. First, every personality pattern is *unique* in that it varies in the combination and organization of the traits that constitute the pattern, in the strength of the different traits, and in the self-concept—the core of the pattern. Because no two individuals have the same hereditary endowment—ex-

cept in the case of identical twins—or the same social environment, they show increasingly different personality patterns with each passing year (8,58,326,446).

Uniqueness in personality patterns means differences in *kind* rather than differences in amount. While there are certain common personality traits in a social group, owing to cultural values and child-training methods used to produce patterns of behavior that will conform to these values, these traits are expressed in different ways by different individuals (446,517). As Allport (8) has pointed out:

No two persons ever have precisely the same trait. Though each of two men may be aggressive (or esthetic), the style and range of the aggression (or estheticism) in each case is noticeably different. What else could be expected in view of the unique hereditary endowment, the different developmental history, the never-repeated external influences that determine each personality? The end product of unique determination can never be anything but unique.

The major reason for uniqueness can be traced to individuality in self-concepts. Even though two children may be brought up in an identical physical environment, each will be influenced differently by the interpersonal relationships he experiences. One adolescent, for example, may have grown up with people who have instilled in him the belief that he owes the world nothing and should think of himself first. He may be generous with his money and material possessions as a means to an end— a way of "buying popularity."

Another adolescent learns from earliest childhood to believe that he does owe the world something; his generosity is inspired by the belief that he should help others less fortunate than he. In the first case, generosity will be expressed only when it counts. In the second, by contrast, generosity will be influenced by the belief that those who deserve it most are least likely to be able to repay.

The second characteristic of the personality pattern is *consistency*. This means that a person behaves in approximately the same way in similar situations and under similar conditions. Because there is an underlying pattern of consistency in a person's characteristic adjustments to life, it is possible to predict his attitudes, opinions, and reactions. However, because the personality pattern is built up through learning rather than as a part of the hereditary endowment, it is susceptible to change. This is likely to happen when there are changes in the environment, in the physical makeup of the individual, or when he has a strong motivation to effect change (8,60,227,446).

Consistency, like individuality, is a matter of degree. When consistency is pronounced, the personality pattern is said to be "rigid." A rigid person shows a tendency to resist conceptual change, to acquire a new pattern of behavior, or to relinquish old and established patterns (4,401). This leads to social introversion, feelings of anxiety and guilt, and intolerance (370).

Consistency also leads to the development of personality syndromes—constellations of related traits. In the authoritarian syndrome for example, the same cluster of traits exists as in the tolerant syndrome, but in different degrees. The difference is that in the former, there is a greater resistance to change in the accepted pattern of behavior than in the latter (178,293,380). In the ascendant syndrome, the individual upholds his rights and defends himself in face-to-face contacts with others. He does not object to being conspicuous and may even enjoy it (185).

The third characteristic of the personality pattern, closely related to the second, is the *degree of stability that exists in the concept of self*. The child, for example, tends to have a relatively unstable self-concept. As a result, he swings from real to ideal and then back to real. The peak of instability usually occurs at the time when there are the most rapid and pronounced body changes—during the puberty period. After that, greater stability is normally achieved (46,65,227,249,278,296,384).

The degree of stability of the self-concept has a marked influence on the characteristic pattern of adjustment the adolescent makes. Adolescents with stable self-

concepts have been reported to have higher levels of self-esteem; they are better liked by the group; they are relatively free from feelings of inferiority and nervousness; they have more friends and are more active socially; they show less evidence of compensatory behavior of a defensive sort, such as withdrawal or shyness; and they make better adjustments than do those who have unstable concepts of self (65). By contrast, those whose self-concepts are unstable make poor social adjustments and show such qualities as negativism, introversion, hyperactivity, dominance-seeking, and other forms of problem behavior (46,65,155,461).

Fourth, in every personality pattern, the core or *self-concept is the dominant element*; it governs the characteristic reactions the individual makes to people and to situations (93,227,249). If, for example, an adolescent believes that he cannot do something, he does not try (497). If, on the other hand, he has feelings of competence and self-worth, he will not only try but will probably achieve the goal he sets out to reach (502).

As the self-concept becomes increasingly more stable, the behavior patterns related to it become habitual. The adolescent then thinks of himself in terms of the concept of self he has developed and assigns to himself a role related to this self-concept. As Shane (421) has explained:

> Children and adults are governed by the concept of self which they develop and make part of themselves. Thus we have boys and girls who assign to themselves the role of clown, good citizen, manager, shrinking violet, little demon, sage, feather-head.

How the concept of self dominates the characteristic role the adolescent learns to play is illustrated in Figure 16–4.

Difficulty in Improving Personality Once the core of the personality pattern becomes fixed and the traits controlled by it become habitual, making a change is far from easy even when the individual wants to do so. It is quite common for the individual to try to change one or two traits which he believes are responsible for his poor adjustments and to replace them with traits he has discovered lead to more successful adjustments. Ignoring the fact that all traits are interrelated and influenced by the core of the pattern, he finds his attempts at improvement lead to scant success.

Changing the core of the pattern—an essential to personality improvement—is far from easy. Any attempt to change it must be done slowly and with care to avoid upsetting the personality balance (58).

The adolescent often resists attempts on the part of others to change his concept of self (494). When the student has learned to think of himself as a slow learner he will put up "Gibraltar-like resistance to learning," even when his teachers and counselors give him evidence to prove that he is capable of learning as much and as quickly as his classmates (497). He is especially likely to reject advice and help if he feels that they are threats to the self-concept he has already established (265,386).

An equally serious obstacle to improving the personality pattern is the reputation the adolescent acquires. One who gains the reputation of being stingy will find it difficult to learn to be more generous when his friends continue to think of him as stingy or when they misinterpret his attempts to be generous as a sign of trying to "buy popularity" (56).

factors influencing self-concept

A number of factors play roles of importance in the development of the self-concept. In general, these factors have high prestige in the eyes of the peer group. Adolescent boys, for example, with superior physical traits usually enjoy greater peer status and are more favorably judged than those with average or below average physical traits (86). Because physical attractiveness has greater prestige for girls, looks play a more important role in the development of the self-concept among girls than among boys (237).

Some of the factors that influence the self-concept are controllable; others are not. There is no known way, for example, to improve the adolescent's intellectual level.

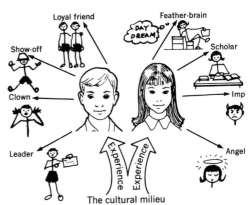

FIGURE 16–4 The concept of self determines the characteristic role the adolescent learns to play. (Adapted from H. G. Shane: Social experiences and selfhood. *Childhood Educ.*, 1957, **33**, 297–298. Used by permission.)

And yet intelligence lower than that of members of the peer group with whom the adolescent is associated day after day in school can play havoc with his concept of self. On the other hand, it is possible, within limits, for the adolescent to improve his looks and, by doing so, to improve the attitudes of others toward him. With this change, his attitude toward himself will improve.

Of the many factors that have been found to be important in the development of the self-concept, the following have been reported to play the major roles.

PHYSIQUE

The physique of the adolescent—especially his size, sex appropriateness, and personal attractiveness—affects the reaction of other people toward him. This, in turn, affects his attitude toward himself. Furthermore, adolescents are aware that many people accept the cultural stereotypes that relate certain physical features to certain personality traits (336,413,414). They know, for example, that a wide mouth is believed to be an indication of friendliness; thick lips, of sensuality; and an imposing stature, of leadership (236,297,474). Figure 16–5 shows how certain personalities are associated in the minds of others with the individual's body build.

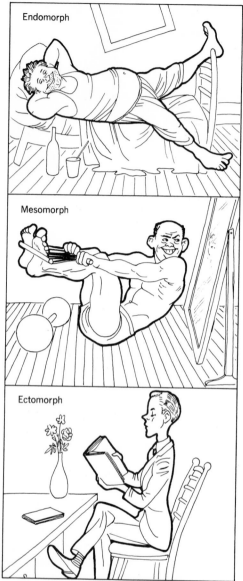

FIGURE 16–5 Many people associate certain personality "types" with the individual's body build.

Every cultural group has its own standards of what is "right" in appearance for members of the two sexes (292). There is, for example, the "right" height for boys and for girls; the "right" weight for members of each sex; and the "right" degree of development of the different secondary sex characteristics. Any physical characteristic that deviates from the cultural norm will be regarded as "wrong." A girl whose breast development is relatively large but whose body is slender will conform to the cultural stereotype of female beauty. Winning favorable reactions from others will help her to develop a favorable attitude toward herself (109,220,238,279,415,467,500).

Any deviation from the culturally approved norm has an unfavorable effect on the adolescent's self-concept. Just as being too fat leads to feelings of inferiority, so does being too thin. Because few adolescents conform to the norms in every respect, they are concerned about the features that deviate and are anxious to correct them. Boys, for example, usually want to gain weight while girls want to lose it (73,190). Being overweight can lead to "a disturbance in the maturation of the total personality" (67). This is illustrated in Figure 16–6. A big nose may be so disturbing to the adolescent that he will seek plastic surgery in the hope of avoiding being judged in a stereotyped way (313).

Some adolescents are mainly concerned about single features that fail to conform to the approved cultural stereotype; others are more concerned about the general impression their bodies make on others (147, 227,406). A boy, for example, may be disturbed primarily because his small stature and delicate features create the impression that he is a sissy. Studies of juvenile delinquents and adult criminals have revealed that they usually have distorted body images, stemming from sex-inappropriate builds. Their antisocial behavior is partially an attempt to compensate for the unfavorable impression they believe they create on others (94,246).

When the physical growth pattern of the adolescent differs from that of members of the peer group, he is likely to become disturbed (133,143,208,234,321,332,440). How seriously such deviations can affect the self-concept has been emphasized thus by Mussen and Jones (333):

Apparently, in our culture, the physically retarded boy is more likely to encounter a sociopsychological environment which may have adverse effects on his personality development. The early-maturer's experiences, on the other hand, seem to be conducive to good psychological adjustment.

Physical Defects Physical defects that were of little consequence during childhood often become the source of embarrassment and feelings of inferiority during adolescence. A slight facial scar or broken tooth, for example, may not disturb a child; his peers pay little attention to it, unless it is conspicuously apparent. But, to an adolescent, this is a serious source of embarrassment; he believes that *everyone* notices it and judges him unfavorably because of it. Thus, it is not the defect per se that influences the adolescent's personality but rather the frustrations and resentments he suffers because of his defect (82,179,284, 342).

When a defect is so serious that the adolescent must be segregated from his peers and put in a special school or home for those with defects similar to his, the effect on his self-concept will be especially damaging. Under such conditions, adolescents have been found to show high neurotic tendencies, to have negative attitudes, to lack self-confidence, and to suffer from generally poor mental health (44,98,179, 342).

While a crippling condition is a source of serious personality damage at any age, it is especially so during adolescence because of the negative attitudes the adolescent develops toward himself and toward members of the peer group who are able to have fun in activities which he cannot participate in. Deafness and blindness, which, like crippling, result in social isolation for an adolescent, lead to poor self-concepts and encourage rigidity due to lack of opportunities on the adolescent's part to communicate with his peers (75,82,259,300,311). By contrast, a defect that does not handicap the adolescent to the point where he is unable to participate in activities that have high prestige value in the peer group will

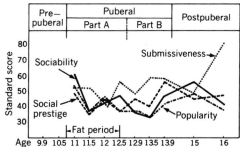

FIGURE 16–6 Being overweight can lead to personality disturbances which are reflected in poor personal and social adjustments. (Adapted from H. R. Stolz and L. M. Stolz: *Somatic development of adolescent boys.* New York: Macmillan, 1951. Used by permission.)

have a less damaging effect on his developing self-concept (45,256,320).

Control of Physical Factors Only within limits can the physical factors that have such a pronounced influence on the adolescent's concept of himself be controlled. Minor physical defects can usually be corrected so that they are barely apparent to others. Major physical defects can often be corrected so that the defective structure can be functionally useful. Poor eyesight, for example, can be made functionally nearly perfect by the wearing of glasses, and amputations can be overcome by the use of artificial limbs. But the adolescent's attitude toward these corrective devices may be so negative that the damage to his personality persists (82,98,284).

Little is known at the present time regarding ways to change the body size and shape to conform to the individual's aspirations. Dieting may make a fat body more slender or a slender body fatter. However, there is no way in which an adolescent who is too short or too tall or who is less sex appropriate in appearance than he would like to be can control the matter. Even though adolescents may, through the use of camouflage, acquire a body that comes close to their aspirations, the psychological damage resulting from their earlier resentments and frustrations may never be completely eliminated.

PHYSICAL CONDITION

Anything that upsets the homeostasis of the body, whether it be a temporary condition —such as fatigue or hunger—or a more prolonged condition—such as a wasting illness—will have an effect on the self-concept, and this will be reflected in the type of adjustment the individual makes to life. Upsets in homeostasis are especially common during periods of rapid and uneven growth. They may, however, occur at any time when health is poor (119,208,429).

Partial starvation, for example, brings with it marked changes in personality. The semistarved person is continually preoccupied with thoughts and dreams of food, shows little interest in things that formerly interested him, and is depressed, irritable, unsocial, and lacking in a sense of humor (184).

Frequent illness in childhood has not been found to have a detrimental effect on the adjustments of adolescents. Instead, it may stimulate the development of wholesome attitudes toward life (192). (See Figure 16–7.) Should poor health or chronic illness develop during adolescence in an individual whose childhood was healthy, changes in the self-concept are almost inevitable. The adolescent who finds himself suddenly unable to take part in the activities of the group and who has to establish new interests and become self-sufficient finds the adjustment very difficult (259,311,320).

Chemique The "chemique," or glandular condition produced by hormones from the endocrine system, has a marked influence on personality. A hyperthyroid condition, for example, will predispose the individual to be nervous, tense, restless, jumpy, irritable, on edge, and ready to fly off the handle at the slightest provocation. Hypothyroidism, by contrast, is primarily responsible for the easygoing, happy-go-lucky, unruffled individual who is lazy and indolent.

Indirectly, endocrine glands also are factors of no slight importance in determining the personality of the individual. Through their influence on physical growth, they influence the attitude toward self. The anterior lobe of the pituitary determines whether the individual will be normal in stature or tend toward giantism or dwarfism. His marked deviation from the average stature of the group is reacted to unfavorably. The more marked the deviation, the more serious its effect on the self-concept.

Control of Physical Condition With modern medical techniques, it is far easier to control the physical condition of the individual than it was when medicine was less advanced. However, if this control is to occur and if upsets in body homeostasis are to be avoided or kept to a minimum, the individual must be motivated to make use of the medical techniques available. To an adolescent, concern about health is a sign of being a sissy. The result is that most adolescents tend to ignore advice about health in an attempt to prove to themselves and others that there is nothing the matter with them.

Even when the adolescent is sick or suffers from some chronic ailment, such as allergies or diabetes, he is likely to be careless about following medical advice. When he is feeling better, for example, he fails to take his medicine or to keep to the diet prescribed for him. This neglect is motivated by a desire to convince others, as well as himself, that he is healthy and can do what others do.

The same disregard for health is shown in the attitude the adolescent takes toward any defect he may have. If the defect is serious enough to prevent him from doing what members of the peer group do, he is likely to take a defeatist attitude and refuse to comply with medical advice that might help him. If, on the other hand, the defect does not incapacitate him, he also ignores medical advice if following this advice will make him conspicuous. When, for example, an adolescent is advised to eliminate certain foods from his diet as an aid to curing acne, he is likely to ignore this advice because he does not want to make himself conspicuous by not eating the snacks his friends eat with such relish.

As adolescence progresses, most boys and girls realize that it is to their personal advantage—not only to the improvement of their looks but also to the improvement of their dispositions—to make use of any medical aids they can. As a result, they become more health-conscious. With this motivation to improve their physical condition they, in turn, improve their self-concepts.

CLOTHES

Clothes, as was stressed earlier (see pages 257 to 262), are important status symbols to an adolescent. As such, they have a profound influence on his concept of self. Furthermore, growing up and adjusting to new social expectations is not easy. For that reason, "clothes may make growing up easier. They may become a symbol of security, an extension of self, a way of identifying with someone, a means of real satisfaction" (367). Morton (322) has further emphasized how important a role clothes play in the adolescent's adjustments to life, and indirectly to his concept of self:

> Clothes help to make us self-confident, self-respecting, jolly, free or they make us self-conscious, shy, sensitive, restrained. They determine how much we go into society, the places we go to, the exercise we take. They help us to get jobs and to hold them, to miss them and to lose them. . . . Clothes, then, make or mar us. They may enhance our personality or be so conspicuous as to subordinate us to them, or they may be just ordinary, nondescript, characterless.

For an adolescent whose physique is a source of concern to him, clothes are especially important because of their camouflage value. Furthermore, because appearance plays such an important role in social acceptance (see pages 169 and 170), the adolescent whose self-concept could be seriously damaged by social rejection can be spared much of this damage if he has clothes that improve his chances for acceptance (29,92).

In a study of high school and college girls, it was reported that clothes had a great effect on attitudes and behavior. Being well dressed made the girls more confident, happier, gayer, and in better spirits, while being poorly dressed made them uncomfortable, worried, fidgety, and nervous.

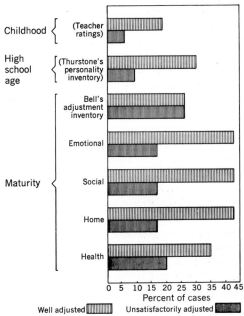

FIGURE 16–7 The effects of frequent illness in childhood on personality development. (Adapted from M. C. Hardy: Adjustment scores of adolescents having a history of frequent illness during childhood. Amer. J. Orthopsychiat., 1937, 7, 204–209. Used by permission.)

Being well dressed made them friendlier, more sociable, more vivacious, and talkative. They were able to behave in a natural, friendly way because they felt they made a good appearance. Those who felt they were poorly dressed tried to withdraw from the group, to be inconspicuous, to avoid talking to people, and to get away from the group as soon as possible (388).

Control of Clothes If clothes are to serve as an aid to improvement of the concept of self, they must be both a status symbol that will add to the adolescent's prestige in the group and a means of enhancing his physique. There is no dearth of clothing available to serve these two major purposes. There are, however, obstacles which prevent the adolescent from taking advantage of the opportunities available to him.

The most serious obstacle is *ignorance* of what clothes will best serve to enhance his physique. Sooner or later, through trial and error or through comments made by others, the adolescent learns to be more selective in the choice of his clothes and to concentrate on those which improve his looks, even though they may not conform to his preferences.

Feelings of insecurity which motivate the adolescent to *conform to the prevailing styles* of the group are almost as serious an obstacle as ignorance. An overweight girl, for example, who wears dresses with ruffles when that is the prevailing style may do serious damage to her self-concept by increasing her sensitivity about her physique and by creating an impression of unattractiveness that militates against social acceptance.

If clothes are to serve as a prestige symbol, they must be "name-clothes"; these often cost more than the adolescent or his family *can afford*. In spite of the affluence of the American family of today, not all adolescents come from homes where family budgets allow for such expenditures. Nor do all parents feel, even when they can afford it, that such expenditures are justified.

NAMES AND NICKNAMES

Young children accept the names their parents give them without thought or criticism. As a result, the child's name has no influence on his personality. As the child grows older, he discovers that people react differently to different names. To some, they react favorably; to others, they react with scorn, ridicule, or rejection. Only then does the child's name or nickname have any effect on his personality (209). See pages 267 to 270 for a more complete discussion of names and nicknames.

How the adolescent feels about his name will determine what effect it will have on his self-concept. And how he feels about his name will be greatly influenced by the attitudes of significant others, or what he *believes* is their attitude, toward his name. Furthermore, he learns that the attitudes of significant people are not always the same; some may have a favorable attitude while others have an unfavorable attitude toward the same name.

To a romantic mother, for example, the son whom she has named "Romeo" will be her dream child—the kind of boy who will develop into the type of man she had always hoped to marry. To his peers, on the other hand, the name is regarded as a joke; it gives rise to constant ridicule and taunts about his sex appeal (209).

Because a name can be a psychological asset or liability, depending on how the bearer of the name feels about it, it is evident that the choice of name or nickname is far more important than most people realize. As Allen et al. (6) have emphasized:

> [The] *choice of a given name to be bestowed upon the child is a matter of no little amount to him in his relations with other individuals, for an unfortunate selection may doom him to recurring embarrassment or even unhappiness.*

Effect of Names   Should the adolescent like his name and feel that it is approved by the social group with which he is identified, it will give him a feeling of superiority. This will increase his self-confidence. The more dissatisfied he is with his name, the greater psychological hazard it becomes. Adolescents who dislike their names and are embarrassed because of them tend to be shy, sensitive, and easily embarrassed when their names are mentioned or when they are introduced to strangers. As a result, they often shun social situations and develop feelings of personal inadequacy and inferiority which contribute strongly to maladjustments (19,127,219,225,397). It has been found, for example, that college students who have unusual names which they strongly dislike have more than their proportion of failures and psychoneuroses (3,219,397). A nickname that suggests ridicule on the part of the peer group has much the same effect on the adolescent; he shuns situations where he can be embarrassed, humiliated, or angered by the name used to symbolize him in the minds of others (186,346,442,453).

In commenting on the effect of names and nicknames on the self-concept of the individual, Murphy (330) has emphasized that it is not the name, per se, that determines what effect it will have but the attitude of the individual toward his name:

> The names of individuals play an important role in the organization of their ego defense patterns and are cathected and utilized from the point of view of ego defenses in a manner similar to an organ or body part. . . . For some, the name may become a part of the core of severe neurosis. . . . The degree of pathological disturbance varies from exaggerated pride or exaggerated shame over one's name, commonly encountered among adolescents, to extremes of psychotic proportions.

Control of Names Only within limits can the adolescent control the name that becomes a symbol of self in the eyes of others. If he likes his name or nickname, or some part of it, he can encourage others to use it, though he cannot force them to do so.

Or if he has two given names, one of which he likes better, he can use the preferred name and drop the other or use an initial in place of the disliked name. He can further add to the distinctiveness of his name and thus inflate his ego by adding "Jr.," "III," or "IV" to his signature (194, 508).

Family names which are a source of embarrassment to the adolescent are not so easy to change. Should the adolescent's parents be divorced and should his mother remarry, he may be embarrassed to have a different name from hers, especially if he is living with her. Under such conditions, the only way to avoid this embarrassment is to be legally adopted by the stepfather—a step that can be taken only with the consent of both parents and the stepfather (330). Adolescents with given or family names that are foreign or which identify them with the stereotyped discrimination associated with their name, can legally change their names *only* with parental consent. But if they meet parental resistance to the change, there is nothing they can do to remove the constant source of embarrassment and accompanying feelings of inferiority their names cause (19,330,339).

INTELLIGENCE

Young children are unaware of their level of intelligence or of the attitudes of the peer group toward those whose intelligence deviates markedly from the norm. Consequently, their intellectual level plays no role in determining what their concepts of self will be. However, shortly after they enter school, they discover that some of their classmates are brighter or duller than others. They also discover that the social group has an unfavorable attitude toward those who deviate.

The attitude toward those *below average* is one of scorn and annoyance because they are slow in grasping meanings; they fail to see the point of jokes others think funny; they tend to be clumsy as compared with their age-mates; and most serious of all, they have unrealistic concepts of their abilities, failing to realize how dull they are. By the time the child reaches adolescence, the mirror image he has developed is very unfavorable (15,241,443,523).

If an adolescent finds that he is unable to do the regular work of the high school and is sent to a vocational school, this further increases his feelings of inadequacy and inferiority (394,395,427). Because of his inability to comprehend situations as quickly and as well as those of normal intelligence, the below-average adolescent has poor social insight. The result is that he says and does many things which cause his classmates to regard him as a pest or a "boob." If the adolescent recognizes that he is disliked, this unfavorable social attitude will be very damaging to his personality. Fortunately, however, most dull adolescents have such poor social and self insight that they fail to recognize how unpopular they are. As a result, the damage to their personality is less than one might anticipate (27,28,135, 204,318,498).

Most adolescents who are *bright* know it and they know others know it. How their peers react to their brightness will depend, to some extent, upon the type of school they attend. If they are in schools where pressure is put on the majority of the students to go to college, they can be assured of the respect, admiration, and envy of their classmates *provided* they are not cocky and "stuck up" toward their less intellectual classmates and *provided* they make some contribution to the school instead of spending all their time on achieving high grades (92,120,289,374).

If bright adolescents behave in such a way as to make others dislike them, their brightness is damaging to their self-concepts. Or if they are self-bound, showing difficulty in talking to others or in expressing their feelings toward others, they are regarded as having a "swelled head" (134,460,485,495).

Because the cultural stereotype of brightness stresses being "queer," the bright adolescent who does not make good social adjustments is likely to develop a self-concept characterized by the belief that he is "different." Then, as a defense against unfavorable social attitudes, he often becomes an intellectual snob—a person who feels socially inferior but intellectually superior. When this happens, his self-concept is characterized by a superiority complex (216,485, 499). Thus, it is apparent that brightness, per se, is neither an asset nor a liability to personality; it depends on the use the adolescent makes of his brightness to win social acceptance.

Average or slightly above average intelligence enables the adolescent to adjust with reasonable success to academic life without being a threat to his classmates. He has enough social insight to size up people and situations adequately to react to them in an acceptable way. As a result, he feels no need to defend himself against unfavorable peer attitudes. Consequently, he is less likely to develop delusions of grandeur because of his superior intelligence or delusions of persecution because he feels inadequate and blames others for misjudging him (120,270,374).

Control of Intelligence There is no known way to produce appreciable changes in the intellectual capacity of the individual (15). However, the use the individual makes of his capacity is controllable. An adolescent who is very bright can learn to accept his intellectual superiority as a legacy from his ancestors, not as an indication of his superiority over those less fortunately en-

dowed than he. He can also learn that his superior intelligence entails a responsibility to use it to make some contribution to society. Instead of spending the major part of his time in an effort to win academic awards which, though ego satisfying, contribute nothing to the social group and are, hence, selfishly motivated, he can participate in extracurricular activities which his less bright peers may not have the time for or the ability to make worthwhile contributions to.

One of the reasons for the prestige associated with athletic achievements in school and college is that they enhance the prestige of the institution while academic achievements enhance only the prestige of the student. The social attitude toward very bright students is always more favorable if they are well-rounded individuals, participating in the affairs of their institutions and making some contribution to them than if they spend their time selfishly seeking personal glory through academic achievement and leaving the activities of their institutions for others to take care of (92,134,499).

The psychological damage resulting from low-grade intelligence can be greatly minimized by putting adolescents with limited ability in classes with others of similar abilities. In this way, the likelihood of developing feelings of inferiority will be reduced as a result of elimination of daily competition with those of greater intellectual abilities. Furthermore, as friendships are usually established among those who are in the same school classes, the less-bright adolescent will become identified with a social group where he will have little reason to feel rejected as a "pest" as so often happens when he tries to identify himself socially with peers of higher intellectual abilities than his. The major obstacle to the control of the environment that fosters feelings of inadequacy in adolescents of low intellectual ability is resistance on the part of parents to the acceptance of the fact that they are intellectually handicapped.

LEVELS OF ASPIRATION

The adolescent's level of aspiration has a marked influence on his self-concept. The reason for this is that his level of aspiration will determine whether he will see himself as a success or a failure (470,495,496). See pages 314 to 324 for a complete discussion of levels of aspiration and the importance of objective and subjective success and failure.

Most adolescents, especially young adolescents, set goals beyond their reach. Boys, as a rule, feel a greater need for achievement than do girls. Boys are more likely, then, to have levels of aspiration above their abilities. As a result, they show a greater discrepancy between their achievements and aspirations than girls do (198,242,247,505).

Effect on Self-concept When the adolescent is successful in reaching the goal he sets for himself, he has a feeling of self-satisfaction and self-confidence. This is more characteristic of intelligent and well-adjusted adolescents than of those who are less intelligent and less well adjusted. However, if the adolescent has too many easy successes, owing to setting his levels of aspiration too low for his abilities, he may become cocky and conceited, boasting of his achievements in the hope of winning the approval of others. He may even, on the basis of past successes, raise his goals unrealistically high and then experience a blow to his ego when he fails. While an occasional failure helps the adolescent to keep his feet on the ground and view himself realistically, too many successes can be almost as damaging to his self-concept as too many failures (165,341,518).

Failure to reach the goal he has set for himself undermines the self confidence of the adolescent and leads to feelings of personal inadequacy. It makes him anxious, submissive in his attitudes, and apprehensive about the future. To avoid the ego-deflating experiences of future failures, he may lower his levels of aspiration as unrealistically as he originally raised them. By doing so, he guarantees success at the lower level and the removal of future ego-deflating experiences. Or he may project the blame for his failures on others, thus thinking of himself as a martyr. Whichever path he follows will lead to poor self-concepts, poor adjustment, and unhappiness (164,484,

518). As Symonds has pointed out, the individual who has experienced failures "probably never overcomes the weakness that results from these experiences, and is ever after liable to succumb to stress that he may encounter" (470).

Control of Levels of Aspiration Because of the psychological damage to the personality development of the individual that can come from too many and too severe failures or from too many and too easy successes, the best way to control the condition is to encourage the individual to assess his abilities realistically and to set levels of aspiration which he has a reasonable chance of reaching. Once he has developed the habit of aspiring unrealistically, in either direction, there will be resistance to change. It is understandable, for example, that an adolescent who has experienced satisfaction from frequent and easy successes will not willingly raise his levels of aspiration, requiring him to put forth more effort and jeopardizing future ego satisfaction from possible failure. Admitting that he is aspiring too high is regarded by the adolescent as an admission of failure. He will not, therefore, willingly lower his unrealistically high level of aspiration. If the habit of unrealistic thinking has never been allowed to develop, the problem is easier to solve.

Almost as important a source of control is the discouragement of verbalizations of levels of aspiration. Many parents and teachers believe that expressing a level of aspiration will serve as an important motivation to reach the goal; the adolescent has, literally, signed on the dotted line and must achieve in order to save face. While it is true that talking about his level of aspiration is a way of raising his prestige in his own eyes as well as in the eyes of others, the psychological damage from failure is too great to justify the temporary ego satisfaction the adolescent derives (84,247).

EMOTIONS

There are three important ways in which the emotions affect the concept of self. The first effect comes from the *upset in body homeostasis* which accompanies even mild emotions. This upset in homeostasis, even when the overt expressions of the emotions are controlled, makes the adolescent nervous, jittery, edgy, and ill at ease. This upset state is often accompanied by nervous mannerisms, such as nail-biting and giggling, which create the impression that the adolescent is silly and immature. Because the adolescent wants to create the impression that he is mature, poised, and in complete control of himself, knowing that he has failed to do so leads to feelings of inadequacy and inferiority (286,324,420).

The second way in which the emotions influence the adolescent's self-concept is in the *type of emotions* that are dominant in his emotional repertoire. The adolescent, for example, who experiences more anger and resentment than happiness will soon get the reputation of having a disagreeable personality. Not only will his behavior suggest that he has a chip on his shoulder but his facial expression will strengthen this suggestion. If he has a cheerful smile on his face most of the time and talks and acts as if he enjoyed whatever he did, he will be considered a happy or good-natured person. In the latter case, social reactions to him will be far more favorable (228,275,443,527).

The third and, by far, the most important way in which the emotions influence the concept of self is the adolescent's *characteristic method of expressing his emotions* and the frequency with which he does so. Some adolescents express their emotions on the spot, thus giving the impression that they are immature. Others inhibit the expressions but release the pent-up energy by directing it at some scapegoat; this is regarded by others as poor sportsmanship. Still others learn to inhibit emotional expressions and later release the pent-up energy at an opportune moment and in a socially approved way. They are regarded as mature and well controlled (8,420,446).

Too frequent, too violent, and apparently unjustified emotional outbursts create the impression that the adolescent is immature. If, for example, he has a low level of frustration tolerance, he will explode at inopportune times and in inappropriate places, giving rise to the judgment by others

that he is "acting like a kid" (420,446). Too much control over the expression of his emotions, on the other hand, will make him moody and disagreeable. This will create almost as unfavorable an impression on others as frequent outbursts, especially when his bad moods seem unjustified.

Control of Emotions Because of the psychological damage emotionality can cause to the self-concept, proper handling of the emotions is essential if the adolescent is to improve his personality. Emotional catharsis, both physical and mental, is the only successful way to handle emotions. See pages 105 to 110 for a more complete discussion of this matter. On the other hand, the adolescent can reduce some of the stress that his environment gives rise to by developing a more realistic concept of himself and his abilities and by setting levels of aspiration within his potentials. If he regards his teachers as hostile because they give him poor grades, if he looks upon every examination as a threat, or if he regards some of his classmates as hostile because they find too little in common with him to want him as a friend, he will experience far more emotionality in the school environment than he would if he had a more realistic appraisal of the situations involved.

Most important of all, he must learn appropriate ways of expressing his emotions. If his anger is justified, he will win more approval than disapproval if he shows his resentment in a mature manner. Otherwise, he will be regarded as weak or "afraid to call his soul his own." However, this resentment must be expressed in a manner approved by the group with which he is identified if he is to gain the group's approval. If, for example, he is identified with a lower-class group, a physical attack on an offender would win greater approval than a verbal attack.

Some methods of expressing emotions, however, are condemned by all groups. Bottling up an emotion and then being rude, gruff, uncooperative, snappy, and preoccupied with self will never win approval; the person is too disagreeable for others to want to be with him. Likewise, projecting pent-up emotional energy on a scapegoat is never approved of; it always leads to the judgment that one is a poor sport.

CULTURAL PATTERNS

Each culture has its own pattern for the approved behavior of its members. Every child is subjected to pressures in the home and outside the home to develop a basic personality pattern that will conform as closely as possible to this standard. The "basic personality pattern" is the organization of drives and emotions, the deeper-lying parts of mental behavior. It includes inner feelings toward family members and toward members of both sexes and emotional reactivity, such as guilt and hostility. Many of these feelings are unconscious but they still have a profound influence on the individual's behavior (38,308).

The approved personality pattern of members of the orthodox Hindu culture, for example, emphasizes strict conformity to authority rather than personal initiative (430,477). Japanese adolescents develop a personality pattern characterized by self-sacrifice, cooperation, loyalty, and an unrealistic concept of themselves and their roles in life (169). Arabs are trained to be group-oriented rather than self-oriented (360); the Indonesians to be independent and self-sufficient (101,102); the Puerto Ricans to be family-oriented (175); the East Indians to be future-oriented and self-controlled (317); the American Indians to be reserved, uncompetitive, and nondemonstrative (130,444); the Germans and Swedes to be authoritarian and somewhat rigid (364,513); and the French to be family-oriented, thrifty, and conservative (449).

In America, there are three major types of cultural systems, each of which puts emphasis on certain values in the basic personality pattern structure. These are the *general American system* of cultural behavior, the *social class cultures*, and the *ethnic group cultures* (103,161,197). The values of the general American system, for example, put strong emphasis on egocentrism, realism, autonomy, and monetary value (169,430). It has been said that in "our own society, personality, like other commodities, has a price associated with it" (280). In addition to these general American cultural values, there are regional differences. In the Southeast, for example, family social status and power are highly valued; in the Far West, low value is placed on family status and high value on individual achievements and social mobility (161). Within a regional group, values differ for suburban, urban, and rural groups. There is, for example, greater emphasis on "protection" of youth from contacts with the world in the suburban than in the urban or rural groups (510).

While each ethnic group within the American general culture has its own values, these are overshadowed by social-class cultural values. In fact, the social-class cultures are so powerful that they tend to influence the general American system of culture (188,200,251,261,363,383).

In every culture and in every subgroup within a culture, there are certain culturally approved patterns of behavior for members of the two *sexes*. Each individual is expected to develop a basic personality pattern that conforms to the approved pattern for his sex. A girl, for example, must avoid all behavior patterns which suggest aggressiveness; a boy must avoid those which suggest weakness of either a physical or psychological nature (40,172,211,407,423). See pages 562 and 563 for a more complete discussion of the culturally approved sex roles.

Effects on Personality Personality is "shaped and changed by interactions with the culture in which the individual lives" (430). Cultural values are reflected in the training of the adolescent from his earliest childhood days. Through this medium, they leave their mark on his personality (282, 316). Adolescents trained to conform to upper-class values, for example, put more value on "being" than "doing," on their families, and on family achievements in the past than do adolescents trained by middle-class parents to conform to the values approved by their group, especially achievement striving and conformity to the group (301,302).

Unquestionably the most pronounced

influence of cultural values on personality comes from values related to sex appropriateness. Playing the approved role for one's sex leaves its mark on the self-concept and on one's characteristic patterns of adjustment to life. In a study of what concepts men and women develop of themselves as a result of playing approved sex roles, it was found that by the time boys and girls reach adolescence, the characteristic self-concepts of members of the two sexes were markedly different.

Some of the major differences in qualities women felt to be more characteristic of them than of men were greater *social benevolence*, as seen in social empathy, warmth, and unselfishness; greater *social propriety*, as shown in social morality, honesty, and absence of social coarseness; greater *personal inadequacy*, as seen in imprecision, impetuousness, and personal fear; greater *personal satisfaction*, as seen in happiness and euphoria; greater *controlled rage*, as seen in less overt aggressiveness and more covert hostility; less *personal maturity* and less *personal conviction*; and greater *democratic* and *domestic feelings* (40). These sex differences in self-concepts are shown in Figure 16–8.

Control of Cultural Influences Because personality is a product of cultural influences and is shaped from earliest childhood by pressures from the social group, this means that as "cultures differ, so do the personalities embedded in these cultures" (449). Even more important, because the personality is "embedded" in the culture in the sense that the individual has learned to think of himself and to behave in a manner approved by the social group to the point where this has become habitual, it is a truism, as the old saying goes, "You can take the individual away from his culture but you cannot take the culture away from him."

Without question, if the motivation is strong enough the adolescent can break away from his earlier cultural influences just as he can break any well-learned habit. This he can and must do if his family is socially mobile. But, as was stressed earlier (see pages 369 to 374), this is a long, difficult, and often only partially satisfying experience.

Should the adolescent, on the other hand, remain in the same or a similar cultural group, he will learn that it is to his personal advantage to develop a personality pattern that conforms to group expectations. If he refuses to accept the values of the group he will become a cultural misfit. Failure to come up to social expectations leads to conflict, accompanied by feelings of guilt and shame; this affects the self-concept unfavorably (255,331). The more he rejects the cultural pattern, as in the case of the rugged individualist, the more he will be socially disapproved and the more damage there will be to his self-concept (210,252, 273).

At no time is this more serious than failure to conform to standards of sex appropriateness. For example, because daring does not have high prestige for girls, as it does for boys, a daring girl is likely to win social disapproval (276). So long as adolescents conform to the approved pattern for their sex, they will be more socially approved and accepted, happier, and better adjusted (485,503).

Thus, it is apparent that if the adolescent wants to improve his personality, he must learn to conform to the approved social standards for *his* group. He cannot change those approved standards to conform to his personal wishes nor can he violate them and hope to win the approval of the group. If, on the other hand, he cannot or will not conform to the standards of the group, the only way he can hope to improve his self-concept is to identify himself with a social group whose values are more to his liking and which he can wholeheartedly accept as his own.

SCHOOL AND COLLEGE
As soon as the child enters school, the school environment begins to exert an influence on the development of his personality. This influence comes more from social relationships with teachers and classmates than from studies or extracurricular activities. As Solomon has stressed, "The schoolroom must be looked upon as a force sec-

ondary in importance only to the home in the development of human personality" (441).

Each year, as the child grows older, he spends a larger portion of his waking time in school or in activities related to school. By adolescence, he is in the school or college environment more than he is in any other environment. The people in these environments thus become the significant people in his life. It is they, more than family members, who determine the mirror image he has of himself.

That the environment of the school or college is an important factor in the adolescent's personality development may be seen by the results of studies in which adults were asked to recall memories of their school and college experiences. Many unpleasant memories were reported as relating to situations in which they felt inadequate due to some physical or economic handicap, to such personality difficulties as shyness or feeling insecure because of clothes or appearance, and to social awkwardness resulting from ignorance of the approved patterns of behavior in social situations. Such memories, persisting into adult life, indicate how dominant an influence school and college experiences must have had on the personalities of these individuals (70,217).

Areas of Influence   As a general rule, one can say that the areas of school or college life that have the greatest influence on the personality development of the adolescent are those which have the highest prestige in the eyes of the members of the school or college group with which the adolescent is identified. How he rates in activities related to these areas in comparison with his classmates will have a marked influence on how he rates himself.

Because different schools and colleges rate various aspects of their environment differently, no general statements can be made about their relative importance in the personality development of the adolescent. However, certain aspects of *every* educational environment affect the adolescent's concept of himself. Of these, the following are the most important.

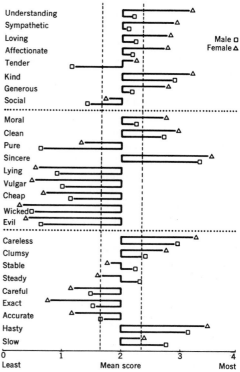

FIGURE 16–8 Sex differences in the self-concepts of adolescents, indicating that girls perceive themselves as having traits considered appropriate for their sex while boys perceive themselves as having traits regarded as "masculine." (Adapted from E. M. Bennett and L. R. Cohen: Men and women: personality patterns and contrasts. *Genet. Psychol. Monogr.*, 1959, **59**, 101–155. Used by permission.)

teachers   In childhood, the teacher is unquestionably the most important aspect of the school environment so far as personality development is concerned. By adolescence, this is infrequently true, partly because each teacher comes in contact with the students only when teaching the subject of her specialty and partly because the peer-group attitude toward an adolescent who has a close relationship with any teacher is unfavorable. As a result, few adolescents have enough contact with their teachers to be markedly influenced by them (144,441). In colleges and in professional training schools, the adolescent's contacts with his teachers are even more limited than in high school.

However, the influence of teachers on personality development during the adolescent years is important. It may, first, come from the way the adolescent believes the teacher judges him. If he believes the teacher thinks he is a poor student or a "pest" in the classroom, this will have an unfavorable influence.

The second influence comes from the way the teacher treats the adolescent. If the teacher is interested in the adolescent and his problems and is willing to discuss them, help find solutions, and advise him about his plans for the future, his self-concept will be improved—partly by becoming a better-adjusted person and partly by feeling important because the teacher thinks he is important enough to devote valuable time to (77,85,263,309,457,526).

Third, the teacher's influence is felt in the method used to motivate students to study. If emphasis is placed on the use of praise, the adolescent who is the recipient of the teacher's praise will improve his self-concept. Should the teacher emphasize the use of blame, reproof, and punishment as ways of motivating students, the adolescent who is the victim of these motivational forces will think of himself as a failure (497).

Finally, the teacher's influence comes from the type of person the teacher is. An attractive, well-adjusted, able person may become the adolescent's ideal. An unattractive, poorly adjusted, and disinterested teacher, on the other hand, is responsible for an unhealthy emotional climate in the classroom. This is damaging to all students, but most especially to those who are already poorly adjusted (9,223,426,492,512).

extracurricular activities As was emphasized earlier (see pages 178 and 179), most adolescents would rather be remembered for their extracurricular achievements than for their academic. Because athletic achievements are most prestigeful for boys and social achievements for girls, those who stand out as successful in these areas will develop more favorable self-concepts than those who, through physical, economic, or other handicaps are prevented from participating in such activities (70,92,461).

bull sessions Adolescents devote much of the time they are with their friends to talking about their interests, their values, other people, and themselves. These intimate conversations help the adolescent to get a new insight into his own problems and to realize that his problems are not unique but are shared by others. Bull sessions become an outlet for pent-up emotions and serve as a form of emotional catharsis. (Refer to pages 221 to 224 for a more complete discussion of adolescent conversations.) In addition, bull sessions give the adolescent an opportunity to exchange views on different problems with his agemates. This helps to break down any rigidity in his thinking that may have developed in the home (16,221,222). As a result, he not only sees himself but others in a new light. This helps him to change his concept of self.

prestige of institution The adolescent is aware of the degree of prestige associated with his school or college and his self-concept reflects this degree of prestige. If he is in a school that has high prestige in the community because of its high academic rating, its successes in athletics, or its "exclusiveness" in student makeup, this is ego inflating to him.

Different types of schools have different degrees of prestige in the eyes of the American people. Private or "independent" schools, while often labeled as "snob schools," have greater prestige than public schools; their exclusiveness gives them this prestige rather than their excellence as educational institutions. Church-related schools have different levels of prestige, depending on the religious affiliation of the school. In recent years, college preparation has acquired the reputation of being more prestigeful than preparation for skilled work. As a result, the "college-prep" high school has greater prestige than the vocational high school (91,347,427).

Similarly, Ivy League colleges have greater prestige than state-supported uni-

FIGURE 16-9 The prestige of the adolescent's school influences his self-concept.

versities. Some departments within these colleges have greater prestige than others. Majoring in a subject that is prestigeful influences the older adolescent's self-concept favorably even if he receives poorer grades than he would receive in a less prestigeful subject (492). Figure 16-9 shows some of the ways in which the prestige of the school or college influences the adolescent's self-concept.

grades Because the grades given for academic achievement are used by schools and colleges to assess the student's abilities, the adolescent uses the same measuring rod and judges himself in terms of his grades (79). The more stress a school or college puts on grades and the more awards it gives for academic achievement, the greater will be the influence on the adolescent's self-concept. The adolescent whose self-concept is inflated by going to a prestigeful school or college may experience a deflation of his ego if he discovers that his ability to compete successfully with the other students is limited and if he receives grades that encourage him to think of himself as inferior (79,287,371,480,495). In discussing the effect of grades on the student's evaluation

of his abilities and, indirectly, of himself, Symonds (471) has pointed out:

> Marks make a tremendous difference to a pupil. They influence his estimate of himself; they serve as a sign to him that he is liked or disliked; they determine whether he is to remain with classmates or instead to become (what he considers) an outcast and forced to join a group of strange pupils in another class. They indicate success or failure; they determine promotion; they indicate the probability of future success; they influence his parents' attitudes toward him. Marks help to determine whether a pupil thinks of himself as successful, smart, or as a failure, an outcast, stupid, a nitwit.

popularity That extracurricular activities influence the self-concept has been shown by the reports of adult memories of school experiences. Many adults who reported happy memories of their school days stressed the fun they had with their classmates and the enjoyment they derived from participation in the social affairs of their schools or colleges. By contrast, those whose memories were unhappy put more stress on social than on academic failure (70,217).

While reasons given for dropping out of school are myriad, stress is more often placed on social than on academic failure. This was discussed in detail on pages 348 and 349.

Control of School Influences No adolescent can change the established pattern of school or college life or the values held by the majority of the students. Therefore, if he is in an institution that is frustrating and damaging to his personality, one of two things must be done: either he must adjust to things as they are—whether it be to his teachers, his classmates, or to the values they consider important—or he must change schools. In public schools, this is difficult unless the family moves into a new district in the community or to another community.

Changing colleges is usually easier than changing schools, though this is not always true. Parents, for example, may not be able to afford to send their sons and daughters away to college if they are unhappy in the college in their community. An adolescent whose ego satisfaction is damaged by attending a low-prestige college may not have high enough grades to be accepted in a college with higher prestige.

A more practical way to control the influence a school or college has on the adolescent's personality development is to encourage him to change and to help him to do so. A student, for example, whose achievement is below his capacities because of poor reading ability can, through remedial reading, be helped to improve this ability. By doing so, he can reduce the amount of time he must spend on his studies and improve his grades (366). Similarly, a student who feels inadequate because he lacks the social skills needed to become a part of the social group that participates in extracurricular activities can be helped to improve these skills (59).

Even more important, the adolescent can be helped to assess himself and his abilities more realistically. This will eliminate the causes for constant feelings of academic and social failure. A more realistic attitude toward himself and his abilities will make his school experiences happier and

forestall the temptation he has, when he feels that he is a failure, to drop out before he has received his diploma. While dropping out may be a temporary solution to the problem of conditions which are damaging to the self-concept, the solution is never more than temporary; the dropout inevitably feels that he is a failure.

SOCIAL STATUS

How much the social status of the adolescent in the peer group will affect his self-concept will depend on many factors. First, long before childhood ends, the child is well aware of how he rates with his peers and the adolescent is more so. Even though adolescents may rationalize their status in the group, if it is unfavorable, they still have to contend with the realization that they are not so popular as they would like to be. When self-conflicts occur, owing to differences in the way the adolescent rates himself and the way the group rates him, they make for poor personal and social adjustments and have a damaging effect on the self-concept (170,233,305,476).

Second, the stronger the adolescent desires high status in the peer group, the stronger and more persistent the effects of the emotions aroused by the thwarting of this desire. And, in turn, the more damaging will be the effect to body homeostasis and to the self-concept. Furthermore, complaining about being deprived of the status he craves will lead to social condemnation of being a poor sport. Having no wholesome catharsis for his pent-up emotions, he experiences the damaging effects of persistent and intense emotional strain which adds to the already serious effects of being frustrated.

Third, the adolescent who is in a school or college that puts higher value on being popular and socially active than on scholarship will be more affected by the status he has in the peer group than will the adolescent who attends an institution where social status is secondary to academic and other achievements (58,92,461).

Finally, of all the factors that influence how great an effect social status will have on the adolescent's concept of himself, *change in status* from that he had in childhood is unquestionably one of the most important. The child who was popular and played leadership roles in childhood cannot be sure that he will have the same status in adolescence. New factors of relative unimportance in childhood come to be important in the social lives of adolescents. Socioeconomic status, religion, racial background, and many other factors begin to affect the attitudes of his peers toward him (92).

Effects on Self-concept Studies of the effects of different social statuses on the self-concept have revealed that certain personality characteristics are commonly associated with these statuses (110,131,212,369, 521). Adolescents who are *reasonably popular* become extroverted, friendly, poised, self-confident, relaxed, independent in thinking and actions, and happy. As a result of these personality traits, they increase their popularity. This, in turn, increases the favorable concepts they have of themselves. The *very popular* adolescents, as was pointed out earlier, are less happy and tend to be somewhat aloof and self-centered, partly because they do not want to offend anyone by having favorites and partly because they tend to get exaggerated opinions of their importance as a result of the social acclaim they have received (274,381). Unfortunately, only a small number of adolescents are popular enough to feel good about themselves. This is not because so few are popular but rather because only a few achieve as much social acceptance as they would like to have (92).

Even fewer adolescents are selected to play *leadership* roles. Those who are unselected often develop the unfavorable personality qualities that go with feelings of failure—resentment, anger, jealousy of those more successful than they, and unhappiness. On the other hand, those who are selected as leaders develop favorable self-concepts even to the point of exaggerating their self-importance if they are chosen many times for leadership roles. Under such conditions, their self-concepts are colored by delusions of grandeur (23,80,373,524).

The type of *unpopularity* the adolescent experiences will determine the type of influence it has on his self-concept. The adolescent who is disliked develops a chip-on-the-shoulder attitude which causes him to become uncooperative, selfish, and aggressive in his behavior and speech (125). As Coleman (92) has pointed out, the adolescent will not "sit still while his self-evaluation is being lowered by the social system of the school." Instead, he may try to win status by acts that give status but he is more likely to retaliate and try to get even with those who have rejected him (8,92, 245,251,361,446).

Adolescents whose unpopularity takes the form of being overlooked and neglected have many of the same frustrations and resentments as those who are rejected. But, in addition, they come to think of themselves as "different" or oddballs. This leads them to believe that they have nothing to offer the group. The result is that they become shy and retiring, leading further to their being overlooked (92,153).

In commenting on the damaging effects of unpopularity, Friedenberg (153) has emphasized its seriousness thus:

> *Adolescents lack reserves of self-esteem to sustain them under humiliating conditions. . . . Adolescents are dreadfully concerned about society's appraisal of them and their worth. . . . They cannot easily assimilate an attack on their dignity or worth, for it produces not merely resentment but intense anxiety. The self is threatened while still ill-defined and in its early stages of construction.*

While the *voluntary isolate* may be liked by the social group and would be accepted as a member if he wanted to be, he feels that he has little in common with them and that he is "different." This unfavorable self-concept is reflected in an indifference toward peers and the shunning of social activities—behavior which leads others to conclude that he *is* an oddball. This social attitude is then mirrored in his self-concept (37,154).

The insecure status of the *fringer, clinger,* or *climber* is reflected in insecurity.

This leads to anxiety and a strong motivation to do and say what the group approves of. Most adolescents in this precarious social status become "me-too" personalities (158, 233,446,476).

Improving Social Status Because social status is used by adolescents as a measuring rod for their worth, an improvement in status would, unquestionably, lead to an improvement in the self-concept. This, unfortunately, is one of the factors affecting the self-concept that is difficult or impossible to control. As was pointed out in detail earlier (pages 186 to 189), improving social status is far from easy; rarely is it to the adolescent's satisfaction.

One way to improve the adolescent's self-concept by improving his social status is to change the environment so that the adolescent will have opportunities to associate with other adolescents whose interests, abilities, and backgrounds are more similar to his (222). It is hard, for example, for an adolescent who is constantly associated in school with peers of different religions, races, and social backgrounds who regard him as "inferior" to do anything but think of himself as inferior (113,123,340,493,507).

If poor social acceptance does not come from being different but from unrealistic levels of aspiration, changing the environment alone will not lead to an improved self-concept. If the adolescent lacks what is needed for acceptance by the leading crowd in his class, he can improve his social acceptance *only* if he is willing to be friends with members of the peer group whose abilities and backgrounds are similar to his (222). Similarly, if he lacks the abilities to be a leader, encouraging him to aspire to being a cooperative, loyal follower will increase his social acceptance. With it, there will be an improvement in his self-concept (34,59,124,365).

FAMILY INFLUENCES

Because the people who live with the adolescent longest have the greatest influence on him, his family becomes the "looking glass" in which he sees himself through the eyes of the family members (483,504).

Retrospective reports of male college freshmen of parental behavior during their childhood and early adolescence suggest how powerful they felt the influence of their parents was in shaping their personalities. Strict, punitive, demanding, and inhibiting parents, for example, cause impulsiveness in the adolescent because he is not encouraged to build internalized controls. Warm, affectionate parents encourage adolescents to develop into gregarious and social people, while cold and indifferent parents encourage them to be gloomy, seclusive, or socially withdrawn (431). The effect of relationships with parents on the adolescent's personality is illustrated in Figure 16–10.

When the home environment meets the needs of the child as he passes into adolescence and then into adulthood, the result will be a healthy, well-balanced personality. Affectional family relationships, combined with an interest in the adolescent's friends and activities and an environment suited to the needs of the individual are more important than any other aspects of the family relationships (139,383,459). As Symonds (469) has pointed out:

> If an individual possesses a healthy, stable, courageous, and loving father and mother, the chances are that he will be a good student, a good worker, a good husband or wife, a good leader, and a good citizen.

When there is less than adequate affection from their fathers, adolescent boys are less relaxed, less secure, less calm, less self-confident, and less happy than when they feel their needs for approval and affection have been adequately met. If the needs are not met, the adolescents make poor social adjustments. This further affects their already unfavorable self-concept (334).

Emotional problems of adolescents can often be traced to feelings of insecurity on the part of the mother, resulting from her lack of training for the parental role and her confusion about how to bring up her children (243,412). Parents with limited education, it has been found, tend to be irritable and to exercise less emotional control than do better-educated parents. Many personality disturbances in adolescents closely resemble those of their parents, especially the mother (139,379,431).

Areas of Influence   Of the many ways in which the family influences the adolescent's self-concept, the following have been found to be the most important.

parental power   The *amount* of autonomy parents are willing to grant the adolescent will greatly affect his self-concept. If his parents are confident that he can handle his affairs successfully, he will be confident also (207,328). As Rosenberg has pointed out, in discussing parental control over adolescents and the attitudes that accompany this control, "The feeling that one is important to a significant other is probably essential to the development of a feeling of self-worth" (383).

The *type* of control exerted by parents is as important as the amount. Adolescents who grow up in a mother-dominant family have been found to have a high level of performance in achievement-oriented roles, but this is accompanied by high anxiety and parental rejection. In the father-dominant family, there is less anxiety, lower performance, and a more wholesome attitude toward parents. In companionate families in which each member is autonomous in relation to his abilities, there is low anxiety, low parent rejection, but the highest achievement (462). Figure 16–11 shows how different types of control affect the adolescent's personality.

family friction   Family friction affects the adolescent's personality unfavorably in two major ways. First, it upsets body homeostasis. Emotional tension will then be expressed in anxiety, resentments, and insecurity. Second, friction is generally accompanied by verbal attacks which, because spoken in anger, are usually exaggerated and, hence, especially damaging to the adolescent's self-esteem. See pages 591 and 592 for a more complete discussion of the effects of family friction. When friction is reduced or eliminated by a break in the family, much of the psychological damage from friction is eliminated (71).

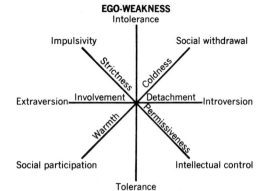

FIGURE 16–10   Effects of relationships with parents on personality development. (Adapted from P. E. Slater: Parental behavior and the personality of the child. *J. genet. Psychol.*, 1962, **101**, 53–68. Used by permission.)

family size   While adolescents from large families may be able to adjust to the changing vicissitudes of a realistic world better than those from smaller families, they do not make as successful adjustments to people and to life in general as adolescents brought up in smaller families. By adolescence, there is generally more maladjustment among those from large families. The adolescent from a one-child family, contrary to popular belief, normally develops a more wholesome self-concept than adolescents who have siblings, because he is spared the rivalries and frictions that are so damaging to the self-concept (21,52,253,343).

status in family   Many years ago, Freud pointed out that the individual's "position in the sequence of brothers and sisters is of very great significance for the course of his later life" (151). The reason for this is that status in the family has a marked influence on self-concept. *Firstborn* children become adult-oriented and are under constant pressure to live up to adult expectations. As a result, they become serious, sensitive, conforming, anxious, dependent, and withdrawn. Because they find it difficult to live up to adult expectations, they often develop feelings of personal inadequacy (33,177,187, 283,303,398,506). If, after a year or two of being the center of his universe, the child

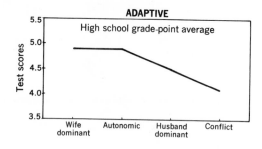

ADAPTIVE

High school grade-point average

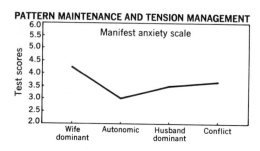

GOAL ATTAINMENT

Active-future value orientation scale

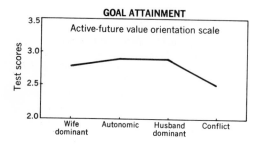

PATTERN MAINTENANCE AND TENSION MANAGEMENT

Manifest anxiety scale

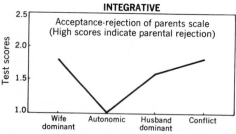

INTEGRATIVE

Acceptance-rejection of parents scale
(High scores indicate parental rejection)

FIGURE 16–11 Effects of different types of parental control on the adolescent personality pattern. (Adapted from M. A. Straus: Conjugal power structure and adolescent personality. *Marriage fam. Living,* 1962, **24,** 17–25. Used by permission.)

is displaced by a sibling, these unfavorable self-attitudes are accompanied by resentments. What effect such displacement has on his self-concept has been described thus by Strauss (463):

> *He will walk constantly as if with a chip on his shoulder. This he will do because he must constantly be on his guard. He has learned from bitter experience that he may be displaced. In line with this, a general attitude of pessimism is common among first born.*

Because the "psychological position" of later children is different from that of the firstborn, they will develop different self-concepts (177,268,384,465). Owing to the fact that later-born children are more peer- than adult-oriented, they are less anxious, more cheerful, friendly, and competitive; they show more empathy and sympathy in their relationships with others; they have more initiative and self-confidence; and they are more overt, competitive, and aggressive in their behavior. They tend to be more popular with their peers; this has a favorable effect on their self-concepts (187,283,303, 391,435,454,455).

socioeconomic status The socioeconomic status of the family affects the personality of the adolescent both directly and indirectly. *Directly,* the effect on personality comes from the type of control the parents exercise over the child when he reaches the adolescent years. Middle-class families, for example, who emphasize the importance of conformity to group standards, produce in their children a personality pattern that is characterized by feelings of insecurity and anxiety (197,282). *Indirectly,* the socioeconomic status of the family has an even greater influence. The adolescent compares his family's home and his possessions with those of his peers. How they compare determines how he feels about himself (104, 218,269,280,403,419,428,451).

Scott Fitzgerald, in writing about "The Rich Boy," explained why the personality patterns of adolescents from rich families are different from those of adolescents whose families are poor or only comfortably well-off. According to his explanation, the difference is to be found in the different types of self-concept developed in those of different degrees of wealth. This is how he explained it (140):

> Let me tell you about the very rich. They are different from you and me. They possess and enjoy early, and it does something to them, makes them soft where we are hard, and cynical where we are trustful in a way that, unless you were born rich, it is very difficult to understand. They think, deep in their hearts, that they are better than we are because we had to discover the compensations and refuges of life for ourselves. Even when they enter deep into our world or sink below us, they still think they are better than we are. They are different. . . .

Control of Family Influences Of all the factors that influence the adolescent's self-concept, control of family influences is, unquestionably, the most difficult. So long as his parents are in power, he must be governed by their wishes, whether it be to live in one area rather than another or to go to a school of their choosing rather than of his. He cannot control the way his parents treat him and his siblings nor can he change the type of training methods they use. Within limits, he can exert some influence over the frictional relationships that exist in the home. But this influence is limited. He alone is not responsible for them, even though he may contribute his share or more.

Many parents, unfortunately for the adolescent, do not recognize the psychological damage that comes from conditions within the home. Unless it is disturbing to them personally, they far too often adopt a hands-off policy and allow the children of the family to cope with the situations as best they can. This is well illustrated in the verbal fighting of siblings. If it proves to be annoying to the parents, they will put a stop to it. But if they feel that this is an inevitable accompaniment of growing up, they will do nothing. As a result, they unwittingly allow the adolescent's self-concept to be damaged.

Fortunately for most adolescents, their parents sooner or later realize that treating their sons and daughters like near adults instead of like children reduces family friction and brings about an improvement in the home climate. They recognize, also, that it improves the dispositions of the children of the family and encourages a more mature pattern of behavior. This provides them with the necessary motivation to take a firmer control of the family-relationship problems. As a result, they control the conditions that have been so damaging to the adolescent's self-concept.

how great is the improvement?

Few adolescents are as successful at improving their personalities as they would like to be. The reason for this is that even in the early years of childhood the pattern of personality begins to take on a characteristic form that is readily identifiable. The combined influences of heredity and environment result in the development of individual personality patterns (202,450).

Because adolescence is characterized by profound and frequently sudden physical, mental, and emotional changes, it is logical to anticipate that some change will occur in the individual's personality at this time. Furthermore, new environmental factors enter into the adolescent's life. They, too, leave their mark on his personality. Adolescence, then, may be regarded as a critical time in the development of personality; these years determine whether the individual will become a mature, resolute, socially conscious individual or one who is frustrated, unsocial, and dependent (79,248,375,520).

To determine how much improvement takes place in the individual's personality during adolescence, it is essential to examine evidence from studies of persistence and change in personality to see how much change occurs, what causes it, and what form it takes.

MEANING OF IMPROVEMENT
"Change" and "improvement" are not synonymous. To "change" means to "alter" or to "vary"; it does not necessarily mean that the alteration or variation will be complete.

Even more important, it does not necessarily mean that the change will be for the better. In fact, change can be for the worse. To "improve," on the other hand, means a change for the better. No adolescent, of course, wants to change for the worse; he wants to change for the better.

Changes can be quantitative or qualitative. In *quantitative* changes, there is a weakening or a strengthening of a trait or traits already present. These changes are shifts in the direction of traits already present. Undesirable traits, for example, such as selfishness or cowardice, become less undesirable as children have stronger desires to conform to socially approved standards of behavior. The result is that, by adolescence or adulthood, these traits closely approach the mean though they are rarely replaced with socially desirable traits, such as generosity or courage.

In the same way, socially desirable traits are strengthened. This creates the impression that the individual's personality has been improved. Improvement has come, thus, from weakening the socially undesirable traits and strengthening the desirable. It is unusual, especially in adolescence or adulthood, for *qualitative* changes—or changes in which a socially undesirable trait is eliminated and replaced by a socially desirable one—to occur (58,90,257,438).

Improvement in the adolescent's characteristic methods or adjustment may suggest that his personality has changed and that the change has been for the better. This may not be the case; his improved behavior may be merely a front or a cloak to win greater social approval. He may be generous with peers whose favor he craves but revert to his characteristically stingy patterns with peers he cares little about or with family members. Under such conditions, he has not actually changed his personality even though he gives the impression of having improved it. Under stress, he is likely to drop the cloak and revert to his characteristic pattern of adjustment (55,466,475).

When improvement in personality occurs it is more likely to be in *specific traits* than in the total personality pattern. The core of the pattern—the concept of self—is least likely to change, either for the better or for the worse. With each passing year, this core becomes more fixed. It may, however, express itself in different ways, varying with the environmental situations in which the adolescent finds himself. A timid, shy adolescent, for example, may put up a front when with peers, doing things that will win their approval even though he is quaking in his boots. Quantitative changes in traits, on the other hand, are more common and, for the most part, they are in the direction of improvement (55,257,375,438,459).

Causes of Improvement There is ample evidence that repetition serves to reinforce attitudes and patterns of behavior, thus developing deeply rooted habits that are difficult to change. Improvement can occur only with *relearning*. Relearning is always long, difficult, and time- and energy-consuming. If the adolescent wants to improve his personality enough to put forth the time and effort needed, he must be willing to accept two essentials to reach his goal: he must have the necessary *motivation* to drive him on, regardless of how many obstacles he may encounter, and he must be patient and realize that improvements *take time* as well as effort. Marked changes, it is true, do occur in personality in a short period of time. But they are almost always changes for the worse and they are an indication of mental illness; they are not found in normal people (420,446).

Of the many conditions that lead to changes in personality, the following four have been found to be the most important.

physical condition After the major physical and glandular changes of puberty have been completed, homeostasis is restored; the adolescent then feels better. Many of the temporary physical conditions that plagued him during the transformation period are cleared up and he now has energy and zest for life which were lacking while his energy was expended in growth. Furthermore, most adolescents come closer to their ideal physical selves as their bodies change. A pubescent boy, for example, who developed an unfavorable self-concept during the time of the puberty fat period will improve his self-concept as his body becomes taller, thinner, and more masculine.

Not all adolescents improve their looks with puberty changes, nor do they come up to their ideal physical selves. They unquestionably are more attractive looking when the puberty changes are completed than they are when they are part child, part adult. Added to this is their greater knowledge of how to camouflage unfavorable and to accent favorable physical features with clothes which further enhance their attractiveness. Only when physical changes fall far short of the adolescent's expectations and, hence, widen the gap between his real and ideal physical self-concepts will the changes not contribute to personality improvement (10,119,232,332,471).

changes in environment Personality changes are dependent upon changes in ideologies and value systems (16,221). To enable the adolescent to come up against significant life experiences and to learn about others' experiences as a basis for insight into his own problems, he must have new environmental opportunities. If these changes are to be in the direction of improvement, the changed environment must provide the adolescent a more realistic insight into his own problems and an encouragement to reevaluate his aspirations so as to set more realistic goals (126,128).

Studies of the effects of college on personality have revealed that the change from the narrow, restricted environment of childhood to the broader, more varied environment of the college campus tends to change the adolescent's concept of self; the college student is a less dependent, more autonomous person, and his self-concept reflects this change in status. College has a democratizing effect on personality; contact with people whose values and ideologies are different breaks down the rigidity and authoritarianism that so often develop in a more restricted environment (16,221,266). When, in addition, the adolescent assumes important social roles in college, when he is able to compete satisfactorily with his classmates in athletics and academic work, and when

he finds himself capable of being autonomous, this enables him to improve his self-concept (62,79,149,176,266,392,393).

A change in the environment which enables the adolescent to more closely approximate his ideal self will, inevitably, improve his self-concept. If, for example, having status symbols that win the attention, admiration, and envy of his peers plays an important role in ideal self-concept, change from the status of a family dependent to a worker with independence to do as he pleases with his earnings will go a long way toward making his real self-concept more closely approximate his ideal (268,384,490). Figure 16–12 shows how improvement in optimism and a more wholesome outlook on life come with improvement in economic conditions.

Changed environmental conditions will not guarantee improvement in personality; they may have the opposite effect. Going to

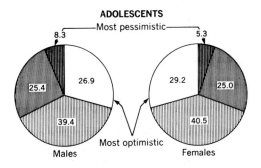

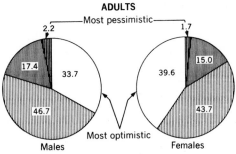

FIGURE 16–12 With improvement in economic conditions comes improvement in optimism and a more wholesome outlook on life. (Adapted from R. D. Tuddenham: Constancy of personal morale over a fifteen-year interval. *Child Develpm.*, 1962, **33**, 663–673. Used by permission.)

college, for example, will not lead to an improved self-concept if the conditions on the college campus lead to feelings of personal inadequacy (79). Nor will going into the armed services where life is far more regimented than it was at home lead to as favorable a self-concept as was present when the adolescent was given more autonomy in the home, the school or college, or on the job.

To improve the self-concept of the adolescent, the change in environment must do two things: first, improve his status, and second, help him to be more in equilibrium with his environment. If his status is worsened instead of improved by the environmental change, as so often happens in social mobility, or if he is more "out of focus" with his new environment than he was with the old, the change in his self-concept will be for the worse. As a result, the change in his personality will be in the direction of deterioration rather than in the direction of improvement (159,473,481).

social pressures The adolescent has discovered from his childhood experiences that people are "liked or disliked not on the basis of one or two or a half dozen traits but on the basis of the impression they make as total individuals" (50). As a result, he concentrates on improving the traits that are most highly approved by the group with which he wants to be identified (252,438, 448,486).

How great the motivation will be to improve the personality pattern will depend partly on how anxious the adolescent is to win social approval and acceptance, partly on whether his social insight is good enough to enable him to know what the group expects of its members, and partly on how strong the social pressures are (174,481, 522). If he is perceived favorably by members of the social group, the adolescent has less motivation to change his personality than if the reactions of the group members toward him are unfavorable (22,288).

self-insight Because the self-concept is the core of the personality pattern, improvement in personality can occur best if the

self-concept is improved. This requires self-insight; the adolescent must see himself as he is and as he is perceived by others. Any adolescent *can* gain greater self-insight by the use of introspection; through introspection, he can see himself as he is in relation to others. But the habit of seeing himself in a particular way is often so firmly established by the time the individual reaches adolescence that he needs guidance and help in this matter (362,475).

Some adolescents get greater self-insight from reading books on the subject. Some are able to work out their problems by comparison of their self-concepts with what they know are the concepts significant people in their lives have of them. Most, however, can achieve the goal of personality improvement best by individual or group psychotherapy.

Professional guidance through psychotherapy includes helping the adolescent to gain insight into the cause or causes of his unfavorable self-concept; to have a better understanding of how rational or irrational his self-concept is; to recognize the role the self-concept plays in determining the quality of his behavior; and to guide him in making changes in the self-concept to avoid upsetting the entire personality pattern (55, 432).

Gaining greater personal insight, even when accompanied by strong motivation to improve, is not necessarily enough. No adolescent, for example, can improve his self-concept, regardless of self-insight and motivation, if he is constantly made to feel inferior by prejudice directed against him because of his race, nationality, or religion (340,493,507). Similarly, constant feelings of failure because of unrealistic levels of aspiration imposed on him by overly ambitious parents will counteract the building up of self-confidence that comes with better self-insight (79,266). Only when he can change to a more wholesome environment will these counteracting influences be removed (277,307).

MEANING OF PERSISTENCE

Improving the personality is difficult and often impossible; this suggests that the personality pattern, established in childhood, has become persistent by adolescence. "Persistence" means "enduring" or "constantly recurring"; it does not mean that no change occurs. Instead, it means that there is a tendency for certain traits to remain in an unchanged, or relatively unchanged, form. The important thing about personality is "its relatively enduring and unique organization" (8). As Cole and Hall (90) note:

One's personality is not fixed by heredity; it grows, sheds some traits, acquires others, is sometimes supported by environmental pressures and sometimes warped by them, and is quickly affected by illness, disease, or unusual emotional strain.

Changes in personality are more frequent and more pronounced in early childhood than during late childhood or adolescence, and very much more frequent and pronounced than in adulthood (257,450). To emphasize this point, Peck and Havighurst (351) have explained:

Some individuals are markedly inconsistent —now considerate, now callously selfish: responsible here, irresponsible there. Such a pattern has its own "consistency," though. It is an enduring, predictable kind of pattern that sets the person off from other people of different character. . . . It has been found that most individuals tend to maintain the same attitudes and motives through the years. . . . The child who is deeply friendly and affectionate at ten, for instance, is most likely to show the same warm trustful feelings for people at 16 or 17. Conversely, the child who is deeply cowed, submissive, and yet covertly resentful toward people at 10 is most apt to show just about the same reaction pattern at 17, even allowing for all the pressures and encouragement to become more independent as adolescence progresses. . . . Numerous details of attitude and behavior normally do change during the course of adolescent development and allowance must be made for these maturational changes; but once such allowance is made for the changes "everybody" undergoes, it is remarkable how little alteration there is in the basic motive pattern of most adolescents.

Persistence of personality is further emphasized by Thompson (481):

Only rarely does there occur a maverick, one whose life experience somehow made him a rebel rather than a conformist. But even then the degree of his deviation is not permitted to be unlimited. Beyond a certain point, society forbids his deviation and few can survive that degree of disapproval.

There are, however, Thompson further explains, two conditions under which persistence will be replaced by change in the personality pattern: first, under circumstances of great stress and temptation unacceptable patterns of behavior may erupt, and second, when significant people in the individual's life change, he will try to adapt to the new situation (481).

Persistence of Core The fundamental reason for persistence in the personality pattern is to be found in the stability of the self-concept, based on persisting ways in which the individual sees himself (69,352, 475). This is well illustrated in feelings of inadequacy, inferiority, and martyrdom that develop as a result of constant exposure to prejudice and discrimination (244). The long-term effects of prejudice have been vividly described by the Group for the Advancement of Psychology thus (182):

Wherever segregation occurs, one group, in this instance the Negroes, always suffers from inferior social status. The damaging effects of this are reflected in unrealistic inferiority feelings, a sense of humiliation, and constriction of potentialities for self-development. This often results in a pattern of self-hatred and rejection of one's own group, sometimes expressed by antisocial behavior toward one's own group or the dominant group. These attitudes seriously affect the levels of aspiration, the capacity to learn, and the capacity to relate in interpersonal situations.

While unquestionably the self-concept is the most persistent aspect of the personality pattern, some traits of this pattern are markedly persistent also. Those associated with intelligence, physical development, and

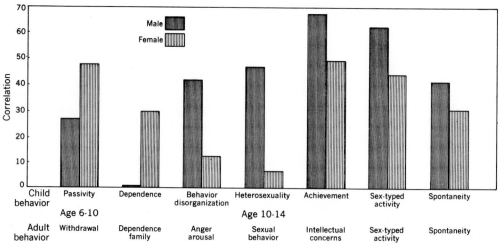

	Child behavior	Passivity	Dependence	Behavior disorganization	Heterosexuality	Achievement	Sex-typed activity	Spontaneity
		Age 6-10				Age 10-14		
	Adult behavior	Withdrawal	Dependence family	Anger arousal	Sexual behavior	Intellectual concerns	Sex-typed activity	Spontaneity

FIGURE 16–13 Persistence in different personality traits from childhood into early adulthood. (Adapted from J. Kagan and H. A. Moss: *Birth to maturity: a study in psychological development*. New York: Wiley, 1962. Used by permission.)

temperament have been found to be most persistent, while those related to social situations, such as introversion or extroversion, values, and attitudes, have been reported to be less persistent (8,248,323,438). Traits that are traditionally sex appropriate for members of the two sexes have been found to be more persistent than other traits (240, 489). Persistence in different personality traits is illustrated in Figure 16–13, which shows behavior ratings for the same males and females in childhood and in adulthood.

Evidence of Persistence   That the personality pattern is persistent has been shown by a number of genetic studies covering a wide range of ages in the lives of the same individuals (155,349,387). "Shirley's babies," who were found to show consistent patterns of personality during the first two years of their lives, showed patterns so similar to their original patterns 15 years later that they could readily be identified by the uniqueness of their personality patterns (337,424). A study of six individuals, rated on 35 personality traits 50 years after judgments about them had been recorded in

their mother's diary, revealed that even after that length of time there was marked persistence in 70 percent of the traits (438). Dependent behavior, striving for achievement, and recognition through competence in intellectual or athletic attainments or through improved economic and cultural milieus have likewise been found to be persistent from the early school years into adulthood (239,323). Personality patterns of early and late maturers, developed as a result of the way they were treated because of their physical status at puberty, have been found to persist into the early thirties (14, 232,332). Refer to pages 66 and 67 for a more complete discussion of the effects of deviant sexual maturing on personality.

Unquestionably the best evidence of the difficulties the adolescent faces when he wants to improve his personality comes from studies of the persistence of *maladjustive behavior*. Records of patients in mental hospitals have revealed that they have shown poor adjustment since their childhood days. Those who are excitable as adults were excitable as children; those who are schizophrenic as adults have been apathetic since they were children (146,148,260,484). Adults who have psychosomatic disorders have been found, in one study, to have made poorer adjustments during childhood and adolescence than did a symptom-free group used for comparison (452). This is illustrated in Figure 16–14. Children and adolescents who make good social and personal adjustments tend to make better adjustments in adulthood than do those who were poorly adjusted when they were younger. They are also far less likely to become involved in delinquent and criminal behavior (26,148,314,376,377,378).

Causes of Persistence Because the personality pattern tends to remain relatively unchanged over the years, it would be logical to conclude that personality is a product of heredity. While it is unquestionably true that any trait that is related, either directly or indirectly, to the individual's hereditary endowment will be more stable over the years than traits that have little relationship to the hereditary endowment, the core of the personality pattern and many of the characteristic patterns of adjustment influenced by this core are the product of environmental influences during the early, formative years of life (15,349,425).

Home training throughout the formative years of childhood has a marked influence on the self-concept the individual develops and the patterns of adjustment he uses. Because this training is persistent, the self-concept and patterns of behavior become reinforced over the years. They then develop into well-established habits (7,43, 295,400). Parents, for example, who want their daughters to develop dependent behavior, in the belief that this will produce the admired feminine personality pattern, train their daughters to be dependent and repress any attempts on their part to become too independent (239). In the same way, they pressure their sons to strive for achievement and social recognition in the belief that this will develop personality patterns that will lead to success in life (323).

Social interactions, both in the home and outside the home, tend to be persistent. This factor helps to reinforce self-concepts and patterns of adjustive behavior developed through child-training methods. As Stott (456) has pointed out, the child's:

. . . *basic personality structure—his indi-*

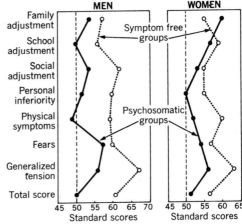

FIGURE 16–14 Poor adjustments in childhood and adolescence often lead to psychosomatic disorders in adulthood. (Adapted from L. H. Stewart: Social and emotional adjustment during adolescence as related to the development of psychosomatic illness in adulthood. *Genet. Psychol. Monogr.,* 1962, **65**, 175–215. Used by permission.)

viduality—very early begins to form as he, with his particular inherent temperamental nature interacts with the particular environment into which he is born.

Burgess and Locke (72) go further, stating that the persistent qualities of personality:

. . . *develop in the interpersonal relations of the family. They arise more or less spontaneously in the social interaction of the child with his parents. . . . Once fixed, they are not subject to any great modification.*

In the home, the child becomes accustomed to play a certain role and to think of himself as the family members think of him. Through the years, there will not be an appreciable change in this role, nor will there be likely to be marked changes in the attitudes of family members toward him (52,199,254). This pattern, once established in the home, is carried outside the home and influences interpersonal relationships. For many children, the "first four years of contact with the school and peer environments (i.e., during the ages 6 to 10) crystallize behavioral tendencies which are maintained through young adulthood" (240).

Once established, the personality pattern determines the *type of environment* the adolescent will select and the type of people he will associate with (17,363). He will, for example, select as friends those whose concept of him causes them to treat him in accordance with his concept of himself. If he thinks of himself as important, he will associate only with those who have a similar concept of him (22). This further reinforces his self-concept.

When not free to choose his environment, on the other hand, he may be forced to change his concept of self to coincide with the concept others have of him. Minority-group adolescents often develop unfortunate self-concepts as a result of the constant prejudice and discrimination they are subjected to in school. This leads to defensive reactions which result in maladjustments. These, in turn, are constantly reinforced by environmental pressures that lead to a crystallization of the unfavorable self-concepts (106). This has been further illustrated in the case of adolescents who spent their early years in institutions. As a result of lack of warm, personal relationships of the type noninstitutional children normally experience, these adolescents showed "extreme difficulty in meeting adults on a meaningful, reciprocal level" and had personality patterns characterized by rigidity and inflexibility (156,166,344).

DEGREE OF IMPROVEMENT ACHIEVED

Because the conditions that foster persistence are so strong, the likelihood is that there will be less change in personality than the adolescent may have hoped for. On the positive side, this is an advantage because it enables adults to predict at an early age what the mature personality of a given child will be and what sort of adjustment he will make to life (271). Centuries ago, Plato emphasized this when he said, "He who is of a calm and happy nature will hardly feel the pressures of old age, but to him who is of an opposite disposition, youth and old age are equally a burden."

Knowing that the kinds of adjustments the young child makes are likely to be persistent allows parents and teachers to check unhealthy attitudes toward self and patterns of behavior that will lead to maladjustment. Anxiety and worry, for example, generally lead to neuroticisms as time passes unless something is done to help the individual develop more realistic levels of aspiration. If he becomes a compulsive worker in childhood, the chances are that he will have a well-developed "busy complex" by the time he reaches adolescence. He will then feel guilty if he takes time to enjoy the normal activities of his peers. Children who show signs of unsocial and antisocial behavior are more likely to develop into juvenile delinquents than are those whose behavior conforms more closely to social expectations (484,509). This knowledge is important because it stresses the fact that one cannot expect a child to "outgrow" unfavorable self-concepts and patterns of behavior (248,471).

Because most adolescents hopefully expect to improve their personalities, many are disappointed when the desired improvements do not occur (13,14). As Kelly has pointed out, "Even though in retrospect few of these desired changes may have occurred, it's comforting to think that one *can* change if one tries hard enough" (248). Many adolescents, unfortunately, do not take this philosophical attitude. When the improvements in personality they had hoped for do not materialize, they are disappointed. They then become so discouraged that much of the motivation they originally had to make the improvements is lost. As a result, they do not try hard enough to make the changes.

self-acceptance and self-rejection

Because few adolescents are satisfied with their personalities or with the improvements they are able to make, many find it difficult to like and accept themselves. "Self-acceptance" is the degree to which an individual, "having considered his personal characteristics, is able and willing to live with them" (348). This he can do without "feeling too guilty, anxious, or hostile, without being self-defeated or destructive of others" (142). A person who is self-acceptant (228):

> . . . *respects himself and lives comfortably with himself; he is able to recognize his own wishes, hopes, fears, and hostilities and to accept his emotional tendencies not in the sense of being smugly self-approving but in the sense of having freedom to be aware of the nature of his feelings; he is freer to make his own decisions and assume responsibility for them.*

Because of these self-acceptant attitudes, he "likes" himself and feels that others find qualities in him that are likable. His positive self-regard is stable; it does not fall or rise indiscriminately in relation to criticism or praise from others (93,228,445).

Many more adolescents are self-rejectant than self-acceptant. This is especially true in the early years of adolescence. It is also more true of boys than of girls (10,11,288). The *self-rejectant* person dislikes himself; he tends to be self-derogatory and condemns himself for his shortcomings; his self-regard vacillates with the attitudes of others toward him; he feels that others view him with hostility and disparagement; he does not trust his own feelings and attitudes; and he has a grudging attitude toward himself, as shown by an unwillingness to spend money on himself (445,461). Self-rejection comes mainly from having a real self-concept that falls far short of the ideal self-concept. Even older adolescents, as has been revealed by a study of college freshmen, have a strong tendency to have unrealistic objectives and aspirations and to come to college with grandiose expectations. This disparity between what they are and what they would like to be makes it difficult for them to accept themselves (298, 491,516).

Self-rejection does not begin in adolescence. In fact, many children reject themselves. But the tendency to be self-rejectant increases in adolescence because the adolescent hopes to outgrow undesirable personality traits or he believes that if he wants to improve his personality he can do so. When he discovers that he has not outgrown his undesirable traits and that he has not improved his personality as much as he had hoped to, he likes himself even less than he did in childhood.

That self-rejection continues over a long period of time has been stressed by Jersild (226) thus:

> A large proportion of children will move into adulthood troubled and unhappy about many things. . . . Many, as adults, will suffer from attitudes of hostility, vindictiveness, and defensiveness which are not a response to hostile forces in the outside world but represent attitudes carried over from unresolved childhood struggles. Many persons similarly will acquire persisting feelings of inferiority or other unhealthy attitudes regarding their personal worth which represent either an irrational estimate of themselves or a failure to accept themselves realistically as they are. In numerous ways there is a vast carry-over of unhealthy attitudes regarding self and others from childhood and adolescence into adult life.

Relation to Adjustment   The degree to which the adolescent accepts himself will determine the type of adjustment he makes to life. No one, at any age, can hope to make good adjustments if he dislikes and rejects himself. On the other hand, if he is reasonably self-acceptant, he will behave in such a way that others will like and accept him. This will increase his self-acceptance (491,516). Because self-acceptance and self-rejection become self-perpetuating, maladjustive or adjustive behavior likewise becomes self-perpetuating.

How self-acceptant or self-rejectant the adolescent is will be influenced markedly by the type of environment in which he finds himself. If he is forced to remain in a school year after year where he is constantly subjected to prejudice and discrimination, or if he lives in a home where parents believe that the best way to discipline children is to emphasize their weaknesses and ignore their good qualities, the adolescent will find that self-rejection outweighs self-acceptance (491,516).

The importance of *consistency* in determining the degree of adjustment the adolescent will make was emphasized by Jersild (226) when he discussed the relationship between self-acceptance and adjustment:

Self-acceptance denotes a predominant trend or direction in a person's life rather than a state in which everything is rosy. An adolescent who is whole-hearted in accepting some aspects of his life may be in doubt or difficulty with respect to others. The prevailing bent, however, is in the direction of self-acceptance.

Self-acceptance is easiest when the attitudes of others, especially significant people in the individual's life, are favorable; self-acceptance is most difficult when the attitudes of significant people are unfavorable. A baby, for example, has little difficulty in accepting himself because "everyone loves a baby." The troublesome teen-ager, on the other hand, finds that significant people in his life have derogatory attitudes toward him as a member of the stereotyped group that has won the reputation of being "terrible teens," the "potential juvenile delinquents," or the "smart alecks who know it all" (92, 205,440).

EFFECTS OF SELF-REJECTION

When a person rejects himself, he makes poor personal and social adjustments. Maladjustments are far more common in adolescence than is usually realized. Popular attention was first focused on this problem during the Second World War when more young men were rejected by the armed services for psychological than for physical reasons (464). Today, it is a recognized fact that juvenile delinquents are maladjusted. It is also recognized that many so-called "normal" adolescents are difficult to live with; many are serious underachievers; others do poor work in school and on the job; most have few friends; and almost all are quarrelsome and unhappy at home and in their social relationships outside the home.

Most adolescents who are maladjusted are aware of it and would like to improve. And yet some adolescents are so poorly ad-

justed they seem unable to make the change they so strongly desire. Sometimes they are so unhappy about themselves that they threaten suicide or even carry out the threat; sometimes they become drug addicts to help them "to forget their problems"; sometimes they retreat into the daydream world as a compensation for the unhappiness life has offered them; sometimes they suffer from nervous breakdowns; and sometimes they are so badly adjusted that they become institutional cases (83,118,164,215, 224,299,338).

In the process of adjusting himself to the adult world, the individual may pass through this adjustment period without undue stress or he may fall the victim of mental disease. Those who break under the strain almost always have shown symptoms of emotional disturbance in childhood (36, 231,283,355). As Yellowlees (519) has pointed out:

Trouble in adolescence rarely comes out of the blue. It is, as a rule, the strongest possible evidence that the mischief has been done, that possible danger signals have been ignored.

Danger Signals When maladjustment exists, there are always "danger signals." Not one of these alone will necessarily be a portent of future trouble. However, when several appear in the same individual and when they seem to fit into a "personality picture," they can no longer be ignored (491,516).

Of the many behavior patterns that can be regarded as danger signals, the following are the most serious during the adolescent years: irresponsibility, aggressiveness, feelings of insecurity, martyr complexes, homesickness, excessive daydreaming, regression, rationalization, "clowning", excessive "worriedness" and anxiety, hypersensitivity to real or imagined slights, a perfectionistic attitude toward everything undertaken, excessive concern or lack of concern about appearance, hostility toward all in authority, accident-proneness, sour-grapes attitudes, indecisiveness even in minor choices, imaginary invalidism, and displacement of aggressiveness against those incapable of defending themselves (42,49, 88,181,214,250,329,357,420,446,484).

Whatever form the maladjustive behavior of the adolescent takes, its fundamental purpose is to protect his ego (137, 497). As Washburn has stressed, "Just as an individual evolves many responses to protect his body, so he does to protect his ego" (501). The smaller the discrepancy between real and ideal self-concepts, the less self-rejectant the adolescent will be and the less need he will have to protect his ego (47,48,491,516).

Not only must the adolescent who has a self-rejectant attitude protect his ego, but he must do so with patterns of behavior that compensate for the dissatisfaction that comes with self-rejection. As Lane (258) has explained:

> The human personality, as well as the body, is subject to malnutrition. Lacking essential nutrients and conditions for growth the personality develops crookedly. The greater number of malnourished personalities become dull. These cause us little trouble, grow up to do work we do not like to do. Others become neurotic. They don't think straight, are undependable and unpredictable but are bothersome principally to their families and immediate neighbors. A smaller portion of the malnourished become aggressive. They strike out, rarely back, in response to deprivation. They are the disorderly ones.

Types of Maladjustment   There are two major types of personality maladjustment. The first involves behavior that is personally satisfying but socially unacceptable; the second involves behavior that is socially acceptable but a source of excessive, continuous, and disturbing conflict to the individual. If the adolescent uses the former, he will gain temporary personal satisfaction by aggressive attacks, either physical or verbal, on others or by projecting the blame for his socially disapproved behavior on others. This temporary satisfaction will be overshadowed by social disapproval. On the other hand, if he retreats from reality by refusing to come to grips with his problems, his behavior will win greater social approval. But it will be personally less satisfying to him (53,105,116,420,461,501).

Most adolescents experience unhappiness to some extent. The maladjusted adolescent not only experiences unhappiness in a more pronounced form but he also experiences it more often. While the problems the maladjusted adolescent faces are not appreciably different from those of the well-adjusted adolescent, his unhappiness stems mainly from the poor adjustments he makes to his problems (52,460). To counteract some of his unhappiness, the adolescent tries to repress memories that are injurious to his concept of the ideal self; he devalues the source of derogatory evaluations of himself by trying to convince himself and others that such evaluations are wrong or unfair; or he denies his responsibility for behavior that leads to these derogatory evaluations. While this kind of response may alleviate some of his unhappiness, it further increases his maladjustments (195,217,497).

Equally as serious is the fact that maladjustive behavior becomes persistent. This has been emphasized by Bennett (39):

> Maladjustive behavior shows a tenacious tendency to remain maladjustive. Forms of activity that succeed in doing the individual far more harm than good remain in operation even in the face of the strongest psychotherapeutic efforts. Minor forms of maladjustive behavior become permanent fixtures in the totality of an individual's behavior and often remain throughout his lifetime.

EFFECTS OF SELF-ACCEPTANCE

The adolescent who sees himself as liked, wanted, acceptable, and fundamentally worthy; who plays his role satisfactorily and derives satisfaction from it; and who is willing to see himself accurately and realistically can accept himself. This leads to behavior that is regarded as well-adjusted (93,235). Combs (93) has described well-adjusted adolescents thus:

> They suffer from no delusions of grandeur or undue humility. They are able to see

themselves for what they are and value themselves in accurate and realistic terms. As a consequence, they do not battle ghosts and goblins but are capable of utilizing themselves as effective instruments for the satisfaction of their own needs and others as well.

The effectiveness of adjustment depends upon the degree to which traits or groups of traits are balanced or integrated. As a result, the well-adjusted adolescent enjoys "inner harmony"; he is at peace with himself just as he is at peace with others (25,262). Because he is capable of accepting himself and others, he does not find it necessary to defend himself. Instead, he accepts himself as he is and governs himself accordingly. This does not mean resignation or defeatism; it means simply *realism* (93).

Characteristics of Self-acceptant People
There are certain forms of behavior found in people who accept themselves and who, as a result, are described as well-adjusted. Lawton (262) has suggested the following 20 forms of behavior characteristically found in those who are well adjusted:

1 *The well-adjusted person is both able and willing to assume responsibilities appropriate to his age.*
2 *The well-adjusted person participates with pleasure in experiences belonging to each successive age level. . . .*
3 *The well-adjusted person willingly accepts the experiences and responsibilities pertaining to his role or position in life. . . .*
4 *The well-adjusted person attacks problems that require solution. . . .*
5 *The well-adjusted person enjoys attacking and eliminating obstacles to his development and happiness. . . .*
6 *The well-adjusted person can make decisions with a minimum of worry, conflict, [and] advice-seeking. . . .*
7 *The well-adjusted person abides by a choice he has made until new factors of crucial importance enter the picture.*
8 *The well-adjusted person finds his major satisfactions in accomplishments and ex-periences in real life, not in the realm of daydreams.*
9 *The well-adjusted person's thinking is a blueprint for action, not a device for delaying or escaping action.*
10 *The well-adjusted person learns from his defeats instead of finding excuses for them.*
11 *The well-adjusted person does not magnify his successes nor extend their applications from the areas in which they originally occurred.*
12 *The well-adjusted person knows how to work when working and how to play when playing.*
13 *The well-adjusted person can say "No" to situations which, over a period of time, run counter to his best interests. . . .*
14 *The well-adjusted person can say "Yes" to situations that will ultimately aid him even though they may be momentarily unpleasant.*
15 *The well-adjusted person can show his anger directly when injured and act in defense of his rights with indignation and action that are appropriate in kind and amount to the injury.*
16 *The well-adjusted person shows his affection directly and gives evidence of it in acts that are fitting in amount and kind.*
17 *The well-adjusted person can endure pain and emotional frustration whenever it is not in his power to alter the cause.*
18 *The well-adjusted person has his habits and mental attitudes so well organized that he can quickly make necessary compromises called for by difficulties he meets.*
19 *The well-adjusted person can bring his energies together and concentrate them on a single goal he is determined to achieve.*
20 *The well-adjusted person does not try to change the fact that life is an endless struggle. . . .*

One of the major reasons why adolescents can accept themselves is that others accept them. A well-adjusted adolescent makes good *social adjustments*; he is able to identify with other people and to have harmonious relationships with them. He is willing to conform to what others value; he is not jealous of others, nor does he try to undermine them; he is not unduly aggressive, unkind, or critical of others; nor does he lose his temper or get easily depressed when things do not go as he wants them to go (92,93,285). In addition, he does not "distort himself to please others, nor does he use them as scapegoats for self-dissatisfaction" (30). Because the well-adjusted adolescent behaves in a manner that makes others like and accept him, there is an increase in his acceptance of self and a decrease in his wanting to be someone else (92,345,369). This is illustrated in Figure 16–15.

The adolescent who does not perceive his social acceptance realistically will behave in a manner that will decrease his social acceptance. The adolescent who overaccepts himself believes that he is more popular than he is; to be able to continue to believe this, he becomes intolerant of others and develops an exaggerated attitude of superiority. Adolescents, on the other hand, who have low self-acceptance depreciate themselves in favor of others and act in accordance with this belief. This decreases the social acceptance they would have had they had more realistic social insight (137,403).

Well-adjusted adolescents are not only happier than poorly adjusted adolescents, but they suffer less from psychosomatic illnesses then and as they grow older (452). This is illustrated in Figure 16–14, page 681. Because people who suffer from psychosomatic illnesses are less happy and less efficient in their activities than are those who are healthier, one can conclude that self-acceptance which leads to good adjustment will also lead to good health, happiness, and efficiency.

suggestions for improving self-acceptance

Because of the close relationship between the type of adjustment the adolescent makes and the degree to which he accepts himself, it is obvious that improvement in adjustment can come only with improvement in self-acceptance. Fundamentally, this resolves

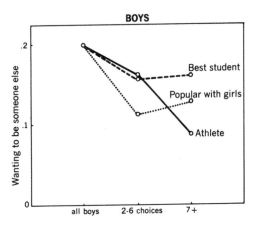

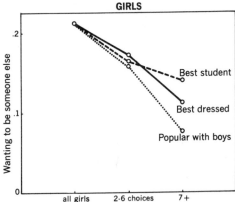

FIGURE 16–15 Decrease in wanting to be "someone else" comes with increase in social acceptance. (Adapted from J. S. Coleman: *The adolescent society.* New York: The Free Press of Glencoe, 1961. Used by permission.)

itself into bringing the real and ideal self-concepts closer together (107,183,191,335, 437,491,525). Difficult as it is, this gap can be closed. However, it is easier to do in childhood than when the child reaches the romantic or unrealistic age of adolescence.

AIDS TO IMPROVED SELF-ACCEPTANCE
To close the gap between the real and the ideal self-concept—an essential to increased self-acceptance—the following aids have been found to be helpful:

1 Convince the adolescent that he will *not outgrow undesirable traits* nor will his personality pattern automatically change for the better as his body changes.

2 Help the adolescent to *increase his self-insight* so that he has a better understanding of his strengths and weaknesses (74,93,235,265).

3 Help in increasing *social insight* can be achieved best by improved self-insight so that the adolescent will act in accordance with the way others see him, not as he hopes they see him (56,137,174,522).

4 Increase in the *stability* of the self-concept leads to greater social acceptance. For that reason, every adolescent needs help to see himself consistently in one way. When a small gap exists between the real and ideal self-concepts, stability of the self-concept is increased; a large gap, on the other hand, encourages instability. To increase self-acceptance, therefore, the self-concept must be *both stable and favorable* (95, 437).

5 To improve self-acceptance, the adolescent must be constantly on the *alert for minor disturbances* and must take remedial steps at once to correct them before they develop into habits. To nip such minor disturbances in the bud may necessitate a change of environment (63).

self-acceptance and happiness

Happiness and adjustment go hand in hand; unhappiness and maladjustment are equally closely correlated. Furthermore, because good adjustment depends upon self-acceptance, happiness can be achieved only when a person is reasonably satisfied with himself. Much of the unhappiness the adolescent experiences could be eliminated or reduced to a minimum if he had healthier and more realistic concepts of himself. The adolescent who can see himself as he actually is, not as he would like to be or as his family and friends would like him to be, will make far better adjustments to life than will the adolescent whose concept of self has been distorted by wishful thinking. And because he makes better adjustments, he is better satisfied and happier.

While early adolescence is a period when many difficult adjustments must be made, the adolescent who progresses satisfactorily through this period should find his happiness increasing with each passing year. Studies of memories of different ages in the life span have indicated that the periods in which the individual was happiest were those in which he felt he made the best adjustments (31,439,482,488). The happy adolescent has a philosophy of life that enables him to take the good with the bad, enjoying the good and not being overly disappointed when things are not to his liking.

TRADITIONAL BELIEFS ABOUT HAPPINESS

According to tradition, one can best be happy if one is *carefree*. Childhood is looked upon by people in all cultures as the "golden days" when the individual can be carefree as will never again be possible (385). The reason for this belief is that responsibilities are regarded by most people as frustrating and anxiety provoking. They argue, then, that if one can be free from responsibilities, one can be free from frustration and anxiety and, thus, happy.

Studies of children and adolescents have disproved this belief. Not having an opportunity to assume responsibility means two things to both children and adolescents: first, the belief of significant people in their lives that they are incapable of handling responsibilities successfully, and second, that they must remain dependent on others. No one who is constantly fighting for his rights can hope to be happy. Nor can he have a favorable concept of self if he believes that the significant people in his life think that he is incapable of handling independence of the degree that his agemates enjoy (117,193,203,272,323,447).

An equally common traditional belief about happiness is that *material possessions* lead to happiness. This belief has been fostered by different forms of mass media which depict poor people as unhappy and rich people as happy. Furthermore, because of the high prestige value of material possessions as status symbols, parents believe that children must have material possessions to be happy. They also believe that more and costlier material possessions make the person more happy.

Material possessions and money to use as they please are unquestionably important to adolescents. Furthermore, they contribute to the social acceptance of the adolescent and, indirectly, to his happiness. On the other hand, there is ample evidence that material possessions and money will not "buy" social acceptance. There is also evidence that the more the adolescent has, the more likely he is to be envied and regarded as conceited. Studies of socially mobile families have likewise shown that children and adolescents whose families better themselves tend to be less happy than those whose families are more static. Thus, it is apparent that material possessions will not bring happiness *unless they increase the social acceptance* of the individual.

A third commonly accepted traditional belief is that a *happy childhood* will guarantee happiness throughout life. Studies of happiness throughout the life span, referred to earlier, indicate that such is not the case. Many happy children become unhappy, neurotic, maladjusted adolescents, adults, or elderly citizens. Many whose childhood was unhappy, on the other hand, become happier as life progresses. As was stressed earlier, happiness at any age does not depend upon the period in the life span, but rather upon the type of adjustment the individual makes to social expectations at that age. If, for example, he conforms to social expectations, he will be happy, regardless of whether he is a child, an adolescent, or an adult. The only way that a happy childhood can guarantee happiness in the remainder of the life span is to train the individual to adjust to social expectations. This can be done only if he learns to assess himself and his abilities realistically and to accept and utilize his abilities to their full extent.

THE THREE A'S OF HAPPINESS

There are three factors that contribute to self-acceptance which is at the basis of good adjustment; good adjustment, in turn, is at the basis of happiness. These are acceptance by others, affection, and achievement—the "Three A's" of happiness. A person, regardless of his age, can be happy only if he feels that others like and accept him. This is especially true in a culture such as the American culture of today where high value is placed on *social acceptance.* Just being popular is not enough; to be happy, an adolescent must be accepted by the people he *wants* to be friends with. If he aspires unrealistically high, he is doomed to be disappointed. This will lead to poor self-concepts and self-rejection (92,115).

Social acceptance is accompanied by *affection*—the degree of affection depending on the degree of acceptance the individual enjoys. Affection of others contributes to "ego strength"—the individual's ability to cope with the problems of reality (7). As is true of social acceptance, the adolescent can be happy only if he receives affection from the people who are *important to him.* A girl, for example, will be unhappy if she is loved by a boy who means little to her while being ignored by a boy she claims she is madly in love with. Similarly, if an adolescent wants affection in the form of romantic love, he will be unhappy if it is the more mature type—companionship love (107).

The third "A" of happiness is *achievement.* To contribute to happiness, achievement must have two important qualities: First, it must conform to the adolescent's expectations, and second, it must be in an area that is prestigeful in the eyes of significant people in his life, especially his peers. If the adolescent has realistic levels of aspiration, the chances are that he will achieve what he sets out to achieve. This will make him happy. If he does better than he anticipated, he will not only be happy but he will also be elated—he will literally "walk on the clouds."

How much satisfaction an adolescent derives from his achievements will depend to a marked extent upon the prestige associated with them. As has been stressed repeatedly, the American adolescent peer group of today puts high value on athletic and social achievements for boys and on social success for girls. Achievements that have low prestige value in the eyes of the peer group, as in the case of academic achievements, will lead to some satisfaction but far less than those that have high prestige value.

In conclusion, then, it becomes apparent that to be happy, an adolescent must be realistic about the achievements he is capable of, about the social acceptance he can expect to receive, and about the type and amount of affection he will receive. Of the three, social acceptance is the most important. A well-accepted adolescent will automatically receive affection from those who accept him and his achievements will win their approval if not their acclaim. Fortunately, happiness is possible for all adolescents *provided* they are willing to see life and themselves as they are rather than viewing them through rose-tinted glasses and provided they are willing to accept themselves as they are instead of wanting to be someone else.

BIBLIOGRAPHY

1 ABBE, M.: Ideal personalities of pupils and teachers judged by pupils. *J. Psychol.*, 1950, **20**, 37–43.

2 ABU-LABAN, B.: Self-conception and appraisal by others: a study of community leaders. *Sociol. soc. Res.*, 1963, **48**, 32–37.

3 ADELSON, D.: Attitudes toward first names: an investigation of the relation between self-accepance, self-identity, and group and individual attitudes toward first names. *Dissert. Abstr.*, 1957, **17**, 1831.

4 AINSWORTH, L. H.: Rigidity, insecurity and stress. *J. abnorm. soc. Psychol.*, 1958, **56**, 67–74.

5 ALEXANDER, F.: The dynamics of personality development. *Soc. Casewk*, 1951, **32**, 139–143.

6 ALLEN, L., L. BROWN, L. DICKINSON, and K. C. PRATT: The relation of first name preferences to the frequency in the culture. *J. soc. Psychol.*, 1941, **14**, 279–293.

7 ALLEN, M. G.: Psychoanalytic theory on infant gratification and adult personality. *J. genet. Psychol.*, 1964, **104**, 265–274.

8 ALLPORT, G. W.: *Pattern and growth in personality.* New York: Holt, 1961.

9 AMATORA, SISTER M.: Similarity in teacher and pupil personality. *J. Psychol.*, 1954, **37**, 45–50.

10 AMATORA, SISTER M.: Comparisons in personality self-evaluations. *J. soc. Psychol.*, 1955, **42**, 315–321.

11 AMATORA, SISTER M.: Validity in self-evaluation. *Educ. psychol. Measmt.*, 1956, **16**, 119–126.

12 AMATORA, SISTER M.: Developmental trends in pre-adolescence and in early adolescence in self-evaluation. *J. genet. Psychol.*, 1957, **91**, 89–97.

13 AMES, L. B.: Longitudinal survey of child Rorschach responses: younger subjects aged 2 to 10 years. *Genet. Psychol. Monogr.*, 1960, **61**, 229–289.

14 AMES, L. B.: Longitudinal survey of child Rorschach responses: older subjects aged 10 to 16 years. *Genet. Psychol. Monogr.*, 1960, **62**, 185–229.

15 ANASTASI, A.: Heredity, environment, and the question "how?" *Psychol. Rev.*, 1958, **65**, 197–208.

16 ANDERSON, C. C.: A developmental study of dogmatism during adolescence with reference to sex differences. *J. abnorm. soc. Psychol.*, 1962, **65**, 132–135.

17 ANDERSON, J. E.: Personality organization in children. *Amer. Psychologist*, 1948, **3**, 409–416.

18 ANDERSON, J. E.: The relation of attitude to adjustment. *Education*, 1952, **73**, 210–218.

19 ARTHAUD, D. L., A. N. HOHNECK, C. H. RAMSEY, and K. C. PRATT: The relation of family name preferences to their frequency in the culture. *J. soc. Psychol.*, 1948, **28**, 19–37.

20 ASCH, S. E.: Forming impressions of personality. *J. abnorm. soc. Psychol.*, 1946, **41**, 258–290.

21 ASHLEY-MONTAGU, M. F.: Sex, order of birth, and personality. *Amer. J. Orthopsychiat.*, 1948, **18**, 351–353.

22 BACKMAN, C. W., P. F. SECORD, and J. R. PIERCE: Resistance to change in the self-concept as a function of consensus among significant others. *Sociometry*, 1963, **26**, 102–111.

23 BAILEY, R. P.: College leaders remember high school. *Sch. Soc.*, 1956, **84**, 89–91.

24 BAILYN, L.: Mass media and children: a study of exposure habits and cognitive effects. *Psychol. Monogr.*, 1959, **73**, no. 1.

25 BAIN, R.: Making normal people. *Marriage fam. Living*, 1954, **16**, 27–31.

26 BAKER, J. W., and A. HOLZWORTH: Social histories of successful and unsuccessful children. *Child Develpm.*, 1961, **32**, 135–149.

27 BALDWIN, W. K.: The social position of the educable mentally retarded child in the regular grades in the public schools. *Except. Children*, 1958, **25**, 106–108, 112.

28 BARBE, W. E.: Peer relationships of children of different intelligence levels. *Sch. Soc.*, 1954, **80**, 60–62.

29 BARBER, B., and L. S. LOBEL: "Fashion" in women's clothes and the American social system. *Soc. Forces*, 1952, **31**, 124–131.

30 BARRETT-LENNARD, G. T.: The mature person. *Ment. Hyg.*, N.Y., 1962, **46**, 98–102.

31 BARSCHAK, E.: A study of happiness and unhappiness in the childhood and adolescence of girls in different cultures. *J. Psychol.*, 1951, **32**, 173–215.

32 BECKER, S. W., and J. CARROLL: Ordinal position and conformity. *J. abnorm. soc. Psychol.*, 1962, **65**, 129–131.

33 BECKER, S. W., M. J. LERNER, and J. CARROLL: Conformity as a function of birth order, payoff, and type of group pressure. *J. abnorm. soc. Psychol.*, 1964, **69**, 318–323.

34 BEER, M., R. BUCKHOUT, M. W. HOROWITZ, and S. LEVY: Some perceived properties of the difference between leaders and non-leaders. *J. Psychol.*, 1959, **47**, 49–56.

35 BEIER, E. G., and J. STUMPF: Cues influencing judgment of personality characteristics. *J. consult. Psychol.*, 1959, **23**, 219–225.

36 BEILIN, H.: Teachers' and clinicians' attitudes toward the behavior problems of children: a reappraisal. *Child Develpm.*, 1959, **30**, 9–25.

37 BELL, W.: Anomie, social isolation and the class structure. *Sociometry*, 1957, **20**, 105–116.

38 BENEDICT, R.: Child rearing in certain European countries. *Amer. J. Orthopsychiat.*, 1949, **19**, 342–350.

39 BENNETT, E. M.: A socio-cultural interpretation of maladjustive behavior. *J. soc. Psychol.*, 1953, **37**, 19–26.

40 BENNETT, E. M., and L. R. COHEN: Men and women: personality patterns and contrasts. *Genet. Psychol. Monogr.*, 1959, **59**, 101–155.

41 BENNETT, E. M., and D. E. JOHANNSEN: Psychodynamics of the diabetic child. *Psychol. Monogr.*, 1954, **68**, no. 11.

42 BERGER, E. M.: The relation between expressed acceptance of self and expressed acceptance of others. *J. abnorm. soc. Psychol.*, 1952, **47**, 778–782.

43 BETTELHEIM, B.: Mental health and current mores. *Amer. J. Orthopsychiat.*, 1952, **22**, 76–78.

44 BICE, H. V.: Some factors that contribute to the concept of self in the child with cerebral palsy. *Ment. Hyg.*, N.Y., 1954, **38**, 120–131.

45 BIDDULPH, L. G.: Athletic achievement and the personal and social adjustments of high school boys. *Res. Quart. Amer. Ass. Hlth. Phys. Educ. Recr.*, 1954, **25**, 1–7.

46 BIERI, J., and R. LOBECK: Self-concept differences in relation to identification, religion, and social class. *J. abnorm. soc. Psychol.*, 1961, **62**, 94–98.

47 BILLS, R. E.: A validation of changes in scores on the index of adjustment and values as measures of changes in emotionality. *J. consult. Psychol.*, 1953, **17**, 135–138.

48 BILLS, R. E.: Self-concepts and Rorschach signs of depression. *J. consult. Psychol.*, 1954, **18**, 135–137.

49 BLAIR, G. M., R. S. JONES, and R. H. SIMPSON: *Educational psychology.* 2d ed. New York: Macmillan, 1962.

50 BONNEY, M. E.: A study of the relation of intelligence, family size, and sex differences with mutual friendships in the primary grades. *Child Develpm.*, 1942, **13**, 79–100.

51 BORG, W. R.: Personality characteristics of a group of college art students. *J. educ. Psychol.*, 1952, **43**, 149–156.

52 BOSSARD, J. H. S., and E. S. BOLL: *The sociology of child development.* 3d ed. New York: Harper & Row, 1960.

53 BOWER, E. M., T. A. SCHELLHAMER, and J. M. DAILY: School characteristics of male adolescents who later became schizophrenic. *Amer. J. Orthopsychiat.*, 1960, **30**, 712–729.

54 BOWERMAN, C. E., and J. W. KINCH: Changes in family and peer orientation of children between the fourth and tenth grades. *Soc. Forces*, 1959, **37**, 206–211.

55 BRANDT, R. M.: Self: the missing link for understanding behavior. *Ment. Hyg.*, N.Y., 1957, **41**, 24–33.

56 BRANDT, R. M.: The accuracy of self esti-

mate: a measure of self concept reality. *Genet. Psychol. Monogr.*, 1958, **58**, 55–99.

57 BRANSON, B. D.: Anxiety, discrimination and self-ideal discrepancy. *Personnel Guid. J.*, 1960, **38**, 373–377.

58 BRECKENRIDGE, M. E., and E. L. VINCENT: *Child development.* 5th ed. Philadelphia: Saunders, 1965.

59 BRETSCH, H. S.: Social skills and activities of socially accepted and unaccepted adolescents. *J. educ. Psychol.*, 1952, **43**, 449–458.

60 BRONSON, G. W.: Identity diffusion in late adolescents. *J. abnorm. soc. Psychol.*, 1959, **59**, 414–417.

61 BRONSON, W. C.: Dimensions of ego and infantile identification. *J. Pers.*, 1959, **27**, 532–545.

62 BROW, D. R., and D. BYSTRYN: College environment, personality, and social ideology of three ethnic groups. *J. soc. Psychol.*, 1956, **44**, 279–288.

63 BROWER, D.: Child psychology: a look at tomorrow. *J. genet. Psychol.*, 1963, **102**, 45–50.

64 BROWN, D. G.: Sex-role development in a changing culture. *Psychol. Bull.*, 1958, **55**, 232–242.

65 BROWNFAIN, J. J.: Stability of the self-concept as a dimension of personality. *J. abnorm. soc. Psychol.*, 1952, **47**, 597–606.

66 BROZEK, J., H. GUETZKOW, and A. KEYS: A study of personality of normal young men maintained on restricted intakes of vitamins of the B complex. *Psychosom. Med.*, 1946, **8**, 98–109.

67 BRUCH, H.: Developmental obesity and schizophrenia. *Psychiatry*, 1958, **21**, 65–70.

68 BRUNER, J. S., and H. V. PERLMUTTER: Compatriot and foreigner: a study of impression formation in three countries. *J. abnorm. soc. Psychol.*, 1957, **55**, 253–260.

69 BUGENTAL, J. F. T., and E. C. GUNNING: Investigations into self-concept: II. Stability of reported self-identifications. *J. clin. Psychol.*, 1955, **11**, 41–46.

70 BÜHLER, C.: School as a phase of human life. *Education*, 1952, **73**, 219–222.

71 BURCHINAL, L. G.: Characteristics of adolescents from unbroken, broken, and reconstituted families. *J. Marriage Fam.*, 1964, **26**, 44–50.

72 BURGESS, E. W., and H. J. LOCKE: *The family.* New York: American Book, 1956.

73 CALDEN, G., R. M. LUNDY, and R. J. SCHLAFER: Sex differences in body concepts. *J. consult. Psychol.*, 1959, **23**, 378.

74 CAPLAN, S. W.: The effect of group counseling on junior high school boys' concepts of themselves in school. *J. counsel. Psychol.*, 1957, **4**, 124–128.

75 CARLSEN, A. H.: Vocational and social adjustment of physically handicapped students. *Except. Children*, 1957, **23**, 364–367, 398.

76 CARLSON, A. J., and E. J. STIEGLITZ: Physiological changes in aging. *Ann. Amer. Acad. pol. soc. Sci.*, 1952, **279**, 18–31.

77 CARLSON, R. O.: Variation and myth in the social status of teachers. *J. educ. Sociol.*, 1961, **35**, 104–118.

78 CARTER, D. C.: The influence of family relationships and family experience on personality. *Marriage fam. Living*, 1954, **16**, 212–215.

79 CARTWRIGHT, R. D.: Self-conception patterns of college students, and adjustment to college life. *J. counsel. Psychol.*, 1963, **10**, 47–52.

80 CATTELL, R. B., and G. F. STICE: Four formulae for selecting leaders on the basis of personality. *Hum. Relat.*, 1954, **7**, 493–507.

81 CATTELL, R. B., G. F. STICE, and N. W. KRISTY: A first approximation to nature-nurture ratios for eleven primary personality factors in objective tests. *J. abnorm. soc. Psychol.*, 1957, **54**, 143–159.

82 CENTERS, L., and R. CENTERS: Peer group attitudes toward the amputee child. *J. soc. Psychol.*, 1963, **61**, 127–132.

83 CHESSICK, R. D., D. H. LOOF, and H. G. PRICE: The alcohol-narcotic addict. *Quart. J. Stud. Alcohol*, 1961, **22**, 261–268.

84 CHILD, I. L., and M. K. BACON: Cultural pressures and achievement motivation. In P. H. Hock and J. Zubin (eds.), *Psychopathology of childhood.* New York: Grune & Stratton, 1955, pp. 166–176.

85 CHRISTENSEN, C. M.: Relationships between pupil achievement, pupil affect-need, teacher warmth, and teacher permissiveness. *J. educ. Psychol.*, 1960, **51**, 169–174.

86 CLARKE, H. H., and D. H. CLARKE: Social status and mental health of boys as related to the maturity, structural, and strength characeristics. *Res. Quar. Amer. Ass. Hlth. Phys. Educ. Recr.*, 1961, **32**, 326–334.

87 CLARKE, T. W.: Allergy and the "problem child." *Nerv. Child*, 1952, **9**, 278–281.

88 COBLINER, W. G.: Social factors in mental disorders: a contribution to the etiology of mental illness. *Genet. Psychol. Monogr.*, 1963, **67**, 151–215.

89 COLE, D. L.: The perception of Lincoln: a psychological approach to the public's conception of historical figures. *J. soc. Psychol.*, 1961, **55**, 23–26.

90 COLE, L., and I. N. HALL: *Psychology of adolescence.* 6th ed. New York: Holt, 1964.

91 COLEMAN, J. S.: Athletics in high school. *Ann. Amer. Acad. pol. soc. Sci.*, 1961, **338**, 33–43.

92 COLEMAN, J. S.: *The adolescent society.* New York: Free Press, 1961.

93 COMBS, A. W.: New horizons in field research: the self concept. *Educ. Leadership*, 1958, **15**, 315–319, 328.

94 CORSINI, R. J.: Appearance and criminality. *Amer. J. Sociol.*, 1959, **65**, 49–51.

95 COWAN, E. L.: The "negative self concept" as a personality measure. *J. consult. Psychol.*, 1954, **18**, 138–142.

96 COWAN, E. L., and P. N. TONGAS: The social desirability of trait descriptive terms: application to a self-concept inventory. *J. consult. Psychol.*, 1959, **23**, 361–365.

97 CRANE, A. R.: Stereotypes of the adult held by early adolescents. *J. educ. Res.*, 1956, **50**, 227–230.

98 CRUICKSHANK, W. M., and G. O. JOHNSON: *Education of exceptional children and youth.* Englewood Cliffs, N.J.: Prentice-Hall, 1958.

99 DAI, B.: A socio-psychiatric approach to personality organization. *Amer. sociol. Rev.*, 1952, **17**, 44–49.

100 DANZINGER, K.: Choice of models among Javanese adolescents. *Psychol. Rep.*, 1960, **6**, 346.

101 DANZINGER, K.: Independence training and social class in Java, Indonesia. *J. soc. Psychol.*, 1960, **51**, 65–74.

102 DANZINGER, K.: Parental demands and social class in Java, Indonesia. *J. soc. Psychol.*, 1960, **51**, 75–86.

103 DAVIS, A., and R. J. HAVIGHURST: *Father of the man.* Boston: Houghton Mifflin, 1947.

104 DAVIS, J. A.: Status symbols and the measurement of status perception. *Sociometry*, 1956, **19**, 154–165.

105 DAVIS, J. M.: A reinterpretation of the Barker, Dembo, and Lewin study of frustration and aggression. *Child Develpm.*, 1958, **29**, 503–506.

106 DAVITZ, J. R.: Contributions of research with children to a theory of maladjustment. *Child Develpm.*, 1958, **29**, 3–7.

107 DEAN, D. G.: Romanticism and emotional maturity: a preliminary study. *Marriage fam. Living*, 1961, **23**, 44–45.

108 DE JUNG, J. E., and E. F. GARDNER: The accuracy of self-role perception: a developmental study. *J. exp. Educ.*, 1962, **31**, 27–41.

109 DENO, E.: Self identification among adolescent boys. *Child Develpm.*, 1953, **24**, 269–273.

110 DEUTSCH, M.: The interpretation of praise and criticism as a function of their social context. *J. abnorm. soc. Psychol.*, 1961, **62**, 391–400.

111 DEUTSCH, M., and L. SOLOMON: Reactions to evaluations of others as influenced by self-evaluations. *Sociometry*, 1959, **22**, 93–112.

112 DICKENS, D.: Social participation as a criterion for determining scientific standards in clothing. *Rural Sociol.*, 1944, **9**, 341–349.

113 DIEN, D. S., and E. W. VINACKE: Self concept and parental identification of young adults with mixed Caucasian-Japanese parentage. *J. abnorm. soc. Psychol.*, 1964, **69**, 463–466.

114 DIXON, J. C.: Development of self recognition. *J. genet. Psychol.*, 1957, **91**, 251–256.

115 DOLL, E. A.: Evaluating social maturity. *Education*, 1957, **77**, 409–413.

116 DORIS, J., and S. SARASON: Test anxiety and blame assignment in a test situation. *J. abnorm. soc. Psychol.*, 1955, **50**, 335–338.

117 DOUVAN, E.: Independence and identity in adolescence. *Children*, 1957, **4**, 186–190.

118 DUBLIN, L. I.: *Suicide: a sociological and statistical study.* New York: Ronald, 1963.

119 DUNBAR, F.: Homeostasis during puberty. *Amer. J. Psychiat.*, 1958, **114**, 673–682.

120 DURR, W. K.: Characteristics of gifted children: ten years of research. *Gifted Child Quart.*, 1960, **4**, 75–80.

121 EAGELSON, O. W.: Students' reactions to their given names. *J. soc. Psychol.*, 1946, **23**, 187–195.

122 EIDUSON, B. T.: Artist and nonartist: a comparative study. *J. Pers.*, 1958, **26**, 13–28.

123 EISENMAN, R., and S. N. COLE: Prejudice and conservatism in denominational college students. *Psychol. Rep.*, 1964, **14**, 644.

124 ELKIN, F.: Socialization and the presentation of self. *Marriage fam. Living*, 1958, **20**, 320–325.

125 ELKINS, D.: Some factors related to the choice-status of ninety eighth-grade children in a school society. *Genet. Psychol. Monogr.*, 1958, **58**, 207–272.

126 ELLIS, A.: Requisite conditions for basic personality change. *J. consult. Psychol.*, 1959, **23**, 538–540.

127 ELLIS, A., and R. M. BEECHLEY: Emotional disturbances in children with peculiar given names. *J. genet. Psychol.*, 1954, **85**, 337–339.

128 ENGEL, M.: The stability of the self concept in adolescence. *J. abnorm. soc. Psychol.*, 1959, **58**, 211–215.

129 ENTY, J. E.: *The effect of clothing on the social adjustment of the adolescent girl.* Washington, D.C.: Howard University, 1950.

130 ERIKSON, E.: *Childhood and society.* New York: Norton, 1950.

131 EYSENCK, H. J.: Personality and social attitudes. *J. soc. Psychol.*, 1961, **53**, 243–248.

132 FARBER, M. L.: English and Americans: values in the socialization process. *J. Psychol.*, 1953, **36**, 243–250.

133 FAUST, M. S.: Developmental maturity as a determinant in prestige of adolescent girls. *Child Develpm.*, 1960, **31**, 173–184.

134 FEINBERG, M. R.: Relation of background experience to social acceptance. *J. abnorm. soc. Psychol.*, 1953, **48**, 206–214.

135 FEINBERG, M. R., M. SMITH, and R. SCHMIDT: An analysis of expressions used by adolescents at varying economic levels to describe accepted and rejected peers. *J. genet. Psychol.*, 1958, **93**, 133–148.

136 FERNBERGER, S. W.: Persistence of stereotype concerning sex differences. *J. abnorm. soc. Psychol.*, 1948, **43**, 97–101.

137 FEY, W. F.: Acceptance of others and its relation to acceptance of self and others: a revaluation. *J. abnorm. soc. Psychol.*, 1955, **50**, 274–276.

138 FEY, W. F.: Correlates of certain subjective attitudes toward self and others. *J. clin. Psychol.*, 1957, **13**, 44–49.

139 FINNEY, J. C.: Some maternal influences on children's personality and character. *Genet. Psychol. Monogr.*, 1961, **63**, 199–278.

140 FITZGERALD, F. S.: The rich boy. In M. Cowley, *The stories of F. Scott Fitzgerald.* New York: Scribner, 1951, pp. 177–208.

141 FLUGEL, I.: On the significance of names. *Brit. J. med. Psychol.*, 1930, **10**, 208–213.

142 FRANK, L. K.: Genetic psychology and its prospects. *Amer. J. Orthopsychiat.*, 1951, **21**, 506–522.

143 FRANK, L. K.: Personality development in adolescent girls. *Monogr. Soc. Res. Child Develpm.*, 1951, **16**, no. 53.

144 FRANK, L. K., and M. H. FRANK: Teachers' attitudes affect children's relationships. *Education*, 1954, **75**, 6–12.

145 FRANK, L. K., and M. H. FRANK: *Your adolescent, at home and in school.* New York: Viking, 1956.

146 FRAZEE, H. E.: Children who later became schizophrenic. *Smith. Coll. Stud. soc. Wk.*, 1953, **23**, 125–149.

147 FRAZIER, A., and L. K. LISONBEE: Adolescent concerns with physique. *School Review*, 1950, **58**, 397–405.

148 FREEDMAN, A. M., and L. BENDER: When the childhood schizophrenic grows up. *Ment. Hyg., N.Y.*, 1957, **27**, 553–565.

149 FREEDMAN, M. B.: Influence of college experience on personality development. *Psychol. Rep.*, 1961, **8**, 21–22.

150 FRENCH, R. L., and I. N. MENSH: Some relationships between interpersonal judgments and socioeconomic status in a college group. *Sociometry*, 1948, **11**, 335–345.

151 FREUD, S.: *The standard edition o, he complete psychological works of Sigmund Freud.* London: Hogarth, 1953–1962.

152 FRIED, E.: Ego functions and techniques of ego strengthening. *Amer. J. Psychother.*, 1955, **9**, 407–429.

153 FRIEDENBERG, E. Z.: *The vanishing adolescent.* Boston: Beacon Press, 1959.

154 FROMM-REICHMANN, E.: Loneliness. *Psychiatry*, 1959, **22**, 1–15.

155 GAIER, E. L.: Selected personality variables and the learning process. *Psychol. Monogr.*, 1952, **66**, no. 17.

156 GARDNER, D. B., G. R. HAWKES, and L. G.

BURCHINAL: Noncontinuous mothering in infancy and development in later childhood. *Child Develpm.*, 1961, **32**, 225–234.

157 GARRISON, K. C.: *Growth and development.* 2d ed. New York: Longmans, 1959.

158 GERARD, H. B.: Some effects of status, role clarity, and group goal clarity upon the individual's relations to group process. *J. Pers.*, 1957, **25**, 475–488.

159 GESELL, A., F. L. ILG, and L. B. AMES: *Youth: the years from ten to sixteen.* New York: Harper & Row, 1956.

160 GILLIN, J.: Personality formation from the comparative cultural point of view. In C. Kluckholm and H. Murray (eds.), *Personality in nature, society, and culture.* New York: Knopf, 1949.

161 GILLIN, J.: National and regional cultural values in the United States. *Soc. Forces,* 1955, **34**, 107–113.

162 GLASNER, RABBI S.: Family religion as a matrix of personal growth. *Marriage fam. Living,* 1961, **23**, 291–293.

163 GLÖCKEL, H.: A comparative study of the self-ideal in youth. *Child Develpm. Abstr.,* 1960, **34**, no. 649.

164 GOLD, M.: Suicide, homicide, and the socialization of aggression. *Amer. J. Sociol.,* 1958, **63**, 651–661.

165 GOLDBERG, M. L.: Motivation of the gifted. *57th Yearb. Nat. Soc. Stud. Educ.,* 1958, part 2, 87–109.

166 GOLDFARB, W.: The effects of early institutionalized care on adolescent personality. *J. exp. Educ.,* 1943, **12**, 106–129.

167 GOLLIN, E. S.: Organizational characteristics of social judgment: a developmental investigation. *J. Pers.,* 1958, **26**, 139–154.

168 GOODCHILDS, J. D., and E. D. SMITH: The wit and his group. *Hum. Relat.,* 1964, **17**, 23–31.

169 GOODMAN, M. E.: Japanese and American children: a comparative study of social concepts and attitudes. *Marriage fam. Living,* 1958, **20**, 316–319.

170 GOSLIN, D. A.: Accuracy of self-perception and social acceptance. *Sociometry,* 1962, **25**, 283–296.

171 GOTTESMAN, I. L.: Heritability of personality. *Psychol. Monogr.,* 1963, **77**, no. 9.

172 GOUGH, H. G.: On making a good impression. *J. educ. Res.,* 1952, **46**, 33–42.

173 GOUGH, H. G., and D. R. PETERSON: The identification and measurement of predispositional factors in crime and delinquency. *J. consult. Psychol.,* 1952, **16**, 207–212.

174 GRATER, H.: Changes in self and other attitudes in a leadership training group. *Personnel Guid. J.,* 1959, **37**, 493–496.

175 GREEN, H. B.: Comparison of nurturance and independence in Jamaica and Puerto Rico, with consideration of the resulting personality structure and transplanted social patterns. *J. soc. Psychol.,* 1960, **51**, 27–63.

176 GREENBERG, H., and D. FARE: An investigation of several variables as determinants of authoritarianism. *J. soc. Psychol.,* 1959, **49**, 105–111.

177 GREENBERG, H., R. GUERINO, M. LASHEN, D. MAYER, and D. PISKOWSKI: Order of birth as a determinant of personality and attitudinal characteristics. *J. soc. Psychol.,* 1963, **60**, 221–230.

178 GREENBERG, H., C. MARVIN, and B. BIVINS: Authoritarianism as a variable in motivation to attend college. *J. soc. Psychol.,* 1959, **49**, 81–85.

179 GREENBERG, H. M., L. ALLISON, M. FEWELL, and C. RICH: The personality of junior high and high school students attending a residential school for the blind. *J. educ. Psychol.,* 1957, **48**, 406–410.

180 GREENBERG, P., and A. R. GILLILAND: The relationship between basal metabolism and personality. *J. soc. Psychol.,* 1952, **23**, 3–7.

181 GREENFIELD, N. S.: The relationship between recalled forms of childhood discipline and psychopathology. *J. consult. Psychol.,* 1959, **23**, 139–142.

182 Group for the Advancement of Psychology Report: *Psychiatric aspects of school desegregation.* New York: Group for the Advancement of Psychology, 1957.

183 GUERNEY, B., and J. L. BURTON: Relationships among anxiety and self, typical peer, and ideal percepts of college women. *J. soc. Psychol.,* 1963, **61**, 335–344.

184 GUETZKOW, H. S., and P. H. BOWMAN: Men and hunger. Elgin, Ill.: Brethern Publishing Co., 1946.

185 GUILFORD, J. P., and W. S. ZIMMERMAN: Fourteen dimensions of temperament. *Psychol. Monogr.,* 1956, **70**, no. 10.

186 HABBE, S.: Nicknames of adolescent boys.

Amer. J. Orthopsychiat., 1937, **7**, 371–377.

187 HALL, R. L., and B. WILLERMAN: The educational influence of dormitory roommates. *Sociometry*, 1963, **26**, 294–318.

188 HALLER, A. O., and S. THOMAS: Personality correlates of the sociometric status of adolescent males. *Sociometry*, 1962, **25**, 398–404.

189 HANDSCHIN-NINCK, M.: Aeltester und Jüngster in Märchen. *Prax, Kinderpsychol. Kinderpsychiat.*, 1956, **7**, 167–173.

190 HANLEY, C.: Physique and reputation of junior high school boys. *Child Develpm.*, 1951, **22**, 247–260.

191 HANLON, T. E., P. R. HOFSTAETTER, and J. P. O'CONNOR: Congruence of self and ideal self in relation to personality adjustment *J. consult. Psychol.*, 1954, **18**, 215–218.

192 HARDY, M. C.: Adjustment scores of adolescents having a history of frequent illness during childhood. *Amer. J. Orthopsychiat.*, 1937, **7**, 204–209.

193 HARRIS, D. B., A. M. ROSE, K. E. CLARKE, and F. VALASEK: Personality differences between responsible and less responsible children. *J. genet. Psychol.*, 1955, **87**, 103–106.

194 HARTMAN, A. A.: Name styles in relation to personality. *J. gen. Psychol.*, 1958, **59**, 289–294.

195 HARVEY, O. J., H. H. KELLEY, and M. M. SHAPIRO: Reactions to unfavorable evaluations of the self made by other persons. *J. Pers.*, 1957, **25**, 393–411.

196 HAVIDSON, H. H., and L. P. KRUGLOV: Some background correlates of personality and social attitudes. *J. soc. Psychol.*, 1953, **38**, 233–240.

197 HAVIGHURST, R. J.: Social class and basic personality structure. *Sociol. soc. Res.*, 1952, **36**, 355–363.

198 HAVIGHURST, R. J.: *Human development and education.* New York: Longmans, 1953.

199 HAVIGHURST, R. J.: The social competence of middle-aged people. *Genet. Psychol. Monogr.*, 1957, **56**, 297–375.

200 HAVIGHURST, R. J.: Social-class influences on American education. *60th Yearb. Nat. Soc. Stud. Educ.*, 1961, part. 2, 120–143.

201 HAVIGHURST, R. J., and D. V. MAC DONALD: Development of the ideal self in New Zealand and American children. *J. educ. Res.*, 1955, **49**, 263–273.

202 HAVIGHURST, R. J., and H. TABA: *Adolescent character and personality.* New York: Wiley, 1949.

203 HEATHERS, G.: Acquiring dependence and independence: a theoretical orientation. *J. genet. Psychol.*, 1955, **87**, 277–291.

204 HEBER, R. F.: The relation of intelligence and physical maturity to social status of children. *J. educ. Psychol.*, 1956, **47**, 158–162.

205 HECHINGER, G., and F. M. HECHINGER: *Teenage tyranny.* New York: Morrow, 1963.

206 HEILBRUN, A. B.: Parental model attributes, nurturant reinforcements, and consistency of behavior in adolescents. *Child Develpm.*, 1964, **35**, 151–167.

207 HEILBRUN, A. B., and R. MC KINLEY: Perception of maternal child rearing attitudes, personality of the perceiver, and incipient psychopathology. *Child Develpm.*, 1962, **33**, 73–83.

208 HELLERSBERG, E. F.: Unevenness of growth in its relation to vulnerability, anxiety, ego weakness and schizophrenic patterns. *Amer. J. Orthopsychiat.*, 1957, **27**, 577–586.

209 HELPER, M. M.: Learning theory and the self concept. *J. abnorm. soc. Psychol.*, 1955, **51**, 184–194.

210 HELPER, M. M., and L. L. MC QUITTY: Some relations of personality integration to occupational interests. *J. soc. Psychol.*, 1953, **38**, 219–231.

211 HESS, R. D., and G. HANDEL: Patterns of aggression in parents and their children. *J. genet. Psychol.*, 1956, **89**, 199–212.

212 HICKS, J. M.: The influence of group flattery upon self evaluation. *J. soc. Psychol.*, 1962, **58**, 147–151.

213 HILL, T. J.: Attitudes toward self: an experimental study. *J. educ. Sociol.*, 1957, **30**, 395–397.

214 HILLSON, J. S., and P. WORSHEL: Self-concept and defensive behavior in the maladjusted. *J. consult. Psychol.*, 1957, **21**, 83–88.

215 HIRSH, J.: Suicide. *Ment. Hyg., N.Y.*, 1959, **43**, 516–525.

216 HOLLINGWORTH, L. S.: Personality and adjustment as determiners and correlates of intelligence. *39th Yearb. Nat. Soc. Stud. Educ.*, 1940, 271–275.

217 HOROWITZ, E.: Reported embarrassment memories of elementary school, high school, and college students. *J. soc. Psychol.*, 1962, **56**, 317–325.

218 HOULT, T. F.: Experimental measurement of clothing as a factor in some social ratings of selected American men. *Amer. sociol. Rev.*, 1954, **19**, 324–328.

219 HOUSTON, T. J., and F. C. SUMNER: Measurements of neurotic tendency in women with uncommon given names. *J. gen. Psychol.*, 1948, **39**, 289–292.

220 ILIFFE, A. H.: A study of preferences in feminine beauty. *Brit. J. Psychol.*, 1960, **51**, 267–273.

221 IZARD, C. E.: Personality change during college years. *J. consult. Psychol.*, 1962, **26**, 482.

222 IZARD, C. E.: Personality similarity and friendship: a follow-up study. *J. abnorm. soc. Psychol.*, 1963, **66**, 598–600.

223 JACKSON, J.: The effect of classroom organization and guidance practice upon the personality adjustment and academic growth of students. *J. genet. Psychol.*, 1953, **83**, 159–170.

224 JACO, E. G.: Social factors in mental disorders in Texas. *Soc. Probl.*, 1957, **4**, 323–328.

225 JAHODA, G.: A note on Ashanti names and their relationship to personality. *Brit. J. Psychol.*, 1954, **45**, 192–195.

226 JERSILD, A. T.: Self understanding in childhood and adolescence. *Amer. Psychologist*, 1951, **6**, 122–126.

227 JERSILD, A. T.: *In search of self.* New York: Teachers College, Columbia, 1952.

228 JERSILD, A. T.: *Child psychology.* 5th ed. Englewood Cliffs, N.J.: Prentice-Hall, 1960.

229 JERSILD, A. T.: *The psychology of adolescence.* 2d ed. New York: Macmillan, 1963.

230 JOHNSON, W.: The semantics of maladjustment. In L. A. Pennington and I. A. Berg (eds.), *An introduction to clinical psychology.* New York: Ronald, 1948, chap. 20.

231 JONES, H.: Maintenance of mental health. *Ment. Hlth., London*, 1951, **10**, 40–42.

232 JONES, M. C.: The later careers of boys who were early- or late-maturing. *Child Develpm.*, 1957, **28**, 113–128.

233 JONES, M. C.: A study of socialization patterns at the high school level. *J. genet. Psychol.*, 1958, **93**, 87–111.

234 JONES, M. C., and P. H. MUSSEN: Self-conceptions, motivations, and interpersonal attitudes of early- and late-maturing girls. *Child Develpm.*, 1958, **29**, 491–501.

235 JOURARD, S. M.: Healthy personality and self-disclosure. *Ment. Hyg., N.Y.*, 1959, **43**, 499–507.

236 JOURARD, S. M., and R. M. REMY: Perceived parental attitudes, the self, and security. *J. consult. Psychol.*, 1955, **19**, 364–366.

237 JOURARD, S. M., and R. M. REMY: Individual variance score: an index of the degree of differentiation of the self and the body image. *J. clin. Psychol.*, 1957, **13**, 62–63.

238 JOURARD, S. M., and P. F. SECORD: Body-cathexis and the ideal female figure. *J. abnorm. soc. Psychol.*, 1955, **50**, 243–246.

239 KAGAN, J., and H. A. MOSS: The stability of passive and dependent behavior from childhood through adulthood. *Child Develpm.*, 1960, **31**, 577–591.

240 KAGAN, J., and H. A. MOSS: *Birth to maturity: a study in psychological development.* New York: Wiley, 1962.

241 KAGAN, J., L. M. SONTAG, C. T. BAKER, and V. L. NELSON: Personality and IQ change. *J. abnorm. soc. Psychol.*, 1958, **56**, 261–266.

242 KAHL, J. A.: Educational and occupational aspirations of "common man" boys. *Harv. educ. Rev.*, 1953, **23**, 186–203.

243 KANNER, L.: Emotional and cultural impacts on contemporary motherhood. *J. child Psychiat.*, 1951, **2**, 168–175.

244 KATZ, I.: Review of evidence relating to effects of desegregation on the intellectual performance of Negroes. *Amer. Psychologist*, 1964, **19**, 381–399.

245 KATZ, I., and L. BENJAMIN: Effects of white authoritarianism in biracial work groups. *J. abnorm. soc. Psychol.*, 1960, **61**, 448–456.

246 KAUFMAN, I., and L. HEIMS: The body image of the juvenile delinquent. *Amer. J. Orthopsychiat.*, 1958, **28**, 146–159.

247 KAUSLAR, D. H.: Aspiration level as a determinant of performance. *J. Pers.*, 1959, **27**, 346–351.

248 KELLY, E. L.: Consistency of the adult personality. *Amer. Psychologist*, 1955, **10**, 659–681.

249 KINCH, J. W.: A formalized theory of the self-concept. *Amer. J. Sociol.*, 1963, **68**, 481–486.

250 KING, G. F., and M. SCHILLER: Ego strength and type of defensive behavior. *J. consult. Psychol.*, 1960, **24**, 215–217.

251 KLAUSNER, S. Z.: Social class and self-concept. *J. soc. Psychol.*, 1953, **38**, 201–205.

252 KLINEBERG, O.: Cultural patterns in personality adjustment of children. *Amer. J. Orthopsychiat.*, 1953, **33**, 465–471.

253 KOCH, H. L.: The relation of certain formal attributes of siblings to attitudes held toward each other and toward their parents. *Monogr. Soc. Res. Child Develpm.*, 1960, **25**, no. 4.

254 KOPPITZ, E. M.: Relationships between some factors and children's interpersonal attitudes. *J. genet. Psychol.*, 1957, **91**, 119–129.

255 LA BARRE, W.: The age period of cultural fixation. *Ment. Hyg.*, N.Y., 1949, **33**, 209–221.

256 LAIRD, J. T.: Emotional disturbances among the physically handicapped. *Personnel Guid. J.*, 1957, **36**, 190–191.

257 LANDIS, J. T.: Personality: a 1954 view. *J. Home Econ.*, 1954, **46**, 459–462.

258 LANE, H.: The meaning of disorder among youth. *Education*, 1955, **76**, 214–217.

259 LANTZ, B.: Children's learning, personality, and physiological interactions. *Calif. J. educ. Res.*, 1956, **7**, 153–158.

260 LANTZ, H. R.: Number of childhood friends as reported in the life histories of a psychiatrically diagnosed group of 1,000. *Marriage fam. Living*, 1956, **18**, 107–109.

261 LASSWELL, T. E.: Social class and stereotyping. *Sociol, soc. Res.*, 1958, **42**, 256–262.

262 LAWTON, G.: *Aging successfully.* New York: Columbia, 1951.

263 LAYCOCK, S. R.: Effect of the teacher's personality on the behavior of pupils. *Understanding the Child*, 1950, **19**, 50–55.

264 LAYCOCK, S. R.: Counseling parents of gifted children. *Understanding the Child*, 1956, **23**, 108–110, 134.

265 LECKY, P.: *Self-consistency: a theory of personality.* New York: Island Press, 1951.

266 LEHMANN, I. J., and I. K. PAYNE: An exploration of attitude and value changes of college freshmen. *Personnel Guid. J.*, 1963, **41**, 403–408.

267 LEICHTY, M. M.: The effect of father-absence during early childhood upon the Oedipal situation as reflected in young males. *Merrill-Palmer Quart.*, 1960, **6**, 212–217.

268 LEVIN, P. L.: How to succeed as a teen-ager. *The New York Times*, Apr. 18, 1965.

269 LEWIS, L. S.: Class and the perception of class. *Soc. Forces*, 1964, **42**, 336–340.

270 LIDDLE, G.: Overlap among desirable and undesirable characteristics in gifted children. *J. educ. Psychol.*, 1958, **49**, 219–223.

271 LIEF, H. I., and W. C. THOMPSON: The prediction of behavior from adolescence to adulthood. *Psychiatry*, 1961, **24**, 32–38.

272 LIFSHITZ, A. D., and J. SAKODA: Effect of summer camp on adolescent maturity. *J. child Psychiat.*, 1952, **2**, 257–265.

273 LINDGREN, H. C.: The development of a scale of cultural idealization based on the California Test of Personality. *J. educ. Psychol.*, 1952, **43**, 81–91.

274 LINDZEY, G., and J. A. URDAN: Personality and social choice. *Sociometry*, 1954, **17**, 47–63.

275 LIPSITT, L. P.: A self-concept scale for children and its relationship to the children's form of the manifest anxiety scale. *Child Develpm.*, 1958, **29**, 463–472.

276 LIVSON, N., and W. C. BRONSON: An exploration of patterns of impulse control in early adolescence. *Child Develpm.*, 1961, **32**, 75–88.

277 LODGE, H. C.: The influence of the study of biography on the moral ideology of the adolescent at the eighth grade level. *J. educ. Res.*, 1956, **50**, 241–255.

278 LOWE, C. M.: The self-concept: fact or artifact. *Psychol. Bull.*, 1961, **58**, 325–336.

279 LOWREY, G. H.: Obesity in the adolescent. *Amer. J. Pub. Hlth.*, 1958, **48**, 1354–1358.

280 LUFT, J.: Monetary value and the perception of persons. *J. soc. Psychol.*, 1957, **46**, 245–251.

281 LUND, F. H.: Biodynamics as Freudian psychodynamics. *Education*, 1957, **78**, 41–54.

282 MAAS, H. S.: Some social class differences in the family systems and group relations of pre- and early adolescents. *Child Develpm.*, 1951, **22**, 145–152.

283 MACFARLANE, J., L. ALLEN, and M. P. HONZIK: *A developmental study of the behavior problems of normal children between twenty-one months and fourteen years.* Berkeley, Calif.: University of California Press, 1954.

284 MAC GREGOR, F. C.: Some psycho-social problems associated with facial deformities. *Amer. sociol. Rev.*, 1951, **16**, 629–638.

285 MALM, M., and O. G. JAMISON: *Adolescence.* New York: McGraw-Hill, 1952.

286 MALONE, A. J., and M. MASSLER: Index of nail-biting in children. *J. abnorm. soc. Psychol.*, 1952, **47**, 193–202.

287 MALPASS, L. F.: Some relationships between students' perceptions of school and their achievement. *J. educ. Psychol.*, 1953, **44**, 475–482.

288 MANIS, M.: Social interaction and the self-concept. *J. abnorm. soc. Psychol.*, 1955, **51**, 362–370.

289 MANN, H.: How *real* are the friendships of gifted and typical children in a program of partial segregation? *Except. Children*, 1957, **23**, 199–201, 206.

290 MARGOLES, M. S.: Mental disorders in childhood due to endocrine disorders. *Nerv. Child*, 1948, **7**, 55–75.

291 MARKEL, N. N., M. MEISELS, and J. E. HOUCK: Judging personality from voice quality. *J. abnorm. soc. Psychol.*, 1964, **69**, 458–463.

292 MARTIN, J. G.: Racial ethnocentrism and judgment of beauty. *J. soc. Psychol.*, 1964, **63**, 59–63.

293 MARTIN, J. G., and F. R. WESTIE: The tolerant personality. *Amer. sociol. Rev.*, 1959, **24**, 521–528.

294 MARTIN, W. E.: Learning theory and identification: III. The development of values in children. *J. genet. Psychol.*, 1954, **84**, 211–217.

295 MARTIN, W. E.: Effects of early training on personality. *Marriage fam. Living*, 1957, **19**, 39–45.

296 MARTIRE, J. G., and R. H. HORNBERGER: Self-congruence, by sex and between the sexes, in a "normal" population. *J. clin. Psychol.*, 1957, **13**, 288–291.

297 MASON, D. J.: Judgments of leadership based upon physiognomic cues. *J. abnorm. soc. Psychol.*, 1957, **54**, 273–274.

298 MATTESON, R. W.: Self-estimates of college freshmen. *Personnel Guid. J.*, 1956, **34**, 280–284.

299 MAURER, D. W., and V. H. VOGEL: *Narcotics and narcotic addiction.* 2d ed. Springfield, Ill.: Charles C Thomas, 1962.

300 MC ANDREW, H.: Rigidity and isolation: a study of the deaf and blind. *J. abnorm. soc. Psychol.*, 1948, **43**, 476–494.

301 MC ARTHUR, C.: Personalities of public and private school boys. *Harv. educ. Rev.*, 1954, **24**, 256–262.

302 MC ARTHUR, C.: Personality differences between middle and upper classes. *J. abnorm. soc. Psychol.*, 1955, **50**, 247–254.

303 MC ARTHUR, C.: Personalities of first and second children. *Psychiatry*, 1956, **19**, 47–54.

304 MC GUIRE, C.: Family and age-mates in personality formation. *Marriage fam. Living*, 1953, **15**, 17–23.

305 MC GUIRE, C., and G. D. WHITE: Social-class influences on discipline at school. *Educ. Leadership*, 1957, **14**, 229–231, 234–236.

306 MC KEACHIE, W. J.: Lipstick as a determinant of first impressions of personality: an experiment for the general psychology course. *J. soc. Psychol.*, 1952, **36**, 241–244.

307 MC KINNON, J. K. M.: Consistency and change in behavior manifestations. *Child Develpm. Monogr.*, 1942, no. 30.

308 MEAD, M.: *Male and female.* New York: Morrow, 1952.

309 MEDLEY, D. M.: Teacher personality and teacher-pupil rapport. *J. teacher Educ.*, 1961, **12**, 152–156.

310 MEISSNER, W. W.: Some anxiety indications in the adolescent boy. *J. gen. Psychol.*, 1961, **64**, 251–257.

311 MERRIMAN, J. B.: Relationships of personality traits to motor ability. *Res. Quart. Amer. Ass. Hlth., Phys. Educ. Recr.*, 1960, **31**, 163–173.

312 MERRY, F. K., and R. V. MERRY: *The first two decades of life.* 2d ed. New York: Harper & Row, 1958.

313 MEYER, E., W. E. JACOBSON, M. T. EDGERTON, and A. CANTER: Motivational patterns in patients seeking elective plastic surgery. *Psychosom. Med.*, 1960, **22**, 193–203.

314 MICHAEL, C. M., D. P. MORRIS, and E. SOROKER: Follow-up studies of shy, withdrawn children: II. Relative incidents of schizophrenia. *Ment. Hyg., N.Y.*, 1957, **27**, 331–337.

315 MILLER, H., and D. W. BARUCH: A study of hostility in allergic children. *Amer. J. Orthopsychiat.*, 1950, **20**, 506–519.

316 MILNER, E.: Effects of sex role and social status on the early adolescent personality. *Genet. Psychol. Monogr.*, 1949, **40**, 231–325.

317 MISCHEL, W.: Preference for delayed rein-

forcement: an experimental study of a cultural observation. *J. abnorm. soc. Psychol.*, 1958, **56**, 57–61.

318 MITCHELL, A. C.: A study of the social competence of a group of institutionalized retarded children. *Amer. J. ment. Defic.*, 1955, **60**, 354–361.

319 MIYAMOTO, S. F., and S. M. DORNBUSCH: A test of interactionist hypotheses of self-conception. *Amer. J. Sociol.*, 1956, **61**, 399–403.

320 MOODY, C. B.: Physical education and neurotic behavior disorders. *Understanding the Child*, 1952, **21**, 20–24.

321 MORE, D. M.: Developmental concordance and discordance during puberty and early adolescence. *Monogr. Soc. Res. Child Develpm.*, 1953, **18**, no. 1.

322 MORTON, G. M.: Psychology of dress. *J. Home Econ.*, 1926, **18**, 584–586.

323 MOSS, H. A., and J. KAGAN: Stability of achievement and recognition seeking behaviors from early childhood through adolescence. *J. abnorm. soc. Psychol.*, 1961, **62**, 504–513.

324 MOULTON, R.: Oral and dental manifestations of anxiety. *Psychiatry*, 1955, **18**, 261–273.

325 MULL, H. K., M. KEDDY, and M. KOONCE: Some personality differences in northern and southern college students. *Amer. J. Psychol.*, 1945, **58**, 555–557.

326 MUNN, N. L.: *The evolution and growth of human behavior*. 2d ed. Boston: Houghton Mifflin, 1965.

327 MUNSTERBERG, E., and P. H. MUSSEN: The personality structure of art students. *J. Pers.*, 1953, **21**, 457–466.

328 MURPHY, E. B., E. SILBER, G. V. COELHO, D. A. HAMBURG, and I. GREENBERG: Development of autonomy and parent-child interaction in late adolescence. *Amer. J. Orthopsychiat.*, 1963, **33**, 643–652.

329 MURPHY, L. B.: Coping devices and defense mechanisms in relation to autonomous ego functions. *Bull. Menninger Clin.*, 1960, **24**, 144–153.

330 MURPHY, W. F.: A note on the significance of names. *Psychoanal. Quart.*, 1957, **26**, 91–106.

331 MUSGROVE, F.: Role-conflict in adolescence. *Brit. J. educ. Psychol.*, 1963, **33**, 34–42.

332 MUSSEN, P. H., and M. C. JONES: Self-conceptions, motivations and interpersonal attitudes of late- and early-maturing boys. *Child Develpm.*, 1957, **28**, 243–256.

333 MUSSEN, P. H., and M. C. JONES: The behavior-inferred motivations of late- and early-maturing boys. *Child Develpm.*, 1958, **29**, 61–67.

334 MUSSEN, P. H., H. B. YOUNG, R. GADDINI, and L. MARANTE: The influence of father-son relationships on adolescent personality and attitudes. *J. child Psychol. Psychiat.*, 1963, **4**, 3–16.

335 NAHINSKY, I. D.: The relationship between the self-concept and the ideal-self concept as a measure of adjustment. *J. clin. Psychol.*, 1958, **14**, 360–364.

336 NASH, H.: Stereotyped associations to schematic faces. *J. genet. Psychol.*, 1958, **93**, 149–153.

337 NEILON, P.: Shirley's babies after 15 years: a personality study. *J. genet. Psychol.*, 1948, **73**, 175–186.

338 *New York Times* Report: Jersey study finds loneliness a factor in 41 child suicides. *The New York Times*, Apr. 2, 1964.

339 *New York Times* Report: What's in a name? *The New York Times*, Nov. 10, 1964.

340 NOEL, D. I., and A. PINKNEY: Correlates of prejudice: some racial differences and similarities. *Amer. J. Sociol.*, 1964, **69**, 609–622.

341 NORMAN, R. D.: The interrelationships among acceptance-rejection, self-other identity, insight into self, and realistic perception of others. *J. soc. Psychol.*, 1953, **37**, 205–235.

342 NORRIS, H. J., and W. M. CRUICKSHANK: Adjustment of physically handicapped adolescent youth. *Except. Children*, 1955, **21**, 282–288.

343 NYE, F. I.: Adolescent-parent adjustment: age, sex, sibling number, broken homes, and employed mothers as variables. *Marriage fam. Living*, 1952, **14**, 327–332.

344 O'CONNOR, N.: The evidence for the permanently disturbing effects of mother-child separation. *Acta psychol., Amsterdam*, 1956, **12**, 174–191.

345 OMWAKE, K. T.: The relation between acceptance of self and acceptance of others shown by three personality inventories. *J. consult. Psychol.*, 1954, **18**, 443–446.

346 ORGEL, S. Z., and J. TUCKMAN: Nicknames of

institutionalized children. *Amer. J. Orthopsychiat.*, 1935, **5**, 276–285.

347 PACKARD, V.: *The status seekers.* New York: Pocket, 1961.

348 PANNES, E. D.: The relationship between self-acceptance and dogmatism in junior-senior high school students. *J. educ. Sociol.*, 1963, **36**, 419–426.

349 PAULSEN, A. A.: Personality development in the middle years of childhood: a ten-year longitudinal study of thirty public school children by means of Rorschach tests and social histories. *Amer. J. Orthopsychiat.*, 1954, **24**, 336–350.

350 PAYNE, D. E., and P. H. MUSSEN: Parent-child relations and father identification among adolescent boys. *J. abnorm. soc. Psychol.*, 1956, **52**, 358–362.

351 PECK, R. F., and R. J. HAVIGHURST: *The psychology of character development.* New York: Wiley, 1962.

352 PERKINS, H. V.: Changing perceptions of self. *Childhood Educ.*, 1957, **34**, 82–84.

353 PERKINS, H. V.: Factors influencing changes in children's self-concepts. *Child Develpm.*, 1958, **29**, 221–230.

354 PERLMUTTER, H. V.: Relations between the self-image, the image of the foreigner, and the desire to live abroad. *J. Psychol.*, 1954, **38**, 131–137.

355 PETERSON, D. R.: Behavior problems of middle childhood. *J. consult. Psychol.*, 1961, **25**, 205–209.

356 PETERSON, D. R., W. C. BECKER, D. J. SHOEMAKER, Z. LURIA, and L. A. HELLMER: Child behavior problems and parental attitudes. *Child Develpm.*, 1961, **32**, 151–162.

357 PHILLIPS, B. N., E. HINDSMAN, and E. JENNINGS: Influence of intelligence on anxiety and perception of self and others. *Child Develpm.*, 1960, **31**, 41–46.

358 PLOTTKE, P.: The child and his name. *Indiv. psychol. Bull.*, 1950, **8**, 150–157.

359 POLLOCK, G. H., and J. B. RICHMOND: Nutritional anemia in children. *Psychosom. Med.*, 1953, **15**, 477–484.

360 PROTHRO, E. T.: Arab students' choices of ways to live. *J. soc. Psychol.*, 1958, **47**, 3–7.

361 RADKE-YARROW, M., and B. LANDE: Personality correlates of differential reactions to minority group belonging. *J. soc. Psychol.*, 1953, **38**, 253–272.

362 RAINES, G. N.: Adolescence: pattern for the future. *Geriatrics*, 1956, **11**, 159–162.

363 RAINWATER, L.: A study of personality differences between middle and lower class adolescents: the Szondi Test in culture-personality research. *Genet. Psychol. Monogr.*, 1956, **54**, 3–86.

364 RAINWATER, L.: Some themes in the personalities of German men. *Genet. Psychol. Monogr.*, 1960, **61**, 167–195.

365 RATH, R.: Subjective factors in judging personality traits. *J. soc. Psychol.*, 1961, **55**, 85–96.

366 RAYGOR, A. L.: College reading improvement and personality change. *J. counsel. Psychol.*, 1959, **6**, 211–217.

367 READ, K. H.: Clothes help build personality. *J. Home Econ.*, 1950, **42**, 348–350.

368 REEDER, L. G., G. A. DONOHUE, and A. BIBLARZ: Conceptions of self and others. *Amer. J. Sociol.*, 1961, **66**, 153–159.

369 REESE, H. W.: Relationships between self-acceptance and sociometric choice. *J. abnorm. soc. Psychol.*, 1961, **62**, 472–474.

370 REHFISCH, J. M.: A scale for personality rigidity. *J. consult. Psychol.*, 1958, **22**, 11–15.

371 RESNICK, J.: A study of some relationships between high-school grades and certain aspects of adjustment. *J. educ. Res.*, 1951, **44**, 321–333.

372 RHODES, I. G.: Allergic causes of emotional disturbances in children. *Nerv. Child*, 1952, **9**, 369–377.

373 RICHARDSON, H. M., and N. G. HANAWALT: Leadership as related to the Bernreuter personality measures: V. Leadership among adult women in social activities. *J. soc. Psychol.*, 1952, **36**, 141–153.

374 RINGNESS, T. A.: Self-concepts of children of low, average and high intelligence. *Amer. J. ment. Defic.*, 1961, **65**, 453–461.

375 ROBERTS, K. E., and V. V. FLEMING: Persistence and change in personality patterns. *Monogr. Soc. Res. Child Develpm.*, 1944, **8**, no. 3.

376 ROBINS, L. N., and P. O'NEAL: Mortality, mobility, and crime: problem children thirty years later. *Amer. sociol. Rev.*, 1958, **23**, 162–171.

377 ROBINS, L. N., and P. O'NEAL: The marital history of former problem children. *Soc. Probl.*, 1958, **5**, 347–358.

378 ROBINS, L. N., and P. O'NEAL: The adult prognosis for runaway children. *Amer. J. Orthopsychiat.*, 1959, **29**, 752–761.

379 ROFF, M.: Intra-family resemblances in personality characteristics. *J. Psychol.*, 1950, **30**, 199–227.

380 ROKEACH, M.: Political and religious dogmatism: an alternative to the authoritarian personality. *Psychol. Monogr.*, 1956, **70**, no. 18.

381 ROSE, A. M.: Attitudinal correlates to social participation. *Soc. Forces*, 1959, **37**, 202–206.

382 ROSEN, B. C.: Race, ethnicity, and the achievement syndrome. *Amer. sociol. Rev.*, 1959, **24**, 47–60.

383 ROSENBERG, M.: Parental interest and children's self-conceptions. *Sociometry*, 1963, **26**, 35–49.

384 ROSENBERG, M.: *Society and the adolescent self-image*. Princeton, N.J.: Princeton, 1965.

385 ROSENZWEIG, S., and L. ROSENZWEIG: Agression in problem children and normals as evaluated by the Rosenzweig Picture-Frustration Study. *J. abnorm. soc. Psychol.*, 1952, **47**, 683–688.

386 ROTH, R. M.: The role of self concept in achievement. *J. exp. Educ.*, 1959, **27**, 265–281.

387 RYAN, M. E.: Social adjustment of kindergarten children ten years later. *Smith Coll. Stud. soc. Wk.*, 1949, **19**, 138–139.

388 RYAN, M. S.: *Psychological effects of clothing*. Ithaca, N.Y.: Cornell University Agricultural Experimental Station, 1952, Bulletin 882; 1953, Bulletin 900.

389 RUSSELL, D. H.: What does research say about self-evaluation? *J. educ. Res.*, 1953, **46**, 561–573.

390 SAEGNER, G., and S. FLOWERMAN: Stereotypes and prejudicial attitudes. *Hum. Relat.*, 1954, **7**, 217–238.

391 SAMPSON, E. E.: Birth order, need achievement, and conformity. *J. abnorm. soc. Psychol.*, 1962, **64**, 155–159.

392 SANFORD, N.: Personality development during the college years. *Personnel Guid. J.*, 1956, **35**, 74–80.

393 SANFORD, N., H. WEBSTER, and M. FREEDMAN: Impulse expression as a variable of personality. *Psychol. Monogr.*, 1957, **71**, no. 11.

394 SARASON, S. B.: Mentally retarded and mentally defective children: major psycho-social problems. In W. M. Cruickshank (ed.), *Psychology of exceptional children and youth*. Englewood Cliffs, N.J.: Prentice-Hall, 1955, pp. 438–474.

395 SARASON, S. B., and T. GLADWIN: Psychological and cultural problems in mental subnormality: a review of research. *Genet. Psychol. Monogr.*, 1957, **57**, 3–290.

396 SARBIN, T. R.: A preface to a psychological analysis of the self. *Psychol. Rev.*, 1952, **59**, 11–22.

397 SAVAGE, B. M., and F. L. WELLS: A note on singularity in given names. *J. soc. Psychol.*, 1948, **27**, 271–272.

398 SCHACTER, S.: *The psychology of affiliation*. Stanford, Calif.: Stanford, 1959.

399 SCHACTER, S.: Birth order and sociometric choice. *J. abnorm. soc. Psychol.*, 1964, **68**, 453–456.

400 SCHAEFER, E. S., and R. G. BELL: Development of a parental attitude research instrument. *Child Develpm.*, 1958, **29**, 339–361.

401 SCHAIE, K. W.: Differences in some personal characteristics of "rigid" and "flexible" individuals. *J. clin. Psychol.*, 1958, **14**, 11–14.

402 SCHEINFELD, A.: *The human heredity handbook*. Philadelphia: Lippincott, 1956.

403 SCHIFF, H.: Judgmental response sets in the perception of sociometric status. *Sociometry*, 1954, **17**, 207–227.

404 SCHMUCK, R.: Sex of sibling, birth order position, and female dispositions to conform in two-child families. *Child Develpm.*, 1963, **34**, 913–918.

405 SCHNEIDER, D. M., and G. C. HOMANS: Kinship terminology and the American kinship system. *Amer. Anthropologist*, 1955, **57**, 1194–1208.

406 SCHNEIDERMAN, L.: The estimation of one's own bodily traits. *J. soc. Psychol.*, 1956, **44**, 89–99.

407 SCHOEPPE, A.: Sex differences in adolescent socialization. *J. soc. Psychol.*, 1953, **38**, 175–185.

408 SCHONFELD, W. A.: Deficient development of masculinity. *Amer. J. Dis. Children*, 1950, **79**, 17–29.

409 SCHONFELD, W. A.: Gynecomastia in adolescence. *Amer. Arch. gen. Psychiat.*, 1961, **5**, 46–54.

410 SCHONFELD, W. A.: Body-image disturbances in adolescents with inappropriate sexual development. *Amer. J. Orthopsychiat.*, 1964, **34**, 493–502.

411 SCHWARTZ, E. K.: A psychoanalytic study of the fairy tale. *Amer. J. Psychother.*, 1956, **10**, 740–762.

412 SEARS, R. R., E. E. MACCOBY, and H. LEVIN: *Patterns of child rearing.* New York: Harper & Row, 1957.

413 SECORD, P. F., W. BEVAN, and W. F. DUKES: Occupational and physiognomic stereotypes in perception of photographs. *J. soc. Psychol.*, 1953, **37**, 261–270.

414 SECORD, P. F., W. F. DUKES, and W. BEVAN: Personalities in faces: I. An experiment in social perceiving. *Genet. Psychol. Monogr.*, 1954, **49**, 231–279.

415 SECORD, P. F., and S. M. JOURARD: The appraisal of body-cathexis: body-cathexis and the self. *J. consult. Psychol.*, 1953, **17**, 343–346.

416 SECORD, P. F., and S. M. JOURARD: Mother-concepts and judgments of young women's faces. *J. abnorm. soc. Psychol.*, 1956, **52**, 246–250.

417 SECORD, P. F., and J. E. MUTHARD: Personalities in faces: IV. A descriptive analysis of the perception of women's faces and the identification of some physiognomic determinants. *J. Psychol.*, 1955, **39**, 269–278.

418 SEWELL, W. H.: Infant training and the personality of the child. *Amer. J. Sociol.*, 1952, **58**, 150–159.

419 SEWELL, W. H., and A. O. HALLER: Social status and the personality adjustment of the child. *Sociometry*, 1956, **19**, 114–125.

420 SHAFFER, L. F., and E. J. SHOBEN: *The psychology of adjustment.* 2d ed. Boston: Houghton, Mifflin, 1956.

421 SHANE, H. G.: Social experiences and selfhood. *Childhood Educ.*, 1957, **33**, 297–298.

422 SHERIF, M., and H. CANTRIL: *The psychology of ego-involvements.* New York: Wiley, 1947.

423 SHERRIFFS, A. C., and R. F. JARRETT: Sex differences in attitudes about sex differences. *J. Psychol.*, 1953, **35**, 161–168.

424 SHIRLEY, M. M.: *The first two years.* Minneapolis: University of Minnesota Press, vols. II and III, 1933.

425 SHIRLEY, M. M.: The impact of the mother's personality on the young child. *Smith Coll. Stud. soc. Wk.*, 1941, **12**, 15–64.

426 SHUMSKY, A., and W. L. MURRAY: Student teachers explore attitudes toward discipline. *J. teacher Educ.*, 1961, **12**, 453–457.

427 SILVERMAN, D.: An evaluation of the relationship between attitudes toward self and attitudes toward a vocational high school. *J. educ. Sociol.*, 1963, **36**, 410–418.

428 SILVERMAN, S. S.: Clothing and appearance: their psychological implications for teen-age girls. *Teach. Coll. Contrib. Educ.*, 1945, no. 912.

429 SIMPSON, S. L.: Hormones and behavior pattern. *Brit. med. J.*, 1957, **2**, 839–843.

430 SINGH, P. N., S. C. HUANG, and G. G. THOMPSON: A comparative study of selected attitudes, values, and personality characteristics of American, Chinese, and Indian students. *J. soc. Psychol.*, 1962, **57**, 123–132.

431 SLATER, P. E.: Parental behavior and the personality of the child. *J. genet. Psychol.*, 1962, **101**, 52–68.

432 SLOBETZ, F., and A. LUND: Some effects of a personal developmental program at the fifth grade level. *J. educ. Res.*, 1955, **49**, 373–378.

433 SMELSER, W. T.: Adolescent and adult occupational choice as a function of family socioeconomic history. *Sociometry*, 1963, **26**, 393–409.

434 SMITH, A. J.: Similarity of values and its relation to acceptance and the projection of similarity. *J. Psychol.*, 1957, **43**, 251–260.

435 SMITH, E. E., and J. D. GOODCHILDS: Some personality and behavioral factors related to birth order. *J. appl. Psychol.*, 1963, **47**, 300–303.

436 SMITH, G. H.: Personality scores and the personal distance effect. *J. soc. Psychol.*, 1954, **39**, 57–62.

437 SMITH, G. M.: Six measures of self-concept discrepancy and instability: their interrelations, reliability, and relations to other personality measures. *J. consult. Psychol.*, 1958, **22**, 101–112.

438 SMITH, M. E.: A comparison of certain personality traits rated in the same individuals in childhood and fifty years later. *Child Develpm.*, 1952, **23**, 159–180.

439 SMITH, M. E.: Childhood memories compared with those of adult life. *J. genet. Psychol.*, 1952, **80**, 151–182.

440 SMITH, W. D., and D. LEBO: Some changing aspects of the self-concept of pubescent males. *J. genet. Psychol.*, 1956, **88**, 61–75.

441 SOLOMON, J. C.: Neuroses of school teachers. *Ment. Hyg., N.Y.*, 1960, **44**, 79–90.

442 SONTAG, L. W.: Some psychosomatic aspects of childhood. *Nerv. Child*, 1946, **5**, 296–304.

443 SONTAG, L. W., C. T. BAKER, and V. L. NELSON: Mental growth and personality development: a longitudinal study. *Monogr. Soc. Res. Child Develpm.*, 1958, **23**, no. 2.

444 SPINDLER, G. D., and L. S. SPINDLER: American Indian personality types and their sociocultural roots. *Ann. Amer. Acad. pol. soc. Sci.*, 1957, **311**, 147–157.

445 SPIVACK, S. S.: A study of a method of appraising self-acceptance and self-rejection. *J. genet. Psychol.*, 1956, **88**, 183–202.

446 STAGNER, R.: *Psychology of personality.* 3d ed. New York: McGraw-Hill, 1961.

447 STAINS, K. B.: Developing independence in children. *Understanding the Child*, 1951, **20**, 49.

448 STEINER, I. D.: Some social values associated with objectively and subjectively defined social class membership. *Soc. Forces*, 1953, **31**, 327–332.

449 STENDLER, C. B.: The learning of certain secondary drives by Parisian and American children. *Marriage fam. Living*, 1954, **16**, 195–200.

450 STEVENSON, I.: Is the human personality more plastic in infancy and childhood? *Amer. J. Psychiat.*, 1957, **114**, 152–161.

451 STEWART, L. H.: Relationship of sociometric status to children's occupational attitudes and interests. *J. genet. Psychol.*, 1959, **95**, 111–136.

452 STEWART, L. H.: Social and emotional adjustment during adolescence as related to the development of psychosomatic illness in adulthood. *Genet. Psychol. Monogr.*, 1962, **65**, 175–215.

453 STOLZ, H. R.: Shorty comes to terms with himself. *Progressive Educ.*, 1940, **17**, 405–411.

454 STOTLAND, E., and R. E. DUNN: Empathy, self-esteem, and birth order. *J. abnorm. soc. Psychol.*, 1963, **66**, 532–540.

455 STOTLAND, E., and J. A. WALSH: Birth order and an experimental study of empathy. *J. abnorm. soc. Psychol.*, 1963, **66**, 610–614.

456 STOTT, L. H.: The persisting effects of early family experiences upon personality development. *Merrill-Palmer Quart.*, 1957, **3**, 145–159.

457 STOUDT, V. M.: Character formation is the teacher's business. *Education*, 1957, **77**, 198–202.

458 STOUGHTON, M. L., and A. M. RAY: A study of children's heroes and ideals. *J. exp. Educ.*, 1946, **15**, 156–160.

459 STOUT, I. W., and G. LANGDON: A report on follow-up interviews with parents of well-adjusted children. *J. educ. Sociol.*, 1953, **26**, 434–442.

460 STRANG, R.: Psychology of gifted children and youth. In W. M. Cruickshank (ed.), *Psychology of exceptional children and youth.* Englewood Cliffs, N.J.: Prentice-Hall, 1955, pp. 475–519.

461 STRANG, R.: *The adolescent views himself.* New York: McGraw-Hill, 1957.

462 STRAUS, M. A.: Conjugal power structure and adolescent personality. *Marriage fam. Living*, 1962, **24**, 17–25.

463 STRAUSS, B. V.: The dynamics of ordinal position effects. *Quart. J. Child Beh.*, 1951, **3**, 133–145.

464 STRECKER, E. A.: *Their mothers' sons.* Philadelphia: Lippincott, 1946.

465 STROUP, A. L., and K. J. HUNTER: Sibling position in the family and personality of offspring. *J. Marriage Fam.*, 1965, **27**, 65–68.

466 SULLIVAN, C., M. G. GRANT, and J. D. GRANT: The development of interpersonal maturity: applications to delinquency. *Psychiatry*, 1957, **20**, 373–385.

467 SUMMERSKILL, J., and C. D. DARLING: Emotional adjustment and dieting performance. *J. consult. Psychol.*, 1955, **19**, 151–153.

468 SYMONDS, P. M.: Happiness as related to problems and interests. *J. educ. Psychol.*, 1937, **28**, 290–294.

469 SYMONDS, P. M.: Essentials of good parent-child relations. *Teach. Coll. Rec.*, 1949, **50**, 528–538.

470 SYMONDS, P. M.: Pupil evaluation and self evaluation. *Teach. Coll. Rec.*, 1952, **54**, 138–149.

471 SYMONDS, P. M.: What education has to learn from psychology: IX. Origins of personality. *Teach. Coll. Rec.*, 1960, **61**, 301–317.

472 TAGIURI, R., R. R. BLAKE, and J. S. BRUNER: Some determinants of the perception of positive and negative feelings in others. *J. abnorm. soc. Psychol.*, 1953, **48**, 585–592.

473 TANNENBAUM, A. S.: Personality change as a result of experimental change of environmental conditions. *J. abnorm. soc. Psychol.*, 1957, **55**, 404–406.

474 TAYLOR, C., and G. G. THOMPSON: Age trends in preferences for certain facial proportions. *Child Develpm.*, 1955, **26**, 97–102.

475 TAYLOR, D. M.: Changes in the self concept without psychotherapy. *J. consult. Psychol.*, 1955, **19**, 205–209.

476 TAYLOR, F. K.: Awareness of one's social appeal. *Hum. Relat.*, 1956, **9**, 47–56.

477 TAYLOR, W. S.: Basic personality in orthodox Hindu culture patterns. *J. abnorm. soc. Psychol.*, 1948, **43**, 3–12.

478 TEAGARDEN, F. M.: *Child psychology for professional workers*. Rev. ed. Englewood Cliffs, N.J.: Prentice-Hall, 1946.

479 TERMAN, L. M.: The discovery and encouragement of exceptional talent. *Amer. Psychologist*, 1954, **9**, 221–230.

480 THISTLEWAITE, D. L.: Effects of social recognition upon the educational motivation of talented youth. *J. educ. Psychol.*, 1959, **50**, 111–116.

481 THOMPSON, C.: Concepts of the self in interpersonal theory. *Amer. J. Psychother.*, 1958, **12**, 5–17.

482 THOMPSON, G. G., and S. L. WITRYOL: Adult recall of unpleasant experiences during three periods of childhood. *J. genet. Psychol.*, 1948, **72**, 111–123.

483 TOMAN, V. V.: Family constellation as a basic personality determinant. *J. indiv. Psychol.*, 1959, **15**, 199–211.

484 TOPP, R. F.: Preadolescent behavior patterns suggestive of emotional malfunctioning. *Elem. Sch. J.*, 1952, **52**, 340–343.

485 TRUMBULL, R.: A study of relationships between factors of personality and intelligence. *J. soc. Psychol.*, 1953, **38**, 161–173.

486 TRYON, C. M.: Evaluation of adolescent personality by adolescents. *Monogr. Soc. Res. Child Develpm.*, 1939, **4**, no. 4.

487 TRYON, C. M., and W. E. HENRY: How children learn personal and social adjustment. *49th Yearb. Nat. Soc. Stud. Educ.*, 1950, part 1, 156–182.

488 TUCKMAN, J., and I. LORGE: Old people's appraisal of adjustment over the life span. *J. Pers.*, 1954, **22**, 417–422.

489 TUDDENHAM, R. D.: The constancy of the personality ratings over two decades. *Genet. Psychol. Monogr.*, 1959, **60**, 3–29.

490 TUDDENHAM, R. D.: Constancy of personal morale over a fifteen-year interval. *Child Develpm.*, 1962, **33**, 663–673.

491 TURNER, R. H., and R. H. VANDERLIPPE: Self-ideal congruence as an index of adjustment. *J. abnorm. soc. Psychol.*, 1958, **57**, 202–206.

492 TYPERMAN, M. J.: A research into truancy. *Brit. J. educ. Psychol.*, 1958, **28**, 217–225.

493 VAUGHAN, G. M.: Ethnic awareness in relation to minority group membership. *J. genet. Psychol.*, 1964, **105**, 119–130.

494 VIDEBECK, R.: Self-conception and the reactions of others. *Sociometry*, 1960, **23**, 351–359.

495 WALSH, A. M.: *Self-concepts of bright boys with learning difficulties*. New York: Teachers College, Columbia, 1956.

496 WALTER, L. M., and S. S. MARZOLF: The relation of sex, age, and school achievement to levels of aspiration. *J. educ. Psychol.*, 1951, **42**, 285–292.

497 WALTERS, SISTER A.: The role of the school in personality development. *Education*, 1957, **77**, 214–219.

498 WANG, J. D.: The relationship between children's play interests and their mental ability. *J. genet. Psychol.*, 1958, **93**, 119–131.

499 WARREN, J. R., and P. A. HEIST: Personality attributes of gifted college students. *Science*, 1960, **132**, 330–337.

500 WASHBURN, W. C.: The effects of physique and intrafamily tension on self-concepts in adolescent males. *J. consult. Psychol.*, 1962, **26**, 460–466.

501 WASHBURN, W. C.: Patterns of protective attitudes in relation to differences in self-evaluation and anxiety level among high school students. *Calif. J. educ. Res.*, 1962, **13**, 84–94.

502 WATTENBERG, W. W., and C. CLIFFORD: Relation of self-concepts to beginning achievement in reading. *Child Develpm.*, 1964, **35**, 461–467.

503 WEBB, A. P.: Sex-role preferences and adjustment in early adolescents. *Child Develpm.*, 1963, **34**, 609–618.

504 WECHSLER, H., and D. H. FUNKENSTEIN: The family as a determinant of conflict in self-perceptions. *Psychol. Rep.*, 1960, **7**, 143–149.

505 WEINGARTEN, S.: Reading as a source of the ideal self. *Reading Teacher*, 1955, **8**, 159–164.

506 WELLER, L.: The relation of birth order to cohesiveness. *J. soc. Psychol.*, 1964, **63**, 249–254.

507 WELLER, L.: The relationship of personality and nonpersonality factors to prejudice. *J. soc. Psychol.*, 1964, **63**, 129–137.

508 WELLS, F. L., and H. R. PALWICK: Note on usage of male personal names. *J. soc. Psychol.*, 1950, **31**, 291–294.

509 WERNER, E., and E. GALLISTEL: Prediction of outstanding performance, delinquency, and mental disturbance from childhood evaluations. *Child Develpm.*, 1961, **32**, 255–260.

510 WESTLEY, W. A., and E. ELKIN: The protective environment and adolescent socialization. *Soc. Forces*, 1957, **35**, 243–249.

511 WHEELER, D. K.: Development of the ideal self in Western Australian youth. *J. educ. Res.*, 1961, **54**, 163–167.

512 WHITLEY, H. E.: Mental health problems in the classroom. *Understanding the Child*, 1954, **23**, 98–103.

513 WILLIS, R. H.: Political and child-rearing attitudes in Sweden. *J. abnorm. soc. Psychol.*, 1956, **53**, 74–77.

514 WINICK, C.: Trends in the occupations of celebrities: a study of news magazine profiles and television interviews. *J. soc. Psychol.*, 1963, **60**, 301–310.

515 WINKER, J. B.: Age trends and sex differences in the wishes, identifications, activities, and fears of children. *Child Develpm.*, 1949, **20**, 191–200.

516 WINKLER, R. C., and R. A. MYERS: Some concomitants of self-ideal discrepancy measures of self-acceptance. *J. counsel. Psychol.*, 1963, **10**, 83–86.

517 WOODWORTH, R. S., and D. G. MARQUIS: *Psychology*. 5th ed. New York: Holt, 1947.

518 WORRELL, L.: Level of aspiration and academic success. *J. educ. Psychol.*, 1959, **50**, 47–54.

519 YELLOWLEES, H.: The problems of adolescence. *Lancet*, 1940, **238**, 233–235.

520 ZACHRY, C. B.: Customary stresses and strains of adolescence. *Ann. Amer. Acad. pol. soc. Sci.*, 1944, **236**, 136–144.

521 ZANDER, A.: Group membership and individual security. *Hum. Relat.*, 1958, **11**, 99–111.

522 ZANDER, A., and G. RASMUSSEN: Group membership and self evaluation. *Hum. Relat.*, 1954, **7**, 239–257.

523 ZANDER, A., and E. VAN EGMOND: Relationship of intelligence and social power to the interpersonal behavior of children. *J. educ. Psychol.*, 1958, **49**, 257–268.

524 ZILLER, R. C.: Leader acceptance of responsibility for group action under conditions of uncertainty and risk. *J. Psychol.*, 1959, **47**, 57–66.

525 ZIMMER, H.: Self-acceptance and its relation to conflict. *J. consult. Psychol.*, 1954, **18**, 447–449.

526 ZIMMERMAN, K. A., and E. LEWTON: Teacher personality in school relationships. *Educ. Leadership*, 1951, **8**, 422–428.

527 ZUK, G. H.: The influence of social context on impulse and control tendencies in preadolescents. *Genet. Psychol. Monogr.*, 1956, **54**, 117–166.

index

Juvenile delinquency, seriousness of, 486
    traditional beliefs about, 471–472
    variations in, 486–487
Juvenile mustache, 52

Keepsakes, 554

Large families, 608
Latchkey problems, 277
Leaders, 135, 189–201
    attitudes and behavior of, 202–203
    characteristics of, 194–198
    function of, 191
    making of, 192–194
    meaning of, 190–191
    persistence of, 198–201
    status of, 189–190
    types of, 191–192
Leadership, 189–201, 671
    effects of, on attitudes and behavior, 202–203
    on personality, 671
    persistence of, 198–201
Legs, changes in, 46
Length of acquaintance, 174
Level of aspiration, 293–330, 662–663
    effect, of failure on, 320–321
    on self-concept of, 662–663
    of success on, 316–317
    how developed, 299–304
    meaning of, 297–298
    methods of study of, 298–299
Levels of acceptance, 165–168
    designations of, 168
Liberalism, 141–142
    variations in, 142
Life after death, concept of, 406
Linguistic snob, 263
Loafing, 224–225
    evaluation of, 224–225
    places for, 224
Loafing spots, 224
Love, learning to express, 552–561
    puppy (see Puppy love)
Lying, 439

Magazines, 234–235
Maladjustment, types of, 685
Male sex organs, 48–49
Manner of dressing, 548
Marginal status, 184
Marital relationships of parents, 603–604
    deterioration in, 603–604
Marriage, 532–536, 632
    early, 532–536

Marriage, interfaith, 417–419
    factors influencing, 418–419
    reasons for, 417–418
Mass media, 301–302, 430, 458–459, 477–478, 509
Masturbation, 572–573
    psychological effects of, 573
    variations in, 572–573
Mate selection, 545–552
    characteristics, with high value in, 548–550
    with low value in, 550–551
    establishing values in, 546–548
    obstacles to, 545–546
Material possessions, 270–272
    expression of interest in, 270–271
    sex differences in symbolism in, 271–272
Maturity, 1–2, 252, 255, 259–260, 264, 280, 282
    of behavior, 631
    emotional, 109–110
    moral, 427
Menarche, 35, 49
    concern about, 56
Menstruation, 49–50
    concern about, 56
Mental catharsis (see Catharsis)
Mental health, 216
Miracles, concept of, 406
Misbehavior, 345
Misdemeanors, 461–468
    age of, 461–462
    causes of, 462–463
    common forms of, 463–466
    effects of, 467–468
    variations in, 466–467
Misunderstanding, 595
    effects of, on family relationships, 595
Mobility (see Social mobility)
Money, 272–275
    amount needed, 275
    qualities symbolized in, 273–275
Mood swings, 78
Moodiness, 79–80
Moods, 103
"Moral," meaning of, 427
Moral alternatives, 428–431
Moral behavior, 457–499
    versus moral knowledge, 458–459
Moral character, 431
    types of, 431–432
Moral concepts, 436–441
    changes in, 436
        time of, 436–437
        type of, 437–438
    education in, 441
    specific forms of, 438–441
Moral decisions, 428

Reading, favorite media of, 233–237
favorite topics of, 233
Realism, 11–12, 357, 358
degree of, 11–12
Recreations, 215–247
adolescent needs in, 243–244
benefits of, 216–217
changes in, 217–218
common forms of, 221–243
factors influencing, 218–221
importance of, 216
types of, 215–216
Reform, attempts at, 139–141, 344–345
Rehabilitation of juvenile delinquents, 487–488
Relatives, 613
Religion, 145, 390–425
meaning of, 390
Religious awakening, 395–397
age of, 396
effects of, 397
factors influencing, 396–397
types of, 395–396
Religious beliefs, 403–408
changes in, 403–404
age of, 404–405
areas of, 405–407
reactions to, 407–408
revision of, 401
Religious dogmatism, 400
Religious doubts, 81, 397–403
age of, 398
causes of, 398–400
effects of, 401–402
meeting, 402–403
pattern of, 400
variations in, 400–401
Religious faith, 402, 548
changes in, 411, 417
Religious interest, 391–392, 407
decrease in, 407
evidence of, 391–392
Religious needs, 393–395
types of, 393–394
variations in, 394–395
Religious observances, 390, 402, 408–416
decrease in, 402
in home, 414
Religious reconstruction, 407
Religious tolerance, 416–419
effects of, 416–419
variations in, 416
Religious training, 398, 479–480
Reputation, 170–171, 188
improvement of, 188
Residential propinquity, 550
Resistance to adult authority, 139
Resolutions, 299

Respiratory system, 48
Responsibility, 440
Restlessness, 61
Rewards, 441–442, 450
evaluation of, 450
Role, of child, 624–625
of father, 623–624
of mother, 624
of parents, 622–623
of relatives, 625
Role playing, 530–531
Romanticism, 530

Sabbath, concept of, 406–407
Satisfaction, 318, 342–344
with education, 342–344
School, 357, 411, 508–509, 666–670
attitude toward, 473–474
influence of, on personality, 670
prestige of, 668–669
(See also Education)
School failure, 81
School misdemeanors, 463–465
Secondary sex characteristics, 50–52, 55
of boys, 52–53
concern about, 55
of girls, 50–52
pattern of development of, 50
Self-acceptance, 682, 685–690
characteristics of, 686–687
effects of, 685–686
and happiness, 688–690
improvement in, 687–688
relation of, to adjustment, 683–684
Self-assertiveness, 138–139
Self-concept, 188, 651, 655–675
factors influencing, 655–675
ideal, 651
Self-confidence, 188
Self-image, physical, 651
psychological, 651
Self-insight, 188, 678
influence of, on personality, 678
Self-realism, 321–322
Self-rejection, 682–685
danger signals of, 684–685
effects of, 684
relation of, to adjustment, 683–684
Servants, 612
Services for loved one, 554
Sex, adjustment to other sex, 81
influence of, 145, 220, 309–310, 356–357, 411
Sex antagonism, 511–512
Sex-appropriate appearance, 170

Socialized delinquent, 480
Socialized speech, 266
Socially isolated people, preponderance of, 184–185
Socioeconomic status, 175–177, 195–196, 220–221, 258–259, 273–274, 278, 280, 284–285, 412, 674–675
    effects of, 175–177
        on personality, 674–675
    of family, 615–616
Socioempathy, 166
Solo home, 604–605, 617
Solo parent, 604–605
Speech, 262–267
    content of, 265–266
    quality of, 266–267
    status clues in, 262–264
Sports, 227–228
    favorite, 227–228
Stability of friendships, 134–135
Status, ambiguous, 11
    in family, 673–674
    effects of, on attitudes and behavior, 202–203
    social (see Social status)
    socioeconomic (see Socioeconomic status)
Status symbols, 251–292
    importance of, 254
    meaning of, 252
    qualities symbolized in, 252–253
    types of, 254–285
    variations in, 253–254
Status variations, 610–611
Steady dating (see Going steady)
Stealing, 439–440
Stepparents, 605–606, 614–615
Stepping stones, 332
Stereotypes, 54, 146–147, 358–360, 562–563, 648–649
    of adult sex roles, 562–563
    of feminine role, 562–563
    of male role, 562
    of personality, 648–649
Storm and stress, 76
Sturm und Drang, 76
Style, 261
Subcultural ideals, 305–306
Subdivisions of adolescence, 2–3
    labels of, 3
Sublimation, 104
Success, 308–309, 314–318
    effects of, 316–318
    factors contributing to, 315–316
    meaning of, 315
    objectively judged, 315
    obstacles to, 316
    subjectively judged, 315

Success complex, 317
Suffering-hero daydream, 231
Swearing, 264
Sweat glands, 51–52
Syndrome, 172
    acceptance, 172
    alienation, 172

Tabloids, 235
Tabooed pleasures, 280–285, 463, 466–467
    areas of, 281–282
    status value of, 282–285
Talking, 127
Teachers, 341, 667–668
    attitudes toward, 341
    effects of, on personality, 667–668
Teaching techniques, 341–342
Telephoning, 221–222
Television watching, 240–243
    effects of, 242–243
    variations in, 241–242
Tension, emotional, 401, 605
    nervous, 78
Togetherness, 599–602
    breakdown in, 600–601
    effects of, on home climate, 601–602
    variations in, 600
Traditional beliefs, 4–5, 471–472, 647–648
    about adolescence, 4–5
    about juvenile delinquency, 471–472
    about personality, 647–648
Traditional sex roles, 566–567
    effects of, on boys, 566
        on girls, 566–567
Transition, 1–26
    age of, 1–26
    aids in making, 24–26
    from childhood to adulthood, 8–9
    difficulties in making, 9–12
    effects of, 12–22
    in primitive peoples, 23–24
    in religion, 390–425
        long-term effects of, 419–420
    in socialization, 116–162
        difficulties in making, 118–122
        major areas of, 122–152
            friends (see Friends)
            leaders (see Leaders)
            social attitudes and behavior, 135–152
            social groupings, 122
                types of, 123–130
    success in making, 22–26
Troublesome behavior, 605
Trunk changes, 46